SOCIAL PSYCHOLOGY

FIFTH EDITION

James A. Wiggins
University of North Carolina, Chapel Hill

Beverly B. Wiggins
University of North Carolina, Chapel Hill

James Vander Zanden
Emeritus, The Ohio State University

McGraw-Hill, Inc.

New York St. Louis San Francisco Auckland Bogotá Caracas
Lisbon London Madrid Mexico City Milan Montreal
New Delhi San Juan Singapore Sydney
Tokyo Toronto

SOCIAL PSYCHOLOGY

Photo Credits appear on page 609, and on this page by reference.

This book is printed on acid-free paper.

5 6 7 8 9 0 DOC/DOC 9 9 8 7 6

ISBN 0-07-066980-5

This book was set in Janson by Better Graphics, Inc.
The editors were Phillip A. Butcher, Melissa Mashburn, and Linda Richmond;
the designer was Jo Jones;
the cover was designed by Rafael Hernandez;
the production supervisor was Friederich W. Schulte.
The photo editor was Barbara Salz.
R. R. Donnelley & Sons Company was printer and binder.
Cover photo by Renato Rotolo/Gamma Liaison.

Library of Congress Cataloging-in-Publication Data
Wiggins, James A.
    Social psychology. — 5th ed. / James A. Wiggins, Beverly B.
Wiggins, James Vander Zanden.
        p.   cm.
    Rev. ed. of: Social psychology / James W. Vander Zanden. 4th ed.
c1987.
    Includes bibliographical references (p.   ) and index.
    ISBN 0–07–066980–5
    1. Social psychology.   I. Wiggins, Beverly B.   II. Vander Zanden,
James Wilfrid.   III. Vander Zanden, James Wilfrid.   Social
psychology.
HM251.W597   1994
302 – dc20   93–27414

INTERNATIONAL EDITION

When ordering this title, use ISBN 0-07-113763-7.

ABOUT THE AUTHORS

James A. Wiggins is Associate Professor of Sociology at the University of North Carolina at Chapel Hill where he teaches introductory social psychology, social psychological theory and methods, and sociology of the family. He received his doctorate in Sociology at Washington University. Wiggins has done research on a range of topics including education, sports, alcohol use, and the principles of social exchange. He and his wife, Beverly Wiggins, have coauthored articles on alcohol use among college students.

Beverly B. Wiggins is Associate Director for Research Development at the Institute for Research in Social Science at the University of North Carolina at Chapel Hill. She received her doctoral degree in Sociology from the University of North Carolina at Chapel Hill. She has done research on affect control theory and alcohol use among college students. Wiggins has served as president of the Southern Association for Public Opinion Research and is chairperson of the National Network of State Polls.

   Jim and Bev are married and have two grown-up children, Breck and Whitney, who have been the subjects of much social psychological analysis. They live in a rural area near Chapel Hill, North Carolina, with their two cats. They enjoy snorkeling, gardening, and "doing" social psychology together.

James Vander Zanden is Professor Emeritus in the College of Social and Behavioral Sciences at The Ohio State University and previously taught at Duke University. His doctorate is from the University of North Carolina at Chapel Hill. Professor Vander Zanden's published works include more than twenty professional articles and eight other books. He has two sons who attest to having benefited from their father's devotion to the discipline of social psychology.

This book is dedicated
to our parents
Mary Alice Fugate Bridges
George Foster Pierce Bridges, Jr.
Mary Harriet Gross Wiggins
and
Arthur Lyle Wiggins
who gave us safe and happy starts in life
and to our teachers
Robert L. "Doc" Hamblin
David R. Heise
Sugiyama Iutaka
and
Larry J. Severy
who helped us become social psychologists.

CONTENTS

PREFACE

*B*eginning with the first edition of this book in 1977, James Vander Zanden worked to present a spirited blend of social psychological theories and research. He successfully conveyed his own fascination with the discipline of social psychology—making social psychology "come alive" for students by showing how it allows us to understand human behavior and to lead richer lives. James Vander Zanden did not work on or contribute to this fifth edition, but we have endeavored to build upon the strengths of Vander Zanden's approach while significantly updating the work and bringing to it our own viewpoints and style. Drafts of this edition have been "pretested" by students in our classes over four semesters and have benefited considerably from their reactions and recommendations.

Features Preserved From Earlier Editions

Reviewers of earlier editions of Vander Zanden's text identified several features they particularly valued. We put a high priority on preserving and expanding these qualities in the fifth edition. Among these are:

- the use of Student Observations (which Vander Zanden called Student Journal Entries) to capture student interest and provide vivid and readable illustrations of the provocative insights into human behavior offered by social psychology and its applicability to the world in which we live. The fifth edition contains even more student observations per chapter than previous editions – all provided by student readers of the text.

- the scientifically sound presentation of a wide variety of social psychological theories and research that balances sociological and psychological interests. Assisted by reviewers representing a wide range of social psychological perspectives and academic settings, we have broadened the coverage of theoretical and methodological perspectives in the fifth edition. Some chapters necessarily emphasize psychological interests and research while others emphasize sociological interests and research. Care has been taken, however, to weave this material into a meaningful and coherent whole.

- a readable writing style. Reviewers of the fifth edition praised its "down-to-earth" style, which presents material in everyday language that is easy to understand, and the use of clear, practical examples that clarify the conceptual discussion and make it applicable to everyday life. Reviewers also applauded the book's use of interesting introductions and its "connectedness"—the smooth and logical transitions from one topic and one chapter to another.

Major Changes in the Fifth Edition

Many exciting changes have occurred in social psychology since the publication of the fourth edition of this text in 1987. To reflect the contemporary discipline and to address what reviewers saw as weaknesses in previous editions, we have extensively revised the organization and contents of the text.

- Throughout the text, we have tried to produce chapters that are more theory based and better integrated. Each chapter makes use of several theoretical and methodological perspectives. Theories added to the fifth edition include affect control, differential association, reasoned action, and social control.
- We make more frequent use of illustrations of qualitative research, which reviewers of previous editions believed to be underrepresented. See, for example, our coverage in Chapter 11 of a study by researchers Robin Simon, Donna Eder, and Cathy Evans (1992) that examined the peer culture of adolescent girls to uncover norms involving romantic love and in Chapter 10, our discussion of Arlie Russell Hochschild's (1989) observations of the value norms of two married couples.
- We have added chapters on socialization over the life course and on deviance and stigmatization. The sociology of emotion, an exciting area receiving much attention in the current social psychological literature, receives coverage in almost every chapter of the fifth edition.
- The fourth edition's chapters on roles and the physical environment have been deleted. (Limited material from the physical environment chapter has been included in the chapter on communication. Roles are discussed throughout the text.) The discussions of the development of language and the development of self (discussed in separate chapters in the fourth edition) have been incorporated into the chapter on early socialization. The attitude change literature is now discussed in the chapter on social power.
- We have integrated the coverage of gender and race into *every* chapter of the text, rather than limiting their coverage to separate chapters. Sexism and racism are treated under the more general concepts of inequality and discrimination. Prejudice is addressed in the chapter on social attitudes. Homosexuality is explored in the chapters on close relationships, deviance and stigmatization, and social movements.
- Chapters have been reorganized into four new sections to better reflect contemporary social psychology:
  Culture: Socialization and Negotiation
  Identities, Attitudes, and Behavior
  Forms of Social Interaction
  The Struggle Over Social Definitions

Chapter Highlights

Our revision for *Social Psychology*, 5th edition, was extensive. We have not just patched the fourth edition with inserts and updates. We have rewritten every chapter to incorporate contemporary research and to achieve the clearest possible presentation. We have tried to respond to the helpful suggestions of many users of previous editions. Here are some of the highlights:

Chapter 1: Perspectives and Methods in Social Psychology Several theories are presented in the historical context of four general perspectives—behavioral, cognitive, structural, and interactionist. These perspectives offer different answers to two basic questions: "How much attention should social psychologists give to mental activities in their attempts to understand social behavior?" and "How active are individuals in shaping social interaction?" There is a new section on ethical considerations.

PART I: CULTURE: SOCIALIZATION AND NEGOTIATION We begin our discussion of how social psychologists view behavior by focusing on the relationship that exists between our society and ourselves. This relationship is shaped by two processes—socialization and negotiation. Because our behavior is shaped by our society's culture, the chapters in this section discuss socialization—the process by which we learn the ways of thinking, feeling, and interacting that are essential for effective participation with a particular group of people, and by which we are instilled with the fundamental elements of the group's culture. But we are not only the *products* of culture. We are also the *producers* of culture. In the course of our interaction with others—through a process called negotiation—we help create a culture that influences our subsequent interactions. Thus, the chapters in this section illustrate that culture both shapes, and is shaped by, us.

Chapter 2: Early Socialization This chapter shows that culture shapes both *what* is learned and *how* it is learned. There is also expanded discussion of social learning and of developmental and symbolic interaction theories. Treatments of the development of self and of language learning were moved from other chapters in the fourth edition and have been integrated with the concept of early socialization. Also discussed are the limits of socialization, the reciprocal relationship between socializing agents and children as the targets of socialization, and subcultures.

Chapter 3: Socialization over the Life Course This chapter emphasizes the concept of role and illustrates how cultural expectations differ for different categories of people—for example, those different in age, sex, race, and social class. It also discusses the difficulties people have in meeting these expectations and the impact of historical events on culture. A box on what parents and adolescents argue about is included.

Chapter 4: Social Relationships and Groups This chapter integrates the discussion of social relationships and groups—some of the subunits of society that have cultures of their own. We examine the different kinds of bonds uniting members of relationships and groups. We also discuss the components of group culture and how they affect us, how we experience and manage the multiple cultures that impinge upon us, and how these cultures are constructed through a process of negotiation as group members interact. New topics include networks, internal and external culture, as well as boxes on sociometry, social support and health, and the group bonds of a college basketball team.

Chapter 5: Communication Detailed attention is given to the process by which people interact and interpret their interactions, including negotiations. We discuss what gets communicated and how—and how the styles of communication used by different people are shaped largely by culture. New or expanded topics include nonverbal communication; the rules of communication; and race, class, and gender differences in communication. There are boxes on warspeak (a military jargon), student accounts for absences from class, and race as unintended communication.

PART II: IDENTITIES, ATTITUDES, AND BEHAVIOR The chapters in this section emphasize the implications of mental activities for behavior. We look at the processes by which we categorize and interpret information about ourselves and others, and analyze how mental activity is related to behavior.

Chapter 6: Social Attitudes and Attributions Here we focus on how we form impressions of and make decisions about other people on the basis of limited information about them: identities, categorization, social attitudes and schema, stereotypes, attributions. The chapter provides concrete examples of stereotypes (ethnic, racial, gender, family, physical) and attribution (about crime, poverty, homelessness). We also include boxes on stereotypes of professors, eyewitness testimony, symbolic and traditional racism, and the attribution of responsibility for obesity.

Chapter 7: The Social Nature of Self Our notions of who we are also have a social basis. We examine how social structure affects how we think and feel about ourselves and the processes involved—self-reflection, social comparison, and social influence. We also take an active role—through a process called impression management—in shaping the self that others see. There is a box on self-monitoring.

Chapter 8: Attitudes and Behavior Social psychologists are, for the most part, interested in attitudes because they assume they are powerful predictors of behavior. We discuss three theories that attempt to explain the relationship between attitudes and behavior—reasoned action, balance and cognitive dissonance, and affect control theories. We also discuss the special case of low self-esteem.

PART III: FORMS OF SOCIAL INTERACTION This section provides an intensive examination of the kinds of interaction that have received special attention from social psychologists: performance, conformity, and cooperation; helping and reward exchange; attraction and intimacy; aggression and conflict; and social power.

Chapter 9: Performance, Conformity, and Cooperation Here we discuss the influence of others on task performance. This chapter integrates a diverse literature in a way understandable to students. Social facilitation and inhibition, groupthink, polarization, social dilemmas, and interdependence of outcomes are some topics we include. Boxes focus on binge eating, jury decisions, and the classic bank wiring room observation group.

Chapter 10: Helping and Reward Exchange This chapter focuses on individual and structural factors affecting helping, steps involved in helping, reward exchange and social exchange theory, and trust and shared value norms. A box on helping in drunk–driving situations is included.

Chapter 11: Close Relationships: Attraction and Intimacy Characteristics and types of close relationships (including kinship, friendship, and both homosexual and heterosexual romantic relationships) are discussed, as well as factors affecting attraction and the life course of close relationships. We include boxes on jealousy in American culture, children and divorce, and successful marriages.

Chapter 12: Aggression and Conflict Theoretical explanations of aggression are given. Reciprocal aggression (conflict), competition, and factors affecting escalation and deescalation are other topics we discuss. Boxes focus on family violence, the social definition of rape, and victimization.

Chapter 13: Social Power: Behavior and Attitude Change This chapter discusses power resources and the process of social power — behavior aimed at changing another person's attitudes or behavior in the face of resistance from that person. Examples of power in laboratory experiments, families, and organizations are given. Box topics include the power to make others wait and image-building by political candidates.

PART IV: THE STRUGGLE OVER SOCIAL DEFINITIONS While members of our society share many aspects of culture, they disagree about other important aspects. The good things in life are unequally distributed. Members of society disagree about whether such inequality is caused by equity (where each person gets what he or she "deserves") or by discrimination. We analyze this disagreement in Chapter 14, "Inequality and Discrimination." In Chapter 15, we examine the consequences of varying definitions of what is right or good—stigmatization and deviance. And in Chapter 16, we discuss how some clashes over social definitions result in collective action and social movements.

Chapter 14: Inequality and Discrimination: The Examples of Racism and Sexism In this chapter we discuss inequality in American society and American attitudes toward this inequality, specifically the disagreement about whether inequality among major social groups (such as between men and women and blacks and whites) is the result of equity or discrimination. We discuss institutional racism and sexism (in occupations, education, and families), as well as efforts to reduce discrimination (such as affirmative action). Boxes focus on unequal justice, sexual harassment, and excuses given by male chauvinist husbands.

Chapter 15: Deviance and Stigmatization This is a new chapter that covers the social definition of deviance, the effects of negative social definitions, how we use accounts as repair work, passing and covering, and self-fulfilling prophecies. There are major sections on motivational explanations of and group influences on criminalized behavior. Boxes discuss the savings and loan scandal, organizational crime in the 1980s and 1990s, and excuses in traffic court.

Chapter 16: Collective Action and Social Movements This chapter has been totally reworked to reflect major changes in the social psychological view of collective action. It covers the nature and origins of collective action, factors affecting participation in collective action (including influences over the life course, using as an example 1960s activists), interactions between and within movements and countermovements, and the outcomes of collective action. There is a box on religious cults.

New Instructor's Manual

The Instructor's Manual for the fifth edition is more than a test bank. In addition to approximately 50 test items per chapter (including multiple choice, true-false, matching, and essay), the manual contains an introduction to each chapter, a tear-away study sheet that contains a chapter outline instructors may give to students, many suggestions for lectures and class discussions (some with detailed lecture material provided), and student exercises (many with tear-away handouts included). A computerized test bank is also available.

Thanks and Acknowledgments

First and most importantly, we want to thank our students, whose comments, questions, and observations contributed greatly to both the richness of the text and our pleasure in producing it.

We are fortunate to have had the thoughtful suggestions of several academic reviewers, whose responses to the previous edition and to our proposed outline for the fifth edition and whose comments on chapter drafts were immensely helpful. The reviewers reinforced our notion of the two requirements of a good textbook — student interest and academic integrity. This revision benefited from the wisdom they brought from their varied teaching experiences and areas of expertise. Reviewers included: Robert Brisson, North Carolina State University; Dorothy D. Dubose, North Carolina State University; Stanford W. Gregory, Kent State University; Wanda I. Griffith, University of Colorado, Denver; John Lynxwiler, University of Central Florida; David R. Maines, Pennsylvania State University; Mari J. Molseed, Drake University; Clifford Paynton, California State University, San Bernadino; Judith Raiskin, University of Oregon, Eugene; Christian Ritter, Kent State University; Edward J. Silva, El Paso Community College; J. William Spencer, University of New Orleans; Stephen P. Spitzer, University of Minnesota; Clifford Staples, University of North Dakota; Sheldon Stryker, Indiana University; Marilyn Whalen, University of Oregon; Ronald Wohlstein, Eastern Illinois University; and William C. Yoels, University of Alabama.

We are grateful to the members of the McGraw-Hill College Division staff for their support and collaboration of this project. We owe special thanks to Melissa Mashburn, our assistant editor, who not only provided sound feedback and suggestions but also nurtured us through sometimes difficult times. We also appreciate the support of Linda Richmond, editing supervisor, Phil Butcher, executive editor, and Kathy Bendo, photo researcher for their many contributions. Thanks also to our University of North Carolina colleagues: Craig Calhoun, who encouraged us to undertake this project; Alecia Holland, who managed the onerous process of obtaining permissions; Gary Gaddy, whose willingness to share word processing expertise saved us endless hours and much frustration; Anne Hastings, who undertook the preparation of the instructor's manual with enthusiasm and proficiency; Roberta Engleman, who produced the index; and teaching assistants, Kathleen Nebeker and Yuan Wei who helped develop test items.

An Invitation to Instructors

We have put forth our best effort to produce the fifth edition of *Social Psychology* and are pleased with the result. Undoubtedly, however, the very next time we read it or discuss it in class we will discover areas that could be improved or updated. And other instructors who adopt the book will bring to its use different perspectives and experiences with students from different backgrounds that will lead them to identify potential improvements that may not occur to us. Because we hope that the fifth edition of *Social Psychology* will not be the last, we invite instructors to send us their suggestions for improvements, as well as, we hope, reports of their experiences with aspects of the book that they think should be preserved in future editions. Please send suggestions or comments to:

Beverly Wiggins
Institute for Research in Social Science
Manning Hall, CB#3355
University of North Carolina at Chapel Hill
Chapel Hill, North Carolina 27599–3355
fax: 919–962–4777
email: BWIGGINS. IRSS@MHS.UNC.EDU

Jim and Bev Wiggins

CHAPTER 1

PERSPECTIVES AND METHODS IN SOCIAL PSYCHOLOGY

*I*n recent years there has been a deluge of violent car hijackings in my suburb. Especially interesting is the reaction to such horrible occurrences. Invariably, people ascribe the event to the victim's stupidity. For instance, the driver failed to lock his door, did not have the windows rolled up, drove on "such and such" a road, or simply was foolish enough to drive a BMW. Pretty unreasonable assertions, but they *do* serve a purpose. By proposing that the innocent victim actually deserves such suffering through a fault of his own, we maintain our view of the world as just. Consequently, the uncomfortable prospect that we too could suffer such random misfortune is denied. This is an example of *derogating the victim*.

I am suffering a *role-person merger*! I am a Phonathon supervisor, and that role is invading the rest of my life! I'll explain. I work at the UNC Phonathon, supervising students who call UNC alumni and ask them to contribute money to Carolina academics. My main responsibility is to motivate our callers—excite and enthuse them in their, at times, none-too-rewarding job. In short, I get paid to be perky. Well, I'm about to drive my roommate crazy because my Phonathon perkiness is seeping over into the rest of my existence. Even at 6:30 in the morning when a prank call jolts me out of a sound sleep, I just chime, "Good morning! . . . Oh, I'm afraid you have the wrong number. Have a good day!" in my most congenial telemarketer voice. My salient Phonathon supervisor identity is

becoming so dominant that its effects are spilling over—much to my friends' dismay—to my other identities.

I have to be recertified for CPR and basic first-aid next month. In reviewing my old manual and workbook this week, I encountered a section that is aimed at eliminating *diffusion of responsibility*. Whenever you are performing CPR and requesting that a bystander call 911, the manual instructs that you should never say, "Someone call 911." Instead, it advises that you point your finger at a particular person and say something like, "You—in the red sweater—call 911." This helps to alleviate diffusion of responsibility among the bystanders—a condition which may lead each to assume that someone else will call 911 if he or she does not.

These observations were made by students who were applying to their own experiences ideas discussed in this text. We hope that you will be doing the same thing. Indeed, our goal in writing this book has been to offer readers new ways of looking at their own behavior, as well as others' behavior. How behavior is influenced by and influences other people is the substance of **social psychology**—the study of the behavior, thoughts, and feelings of an individual or interacting individuals and of their relationships with larger social units. Social psychology, then, is the study of people — loving, hating, working, helping, trusting, fighting, communicating. It focuses on the entire drama of our daily lives, all our activities in relation to one another. As such, it studies the trivial and the vital, the joyful and the painful, the temporary and the enduring.

Perspectives in Social Psychology

EARLY ROOTS OF SOCIAL PSYCHOLOGY

Although social psychology is an ancient discipline (some point to either Plato or Aristotle as its founder), it was officially launched as a separate field only in 1908. In that year the first two English-language textbooks on the subject appeared — William McDougall's *Introduction to Social Psychology* and E. A. Ross's *Social Psychology: An Outline and Source Book*. McDougall was a psychologist; Ross, a sociologist.

The prevailing question among early social psychologists was, "How can we explain the influence that other people have on our behavior?" In France, social analysts, keenly aware of their country's bloody revolution, asked why people behaved less "rationally" or more emotionally when they were participating in crowds — for example, during riots, strikes, and revolutions. In Germany as well as at the University of Indiana in the United States, early researchers examined why the presence of other people enhanced individuals' normal solitary performances — for example, the speed of bicycle racers or the quality of children's schoolwork. Moreover, on both continents, psychologists, sociologists, and philosophers were interested in child development and in the apparent conflict between individual freedom, on the one hand, and the need to transmit society's standards from one generation to the next, on the other.

Early theorists focused on two possible explanations for the impact of other people on behavior: (1) the experiences of our ancestors, which we acquire through heredity in the form of biological instincts — the "nature" explanation — and (2) our own experiences with other people throughout our lifetimes — the "nurture" explanation. The doctrine of natural selection, formulated by the nineteenth-century English scientist Charles Darwin, dominated the thinking of early social psychologists. Darwin's theory proposed that the explanation of all behavior lay in the evolutionary array of instincts serving the survival of the species — a "nature" explanation. Social psychologists used words like "suggestion" and "imitation" to refer to the instincts they felt cause us to behave the way we do in the presence of others. In fact, McDougall believed that all social behavior could be based on this view of instincts.

But many social analysts and researchers did *not* believe that instinct explained most social behavior. These early workers in the field disagreed with the notions that heredity is the sole cause of social behavior and that such behavior is enduring and changeless. For example, William James (1890), an early psychologist, believed that although evolution-based instincts do influence our social behavior, the primary explanation is "habit" — patterns of behavior acquired through repetition *during a person's lifetime* — a "nurture" explanation.

John Dewey, another early social psychologist, proposed a modified, more flexible, view of habit. According to Dewey (1922), our behavior is not simply a function of the number of times we have performed that behavior in the past. Instead, our behavior is sustained or changed by our environment — "our situation" — including, of course, other people. Dewey left it to others to specify how this actually occurred.

Several alternatives to the instinct and habit explanations of human behavior were developed, and they have survived — in revised form — to this day. We will call them social psychological **perspectives** — sets of basic assumptions about the most important things to consider when trying to understand social behavior. We'll look at four main perspectives — behavioral, cognitive, structural, and interactionist.

The behavioral and cognitive perspectives — used more often by social psychologists in psychology — offer different answers to the question,

"How much attention should social psychologists give to mental activities in their attempts to understand social behavior?" The **behavioral perspective** emphasizes that we can better understand people's behavior if we ignore information about "what a person is thinking" and focus only on the behaviors that can be verified by our own observations. A person's own accounts of his or her mental processes do not help us understand that person's behavior, according to this perspective, because frequently people are *unreliable* reporters of their own mental processes. On the other hand, the **cognitive perspective** emphasizes that we cannot understand people's behavior without understanding their mental processes. People do not respond automatically to their environment. Instead, their behavior depends on how they *perceive and think about* their environment. Thus, getting reliable information about these processes, according to the cognitive perspective, is critical to our efforts to understand social behavior.

The structural and interactionist perspectives — used more often by social psychologists in sociology — take different positions on the question, "How active are individuals in shaping social interaction?" The **structural perspective** emphasizes that people's behavior can best be understood in terms of the different expectations that society imposes on its members. People's behavior, they argue, is largely a *reaction* to or is constrained by these expectations. On the other hand, the **interactionist perspective** emphasizes that people are active agents in determining their own behavior and establishing social expectations. People negotiate with each other to *construct* their interactions, expectations, and interpretations.

In the following sections, we will look in more detail at each of these social psychological perspectives by briefly describing several theories that start from each one. A **theory** is a set of ideas that summarize, organize, and explain observations parsimoniously, or efficiently. It gives us a general blueprint by which to see relationships among observations and uncover implications not otherwise evident in isolated bits and pieces of information. A theory guides researchers' thinking about a topic of study, leading them to ignore some aspects and focus on others. A theory may suggest possible causes for and consequences of a particular event, allowing researchers to make predictions that may be tested through research.

While the theories we will discuss in this text are widely accepted by those who consider themselves to be social psychologists, it may help you to understand the uses of theory to note that we all use theories of a more everyday sort as we go about our daily lives. Many "folk wisdoms" are everyday theories for understanding, predicting, and dealing with social behavior: "Birds of a feather flock together," or "One rotten apple can spoil the whole barrel." In this sense, we are all amateur social psychologists. As we will see in subsequent chapters, some common folk theories are supported by social psychological research, while others are not.

For now, our purpose in describing various social psychological theories is to familiarize you with the four perspectives on which these theories are based. The theories illustrate the distinctions among the four perspectives. We will discuss the theories in more detail in later chapters, where we will show how they shape social psychological research.

THE BEHAVIORAL PERSPECTIVE

Initially articulated by John B. Watson (1914, 1919), the behavioral perspective occupied the center stage in psychological work between 1920 and 1960. When Watson began his research early in this century, he was proposing not only an alternative to the instinct explanation of social behavior but also an alternative to another explanation of the period, which focused on people's introspective accounts of their mental states — the mind, image, and consciousness. Watson rejected this kind of information, labeling it "mystical," "mentalistic," and "subjective." He called for a totally objective psychology, one that would deal only with the *observable* activities of organisms — their "doings and sayings." In this respect, Watson differed from James and Dewey, both of whom believed that mental processes as well as observable behavior could be explained in the same manner.

Behaviorists segment behavior into units called *responses*, and they divide the environment into units called *stimuli*. A particular stimulus and a particular response, according to behaviorists, may be "associated" with one another, producing a functional relationship or linkage between them. For example, a stimulus, such as a friend coming into one's visual field, elicits a response, such as a smile. The behaviorists believe that stimuli and responses can be connected without reference to inner mental considerations. It is not surprising, therefore, that extreme behaviorism is often termed a "black box" approach. Stimuli enter the "box" (the organism), and out come responses. Mechanisms within the black box — the internal structures or mental processes that intervene between the stimulus and the response — since they are not directly observable, are of no interest to traditional behaviorists.

Later, B. F. Skinner (1953, 1957, 1974) helped change the focus of behaviorism through his examination of operant behavior and reinforcement. *Operant behavior* is any behavior that *operates on the environment* in such a way as to produce some consequence or change in the environment. For example, smiling at others as we encounter them may generally result in their smiling back and greeting us. In this example, smiling at others is an operant behavior. *Reinforcement* is the process in which a consequence or change in the environment strengthens the *future* probability of a particular behavior. For example, if whenever we smile at strangers, they smile back and are friendly, this may increase the probability that we will smile at strangers in the future. A good illustration is provided by Benjamin Franklin. Two centuries ago a minister on a ship complained to Franklin that the sailors rarely attended prayer meetings. Franklin suggested that the minister take charge of passing out the daily ration of rum and dispense it immediately after the prayers. The minister did what Franklin recommended, and "never were prayers more generally and more punctually attended" (Franklin, 1969).

Social Learning Theory

In 1941, psychologists Neil Miller and John Dollard reported a series of experiments which showed that imitation among humans was not caused by instinct or biological programming. Miller and Dollard's studies indicated that we *learn* to imitate the behavior of others and that this learning occurs according to the principles of behavioral theory — a process Miller and Dollard called "social learning." Our imitative behavior occurs because we have been rewarded when we imitate and not rewarded (or punished) when we do not. In order to learn the standards prescribed by society, "individuals must be trained, in many situations, so that they will be comfortable when they are doing what others are doing and miserable when they are not" (Miller and Dollard, 1941: 10).

In their experiments, Miller and Dollard showed that children can learn to imitate or not to imitate a person in order to get a reward of candy. The experiments also indicated that children can learn to discriminate between persons and thus imitate one person (e.g., a man) and not imitate another (e.g., a woman). Furthermore, once imitative behavior is learned, this learning sometimes generalizes to similar stimuli. For example, the children were more likely to imitate persons who were similar, rather than dissimilar, in appearance to the individual whom the children were initially rewarded for copying. Thus, we learn many "new" behaviors by repeating behaviors we see others perform. We copy the behavior of certain others because we have been rewarded for imitating those or similar persons in the past.

Twenty years later, psychologists Albert Bandura and Richard Walters (1959, 1963) proposed a revision in Miller and Dollard's ideas about learning through imitation. Bandura and Walters suggested that we learn many behaviors through imitation even *without reinforcement*. We learn some behaviors just by observing how models behave and what consequences an action has for them. Such learning is called *observational learning*. However, whether we actually *perform* a behavior learned through observation is influenced by the consequences we experience for our own performance. For example, experiments by Bandura and Walters indicated that although reinforcement influences children's performance of aggressive behavior, the original learning of such aggression can occur through the children's merely *observing* aggressive models, such as human adults in person or on film or even cartoon figures on film. Similarly, children can learn to inhibit their own aggression by observing inhibition of aggression by models. (Before reading further, see the Student Observation: "Social Learning Theory.")

Bandura (1971) later proposed that social learning theory should be revised even further. This time he suggested that social learning theory abandon the strict behavioral approach, which avoids consideration of unobservable mental processes. He proposed that we might better understand human behavior by taking thinking capacity into account and looking at the *reciprocal* relationship between behavior and the environment. He stated:

> People can represent external influences symbolically [in thought] and later use such representations to guide their actions; they can solve problems symbolically without having to enact various alternatives; and they can foresee the probable consequences of different actions and alter their behavior accordingly. (Bandura, 1971: 2–3)

Thus, Bandura's version of social learning theory examines (1) how our behavior is influenced by our environment through reinforcement and observational learning; (2) the way we perceive and think about this information; and (3), in turn, how our behavior influences our environment to create reinforcement and observational opportunities.

Social Exchange Theory

While Bandura and Walters were developing their ideas about social learning theory, psychologists John Thibaut and Harold Kelley (1959) and sociologists George Homans (1961), Richard Emerson (1962), and Peter Blau (1964) formulated what they called "social exchange theory." According to this theory, we enter into exchange relationships with others because we derive rewards from doing so.

Like Bandura's social learning theory, social exchange theory sees behavior and environment as linked in a reciprocal relationship, each influencing the other. Because our environment usually involves other people, we and these others are viewed as engaging in *reciprocal* behaviors as a

---

STUDENT OBSERVATION

Social Learning Theory

I remember, back when I was nine years old, running around the house making noises, throwing things and generally just getting on my mom's nerves as she was trying to fix dinner. She handled this like all moms do by saying, "Go help your dad; he is in the garage." Of course, when I got down to the garage and found Dad working on the car, he tried to get rid of me too. But I promised I would stay out of his way and just watch, so he let me stay. While he was working under the hood, he stood up straight and smashed his head on the underside of the car hood and guess what he said . . . "Damn!" The next day I was again running through the house (I did that a lot), and I slipped on the kitchen floor and cracked my head on the cabinet, so I appropriately screamed "Damn!" Mom made me wash my mouth out with Ivory soap. I never said "damn" (in front of my mom) again. This is a good example of social learning because I learned to say "damn" from observing my father, but my behavior was altered by the consequence of having to eat soap.

Trying to be the best he can be — a youngster tries to copy the salute of a marine at a Veterans Day service. We learn some behaviors just by observing how models behave and what consequences an action has for them.

consequence of rewards, costs, and profits. *Rewards* are anything that human beings will incur costs to obtain. *Costs* are whatever human beings attempt to avoid. And *profits* are rewards less costs. Thus social behavior consists of an exchange of behaviors between at least two people that is perceived by each person as being more or less rewarding or costly. Such patterns of behavior — which may occur within the context of a job, a love affair, a marriage, a friendship — will continue only if they are profitable to both parties relative to alternative activities.

To illustrate, let us assume that you and I are co-workers. I frequently ask you for advice; you frequently provide it. We are engaged in social exchange. I exchange my approval, recognition, and gratitude for your help. You exchange your help for my approval, recognition, and gratitude. Through this arrangement, we both derive important rewards. But we also experience costs: I suffer in self-esteem; you discover that I interfere with your getting your work done. As long as we both find profit (reward minus cost) in the relationship, we will probably continue it, just as in marketplace decisions. But unless each of us derives a certain minimum benefit, the interaction will cease, and no benefit will come to either of us. (Before reading further, see the Student Observation: "Social Exchange Theory.")

Social learning theory and social exchange theory illustrate the behavioral perspective's primary focus on observable behavior. Although some theorists depart from the most extreme black box approach — which gives *no* attention to mental

STUDENT OBSERVATION

Social Exchange Theory

*I*n my computer science class we have a good many tough assignments. One guy in class, Mike, seems to be quite bright and isn't at all reluctant to let everyone know that he's got the "smarts." In fact, he showboats all over the place, and he has succeeded in alienating a lot of us. By the end of the first week of classes, another guy, Dave, managed to take over the seat next to Mike. Dave made it a practice to "ego massage" Mike before classes, and soon Mike was letting Dave copy his homework. The copying went on well into the third week. Then yesterday we got back our latest homework assignment, and Mike had 5 points taken off because he had allegedly copied the work from Dave. Mike was furious and told Dave to go see the instructor and own up. But Dave told Mike to take a "flying jump," and the relationship has now ended. Here is a good illustration of social exchange theory. Each individual got something from the relationship: Mike got an ego massage, and Dave got homework. But when the cost became too high for Mike (and for Dave, had he owned up to his copying Mike's homework), the relationship blew apart.

processes — all theories influenced by this perspective emphasize the relationship between directly observable behavior and the environment.

THE COGNITIVE PERSPECTIVE

Let's go back again to the turn of the century, when social psychology was just beginning to develop. We have already indicated that a habit explanation had been touted as an alternative to the dominant instinct explanation of social behavior, particularly for imitative behavior. But some social analysts believed that both the instinct and the habit explanations were too extreme — ignoring humans' mental activities.

Psychologist James Baldwin (1897) proposed that there are at least two forms of imitation — one based on our habits (nondeliberative) and the other based on our insight into what we and the person we are imitating are doing (deliberative). Echoing Baldwin's observations, sociologist Charles Cooley (1902) proposed a distinction between "suggestion" and "choice." Suggestion referred to comparatively mechanical or habitual actions elicited by a person. In contrast, choice referred to "an elaborate process of mental organization or synthesis" resulting, Cooley felt, from the complex social relations that typify modern society. Baldwin and Cooley focused their attention on social behavior that involved mental, or *cognitive*, activity (deliberation or choice).

Soon, many social psychologists settled on the concept of *attitude* to identify this deliberative mental activity. For example, in their 1918 study of Polish peasants, sociologists W. I. Thomas and Florian Znaniecki defined social psychology as the study of "attitudes," by which they meant the individual mental processes that determine both the actual and the potential responses of each person in the social world. "Preliminary to any self-determined act of behavior," Thomas pointed out, "there is always a stage of examination and deliberation which we may call the definition of the situation" (1937: 42). Such definitions influence our behavior: "If human beings define situations as real, they are real in their consequences" (Thomas, 1931: 189). World War I provided an impetus to the adoption of the concept of attitude. Patriotism, propaganda, and prejudice became particularly fascinating to social psychologists. By 1935, George Gallup had begun his Gallup Poll to regularly survey American public opinion.

Field Theory

Psychologist Kurt Lewin (1935, 1936) fled to the United States during Hitler's rise. Lewin's approach was based on the concept of *field*, or "life space." Traditionally, psychologists had focused on the characteristics of individuals (instincts and habits) relatively independently of the situations in which the individuals were operating. But, according to Lewin, explanations of behavior that do not take the immediate situation into account are incomplete. He felt that all psychological events, be they acting, thinking, dreaming, hoping, or whatever, are a function of *life space* — the person *and* the environment viewed as one constellation of interdependent forces. Life space consists of all past, present, and future events, since all three aspects of life can influence behavior in any single situation.

One of Lewin's most famous studies concerned behavior in various kinds of leadership environments (Lewin, Lippitt, and White, 1939). The study looked at the effects of democratic and authoritarian leadership on the productiveness and behavior of a group of boys. Authoritarian leadership was found to be accompanied by high levels of frustration and some degree of aggression toward the leader. When the leader was present, productivity was high; when he was absent, it was low. In contrast, democratic leadership was associated with greater individual happiness, more group-minded activity, greater productivity (especially in the leader's absence), and fewer aggressive displays.

During World War II, Lewin embarked on a series of studies to investigate ways of persuading homemakers to use unusual but edible foods (such as kidney, tongue, and brain) to conserve resources for the war effort. People's eating habits, he discovered, were more effectively changed when information was given to them through group discussion and group decision procedures than when it was presented in a lecture format. Again, *situation* made a difference.

Attitude Consistency and Attribution Theories

Hitler and World War II also brought to the United States another psychologist — Fritz Heider (1946, 1958). Heider proposed that we tend to organize our attitudes so that they are not in conflict. For example, if we favor abortion rights and like other people who also support this position, our attitudes are consistent, or "balanced." Heider suggested that when we find our attitudes to be inconsistent or imbalanced (for example, we favor abortion rights, but our best friend opposes abortion under any circumstances), we feel stress and discomfort and, consequently, seek to reconcile our conflicting attitudes in order to restore a state of consistency. For example, we may decide that we don't feel strongly about our support of abortion rights or that our best friend really isn't our *best* friend. (Before reading further, see the Student Observation: "Balance Theory.")

Heider also proposed that we organize our thoughts in terms of cause and effect. In order to carry on our activities and fit our actions to those around us, we interpret information to decide what caused the behavior of ourselves and others. In everyday life, we typically distinguish between two types of causation — internal and external. *Internal causality* involves attributing responsibility for events to the personal qualities and traits of the individual. *External causality* involves attributing responsibility for events to environmental and situational circumstances that lie outside the individual. For example, we may attribute the friendliness of a new acquaintance to her genuine liking for us (internal) or to an effort to get us to join her organization (external). Or we may attribute the A we received on an important exam to our own intelligence (internal) or to the professor's being an easy grader (external). During the 1950s and 1960s, social psychologists, primarily in psychology, expanded Heider's basic ideas about attitude consistency and causal attribution.

A Social Learning Theory of Attitudes

We noted previously that Albert Bandura modified social learning theory, a behavioral perspective, by incorporating some ideas from the cognitive perspective. Our behavior, he suggested, is influenced by reinforcement, imitation, *and* cognition. Psychologist Carl Hovland and his

---

STUDENT OBSERVATION

Balance Theory

I used to despise country music. In high school, one of my teachers tried to get our class to listen to country music and learn to appreciate it. No way. I listened, but still hated it. However, when I got to college, a girl on my hall loved country music. We became fast friends, and our only point of disagreement was musical taste. The closer Alice and I became, the more out of balance my attitude toward country music was. By the end of the semester, I began to listen to country music and even started to enjoy it. I changed my attitude to be in balance with my positive feelings toward Alice and her positive attitude toward country music. As balance theory points out, I did not alter my attitude when my high school teacher liked country music because I did not care much about her. However, when a close friend liked country music, I changed my attitude to restore balance.

---

associates (1953) revised learning theory even further — proposing that our attitudes are learned in much the same way as our behavior — following the principles of behaviorism. We learn to associate a particular stimulus with certain information and feelings. For example, you probably have unpleasant feelings toward poor grades. If you consistently receive such grades from a particular professor, you may mentally "transfer" these negative feelings to the professor. Consequently, for you, seeing the professor may evoke unpleasant feelings. Alternatively, your negative attitude toward your professor may have been learned through reinforcement — for example, your friends may agree with you whenever you express dislike toward the professor — or you may simply be imitating your friends' negative attitudes.

Contemporary Cognitive Theory

Beginning in the 1980s, the concept of *cognition* largely preempted the concept of attitude. The term "cognition" is used to refer to all the mental processes that transform sensory input in some meaningful fashion — processes that code, elaborate, store, retrieve, and appropriately use it. Contemporary cognitive theorists view people as active agents in receiving, using, manipulating, and transforming information. We engage in thinking, planning, problem solving, and decision making — mentally manipulating images, symbols, and ideas.

The primary focus of contemporary cognitive theorists is on how we mentally represent social knowledge (Markus and Zajonc, 1985; Morgan and Schwalbe, 1990; Fiske and Taylor, 1991). The human organism processes information in such a way that an image, a symbol, or an idea comes to stand for something else, for instance, an act, an object, an emotion, a sound, or an internal state. Information is processed by some type of internal, or mental, structure — termed a *cognitive structure* or *schema* — that receives and organizes it. Such structures are organized stores of information (mental representations) that we have developed as a result of prior information processing. They operate as frameworks for interpreting our current social experiences. These structures simplify perceptual inputs that would otherwise overwhelm us by their volume and complexity. And the structures fill in where there is too little information from the environment, allowing us to make sense of otherwise ambiguous situations. Thus cognitive structures help us achieve some coherence in our environment, and they assist us in the construction of social reality. Our memory systems are assumed to contain countless knowledge structures.

Cognitive theories share a focus on how we mentally structure and process information coming from the environment. We can't understand social behavior, according to the cognitive perspective, without getting reliable information about these processes. Information about the objective, external environment is not enough.

THE STRUCTURAL PERSPECTIVE

Let's return again to the turn of the century to trace the development of still another social psychological perspective. We have noted that social scientists at that time were debating the relative contributions of instinct, habit, and mental processes to the explanation of social behavior. They were interested in the best way to describe the relationship between society and individuals. Scholars such as William James and John Dewey emphasized the habit explanation, but they also noted that individual habits reflect collective habits—the customs of a society or group—or *social structure*. As sociologists conceive of social structure, it consists of the interweaving of people's interactions and relationships in recurrent and stable ways. We "inherit" social structure in that patterns of behavior are handed down from one generation to the next—but, in this case, through socialization instead of genes. By virtue of social structure, we experience social life as orderly and patterned. James described the important impact of social structure on *self*—our feelings about ourselves. Society's influence on self, he believed, results from our reflecting on how others feel about us.

Sociologist Robert Park studied under both James and Dewey and later became a professor at the University of Chicago. In Park's view, society organizes, integrates, and directs the energies of individuals composing it. It is in *roles*, he suggested, that we come to know ourselves. We are parents and children, teachers and students, men and women, Christians and Jews. Our conceptions of ourselves are dependent on the roles we perform, which in turn are built upon society's definitions of these roles.

During World War I, many Americans were surprised to learn that European immigrants had very different life styles and customs from those of other Americans. Some demanded that immigrants, particularly German-Americans, be instantly "Americanized." However, others recognized that this could endanger Americans' traditional civil liberties. As part of a series of "Americanization studies," Park directed a study of the foreign-language press (1922) that demonstrated how these papers helped many immigrants adjust to the new roles they encountered in American society.

Role Theory

Although Park explained the impact of society on our behavior in terms of roles, it was left to anthropologist Robert Linton (1936) to develop a role theory. *Role theory* portrays social interaction in terms of actors who play their assigned parts in accordance with a script specified by culture. According to this theory, role expectations are shared understandings that tell us what actions we can anticipate from one another as we go about our daily activities. By virtue of roles, we mentally classify people on the basis of their common attributes, their common behavior, or the common reactions they elicit. Thus, we collapse or telescope a range of behaviors into manageable bundles, specifying who does what, when, and where. In sum, roles specify the social expectations that apply to the behavior of specific categories of people in particular situational contexts (e.g., doctors, students, uncles, elderly women, neighbors, shoppers).

Later, sociologist Glen Elder (1975) helped expand the use of role theory. His *life-course* approach emphasized that all societies have role expectations that classify individuals into age categories, dividing our lives into meaningful stages and establishing timetables for major life events. For example, most of us in the United States become students at age four or five, voters at age eighteen, full-time workers and spouses between ages seventeen and twenty-seven, and retirees at sixty-five. This is called *age grading*. In contem-

All societies have role expectations that classify individuals into age categories, dividing our lives into meaningful stages and establishing timetables for major life events. In contemporary America, our life course is divided into childhood, adolescence, adulthood, and old age, with each stage having various subdivisions.

porary America, our life course is divided into childhood, adolescence, adulthood, and old age, with each stage having various subdivisions.

Expectation-States Theory

While the life-course version of the structural perspective focuses broadly on the impact of society's role expectations on our behavior throughout our lives, expectation-states theory, formulated by sociologist Joseph Berger and his colleagues at Stanford University, focuses more narrowly on the interaction occurring in task groups (Berger, Cohen, and Zelditch, 1972; Berger, Wagner, and Zelditch, 1985; Berger, Fisek, and Norman, 1989). According to this theory, group members form expectations concerning their own and other members' task-relevant abilities, and these expectations affect the members' interaction styles. Of course, the attributes most strongly affecting performance expectations are those directly related to task skill. Members judged to have the motivation and skill necessary to contribute to the accomplishment of the group's task are expected to perform well.

However, we often lack information about task-relevant abilities, and even when we have such information, it appears that we *also* base our expectations on personal attributes of group members, such as sex, race, and age. In our society, some personal attributes are more highly valued than others: being a male (versus a female), a white (versus a black or a Hispanic), and an adult (versus a child). Berger calls these "diffuse status characteristics." These status characteristics affect performance expectations in many different circumstances. Group members with highly valued status characteristics are expected to make greater contributions to the group's task. High-status members are given and take more opportunities to contribute to task solutions; that is, they often assume leadership positions. The contributions of high-status members are also more likely to be valued by other group members. Diffuse status characteristics such as sex, race, and age therefore have a powerful influence on social interaction and the rewards that social groups base on perceived competence.

Postmodernism

Both role theory and expectation-states theory explain social behavior in terms of society's *contemporary* role expectations. Other social psychologists seek a more *historical* explanation. Postmodernism theory, for example, proposes that during the course of the twentieth century, members of the modern world have gradually lost their individuality—their autonomous selves, self-concepts, or real selves (Denzin, 1986; Murphy, 1989; Dowd, 1991; Gergen, 1991). In this view, our efforts to fulfill the roles assigned to us by society have resulted in the replacement of our more enduring individuality by a collection of *self-images*, each of which we wear for a while and then discard. "Under postmodern conditions, persons exist in a state of continuous construction and reconstruction; it is a world where anything goes that can be negotiated" (Gergen, 1991: 7).

According to postmodernism, the gradual erosion of individuality coincided with the rise of capitalism and rationality. These factors, postmodernists argue, reduced the importance of personal relationships and emphasized impersonal aspects. Capitalism, according to this view, caused people to be viewed as commodities—valued on a common yardstick according to what they could produce. After World War II, people increasingly came to be viewed as consumers as well as producers. The advertising industry and the mass media created commercial images that reduced individual diversity to a few common denominators: personalities became styles. People are increasingly judged, postmodernists suggest, by how well they copy a style. What we consider "our own autonomous choices" of music, food, clothes, and so forth, are actually a set of acquired cultural preferences compatible with our place in the economic structure of our society.

Role, expectation-states, and postmodernism theories illustrate the structural perspective's focus on the influence of societal expectations on social behavior. According to this perspective, social structure—recurrent patterns of interaction—largely *constrains* and shapes individual behavior. In this view, individuals play a relatively passive part in determining their behavior. Instead, they are *acted upon* by structural forces to which they react in fairly predictable ways.

THE INTERACTIONIST PERSPECTIVE

At the same time that Robert Park was teaching sociology at the University of Chicago, George Herbert Mead (1934) was teaching a course in social psychology in the university's philosophy department. Mead believed that our membership within a social group produces common, shared behaviors — a culture. At the same time, he recognized that individuals who hold different positions within the group have different roles and that the particular role we take on creates differences in our behavior. For example, leaders behave differently than followers. In this respect, Mead was a structuralist. But he opposed the view that our behavior is a result of *only* our environment — whether our environment is a stimulus (according to the behavioral perspective) or the greater society (according to the structural perspective). To the contrary, Mead believed that we have some say in which parts of the environment we pay attention to; in essence, we help *create* our environment. Moreover, he noted that although we are aware of our community's standards (common attitudes), this does not mean that we will behave in conformity to them. For example, a baseball player knows that his team expects him to field a ball hit in his direction, but it may be hard to predict whether he will make a brilliant play or an error.

Although they were good friends, Mead disagreed with John Watson's version of behaviorism, which dealt only with *external*, observable behavior. Instead, Mead took a behavioristic view of *internal* behavior, seeing attitudes as physiological responses of our internal central nervous system and, therefore, just as real and worthy of study as our external behavior. Because he was interested in the behaviors (internal and external) of two or more *interacting* individuals, he called his behaviorism "social behaviorism."

Symbolic Interaction Theory

Mead wasn't particularly interested in behavior

that failed to include conscious thought (internal behavior). He was most interested in those interactions in which the connection between a particular gesture and its meaning may become a matter of the parties' thoughts. For example, a professor decides that she will accuse a student of cheating; but because the accusation should deter him from future cheating, she will not pursue further disciplinary action. She is conscious of the meaning of her own behavior. The student may also believe that if the professor confronts him about his cheating, she will not pursue further disciplinary action.

In this instance, both the student and the professor share similar meanings of the professor's initial accusation. In Mead's terminology, a gesture whose meaning is shared by those involved in the interaction is a "significant symbol." Words and other vocal sounds, physical movements and body language, clothing, and social roles (e.g., professor, student, mother) can all serve as significant symbols. (Before reading further, see the Student Observation: "Symbols.")

Mead was interested in social *interaction* in which two or more persons present potentially significant *symbols* to each other — thus the designation of his proposals as *symbolic interaction theory*. Instead of focusing on one person as being the cause of another's behavior, this theory views both parties as influencing one another. In its emphasis on the *reciprocal* nature of interaction, symbolic interaction theory is similar to social exchange theory.

The interaction in the above example was unproblematic in that the parties shared the same meanings for their various gestures, and, therefore, their interaction proceeded smoothly. This probably results from their being members of the same culture or having previously resolved any differences in the meanings. But interaction may not always occur as smoothly as in the example. Parties to an interaction may not be using gestures that are significant symbols; that is, the parties may not share the same meanings for certain gestures. Consequently, people must continually fashion meanings and devise ways to fit their actions together. Much of human behavior has a

---

STUDENT OBSERVATION

Symbols

It seems like the better you know a person, the more symbols you come to share. Kim was one of the first people I met when I came to college. Before too long, Kim and I had practically created our own language. We made up new words for things or assigned new meanings to preexisting words. Now, two years later, Kim and I have so many "inside references" that many times a third listener has no idea what we're talking about.

If we liked a particular guy, we'd call him our "ultimate" (the *ultimate* love of my life). After designating our "ultimates," we would seldom use their proper names when talking about them. If an extremely good-looking guy passed by, we'd probably watch him pass and then declare him "malignant." This one word sums up a large train of thought. The popular term for an attractive person these days is "hot." What is the primary source of heat? The sun. The sun gives off heat along with radiation (Kim and I might say that a good-looking guy "radiates"). If you get too much of this radiation, there is a chance that you will get cancer. What is the term for a cancerous tumor? "Malignant."

These are only a couple of our shared symbols. It would really be impossible to compile a complete list.

---

tentative and developing quality: people map, test, devise, suspend, and revise their overt acts in response to the actions of others. According to this view, individuals *negotiate* interaction as they fit their own behavior to the developing actions of others.

Identity theory. More recently, social psychologist Sheldon Stryker (1980; Stryker and Statham, 1985) has proposed an *identity theory* that focuses on the reciprocal relationship between the individual (and interactions between individuals) and the larger social structure (society). Individuals and society are viewed as "two sides of the same coin."

Stryker believes that whatever the potential of a particular interaction for the creation of novel behaviors, most interactions involve the same or slowly changing sets of individuals doing the same things repeatedly. "Persons do not come together randomly. Nor are the opportunities for, and the circumstances of, social relationships randomly distributed. The person is shaped by interaction, but social structures shape interaction" (Stryker and Statham, 1985: 345). In this sense, Stryker appears to be in agreement with the structural perspective, especially role theory.

But role theory, Stryker suggests, is too insen-sitive to the creativity of individuals seeking solutions to the problems encountered in their interactions with one another. Its conception of individuals and their interactions is too deterministic — "oversocialized" — suggesting that we behave largely according to our culture's scripts. While cultural expectations are important, Stryker notes, we still have considerable latitude in constructing our interactions with others.

Stryker's theory combines the concepts of role from role theory and self from symbolic interaction theory. For each role that we perform in our interactions with others, we have a distinct definition of ourselves, which Stryker calls an "identity." If we assume many roles, we have many identities. Our behavior in a particular interaction is influenced by role expectations and our own identities, as well as by the behavior of those with whom we are interacting.

Everyday understandings and the dramaturgical school. Erving Goffman (1959, 1963a, 1971, 1981) received his Ph.D. in sociology from the University of Chicago in 1953. His major contribution was to draw our attention to the implicit understandings of face-to-face, everyday interaction, what he called "conventions" or "routines." Like the formal expectations of social institutions studied by Stryker, these implicit understandings influence our behavior. Sometimes when we violate these understandings, other understandings influence us to engage in some kind of "repair work." For example, a belch or sneeze requires an apology. Cutting in front of someone standing in line or failing to reciprocate an invitation to dinner may also represent breeches of common understandings.

Frequently, these understandings, or routines, are so taken for granted that we aren't consciously aware of them. In other instances, our conscious *interpretation* of particular events is shaped by these understandings. In Goffman's terms, the cultural understanding provides a "frame" for our interpretation. We examine our experience, judging our own behavior as well as the behavior of others, in light of such frames.

Goffman also sees us as active agents in creating particular interpretations. We are not assigned a particular role by our cultural script. Rather, we actually *select* a role from among several choices in order to achieve our own goals. Although he adopted the concept of role, Goffman used the term to focus upon the ways that we ("actors") manipulate gestures to create impressions of ourselves ("roles") in a particular social situation ("scene"). These terms suggest the source of the name given to Goffman's brand of interactionism: the *dramaturgical school* (Goffman, 1967).

If, as symbolic interactionists believe, social interaction is based on gestures and the meanings they convey, then we possess the potential for manipulating various aspects of our performances in order to produce an outcome we desire. Although we have ideas about who and what we are, we also have ideas about ourselves that we seek to present to others. On some occasions these are one and the same (the authentic self); on other occasions they are different (fabrication). Goffman used the term "impression management" to refer to our efforts to affect others' impressions by presenting gestures that will lead them to act in accordance with our plans (Goffman, 1959, 1963a, 1971, 1981). (Before reading further, see the Student Observation: "Impression Management.")

There are some limits, Goffman acknowledged, on our ability to choose roles during our interactions with others. For one, our selection is constrained by our interpretation of "what's going on" in an interaction with others. Our interpretation is influenced by the behavior of others who are engaged in trying to manage *our* impressions of *them*. When we are interacting with someone with whom we have an established relationship, our role selection is also constrained by our previous selection of roles, as well as by the bonds that tie us to the relationship.

Ethnomethodology

Sociologist Harold Garfinkel (1967) and some of his colleagues and students evolved an approach to social phenomena that they term "ethnomethodology." *Ethno*, borrowed from the Greek,

STUDENT OBSERVATION

Impression Management

This past weekend I attended a beach retreat with a religious campus group. During my time with those people, I never openly used profanity, made an off-color remark, or displayed any prejudiced attitudes. I was open, friendly, humble, and reverent. When I returned home to my not-so-religious roommate, I soon joined right in with his profanity. When I went to class the next day, I paid close attention to the professor and did not socialize with my peers. When I worked last night for a fund-raising telephone campaign, I used a pleasant, enthusiastic voice and attended to my conversations very closely and listened actively. In each of these situations I was attempting to manipulate a certain perception of me in others to fit the circumstances for my personal gain.

Our ideas about who and what we are do not always match the image of ourselves that we seek to present to others. We possess the potential for manipulating various aspects of our performances in order to produce an outcome we desire. Such attempts to affect others' impressions are known as impression management.

means "people" or "folk" and is used in the formation of compound words such as "ethnomedicine," "ethnobotany," and "ethnophysics." Anthropologists commonly use such terms to refer to a people's folk beliefs and practices. For instance, ethnomedicine has to do with the explanations that a particular people advance for illness and the remedies they employ. *Methodology* concerns procedures by which something is done or analyzed. Hence, *ethnomethodology* in its most literal sense refers to the activities and mental procedures people employ in making social life and society intelligible and understandable to themselves. Ethnomethodologists are particularly concerned with the methods we use to produce and sustain a sense of order and structure — the process by which we go about "structuring" structure through our interpretations and behavior.

Ethnomethodologists emphasize the methods whereby individuals construct *interpretations* of social interaction. In this respect, ethnomethodologists bear some kinship to those social psychologists who advocate the cognitive perspective. But unlike cognitive social psychologists, ethnomethodologists emphasize the *similarity* between the interpretations of social psychologists and the interpretations of the people studied by social psychologists. People (social

psychologists and others alike) work together to construct ideas about the enduring and orderly features of human behavior. We try to explain (offer reasons for or interpret the "causes" of) people's behavior using terms such as "heredity," "role expectations," "social structure," "personality," and "the real self." According to ethnomethodologists, social psychological theories, like folk theories, are only interpretations — socially constructed and designed to bring some order to our social lives. For example, we construct distinctions between persons being "responsible" or "not responsible" for their behavior. We even distinguish between true reasons (the "real reason") and false reasons (a "rationalization" or an "excuse") people offer for their behavior (Coulter, 1989).

According to ethnomethodologists, the formal rules and roles emphasized by the structural perspective provide inadequate guidelines for our behavior. We are presented with too wide a range of situations for such rules to encompass. Instead, we *actively work to produce* a sense of order and normality by negotiating (constructing) informal rules with others. This may even involve using formal rules in ways other than those intended. For example, we may use a formal rule to justify behavior that we arrived at through an entirely different set of rules that are not explicit (Maynard and Clayman, 1991). Police officers and other justice officials, for instance, may arrest and officially process a youth who appears to them to have insufficient adult supervision, while merely warning a youth whose family the officials judge to be responsible and in control — even though both have committed the same "delinquent" act. This informal standard of judgment may not be among the formally recognized standards for making such decisions. It may even be formally disapproved. But the officials may use it anyway and then use officially recognized standards — such as the demeanor of the youth when apprehended — to *justify* their decision.

Symbolic interactionism and ethnomethodology illustrate the interactionist perspective's focus on the active part that people play in determining their own behavior and establishing social expectations. While the perspective does not deny the influence of social structure, it views social structure as an inadequate explanation of social behavior — one insufficiently sensitive to the creativity of individuals seeking to work through the problems they encounter in everyday social interaction.

THEORETICAL OVERVIEW

Let's take a break here to summarize the information presented so far. We have discussed four perspectives in social psychology. A perspective specifies the most basic assumptions that support a particular approach to social psychology; it suggests what is important and interesting to study and gives some basic ideas about how to explain those phenomena. The behavioral and cognitive perspectives differ in their emphasis on observable behavior or mental activity as the key to explaining social behavior. The *behavioral perspective* suggests that our social behavior can be best understood by focusing on directly observable behavior and the environment that causes our behavior to change. The *cognitive perspective* explains our social behavior by focusing on how we mentally structure and process information coming from our environment. The structural and inter-

actionist perspectives differ in their views of the relative importance of social structure and individuals as active agents in shaping social behavior. The *structural perspective* focuses on socialization — how our behavior and views are shaped by the multiple and changing roles prescribed by our society. And finally, the *interactionist perspective* focuses on how we negotiate with others to construct our interactions.

Each of these four perspectives has its own definition of social psychology that reflects the unique aspects of the particular perspective. Here we will try to cast a net large enough to cover all of them by defining *social psychology* as the study of the behaviors, thoughts, and feelings of an individual or interacting individuals and of their relationships with larger social units. This definition is also broad enough to include both those social psychologists who identify primarily with sociology and those who identify primarily with psychology. In sociology departments, social psychologists are distinguished from other sociologists by interests that include separate individuals. Other sociologists are interested only in social units that lump individuals together — groups, institutions, and societies. In psychology departments, social psychologists are distinguished from other psychologists by their exclusive focus on social behavior or the social environment.

The details of many social psychological theories will become clearer as we encounter them in the chapters to come. Before proceeding, however, it might be a good idea to pause and respond to the questions students often raise about theories: "Which theory is correct?" or "Which theory is the best?" In all candor, many social psychologists would answer that none of these theories is necessarily correct, wrong, better, or worse. Theories are simply *tools* — mental constructs that allow us to visualize, describe, and analyze social life. By its nature, a theory limits the viewer's experience, presenting a tunnel perspective. But a good theory also extends the vision of what *is* seen, much as a pair of binoculars helps us focus on a part of the landscape.

Different theories draw our attention to different aspects of the same phenomenon. In studying aggression, for instance, a behaviorist might focus on the learning experiences that reinforce aggressive behavior — on how parents, teachers, coaches, and others unwittingly reward a person for aggressive behavior. Cognitive social psychologists might be interested in how people perceive, interpret, and think about aggressive behavior. Social psychologists using field theory might concern themselves with the interplay between an individual's characteristics and features of the situation that activate aggressive behavior. Social exchange theorists might focus on the social rewards people gain by using aggression. Role theorists might be drawn to the social expectations that specify aggressive or nonaggressive behaviors for persons in particular social positions. Symbolic interactionists might consider the social meanings individuals assign to their acts as they contend against one another and go about formulating their courses of action. And ethnomethodologists might examine the methods people employ in interpreting aggression and applying certain rules to specific acts of aggression.

Each approach, then, offers a somewhat different insight. Moreover, each theory provides a more effective approach, a better "fit," to *certain* kinds of data — *certain* aspects of behavior — than the other theories do. Consequently, the fact that one theory has merit does not necessarily preclude the accuracy of another theory in explaining given data or predicting given outcomes. Indeed, each theory is useful because it presents us with one piece of information in the exceedingly complex puzzle of human behavior.

Methods of Social Psychological Study

Science presupposes the existence of an empirical world; it rests on the assumption that a universe prevails apart from our experience of it. Since this universe has a real existence, it must be knowable. The task of science is to make the world intelligible to us. Scientists undertake to fathom and depict, to detect and establish, the *what is*. Theories are one side of the scientific endeavor. Social psychological theories provide alternative summaries and interpretations of information (data) about our behavior, attitudes, and feelings. But where do the data come from? The answer is **research methods** — procedures for acquiring and analyzing information (Babbie, 1992; Frankfort-Nachmias and Nachmias, 1992). Thus, methods are another tool of social psychological research.

The relationship between theory and methods involves two processes — induction and deduction. *Induction* begins with concrete, specific observations and seeks to identify general principles governing what is being observed. For example, you might observe that students tend to sit in the same general area of a classroom each class period, and you might try to determine the ways in which students who sit near the back differ from those who sit near the front. *Deduction*, in contrast, begins with general principles — sometimes in the form of a theory — and uses observation as a way to test the validity of the general principles. It does this by developing from the general principles *hypotheses*, or expectations about what should be observed. The hypotheses are compared to actual observations to see whether they are supported or refuted. For example, we may suspect that students' behavior is determined largely by the relative importance of their student versus partygoer identities. This would lead us to hypothesize that those for whom it is more important to "be a good student" will be more likely to sit near the front of the class than those for whom it is more important to "be well-liked and sociable." To test our hypothesis, we would need to observe where individuals sat in class over several class periods and also to measure the relative importance of their student versus partygoer identities.

Inductive and deductive processes, applied to the same topic in numerous studies, lead to the refinement of theory. Observations may lead to theory, which produces hypotheses, which are tested through observation, which leads to refinements of the theory, which lead to modified expectations, more tests, and so on. We've discussed a number of theories that guide social psychological research. Let's turn now to a discussion of three major methods employed by social psychologists: experiments, field research, and surveys.

EXPERIMENTS

By far the most frequently used method employed by social psychologists is the **experiment**. An experiment is a study in which the investigator manipulates one or more factors within a situation and measures subsequent changes in other factors. The experiment constitutes the most effective method of testing a hypothesis that one variable (x) causally influences another variable (y). The logic behind an experiment is this: If in the presence of variable x certain changes occur in another variable, y, and if these changes in y do not occur in the absence of variable x (all other or extraneous elements having been controlled so that they do not intervene), then the changes in y must be due to variable x.

In an experiment, investigators try to discover whether a relationship exists between two specific variables (x and y). First, they systematically vary the first variable (x). Second, they observe the effects of such variation on the second variable (y). We refer to the manipulated factor as the **independent variable** (x); it is independent of what the subject or subjects do. The independent variable is assumed to be the causal factor or determining condition in the relationship being studied. We call the affected factor — the one that occurs or changes as a result of such manipulation — the **dependent variable** (y); it is usually some measure of the subject's or subjects' behavior. If, for example, students talk noisily when the teacher is out of the classroom but become quiet when he or she enters, the change in the level of the classroom noise (the dependent variable) is caused by the teacher's presence or absence (the independent variable).

Laboratory Experiments

Most social psychological experiments are carried out in specially constructed facilities — equipped with one-way mirrors, communication systems, computers, or other devices and located in a uni-

versity or a research institute — and hence are called **laboratory experiments**. A laboratory allows the investigator to control conditions more carefully and to take measurements more precisely than is commonly possible in real-world settings. A good illustration of a laboratory experiment is one conducted by sociologists Dawn Robinson and Lynn Smith-Lovin (1992). The researchers were interested in this question: "In selecting interaction partners, are we more likely to choose someone who has previously provided feedback which (1) *enhanced* or (2) *confirmed* our self-image?" Of particular interest was the choice that would be made by those who have a negative picture of themselves (low self-esteem). Their options were positive feedback (which does not match their picture of themselves) and negative feedback (which does). What choice would they make? The researchers hypothesized that we will choose to interact with those who provide us with information that best *confirms* our own image of ourselves — even if that image is negative.

The experimental subjects were seventy-eight undergraduate students who volunteered to participate in the study in exchange for extra course credit. The experimental setting was a large, comfortable room with two one-way mirrors on one wall. Next to the experimental room, on the other side of the one-way mirrors, were two connecting rooms, each with a view of the experimental room.

Subjects were told that the purpose of the study was to compare the accuracy of first impressions based on nonverbal cues with the accuracy of first impressions based on verbal cues. They were asked to fill out "background information sheets" that included a measure of self-esteem. Next, each subject was asked to deliver a prepared speech (a passage from *Jonathan Livingston Seagull*) and told that he or she would be watched and evaluated by two observers from behind the one-way mirrors, who would be able to see, but not hear, the subject. The subject was told that after the speech he or she would be allowed to see the ratings of both observers.

After the speech, the experimenter told the subject about the second phase of the experiment, which was said to involve a study of the accuracy of first impressions that are based on verbal behavior. The experimenter explained that the subject would be asked to hold with another student a conversation that would be tape-recorded for analysis at another time. Then the experimenter left the experimental room and returned with two rater-feedback summary sheets, presumably from the observers who had watched from behind the mirrors. In actuality, the feedback sheets constituted the manipulation of the independent variable in the study—enhancing or confirmatory feedback. They were prepared ahead of time and were the same for all subjects. On the positive feedback sheet, rater A characterized the subject as high on social expertise, communication skills, and confidence and slightly less high on interpersonal sensitivity and leadership ability. The subject was described as poised, graceful, and at ease in social situations. On the negative-feedback sheet, rater B characterized the subject as low on leadership ability, communication skills, and confidence. The subject was described as nervous, uncomfortable, and probably awkward around groups of people.

The subject was allowed to read both feedback sheets. Then the experimenter offered the subject a choice:

> In this part of the study we will be audiotaping a conversation between you and another participant to be rated at a future time by different raters who have not been exposed to your nonverbal behavior. I am going to ask one of the raters to come in and serve as a participant in this second part of the study. Because we will be using the tape to generate a second set of first impressions of you, I would like you to choose the rater that you would be most comfortable talking with for the next few minutes. (Robinson and Smith-Lovin, 1992: 23–24)

So which of the raters did the subjects choose to interact with? Remember, the researchers' hypothesis was that subjects would choose the rater who provided feedback *consistent* with the subject's self-esteem. For high-self-esteem subjects, this would be the positive rater (A); for low-self-

esteem subjects, it would be the negative rater (B). So the researchers divided the subjects into three categories based on their responses to the self-esteem measure. They determined that there were twenty-four subjects with high self-esteem, forty-five subjects with moderate self-esteem, and nine with low self-esteem. The analysis showed that the rater who provided negative feedback was, indeed, much more likely to be chosen by subjects with low self-esteem (89 percent) than by subjects with moderate self-esteem (24 percent) or high self-esteem (33 percent). Thus, the findings supported the researchers' initial hypothesis that we select as interaction partners those whose feedback matches the way we view ourselves.

It is important to note that following each subject's choice of an interaction partner, the subject was *debriefed*; that is, the true nature and purpose of the experiment was explained. Debriefing is an important aspect of experimentation, because when it is done effectively, it minimizes potential negative effects that subjects may experience.

Field Experiments

Sometimes a creative and imaginative experimenter uses the "real world" as a laboratory; he or she is conducting a **field experiment**. In field experiments, the researcher introduces the independent variable into a natural setting to determine its impact on behavior. Sociologists Sandra Ball-Rokeach, Milton Rokeach, and Joel Grube (1984) conducted a very ambitious field experiment. Their study was designed to test the hypothesis that if we are faced with information suggesting that our specific behaviors and beliefs are inconsistent with our view of ourselves as competent and moral people, we will change our behavior or beliefs to be more consistent with our view of ourselves. Specifically, the researchers had two questions: (1) Could they influence people's behavior by exposing them to information suggesting that particular behaviors are more consistent with being a moral and competent person? (2) Could this effect be achieved by providing the information through television?

The researchers started with the idea that most Americans view themselves as good and competent people and, therefore, would want to align themselves with such socially desirable values as regard for "a world of beauty," as opposed to such less socially desirable values as concern with "a comfortable life." In order to test their hypothesis, the researchers used television to present information to the people in one community (the experimental group) suggesting that certain (pro-environmental) behaviors were more consistent with valuing "a world of beauty" than with being concerned about "a comfortable life." Another, similar community that did not receive the information served as a control group for comparison purposes. If later behavior measures indicated more pro-environmental behaviors in the experimental community than in the control community, the researchers could conclude that this was probably the result of the information they had presented.

The source of information in the researchers' experiment (the experimental treatment) was a thirty-minute television program entitled "The Great American Values Test," written and produced by the researchers. The program was simultaneously broadcast to people living in the Tri-Cities area of eastern Washington State on the local CBS, NBC, and ABC stations. Thus, this area was the "experimental city," while a similar city nearby, which did not receive the broadcast, was the "control city." The program was co-hosted by actor Ed Asner and Sandy Hill, who at that time was anchorperson of ABC's *Good Morning America* show. Asner opened the program with a voice-over scene of everyday people walking and talking:

These are people. People like you and me. Americans who work, relax, and live life with all of its anxieties and pleasures . . . and all of us, no matter what we do or who we are, have a definite set of human values. For the next 30 minutes, we're going to take a close look at our values. "The Great American Values Test" will help us find out what our own values are and how similar or different they are from

the values of other Americans. (Ball-Rokeach, Rokeach, and Grube, 1984: 73)*

The two values targeted on the program involved the environment and civil rights. For purposes of illustration, we'll discuss only the environment. The first part of the experimental treatment involved Hill's discussion of the results of a national survey of Americans. Here is an excerpt:

Young people start out with a natural appreciation of beauty. But in the process of growing up we somehow knock this appreciation out of them. Eleven year olds rank "a world of beauty" seventh in importance. Fifteen year olds rank it fourteenth. And by the time they reach adulthood, "a world of beauty" has plummeted to seventeenth down the list of importance . . . and there it remains for most adult Americans. [A full-screen graphic of these statistics was shown.] Maybe that explains why so many Americans are willing to live with pollution and ugliness. . . . But the values underlying consumer preferences for cars and other things are now undergoing change. Increasingly, people see conflict between "a comfortable life" and "a world of beauty." Studies show that those unconcerned with the environment rank "a comfortable life" higher than they rank "a world of beauty." But it is the other way around when you survey environmentalists. They rank "a world of beauty" sixth on the average and "a comfortable life" seventeenth. (Ball-Rokeach, Rokeach, and Grube, 1984: 76)*

Asner's concluding remarks included the following comment: "Also, people who prefer products that can be recycled place a higher value on 'a world of beauty.' So do people who favor laws to ban throw-away beverage containers" (Ball-Rokeach, Rokeach, and Grube, 1984: 77).

The researchers divided the respondents into four groups. The first group lived in the control city, where the program had not been broadcast

*From *The Great American Values Test* by Sandra Ball-Rokeach, Milton Rokeach, and Joel Grube. Copyright © 1984 by Sandra Ball-Rokeach, Milton Rokeach, and Joel Grube. Reprinted with the permission of The Free Press, a Division of Macmillan, Inc.

($N = 699$). The other three groups (all from the experimental city) were determined by how they had responded to a telephone interview that immediately followed the broadcast. Trained interviewers (associating themselves with the television station rather than with the specific program) asked each respondent whether he or she had (1) watched the program uninterrupted ($N = 178$), (2) watched only part of the program ($N = 157$), or (3) not watched the program at all ($N = 953$).

Did the television information affect the viewers' pro-environment behaviors? Two to three months after the program aired, a solicitation was mailed to samples of households in the experimental and control cities. The solicitation made no mention of the television program. Included were requests to be put on the organization's mailing list; to agree to vote for a particular pro-environmental bill; and to contribute time, materials, transportation, and money. How did the people of the two cities respond to the solicitation?

Analysis of the results of the solicitation showed that a positive response to the solicitation was obtained from 9 percent of the uninterrupted viewers, 6.4 percent of the interrupted viewers, 5.8 percent of the nonviewers in the experimental city, and 4.2 percent of those from the nonbroadcast control city. Uninterrupted viewers contributed on the average about four to six times as much money as did those in the other groups. Thus, the researchers concluded that this field experiment supported their hypothesis that people's behavior can be influenced by exposing them, via television, to information suggesting that particular behaviors are more consistent with being a moral and competent person.

Laboratory experiments and field experiments offer different advantages. Laboratory experiments offer the researcher a high degree of control over *treatments*, or manipulated variables. They also allow the random assignment of subjects to conditions, thereby increasing the certainty that differences between experimental groups are indeed due to treatments and not to other differences between the groups. Field experiments, on the other hand, facilitate the use of participants other than college students (who are most often the subjects of laboratory experiments), and the experimental situations sometimes better reflect those found in the real world. In addition, researchers may study, under real-life conditions, stressful events that it would be unethical to create within laboratory settings. For example, a field experiment might compare the willingness to donate to a cancer charity of persons who have recently had a relative die of cancer with that of persons who have had no such experience. The experience of having a relative die of cancer might be one of interest to researchers but certainly is not one that can be manipulated in a laboratory.

Problems in Experimentation

Experiments, especially of the laboratory variety, offer substantial advantages over other techniques. Investigators can control outside influences and arrive at causal relationships. But experiments are not without their problems. There are two principal kinds of bias that may intrude into social psychological experiments: bias arising from the demand characteristics of the experiment itself and bias deriving from the unintentional influence of the experimenter.

The bias associated with the *demand characteristics* of the experimental situation (cues that inadvertently guide and direct the responses of a subject) parallels the placebo problem in medical research. Subjects know that they are part of an experiment, that their behavior is being scrutinized, and that certain things are expected from them. "Good subjects" try to figure out the purpose of the research and then undertake to "help" the experimenter by confirming the hypothesis. "Faithful subjects" believe that a high degree of docility is required by research settings and that they should follow experimental instructions scrupulously. "Negativistic subjects" attempt to invalidate or sabotage the experiment. And "apprehensive subjects" worry about the adequacy of their performance and how the experimenter will evaluate their abilities or emotional adjustment. In any of these cases, extraneous considerations intervene to shape the responses of a subject and contaminate the experimental results.

Martin Orne (1962) was one of the first to point out that subjects participating in experimental studies tend to be unusually compliant. In one of his experiments, Orne had the subjects perform psychologically noxious, meaningless, and boring tasks over several hours. Despite the senseless nature of the behavior required of them, the subjects presumably interpreted the experiment as a test of their cooperation and took this fact into account, going to great lengths to behave in a compliant way.

Bias associated with *experimenter effects* concerns distortions in experimental outcomes resulting from the behavior or characteristics of the researcher. Some years ago, Robert Rosenthal (1966) reported on a number of rat experiments he had undertaken with the assistance of student handlers. Rats performed better in carefully controlled tests if their handlers were told, falsely, that the rats had been especially bred for intelligence. The same kind of rats consistently turned in poor performances when the handlers had been told that the rats were dull. Some social psychologists claim that in human experiments somewhat similar contaminating effects are produced by experimenters through subtle body movements, tone of voice, and facial cues (e.g., shifting posture, changing voice intonation while reading directions, or providing a fleeting glance at a critical juncture). Similarly, the age, sex, race, and social status of researchers is thought to affect subjects and their responses.

Various techniques have been employed to minimize experimenter bias. One procedure is to have an assistant who is unaware of the nature of the experiment's hypothesis deal with the subjects and collect data. Of course, this is simply one precaution and not a guarantee of objectivity. (Like subjects, the "blind" experimenter may formulate his or her own hypothesis about the research and unknowingly bias the subjects.) Another procedure is to employ mechanical equipment, such as taped instructions. Yet this technique often depersonalizes the experiment and reduce the subjects' interest and motivation,

merely substituting one type of bias for another type.

Bias may also result from the experimenter's misinterpretation of the data collected. The possibility of misinterpretation can be reduced by obtaining the interpretations of more than one experimenter. Videotape records of behavior are commonly used by social psychologists to allow repeated examination of the behavior under study, in order to reduce the possibility of misinterpretation (Katovich, 1984; Couch, 1987). Thus, researchers need not only to be alert to the problem of bias but also to introduce appropriate measures within the specific context of their experimental situation to control it.

FIELD RESEARCH

At times, researchers undertake intensive observation and recording of people's behavior in a natural setting; this method is known as **field research**. Instead of concentrating on cause-and-effect relationships among a limited number of factors, field researchers attempt to maximize their depth of understanding of a particular social interaction — to capture the details of people's behavior as it spontaneously occurs and to measure the understanding that participants have of the interaction. The approach often entails **participant observation**, a procedure in which the researcher spends a good deal of time actually interacting with the people he or she is studying. Participation may increase the researcher's access to information, particularly detailed or sensitive information. Given that field researchers are not confined by questions on a questionnaire or a specified set of observation categories, they have the flexibility to pursue the leads of the moment. In-depth interviews may be conducted to supplement observations.

But field research also has its problems, particularly if it involves participant observation. As with experimenters, the presence of the observer may unintentionally but subtly modify the behavior of the subjects. And the experience of being a participant probably influences the interpretations of the observer. This does not make the

One of these poker players might actually be a researcher who is studying the group. In participant observation the researcher spends a good deal of time interacting with the people he or she is studying. This method allows access to detailed and sensitive information and provides the flexibility needed to pursue unanticipated leads. However, the presence of the observer may unintentionally modify the behavior of the subjects, and participation may influence the observer's interpretations.

interpretations invalid, but it may make them *different* from those of nonparticipatory observers.

Perhaps the best-known sociological study employing participant observation is William Foote Whyte's *Street Corner Society* (1943). Whyte lived in a lower-class Italian neighborhood of Boston for three and one-half years. For eighteen months he lived with an Italian family to gain an intimate view of family life and to establish contacts within the community. To be able to talk with the first-generation Italian immigrants, Whyte learned their language. He joined the second generation's activities. These included bowling, playing baseball, shooting pool, playing cards, eating and drinking, and otherwise "hanging out" with a group of young men known as "corner boys" and "the Norton gang."

One of the most important of Whyte's findings had to do with the impact of the Norton gang on its members' self-images. Frank, for instance, on the basis of general athletic ability, should have been an excellent bowler (indeed, he had been a semiprofessional baseball player); but he performed poorly when he bowled with the gang. Alex was an outstanding bowler when he played "for the fun of it" on weekday evenings against the members of other groups; but on Saturday nights, when he played with the Norton gang, he

would perform poorly. Why? Whyte discovered that both Frank and Alex ranked low on social status in the Norton gang. For either Frank or Alex to have defeated Doc, Mike, or Danny, who made up the leading clique, would have been viewed as inappropriate. Bowling performance was related to the status the individual held within the group.

Harold Garfinkel (1964, 1967), the ethnomethodologist we mentioned earlier, employed in his studies an interesting variation on observational techniques. He calls his method the *demonstration experiment*. This method entails introducing a "nasty surprise" in a situation or disturbing an interaction to reveal the underlying expectations of which we are normally unaware. Garfinkel disturbed others by simply not performing acts they expected or by performing acts they did not expect. In one experiment he had his students behave as though they were guests in their parents' homes rather than sons or daughters. The students' small acts of kindness and overall politeness were interpreted by their parents as displays of hostility, antagonism, or fatigue. Asking their parents whether they might look in the refrigerator for something to eat or asking permission to eat in the first place generated parental confusion and surprise. Through such methods, Garfinkel seeks to reveal the "background understandings" that are taken for granted in commonplace conversations and interactions.

SURVEYS

Prominent in the social psychological arsenal of methods is the **social survey**, a method of obtaining information using questions in an interview or a written questionnaire. Social psychologists are often interested in obtaining information about such matters as the extent of drug use within a population, the impact of an advertising campaign, the incidence of abortion, political attitudes, the process whereby a new fad is diffused, or public reactions to an assassination. In contrast to experiments and field research, which focus on gathering information as it occurs, surveys frequently ask participants to recall or reconstruct a past event.

Survey researchers use two basic question formats. *Open-ended questions* ask the respondent to provide her or his own answer, while *closed-ended questions* ask the respondent to select an answer from among a list provided by the researcher. A major problem of open-ended questions is that some respondents may give answers that are irrelevant to the researcher's interests. In addition, since several respondents may say basically the same thing in different ways, the researcher must impose some kind of coding or interpretation scheme on the responses in order to summarize them. This can be a time-consuming task. On the other hand, a problem with closed-ended questions is that the researcher's list of possible answers may overlook some important answers or may even be irrelevant to the way the respondent views things.

Survey researchers realize that a respondent's answers to their questions are a result of several factors: (1) the respondent's "true" information (what the researcher really wants to know); (2) the answer the respondent *thinks* the researcher prefers—the "socially desirable answer"; and (3) the wording of the question and the ordering of the questions—which influence the respondent's understanding of the question or way of thinking about the answer. Question wording is very significant. If questions (closed- or open-ended) are vaguely stated, respondents will be uncertain about what is being asked. If questions are too long, respondents might forget what was at the beginning of the question by the time they get to the end. A negative in a question may create a misinterpretation. For example, respondents asked to agree or disagree with the statement, "The Congress should not cut back on defense spending" may read over the word "not." Or respondents may be asked to give a single answer to a combination of questions. For example, they may be asked to agree or disagree with the statement, "The Congress should cut back on defense spending and use that money to support domestic programs." This statement is really two statements (what researchers call "double-barreled"): (1) The Congress should cut back on defense spending, and (2) it should use that money to support domestic programs. A respondent who agrees with one part and disagrees with the other may not be sure how to answer.

Questions that encourage respondents to answer in a particular way are called *biased*. To begin a question with "Don't you agree" is obviously biased. The choice of a single word can affect the responses to a question. For example, more respondents probably would indicate their support for "assistance" to the poor than would support "welfare." Even the order of questions can affect respondents' answers. For example, if an early question asks respondents to indicate their political ideology (e.g., conservative, liberal, libertarian), their answers to later questions may be aimed at being consistent with their earlier answer. Many studies have found that respondents give different answers to the question, "Overall, how happy would you say you are these days?" when they are asked this question by itself (or first in a series of questions) and when they are asked this same question after being asked questions about how satisfied they are with their marriage and family life, their job, their neighborhood, and their health (McClendon and O'Brien, 1988; Schwartz, Strack, and Mai, 1991; Tourangeau, Rasinski, and Bradburn, 1991). Apparently, what happens is that answering all the questions about various aspects of their lives makes respondents think about their happiness more and give greater weight to things that they don't consider when asked the "overall" question alone. This is an example of how question order can affect respondents' answers.

Survey data can be gathered in several ways. People are sometimes interviewed by a researcher who reads them questions from a prepared questionnaire and records their answers. Such *interviews* may occur face-to-face or by telephone. Other surveys are *self-administered*. These are conducted by having individuals fill out a questionnaire (recording their *own* answers) in groups (you may have filled out a questionnaire in one of your classes), individually in the presence of the researcher, or alone. Printed questionnaires are sometimes delivered to respondents through the mail. *Computer-assisted* surveys gather data using a computerized questionnaire. Most often, the interviewer reads questions to the respondent from a computer screen (either face-to-face with the respondent or over the telephone) and records the respondent's answers on the computer. Alternatively, respondents may read the questions from the computer screen themselves and record their own answers.

Each data-gathering technique has it advantages and disadvantages. Generally, self-administered questionnaires are cheaper and quicker than interviews. They may also provide more truthful answers to questions about sensitive issues because of the greater anonymity they offer. Interviews also have their advantages. An interviewer can keep respondents from skipping questions inadvertently. Computer-administered questionnaires have the same advantage. Interviews also afford greater opportunity to deal with complex information as well as with important information that was not anticipated when the questionnaire was originally designed. In other words, they are more flexible. The downside to interviews is that

the appearance and demeanor of interviewers may influence the information they receive from the respondents. As a general rule, interviewers should behave in a pleasant manner that does not suggest a preference for any particular answers to their questions.

Conducting a massive number of interviews or mailing a good many questionnaires, however, is exceedingly expensive and often also impractical. For this reason, social psychologists use *samples* — that is, they question relatively small numbers of people — to arrive at broad generalizations. Similarly, public opinion pollsters (such as those who work for Gallup, Harris, CBS, and NBC) employ a small sample of approximately 1,500 to tap the opinion of 250 million Americans with only a small margin of error.

You may find it surprising that the conclusions based on the responses of a relatively small sample of a larger group can be accurate. Consider, for example, a jar filled with 100,000 green and yellow marbles. We need not count all the marbles to know the proportion that is green or yellow. A sample of just 1,000 would allow us to estimate the ratio of green to yellow with great confidence, within a small margin of error, *as long as each marble had an equal chance of being counted*. Doctors proceed on the same assumption when they test our blood: rather than draining all of it for testing, they take a small sample. When it comes to social behavior, however, the situation is not as simple as it is with marbles and blood. Accordingly, methodologists and statisticians have evolved various techniques for arriving at a representative sample. These techniques are usually taught only in more advanced courses. This is not to say that surveys are always correct; they can be disconcertingly inaccurate at times.

Ethical Considerations

Over the past two decades, a number of studies have generated heated debate regarding the ethics of social psychological research. Among these studies have been the following:

- In his field research, Laud Humphreys (1970) studied the lives of homosexual men. He actually observed them in homosexual acts in public restrooms in parks ("tearooms") by offering to serve as a lookout ("watchqueen"). In order to study other aspects of their lives, Humphreys noted the license numbers of their cars and used the numbers to locate the names and addresses through the police. He then visited the men at their homes in order to interview them, but he disguised himself enough to avoid recognition. Humphreys was criticized for invading the subjects' privacy, for deceiving them by leading them to think that he was only acting as a lookout, and for disguising himself in his interviews. Many thought his use of subjects' license numbers to trace them to their homes was unethical.

- In his laboratory experiments into the study of obedience to authority, Stanley Milgram (1974) led subjects falsely to believe they were participating in a "learning study." Subjects were told to teach another subject to match words by administering various levels of electric shocks to the subject (actually a confederate) when he made a mistake. Each shock-delivering switch had a label indicating a different number of volts (15 to 315), while some labels also included such phrases as "Extreme-Intensity Shock," "Danger — Severe Shock," and "XXX." During the experiment, subjects were instructed to give progressively more intense shocks to the other subject in the adjoining room, even though he would scream, kick the wall, and beg for the experiment to stop. Critics of Milgram's experiments argued that the experience produced as much pain for the real subjects as the confederate subject pretended to experience. Many subjects became nervous and upset and pleaded with the experimenter to let them stop giving shocks.

- In a field experiment, Steven G. West, Stephen P. Gunn, and Paul Chernicky (1975) induced subjects to agree to commit to a lawbreaking, Watergate-type burglary. The experimental conditions involved several rationales for the burglary that had been used as various explanations for the 1972 burglary of the Democratic Watergate headquarters. Critics have argued that encouraging subjects to engage in illegal acts (even though the acts are not carried out) is unethical.

- Neil M. Malamuth, Maggie Heim, and Seymour Feshbach (1980) investigated the sexual arousal of individuals confronted with portrayals of sexual violence. They provided male and female students in two undergraduate psychology classes with booklets containing rape stories. Despite the debriefing of the subjects after the experiment (when the researchers described its true nature), critics have expressed concern that the women in the study may have become more worried about rape and limited their activities in a quest for safety. They also question the effects such an experiment might have on young men who discover that they are aroused by a description of orgasm under cruelly violent circumstances.

- In their book *Small Town in Mass Society*, Arthur Vidich and Joseph Bensman (1960) described the sometimes embarrassing details of the lives of residents of a small upstate New York town in the 1950s. Even though the town and its residents were given fictitious names, those involved easily recognized themselves and their neighbors. To show their displeasure, the townspeople staged a parade in which each wore a mask with the fictitious name given to them by the researchers. At the end of the parade was a manure spreader, with effigies of the researchers looking into the manure (Diener and Crandall, 1978).

- In the fall of 1986, the Louis Harris and Associates polling organization conducted a national survey on public attitudes toward the civil justice system and tort law reform. The survey was commissioned by Aetna Life and Casualty, an insurance company which was frequently involved in civil litigation and which favored changes in some regulations governing civil lawsuits. In the Harris report summarizing the survey findings, and in press releases and media reports, the survey was characterized as indicating that the public favored many of the reforms desired by Aetna. Critics later noted that in reporting the findings, Harris failed to use the exact wordings of the questions asked of respondents. For example, on some questions, the report indicated that results showed "very strong support" for proposed changes, when, in fact, a large proportion of respondents said they found the changes "somewhat acceptable." A later study demonstrated that when the word "support" was substituted for "acceptable," the percentage of respondents agreeing dropped substantially — a finding which indicates that the published summaries of the Harris study most likely overstated public support for the changes advocated by the survey's sponsor (Krosnick, 1989).

COERCING PARTICIPANTS

As we have noted, critics have raised a variety of ethical questions about studies such as those discussed above. One criticism aimed at some research is that participants' involvement is not voluntary. In the past, many people — particularly those in institutions, such as military personnel, prisoners, the mentally disabled, and students — have not been allowed to refuse to participate in research projects supported by those institutions. In some field studies, the persons being studied are unaware that they are the subjects of research. In other instances, individuals who initially agree to participate are not allowed to drop out when they wish to do so. In their zeal to conduct a good study, some researchers put pressure on people to participate.

More recently, *informed consent* has become an important condition of social research. Federal regulations require that subjects, "to the degree that they are capable, be given the opportunity to choose what shall or shall not happen to them" (National Commission for the Protection of Human Subjects of Biomedical and Behavioral Research, 1979: 6). Regulations require that potential subjects be given sufficient information to

make an informed decision about whether to participate and that this information be presented in a way that is understandable to the subjects.

Because even well-informed participants may feel coerced, the regulations also say that "an agreement to participate in research constitutes a valid consent only if voluntarily given" (National Commission for the Protection of Human Subjects of Biomedical and Behavioral Research, 1979: 6). For example, college students who are asked by an instructor to participate in an experiment or a survey may fear that nonparticipation will somehow affect their grade, even if they are told that their participation is completely voluntary. To reduce this possible source of coercion, many institutions require that information about which particular students participate be unavailable to the professor making the request.

Coercion can also take a positive form. Consequently, the regulations protecting human research subjects also prohibit the use of "undue influence . . . through an offer of an excessive, unwarranted, inappropriate, or improper reward . . . in order to obtain compliance" (National Commission for the Protection of Human Subjects of Biomedical and Behavioral Research, 1979: 6).

DECEIVING PARTICIPANTS

The idea that potential subjects have the right to information about a study in order to decide whether to participate in the research seems simple enough. Yet we all know that people act differently when they know they are being studied than when they are unaware of the researcher's interest. For example, in Milgram's study, described previously, it is unlikely that the subjects would have delivered high levels of shock to a person begging to be released from the study if they had been told the true purpose of the experiment. The subjects *believed* they were taking part in a study of learning. If Milgram had told them the true purpose of the study — that he wanted to know just how much harm they would inflict on another when ordered to do so by an authority figure (the experimenter) — they probably would have behaved differently. Similarly, the field researcher who asks to join a group in order to study it is likely to make different observations if she reveals that the *specific* focus of her study is gossiping among the members.

Psychologist Diana Baumrind (1985) contends that this sort of intentional deception in the research setting is unethical, imprudent, and unwarranted scientifically. And she maintains that even when subjects are debriefed, they gain a view of themselves as gullible and naive, and that this recognition invariably lowers their self-esteem and undermines their trust in scientific endeavors. Baumrind insists that concern for the rights of human beings is morally superior to freedom to seek knowledge and should take precedence over it. She argues that all consent must be based on complete and total information. Defenders of deceptive research procedures do not necessarily find these arguments convincing. Deception is morally justified, they argue, as long as the risks or costs to the participants are outweighed by the benefits to humanity.

Social psychologists, like scientists in other disciplines, disagree about the degree to which researchers should be allowed to use deception (telling subjects that the focus of their research is one thing when it is really something else) or even incomplete information (not telling subjects the specific focus of one's research). Some, like Baumrind, find these practices unethical. Others disagree with their use for more practical reasons. Some social psychologists who study memory or information processing, for example, feel that their results are unaffected by telling subjects the truth and the whole truth about the nature of their investigations. These researchers feel that the use of deception and incomplete information by other social psychologists gives research "a bad name" and may even adversely affect their own studies by leading subjects to disbelieve the researchers' accounts and engage in efforts to figure out their "true" purpose. Still other social psychologists believe that deception and incomplete information are acceptable, as long as harm to

subjects is minimal and potentially beneficial knowledge may result from the study.

HARMING PARTICIPANTS

A serious criticism of some social psychological research is that it exposes participants to psychological trauma and even to physical, mental, and emotional impairment. Participants are sometimes asked to reveal deviant behavior, unpopular attitudes, or demeaning personality characteristics. They may thus derive a devastating reflection of themselves as thieves, sadists, perverts, or potential murderers. And, as in the case of the rape study cited previously, individuals may become fearful and alter their behavior. Minimally, many studies cause participants to feel embarrassed, guilty, or anxious about their actions. On the other hand, other social psychologists note that the ordinary testing of college students as part of the procedure for passing a course also generates anxiety — frequently substantially greater and more pervasive anxiety than that produced by social psychologists.

In defense of his procedures in the shock study described earlier, Stanley Milgram pointed out that a follow-up study revealed that participants felt positively about the experiment: 84 percent of the subjects stated they were glad to have participated in the study; 15 percent indicated neutral feelings; and only 1.3 percent indicated negative feelings. In addition, four-fifths of the subjects felt that more experiments of a similar sort should be carried out, and 74 percent indicated that they had learned something of personal importance from the study. Moreover, similar follow-up studies made after other such experiments have failed to demonstrate long-term negative consequences of the experimental manipulations (Clark and Word, 1974; Zimbardo, 1974).

Nonetheless, it should be recognized that research can have an impact on the subsequent behavior of participants. Shalom H. Schwartz and Avi Gottlieb (1980a, b, 1981) followed up an earlier study that they had conducted in order to investigate this matter. In the earlier research they had attempted to determine whether subjects would attempt to assist another "subject" (in reality a confederate) whom they had witnessed being attacked over closed-circuit television. Eighty-nine percent of the subjects had helped, either by directly trying to aid the victim or by calling the experimenter. When confronted with another bystander-intervention situation some six to ten months later, the subjects were less likely to help a seemingly distressed and injured victim than were control-group subjects. But subjects who were confronted with the situation eleven to twenty months later were more willing to provide the victim with assistance than were subjects in the control group. Schwartz and Gottlieb conclude that their original experiment had induced simultaneous cognitions in their subjects about the possible inauthenticity of need and generalized beliefs about the value of helping. With the passage of time, the former faded and the latter became more salient.

Another type of harm to participants may occur if others gain access to the specific information they have provided to the researchers. For example, authorities may want to know the identities of those participants who report their involvement in illegal activities, such as cheating in the classroom, evading taxes, or using drugs. The surest way to prevent harm of this kind is to protect the participant's identity. Two techniques are essential in this regard — anonymity and confidentiality.

A participant is considered *anonymous* when the researcher *cannot* identify which participant provided a given bit of information. Thus, participants would be anonymous in a self-administered survey in which no identifying information is included. Identifying information includes such obvious identifiers as names and Social Security numbers, but other information may also serve as identifying data. In a classroom with only a few females or only a few Hispanics, for example, information about gender or ethnicity may function as identifying information.

Participants are never totally anonymous if they have provided their information when the researcher is present, as is the case in most interview surveys, experiments, and field studies. But a participant's identity can be protected even in these situations. Names and other identifying information are usually removed from data records, and then the information from several participants is combined. Students (and research subjects) often wonder how the information can be useful if researchers don't know who said (or did) what. In fact, social psychologists are not interested in the performance or opinions of individuals per se. For example, Milgram was not interested in how any of his *particular* subjects responded. Instead, he wanted to answer such questions as: How many subjects will give shocks after the confederate has pleaded to be released? What's the maximum shock level that any subject will give? Are younger people more likely, or less likely, or just as likely as older people to obey authority figures? To answer these questions, it is not necessary to know the identity of a particular subject.

A participant's information is considered *confidential* when the researcher is able to identify the source of the information but takes steps to prevent anyone else from identifying the source. All names and addresses are removed from the information records and replaced by identification numbers. A separate file is created linking the numbers to the names. Regulations require high levels of security for such files, such as keeping them in a locked file cabinet to which only authorized researchers have access.

Confidentiality, rather than anonymity, is used when it is necessary to identify individual respondents for some reason. This is the case when a study requires that participants be contacted again at a later time. In such cases, the researcher must be able to link the information given by a particular respondent on one occasion with that provided later.

MISREPRESENTING RESULTS

The ethical obligations we have been discussing are those of the researcher toward the research subjects. But researchers also have obligations toward their colleagues and the public. These obligations generally have to do with being open and honest about their research. For example, researchers have the obligation to acknowledge any shortcomings of their studies to their readers. If mistakes are made in carrying out a study, the researcher should admit them. And it is the researcher's responsibility to describe the results of a study clearly and completely, avoiding presentations that may mislead readers about the conclusions that the study supports. The Louis Harris study discussed earlier was criticized for implying that the results suggested stronger public support than there actually was for changes desired by the client company that paid for the survey.

CODES AND REGULATIONS

Concern regarding the ethics of medical and behavioral research led Congress to enact the 1974 National Research Act. In response to this legislation, various federal agencies have established regulations governing the use of human subjects (i.e., research participants). Before a study can be conducted, an institutional review board (IRB) must review and approve the project. Located at universities, research centers, and related institutions, institutional review boards are committees composed of researchers, administrators, and community representatives. The review process seeks to safeguard the welfare and rights of participants of government-supported research, protecting them from risk to mental and physical health and from deceit.

Many social scientists felt that the early regulations unnecessarily encumbered behavioral research and posed a threat to academic freedom and free inquiry. Whole lines of research were no longer possible. Consequently, in January 1981, the Department of Health and Human Services (DHHS) modified its earlier regulations and made some allowances for social and behavioral studies in which there is little risk to the participants and in which participants provide their informed consent. Further, incompletely informed

consent was held acceptable if, in the view of the IRB, it involved "minimum risk to the subject" and if the research "could not practically be carried out" otherwise.

Social psychologists have attempted to resolve their ethical dilemmas in a manner that avoids the extremes of (1) eliminating experimentation altogether and (2) failing to consider the rights and dignity of research participants. Most of the professional associations to which social psychologists and other behavioral scientists belong have created and published formal codes of conduct describing what is considered acceptable and unacceptable research behavior.

Summary

1. Social psychology is the study of the behaviors, thoughts, and feelings of an individual or interacting individuals and their relationships with larger social units.

2. At the turn of this century, the prevailing question asked by social psychologists was, "How can we explain the influence that the presence of others has on our behavior?" Charles Darwin's doctrine of natural selection led some to propose that the answer to this question lay in evolution and instincts. This proposal has been challenged by four social psychological perspectives, each with its own basic assumptions—the behavioral, cognitive, structural, and interactionist perspectives.

3. The behavioral and cognitive perspectives represent different answers to the question, "How much attention should social psychologists give to mental activities in their attempts to understand social behavior?" The behavioral perspective focuses on directly observable behavior and on the environment that causes our behavior to change. The cognitive perspective focuses on how we mentally structure and process the information that we receive from our environment.

4. The structural and interactionist perspectives represent different positions on the question,

"How active are individuals in shaping social interaction?" The structural perspective concentrates on how our behavior and views are shaped by the multiple and changing roles prescribed by our society. The interactionist perspective proposes that social behavior is best understood by studying how individuals negotiate with others to construct their interactions.

5. A theory is a set of ideas about a subject matter that summarize, organize, and explain it.

A method is a procedure for acquiring and interpreting information. Social psychological methods include social surveys, experiments, and field research.

6. In designing and conducting research, social psychologists must balance the value of the information gained from the research against concern for the rights and dignity of the participants in the research. Participant rights preclude the participant's being coerced, deceived, or harmed.

PART ONE

CULTURE: SOCIALIZATION AND NEGOTIATION

CHAPTER 2

EARLY SOCIALIZATION

*B*abies are born knowing nothing of the ways of society, but they have the potential to learn. *What* they learn depends primarily upon the group they are born into. One will learn to speak English; another, Russian or Japanese. One will eat rice with chopsticks; another, with a fork. Different cultures have different rules about what is appropriate in various situations, such as when to speak and when to be silent, how to greet strangers, and how to show or conceal emotion in different settings.

Socialization is a broad concept that encompasses the process by which we learn, through interaction with other people, the ways of thinking, feeling, and acting that are essential for effective participation within a particular group of people. It is the process by which a mere biological organism becomes transformed into a social being. Compared with other organisms, we are remarkably "open" or "unfinished" beings. Thus our humanness is bestowed and sustained through social interaction. Socialization is a process that continues through life: an initiate is socialized within the League of Women Voters; a new patient, within a hospital ward; a bride and groom, within marriage; a senior citizen, within a Golden Age Village; an upwardly mobile person, within a

new social class; a religious convert, within a new religion; an accounting student, within his or her profession; and a new employee, within a corporation. We will illustrate the lifelong nature of socialization in Chapter 3, "Socialization over the Life Course." In this chapter we'll explore the special tasks of early childhood socialization.

Preconditions for Socialization

Socialization makes two fundamental contributions to human life. First, it provides the foundation for effective participation in society. As infants, we enter a society that is already an ongoing concern. Indeed, not only are the society and its culture in operation when the infant arrives, but also they continue in operation after the individual's death. Hence the human organism needs to be fitted and to fit itself into a social environment, that is, to take on the ways of its society's people and to fashion a competence for controlling and shaping its own fate.

Second, socialization makes society possible. In the absence of socialization, society could not perpetuate itself beyond a single generation, and culture would be nonexistent. Through socialization, vast numbers of organisms — human beings — are able to fit their actions to the developing actions of others. Common understandings of life's activities provide a map telling us in broad terms what we can expect of others and what they can expect of us. These coordinated actions and common understandings are transmitted through socialization.

In sum, the individual and society are twin-born. The needs of the individual and society are mutually dependent on the success of socialization. However, human socialization presupposes the existence of an appropriate biological endowment and an appropriate social environment. There is an old notion that each of us enters the world with a clean slate (*tabula rasa*) upon which parents and others inscribe the rules of social life. While the imagery is dramatic, it is nonetheless inaccurate. None of us is born with a clean slate. We have a double inheritance, one biological and the other social. In the absence of either, humanness would not arise.

BIOLOGICAL INHERITANCE AND MATURATION

The nature of the human animal both allows and requires socialization. Humans are helpless and dependent at birth and remain so for a longer time than any other species. Unlike other species that are equipped with many instincts (built-in responses to their environments), humans are born with fewer instincts but with a great capacity to learn from experience. This biological inheritance permits socialization and enables us to adapt to an enormous range of environments in flexible

Humans are helpless and dependent at birth and remain so for a longer time than any other species. Humans are born with fewer instincts than other species but with a great capacity to learn from experience. This biological inheritance permits socialization and enables us to adapt to an enormous range of environments in flexible and complex ways.

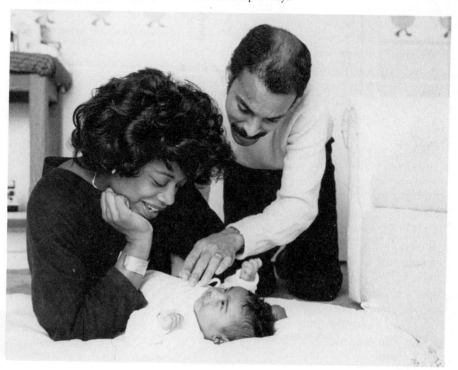

and complex ways. It allows us to understand the ongoing society, to function within it, to judge it, and to modify it.

But our biological inheritance also sets limits on socialization. Studies with chimpanzees have shown that even a rich environment cannot overcome the limits imposed by genetic endowment. For example, despite impressive achievements, such as learning to communicate with sign language, chimps lack an inherent biological capacity to learn the complexities of human language. Similarly, among humans, biological impairments such as brain damage, deafness, blindness, or other physical disabilities can profoundly affect an individual's socialization. For example, a child born deaf cannot learn language in *the same way* that a child with normal hearing does, because the deaf child cannot hear his or her own voice or the voices of others.

The extent to which a biological deficit interferes with socialization depends not entirely on the defect itself but on society's response to it as well. In the past, persons with such disabilities as deafness, blindness, and mental retardation have been assumed to be "hopeless cases" — unable to learn much about their society or how to function in it. More recently, expectations for these persons have changed, and the institutions that once were charged with custodial care are now discovering and implementing ways to minimize the impact of physical and mental disabilities on socialization.

The development of certain human capacities results from both children's experiences with their social environments and their **biological maturation**—the more or less automatic unfolding of biological potential in a set, predictable sequence. In this view, the impact of the social environment is limited by the child's biological maturation. For example, the ability to interact with others depends in part on the development of adequate visual and auditory discrimination. The development of discrimination skills seems to be governed by a biological timetable. For example, as early as four weeks of age, many infants relax in

response to close physical contact. At sixteen weeks, most can discriminate the human face and often smile in response. They also show signs of recognizing the voice of the usual caregiver. By twenty-eight weeks, most infants can clearly distinguish individual people, often showing fear in the presence of strangers and responding to variations in facial expression and tone of voice. At one year, most children show a definite preference for some persons, seeking out interaction by going to them and tugging on clothing.

Our biological inheritance also establishes a timetable for early socialization. We all recognize that a three-month-old infant is not physically ready to walk, and we wouldn't waste much energy trying to teach the infant to read, to do calculus, or to dress or eat unassisted. We realize that a certain level of physical or mental development, determined largely by biology, is a necessary precondition for the child's learning of these skills. Thus biological maturation — the more or less automatic unfolding of biological potential in a set, predictable sequence — is a precondition for some socialization outcomes.

AN APPROPRIATE ENVIRONMENT

Maturational processes are usually not sufficient for the emergence of complex social behavior. Socialization also presupposes an appropriate environment — one that includes social interaction. This fact is starkly illustrated by cases involving extremely isolated and deprived children.

Susan Curtiss (1977) stirred interest in social deprivation cases with her report on Genie. In 1970, California authorities discovered Genie when Genie's fifty-year-old mother ran away from her seventy-year-old husband after a violent quarrel and took the child with her. Genie was thirteen years old and had been isolated in a small room, rarely having contact with anyone. The social worker in the welfare office where Genie's mother applied for public assistance immediately took note of Genie's condition. She notified her supervisor, who called the police. Genie was hospitalized, and her parents were charged with willful abuse. However, on the day he was to appear in court, Genie's father committed suicide.

When Genie was admitted to the hospital, she was a malformed, incontinent, unsocialized, and malnourished youngster. On various maturity and attainment tests she scored as normal one-year-old children score. Psychologists, linguists, and neurologists at nearby UCLA designed a program to rehabilitate and educate Genie. In time, she began to use two phrases that she employed in a ritualized way, as though they were single words: "stopit" and "nomore." Somewhat later she began to string two words together on her own, such as "big teeth," "little marble," and "two hand." However, unlike normal children, Genie never acquired the ability to ask questions, and her understanding of grammar remained limited. Four years after she began stringing words together, her speech remained slow and resembled a garbled telegram.

Psychologists and linguists are uncertain why Genie failed to learn the kind of grammatical principles that underlie human language. Genetic factors do not appear to underlie her deficiencies. Nor can her difficulties be attributed to the absence of competent teachers. Since her discovery and until she reached the age of twenty, Genie enjoyed an enriched environment and the services of accomplished speech therapists. In 1978, Genie's mother was awarded legal guardianship of her daughter, and she filed suit against UCLA researchers for subjecting Genie to "unreasonable and outrageous" testing, which she alleged was not conducted for treatment but was done to exploit Genie for personal and economic benefits. The damage suit brought to a halt research on Genie's development. One hypothesis that psychologists have advanced to account for Genie's language deficiencies is that there are critical periods in the development of language capabilities and that these periods cannot be successfully passed through once children enter puberty.

Less extreme cases of deprivation also provide evidence of the importance of environment for successful socialization. Rene Spitz (1945, 1946) studied babies in an orphanage who received adequate nutrition and medical care but little personal attention. Six nurses cared for forty-five infants under eighteen months old. For most of the day, the infants lay on their backs in small cubicles without human contact. The babies hardly ever smiled or cried and did not try to speak. Their scores on developmental tests fell dramatically within the first year. Two years later, a follow-up study found that over one-third of the ninety-one children at the institution had died and that the ones who remained at the institution were severely retarded—even though at age fifteen months they had been provided with more nurses and more opportunities for joint play. Spitz concluded that the conditions of the first year were so detrimental both physically and psychologically that the more favorable conditions introduced later did not counteract the damage. It appears that infants need a secure attachment—a warm, close relationship with an adult who provides a sense of security and offers stimulation—in order to develop the interpersonal and cognitive skills necessary for normal development.

CULTURE: THE CONTEXT AND CONTENT OF SOCIALIZATION

Children are born into a social world that already exists. They are *new members* of an ongoing society. From the point of view of society, the function of socialization is to transmit to new members the knowledge and motivation needed to participate in established social relationships. There are a number of important features of societies that, in large part, define the social environment into which the child is socialized and comprise many of the things he or she will be expected to learn.

We experience much of life as relatively stable and predictable. Consider that we usually have little difficulty in attuning ourselves to new classmates and professors each semester; much of academic life is a replay of itself. Consider the recurrent and orderly flow of traffic into the city each morning and its outward flow to the suburbs in the evening. Consider the store clerks smoothly carrying out innumerable transactions with streams of customers. Consider the layout of the city, with the central business district, ghetto areas, "automobile row," manufacturing district, and middle-class suburbs. As we observe human behavior, it seems in large measure to be organized and focused rather than haphazard and random.

This order — this regularity and stability that develops out of human interaction — is embodied in **culture**. A culture is the aggregate of things that a given social unit has created and to which the unit's members attach similar meanings: their beliefs, values, norms, knowledge, language, and patterns of behavior and interaction, as well as physical objects such as books, clothing, buildings, cars, and personal computers. All cultures have these elements, even though the content varies greatly from one culture to another. Let's look more closely at these elements of culture and how they are involved in socialization.

COMPONENTS OF CULTURE

Values are ethical principles to which people feel a strong emotional commitment and which they employ in judging behavior. They are general ideas that people share about what is good or bad, desirable or undesirable. Values transcend particular situations and are applied in many social contexts. For example, our culture values freedom. This is reflected in our economic practices ("the free market"), our political practices (freedom of speech), our educational philosophies (every child's right to a basic education), our laws about marriage (freedom to choose a mate), and our child-rearing practices (the parents' right to determine most aspects of their child's life). This is not to say that all aspects of American culture are entirely consistent with the value of freedom. Other values may generate inconsistencies. This is because the rules governing a particular situation are often not derived from a single value.

New members of a society are expected to come to share its values and to learn accepted ways of reconciling inconsistencies among them.

Values provide the framework within which people in a society develop norms of behavior. Less general than values, **norms** are standards for behavior that members of a social unit share, to which they are expected to conform, and that are enforced by positive and negative sanctions. These are the "shoulds" of a society. In our society there are many norms that the newcomer must learn. For example, mainstream American society believes that we *should* eat with utensils rather than hands, wear clothes in public, be polite to most other people, and respect the property of others. Part of the process of acquiring a culture — of becoming socialized — is learning exactly when to obey each of the norms that are part of our culture. For example, we typically are expected to raise a hand and wait to be called upon to speak in a classroom, but this behavior is considered inappropriate in a group of friends. Group members will impose the group's rules of behavior on a new member and will expect him or her, in time, to come to understand and share these norms.

Norms specify *a range of acceptable behavior*; some specify a more narrow range of acceptable behavior than others. Norms also vary in the importance that people assign to them. *Folkways* are everyday habits and conventions that people follow without giving them much thought. For example, most Americans subscribe to norms specifying that they should chew with their mouths closed, greet acquaintances with whom they come into contact, and wear casual or business clothes (but not evening clothes) to class. People who violate folkways may be labeled eccentric or rude, but their violations are usually not strongly sanctioned.

In contrast, *mores* are the norms we consider vital to our well-being and our most cherished values. Examples are the prohibitions against murder, theft, and sexual abuse of children. Violations of mores provoke intense reactions — ostracism, imprisonment, execution. *Laws* are norms that are written down, formalized, and enforced by governments. Laws may formalize folkways (as some traffic regulations do) or mores (as laws against murder and the sexual abuse of children do).

Roles are the normative requirements, or expectations, that apply to the behavior of a specific category of people in a particular situation. Role expectations specify who does what, when, and where. Members of the society can cooperate with one another because they know their own rights and obligations as well as those of others with whom they come into contact. Our socialization is affected in two ways by roles: First, role expectations determine much of the behavior of those who socialize us, and, second, much of our socialization, especially as adults, is concerned with learning role expectations appropriate to the positions we hold in social groups.

Even young children are expected to learn some role expectations. Among the first and most important roles we learn are gender roles — expectations associated with being male or female in our society. Role expectations are also associated with children's positions in their family units, such as youngest son, oldest daughter, cousin, and grandchild. For example, the oldest child may be expected to take some responsibility for the safety and care of younger siblings. Later, children must learn the role expectations for student and classmate, and the associated expectations for teacher and principal. Still later in life, most of us learn the role expectations for husband or wife, parent, and grandparent, as well as specific expectations for occupations such as police officer, banker, physician, truck driver, secretary, attorney, and production supervisor. Chapter 3, "Socialization over the Life Course," will illustrate how the role expectations held by others in our society affect all of us.

In summary, in order to become a member of society, we must acquire at least a minimal amount of knowledge about the world we were born into, including what our culture defines as appropriate behavior and feelings. We must know what to expect from other people in various roles, how we ourselves fit in with others, and what is considered proper and improper in various situations. This is the knowledge that our socializers, knowingly or unknowingly, pass on to us.

AGENTS OF SOCIALIZATION

Institutions are social units that focus on particular societal needs. For example, schools are institutions which exist to transmit certain kinds of knowledge to the youth of a society. Schools have norms relating to attendance, sports events, courses, and holiday celebrations. Role expectations define relationships among teachers, students, principal, and cleaning staff. Churches, hospitals, factories, and courts are also institutions. Most institutions, like societies, continue to operate over a long period of time even though the individuals who pass through them change regularly. Institutions illustrate the stability of society and the effectiveness of socialization. They can remain relatively unchanged, even though the individuals within them are changing, largely because new recruits are socialized into the appropriate patterns of behavior.

We just noted that schools are institutions having the societal responsibility to socialize children by passing on particular kinds of knowledge — reading, writing, arithmetic, science, and so on. Other institutions also play a large part in the socialization of children. The mass media, for example — which consists of television, radio, newspapers, and magazines — is also influential, even though it does not exist for the sole purpose of transmitting knowledge about the culture to the younger generation. Individuals and groups, as well as institutions, socialize children. By virtue of their particular relationships with children, some people, such as parents and other family members, are especially significant in children's development. The individuals, groups, and institutions that play a part in the transmission of culture to the new generation are referred to by social psychologists as **agents of socialization**.

Agents of socialization usually act toward a particular child in terms of their image of him or

Agents of socialization are the individuals, groups, and institutions that play a part in the transmission of culture to the new generation. Here, a mother lights Hanukkah candles with her child at a temple and a second-grade teacher instructs her class.

her. That image is derived in part from general conceptions in the society and in part from the child's particular characteristics — for example, the level of independent behavior judged appropriate for someone of the child's age and gender. Agents of socialization teach role behavior. For instance, they may show the child how to pitch a softball or be a good friend, or they may explain what a fire fighter or doctor does. Sometimes they emphasize norms or values, such as "Big boys don't cry" or "Always tell the truth."

But much of the agents' instruction is not consciously planned by them. The mother who threatens a spanking if her child won't stop screaming probably has no important long-term lesson in mind. Rather, her action is a response to the immediate, annoying situation. The father who is pleased when his daughter kisses her younger sister may not realize the effect of his happy smile. But these everyday events, intentional or unintentional, also teach the child important lessons that become organized into roles and values.

Because children seek the approval of their socializing agents, they are often motivated to behave the way those agents wish.

So far, we have highlighted the necessity of a process of socialization and have identified some of *what* must be learned and *who* is likely to transmit that information to the child. Now let us look at the learning processes involved in socialization — *how* does socialization take place.

Learning Processes Involved in Socialization

Socialization involves learning. Learning is basic to the human condition. It enables the human organism to adapt itself to its environment. Accordingly, learning is not restricted to what takes place in formal education but is an ongoing, lifetime process. By *learning* we mean a more or less permanent modification in an organism's behavior or capability that results, at least in part, from its experience in the environment.

Social psychologists look at the process of socialization from a number of different theoretical viewpoints. In the discussion of the process of socialization that follows, the strong influence of three theories will be evident: the social learning, developmental, and symbolic interaction theories. Social learning theory focuses on how learning results from the rewarding or punishing consequences of a person's behavior. The processes involved are conditioning and observational learning. On the other hand, developmental theory emphasizes the role of maturation and developmental stages in the learning process. Symbolic interaction theory focuses on how we reflect on our own behavior and negotiate our interests with others. Each theory emphasizes different factors as important to socialization, taking for granted or glossing over factors emphasized by the others. All three theories agree that human individuality is achieved through socialization and that socialized behavior is learned, often incidentally and unintentionally, in the course of social interac-

tion. Let's turn now to a discussion of the processes by which learning occurs. We will give particular attention to how children learn (1) language and communication and (2) standards of right and wrong.

CONDITIONING AND OBSERVATIONAL LEARNING

Social learning theorists are concerned with learning processes that result from our experience with the environment. They describe how we, as a result of our experience, establish an association, or linkage, between two events. For instance, you very likely have formed an association between a hot stove and a painful, burning sensation, between attending class and passing a course, and between showing up late and upsetting your friends. The process by which this association or linkage occurs is called *conditioning*.

Social Contingencies

No psychologist was more closely identified with the study of conditioning than B. F. Skinner (1953). Much of Skinner's scientific reputation derives from his studies of **operant conditioning** — a type of learning in which the association between a behavior and the environmental change it produces affects the *future* probability of that behavior.

Many of Skinner's ideas about operant conditioning resulted from his experiments on rats and pigeons. For example, he would place a hungry pigeon in an experimental chamber, and in about two to three minutes, he would teach the pigeon to turn in a full circle. Here's how he did it: The hungry bird strutted about the chamber under Skinner's watchful eye. Once the pigeon made a slight clockwise turn, Skinner instantly gave it a food pellet. Again the pigeon strutted about, and when it made another clockwise turn, Skinner repeated the procedure. When the bird mastered making a full circle, Skinner gave the bird the food pellet only when it moved in the opposite direction. Then he waited until it made a clockwise circle followed by a counterclockwise circle. In about fifteen minutes, Skinner taught the bird to do a perfect figure eight. Additionally, Skinner taught pigeons to do such humanlike activities as dancing with one another and playing Ping-Pong. (Before reading further, see the Student Observation: "Operant Conditioning.")

In these experiments, Skinner established an association between the pigeon's behavior (e.g., turning) and its receiving food pellets; that is, it received a food pellet *only* when it performed the behavior. This association modified the bird's subsequent turning behavior by making future turning behavior more likely. Such behavior-altering associations between an organism's behavior and a subsequent change in its environment are called *contingencies*. If the environmental change involves the conduct of another person (e.g., Skinner in the case of the pigeon) or a social group, the contingency is called a **social contingency**. On the other hand, if the change in the environment (e.g., delivery of the food pellet) is *not* associated with a particular behavior—that is, if the change occurs whether the behavior is performed or not (e.g., the pellet is delivered whether the pigeon turns or not)—there is no contingency and the future likelihood of the behavior will not be affected.

According to **social learning theory**, social contingencies are a primary source of socialization or, for that matter, a primary source of learning any behavior (Baldwin and Baldwin, 1986; Modgil and Modgil, 1987; Lee, 1988). An infant

child's "da-da" may produce a parent's hug, which increases the future probability of the child's making "da-da" sounds. Appropriate work behavior by employees may result in the employer's giving them salary increases, which makes the future probability of appropriate work behavior more likely. Patients who feel better following a visit to the doctor are more likely to return for additional treatment.

But any single social contingency is frequently just one-half of the picture. The relationship is actually reciprocal (Gewirtz, 1990). In Skinner's experiments, who is conditioning whom? Isn't the pigeon's turning behavior (which follows Skinner's pellet-giving behavior) the environmental consequence that increases the future occurrence of Skinner's pellet-giving behavior? Similarly, an infant's repeated smiles (after the parents' hugging behavior) create contingencies that increase the parents' future hugging behavior. And the parent who gives a child candy so that the youngster will stop a temper tantrum not only is *teaching* the child to throw future tantrums but also is *being conditioned*, by the child's "shutting up," to continue to reward temper tantrums.

Contingency effects. Social learning theorists distinguish contingencies in terms of their *effects* and their *scheduling*. First, let's look at how contingencies differ in their effects. Some contingencies produce an increase in the occurrence of a behavior in the future. These are called *reinforcement contingencies*—contingencies that *strengthen*

STUDENT OBSERVATION

Operant Conditioning

A couple of days ago my four-year-old sister complained of a stomachache, so I bought some Tums and gave her a few. Yesterday the same thing happened, and again I gave her some Tums. I guess she thought they tasted pretty good, because today she is faking another stomachache. This is a good illustration of operant conditioning. The frequency of her behavior was changed according to the event that followed it. The candy reward served to reinforce the "stomachache" behavior.

the behavior. On the other side of the coin are *punishment contingencies* — contingencies that *decrease* the occurrence of a behavior in the future.

Reinforcement contingencies can be created by altering the child's environment. For example, a parent may increase the future occurrence of a particular behavior of the child, such as talking, by *adding* something to the child's environment (such as smiling, saying "Good girl," or remaining longer with the child) or by *subtracting* something from the child's environment (such as stopping the teasing of an older sibling).

Of course, parents can also create punishment contingencies by adding or subtracting something from the child's environment. In either case, the child's future talking behavior will decrease. For example, if a child's talking is always followed by a correction from the parent (such as telling the child to talk louder, slower, or clearer), the future talking behavior may decrease. This is an example of adding something that subsequently decreases the behavior. If the parent subtracts something from the child's environment (e.g., leaves the room or looks away while the child is talking), the parent may also decrease the child's future talking behavior.

You should note that whether a contingency is reinforcing or punishing depends entirely on its *effect*, that is, on whether it increases or decreases the behavior. Students sometimes find this confusing because, in common usage, we think of reinforcers as "good" things and punishers as "bad" things. This is not the way social learning theorists use these terms. For example, if a child's tantrum behavior is usually followed by scolding from the mother, and the tantrum behavior increases, we have a *reinforcement contingency* — despite the fact that we usually think of scoldings as "bad" or negative. Being aware of the difference between common, everyday usage of these terms and the way the theory uses them can help reduce confusion.

Consequences that have previously modified a child's behavior can be expected to have similar effects on other behaviors of that child. Apart from noting that "what worked in the past should continue to work," social learning theory does not specify what particular consequences can consistently change behavior for any specific child. Praise from a parent may reinforce one child's polite behavior but fail to affect the behavior of a sibling. The criticism of a teacher may curtail (by establishing a punishment contingency) some students' rowdy behavior and not affect the behavior of other students. It is probably safe to assume that food (though obviously not all foods), possibly hugging (though not necessarily by just anyone), and pain can create contingencies that reliably alter most children's behavior.

Contingency schedules. The *scheduling* of reinforcement or punishment is also important in learning. The schedule refers to the ratio of consequences (environmental events) to behaviors across repeated occasions of a contingency. For example, during the early phases of socialization (particularly with a first-born), parents frequently attend to everything that their child does. Every time the child babbles, the parents may be right there to coo and smile and play with the child. Every time the child cries, the parents may be there to take away a wet diaper or give the child food. This *one-to-one* ratio between the behavior of the child and the parents' consistent reaction is called a *continuous schedule*. In other words, *every* occurrence of the child's babbling (or crying) is followed by an attentive response from the parent. (Again, whether it is a reinforcement or punishment contingency depends on the contingency's effect — whether it increases or decreases the child's babbling or crying behavior.)

At the other extreme, if the child performs the behavior (babbling) but the parents stop giving an attentive response (perhaps because the behavior doesn't seem as cute as they once thought), the child's behavior will return to the level of occurrence that existed before the parents established the contingency. This is called *extinction*. Extinction involves the discontinuation of a contingency. In this example, the child's babbling behavior and the attentive response of the parents are no longer associated.

In between these two extremes of *always* or *never* following the child's behavior with a particular environmental response are many contingency schedules in which the behavior is *sometimes* followed by the environmental response. These schedules are collectively referred to as *intermittent schedules*. For example, after some of the novelty of a babbling infant has worn off, parents may only occasionally give the babbling infant attention. The rest of the time, the infant's babbling behavior goes unattended.

Social learning theorists distinguish among these kinds of schedules because they have different effects on learning behavior. Children *learn new behaviors faster* when reinforcement is continuous than when it is intermittent. Once the behavior is well established, both continuous reinforcement and intermittent reinforcement have the same effect on the *persistence* of the behavior, as long as the contingency is maintained. However, if the contingency is entirely extinguished, the behavior will persist longer if it was previously reinforced intermittently than if the reinforcement was continuous.

Discriminative stimulus. Behavior that was initially learned in one situation can occur in other situations. Aggressive behavior learned at home can be duplicated in a preschool, for example. However, in many instances, the environment not only reinforces or punishes a person's behavior but also gives the person signals about when a particular contingency is going to be in operation and when it is not. For example, a child's talking will result in her father's attention only when the father is in the room, looking at her and smiling. These conditions may come to signal to the child that the contingency is "on": the child knows from past experience that if she talks under these conditions her father will pay attention and respond with interest. On the other hand, the child may learn that if the father is talking to another adult, reading a book, or watching TV, he is less likely to attend to her talking. Consequently, these conditions come to signal to the child that

the contingency is "off." As a result, the child's talking behavior will increase under the former conditions and decrease under the latter. The child is not only learning to talk by learning the association between her talking behavior and the response by her father that follows. She is also learning *when* to talk by associating environmental signals that precede her behavior with the consequences.

Contingencies like the one we just described are more complicated and take longer to learn than other contingencies as they have three components instead of two. Instead of learning the association between their behavior and a resulting environmental change, children must learn the association between their behavior, the environmental change following their behavior, *and* an environmental change that precedes their behavior. Social learning theory refers to the environmental signal that precedes the behavior as the *discriminative stimulus*, while the one following the behavior is called the *consequence* (the reinforcing or punishing stimulus).

Conditioned consequences. Social learning theory also describes how a neutral environmental stimulus — one that initially has no effect on behavior — can become an effective consequence — one capable of modifying behavior. Again, the concept of association is critical. The neutral stimulus becomes an effective consequence by being associated with a stimulus that is *already* an effective consequence. For example, a mother can probably effectively reduce her three-year-old's behavior of playing with the television controls by slapping his hand or bottom. However, this consequence (spanking) does not occur as an isolated event; rather, the mother may frown at and scold the child at the same time. Initially the mother's frowning and scolding may be neutral stimuli in that they would not function by themselves to modify the child's behavior. However, with repeated associations of the neutral stimuli with the effective consequence of spanking, the neutral stimuli can become *conditioned consequences* capable of independently modifying the child's behavior. Discriminative stimuli often acquire this capability.

A review. Let's pause to review what we've been discussing. Social learning theory describes how a child's behavior is learned as the result of several kinds of associations, or linkages, among events. The most basic association is a contingency between a particular behavior and its consequences, that is, the environmental change or changes the behavior produces. A contingency may increase (reinforcement) or decrease (punishment) the *future* probability of a behavior. More complex, three-component contingencies involve (1) the behavior, (2) the environmental change it produces, and (3) an environmental cue (a discriminative stimulus) that precedes the behavior and signals that the environmental change will occur if the behavior is performed. Another kind of association pairs an already effective consequence (environmental change) and a previously neutral environmental stimulus. This association increases the likelihood that the stimulus will acquire the same capacity as the effective consequence, that is, as part of social contingencies, it can affect the future probability of behaviors.

Shaping. Some critics note that social contingencies can explain only modifications (increases or decreases) in behaviors already in the child's repertoire. In other words, it is not possible to reinforce or punish a behavior *until it occurs*. So how do children learn *new* behaviors? Social learning theorists agree that a contingency that goes into operation only after the child performs a new behavior will take a long time to modify the behavior if the initial chance of the behavior's occurrence is low. Social learning theory proposes that the contingency will be more effective if it starts with a behavior that the child can already perform and then gradually changes the behavioral requirement in a series of successive approximations in which the child's behavior resembles more and more closely the desired new response.

This is exactly how Skinner got the pigeon to turn in a circle in the study we described earlier. Teaching a child how to write, ride a bike, or swim sometimes follows such a process, which social learning theory calls *shaping*. For example, it is common for parents to give their child a lot of attention when the child initially says anything that could be remotely interpreted as "Daddy" or "Mommy." However, over time the child must make closer approximations of these words to get the parents' attention. A similar process is often involved in toilet training. At first, the child is rewarded with praise or goodies if he or she makes it through an afternoon nap without wetting the diaper. As time passes, the reward occurs only if the child "stays dry" for longer and longer periods of time.

Observational Learning

It might have occurred to you that if we depended solely on direct experience for learning new behaviors — relying exclusively on the rewarding and punishing consequences of behavior — most of us would not survive our formative years. Learning to cross a busy street in traffic is one of many behaviors best learned by following someone's example. We can avoid tedious, costly (even fatal), and haphazard trial-and-error experimentation by imitating the behavior of socially competent models. By observing others, we learn novel responses without necessarily having to depend on the availability of an environment carefully organized around shaping procedures. Social psychologists refer to this process as **observational learning**. At times the terms "imitation," "identification," and "modeling" are used interchangeably with "observational learning." All these terms refer to the tendency of individuals to reproduce the actions, attitudes, or emotional responses displayed by real-life or symbolized models.

The social learning theorist most often associated with the notion of observational learning is Albert Bandura. Bandura disagrees with the social learning theorists who believe that observational learning is just a special case of discrimination learning in which a child matches her or his behavior to that of another person (the model) because the child has learned that the model's presence (or behavior) is the occasion on which such behavior will be rewarded. Bandura believes that although contingencies play a major role in the *continuation* of behavior, they are not necessary for the *initial learning* of a behavior by observation. This is seen best in a case where some time lapses between the model's conduct and the imitation behavior of a child. Parents who use the word "damn" or other expletives when they break or drop something are often distressed to hear their young child exclaim "damn" in a similar situation. Bandura would say that the child *learns* the behavior when she or he observes it but *performs* the behavior later, when the situation seems appropriate. Whether the behavior is repeated depends on the consequences that follow it—in this example, the parent's reaction. Thus, Bandura proposes a two-stage learning model: (1) establishment comes though imitation, and (2) maintenance comes about through reinforcement.

In one interesting study, Bandura (1965) had nursery children watch a film in which an adult actor (the model) attacked a large, inflated rubber Bobo doll. The children were divided into three groups, and each group was shown a different version of the film. In the first version, the model was given soft drinks and candy after attacking the doll. In the second version, the model was spanked with a magazine by another adult. In the third version, nothing happened to the model. Later, each child was left alone to play with various toys, including a Bobo doll. Bandura observed that the children who watched the model being spanked with a magazine were much less likely to punch and kick the doll than were the other children. We might conclude from this that these children had not learned the aggressive behavior. To test this notion, Bandura then offered each child a reward for each act of the model that the child could reproduce. He found that children in all three groups were equally able to reproduce the model's acts. In other words, all the children had "learned" the acts, but those who saw the model being punished for his aggression failed to "perform" the acts. (Before reading further, see the Student Observation: "Learning Through Modeling.")

Bandura's study illustrates that modeling may inhibit behavior if the observer sees that the model experiences punishing consequences for the behavior. For example, teachers often punish one child in the presence of classmates to achieve a deterrent effect. And, of course, inhibition be-

---

STUDENT OBSERVATION

Learning Through Modeling

I am quite upset as I write this. Over the past year I have been baby-sitting with Debbie, my neighbor's four-year-old daughter. The mother is about twenty years old and unmarried, lives alone except for Debbie, and clearly has more than she can handle emotionally or financially. When I have taken care of Debbie, it has disturbed me how violent she is with her dolls. I have seen her reprimand her "baby" by grabbing the doll by the arms or legs, swinging the "baby" about, and pounding the "baby's" head against the floor or a table. As she does it, she exclaims, "Bad baby, bad baby." Well, today while I was at school, a neighbor discovered that the mother is a child abuser and has been beating Debbie. The local authorities are now investigating the case. Debbie has been "learning" her mother's behavior toward children—I never realized that she was imitating what she herself had been experiencing. I now can see how patterns of child abuse can be transmitted from one generation to the next through socialization and child-rearing practices.

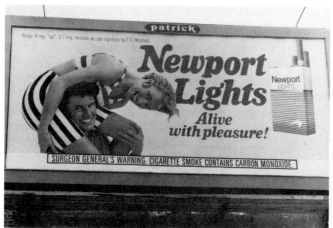

Advertisers have long recognized that they can increase the sales of a product by associating it with attractive people having a good time. More recently, antidrug, antismoking, and anti-drunk-driving ads have used the opposite tactic, associating drugs, smoking, or drinking with ugly, negative consequences in an effort to influence young people through observational learning.

comes weaker if a model is observed to be rewarded for a prohibited behavior. For instance, students who witness other pupils successfully violating school rules are themselves more likely to do so. In other words, children do not simply learn the behaviors they see others perform. They also learn the *contingencies* they observe.

Social Learning Theory's View of Language and Communication

The social learning theory of language acquisition is closely identified with the early formulations of B. F. Skinner. In his book *Verbal Behavior* (1957), Skinner drew attention to three ways in which a speech response may arise in small children. First, there are *mand* responses—a term Skinner coined, drawing it originally from such words as "command" and "demand." The mand response may start out as simply a babbling noise, a random utterance, but that noise creates a reinforcement contingency. Thus, for example, the child may emit a sound that makes the parent think the child is asking for (*manding*) water. The parent accordingly provides the child with water and satisfies the thirst. Such a sequence, when repeated on

several occasions, enhances the probability that "wa-wa," "water," or something like this will be uttered by the child whenever he or she is thirsty and wants water.

Second, there are *tact* responses, a term suggested by "contact." This response arises when the child is in actual contact with an object or event. In this case, the child may be babbling in the presence of water and may randomly utter a "wa-wa" sound. The parent in turn associates "wa-wa" with water (an association not as yet made by the child) and rewards the child. When the sequence is repeated, the child learns to make this response whenever she or he comes into contact with the relevant stimulus—in this case, water.

Third, there are *echoic* responses (from "echo"). The child *imitates* the sound that parents make in relation to a given stimulus. For example, the child may repeatedly hear his or her parents refer to a clear liquid as "water" and in turn may undertake to echo the response, producing "wa-wa." He or she is then rewarded by the parents (perhaps by a smile, a hug, or attention) for having made this particular utterance.

When talking to infants and young children, parents typically speak *motherese*, or *baby talk* — a simplified, redundant, and highly grammatical form of language that is similar to the form of speech we use when talking to our pets or the senile elderly (Furrow and Nelson, 1986). Mothers and fathers typically restrict their utterances to the present tense, to concrete nouns, and to comments on what the child is doing or experiencing — for example, statements pertaining to what objects are called, what color they are, and where they are located (Baron, 1992). Motherese includes such statements as "That's a duck, Sara. See the duck?" A mother might say "That's Mommy's," rather than "That's mine," so that the child wouldn't have to figure out the referent of the pronoun "mine" (Mann and Boyce, 1982).

Adults also respond to children's speech with *speech expansion* — rephrasing the child's utterance in an expanded and more culturally acceptable form. In response to "Go store," a mother might say "We're going to the store." If the child says "See Daddy," the mother might say "I see Daddy." Some speech expansion probably results from adults' efforts to determine the child's specific meaning. For example, when a young child says "doggie," he or she may mean "I see a doggie," "Look at the doggie," "Where is the doggie?," or "Give me my toy doggie." To determine the child's meaning, the adult often engages in a trial-and-error process of offering several responses in succession until the child seems satisfied (Ochs, 1988, 1991). Children may be motivated to improve the precision of their speech when others do not initially respond "correctly." They learn a specific sentence, such as "I want a cookie," and find that they can substitute words to produce other sentences, for example, "I want some juice," or "I want the doll." By providing a model for how to convey meanings more effectively, speech expansion contributes to language acquisition.

Studies suggest that parents usually don't *explicitly* correct young children's grammar but that they do provide *implicit* feedback (Demetras, Post, and Snow, 1986). When a child's utterance is grammatically correct, parents usually "move on": they begin a new topic or add to the last one without repeating or questioning the child's previous statement, or they follow the correct utterance with an exact repetition of the child's statement. When the child's utterance is not well formed, parents more often ask a clarifying question or repeat the child's statement with something added (speech expansion). Move-ons and exact repetitions can be viewed as a form of confirmation, which may function as a reinforcing consequence. Clarifying questions and extended repetitions model correct grammar and prompt the child to produce correct utterances. Research suggests that parents use these implicit strategies to correct only the particular features of language that they perceive the child to be mastering at the time — ignoring more complicated errors until later in the child's development (Demetras, Post, and Snow, 1986).

Learning how to participate in a conversation is part of learning how to talk. When we carry on a conversation with someone else, we follow certain rules — commonly accepted ways of interacting. For example, we use strategies for getting a conversation going, taking turns, maintaining the conversation, and changing topics or ending the conversation. We'll discuss these strategies in more detail in Chapter 5, "Communication." For now, let's focus on how children learn these strategies.

When they are two to two-and-a-half years old, toddlers begin to use certain verbal strategies for opening conversations. They may ask a question, give a command, or comment on what the listener is doing; get the listener's attention by looking at him or her; stand relatively close to the listener; and use attention-getting gestures and utterances, such as "Hey!" or "Guess what?" These strategies are very similar to the approaches mothers take in communicating with their infants, beginning late in the first year. Once toddlers have a listener's attention, however, they often don't know how to keep the conversation going. They respond to comments and questions, but they don't ask questions or link their comments to the partner's previous remarks (Kaye, 1982). These conversational skills are developed later.

Like children's speech, their conversation skills can also be expanded as a result of contingencies. Children's earliest communications with others involve single-turn conversations. The child uses a small number of "words" that are followed by a response from another person. For example, a child may have learned to say "Go potty" because her mother responds to this request by saying "Good girl!" and taking her to the bathroom. (Of course, the mother's part of the conversation is rewarded by her child's successful toilet training.)

But how do children come to develop a more expanded conversational style that involves turn taking? One type of expansion occurs when the child learns that her simple requests are more successful if she first gets her mother's attention, particularly when her mother is closely attending to someone or something else. She learns that if she first says "Mommy" and then waits for her mother to look at her and say "Yes, what dear?" it is more likely that her continued speech ("Go potty") will produce the intended response from her mother. Speaking without first getting her mother's attention or getting her attention by slapping her on the leg may not produce desirable results. An important part of learning language is learning what language style is appropriate to a given situation. By the time children are only three or four, they usually know that some situations call for being quiet, and they know how to whisper. By this age, they also use baby talk to speak to infants.

Additional conversational expansion occurs if the child learns that a good time to ask "May I *please* have a cookie?" is while her mother is pleased by her successful potty behavior. She learns this if *under these conditions* her mother more often than not responds "Yes — for being such a good girl" and gives her a cookie. The child may learn to extend her conversation a step further if she learns that saying "Thank you" after receiving the cookie (even if prompted by her mother's "What do you say?") pleases her moth-

er. Through these backward and forward expansions of verbal responses children learn to use language to carry on conversations with others.

Social Learning Theory's View of Internalization and Conscience

Now let's turn to a discussion of how the processes of conditioning and observational learning are involved in what we refer to as **internalization** — the process by which we incorporate within our personality the standards of behavior that are prevalent within our society — and result in **conscience** — the internal operation of values that control or inhibit the actions and thoughts of an individual. For young children, conformity to the expectations of others is largely a product of external controls. Standards for behavior — judgments of right and wrong, evaluations of good and bad, and assessments of desirable and undesirable — are foreign to infants. The members of society have a considerable stake in shaping children within the "proper" cultural mold.

As children grow older, an increasing proportion of their behavior becomes independent of *external* control; to a considerable extent, it gradually comes to be governed by *internal* monitors. These internal monitors carry on many of the functions previously performed by the external controls. In brief, internalization occurs: social control (external control) becomes *self*-control. (Before reading further, see the Student Observation: "Learning Appropriate Moral Values.")

Social learning theorists believe that children internalize norms and acquire a conscience in the same manner that they learn any other behavior — through conditioning and imitation. Note though that we said "behavior." It may seem strange to you to think of internalization or the conscience as behavior, but according to social learning theory, the conscience consists of not one behavior, but several: (1) the situationally specific performance of moral behaviors, (2) verbal expressions of moral standards, and (3) self-imposed contingencies involving moral behavior.

First, conscience involves the situationally specific performance of moral behavior. Social learn-

STUDENT OBSERVATION

Learning Appropriate Moral Values

When I was in kindergarten, I made the mistake of being "too honest." My parents had stressed to me during my early years the importance of always telling the truth and not lying. On one occasion, which I still vividly remember, my parents were visiting with a neighbor lady who must have weighed at least 300 pounds. I commented that she was a fat lady. I had not intended to insult the woman. I was merely making an observation, and an honest observation at that. My parents were very upset. They scolded me and made me apologize to the lady. All of this highlights the fact that morality is not a simple matter. Much depends on the situation. Children must learn when it is and is not appropriate to tell the truth. Many times in life we are expected to tell "white lies."

ing theorists see moral behavior (like all behavior) as dependent on situational contexts. Thus, depending on the circumstances, a person may steal an item or cheat on an examination in one situation and be scrupulously honest in another. This is hardly surprising, since most actions lead to positive consequences in some situations and not in others. Consequently, individuals develop highly discriminating and specific response patterns that do not generalize across all life situations. Similarly, a person who has internalized norms against cheating has not necessarily internalized norms against aggression or norms that promote helping others. The consistency and breadth of moral behavior results from the consistency and breadth of learning, not from a single unified conscience.

Second, conscience involves the verbal expression of moral standards or of remorse. "I'm sorry, Mommy, that I broke your mirror. I know I did wrong." "I really feel guilty for lying to her." "I think you should love your parents." One girl tells a friend, "I think you should be ashamed for tattling on your brother." These are all verbal expressions of moral standards by which we *may* judge a child's conscience. These verbalizations are behaviors that a child learns to perform, particularly under certain conditions, such as having broken someone's rule. (Do you think that a child can also learn to *look* ashamed or sorry?)

Third, conscience consists of self-imposed contingencies involving moral behavior. What could be a more dramatic test of a child's conscience than a child who, when he breaks his parents' rules, reports his misdeed to his parents, "sends himself" to his room, or tells himself he has been a bad boy. The child has, in effect, punished his own misbehavior. You just want to love a child like that—or feel sorry for him. So what do you do? You probably hug him—which does what? It may create a reinforcement contingency that increases the occurrence of such self-punishing behavior in the future; in other words, it may strengthen his conscience.

Since social learning theory views the conscience as behavior, it is not surprising that the learning theorists believe that learning of conscience results from the same factors influencing the learning of other behaviors—social contingencies and the imitation of models. Because it is possible for there to be different social contingencies and models for each type of conscience behavior, there may be contradictions among them. A child may verbally express a moral standard while performing immoral behaviors. Or a child may report a misdeed to her or his parents even though the child continues to perform the misdeed.

Social learning, whether it is the result of social contingencies or observation, does not necessarily result in socialization. Remember, socialization is the process by which we learn the culture of the groups we live in. Social learning may result in behavior *contrary to* the norms of a society, an institution, or an agent of socialization. Social learning theory is "content-neutral": it proposes that contingencies and models influence behavior whether the behavior is normative or deviant. Contingencies and imitation will produce normative behavior when the contingencies reward normative behavior and punish deviant behavior and when models display and are rewarded for normative behavior. Of course, society's agents of socialization try to do just that.

DEVELOPMENTAL STAGES

Developmental theories of socialization stress that early socialization involves a series of successive *developmental stages*, rather than a continuous process. The **stage model of development** is based on two premises. First, according to this view, each stage is marked by discontinuities or abrupt changes from the previous one. The kind of learning that takes place changes from one stage to the next in a manner analogous to biological maturation. Second, all individuals pass through the *same stages in the same order*, except those individuals who do not complete the entire sequence of stages due to biological or environmental deficits. Thus, our current stage of development determines how we adjust to the world in which we live.

Erikson's Theory of Development

Let's illustrate the idea of developmental stages by summarizing a frequently cited theory—Erik Erikson's (1950) theory of development. Erikson's stages of development emphasize a series of crises. In his view, development is enhanced or retarded by a person's experiences in confronting and handling each crisis brought about by the combination of maturational development and social conditions. Although he views development as continuing throughout a person's life, the first five stages involve childhood socialization.

Stage 1: Trust versus distrust. The first stage focuses on how infants develop a sense of basic trust or distrust in the environment. Children at this stage are very dependent on their parents to

meet their basic needs. When parents meet these needs consistently, the child develops a sense of trust. When parents fail to consistently meet the child's needs, the child becomes distrusting. Because mothers are the primary caretakers in our society, they are seen as most important for determining a child's sense of trust or distrust.

Stage 2: Autonomy versus shame and doubt. The second crisis stage (about eighteen months to three years) focuses on developing a sense of autonomy as opposed to continued dependence on others. The outcome of this crisis is influenced by the approach that parents take to the child's efforts to perform such activities as personal care (washing, toileting, or dressing) and other tasks (cutting with scissors or opening doors). If the child is allowed to move around, touch objects, and explore, and if toilet training is not severe, the child develops a sense of being able to make choices—autonomy. On the other hand, parental interference with these activities in order to show the child the "right and wrong way" to perform them fosters the child's continued dependence and parental control, producing in the child a sense of doubt and shame. In this stage, the father often becomes increasingly important because he lessens the intensity of the child's attachment to the mother and consequently increases the child's sense of autonomy and broadens the child's trust of others.

Stage 3: Initiative versus guilt. The third through sixth years of a child's life are characterized by exploration or "getting into things." This is a result of the child's increased capacity to move about and to communicate with others. The child's social world has grown to include other members of his or her family—siblings, grandparents, cousins, and other relatives. The crisis at this stage occurs as the child finds out whether his or her initiatives will be successful or will fail, that is, be rewarded or punished. If the initiatives are rewarded, the child will develop an attitude of "I can"—a sense of initiative. If, on the other hand, the child is punished for his or her initiatives, the child will develop a sense of guilt. The child will learn that it is safer not to try too many different things.

Stage 4: Industry versus inferiority. From about six to twelve, the child's life is characterized by a determination to master what he or she is doing, both materially and socially. Teachers and schoolmates are added to the child's social environment. Children begin to compare themselves to, as well as compete with, their peers — academically, socially, athletically, and so forth. They want to do something well — sometimes to be the best. Again, the crisis comes in the form of a child's success or failure. If the child is successful, he or she develops a sense of industry. If not, the child will develop a feeling of inferiority.

Stage 5: Identity versus role confusion. The fifth stage of a child's development begins with puberty and lasts through the adolescent years. The challenge of this stage involves establishing the answer to the question "Who am I?" Through an ever-widening network of contacts with family members, teachers, peers, and others, the adolescent is exposed to a wide variety of different roles and relationships. For adolescents, the problem becomes one of *integrating* these diverse experiences into a clear picture of themselves and relationships with others — a wholeness of self — as they enter adult life. Again, an adolescent may be more or less successful. If successful, the adolescent will develop a sense of identity. Failure to integrate his or her various roles into a composite will produce a sense of role confusion.

Although it does not concern us here, Erikson extends his idea of development into the years of adulthood and aging.

The Developmental View of Language and Communication

Earlier we described social learning theory's view of how children learn to speak and communicate with others. That theory focused on the learning that results from the child's observation of models and social contingencies — contingencies that affect both the child and the socializing agent. In contrast, developmental theory focuses on the discrete stages through which the learning of language takes place. Learning, according to this view, is affected by both nature and nurture, with each stage requiring a certain level of maturational development *and* particular social experiences. Thus, each stage is a prerequisite to the next.

According to the developmental view, the *capacity* for language has deep biological roots, but the *exercise* of that capacity depends upon our coming to understand ways of acting and thinking that exist not in our genes but in our culture. Developmental theorist Noam Chomsky proposes that all children are born with a predisposition to learn language — a language acquisition device (LAD) — that enables them to master any language (Chomsky, 1968, 1975). According to Chomsky, *mere exposure* to language activates the innate learning device. Born with this predisposition, children simply reproduce the *particular* language they are exposed to in their environments.

Other developmental theorists propose that infants are born with a cognitive endowment that makes language possible (Bruner, 1983). For example, infants are biologically predisposed to find social interaction rewarding. The predispositions provide the foundation for language acquisition. They do not generate language, but they make the infant sensitive to the features of human communication that make language learning possible. In this view, the input required by the child's biological predisposition is not mere exposure to a shower of spoken language (Bruner, 1983). Instead, the child's limited capacity for processing information requires that his or her exposure to language occur in special settings and formats. Motherese, for example, may get a baby's attention and allow more of the adult's message to be understood.

How does a child progress from a three-month-old babbling in the crib to a ten-year-old arguing with a peer about what it means to act as a "good friend"? Developmental theory tries to identify the steps a child takes during this process. It's an uncertain business. Developmental theorists disagree about the number of stages and the specific behaviors that mark each stage (Piaget, 1954; McTear, 1985; Vygotsky, 1987; Levine and

Mueller, 1988; Doval, 1990). We'll describe some features of the process.

First year: The prelinguistic stage. Vocal behavior during an infant's first year is called *prelinguistic* because it contains no actual words. While the infant's first vocalization is crying, other vocalizations appear soon after birth — for example, cooing. Developmentalists note that this is because of the shape and structure of the vocal tract of infants, which differs substantially from that of adults (Baron, 1992). "Aaaah" and "ooooo" sounds are common — hence the "ga-ga" and "goo-goo" repetitions of adults to infants at this stage. The ability to coo disappears with normal maturation of the vocal tract. At four or five months, coos turns to babbles — sounds containing consonants and vowel strings — such as "dadadadada." At about ten or twelve months, babbles are shortened to one or two repetitions of a syllable, such as "da-da." Infants also use gazing, smiling, and grasping in interacting with adults. Frequently, these behaviors mirror those of the adult with whom the infant is interacting.

Of course, infant-adult interaction does not always go smoothly, as the adult may misread the baby's signals or choose to ignore them. Not sure of the meaning, an adult may respond with a raised eyebrow or quizzical look and baby talk such as "Does your tummy hurt?" If there is an object of attention — for example, a milk bottle or drinking cup — the adult may point a finger at it, move his eyes between the child and the object, or move the object closer to the infant. These nonverbal gestures may be combined with verbal comments: "What? Milk? Do you want milk?" Infants are not very adept at responding to other infants. Signals from another infant are usually ignored. When infants do respond to one another, the response is likely to be simple: one child may gaze at the other or take an offered toy and then turn his or her attention to something else.

Toddlers: Shared-meaning stage. Soon after a child's first birthday, communication skills begin to diversify. Children's utterances begin to take on meaning; specific utterances are used to refer to objects and express intentions. Sometimes children's words approximate adult words ("ku" to refer to cookie); other times children use bablelike sounds ("ga-ga" to refer to blanket). They usually use one or two words instead of word sequences. A surprising amount of adult-child communication is possible even when a child's use of words is very restricted. A common word used by many toddlers is "Dat?" — meaning "What is that?" Once the child realizes that things have names, he or she may point to object after object asking "Dat?" With a cooperative partner, this naming game can result in the rapid acquisition of new words (Kamhi, 1986). The adult may accept the child's use of an imperfect word or demand a closer approximation of the adult word — "Say 'cookie' and you can have one." Children use "there" to draw someone's attention to an object, or the infamous word "no" to complain or refuse a request.

Usually, toddlers accompany attention-getting verbalizations with the same nonverbal gestures used by adults — moving close to the adult, pointing a finger, or moving the eyes between the adult and the object of attention (cookie jar, book, untied shoelace, or bruise). Adults must rely largely on nonverbal gestures to know exactly what the child means. Similarly, toddlers seem to be able to understand more words than they can say, but they use clues from nonverbal gestures to understand their meaning. For example, a child may seem to understand his mother's request "Give the block to Mommy." However, he may be responding, in part, to her holding out her hand to receive the block and focusing her gaze on the block. In the absence of these cues, he may *not* understand the verbal request. Thus, both adults and toddlers use context and nonverbal gestures to communicate.

Toddlers learn something about conversations. They begin to take turns talking and will respond to conversations initiated by adults, but they seldom take the initiative to sustain the conversation themselves. Successful communication at this stage depends heavily on the adult partner's willingness and ability to do "extra" work in order to

Once a toddler realizes that things have names, he or she may point to object after object asking "Dat?"—meaning "What is that?" With a cooperative partner, this naming game can result in the rapid acquisition of new words.

make sense of the toddler's utterances. Thus, it is not surprising that child-child interaction during this period is often less fruitful. Initiatives taken by one child toward another frequently involve demanding toys. When these demands are not met, children may resort to hitting or biting to get what they want. Instances of sustained interaction between toddlers are rare. When they occur, they usually involve simultaneous or sequential imitations of a behavior. Adults play a major role in children's sustained interactions with one another by teaching them games or other cooperative activities.

Preschoolers: Conventional communication stage. In the earlier stages of language development, many of the words and phrases children use to communicate with their family members have little meaning outside the child's family. Between the age of three and the time they begin school, most children's language expands and becomes more conventional, matching that found in the child's community. The significance of this is that it allows children to communicate more successfully with others beyond their family members. Preschoolers' sentences become longer and more complete, though not necessarily grammatically correct. Sentences are punctuated with idiosyncratic words as well as errors in verb tense ("runned," "have went"), plurals ("tooths," "mouses"), omitted words ("Where goes the wheel?"), and word order ("Where she is going?"). Children have difficulty using relational expressions ("in," "under," "between," "more," "less"). As their verbal communication becomes more effective, so does the incidence of verbal aggression, and arguments among preschoolers are common.

Preschoolers are more able to initiate and sustain communication over a period of time than are toddlers. They get some practice by the telling of jokes or riddles. The child knows that when telling a knock-knock joke, he or she (1) says "knock-knock," (2) waits for the other person to ask "Who's there?," (3) provides an answer, (4) waits for another question, and then (5) provides the punchline. Although children in this stage are aware of the turn-taking aspects of communication, they have not yet learned how to create new jokes or riddles. They know the communication routine, but they don't know what makes jokes funny.

School age: The adaptability stage. Going to school entails greater developmental challenges for some children than for others. Children whose first language is not English have an especially difficult adjustment to make when they enter school. Many children come from homes where the dominant language is Spanish, Chinese, Vietnamese, or some other non-English language. Others come from homes in which different dialects of English are spoken. For example, in so-called "black English" the present tense of the verbs "come" and "say" is sometimes used for the past tense. A person might use "He say" rather than the teacher's preference for "He said." Auxiliary verbs may be dropped, as in "What you mean?" rather than the preferred "What do you mean?"

In addition, many children enter school having learned different styles of communication, some of which conflict with those expected by their teachers. For example, they freely interrupt teachers and classmates without raising their hands and waiting to be recognized by the teacher. Others are not familiar with the teacher-question-followed-by-student-answer routines typical of most classrooms.

In schools, children also experience greater contact with other children who have different language and communication styles. We have already mentioned some racial and ethnic differences. There are also gender differences. For example, girls orient themselves more directly toward one another in conversation than boys do. Girls sit close together, looking straight into one another's eyes. During conversation, boys sit far-

ther apart, shoulder to shoulder, with a minimum of eye contact. These racial, ethnic, and gender differences in communication styles sometimes result in the perpetuation of group segregation, with members of different groups using their limited style of communication with one another and avoiding contact with members of groups whose styles are different. However, in other cases, children become more skillful in adapting their verbal and nonverbal behavior to achieve greater success in communicating with others whose styles differ from their own. These skills allow children to resolve conflicts with peers through conversation, in which they offer explanations and criticisms as well as expressions of their awareness of how peers think and feel about their positions.

Thus, the developmental view of language acquisition stresses the interaction of biological and environmental forces. Children master aspects of language learning as they become physically and cognitively mature enough to do so—and as their environment poses the right challenges and supports. More complex aspects of language usage are accomplished only after simpler aspects are mastered. Thus, later stages build upon earlier ones.

The Developmental View of Internalization and Conscience

Social learning theorists conceive of internalization and the development of conscience as a cumulative process that builds upon itself gradually and continuously. In sharp contrast, developmental theorists like Lawrence Kohlberg (1984), a Harvard psychologist, say that such development—which he calls "moral development"—takes place in stages, each reflecting a different mode of reasoning. Kohlberg claims that children pass, step by step, through a sequence of culturally universal and invariant stages in moral development. Reaching any stage necessitates passing through the preceding series of stages. Moreover, each successive stage is considered to be morally superior to the preceding stages.

Kohlberg developed his ideas about these stages by asking subjects questions about hypothetical moral dilemmas. One of the situations he presented has become famous as posing a particularly difficult dilemma:

> In Europe, a woman was near death from a special kind of cancer. There was one drug that the doctors thought might save her. It was a form of radium that a druggist in the same town had recently discovered. The drug was expensive to make, but the druggist was charging ten times what the drug cost him to make. He paid $200 for the radium and charged $2,000 for a small dose of the drug. The sick woman's husband, Heinz, went to everyone he knew to borrow money, but he could only get together about $1,000, which is half of what it cost. He told the druggist that his wife was dying, and asked him to sell it cheaper or let him pay later. But the druggist said, "No, I discovered the drug and I'm going to make money from it." Heinz got desperate and broke into the man's store to steal the drug for his wife. Should the husband have done that? (Kohlberg, 1963: 18–19)

On the basis of children's and adults' responses to dilemmas of this sort, Kohlberg has arrived at six stages in the development of moral judgment or conscience. He groups these stages into three major levels: the preconventional level, the conventional level, and the postconventional level. The stages and levels are not based on the moral decision of whether Heinz should or should not have stolen the drug. Rather, Kohlberg is concerned with the *style of reasoning* the individual employs in reaching a decision.

Each of Kohlberg's levels reflects a different type of relationship between an individual and social norms. The first level, the *preconventional level*, characterizes individuals who respond to social norms in order to achieve rewards and avoid punishment. Social norms remain *external* to such individuals — something imposed by other people. For example, a child at this stage of reasoning might justify Heinz's theft of the drug "because the wife needs the drug and Heinz needs his wife's companionship." Alternatively, a child might condemn Heinz's theft "because he will get caught and go to jail." The preconventional level

characterizes young children, some adolescents, and many criminals. Some people do not develop beyond this initial level.

The second level, the *conventional level*, is typical of most adolescents and adults. Individuals at this level have *internalized* the social norms, adopting others' norms as their own. The behavior of persons operating at this level reflects an orientation toward the needs of others and respect for authority. At the *postconventional level* (the highest level of moral development), the individual creates a set of *personal* principles by which the person judges her or his own behavior. According to Kohlberg, these principles emphasize a respect for the rights of all people — the individual's own and others' — a balancing of conflicting interests. The principles are embodied in such words as "justice" and "equality." Kohlberg believes that only a minority of Americans attain the postconventional level.

The developmental psychologist Carol Gilligan (1982*a*, *b*), who worked with Kohlberg for more than a decade, contends that Kohlberg's moral dilemmas capture men's but not women's moral development. She finds that men and women make different moral judgments. Men typically define moral problems in terms of rights and rules — justice. Women are more likely to conceive of morality as an obligation to help and to avoid hurt — caring. Thus, while both men and women may come to the aid of a suffering person, they may do so for different reasons. Men are likely to intervene in order to prevent injustice or inequity; thus their judgment is based on rules applied to both the sufferer and themselves. On the other hand, women are more likely to give aid because of the sufferer's needs, which may be unrelated to their own needs.

Gilligan explains this proposed difference in terms of the types of relationships typical of men and women. Men's relationships tend to be competitive because men value the pursuit of individual goals and strive to maintain the autonomy of each individual involved in a relationship. Accordingly, men see morality as a system of rules for guiding competition, taming aggression, and adjudicating the rights of the separate participants. Women more typically see relationships themselves as important — as ends in themselves. Consequently, they think of morality in terms of protecting the integrity of relationships and maintaining human bonds. Gilligan's proposal has given rise to considerable controversy (Deaux, 1985). Does her distinction between the moral judgments of men and women seem reasonable to you?

While the studies of moral development by Kohlberg and Gilligan focus on moral *reasoning*, other studies focus on moral *behavior*. Some researchers look at how children allocate rewards among their peers. This emphasis reflects Kohlberg's concern with justice. Young children typically give themselves greater rewards (the biggest piece of cake or the bag with the most marbles, for example). Later, they are more likely to distribute rewards equally (equality) or give greater rewards to those children who make greater contributions (equity). A second research focus reflects what Gilligan describes as the caring type of morality that is typical of females. This research looks at when children begin to come to the aid of others in need or distress in different situations. Finally, still other researchers study how children fix responsibility or blame for harm done to others. In their research, the question under investigation is whether children consider mitigating factors in deciding to blame or punish an "accused." For example, did the accused *intend* to harm the person? Did the accused *foresee* the harm he or she caused? Was the accused *justified* in causing the harm; that is, was the accused provoked or just doing his or her duty? Perhaps, the most important finding of all this research has been that children begin to develop moral behavior at a very early age, as early as two or three years old (Darley and Schultz, 1990).

REFLEXIVE BEHAVIOR AND NEGOTIATION

Thus far, our discussion has focused on social learning and developmental theories. And although they are of interest to most social psychol-

ogists, their origins are in psychology. The theory of socialization that has more sociological origins is **symbolic interaction theory** — a theory that focuses on how individuals interpret and give meanings to their social interactions. Symbolic interactionists point out that just as two interacting individuals can perceive, evaluate, communicate with, motivate, and attempt to control each other, they can also take these same actions toward themselves through self-evaluation, self-communication, self-motivation, and self-control. Behavior of this type is called **reflexive behavior**. To have a **self** is to have the capacity to engage in reflexive actions — to observe, plan, guide, and respond to our own behavior. The development of a child's self and the child's subsequent use of reflexive behavior are important aspects of the process of socialization. Reflexive behavior is important because it is through this process that children learn to modify their own behavior.

The Development of the Self

George Herbert Mead (1934) described a three-stage process through which the self develops and the child becomes able to fully participate in social life. His description of the origins of the self is a developmental theory, analogous to Kohlberg's theory of moral development.

In the *preparatory stage*, children do not have the ability to view their own behavior. They imitate specific actions that they observe around them. For example, a child may hold up a newspaper or book as though she or he is "reading" it, may clap and cheer an action viewed on the television, or may blow a kiss and wave "bye-bye." Preverbal children learn behaviors that arouse particular responses in others. For example, a child may have the repeated experience of crying and being fed. According to Mead, the child learns the sequence of events in the form of a *mental image* of the sequence. The *meaning* (to the child) of the crying is that it brings food. Children learn the meanings of objects in their environment. For example, a father may dangle a rattle so that his child can see it. If the child strikes the rattle, the behavior may cause the rattle to move back and forth, make a noise, and produce a smile on the face of the father.

Through repeated social interactions like this, the child learns the connections among these events — the mental image of the sequence. When the object rattle is presented, it will produce this mental image. The mental image provides the meaning of the object rattle — something to strike that produces motion, noise, and a smile. Other people and their gestures may become meaningful objects. The mother's act of bringing food when the child cries gives meaning to the mother. The dangling of the rattle by the child's father gives meaning to him.

Children begin to learn the meaning of words in the same manner. With repeated experiences, for example, a child may learn (develop a mental image) that his saying "juice" can produce a drink. Or that if a parent says "juice" and he says "goo," he will get a drink. With the exception of Mead's focus on learning in terms of mental images, his description of the process of learning is very similar to the learning by contingencies proposed by social learning theory.

The second stage in Mead's account of the development of self is the *play stage*. In this stage, children assume the role of *one* person at a time and attempt to enact the behavior associated with the role, such as mother, cowboy, police officer, or teacher. Very often the model is a *significant other* — a particular person who has considerable influence on our self-evaluation and our acceptance of given social norms. For instance, a two-year-old child may examine a doll's undergarment, pretend to find it soiled, reprimand the doll, and take the doll to the bathroom. The child is proceeding from the perspective of a particular person — in this case, very likely the mother — and then responding to the situation as the mother would respond. At first, this takes the form of play, a little skit in which the child imitates the behavior of another person she or he has observed. Eventually, the child develops the capacity to *think about* the other's perspective without acting it out.

By playing at a variety of behaviors associated with a single role, the child learns the overall pattern of conduct that constitutes the role. Even though many of the roles children "play at" are not ones they will ever have in real life, children will be called upon many times to adopt new roles. The play process teaches them *how* to learn and play roles.

In the play stage, children assume the role of only one other person at a time. Mead's third stage, the *game stage*, involves additional social skills. Children find themselves in situations in which they must respond to the expectations of several people at the same time. To participate in a baseball or soccer game, for example, the child must be aware of the possible actions of each player. In a game such as football, all eleven roles are closely and tightly interwoven. If the play involves a sweep to the right, the end has to coordinate his or her behavior with that of the halfback, the quarterback, the tackle, and the guard in a way quite different from that involved in a passing play. All the players must know the responses associated with the other positions and take these responses into account in devising their own behavior. The game entails a social situation that links people within a network of role relationships and a web of role demands. Consequently, games socialize and prepare children to participate in cooperative, coordinated endeavors as group members.

The same principle applies to other tasks that involve collaboration or a division of assignments. To function in these more complex social interactions, children are required to view themselves from the position of the larger group. They now gain a synthesized overview of the cultural workings of their community and view themselves from the perspective of the *generalized other* — the community as a whole. The generalized other is reflected in internalized standards (norms) by which the child views and judges her or his own behavior. Games and similar social interactions lead to the internalization of such basic social rules as "playing fair" and "taking turns." At this

---

STUDENT OBSERVATION

The Generalized Other

*L*ast evening a group of us went to see an X-rated movie. I had never seen one before. We had to wait in line along the sidewalk outside the theater. The theater is in the campus district, and I felt exceedingly uncomfortable. I was ashamed of what I believed other people would think of me if they saw me going to a porno movie. I worried that my professors or someone who knew my parents might observe me. This is a good example of the generalized other. Through socialization processes, I had come to take over the view of the larger society that porno movies are licentious and reveal lewd, carnal appetites — deviant sexuality. The conceptions I hold of the expectations others have of me tell me that if I am seen as watching porno movies, others will disapprove of me.

---

point the child has developed expectations for her or his own behavior as well as expectations for others. (Before reading further, see the Student Observation: "The Generalized Other.")

Language and Private Speech

Mead and later theorists emphasize the role of language and "private speech" in the development of the self (Vygotsky, 1978; Wertsch, 1991). Private speech is the use of language as a tool of thought — talking to one's self. Thus, children use language not only for social communication but also for planning, guiding, and monitoring their own behavior — for self-regulation. In this view, private speech is an intermediate step between the regulation of the child's behavior by others and its regulation by thought.

Children's use of private speech to control their own behavior follows a development pattern. At first, private speech comes after the child's behavior. Later, it occurs simultaneously with the behavior. Finally, it precedes action and assumes a self-regulatory function, affecting behavior on a moment-by-moment basis as the child grapples with challenging tasks. Eventually, private speech becomes abbreviated, and the child begins to "think" words instead of saying them aloud (Berk, 1992). Young children use private speech in their pretend play, practicing self-regu-

lation of their behavior and contributing to cognitive development (Smolucha, 1992).

Role-taking

Once children have acquired a self — the capacity to act toward themselves — they begin to develop concepts of themselves and to modify their own behavior. This process, sometimes called "the selfhood process," involves children's looking at their behavior and responding to what they see. For example, a child may want to go out to play. But the child mentally "takes a look at this behavior" and sees that if she goes out, she will miss her favorite TV show. Consequently, the child might decide to stay at home and go out to play later, but then she sees that doing so means that all her friends will be gone. Through the alternating process of reflexive behavior the child guides her own behavior.

The "self," as the word is used in the social sciences, does not refer to a corporeal body or even to part of it; the self lacks a real physical existence. Rather, the self is a psychological process consisting of mentally constructed images each individual has regarding his or her behavior. The self represents a way of thinking and speaking about our experience rather than a physical thing or a psychic entity.

Children's reflexive behavior may sometimes

involve looking at their own behavior "from their own point of view." Of greater interest to symbolic interactionists is reflexive behavior in which children look at their own behavior "from the point of view of other people." This is called **role-taking**. Charles Horton Cooley (1902) had his own name for it — the *looking-glass self*. In this view, children's conceptions of themselves are influenced by seeing themselves reflected in other people's attitudes and behaviors toward them.

According to Cooley, the looking-glass self has three parts: how we think we appear to others, how we think they judge what they see, and how we feel about their judgments. For example, from other people's comments and actions, a boy may think that his peers see him as relatively larger and more developed than they are. He may think that they see him as a freak, and he may be embarrassed by this. Or he may think that they judge his size as evidence of athletic ability and skill and be pleased by this. Or he may think that they are afraid of him because of his larger size. He might be glad about this and see it as a source of power over them, or he might be confused and hurt that they don't treat him like "one of the guys." Thus the looking-glass self is a mixture of observation, imagination, and subjective interpretation. The ability to take the perspective of another person is a basic requirement of all social behavior (Hass, 1984). (Before reading further, see the Student Observation: "Taking the Role of the Other.")

Mead (1932, 1934, 1938) later elaborated upon Cooley's ideas and contributed many insights of his own. Mead called reflexive behavior "taking the role of the other." The phrase "taking the role of the other toward ourselves" does not mean that at some point we cease being ourselves. Rather, we assume a *dual* perspective: simultaneously, one is the *subject* doing the viewing and the *object* being viewed. In imagination, one steps out of oneself, so to speak, into the position of another and looks back upon the self from this standpoint — a reflexive process. Thus, taking the role of the other toward ourselves is nothing more than responding to ourselves in the same way in which other people might respond to us: just as they might become angry with us, so we become angry with ourselves; just as they might rebuke us, so we rebuke ourselves; just as they might argue with us, so we argue with ourselves; and so on. Thus we may feel "proud of ourselves" or "ashamed of ourselves" or may "talk to ourselves." Only by seeing ourselves as objects can we designate to ourselves that we are or are not acting appropriately. It is our self — the ability to take ourselves as objects — that allows us to imaginatively

---

STUDENT OBSERVATION

Taking the Role of the Other

When I was in high school, my teachers used to compliment me often, so I knew that they thought I was a pretty good kid. However, there was one time that I got caught "helping" a friend on a test. The teacher called the two of us up to her desk at the end of the class. I was so nervous because I knew she had seen us cheating. I was trying to figure out a way to get out of this. I said to myself, "If I was in her shoes right now, what would I be thinking about me?" I figured that she would probably still think I was a good kid and say to herself that I just "messed up" this one time. So I decided that the best thing to do would be to put on the most pitiful, sorry face that I could — hang my head low and act ashamed. I think it worked. At first she talked to my friend and me together and told us that she was going to give us both a zero on the test. Then later that day, when I saw her, she said that she had decided that on *my* test she would take off 20 points — which still left me with a 75 on the test. I guess it paid off to take a little time to step outside myself and look at things (me) though her eyes in order to determine how I should act.

rehearse possible future actions, judge them, and revise them.

Symbolic interaction theorists view role-taking as the principal learning process in socialization. What social contingencies are to social learning theory and maturational stages are to developmental theory, role-taking is to symbolic interaction theory. In this view, children learn culture through role-taking.

Communication

In role-taking, we view ourselves from another's point of view. However, our perception of how the other expects us to behave may be accurate or inaccurate. The accuracy of our perceptions is strongly affected by communication. Communication requires *significant symbols*—a repertoire of signs, gestures, and eventually language shared by members of a society or groups—in this case, children and their agents of socialization. In fact, role-taking may not occur at all until children learn the pronouns "you" and "I," which facilitate their distinction between themselves and others. Most children master the use of these pronouns by age two and one-half (Clark, 1976). With experience, children learn that some things stand for other things. Holding out my hands means I want to be picked up. "Ba" means ball (or "I want my ball"). Frowning means "I have to go to the potty." "Shush" means to be quiet. "Be good" means to stand still.

When using or responding to symbols, children engage in role-taking in order to anticipate how a socializing agent will respond to them or how the socializing agent wants them to respond. If the child and the socializing agent share the same understanding of the symbols, communication is possible and the chances of accurate role-taking are enhanced. Most children learn their first symbols from their parents; and because of their shared meaning, children can engage in role-taking with considerable accuracy. But when the child comes into contact with others— Grandma, Uncle Joe, neighbor Mr. Wilson, or the waiter at the local restaurant—these adults may not understand that frowning means "I have

to go to the potty." And the child may not understand that "whoa" means to stand still and that "Be good" means to act happy. The child may misinterpret the adults' symbols. In such circumstances, the child may have the *capacity* to role-take but not understand how the socializing agent wants him or her to respond. The child's behavior in response to such inaccurate interpretations will appear "unsocialized."

Negotiation

Even if children correctly understand adults' communications, we can't be sure that they will "do the right thing." They may be motivated to ignore what the socializing agent wants and do something else. If, thinking reflexively, children perceive that doing the right thing—what the adult wants—would mean not getting to watch TV, eat candy, or play with their friends, they may not follow the adult's instructions. This should give you some understanding of why symbolic interaction theorists see children, as well as adults, as *active* participants in the socialization process.

But socialization will not fail just because a child is motivated to ignore what a socializing agent wants. Ultimately, socialization depends on the outcome of a **negotiation** of the conflicting interests of the child and the socializing agent—a bargaining process through which they settle on the terms of a transaction or an agreement. Social learning theorists would say that negotiation involves "reciprocal social contingencies": *each* person's behavior produces its own consequence in the form of the other's behavior. Symbolic interactionists would say that negotiation involves the parties' efforts to influence each other's "definition of the situation."

Often the issue under negotiation involves whether the child's behavior is wrong and deserves punishment (the agent's interpretation) or not wrong and undeserving of punishment (the child's interpretation). Researchers give particular attention to children's efforts to establish their own interpretation of the situation by offering explanations for their behavior, called *accounts*.

For example, a child may deny ever committing the behavior (*refusal*): "Mommy, I didn't hit her. She's lying." Or the child may admit committing the act but try to establish the interpretation that the behavior was justified (*justification*): "She was pinching me, so I hit her to make her stop." Researchers have found that children learn these methods of negotiation when they are as young as two years old (Dunn, 1987).

Cultural Routines

Much of children's learning occurs in negotiations during play with their peers. For example, to initiate interactions with one another, children often use "access rituals," following and watching other children at a "safe" distance, repeatedly imitating other children's behavior, or pleading to be included in their activities (Mandell, 1988, 1991). Research shows that young children may develop a peer culture, which consists of *routines* — activities that the children consistently produce together — for example, verbal disputes, insults and teasing, protection of play areas, and ridicule of adult roles (Corsaro and Rizzo, 1988). Through such activities, even very young children learn that there is a status hierarchy — in other words, that some children have more power over their peers than others do (Corsaro, 1979). Differences in ages ("big kids" versus "little kids") are frequently understood as the basis for differences in power and expertise (Passuth, 1987). The peer cultures of young children frequently include conflict rituals much like those of adolescents and adults. The purpose of such conflict rituals is to demonstrate the participants' competence (e.g., who is best at insulting) rather than to resolve some larger issue (Corsaro and Rizzo, 1988, 1990).

While some of the routines of children's groups *reflect* the adult culture, other routines consist of creative methods of *evading* the adult culture. This is illustrated by William Corsaro's studies (1992) of nursery school children. In some classrooms, the children employed several concealment strategies to evade the teachers' rule that prohibited bringing toys or other personal objects from home to school. The teachers saw this rule as necessary to prevent them from constantly having to settle disputes about sharing these items. The children adopted the method of bringing small objects that they could conceal in their pockets to show one another without attracting the teachers' attention. Just as a child can influence an adult, so too can children's culture influence adult culture. In some of the classrooms that Corsaro studied, the children's desire to bring personal objects to class led the teachers to add a new element to their curriculum — a designated "show and tell" routine aimed at developing the children's communication skills.

A SUMMARY OF THE THEORIES

We have been discussing three views of how socialization occurs during early childhood. Let's review the processes of socialization according to the three theories we have examined. Social learning theory proposes that learning occurs in two principal ways — through conditioning and imitation. Conditioning describes the process whereby individuals, as a result of their experience, establish an association, or linkage, between two events. Through observational learning, or imitation, individuals can acquire new patterns of behavior, as well as strengthen or weaken inhibitions of previously learned behavior. In contrast, developmental theories stress that early socialization involves a series of successive stages. According to this view, each stage is marked by discontinuities or abrupt changes from the previous one in the kinds of learning that take place. Developmental theories also assume that all individuals (except for those with biological or environmental deficits) pass through the same stages in the same order and that a person's stage of development determines how he or she adjusts to the environment. Symbolic interaction theorists emphasize the active role of children in the socialization process. These theorists are concerned with reflexive behavior — the ability to observe, plan, guide, and respond to our own behavior. Through reflexivity, the child views and judges her or his own behavior in terms of the generalized other.

So which theory correctly accounts for socialization? The answer is, of course, that it depends on the research question we are trying to answer. The three theories we have discussed contradict one another less than it may first appear. Rather, they focus on different aspects of the same phenomenon — in this case, socialization. Let's look at what the theories have to say about language learning, for example. Symbolic interaction theory has little to say about *how* children learn language, but it proposes that the reflexive process — the key to socialization according to this approach — requires language. To take ourselves as objects, we must be able to symbolize ourselves to ourselves, and we do this through language. We noted that role-taking probably does not occur at all until we know the pronouns "you" and "I," which allow us to distinguish between ourselves and others. Similarly, developmental psychologists assume that the failure to learn language at the appropriate time will interfere with other important kinds of learning that normally take place in later stages. But in the developmental view, biological, psychological, and social factors combine to produce a time during which children are most receptive to various aspects of language learning. According to social learning theorists, we learn language the way we learn any other behavior — through social contingencies and imitation. Once learned, language can serve as any part of a social contingency — behavior, consequence, or discriminative stimulus.

The three theories we have discussed have in common an opposition to the view that learning means perfect socialization, which social psychologists sometimes call "oversocialization." We have pointed out, for example, that children may learn something other than what is intended by their agents of socialization. Social learning theory notes that deviant behavior — behavior contrary to the norms of the culture — may be supported by social contingencies and by displays of deviant behavior by models. Developmental theory points out that some people fail to progress beyond the early stages of development. And symbolic interaction theory emphasizes the effects of inaccurate role-taking, contrary motivation, and negotiations. All these factors may contribute to a diversity of learning outcomes, some of which will not be consistent with prevailing social norms.

Subcultures and Social Change

There is yet another factor contributing to the diversity of learning outcomes. Although we sometimes speak of *society* and *culture* as though all members subscribed equally to their values and norms, this is not the case. Especially in large, complex, modern societies, the larger society is subdivided in a number of different ways. One important subdivision is *social class* — a categorization of members of a society in terms of the amount of wealth, prestige, and power they possess. Associated with variations in social class are differences in values and ways of life, including child-rearing practices. As we shall see in the next chapter, our social class can affect not only *how* we are socialized but also *what* we are taught.

Other major subdivisions in our society are *racial* and *ethnic* groups. The United States has been populated by immigrants from many countries. Some, because of their appearance, names, language, traditions and rituals, religion, or other distinguishing characteristics are thought of as "different" by both others and themselves. Such groups often have some values, norms, and roles that differ from those of the larger, **dominant culture** — the culture of the group whose values, norms, traditions, and outlooks are imposed on the society as a whole. When the perspective and life style of a subgroup of society differ significantly from those of the dominant culture and when its members identify themselves as different, the subgroup is said to have a **subculture**.

Subcultural differences are important for the socialization of new members of subgroups, who may receive conflicting messages about what behavior is appropriate, or what "works" best. We have noted, for example, that children's peer groups often develop subcultures that clash in some ways with the dominant culture represented by adults. Each group applies its own pressures to ensure adherence to its own norms. You can probably recall an experience from your own childhood in which your parents and friends disagreed about the appropriateness of some behavior — how to dress or wear your hair, perhaps.

Children growing up in different subcultures, then, have different socialization experiences. To some degree, at least, they learn different things. Consider how subculture might shape the experiences of children growing up in the Appalachian Mountains in eastern Kentucky or western North Carolina compared with the experiences of children growing up in New York City, Chicago, or San Francisco. Similarly, the subculture to which

children growing up in urban housing projects are socialized differs from the one their suburban counterparts experience. And children growing up on the Navajo reservation in Arizona are not exposed to the same culture as the children of Mormons in Salt Lake City, the children of Irish immigrants in Boston, or the children of families recently immigrating from Mexico to Los Angeles.

Although these subcultures have accommodated many of the features of the dominant culture — particularly as a result of most children's being exposed to our dominant culture's "universal education" — the differences that exist may make it difficult for a child from one subculture to function well in another. A child socialized in Appalachia will probably be more successful in

When the perspective and life style of a subgroup of society differ significantly from those of the dominant culture and when its members identify themselves as different, the subgroup is said to have a subculture. Each group or subgroup applies pressures to ensure adherence to its own norms. Thus, the socialization experience of subgroup members may differ from those of members of the dominant culture.

Appalachia than in New York. Of course, the reciprocal is also true: a child socialized in New York will probably be more successful there than in Appalachia. This is because subcultures are people's adaptations to their physical and social circumstances. In addition to reflecting what people value, a subculture reflects what they believe to be "realistic" or "necessary," given their circumstances. Thus, the greater emphasis of middle-class persons, compared with lower-class persons, on career success may indicate a difference in values, *or* a realistic adaptation by lower-class people to their very restricted chances of achieving success.

When a child moves from one culture or subculture to another—for example, from the family's culture to the school's culture and back again or from one region of the country to another as a result of a family move—the child may experience conflicting messages about what is expected. These different messages may generate confusion for the child. Thus, the children of recent immigrants from Mexico, the Caribbean, Vietnam, and elsewhere not only face the problems of transition from one society to another but also must manage potential conflicts between the subcultures embraced by their families and their schools.

The concepts of culture, institution, agents of socialization, and subculture are useful in that they help us understand both the process and the content of the socialization we all experience. However, we do not mean to imply that the society into which a child is born is static. Instead, basic alterations occur over time in the behavior patterns, culture, and structure of a society—alterations known as **social changes**. Some examples of these changes are the increasing number of working mothers and one-parent families, the development of new occupational roles in response to new technologies, and movements to end discrimination on the basis of race, sex, and handicaps. Obviously, the socialization of new members of the society both affects and is affected by social change.

This chapter has illustrated how socialization into an ongoing society begins with infants. Successful early socialization results in behavior that is consistent with the culture's norms and values, a conscience that internalizes many of these norms and values, linguistic and cognitive competence, the emergence of self, and the learning of some basic roles of the society. The success of later socialization depends upon the accomplishment of these goals of early socialization. We often think of socialization as something that takes place during childhood and ends with adulthood. Yet as noted at the beginning of the chapter, socialization is a lifetime process. In the next chapter, "Socialization over the Life Course," we provide a more detailed picture of what social psychologists see when they look at socialization beyond infancy.

Summary

1. Socialization helps us to understand two kinds of phenomena: (1) how a person becomes capable of participating in society and (2) how society is possible. *Both* an appropriate biological inheritance and a favorable environment are essential for producing a human personality.

2. Children are born into a social world that already exists. The cultures of the society and subgroups into which children are born define the social environment into which they will be socialized and comprise many of the things they will be expected to learn. Culture is composed of values, norms, roles, symbols (including language), and physical objects.

3. According to social learning theory, learning occurs in two principal ways: (1) conditioning and (2) imitating the behavior of another. Conditioning describes the process whereby individuals, as a result of their experience, establish an association, or linkage, between two events. Through observational learning, individuals can acquire new patterns of behavior,

as well as strengthen or weaken inhibitions of previously learned behavior.

4. The stage model of development stresses that early socialization involves a series of successive stages. According to this view, each stage is marked by discontinuities or abrupt changes from the previous one in the kinds of learning that take place. A second basic premise of the stage approach is that all individuals pass through the same stages in the same order, unless they experience biological or environmental deficits. Thus, our current stage of development determines how we adjust to the world in which we live.

5. Symbolic interaction theorists emphasize the active role of the child in his or her socialization process. They are concerned with reflexive behavior — the ability to observe, plan, guide, and respond to our own behavior — and negotiations between the child and socializing agents.

6. Social psychological theories caution against the view that learning means perfect socialization, which social psychologists sometimes call "oversocialization." The theories identify the factors contributing to a diversity of learning outcomes, some of which will not be consistent with prevailing social norms.

7. Social class, racial, ethnic, and other groups are said to comprise subcultures when they have norms, values, and roles that differ from those of the dominant culture. Subcultural differences are important for the socialization of new members of subgroups because they may provide conflicting messages about what is good or how to act.

CHAPTER 3

SOCIALIZATION OVER THE LIFE COURSE

All the world's a stage,
And all the men and women merely players.
They have their exits and their entrances;
And one man in his time plays many parts,
His acts being seven ages.
At first the infant,
Mewling and puking in the nurse's arms.
Then the whining school-boy, with his satchel
And shining morning face, creeping like snail
Unwillingly to school: and then the lover,
Sighing like furnace, with a woeful ballad
Made to his mistress' eyebrow: then a soldier,
full of strange oaths and bearded like the pard,
Jealous in honour, sudden and quick in quarrel,
Seeking the bubble reputation
Even in the cannon's mouth: and the justice,
In fair round belly with good capon line,
With eyes severe and beard of formal cut,
Full of wise saws and modern instances,
And so he plays his part. . . . The sixth age
    shifts
Into the lean and slippered pantaloon,
With spectacles on nose and pouch on side,
His youthful hose, well saved, a world too wide
For his shrunk shank, and his big manly voice,
Turning again toward childish treble, pipes,

And whistles in his sound. . . . Last scene of
    all,
That ends this strange eventful history,
In second childishness, and mere oblivion,
Sans teeth, sans eyes, sans taste, sans
    everything.

As You Like It, William Shakespeare

The Life-Course Perspective

ROLE EXPECTATIONS AND THE LIFE COURSE

How the "mewling and puking infant" becomes the lover, the soldier, and the justice and finally enters "second childishness, and mere oblivion" has been of great interest to social psychologists. All societies have norms that classify individuals into age categories, dividing individuals' lives into meaningful stages and establishing timetables for major life events. This is called **age grading**. Societies differ in the number of stages they recognize, in where they draw the boundaries between one stage and another, and in the role expectations that are associated with each stage. For example, many contemporary Americans divide life into childhood, adolescence, adulthood, and old age, with each stage having various subdivisions. Some social psychologists are interested in how people learn and adapt to the socially patterned sequence of changes in roles that defines the journey from life to death — the **life course.** This particular interest is called the life-course perspective (Clausen, 1986; Elder, 1987; O'Rand and Krecker, 1990).

In Chapter 2, "Early Socialization," we introduced the concept of **role** — the normative expectations that apply to the behavior of a specific category of people in a particular situation. It is of particular interest to life-course researchers that *role expectations are age-graded.* In our society, for example, we don't expect a ten-year-old to be a physician or a middle-aged man to be a kindergarten student. All societies have norms that prescribe certain role behaviors for certain stages of the life course. In some instances, the age marking a change in role expectations is very specific. For example, the laws of most U.S. states say that you can legally purchase liquor at age twenty-one. In other cases, societal norms specify a range of ages within which particular roles should be exited or entered. For example, in our society, most people are expected to leave school and begin work

between the ages of sixteen and twenty-five. Societies differ in the role expectations they impose on their members, as well as in how these expectations are associated with age. (Before reading further, see the Student Observation: "Age Grading of Role Expectations.")

Within any society, age-graded role expectations may change over time. A century ago, our society expected most of its members to begin work at a very young age and to work until they were physically unable to continue. Today, we exempt children, adolescents, and retirees from work expectations. Over time, the ages marking the boundaries of the work role have converged: people now enter work later and leave earlier. Only a few decades ago, most male members of our society were expected to spend some time in the soldier role, and most females were expected to be housewives.

The latter point suggests that all members of a society do not face the same role expectations. In all societies, role expectations differ by gender. Social psychologists call these different patterns of expectations **sex roles.** The differential imposition of role expectations by gender is of particular significance because societies use roles to allocate privileges and responsibilities. Many sex-role differences produce social inequalities between the

---

STUDENT OBSERVATION

Age Grading of Role Expectations

I am a "nontraditional" student in that I have returned to college as a married twenty-nine-year old to finish my undergraduate degree. The traditional role expectation for a college student is to graduate at twenty-one or twenty-two years old and then to go on to graduate school or work. The majority of people my age are in a different role in life.

I receive many different responses depending on the "age grade" I am talking with about my return to college. The traditional student wants to know why I didn't finish college "on time" and why I came back to school. People closer to my own age, or older, have one of two responses. Those who finished college "on time" tell me that they admire me for going back to college "at my age" to finish. The others, many of whom would like to go back to school themselves, say they would feel "too old and out of place" to go back to school "at my age." It is our society's timetable of life stages that provides an image of what a college student should be.

sexes, or **sexism,** because they legitimize social arrangements and patterns by which members of one gender group realize more benefits and fewer burdens than members of the other gender group. Most commonly, sexism has operated to the advantage of men and to the disadvantage of women. Sexism will be the focus of some discussion in Chapter 14, "Inequality and Discrimination." In this chapter, we will see how sex roles are learned and how differently the life course is experienced by men and women in our society.

Similarly, the life course is experienced differently by members of different races and social classes. For example, in the middle class, adolescence often is considered to last until graduation from college at age twenty-one or twenty-two. Among the working class, it is common for adolescence to be seen as ending shortly after graduation from high school — with entry into full-time work and marriage roles. While this chapter will focus on roles that differ by age, sex, race, and social class, other factors also provide the basis for subcultural differences in our society. For example, certain religious sects prescribe periods of missionary work before adult work and family roles are entered.

ROLE STRAIN

Because roles are age-graded, we are not provided at birth with a set, rigid script, carved once and for all time in granite. Rather, as we age, we are compelled to modify our behavior as we exit some roles and acquire others. Work, marriage, and parenthood represent major roles for most people. The history or path taken by each of a person's roles is called the role's **trajectory.** The major shifts or changes in the stages of each role are called **transitions.** The multiple trajectories of these changing roles affect one another over the life course (Elder, 1985). For example, an individual's parent role may have some impact on his or her employment role. It is hardly surprising, therefore, that from time to time we should encounter difficulties in hammering out our courses of action and experience these difficulties

as stress. **Role strain** is the term social psychologists apply to those problems we experience in meeting the requirements of our roles.

Some role strain has to do with failure to meet the timing requirements of a role. American society is much more flexible than most other societies with respect to its timing requirements. Nevertheless, generally accepted *timetables* and *age expectations* govern major life transitions, such as finishing school, becoming economically independent, marrying, having children, and retiring. Some individuals fail to acquire roles when our society's norms say they "should" or acquire them at the "wrong" time. Similarly, exiting a role too early or failing to exit by the generally accepted time can create problems. The woman who marries for the first time at age forty-two would be said to have married "late." The forty-year-old man who has never been promoted from the entry-level job he started in his twenties is likely to be judged a "failure." The teenage girl who drops out of school and gives birth has, in many people's minds, acquired the role of mother and exited the student role "too early."

In some ways, society is organized to minimize role strain for those members who acquire and exit roles according to its timetable. Before role acquisition, roles are often anticipated and rehearsed. The phase of socialization during which we fantasize about, experiment with, and try on the behavior associated with a future role is referred to by social psychologists as **anticipatory socialization.** At the point of role acquisition, public ceremonies or rituals — **rites of passage** — may mark the person's new status. Rites of passage are important because they highlight expectations for changes in social relationships — in role expectations.

Individuals usually find it easier to adjust to role transitions that take place "on time" according to the society's timetable. Failure to be in the right role at what society considers to be the right time can increase the likelihood of role strain. Indeed, some research indicates that when life events do *not* occur on schedule, they are more likely to cause stress (Rindfuss, Swicegood, and

---

STUDENT OBSERVATION

Rite of Passage

While staying in Texas this summer, I had a chance to observe a Spanish-Mexican ritual called the *quincinara*. This Catholic ceremony is meant to officially recognize and induct all fifteen-year-old Catholic girls into the church. The ritual signals to the eligible bachelors that the girl can now date. It is generally required of all the girls within the community and planning for the event takes months, sometimes even a year! The girls are expected to wear long, formal white gowns, to invite all family members and friends, and to offer lots of food and drink to those attending. This elaborate (and expensive) ceremony is a *rite of passage* for these girls — marking their recognition as young women. Its significance was evident within the community; it was valued as an indicator of the girls' new status.

Rosenfeld, 1987). There is also evidence that there are long-term negative consequences for being "out of sync." For example, men who marry "too early" complete fewer years of education, hold lower-status jobs, and earn less income (Teti, Lamb, and Elster, 1987). These effects are evident *forty years* after marriage. (Before reading further, see the Student Observation: "Rite of Passage.")

In other ways, society makes some degree of role strain almost inevitable. People may be encouraged to acquire combinations of roles that lead to *role overload* — the kind of role strain that occurs when the expectations for roles held simultaneously are incompatible in terms of time, energy, or resources. For example, women may be expected to be "super-moms" — to excel in both employment and parental roles. How super-moms and others like them respond to role overload is of great interest to life-course researchers. We'll see examples of resolutions to role strain in the following sections of the chapter.

HISTORICAL EVENTS

Historical events can also affect roles. For example, such events may cause changes in age-graded roles. Consider the changes in our society's age-graded roles for men and women caused by termination of the military draft and expansion of employment opportunities for women. Age-graded roles are shaped, in part, by the particular economic, political, and social conditions that we share with the category of people who were born about the same time we were — our **birth cohort** (Riley, 1987).

Life-course researchers point out that various cohorts, and even subcategories of cohorts, may experience the life course quite differently. They study birth cohorts in two different ways in order to examine how historical events affect age-graded role behavior. First, they look at the different events facing two different cohorts when the cohorts were the *same age*. For example, what historical events confronted your grandparents and parents when they were the age you are now? How did those events differ from events facing you now? Research indicates that the events having the greatest impact on *memorableness* occur during a cohort's late adolescence and early adulthood; the process is called *generational imprinting* (Schuman and Scott, 1989). For one cohort, the event could be the Great Depression or the bombing of Pearl Harbor; for another cohort, the event might be the assassination of President Kennedy or Martin Luther King, Jr.; and for still others, it might be the Vietnam War or the destruction of the Berlin Wall.

Consider the experiences of the birth cohort entering young adulthood during the Vietnam War (1964–1973). Young adults in this cohort faced the draft and protests against the war. For some, the war meant deviation from age-graded roles. Because of serving in the military, they may have had to enter college, the work force, or even marriage later than would normally be expected. Some had husbands, boyfriends, brothers, or friends killed or injured in the war. Others had ties with individuals who left the country to avoid being drafted. How do their experiences compare with those of individuals who entered young adulthood in the early 1980s? And with those of persons who entered this life stage in the 1990s?

There are other, more subtle cohort differences that make the life experiences of cohorts quite different. Compare, for example, the experiences of people who grew up in the "baby-boom" generation of the 1950s with the experiences of those who grew up in the 1970s. The baby-boom generation was produced by a rising birthrate that followed the return of GIs from World War II. The life-course experiences of members of this birth cohort have been influenced a great deal by the cohort's relatively large size. For example, some have had to settle for less prestigious jobs than they had planned for because so many well-educated baby-boomers entered the job market at the same time.

By contrast, baby-boomers have waited longer to have families of their own and have had fewer children, so *their* children are part of a smaller cohort and will have very different socialization experiences. Because the 1950s cohorts were much larger than those of the 1970s, the 1970s cohorts will face a very different world than the 1950s cohorts faced at the same ages. Their smaller numbers will mean less competition in school, for jobs, and for houses. However, they will face the largest percentage of elderly in recorded history—a situation that may dramatically affect the Social Security taxes of the 1970s children and the baby-boomers' quality of life in old age.

The second way that life-course researchers look at birth cohorts is by comparing how the *same*, societywide event affects members of different cohorts. One cohort might experience an event differently than do other cohorts. For example, the Vietnam War was experienced by different cohorts (children, young adults, older

adults) in different ways. The recent AIDS epidemic is more of a threat to young, sexually active singles than to older, married persons who are sexually monogamous.

Of course, not all members of a cohort experience historical events in the same way. Our Vietnam War example can be used to illustrate that some historical events affect men and women of the same cohort differently. Men faced the prospect of the draft and military service directly. Most women experienced the indirect consequences of the war through its effects on loved ones. Social psychologists are particularly interested in how the same historical event can have a differential impact on cohort members of different races and social classes. For example, research has indicated that college and noncollege youth of the same cohort had very different attitudes toward the Vietnam War (Braungart, 1975). The Great Depression of the 1930s affected the occupational and family experiences of children from deprived families and those from relatively privileged families very differently (Elder, 1974). Of course, individuals can also experience significant events, such as serious illness, divorce, or bankruptcy, that are not experienced by everyone. Life-course researchers are also interested in how such events affect individuals' experience of the life course.

In the rest of this chapter we'll take a closer look at our own society's role expectations over the life course and the influence they have on our role behavior. We shall see that modern American life entails a continuous process of adjustment to new developments and new demands. Role strain, historical events, and individual factors may interfere with our attempts to meet society's role expectations—and may result in negative consequences for us as individuals. If enough of us experience these negative consequences, our reactions may produce a change in the role expectations themselves. Thus, although the larger society's role expectations exert considerable influence on our behavior, we, as individuals or small groups, can in turn influence our society's expectations. For example, consider how American life has been changed as a result of the civil rights movement.

If you haven't already done so, we suggest that you take some time now to think about how well the concepts in this section fit *your* life.

Role Socialization During the Childhood Years

SOCIALIZATION INTO CHILDHOOD ROLES

As we discussed in Chapter 2, much of early childhood socialization is concerned with the learning of behavior consistent with basic societal values and norms. Adult socialization builds upon this foundation and focuses more on teaching specific social roles. However, while not as extensive as it is in adulthood, socialization in childhood does involve some role learning. Age-graded role expectations apply even to newborns.

The Good-Baby Role

Role socialization begins at birth. The adult members of the society have certain expectations for the behavior of the newborn, and the adults modify their own behavior accordingly. In our culture, it is expected that very young babies will cry when uncomfortable, sleep when sleepy, and excrete whenever the urge arises. Because of babies' extreme dependence, infants' experiences of the social and physical worlds are mediated by parents or others who keep them fed, warm, dry, and safe. In doing so, these caretakers begin their role as agents of socialization by imposing social patterns on the largely nonsocial infant. For example, different societies and subcultures have different notions of when an infant should be hungry and what feeding schedules (and other infant-care techniques) are proper. Whether infants are breast-fed or bottle-fed, and whether they are fed on demand (whenever they cry) or on a strict schedule, depends on the culture of their caretakers. An infant is judged to be a "good baby" if he or she adjusts to the feeding schedule. An infant who takes a long time to learn *when* to

be hungry is viewed as "a difficult baby." In this sense, social patterns are being imposed on our behavior from our very first moments of life. Even our basic, biological behavior must meet socially approved standards.

Gender Roles in Childhood

While gender would seem to be relatively unimportant for very young babies, studies have shown that caretakers' expectations for their behavior differ by gender. At birth, the first words used to describe the baby are normally something like, "It's a boy (girl)!" From the moment this labeling occurs, it is repeated countless times each day and has important effects on the treatment of the child. For example, parents typically decorate the rooms of their daughters with ruffles, lace, and flowery motifs and give the girls dolls, doll houses, and toys such as little brooms, irons, and cooking utensils. In contrast, they usually decorate their sons' rooms with animal motifs and give the boys sports equipment, toy cars and guns, and mechanical toys (Rheingold and Cook, 1975; Pomerleau et al., 1990). Many researchers suggest that toys have important implications for learning and social development in boys and girls (Peretti and Sydney, 1985; Miller, 1987; Robinson and Morris, 1987; Tracy, 1987).

Parental reinforcement of sex-role behavior. Apparently, a child's sex shapes the parents' views and treatment of the child from birth. In one study, researchers interviewed mothers and fathers of newborn infants on the day of the child's birth (Rubin, Provenzano, and Luria, 1974). The fathers, interviewed almost immediately after the birth, had not handled the babies but had viewed them through the display window of the hospital nursery. The mothers, interviewed within twenty-four hours after the birth, had held and fed the infants. Each set of parents was asked to describe their baby as they would to a close friend or relative and also to rate the baby on an eighteen-item scale, on which they were to choose between adjectives such as "strong" versus "weak," "noisy" versus "quiet," "cheerful" versus "cranky," and "active" versus "inactive." Both mothers and fathers described sons as firmer, stronger, hardier, larger featured, better coordinated, and more alert. They described daughters as softer, weaker, smaller, prettier, finer featured, more awkward, and more inattentive. Although both mothers and fathers attributed sex-differentiated characteristics to their children, fathers were more likely to do so. In other words, when parents of male and female children were compared, fathers labeled the sexes farther apart than mothers did on the adjective pairs.

Did the perceived differences between the male and female infants reflect real differences between the children? It appears not. The sample of newborn male and female infants did not differ in average length, weight, or measures of the infants' basic mental and physical functioning. The researchers concluded that sex-role socialization begins at birth and may well affect subsequent expectations for both the parents' and the infant's behavior. Fathers, especially, seem to be particularly gender-conscious in their treatment of their sons (Snow, Jacklin, and Maccoby, 1983). Other studies provide additional evidence that adults do, in fact, treat very young male and female children differently (McDonald and Parke, 1986; Leone and Robertson, 1989; Ross and Taylor, 1989; Stern and Karraker, 1989).

The differential treatment of infants and young children according to their sex produces different behavior in boys and girls. A study of children age thirteen to fourteen months found that parents responded differently to the same behaviors depending upon whether they were performed by a boy or a girl (Fagot et al., 1985). For example, parents paid more attention to girls' attempts to communicate with adults and more attention to boy's physically active behavior. When the same children were observed in play groups eleven months later, girls talked to their teachers more and boys were more assertive.

These studies illustrate that sex-role socialization begins before the child is even aware of a sexual identity. They suggest that cultural assumptions about what is "natural" for a boy or for a girl are so deeply ingrained that adults may treat children differently without even being aware of it (Weitzman, Birns, and Friend, 1985). Thus, wittingly or unwittingly, parents encourage and reinforce culturally desired sex-role behavior.

Media influences on sex-role behavior. But parents are not the only source of sex-role socialization. In the 1970s, Weitzman and her colleagues (1972) examined the treatment of sex roles in children's books identified as the "very best"—winners of the Caldecott Medal. They found that there were eleven pictures of males for every picture of a female. Females were underrepresented in titles, central roles, pictures, and stories. Most of the books were about boys, men, and male animals, and most dealt exclusively with male adventures. The female characters who did appear were most often insignificant or inconspicuous.

Weitzman found that the girls in the 1970s books were portrayed as "passive and doll-like," engaging in service activities directed at pleasing and helping their brothers and fathers. Mothers were depicted as housebound servants who cared for their husbands and children. Not a single adult female character had a job. In fact, the only adult female with an active leadership role was a fairy godmother—clearly not a normal woman. On the other hand, boys were shown as active and adventuresome, engaged in a variety of tasks requiring independence and self-confidence. The men played varied, interesting roles, such as storekeepers, house builders, storytellers, monks, fighters, fishermen, policemen, soldiers, adventurers, fathers, cooks, preachers, judges, farmers, kings, and gods.

The researchers concluded that "little girls receive attention and praise for their attractiveness, while boys are admired for their achievements and cleverness. . . . Girls are taught to have low aspirations because there are so few opportunities portrayed as available to them" (Weitzman, 1979: 9).

Another group of researchers replicated Weitzman's study, giving attention to the award-winning books of the 1980s (Williams et al., 1987). In contrast to Weitzman's findings, the later study found that male and female characters were about equally represented. Of leading characters, about one-third were female. Still, only one female character worked outside the home (she was a waitress). Thus, while female characters in children's books have become more visible, they are still portrayed in line with traditional roles.

The portrayal of sex roles is also a controversial aspect of television programming. For example, on children's shows, there are over twice as many male characters as females, and males are portrayed as more active, constructive, and rewarded. Females are shown as more deferential and manipulative (Basow, 1986). Prime-time programs also show females in subordinate roles (Durkin, 1985; Signorielli, 1989). They are less likely than male characters to hold jobs, and when they do, their occupations are usually gender-stereotyped (secretary, nurse, teacher). Male characters are twice as likely to be portrayed as competent and self-assured and are much more likely to have adventurous roles (such as detective and police officer). Even television commercials maintain these stereotyped images (Bretl and Cantor, 1988; Lovdal, 1989). Pay attention to the next few commercials you watch — how often is the competent, authoritative voice describing the product's virtues the voice of a female?

Student and Citizen Roles in Childhood

Before the sixteenth century, childhood was not considered an important stage of life. Rather, it was seen simply as a biologically necessary prelude to adulthood, which began much earlier than it does today. As soon as most youngsters were able to perform useful chores, they worked alongside adults (Zelizer, 1987).

By the eighteenth century, most upper-class families had come to view childhood as a clearly marked-off period of life, during which children should be nurtured and allowed to learn and play. This view had been widely accepted among the growing middle classes by the end of the nine-

teenth century. But not until the early decades of the twentieth century did life change much for lower-class children. Like adults, they worked long hours in factories, fields, and mines. In the 1920s, laws banning child labor and making schooling compulsory became widely enforced, making childhood a reality for most American youngsters.

Today, we see childhood as an extended period of learning and growth. Most children are cherished, nurtured, and protected from a separate adult world. Childhood is a time to learn, explore, and play — a period in which children must acquire many of the skills needed to function in the adult world. However, there is some evidence that all children were not equally affected by these historical events. Even now, some children, such as children of migrant workers, have very shortened childhoods and enter the adult world of work at an early age.

Classroom experiences. In our society, most children, at about five or six years old, begin to attend school. This marks the beginning of another important influence in the child's life. Before children attend school, the family largely defines the social world of the child. Schools introduce children to impersonal, bureaucratic organizations, where rules must be obeyed and fewer adjustments are made for individual differences.

The school and family have in common the explicit mission of socializing the child, and the child's involvement with both institutions is largely involuntary. But in other respects the family and classroom provide quite different socialization experiences for the child (Gecas, 1981). When they go to school, children must learn the student role, which differs greatly from their family roles. For one thing, the ratio of children (students) to adults (teachers) in school is greater than the ratio of children to parents at home. The relationship between teacher and student is of shorter duration and is more limited in scope than the relationship between parent and child. In school, children learn to compete on an individual basis with other students. They learn that they

Until late in the nineteenth century, most children were put to work as soon as they were able. Today, childhood is seen as an extended period of learning and growth, and children are protected from a separate adult world. Even now, some children, such as the children of migrant workers, have abbreviated childhoods and enter the adult world of work at an early age.

must comply with authority and that the majority does not rule in all matters.

An especially important feature of classroom structure is the homogeneous age composition of the class, which provides both the student and the teacher with a standard of comparison for the student's competencies. Evaluation of performance in the classroom tends to be formal and public. Grades are the official signs of approval or disapproval of the student's performance. But grades are also used to reward conformity with expectations of the student role, such as punctuality, tact, perseverance, and drive to achieve. Such lessons are part of what Talcott Parsons (1959) called the "hidden curriculum" — they are built into the structure of the classroom. How well children do in school depends in part on how well they learn to play the role of student.

Schools as transmitters of cultural values. Our society gives a major part of the responsibility for producing good citizens to schools. Not surprisingly, the textbooks used in elementary schools usually reflect what society views as the expectations for all its citizens. For example, the nineteenth-century American reading texts, the *McGuffey Readers*, expounded the predominantly middle-class values of self-reliance, hard work, thrift, free enterprise, individualism, nationalism, and religiosity. The perceived significance of textbooks is reflected in continued debates over the teaching of such subjects as evolution as opposed to biblical views of creation, sex education, and many other topics.

Schools instill political values through nationalistic rituals, such as salutes to the flag, the Pledge of Allegiance, and patriotic songs. Children are taught national loyalty and reverence for democracy, as well as information about the structure of our government and the rights and obligations of both authorities and citizens. They are also taught to respect leading figures in U.S. history, particularly the founding fathers and various U.S. presidents. Students associate "America" with symbols such as the flag and the Statue of Liberty.

The Peer Role

When children attend school, their contacts with their peers usually increase. Peers play a unique and important role in socialization (Corsaro and Eder, 1990). Unlike the child's relationships with more powerful adults, peer relationships give the child opportunities to practice both superordinate and egalitarian roles. Peers "stand in the same relation to persons of authority" and "see the world through the same eyes" (Davis, 1949: 217). Children have the opportunity to take on roles with their peers — such as helper, teacher, leader, expert, bully, and confidant — that, because of the power differential, they rarely play with adults. As we discussed in Chapter 2, an important part of peer culture involves children's resistance to and challenging of adult rules and authority. Children cooperatively produce routines in which they both mock and evade adult authority (Dunn, 1988). Another way that peer relationships differ from family relationships is that children have some control over choosing their friends. They learn from peers, for example, that social interaction does not always go smoothly and that friendship is not automatic. It is in the course of shared play that the concepts of friend and peer arise (Corsaro, 1985; Rizzo, 1989).

In children's interactions with adults, it is the adult who usually defines the rules and has the power to enforce them. In peer interactions, the child can participate in the creation and enforcement of norms. Gary Fine's (1987) observations of Little League teams illustrate that the socialization the child experiences with adults and peers can result in two sets of role expectations.

According to Fine, adults believe that they have an obligation to teach children correct values, and they create opportunities to do that. But, parallel to the adults' socialization efforts are a set of standards applied by peers to one another. Fine found that the Little Leaguers expected one another to display appropriate emotions (e.g., to be appropriately elated when the team wins and appropriately humble when one strikes out). The boys also imposed an expectation of self-control (anger is to be kept within limits, crying is not tolerated, and pain is to be borne stoically). Team members scorned those who did not display a strong desire to win. They expected involvement, hustle, and dressing the part. Loyalty was demanded, and "ratting" to an adult on a peer was a major offense. Acting superior to peers was also against the group's informal rules.

Peer socialization often reinforces cultural norms. When a child violates gender-role expectations, for example, peers may criticize, complain, withdraw attention, or even use physical force. For instance, a study of junior high school girls found a strong norm of heterosexuality (Simon, Eder, and Evans, 1992). Homosexuality was viewed very negatively, and this label was applied to girls who did not express a romantic interest in boys or who had gender-atypical interests. The girls also frequently teased one another about behavior that could be interpreted as homosexual, such as close physical contact between friends. In contrast, behavior in line with gender stereotypes is often praised and imitated (Lamb, Easterbrooks, and Holden, 1980). Peers are also a source of information about subjects adults consider sensitive or taboo, such as sex.

Social psychologist William Corsaro (1988, 1992) suggests that young children often fail to fully understand their interactions with adults and that they work out their confusion and uncertainties in peer-group activities. By interacting with playmates, children produce a peer culture in which inputs from the adult world are interpreted. Thus, in peer groups, childhood knowledge and practices gradually are transformed into the knowledge and skills necessary to participate in adult life.

ANTICIPATORY SOCIALIZATION INTO ADULT ROLES

Part of learning a new role involves fantasizing about, experimenting with, and trying on the behaviors associated with a role to be assumed in the future. Social psychologists call this *anticipatory socialization*. Anticipatory socialization for work and adult family roles begins in childhood. Pre-paratory learning takes place in the family, at school, with peers, and through the media. The outcomes of this anticipatory socialization range from the internalization of broad orientations, such as self-direction or caring, to specific skills, such as language, math, or physical coordination. Often, children try out some of the skills and perspectives acquired through early socialization in actual work or family situations. Job skills, for example, may be practiced through a variety of unskilled and temporary jobs, such as newspaper routes, baby-sitting, weekend jobs, or summer employment.

Social Class and Employment Roles

The child's family status has strong and important effects on how others — neighbors, teachers, and peers, for example — see the child. In addition, the family's values, attitudes, and life style reflect the social class, ethnic group, religion, region, and country of which it is a part. The socialization of the child is shaped by her or his family's position and experiences in society. Thus, socialization plays a part in perpetuating social differences across generations.

Let's focus on the case of social class. Most people end up, as adults, in the same social class into which they were born. What part does socialization play in this? Researchers comparing lower- and middle-class families have found differences in how children are socialized. Some of these differences have to do with language and communication skills. For example, the higher the mother's pay and the greater the complexity of her work activities, the better is her child's verbal facility (Parcel and Menaghan, 1990). Other differences involve *values* — the ethical principles to which members of a group feel a strong commitment and which they employ in judging behavior. It appears that both kinds of differences may tend to channel children into the same kinds of occupations, and hence the same social class, as their parents.

Class differences in language and communication skills. Basil Bernstein and his colleagues

(1971, 1977, 1981) have found important differences between the language systems used in working-class and middle-class families. Bernstein describes working-class families as characterized by *restricted speech codes* — abbreviated speech patterns that are based on the assumption that the listeners share most of the information, assign the same meanings, and generally have the same views as the speaker. All of us tend to use a restricted speech code when we are with people we know very well. Bernstein suggests that members of the working-class tend to use the restricted pattern in all situations. He sees this pattern of speech as related to the kind of social structure found in many working-class families, which tends to discourage questioning and discussion. In such families, members are simply expected to accept their positions. A parenting style in which children are told what to do with little explanation ("because I said so") is a common feature of these households. Restricted speech patterns are adequate for the kind of interaction found in such settings and, perhaps, for the interactions characteristic of many working-class occupations.

On the other hand, Bernstein says that most middle-class parents have had educational and occupational experiences that have led to the development of an *elaborated speech code*. An elaborated code is used to express ideas and meanings different from those of our listeners. It is more complex and detailed, more logical and precise, than restricted speech. Related to this is the finding that children in middle-class families are given more discretion in their choice of roles. Individuality and personal choices become frequent topics of discussion. Similarly, the parenting style that often characterizes such families requires discussions of why a request has been made. For communications of this sort, an elaborated speech code is required.

Children learn these speech codes, in large part, from their parents. Bernstein believes that children who have acquired an elaborated speech code and have experienced a family structure that encourages them to be more open-minded, analytical, and independent have more opportunity to develop a sense of individuality and will be more independent in their thinking as well as in their relationships with others. These traits are important in most middle-class occupations. In contrast, it appears that the style of language and modes of interaction used in working-class families do not provide children with the skills needed to compete for middle-class occupations and thus lead to the perpetuation of social class from one generation to another.

Class differences in values. There is evidence that the values that parents hold and teach to their children differ by social class (Kohn, 1959; Kohn and Schooler, 1983). Sociologist Melvin Kohn and his colleagues have studied these differences extensively. They have found that working-class parents stress manners, neatness, the importance of being a good student, honesty, and obedience. Middle-class parents stress consideration of others, interest in why and how things happen, responsibility, and self-control. Kohn summarizes these differences by suggesting that working-class values stress *conformity to external authority* and that middle-class values stress *conformity to internal standards* (self-direction). (This should remind you of our discussion in Chapter 2 of Kohlberg's stages of moral reasoning.) Kohn notes that these differences are reflected in the parenting styles of the two classes. Working-class parents are more likely to focus on the consequences of the child's action. If a rule is broken, the child is likely to be punished. On the other hand, middle-class parents tend to be more concerned with the child's motives and intentions and take these into account when deciding whether to punish. As Bernstein noted, they are also more likely to reason with their child, since they are concerned with having the child understand *why* he or she should or should not do something.

Kohn's research has shown that these class differences in values and child-rearing techniques are directly related to the parents' work experiences (Kohn, 1976; Kohn, 1978; Kohn and Schooler, 1981). Middle-class adults have jobs that lack close supervision, involve information or people instead of things, and are complex enough to allow a variety of approaches (rather than being standardized). Such jobs provide opportunities for and require independent thought, initiative, and judgment, fostering the values of self-direction, self-initiative, and self-reliance. Working-class jobs require following procedures and supervisor's orders, fostering the values of obedience and conformity. In other words, parents tend to value the characteristics that determine success in their jobs. Kohn's description of the relationship between occupational conditions and values has received wide support (Kohn, 1977; Lee, 1977; Gecas, 1979). The influence of work-generated values on parental practices provides an important link between the occupational and family contexts of socialization.

Other researchers have examined whether the values stressed by parents really affect the traits children develop. Kohn noted that parents who value self-direction tend to support and encourage their children more than do parents who value conformity. One study of father-son relationships indicates that the father's encouragement and support is related to the son's self-competence and involvement in work (Mortimer, Lorence, and Kumka, 1986). Both these traits are found in people who pursue high-status careers. Mothers whose jobs involve complex work were found to provide more cognitive stimulation and warmth to their young children (Menaghan and Parcel, 1991), leading to better verbal development (Parcel and Menaghan, 1990) and fewer behavior problems (Rogers, Parcel, and Menaghan, 1991).

Contested versus sponsored mobility. Schools share with families the responsibility of socializing young people for the world of work. Because different students must learn how to fill different occupational roles, occupational socialization involves some degree of sifting and sorting students into subgroups that are directed toward paths leading to different occupations. There are two general models about how this sifting and sorting takes place. The first model views schools' attempts at occupational socialization as an effort to give every student an equal opportunity to gain the skills for any job consistent with his or her abilities. According to this model of **contested mobility**, higher-income occupations go to those who demonstrate the appropriate skills in competition with other students. In such a *merit* system, a student with ability has a good chance to compete successfully for high-income occupations, regardless of his or her family background.

On the other hand, the second model posits that even though we claim that our schools operate on a merit system, the real outcome of schools' socialization is the reproduction of the present stratification structure. According to this model, children from wealthier families are given instruction that makes it more likely that they will achieve occupational success. At the same time, those from poorer families, nonwhites, and females are steered toward occupations lower on the scale of prestige and income. This is called **sponsored mobility**.

In a 1980 study, researcher Jean Anyon observed differences in socialization at several schools that would make it likely that most students at a particular school would enter the labor force in occupations similar to those of their parents. Anyon found that socialization practices differed substantially by school, depending upon the occupational classification of most students' parents.

Individual students in a racially or socio-economically mixed school may also be treated differently. Teachers and guidance counselors have a large "gatekeeping" role in guiding students toward particular occupational tracks (Erickson, 1975). If they have different expectations for students from different backgrounds, differential socialization may result. *Curriculum tracking* sorts students into categories that are directed toward particular occupational types. There is evidence that students' participation in tracks is influenced by their social class, race, and sex (Gouldner, 1978; Gaskell, 1985; Colclough and Beck, 1986; Vanfossen, Jones, and Spade, 1987). For example, working-class girls are disproportionately represented in the business track;

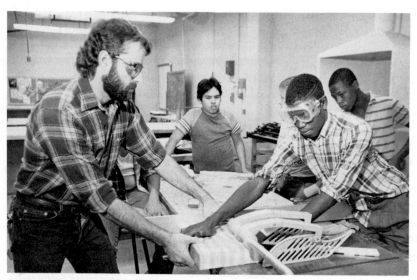

Curriculum tracking sorts students into categories that are directed toward particular occupational types. There is evidence that students' participation in tracks is influenced by
their social class, race, and sex. For example, working-class girls are disproportionately
represented in the business track; African-Americans and other minorities are overrepresented in vocational tracks and vocational schools but underrepresented in private
schools and four-year colleges.

African-Americans and other minorities are overrepresented in vocational tracks and vocational
schools but underrepresented in private schools
and four-year colleges. Racial integration of
schools was supported by some as a way to increase the academic achievement of African-
Americans by reducing racial tracking. But racial
tracking still occurs in integrated schools.

Christopher Jencks and his colleagues concluded, on the basis of their research, not only
that family background has a strong effect on
success in school but also that schools do little
to change children's ultimate status in society
(Jencks et al., 1979). These conclusions created
controversy, anger, and denial. Many citizens
were disturbed to hear that one of their most
sacred institutions was not performing according
to their ideological belief that schools operate on
a merit system — providing equal opportunity for
each student to achieve according to his or her
ability and effort.

Socialization for "Men's and Women's Work"

In our earlier discussion of childhood socialization, we noted that socialization differs markedly
by gender. Almost immediately after birth, parents and other family members respond differently to boys and girls. As children grow older,
they tend to play with other same-sex peers in
ways that highlight and compound gender differences. Janet Lever (1978) argues that boys' games
are more complex than girls' games and thus give
men a later advantage in occupations that share
structural features of these games — occupations
that tend to have higher status and pay. Other
researchers suggest that girls' games are just as
complex as boys' but that the two types are different in that boys' games focus on skill while girls'
games focus on affiliation or popularity (Goodwin
and Goodwin, 1987; Eckert, 1990). Deborah
Tannen (1990) suggests that boys and girls learn
to handle complexity in different arenas — boys in

terms of complex rules and activities, and girls in terms of complex networks of relationships and complex ways of using language to mediate those relationships. Thus, boys and girls learn different ways of interacting and different skills that may influence the occupations they choose or are steered toward later in life.

When children go to school, this process is intensified. Schools negatively influence the occupational destinies of females, as compared with males, through a variety of social arrangements and processes (Fox and Hesse-Biber, 1984). First, there is a process that involves *segregating, tracking,* and *funneling* boys and girls into different groups, activities, classes, and courses. (Interestingly, whereas all-black schools are considered a disadvantage to black children, some researchers argue that all-female schools are advantageous to females, allowing them to escape the sex tracking that occurs in sex-integrated schools [Lee and Bryk, 1986].) Second, books, texts, and readers *depict girls and women in stereotypic sex roles* (Fox and Hesse-Biber, 1984). Fox example, math problems involving girls often show them buying clothes, cooking, sewing, and calculating the grocery bill. Third, schools provide role models reflecting a structure of power and authority in which males are in superordinate and females in subordinate positions. Eighty-five percent of elementary school teachers are women; 79 percent of principals are men (Baker, 1984). First-graders whose schools had female principals generally had less stereotyped views of gender role than children whose schools had male principals (Paradiso and Wall, 1986). Fourth, teachers interact more actively with boys, giving them more instruction, attending more carefully to their questions and responses, and providing more opportunities for them to respond (as well as reprimanding them more often). And fifth, both teachers and guidance staff reinforce, covertly and overtly, traditional, cultural definitions of masculinity and femininity. For example, studies of teachers' relationships with boys and girls in the classroom reveal that teachers encourage boys to be more assertive (Sadker and Sadker, 1985; Rice, 1989).

Researchers argue that these processes tend to lower women's esteem and confidence and that girls consequently become less assured about their own accomplishments and those of other females (Danziger, 1983; Simmons and Parsons, 1983; Alishio and Schilling, 1984). These socialization practices restrict the development among females of mathematical, technical, and scientific skills, which are very important in both higher education and well-paying jobs.

Self-fulfilling Prophecy

Does it matter that parents, teachers, and others have different expectations for boys and girls, for African-American and white children, and for middle- and lower-class children? Social psychologists think it does. They believe that expectations or beliefs (even false ones) can evoke behaviors that conform to the original belief. This phenomenon is known as a **self-fulfilling prophecy** or an **expectancy effect**. The notion derives from W. I. Thomas's insight: "If men define situations as real, they are real in their consequences" (1928: 527). Robert Merton (1957) elaborates:

> The self-fulfilling prophecy is, in the beginning, a "false" definition of the situation evoking a new behavior which makes the originally false conception come "true." This . . . perpetuates a reign of error. For the prophet will cite the actual course of events as proof that he was right from the very beginning. (p. 423)

Merton's statement implies that self-fulfilling prophecies are always negative. The literature on race relations, deviance, and gender stereotyping suggests that they often are. But research on self-fulfilling prophecies in the classroom demonstrates that they can lead to positive as well as negative consequences, depending upon the expectation (Jussim, 1990).

Rosenthal and Jacobson's landmark study on this topic, *Pygmalion in the Classroom* (1968), tested the proposition that children would show more scholastic improvement if their teacher expected it than if their teacher did not. The researchers conducted an experiment in an elementary school with high percentages of lower-class and Hispanic students. First, they gave a nonverbal "test for intellectual blooming" to all students in Grades 1 through 6. Then they randomly selected some students to be in the experimental condition. They gave the names of these students to their teachers, indicating that these students' scores on the test for intellectual blooming showed that they would make unusual intellectual gains during the year. In actuality, of course, according to the information available to the researchers, the students in the experimental condition were no more likely than any others to make such gains. The only difference between them and the other students was that they had been (falsely) identified to the teachers as having scores that promised intellectual achievement during the year. The researchers found that the teachers' performance expectations for first- and second-grade students had significant effects on the pupils' IQ gains. This effect was not found for third-, fourth-, and fifth-graders.

Especially in schools that are racially or socioeconomically mixed, parents and policy makers fear that teachers may have *lower* expectations for minority and lower-class students. If, through differential treatment, these lower expectations are communicated to the child, a self-fulfilling prophecy may result.

Of course, parents' expectations for their children also have important expectancy effects. For example, studies have found that many parents believe that males are better at math than females. They hold this view despite the fact that their male and female children do equally well in math both in school grades and on standardized tests (Alexander and Entwisle, 1988). The parents' expectations for their children's competence in math seems to affect the children's own perceptions of their math ability. Because children spend more time engaged in activities that they think they are good at, the original expectancy becomes true—a self-fulfilling prophecy. Similar effects have been found for learning English and sports (Eccles, Jacobs, and Harold, 1990).

How do adults' expectations affect children's self-perceptions and subsequent performance? Researchers believe that adults' stereotypes cause them to expect certain differences among children (on the basis of gender or race, for instance). These different expectations cause the adults to

---

STUDENT OBSERVATION

Sex Roles

I am engaged to be married. My fiancé, Chris, loves to cook, while I can barely make toast (and I don't mind that particular deficiency—I don't like to cook). Also, when we are married, I will be working on a Ph.D. in psychology, which will demand an exorbitant amount of my time and energy. Chris will be working nine to five and have much more spare time than I will. I am very close to Chris's sister, and therefore she knows our preferences and future occupational situation. On a recent visit, she excitedly presented *me* with a gift to prepare me for "married life" (in other words, for my "expected role *as the female in married life*")—an apron. This is a classic example of a sex role—a normatively prescribed behavior (cooking) is expected of me on the sole basis of my sex (female) when I enter a given position in society (marriage). If any other factors had been considered, such as personal preference for or relative amount of time available for the behavior, the apron would have gone to Chris.

P.S. How did I respond? I thanked her and said that Chris would enjoy it. She then laughed at the way she had so automatically assumed that the sex-role stereotype would be appropriate, and she vowed to be more conscious of it in the future. *Good.*

react differently to the children's performances, to attach differing importance to the acquisition of particular skills, to give different advice, and to provide different activities and toys for the children. In turn, these factors influence the children's confidence in their abilities, their interest in mastering certain skills, their enjoyment of various activities, and the amount of time and effort they devote to mastering particular skills (Eccles, Jacobs, and Harold, 1990).

Family Roles

Young children respond to parental encouragement and acquire gender expectations at a very early age. It appears that much of our early socialization is taken up with preparing us to assume adult family roles that differ by gender — for females, to be attentive, nurturing wives and mothers; for males, to be responsible, hard-working husbands and fathers. Today's children are more likely than those of earlier generations to have as a role model a mother who works outside the home. However, when it comes to household tasks, it appears that a traditional sex-typed division of labor is still the model they will observe. Studies show that children's participation in household tasks is also largely sex-typed (Brody and Steelman, 1985). A study of two-parent, two-child (six to seventeen years old) families revealed that the majority of children participated in at least one household task (Cogle and Tasher, 1982). Boys were unlikely to do or help with dishwashing and girls were unlikely to participate in tasks involving maintenance of home, yard, car, and pets. (Before reading further, see the Student Observation: "Sex Roles.")

EXITING CHILDHOOD: ADOLESCENCE

In 1900, only about 6 percent of Americans graduated from high school. The end of childhood and the beginning of adulthood was easily identified by departure from home, economic independence, and, especially, marriage. It is only in this century that large numbers of teenagers have postponed entry into the adult world by staying in

high school or attending college. Currently, over 86 percent of Americans twenty-five to thirty-four years old have graduated from high school (U.S. Bureau of the Census, 1992*a*). There are a number of reasons for this increase. The United States was becoming more industrialized and urbanized, making education more important for finding work. And, during the Great Depression, young people were encouraged to stay in school to keep them out of the overcrowded job market.

These historical events set the stage for the development among subsequent birth cohorts of what we call "adolescence." Sociologist James Coleman (1961) argues that the segregation of young people in schools in the 1940s and 1950s fostered the development of an adolescent subculture, with its own tastes and standards. Post–World War II affluence gave many teenagers access to cars, which removed dating and other teenage interactions from adult surveillance.

But these historical events have not affected all members of recent birth cohorts to the same degree. There is considerable diversity in peer subcultures (MacLeod, 1987; Eckert, 1988; Lesko, 1988). The "achievement" subculture awards status on the basis of academic performance. The "popular" subculture emphasizes friendships. The "growing-up" subculture focuses on having a romantic relationship. In the "tough" subculture, status is determined by displaying courage and skill in physical fighting, defying authority, and breaking the rules. And the "burnout" subculture involves the pursuit of pleasure through drinking, smoking, having sex, and "bumming around." There is also substantial variation among individuals in the specific ages at which they exit the child role and take on adult roles. For example, middle-class youth generally leave school and assume adult roles at a later age than do working-class youth.

Adolescence is a transitional stage, one bridging the gap between dependent child roles and independent adult roles. In more traditional societies, no such stage exists. Instead, specific events or ceremonies — rites of passage — clearly mark the transition to adulthood. In more complex, modern societies such as our own, the transition is more gradual, creating opportunities for several types of role strain.

For example, adolescents may experience what appear to be contradictory expectations. Parents may expect the adolescent to display increased independence and responsibility in some behavior domains, such as getting to appointments on time without the parents' assistance, helping out around the house, or earning some of his or her own spending money. On the other hand, the parents may continue to want to control such decisions as where the adolescent "hangs out" with friends and how late he or she is allowed to stay out at night. This type of role strain is called **intra-role conflict**: the expectations associated with a single role contain inconsistencies.

Adolescents' continued financial dependence on their parents may clash with their yearning to leave childhood behind. Hence, an adolescent's demands for increased control may be met with a version of "As long as I put the food on the table and the roof over your head, I'll decide." And the adolescent's own feelings may be ambivalent. While the independence of adulthood may usually seem attractive, it is likely that there are times when the stresses and strains of making important choices and developing new relationships make the old childhood role seem secure and inviting. This type of role strain is called **role discontinuity**: expectations associated with the old role (childhood dependency) conflict with expectations associated with the new role in a sequence (adult independence).

Adolescents may also experience inconsistencies among the expectations of various others. The type of role strain that involves inconsistencies among the expectations of various others is called **role dissensus**. For example, the family's traditional "family dinner" on Friday may conflict with Friday-night basketball games. Parents may expect the adolescent to be home for dinner with the rest of the family, while peers place importance on being together for the game. Parents and peers may send conflicting signals when it comes to a Mohawk haircut, purple hair, a ring in the

nose, or a tattoo on the shoulder. Of course, these may be just the standards set by the peer group as indicators of membership and belonging.

It is not surprising that adolescence is experienced by many — both adolescents and parents — as a difficult time. Our society does not provide clear, standardized expectations for adolescent behavior. Because of this **role ambiguity**, neither parents nor adolescents have a clear idea of what is expected of them. Both may act inconsistently, leading to low predictability for one another and increased conflict as they try to negotiate their own role definitions. (See the box "What Parents and Adolescents Argue About.")

Parental influence declines as peers support one another's steps toward independence, but, for most teenagers, both parents and peers remain important sources of norms and values (Troll and Bengtson, 1982). Peer preferences seem to be most influential when the topic involves music, dress, entertainment, smoking, drinking, marijuana use, or cheating in school. Parental preferences are usually more important when future life goals or values are involved — areas in which adult advice seems to be more relevant (Davies and Kandel, 1981; Krosnick and Judd, 1982; Youniss and Smollar, 1985). Was your adolescence characterized by any of the kinds of role conflict we have just discussed?

Socialization During the Adult Years

As we enter adulthood, we are expected to adopt new roles — some of which we were prepared for through anticipatory socialization in childhood or adolescence. Many adult roles involve employment or family. Let's examine each in some detail to see how socialization continues during the adult years.

EMPLOYMENT ROLES

For most employees in the United States, work takes place in the context of an organization. **Organizational socialization** is the process by which a person learns the values, norms, and re-

WHAT PARENTS AND ADOLESCENTS ARGUE ABOUT

The interactions between adolescents and their parents are sometimes disagreeable and stressful. Social psychologists studying the nature of this conflict have made some interesting discoveries.

What are the arguments about? First, a notable feature of the arguments that adolescents have with their parents is that they rarely argue about such "big" topics as sex, drugs, religion, or politics. The absence of conflict about these issues is surprising, given that great differences often exist between the attitudes of parents and adolescents on these topics. Researchers speculate that these generational differences do not lead to much intra-family conflict because they do not directly affect many day-to-day interactions among family members. It appears that what is not relevant to daily life is not discussed. For example, there is much evidence that adolescents are more sexually active today than were their parents at the same age, but this difference does not produce as much conflict as we might expect because parents and adolescents rarely discuss sexuality (Thornburg, 1981).

So, if most potentially explosive generational differences are silently ignored, what *does* produce parent-adolescent conflict? Most studies show that the majority of arguments between parents and their adolescent children are about normal, everyday, mundane family matters such as schoolwork, social life and friends, chores, disobedience, disagreements with siblings, and personal hygiene (Montemayor, 1986; Hill, 1988; Powers, Hauser, and Kilner, 1989). Does this match your own experience?

Montemayor (1983) examined seventeen studies conducted between 1929 and 1982 and found that, over the years, very little has changed in what parents and adolescents argue about. The same problems, all dealing with daily family functioning, appear in study after study. Even the studies conducted during the late 1960s and early 1970s, when conflict over such issues as civil rights, the Vietnam War, and college protests might have been expected, found that these issues were not mentioned. In spite of the many changes in modern family life that have occurred over the last fifty years, adolescents appear to have the same kinds of disagreements with their parents that their parents had when they, themselves, were adolescents.

The reasons offered by adolescents and parents to justify the correctness of their own positions during arguments suggest that the basic issue is the conflict between the autonomy of the adolescent and the authority of the parents. Psychologist Judith Smetana and her colleagues (1991) studied both two-parent and divorced, single-parent families with children ranging from fifth-graders to twelfth-graders. Their sample was primarily white and well educated. The researchers asked parents and adolescents how they justified their respective positions in arguments.

Adolescents in two-parent families saw their arguments with their parents as resulting from the conflict between their own desire to exercise personal autonomy and their parents' desire to maintain control. Their justifications focused on their "right" to exercise autonomy— "It's my room and I should be able to decide how it looks," or "I'm just expressing who I am." Parents also saw the issue as one of autonomy versus authority, but they focused on their "right" to exert control— "I'm your mother and I told you to do it," "It's rude to talk to your mother like that," or "You need to learn some responsibility." Parents sometimes also justified their position in terms of the needs of the family as a whole— "We're all part of the family, so we all have to chip in and help," "With your mother working, we all have jobs so that things will get done around here." Interestingly, both parents and adolescents could take the other's perspective and could articulate it even though they disagreed with it.

In single-parent families, on the other hand, these kinds of autonomy-versus-authority justifications were used infrequently by both adolescents and parents, particularly during early adolescence. This finding is consistent with the results of other studies which show that adolescents in divorced families are more independent and that their mothers are less controlling than mothers in intact families (Dornbusch et al., 1985; Hetherington, 1989).

quired behaviors that permit him or her to participate as a member of an organization. This process continues throughout the individual's career with the organization and determines the individual's attachment, productivity, and satisfaction with the organization (Van Maanen, 1976). Most people choose to work within a particular organization and are therefore strongly motivated to discover and meet the expectations of the organization. Some organizations leave nothing to chance: they use selection devices to identify recruits who already have the proper attitudes, values, and motivations required for membership and who will therefore require little socialization. Some even make it a practice to "raid" their competitors for good recruits who have the skills required by organizations in their particular field.

Organizational Socialization

If an organization cannot meet its needs by recruiting individuals who are already socialized to their particular job expectations, it must perform the task of organizational socialization itself. Organizations differ in terms of how they approach this task. First, organizations vary in the degree of *formality* of the initial socialization process. When socialization is formal, the recruit is given a special designation such as "trainee" or "apprentice" and assigned to a "trainer" or an "instructor."

Second, organizations differ in the degree to which they make use of the simultaneous socialization of several recruits in a class or *peer group* to ease the individual's transition into the organization. Collective-socialization settings put recruits "in the same boat" and encourage the development of group solutions to the problems of everyday life in the organization. Another version of the use of a peer group is to place the recruit "under the wing" of others in the organization who have previously undergone the same socialization process. Such "big brothers and sisters" can reduce role discontinuity by being a source of expert advice. Even in organizations without any formal efforts to socialize recruits, most new members become part of small, ongoing groups of workers that constitute a key source of socializa-

tion. Although peer-group socialization can be an effective method of socializing recruits, it does not always work out this way. Peer groups can develop subcultures that *oppose* the larger organization's rules. They sometimes devise new solutions to work problems that are unacceptable to the organization. Or longtime workers can pass their low morale on to new recruits.

A third way that organizations differ in their approach to socializing new recruits is in the type of *motivation* they offer. Some organizations can rely on *intrinsic motivation*, or motivation that comes from the task itself, as the primary socializing force. Tasks that are intrinsically motivating tend to allow the worker to use a variety of skills and to exercise independence and discretion in carrying out work assignments. Other organizations must rely on *extrinsic motivation*, or rewards, such as pay, that are not inherent in the task. Some organizations emphasize the great reputation of the organization ("We're number one") or the collegial relationship between management and labor.

Finally, organizations also differ in terms of the extensiveness, or *totality*, of the control they have over the recruits' lives. For example, Diane Margolis (1979) has argued that some work organizations use a socialization process that deliberately transfers young executives from one area to another to weaken outside ties and make managers more dependent upon the corporation. Similarly, by demanding long hours of work, the organization disrupts commitments to family, friends, community, and other interests that might be the source of conflicting pressures on the manager. Likewise, because the military desires to teach its recruits a role that differs dramatically from their civilian roles, it structures a socialization experience—boot camp—to exert maximum control over the recruits' lives.

Erving Goffman (1961a) has noted four common traits of "total institutions" such as the military boot camp. First, all aspects of life are conducted in the same setting and under the control of a single authority. Second, all aspects of daily life are conducted in the company of others who are in the same circumstances. There is little privacy, and contact with the outside world is strictly regulated. Third, all activities are scheduled without consulting the participants. Often, formal routines specify such details of life as when to get up or go to bed, what to wear, when and what to eat, what work is to be done, and what leisure activities are offered. Finally, all activities in such a controlled environment are designed to meet a goal of the organization.

Occupational Careers

The organizational socialization process — which emphasizes the transfer of knowledge, abilities, and motivation — also involves the creation of expectations about careers. **Occupational careers** are patterned paths of mobility within the organization. Organizational expectations define various positions within the organization and set timetables, as well as acceptable paths for moving through these positions. There are often several acceptable routes to a particular position, but some paths will be thought of as unacceptable. It is possible for a person to become "stuck" in a position. Movement through some career paths, on some timetables, will be defined by the organization and the participants as "success," while movement through others will be taken to indicate "failure."

Organizational socialization is likely to be especially intense just before and just after an individual's transition from one status to another in the career path. Rites of passage may mark transitions, indicating to the initiate that she or he has been granted full membership in the new status and developing the initiate's sense of belonging. These rites may involve giving the member a new title, providing extra rights (such as a bigger office or more secretarial support), or sharing information that previously had been withheld (e.g., by including the person at staff meetings from which she or he had been previously excluded). They signify to everyone that the member now has the skills, knowledge, and motivation to occupy the new role.

Socialization for work is a continuous process, even for workers whose jobs do not involve participation in organizations. This is well illustrated by Howard Becker's (1982) analysis of the work of artists. We often think of artists as among the most solitary and independent of workers. However, Becker shows that artists learn their roles in interaction with others. Even artists who don't follow the existing artistic conventions of their day learn their roles in interaction with other artists, art critics, and the public (Hall, 1986).

Gender and Employment Roles

Even today in the United States, women tend to be segregated in jobs that society considers appropriate for women. Women accounted for less than 10 percent of engineers, dentists, pilots, fire fighters, mechanics, and clergy in 1989 but made up more than 95 percent of secretaries, dental hygienists, kindergarten teachers, and nurses (U.S. Bureau of the Census, 1991a). In virtually every industry in which both men and women work, women tend to be concentrated in the lower-paying, lower-prestige jobs, while men tend to monopolize the higher-paying, higher-prestige jobs. As women become trained in the professions, more are becoming doctors, attorneys, and business executives. But in these occupations dominated by men, women still face obstacles to mobility (Blum and Smith, 1988).

While many social psychologists point to early sex-role socialization to explain the characteristics of women in work organizations, Rosabeth Moss Kanter (1977) argues that the structure of the work organization itself contributes to women's relative lack of success on many work-related measures. Kanter argues that individuals' adaptation to their work circumstances is largely determined by their positions in three structural features of the work organization: *opportunity*, *power*, and *relative numbers*. She finds that women's disadvantaged positions in all three of these structural dimensions produce such self-defeating attributes in the job situation as pettiness, low aspirations, loyalty to the immediate work group instead of the larger organization, and concern with emotional ties to other workers.

For example, women often work in situations that provide little *opportunity* for advancement. Kanter states: "People relate to the present in part in terms of their expectations for the future . . . to be 'stuck' is a very different work experience than being . . . 'up and coming'" (1977: 251). People who see themselves as 'stuck' tend to limit their aspirations, seek satisfaction from nonwork activities, give precedence to interpersonal relations and strong peer associations, and develop loyalties to their immediate work group rather than to the larger organization. Having little *organizational power* causes women to behave in a petty, authoritarian fashion, to use subordinates for their frame of reference, and to rely more on coercive rather than persuasive techniques of control. Even women in management positions are disadvantaged because they are in the *minority* among their peers. They find it harder to be taken seriously, are more isolated and excluded from informal peer networks, and, as a result, are less effective.

According to Kanter, placement in low-power, dead-end jobs promotes self-defeating behavior, which leads to further disadvantage. Breaking this cycle is difficult because the perceptions and expectations that others have of the individual become solidified. Kanter notes that although women are more likely to be in structurally disadvantaged positions, men placed in similar positions also develop self-defeating behavior. In short, she argues that men and women do not have different personalities, skills, and values: they react the same way when placed in the same structural positions and given the same opportunities. But women do not often find themselves in the same structural positions with the same opportunities as men. It is this structural disadvantage, Kanter suggests, that *produces* the work-related behaviors and attitudes that are typically viewed as "female" traits.

FAMILY ROLES

Despite the great importance given to the roles of spouse and parent in American society, these seem to be two of the roles for which we are least prepared. Anticipatory socialization for marriage and parenthood — observing your parents, playing

mommy and daddy during childhood, caring for younger siblings, baby-sitting — seems minimal and haphazard compared with the preparation for other adult roles, such as occupational roles. Although children observe their parents over a period of many years, much of marital behavior is hidden from them. Parents do not engage in sex in front of their children, and many parents also carry out serious discussions and decision making in private. Most businesses would not consider putting a salesclerk, cashier, or waitress to work without some training. Yet, even during engagement, most couples' preparation for marriage is limited to such activities as talking with a minister, furnishing a home, and, possibly, engaging in increased sexual intimacy. During pregnancy, a couple's preparation for parenthood is usually limited to such things as reading, consulting with friends and family, having discussions with each other, and preparing a place in the household for the child (Rossi, 1980).

The Transition from the Single to the Marital Role

It is estimated that only 8 to 9 percent of men and women now in their twenties will never marry. Of the brides embarking on a first marriage, 18 percent are teenagers, 43 percent are twenty to twenty-four years of age, 26 percent are twenty-five to twenty-nine, and only 13 percent are thirty or older (U.S. Bureau of the Census, 1992a). Grooms tend to be older than brides; African-American brides and grooms are generally older than their white counterparts. Age at first marriage is up from 1970, when, for example, 42 percent of brides were teenagers.

In our culture, the rites of passage marking the transition from single to married status often include an engagement and a wedding ceremony. The engagement is an intermediate stage between courtship and marriage. A formal engagement serves notice to others that the couple intend to marry, and it gives everyone an opportunity to adjust to the idea. Bridal showers and bachelor and bachelorette parties give friends and relatives of the couple a chance to participate in the role

STUDENT OBSERVATION

Rite of Passage — Engagement

Last February, two of my best friends, Liz and Steve, became engaged to each other. The engagement itself did not come as a shock, but the way everybody — myself included — began thinking about and acting toward them started to change. For instance, they had been living together for nearly six months, but the situation was not acceptable to either set of parents until after they were engaged. The fact that they officially declared their intention to get married changed the way their parents looked at their living arrangements. When Liz graduated in May, she took a job in another state and Steve went with her. Again, they moved in together, but nobody questioned it because of the engagement. People thought, "Well, they'll be married in a year anyway, so it would be a waste of money to keep two apartments." Also, Liz and Steve began taking their relationship more seriously. They discussed finances and argued over housekeeping rather than what bar to go to or what movie to see. They had already decided to spend the rest of their lives together, but the public announcement of that intention made it seem "real" to everyone involved. The rite of passage of the engagement was a public transition that changed their views about themselves and their relationship, as well as everyone else's views.

transition. Some researchers believe that these parties give all involved a chance to express ambivalent feelings they may have about the transition (Berardo and Vera, 1981). (Before reading further, see the Student Observation: "Rite of Passage — Engagement.")

The wedding ceremony itself is a rite rich in meaning and symbolism (Chesser, 1980). While such rites vary among different religious groups and civil ceremonies, there are some things they have in common. The bride and groom make certain pledges to each other, and they indicate their agreement to abide by civil (and often religious) law. Rings may be exchanged as a sign of the eternal nature of love and a reminder of the vows taken. The marriage license is signed and

A wedding is a rite of passage — a ceremony intended to signify to all participants (the couple, their families, and friends) the importance of the transition from single to married status.

witnessed as evidence that state law has been ful-filled.

The wedding ceremony is intended to signify to all participants — the couple, their families, and friends — the importance of the transition from single to married status. As such, it is an impor-tant part of socialization for the married role. It is meant to change the way the bride and groom think about themselves — "This is an important change. I am now a married person. I will be different. Others will see me differently and act differently toward me." The ceremony is also meant to change the way others think about the couple. For example, the groom's parents must come to think of the person who was "our son's girlfriend" as "our son's wife — our daughter-in-law."

The wedding ceremony is, of course, only the beginning of the couple's life together. During the marriage, each partner will continue to adjust to his or her marital role. These roles are, in effect, negotiated through the interaction of the marital partners with each other and with others who relate to them in their new statuses (mothers- and fathers-in-law, sisters- and brothers-in-law, other relatives, friends, co-workers, and so on). Couples must work out their own balance of power regarding how decisions are made, develop joint friendships and social activities, and learn to coordinate their schedules and share belongings.

Parenthood

In the United States, most married couples have children. Only about 20 percent of women ever married are childless (U.S. Bureau of the Census, 1992a). This percentage has been increasing since the mid-1960s. The percentage is higher among whites and lower among African-Americans and Hispanics. Some couples who remain childless do so involuntarily; they would like to have children, but, because of fertility problems, they are unable to. Other couples are childless voluntarily. Volun-tary childlessness is frequently the result of re-peatedly postponing having children until "time runs out." Although negative attitudes toward childlessness have relaxed somewhat in recent years, those who are voluntarily childless still en-counter negative evaluations and social pressure to become parents (Thornton, 1989). It appears that the social norms of our culture prescribe that most, if not all, married couples *should* become parents.

The stresses of parenthood. The transition to parenthood is often stressful because of its abrupt-ness. One day you are not a parent; the next day you are. Furthermore, the birth of a child is not followed by a gradual taking on of responsibili-ty (as is the case with many occupational roles). Most new parents start out immediately on twenty-four-hour duty, with responsibility for a fragile and mysterious infant totally dependent on their care. The routines they have developed and their patterns of interaction with each other as a marital couple are almost certainly disrupted by the demands of the new family member (Belsky, Lang, and Rovine, 1985; Cowan and Cowan, 1988, 1990; MacDermid, Huston, and McHale, 1990; Wallace and Gotlib, 1990; Cowan et al., 1991). Marital satisfaction tends to decline when a couple become parents. The amount of household work rises, and the mother takes on a dispropor-tionate share. Fathers see child care as the moth-er's primary responsibility and view their role as "helping out" (Cowan et al., 1985; McHale and Huston, 1985). Parents' time together, intimacy, and communication tend to decrease dramatically (Belsky, Lang, and Huston, 1986).

The pressure to be a "good parent" is very great. In most areas of life there is some margin for error — doctors are expected to lose some pa-tients, teachers are expected to fail to teach some students, some marriages are expected to end in divorce — but, increasingly in American society, parents are expected to "succeed" with every child. This higher expectation may be due, in part, to smaller family size. The number of chil-dren per family is declining. The only group hav-ing more children than in the past is unmarried women, particularly teenagers (U.S. Bureau of the Census, 1991b). If you have five or six children, as many of your great-grandparents did, it doesn't seem that terrible to have one (or even two) turn out badly. If you have only one or two children and one turns out badly, the failure seems greater.

While the pressure to "do it right" is great, there are no clear guidelines about how to be successful in parenthood. Despite a proliferation of "expert" advice, there is no clear model for parents to follow. In the past, American parents may have felt comfortable using their own parents as models, raising their children more or less as they, themselves, were raised. Changes in the structure of the family—smaller extended families; more working mothers; higher divorce rates; and more single parents, stepparents, and blended families—often make it impossible for today's parents to rely on their own parents as role models.

Children's influence. The focus of the parental role is the socialization of the child. Perhaps because this process is so dramatic, we sometimes overlook the fact that babies can have as much impact on their parents' socialization to the parental role as parents have on their children's early socialization. In part, the effect of early encounters between parents and an infant depends on how well the child's temperament meshes with the parents' expectations and personalities (Maccoby, Snow, and Jacklin, 1984). For example, an anxious first-time mother may find an easy baby's happy moods and adaptability reassuring and interpret them as an indication that she is a "good mother." The same mother, faced with a difficult baby, will have a very different parenting experience.

Parenting behavior is often guided by the parents' inferences about the reasons for a child's behavior. The way a child's behavior is interpreted depends to some degree on the parents' estimate of the child's level of knowledge and ability—and this depends, in part, on the child's age (Dix and Grusec, 1985). Such estimates must continually be adjusted as the child grows and develops. For example, parents of older children were more likely to view all types of behavior as being intentional and attributable to the per-

sonality dispositions of the child, as opposed to being caused by external or situational factors (Dix et al., 1986). As children grow older, their ability to use language, to respond to reasoning, to use logic, and to develop control of their own behavior is marked by a corresponding change in the ways that parents try to control unacceptable behavior.

The parent and child roles provide a good illustration of the *reciprocal and dynamic nature of socialization*. The parents' interaction with the child not only influences the child but changes the parents as well. As we have seen in our discussion of the child's socialization, the parents change the methods they use to socialize the child as the child ages, grows, and learns. The same is true for the parents' socialization. Parents learn from their interaction with the growing, developing child that they must change their approach to be effective.

As children become adolescents, parents must continue to adjust their responses. Conflicts are common as new roles are negotiated, but they usually are limited to a few areas of disagreement, such as grades, curfews, and household responsibilities. The increased autonomy of teenagers relieves parents of some of their child-care duties. As the youngest child reaches this age, parents report higher levels of marital satisfaction than parents with school-age children, perhaps indicating a reduction in role overload. In anticipation of the reduced importance of their parental role once the last child has entered adulthood, parents may reexamine their marital relationships and move toward a new balance.

Gender and Family Roles

In traditional marriages, a division of labor is taken for granted. It is assumed that the husband will be the wage earner and the wife will take care of the house and children. Contemporary couples have more choices of life style than were available to couples in the past, but they also have fewer guidelines. More aspects of the marital relationship are subject to negotiation: Should the wife work? Should the couple have children? How should household tasks be shared? Whose job opportunities should determine where the couple lives?

In our society, the male's occupational role is at the heart of other male adult roles. The roles of husband and father are largely defined in terms of being a "good provider." Males who are successful in their occupational roles are more likely to be happy with themselves and to feel adequate as husbands and fathers (Osherson and Dill, 1983; Draughn, 1984; Gaesser and Whitbourne, 1985). Females, on the other hand, face a very different situation. To fill the traditional roles of wife and mother, a female is expected to be dependent on her husband for financial support. In return, she is expected to care for the house and children and to provide a supportive atmosphere for the husband so that he can pursue his career without having to worry about these things. Thus, when a woman takes on an occupational role, it is frequently seen as undermining, rather than contributing to, the adequacy of her fulfillment of the roles of wife and mother. Some husbands see their wives' "having to work" as a personal inadequacy — as an indication that they have failed to be good providers (Bernard, 1986).

These gender differences in role priorities are highlighted by emergency situations in which the demands of one role intrude on the time or effort usually devoted to another. Consider, for example, situations in which a family emergency, such as a sick child, demands that someone take time away from work or an important job assignment requires that office work be done at home during times normally reserved for family activities. In such situations, for men, work roles are culturally given priority, while, for women, family roles are (Coser and Rokoff, 1982). In emergencies, women tend to disrupt their occupations and men tend to disrupt their families.

Because of the way traditional male roles are defined, men can work and maintain a family much more easily than can women, whose family roles stress being at home, nurturing, and meeting the needs of others (Rubin, 1983). In fact, the more occupationally successful men are, the more likely they are to marry and to have children.

Women, on the other hand, are more likely to be successful if they are single and childless. (Hull, 1982). In addition to actual role strain, women's occupational outcomes are affected by employers' assumptions of incompatibility between women's family and work roles (Peterson, 1989a).

Sources of Role Strain

Despite the obstacles to doing so, many women today *do* combine occupational roles with their roles as wives and mothers. Between 1900 and 1991, the proportion of women who worked outside the home almost tripled, rising from 20 to 58 percent. One of the historical events during this period that changed the work expectations for all women was World War II. Due to the shortage of men for defense production jobs, women were "temporarily" ushered into unfamiliar jobs. The postwar economy encouraged the continued upward trend of women's participation in the labor force. At the beginning of this century, most working women were single and childless. Today, many not only are married but also have young children at home. In 1991, for example, over 60 percent of American women with preschool children had paid jobs (U.S. Bureau of the Census, 1992a).

Whether they work by choice or necessity, women who try to meet the expectations of both occupational and family roles frequently find it difficult to manage the two sets of responsibilities. One source of strain is internal, resulting from the woman's own ambiguous feelings about the fact that she is working. Especially if a woman works out of necessity, rather than by choice, and if her socialization experiences have stressed more traditional female roles, she may feel tension and guilt about working. In this case, the woman's behavior is at odds with her beliefs about being a "good wife" and "good mother." This kind of strain is called **role conflict** — the expected behavior in one role is contrary to the behavior expected of the same person in a different role. (Before reading further, see the Student Observation: "Role Conflict.")

Another source of strain is having to meet too

STUDENT OBSERVATION

Role Conflict

The United States Field Hockey Association has a national team tryout camp every December. The best hockey players in the country are invited. The environment is very competitive, and field hockey is the only emphasis. While I was at the camp last year, my boyfriend called to say that he had some free days and wanted to know if he could come visit me at camp. I happily agreed. But when he arrived, I experienced a lot of disturbing feelings. Both being a national hockey player and being in a relationship with my boyfriend were very important to me. I wanted to excel at the camp and continue my membership on the national team. I also wanted to spend "quality" time with my boyfriend. I had trouble deciding which identity — field hockey player or girlfriend — should take precedence. In short, I experienced role conflict.

---

many role demands at once — a condition called **role overload**. A woman who works full-time, who is raising one or more children, and who tries to meet the needs of her husband has taken on a great deal of responsibility. With over half of all married women gainfully employed outside the home, we might expect that husbands would share more responsibility for housework and child care. A study of the ten-year period from 1965 to 1975 revealed few changes in the amount of time husbands spend in housework and child care even though wives' participation in the labor force increased considerably during the same period (Coverman and Sheley, 1986). More recent studies indicate that egalitarian roles still are not common (Thompson and Walker, 1989). One study revealed that, overall, wives performed about 79 percent of the housework that was done in their homes (Berardo, Shehan, and Leslie, 1987). Even in families where both husband and wife worked, the wives performed about 70 percent of the housework.

When we take on roles can also affect the strain they produce. Earlier in this section, we referred to the increasing number of adolescent mothers. Our society generally regards teenagers as "too young" to become parents. Whereas in the past many unmarried teenage mothers gave their babies up for adoption, currently, about 90 percent decide to keep their babies. Early motherhood also has implications for performing other roles. The younger women are when their first child is born, the less formal education they complete.

While having children in the teenage years appears to be stressful, some evidence suggests that there is also a "too late" period. Women who become mothers relatively late in life report more difficulties in carrying out the mother role. Rossi (1980) notes that part of the difficulty reported by older mothers may be related to their being "out of sync" with other, same-age mothers who had children earlier — whose behavior was closer to role expectations.

Reducing Role Strain

Our efforts to deal with role strain may take several forms. If the strain is primarily one of role overload, we might establish **role priorities**: we avoid or reduce our involvement in one or more of the roles producing the overload. For example, to avoid role overload involving employment and marital roles, some women choose to delay marriage. If the overload involves employment and parent roles, the woman may give priority to her employment role and choose to remain childless, may limit the number of children she has, or may renegotiate family responsibilities, especially with her husband. If, on the other hand, she gives priority to her parent role, she may reduce work when her children are young or choose an occupation with a flexible work schedule. Many employed women drop out of the labor force when they have children. The current trend is for such women to stay out of the labor force for a shorter time than earlier cohorts did.

Role strain involving role conflict can be resolved through **compartmentalization** — the process of subdividing our lives so that in one context we act one way and in another context we act another way. For example, a woman may feel that, as a mother, she should be very warm and nurturing toward her children. With her work colleagues, she may not want to show this warm and nurturing side; she may fear that she will be taken less seriously if she lets down her professional demeanor even momentarily. Role strain would occur if this woman were in the presence of her children and colleagues at the same time. If she made sure that this never happened, she would be using compartmentalization to avoid role strain. Of course, men too may experience role strain and resolve it using the strategies we have just discussed.

Exiting Marital Roles: Divorce

Currently, one-third of married women end their first marriage before age forty. Research indicates that marriages which begin during the teenage years ("too early") and after age thirty ("too late") have greater chances of ending in divorce than those beginning between twenty and twenty-nine years of age (Booth and Edwards, 1985). With the exception of a post–World War II "divorce boom," the divorce rate increased steadily until some leveling began to occur during the 1980s. Much of the increase in divorce has been attributed to historical events such as the advent of "the pill" and the rising employment of women (Cherlin, 1981). Between 1962 and 1980, Americans' attitudes toward divorce became more approving (Thornton, 1989). Still, divorce is a life change that can involve considerable stress.

Divorce usually means lower economic standards for women and children but higher standards for men (Pett and Vaughan-Cole, 1986; Peterson, 1989b). Fifty percent of single mothers, many of them divorced, live in poverty. These economic conditions force many divorced moth-

ers into the labor force, creating strains due to role overload (Berman and Turk, 1981). Divorced fathers with custody of their children experience the same pattern of role overload regarding job, parenting, and household management (Smith and Smith, 1981). Men who assumed no household tasks prior to divorce generally experience more stress. Noncustodial parents must negotiate new relationships with their children (Seltzer and Bianchi, 1988).

There are also difficulties associated with establishing new romantic relationships after divorce. One study found that both men and women tend to respond in one of two patterns (Ebaugh, 1988). A minority feel elated at being "free" and throw themselves into the dating-and-sex game for one to two years, after which they begin to slow down. The majority feel that they are "failures," and they are very shy about dating. Social support is an important factor in reducing or avoiding these difficulties. Those who had new romantic relationships established *before* the divorce had easier adjustments than those who did not.

Approximately three-fourths of the people who divorce each year remarry eventually (Pasley and Ihinger-Tallman, 1988; Bumpass, Sweet, and Martin, 1990). Indeed, remarriages currently comprise almost half of all marriages (U.S. Department of Health and Human Services, 1990). Remarriage often creates still other sources of stress, such as blended families that include step- and half-relationships. There is little anticipatory socialization for these roles, so those who become members of blended families have to work out their own role expectations in interaction with one another.

Socialization in Later Life

In later life, most adults experience a number of important changes in roles that require continuing adjustment and socialization. Parental roles continue to change as children themselves become adults and take on new roles. Work roles are relinquished, and marital roles may end in widowhood. Let's look at some of these changes in more detail.

REVISING THE PARENT ROLE

When children grow up, their parents do not cease to be parents, but the expectations associated with being the parent of an *adult* child are different. The parental role becomes much less important in the parent's daily life.

The Empty-Nest Transition

The period of family life experienced by parents when the last child leaves home has been called the **empty-nest stage**. The use of this term is based on the assumption that parents, especially mothers, will feel lonely and useless once their children have left home. Many studies suggest that this is not the case (Borland, 1982; Bell and Eisenberg, 1985; Adelmann et al., 1989). Many women look forward to the time when their youngest child leaves home as a time when they can begin new jobs, return to school, or pursue other opportunities for self-fulfillment (Robertson, 1978; Rubin, 1978). There is also some evidence that the parents' marital relationship improves after their children leave home (Schram, 1979; Glenn and McLanahan, 1982; Anderson, Russell, and Schumm, 1983; Glenn, 1991).

In fact, research has indicated that the transition to the empty-nest stage is more stressful if the children leave home unexpectedly early or "too late." Having young-adult children who don't become independent as early as their parents anticipated—or who return to live with their parents because of divorce or financial difficulties—is a problem faced by a growing number of families today (Mancini and Blieszner, 1991). About 61 percent of never-married men and 48 percent of never-married women age eighteen to twenty-four live with their parents (Saluter, 1989). Most parents—about 80 percent of those with children twenty-two and over, according to one study—expect their adult children to be "up, gone, and on their own" by that age, and half of the parents reported that living with adult children caused serious conflict (Clemens and Axel-

son, 1985). Middle-class parents report more problems associated with having an adult child living with them than do lower-class parents (Aquilino, 1991). Couples in this period of life may also experience strain caused by the failing health of their own parents (Pillemer and Wolf, 1986).

Relationships with Adult Children

Americans' stereotyped view of old age portrays the elderly as confined to nursing homes and dependent on their middle-aged children or as neglected and alone. Actually, the great majority of the elderly—even those age eighty-five and older—maintain their own homes or apartments. Less than 1 percent of older people say that they would want to live with their children (Horn and Meer, 1987). Most older Americans maintain relationships with their children while continuing to live as independently as possible. Research shows that most older persons are not isolated from their children (Montgomery, 1982; Bengtson et al., 1985). About three-fourths of elderly parents have been in contact with their children—by telephone, letter, or visit—in the past week (Kovar, 1986; Aldous, 1987).

Financial dependence on children does not appear to be widespread. In fact, a 1987 poll by Louis Harris and Associates found that older Americans are four times more likely to *give* financial aid to their children than to receive it (Harris, 1987). A study by Joan Aldous (1987) found that older parents provide assistance to their adult children—in the form of loans, gifts, child care, housekeeping services, and emotional support—quite frequently. The parents studied gave the most assistance to their adult children who were single or divorced, especially single mothers. Their adult children reciprocated by assisting the parents with physical chores, such as household and yard work, and helping out when a parent was ill. When older adults do need care, it is most often women—generally daughters or daughters-in-law—who provide it (Mancini and Blieszner, 1991).

Family members are not the only source of support for the elderly. Just as they are for other age groups, friends are an important source of social support and satisfaction. Half of the elderly respondents in one study said they had more than ten friends they could call on for assistance in their daily lives (Quadagno, 1986). These relationships appeared to be reciprocal — based on an exchange of kindnesses. For example, one person might read to a friend with eye trouble; another might drive friends to church or to stores; still another might cook more than she needed and share the excess with friends.

ENTERING THE GRANDPARENT ROLE

Adults today can expect to spend nearly one-half of their lives as grandparents (Barranti, 1985). For most, grandparenthood begins in middle age and lasts several decades, usually well into the grandchild's adulthood (Thompson and Walker, 1987). Because adults live longer, more children today have living grandparents. Distance appears to be the most important factor affecting the amount of interaction between grandparents and grandchildren (Cherlin and Furstenberg, 1986). In a recent study of college students (Kennedy, 1990), almost half had at least one grandparent living in the same town, and another one-fifth had a grandparent living within 50 miles. More than half of the students reported that they felt very close to at least one grandparent.

Individuals' experiences with their grandparents may sometimes provide models for their own grandparenting behavior. However, in many cases these models may not be appropriate, because today's grandparents are younger and healthier than those of previous generations. Other changes in family structure have complicated the picture. Stepfamilies have created step-grandparents, who must define their own relationship with their step-grandchildren. Divorce often causes conflict or strain between grandparents and a custodial parent (Bray and Berger, 1990). As with many other family roles, socialization for the grandparent role is largely on-the-job training. When people feel that their transition to the grandparent role is "on time," they seem to adjust more easily to learning the expected behaviors.

For example, the infants of teenage mothers are frequently cared for by the infants' grandmothers. This creates role overload for many of the young grandmothers, particularly for those who have young children themselves (Burton and Bengston, 1985).

One study of 125 grandmothers found that 80 percent enjoyed their grandparent role and most thought being a grandmother was easier than being a mother (Robertson, in Quadagno, 1980). Grandparents have more time than busy parents to play with children, and some researchers suggest that the companionate style of grandparenting, in which the grandparent and the grandchild are pals, is increasing (Cherlin and Furstenberg, 1986).

EXITING THE EMPLOYMENT ROLE AND ENTERING RETIREMENT

In some societies the elderly are revered. In Japan, for example, despite industrialization and rapid technological change, younger people defer to their parents on family matters, seek the opinions of the elderly, and expect their aging parents to live with them. These attitudes result from longstanding religious and cultural traditions. By contrast, Americans tend to idealize youth and to reject the elderly. A system of negative beliefs about the elderly is part of our culture. In this stereotyped view, old age means inevitable physical, mental, and sexual decline; lack of adaptability; and disinterest in and withdrawal from the world. Polls consistently show that Americans under age sixty-five hold negative stereotypes of the elderly. Those over sixty-five have the same negative stereotypes, but they often see themselves as exceptions to the rule (Harris, 1981). No wonder most of us dread the idea of getting old ourselves!

Old age, like childhood and adolescence, is a relatively recent invention. At the beginning of this century, life spans were shorter and retirement was less common — few persons lived long after their working lives were over. Today, three out of four Americans live to be at least sixty-five years old; in 1900, the figure was only two out of

Today's grandparents are younger and healthier than those of earlier generations. Researchers suggest that the companionate style of grandparenting is increasing.

five. Today, only one out of six men age sixty-five and older (and one out of ten women of that age) is employed; in 1900, two out of three older men were still in the work force (U.S. Bureau of the Census, 1991*a*).

The numbers of working elderly were significantly reduced by two historical events. The first was the passage of the Social Security Act in the 1930s. The act provided assistance to unemployed people, thereby encouraging older workers to retire and opening up desperately needed opportunities for younger workers. Since its passage, benefits under the act have been extended, particularly by the inclusion of Medicare, a mandatory health insurance program for those sixty-five and older. These benefits have improved older Americans' standard of living, although for many the standard is just above the poverty level.

The second historical event that reduced the number of working elderly was the advent of mandatory retirement agreements. In modern industrial societies, rapid technological change makes the knowledge and skills of older members of the society obsolete, and generational competition for jobs leads to pressures on the elderly to retire. About 80 percent of American workers face mandatory retirement at age sixty-five or seventy, even though at least 30 percent would prefer to keep working (Quadagno, 1986). Mandatory retirement was originally instituted as part of a package designed to protect older workers. In exchange for job security for workers in their fifties, unions accepted mandatory retirement at age sixty-five. More recently, mandatory retirement has come to be viewed as one example of **ageism** — society's denial of privileges to a category of people because of their age. A law banning mandatory retirement was passed by Congress in 1986, but it is being phased in gradually and will not cover all workers until 1994.

Retirement is an important transition in the life course, and it can be very stressful. This is especially true for those men and women who derive much of their identity from their occupational status. For them, a job is not only a source of income but also an important source of pride and meaning. It provides structure in their lives, is a source of social contacts, and often provides opportunities for creativity and personal fulfillment. Persons for whom work has been very important might, understandably, look to retirement with some apprehension. However, most studies show that a majority of older Americans look forward to retirement (Quadagno, 1986). Perhaps the growing number of older Americans who are experiencing this time of life positively—having both time and money to enjoy leisure activities—will work against the negative stereotypes. Many surveys have found that Americans sixty-five and over are more highly satisfied with their standard of living than are those in younger age groups (Gallup, 1983).

The husband's retirement marks a transition for the full-time homemaker-wife as well. Such wives may find it difficult to share the house that has long been their exclusive territory during the day, and many don't want to share the housework with their retired husbands. Both members of the couple must adjust to a new pattern of increased "togetherness" by negotiating new roles. Nevertheless, marital satisfaction increases for many couples during this time (Zube, 1982; Kozma and Stones, 1983).

We do not intend to perpetuate the myth that old age is a perfectly serene time in which the stresses and strains of everyday life magically disappear. Most people experience a reduction in income during old age, and some experience extreme economic hardship. The most likely to suffer are women and members of minority groups because they earn less than white males during their lifetimes. As a result, they receive less in Social Security benefits and other pensions. Eight percent of households headed by males age sixty-five and older have incomes below the poverty line, compared with 15 percent of households headed by females the same age. Elderly African-Americans and Hispanics are three times as likely to be living in poverty as elderly whites (Quadagno, 1986). Poverty tends to increase with age. For example, those eighty-five and older are twice as likely to live in poverty as those age sixty-five to sixty-nine. Ninety-six percent of Americans age eighty-five and older have no income other than Social Security benefits. For these disadvantaged older Americans, the elderly role is most likely a difficult one.

EXITING THE MARITAL ROLE AND ENTERING WIDOWHOOD

Because American females have a longer life expectancy and typically marry men a few years older than themselves, most outlive their husbands by several years. Therefore women are more likely than men to have to face the death of a spouse before confronting death themselves. Only 15 percent of men age sixty-five and older but 48 percent of women the same age are widowed. By age seventy-five, 66 percent of men but only 24 percent of women are still living with a spouse (U.S. Bureau of the Census, 1992a).

The death of a spouse is one of life's most traumatic events. Both widows and widowers mention loneliness as their biggest problem of adjustment (Clark, Siviski, and Weiner, 1986). As is true for so many other roles, the experience of widowhood differs greatly for men and women.

In some ways, adjustment to widowhood may be more difficult for males. With the wife's death, many men lose a system of emotional and domestic support that they have always taken for granted. Especially for men who are elderly today—whose marriages were most often based on traditional gender roles—cooking and certain household chores may be totally unfamiliar tasks. This can even lead to physical decline due to poor nutrition. Men may be reluctant to ask for help, since this clashes with their self-definitions as independent and resourceful. Men have often relied on their wives to maintain close contacts with friends and relatives and may receive less support from these sources following the death of the spouse (Longino and Lipman, 1981).

Men are also more likely than women to escape widowhood through remarriage. Men age sixty-five and older are eight times more likely to remarry than women the same age (Horn and Meer, 1987). This is due, in part, to the much smaller pool of unmarried men in the older age group. The more education a man has, and the higher his income, the more likely he is to remarry. Interestingly, the reverse is true for women (Hagestad, 1986).

Widowhood is more likely to bring a decline in standard of living for women than for men. Most of today's elderly widows were full-time housewives who worked for pay sporadically, if at all. They are unlikely to have pension plans or savings. Even women who worked most of their lives earned much less than men and therefore receive less in Social Security benefits after the husband's death. Widows whose marriages were very traditional may have little experience with driving, home repairs, and financial management. The more central the role of wife has been for the woman, the more adjustment may be required to widowhood as she tries to find other roles to give her life meaning (Rice, 1986).

DEATH: THE FINAL EXIT

Just as we learn how to live, we must learn how to die. In the past, death came at unpredictable times. Today, most deaths occur among the old. This has changed the meaning of death, both for individuals and for society. Our society segregates the young and healthy from the old, sick, and dying, who are kept in hospitals and old-age homes. Most of us, as a result, have little opportunity to learn about death through personal observation. Even in conversation, death is not a topic to be dwelled upon, so it is difficult to know what is expected of us in the terminally ill or dying role.

This situation is changing to some degree. As recently as twenty-five years ago, most physicians felt that it was best not to tell a patient that he or she was terminally ill. Even when everyone guessed the truth, patients were expected to act as though they were going to get better. In 1969, Elisabeth Kübler-Ross, in her book *On Death and Dying* (1969), provided the dying and those who care about them with some sense of what the final stage of life is like. Based on observation and interviews with the terminally ill, she described five stages in the process of dying: denial, bargaining, anger, depression, and acceptance. She argues that it is cruel to prevent the dying and their loved ones from working through these stages. The idea that there are stages of dying that are similar to the stages of adaptation to other stressful situations seems to have gained acceptance (Leming and Dickinson, 1985). Physicians now acknowledge that patients have a right to know their condition, and hospices — facilities that provide care and support for the terminally ill and their families — have gained support.

The development of medical technologies that prolong life and the increasing cost of health care have raised concerns about such issues as the right to refuse treatment, the right to die, the need for care and support for the terminally ill and their families, and how to distribute scarce medical resources among those who need them. The ways these dilemmas are solved will influence the meaning of death in our society and affect how we all must learn to face it.

To paraphrase an old television program "This is your life course." As successive cohorts move through the life course, their unique experiences both reflect and cause changes in social conditions (Elder, 1978; Riley, 1987). The life-course perspective makes us aware that socialization over the lifetime is characterized by both continuity and change. Continuity is provided by age grading and the sequencing of role transitions so that each transition builds, to some extent, on earlier ones. Changes result when a cohort experiences a unique combination of factors that shape socialization experiences and, perhaps, alter the society's norms about the timing of role transitions and other life-course patterns. Thus, although socialization perpetuates the existing ideology, norms, roles, and values of the society, it also contains the seeds for change (Turner, 1990).

Summary

1. The life-course perspective emphasizes the importance of the socially patterned sequence of changes in role expectations that defines the journey from life to death. Because many roles are age-graded, we must, as we age, continually modify our behavior as we exit some roles and acquire others. The trajectories of our changing roles affect one another over the life course. From time to time, we encounter difficulties in meeting the requirements of our roles and experience role strain. Life-course researchers are particularly interested in how historical events affect the role behavior of various birth cohorts. They point out that various cohorts, and even subcategories of cohorts, may experience the life course quite differently.

2. Childhood socialization is concerned with the learning of behavior consistent with basic societal values and norms. Gender roles are imposed on the infant at birth and pervade both childhood and adult work and family roles. Schools introduce children to impersonal, bureaucratic organizations, where they learn to compete with other students. Peers play a unique and important role in socialization because they give children the opportunity to practice roles with others whose power is equal to or weaker than their own and because they give children a chance to participate in the creation and enforcement of norms.

3. Childhood is also a time for preparing for adult roles. The child's family status has strong effects on the child's socialization. Speech codes, child-rearing practices, and values are affected by social class and, in turn, perpetuate social class differences across generations. Schools also play a part in perpetuating class and gender differences. The role expectations for adolescents are not clearly defined in our society, and the period is characterized by various types of role strain for both adolescents and parents.

4. Much of adult socialization is on-the-job training. Work roles often involve socialization into organizations, whose socialization efforts differ in formality, totality, peer-group involvement, and motivational inducements.

5. Despite the importance given to the marital and parental roles in American society, these seem to be two of the roles for which we are least prepared. The transition to parenthood is often stressful because of its abruptness. The parent-child role illustrates the reciprocal and dynamic nature of socialization. Both the child and the parents are changed in the process, and both must continually make adjustments to one another.

6. Later adulthood is characterized by role exits. The active parent role is revised when the last child leaves home. Occupational roles are exited and the retirement role acquired. Marital roles may be exited through divorce or widowhood.

CHAPTER 4

SOCIAL RELATIONSHIPS AND GROUPS

*W*hen you first went away to college, did you sometimes feel lonely or lost in the crowd? For many people, the excitement of beginning college is tempered by a feeling of loneliness for the family and friends left behind. A study by Carolyn Cutrona (1982) of students entering UCLA found that 75 percent experienced at least occasional loneliness during their first few weeks on campus. More than 40 percent reported their loneliness to be "moderate" to "severe." Even after seven months on campus, 25 percent of the students reported they were lonely.

In a similar study, Shaver, Furman, and Buhrmester (1985) examined the loneliness of students *before* and *after* going to college. Students' old relationships back home, they found, declined in both number and perceived quality during the students' first few months at college. For example, all romantic relationships involving a partner back home experienced stress, with almost half (46 percent) coming to an end altogether. Transition to college was particularly stressful for males. Men's loneliness increased *four times* more than women's, perhaps because males'

dating frequency declined more than females'. The researchers speculate that the difference in dating may have resulted from freshman males having a smaller pool of dates available to them. Cultural norms discourage women from dating men younger than they are, so the dating pool available to freshman males is restricted to mainly freshman females. Women, on the other hand, are "free" to date older men, so the pool available to freshman women includes all upper-class men.

Loneliness and aloneness are not the same. *Loneliness*, or estrangement, refers to the psychological discomfort of *feeling* distant or isolated from other people. One can feel uncomfortable with having no friends, too few friends, or the wrong kind of friends. Psychologist Robert Weiss (1973) distinguishes between two types of loneliness: *emotional loneliness*, resulting from the absence of intimacy, and *social loneliness*, resulting from the lack of a sense of social integration or community. Some evidence suggests that women are more likely to experience emotional loneliness, while men are more likely to experience social loneliness (Stokes and Levin, 1986). Sociologists frequently interpret loneliness as one type of "alienation." One can be alienated—feel distant—from many things: people, community, school, work, rules, and so forth.

Aloneness, in contrast, is *being* apart from others. It can produce either distressing feelings of loneliness or pleasant feelings of happiness. The association between aloneness and loneliness is actually probably weak. We can feel happy when alone and lonely in the company of others.

Units of Social Interaction

In Chapter 3, "Socialization over the Life Course," we discussed how our behavior is shaped by the norms and roles of the society in which we live. But our behavior is shaped by other, more immediate, forces as well. Much of human life consists of **social interaction**—any process directed toward, or influenced by, another person or persons. The way we behave is in large measure determined by our relations with one another. In our daily lives we continually encounter others, cooperate with them, conform to their wishes, irritate or ignore them, violate their standards, and compete with them. Social psychologists distinguish among three major types of interacting units that affect our behavior differently: aggregates, social relationships, and groups.

AGGREGATES

An **aggregate** is two or more persons whose social interaction is minimal. What defines a collection of people as an "aggregate" is that they are merely in the same place at the same time—maybe, but not necessarily, doing the same thing. Residents of a dormitory or city block, shoppers at a department store, riders on a bus or an elevator, patients in a waiting room, and students in a large class are all examples of aggregates.

Note that we say the interaction is "minimal"—not nonexistent. Social psychologists take some satisfaction in describing the interaction that takes place in situations where most people see no interaction. Most of us notice interaction

only where we observe others *talking* to one another. Social psychologists are aware that social interaction often occurs even without the exchange of words. We space and position ourselves when walking down the sidewalk, riding on a bus, or sitting in the library. Such conduct indicates to strangers what we are going to do and what we expect of them (e.g., that we do not want them to talk to us).

In such cases, although the interaction is minimal, our behavior *is* affected by the presence of others. The avoidance of more involved interaction in these settings is prescribed by the cultural expectations of our society, as are the symbols for indicating the desire to avoid more interaction. A single nonverbal characteristic of a person—for example, gender, race, or body type—can cause us to draw about that person inferences that affect our actions toward him or her. In these cases, the other person needn't *do* anything to affect our behavior. If, for example, we observe that the person's race is different from our own and this leads us to avoid him or her, minimal interaction has taken place because the other person, without doing or saying anything, has affected our behavior.

SOCIAL RELATIONSHIPS

When people become linked by a relatively stable set of expectations and pattern of interaction, social psychologists say that the participants are partners in a **social relationship**. We usually think of ourselves as "having a relationship" with persons whom we interact regularly with over some length of time. A number of our social interactions have this enduring quality. A chance afternoon game of touch football in the corner lot may lead to a Saturday-afternoon routine. Signing up for a college class usually entails multiple meetings with the same professor over a number of weeks. A retail jeweler's order to a wholesaler may evolve into a standing business arrangement. Still other interactions involve an even longer period of time. A chance assignment of roommates may develop into a long-term friendship.

An encounter at McDonald's may lead to a date and grow into a romantic relationship or even a marriage.

Many of our social interactions, however, are casual, one-time encounters. In buying a pair of shoes, taking a seat on a bus, going to a movie, buying lunch, and checking a book out of the library, we deal primarily with strangers. These interactions are more than minimal but generally lack continuity through time, so we invest little of ourselves in them. Nonetheless, we still need to "plug" ourselves into the world of these others — to coordinate our actions with theirs. Thus, at the very least, we need to identify and appraise them, attune ourselves to the meaning of their actions, do our best to figure out what they intend to do, and adjust or respond to whatever action they take toward us. Although brief, such interactions also constitute a type of social relationship.

Dyads

When we think about relationships, we usually think about the interaction between two people — a *dyad*. Husband-wife, student-teacher, parent-child, doctor-patient, employee-employer, customer-salesperson, and self–best friend are all dyadic relationships. What distinguishes dyads is the directness of their interaction. Each person has an effect (usually immediate) on the other, with no buffer between them. Georg Simmel, an early sociologist, noted that the directness of dyadic relationships creates unique positive as well as negative effects (Wolff, 1950). The directness creates an opportunity for closeness or intimacy, which is difficult to achieve in interactions involving more than two people. This closeness may provide a basis for the continued stability of the relationship. On the other hand, if bad feelings develop between the parties, directness may

Even casual, one-time encounters constitute social relationships when such interactions involve a relatively stable set of expectations and pattern of interaction.

increase the opportunity for interpersonal conflict. And if one person chooses to exit, the relationship is finished.

Triads

Simmel pointed out the significance of adding a third person to a dyad to create a triad. A dyad consists of a single relationship. A *triad* consists of three relationships: A↔B, A↔C, and B↔C. Furthermore, whereas a dyad has only a *direct* relationship, when a third party is added, the original two parties also have an *indirect* relationship through the third party. To illustrate, Simmel uses the example of the married couple who have their first child. When a child is born to a couple, they retain their direct relationship (as spouses) to each other. However, they also sometimes interact in terms of their relationship to the child (as mother and father). The child can have two effects on the relationship between the parents. The new baby may bind them together—increasing their commitment to maintain their marriage—because of their shared concern for the welfare of their child. But the child may also interfere with the direct intimacy of the parental dyad by focusing the attention of each parent away from the other and toward the child. Although the baby provides a link, or bridge, between the parents, it also increases the distance between them.

A third person, Simmel suggests, can increase *or* decrease the stability of the relationship between another two parties. Three-person interactions are prone to *coalition formation*—a circumstance in which three persons become two persons against a third. "No matter how close a triad may be, there is always the occasion on which two of the three members regard the third as an intruder" (Wolff, 1950: 135–136).

Thus, any person in a triad can play three possible roles relative to the other two parties: (1) mediator, (2) opportunist, and (3) one who "divides and conquers." Acting as a mediator, the third person helps increase the stability of the dyadic relationship by assisting the other two conflicting parties to resolve their differences. The mediator forces the parties to confront their dif-

ferences objectively, instead of emotionally and antagonistically, thereby facilitating a negotiated settlement. Sometimes this is more easily said than done. Each of the conflicting parties is likely to pressure the third person to take his or her side rather than remain strictly neutral. Children of divorcing parents are sometimes put in this position. So are teaching assistants.

The opportunist may contribute to the *instability* of a dyadic relationship. Instead of attempting to settle the dispute between the other two parties, the third person may try to exploit the fact that each conflicting party wants his or her support in the dispute. The little girl whose parents are divorcing may try to get what she wants by strategically taking the side of the parent with the best offer. Or a man who offers to help mediate the dispute between a friend and his girlfriend may be motivated by the desire to be in a position to receive the girl's affection should the original intimate relationship dissolve.

Instead of simply taking advantage of an existing conflict, the third person may try to "divide and conquer" by actively seeking to instigate a dispute between the other two parties in order to prevent their forming a coalition with power over her or him. A ten-year-old boy may try to pit one sibling against another in order to prevent them from ganging up on him. An employer may tell two employees they are competing for the same job promotion in order to keep them from collectively resisting his orders. But this requires a bit of a balancing act. The third person usually does not want to create so much conflict as to cause the parties to quit the triadic relationship, leaving the third person with no one to have power over.

Simmel's analysis of triads illustrates how complex the analysis of relationships can become even when only three persons are involved. Of course, many of our interactions involve more than three people. (Before reading further, see the Student Observation: "Coalition Formation in Triads.")

Networks

Beyond its dyadic and triadic relationships, human life encompasses multiple relationships or-

Triads are prone to coalition formation.

ganized into **networks**. These are webs of social relationships that center on a single individual and tie him or her directly to other individuals and indirectly, through these other individuals, to still more people. Take an individual named Arlene Tracy. She may be linked in direct relationships with three people — Ida Block, John Ford, and Isaac Kramer. In turn, she may be indirectly linked to Bob Werner through Ida Block and to Fran Walton through Bob Werner. Each of us is in touch with a number of other people, some of whom are directly in touch with one another and

STUDENT OBSERVATION

Coalition Formation in Triads

Living in a triple [a suite shared by three people] for the past two years, I have had quite a bit of experience with the coalition formation which triads are prone to. More often than not, although we were all close friends, the three of us would become two against one. For example, on Thursday night, one of my roommates and I came in very late, disrupting the third one from sleep. It was us against her as we argued that she sleeps too much anyway. The next morning, I had a major assignment to concentrate on, and my two roommates were running around being loud — leading to a conflict between me and them. Then, that very same afternoon, I was having a serious conversation with my roommate who sleeps all the time when our other roommate walked in, and we immediately got quiet. We felt that she had intruded on our privacy, causing her to be upset with us and vice versa. Within our triad, all in one day, we formed three different coalitions.

some of whom are not. (John Ford may also have a direct relationship with Isaac Kramer but not necessarily with Ida Block.) (See the box "Sociometry" for a discussion of one method for assessing patterns of attraction, rejection, communication, or indifference among members of a group.)

Networks play an important part in our everyday lives. Consider, for instance, our search for help in times of difficulty. When visited by misfortune — illness, mental turmoil, grief, loneliness — we may seek assistance from those who professionally help people in trouble: doctors,

psychologists, marriage counselors, ministers, chiropractors, and others. Yet often we lack personal acquaintance with specific professionals and tend to distrust those whom we do not personally, directly, know. Under these circumstances we commonly turn to our own "lay referral systems." For example, an acquaintance who got help for a "bad back" from a certain chiropractor will recommend that professional to us.

Similarly, social networks are the primary source for the diffusion of new medical procedures, technologies, and medications among

SOCIOMETRY

Sociometry, one method of studying networks, is an objective method for assessing patterns of attraction, rejection, or indifference among group members. The technique has been widely employed in the study of influence and power, friendship, social adjustment, morale, group structure, race relations, political divergences within a community, and social status. Its usefulness has been demonstrated in studies of fraternities, graduate schools, high schools, college student bodies, summer camps, units of the armed forces, factories, and even entire communities.

The basic technique involves a sociometric questionnaire or interview in which people are asked to name the three (or five) individuals in the group whom they would most like to sit next to (or eat with, have as a close friend, live next to, go camping with, have on their team, and so on). Or the study can trace patterns of discrimination, rejection, or antagonism by asking people whom they would least like to interact with in a given context. Each person is assured that his or her choice will be kept confidential.

The data secured from sociometric questionnaires can be represented in a *sociogram*, which graphically shows the patterns of choice existing among members of a group at a given point in time (see Figure 4-1). Unreciprocated choices are represented by one-way arrows (→), while reciprocated choices are symbolized by two-way arrows (↔). A

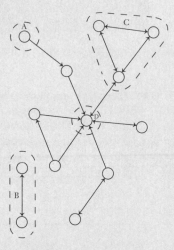

FIGURE 4-1 SOCIOGRAM
Patterns of attraction, rejection, or indifference among members of a group can be uncovered by sociometric questionnaires and mapped in this simple form.

person who is chosen by no one is considered an "isolate" (see A). Two individuals who choose each other, possibly to the exclusion of others, comprise a "mutual pair" (see B). Similarly, three or more people who choose one another constitute a "clique" (see C). An individual who is chosen by many others is considered a "star" (see D).

physicians. Physicians tend to be skeptical of published sources of information and rely on the experiences of their colleagues when deciding on new methods of treatment (Anderson and Jay, 1985).

Job seekers likewise commonly turn to informal acquaintance networks. Indeed, research shows that a person's social network can significantly affect his or her career (Granovetter, 1973). Often, employers view individuals who list themselves in "situations-wanted" columns or with employment agencies as being at the "bottom of the barrel." Similarly, job seekers often find that employment agencies list jobs that turn out to be "dogs." Both prospective employers and job seekers, then, prefer to rely on informal acquaintance networks. By reaching out to relatives, friends, and acquaintances and advising them of our job skills and desires, we accomplish three tasks: (1) We learn about unadvertised job openings. (2) We have someone (our contact) who can speak for us and speak well of us prior to a job interview. (3) We are able to bypass the personnel department and secure interviews directly with people empowered to hire us (Fader, 1984).

Common sense might suggest that those to whom our ties are strongest are likely to be the best source of job leads. After all, the people we are closest to are the most motivated to help us. However, research shows that, generally, those most useful in providing us with job leads are people whom we do not see often and with whom we have weak ties (Granovetter, 1984). Why? Because those to whom we are closest know many of the same people we know. Those with whom our connections are weaker have ties to people we do not know. Therefore, they are more likely to turn up information that we don't already know about.

Research suggests that finding a job through someone we are weakly connected with is more common among persons with higher levels of education, who are seeking managerial or professional positions. This is partly because such people tend to have larger networks, giving them access to information about job openings in a wide variety of places (Bridges and Villemez,

1986; Marsden and Hurlbert, 1988). Such people also tend to be linked to high-status others, who are generally more likely to know about and have influence over job openings (Lin, Ensel, and Vaughn, 1981).

Extensiveness. One approach to networks has emphasized the paths, or threads, that prevail in a single network. Social psychologists with this interest focus on how long chains of contact wind their way through large social systems. Stanley Milgram's "small-world" studies illustrate this approach.

When you were in some distant city or state, how often have you met someone who had a mutual acquaintance with you back home? And then you both exclaimed, "My, it's a small world!" Indeed, as part of the process of becoming acquainted, college students usually ask one another what their hometowns and academic majors are and then turn to the "small-world game": "Do you know . . . ?"

Stanley Milgram and his associates (Milgram, 1967; Travers and Milgram, 1969; Korte and Milgram, 1970) experimentally studied social networks involving unexpected strands linking people widely separated by physical or social space. They selected an arbitrary "target person" (the wife of a divinity-school student who lived in Cambridge, Massachusetts, or a stockbroker who worked in Boston and lived in Sharon, Massachusetts) and a group of "starting persons" (individuals who lived in Wichita, Kansas, and Omaha, Nebraska). Each starter was given a booklet telling the target person's name, address, and occupation, as well as a few other facts. The starter was instructed to begin moving the booklet on by mail toward the target. The booklet, however, could be sent only to a first-name acquaintance. Each person in turn was to advance the booklet in this manner until ideally the chain reached its target.

As might be expected, in most cases the booklet failed to reach the target person. The proportion of chains completed ranged from 12 to 33 percent in the different studies. That some were successful testifies to the strength of indirect linkages among people. The number of links in the completed chains ranged from two to ten, with averages between five and eight. Milgram describes one case involving two intermediate links:

> Our first target person was the wife of a student living in Cambridge. Four days after the folders were sent to a group of starting persons in Kansas, an instructor at the Episcopal Theological Seminary approached our target person on the street. "Alice," he said, thrusting a brown folder toward her, "this is for you." At first she thought he was simply returning a folder that had gone astray, but . . . we found to our pleased surprise that the document had started with a wheat farmer in Kansas. He had passed it on to an Episcopalian minister in his home town, who sent it to the minister who taught in Cambridge, who gave it to the target person. (1967: 64)

Most people are surprised to learn that only five to seven intermediaries typically suffice to link any two randomly selected individuals, wherever they happen to live in the United States. But although we deal with only a small number of intermediaries, behind each of them stands a much larger group of 500 to 2,500 individuals. Each sender, in other words, has an acquaintance pool of 500 to 2,500 people from which he or she selects the person believed best able to advance the chain. Thus a screening procedure operates. Further, a process of geometric progression is implicit in the research procedure. (Analogously, if you earn a penny a day and the sum is doubled each day, you will have more than $10 million at the end of thirty working days.) Elements of geometric progression, with an increase rate far more powerful than mere doubling, underlie the small-world scheme; thus, with just a few links in the network, the search extends to an enormous number of individuals.

Density. Another approach has stressed the "knittedness" of interconnections within a network. This interest has led to the study of network *density*. Density is a measure of how nearly a network approaches a state in which each individual is directly linked to every other individual. More precisely, density is the ratio of *observed* to *possible* direct relations between people in a network. This approach has been employed in studying people's "sense of community." Research suggests that a crucial part of "belonging" comes from having a dense network of social ties, a place in which we constantly encounter familiar, friendly faces in the course of everyday life. To the extent that such multibonded relationships overlap and crisscross, they provide an encompassing web — a meshed fabric — knitting and integrating people within a larger social whole. The social bonds provided by dense networks act as support systems in times of stress (House, Landis, and Umberson, 1988).

GROUPS

Social psychologists use the term "relationship" when focusing on the interaction *between individuals*. But social psychologists are also interested in how individuals *collectively* interact with their environment. Their shift in focus is marked by a change in terminology, from "relationship" to "group" — a family, a childhood gang, a class, a team, an organization, a factory, or a government department. A **group** is defined as two or more people linked by a social relationship who are interdependent with respect to their environment (including other individuals and groups) and who are identified as "one." Let's look at each of the aspects of this definition.

Groups as Interdependence

What do we mean when we say that two or more individuals are *interdependent with respect to their environment*? Interdependence can take two forms. First, we can be interdependent in our actions *toward* the environment. That is, we attempt to coordinate our behaviors in an effort to affect our environment. A basketball team displays this kind of interdependence when its members coordinate the activities of moving the ball around the court, setting picks, executing a pick and roll, moving without the ball, shooting, blocking out, rebounding, switching, and taking the charge. A family is also interdependent in that its members coordinate the activities of earning money, doing housework, eating, caring for the sick, utilizing transportation, relaxing and entertaining, doing homework, having family discussions, sharing intimacies, or scheduling the use of too few bathrooms. A work group is interdependent in that its members coordinate their actions to produce a product or service.

Second, we can also be interdependent in terms of the environment's actions *toward us*. This means that the environment does not distinguish among particular individuals; the environment either rewards or punishes all of us alike. Members of a labor union are interdependent in this respect in that all members either "win or lose" in their contract negotiations with management. Members of a college wrestling or gymnastics team are similarly interdependent. Although these are "individual" sports in the sense that the team members only minimally coordinate their activities, the team members are just as interdependent as the members of a basketball team when it comes to the *team's* winning or losing. From these examples, you can see that some groups are interdependent with respect to their environment in both ways — their actions toward the environment and the environment's actions toward them.

Groups as Identity

Groups are also states of mind, mental models, or images. We fabricate groups in the course of social interaction by clustering people together in social units: families, teams, cliques, parties, organizations, unions, fraternities, and the like. Groups, then, are products of social definitions — sets of shared ideas; they are human-constructed "realities." In short, we conceptualize groups; we attribute real substance to them and treat them *as if* they were real and exact things. For whatever historical reasons, people become lumped together on the basis of some shared physical attribute — perhaps their skin color, hair texture, head shape,

stature, or facial features — or their way of life — say, their language, dress, diet, religious beliefs, or social customs. Groups distinguished by hereditary physical traits are called *racial groups* (for instance, African-Americans and whites in the United States). Groups distinguished by socially acquired lifeways are called *ethnic groups* (for instance, Hispanics, Italians, Irish, and Jews in the United States).

Races present the clearest example of the social nature of groups. Although we commonly conceive of races as separate, sharply delimited biological categories, in point of fact populations throughout the world grade into one another. It is next to impossible to say where one population ends and another begins. Similarly, "black" and "white" are not naturally occurring biological or genetic categories but human-constructed pigeonholes for placing people. This is illustrated by the fact that societies differ greatly in how they categorize the races. Thus in Barranquilla, Colombia, the term "Negro" is applied only to slum dwellers of the city. In northern Colombia, distinctions are made according to a person's hair and eyes and to a certain extent according to stature. Skin color and the shape of the lips or nose are hardly taken into account. A person whose features are predominantly "Negroid" but whose hair is long and wavy is considered a "Spaniard." Someone with predominantly Caucasoid features and light skin, but with straight hair, slightly oblique eyes, and small stature, is an "Indian" (Pitt-Rivers, 1967).

By mentally grouping certain persons together into social units, we fashion and create an existence *beyond* the individuals involved (Hogg and Abrams, 1988). Thus, groups have an existence as social entities *apart from* the particular relationships individual people have with one another. For example, a school's parent-teacher association has continuity through time as a distinct, recognizable, and enduring entity, even though its membership changes from year to year. The same holds for ethnic groups, religious orders, political parties, labor unions, business corporations, colleges, and nation-states, each of which has an existence extending beyond the life spans of specific people.

Groups are not only the social constructions of "outsiders." Group members can have an awareness of their common self-identity—a "consciousness of oneness," a feeling of "we-ness."

Ingroups and outgroups. We often categorize people according to whether we see ourselves as having group membership in common with them. An **ingroup** is a social unit that we either belong to or identify with. An **outgroup** is a social unit that we neither belong to nor identify with. Sometimes ingroups are termed *we-groups* and outgroups, *they-groups*. The mere conceptualization of our world into "us" and "them" is enough to arouse ingroup sympathies and bias. The presence of an outgroup increases our consciousness of the ingroup and promotes conformity to ingroup norms (Lauderdale et al., 1984; Wilder and Shapiro, 1984).

Social categorization may produce ingroup-outgroup biases even when the basis for categorizing people into groups is arbitrary or trivial. A classic study by Henri Tajfel (1970; Tajfel et al., 1971) illustrates this. When they arrived for his study, Tajfel showed English high school students several slides containing a large number of dots and asked them to estimate how many dots were on each slide. Some of the students were told that they had consistently overestimated the number of dots, while others were told that they had underestimated. Later, the students played a game that allowed them to allocate money as a reward to two other students. They were told that one of the students had made the same kind of error in dot guessing that they had made (the ingroup member) and that the other student had made the opposite kind of error (the outgroup member).

The students favored the ingroup member in the rewards they gave during the game. Clearly, the kinds of errors we make in guessing the number of dots on a slide is a trivial matter. But the information was sufficient to create a conceptual-

ization of "us" and "them," which was translated into favoritism toward the ingroup and discrimination against the outgroup. In other studies, the researchers told subjects that they were being assigned to groups on a *random basis* and even showed them the coin toss or lottery drawing that determined their assignment to groups with meaningless names like the "A's" and the "B's" (Billig and Tajfel, 1973; Locksley, Oritz, and Hepburn, 1980). Still, the subjects showed a strong ingroup favoritism.

We come to assume that members of the *same* group are more similar than are members of *different* groups. In other words, we stereotype group members (Messick and Mackie, 1989; Simon, Glassner-Bäyerl, and Stratenwerth, 1991). We tend to hold extreme or polarized appraisals of *out*group members and are more likely to act toward them in an unfriendly and negative fashion. On the other hand, when we see others as part of our *in*group, we tend to focus on their attractiveness and to favor them in the allocation of rewards (Linville and Jones, 1980; Holtz and Miller, 1985). We come to assume that our inner experiences and emotional reactions are closer to those of ingroup members than they are to those of outgroup members (Allen and Wilder, 1975). Moreover, since we expect differences between ourselves and members of an outgroup, we behave so as to create such differences (Markides and Cohn, 1982). Consequently, we become set apart from others with whom we do not share group membership—those who are not "one of us." We experience **social distance** from them. Social distance refers not so much to spatial separation as to a *subjective sense* of being set apart from (as opposed to being near to) a *particular outgroup:*

> We commonly experience high social distance from people who engage in quite different practices and customs. Under such circumstances, it is not difficult for us to perceive outsiders as objects of loathing. The outsider is a symbol of strangeness, evil, and danger to the community as a whole. His existence disturbs the order of life in the sense in which order is understood and experienced by the in-

group. His customs are scandalous, his rites sacrilegious. His laws are incomprehensible, so that he appears to be lawless. His gods are false gods. (Speier, 1941: 445)

Ethnocentrism. Thus we often see outsiders as deviants — not just different, but *undesirably* different. **Ethnocentrism** is the tendency to view our own group as the center of everything and to judge all other people with reference to it. While ethnocentrism promotes ingroup bonds, such as group identity and pride, it also promotes outgroup discrimination (Brown, 1986).

Many of our "social problems" derive from a conceptual scheme in which we create social entities that include some people and exclude others: capitalists-workers, whites-blacks, Gentiles-Jews, honest citizens–criminals, sane-insane, young-old, rich-poor, heterosexual-homosexual, and so on. We draw social boundaries between "us" and "them." We carve up the world, organize it into categories, and assign meanings to it; we impose lines of demarcation on the great range of human behaviors. But in doing so, we create the sort of social problems that derive from insider-outsider divisions.

We see this principle highlighted in the nationalist and ethnic-group frictions that have underlain many wars. Consider Europe, for example. Almost every European territory has at one time or another combined with almost every one of its neighbors. It is impossible to align each European ethnic nationality with a distinct territory. Ethnic groups are found in segmented local pockets or scattered by residence and place of occupation throughout the territory of the dominant group. Most European nation-states contain multiple nationality groups: Great Britain (English, Welsh, Scotch), Switzerland (French, Italians, Germans), Belgium (Flemish and Walloons). Therefore, political self-determination for one people is incompatible with political self-determination for others.

National and ethnic-group conflicts are not inherent in human affairs. Rather, they are *created by* an ingroup-outgroup awareness, which causes us to include some people in, and exclude others from, certain flows of interaction. They derive from an image — a social definition — of what a "society" or "nation-state" is (a conception of "my kind of people"). Hence we *create* national or ethnic-group "problems," such as those between Czechs and Slovaks in dividing the former nation of Czechoslovakia or among the Serbs, Croatians, Slovenes, Macedonians, and Montenegrins in changing the nation of Yugoslavia.

Let's pause here to summarize our discussion of the various units of social interaction. Social psychologists distinguish among aggregates, social relationships, networks, and groups. Aggregates involve only minimal interaction. Relationships link two persons in patterned interaction that may range from casual, one-time encounters to intimate, enduring relationships. Networks are the webs of relationships that link us directly to some people and, through them, indirectly to others. Groups are collections of individuals connected through interdependence and a subjective sense of oneness.

Sources of Bonds and Cohesion

Why do we participate in relationships and groups? What is it that ties or glues people together? What is the process that links people together in a relationship or group? Social psychologists have used two terms to refer to this process. They call it **bonding** when describing the effort or desire to maintain a relationship and **cohesion** when describing the effort or desire to be a member of a group. Because the process is essentially the same whether one is talking about relationships or groups, we will use the terms interchangeably. The bonds of a relationship and the cohesion of groups can be based on one or more characteristics of the relationship or group. Social psychologists have paid particular attention to four characteristics: members, goals, norms, and external oppression.

EXPRESSIVE BONDS

Our bonds to a relationship or group may be based on our attraction to its other member or members. Through certain other people we satisfy our needs for security, love, acceptance, companionship, and a sense of worth. Accordingly, many gratifications require sustained social interaction in which we are deeply involved in relationships with *particular* other persons. Bonds based on our attraction to particular others are called **expressive bonds**. Social interactions based primarily upon expressive bonds among people are called **primary relationships** or **primary groups**. We view these relationships as ends in themselves, valuable in their own right. Within them we experience warmth, oneness, familiarity, and closeness. We relate to others in such relationships in direct, intimate, personal ways. We can have primary relationships with kin, friends, lovers, neighbors, and co-workers.

The formation of primary groups is encouraged by (1) physical proximity involving face-to-face contact, (2) a small number of people, and (3) intense and frequent interaction (McGrath, 1984). Physical proximity permits intimate communication; when people can see and talk with one another, they can carry on a subtle exchange of moods, feelings, and opinions. Size is important simply because large numbers of people cannot relate to one another directly and personally. And finally, the duration and intensity of the interaction are critical. Other things being equal, the more often we are together, the more numerous and more profound the ties between us. As we associate with one another, we evolve interlocking habits that bind us together.

One reason primary groups are "primary" is that they provide various social satisfactions. Within them we find companionship, a feeling of ego worth, affection, acceptance, and a general sense of well-being. We come to appreciate this

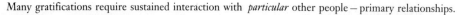

Many gratifications require sustained interaction with *particular* other people — primary relationships.

quality of primary groups when we leave home to attend college, marry, or take a job: we feel home-sick — nostalgic for a primary group from which our immediate ties have suddenly been severed. Charles Horton Cooley, the social psychologist who originated the concept of primary groups, observed:

> The result of intimate association, psychologically, is a certain fusion of individualities in a common whole, so that one's very self, for many purposes at least, is the common life and purpose of the group. Perhaps the simplest way of describing this whole-ness is by saying that it is a "we"; it involves the sort of sympathy and mutual identification for which "we" is the natural expression. One lives in the feeling of the whole and finds the chief aims of his will in that feeling. (1909: 23–24)

Most of us recognize that a large part of our lives centers on our connections to others. When we are asked what it is that makes our lives most meaningful, we typically answer in terms of our relationships with friends, relatives, and lovers. And we commonly stress the significance of "feel-ing loved and wanted." Public opinion surveys reveal that we believe our personal happiness is integrally bound to the state of our intimate rela-tionships (Glenn and Weaver, 1981; Benin and Nienstedt, 1985). We consider it important to have "a happy marriage," "a good family life," and "close friends."

Studies show that social support from primary relationships contributes to our psychological and physical well-being by reducing the adverse con-sequences of a wide variety of stressful events. It is not surprising, therefore, that a strong association exists between marital disruption and physical and emotional disorder (Haring-Hidore et al., 1985; Williams, 1988). Divorced adults are at much greater risk than married adults for mental and physical illness, automobile accidents, alcoholism, and suicide. A recent study suggests that the posi-tive relationship between marriage and reported life satisfaction may have recently declined some-what, perhaps due to the increased acceptability of intimate relationships outside of marriage (Glenn and Weaver, 1988). The primary group, then, satisfies a variety of social needs and gives us a sense of belonging. See the box "Social Support and Health." Because of the importance of ex-pressive bonds, we will explore in detail the devel-opment of these relationships in Chapter 11, "Close Relationships."

INSTRUMENTAL BONDS

Life confronts us with countless circumstances in which we need others, besides those we are inti-mately involved with, to achieve certain goals. Attachments to others that are based on our needs for achieving goals are called **instrumental bonds**. Sometimes such attachments may entail working with our enemies, as in the old political saying, "Politics makes strange bedfellows." More often, they simply reflect the situation in contem-porary societies, in which large, complex net-works interlink the diverse actions of diverse people — for instance, the division of labor ex-tending from the farmers who grow wheat to the grocers who sell bread.

Social interactions that rest primarily on in-strumental bonds among people are called **sec-ondary relationships** or **secondary groups**. We view such relationships as means to ends, rather than as ends in their own right. In secondary relationships, our commitment to or involvement with others is limited to the particular task at hand — seeing that customers receive good ser-vice, working on a class project, winning the foot-ball game, getting our annual physical, registering for classes. Typically we invest only a segment of our lives and personalities in secondary groups — the portion most relevant for the achievement of the group goal — not our total selves, as in pri-mary groups. Secondary groups are often special-interest groups that perform particular functions: educating youth (schools), producing goods (cor-porations), protecting the country (the military), and worshipping (churches). The University of North Carolina, the U.S. Air Force, General

SOCIAL SUPPORT AND HEALTH

The quality of our lives depends largely on our interpersonal relationships. As social beings, we meet our needs though interaction with others. Our patterns of health and illness offer striking evidence of our need for such interaction (Shumaker and Brownell, 1984; Cohen and Symes, 1985). One strength of the human condition is our propensity for providing support to one another.

People with social ties live longer and have better physical and mental health than do those without such ties (Berkman and Breslow, 1983; House, Landis, and Umberson, 1988). Research on a vast range of illnesses, from depression to arthritis to heart disease, shows that the presence of interpersonal support helps people fend off illness, while the absence of such support makes poor health more likely (Cohen and McKay, 1984; Ruberman et al., 1984; Reis et al., 1985). Similarly, death from all causes is greater among people with relatively low levels of social support (Blazer, 1982; House, Robbins, and Metzner, 1982).

People with strong support systems appear better able to cope with major life changes and daily hassles. Social support cushions stress in a number of ways (Cohen and Wills, 1985; Seeman, Seeman, and Sayles, 1985). First, friends, relatives, and co-workers may let us know that they value us. Our self-esteem is strengthened when we feel accepted by others despite our faults and difficulties. Second, other people often give us informational support. They help us define and understand our problems and discover solutions to them. Third, we typically find social companionship supportive. Engaging in leisure-time and recreational activities with others helps us meet our social needs while simultaneously distracting us from our worries and troubles. Fourth, other people may supply us with instrumental support — financial aid, material resources, and needed services — that reduces stress by enabling us to resolve and cope with our problems.

Electric, and the Roman Catholic church are examples of large secondary groups. We can also be involved with smaller secondary groups, such as one that meets monthly to deliver food to the poor, meets once a week to play tennis, or meets daily to put out the school newspaper. In sum, interaction in secondary groups is more impersonal than that in primary groups; that is, secondary-group interaction is goal-oriented, not person-centered.

Studies of nonsupervisory workers and their commitment to their organization customarily focus on instrumental bonds. Workers have been studied in organizations such as restaurants, elementary schools, a plastic factory, an order-processing firm, a law enforcement agency, a hospital, and a university (DeCotiis and Summers, 1987; Luthans, Baack, and Taylor, 1987; Mottaz, 1988). These studies show that workers' commitment to their organization is associated with such factors as (1) workers' compensation and promotion opportunities, (2) work assistance from their co-workers, (3) work that is perceived to be significant and interesting, and (4) a relationship with their supervisor that is clearly defined but that allows workers some autonomy in performing their jobs. Workers' perceptions of the significance, interest, and autonomy of their jobs play a larger role in their commitment than does the compensation or assistance they receive in their jobs. This is true of *both* professional and blue-collar workers, although *more* true among professionals than among blue-collar workers.

NORMATIVE BONDS

More than a century ago, Henry Thoreau pointed out that the apparent nonconformist — the person out of step with the procession — may merely be marching to the tune of a different drummer. Implicit in Thoreau's observation is the idea that an individual may adopt the standards of a particular group to define and evaluate his or her own behavior. Such a person's bond to the group is based on the group's norms; hence, it is called a **normative bond**.

When a person's bond to a group is primarily normative, social psychologists refer to the group as a **reference group**. A reference group may or may not be a social unit to which an individual actually belongs — in terms of how others socially identify her or him. Reference-group affiliation derives mostly from *self-identification*. It helps explain seemingly contradictory behavior: the upper-class revolutionary, the renegade Catholic, the reactionary worker, the shabby gentleman, the assimilated immigrant, and the social-climbing chambermaid. Such an individual has taken as a reference group people other than those in his or her own membership group. Many college students aspiring to membership in various professions also fit this description. Indeed, their schooling is a form of *anticipatory socialization:* they are cultivating the behaviors (professional skills, manner, ethics, and outlook) associated with full-fledged nurses, doctors, engineers, law-

yers, accountants, scientists, and so on. Each one hopes to ultimately become an actual member of his or her reference group.

Reference groups perform two functions. First, they provide us with norms and attitudes — a frame of reference for guiding our behavior. Social psychologists call this the *normative function* of reference groups. We view ourselves as being members in good standing within a certain group or as wishing to be members in good standing. Hence we take on the group's political views, clothing and hair styles, religious beliefs, sexual practices, or drug-using behaviors. The group's views and norms become our views and norms. In this sense our behavior is group-anchored.

Second, reference groups provide a *comparison function:* they serve as a standard, or comparison point, against which we judge or evaluate ourselves. We continually make self-assessments regarding our physical attractiveness, intelligence, health, social ranking, and standard of living relative to those of others. When we compare unfavorably with our reference group, we may experience a sense of *relative deprivation* —

Secondary-group interaction is goal-oriented, not person-oriented.

dissatisfaction derived from the gap between what we have and what we believe we should have (the conditions or circumstances of our reference group). In contrast, a sense of *relative gratification* may render us satisfied with the "system" (Singer, 1981). For example, if the personnel manager of a small company in a tiny Southern town has as her reference group a national association of personnel managers, she may find that her salary is well below average for that group and, consequently, experience relative deprivation. But if her reference group consists of the other workers at her company, or of other managerial workers in her community, she might be among the highest paid in that group and therefore experience relative gratification.

When discussing reference groups, social psychologists differentiate between negative and positive reference groups. *Negative reference groups* are groups with which we compare ourselves in order to emphasize the *differences* between ourselves and others. For Cuban-Americans in southern Florida, the Castro regime functions as a negative reference group (Carver and Humphries, 1981). Most of them fled their homeland after the 1959 revolution, which brought Fidel Castro to power. Opposition to Castro's Cuba helps the Cuban-Americans decide what they believe in and determine who they really are. The negative reference group also provides a mechanism of social cohesion, a vehicle by which the exile community knits itself together. It facilitates acceptance within the community and ensures exiles that they will have the benefits of social interaction with like believers. (Before reading further, see the Student Observation: "Reference Groups.")

OPPRESSION BONDS

People in modern societies are evaluated and rated according to a great many attributes, including race, ethnic membership, gender, occupation, income, education, accumulated wealth, age, physical attractiveness, and social skills. Thus, individuals and groups are ranked from high to low and from better to worse, which results in differences in power, privilege, and status.

Sometimes people low in power, privilege, and status may develop a group bond based on their common oppression by another group; this type

---

STUDENT OBSERVATION

Reference Groups

I spent Memorial Day with my best friend. Tony has been a truck driver for the past year, hauling livestock. I noticed a tremendous change in his behavior during this time. Previously, he was a dignified, middle-range executive with the regional IBM office. When he was with IBM, he played golf, loved bridge, attended middle-class social gatherings, drank bourbon, and dressed in a suit with a white shirt and a tie. Now that he has become a truck driver, his behavior has drastically changed. He sold his golf clubs, plays little bridge, no longer attends middle-class social gatherings (preferring the company of truckers and blue-collar workers), and mainly drinks beer. I never see him in "business" suits anymore. Now he wears only Levis, a Western shirt, cowboy boots, and, to top it all off, a $40 cowboy hat. Even his accent now has a drawl like the Texas cattlemen he is in contact with, and his speech reflects the "toughness" of truck drivers. Tony conforms to the patterned behavior characteristic of his trucking associates. He is "in" with the truckers and "out" with the local businessmen.

We can understand the shift in Tony's behavior in terms of reference groups. When he worked for IBM he had the business community as his reference group. When he became a truck driver, he attached himself to a new reference group. This explains the very marked change in his behavior.

of attachment is known as an **oppression bond**. A group whose members suffer oppression and various disabilities because of their treatment by another group is called a **minority group** or an **oppressed group** (Meyers, 1984). As a consequence of their power disadvantage, some groups — minorities — discover that they are similarly disadvantaged in terms of privilege and status relative to the dominant group. But it is not simply a matter of disadvantage. The minority is the *source* of the dominant group's advantages. The oppression of one people confers privilege on another.

A minority is not merely exploited; it is commonly victimized by prejudice, discrimination, and racism. Its members are physically and psychologically degraded, abused, and humiliated. The functioning of the dominant group's social order continually confronts the members of the disadvantaged group with a social definition of their worthlessness, ignorance, despicableness, and bestiality. At times the group's members may be hounded, persecuted, lynched, murdered, imprisoned, segregated, tortured, and raped with relative impunity.

The concept "minority" lacks any numerical connotation. Despite the literal meaning of the word, a minority is not a statistical unit. In many cases a minority is *larger* in population than the dominant group. For example, blacks form a majority of the population in the Republic of South Africa and in some American cities and southern counties. And until recently, small numbers of Europeans dominated "minority peoples" throughout Africa, Asia, and the Pacific islands. "Minority," then, is a social, not a numerical, concept.

A minority group is symbolically identified by certain traits having high social visibility. As is true generally of groups, a minority is a socially constructed reality. It is *not* a naturally self-constituted or self-contained entity; rather, it is a mental model fabricated through the process of social interaction. A person usually does not voluntarily become a member of a minority; he or she is born into it. Often, if only one parent is a member of a minority, the children of that family also belong.

Sometimes, a single grandparent or great-grandparent is enough to confer membership. In Nazi Germany, for example, it did not matter if a "Jew" looked like thousands of German non-Jews, had been converted to Christianity, and had married a Christian; by Nazi definition, he or she was a "Jew." Similar rules operate in many communities of the United States, where a person with all "white" ancestry except for a "black" grandparent is almost always grouped with "blacks."

Minorities are self-conscious social units; they have a consciousness of oneness. Members of a minority frequently experience an intense social and psychological affinity with others like themselves. They may possess a strong sense of kinship, a solidarity springing from the roots of a real or mythical common ancestry. Frequently, they are so strongly bound together by a common identity that all other differences and conflicts become submerged in a spiritual loyalty and allegiance to the "people" — "my people": the Jews, Turks, African-Americans, Armenians, or Greeks.

Such feelings of spiritual allegiance tend to be solidified by common suffering, a sense of isolation, and a common sense of burden. It is said, for example, that Jews have survived as a people *because* of their persecution, not despite it. Persecution highlights a group's boundaries, setting "us" off from "them." It solidifies the membrane that filters out "foreign" and "alien" ways and plugs the pores by which assimilation might otherwise occur. Thus as anti-Semitism has declined in the United States, Jewish group existence has become endangered. Nahum Goldmann of the World Zionist Organization insists that assimilation, "if not halted and reversed, threatens Jewish survival more than persecution, inquisition, pogroms and mass murder of Jews did in the past" (Vander Zanden, 1983). (Before reading further, see the Student Observation: "Minority Group.")

PREDOMINANT BOND AND BOND PROFILE

We have discussed four types of bonds that tie people together in relationships or groups: ex-

STUDENT OBSERVATION

Minority Group

*I*was not born in North Carolina, but I attended high school there in a small town at the base of the Appalachian Mountains. The majority of the students were white and were born in that region from old-traditional "mountain folks." Although the race that these students belonged to comprised more than 85 percent of the population in that county, they were considered a minority group, an ethnic category known as "Appalachian whites." In applying to college, my classmates were even able to apply under special minority considerations even though they were white and members of the dominant group in our society.

This illustrates the idea that a minority is not a statistical or numerical unit but more of a social concept. It was obvious that my classmates belonged to a race that was the dominant group. However, the members of the group that my classmates belonged to feel a strong urge to bond together as a subunit of a broader category because their subculture was being threatened by the progressive urban "whites." Their simple way of life was being looked down on by the expanding, mainstream, white culture that was slowly penetrating the rural areas from the cities.

Thus, rightly so, the "Appalachian whites" can be referred to as an oppressed group because of the common oppression they have suffered at the hands of the incoming, dominant whites. Their "minority" label is clearly not due to racial or genetic factors but strictly to the constructed social stigma placed on them by the dominant group culture.

pressive, instrumental, normative, and oppression. Frequently, social psychologists talk about a relationship or group as though it were based on only a single type of bond: "The family is a primary group," "The sociology department is a secondary group," "The Republican party is a reference group," or "Homosexuals are a minority group." Such statements are somewhat misleading, as obviously any group may be based on more than a single type of bond or cohesion. For example, we might analyze a particular family and find it to be based on expressive, instrumental, and normative bonds, with the strongest, or the *predominant bond*, being expressive. If we find this to be generally true of American families, we may conclude that the American family is *more* a primary group than either a secondary or a reference group.

As an alternative to classifying relationships and groups according to their predominant bond, we might describe them by using a *bond profile*—a description of the degree to which each of the four types of bonds is a basis for a person's attachment to a relationship or group. Athletic teams frequently represent an interesting combination of bonds. To outside observers, they are obviously based on instrumental bonds—they exist to achieve something, to win—making them examples of secondary groups. But team members sometimes refer to themselves as "family," indicating the presence of expressive bonds that may rival the instrumental ones.

Different members may be attracted and bonded to the group for different reasons. Thus, within a single family, the bond profiles of the members may differ substantially. Let's look at two members of a hypothetical four-person family consisting of a father, mother, fifteen-year-old daughter, and six-year-old son. While most of the fifteen-year-old daughter's instrumental needs are still met by the family, she looks to her peer group for friendship and affection, so her expressive ties to her family are less extensive than her younger brother's. Similarly, her peers are her reference group for such matters as appearance and dating, though on matters of religion her family serves this function. Conflict with her parents over many issues is great, and she is bonded to her peer group by oppression ties as well. She sees herself as part of a younger generation that the old folks just don't understand.

As for the mother, her instrumental needs are met partly by her immediate family but also partly by a broad network of extended family, friends, and business colleagues. She has expressive ties to a number of others, including several close friends, a few business colleagues, and members of her own and her husband's extended families, as well as to the nuclear family, which includes herself, her husband, and their two children. Her normative bonds to many of these same groups are strong. None of her relationships is based on oppression bonds.

RITUALS

The social bonds of a relationship or group may be established, heightened, and rejuvenated by means of **rituals** — social acts of symbolic significance that are performed on certain occasions prescribed by tradition. The social sciences owe much to Emile Durkheim (1954), a pioneer French sociologist (1858–1917), for an understanding of the part rituals play in human life.

Rituals assume many forms: communion, flag salutes, the singing of the national anthem before sporting events, Fourth of July parades, Thanksgiving and Christmas festivities, graduation exercises, marriage and funeral ceremonies, birthday parties, sports events like the Kentucky Derby and the Super Bowl, and, in some countries, public executions. All such activities, according to social psychologists, have a common function: they recharge our sense of collective solidarity. Rituals symbolize the reality of the group and our relation to it.

We engage in these stereotyped actions in a collective setting and manner. We perform them with an appropriate sense of sacredness, awe, and reverence, all of which evoke a single definition of reality and a mutually held emotion. The rituals identify group boundaries.

For example, colleges employ athletic events, especially basketball and football games, as rituals to achieve a collective consciousness among students, faculty, and alumni. Traditional games, such as a homecoming game or a game against a longtime rival, cement group ties. The events and activities associated with a game between two schools take place in a patterned way that gives them structure. There are crowd members, the opposing teams, referees, coaches, concession-stand workers, ushers, security personnel, media people, and maintenance workers, all with unique roles for the event. Players wear uniforms that bear the school colors, and the home court and many of the home fans are decked out in the same colors. Fans sing the school's alma mater (particularly if they win) and related "fight" songs. Cheerleaders orchestrate cheers, the "wave," chants, and other expressions of school loyalty. A mascot — a badger, wolverine, lion, cardinal, Trojan, hawkeye, ram — symbolizes the intangible university and gives it a tangible existence.

The net result of these activities is that the boundaries between "our" school and "their" school are highlighted. Students, faculty, staff, and alumni mentally come to think of themselves as a social unit and act toward this social unit as if it were real (making it a social reality). And a consciousness of oneness is awakened and solidified. Consequently, people who have very little else in common find themselves bonded together in a larger social enterprise — the group or social structure that we term the "university."

Romantic partners, families, and friendship groups also have rituals: dining by candlelight and giving roses to mark a wedding anniversary, kissing when a partner leaves for and returns from work, sleeping late and having sex on weekend mornings, singing "Happy Birthday" and serving cake for family birthdays, gathering together on holidays, flipping a coin to see who buys the beer, going out to dinner on Friday nights. Think about your own family and what its rituals are. The importance of these for the group's feeling of oneness is highlighted by the members' reaction when one member fails to play his or her part in the ritual. Consider how your family members would react if you announced that you were not going to be at the next holiday gathering — or the one after that.

Durkheim (1954) observes that if we are left to ourselves, our individual consciousnesses — our internal states — are closed to one another. Our separate minds cannot come in contact and communicate with one another except by "coming out of themselves." We accomplish this by making external what is internal. Our inner consciousness is transformed into a *collective* consciousness through the symbolic device of rituals. By uttering the same cry, pronouncing the same word, or performing the same gesture, we inform one another that we are in harmony and are aware of our unity. Additionally, through the collective representations of rituals, we fuse ourselves in real communion; we experience a fellowship of sentiment (a common emotional bond) as we create in unison through ritualistic symbols a shared state of mind. In sum, rituals operate in two directions: First, they function as instruments or vehicles for *revealing* our individual mental states. Second,

they *create* common, shared mental states. (Before reading further, see the Student Observation: "Ritual.")

SEGREGATION

Rituals are but one way of reinforcing our social bonds. Segregation is another. The human group is territorial: a family has its home; a juvenile gang, its "turf"; an ethnic group, its neighborhood (or schools, restaurants, restrooms, drinking fountains); the sexes, their jobs and clubs; a state, its national territory. Virtually every piece of the earth's surface is claimed by one group or another.

Segregation is the physical separation of groups — whether the separation is based on geographic location (e.g., neighborhoods), facilities (e.g., schools, restrooms), or activities (e.g., jobs). (Don't confuse segregation — the physical separation of *groups* — with aloneness — which refers to

Rituals symbolize the reality of the group and our relationship to it. Through the collective representations of rituals, we experience a common emotional bond as we create a shared state of mind.

STUDENT OBSERVATION

Ritual

My roommate and I share a ritual that helps maintain the close relationship we have. Every two weeks or so, we will go out to dinner together, taking turns as to who picks up the tab. We always go to the same restaurant (Breadmen's), and we always order the same thing (the vegetable plate). This dinner allows my roommate and me to catch up on everything that's been going on with us, which is very nice since we don't usually have time to have any long talks during the week. Our dinner also serves as a great excuse to get away from studying, at least for a little while. By talking to my roommate, I am able to learn what he's been up to, and at the same time I can sort through my own feelings by verbalizing them. We always leave the restaurant feeling closer, like better friends, and I personally feel more relaxed and less stressed out after our dinner. It is always nice to talk to a good friend, and our ritualistic dinners give my roommate and me the perfect opportunity to do so.

---

one *individual's* being apart from others.) *Territorial behavior* is behavior in which individuals or groups maintain, mark, and defend certain areas against intrusion by others. It has long been recognized that birds and many animals have a strong sense of territory. But many resemblances exist between hedges, fences, and flower beds in human communities and territorial boundaries in the animal kingdom.

All of us have observed and experienced segregation. Most of us spent years in an educational system that segregated people by age. Students of different ages were assigned to different classrooms or even different school buildings. Your college may have some dormitories that are segregated by gender — either entire buildings designated as male dorms or female dorms or different wings or sections of buildings restricted to one gender or the other. Jobs are often segregated by race and sex. We'll discuss this more thoroughly in Chapter 14, "Inequality and Discrimination: Racism and Sexism." Communities are often segregated by race, ethnicity, and social class. The most extreme form of segregation establishes legal, social, or economic barriers that restrict members of minority groups to particular areas, sometimes called "ghettos."

Segregation is one means by which elites appropriate privilege. Not only are their homes and offices located in the most desirable places, but their command of territory — mines, factories, and plantations — makes them gatekeepers in the distribution of good things. In American society, for example, African-Americans, women, institutional inmates, and young people are especially deprived of territorial control. The disadvantaged can be relegated to "reservations" — African-Americans to ghettos; women to kitchens; "deviants" to prisons and mental institutions; and young people to campuses, where a growing army of young adults is diverted, managed, and kept off the streets without threatening the jobs of the working population. Hence, subject peoples, besides forfeiting the full fruits of territory, are controlled through segregation.

One facet of territoriality is that the "home team usually wins." Among captive animals — fish, lizards, mice, chickens, and monkeys — a *home-cage effect* operates: the "owner" of the cage, even if it has been there only a short period, is usually victorious over a newcomer. In general, the winner of a fight is likely to be the animal that is on its home territory rather than the animal that is bigger and stronger.

Evidence also suggests that a home-cage effect operates among human beings. The great Russian novelist Count Leo Tolstoy (1828–1910) portrayed territorial dominance as contributing to the outcome of epic human battles, including the retreat from Moscow of the French forces under Napoleon. In professional and college sports, coaches are well aware of the advantage of the "home" court, park, and field: in professional baseball, the home team wins about 53 percent of the time, compared with 58 percent in professional football, 60 percent in college football, 64 percent in professional hockey, and 67 percent in professional basketball (Schwartz and Barsky, 1977). A ten-year survey of the performance of basketball teams in the Atlantic Coast Conference found that on the average the teams won 66 percent of their home games but only 34 percent of their road games (Varca, 1980).

How do social psychologists explain the home advantage? Crowd hostility to visiting teams causes the visiting players to perform below their normal level, while crowd support gives a lift to the home team (Greer, 1983). (However, when a title is on the line, exuberant home crowds can lead home-team players to "choke.") Children too often display the home-cage effect in play and at school. Police interrogation is based on the

GROUP BONDS: THE EXAMPLE OF A COLLEGE BASKETBALL TEAM

Researchers Patricia and Peter Adler (1988) closely observed the members of a major college basketball team (players and coaches) over a five-year period. He went "inside" in the role of "team sociologist" to gather information, while she stayed "outside" in order to debrief him at the end of each day. Working jointly, they were able to piece together a picture of the forces contributing to the athletes' loyalty to their team — a picture illustrating several different kinds of bonds and the structural features reinforcing those bonds.

The bonding process begins with a "contract." At the end of high school, players sign letters of intention to play for a particular team for four years. Although these letters are not legally binding, they are nevertheless taken seriously by the National Collegiate Athletic Association (NCAA) and the athletic community. The NCAA's intention in instituting the contracts was to limit the intense recruiting of talented players, but a side effect is that the contracts make it difficult for a player to change his or her mind. Another "contractual" aspect maintains this arrangement: once a player has signed a contract, transferring to another school can involve having to sit out a year before being allowed to play on another NCAA team. These rules provided at least a minimal commitment to the team.

Once a player joined the basketball program, instrumental bonds were established on several levels. Players became dependent on the coach for almost all their daily needs and responsibilities, such as food, lodging, friendships, and sense of well-being. The coach controlled their daily schedules, including classes, practices, study halls, meals, and booster functions. And, of course, the coach controlled rewards and punishment such as playing time, practice drills, and even suspension from the team.

The Adlers observed that the players' dependence on the coach was facilitated by weakened or severed ties with other providers. The players' ties with their own pasts were severed. They were no longer high school stars, allowed to play in a loose, undisciplined manner. Subordination was an important feature of players' commitment. They went through a rigorous training process in which they abandoned the old ways in favor of a single *team* identity. What was "good" for a player was what was good for *the team*. One player explained:

> I don't care who shoots, I'm gonna get the ball when I can; I'm gonna dive for it when I see it. When I say complete player, I mean a team player. . . . In college ball, you learn that you have to rely on so many people. (Adler and Adler, 1988: 407)

Players wore identical uniforms, even school blazers, when traveling together. Deviance was believed to reflect on the team, coach, and school, and same principle: Never question suspects on their home ground; always do it on the detective's home ground—at the police station (Inbau and Reid, 1962). There may be profound truth in the saying that one's home is one's castle, since on home territory we enjoy a special sovereignty we may not possess elsewhere.

The various bonds and reinforcing mechanisms that we have discussed in this section are examined in a real-life setting in the box "Group Bonds: The Example of a College Basketball Team."

Group Culture and Its Negotiation

In Chapters 2 and 3, "Early Socialization" and "Socialization over the Life Course," we discussed how culture influences our behavior. We noted that the regularity and stability that develops out of human interaction is embodied in *culture*—the aggregate of things that a given social unit has created and to which its members attach similar meanings: their beliefs, values, norms, knowledge, language, and patterns of behavior

those who deviated were told to "get with the team." In the words of one player,

> I was in the public eye. A college basketball player has to represent not only himself but the University, because you've got to think about the media, what they can do if they see you drinking a beer in public, or getting into a fight, how that make your school look, how that make your coach look, how that make your team look. (Adler and Adler, 1988: 408)

Although the coach's behavior contributed significantly to the players' instrumental bonding, it occasionally also contributed to both expressive and oppression bonds. On some occasions, the coach was very paternalistic, treating players as part of his extended family. He counseled players on personal problems and invited them to join his family for dinner; he emphasized that family members were loyal to one another. On other occasions, he would severely criticize players in private and in public shaming rituals. During these degradation ceremonies, he would openly denounce players in front of the whole team, calling them "hopeless cases" or "candy-asses." As the coach put it,

> The pressure is on them every day to compete against each other to impress me for the starting jobs on the team. Now when I come out and start running them and screaming, they're not trying to impress me anymore; I'm the real enemy right there. That's how you make a team become clos-

er together—by them hating the coach. Once I become the enemy I take the pressure off of them. (Adler and Adler, 1988: 410)

Younger players were taken "under the wing" of veteran players and shown how to conduct themselves—how to avoid the wrath of the coach and minimize the stresses of their new environment.

Segregation contributed to the players' commitment to the team. Even during the summer players worked at jobs provided by boosters, practiced in the gym daily, and hung around with other athletes. Once school began, they lived in an athletic dorm located on the far side of the campus, away from the other students. They had little time to socialize with other students, and their physical size and race (mostly African-American) restricted the contact initiated by other students.

The Adlers found that, with all these factors operating at once, the loyalty of players to their team was very intense. This level of commitment is more akin to that found in many families, military units, or religious cults than it is to that typically found in the occupational organizations to which athletic teams are often compared.

Quotes reprinted from "Intense Loyalty in Organizations: A Case Study of College Athletics" by Patricia A. and Peter Adler, published in Administrative Science Quarterly *Volume 33, by permission of* Administrative Science Quarterly. © *1988 by Cornell University.*

and interaction, as well as physical objects. The culture we focused on in those earlier chapters was, for the most part, societal culture. We noted, however, that smaller social units within a society may also have their own cultures, which differ in some respects from the societal culture. The cultures of these subunits of society are called *subcultures* when the focus is on how they differ from the larger, societal culture.

Social relationships and groups are among the subunits of society that have cultures of their own. In this section, we'll look at the components of group culture and how they affect us, how we experience and manage the multiple cultures that impinge upon us, and finally how these cultures are constructed through a process of negotiation as group members interact.

COMPONENTS OF GROUP CULTURE

In Chapter 2, "Early Socialization," we discussed culture as the "context and content of socialization." Culture not only is *what* we learn but also determines *how* we learn it. Culture also provides the context and content for *interaction*. Culture both reflects and contributes to our experience of social life as relatively stable and predictable. Culture consists of the regularity and stability that develops out of human interaction, and its existence allows us to project this experience to future events. Like societal cultures, group and relationship cultures consist of values, norms, knowledge, language, and patterns of behavior and interaction, as well as physical objects. Social psychologists give particular attention to three components of group culture: norms, identities, and roles.

Group Norms

One way in which we achieve a sense of social order is through shared expectations prescribing behavior for us in terms of do's and don'ts: thou shalt be quiet and attentive while a professor is lecturing; thou shalt not cheat on examinations; thou shalt not walk out of class simply because the lecture is boring. Such social requirements are **norms** — standards for behavior that members of a social group share and are expected to follow and that are enforced by positive and negative sanctions. Norms provide guidelines whose contours tell us what action is appropriate in specific situations.

Day by day, we are able to act together with relative ease because we share common understandings about what each of us is supposed to do. When we all take the same things for granted, we discover that cooperation is facilitated. We are prepared to wait in line at the supermarket, the bank, or the ticket office, on the assumption that we will be served when our turn comes (Dullea, 1982). On the assumption that we can exchange the money later for the goods and services we want, we are willing to be paid for our work in pieces of paper having no inherent value. Thousands of such shared assumptions characterize social life. Social relationships are possible precisely because of the faith we place in our mutual willingness to act upon them.

Some norms are precise and explicit. For example, a family may have an explicit rule that all family members must be present for Sunday dinner. Athletic contests are usually regulated by explicit, written rules. Business organizations tend to have written rules about such matters as when employees should arrive for work, how long they can take for lunch, when and where smoking is allowed, and so forth. But most norms are not expressed in an official code. Rather, they are an abstract synthesis of the many separate times that the members of a group express their sentiments on a given issue by behaving in a particular fashion. They are the accumulated understandings reached through time that become precedents for future understandings. For example, most of us follow such unwritten rules as "Don't stare at strangers in elevators," "Don't arrive early for a dinner party," "Don't wear shorts to church," and "Don't talk when the professor is lecturing."

Whether norms are explicit or implicit, formal or informal, most people conform to most norms most of the time.

Identities and Roles

Social psychologists have often suggested that there is an analogy between human behavior and the theater. Much of social life resembles the acting on the stage of a theater, with its varied scenes, parts, masks, and airs. As actors perform their theatrical roles, they are governed by the script, what the other actors say and do, and the reactions of the audience.

The analogy of the stage, of course, has its shortcomings. Our parts are real, whereas the theater is a world of make-believe. Life often presents us with actual scenes and players who are poorly rehearsed (Goffman, 1959, 1981). The scripts our culture offers us are far too broad to cover many of the details and eventualities of social interaction. Indeed, few situations in everyday life supply us with a fixed script. Instead, as we experience much of life, we must continually write our own lines as we devise our courses of action (Hewitt, 1984). Hence, there is an element of tentativeness in our relations with other people.

We noted in Chapter 3, "Socialization over the Life Course," that in going about our everyday activities, we mentally place people in various social categories: neighbor, grandfather, baby, motorist, salesclerk, Jew, physician, drug addict, Democrat, friend, and so on. We classify not only individuals but settings as well. For example, you and your social psychology instructor might agree that you are "the student" and she is "the professor"; that collectively, the two of you and the other students make up "Sociology 101: Introductory Social Psychology"; and that Sociology 101 is a course at the "University of North Carolina." The social categories we apply to people and settings are called **identities**.

That so much of social life is routine and repetitive permits us to treat certain activities and situations as things or objects. By attending classes and interacting with deans, faculty, and students, we give existence to the University of North Carolina. By acting toward one another in certain ways, we "are" the University of North Carolina. Additionally, since we are aware, or conscious, of these patterned relationships, we label them "the University of North Carolina." We can act toward these and related activities as an object: "I will graduate from the University of North Carolina next June"; "The University of North Carolina defeated the University of Michigan in a basketball game"; "The University of North Carolina is closed for the Christmas holidays."

While different identities may be applied to different members of a group or relationship, a single identity may also be applied to all members of the group. For example, faculty, students, administrators, and staff may be identified collectively as "the university." Similarly, wife/mother, husband/father, children, and grandparents are identified as "the family."

We establish identities in order to identify the set of expectations that will operate in the relationship — what we can expect of others and what they can expect of us. These expectations are called **roles**. Roles specify the normative requirements applying to the behavior of specific categories of people in particular situational contexts. Roles, in other words, specify *who does what, when, and where.*

Identities and roles permit us to formulate our behavior mentally, allowing us to fit our action to that of others. Through identities and roles we are able to collapse, or telescope, a range of behaviors into manageable bundles, collecting the particulars of an unfolding social scene under more general categories or classes. And identities enable us to assume that in certain respects we can ignore personal differences, that individuals who share an identity are interchangeable, and that as a practical matter we can deal with them in almost identical ways. We know what to expect of one another in certain situations because we "know" that particular "types" of people behave in typical ways under such circumstances. For instance, every member of a sports team "knows" that a coach is expected to direct team practice and competition.

Identities involve a categorizing process. By means of identities we structure our social world in terms of classes or categories of potential coactors (individuals with whom we may interact). Of course, the process of categorization involves a social loss. As Georg Simmel points out: "Man distorts the picture of another. He both detracts and supplements, since generalization is always both less and more than individuality is" (1971: 2).

The Reciprocal Nature of Identities and Roles

Identities and roles do not exist by themselves (Athay and Darley, 1982; Stiles et al., 1984). Both are defined in terms of the identities and roles of others. Without students there are no professors; without clients, no lawyers; without husbands, no wives; without Jews, no Gentiles; without "offenders," no police; without "psychotics," no psychiatrists. And vice versa: without professors there are no students; without lawyers, no clients; and so on through the list.

Roles impinge upon us as sets of norms defining our *obligations* — the actions others can legitimately insist we perform — and our *expectations* — the actions we can legitimately insist others perform (Goffman, 1961*b*). Every role is linked to at least one other role and is reciprocal to the linked role (or roles). Thus the obligations of the student role (to read assigned materials, take exams, attend classes) are the expectations of the professor role. The expectations of the student role (to receive authoritative material from lectures; be given fair examinations; be graded on the basis of merit without regard to personal attributes, race, sex, or religion) are the obligations of the professor role. Social relationships are characterized by peculiarly intricate complexes of interlocking roles, which we sustain in the course of interaction with one another. We experience these patterns of interaction and expectations as social order.

THE MESHING OF MULTIPLE CULTURES: NESTING AND LINKAGE

We have been discussing relationships and groups as if they existed in isolation. Of course, they do not. Most of us participate in numerous relationships and groups in the course of a single day. Frequently, these relationships and groups are embedded within other, larger groups; all are subunits of the larger society. Social psychologists call this *nesting* and refer to the smaller unit as a *subgroup*. For example, a mother-son relationship is embedded, or nested, within a larger family group. A friendship clique may be nested within a fraternity. Departments are nested within organizations. A subgroup's most immediate environment is the larger group in which it is nested. The mother-son relationship is affected most by, and affects, the rest of the family.

Naturally, within the subgroup there is even a smaller unit — the individual person. Social psychologists are interested in how all of these "layers" — an individual within a subgroup within a larger group within a society — affect the individual and interaction. For example, you are an individual within a social psychology class within a department of sociology within a college or university. You may also be an individual member of a friendship clique within a large residential unit within a town within a region within the United States.

Social psychologists are particularly interested in the **linkage**, or connection, that a subgroup provides between an individual and a larger group. They point out that much of our experience with larger groups is *mediated* by smaller groups. That is, we do not always experience the larger group directly. For example, much of your experience as a student at your college or university is mediated through the smaller groups in which you participate — the various classes you take, the extracurricular clubs you participate in, the friendship groups you attend sports events with, and so on. To be sure, the culture of the larger organization, the university, shapes our experience to a great extent, but most of our interactions take place in the context of the smaller groups, and it is through those groups that we are linked to the larger organization and, finally, to our society.

Primary Groups as Links

Social psychologists believe that primary groups provide a particularly important linkage between individuals and society. We live our lives within large, complex societies and formal organizations characterized by impersonal, secondary relationships and groups. Within this context, primary groups provide an essential bridge between the individual and the "great society." Primary groups function to transmit, interpret, and, in the end, sustain society's norms. Primary groups are the principal carriers and repositories of a people's cultural ways. In this sense, primary groups perform a mediating function, binding individuals to the larger society.

It is not surprising that primary subgroups often play a critical part in mobilizing people to work for the goals of larger organizations. An army is a case in point. Why should people endure situations in which they can be killed and in which they have to kill others? In brief, why do soldiers enter combat—behavior that is extremely hazardous to life and limb? Part of the answer is to be found in the functioning of small face-to-face groups and the sense of solidarity they encourage (Moskos, 1984). Much research suggests that the stronger the primary-group ties of the troops fighting together, the better their combat record.

In a study of the German army during World War II, Edward A. Shils and Morris Janowitz (1948) found that the Wehrmacht's fighting effectiveness stemmed from its ability to reproduce in the infantry unit the intimacy and ties previously furnished by the soldiers' civilian primary groups. Except among a minority of hard-core Nazis, political and ideological convictions had little impact on determination to fight. As one captured German said, "Nazism begins ten miles behind the front line." Unlike the Americans, the German soldiers who trained together went into

battle together. And whereas American fighting units were kept up to strength through individual replacements, German units were "fought down" and then pulled back to be formed anew (Van Creveld, 1982). The result was that the German units often fought better than their American counterparts.

The German soldiers showed considerable ignorance and apathy about the course of the fighting. Shils and Janowitz report:

> For the ordinary German soldier the decisive fact was that he was a member of a squad or section which maintained its structural integrity and which coincided roughly with the *social* unit which satisfied some of his major primary needs. He was likely to go on fighting, provided he had the necessary weapons, as long as the group possessed leadership with which he could identify himself, and as long as he gave affection to and received affection from the other members of his squad and platoon. In other words, as long as he felt himself to be a member of his primary group and therefore bound by the expectations and demands of its other members, his soldierly achievement was likely to be good. (1948: 284)

Studies of American soldiers after World War II reveal similar motivations (Shils, 1950; Moskos, 1969). Influenced by social psychological research, the U.S. Army has moved decisively toward keeping soldiers together throughout their military careers. It has concluded that "a soldier's loyalty is to the primary group with which he identifies and interacts." The army anticipates that stabilization in a regiment will "overcome the transitory nature of soldiers in units and will provide a solid basis for cohesion and bonding" (Middleton, 1983: 10).

External and Internal Culture

We have observed how subgroups may function as *intermediaries* binding individuals to a larger group. But they can also operate to *undermine* the larger group's official goals and commands. Gary Fine (1979) describes how subgroups can act as both transmitters and buffers of the culture of the larger group. The culture of the larger group, such as our society, supplies a set of normative "blueprints" to its members outlining how particular kinds of subgroups should operate — a family, a romantic relationship, a class, a committee, or a gang. However, each subgroup "overlays" the blueprint with its own unique culture — Fine calls it "idioculture" — including language, dress, and behavioral patterns unique to that subgroup. In other words, we come to interaction with certain common, socially created beliefs, meanings, experiences, and rules. However, as we apply these beliefs and rules to the specific events of interaction, we combine and reshape their implications in ways that are distinctive to the particular encounter. Thus, we actively *construct* the culture of our social relationships and groups through interaction (Ridgeway, 1992).

If you studied five sororities on the same university campus, for example, you would undoubtedly discover that they share many aspects of the larger culture and even many aspects of "sorority culture." But each sorority probably also possesses its own idioculture. One may have a norm that members should "dress" for dinner and sorority meetings, while another has a norm that members should wear their most comfortable, homey clothes for group meals and meetings. One might have norms that rank fraternities on a the basis of their members' desirability as dates, while another views dating as "not a sorority concern." Women in one sorority might frequently use a particular word or phrase that has a special meaning in their idioculture, while members of the other sororities never do so. One of the sororities might have a tradition of recruiting college athletes and encouraging participation in sports, while another looks down on athletics and has a negative stereotype of female athletes, and the rest view college athletics as irrelevant to sorority life.

Occasionally, the larger culture may adopt elements of an idioculture. For example, in Chapter 2, "Early Socialization," we discussed how the subculture of preschool children — which involved their smuggling small toys into their classrooms to show one another — caused their teachers to change their own culture by adding a "show-and-tell" segment to the curriculum. This also occurs when the idioculture is transmitted from one subgroup to another until a societywide social movement is successful in causing social change. We will discuss this topic in our final chapter, "Collective Action and Social Movements."

A subgroup may be a "countergroup," working against the goals of the larger group it is part of. This can often be seen in *informal groups* — groups that evolve within a formal organization although they are not shown on its organization chart. For example, informal groups that arise in work settings develop norms enabling workers to increase their control over the work environment and lessen their dependence on management. Peter M. Blau and W. Richard Scott have summarized some of these group norms and the measures employed to support them:

> In the course of interaction a set of common rules of conduct emerged, which included the following prohibitions: Don't be a rate-buster by working too fast. Don't be a chiseler by working too slow. If you are a straw boss, act like a regular guy; don't try to get bossy. Don't be a squealer. Conformity to norms was rewarded by approval that bestowed a relatively high position in the informal status structure. Norm violations were punished by group members in a variety of ways. Minor violations might be met with "binging" — striking the offender on the upper arm — or with ridicule. Continued violation of important norms resulted in a loss of popularity, a reduction in social interaction, and ultimately in complete ostracism. One worker was isolated because he violated the most serious group norm: he "squealed" on his fellows to the foreman. (1962: 92)

In prisons, military units, the postal service, hospitals, schools, and factories, studies have revealed elaborate patterns of "kidding," gambling, illicit drug trafficking, unauthorized work breaks, and "goldbricking," all derived from informal-group norms.

Thus, there are two sources of group culture. Some of the culture originates outside the group — **external culture** — and some of it emerges from within — **internal culture** (Turner, 1988). *External culture* gives us some expectations for interaction when we begin a new relationship or join a new group. Even though we have had no previous interaction with the particular partners the new membership will bring us into contact with, we know, more or less, what to expect because we have learned the relevant roles from other people and from previous experience in the same role. For example, when you and your social psychology professor met for the first time, both of you already had some information on how to act toward each other. This information came partly from your earlier student-professor experiences at your university. But even before that, you had learned from the larger culture something about the ways that students and professors are expected to act toward one another. Similarly, you learned enough about dating from other people to know how you should act on your first date. This information was probably modified and elaborated as you gained experience with dating. So, when you initially dated your current partner or spouse, your expectations for the interaction were considerably influenced by external culture.

Thus we can become involved in a relationship with a particular partner without any previous interaction with that person because we have previously learned the relevant roles from other people. However, repeated interaction with particular partners may modify our relationships with them. When we acquire new information through our interaction with one another, an *internal culture* develops. For example, the external culture — what you have learned from others and your previous experience in the student role — may lead you to expect that a particular professor (like all the others you know) will post office hours and see students outside of class only during those hours. You might learn, however, that this particular professor does not post office hours and will see students only by appointment or that he will stay after class to answer student questions.

Think of elements in your relationship with your current partner or spouse that are unique to that particular relationship, compared with other such relationships you have had. Are there particular affectionate names that you and your partner call each other that you have never used with anyone else? Are there other words or phrases that have a special meaning for you and your partner — ones that others wouldn't understand? How do your own and your partner's unique likes and dislikes (for music, food, entertainment, affection, and so on) shape your interaction? If you are able to identify ways of interacting between you and your partner that have developed as a result of getting to know each other's unique and personal qualities, then your relationship has developed an internal culture.

Actual relationships are based on a mix of external and internal culture. The balance of the two kinds of culture varies from one group to another. Some relationships are based primarily on external culture; these are called **role relationships**. In these we need know little about the peculiarities of our partner in order to successfully interact. Other relationships, known as **personal relationships**, depend largely on the development of an internal culture. In personal relationships the particular other is very important. Your relationship with your social psychology professor is probably closer to a role relationship, while your relationships with your close friends and romantic partner or spouse are closer to personal relationships. (Before reading further, see the Student Observation: "Internal Culture.")

NEGOTIATING AND RENEGOTIATING INTERNAL CULTURE

The preceding discussion suggests that culture is worked at and fashioned as we repeat, reaffirm, and reconstruct social acts. We arrive at mutually shared agreements, tacit understandings, binding contracts, unhappy compromises, and coerced accommodations. And we do all this through processes of manipulation, persuasion, inducement, diplomacy, and bargaining. Culture is *negotiated*

STUDENT OBSERVATION

Internal Culture

Internal culture is a way of interacting that has developed as a result of two partners' getting to know each other. This is often marked by each person learning unique and personal things about the other. My girlfriend and I have developed an internal culture. For example, I often call her by unique and strange names such as "nanerhead." To others this would have no meaning, but to us it has developed from our getting to know one another in our personal relationship. We also have special ways of expressing our affection for each other, such as giving gifts that would delight one another but seem unusual to someone else.

---

out of a conflict of interests and sentiments in the process of social interaction.

Negotiations in Primary Groups

For example, consider the interaction between the adult members of a newly established family. They probably entered marriage (and parenthood) with taken-for-granted ideas about their respective roles, which they have acquired through the kinds of socialization experiences we discussed in Chapter 3, "Socialization over the Life Course." These expectations originate outside their marital relationship and thus constitute part of the relationship's external culture. However, there is evidence that such general expectations about family roles will not provide a sufficient basis for smooth marital interaction. Instead, the marital partners will have to arrive at their own understandings for various aspects of their relationship. For example, they have to work out a division of labor by which they deal with the problems of surviving economically, maintaining a household, and possibly providing child care.

Research suggests that young men and women do not share the same assumptions about *how* their employment, household, and child-care activities will be coordinated. That is, gender differences in external culture may lead to difficulties in negotiating an internal culture for the marital pair. Researchers David Maines and Monica Hardesty (1987) interviewed upper-undergraduate students at a Midwest university. About one-

third of the men interviewed indicated either (1) they had not thought about how they and their future wives would coordinate home and work activities, or (2) they saw the issue as unproblematic. Comments included, "If we were to have kids, I don't know if she's going to quit her job or what. I don't even want to think about that," and "I really don't think that there would be any problems. If you find the right girl. . . ." About another third of the males interviewed said they would opt for a traditional division of labor: "If we really don't need the money badly, I don't see why she should work." In contrast, *none* of the women interviewed gave such responses. *All* anticipated problems in resolving home and work activities, and *none* desired a traditional division of labor as a solution.

Data like these suggest there is a strong chance that couples have to undertake some serious negotiation when they establish their families. And *renegotiation* will likely be necessitated by changes resulting from a family's moving through its "life cycle" — for example, when new family members are added or young members grow up and leave home. Each family must work out the particular division of labor that meets the members' individual needs and situation. Research suggests that couples' division of employment and housework is more diverse than their division of child-care responsibilities. Couples are more likely to divide housework than child care, which is almost always the responsibility of the woman (Ehrensaft, 1987; Hochschild, 1989).

Although internal culture develops out of negotiations engaged in by the relationship partners, the outcome of negotiation is *constrained* in varying degrees by features both external and internal to the relationship (Hall, 1987). As we noted in Chapter 3, "Socialization over the Life Course," society prescribes roles based on age, race, sex, and social class. These prescriptions affect our choice of interaction partners, as well as our expectations for particular relationships. If the relationship is embedded in an organization, the organization's role expectations will also impinge on the interaction partners. The relationship itself may have a history that includes a previously negotiated order that at least one member of the relationship is reluctant to relinquish. The unique personal history of each member of the immediate relationship may also limit individual expectations. Individual members may be unequal in terms of their capacity to influence one another in pursuit of their own interests.

Let's use families to illustrate how external culture, existing internal culture, and even individual personal history constrain negotiations about division of labor in the family group. The division-of-labor options available to a family can be constrained by many factors (Pestello and Voydanoff, 1991). Many division-of-labor alternatives are virtually eliminated by these constraints. Some of these factors originate at the societal level. Our society provides cultural scripts for acceptable patterns of division of labor in American families. These scripts favor the husband taking the role of primary income producer and the wife either staying at home to care for the house and children or taking a secondary employment role. Other alternatives — such as an equal division of household and income-producing roles or a reversal of the traditional roles (the husband stays home to care for house and children, and the wife takes the primary income-producing role) — are discouraged. Laws and policies reinforce the acceptable scripts. For example, men are generally paid more for their work than women are. Efforts to change these scripts — for example, proposed laws that require employers to offer family leaves or that allow parents to deduct child-care expenses from their income taxes — are met with resistance.

Communities also differ in their support for traditional or nontraditional division of labor in families. For instance, some communities have community centers or religious institutions that provide day-care services for working parents, making it easier for mothers to assume income-producing roles. Communities also differ in the degree to which they encourage fathers to assume household and child-care responsibilities.

At an even more immediate level, a family's relatives and friends can provide more or less support for nontraditional division-of-labor alternatives. For example, they may provide child care, allowing the mother to work, or may indicate disapproval if she does not stay home with her children. Similarly, employers may make it easy or more difficult to establish a particular division of labor. Employers differ in their offer of family leaves, on-site day-care facilities, part-time work opportunities, and flexibility in work hours and work locations. For example, work that can be done at home provides a viable alternative to the traditional division of labor (Beach, 1988). And finally, individual family members control different resources — income, expertise, contacts, affection, attractiveness — that can be used to influence one another in negotiations over their division of labor.

All these factors constrain the options available to family members. Thus, although negotiation is required to work out the particulars of the family's internal culture, the negotiations do not take place in a vacuum. Instead, they are constrained by the cultures of the various larger groups in which the family is nested, by the family's own previously negotiated internal culture, and by individual differences.

Negotiations in Secondary Groups

Negotiations are not limited to primary relationships and groups. Secondary relationships nested in formal organizations also develop internal culture through negotiations. Mark Mesler (1989) studied the attempts of pharmacists in two hospital settings to negotiate their relationships with physicians. These pharmacists wanted greater responsibility for patient care. Prior to World War II, pharmacists played a major role in patient care, counseling patients about their illnesses when mixing the necessary compounds to create a remedy. As more and more powerful drugs were discovered during and following the war, the pharmacists' traditional function of creating compound remedies was taken over by manufacturers who could mass-produce high-quality drugs inexpensively. The pharmacists' role changed to one of filling doctors' prescriptions. Thus pharmacists came to be seen more as "counters and pourers — lickers and stickers" than as true members of the medical team.

The pharmacists in Mesler's study were trying to regain their more traditional clinical roles by emphasizing the importance of drug therapy. They sought to become the primary source of information for medical teams on all matters pertaining to drugs and drug dosage. This expansion of the pharmacists' role would come at the expense of the physicians' role, therefore necessitating negotiation between pharmacists and physicians.

Mesler observed that the pharmacists used three general strategies in their negotiations. The first strategy they used was role-taking — trying to see themselves as the physicians saw them and to align their actions accordingly. Physicians differed in their acceptance of outside input; factors such as their age, status, clinical experience, type of practice, and medical training influenced their reactions. Thus, pharmacists' clinical advice giving was selective. As one pharmacist reported, "Sometimes you pick the person to speak to depending on your relationship with them, and what kind of person you perceive them to be, or what kind of person you've been told they are." The second strategy used by the pharmacists was deference — offering therapeutic input in a manner mindful of the physician's superior status. A pharmacist reported, "So, a lot of times I take the tack of — 'I want you [the physician] to tell me why you're doing this this way, I want to learn' — and

then, as that comes out, I try to explain why I think this should be done differently." The third negotiation strategy involved rotating the graduate pharmacy students through internships in various areas of specialization, thereby socializing *physicians* into the benefits of clinical pharmacy. The director of one of the hospital's pharmacy programs reported, "Of course we're always hopeful that wherever we place a fellow [pharmacy student], the physician will get so excited that they demand to have one of their very own."

The pharmacists' negotiation efforts were influenced (constrained) by several factors. First, they were constrained by the now-traditional roles of the physician and pharmacist — the physician doing the clinical work and the pharmacist dispensing the physician-designated drugs. Second, the pharmacists' attempts to expand their clinical programs were taking place during an era of cost controls in American medicine. Hospitals were not interested in developing new programs of questionable cost effectiveness. This situation was also translated into a shortage of labor in the individual hospital departments studied by Mesler. The unavailability of labor required that each pharmacist cover several floors to distribute drugs and limited the time available to the pharmacists for pursuing greater involvement in clinical patient therapy.

In spite of these constraints, the result of the negotiations between the pharmacists and physicians in Mesler's study was that other members of medical teams actually welcomed, and came to depend upon, the pharmacists' input. One physician reported, "Well, it's a give and take of a discourse between the physician and the clinical pharmacists. . . . That is, discussion about dosages, discussion about contra-indications for the drug, discussion about therapeutic effects that can be expected. . . . So, I think the interaction is one of simple peer relationship; in other words, . . . where management of the patient is discussed on an equal basis." Statements such as this indicate that the pharmacists were successful in their efforts to negotiate a new standard of patient care that gave themselves greater input.

Negotiations in a Total Institution

Let's look at one final situation — the negotiation that takes place in total institutions, such as prisons. We might expect prisons to emphasize constraint and to allow minimal negotiation. If this is your view, then the research by Jim Thomas (1984) in a Midwest maximum-security prison might be illuminating.

As we might expect, Thomas did find many constraints on negotiation within the prison. One source of constraint was the official prison structure reflected in the prison's organization chart. This structure specified the official lines of authority among administrators, line staff, and inmates. Although this structure determined the official power of the prison officials and inmates, Thomas discovered that, in actual practice, power was largely negotiated. For example, about 75 percent of the inmates belonged to inmate gangs, whose leaders served as liaisons between prisoners and administrators in mediating disputes, often in return for favors for themselves or the other prisoners. The gang structure partially neutralized the official structure by providing an alternative power hierarchy. In a sense, although the gang structure itself arose out of negotiation, it also served as a second source of constraint on subsequent negotiations. For example, once inmate leaders were recognized to have the power to mobilize other inmates, it became difficult for guards to treat all inmates alike. A third source of constraint from within the prison consisted of the specific rules regulating interaction. As we might expect in a total institution such as a prison, official rules regulated almost every aspect of the inmates' existence. Rules specified when and where and how inmates were to eat, sleep, shower, exercise, and so on. But negotiations did take place between the guards and the inmates regarding the degree to which the rules would be enforced.

Although the guards had most of the official power, the inmates found ways to make rule enforcement costly for the guards. For example, Thomas observed inmates raiding an ice cream cart as it was pushed down a corridor by another inmate — all in full view of a guard. The guard explained to Thomas that it wasn't "worth it" to stop them. To enforce the rule, the guard would have had to fill out paperwork for each inmate's offense, and the inmates might have given the guard a hard time later. So he let the rule breaking occur. When, on the other hand, guards felt that inmates were "getting out of line," they sometimes fabricated evidence of transgressions, just to show inmates that the guards could "get them" if they wanted to. Guards and inmates saw themselves as trying to work out a compromise arrangement in which rules were *selectively* enforced. As one inmate put it:

> I'm not causin' no problems, they don't cause me none. It's understood that I can make any job hard, and it's understood with me that they can make my time hard. So we compromise. (Thomas, 1984: 220)

In summary, we have discussed three types of relationships. These are husband-wife, pharmacist-physician, and inmate-guard. In each case, the participants negotiated the patterns of interaction and expectations — the internal culture — that shaped their future interaction. This negotiation was constrained by the external cultures of the larger networks, organizations, and societal institutions in which the relationships were nested. It should also be clear that the members of these larger social units are engaged in negotiating their own internal culture. Here we have emphasized how the cultures of larger social units constrain the negotiations within smaller ones. In Chapter 16, "Collective Action and Social Movements," we will discuss how the reverse can also be true — how negotiation in relationships and groups can create organizational and societal change.

Summary

1. We distinguish among aggregates, social relationships, networks, and groups according to their various characteristics of interaction. Ag-

gregates involve only minimal interaction. Relationships link two persons in interaction that may range from casual, one-time encounters to intimate, enduring relationships. Networks are the webs of relationships linking us directly to some people and, through them, indirectly to others. Groups connect people through interdependence and a subjective sense of oneness.

2. Four sources of attachment to relationships and groups are members, goals, norms, and oppression. Expressive bonds, based on our attraction to particular others, form the basis of primary relationships and groups. Instrumental bonds derive from our need for others in reaching certain goals and constitute the basis of secondary relationships and groups. Reference groups are based on normative bonds — our adoption of other's norms or standards to define and evaluate our behavior. Oppression bonds are based on common oppression by another person or group.

3. Rituals are social acts of symbolic significance that are used to establish or enhance group identities. Group identities are also reinforced through segregation and territorial behavior. Identifying with a group sometimes makes us feel very different from nonmembers. This subjective sense of one group being set apart from other groups is called social distance.

4. Relationships and groups are characterized by relatively stable sets of expectations and patterns of interaction that are part of their culture. Norms specify a range of acceptable behavior and allow us to act together with others with relative ease. Roles specify the norms that apply to the behavior of specific categories of people in particular situations.

5. Often, a relationship or group is embedded, or nested, within another, larger one. The smaller unit in such situations is referred to as a subgroup. Subgroups can act as both transmitters and buffers of the culture of the larger group.

6. Some of a group's or relationship's culture may come from outside the relationship. External culture allows interactants to become involved in a relationship even though they have had no previous interaction with each other. Through our interaction with a relationship partner, however, we acquire new information, and an internal culture develops. The balance of external and internal culture varies from one relationship to another.

CHAPTER 5

COMMUNICATION

*I*n Chapter 4, "Social Relationships and Groups," we discussed how people are linked by social relationships — patterns of social interaction and sets of expectations (norms and roles) reflecting and shaping these interaction patterns. We noted that social relationships go through cycles of negotiation and renegotiation. But we said very little about *how* this is accomplished. In this chapter we will focus on the important contribution of **communication**, the process by which people interact and interpret their interactions.

Symbols

When people interact, much of the language, behavior, and appearance of each party constitutes **symbols** — objects or actions that, by social convention, stand for or represent something else. Symbols are *arbitrary* stand-ins for other things; their meanings are not *givens*. Rather, they come to have meaning by virtue of socially shared conventions, that is, understandings between users. For example, you and a friend might agree that if you wink at him at a party, the wink means you're having a good time and want to stay longer. You could just as easily agree that the wink means

you're bored and want to escape as soon as possible. Through socialization we learn the meanings assigned by our culture to many symbols. Spoken and written words, for example, are symbols, as are clothing styles and actions such as handshakes and frowns. The traditions and consensus within a society give symbols their meanings. As a result, many symbols have different meanings in different cultures.

Sometimes the parties to an interaction interpret aspects of it differently, and as a consequence, their interaction does not run smoothly. What interests social psychologists is how we negotiate meanings and the implications of this process for our continued interaction. Consider the following newspaper account:

> Stockton, Calif. — The worst possible fate befell two young masked robbers last night. They tried to hold up a party of thirty-six prominent, middle-aged women, but couldn't get anybody to believe they were for real.
>
> One of the women actually grabbed the gun held by one of the youths.
>
> "Why," she said, "that's not wood or plastic. It must be metal."
>
> "Lady," pleaded the man, "I've been trying to tell you, it is real. This is a holdup."

"Ah, you're putting me on," she replied cheerfully.

The robbers' moment of frustration came about 9:00 p.m. at the home of Mrs. Florence Tout . . . as she was entertaining at what is called a "hi-jinks" party. Jokes and pranks filled the evening. Thus not one of the ladies turned a hair when the two men, clad in black, walked in.

"All right now, ladies, put your rings on the table," ordered the gunman [the women were prominent in Stockton social circles].

"What for?" one of the guests demanded.

"This is a stickup. I'm serious!" he cried.

All the ladies laughed.

One of them playfully shoved one of the men. He shoved her back.

As the ringing laughter continued, the men looked at each other, shrugged, and left empty-handed. (*San Francisco Examiner*, April 4, 1968)*

In this example, interaction was problematic because the participants did not share meanings. The failure of the robbery attempt can be attributed to the *different meanings* that the robbers and the women at the party assigned to the robbers' message. The robbers thought that their symbols — masks, guns, and the words "This is a stickup" — would lead the partygoers to define the situation as a robbery and to give up their valuables.

But that's *not* how the women interpreted the symbols. They saw the masks and guns and heard the words, but these happened in the context of a "hi-jinks" party, where several pranks had already occurred. The women interpreted the robbers' symbols as part of still another joke. Moreover, in the women's minds, the joke did not call for them to actually hand over their valuables. In other words, the robbers and the women arrived at different meanings for the same symbols because they interpreted them in terms of different definitions of the situation. A **definition of the situation** is the meaning we give to an entire situation.

* Reprinted with permission from the San Francisco Examiner. © 1968 San Francisco Examiner.

DEFINITIONS OF THE SITUATION

What we are trying to arrive at when we send and receive various types of symbols is a definition of the situation. We might, for example, have definitions for such situations as a prayer meeting, a camping trip, an accident, an argument, a seduction, a friendly conversation, a tennis match, a robbery, a party, a social psychology class, and so forth. We use whatever information we can to help us define the situation we are in or are about to enter. Some of this information comes in the form of symbols provided by others — communication. Once we arrive at a definition of the situation, we interpret other information in terms of that definition. In other words, the definition of the situation constitutes a type of context for our interpretation of events. If we define the situation as a wedding, for example, and observe that a woman in the front row is weeping, we may interpret her tears as tears of joy. If we define the situation as a funeral, we may be more likely to define her tears as tears of grief.

Arriving at a definition of a situation gives us insight as to the roles people are going to play — allowing us to anticipate the actions of others and adjust our own actions accordingly. Much human interaction occurs among people who do not know one another and who, consequently, have no direct experience on which to base predictions about one another's behavior. *Scripts* are mental representations of sequences of interaction over a period of time. They allow us to quickly and easily fit our behavior with that of others in a situation. We feel quite comfortable going to an appointment with a new dentist, going to a new restaurant, or attending a class for the first time because we know the scripts. This allows us to take for granted certain expectations for our own behavior and the behavior of others in the situation.

When behavior follows a script, interaction proceeds smoothly. This is highlighted by cases in which we *don't* know the script for the situation. If we received an invitation to a state dinner at the White House and planned to attend, we would probably try to find out as much as we could about the script for state dinners. We'd want to know "who does what when?" (See the Student Observation: "Scripts.")

We are, of course, also interested in information not provided by the script for a particular definition of a situation. When visiting the dentist, for example, a patient might also be attentive to symbols indicating whether the dentist intended to carry out a complicated procedure, liked him, seemed competent and professional, or was in a bad mood. He would use this additional information to modify his interaction in that particular encounter with the dentist.

SIGNIFICANT SYMBOLS— SHARED MEANINGS

Because appearances and behaviors — indeed, all the things that can serve as symbols in communication — are interpreted, people may perceive and interpret the same information in different ways. Interpretation provides meaning for the symbol. When a symbol is interpreted similarly by several persons, the symbol is said to be a significant symbol. In other words, **significant symbols** are symbols whose meaning is *shared* by the parties in question. For example, for most Americans, the American flag stands for the country and our pride in it. But for some, it stands for aspects of the American government to which they object. When members of these two groups interact, the American flag will not be a significant symbol. In other words, they will not agree on its meaning.

Significant symbols are important because they allow us to anticipate one another's behavior and, therefore, to coordinate our behaviors. If the symbols we choose are *not* significant symbols — if their meanings are not shared — the chances of coordinating our actions with those of others is greatly diminished.

Subgroups within language groups often have specialized vocabularies or other symbols that emphasize the concepts that are most important to them. In this course, you are learning many of terms which social psychologists use regularly but which are relatively unknown to others. Similarly, physicists, farmers, truck drivers, cooks, physicians, and construction workers all have special vocabularies that allow them to efficiently communicate with one another about the things that are important to them.

STUDENT OBSERVATION

Scripts

People fail to realize how important scripts are until they come into a situation for which they don't have one. A few weeks ago I was reminded of this fact when I attended a retreat of the co-chairs of the committees of the Campus-Y. I was one of the very newest members of the Y, and I didn't know any of the other co-chairs. I had never been to one of the retreats before. When I arrived at the campground, I was painfully aware that I had no *script* — no mental representation of sequences of behavior over time — for this occasion. As all the other committee chairs boldly slung their bags and other gear in a corner of the big log cabin meeting room and laughed and hugged one another in a presumably Campus-Y co-chair fashion, *I was so uncomfortable!* I did not know what an appropriate greeting would be for me, a new, unfamiliar member, nor had I the faintest idea what to do with my camping stuff. I stood very awkwardly — scriptless — until a facilitator, someone who obviously had a script, introduced herself and kindly showed me where to put my backpack and sleeping bag. After watching the others for a while, I began to piece together a script so that I could fit my behavior to theirs. However, I was never more grateful for directions than I was those first minutes at the rustic retreat.

THE TWO SIDES OF WARSPEAK

During the 1991 Persian Gulf War, a *Time* magazine article pointed out that the top brass and the GIs seemed to be speaking two different languages, neither of them English. William Lutz, a Rutgers University English professor, noted that military strategists seemed to have adopted M.B.A.-style buzzwords that reflected an "emphasis on managerial skills," a depersonalization of the enemy, and a distancing from violence, while the men and women in the ranks adopted a more colorful and less distanced way of communicating. Here's a sampler:

Top Brass

Incontinent ordinance: Bombs and artillery shells that fall wide of their targets and hit civilians.
Area denial weapons: Cluster bombs with the ability to wreak great damage over a particular zone.
Ballistically induced aperture in the subcutaneous environment: A bullet hole in a human being.
Coercive potential: The capability of bombs to harm and demoralize soldiers.
Suppressing assets: The destruction of sites containing antiaircraft weaponry.
Unwelcome visit: British term for any foray into enemy territory.

Scenario-dependent, post-crisis environment: Conditions after the war.

Grunts

Echelons beyond reality: The source of orders from superior officers.
High speed, low drag: Phrase indicating that an operation went exactly according to plan.
Micks: Abbreviation of minutes, as in "Give me five micks."
9-4: A more chummy version of the traditional "10-4" radio sign-off.
Suicide circles: Nickname for Saudi traffic roundabouts. A number of allied soldiers died in road accidents in Saudi Arabia.
180 out: The coordinate-minded soldier's term for the wrong answer — 180 degrees from the truth.
Strack: To get on the right track, or frame of mind, for battle.

Source: Reprinted from D. Ellis, "The Two Sides of Warspeak," *Time,* February 25, 1991 p. 13. Copyright 1991 Time, Inc. Reprinted by permission.

These special vocabularies are sometimes disparagingly referred to as *jargons,* because the meanings these words have are not shared by the larger population. Thus, although they increase the efficiency of communication among those who share them, they are not effective symbols for communication with those who don't. During the 1991 war against Iraq in the Persian Gulf, the public was exposed to military jargon during the many briefings on the progress of the war. Interested observers noted that the jargons of the commanders and those of the lower-level soldiers differed, perhaps reflecting the two groups' different concerns and perspectives on the situation (see the box "The Two Sides of Warspeak").

KINDS OF SYMBOLS—CHANNELS OF COMMUNICATION

Talking and listening are the activities that we most often associate with communicating. But speech is only one of the kinds of symbols we use to communicate with others. Besides using words, we communicate with qualities of our voices and through nonverbal channels — our facial expressions, body movements, the distances and orientations with which we position ourselves relative to others, and our physical appearance and such personal attributes as hair styles and clothing. Social psychologists and linguists note that these kinds of symbols constitute the *channels of communication* available to us. They distinguish between the verbal and nonverbal channels.

Verbal Symbols

Verbal symbols are of two main types: language and paralanguage. **Language** is our principal vehicle for communication, finding expression in speech and writing. Language allows us to denote abstract ideas and events that are distant in time or place. A single word may have a complex meaning. For example, you may associate the word "home" not only with the house you live in but also with your family and dinnertime, with conflict or happiness and security. So the word "home" may represent more than "bricks and mortar" if it pertains to these other things as well.

We learn words and their meanings from agents of socialization (see our discussion in Chapter 2, "Early Socialization," for details). Because these meanings are largely shared, we are able to communicate with others in our language group. However, we sometimes create new symbols, such as new words, or assign words new meanings that are shared only by members of a particular relationship or group. Such symbols are part of the internal culture of our relationships and groups. They are significant symbols for members of the group, but not for others. For example, you may have a special name for a loved one that stands for your special feelings for that person. (We discussed internal culture in Chapter 4, "Social Relationships and Groups.")

Paralanguage consists of the nonsemantic aspects of speech — the stress, pitch, and volume of speech — by which we communicate meaning. Paralanguage has to do with *how* we say something, not with *what* we say. Tone of voice, inflection, pacing of speech, silent pauses, and extralinguistic sounds (such as sighs, screams, laughs) constitute paralanguage. Paralanguage is what we are referring to when we say, "It wasn't *what* she said; it was the *way* she said it." Consider, for instance, the difference in the meaning of the response "Oh yeah" under the following circumstances:

1. As a retort to the threat "Stop it or I'll smash you!" (hostile intonation)
2. As a response to the sexual invitation "Let's make love." (seductive intonation)
3. As a response to the suggestion "Won't it work if you hold that button down?" (embarrassed acknowledgement)
4. As a response to the question "Are you coming with us?" (affirmation)

Baby talk is a type of paralanguage (Caporael, 1981, Caporael and Culbertson, 1986; DePaulo and Coleman, 1986). While baby talk contains unique words (for example, "choo-choo" for train

---

STUDENT OBSERVATION

Paralanguage

My roommate provides a good example of the use of paralanguage in his telephone conversations. When he talks to his relatives, he speaks at a higher volume than in normal conversation. He also uses a higher pitch and a very happy tone of voice. When he talks to his girlfriend, he raises his pitch still higher and slows his rate of speech. When speaking to friends, he lowers his pitch and varies his tone of voice more frequently. The variation in paralanguage is really evident when one of his male friends calls when he is expecting his girlfriend. He answers with a high-pitched "Hey!" — but quickly "corrects" his pitch and tone when he realizes who the caller actually is.

and "tum-tum" for stomach), it is also distinctive in its paralinguistic features, especially its high pitch and exaggerated intonations. Indeed, baby talk has been documented in numerous languages. The higher pitch of baby talk may serve to hold babies' attention. Studies show that babies prefer to listen to baby talk (Fernald, 1985). (Before reading further, see the Student Observation: "Paralanguage.")

Nonverbal Symbols

Suppose you can see, through a window across the street, a young man and woman interacting in an apartment. Because of the noise of the traffic below, you can't hear their words, or even their voices, but you can see their faces and movements quite clearly. Without any verbal or paralinguistic cues, do you think you could tell whether the couple was having an argument or beginning a romantic evening together? Your guess just might be correct. This is because, besides speech and paralanguage, we use several kinds of nonverbal symbols to convey or amend meaning. These include body language, interpersonal spacing, and physical characteristics and personal effects. (Before reading further, see the Student Observation: "Symbols.")

Body language (also called **kinesics**) is the nonverbal communication of meaning through physical movements and gestures. We tap our fingers to show impatience. We shrug our shoulders to indicate indifference. We nod our heads to mean "yes" or "um-hum, I'm paying attention." We scratch our heads in puzzlement. We maneuver our bodies to negotiate a crowded setting without touching others. We avoid eye contact to indicate an unwillingness to interact. Through the motions of our bodies, limbs, faces, and eyes we communicate information about our feelings, attitudes, and intentions. This is not to say that we easily decipher the motions, wiggles, and fidgets accompanying ordinary speech. A nonverbal behavior may represent many different meanings, depending on the context in which it occurs—its timing and intensity, and its combination with other verbal and nonverbal behaviors (Zuckerman et al., 1981; Harper, 1985; O'Sullivan et al., 1985).

Eye contact frequently functions as a type of body language. Depending on how people define the situation, eye contact may signal an aggressive or dominating intent, as in a staredown; intimacy or close bonding, as among lovers; or a fervent call for assistance, as with a prisoner of war ap-

---

STUDENT OBSERVATION

Symbols

When I was about four years old, I attended a wonderful playschool. However, one afternoon my mother was late picking me up. Of course, I was hysterical—I thought my mother was never coming back to get me! From that point on, the playschool was a terrifying place to me. I began to have temper tantrums in the mornings before going, and I cried all day until my mother came to pick me up. Finally, my mother figured out a plan to ease my fear of being left and forgotten. She devised a symbol to represent the fact that she wasn't going to forget about me in the afternoons—she might be late, but she wasn't going to forget and leave me.

The symbol was nothing but a simple lipstick kiss on the back of my hand. It may sound silly, but it worked. Every day when she left me at the playschool, my mother would kiss my hand and leave her lipstick print. This "silly" mark meant the world to me. It was a symbol of security, of my mother's love, and of her promise that she would never forget me.

STUDENT OBSERVATION

Civil Inattention

One interesting example of civil inattention takes place in automatic teller lines. In lines for other kinds of service, people tend to stand with about 1 or 2 feet between them. In automatic teller lines, however, the distance between the person completing the transaction and the next one in line greatly increases. The "next up" must stand at least 4 to 5 feet away and make an obvious effort to gaze at something other than the person completing the transaction, in effect saying, "Don't worry about me. I'm just waiting for my turn—I'm not trying to see your number or how much money you're taking out. I'm no threat."

The other day I was in one of these lines. The next-up man was obviously in a hurry and violated the interpersonal spacing norms either out of carelessness or an effort to hurry the woman completing her transaction. She looked over her shoulder with a sharp, nervous expression on her face, obviously perceiving the opposite of the benign, adequately spaced message: "I'm too close to be normal—I'm looking to see your number or how much money you are taking out. I'm a threat." As soon as he saw her look back, the man sheepishly backed up to the appropriate distance—now saying, "No, I'm really *not* a threat. Sorry!" —and concentrated on the bush to the left, looking embarrassed about having communicated such a threatening message unintentionally.

---

pearing before a television camera. Gazes come in many variations. We can glare, gawk, ogle, or leer. We alter the symbolism of a gaze by tilting our heads, widening or narrowing our eyes, or lowering or raising our eyebrows. For instance, we typically perceive the lowering of brows as more assertive and domineering than the raising of brows (Mazur et al., 1980).

Eye contact assumes considerable importance in public settings. We employ it to assess strangers and define their intentions. Consider our behavior on a city bus, a subway, or an elevator. We view these forms of public transportation as means of moving from one place to another. Therefore, within such contexts we usually aim to protect our own rights and to maintain a proper social distance from strangers.

One way to achieve these outcomes is through **civil inattention**: we give others enough visual notice to signal to them that we recognize their presence, but then we quickly withdraw visual contact to show that we pose no threat to them and that we do not wish to interact. We do this by cutting off eye contact, a maneuver of civil inattention that Erving Goffman dubs "a dimming of the lights" (1963b: 84). Thus, despite the closeness of our bodies and our mutual vulnerability, little focused interaction occurs, few of us are accosted, and few friendships arise. We project cues to ensure that these things *do not take place*. (See the Student Observation: "Civil Inattention.")

Social contexts vary in permissible *looking time*—the amount of time that we can hold another person's gaze without being rude, aggressive, or intimate. The permissible looking time is zero on an elevator; it is a little longer in a crowded subway or bus; and it is still longer out on the street. Apparently, greater leeway is permitted to pedestrians in "looking one another over."

Interpersonal spacing (also termed **proxemics**) is nonverbal communication involving the distances and angles at which people position themselves relative to others. We invite interaction by angling our bodies toward others and discourage it by angling away. We position ourselves closer to those we like and farther from those we don't like.

We also use *markers*—signs that communicate the fact of ownership or legitimate occupancy to keep others at a distance from the territory we want to claim. As markers we use symbols such as nameplates, fences, hedges, and personal belongings. We place a book, handbag, or coat on a table or an empty chair to reserve a place in the library, sunglasses and lotion on a towel to lay claim to a spot on the beach, and a drink on a bar to assert "ownership" of a bar stool (Becker, 1973; Shaffer and Sadowski, 1975). We also use touch to communicate territorial control. For instance, at a game arcade, others are less likely to attempt to use a machine if a person stands near it and touches it than if a person stands off and does not touch it (Werner, Brown, and Damron, 1981).

Physical characteristics and personal effects. We also communicate through the way we look. This includes not only our physical characteristics (such as hair color, skin color, body build, height, the way we groom our bodies) but also the personal effects we choose and display (clothing, jewelry, makeup, choice of beverage, car, the way we decorate our living quarters, and so on). A ring on the fourth finger of the left hand suggests, in our culture, that a person is married. A uniform communicates that the wearer occupies a specific role, such as police officer, airline attendant, or physician. Thus, the uniform sets our expectations for the behavior of the wearer.

Note that some of these aspects of appearance are easily changed. We *choose* our clothing, makeup, grooming styles, and sometimes even hair color. Other aspects of our appearance are not easily changed—such as skin color, height, and body build. Even those aspects of our appearance over which we have little control are used by others to make judgments about us. Black males, for example, sometimes find that their race and gender are viewed as symbols of threat or danger (see the box "Just Walk on By: A Black Man Ponders His Power to Alter Public Space").

Norms define what is considered to be "appropriate dress" in various situations. That's why we tend to have different clothes for different occasions—some for work, some for leisure, some for dress-up nights out. For example, we would think it very odd if a friend attended our backyard cookout in sequined evening dress or a job applicant showed up for an interview in swim trunks and flip-flops. We would probably think such persons socially inept.

Within the range considered situationally appropriate, individuals choose their clothing and other personal effects partly to make a statement about who they are. A woman who wants to be taken seriously as a supervisor at work probably should not wear childish clothing. A manager who

If others attribute meaning to such social characteristics as race and gender, aspects of our appearance serve as symbols for these social categories and communicate information about us.

JUST WALK ON BY: A BLACK MAN PONDERS HIS POWER TO ALTER PUBLIC SPACE

My first victim was a woman — white, well dressed, probably in her early twenties. I came upon her late one evening on a deserted street in Hyde Park, a relatively affluent neighborhood in an otherwise mean, impoverished section of Chicago. As I swung onto the avenue behind her, there seemed to be a discrete, uninflammatory distance between us. Not so. She cast back a worried glance. To her, the youngish black man — a broad six feet two inches with a beard and billowing hair, both hands shoved into the pockets of a bulky military jacket — seemed menacingly close. After a few more quick glimpses, she picked up her pace and was soon running in earnest. Within seconds she disappeared into a cross street.

That was more than a decade ago. I was 22 years old, a graduate student newly arrived at the University of Chicago. It was in the echo of that terrified woman's footfalls that I first began to know the unwieldy inheritance I'd come into — the ability to alter public space in ugly ways. It was clear that she thought herself the quarry of a mugger, a rapist, or worse. Suffering a bout of insomnia, however, I was stalking sleep, not defenseless wayfarers. As a softy who is scarcely able to take a knife to a raw chicken — let alone hold it to a person's throat — I was surprised, embarrassed, and dismayed all at once. Her flight made me feel like an accomplice in tyranny. It also made it clear that I was indistinguishable from the muggers who occasionally seeped into the area from the surrounding ghetto. That first encounter, and those that followed, signified that a vast, unnerving gulf lay between nighttime pedestrians — particularly women — and me. And I soon gathered that being perceived as dangerous is a hazard in itself. I only needed to turn a corner into a dicey situation, or crowd some frightened, armed person in a foyer somewhere, or make an errant move after being pulled over by a policeman. Where fear and weapons meet — and they often do in urban America — there is always the possibility of death. . . .

The fearsomeness mistakenly attributed to me in public places often has a perilous flavor. The most frightening of these confusions occurred in the late 1970s and early 1980s when I worked as a journalist in Chicago. One day, rushing into the office of a magazine I was writing for with a deadline story in hand, I was mistaken for a burglar. The office manager called security and, with an ad hoc posse, pursued me through the labyrinthine halls, nearly to my editor's door. I had no way of proving who I was. I could only move briskly toward the company of someone who knew me. . . .

I began to take precautions to make myself less threatening. I move about with care, particularly late in the evening. I give a wide berth to nervous people on the subway platforms during the wee hours, particularly when I have exchanged business clothes for jeans. If I happen to be entering a building behind some people who appear skittish, I may walk by, letting them clear the lobby before I return, so as not to seem to be following them. I have been calm and extremely congenial on those rare occasions when I've been pulled over by the police.

And, on late-evening constitutions along streets less traveled by, I employ what has proved to be an excellent tension-reducing measure: I whistle melodies from Beethoven and Vivaldi and the more popular classical composers. Even steely New Yorkers hunching toward nighttime destinations seem to relax and occasionally they even join in the tune. Virtually everybody seems to sense that a mugger wouldn't be warbling bright, sunny selections from Vivaldi's *Four Seasons*. It is my equivalent of the cowbell that hikers wear when they know they are in bear country.

Source: Brent Staples, "Just Walk on By: A Black Man Ponders His Power to Alter Public Space," *Ms.*, September 1986, pp. 54, 88. Used by permission of the author.

wants to be seen as "one of the guys" probably should not dress too differently from them.

INTENDED AND UNINTENDED SYMBOLS

Communication involves a behavior or an attribute capable of being perceived by someone else — something that can serve as a symbol. Sometimes we *intend* for our behavior or attribute to be interpeted by others; sometimes we do not. Sociologist Erving Goffman (1959) distinguishes between *expressions given* — intended symbols — and *expressions given off* — symbols we transmit unintentionally. Communication occurs whenever some other person perceives and interprets a symbol we transmit, whether we *intended* to transmit that symbol or not.

We usually consider communication to be an intentional process, and it often is. For example, a graduate who majored in accounting may explain to a job interviewer, "In addition to my coursework, I did the accounting for student government during my junior and senior years at college. I think this experience makes me more prepared than many other graduates to enter a job with substantial responsibility." Here, the speaker is sending verbal signals that she hopes will serve as symbols of her suitability as a job candidate. She is also likely to have sent nonverbal messages intended to convey the same meaning — such as dressing in a suit, presenting a neatly prepared résumé, and being punctual for the interview.

But a sender may also deliver messages *without* intending to. The woman in our example almost certainly does *not* intend to send signals indicating that she is extremely nervous during the job interview. Nevertheless, her unsteady voice and trembling hands might communicate her nervousness to the interviewer. Similarly, the woman's wedding band might communicate her maturity and responsibility to the interviewer, even though she hasn't thought about communicating this or may not even be aware that her wedding band has been noticed by the interviewer. In most situations, we both give and give off expressions — through our appearance and behavior — that are interpreted by others. We communicate both intentionally and unintentionally.

MULTICHANNEL COMMUNICATION

Ordinarily, communication takes place through several communications channels simultaneously. Even on the telephone, both linguistic and paralinguistic cues are available to us, although body movements, facial expressions, spacing, and personal effects are not. In face-to-face conversation, we may use all the channels of communication. Sometimes, the information provided by a single channel can be interpreted in more than one way. For example, intense looking may indicate either love or hostility. A tense body posture may signal respect or hostility. The meaning of such behaviors is usually clarified when we look at the context provided by additional behavior channels. Thus we often impute love to an intense gaze when it is combined with close distance and relaxed posture (Schwarz, Foa, and Foa, 1983). In contrast, intense gaze coupled with loud speech and negative facial expression would probably be interpreted as anger. Thus, we decode most accurately when multiple communication channels convey what appears to be consistent information.

But if we had access to only a single channel of communication, which channel would give us the best (most accurate) assessment of a person's emotion? Research suggests that judgments based on verbal content are the most accurate. One such study presented subjects with passages from the 1976 televised debate between vice-presidential candidates Walter Mondale and Robert Dole. The researchers selected twelve passages for each speaker, half of which seemed to convey positive emotions and half negative. Subjects were presented with only one of several channels of communication available in the standard videotape of the passages: (1) verbal only — a written transcript; (2) video only — with audio removed; or (3) paralinguistic only — the audio track with content filtered out but with paralinguistic features such as pitch, loudness, rate, and so forth, preserved. The subjects' judgments about the positivity or negativity of the emotions being expressed were compared to those of another group of subjects who viewed the standard videotape, which contained both audio and video. The judgments of subjects who read the written transcript — the verbal content — most closely matched the judgments of subjects with complete information (Krauss et al., 1981). The results of this study indicate that when the information provided by various channels is reasonably consistent, the verbal channel contributes most to the *accuracy* of our judgments of positivity and negativity of emotion.

But sometimes the information conveyed through various channels appears *inconsistent*. What do we do when that happens? Albert Mehrabian (1972) designed a study to answer this question. He had actors display contradictory verbal, paralinguistic, and facial cues. In deciding which emotions were the true ones, subjects judging the actors' emotions assigned the most importance to facial cues, less to paralinguistic cues, and the least importance to verbal cues. Although they may disagree on the exact proportion of meaning attributable to verbal and to nonverbal cues, many researchers have found evidence that when observers are faced with inconsistent information, they weigh nonverbal symbols most heavily and tend to give very little weight to verbal symbols (Argyle, Alkema, and Gilmour, 1971; Archer and Akert, 1977; DePaulo, et al., 1978). Perhaps we believe that nonverbal channels are more likely to reveal a person's "true" feelings when we don't trust the verbal channel.

In real life, of course, much depends on the situation, the kind of behavior being judged, and the availability of multiple channels of information. Studies suggest that, when they are available, we make use of multiple channels of information, interpreting each within the context of the others (Zuckerman, Depaulo, and Rosenthal, 1981; Harper, 1985; O'Sullivan et al., 1985).

What We Communicate

The previous section focused on the different types of symbols we use to communicate with others. Now let's turn to *what* we communicate — the various types of meaning we can convey through the use of symbols.

TASK INFORMATION

Some communicative behavior is, of course, task-oriented, or aimed at getting something done. For example, a boss communicates on the job in order to coordinate her actions with those of co-workers to produce a product, such as an automobile or a report. Thus, the boss tells her secretary when a report is needed and specifies the typeface and margins she requires. Or you might communicate with your friends about plans for a party in order to coordinate your actions with theirs so that everyone knows when and where the party will be and so that you don't end up with lots of munchies but no beer. A student calls his parents to tell them that he is working hard, but that this is a particularly difficult semester, in order to prepare them for the disappointing grades he anticipates.

Task information is perhaps the most obvious kind of information we communicate. But we inevitably communicate several kinds of meanings at once. Our communicative behavior reflects the intimacy of our relationships with other persons, reflects and reinforces our relative status in the group, and provides information about ourselves (Patterson, 1988).

EXPRESSIONS OF INTIMACY

Relationships vary in terms of intimacy, or closeness, and we provide symbols to communicate degrees of intimacy and liking to our partners and other, third-party observers. For example, a man might choose particular verbal and nonverbal behaviors to encourage observers of his interaction to perceive him as a loving spouse, a devoted friend, or a disinterested date.

Relationship partners sometimes cooperate to present a particular image of their relationship. A feuding marital couple might agree to present a harmonious image when they are in public. Their nonverbal behaviors, such as hand-holding and mutual gazing, serve to promote the desired image of their relationship. When partners in a close relationship enter a setting where their closeness is unknown to others, they often display "withness cues" (Scheflen and Ashcraft, 1976) or "tie-signs" (Goffman, 1971) to signal that they are a "couple." A jealous partner may initiate higher levels of nonverbal involvement toward his or her partner in order to "stake a claim" to the partner. On the other hand, exaggerated noninvolvement, such as sitting far apart, may be used to signal to others that the relationship is *not* a close one.

We use both verbal and nonverbal symbols to express and promote intimacy.

Intimacy with Words

Some languages, such as French and Spanish, have formal and familiar forms of second-person pronouns. In intimate relationships, the familiar form is used. Similarly, in most languages, forms of address indicate intimacy. We frequently use only first names in interactions with intimates, while titles and last names are more commonly used with strangers or those with whom we have only formal relationships. Imagine your mother's reaction if you were to insist on addressing her as "Mrs." followed by her last name — a more intimate form of address for your own mother is expected. But when you first meet a friend's mother, the formal "Mrs." would be considered appropriate.

Intimacy also affects conversational style. Analyses of telephone conversations have showed that, in comparison to strangers and casual acquaintances, friends use more implicit openings, such as "Hi" or "Hi. It's me." They also introduce more topics into their conversations and are more responsive to their friends (Hornstein, 1985). Other studies suggest that as closeness in-

creases, partners develop communication patterns (part of their internal culture) — including speech rhythms, pitch, and movements — that are increasingly personalized, synchronized, and efficient (Baxter and Wilmot, 1985).

Intimates often develop their own jargon — private symbols, including words and phrases commonly used by others, that have special meanings for them. When these words or phrases are used publicly, intimates may exchange a knowing glance, a wink, or a smile. A person is likely to feel disappointment if her or his partner uses these special words or way of talking with someone else.

Intimacy Without Words

Nonverbal behaviors can also indicate the closeness of relationships. In several studies, observers inferred stronger liking and higher levels of sexual involvement between partners whose level of reciprocated gaze was higher (Kleinke, Meeker, and LaFong, 1974; Thayer and Schiff, 1977). Other studies suggest that postural congruence or matching — in which participants assume postures that are carbon copies or mirror images of one another — reflect greater rapport or the desire to promote a closer relationship (LaFrance and Ickes, 1981).

In close relationships touch signals positive affect, such as support, appreciation, inclusion, sexual involvement, or affection (Jones and Yarbrough, 1985). Support touches are intended to nurture or reassure the other. Appreciation touches, which signal gratitude, are often accompanied by a verbal expression of thanks. Inclusion touches, such as holding hands or putting an arm around a partner, emphasize closeness. Touches signaling sexual interest usually involve holding or caressing the partner on the chest, pelvis, or buttocks. Affection touches are used to express general positive regard toward the partner.

EXPRESSIONS OF STATUS

An individual's status is his or her relative standing vis-à-vis others, and a person's status may differ from one social situation to the next. A

Touch is often used in close relationships to signal positive affect, such as support, appreciation, inclusion, sexual involvement, or affection. Can you tell which kind of affect is being communicated in each photo?

college sophomore may have relatively low status compared with seniors but high status relative to freshmen. The same person may have high status among the friends with whom he plays poker on Thursday nights but lower status among those with whom he plays softball on Tuesday afternoons. In social situations, persons with higher status generally exercise greater power and control. Status is reflected and reinforced through communicative behaviors.

Status with Words

Relative status in relationships is clearly communicated by forms of address. People with lower status use formal forms of address for those with higher status. People with higher status often use familiar forms to address those whose status is lower. Two people with equal status tend to employ the same form of address with each other. Both will use either formal ("Dr.," "Mrs.," "Ms.," "Professor") or familiar ("John," "Pat") forms, depending on how well they know each other. When we are unsure about our status relative to someone else, we are faced with a dilemma. A familiar example is the problem of what to call our in-laws — "Mr. and Mrs."? "Mom and Dad"? or (after the arrival of grandchildren) "Grandma and Grandpa"? When we feel uncertain about how to address someone, we sometimes avoid calling him or her anything at all (Little and Gelles, 1975). Other strategies for masking our uncertainty without using a formal title that confers too much status or a familiar address that confers too little include using ambiguous forms of address (such as "Sir," "Miss," "Ma'am," or "Ms.") or inventing an in-between form (such as "Doc" for a physician or professor).

Our choices of vocabularies and pronunciations reflect our relative status and, consequently, influence our relationships. We often adjust our speech to express status differences appropriate to changing situations (Stiles et al., 1984). For example, there are words and phrasings we would use with our children but not with our spouses, and vice versa. A person might tell a child, "Pick up all those magazines you left in the living room, right now!" but the same person would probably address a spouse more politely: "The living room sure is getting messy." In our culture, polite, indirect phrasing is considered more appropriate between equal-status adults.

Similarly, social class and racial, ethnic, and regional differences in vocabulary, pronunciation, and speech style can have a large impact on communication. Recall our discussion in Chapter 3, "Socialization over the Life Course," regarding class differences in communication styles that not only reflect but also perpetuate status differences from one generation to the next.

Paralinguistic behaviors also communicate status. Higher-status speakers talk more frequently, longer, and more loudly and interrupt their partners more in conversations than do lower-status speakers (Brown, 1980; Street and Brady, 1982; Cappella, 1985; Street and Cappella, 1985; Weimann, 1985; Street and Buller, 1988). People with lower status show that they are paying attention by such responses as "Mmmm" at appropriate times. When people of the same status interact, they use these paralinguistic cues more equally (Leffler, Gillespie, and Conaty, 1982). Studies suggest that influence is enhanced by using the paralinguistic behaviors deemed appropriate to one's status in the group (Ridgeway, 1987).

Status Without Words

Status is also communicated through body language (Mazur et al., 1980; Edinger and Patterson, 1983; Givens, 1983). When a person in authority talks to a subordinate, the lower-ranking person listens intently and keeps his or her eyes riveted to the superior. Looking about would indicate disrespect. But when the subordinate is speaking, it is deemed appropriate for the boss to look around or gaze at his or her watch. And people in submissive roles tend to crouch slightly and display self-protective stances (e.g., folding their arms or hugging themselves, crossing their legs, or reaching up and touching their throats). People in dominant roles typically use more expansive gestures, (such as spreading their arms and legs, thereby creating an air of assurance) (Leffler, Gillespie, and Conaty, 1982).

A person can convey his or her higher status by patting a low-status person on the back or shoulder, a behavior not permitted to a person of subordinate rank. And the high-status person takes the lead. If he or she remains standing, then the subordinate is also expected to stand. Only when the high-status person sits can the lower-status person feel free to sit down.

INFORMATION ABOUT OURSELVES: FACEWORK

Some of our communication behavior is designed to deliberately present or enhance an identity or image we have of ourselves or of our relationships. Such actions illustrate that meanings are not fixed entities that set in motion an automatic unfolding of behavior. The activities of others enter as factors in the formation of our own conduct.

The need for the negotiation occurs when interactants do not share definitions of the situation. For example, suppose that Linda, the chairperson of a committee, is making a request of Paul, an older colleague on the committee. If Paul defines the situation as one in which he, an older, experienced committee member, should be advising an inexperienced younger committee member, he and Linda are likely to see each other as being too directive. When this happens, each is likely to ask, "What's going on here?" By getting additional information from each other and making adjustments, Linda and Paul may reach a shared definition of the situation — or they may not. The flow of the interaction will be affected by their ability or inability to arrive at a single script to govern the interaction.

Upon discovering that something is wrong — in this case, each one's thinking that the other is being too directive — Linda and Paul might respond by providing additional information about their own meanings. Linda might say, "Well, as chair of the committee, I think we should . . . ," or Paul might say, "If you had more experience, I think you would see that. . . ." These phrases would at least let each of them know where the other was "coming from."

From here, they might come to agreement by either one's giving up his or her own position in favor of the other's or by reaching a compromise (e.g., the young, inexperienced chair of the committee is making a polite request of the older, experienced, distinguished member of the committee). On the other hand, each might cling to his or her early meanings or adjust them so that they are even more discrepant. For example, Linda might change her definition of the situation to portray herself as the young, promising chair of the committee arguing with an old stick-in-the-mud committee member. Paul's definition might depict himself as the experienced, distinguished committee member being insulted by the uppity young chairperson. Whether Linda's interaction with the older committee member proceeds smoothly or problematically or is terminated altogether depends in part on whether she and Paul can arrive at a mutually acceptable definition of the situation.

In Chapter 1, we first mentioned sociologist Erving Goffman and his ideas about "impression management" — the routine ways in which we try to manage the impressions of ourselves as well as those of others. In everyday life, we often explain our own and other people's behavior through appeals to "face" (Tracy, 1990; Holtgraves, 1992): I was trying to give him a way to *save face. Face* is a social phenomenon referring to our concern with personal reputation — the public images we claim for ourselves or attribute to others. The communication strategies we use to enact, support, or challenge these public images are called **facework** (Goffman, 1955). Facework is one of the ways we negotiate with others about the meanings of our actions. The goal of such conduct is to enhance or protect our own face claims and/or to support or challenge others' face claims. According to Goffman (1971), these strategies are either "corrective" or "preventive."

Corrective Facework

Corrective facework consists of practices we employ to restore face *after* it has been attacked or threatened. Sociologist C. Wright Mills noted, in a classic article, that along with learning norms of action for various situations we learn acceptable explanations, which he called "vocabularies of motive" (1940: 909). For example, we often use *accounts* — explanations we offer to make our inappropriate behavior appear more reasonable (Cody and McLaughlin, 1985; Snyder, 1985). Accounts take four forms: excuses, justifications, concessions, and refusals. *Excuses* are statements admitting the inappropriateness of our behavior or its consequence but denying our responsibility for it. For instance, "I know you had to wait a long time because I was late, but I had a flat tire." *Justifications* are statements we provide that admit responsibility for our behavior or its consequence but deny its inappropriateness, reinterpreting it in a more socially acceptable manner: "You would have hit him too if he had said that about your wife."

In a *concession*, we neither deny responsibility nor attempt to justify our conduct. Rather, we simply admit to the failure in question and frequently offer an apology or expression of remorse or offer to make restitution: "I acted foolishly; I'm sorry." On the other hand, *refusals* involve denying that the act in question was actually committed: "I was *not* late! I said I'd be here at 3:30!" Refusals may also include a denial of the other party's right to punish; "Don't you dare scold *me* for being late! How late were *you* last night?" Accounts are discussed further in the box "Facework by Students: Accounts for Absences."

To minimize threats to others' face, we are often studiously inattentive to small lapses in their behavior (Edelman, 1985; Cupach, Metts, and Hazelton, 1986; Knapp, Stafford, and Daly, 1986). For example, we might pretend not to notice the quiet burp emitted by the person seated next to us at the table. We sometimes provide facework to protect the reputations of others. "It's OK, I know you are busy" may give a spouse a (corrective) excuse for her or his failure to pick up the dry cleaning.

Preventive Facework

Whereas corrective facework consists of the practices we engage in *after* our face is damaged or threatened, *preventive facework* consists of the things we do *when we anticipate* damage to face. We use such practices to avoid punishment for a future behavior or to assess the consequences of our actions. For example, asking someone to do something for us reduces our face if we are seen to have acted inappropriately. We can reduce the face threat of making such requests in several ways: (1) by seeking permission to make the request in the first place — "May I ask you a favor?"; (2) by offering an excuse for making the request — "I'm going to *have* to miss our next class because I have a job interview at that time"; or (3) by pleading — "Please, this is very important to me."

We also protect our face by using *disclaimers* intended to convey that, despite our present behavior, we normally abide by the rules: "I normally wouldn't ask to be excused from class, but. . . ." When making what another person might consider a negative statement or criticism, we might use a disclaimer such as, "I know I shouldn't say this, but . . ." or "I'm not prejudiced, but. . . ." When offering advice that may not be well received, we might say, "I know I'm not an expert, but . . ." or "I know it's none of my business, but. . . ." These tactics take away the other person's ability to damage our face by pointing out our weakness: "You're no expert!" or "It's none of your business!"

We may protect the face claims of ourselves and others by preceding a request with a question that suggests to them an excuse for their refusal. For example, "Are you going to be home tonight?" allows the person to answer "No" (without embarrassment to either party) before being placed in the position of refusing a request to pay the person a visit.

Individuals differ in the face concerns they bring to each interaction (O'Keefe and Shepherd, 1987; O'Keefe, 1988). An insecure person may approach the interaction hoping only to avoid embarrassment, while a confident, outgoing person may want to be the focus of attention. And the face wants that individuals pursue may be different in different contexts. For example, sometimes we want to be seen as fun and likable, and other times we want to be seen as firm or even intimidating. This means that communicators need to

FACEWORK BY STUDENTS: ACCOUNTS FOR ABSENCES

Kathleen Kalab (1987) studied the "vocabularies of motive" provided by students when they missed her introductory sociology and social psychology classes. She told her students on the first day of class that they would be expected to give her a written reason for any missed class. Over two semesters, she received 270 notes.

When she analyzed the notes, Kalab found that only about 8 percent contained *justifications*. All of the justifications used by Kalab's students were "appeals to higher loyalties." They suggested that although the student was responsible for missing class—normally a bad thing—doing so was necessary because obligations to relatives and friends had to be placed ahead of the obligation to be in class on a particular date: "The reason I wasn't in your class last Friday and Monday is because my grandmother had a stroke and I had to fly home early." "On [date] I had to attend the funeral of a friend's mother." "Here we go again! I really am sorry to have missed your class [date]. Believe it or not, a friend of mine (not myself) got stranded? at a motel. She called me up Friday morning and like a fool I missed class to pick her up in Russellville. What else could I do?" (Kalab, 1987: 74–75).

Most of the accounts Kalab received were *excuses*. In these notes students admitted to the negative aspect of missing class but attempted to lessen their individual responsibility through the use of five major themes: reference to biological factors, control by another person, oversleeping, other coursework, and accidents. It is not surprising that students made illness their number-one excuse, because illness is commonly recognized as an excuse for not fulfilling various social obligations. It is also an excuse that can be used more than once without being viewed skeptically—and it was used more than once by many of Kalab's students.

Excuses involving control by another person included organizational demands ("The reason for missing your class on Friday, [date] was because I had a cross-country meet to run and we left at 10:30 a.m."); appointments set by others with higher status ("I missed your class on Friday in order to make a doctor's appointment."); and ride providers ("I was absent Friday [date] because my only ride home was leaving at 1:00. I hadn't been home in an awfully long time. Thanks.").

A third, and less common, theme among excuses was oversleeping. Intentional wit and humor were more likely to be used in notes about oversleeping than in those for other excuses. One student wrote, "I'm sorry I missed Friday. My id took over and wouldn't let my superego in until it was too late. Basically I overslept. (I had no intention of missing.) Thank you." Most students who used oversleeping as a reason seemed to recognize it as a rather weak excuse for missing class; very few students used it as an excuse more than once.

Some students' excuses involved missing class in order to do other classwork: "I am sorry that I was not in class on Wednesday [date]. I was studying for a very very important test. Thank you." When using the "other classwork" excuse, students were more serious than when writing about oversleeping. Only one student used this excuse more than once.

The final, and least used, type of excuse Kalab identified in her study involved accidents. Accounts that attribute responsibility to accidents emphasize hazards in the environment. The appeal to accidents often works because we all know that we cannot totally control our environment. Almost half the students' accident notes referred to faulty alarm clocks. The most unique excuse Kalab received was in the accident category:

> I was absent Friday, [date] because the dye I used Thursday night to turn my hair black somehow changed to green when I washed it Friday morning. I'm talking green-bean green! I spent 3 hours and 36 dollars to return my hair to a normal hair color. (Kalab, 1987: 80)

As with oversleeping and other coursework, accident excuses were not used more than once. Kalab notes that accident excuses are not likely to work if they are overused. We honor such excuses precisely because they do not occur often.

A few of the notes Kalab received provided neither excuses nor justifications for missing class. For whatever reason, on these occasions, the students didn't try to explain their negative act in a way designed to protect or restore their face. One note said:

> Yes, I was absent from your class on Friday, [date]. (Bet it was a whole lot quieter!) I have no good excuse. I didn't go home. I blew off *all* my classes Friday. And I'll be honest—I enjoyed every minute of it. Thank you. (Kalab, 1987: 82)

And another simply stated, "I can't remember why I was absent Wed."

decide which aspect of another's identity is governing the other's face claims in a particular situation. In fact, orienting remarks to a contextually inappropriate face of the other may be (or may be seen as) a strategy to attack the other or to enhance one's own face.

Even in a single situation, our face needs may conflict. We want to be connected to, and intimate with, others, but we also want to be independent and autonomous. We might want to be both fair and firm. We want to be honest *and* considerate. Behaviors that support one of the face needs can undermine the other. We sometimes deal with such conflict through a kind of facework called *equivocating* (Bavelas, 1983, 1985; Bavelas and Chovil, 1986; Bavelas et al., 1988). For example, if someone gives us a gift that we don't really like, we might equivocate by responding, "Oh, how thoughtful of you!"

Social situations also sometimes involve tensions between the face needs of interactants. In some situations, to protect our own face, we must challenge someone else's (Craig, Tracy, and Spisak, 1986). For example, to protect her identity as a competent student, a woman who has just received a failing grade on an exam might portray her professor as incompetent by suggesting that he gave inadequate instructions about what the exam would cover, wrote unclear questions on the exam, or misgraded.

Nothing guarantees that our facework, whether corrective or preventive, will soothe the interaction and allow us to avoid or reduce the disruptive consequences of our actions. Instead, the facework itself may become a *second* source of controversy: "You are always late! I'm sick of your excuses!"

We have seen that communication takes place through the exchange of various types of symbols, both verbal and nonverbal, which convey various types of meaning—about tasks, intimacy, status, and self. We noted that communication involves the negotiation of meanings and have discussed some of the processes through which negotiation takes place. Now let's turn to a discussion of *how* we communicate—the rules of conversation.

How We Communicate:
Rules of Conversation

All human encounters involve, in one way or another, the transfer of information. If we were capable of sending and receiving information simultaneously, regardless of the complexity and amount of information presented, we would not need rules governing the flow of information. However, because humans have finite information-processing capacities, human interactions must be governed by some rules of procedure that control the flow of information and signal when speaking and listening roles are to be switched. Besides solving technical problems of sequencing, so that communication can take place more smoothly, these rules of procedure also influence our impressions of who is in control of a situation, who is a competent social actor, who is friendly, and who is shy. Thus, interpersonal power, status, competence, and attraction depend, at least partly, on our ability to control speaking and listening roles (Cappella, 1985).

Both verbal behavior and nonverbal behaviors such as gaze, touch, facial expressions, postural shifts, gestures, and paralinguistic cues often signal immediate or impending changes in the state of conversation (Button and Lee, 1987; Leeds-Hurwitz, 1989; Goodwin and Heritage, 1990; Boden and Zimmerman, 1991; Maynard and Clayman, 1991). The regulation of conversation, such as who should speak when and about what, usually occurs without our awareness. As an analogy, consider how we navigate a crowded sidewalk. Through mutual glances and gestures we communicate with one another about our speed and direction of movement so as to minimize collisions. In effect, these glances and gestures function as routing or crash-avoidance devices. Just as we want to avoid collisions on sidewalks and streets, it is desirable to avoid simultaneous talking in conversations. Typically, we take turns in speaking and listening. We spend relatively little time in mutual silence or simultaneous talking, and usually the transitions from one speaker to another are without perceptible speaker overlap or pause (Trimboli and Walker, 1982, 1984).

How do we manage to avoid verbally bumping into one another in our conversations? The answer lies in the rules and signals with which we regulate conversation.

INITIATING CONVERSATIONS

When and how to start a conversation is governed by several rules. *Initiation rules* encourage us to initiate conversations in some situations and discourage us from doing so in others. For example, whenever we encounter friends or acquaintances we are almost always expected to say "Hi" and are frequently expected to initiate small talk or conversation. We are expected *not* to begin conversations with strangers in the same settings.

Conversations may be initiated with an *attention-getting sequence* such as a greeting, question, knock on the door, or ring of the telephone. Such efforts may be successful or not. In response to an attention-getting attempt, the person being addressed may signal that he or she is paying attention and is ready to interact. In face-to-face interaction, eye contact is a critical signal of availability. For example, a voice from down the hall calls "Sally!" Sally looks toward the voice and sees John, and she returns the greeting, "Hi, John!" John smiles and waves and then turns his gaze back to the bulletin board in front of him. No further interaction takes place. If John smiles and waves and *holds* Sally's gaze, Sally is under an obligation to interact further (Goffman, 1981). When people ignore our attention-getting attempts — violating the rules of conversation — we consider them rude, snobbish, or psychologically absent (absorbed in other thoughts, asleep, intoxicated, and so on).

If the attention-getting sequence is successful, it will probably be followed by a *"how are you" sequence* before another topic is introduced. For example:

J: Sally!
S: Hi, John! What's up?
J: Not much. What about with you?
S: Been studying for my physics exam. Are you going to the party on Friday?

Most telephone conversations begin with an attention-getting/answer sequence, followed by an *identification-recognition sequence*, and then by a "how are you" sequence, before another topic is introduced (Schegloff, 1979):

[Ring]
W: Hello.
S: Dr. Wiggins?
W: Yes.
S: Hi. This is Mary Jenkins . . . from your Soc. 51 class. How are you?
W: Fine, thanks, Mary. What can I do for you?
S: Well, um . . . I'm not going to be able to be in class on Friday for the exam.

In face-to-face situations that do not offer us much information about *who* the other person is (such as at a large party where most of the other guests are strangers to us), we may also proceed with an identification-recognition sequence, in part as a search for an opening topic of conversation:

A: Hi, I'm Todd Baker.
B: Hello, I'm Joanne Summers.
A: Are you a friend of Joe's [the party's host]?
B: I guess you could say so. I'm his fiancée. What about you?
A: Oh, I just met Joe. I came to the party with a mutual friend — Paul Andrews.

This sequence offers enough information to continue the conversation if the two participants desire to do so. For example, Todd could ask Joanne about her wedding plans. Joanne could ask how Todd knows Paul Andrews or how Paul Andrews knows Joe. On the other hand, Todd may be hoping for a romantic encounter with someone at the party, and discovering that Joanne is Joe's fiancée may squelch his interest in pursuing the conversation. Similarly, if Joanne doesn't know Paul Andrews, Todd and Joanne's conversation topics are limited, and they may begin to look elsewhere for conversation partners.

In special situations, we dispense with most, if not all, of these initiation sequences. We seldom engage in them with our intimates. In emergencies, we dispense with them even when initiating a conversation with a stranger. For example, Whalen and Zimmerman (1987) have observed that emergency phone calls dispense with greetings in order to get more quickly to the reason for the call:

[Ring]
P: Newton Police.
C: I'd like to report a stolen car.
P: Your name?
C: Jack Jones.
P: Address?

The first response to the attention getter (ring) also verifies for the caller that he has reached the intended party (the police). The caller immediately states his reason for calling. Then the police officer asks questions to obtain the critical information needed to respond to the request for help. A similar modification of face-to-face interaction patterns occurs in emergency situations:

A: Hey! I can use some help here. This woman has fainted.
B: Have you called an ambulance?

Some role relationships allow us to skip initiation sequences. For example, it is acceptable for a waiter to skip the initiation rituals and ask a customer, "Are you ready to order?" Although the customer is otherwise a stranger, his or her strangeness is not absolute. The waiter and customer each are aware of the role of the other, and being in these reciprocal roles makes an initiation ritual unnecessary.

Initiation rules also *discourage* us from initiating conversations in some situations. For example, most of us are hesitant to interrupt when someone is busy, to initiate conversations with strangers, or to talk during class, a movie, or a church service.

However, violations of these rules may be excused if prefaced by *intrusion sequences* which offer an acknowledgment or apology for the intrusion:

"Excuse me" or "Sorry to bother you." This may be followed by a signal from the person being addressed which indicates that the speaker can proceed with her or his intended conversation ("That's OK, what is it you want?") or by a signal indicating that the intrusion is not welcome ("I'm busy. What do you want?")

In some encounters with strangers, the rules against initiating conversations are relaxed. Simply sharing a situation with others provides us with some information about them, offering us an excuse for initiating conversation. For example, we may be attending a party, waiting in line for a bus or basketball tickets, or sharing a view of the Grand Canyon. In such situations we probably could comment on the particular situation we are currently sharing without breaching an intrusion rule: "Why don't they stop those guys from breaking into the line?" "Nice camera!" While these comments probably would not be considered offensive, they may or may not lead to an extended conversation, and we would be expected to respect the other's privacy if he or she did not encourage us to pursue the conversation.

KEEPING CONVERSATIONS GOING

We have described how we initiate conversations, but how do we keep them going? Communication is a shared social accomplishment. Through verbal and nonverbal feedback, listeners help us assess how effectively we are communicating. Any subtle vocal or nonverbal response that a listener makes while a speaker is talking is called **back-channel feedback**. This feedback helps us know whether we are keeping our listeners' interest and being understood. Listeners may signal their *attention* to us by simply looking at us, perhaps occasionally nodding their heads. To indicate that they *understand* us, they may use brief vocal insertions such as "Oh," "Yeah," "OK," or "I see"; complete our unfinished sentences; or restate in a few words our preceding thoughts (Kraut, Lewis, and Swezey, 1982; Jefferson, 1984; Heritage, 1984b). Smiles and laughs as well as frowns and tears may indicate understanding *if they are appropriate to the speaker's topic*. For example, a listener's laugh following a speakers's joke indicates under-standing. However, if it follows a serious com-ment, it indicates that the listener does not understand or is trying to disrupt the speaker's talking (Jefferson, 1985; Drew, 1987). Listeners also unconsciously display subtle rhythmic body movements — such as swaying, rocking, and blink-ing — that are precisely synchronized with the speech sounds of the speaker when communica-tion is going well (Kendon, Harris, and Key, 1970).

The timing of feedback is also important, often occurring when the speaker pauses or turns his or her head toward the listener. When listener feed-back is mistimed or absent, the speaker may un-dertake some "repair work" in order to regain the listener's attention and involvement — by insert-ing "You know," "You see," or "Understand?" prior to or after pauses (Fishman, 1980) or by asking simple yes-no questions such as "OK so far?" or "Are you with me?" (Goodwin, 1987a). If we feel the listener is not paying attention or doesn't understand, we may restart the conversa-tion with such phrases as "What I mean to say . . ." or "My point is. . . ." If these efforts fail to repair the conversation, our speech is likely to deteriorate, becoming more wordy, less efficient, and more general. We may hesitate or even stop talking.

REGULATING TURN TAKING

As speakers, we are interested not only in main-taining our listeners' attention and understanding but also in keeping the floor. We do not want to be interrupted until we have made our points, and we exhibit cues that maintain our turns. One way to do this is to verbally indicate that we intend to make a series of remarks, for example, "First of all" or "To begin with," followed by "Another thing." We may signal our desire to keep speak-ing by maintaining the same voice pitch and keep-ing our heads straight, our eyes unchanged, and our hands gesturing. As we near what would nor-mally be the point where someone else would talk, we may talk faster, filling the pauses with sounds such as "uh" and "umm" or deliberately avoid

finishing a sentence by ending each utterance with "and . . ." or "but the umm. . . ." At the same time, our listeners signal their willingness to allow us to continue speaking by using some of the same cues they use to indicate attention and understanding — for example, an "mm-hmm" or a nod of the head (Schegloff, 1987a, b).

However, turns at talking do not always pro-ceed smoothly. Sometimes we are interrupted. As with intrusions in initiating conversations, some interruptions of ongoing talk evoke an apology — an intrusion ritual; others do not. When seeking a point of clarification, a listener may interrupt a speaker by raising a hand and/or saying, "Excuse me. What do you mean?" When attempting to challenge a speaker's information, a listener for-goes the pleasantries of an intrusion ritual; the intruding listener may try to complete the speak-er's sentence and then continue on with his or her own sentence, may say something like "Just wait a minute. Do you really believe that? That's ab-surd," or may laugh when the speaker is obviously being serious. Of course, a speaker can attempt to rebuff an interruption with a raised hand, indi-cating "Let me finish," or may increase the vol-ume of her or his voice to drown out the in-terruption.

Some interruptions are more permanent than others. An interruption that takes the floor from the original speaker for a brief time and then returns it to the speaker is called a *side sequence*. A side sequence may be initiated by a listener. For example, a listener might attempt to correct a speaker with a brief phrase: "Classes begin on *Wednesday*, not *Monday*." The length of the side sequence depends on how the speaker responds to the correction. The speaker might accept the cor-rection immediately and proceed without missing a beat, or the speaker could reject the correction, diverting the original conversation to a discussion of the side sequence (Jefferson, 1987; Cheepen, 1988).

A side sequence can be initiated by the speaker as well as the listener. For example, as speakers, we might initiate a side sequence if we are forget-ful or uncertain about a piece of information we need to continue talking (Goodwin, 1987a). We may turn to a potentially knowledgeable person and invite that person (with nothing more than a gaze) to share in our search for the information. This has the effect of elevating the status of listener to that of informed speaker. Or when a telephone call interrupts a conversation, the speaker may use an expression such as "Excuse me, please" to initiate the side sequence and another such as "Sorry. Now where were we?" to mark its end and the return to the original conversation.

Having taken a turn at conversation, we can signal that it is the listener's turn to talk. Turn-taking signals involve a number of behavioral cues that are displayed either singly or simultaneously during a conversation. A speaker can indicate a willingness to yield a turn by any of the following signals (Duncan, 1972; Schegloff, 1987*a*; Sachs, 1990):

1. *Gaze:* The speaker gazes directly at the listener toward the end of an utterance.
2. *Body motion:* The speaker ends the hand gesturing he or she used while talking or relaxes tensed hands. If the speaker asks a question such as "What time is it?" or "Where are you going?" his or her head comes up on "it" or on the *ing* in "going." The speaker's eyes also tend to open wider with the last note of a question, as a signal for the other person to start his or her answer.
3. *Paralingual drawl:* The speaker utters the final syllable or a stressed syllable of a terminal clause in a slow, drawn-out manner.
4. *Intonation:* The speaker raises or lowers his or her voice as evidence of a terminal (ending) clause. An example would be raising the voice on "this" in the question "Do you like this?"
5. *Verbal clues:* The speaker utters a stereotyped expression — "but uh" or "you know" — followed by a phrase: "But uh, I guess that's just the way he is." Questions are also an important turn-yielding signal.

Listeners can signal that they are seeking a turn through cues such as inhaling audibly, gesturing

with their hands, beginning a vocalization while shifting their heads away from us, or expressing especially loud vocal responses indicating interest — "Yes!" Such subtle and taken-for-granted (unconscious) mechanisms make communication easier. They make possible back-and-forth exchange without the need of saying, "Are you finished? Now I will talk."

Because of the absence of nonverbal cues, we might expect more turn-taking problems in telephone conversations. However, research does not support this expectation (Rutter, 1987). In fact, the only clear difference supported by research is that there are *fewer* interruptions on the telephone. Thus, although successful turn taking can be accomplished using nonverbal cues, such cues are not necessary, as interruptions can be avoided through the exclusive use of verbal cues.

TERMINATING CONVERSATIONS

We do not conclude conversations any more arbitrarily than we begin, continue, or interrupt them. Two people do not simply stop talking and abruptly walk away from each other. Just as there are initiation rituals, there are also *termination rituals*. Some rituals are short; others, particularly those that require the negotiation of a conversation closure, take more time (Button, 1987). The length of the termination ritual is influenced by such factors as the status of the participants, the setting, and the willingness of a participant to violate the termination rules.

Termination rituals between persons of equal status usually involve some prepping before the final goodbyes. Such rituals are initiated by one of the participants and may involve many components. For example, a person might close a conversation with an acquaintance by saying, "I'd better be going. Nice talking with you. See you." In this case, the final goodbye was preceded by an initiation of the closing ("I'd better be going") and an appreciation statement ("Nice talking with you").

With friends or intimates, a termination ritual might be more elaborate. For example, a student might say, "Sorry! Gotta run. Okay? Thanks for the help. See you after class. Bye." In this example, not only did the closing include an initiation ("Gotta run"), an appreciation ("Thanks for the help"), and a final goodbye ("Bye"), but it was extended by a request for the friend to approve terminating the conversation ("Okay?") as well as an arrangement for initiating the next conversation ("See you after class"). Some termination rituals might be punctuated with a hug or kiss.

In some situations we terminate conversations with friends or intimates more abruptly. For example, if two friends are accustomed to routinely terminating their conversations at a particular point — during a walk to class or work together, for instance — their termination ritual may be as brief as a nod of the head, "Bye," or "See ya." Other components of the ritual are assumed and therefore not spoken; for example, there is no need to include the explanation for closing and an arrangement for reopening the conversation in the future. On another occasion, the closing may be no more than "Oh, no! I forgot about the pie in the oven!" as the person turns and dashes away. Although the words suggest an explanation for the departure, the loss of eye contact suggests that the person is not asking for anyone's approval to leave (Goodwin, 1987*b*).

A termination attempt may be resisted whether or not it includes an actual request of the other party to approve it. It may be countered with "Oh, just one more thing. . . ." Such resistance is usually hard to overcome, whether it occurs in a face-to-face conversation or on the telephone. There isn't much the participant making the attempt can do other than repeat the termination ritual, emphasizing his or her explanation. The person might suggest another conversation in the near future: "I'll call you back tomorrow." In a face-to-face conversation, he or she can slowly decrease eye contact and move farther away from the other person. But abruptly turning away — or hanging up — without waiting for the other person's goodbye is "against the rules" and therefore requires repair work in the next conversation.

Termination rituals are somewhat different when the parties are of unequal status. For example, a superior may conclude a conversation with a subordinate abruptly, with little fanfare. On the other hand, you know your status is higher when the other person — instead of closing the conversation abruptly — asks if you want to extend the conversation. This occurs, for example, when a salesperson asks, "Can I help you with anything else?"

However, other factors may override the effects of status differences. Television news interviews, for example, usually operate with pre-specified closing times (Clayman, 1989). It would be considered rude for either the interviewer or the interviewee to leave early. However, once the agreed-upon ending time arrives, it is often the higher-status person who exercises the right to terminate the interaction. You have probably noticed that it is not uncommon for the president to leave his press conferences with the press's questions still ringing in his ears.

TALK IN INSTITUTIONAL SETTINGS

The conversational rules we have been discussing apply to mundane (everyday) conversations; thus they apply to a diversity of roles and conversation topics. In social institutions, which involve a narrower range of topics and relatively specialized identities, these conversational rules are often modified to better address the interactional contingencies of the particular setting (Heritage, 1984*a*; Whalen and Zimmerman, 1987; Zimmerman and Boden, 1991). For example, turn taking is governed by different rules within the settings of particular institutions, such as classrooms, courtrooms, emergency rooms, and corporate boardrooms. Institution-specific rules may specify the order of speakers as well as how long each can talk, who can interrupt whom in what manner, and, sometimes, what the topic of conversation is (West and Frankel, 1991). The rules may also specify who can make or enforce these kinds of rules, for example, the judge in a courtroom (Philips, 1990). The incumbents of particular roles such as police officers, teachers, doctors, lawyers, and interviewers typically begin the conversation, ask the questions, sometimes interrupt or select the next speaker, and decide when the conversa-

In social institutions, conversational rules are often modified to better address the interactional contingencies of the particular setting.

tion will end. These are the people in charge. On the other hand, others such as students, patients, witnesses, and interviewees follow the formers' initiatives. In some instances, the question-answer activities are reversed. For example, in a classroom or at a press conference the teacher or the politician/expert becomes the interviewee, while the students or the press become the interviewers. However, the teacher or politician still initiates the conversation by selecting the questioner and probably sets most of the agenda of the interview.

To the extent that participants in an institutional setting, such as a courtroom, organize their conversations in a way that is distinctive from everyday conversation, they are both *displaying* and *creating* the unique institutional character of that setting (Heritage and Greatbatch, 1991). Each institution has its own unique pattern of modifications. These vary from culture to culture, and they are subject to processes of social change.

THE COOPERATIVE PRINCIPLE

To make their purposes understood, speakers sometimes explicitly state their intent: "I am asking for your help." "I am telling you to stop right now." "I insist that you leave now." "I invite you to come tomorrow." "I apologize for being late." "I promise to get the paper." "I'm warning you that it is not enough." Most languages also provide standard ways of combining words and intonation to convey a speaker's purpose. In English, for example, there are standard ways of using word order, verb forms, and intonation to convey asking ("Is Wendy here?"), telling ("Wendy is here"), and commanding ("Come here, Wendy!").

More often, however, we indicate our intentions much more indirectly. For example, when Carol telephones Tricia and Jonathan answers, she might ask, "Is Tricia there?" Carol expects Jonathan to understand from this that she wants to speak to Tricia; she isn't simply asking for a yes or no answer. If Tricia is home, Carol expects Jonathan to reply, "Yes, I'll get her." If she isn't home, Carol expects something like, "No, may I take a message?" or "No, she'll be back about nine." These answers acknowledge that Carol wants to speak to Tricia, even though she didn't say so directly. Similarly, when you say to your roommate, "I'm hungry," you expect him to know that you are not simply stating a fact but want the two of you to start doing something about it. Depending on the setting, you might mean "Is there anything in the refrigerator that I could eat?" or "Let's stop what we're doing and go get some dinner."

Obviously, people often mean much more than they actually say. How do listeners figure out the more indirect meanings? Philosopher H. Paul Grice (1975, 1978) has argued that we do this, partly, by relying on a **cooperative principle** — an assumption that speakers are trying to be (1) informative (but not overly informative), (2) truthful, (3) relevant, and (4) clear (unambiguous and brief).

Consider this example: Adam is standing by a car on the side of a dusty rural road as Bob comes along on foot. Adam says, "I'm out of gas." Bob replies, "There's a fruit stand around the corner and another one a little farther down the road on the left." How should Adam interpret Bob's reply? Taking Bob's remarks at face value, Adam might think that Bob is entirely unconcerned with his problem and wants him to buy some fruit at the local stand. But if Adam relies on the cooperative principle, his thinking may be along these lines: Bob thinks the fruit stands are my closest sources of help (he is trying to help by giving good information; he knows and is being truthful about where they are). Maybe the fruit stands also sell gas or have a phone I can use to call for help (they must be relevant to my being out of gas). Why did Bob mention two fruit stands? He must think it's possible that the closest stand won't solve the problem (it might be closed), so he gave me more information, just in case. (Adam assumes Bob wouldn't give unnecessary information because the principle of cooperation says speakers should be brief.)

Suppose you point toward a group of ten dancers and say to the friend next to you, "*That* is Sandra's brother." Your friend assumes that, if you are acting cooperatively, you have given her all the information she needs to pick out the unique dancer to whom you are referring. If nine of the dancers are female, your friend will know that Sandra's brother is the sole male dancer. But what if all the dancers are male? She will look for something that sets one dancer apart from the others. ("Really? The *naked* one?")

Cooperation is essential to language use and, more generally, to all communication. Speakers say what they say intending it to be understood a certain way by their listeners. We talk to convince, request, apologize, warn, and promise. To succeed, we have to rely on the cooperative principle (Clark, 1985; Schiffrin, 1990).

Group Differences in Communication

Not everyone uses the same style of communication. We do not all share the same interpretation of particular cues; in other words, not all cues are significant symbols. Nor do we necessarily interact using the same rules of conversation (e.g., some of us use repair work, which others ignore). Some of these differences occur between individuals; others are differences between groups of people. There are several explanations for the communication differences that distinguish groups (Coupland, Giles, and Weimann, 1991): (1) People use different communication styles (including different languages and jargon) because they come from different cultures or have specialized socialization and training. (2) Different developmental levels of the "same" language may account for different communication styles, such as those seen in conversations between adults and children. (3) People may use different channels of communication because of physical restriction; for example, the sight-, hearing-, or speech-impaired who cannot receive or send information through particular channels and, at the same time, may use cues that the nonimpaired have difficulty interpreting. (4) Biological explanations suggest that genetic differences between categories of persons result in different communication styles. (5) As we have discussed previously, communication differences can be a vehicle for the display of one person's power or status over another. When we encounter someone whose symbols or communication style is different from our own, we often make the judgment that our own style of communication is "the correct one" and other styles are "deviant" — not just different, but bad or *inferior* (Henley and Kramarae, 1991).

Obviously, communication differences, whatever their source, can lead to communication problems between people who have occasion to interact with one another. Our reactions to others whose communication styles are different vary. Sometimes we lower our expectations of the abilities of those using other styles; for example, we may use baby talk when interacting with children, the elderly, the impaired, and even those whose native language is different from our own. Sometimes we attempt to change the communication styles of those whose styles differ from our own; for instance, we may oppose bilingual education. A third way we react to these differences is by avoiding opportunities to interact with dissimilar others; for example, we may adhere to the segregation of ingroup and outgroup members (a topic discussed in Chapter 4, "Social Relationships and Groups"). Of course, segregation can be the *cause* as well as the *effect* of communication differences.

We expect differences when we talk to people who grew up in a different country but not when we talk to people who grew up in "the same culture" and who speak "the same language" as ourselves. So it is perhaps surprising that social psychologists devote a great deal of attention to gender differences in communication.

GENDER DIFFERENCES IN COMMUNICATION

Folklore has long attributed "female intuition" to women. According to this view, women are more adept than men in nonverbal communication. An accumulating body of research supports this popular belief (Hall, 1984). On the whole, psychologists find that women are more visually attentive to other people than are men. And women are better judges than men of the meanings behind voice tones, facial expressions, and body movements — the sorts of cues people cannot or will not put into words.

One explanation for women's superior nonverbal decoding skills and different conversational style is that they are socially oppressed and hence must give greater attention to an accurate reading of the needs and demands of more powerful others. Another speculation is that women in male-dominated societies usually find themselves watching and listening and might therefore develop greater nonverbal ability through sheer practice. Still another is that the ability is genetic, or "prewired," because nonverbal sensitivity on a mother's part might permit her to detect distress in her children or threatening signals from adults, thus enhancing the survival chances of her offspring.

In contrast to these "oppression" and "biological" explanations, another thesis is that gender differences in communication styles emerge from male and female *subcultures* whose norms are learned from, and reinforced by, gender mates from early childhood on (Maltz and Borker, 1982; Maccoby, 1990; Tannen, 1990). According to this explanation, gender differences in communication behavior stem from adherence to the norms of one's own gender group, not so much from status differences that may become salient when men and women interact with one another.

Women's style is seen as reflecting females' greater concern with *intimacy*, or connection with others. This style focuses on minimizing differences and avoiding the appearance of superiority, which would highlight differences among the members of complex networks of friends. Communication, for women, is frequently directed toward establishing connections with others, building relationships, and preserving intimacy.

Men's communication style reflects their greater concern with *status* and independence, with being up rather than down in the hierarchical social order. Thus, men's conversations are negotiations in which they try to achieve and maintain the upper hand if they can and protect themselves from others' attempts to put them down or push them around. This is not to say, of course, that women are entirely unconcerned with status or that men are unconcerned with intimacy. The difference is one of focus and degree — women's primary concern is intimacy, while men's primary concern is status — and this leads to dramatic gender differences in communication styles.

Notice that the difference in the concerns of the two genders reflects two of the main "things we communicate" discussed earlier in the chapter — intimacy and status. Men's greater use of filled pauses (which permit them to keep the floor), faster speech, and interruptions follows from their concern with status: they are competing for conversational floor time and respect. Women's greater use of questions, briefer speech, and more direct gazes reflects their concern with egalitarianism and connection. In this view, men and women come together as citizens of different cultures — thinking that they speak the same language when, in fact, they do not (Hall, 1978).

Perhaps because females are more concerned with interpersonal harmony and/or are more skilled at affecting it, both sexes find interactions with women to be more pleasant and satisfying than interactions with men. Social psychologist Harry Reis (1986) suggests that males and females make different contributions to social interaction. He and his colleagues asked subjects — forty-three male and fifty-three female college seniors — to complete a series of ratings for each interaction of ten minutes or longer that they were involved in during a two-week period.

The researchers found that interactions involving at least one female were rated by the subjects of both sexes as more intimate, more pleasant, and more satisfying. In such interactions, subjects indicated that they and the others involved in the interaction disclosed more. Even when a male interacted with his best male friend, the interaction was rated as less intimate, disclosing, pleasant, and satisfying than interactions between females or between opposite-sex partners. Additionally, among both male and female subjects, the more time they spent interacting with females, the less lonely they reported themselves to be. Reiss's study, however, did not attempt to identify the particular behaviors that made interaction with females more positive.

Gender Differences in Meaning

Because of gender differences in communication skills and approaches to interpersonal interaction, males and females sometimes view the same interaction quite differently. For example, backchannel responses such as "yeah" and "um-hum" have different meanings for men and women. For women, these mean "I'm listening, please continue." For men, they mean "I agree." So, in a male-female conversation, the man may think he is listening but not agreeing, but the woman will think he is not listening. Women frequently ask questions to maintain conversations — to show interest and encourage the speaker to continue. Men are more likely to see questions as requests

for information. Women often respond to shared experiences and problems by offering reassurance. Men see the presentation of problems as requests for solutions and respond by giving advice, lecturing, or acting as experts (Aries, 1987). Women who think they are displaying a positive quality — connection — are misjudged by men who see them as lacking independence, which men regard as synonymous with incompetence and insecurity. Men who think they are displaying a positive quality — independence — are misjudged by women who see them as insensitive and uncaring. It is not surprising that communication between men and women is sometimes difficult.

Deborah Tannen, a linguist who has studied gender differences in conversational styles, illustrates how men's and women's different cultural backgrounds can lead to miscommunication:

> When Josh's old high-school chum called him at work and announced he'd be in town on business the following month, Josh invited him to stay for the weekend. That evening he informed Linda that they were going to have a houseguest, and that he and his chum would go out together the first night to shoot the breeze like old times. Linda was upset. . . . Josh had made these plans on his own and informed her of them, rather than discussing them with her before extending the invitation. . . . But when she protests, Josh says, "I can't say to my friend, 'I have to ask my wife for permission'!"
>
> To Josh, checking with his wife means seeking permission, which implies that he is not independent, not free to act on his own. It would make him feel like a child or an underling. To Linda, checking with her husband has nothing to do with permission. She assumes that spouses discuss their plans with each other because their lives are intertwined, so the actions of one have consequences for the other. . . . Linda was hurt because she sensed a failure of closeness in their relationship: He didn't care about her as much as she cared about him. And he was hurt because he felt she was trying to control him and limit his freedom. (1990: 26–27)*

---

* From "Women and Men in Conversation" from *You Just Don't Understand* by Deborah Tannen. Copyright © by Deborah Tannen. Used by permission of William Morrow & Co., Inc.

Miscommunication between the genders is not limited to the interactions of husbands and wives. Antonia Abbey (1982) got her idea for a study about miscommunication between men and women from an encounter she had with strangers. Abbey was with some female friends at a crowded campus bar, sharing a table with two male strangers. While Abbey thought that she and her friends were merely being "friendly," the men appeared to interpret the women's behavior as an indication of sexual interest. She reports that she and her friends finally had to excuse themselves from the table in order to avoid an awkward scene. This made Abbey wonder: Do men often see women's words and actions as more seductive than the women intend?

Abbey designed a study to answer this question. She assigned two males and two females to each of twenty-six four-person groups. When each group arrived for the study, Abbey randomly selected one male and one female to engage in a brief conversation (the actors) while the other male and female observed the conversation from another room (the observers). After the conversation, all four subjects filled out questionnaires indicating their perceptions of the actors' personality traits and chose from among a list of characteristics those that they thought described how each actor was "trying to behave." Although these terms were included with many others, Abbey was particularly interested in how "flirtatious," "seductive," and "promiscuous" the four subjects perceived the two actors to be.

Abbey found that the behavior of the female actor was rated more promiscuous and seductive by both the male actor and the male observer than by either the female actor or the female observer. Overall, the male observers saw the female actors as more interested in and attracted to their partners than did the female observers. The males and females in this study either participated in or observed the same interaction, but both as actors and as observers the males and females perceived it quite differently—mutual understanding was not reached. As Abbey's experience in the bar indicates, this gender difference in "meaning" can lead to problems.

Differences in Conversational "Work" and Control

As we noted earlier in this chapter, the maintenance of a conversation is somewhat problematic and requires the continual, turn-by-turn efforts of the participants. However, this does not mean that there is an equal distribution of work in a conversation. For instance, Pamela Fishman finds that a woman typically carries the greater burden in keeping a conversation moving with a man. Fishman (1978) analyzed fifty-two hours of tapes made in the apartments of three middle-class couples between the ages of twenty-five and thirty-five. The women raised nearly twice as many topics of conversation as the men because many of the women's topics failed to elicit any response. Besides exercising their right to inject new topics, men controlled topics by veto: they would refuse to become full-fledged conversational participants. Both men and women regarded topics introduced by women as tentative, and many of these topics were quickly dropped. In contrast, topics introduced by men were seldom rejected and frequently resulted in a lengthy exchange.

The tapes revealed that the women resorted to attention-getting devices when faced with the men's grunts or long silences. The women asked three times as many questions as did the men. Asking a question is conversational "work"; it is a device used to keep conversation going by eliciting a response from the other party. And more often than the men, the women prefaced their remarks with comments like "D'ya know what?" and "This is interesting"; as talk lagged, the women used the interjection "you know" with considerable frequency. Such phrases function as "go-ahead" signals, indicating that the other party may speak up and that what is said will be heeded.

Deborah Tannen suggests that men see communication as a way to gain status by showing that they know more. Women, on the other hand, see communication as a way to build connections, so they tend to play down their own expertise rather than display it. Because of these differences, men are often more comfortable, and more talkative, in public situations that allow them to "show off." Women are often more comfortable, and more talkative, in private situations that allow them to build rapport. Men are inclined to jockey for position and challenge the authority of others. Women are more likely to avoid confrontation because they feel it is more important to be liked than to be respected. Men see disagreement as more interesting—and more status enhancing—than agreement. Women see disagreement as a threat to intimacy and strive to be more accommodating. Because they are not struggling to compete with others in conversation, women are often seen by men as being powerless or inept.

A number of studies have found that men account for the vast majority of the interruptions in a conversation. One early study found that in cross-sex conversations in public places, over 90 percent of the interruptions were made by men (Zimmerman and West, 1975). A recent study (Smith-Lovin and Brody, 1989) found that, while male and females interrupt at almost identical rates, males are more than twice as likely to interrupt a female as they are to interrupt another male. Females, in contrast, interrupt male and female speakers equally. The men were also found to be more successful at interrupting women.

Some researchers conclude from these findings that women, who do the routine maintenance work in conversations, neither control nor necessarily benefit from the conversational process (West and Zimmerman, 1983; Kollock, Blumstein, and Schwartz, 1985; Pfeiffer, 1985). One explanation for these findings is that widely held beliefs in our society attribute more status, or power, to men than to women and that this difference is reflected in conversational dynamics (Ridgeway and Diekema, 1992). According to this view, differences in communication styles are essential to the maintenance of male dominance (Henley and Kramarae, 1991). A second explana-

tion proposes that these differences are not so much a reflection of or a mechanism for maintaining male dominance but are, instead, another result of the different socialization and resulting cultures of the two genders.

These two explanations are not necessarily mutually exclusive (Smith-Lovin and Robinson, 1992). Both early *socialization* and peer-group interaction may lead boys and girls to develop gender identities that differ substantially in *power*. Although parents don't directly or intentionally socialize children to play or interact differently on the basis of their gender (Maccoby, 1990), they do communicate, subtly, that girls are nicer, less powerful, and less lively than boys. These early experiences shape our views of ourselves and others as males and females. These gender identities are reinforced in same-sex play groups. In adulthood, men's and women's definitions of "male" and "female" differ substantially. When these gender identities are activated, men and women behave differently in carrying out social roles. Thus, according to this view, it is gender-differentiated *identities*, which we hold for ourselves and others, that shape our interactions, including whether we interrupt, encourage someone else to speak, nod attentively, actively disagree, and so on.

Gender Stereotypes and Communication

One conclusion that we might draw from these studies on gender differences in the use of verbal and nonverbal cues is that women should try to adopt the culturally recognized male patterns in order to reap the same rewards. But would they?

When social psychologists began looking for objective cues to identify who would emerge as leader in an initially unstructured group, they found that the emergent leader was often the one centrally located in the group and that group members seated at the ends of the table became leaders more often than those occupying side positions. Psychologist Robert Pellegrini (1971) had subjects rate each person in photographs of five college women seated around a rectangular table, one at the head and two on each side. The woman seated at the head of the table was identified as the most influential, talkative, and leaderlike and as the one who had contributed most to the group. Pellegrini reasoned that we expect the high-status member of a group to be seated at the head of the table in our society, so we automatically attribute status and dominance to the person who occupies that position. The head of the table thus serves as a nonverbal cue to leadership status.

Natalie Porter and Florence Geis (1981) devised a study to determine whether the cues identifying a man as a leader would equally confer leadership on a woman. They decided to use position at the head of the table as the cue they would study, since it would be unlikely that, in photographs of seating position, males and females would seem to be doing this "differently." The research described above showed that the position at the head of the table serves as a leadership cue in same-sex groups. Porter and Geis hypothesized that in *mixed-sex* settings, sex-role stereotypes that define women as nonleaders when a man is available would cause leadership cues to be interpreted differently for males and females.

Using the same procedure that Pellegrini had used, Porter and Geis showed subjects a slide of five individuals seated at a rectangular table, two on each side and one at the head. To make sure that results were not due to a particular stimulus person, the researchers used several slides, with the seating positions of particular individuals varied in each one. Subjects viewed one slide and then rated each group member shown.

As they had predicted, the researchers found that the person at the head of the table was seen as the leader in the all-female, all-male, and mixed-sex groups with a male at the head of the table but not in mixed-sex groups with a female at the head of the table. In fact, a woman at the head of the table in a mixed-sex group was less than half as likely to be seen as the leader as was the person at the head in the other three conditions. This was true among both male and female subjects, including those with feminist as well as those with nonfeminist beliefs. The researchers concluded

that "seeing is not believing" when the objective evidence seen is not consistent with the beliefs encoded in cultural stereotypes. This suggests that women cannot get the same treatment as men simply by displaying the same nonverbal cues.

Men and women are judged differently when they use the same verbal cues as well. Women who attempt to adjust their styles by speaking louder, longer, and more assertively are judged to be acting in an "unfeminine" manner (Tannen, 1990). They may command more attention and respect, but they are likely to be disliked and disparaged as "aggressive" and "unfeminine." A man acting the same way is merely being a masculine male, and he is judged positively as a result. Indeed, women do not have to be particularly aggressive to be criticized.

A study by Harriet Wall and Anita Barry (1985) found that we define success in masculine terms and see these traits as incompatible with femininity. The researchers gave students information about prospective professors — their academic backgrounds, publications, and letters of recommendation — and asked the students to predict how well the candidates would do if hired and what their chances were of winning a distinguished teaching award. Some of the students were given a woman's name and others a man's name for the candidate. Those who believed the materials described a woman candidate were more likely to predict that she would not win the teaching award because, as one student put it, there was "too much business, not enough personality." None of the students who read exactly the same file under a man's name made these negative inferences about personality. In addition, students who believed they were evaluating a woman expected her to be more nurturing and to devote more time to her students outside of class than those who thought they were evaluating a man.

When women use stronger, more direct power cues — cues considered inappropriate to their gender — they often receive negative evaluations (Burgoon and Miller, 1985; Russell, Rush, and Herd, 1988; Heilman et al., 1989; Powell, 1990). This produces a double-bind dilemma for women who aspire to positions of leadership or responsibility. If they use typical female cues, they are ignored — considered "nice mice" who don't possess the necessary leadership qualities. If they use stronger signals, they are viewed as overly emotional, arrogant, and abusive — "dragons" who are trespassing on territory regarded as inappropriate for women. No "right" demeanor can be achieved (Fogarty, Rapaport, and Rapaport, 1971). Consider, for example, the plight of Geraldine Ferraro as the first female candidate for vice president of the United States. The press made much of the fact that in her debate with then Vice President Bush, she had difficulty creating a public image that would be authoritative but not "too masculine" (Epstein, 1988).

Even when journalists set out to praise Ferraro, they often used terms that highlighted the incongruity between her gender and the office she was seeking. Linguist Michael Geis (1987) points out in his book *The Language of Politics* that she was called "spunky" and "feisty" — words, Geis observes, that are used only for small, powerless creatures: for a Pekingese but not a Great Dane, perhaps for Mickey Rooney but not for John Wayne. Our language has built-in gender distinctions that shape our attitudes. It appears that gender is itself a cue that, in some situations, conflicts with or even overrides other communication cues to determine the responses of others (Eagly and Karau, 1991; Eagly, Makhijani, and Klonsky, 1992).

RACE AND CLASS DIFFERENCES IN COMMUNICATION

Race and social class are also sources of communication differences and, as a result, sources of communication problems when members of different races or social classes come together. Although the research literature on racial and social class communication styles is less extensive than that on gender differences in communication, several interesting observations have been made.

In his classic study, anthropologist William Labov (1972) found that African-American males (in this case, young, urban, and mainly lower class) exchanged insults, often in the presence of other peers who served as an audience. This activity was usually competitive in nature, in that each man tried to top the previous insult with one that was more clever, outrageous, or elaborate. The audience members acted as judges in deciding who won the competition of insults. Labov referred to this style of verbal exchange as "ritual insults."

Labov's observations were followed by research aimed at discovering the communication styles of females, whites, and members of the middle class (whatever their gender or race). Researchers observing African-American females found that they adopted the ritual-insult style when interacting with African-American males, and their communication with one another was typified by play songs and cheers that incorporated several aspects of insulting, such as assertive and mocking tones (Goodwin, 1980; Heath, 1983). Studies of white females found that the use of assertive and mocking play songs was not common (Heath, 1983) and that middle-class white females were often intimidated by the more aggressive style of their African-American peers (Schofield, 1982). However, still another study of the interaction among groups of white females found that ritual insulting *was* common among girls who came from working-. or lower-class backgrounds but not among those from the middle class (Eder, 1990). The researcher concluded that social class (not gender or race) was the major determinant of ritual insulting and that communication problems arise when persons from different social classes interact largely because middle-class people interpret working- and lower-class speech styles as both rude and assertive.

In a similar vein, Thomas Kochman (1981) observed differences in the communication styles used by African-Americans and whites in conflict situations. According to Kochman, blacks more frequently use a loud, animated, and confrontational style, while whites more frequently use a quiet, dispassionate, and nonchallenging style. The observations of a second researcher (Donohue, 1985) support those of Kochman: he found that in conflicts between members of the two races, African-Americans tend to be loud while whites are more likely to be extremely solicitous and friendly. Kochman proposes a cultural explanation for the communication differences. He contends that in African-American culture, loudness is viewed as an expression of sincerity and conviction of action — and therefore is positively valued. African-Americans tend to interpret whites' solicitous and friendly style of conflict communication as a mask of hypocrisy and weakness. On the other hand, whites interpret the loudness of African-Americans as overly aggressive and hostile.

Again, however, it is important to note that these studies compare working- and lower-class African-Americans to middle-class whites. Thus, the observed differences in communication styles may reflect *social class* differences rather than *racial* differences. In one study of middle-class college students, males of both races tended to use the quiet, nonchallenging style (there were only a small number of African-American males in the study), and the style differences between the females of the two races were small, although African-American females used the intense, confrontational style somewhat more frequently (Ting-Toomey, 1986).

Several studies suggest that racial differences in the cues that listeners and speakers provide for one another can also cause difficulties in interracial interaction (LaFrance and Mayo, 1976; Erickson, 1979). For example, African-American speakers tend to give fewer and more subtle cues indicating that they expect listener feedback. White speakers tend to look *away* from the listener while talking, whereas African-American speakers look *at* the listener more. White listeners, on the other hand, look at the speaker almost continuously, while African-American listeners look down or away and give fewer and more subtle listening cues (such as nods) than do whites. For example, for white speakers, listening is signaled by gaze, combined with *both* verbal and nonverbal back-channel cues. For African-

American speakers, *either* a vocal ("um-hmm") *or* a nonvocal (head nod) cue signals listening; these cues are rarely given together. White speakers infer from this that the African-American listener is not paying attention or doesn't understand. Consequently, they often repeat points and overexplain, making the African-American listener feel that the speaker thinks she or he is stupid. On the other hand, African-American speakers often feel that a white listener's "staring" indicates hostility.

CULTURAL UNIVERSALS AND DIFFERENCES

As we noted at the beginning of this chapter, the meanings that symbols come to have are arbitrary in the sense that they result from cultural conventions. A symbol can have any meaning that a group of people agree on. This means, of course, that a single symbol may have different meanings for different groups. Our discussion of gender, race, and class differences provides many examples of this. However, there are some commonalities in the use of symbols among various cultures and subcultures. In this section we'll explore both these commonalities and the cultural differences in the use of various kinds of symbols for communication.

Language

Human communities develop languages in order to express thoughts and feelings. All human groups have some features in common, and these are reflected in **linguistic universals** — features common to every language. Every language has nouns and verbs, for example, because all people must refer to objects and actions. Every language has terms for such spatial dimensions as direction (right, left; up, down; front, back), distance, height, and length, because all people use basically the same perceptual capacities to orient themselves to the physical world (Clark and Clark, 1977). Similarly, every language has terms to distinguish between past, present, and future — universally experienced dimensions of time.

Some linguistic universals result from common experiences of social life. These are of particular interest to social psychologists. For example, all cultures have some sort of family structure, although the structures themselves vary. All languages contain terms that allow speakers to distinguish three characteristics of family members — sex, generation, and blood relationship. All languages have precise, simple terms for relatives who spend the most time together, but they usually string together several terms to specify one's exact relationship to relatives who are less central to the family structure. For example, in English, the term "grandmother" designates a female, two generations prior to the referent, and a blood relationship. But the term "cousin" designates only two of the three characteristics — generation and blood relationship but not gender; it takes two words, "female cousin," to completely describe the cousin relationship. All languages have pronouns that facilitate references to self and other — for example, in English, "I/we," "you," and "he/she/they." Other universal language concepts include certain body parts (head, foot, belly, mouth), colors (red, green, black, white), common human actions (eat, sleep, hear, walk), and features of the environment (cloud, earth, rain, moon, fire) (Swadesh, 1971).

All languages have terms for concepts that are central to daily activities. As we have seen, the *common* capacities and experiences of humans lead to the incorporation of certain features in all languages — linguistic universals. But human groups also *differ* in terms of the physical environments they inhabit and the activities they undertake. These differences are also reflected in their languages. The Arabs have some 6,000 different terms for camels. The Hanunoo, a people of the Philippine Islands, have a term for each of ninety-two varieties of rice. Having precise words for frequently needed concepts makes communication easier and more accurate.

When learning to speak a new language, people generally do not pick up all the cultural conventions about how it should be used in different contexts. As a result, they may accidentally send the wrong message. For example, German allows more direct phrasing of requests and complaints than English does (House and Kasper, 1981). Thus, when Germans speak English, they sometimes sound domineering to Americans accustomed to the English convention that considers it impolite to be too direct with status equals. Similarly, research suggests that Israelis are concerned with appearing to be honest and forthright in their communications, while Americans and the British are more concerned with appearing to be polite and considerate (Katriel, 1986). Israeli speakers, in striving to maximize the attributes of honesty and forthrightness, which are valued in their culture, may come across to American and British listeners as rude and inconsiderate.

Body Language

Some gestures have the same or similar meanings in several cultures. An example is the side-to-side head motion meaning "no." However, some behaviors have a specific meaning in one culture but not in another. The French gesture of putting one's fist around the tip of the nose and twisting to signify that a person is drunk is not employed in other cultures. And a gesture may have one meaning in one culture and a different meaning in another culture. Thus, Roman emperors gave the thumbs-up gesture to spare the lives of gladiators in the Colosseum. Today the same gesture is favored by American and Western European airline pilots, truck drivers, and others to mean "all right." But in Sardinia and northern Greece, it is an insulting gesture, paralleling the insulting middle-finger gesture of American society (Ekman, Friesen, and Bear, 1984).

One aspect of body language, however, does seem to have common meanings in different cultures — the *facial expression* of emotion. Paul Ekman (1980) and his associates showed subjects from widely different cultures photographs of individuals' faces that in Western societies are judged to display six basic emotions: happiness, sadness, anger, surprise, disgust, and fear (see photo). The researchers found that college-educated subjects in the United States, Brazil,

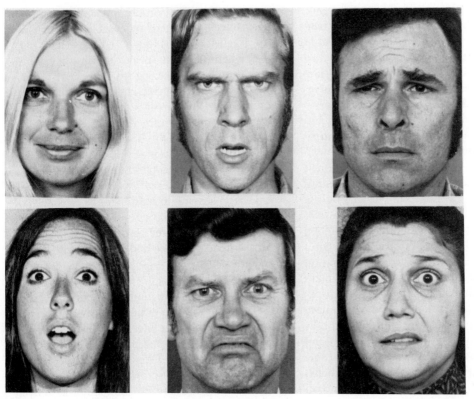

People in many cultures recognize the emotions of happiness, anger, sadness, surprise, disgust, and fear in these photos.

Argentina, Chile, and Japan ascribed the same emotions to the same faces. Moreover, with the exception of their failure to discriminate fear from surprise, even the isolated and preliterate Fore of New Guinea made similar distinctions. (Among the Fore, surprising events are almost always fearful, such as the sudden appearance of a hostile member of another village or the unexpected meeting of a "ghost.")

In a more recent study, Ekman and his colleagues showed photographs depicting the six emotions to college-student observers in ten countries (Ekman et al., 1987). The observers were asked to rate *how intensely* the person in the photo was experiencing the emotion, as well as *which* emotion the person was feeling. Although there were high levels of agreement across cul-

tures about which emotion was being expressed, judgments of intensity showed much lower levels of agreement. The greater variation in intensity than in type of emotion may be a result of cultural differences in "display rules."

Ekman believes this evidence demonstrates that our central nervous systems are genetically prewired for the facial expression of emotion. However, he does not rule out the influence of environment. Learning determines which circumstances will elicit a given emotional expression, and cultures formulate their own display rules to regulate the expression of emotion. For example, in our culture, norms prescribe that even though a guest might feel intense disgust at the thought of eating the specific food served by his hostess, politeness requires that he attempt to mask the expression of this emotion. The guest shouldn't leap back from the table exclaiming, "Oh, yuck, how revolting!" or even sit quietly and wrinkle his nose like the person in the "disgust" photo on page 168. Instead, he should pretend to be delighted by the feast or at least make a polite excuse for not eating the disgusting item ("Oh, that looks delicious, but my doctor has told me I absolutely mustn't eat pickled frog eyes any more") and, at the same time, should make every effort to have his facial expression match his insincere words. Some other cultures might allow freer expression of disgust in this situation.

Interpersonal Spacing

Anthropologist Edward T. Hall (1966) has shown that there are cultural differences in interpersonal spacing. Hall observes that Americans commonly consider Arabs to be pushy and rude. Paradoxically, Arabs also consider Americans to be pushy. This is because interpersonal spacing has different meanings in the two cultures. For example, the visual interaction of Arabs is intense: they stare; Americans do not. Further, Arabs bathe the other person in their breath. To smell another is not only desirable but mandatory; to deny another one's breath is to act ashamed. Whereas Arabs stay inside the olfactory bubble of others, Americans stay outside of it. Hence an American communicates shame to the Arab when, in fact, the American is trying to be polite. These behaviors, Hall explains, derive from the fact that the typical Arab lacks a sense of a private spatial bubble that envelops the body. Rather than viewing a person as extending in space beyond the body, Arabs see the person as existing somewhere down *inside* the body. Thus, they violate the American ego by invading Americans' private space.

In summary, human communication is characterized by both cultural universals and differences. These interest social psychologists because they illustrate the complexity of human experience. On the one hand, we have much in common with others. We inhabit the same earth and are subject to its physical laws. Even some features of social experience are common to all cultures. We all have parents and other kin, for example; we all feel certain basic emotions, and we must all communicate with others in order to negotiate and align our actions.

On the other hand, members of different cultural groups have different concerns and these are reflected in their communications. Different cultural groups have devised different symbols even for the universal aspects of human experience. Consider, for example, all the different words for mother in the world's languages. Subcultures within a cultural group may assign different meanings to certain symbols and may have jargons all their own. Even a brother and sister growing up in the same family, who have in common not only the larger culture but also the group culture of the family itself, may experience the world very differently from each other — and develop different communication styles and concerns — due to a factor such as gender. Why is this so? It is because our culture assigns meanings to such characteristics as gender, race, social class, and physical beauty, and these meanings affect the way we experience the world — how others react to us and how we come to see ourselves. We'll discuss the process by which this occurs in our next two chapters: Chapter 6, "Social Attitudes and Attributions," and Chapter 7, "The Social Nature of Self."

Summary

1. Communication is the process by which people interact and interpret their interactions. Symbols are objects or actions that stand in, or substitute, for something else. Significant symbols are symbols for which several people share meanings. They are important because they allow us to coordinate our behaviors with those of others.

2. We communicate through several kinds of symbols: language, paralanguage, body language, interpersonal spacing, physical characteristics, and personal effects.

3. We communicate multiple meanings with a single message. Besides conveying task information, our communicative behavior reflects the intimacy of our relationships with other persons, as well as our relative status within the group, provides information about ourselves and our feelings, and is used to manage impressions of ourselves and our relationships. We use facework to support or challenge the public images we claim for ourselves or attribute to others.

4. Our behavior also provides cues to regulate the interaction itself: we signal the initiation of interaction, indicate our willingness to stop or start speaking, and provide feedback to the speaker to indicate our interest and understanding. We often indicate our intentions indirectly, relying on the cooperative principle to decipher a speaker's meaning.

5. Different gender, racial, and social class groups have different norms for regulating conversation. Therefore, when members of these different groups interact, miscommunication may result. Some explanations for gender differences in communication styles relate to women's disadvantaged position in society or their biological role as mothers. The socialization or cultural explanation suggests that males and females interact, as children, in same-gender subgroups whose different norms they learn. Working- and lower-class persons use a loud interaction style in conflict situations which middle-class persons interpret as overly aggressive and hostile. Middle-class persons use a friendly and solicitous conflict style which lower- and working-class persons interpret as hypocritical and weak. African-Americans and whites tend to use different speaking and listening cues — sometimes leading to difficulties in interracial interaction.

6. Common human concerns are reflected in linguistic universals — features that exist in all languages. Language differences also reflect the different concerns of various human groups. Even subgroups of a language group have specialized vocabularies which reflect their particular concerns.

PART TWO

IDENTITIES,
ATTITUDES,
AND BEHAVIOR

CHAPTER 6

SOCIAL ATTITUDES AND ATTRIBUTIONS

*Y*ou are alone, walking to your car late at night after spending the evening studying at the library. You are thinking about what you might eat for a snack when you get home. Suddenly you become aware of footsteps a short distance behind you. Your heart beats faster. You know that several students have been attacked in the last few weeks. You turn, wondering what kind of person you will see. When you discover that the footsteps belong to a young woman, carrying books, also hurrying toward the parking lot, you feel relieved.

You want to complain about a course grade and have been told to talk to the chair of the department of sociology. On the way to the chair's office, you begin thinking about how to present your case. What kind of person should you expect?

You get an urgent message on your answering machine from an old roommate, who asks you to go on a blind date that night with a friend from out of town. The only thing your ex-roommate is specific about is that the friend is really good-looking. What kind of person is the potential date likely to be? Do you accept the date or not?

On the first day in your social psychology class, the student sitting beside you asks if you want to study together when preparing for course exams. Do you accept the suggestion? Right now, all you know about the person is what you can see — that the person is an obese, neatly dressed white male. You like the idea of a study partner, but would this person be a good one?

About 11 o'clock one Saturday night, there's a knock at your door. You open the door to find an unfamiliar, skinny teenage girl in a short skirt, holding a young child on her hip. The girl explains that her car has broken down near your house and asks to use your telephone to call a friend for help. Do you let her in? What information do you use to make the decision?

These examples illustrate that many of our everyday experiences require us to make decisions about other people on the basis of limited information about them. How do we make such decisions?

We start with the few solid bits of information we have: the identification of the person as department chair; the friend's description of the blind date as "good-looking"; the personal observation of the individual's appearance — "obese, neatly dressed white male" and "skinny teenage girl . . . holding a young child." This information, provided by the environment, triggers or activates the retrieval of other information that is stored in memory. Our memories provide us with information that goes beyond the initial information we have about a person. For example, in response to your ex-roommate's description of the potential date as "good-looking," you may draw from memory the associations you have for that characteristic — conceited and self-centered. On the other hand, since you respect your roommate, who describes the potential date as a friend, your mental picture is of someone who is friendly, considerate, and fun. Is it possible that the potential date is nice *and* good-looking? You must decide whether you want to go out with the person or not.

Let's say you decide to take the risk. When you meet the date later that evening, you are on the lookout for clues to the kind of person he or she "really" is. Good-looking? Well, your roommate was right about that. Conceited or nice? During the first few minutes of your interaction, you mentally list the evidence: talks a lot, asks lots of questions about you, seems interested in your responses, notes that you have similar taste in music, smiles a lot, and is very attentive. Nice, you conclude, as you feel yourself relaxing and settling into what promises to be an enjoyable evening.

The process by which we interpret sensations that reach us from the environment — sights, sounds, smells, tastes, and touches — in terms of other information we have stored in our memories is referred to by psychologists as *cognition*. *Social* psychologists are interested in how we interpret sensations that reach us from the *social* environment — a process known as **social cognition** (Sherman, Judd, and Park, 1989; Morgan and Schwalbe, 1990; Fiske and Taylor, 1991; Schneider, 1991; Carley and Palmquist, 1992). Social cognition involves perceiving a sensation from the social environment and searching one's

memory for information that might be relevant to it.

Our memories are storehouses of information that we have learned through our own experiences with people as well as from the observed and reported experiences of others. (The processes involved in learning are described in Chapter 2, "Early Socialization.") We store information in our memories and retrieve some each time we think. However, our memories do not store every bit of information that exists in our environment. They store *concepts of select categories* of information. We say "concepts" because, of course, our memories do not literally store the "things" in our environment — lamps, people, behaviors, or places. Instead, they store our ideas, or mental representations, of things — **concepts**. We say "select" because there are many bits of information in our environment that we consistently ignore; we have no concepts of them at all.

We say "categories" because we group together some bits of information in our environment but not others. Our categories are defined to *include* some bits while *excluding* others. For example, you may have a "student athlete" category that distinguishes those students on your campus who are athletes from those who are not. If so, you may lump together all student athletes in this category, making no distinctions among them. *Or* you may make more elaborate distinctions among the campus athletes, using sports categories, gender categories, or a combination of both (football players, basketball players, women basketball players, and so on). We also have concepts that distinguish just one thing from all others — Michael Jordan, my cat Lancelot, Texas, God. In this chapter, we explore the ways we categorize people on the basis of their characteristics and the process by which we associate these characteristics with other information in our memory.

In Chapter 5, "Communication," we noted that symbols such as language, paralanguage, body language, interpersonal-spacing cues, objects, and appearances are — through interpretation — associated with meaning. As the examples

TYPES OF SOCIAL IDENTITIES

Gender, race, ethnicity, age, class: male/female; homosexual/bisexual/heterosexual; black/white/Asian; Hispanic/Anglo; young/middle-aged/old; white-collar/blue-collar; upper-class/middle-class/lower-class.

Group/organization membership (including former membership): Methodist/Baptist/Catholic/Jew/etc.; Democrat/Republican; Harvard/Yale/Brown/etc. alumni; Chi Phi/Kappa/Sigma Nu/etc.; WWII vet/Korean War vet/Vietnam War vet; former president; ex-con.

Position within a group or an organization: boyfriend/girlfriend; parent/child; lawyer/client; professor/secretary/student; doctor/patient; private/sergeant/captain/general; President/representative/Supreme Court justice; guard/inmate; boss/employee; quarterback/end/kicker/etc.

Place of residence: Americans/Japanese/Russians/Canadians/etc.; dorm rat; homeowner/renter/homeless; city slicker/suburbanite/hick; Midwesterner/Southerner/Northeasterner.

Physical characteristics or appearance: tall/short; fat/athletic/skinny; blond/brown/red/black hair; attractive/ugly; well-dressed/shabbily dressed; in-style/tacky.

Personality traits, emotions, behaviors: assertive/passive; warm/cold; happy/sad; calm/nervous; talkative/quiet; organized/disorganized; crazy/normal; racist/sexist/tolerant; narrow-minded/open-minded; generous/stingy; smart/average/stupid.

above show, *any* characteristic of another person can be associated with other information stored in memory. In this chapter we will give more attention to the specifics of the *process* by which we view other people.

Social Identities and Social Attitudes

The process of social cognition often begins with our assigning a person a social identity. **Social identities** are mental concepts or categories that differentiate people on the basis of similarities and differences in one or more characteristics. Social identities can consist of a single trait, such as being white, a student, a feminist, tall, an extrovert, or Southern. They can also consist of a combination of characteristics. For example, white Southerners or tall, athletic males. Social identities are mental concepts that our minds develop and store in memory as a result of our experiences. See the box "Types of Social Identities" for examples of some of the characteristics we use to distinguish social identities.

In memory, each social identity is associated with certain beliefs and feelings — what social psy-

chologists call **social attitudes**. Our social attitudes about a particular social identity constitute the *meaning* of that social identity — our view of the people included in it. Social attitudes represent answers to the question, "What is this person like?" Like all attitudes, social attitudes are composed of two general components — beliefs and feelings. We will discuss these components separately because social psychologists often focus on one or the other. However, we want to stress that beliefs and feelings occur *together*.

THE BELIEF COMPONENT OF SOCIAL ATTITUDES

Social attitudes consist, partly, of the beliefs we have that link a social identity with other characteristics. *Beliefs* are mental associations between two concepts. Beliefs can be expressed in the form "Identity X (are, have, do, behave, and so on) _____." For example, I might believe that white Southerners are racist, quarterbacks are intelligent, obese people are jolly, poor people are lazy, African-Americans prefer to associate with other African-Americans, or men like sex more than women do. Some social attitudes, as in these examples, are based on a single dominant belief. Other social attitudes are more complex in that they involve a *set of beliefs* that link a social identity to several other concepts; in other words, they involve a **schema**. For example, our schema for men would consist of the set of all beliefs we have that link the concept "men" to other concepts: men are muscular, men have penises, men are assertive, men speak loudly, and so on.

A **stereotype** is a schema that attributes a set of characteristics to *most or all* members of a social identity. For example, you may have a stereotype about people who are male, short, assertive, quick-tempered, sexist, and athletic. You may label this social identity "macho" or "redneck." Professors have stereotypes about several types of students — "stars," "hard workers," and "goof-offs" — and students have stereotypes for several types of professors (see the box "Stereotypes of UNC Professors").

The journalist Walter Lippman, who coined the term "stereotype," once observed that since the world is filled with "so much subtlety, so much variety, so many permutations and combinations" we must "construct it on a simpler model" in order to cope with it (1922: 16). In other words, we find it virtually impossible to weigh every characteristic of every person we encounter, minute by minute. Rather, we lump individuals into categories based on some characteristics (while ignoring others). Stereotypes — beliefs about these categories — allow us to make quick decisions based on minimal information. We use them to form impressions of other people and to predict their behavior, and this allows us to plan our own courses of action accordingly. Yet, al-

A stereotype is a schema that attributes a set of characteristics to most or all members of a social identity. Based on the limited amount of information in these photographs, what social identities would you assign to the persons pictured here? If you had to guess, which person would you say probably (1) has the highest education, (2) watches professional wrestling, (3) is a gourmet cook, (4) jogs four miles a day, (5) drinks wine with dinner?

STEREOTYPES OF UNC PROFESSORS

According to Ian Williams, former *Daily Tar Heel* columnist, there are five kinds of professors at the University of North Carolina. They are:

The Ramblin' Man: Professors become professors for a reason, and the Ramblin' Man did it because he

knew more about his subject than anyone else in the solar system. He can't teach for the same reason good musicians can't dance; they know way too much about something to express it naturally. Also known as "Mr. I Wrote the Book," he quotes long, delirious passages from his own textbook in a monotone that would put eighteen-wheel trucks to sleep — and when asked a question, he will ramble on a long, delirious tangent that will send most students into the stratosphere, drooling on their desks with sugar plums dancing in their heads. *Quote:* "And if you'll turn to page one thousand seven hundred and fifty in the textbook, read along with me as we take a voyage through the wondrous world of didactic relativism . . ."

Anal Retentive T. A. from the Ninth Circle of Hell: There are professors in this world who seem to

delight in the academic flogging of their student captives, but much worse are their Igor Teaching Assistants, the Grad Students With Very Serious Attitude Problems. These guys probably had a crudload of sand kicked in their faces in grade school, and now carry this primal sandbox grudge to the poli sci classroom, where they finally have the power over us durn bratty schoolkids. With snake venom spewing from their lips, the T. A. tears through a paper like an angry tiger through a gazelle, gnawing on bad punctuation and flawed argumentation with cackling glee. *Quote:* "Let it be known that attendance to the 8 o'clock recitation section counts as 47 percent of your final grade . . ."

Mr. Everybody's Buddy: This teacher spices his lecture with frequent references to the students' alcoholic and sexual passions, in a vain attempt to "relate" to us kids in our obviously pleasure-driven lives. He'll set up office hours at He's Not Here on Friday evenings, where he'll suck down a brewski and make thinly-veiled sexist comments relating the subject material with boob size, and then get angry

---

though stereotypes are convenient, even necessary — we all have and use them — they are not necessarily accurate. By definition, they are generalizations that ignore some potentially important information.

Our everyday usage of the term "stereotype" highlights the fallibility of such generalizations. We often point out that someone is relying on a stereotype when we believe that her or his inferences about another person are false. While stereotypes, being generalizations, are certainly

subject to this kind of error, they are not *necessarily* false. For example, part of our "female" stereotype may be that females have less upper-body strength than males. In general, this belief is true. As a result, applying this belief — part of our stereotype — to interaction may serve us well *most* of the time. The problem that occurs is that, even though *most* females have less upper-body strength than *most* males, our everyday interaction brings us into contact not with *most* females or males but with individuals. A particular female

when we don't take him seriously as a professor. *Quote*: "I'd schedule a quiz for Friday, but I know you'll be out pillaging all night . . . (*winks*) . . . right, Gloria? Heh heh heh."

Madame Slide: This professor's classroom has a living room quality to it because you talk about the

same stuff you would at three in the morning with drunk housemates. The text for the class is usually a coursepak that consists of three or four newspaper articles vaguely related to each other, all stapled together. Students either get in deep philosophical

discussions or sleep, and the teacher gets in trouble every semester for giving out too many A's; unfortunately, Madame Slide's class never fulfills anything close to being a perspective, so it is commonly known as "Two for One at the Pass/Fail-o-'Rama." *Quote*: "I really don't *believe* in the conventional grading system . . . how do y'all *feel* about that?"

The Academic Superhero: This professor is the veritable god among men, the one teacher that suc-

cessfully combines his own personal intellect with a working knowledge of our own attention span. Passionate yet not a freakazoid, our Superfiend casts off the common shackles of regurgitation list memorizing and lets us learn tough material without leaving us feeling like we just got our teeth cleaned. The Superhero comes along every two years or so in our college career, so look out for them! *Quote*: "I've got a convention in Boulder, so there'll be no class on Thursday."

Source: Ian Williams, "Season of Superheros, Slides, and Sleep," *Daily Tar Heel*, February 28, 1990, 10. Reprinted by permission. Art by Greg Humphreys.

---

may have greater upper-body strength than a particular male or even greater upper-body strength than most males. Stereotypes, then, may be accurate or inaccurate generalizations about a category of people. Even when they accurately describe common characteristics of the category, they may not apply to a particular individual who is a member of that category. (See the Student Observations: "Stereotypes.")

One way social psychologists measure stereotypes is by giving respondents a single-charac-

teristic description of a person (e.g., female, lawyer, aggressive, gay, Jew, or drug user) and asking them to describe other characteristics that they think are typical of people with the given characteristic. Three different methods are used to obtain the descriptions of the other characteristics: (1) *open-ended descriptions*, which allow respondents to use their own words; (2) *adjective checklists*, which provide respondents with a list of characteristics and ask them to indicate *which ones* are typical of people with the specified charac-

STUDENT OBSERVATIONS

Stereotypes

My roommate and I came to Carolina with our own opinions of each other, based on nothing but our names, addresses, and a short phone call. I, being from the North, saw her string of middle names, noticed her Southern accent, and noted the small-town address in North Carolina, and unwittingly labeled her a "redneck." She, in turn, saw my long name and Pennsylvania address, and noticed my very different accent, and groaned about the "pretentious snob" she would have to live with. Upon meeting, we found our stereotypes of each other to be quite wrong. Now we laugh about our earlier impressions of one another, as we have become good friends.

In the summer of 1991 I was fortunate to make friends with a swimmer from the island-nation of Cuba. Before meeting Rodolfo, I had developed a stereotype of Cubans as a whole. I expected him to seem brainwashed, stubborn, and not very worldly. My stereotype could not have been much farther from the truth. Rodolfo was extremely open-minded, receptive to different ideas, and very knowledgeable.

Rodolfo also admitted to me that I was not what he expected from an American. He expected me to be rude, overbearing, and boastful. We often attribute a set of characteristics to the members of a social identity. I am glad that I had the opportunity to discover that my stereotype of Cubans was incorrect.

---

teristic; and (3) *rating scales*, which provide respondents with a list of characteristics and ask them to rate the *degree* to which each one is typical of people with the specified characteristic. In some studies, respondents are given a characteristic that distinguishes two people (e.g., male-female, happy-sad, boss-employee) and are asked to describe other *distinguishing* characteristics of the two people by using one of the above methods.

THE FEELING COMPONENT OF SOCIAL ATTITUDES

The second component of a social attitude is the feelings, or emotions, an attitude holder associates with a social identity or social category. Social psychologists sometimes refer to this feeling component as *affect*. For example, for many people, the idea of associating closely with someone who is infected with the AIDS virus is frightening. We also have feelings about the characteristics we associate with social identities. Consider your own feelings about these characteristics: hateful, stupid, heroic, forgiving. *Whatever* the charac-

teristic we associate with a social identity, we will have some emotional reaction to it.

The aspect of our feelings that social psychologists study most often is evaluation. Our **evaluations** of a social identity are our feelings that the social identity is good or bad, pleasant or unpleasant — a group to be liked or disliked. The *direction* of evaluation refers to whether our feelings toward the social identity are positive or negative. Social psychologists refer to positive evaluations of a social identity as **social esteem** and to negative evaluations as **prejudice**. If you have positive feelings (social esteem) toward students at your school, you will probably associate positive characteristics with them; for example, you are likely to judge them as being intelligent and attractive and as being good sports. On the other hand, if you have negative feelings (prejudice) about students at a competing school, you will probably associate negative characteristics with them: stupidity, rudeness, bad sportsmanship.

The *intensity* of an evaluation refers to its strength, which may range from very weak to very strong. Thus, we may fiercely like or dislike members of certain social identities. Soldiers usually strongly like members of their own units but strongly dislike (hate) members of enemy units. Some people have extremely negative feelings toward flag burners, homosexuals, or liberals. On the other hand, our evaluations of other social identities are less intense: taxi drivers, bystanders, and homeowners generally don't elicit *strong* evaluative feelings.

The intensity with which we react to characteristics associated with social identities also varies. We may have forceful feelings about such characteristics as unpatriotic, filthy, perverted, heroic, and self-sacrificing and less intense feelings about such characteristics as nice, average, chubby, and shy.

Social psychologists have developed a variety of methods to study the evaluative aspect of social attitudes — some direct and some indirect. The evaluation of social identities may be assessed directly by asking respondents how much they like or dislike members (or a member) of a particular social identity.

However, researchers often use more indirect measures, inferring the evaluation of the social identity from the evaluation of the components of the stereotype of the social identity — the evaluation of the characteristics that are linked to the social identity by belief statements. To do this, the researcher first identifies the characteristics associated with the social identity by asking respondents to indicate the characteristics that (1) typify people who share a designated trait (e.g., female) or (2) distinguish two people (e.g., male and female). Next, the researcher has to decide which way to proceed from this point. Some researchers just *assume* the evaluation of the characteristics. In other words, they take for granted that a stereotype that includes the belief that corporate executives are intelligent, ambitious, and hard-working indicates a positive evaluation, while a stereotype that includes the belief that corporate executives are greedy, exploitative, and manipulative indicates a negative evaluation. Other researchers ask respondents to *rate* each characteristic separately for its desirability or undesirability. Afterward, the researchers create a summary measure by averaging the desirability scores or by counting the number of desirable (or undesirable) characteristics.

Still other researchers ask respondents to indicate two things: the *probability* that a member of a social identity will have a certain characteristic (a measure of the belief component) and the *desirability* of that characteristic (a measure of evaluation). Across several characteristics, probability is multiplied by desirability and the products are summed or averaged. This is called the *evaluation likelihood method* (McGuire, 1985). Alternatively, instead of having respondents rate the desirability of *each* characteristic involved in a stereotype, some researchers ask respondents to rate as favorable, neutral, or unfavorable all the characteristics *collectively*. Respondents are asked, for example, "How would you feel about a person who is loud, unintelligent, and overbearing?"

Do all these methods produce the same results? As you might expect, they do not (Gardner et al., 1988; McCauley and Thangavelu, 1991). A person's evaluation of a social identity may not correspond perfectly with his or her evaluation of the characteristics comprising the associated stereotype (McGuire, 1985; Del Boca, Ashmore, and McManus, 1986). For example, we may like Irishmen a lot even though we may have only a moderately positive evaluation of the characteristics we associate with them, such as their being storytellers, fun-lovers, drinkers, emotional individuals, and revolutionaries.

THE STRUCTURE AND ORGANIZATION OF SOCIAL ATTITUDES

Generality and Elaborateness

A social attitude is a schema — a mental structure of beliefs and feelings associated with a social identity. Social attitudes can be distinguished on the basis of their *generality*, that is, the number of people identified by a particular social attitude. Some social attitudes apply to large numbers of people: female, African-American, youth, heterosexual, introvert, Baptist. Other social attitudes apply to smaller numbers: female wrestler, African-American professor, youth offender, fraternity brother, classmate, friend, my family. A **person-attitude** involves a schema that applies to only a single, unique individual. Although many of the characteristics included in a person-attitude are common to other people, the particular *combination* of characteristics, or the inclusion of at least one characteristic not shared by others, distinguishes the individual from all others. For example, among all mothers, each of whom has given birth to a child, only *your mother* gave birth to *you*. Among all First Ladies, each of whom has been married to a President of the United States, only Hillary Clinton is married to President Bill Clinton. Attitudes toward Madonna, Saddam Hussein, Martin Luther King, Michael Jordan, Bill Cosby, and Billy Graham may be included among the many person-attitudes stored in your memory.

Some attitudes are more *elaborate*, or rich, than others; their schemas contain more beliefs. For example, you can probably list more characteristics of *your* mother ("My mother is _____") than you can of single mothers ("Single mothers are _____") or working mothers ("Working mothers are _____") or mothers in general ("Mothers are _____").

Relationships Among Social Attitudes

Stored in our memories, a number of social attitudes share particular characteristics. For example, we may have attitudes about several social identities that involve the characteristic "female." On the one hand, we have a schema that associates the social identity "female" with certain other characteristics, such as "Females are caring," "Females are not physically strong," and "Females are interpersonally skilled." The attitude represented by this schema is likely to be activated when our only information about a person is her female gender. Such an attitude ignores to a large extent the differences among females. For example, we know that some females are more interpersonally skilled than others, but our female schema (or stereotype) generalizes: "[Most] females are interpersonally skilled, so until I get

information to the contrary, I'll assume this one is."

At the same time, we also have several attitudes toward specific types of females, subcategories of the general category "females." Each of these social identities refers to only some females—"Hispanic females," "mothers," "tomboys," "female managers," "traditional females," or "female professors"—and each is represented in memory as a schema having its own collection of associated characteristics. Such attitudes are likely to be activated when we receive more information about a person than her gender. In addition, the characteristic "female" makes up part of our attitudes toward individual people: "(I believe) Dr. Brown, my social psychology professor, is female, fortyish, friendly, a hard grader, a New Englander (and so on)."

Some social psychologists have proposed that our schemas for social identities are arranged *hierarchically*. They mean that the schemas for more general identities, such as "females," which are found at the top of a hierarchy, would contain characteristics common to all females. The schemas for more specific identities, such as "Hispanic females" and "female professors," are at lower levels in the hierarchy and contain all the characteristics of females *plus* some other characteristics that distinguish Hispanic females and female professors from each other. At a still lower, even more specific, level, according to this argument, are *person schemas*—our schemas for *individuals* who fit the categories "Hispanic females" and "female professors." The schemas for these women supposedly have the characteristics common to all females *plus* the characteristics common to Hispanic females or female professors, *plus* some additional characteristics that distinguish each individual from the others.

But most research does not support the view that schemas are organized hierarchically. Instead, evidence suggests that many attitude schemas sharing one or more characteristics contain other characteristics that are not only different but also contradictory. For example, we may have several attitude schemas involving types of males.

Some types of males — husbands, male athletes, and John Wayne types — seem to fit the "male stereotype *plus* other distinguishing characteristics" hierarchical structure. But many other types of males do not. Our schemas for wimps, gay males, and sensitive males, for example, might have some of the characteristics we think typical of males and some characteristics that *contradict* our male stereotype. Thus, in comparing two men, we may draw from memory two different schemas by which we view and respond to the men quite differently — even though they share the characteristic "male." Similarly, how we treat a particular Asian-American person may depend on which schema we use to identify him: "Asian-American," "Asian student," or "Sam Woo — an Asian-American, a student, my roommate (and so on)."

Stereotypes, Social Esteem, and Prejudice

We have suggested that all of us hold beliefs about categories of people — stereotypes — and that we evaluate some groups more positively than others. In this section we will examine some of the social attitudes common in our society, including stereotypes based on personality traits, ethnic identity, physical characteristics, family identities, and gender. We will also look at examples of social esteem and prejudice associated with these stereotypes.

IMPLICIT PERSONALITY THEORIES

Nearly fifty years ago, social psychologist Solomon Asch (1946) drew attention to the fact that we form organized impressions of other people even after brief encounters. In a series of pioneering and influential studies, he demonstrated that we perceive an individual as having a set of interrelated traits that form an integrated personality structure. Asch gave one group of college-student subjects a list of seven personality characteristics

of an unidentified person: intelligent, skillful, industrious, warm, determined, practical, and cautious. Another group of subjects was given the exact same list except that the characteristic "cold" was substituted for "warm." Asch then asked both groups to describe the person by selecting from a different list, which contained pairs of opposite traits, the trait from each pair that they felt best characterized the individual.

Asch found that the portraits provided by the two groups were extremely different. Subjects who were told that the person was *warm* described him as generous, happy, and good-natured. In contrast, subjects who were told that the person was *cold* depicted him as stingy, unhappy, and unpopular. A single bit of information — whether the person was warm or cold — colored entire impressions.

In another version of the experiment, instead of "warm" or "cold," Asch inserted "polite" or "blunt" in the list with the other six words. This time, the subjects' descriptions of the polite or blunt person did not appreciably differ. Table 6-1 shows the results of both experiments. In these two experiments, the warm-cold characteristics elicited two different personality profiles, while the polite-blunt characteristics did not. Thus, the warm-cold characteristics were *central organizing traits* — ones having the greater effect on the overall impression. Different types of information about a person, Asch concluded, have different levels of impact on impressions we form.

Which traits are central depends on what kind of judgment we are making. Warmth appears to be an especially central trait in our evaluations of another person's *sociability*. Yet, when we are evaluating a person's *honesty*, bluntness becomes a central trait and warmth becomes much less important (Wishner, 1960).

Asch's research indicates that our memories contain schemas of traits that we think go together. These trait schemas were used by the subjects in Asch's experiments to fill out the incomplete data given to them by the researcher. Social psychologists call these schemas (our assumptions about how personality traits are related) **implicit**

TABLE 6-1   CENTRAL TRAITS

Stimulus list				
1	**2**	**3**	**4**	**5**
Intelligent	Intelligent	Intelligent	Intelligent	Intelligent
Skillful	Skillful	Skillful	Skillful	Skillful
Industrious	Industrious	Industrious	Industrious	Industrious
Warm	*Cold*	*Polite*	*Blunt*	—
Determined	Determined	Determined	Determined	Determined
Practical	Practical	Practical	Practical	Practical
Cautious	Cautious	Cautious	Cautious	Cautious

% of subjects choosing a trait as characteristic of the unknown person

Overall impression	Warm	Cold	Polite	Blunt	No key trait
Generous	91	8	56	58	55
Wise	65	25	30	50	49
Happy	90	34	75	65	71
Good-natured	94	17	87	56	69
Reliable	94	99	95	100	96
Important	88	99	94	96	88

Source: Adapted from S. Asch, "Forming Impressions of Personality," *Journal of Abnormal and Social Psychology*, 1946, *41*, 258–290.

personality theories — our stereotypes about dispositional (personality) traits.

SOCIAL ATTITUDES ABOUT ETHNIC IDENTITIES

Personality traits are not the only characteristics for which we have stereotypes. Ethnic identities are another. In an early study, Gregory Razran (1950) showed 150 men photographs of 30 young women, all strangers to them. He asked the subjects to rate each photograph on a 5-point scale that would indicate their overall liking for each woman and to rate their assessment of her beauty, character, intelligence, ambition, and "entertainingness." Two months later, he asked the same group to view the identical photographs, but this time each photograph had a surname (label) attached to it. Some of the young women were provided with Jewish names such as Finkelstein and Cohen. To other photographs, Razran affixed Irish surnames such as O'Shaughnessy and McGillicuddy; to still others, Italian surnames such as Valenti and Scadano; and finally to others, old-American surnames such as Davis and Clark.

The surnames had a marked effect on how the men perceived the women. Adding Jewish and Italian surnames resulted in a substantial drop in overall liking and a smaller drop in judgments of beauty and character. The decrease in the likability ratings of the "Jewish" women was twice as great as for the "Italians" and five times as great as for the "Irish." In contrast, the labels contributed to an increase in the ratings of ambition and intelligence for the women with Jewish surnames. Clearly, the labels had a marked effect on the men's perceptions of the photographs and on their assessment of the young women. Apparently the subjects had ethnic social attitudes that the names associated with the photographs activated. Once ethnic identities were associated with the women in the pictures, they were seen as possessing the traits that composed the men's ethnic stereotypes.

Although Razran's study was conducted over forty years ago, ethnic stereotypes are still very much a part of American life. More recent studies show, for example, that Hispanics are seen as ambitious, hard-working, friendly, and ethical (Triandis et al., 1982; Jones, 1991); Native Americans are characterized as silent, passive, drunken, lazy, and immoral (Trimble, 1988); and Asian-Americans are thought to be intelligent but methodical and passive (Borresen, 1982; Bannai and Cohen, 1985; Hurh and Kim, 1989).

In another early study of ethnic stereotypes (Lambert et al., 1960), French- and English-speaking Canadian subjects in Montreal heard ten speakers read the same short passage; some speakers read it in English and some in French. From the tape of each speaker's voice, subjects were to describe the speaker in terms of fourteen characteristics, including height, attractiveness, sense of humor, intelligence, and leadership. What subjects were *not* told was that each speaker was on the tape twice — reading once in English and once in French — so any differences between English and French speakers must be due to language alone. Not surprisingly, subjects whose primary language was English rated the English speakers more positively on seven of the fourteen traits, describing them as taller; of better character; better looking; and more intelligent, dependable, kind, and ambitious than the French speakers. The same speakers, when speaking French, were said to have a better sense of humor than the English speakers.

The surprising finding of the study was that French-speaking subjects *also* rated the English speakers more positively. In fact, they rated them more positively than the English-speaking subjects did, giving the English speakers higher rat-

ings on ten traits. The researchers argued that, in 1960, this reflected the existing social structure in Montreal, where English speakers were clearly in control. Since then, the French-speaking majority in Quebec has gained political power, and French has become the official language of the province. Still, a study similar to Lambert's, conducted in 1985, has found that French Canadians continue to hold negative stereotypes of their own language group (Maurice, 1985). It is possible, then, to hold negative stereotypes about ingroups, as well as outgroups.

Americans are, of course, not the only group to hold ethnic stereotypes. A recent survey of Americans and Japanese found that while Americans characterized the Japanese as competitive, hard-working, crafty, and friendly, the Japanese viewed Americans as friendly, competitive, fair, and prejudiced (Hillenbrand, 1992). See Figure 6-1.

SOCIAL ATTITUDES TOWARD PHYSICAL CHARACTERISTICS

Social psychologists have given a great deal of attention to stereotypes based on physical characteristics. As we noted in Chapter 5, "Communication," like it or not, our physical characteristics *communicate*. In other words, we make judgments about others, and they about us, on the basis of physical appearance cues. In Chapter 5, we said that physical appearance was a *symbol* — something that stands for something else. The something else — the inferences we draw on the basis of a symbol — are said to be its *meaning*. It should be clear by now that the process of communication involves the process of social cognition, that is, the process of interpreting sensations that reach us from the social environment. The meanings we attribute to symbols are determined by the schemas or attitudes we have for them in memory.

In the early 1960s, Wells and Siegal (1961) conducted a study to examine the stereotypes associated with people having different body types. The researchers showed subjects silhouette drawings of people with three different body types: endomorphs, persons whose body type tends

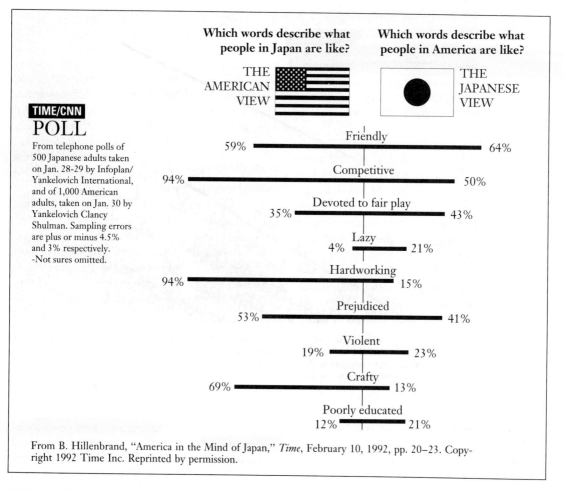

From B. Hillenbrand, "America in the Mind of Japan," *Time*, February 10, 1992, pp. 20–23. Copyright 1992 Time Inc. Reprinted by permission.

FIGURE 6-1 AMERICAN AND JAPANESE ETHNIC STEREOTYPES

toward softness, roundness, or fatness; mesomorphs, those whose body type is more muscular and athletic; and ectomorphs, those whose body type is tall and thin. Subjects were then asked to rate each person on a set of opposite pairs of twenty-four personality characteristics (e.g., intelligent/unintelligent, warm/cool).

Several differences emerged. Endomorphs were believed to be calm (relaxed, even sluggish), sympathetic (warm, even forgiving), and cooperative. Mesomorphs were believed to be active (enthusiastic, adventurous, even reckless), dominant (assertive), and competitive. On the other hand, ectomorphs were believed to be anxious (tense,

reticent), thoughtful (serious, even cautious), and detached (shy, withdrawn).

In addition to body type, physical attractiveness has been much studied by social psychologists. The ancient Greek philosopher Aristotle once observed that "beauty is a greater recommendation than any letter of introduction." Today, social psychologists are finding that in many respects he was right. Indeed, their research suggests that the world is a more pleasant and satisfying place for attractive people because their appearance brings them a decided social advantage (Reis et al., 1982; Webster and Driskell, 1983). Such findings are compatible with the attractive-

Endomorphs are persons whose body type tends toward softness, roundness, or fatness; mesomorphs are more muscular and athletic; and ectomorphs are tall and thin. We tend to stereotype endomorphs as calm, sympathetic, and cooperative. Mesomorphs are believed to be active, dominant, and competitive. Ectomorphs are viewed as anxious, thoughtful, and detached. Do other people's body types influence your judgments about them?

ness stereotype, the belief that "what is beautiful is good."

Physical attractiveness is a characteristic that has a major impact on the impressions that we form of people (Deaux and Lewis, 1984). As unfair and unenlightened as it may seem, we tend to prefer attractive people over their less attractive peers. The *halo effect* refers to our tendency to judge attractive individuals as having a larger number of socially desirable traits than unattractive individuals. Teachers expect attractive children to achieve higher grades than unattractive children, and attractive children do so (Clifford and Walster, 1973). Further, the misdemeanors of good-looking children are judged as less serious than those of unattractive children (Dion, 1972); they are disciplined less severely (Berkowitz and Frodi, 1979); and people predict that they will have more successful careers (Dion, Berscheid, and Walster, 1972). Even young children have these attitudes toward physical attractiveness.

Nursery school children named their good-looking peers as the classmates they liked best and considered their homely classmates to be unfriendly and aggressive (Dion and Berscheid, 1974).

In college, essays ostensibly written by attractive students receive higher grades than do the same essays when they are presumed to be written by homely students (Landy and Sigall, 1974). And attractive adults are thought to have happier marriages, better sex lives, higher status, and better mental health than their unattractive counterparts (Dion, Berscheid, and Walster, 1972; Dermer and Thiel, 1975; Cash et al., 1977). The beautiful-is-good bias prevails even in judgments of newborns, with physically attractive babies being judged smarter, more likable, and less troublesome than unattractive infants (Stephan and Langlois, 1984).

It appears that the attractiveness of one person can even "rub off" onto another person. In one study (Sigall and Landy, 1973), on entering a waiting room, each subject encountered two other people: one was an "average-looking" male who was posing as another subject, and the other was a female who was presented to half of the subjects as the girlfriend of the male and to the other half as someone waiting to see a professor. For half of the subjects who believed the girl to be the other subject's girlfriend and half of those who thought she was waiting to see a professor, the girl was tastefully dressed and made up "so as to accentuate her natural good looks." When seen by the other half of both groups, she wore an unbecoming wig, no makeup, and unflattering clothes. Subsequently escorted to another room, each subject was asked to give his impressions of the "other subject" — the male in the waiting room.

The results of the experiment showed that when the "other subject" just happened to be in the presence of the female who was thought to be waiting to see a professor, her attractiveness did not affect the subjects' perceptions of him. On the other hand, when she was thought to be his girlfriend, her attractiveness did make a difference. When the "other subject" appeared to have an attractive girlfriend, subjects felt they would like him and rated him as more intelligent, self-confident, friendly, and exciting *and as more physically attractive* than when his girlfriend was homely. Another study found that, evidently, attractiveness can also rub off onto *same-sex* friends (Kernis and Wheeler, 1981).

However, many of us also stereotypically attribute negative characteristics to good-looking people. Because physically attractive swindlers are seen as more competent, and therefore as more dangerous, they are given longer sentences (Sigall and Ostrove, 1975). Attractive women are more likely to be seen as vain and adulterous than less good-looking women (Dermer and Thiel, 1975). And what can be viewed as a "positive" characteristic of someone in one situation may be viewed as a "negative" characteristic in another. For example, beautiful women are generally perceived as more feminine than other women. This may be an advantage in dating situations but a disadvantage in occupations where success is associated with stereotypically masculine traits, such as physical strength, independence, and decisiveness (Cash and Janda, 1984).

In addition, in relation to nontraditional jobs, attractive women may be seen as less competent than less attractive women. Thus less attractive women may have an advantage over their more attractive peers when seeking management positions — traditionally a male preserve. Indeed, several "dress for success" books have become bestsellers by advising women to downplay their looks by cutting their hair short, using cosmetics sparingly, and wearing conservative suits if they want to get ahead in business. In brief, in the workplace a sexist prescription for success still holds: If a woman hopes to advance in a man's world, she better not appear too feminine.

The studies we just reviewed indicate that when the only thing we know about a person is his or her physical traits, we quite readily make judgments about other characteristics we have yet to observe. But other research suggests that when we *do* have additional information, other characteristics may influence our judgments more than physical attractiveness. In one study (Solomon and Saxe, 1977), subjects watched a videotape of an attractive or unattractive woman and were told that the woman was either very intelligent (grade point average of 3.75) or not very intelligent (grade point average of 2.25). Later, subjects were asked to rate the personality traits of the woman shown on the tape. Although subjects gave the highest positive rating to the woman who was both attractive and intelligent, intelligence had greater influence on the rating of personality traits than did attractiveness.

SOCIAL ATTITUDES ABOUT GENDER

Since the early 1970s, social psychologists have focused on identifying social stereotypes about gender (Ashmore and Del Boca, 1986). The general question was: "What are the characteristics typically associated with being a male or female?" or "What traits do people believe distinguish males and females?" Typically, "psychological" social psychologists have focused on schemas whose beliefs involve the associations between gender and personality characteristics (e.g., emotional, organized, competent). In contrast, "sociological" social psychologists have tended to focus on schemas whose beliefs involve the associations between gender and occupation/role characteristics (e.g., chairperson, sergeant, lawyer).

Combining both perspectives, Deaux and Lewis (1984) showed that gender stereotypes can include several kinds of characteristics—occupations, role behaviors, and physical as well as personality traits. They found support for this hypothesis by demonstrating that if subjects were given a description of a person that included gender and examples of any one of these kinds of characteristics, they would fill in the remainder of the gender-stereotypic characteristics. For example, if a hypothetical woman was described to subjects as providing emotional support, managing the house, caring for children, and decorating the house, subjects concluded that the woman probably also possessed personality traits such as being emotional, gentle, and understanding of others; physical characteristics such as being dainty and graceful and having a soft voice; and a work role such as occupational therapist or elementary school teacher. In other words, the subjects possessed a traditional-female schema that included *both* personal traits (personality and physical) and role expectations (family and occupation).

Gender apparently plays a key role in many schemas. When the only information we have about a person is gender, we usually anticipate that other differences will distinguish him or her from members of the opposite gender. For example, studies show that employers who know only the gender of a job applicant often believe that women are less in need of and less interested in a job, will keep it only briefly, and are not physically strong enough for it (Reskin and Hartmann, 1986; Eagly, Makhijani, and Klonsky, 1992).

Even when we know that a specific male and a specific female *share* a characteristic that we ordinarily believe distinguishes males from females, we are likely to continue to believe that still other differences separate the two. For example, researchers asked college students to compare male and female murderers. Murderers are believed to have many more traits normally associated with males than with females. Although the respondents rated male and female murderers similarly in terms of personality traits such as aggressive, violent, dangerous, strange, and annoying, they also believed that male (but not female) murderers were ugly, unrighteous, and bad (King and Clayson, 1988).

But when we have information about other characteristics, we may rely less on gender schemas. Deaux and Lewis found that schemas connecting physical characteristics, occupations, role behaviors, and personality traits are sometimes stronger than those connecting gender to any of these characteristics. For example, subjects believed that a person described as having masculine role behaviors (financial provider, leader, person responsible for household repairs) was likely to possess masculine personality traits (independent, active, competitive) and to be in typically "masculine" occupations (truck driver, insurance agent, urban planner) regardless of whether the person was identified as male or female. In addition, physical characteristics (masculine: tall, strong, broad-shouldered; feminine: soft voice, dainty) can sometimes also outweigh gender in determining inferences we make about people.

SOCIAL ATTITUDES TOWARD FAMILY IDENTITIES

Social psychologists, like other social researchers, are increasingly interested in the family. They have found that, even in family life, social attitudes play an important part. Many of us remember reading about the "wicked stepmother" in *Cinderella*. Social psychologists have been curious to see if the words "wicked" and "step" go together in our social attitudes about family identities. To a large degree, research suggests that they do.

Linda Bryan and her associates asked college-student respondents to read one of twenty booklets containing a brief paragraph describing an adult and an adolescent in a family (Bryan et al., 1986). The adults in the paragraphs were portrayed as never-married, married, divorced, step-, or widowed parents. Respondents were then asked to indicate their impressions of the parent and adolescent using several 7-point, bipolar scales — for example, hateful/affectionate, bad/good, unfair/fair, cruel/kind, and severe/lenient. Stereotypes of parents, the researchers found, were not all the same: stepparents, divorced parents, and never-married parents were more negatively evaluated than married or widowed parents. Interestingly, the adolescent children of stepparents and never-married parents were also evaluated more negatively than were the children of married, divorced, or widowed parents.

Researcher Mark Fine (1986) had college-student respondents rate eight family identities (brother, sister, father, mother, stepfather, stepmother, grandfather, and grandmother), using nine evaluative adjective pairs similar to those used by Bryan and her colleagues. The subjects were instructed to respond to the family identities "in general," forgetting any specific person or persons with whom they might be familiar. Fine found that stepfathers and stepmothers were described with more negative adjectives than were fathers and mothers on almost every scale.

Fine also compared the attitudes of three groups of respondents whose personal family structures differed — those from intact, single-parent, and stepparent families. He found that the stereotype of stepfather was more negative than that of biological father in all three groups. However, the stereotype of stepmother was less negative among respondents from stepfamilies and single-parent families than among their counterparts from intact families. This finding suggests that, under some conditions, personal interaction with a social identity, such as stepmother, may modify a negative cultural stereotype.

In another study which suggests that life experiences modify cultural stereotypes, Karen Dugger (1990) compared the social attitudes of white and African-American women toward women's family roles. Using data collected from a national sample of over 3,000 women, Dugger measured attitude toward single parenting through respondents' agreement or disagreement with such statements as "There is no reason why single women shouldn't have children and raise them if they want to." Attitude toward wives' employment (and dual responsibility) was measured by respondents' support for such statements as "a marriage where the husband and wife share responsibilities more — both work, both share homemaking and child responsibilities." And attitude toward nontraditional women was measured by asking respondents, "Which 3 or 4 [of the following] qualities do you admire most in a woman?" Qualities such as intelligence, self-control, frankness, independence, competitiveness, leadership ability, and competence were coded as nontraditional. Gentleness, ability to express emotions, and willingness to compromise were coded as traditional.

Dugger found that African-American women had more positive attitudes than white women toward single parenting, wives' employment, and nontraditional personality traits. Among both African-American and white women, those who were employed, had higher incomes, or were single parents had more positive social attitudes toward those characteristics. This finding suggests that the women's social attitudes may have been influenced by the women's own experiences.

Stereotypes and Causal Attributions

Social attitudes not only affect how we identify a particular person and whether we evaluate him or her positively or negatively. Our attitudes also influence our feelings about that person's capacity to control his or her environment. For example, our stereotype of politicians might include the beliefs that they are intelligent, assertive, powerful, and well connected. On the other hand, our stereotype of high school dropouts might include such characteristics as unskilled, weak, isolated, and unemployed. Thus, our attitudes also include our assessments of the causes of others' behavior. Social psychologists call these assessments *causal attributions.*

TYPES OF CAUSAL ATTRIBUTIONS

Social psychologists have identified two broad types of causation distinguishing our attitudes toward others: internal and external (Heider, 1958). We make **internal attributions** when we attribute responsibility for someone's behavior (or outcomes resulting from the behavior) to the stereotypic characteristics of his or her social identity: "Asian students do well in school because they are intelligent" and "Teenagers get pregnant because they are careless." We make **external attributions** when we attribute responsibility for a person's behavior (or outcomes) to environmental and situational circumstances: "Asian students do well in school because their families pressure them to study hard" and "Teenagers get pregnant because they don't have access to contraceptives."

Internal attributions tend to focus on one of two causes for a behavior or its consequences—ability or effort. External attributions tend to focus on task difficulty and luck as explanations. Suppose you have been watching your favorite basketball team play a game. With three seconds left and the score tied, a player on your team (in your dreams, you are the player!) steals the ball and shoots a 15-foot jumpshot. As the buzzer sounds, the ball swishes through the net, and your team wins the game. A friend, who has been watching with you and pulling for the opposing team, now exclaims, "Were they *lucky*," to which you indignantly respond, "It had nothing to do with luck! That was sheer *ability*." "No way," explains another friend. "Your guys were more psyched up. They just gave it more *effort*." To which a third friend interjects, "It was just an *easy* shot. Anyone could've made it." As you can see, the same behavior has been explained four different ways. Ability and effort are both internal at-

tributions because they attribute the causes of someone's behavior to his or her internal qualities; difficulty and luck are external attributions because they attribute a person's behavior to aspects of the situation or environment.

The distinctions we make, consciously or unconsciously, between internal and external causation or among ability, effort, task difficulty, and luck underlie most of our social attitudes, including those about many contemporary social issues. The way we answer the following questions illustrates this point: Do you believe children do poorly in school because they (1) lack innate ability, (2) aren't motivated or don't try hard enough, (3) are victims of poor schools, inadequate teachers, racism, and poverty? Do you believe that people become criminals because of inner psychological deficiencies, conflicts, and problems or because they live in an environment where social pressures, learning experiences, and poverty propel them into crime? Do you believe that we should hold everybody individually accountable for his or her behavior, thereby rewarding conformity and punishing deviance; or should we hold society responsible for human shortcomings, thereby seeking to remedy unhealthy social conditions through social reforms and direct social change?

Kelley's Theory of Attribution

Building on Heider's work, Harold Kelley (1972) has proposed a theory of causal attribution. Our memories, according to Kelley, include an attribution schema that we use to process information when inferring the cause of someone's behavior. According to this theory, we examine three possible sources of explanations for a behavior or an outcome it produces: one is internal—the person's characteristics—and two are external—an environmental stimulus and the circumstances surrounding the person's encounter with a stimulus. For example, we could attribute Tom's low grade in a social psychology course to (1) Tom's being stupid or not studying, (2) the difficulty of the course, or (3) the interference of another student. But how do we choose among these three causes? Kelley proposes we depend on three kinds of attribution rules: consistency, distinctiveness, and consensus.

Consistency concerns whether the person has responded similarly to the stimulus in the past. For example, were all of Tom's grades in the course low, or was he doing well until he bombed the final? If all his grades were low (high consistency), we are likely to attribute Tom's low grade in the course to his low ability or to the difficulty of the exams. If his grade on the final was different from his grades on the other exams (low consistency), we are more likely to attribute his course grade to the circumstances surrounding his grade on the final. For example, the perceiver might attribute Tom's grade to a recent breakup with his girlfriend.

Distinctiveness concerns whether the person responds in the same way to other stimuli as well. Did Tom receive low grades in most of his courses this term? If Tom's grade in social psychology is similar to his grades in other courses (low distinctiveness), we are likely to attribute the low grade to Tom's (lack of) ability. On the other hand, if the course grade is dissimilar to his grades in other courses (high distinctiveness), we are less likely to attribute the grade to Tom's ability and more likely to conclude that the social psychology course was especially difficult.

Consensus concerns whether other people respond in the same way to the stimulus. Did most students in the course receive the same grade as Tom? If they did (high consensus), we are more likely to attribute Tom's low grade (and everyone else's) to the course: it was "difficult." On the other hand, if Tom's grade was different from the grades of most of the other students (low consensus), we are more likely to attribute Tom's grade to his ability or effort: he "is stupid" or "didn't study" if most of them got higher grades, and he "is bright" or "studied hard" if most of them got lower grades.

Thus, Kelley suggests that our attribution rules indicate internal causality under conditions of high consistency, low distinctiveness, and low consensus. However, to use these rules, we must have information on consistency, distinctiveness, and consensus *before* we attribute the cause or causes of someone's behavior. In fact, we frequently make our causal judgments on the basis of incomplete information. We do this because our social attitudes include information pertinent to causal attributions. Simply having information about a person's characteristics (e.g., sex, race, age, occupation, or personality traits) or behavior can activate a social attitude. On the basis of the additional "information" such a stereotype provides (the other traits associated with it in our memory) we make judgments about causality. So lack of information about causality does not prevent us from drawing causal inferences. (See the box "The Attribution of Responsibility for Obesity.")

Additional research suggests that our judgments about causality are subject to various biases, or kinds of error. Not surprisingly, one of these kinds of error has to do with whether we are making judgments about ourselves or about other people—the fundamental attribution error. Another concerns whether our judgments are about groups with which we identify (ingroups) or those with which we do not (outgroups)—the ultimate attribution error. Let's turn our attention to these kinds of errors now.

Fundamental Attribution Error

Various studies (see, e.g., Watson, 1982) suggest that we generally tend to view internal factors as underlying *other* people's behavior but that we emphasize the extent to which outside forces control our *own* behavior. We believe that we choose our actions to fit particular situational requirements, but we think that others do what they do because of their personality characteristics. Social psychologist Lee Ross (1977) coined the term **fundamental attribution error** to describe our tendency to overestimate the influence of personality factors as causes of other people's actions, while undervaluing the influence of environmental or situational factors.

A study by Richard E. Nisbett and his associates (1973) illustrates the fundamental attribution error. The researchers asked Yale undergraduate

THE ATTRIBUTION OF RESPONSIBILITY FOR OBESITY

Obese people are the object of much prejudice. While many forms of physical unattractiveness are seen as involuntary, obesity is often seen as something the individual could control if he or she chose to. This internal attribution of responsibility for obesity may account for the intensity of negative evaluations toward obese individuals. DeJong (1980) asked 226 women to rate an obese woman on the basis of a photograph and one of three different biographical statements attributed to her. In one of the biographical statements, the woman indicated that her obesity resulted from a minor thyroid problem (presumably a condition the woman did not choose). In the second, she indicated that she had recently lost 25 pounds on a new diet (suggesting that although she may have been responsible for her obesity in the first place, she saw it as undesirable and was trying to do something about it). In the third biographical statement, the woman didn't give any reason for her obesity. The woman was rated most unfavorably when no explanation was given for her obesity. She received more favorable ratings when she mentioned the thyroid condition or the diet.

Even many of the self-help organizations devoted to the obese, such as Weight Watchers, share the view of obesity as socially undesirable, medically hazardous, and remediable. Recently, however, organizations have emerged to defend the interests of the obese and to "fight back" against prejudice and discrimination. Unlike other self-help groups for the obese, these argue that fat is beautiful and that human rights and privileges should not be determined by a person's weight any more than by his or her skin color.

students to write brief explanations of (1) why they liked the women they had dated most frequently in the past year and why they had chosen their majors and (2) why their best friends liked the women they had dated most regularly in the past year and why the friends had chosen their majors.

Judges read the paragraphs written by the students and coded the reasons given as either internal attributions ("I like warm people"; "I want a lot of money") or external attributions ("She's a very warm person"; "Chemistry is a high-paying field"). When describing their *own* reasons for choosing girlfriends, the subjects listed external factors (properties of the girl) twice as frequently as internal factors (reasons associated with their own needs, interests, and characteristics). But when they gave their *best friends'* reasons for selecting girlfriends, the subjects cited internal factors about as often as external factors. In explaining why they themselves had chosen their majors, subjects attributed their reasons almost equally to external and internal factors. (Seemingly, they saw themselves as selecting their majors with deliberation, in contrast to being "carried away" by women.) But subjects attributed their friends' selections of majors to almost four times as many internal as external reasons. Thus, the researchers conclude, people tend to interpret the same behavior differently depending on whether it is one's own or someone else's.

But other studies suggest that we do not *always* attribute others' behavior more often to internal causes than we do our own (see, e.g., Weary, 1980). These studies show that we more often attribute other people's *failures* to their personality characteristics, while we attribute our own failures to the environment, the situation, or the actions of our opponents. On the other hand, we more often believe other people's *successes* to be caused by their environment, while we attribute our own successes to internal causes. Not surprisingly, teachers take causal credit for their students' successes, but attribute students' failures to low intelligence and poor motivation (Johnson, Feigenbaum, and Weiby, 1964; Beckman, 1970;

STUDENT OBSERVATION

Fundamental Attribution Error

*A*s the fundamental attribution error suggests, I more often attribute my roommate's failures to her personality characteristics and my own failures to external factors. Just recently, both my roommate and I failed a Music 21 exam. When she got her test back, I immediately thought, "Well that's what she gets for missing class and going out instead of studying." Then, I got mine back, and my first thought was, "What an unfair test! I can't stand this professor!"

Schopler and Layton, 1972). (See the Student Observation: "Fundamental Attribution Error.")

Social psychologists have suggested that a person's gender influences whether we attribute his or her performance to internal or external factors. Both males and females are more likely to attribute a female's success to luck or effort and a male's success to ability (Deaux and Emswiller, 1974; Feather and Simon, 1975; Nichols, 1975). A female's failure, on the other hand, is more likely to be attributed to lack of ability and less likely to be attributed to bad luck or lack of effort than is a male's failure. These gender differences have been observed even when subjects were asked to give the reasons for their *own* behavior (Deaux, 1981). This tendency to attribute males' success to ability and females' success to luck or effort contributes to the perpetuation of stereotypes depicting women as less powerful and less in control than men.

Ultimate Attribution Error

There is a second source of bias in our causal inferences. Social psychologist Thomas Pettigrew (1979) argues that the performer's membership in an ingroup or outgroup also affects how we explain other people's successes and failures. To social psychologists, the performer is "a member of an ingroup" when we use the same social identity to describe ourselves *and* the performer. The performer is "a member of an outgroup" when we

use different social identities to describe ourselves and the performer. We are more likely to attribute another person's success to internal causes when the person is a member of an ingroup than when he or she is a member of an outgroup. For example, if men were asked why a male movie producer received an Oscar, they would be likely to attribute his success to ability. However, if the producer were a woman, the men would be less likely to attribute her success to ability and more likely to attribute it to outside pressure to recognize women in the movie industry.

This bias toward internal attributions for the success of ingroups and failure of outgroups, on the one hand, and external attributions for the failure of ingroups and success of outgroups, on the other, has been called the **ultimate attribution error** by Pettigrew. He identified four types of explanations that are used to explain the successes of outgroup members while continuing the discreditation of outgroup members:

1. The success is perceived as an exception to the rule. ("I don't think much of women producers as a group, but she deserved the nomination.")
2. The success is attributed to some special advantage, such as affirmative action. ("I guess they figured they had to nominate a woman one of these days.")
3. The success is perceived as overcoming the limitations of members of the performer's

group through effort and hard work. ("She worked really hard on her last three movies, and they were all successful.")

4. The success is attributed to situational factors, such as the demands of the performer's role. ("I'm sure her husband's being such a talented actor gave her the confidence she needed to undertake those films.")

Such attributions, Pettigrew proposed, reinforce our negative stereotypes of (prejudice) and discrimination toward outgroup members.

To illustrate these general ideas about causal attributions, let's look at three examples — causal attributions regarding crime, poverty, and homelessness.

CAUSAL ATTRIBUTION REGARDING CRIME

Social psychologists studying state legislators have distinguished three attribution schemas involving beliefs about the causes of crime and crime prevention (Bynum, Greene, and Cullen, 1986; McGarrell and Flanagan, 1987). The first schema, called by the researchers the "conservative ideology," includes the belief that the immediate causes of crime are such personality traits as laziness, irresponsibility, lack of discipline, and immorality. These personality traits are themselves believed to have been caused by an overly permissive environment that was ineffective in teaching respect for authority and law-abiding values. The second schema, the "liberal ideology," associates crime with poverty and unemployment but attributes both crime and poverty to unequal opportunities and discrimination within society. The third schema, the "radical ideology," sees crime as being committed by both the rich and the poor. In this view all crime can be traced to a capitalist society, which emphasizes economic competition and private property. Believers in the radical ideology attribute the major difference in crimes committed by the rich and the poor to differences in how the criminal justice system deals with crimes committed by the rich and poor. They believe the rich have the political power to ensure that certain

behavior by the poor is more often defined as "crime" and then severely punished than is their own harmful behavior.

Besides their beliefs about the causes of crime, legislators have beliefs about its *prevention* and *reduction*. Conservative legislators argue that irresponsibility and immorality, which they believe cause crime, are best countered by strong deterrence — more police, tougher courts, and longer prison sentences. Liberals contend that unequal opportunity and discrimination, which they believe cause crime, can be reduced through educational programs, job training, and antidiscrimination laws. In contrast, radical legislators assert that crime, which they believe is caused by a capitalist system controlled by the rich, can be reduced only by changing the capitalist system, that is, by reducing competition and private property and making the judicial system more responsive to the poor and less to the rich.

State legislators, the researchers concluded, were a diverse group, with no one of the three ideologies (schemas) dominating. However, most white, Republican, nonurban legislators believed in the conservative ideology, while their nonwhite, Democratic, urban counterparts held either the liberal or the radical ideology.

Characteristics of the Criminal

Research suggests that our causal attributions may be affected by several kinds of information about the performer. For example, we might expect that our attributions about criminals would be most affected by information about the crimes they committed. But in some cases, *other* characteristics of the criminal influence our attributions. In one study (Howard and Pike, 1986), sociology students read descriptions of an arrest for disorderly conduct that included the race (white or black) and social class (working class or middle class) of the arrested person. Respondents then received a questionnaire and were asked to judge the personality traits of the arrested person (very moral/low morals, responsible/irresponsible, impulsive/in control, selfish/not selfish, honest/not honest, and so on) and to indicate whether they would attribute the crime to (1) the person's character, (2) society, or (3) luck.

Respondents judged the white person who was arrested as possessing more negative personality traits and being more responsible for his crime than they did the black person who was arrested. Although the personality traits of the working-class person were judged more negatively than were those of the middle-class person, social class did not affect the attribution of responsibility for the crime.

When respondents read descriptions about unemployment instead of crime, they attributed unemployment to personality traits more often if the unemployed person was working class rather than middle class. Thus, both the person's social characteristics (race and social class) and behavior (disorderly conduct and unemployment) influenced respondents' attributions.

Characteristics of the Perceiver

Characteristics of the perceiver also influence causal attributions. Robert Young (1991) conducted a study to test the hypothesis that blacks' and whites' attitudes toward capital punishment (the death penalty) originate from fundamentally different attributions. White respondents who believed that criminals commit crimes for rational, self-serving — internal — reasons showed more support for the death penalty than whites who believed that poverty — external — causes crime. As we would expect, support for the death penalty was higher among whites who attributed crime to internal as opposed to external factors. These beliefs, however, did *not* affect support for the death penalty among black respondents.

Among black respondents, the only predictor of support for the death penalty was "trust in the police." Black respondents who showed high trust in the police were more likely to support the death penalty than those who showed low trust. For whites, trust in the police was not related to support or opposition to the death penalty.

Young concluded from his study that group membership significantly influences attributions of responsibility for various events. The divergent contemporary circumstances of black and white Americans lead them to view the criminal justice system and the causes of crime differently. These differences are reflected in their different attitudes about the death penalty.

CAUSAL ATTRIBUTION REGARDING POVERTY

Let's now shift our attention from causal attributions regarding crime to those involving poverty. Researchers James Kluegel and Eliot Smith (1986) conducted a large national telephone survey ($n = 2,212$) of beliefs about inequalities in our society. They asked American adults to rate the importance of each of several factors that could be a reason for being either rich or poor. The researchers distinguished between "individual" (internal) and "structural" (external) explanations of economic inequality. They wanted to know if people attribute wealth and poverty more to the individual characteristics of the rich and poor (talent, drive, lack of effort, loose morals) or to the structure of our society (economic system, inheritance, political pull, bad schools, unavailability of jobs, discrimination).

Individual explanations of poverty and wealth were rated as "very important" by more respondents than were structural explanations. On average, the individual explanations for wealth were rated as "very important" by 57 percent of the respondents; the structural explanations, by 42 percent. The individual explanations for poverty were rated as "very important" by 50 percent of the respondents; the structural explanations, by only 34 percent.

In a later study, Kluegel (1990) discovered that respondents' attributions about poverty were related to their opinions about a variety of programs designed to decrease it. People who believed in structural explanations of poverty were more like-

Americans tend to believe that whether a person is rich or poor depends more on individual factors, such as the person's talent and effort, than on structural factors, such as unequal opportunities. These attributions about the causes of poverty and wealth shape our responses to persons we perceive as rich or poor.

ly to support government guarantees of a job and an income above the poverty level to every person who wanted to work. These same respondents were also decidedly more likely to support welfare programs for those who do not have a job than were respondents who favored individual explanations for poverty. Among white respondents, those believing in structural explanations also were more supportive of affirmative action programs that establish quotas setting aside a certain number of positions (e.g., school admissions and jobs) for qualified blacks and other minorities.

Which Americans are most likely to believe in structural explanations of poverty and therefore to support welfare programs? These attributions were more widespread among nonwhites, females, the young, and those with lower incomes — the groups most likely to be affected by poverty.

CAUSAL ATTRIBUTION REGARDING THE HOMELESS

People may use a particular attribution to account for the behavior of the poor in general but use different attributions to explain the behavior of subgroups such as Hispanic poor or single mothers who are poor. Recently social psychologists have begun to investigate the attributions people make regarding another subgroup of the poor —

the homeless. Barrett Lee and his associates interviewed residents of Nashville, Tennessee, about causes of homelessness: (1) "Most homeless people are homeless because they choose that lifestyle"; (2) "Most homeless don't want to work"; (3) "The major cause of homelessness is alcoholism"; (4) "Homelessness is due to forces people can't control, such as housing shortages or changes in the economy"; and (5) "The homeless are victims of bad luck" (Lee, Jones, and Lewis, 1990).

The researchers found that attributions regarding homelessness were in several ways different from attributions about poverty found in the national study discussed above. The individual explanations, which suggest that the homeless choose their lifestyle and don't want to work, were *not* the most frequently cited causes for homelessness, as they were for poverty. Structural explanations, such as housing shortages, changes in the economy, and even bad luck were cited more frequently than reasons focusing on the individual. The difference, the researchers argue, results from a successful effort by advocates, government officials, and the media to define the problem of homelessness (as opposed to poverty in general) in structural terms.

The respondents' attributions about homelessness were found to affect their opinions about the way homeless people should be treated. Although most people surveyed sympathized with the plight of the homeless, those believing in structural causes were more supportive of proposals to increase taxes and provide additional housing as ways to aid the homeless. On the other hand, respondents believing more in individual causes tended to favor the enactment of restrictive laws limiting homeless people's access to downtown businesses and the enforcement of vagrancy laws. Finally, the researchers found that the structural explanation of homelessness was more prevalent among African-Americans, non-Southerners, those identifying themselves as politically "liberal," and the more educated—*not* necessarily the groups most likely to be affected by homelessness.

Pervasiveness and Social Change

Some social attitudes are held uniquely by a single individual, while others are shared by most members of a group and even members of different groups. An attitude's **pervasiveness** is the degree to which it is shared by members of a social group or groups. Attitudes are said to be more pervasive when they are shared by a large proportion of the members of the group and less pervasive when shared by a small proportion.

Social attitudes can change over time. If we look at the social attitudes held by a single individual, over time, some will remain stable while others will change. For example, a woman may be pro-choice at one stage of her life and become pro-life at another. Similarly, the pervasiveness of social attitudes among the members of a social group can change. Over time, some social attitudes will become more widely held and others less widely held among the members of a social group. Sometimes this change occurs relatively quickly; other times change occurs more slowly.

Attitude change does *not* imply that *all* components of an attitude change simultaneously. A change in an attitude may involve only some of its belief components. In other words, a change in the pervasiveness of a social attitude usually involves a reorganizing or restructuring of the attitude.

PERVASIVENESS: THE CASE OF GENDER STEREOTYPES

For example, how pervasive are gender stereotypes? John Williams and Deborah Best (1990) sought to measure their pervasiveness across twenty-five different countries. In other words, the researchers wanted to find out how similar gender stereotypes were in different countries. For each country, data on gender stereotypes had been gathered using the same 300-item adjective checklist. The researchers' criterion for the identification of a gender-linked characteristic was that both women and men respondents associated the characteristic with one gender at least twice as often as with the other gender. The study's findings suggest that gender stereotypes are very pervasive indeed. At least fifty male-associated and fifty female-associated characteristics were identified in all twenty-five countries. For example, active, aggressive, conceited, greedy, lazy, realistic, and steady were some of the characteristics more often associated with males; while affectionate, complicated, fickle, patient, self-pitying, submissive, and understanding were more often associated with females.

Despite these striking similarities in the belief component of gender stereotypes among the twenty-five countries, the researchers found that the feeling component — the evaluation of women and men as good or bad — differed substantially from culture to culture. In some countries (e.g., Japan, South Africa, and Nigeria), males were more positively evaluated than females. Yet, in other countries (e.g., Italy, Peru, Australia, and the United States), women were more positively evaluated.

SOCIAL CHANGE: THE CASE OF ETHNIC AND RACIAL STEREOTYPES

As we have just seen, gender stereotypes are very pervasive. Williams and Best's study showed that there is much agreement across at least twenty-five cultures about the characteristics associated with being male or female. This is not the case for racial and ethnic stereotypes. Indeed, even within the United States, racial and ethnic attitudes have changed a great deal in this century. A good example of changes in the pervasiveness of racial and ethnic attitudes is a study of stereotypes among white undergraduates at Princeton over the middle portion of this century (Karlins, Coffman, and Walters, 1969). Drawing on previous research as well as their own, the researchers obtained information about Princeton students' stereotypes of ten ethnic groups in 1933, 1951, and 1967.

In 1933, beliefs that blacks were superstitious and lazy were very pervasive (held by 84 percent

and 75 percent, respectively, of the respondents). A significant minority of respondents also believed blacks to be happy-go-lucky, musical, ostentatious, very religious, and ignorant. By 1967, the pervasiveness of all but one of these beliefs (that blacks are musical) had decreased to about 25 percent of the respondents. Also, in 1933, the belief was prevalent (79 percent) that Jews were shrewd, and almost half of the respondents saw them as mercenary, grasping, and industrious. By 1967, the prevalence of these beliefs had decreased significantly, and they were replaced by beliefs that Jews were intelligent, ambitious, and materialistic. (See Table 6-2 for the results of several studies on changes in white students' stereotypes of blacks.)

In recent years, a number of social scientists have detected the emergence among relatively affluent, suburban segments of the American white population of a new form of prejudice toward blacks — a perspective that has come to be termed *symbolic, modern,* or *aversive racism* (Brewer and Kramer, 1985; McConahay, 1986). The old racism was (and still is, as it continues to exist) based on beliefs in racial inferiority (e.g., that blacks are genetically unintelligent) and racial segregation (e.g., that blacks and whites should have separate schools). The new racists reject such attitudes as antithetical to their strongly held values of egalitarianism and equal opportunity; they view themselves as antiracist. The new form of racism is based on a schema incorporating beliefs that (1) blacks, contrary to their situation in the past, now have opportunities equal to those of whites, (2) *but* blacks reject cherished values of hard work, individualism, and the delay of gratification, and (3) blacks are too demanding, too pushy, and too militant. (See the box "Traditional and Symbolic Racism.") These stereotypes shape many whites' interpretations of events such as welfare, urban riots, black mayors, crime in the streets, forced busing, affirmative action programs, and quota systems.

The shift that has taken place among American whites from blatant to more subtle forms of prejudice has occurred since World War II (Crosby,

TABLE 6-2   CHANGES IN WHITE COLLEGE STUDENTS' STEREOTYPES OF BLACKS

Stereotype	Princeton[1]			Colgate,[2] 1982	Arizona State,[3] 1982
	1933	1951	1967		
Superstitious	84	41	13	6	9
Lazy	75	31	26	13	18
Happy-go-lucky	38	17	27	15	1
Ignorant	38	24	11	10	9
Musical	26	33	47	29	11
Ostentatious	26	11	25	5	10
Stupid	22	10	4	1	1
Physically dirty	17	*	3	0	1
Naive	14	*	4	4	0

*Trait not included in this study.
Sources:
[1]Adapted from M. Karlins, T. Coffman, and G. Walters, "On the Fading of Social Stereotypes: Studies in Three Generations of College Students," *Journal of Personality and Social Psychology, 1969, 13,* 5. Copyright 1969 by the American Psychological Association. Adapted by permission.
[2]Adapted from J. F. Dovidio and S. L. Gaertner, "Prejudice, Discrimination, and Racism: Historical Trends and Contemporary Approaches," in J. F. Dovidio and S. L. Gaertner (eds.), *Prejudice, Discrimination, and Racism.* New York: Academic Press, 1986, 7.
[3]Adapted from L. Gordon, "College Student Stereotypes of Blacks and Jews on Two Campuses: Four Studies Spanning 50 Years," *Sociology and Social Research,* 1986, 70, 200.

Bromley, and Saxe, 1980). In this interval, white Americans have moved steadily but gradually toward greater liberalism on racial issues. Thus, in 1942, only 30 percent of whites thought that both races should attend the same schools; by 1984, 90 percent of whites favored school integration (Smith and Sheatsley, 1984). Although most whites now oppose educational and occupational discrimination, they draw the line at compensating blacks for past discrimination and disadvantaged backgrounds by employing racial quotas and other preferential treatment.

The Process of Social Cognition

So far, this chapter has focused on social attitudes and their various components. Why do social psychologists give social attitudes so much attention? They do so because social attitudes play an important role in the process of social cognition, the process by which we make sense of our social environment.

Social psychologists view people as continuously facing a potentially problematic environment: "How can I pass this course?" "Should I trust this person?" "Can she do the job?" To answer such questions, we use information from two sources: our environment and our attitudes. Sometimes the environment provides insufficient information, or the information it offers is too expensive — in effort, time, or money — to acquire. For example, we *could* hire a private detective to investigate the background and character of each person we work closely with or think we might establish a friendship with, but we don't. Instead, we supplement the information we are able to acquire from the environment with information from another source — the attitudes stored in our memories. The relevant attitude provides additional information that we apply to our problem-solving efforts. Our attitudes allow us to cut cor-

TRADITIONAL AND SYMBOLIC RACISM

The following lists present examples of questionnaire items used to distinguish between traditional and modern (symbolic) racism. Typically, the items from the two lists are mixed together in random order. Respondents are usually asked to indicate their agreement or disagreement with each statement by using a 5-point scale like the one shown below:

| Strongly agree | Agree | Neither agree nor disagree | Disagree | Strongly disagree |

Traditional Racism Items

1. Black people are generally not as smart as whites. (+)

2. If a black family with about the same income and education as I have moved next door, I would mind it a great deal. (+)

3. Generally speaking, I favor full racial integration. (−)

4. It is a bad idea for blacks and whites to marry one another. (+)

5. I favor laws that permit black persons to rent or purchase housing even when the person offering the property for sale or rent does not wish to rent or sell it to blacks. (−)

6. It was wrong for the United States Supreme Court to outlaw segregation in its 1954 decision. (+)

7. I am opposed to open or fair housing laws. (+)

Modern (Symbolic) Racism Items

1. Blacks are getting too demanding in their push for equal rights. (+)

2. Discrimination against blacks is no longer a problem in the United States. (+)

3. Over the past few years, blacks have gotten more economically than they deserve. (+)

4. Blacks have more influence upon school desegregation plans than they ought to have. (+)

5. It is easy to understand the anger of black people in America. (−)

6. Blacks should not push themselves where they are not wanted. (+)

7. Over the past few years, the government and news media have shown more respect to blacks than they deserve. (+)

Items marked (+) are scored as follows: strongly agree = 5, agree = 4, neither agree nor disagree = 3, disagree = 2, strongly disagree = 1. Items marked (−) are scored as follows: strongly agree = 1, agree = 2, neither agree nor disagree = 3, disagree = 4, strongly disagree = 5. Add the item scores in each list to get the total scores on the measures of traditional and modern (symbolic) racism. The higher the score, the stronger the degree of racism indicated.

Source: J. B. McConahay, "Modern Racism, Ambivalence, and the Modern Racism Scale," in J. F. Dovidio and S. L. Gaertner (eds.), *Prejudice, Discrimination, and Racism.* New York: Academic Press, 1986, 108.

ners and save effort. Social psychologists suggest that we are *cognitive misers* trying to solve the problems posed by life with the minimum amount of information gathering and mental effort.

THE INFLUENCE OF ATTITUDES

Social attitudes have the largest impact on our thinking when the situational information available to us is minimal or ambiguous. Social attitudes take our thinking *beyond* the information our present situation gives us. As time passes after our receipt of the environmental information, the impact of our attitudes increases (Sanbonmatsu, Kardes, and Sansome, 1991). Evidently, with time, we remember less and infer more.

Social attitudes influence our thinking in many ways (Markus and Zajonc, 1985; Stephan, 1985). For one thing, they influence the focus of our *attention* on information in our immediate environment. We tend to pay more attention to information that is most relevant to our attitudes and to ignore other, less relevant data. "Relevant," in this context, does not necessarily mean "consistent." Our attention may be drawn to information that is either consistent or inconsistent with an attitude. For example, if we have a schema that includes the belief that mothers are nurturing, we may pay particular attention to a news story about a mother who murdered her child, but we may ignore the part of the report that describes the mother as living in Minnesota and being married to an engineer because our mother schema does not include characteristics concerning place of residence or husband's occupation. These characteristics are irrelevant.

We also *devote less time* to actively thinking about information provided by our environment when it is consistent with our attitudes. For example, if we encountered information consistent with our mother schema, such as a story about a mother who reads to her young children every night before they go to sleep, we could process this information very quickly. In contrast, we would probably spend a longer time thinking about the woman who murdered her child, in order to make sense of her act. However, this greater amount of time spent thinking about her does not necessarily mean that the information about her will be stored in memory as data conflicting with our mother schema, thereby weakening it. Instead, the inconsistent information makes us mentally review the schema and the past evidence supporting it, thus ironically *strengthening* the schema and decreasing the chances that we will store the contradictory information in memory. On the other hand, consistent evidence may attract attention but basically "go in one ear and out the other."

Attitudes also facilitate our *recall* of information that is consistent with them. During a class discussion of parenting, for example, you might more easily recall having read a story about a nurturing mother than one about an abusive mother. Claudia E. Cohen (1981) found evidence for this effect when she asked two groups of subjects to view a videotape of a wife and husband carrying on a lively conversation while eating dinner and, later, while the woman opened her birthday presents. One group was told that the woman was a waitress; the other, that she was a librarian. On the basis of prior research, Cohen had established that Americans have contrasting stereotypes of women in the two occupations. For instance, they view waitresses as more likely to eat hamburgers, drink beer, enjoy pop music, and receive a nightgown as a gift, whereas they picture librarians as more likely to eat roast beef, drink wine, enjoy classical music, and receive a bestseller as a gift. Although the videotape contained an equal number of "waitress" and "librarian" features, later testing revealed that the subjects selectively remembered those characteristics of the woman that fit the prevailing stereotype of what they believed to be her occupation. Thus, our attitudes can influence our recollections, sometimes producing distortions in memory (see the box "Eyewitness Testimony").

THE INFLUENCE OF THE ENVIRONMENT

The social attitudes we have stored in memory do not totally shape our perceptions (Higgins and Bargh, 1987; Zarate and Smith, 1990, 1992). Information provided by the surrounding environment also affects our thinking. The environment clearly influences *which* schemas we use. Some social characteristics consistently activate the schemas associated with them. Gender and race appear to be among these *priority*, or *master*, *attributes* — characteristics that we take into account in almost all situations.

Our attention also is drawn to environmental characteristics that make a person stand out from others — *distinctiveness* or the *unexpected*. A short person amid a group of tall people is likely to evoke the perceiver's "short-person" schema. We also notice people with obvious physical handicaps and almost always treat them differently, indicating that we have a schema for these characteristics. A person who is unusually quiet in a social setting may elicit a "shy" or "socially unskilled" schema. Of course, it is not necessary that

EYEWITNESS TESTIMONY

Not only do we selectively attend to information that we then store in memory; our recollections of people and events also undergo alterations and distortions in memory. Research by Elizabeth F. Loftus (1979, 1984) shows how information given after an event can influence a person's later eyewitness testimony about it. After viewing a film of a traffic accident, subjects answered questions about the collision. Half of the subjects were asked about the cars' bumping into one another; the other half were asked the same question, but the word "smashed" was substituted for "bumped." Viewers who were asked the "smashed" question estimated that the cars had been traveling faster than did those who were asked the "bumped" question. And those in the "smashed" group were more likely to "remember," erroneously, seeing broken glass after the accident. The difference in the phrasing of the questions continued to affect the answers the subjects gave to another set of questions a week later.

These findings have implications for eyewitness testimony in court cases (Yarmey, 1979; Brigham et al., 1982). Victims often innocently fill in details they think they remember in order to tell a story plausible both to themselves and to their questioners. For instance, when Robert Buckhout showed subjects a film of a violent crime without revealing the face of the attacker, 80 percent of the subjects nonetheless identified the "assailant" from a lineup of faces (Albin, 1981).

In sum, our memories are fallible. Sometimes we invent perceptions even when we do not intend to; indeed, we are frequently unaware that we have done so. To make sense of the scene, we fill in the gaps in our knowledge by plausible constructions of what "must have" or "should have" happened. Moreover, matters are complicated by the questioning that a witness is likely to experience. First the police interrogate a witness; then the attorneys for the prosecution and defense take depositions. Family and friends likewise ask for information. Finally, months or even years later, a witness is expected to testify before a judge and jury about the smallest details. Research suggests that even a trustworthy, well-intentioned witness is subject to errors of memory that may make her or his testimony false.

we *observe* a characteristic in order for it to elicit a schema. We are also influenced by the *labels* that others use for themselves and other people. For example, if we hear a person described as a "genius" (one type of distinctiveness), our genius schema, which includes other associated characteristics, is likely to be activated.

Our environment also affects *how much* we rely on our attitudes. When our rewards and costs depend on paying close attention to our environment, we are more likely to attend to environmental information and to depend less on our own attitudes. For example, as a personnel officer, your decision to hire someone may be reviewed by your supervisor. Knowing this, you will probably pay more attention to the information in the applicant's résumé and interview—relying less on your own stereotypes—than you would if the decision were entirely your own (Tetlock and Boettger, 1989).

We are also more likely to consider information from the environment when we are *not* under time pressure in making our decisions. Time pressure increases our reliance on the attitudes stored in our memories. In one study, subjects judged the suitability of male and female candidates for particular jobs. Under time pressure, those subjects with conservative attitudes toward women tended to discriminate against the female job applicants. However, when conservative subjects had time to consider the evidence, which indicated that the female applicants were at least as well qualified as the male applicants, their discrimination against female applicants considerably decreased (Bechtold, Naccarato, and Zanna, 1986).

Similarly, when our outcomes depend on another person, we spend more time attending to that person—even to information inconsistent with our attitudes—and less time attending to our preconceptions about that person (Darley et al., 1988; Rush and Russell, 1988). For example, as an employee of a company, you are likely to pay close attention to the conduct of that company's manager rather than to rely solely on your attitude toward "bosses" or "managers" in general. Research has also found that people remember more specific information about (1) their competitors and (2) people with whom they anticipate interacting (Judd and Park, 1988; Devine, Sedikides, and Fuhrman, 1989).

Several characteristics of the perceiver also affect which attitudes are activated in specific situations. Group membership is one such characteristic. We tend to use the schema that puts members of a particular outgroup in an unfavorable light relative to members of our own ingroup. For example, when a college plays a nearby rival whose entrance requirements are lower than its own, its students make many jokes and comments about the "intelligence" of the other school's fans and team. In contrast, when the same college plays another nearby rival — a private school with entrance requirements even higher than its own — the jokes and comments are quite different, focusing on the fact that students at *this* rival school tend to be from other states and wealthy families. Our own identities affect our choice of schema. Different schemas may be activated in the roles of stranger, co-worker, friend, lover, and parent. (This will be discussed more thoroughly in Chapter 7, "The Social Nature of Self.") Finally, current mood may influence our choice of schema. In other words, our inferences of others' emotional states are affected by our own feelings of happiness, sadness, fear, and disgust. We typically attribute to others feelings consistent with our own feelings (Clark, Milberg, and Erber, 1984).

PROCESSING COMPLEX INFORMATION

Our perceptions of others are not always (even usually) affected by their characteristics *one at a time*. Usually, our environment provides us with several bits of information simultaneously — bits that we must somehow integrate. Some social psychologists have therefore been interested in the question: "How do we integrate several pieces of information into a single impression?"

Research suggests that, in general, perceivers try to reconcile and integrate the information they have about a person to create a single, unified impression of him or her. For example, Solomon Asch and Henri Zukier (1984) found that if subjects were presented with a pair of discordant personality traits such as shy and courageous, they undertook to reconcile and integrate these seemingly contradictory traits. Taken in isolation, "shy" connotes reticence and withdrawal; "courageous," outgoingness. When the two traits occur together in a single person, however, the meanings are modified. "Courageous" comes to imply more than usual personal determination, whereas "shy" ceases to suggest weakness. We find it easy to imagine a person who acts bravely despite a strong reluctance to be conspicuous — an individual who does not allow shyness to deter his or her action.

By finding a fit between the dispositions, we undertake to see a person as a psychological unit. Thus the contradiction we encounter puzzles us and prompts us to look more deeply. We attempt to establish a coherent impression by looking for some sensible way to bring the characteristics together within a meaningful whole. Sociologist Robert K. Merton observes how a trait may undergo a complete change of evaluation depending on whether it is associated with an ingroup (with its positive evaluations) or an outgroup (with its negative evaluations) schema:

Did Lincoln work far into the night? This testifies that he was industrious, resolute, perseverant, and eager to realize his capacities to the full. Do the outgroup Jews or Japanese keep these same hours? This only bears witness to their sweatshop mentality, their ruthless undercutting of American standards, their unfair competitive practices. Is the in-group hero frugal, thrifty, and sparing? Then the outgroup villain is stingy, miserly, and penny-pinching. All honor is due to the in-group Abe for his having been smart, shrewd, and intelligent and, by the same token, all contempt is owing the out-group Abes for their being sharp, cunning, crafty, and too clever by far. (1968: 428)

Weighted Averaging Model

The bulk of the research evidence suggests that we combine information about persons on the basis of a *weighted averaging model* (Anderson, 1981). According to this model, new information is integrated with already-known information in much the same way as adding a new number to a set of existing numbers changes the average of the set. A new piece of favorable information will not have a favorable impact *unless* the new characteristic has a higher value than the already-known trait has; and then its effect will be diluted by the lower value of the original trait. If the new-found trait is equal in value to the original trait, no change in the evaluation will occur. Moreover, if the new trait is *less* positively valued than the original trait, the overall evaluation of the person will be *lowered* by the additional information.

The model also proposes that not all traits are weighted equally in this averaging process. We assign greater importance to intensely evaluated traits. This is especially true of traits with very negative evaluations, perhaps because we realize that negative information is more difficult to come by given peoples' tendency to present the best possible view of themselves (Ronis and Lipinski, 1985). In our discussion of implicit personality theories, we noted that some traits appear to be more *central* than others; that is, they affect our impressions more.

Under most circumstances, once we have formed an impression of someone, it appears that we rely on our *overall* impression of the person rather than retrieve from memory the specific characteristics associated with his or her identity. Thus we judge any new information we receive in light of these overall impressions (Lodge, McGraw, and Stroh, 1989).

Primacy and Recency Effects

Another factor that appears to influence how we process complex or conflicting information is the timing of our receipt of the bits of information. The popular belief that first impressions are important is true. Indeed, research finds that in forming impressions, we often weight early information more heavily than subsequent information. This tendency is called the **primacy effect** (Luchins, 1957).

Studies suggest that early information is weighted more heavily for two reasons: First, *we interpret later information in light of earlier information* (Zanna and Hamilton, 1977). For example, if you first find out that Sally is honest and Sue is dishonest, and then later both Sally and Sue are very friendly toward you, you are likely to interpret Sally's friendliness differently from Sue's. A second reason for the primacy effect is that, once we have enough information to make a judgment about a person, we *pay less attention to additional information* (Dreben, Fiske, and Hastie, 1979).

Under some circumstances, the primacy effect does not occur. Sometimes, the *most recent* information we receive influences our impressions most strongly; this tendency is called the **recency effect** (Luchins, 1957). Although recency effects are less common than primacy effects in most everyday interactions, they tend to occur when we receive information about traits that are likely to change over time, such as moods, or when so much time has passed that the first impression is largely forgotten.

The amount of time it takes for a first impression to fade may depend in part on the kind of information it is based on. For example, Robert Wyer and his associates (1991) gave subjects two bits of information about a hypothetical political candidate. One bit of information had to do with the candidate's presentation style. For some subjects, he was presented as a forceful, articulate speaker; for others, he was portrayed as a bumbling, fidgeting speaker. The second bit of information concerned the candidate's issue positions. Some subjects were led to believe that the candidate agreed with them; others, that he disagreed. The researchers found that when the two kinds of information were presented to subjects within twenty-four hours of one another, the subjects' evaluations of the candidate seemed to take both into account. However, if at least twenty-four hours separated the bits of information, the subjects' evaluations were influenced only by the information they received last — the information about issue position.

While the exact mechanisms determining how we combine the information from our environment with the information we have stored in memory remain a subject of social psychological research, it is clear that our social attitudes are an essential element of our daily lives. On encountering other people, we typically seek to understand them, to size them up. The focus of this chapter has been the extent to which our social attitudes determine how we come to view others.

But social attitudes are not the only attitudes of importance to our social interactions. We also have attitudes about ourselves. These self-attitudes are the subject of our next chapter. Furthermore, while attitudes are mental structures, they have powerful implications for our *behavior* — a topic to which social psychologists have devoted considerable attention. The relationship between attitudes and behavior will be discussed in Chapter 8.

Summary

1. Social attitudes are composed of belief and feeling components. The belief component consists of beliefs linking a social identity with other characteristics. Such schemas of beliefs about social identities are also called stereotypes. The feeling component of attitudes consists of the feelings, or emotions, an attitude holder associates with a social identity. Social psychologists are particularly interested in our evaluations of social identities. Positive evaluations are referred to as social esteem and negative evaluations as prejudice.

2. Social attitudes are mental structures of belief and affect associated with a social identity. We have schemas — sets of beliefs that link a social identity to other concepts — for social identities that are defined in terms of personality traits; ethnic, gender, and family identities; and physical characteristics. We tend to attribute positive traits to persons who are physically attractive.

3. Our social attitudes not only affect how we identify a person and judge him or her to be acceptable or unacceptable. They also influence our feelings about a person's capacity to control his or her environment. When we believe that responsibility for a person's behavior (or outcomes resulting from it) lies in the characteristics of the person, such as ability or effort, we have made an internal attribution. When we believe that responsibility lies in the environment or situational circumstances, such as difficulty or luck, we have made an external attribution.

4. We tend to overestimate the extent to which the actions of other people are caused by their personality traits. This has been called the fundamental attribution error. We are more likely to attribute our own successes to internal causes and failures to external causes and more likely to make the opposite attributions for the successes and failures of other people. The ultimate attribution error is the tendency to make internal attributions for the success of ingroup members and external attributions for outgroup members.

5. Attributions play a significant role in social policy. If we believe that the cause of a problem is internal, we are likely to conclude that solutions must focus on the person. If, on the other hand, we believe the cause to be external, we are likely to look for structural solutions. In studies of homelessness most respondents cited structural (external) explanations.

6. Our thinking is influenced by both our attitudes and our environment. We selectively focus our attention on attitude-relevant information; but when rewards and costs depend on paying particular attention to the environment, we are more likely to do so and less

likely to rely heavily on the preconceptions stored in the form of attitudes. Our own group membership, roles, and emotional states also affect our selection of attitude schema. We rarely receive only one bit of information about a person on which to base our judgments. Usually, we must process several bits of information simultaneously.

CHAPTER 7

THE SOCIAL NATURE OF SELF

*I*magine, if you can, that you are an amnesia victim. You woke up this morning in a strange hotel room and don't remember how you got there or, indeed, anything else about yourself—even who you are. You are clean and well dressed, but you have no cards or other items that might offer clues about your identity. The hotel clerk remembers that you paid cash for your room and said your name was A. Smith. You don't know who you are. You ask yourself a flood of questions that you are unable to answer: "Am I married?" "Do I have friends? Family?" "What kind of work do I know how to do?" "Am I religious? Educated? Good or evil?" "What kind of person am I?"

Few experiences could be more frightening than this total loss of self-knowledge. In fact, whenever we have difficulty answering the question, "Who am I?"—whenever we lack a set of ready definitions of ourselves—we experience varying degrees of anxiety (Buss, 1980). Consider the discomfort, alienation, and despair revealed in such common statements as "I just can't seem to

find myself," "I can't seem to get my life together," and "I'm unsure about what is right for me."

Just as we form attitudes about other people, we also form them about ourselves. Social psychologists refer to our schemas of beliefs and feelings about ourselves as **self-attitudes** or **self-concepts.** "Who am I?" "Why do I behave, feel, and think the way I do?" Not only do the answers to these questions affect our feelings about ourselves, they also have implications for our interactions with others. In our everyday activities, we base our exchanges with others on our conceptions of them *and of ourselves.* Because we behave toward one another in terms of who we *think* we are, our self-attitudes leave their signature on everything we do. On the one hand, most of us try to be unique—to find differences between ourselves and others (Snyder and Fromkin, 1980). Yet we also realize that to enter into sustained social interaction with others—to participate effectively as members of society—we must establish who we are in terms of meanings that are shared by our interaction partners. Otherwise, as discussed in previous chapters, interaction is likely to be problematic or impossible.

The Components and Organization of Self-Attitudes

You probably feel that you are pretty familiar with your own self-attitudes. So what can social psychology tell you about "you" that you don't already know? Let's find out. For a start, let's identify your own important self-attitudes.

To do that, take out a piece of lined paper and number lines 1 to 20. On each of the numbered lines write a different answer to the simple question, "Who am I?" Respond as if you were giving the answers to yourself, not to somebody else. Write your responses in the order they occur to you. Don't worry about "logic" or "importance."

What you have completed is called the Twenty Statements Test (TST). It is an instrument social psychologists use to measure people's conceptions of themselves. While some social psychologists prefer using open-ended devices like the TST, which allow respondents to employ their own terms rather than the researcher's to describe themselves, there are several other methods for measuring self-attitudes. For example, you might be given a list of characteristics and asked to indicate *which ones* describe you, or you might be given a list of characteristics and asked to indicate *how much* each one describes you. Some of these same methods are used to measure attitudes toward other people; for example, you might be asked to indicate which characteristics you believe describe Jews.

In Figure 7-1, we use a hypothetical person, Jim O'Brian, to illustrate some typical responses to the TST. In many of his answers, Jim describes himself as possessing characteristics that clearly can also describe other people: "male," "Christian," "student," "friendly," "into music," "athletic." Yet some of his other answers pertain uniquely to himself: "Jim O'Brian," "Social Secu-

1. Jim O'Brian
2. Christian
3. male
4. student
5. friendly
6. passive
7. cautious
8. New Yorker
9. an only son
10. into music
11. Mets' fan
12. owner of 1983 Honda
13. Social Security number 343-33-2589
14. husband of Mary O'Brian
15. environmentalist
16. conservative
17. pro-life advocate
18. weight lifter
19. athletic
20. animal lover

FIGURE 7-1 HYPOTHETICAL ANSWERS TO THE TWENTY STATEMENTS TEST

rity number 343-33-2589," "husband of Mary O'Brian."

In Chapter 6, "Social Attitudes and Attributions," we noted that social attitudes consist of two components: beliefs about social identities and feelings toward social identities and their associated characteristics. Similarly, self-attitudes are composed of beliefs about the self and feelings toward the self and associated characteristics.

SELF-IDENTITIES

The beliefs we come to have about ourselves are the characteristics we are most likely to mention when asked to describe ourselves; they are the kinds of things we would probably list on a measure of self-attitudes such as the TST. Beliefs about the self can be expressed in the form, "I am _____." For example, "I am athletic," "I am a Catholic," and "I am an only child" are belief statements involving the self. Thus, the beliefs we have about ourselves associate us with other characteristics. Symbolic interaction theorists call the characteristics we associate with ourselves **self-**

identities. Typically, these theorists distinguish between at least two broad types of self-identities: role identities and dispositional identities. **Role identities** include our beliefs about ourselves in relation to social categories (gender, race, age, and so on), group membership (e.g., religion, family, fraternity), and social roles (student, professor, girlfriend, and the like). **Dispositional identities** include our beliefs about ourselves in reference to character traits (such as optimistic, brave, weak, antisocial) and behavioral tendencies (such as conservative, religious, pro-life). Frequently, we describe ourselves in terms of identities involving combinations of role and disposition: "I'm a dependable son, mediocre athlete, party-loving fraternity brother, passive male."

The distinction between role identities and dispositional identities reflects the difference between sociology and psychology, two disciplines that share an interest in social psychology. Sociology concerns itself more with roles and psychology with dispositions (personality). According to Mark Leary and his colleagues (Leary, Wheeler, and Jenkins, 1986), the behavioral preferences of persons whose self-attitudes emphasize role identities differ from those of persons whose self-attitudes emphasize dispositional identities. For example, adults who described themselves more in terms of role identities preferred team sports, such as volleyball, softball, and basketball, while people whose self-descriptions emphasized dispositional qualities preferred individual sports, such as swimming, running, and aerobics. College students whose role identities predominated preferred occupations offering social rewards, such as status and friendship, while individuals with more dispositional identities preferred jobs offering rewards like personal growth and self-expression.

Louis Zurcher and other researchers (Zurcher, 1977; Snow and Phillips, 1982) have used the distinction between role identities and dispositional identities to study social change in self-identities over time. For example, they found that college students in the 1970s and early 1980s used more dispositional-identity responses and fewer role-identity responses in describing themselves than students in the 1960s did. The researchers interpreted this to mean that college students were increasingly viewing themselves apart from the roles prescribed by society's institutions. If Zurcher were to study today's students, would he find the same results? Look at your own responses — are more of them descriptions of your roles or your dispositions?

Identity Salience

Each of us has multiple self-identities. However, some of our identities are more important to us than others (Rosenberg, 1979). For example, your self-identity as student is probably more important to you than your self-identity as niece or nephew. In fact, our self-identities can be ranked in importance according to the probability of their coming into play in a given situation or across situations (Stryker, 1987). The rank of a particular self-identity on a person's cognitive hierarchy of self-identities is called **self-identity salience**. The Twenty Statements Test represents an effort to identify a person's most salient self-identities. More information, however, is required to determine the *relative* salience, or importance, of the identities revealed by the TST.

The more salient a particular identity is in our hierarchy of identities, the more frequently we will rely on that identity in our perceptions of our environment and our behavior in relation to it. In our earlier example, Jim O'Brian's identity as a Christian may be, to him, the most important of his identities, while his identity as a New Yorker may seem much less significant. If so, he frequently will perceive his own behavior and that of others toward him as reflecting on his identity as a Christian. He also will be more likely to interpret a given situation as representing an opportunity to perform in terms of his Christian identity (Stryker, 1980). And he will more probably cultivate the skills or qualities relevant to his Christian identity — perhaps striving to be forgiving and kind, to "witness" his faith to others, and to avoid "sinful" behavior — than those relevant to less salient identities, such as being a New Yorker. Furthermore, he will be more likely to feel psychological stress when his Christian identity is threatened by his own or others' behavior (Thoits, 1991).

You may know someone for whom the identity of mother, scholar, environmentalist, or homosexual is especially salient. In Chapter 3, "Socialization over the Life Course," we noted that the loss of a salient identity (e.g., identity as wife or husband when one's spouse dies or occupational identity when one retires) can arouse feelings of intense uncertainty. Persons experiencing such changes feel as if they have lost important aspects of who they are. In contrast, the loss of less salient identities may have little effect on people.

Identity salience in any specific situation is determined partly by the cognitive hierarchy of identities stored in our memories and partly by our environment. When you are on campus or elsewhere in your college town, your student identity is probably more salient than your identity as a son or daughter. This is because, in this environment, you rank your student identity highly in your cognitive hierarchy. Moreover, the cues in the environment call for that identity to be enacted. But when you visit your parents' home over the weekend, your son or daughter identity may become more salient than your student identity. The son or daughter identity is probably also near the top of your identity hierarchy, and the cues provided by your parents' presence and your being in the setting of their household push that identity to the fore.

On the other hand, if your parents visit you at college, you may have difficulty determining which of your identities — student or son or daughter — should predominate. Both identities rank high in your cognitive hierarchy and are easily activated by certain environmental cues. When your parents visit your college town, the immediate environment provides *both* kinds of cues. This might explain the discomfort some students experience during their parents' visits to the campus. In effect, lack of clarity about identity salience increases the possibility of *role conflict*. Role conflict (which we discussed in more detail in Chapter 3, "Socialization over the Life Course") is less likely when we feel more certain about which of our identities is most salient in a situation.

Environmental cues available in most situations will not activate identities that are *low* in the cognitive hierarchy of identities. For example, your identity as editor of your high school year-

---

STUDENT OBSERVATION

Identity Salience

During the summer of 1987, I was an exchange student in Japan. My host family lived in a small, traditional city called Oyama. Unlike the situation in major cities such as Tokyo, in this town I was the only American/foreigner. Obviously, my appearance caused me to stand out in the crowd. Wherever I went, people stared and pointed at me (indicating curiosity — not rudeness). Friends and schoolmates always wanted to speak to me in English, and they wanted to know everything about life in the United States: school, music stars, and my boyfriend, to name a few examples. In addition, I was asked to do things such as sing our national anthem, teach kids "American" games, and talk about my feelings on the bombings of Hiroshima and Nagasaki. I wanted to represent my country well, and others did indeed see me as a representative of the United States. Being in Japan made my American-citizen identity more salient for me during my stay there.

book or as star goalie on the intramural soccer team would probably be lower than many other identities in your cognitive hierarchy of identities. If so, you will be unlikely to think of yourself in terms of this identity in most situations. Nevertheless, the environmental cues provided by particular situations might call up such an identity; for example, a reunion of the yearbook staff or an awards banquet for the soccer league might increase the salience of the editor or goalie identity. (See the Student Observation: "Identity Salience.")

In extreme instances, a single, salient identity may become so dominant that its effects spill over to other, less salient identities. In these cases, behavior appropriate to the dominant identity may surface as part of identities for which the behavior is less appropriate. For example, a man with a prominent identity of professor may attempt to *instruct* his wife at home or his neighbors at a cocktail party. Or a woman with a prominent identity of mother may attempt to *nurture* co-workers at the office. This effect is called a *role-person merger* (Turner, 1978). The instructive pro-

fessor becomes an instructive person; the nurturant mother becomes a nurturant person.

SELF-ESTEEM AND SELF-EFFICACY

Just as social attitudes have both belief and feeling components, so do our self-attitudes. Not only do we have beliefs associating ourselves with particular characteristics, we also have *feelings* about our self-identities. We can summarize these feelings along at least two dimensions — evaluation and potency.

Evaluation: Self-Esteem

We evaluate ourselves as good or bad, better or worse, acceptable or unacceptable. Social psychologists call these evaluations **self-esteem**. We evaluate our self-identities, making good-bad judgments about being Hispanic, a student, divorced, or chubby, for instance. But each of us also maintains a general, or *global, self-esteem*, which is a person's evaluation of her or his whole self.

Self-esteem consists of our evaluations of ourselves as good or bad, better or worse, acceptable or unacceptable. We not only evaluate our self-identities but also maintain a general, or global, self-esteem.

Additive measures.   Some researchers measure self-esteem by asking respondents to evaluate, in terms of "goodness" or "desirability," each characteristic they use to describe themselves. Among social psychologists, some disagreement exists about how to combine these ratings of characteristics to form an overall measure of self-esteem. Some researchers just *add* positive evaluations to negative evaluations in order to obtain an indicator of self-esteem. But the additive method of measuring self-esteem has an important limitation: it gives the same score for persons with very different self-schemas. For example, someone with many positively evaluated identities and many negatively evaluated identities may end up with a slightly positive score, while another person with a small number of slightly positive identities may obtain the same score. The additive method, in other words, ignores much of the information about differences between these two persons—differences that might have important effects.

Similarly, the additive method treats evaluations of all identities as equally important. That may or may not be the case, depending on the situation. For example, how positively one person feels about himself might depend almost totally on how well he is doing in school—his student identity may dominate his overall self-esteem—even though his family and friendship identities are evaluated positively. In contrast, another person might give equal weight to her student, family, and friendship identities. Even though the two persons evaluate themselves on the basis of the same identities, each has a different global self-esteem. The additive model does not take this differential weighting of identities into account.

Global measures.   In response to the problems of the additive method, Morris Rosenberg (1965) developed an alternative measure of global self-esteem. His measure also combines positive and negative evaluations; but rather than measuring the evaluation of several self-identities and then adding them, it seeks to get directly at a person's evaluation of his or her whole self. For each state-

ment on the measure, respondents select the answer that best describes how they feel about themselves from among these responses: strongly agree (SA), agree (A), disagree (D), and strongly disagree (SD). The following are some items included in Rosenberg's measure. How would you respond to each one?

1.	I feel that I am a person of worth, at least on an equal basis with others.	SA A D SD
2.	I feel I have a number of good qualities.	SA A D SD
3.	All in all, I am inclined to feel that I am a failure.	SA A D SD
4.	I am able to do things as well as most other people.	SA A D SD
5.	I feel I do not have much to be proud of.	SA A D SD
6.	I take a positive attitude toward myself.	SA A D SD
7.	I wish I could have more respect for myself.	SA A D SD
8.	At times I think I am no good at all.	SA A D SD
9.	On the whole, I am satisfied with myself.	SA A D SD
10.	I certainly feel useless at times.	SA A D SD

Items 1, 2, 4, 6, and 9 are scored in the following manner: strongly agree = 4, agree = 3, disagree = 2, and strongly disagree = 1. Items 3, 5, 7, 8, and 10 are scored in the reverse order: from strongly agree = 1 to strongly disagree = 4. The scores are then summed to produce an overall score. The higher the score, the higher the respondent's self-esteem. (Score your own responses. A score of 30 or above means you have a strongly positive global self-esteem.)

Potency: Self-Attributions

We not only evaluate our goodness or badness, but also judge our potency, or power—our ability to control our environment. In Chapter 6, "Social Attitudes and Attributions," we showed that our attitudes toward other people may include our explanations for their behavior. We tend to explain the behavior of others (or the things that happen to them) as being the result either of their own doing — internal attribution — or of their environment — external attribution. For example, when asked about the causes of poverty, some people blamed it on laziness (internal), while others blamed it on discrimination (external).

Locus of control. We make the same kinds of attributions about the causes of our *own* outcomes. Some people think of themselves as controlling their environment in most situations; others believe themselves to be controlled *by* their environment. The propensity to explain most events in terms of oneself or one's environment is called **locus of control**. Developed by psychologist Julian Rotter (1966), the idea is that people fall into either of two categories: those with internal locus of control perceive that, mostly, they are responsible for what happens to them (both the good and the bad), while those with external locus of control consider their environment to be responsible.

"Internals," then, take credit for their successes, and accept blame for their failures. "Externals" credit the environment for their successes, as well as blame it for their failures. What kind of person are you? Are most of your attributions internal or external? Let's find out. Here are some examples of items that social psychologists use to distinguish between several kinds of self-attributions (Mirowsky and Ross, 1991). For each statement choose the answer that best describes yourself: strongly agree (SA), agree (A), disagree (D), or strongly disagree (SD).

1. There's no sense planning a lot — if something good is going to happen, it will.   SA A D SD

2. The really good things that happen to me are mostly luck.   SA A D SD

3. I am responsible for my own success.   SA A D SD

4. I can just about anything I really set my mind to.   SA A D SD

5. Most of my problems are due to bad breaks.   SA A D SD

6. I have little control over the bad things that happen to me.   SA A D SD

7. My misfortunes are the result of mistakes I have made.   SA A D SD

8. I am responsible for my failures.   SA A D SD

Is your own attributional style mostly internal or external? Here's how to score your responses: "Internals" agree (or strongly agree) with statements 3, 4, 7, and 8, and they disagree (or strongly disagree) with the remaining statements. "Externals" have the opposite pattern of agreement and disagreement: they disagree with items 3, 4, 7, and 8 and agree with the rest. Does your score reflect the way you typically think about yourself?

Attributional bias. Some evidence suggests that most of us are neither true internals nor true externals but are a mixture of the two. Thus, we tend to see ourselves as responsible for our *successes* but attribute our *failures* to our environment. This pattern of self-attribution is said to represent a *self-serving attributional bias* (Fletcher and Ward, 1988; Mullen and Riordan, 1988). For example, football players explain a win as being due to their athletic skills but blame the condition of the field for a loss (Lau, 1984). Similarly, company executives credit good earnings to their research and development efforts but attribute lower profits to unusual national and international economic conditions (Bettman and Weitz, 1983). Do your responses to the previous items suggest that your self-attributions are biased in this manner? If you agreed with statements 3, 4, 5, and 6, while disagreeing with the other statements, you are a "self-defender" and display the self-serving bias.

Self-efficacy. When we describe ourselves as being competent and in control we are said to have high **self-efficacy** (Gecas, 1989). Even when faced with the threat or experience of failure, such individuals are confident that they can ultimately do okay. For example, a person with high self-efficacy who fails an exam is likely to feel confident that, with additional effort, he or she will pass the course. People with very *low* self-efficacy view themselves as either at the mercy of the environment (an external attribution) *or* as incompetent (an internal attribution of responsibility for their frequent failures). Individuals with low self-efficacy are likely to be discouraged by failure and may actively avoid situations perceived as risky.

Victor Gecas and Michael Schwalbe (1986) have developed a measure to assess both global self-esteem and self-efficacy. Respondents rate themselves on a series of scales involving dispositional identities that the researchers believe are indicative of self-esteem and self-efficacy. Here are two of the scales:

___	:	___	:	___	:	___	:	___
Very good		Good		Average		Bad		**Very bad**

___	:	___	:	___	:	___	:	___
Very strong		Strong		Average		Weak		**Very weak**

On each scale, each respondent puts an "X" in the space above the adjective that best describes "how you ordinarily think of yourself." The closer respondents rate themselves to adjectives such as "very good," "very kind," and "very dependable" (which the researchers interpret as positively evaluated identities), the higher their self-esteem. The closer they rate themselves to "very strong," "very powerful," and "can do most things," the higher their self-efficacy.

SELF-SCHEMA

Recently, social psychologists have applied the same social cognition perspective to the study of self-attitudes as they applied to the study of social attitudes (Kihlstrom et al., 1988; Morgan and

Schwalbe, 1990; Fiske and Taylor, 1991; Stryker, 1991). From this perspective, the characteristics we choose to describe ourselves in the TST are not simply a hodgepodge of isolated data. Nor are these characteristics organized solely in a hierarchical fashion, that is, ranked only in terms of their importance. Instead, much of the information we have about ourselves is stored in our memories in the form of several *self-attitudes*, or **self-schemas** — just as our memories include many attitudes, or schemas, organizing information about other people.

As noted in Chapter 6, "Social Attitudes and Attributions," while our *social* attitudes involve categories of people (e.g., males, females, rich, poor, professors, students, introverts, extroverts, jocks, wimps), our *person* attitudes involve only a single person (e.g., my mother, my sister Susan, Michael Jordan, or Jodie Foster). A schema for an individual person often includes some social identities: "Tony, my roommate, is a Native American male and an engineer; he is tall, neat, and friendly." What distinguishes one person attitude from another is, in part, the unique combination of social identities comprising the schema for each person: "My previous roommate was a white male and a student; he was short, messy, and withdrawn."

An individual's self-attitude is one of his or her person attitudes — frequently the most important. As such, it is a "me" schema composed of some identities the individual applies both to others and to self (Asian-American, female, Texan, lawyer, attractive) and other identities he or she applies only to self (daughter of Kirin and Lin Kim, Sam's girlfriend, tallest girl I know). It is the unique combination of these identities that defines each person's unique self-attitude.

Our self-attitudes clearly affect not only how we perceive ourselves but how we perceive everyone else. For example, a man who highly evaluates his own masculinity will be more likely to judge the behavior of another male in terms of masculinity or nonmasculinity (Markus, Smith, and Moreland, 1985). Conversely, our perception of others also influences our perception of ourselves. For instance, we feel good about ourselves when a social identity we identify with is successful — a sports team, political party, or nation.

In rare cases, one social identity comes to so dominate a person's self-attitude that the person nearly loses her or his uniqueness. The individual becomes one-dimensional, thinking of herself or himself solely as a member of that social identity. In Chapter 6, "Social Attitudes and Attributions," we referred to this phenomenon as *role-person merger*. For example, a man may think of himself almost exclusively as a football player or a Vietnam vet, or a woman may think of herself primarily as obese. A person whose self-concept is so dominated by a single identity is likely to think of other people primarily as members or nonmembers of the same social identity.

Problems of Self-Identification

At the conclusion of Chapter 6, we discussed the problems we experience in understanding other people and their conduct and the process of social cognition we use to "make sense of" others. We face a similar problem in coming to understand ourselves. How do we develop and maintain a clear self-attitude? From time to time, most of us ask ourselves, "Who am I?" "Am I a good person?" "Is this the 'real' me?" "Am I the same person I used to be?" We search our environments for information to help us answer these questions. Sometimes the information is limited, producing an "identity vacuum." Other times, the information is contradictory, producing an "identity conflict" (Van der Werff, 1990).

We face these problems of self-definition, in varying degrees, throughout our lifetimes. A major source of such problems are the role strains we discussed in Chapter 3, "Socialization over the Life Course." Some role strains result from our initial socialization into new roles, for example, children's first encounters with the role of student when they enter school. Thus, a boy who has never been disciplined at home for rowdy behavior may experience his teacher's disapproval for

this kind of behavior as punishment for "just being himself." Problems of self-identification also arise from role discontinuity — a type of role strain in which the expectations of an old role conflict with the expectations associated with a new role in a sequence. As we noted in Chapter 3, adolescence is a transitional period in which we are expected to move out of the dependent "child" role and into the independent "adult" role. It is not surprising that such a drastic change might be associated with questions about ourselves. Erik Erikson characterized this period as one entailing "identity crisis."

Problems of self-definition continue during adulthood. Role changes such as becoming unemployed or becoming a parent can cause us to rethink our identities. The transition to old age brings with it expectations for increasing dependence, affecting the sense of control and self-efficacy felt by many older persons. Two changes are particularly significant. Many older persons maintain a sense of self-efficacy by shifting their focus away from attempting to *control* certain physical and social events. Instead, they focus on efforts to *predict* events in order to maintain a sense of control (Rothbaum, Weisz, and Snyder, 1982). For example, a woman may change her belief that her health is under her control and focus instead on predicting the health changes she will undergo, in order to plan for and cope with them. Some adults shift toward a focus on *security*, relying increasingly on others, such as children, neighbors, and physicians, for their positive outcomes (Lawton, 1989).

An elderly person's global self-efficacy may decline very little, despite dramatic declines in self-efficacy as related to specific life experiences — such as health and memory (Rodin, 1987). The person who experiences a decline in control in a specific life area may compensate by reorganizing his or her environment. For example, an elderly man who is homebound may create a "control center" of sorts to maximize his sense of control: he might orient the chair in which he spends most of the day so that he can conveniently reach the

The transition to old age brings with it expectations for increasing dependence, affecting the sense of control and self-efficacy felt by many older persons.

telephone and coffeepot, as well as see the television and look out his front window where people often pass by.

Let's summarize our discussion of the organization of self-attitudes. Self-attitudes have these three components: (1) self-identities (both dispositional and role identities), (2) self-esteem (our evaluation of ourselves), and (3) self-efficacy (our sense of control and competence). Information about ourselves is organized into several self-attitudes. Some of these self-attitudes are more salient than others in *most* situations. Some self-attitudes are salient only in specific situations.

Social Structure and Self-Attitudes

A main focus of sociological social psychology is the association between social structure and individual attitudes and behavior. Chapter 2, "Early Socialization," and Chapter 3, "Socialization over the Life Course," discussed the impact of social structure — for example, social class, gender, or race — on early childhood and role-related behavior throughout people's lifetimes. In this chapter, we are particularly interested in the association between social structure and self-attitudes. How do structural features such as social class, race, and gender shape our self-attitudes?

SOCIAL CLASS AND CLASS IDENTITY

In a national survey conducted during the late 1960s, over 60 percent of Americans identified themselves as middle class and 34 percent as working class, with only 2 percent identifying with either the upper or the lower class (Hodge and Treiman, 1968). The results of this survey are particularly interesting because objective indicators of the respondents' social class — income, education, and occupational prestige — were only weakly related to their class identities (also referred to as *class consciousness*). For example, many people with higher incomes identified themselves in the same, or even lower, social class than some respondents with lower incomes.

There are several possible explanations for the weakness of this association. First, many people feel their position in the social class hierarchy is unclear because there are inconsistencies among the objective indicators of their social class. Hodge and Treiman found this to be true in their study: many respondents were high on one indicator and low on another. Second, compared with many other countries, the United States has fewer symbols of class membership, such as clothing, language, and automobiles, which characterize or are accessible to some classes but not to others. In America, these characteristics are more widely shared, or at least imitated, so that fewer class distinctions exist. And third, a strong egalitarian ideology in the United States may discourage people from publicly expressing social class differences for fear of disapproval.

Yet another reason that class identities are not more closely associated with factors such as education, income, and occupational prestige is that other factors also influence class identities. Ida Simpson and her associates (Simpson, Stark, and Jackson, 1988) suggest that one such factor may be features of a person's workplace. Using information from several large, national surveys conducted during the 1970s, the researchers studied white, married men and women who were employed full-time. As in the Hodge and Treiman study, few people identified themselves with either the upper class or the lower class. Those who did were eliminated from the study, leaving only those who identified themselves with either the middle or the working class. The study corroborated Hodge and Treiman's finding of weak associations between class identity and education, income, and occupational prestige. Interestingly, the class identities of *both* husbands and wives were more closely related to the *husbands'* education and job prestige than to the wives' education and job prestige. Apparently, in America, a family's social standing was, and perhaps still is, determined by the status of the husband.

The study also found that class identities were associated with the conditions of the respondents' workplaces and that the associations were different for women and men. Men tended to identify themselves as "working class" (as opposed to "middle class") when they had manual jobs and were in positions where they more often received than gave orders. On the other hand, women tended to identify themselves as "working class" when they were employed by someone else (as opposed to self-employed) and when they were members of a union. This finding suggests that the sources of class identity are not the same for working men as for working women.

SOCIAL CLASS AND GLOBAL SELF-ESTEEM

Does a person's social class affect his or her global self-esteem? Morris Rosenberg and Leonard Pearlin (1978) hypothesized that certain negative experiences of members of the lower class — occasioned by their lower education, income, and occupational prestige — would cause them to have lower global self-esteem than people in classes above them. Conversely, the researchers reasoned that the positive experiences afforded to those with higher education, income, and occupational prestige (the higher classes) would result in higher global self-esteem.

To test their hypothesis, Rosenberg and Pearlin questioned over 2,000 students, ages eight to eighteen, in the Baltimore area and about the same number of adults in the Chicago area. Their results indicated that the relationship between social class and global self-esteem depended on a person's age. The expected relationship was nonexistent among children, relatively weak among adolescents, and strongest among adults.

Rosenberg and Pearlin interpreted these results as indicating that the impact of social class on global self-esteem varied with the *salience* to the individual of education, income, and occupation identities. These class-related identities develop and increase in importance in adulthood. Thus, adults define themselves more in terms of education, income, and occupation than younger people do. But differences can exist even among adults: some identify themselves more by social class characteristics than others do. Indeed, the association between social class and self-esteem was strongest among adults who said they "strongly agree" that "one of the most important things about a person is the amount of money he makes."

The results of more recent research are consistent with Rosenberg and Pearlin's interpretation. A study of mid-career working men (228 in Washington State) suggests that social class as well as the specific conditions of work affect global self-esteem only if work identity is a salient identity (Gecas and Seff, 1990). The men were asked, "In what kinds of activities do you feel that you are 'most yourself'? That is, in what situations do you feel that the 'real you' comes through?" Among those who answered with work-related responses ("working with customers," "supervising employees," "making decisions on the job"), self-esteem was significantly related to both their social class (education, income, and occupational prestige) and their work conditions (job complexity and control over job). Yet these relationships did not exist (or were very weak) among those who said they were most themselves in nonwork and home situations.

The relationship between adolescents' self-esteem and parents' social class was examined more thoroughly in a study of over 4,000 adolescents which found that their global self-esteem was more strongly related to their *own* achievements than to those of their parents (Wiltfang and Scarbecz, 1990). School grades, group leadership, and close friendships had greater impact on adolescent self-esteem than their parents' education and occupation did. Grades, leadership, and friends are related to more *salient* self-identities for adolescents than are their parents' education and occupation. On the other hand, several social class factors other than parents' education and occupation did have some effect on adolescent self-esteem. Low self-esteem among adolescents was related to the parents' being unemployed, being on welfare, and having a home in a "poor neighborhood."

PARENTAL BEHAVIOR AND GLOBAL SELF-ESTEEM

Researchers have examined whether adolescent self-esteem may also be related to parental factors other than income and occupational prestige. Of particular interest is the kind of relationships parents have with their adolescent children. One recent study (Whitbeck et al., 1991) found that whether adolescents' self-esteem is affected by their parents' economic status depends on their parents' reactions to economic stress. The researchers suggested that adolescents experience economic stress *indirectly* through their parents' reactions. When economic stress causes parents to be more irritable and less warm and supportive

Among adolescents, global self-esteem is more strongly related to their *own* achievements than to their parents' social class. School grades, group leadership, and close friendships had greater impact on adolescent self-esteem than their parents' education and occupation did. Grades, leadership, and friends are related to more *salient* self-identities for adolescents than are their parents' education and occupation.

toward their children, the children's self-esteem is lowered.

In this study of 451 Midwestern two-parent families, a family was considered to be economically stressed if the parents agreed that the family was having problems paying bills, experiencing difficulty in meeting day-to-day material needs, and having to cut back on living expenses to make ends meet. Parental supportiveness was measured by the children's reports, as well as those of researcher observers, of the parents' behavior toward them. Behavior was considered supportive if the parents talked with their children about problems and things going on in the child's life and if they showed trust, approval, and caring. The researchers discovered that it is lack of parental support, rather than economic stress directly, that results in low self-esteem among children (both boys and girls) in economically stressed families. Children whose parents were able to maintain a supportive relationship despite their own economic worries did not suffer from low self-esteem.

Other research has examined the effect of family relationships on children's self-esteem. A study of over 2,500 seventh- through tenth-grade students from one school district in the Midwest (Blyth and Traeger, 1988) found that family intimacy — measured by questions such as "How much does your father (mother) understand what you're really like?" — was associated with positive self-esteem for adolescents of both sexes.

Two smaller studies offer a more detailed look at the effect of parent-child relationships on adolescent self-esteem. In one of the studies, the researchers asked over 600 adolescents whether statements about family support — such as "My family listens to me" and "My family respects my decisions" — were descriptive of their relationships with their own families (Hoelter and Harper, 1987). The researchers found that global self-esteem was higher among adolescents with strong family support *if the adolescents had salient family identities*. Among adolescents whose family identities were not salient, family support seemed to have little impact on self-esteem.

In another study of 128 families, the researchers distinguished between two elements of parental behavior — support and control (Gecas and Schwalbe, 1986). Parental support was measured by statements such as "Over the past several years, I could count on my father (mother) to help me out" and "My father (mother) said nice things about me." Parental control was measured by statements such as "My father (mother) usually tells me exactly how I am supposed to do my work" and "My father (mother) has often complained about what I have done."

The researchers concluded that both support and control by fathers (not mothers) was related to the self-esteem of boys. The stronger a father's support and control, the more positive a son's self-esteem. The data on girls were more interesting. For them, too, the father's support (not the mother's) was important — not for self-esteem but for self-efficacy. The stronger a father's support, the more a daughter viewed herself as being in control of her environment. Thus, this study suggests that the mechanisms promoting self-esteem and self-efficacy may differ by gender of the child.

SOCIAL CLASS AND BLACK SELF-IDENTITY

In 1979 and 1980, a large, national sample of African-Americans was surveyed. Subsequently, several studies have been conducted using the data obtained from this survey (Broman, Neighbors, and Jackson, 1988; Allen, Dawson, and Brown, 1989; Demo and Hughes, 1990). One major focus of these studies has been the effect of social class on "black consciousness," or, in the terms used here, black self-identity. Some African-Americans, in varying degrees, escape discrimination and climb the social class ladder. Is their identification with other blacks stronger or weaker than that of the majority of blacks who remain members of the lower class? All the studies cited above agree that the higher blacks are in social class — education, income, and occupational prestige — the *weaker* their black identity. This may be the result of higher-class blacks' greater contact with whites. The more contact blacks have with whites, the less they emphasize blackness in making decisions (e.g., about dates, purchases, children's names) and the weaker their feelings of closeness to a wide range of blacks (e.g., poor, religious, older, middle class, or professional).

Conversely, lower-class African-Americans apparently identify more closely with other blacks. One explanation for this finding may be that lower-class African-Americans have to rely more on other blacks to survive. Interestingly, lower-class African-Americans not only have stronger black self-identities, but also have more *negative* stereotypes of blacks: they are more likely to say that blacks are lazy, are weak, neglect their families, and give up easily. These respondents are not saying that they themselves have these characteristics, so their negative stereotypes of the group with which they identify do not necessarily lead to low self-esteem. Their negative stereotypes of blacks are *social* attitudes they hold about blacks "in general." Moreover, many of the lower-class black respondents have a schema of blacks that included both positive and negative characteristics.

These studies indicate that other variables are also related to black self-identity. Stronger black identity is associated with religiosity (e.g., church attendance, individual prayer). It is also higher among rural and Southern blacks. But there is no difference in black identity between men and women.

GENDER AND SELF-IDENTITIES

What are the self-attitudes of young children like? Earlier, we noted that young children's global self-esteem is relatively unaffected by their parents' social class and that this is probably because young children do not have salient class identities. But, then, what kinds of self-identities do children possess? And do boys have different self-identities than girls?

Aaron Pallas and his associates (Pallas et al., 1990) asked over 500 Baltimore public school children to rate themselves on thirty-five characteristics during their first, second, and fourth grades. As the students progressed from the first grade to the fourth grade, their self-ratings increasingly clustered into five categories: (1) personal character (polite, obedient, kind), (2) personal responsibility (helpful, take care of self, take care of others), (3) academics, (4) athletics, and (5) physical attractiveness.

However, these five self-identities were not used by boys and girls equally. Boys identified and evaluated themselves more often on the basis of athletics and appearance. In contrast, girls more often identified and evaluated themselves in terms of personal character, responsibility, and academics.

Even among young children, gender seems to shape the identities used for self-evaluation. Boys evaluate themselves more often on the basis of athletics and appearance, while girls use personal character, responsibility, and academics.

What about the gender identities of adults? Do our self-identities continue to develop in a manner that clearly distinguishes masculinity and femininity? In Chapter 6, "Social Attitudes and Attributions," we discussed the social stereotypes people have that distinguish males and females. Men, you may recall, are believed to be hard, tough, and independent; females, soft, tender, and helpless. But do men and women also have similarly distinguishable *self*-identities? Do males view themselves in the same way that men are stereotypically viewed by others? Do females view themselves in the same way that women are stereotypically viewed by others?

Early measures of gender self-identity tended to view masculinity and femininity as mutually exclusive polar opposites: the more you are like one, the less you are like the other. People received a single score on the measure, with high scores indicating masculinity and low scores indicating femininity. In the late 1970s, social psychologists changed their view. They now believe that some people see themselves as having *both* masculine and feminine characteristics (Spence and Helmreich, 1978; Bem, 1981). Consequently, a man or woman can have (1) high scores on both masculinity and femininity ("androgynous"), (2) a high score on masculinity but a low score on femininity ("masculine"), (3) a high score on femininity but a low score on masculinity ("feminine"), and (4) low scores on both masculinity and femininity ("undifferentiated").

Although studies differ in their estimates of the proportion of persons whose self-identities match each of the above types, most agree that a substantial proportion of men and women have self-identities that do *not* match the social stereotypes people hold about their gender. In one study of California college students (Bernard, 1980), about 25 percent of both men and women had androgynous self-identities; 40 percent of both men and women had masculine or feminine self-identities, respectively; 5 percent of the men had feminine self-identities, while 12 percent of the women had masculine self-identities; and, finally, 29 percent

of the men and 21 percent of the women had undifferentiated self-identities.

This finding—that many men and women have self-identities that do not match the cultural stereotype for their gender—has prompted a controversy among social psychologists regarding the association between gender self-identity and global self-esteem. One hypothesis predicts that masculine men and feminine women (those whose self-identities *match* their respective social stereotypes) will have the highest self-esteem, since their conformity to the culture's gender stereotypes will be rewarded. A second hypothesis predicts that androgynous men and women will possess the highest self-esteem, because having both masculine and feminine traits will help them adapt to almost any situation. The third hypothesis predicts that men and women who score high on masculinity (whether masculine or androgynous) will have the highest self-esteem, because our culture rewards masculine traits. Current research seems to favor the third hypothesis (Whitley, 1988; Markstrom-Adams, 1989). This may suggest that self-esteem, in American society, is more closely linked to characteristics that form part of the male stereotype (such as assertiveness, independence, and competence). (Before reading further, look at the Student Observation: "Androgyny.")

SOCIAL STRUCTURE AND ADOLESCENT DEPRESSION

Before we begin our discussion of depression, let's evaluate how you have been feeling recently. The following is a list of problems and complaints that people sometimes have. During the past week, how much were you *distressed* or *bothered* by each item on the list? Choose one of the following responses for each item: 0 = not at all, 1 = a little bit, 2 = a moderate amount, 3 = quite a bit, or 4 = extremely.

    1. Feeling blue   ———
    2. Feeling unusually tired ———

STUDENT OBSERVATION

Androgyny

One of my male friends, Gary, is an unusual individual, probably the closest of any person I know to a self-actualized individual. He is now touring with a ballet company and is rapidly gaining recognition as a first-rate professional. We went to high school together, where he excelled in gymnastics. Gary was also first-string wide receiver on the football team in his senior year. To top it all off, he has a marvelous singing voice. In short, he is truly a gifted individual. Moreover, Gary is quite sensitive, perceptive, and introspective. He is capable of displaying the full range of emotions. I have seen him break down and cry on occasion, as when one of our classmates was killed in an auto accident. Yet I've also witnessed his aggressiveness on the football field, where he won all-conference second-string honors. Gary is an androgynous individual. He seems to enjoy activities that our society labels as "girl" just as much as he enjoys various "boy" activities. Gary seems to find a comfortable integration of roles and is not restricted by societal gender stereotypes.

---

3. Feeling no interest in things _____
4. Feelings of worthlessness _____
5. Feelings of guilt _____
6. Feeling disgusted with myself _____
7. Feeling hopeless _____
8. Thoughts of ending my life _____
9. Crying easily _____
10. Poor appetite _____
11. Avoiding contact with others _____
    Total _____

Total your numerical answers. (The range in possible total scores is 0 to 44.) A researcher would use items similar to these to measure your *symptoms of depression*. The higher your score, the greater your expression of depressive symptoms. In addition to the importance of depression per se, researchers give it added significance because some research indicates that depression in adolescence is associated with poor school performance, poor physical health, aggression, drug use, and delinquency, as well as major depressive episodes in adulthood (Achenbach and Edelbrock, 1981; Harrington et al., 1990; Colten, Gore, and Aseltine, 1991).

But what does this have to do with self-attitudes? A lot. Look at items 4 through 7. Responses to these items indicate how we view ourselves in terms of worthlessness, guilt, disgust, and hopelessness. Negative self-attitudes (low self-esteem and low self-efficacy) are considered to be depressive symptoms.

Gender Differences

A number of researchers are interested in identifying the *predictors* of depressive symptoms. Some have found that depression is equally prevalent among *pre*adolescent boys and girls and that adolescence is the period in which the rates of depression for males and females begin to increase. But the increase is much greater among females than among males, and in adulthood, females continue to have higher rates of depressive symptoms (Kandel and Davies, 1986; Simmons and Blyth, 1987; Petersen, Kennedy, and Sullivan, 1991).

Why might this be so? A possible explanation for the gender difference in depressive symptoms is that females *experience more of the kinds of stressful events* that lead to depression than males do — for example, rejection and overcontrol by parents; controversies with intimates and friends; and problems at school, athletics, or work. Some researchers suggest that puberty, particularly early maturation, is a more stressful experience for females than for males (Brooks-Gunn, 1991). Indeed, research finds that females report more negative events concerning intimates, friends, family, and sexuality than do males. Only in activities such as competitive games and leisure pursuits do males report more negative experiences (Compas and Wagner, 1991; Dornbusch et al., 1991; Larson and Asmussen, 1991; Peterson, Kennedy, and Sullivan, 1991).

A second possible explanation for the gender difference in depressive symptoms is that females may *cope less effectively,* or at least differently, with stressful events than do males. In other words, depression may be a typically female response to stress. Males may respond differently. Some research supports this view. The relationship between stressful events and *depression* is stronger among females than among males. On the other hand, the relationship between stressful events and *deviance* — such as cheating, using drugs and alcohol, smoking, or stealing — is stronger among males (Dornbusch et al., 1991).

Deviance has sometimes been called "masked depression" on the basis of the hypothesis that deviance is the *external* expression of underlying *internal* depressive feelings. According to this hypothesis, boys are just as disturbed as girls but express this disturbance externally rather than internally. Research examining this hypothesis has produced inconsistent findings (Kandel and Davis, 1982; Colten, Gore, and Aseltine, 1991).

Other Vulnerable Groups

Gender is not the only predictor of depressive symptoms. Besides females, other vulnerable groups include adolescents from lower-class families (Gibbs, 1986), from single-parent families (Pearlin and Johnson, 1977), and from disadvantaged minorities (Kessler and Neighbors, 1986). Why? Do these groups experience more stressful events? Or are they less able to cope with stressful experiences? In a study of over 10,000 high school students in California and Wisconsin, sociologist Sanford Dornbusch and his colleagues (1991) found that African-Americans, those from lower-class families, and those from single-parent families reported experiencing more stressful events than their counterparts.

On the other hand, these "high-risk" groups were not necessarily less able to cope with their stresses. For example, although adolescents from lower-class families reported more stressful experiences than their counterparts, their experiences had no greater depressive impact on them than did the stressful experiences of adolescents from middle-class and upper-class families. African-American adolescents were *more* able to cope with their stressful experiences than were those from other racial groups. And adolescents from single-parent families were *more* able to cope with their stressful experiences than were adolescents from two-natural-parent family structures.

These results are especially interesting in light of the studies of adults that sometimes indicate something different. For example, studies show that lower-class adults generally experience a greater depressive impact from their stressful events — they cope less — than do their middle- and upper-class counterparts (Kessler, 1979; Ulbrich, Warheit, and Zimmerman, 1989; McLeod and Kessler, 1990). On the other hand, these studies have found that African-American adults, like African-American adolescents, are better able to cope with certain kinds of stressful experiences than are white adults. For example, African-American adults are better at coping with economic problems, while whites cope better with health problems. We should probably expect some differences in the effective coping of adolescents and adults. Some of their stressful events are different (e.g., school, work, responsibility for family), and adults have had more opportunities to learn effective coping skills.

But what are the specific coping mechanisms that allowed many high-risk adolescents (and adults) to successfully evade the negative effects of their stressful experiences while many of their low-risk counterparts did not? Are some coping mechanisms more effective in dealing with some stressful events than others? Social psychologists are presently investigating such factors as seeking information, having support, reflecting on possible solutions, withdrawing, and talking through problems as potential coping mechanisms for dealing with stressful situations (Bosma and Jackson, 1990; Mattlin, Wethington, and Kessler, 1990; Thoits, 1991).

Processes Affecting Self-Attitudes

We have been discussing research on how our positions in the social structure shape our self-attitudes. Our social class, race, gender, even our positions within our families, powerfully affect our self-identities and self-esteem. But *how* does our position influence our self-attitudes? What are the processes involved? And are we passive or active participants in these processes?

This section discusses three processes by which social structure affects our self-attitudes: self-reflection, social comparison, and social influence. In addition, it describes a fourth process, impression management, in which we take an active role in shaping the self that others see. All of these processes rely heavily on our observing, planning, guiding, and responding to our own behavior — what social psychologists call *reflexive behavior*.

SELF-REFLECTION

In the course of our daily lives, we first extract meaning from the data we receive from our sense organs regarding ourselves and then arrive at innumerable inferences. According to Daryl Bem (1967), we apparently use virtually the same kind of evidence in forming conclusions about ourselves as we do in perceiving others. We come to know our own internal characteristics — dispositional identities such as personality traits, attitudes, motivation, and emotions — by inferring them from our overt behavior, that is, from what we say and do (Tybout and Scott, 1983).

For example, if someone asks you whether a friend of yours likes banana splits, you think over what she usually orders at the ice cream parlor and what she says about desserts, and then you answer, "Yes, she gets banana splits quite often; she must like banana splits." Bem argues that when someone asks you whether you are "in love," you really do not know until you observe or recollect your own behavior and then say, in effect, "Well, I'm always buying presents, waiting in the cold, going out of my way to do nice things for this person — I must be in love." Thus, according to Bem, we infer our own attitudes from scrutinizing situations that provide us with external clues to our internal states. We reach our conclusions on the basis of observations of our own overt behavior and the contexts in which it occurs. This process is called **self-reflection**.

Social psychologists are quick to point out that our self-attitudes help shape our behavior. You go to class and take notes because you see yourself as a student and believe that is the proper behavior for a person so defined. However, behavior also shapes self-concept. When you see yourself behaving like a student (getting out of bed to go to an eight o'clock class, carrying at least five courses, studying on weekends), the role of student will become a more important aspect of your self-identity. Press (1968) found that when medical students began having extensive contact with patients, the proportion who saw themselves as "doctors" showed a marked increase. Similarly, Kadushin (1969) found that as music students began having a greater number of professional performances, memberships in the musician's union, and associations with professional musicians, a greater proportion of the students began to think of themselves as "professionals" instead of students.

Evidence also suggests that our behavior affects self-esteem as well as self-identity. In one experiment (Gergen, 1971), subjects in three groups were asked to complete a measure of self-esteem. Two of the groups were then asked to compose a talk about themselves in a positive way, one that would impress a prospective employer. Next, one group actually delivered the speech. Later, all the subjects were given a second measure of self-esteem. Subjects who had formulated their positive-image talks (whether delivered or not) showed enhanced self-esteem compared with those subjects who had not. In this case, *private* role-playing affected the subjects' self-esteem as much as *public* role-playing.

Internal Information

Another way we derive notions of who we are is from inferences based on our internal thoughts and feelings. For example, a man might think he is "in love" with a particular woman when, in her presence, his heart begins to race and he finds it difficult to think about other things. This type of subjective experience is inherently private, becoming available to others only indirectly when we reveal our feelings.

Indeed, most of us believe that our private thoughts and feelings are more revealing and representative of who we are than is our public behavior. According to one study, we tend to think that other people could learn more about our essential nature through access to our private thoughts and feelings for a single day than they could by observing our overt behavior for several months (Andersen and Ross, 1984). This finding is hardly surprising. First, we experience our thoughts and feelings as spontaneous expressions of the self and, as such, regard them as typically beyond our will and ability to control. Second, we experience our thoughts and feelings as occurring "within us" and as mediating our external words and acts. The existence of these private, inner experiences, and their seeming coherence and continuity, prompts us to conclude that there is an enduring self (Greenwald, 1980, 1982; Tybout and Scott, 1983).

While we also infer our inner states from behavioral cues, our private thoughts and feelings, under some circumstances, overwhelm the external evidence. For instance, some people appear socially adept, yet they continue to perceive themselves as "socially incompetent" or "privately shy" (Zimbardo, 1977; Bandura, 1981). In such cases, people's self-reflections contradict the evidence supplied by their behavior, presumably because their inner thoughts and feelings tell them otherwise. Thus we make self-inferences from covert as well as from overt information.

Norms of Self-Reflection

Let's reconsider Daryl Bem's self-perception theory. Individuals infer their attitudes and inner states, he says, from observing their own behavior and the contexts in which it occurs. But Richard B. Felson (1981) suggests that the self-reflections described by Bem require that people already possess standards or criteria for interpreting their observations. In large measure, each of us acquires such standards or criteria from others through socialization. How do we decide if we are in love? According to Averill (1985), society provides us with a set of criteria—sexual excitement, sacrifices, separation distress—against which we can match our own experiences. In brief, self-reflection frequently involves the application of cultural standards and group norms to ourselves.

Consider, for example, people who have homosexual inclinations but who hide their sexual preferences from others. They avoid, therefore, the direct negative feedback of others. Nonetheless, they cannot totally escape from dominant American cultural definitions about what constitutes homosexuality or from society's highly value-laden judgments regarding homosexuality. Conceivably, closet homosexuals may acquire a homosexual self-identity and a negative self-esteem without receiving direct communications from others about their *own* sexual preferences (Humphreys and Miller, 1980; Cass, 1990). Self-attitudes regarding mental illness may sometimes develop similarly.

SOCIAL COMPARISON

Self-reflection of our overt behavior and covert thoughts and feelings represents one process through which our positions in social structures influence our self-attitudes. A second process is **social comparison**—the process of comparing ourselves with others.

Distinctiveness and Similarity

Sometimes we focus on the aspects of ourselves that make us different from other people.

Sometimes we focus on the aspects of ourselves that make us different from other people when we compare ourselves to others and make judgments about ourselves.

William McGuire and his associates (McGuire and Padawer-Singer, 1976; McGuire et al., 1978; McGuire, McGuire, and Winton, 1979) asked students to describe themselves for five minutes. Students were more likely to describe themselves in terms of characteristics that distinguished them from their classmates — characteristics that placed them in a minority within their group. For example, African-Americans and Hispanics mentioned their race more frequently than did whites, and redheads mentioned their hair color more frequently than did students with more common hair colors. The self-descriptions revealed that comparisons were not limited to classmates. For example, male students who were the only males in their households — those who lived with only a mother and sisters — mentioned their sex more frequently than those whose gender did not distinguish them from other members of their families.

Self-esteem may also be influenced by how we compare ourselves with the majority in reference to a specific characteristic. A national study of employees in the United States found, as ex-

pected, that job loss decreased workers' self-esteem (Cohn, 1978). But unemployed workers living in neighborhoods with little unemployment suffered a *greater* loss of self-esteem than did unemployed workers living in neighborhoods where many people shared their unemployed status. Again, our sense of distinctiveness shapes our self-esteem.

A study of job applicants clearly demonstrates how our sense of distinctiveness — even in comparison with one other person — can affect our self-esteem (Morse and Gergen, 1970). Male college students were interviewed for a summer job. Each applicant filled out several forms, including a measure of self-esteem. When the applicant had completed half of the self-esteem scale, a second applicant entered the room. This person, actually an accomplice of the researchers, appeared in one of two guises. For half of the participants, he wore a dark business suit, carried an attaché case containing a philosophy book and slide rule (if the study were done today, a laptop computer would probably replace the slide rule), and communicated with an aura of competence. For the other half of the participants, the same collaborator wore a smelly sweatshirt, torn pants, and no socks and had several days' growth of whiskers. He looked dazed and carried a dog-eared copy of a cheap sex novel. The researchers privately designated the two guises "Mr. Clean" and "Mr. Dirty."

After the accomplice seated himself, the real applicant completed the second half of the self-esteem measure. In the presence of Mr. Clean, applicants' self-esteem scores showed a marked decline from the first to the second half of the measure. In the presence of Mr. Dirty, self-esteem scores markedly *increased*. The study shows not only that self-esteem was shaped by applicants' comparisons to the accomplice but also that applicants focused on the *differences* between themselves and the accomplice. According to some researchers, the social comparison effect exemplified by Morse and Gergen's study accounts for the lowered self-esteem of many women who are exposed to advertisements portraying highly attractive models (Richins, 1991).

Another early study also found that the characteristics of one person are sufficient by themselves to influence the self-esteem of another person (Gergen and Wishnov, 1965). Young college women were asked to write descriptions of themselves. About a month later each was informed that her self-description had been exchanged with another coed's, whose identity was unknown to her, and that her "partner's" self-description was being returned to her. In fact, what each subject received was an evaluation prepared in advance by the experimenters. One-half of the subjects found themselves reading the self-report of a braggart: this coed enjoyed her work, loved school, had enjoyed a marvelous childhood, had a superb dating life, was beautiful as well as intelligent, and saw herself as having no faults. The other half read the self-report of a student who might have been a dropout from psychotherapy: she was a whiner, and she was unhappy, ugly, and not particularly bright; she had had a miserable childhood, hated school, and was intensely fearful about the future.

The experimenter then asked each of the subjects to complete the same self-evaluation she had completed a month earlier. Self-ratings became much more positive among those who had read the egotist's statement; these women discovered positive qualities in themselves that they had not discussed in the earlier self-descriptions, and they left out negative ones that they had mentioned earlier. It was as if they were saying, "You think you're so great; well, I'm pretty terrific too!" In contrast, those who had received the humble self-evaluation portrayed themselves as much more fault-ridden. They seemed to be saying, "I know what you mean; I've got problems too." Our self-esteem, then, tends to be influenced by the comparisons we make of ourselves with others.

In contrast to other studies we discussed, in Gergen and Wishnov's experiment the comparison process increased the perceived *similarity* between the parties. Collectively, these early studies show that comparing ourselves with others affects our self-attitudes. More recent research supports this conclusion (Gibbons and McCoy, 1991; Suls, Marco, and Tobin, 1991; Wheeler and Miyake, 1992).

Selectivity and Social Structure

The question the studies described above *don't* answer is: When do we focus more on characteristics that distinguish us from others, and when do we focus more on those that make us more similar to them? Still other studies suggest that we actually *select* others to interact with and compare ourselves with. We make these selections in order to influence our own self-attitudes in particular ways. Whom we choose to compare ourselves with and whether we focus on similarities or differences are influenced by our goals, as well as other personal and situational factors (Wood, 1989; Bandura and Jourden, 1991; Duval, Duval, and Mullis, 1992; Kulik and Ambrose, 1992).

Frequently we inflate our self-esteem by comparing ourselves with those "less fortunate" than we are. As a result, we tend to overrate our standing relative to others (Felson, 1981; Taylor and Lobel, 1989). We may avoid comparisons with "superior" people (the star athlete, BMW owner, class president, people in the big house) because such comparisons may deflate our self-esteem. But if we want to improve our performance of a task or our status in a group (rather than to protect our self-esteem), we may seek out superior people to compare ourselves with, believing that these people can provide clues about how to achieve such goals. When we aspire to change, we realize that comparisons with people similar to ourselves may serve only to maintain the undesired status quo (Taylor and Lobel, 1989; Gibbons et al., 1991).

We exert some control over the comparisons we make with others by *selective interaction* with other people. If we want to protect our self-attitudes, we can interact with people who support them and avoid people who do not. This may explain why we tend to associate more frequently with people whom we perceive as agreeing with our self-attitudes (Newcomb, 1956, 1961, 1963; Backman and Secord, 1962). If we have low self-esteem and want to improve it, we may choose to associate with people who have a more favorable view of us than we do (Walster, 1965). However, we will avoid self-enhancing associations if they appear insincere, dishonest, or ingratiating (Jacobs, Berscheid, and Walster, 1971; Brown and Gallagher, 1992). In fact, it appears that people with low self-esteem prefer to interact with others who seem to share their low opinion of themselves, even though they feel bad about the criticism they receive (Robinson and Smith-Lovin, 1992).

Although we influence and are influenced by the judgments of others, our opportunity to interact with people possessing a wide range of such judgments is limited by our society's social structure. For example, segregated schools, jobs, and neighborhoods tend to restrict our interactions to people who are in many ways similar to us. Whites interact with whites more than with people of other races. Catholics interact with Catholics more than with people of other religions. The poor interact with the poor more than with people of other socioeconomic statuses. Thus, peo-

ple's self-attitudes are generally shaped by association with people similar to themselves.

In contrast, obviously, persons in integrated environments are exposed to people who are dissimilar to themselves. How does this affect their self-attitudes? Some studies suggest that African-American children attending segregated schools have higher self-esteem than their peers attending integrated schools (Rosenberg and Simmons, 1972; Stephan, 1985). Jewish children raised in predominantly Gentile neighborhoods have lower self-esteem than Jewish children raised in predominantly Jewish neighborhoods (Rosenberg, 1965). One study even found that *middle- and upper-class* children who attended predominantly lower-class schools had lower self-esteem than their peers who attended schools in which their own class predominated (Rosenberg, 1975). Thus, whether an environment restricts interaction to similar or dissimilar people, it affects the resulting content of self-attitudes.

SOCIAL INFLUENCE

Besides being affected by the processes of self-reflection and social comparison, our self-attitudes are influenced by others' attitudes and by their actions toward us—a process we call **social influence**. For example, you will probably ask the question "Who am I?" at least once in your life. But, to some degree, the answer comes before the question (Yinger, 1965). From the moment of birth, each of us is told: "You are a girl (boy)." "You are my daughter (son)." "You are Catholic (Protestant, Jewish, Muslim)." "You are black (white, Chinese, Chicano)." These initial identities place us into a position within society's social structure. This position influences our subsequent experiences, most notably by limiting our contact with people in different positions and the diversity of judgments they represent.

In this sense we hold the keys to one another's self-attitudes. If we are accepted, approved, and liked for what we are, we tend to acquire positive self-esteem. If we are belittled, blamed, and rejected, we will probably develop unfavorable attitudes toward ourselves. Miyamoto and Dornbusch (1956) found support for this hypothesis in a study of members of ten groups — two fraternities, two sororities, and six sociology classes. Subjects rated themselves on a 5-point scale for each of four characteristics: intelligence, self-confidence, physical attractiveness, and likableness. The students also rated every other member of their group on the same scales. The researchers found that the students highly esteemed by others had higher self-esteem than poorly regarded students.

Actual versus Reflected Appraisals

The studies on social influence and self-attitudes suggest that we tend to see ourselves as others see us. But which is more important: the way others *actually* see us or the way we *think* they do? This is the question addressed by a study of 594 first-year and 432 second-year dental students in a Midwestern university (Quarantelli and Cooper, 1966). On a 10-point scale representing an arbitrary distance between the identities of "dental student" and "dentist," the students indicated where they placed themselves at present. The researchers were interested in whether the subjects saw themselves as being closer to a dental student or closer to a dentist. The subjects also indicated where they thought their parents, classmates, upperclassmates, friends, and members of the dental faculty would place them on the scale. Faculty members also rated the students according to where they thought the students stood in their dental careers.

As in the studies just discussed, the researchers concluded that students (in this case, dental students) who felt their classmates and faculty had a high estimation of them — that is, believed them to be closer to a dentist than to a dental student — rated themselves as closer to a dentist than did their peers who felt their classmates and faculty had a low estimation of them. Perhaps even more significantly, the researchers also discovered that students' self-attitudes were more closely related to their *perceptions* of how the faculty rated them than to how the faculty actually did rate them.

Overall, this study suggests that the *perceived response* of others is more strongly associated with self-attitudes than is their *actual response*. Other research supports this conclusion (Rosenberg, 1979; Shrauger and Schoeneman, 1979; Marsh, Barnes, and Hocevar, 1985; Schafer and Keith, 1985). Thus, many of our self-appraisals are **reflected appraisals,** based on how we *believe* others perceive us. (See the Student Observation: "Reflected Appraisals.")

We may explain the weakness of the association between others' actual appraisals of us and our own self-attitudes in several ways. First, considerable deception characterizes social life. People are reluctant to evaluate others openly in face-to-face encounters, particularly if the assessments are negative or if the other party is not known well. Indeed, most of us tend to believe that revealing to an employer, a supervisor, or a teacher our real feelings about him or her entails considerable risk. People usually inform even a close associate of unfavorable evaluations only if these are directly solicited and if the friend has already made some negative self-appraisal.

Second, not all others are **significant others** — persons exerting considerable influence on our self-attitudes. Nor is everyone "equally significant" to us (Gecas, 1982; Hoelter, 1984). According to research, the importance of others' perceptions of us for our own self-attitudes depends on the combination of (1) the other person's role and (2) the domain of the perception. For example, Felson and his associates (1985; Felson and Reed, 1986) conclude from their research that parents affect children's self-attitudes in the areas of academic and athletic ability, while peers have a greater influence on self-attitudes involving physical attractiveness. Similarly, according to another study, which involved 6,500 adolescents, parents had a greater influence on adolescents' self-appraisals of being over- or underweight than did the adolescents' physicians (Levinson, Powell, and Steelman, 1986). (Males judged themselves to be underweight, whereas females judged themselves to be overweight.) These studies suggest that our *social* attitudes toward others affect the oth-

STUDENT OBSERVATION

Reflected Appraisals

Today I went over to the gym for freshman basketball practice after missing three days of practice because of a viral infection. For some reason the guys assumed that I had been moved up to the varsity team and that was why I hadn't been around. As a result, the guys were somewhat in awe of me and were seeing good points in my game that the coach has yet to notice. Anyway, their comments made me feel very good, and as practice wore on, I played better than I have ever done before. This just goes to show how our self-conceptions are "reflected appraisals." We gain our self-attitudes on the basis of the feedback others give us about ourselves. And, in turn, how we feel about ourselves (our self-attitudes) affects our behavior.

ers' capacity to influence our attitudes about ourselves.

Third, others' actual appraisals of us may not strongly influence our self-attitudes because our self-attitudes, once established, become selective mechanisms that filter incoming information. They influence which social appraisals we pay attention to, interpret, and remember (Bornstedt and Felson, 1983). In other words, we are more likely to pay attention to and remember appraisals that *confirm* rather than *disconfirm* our self-attitudes (Swann and Read, 1981*a, b*; Swann and Ely, 1984). We recall our successes and positive characteristics more often than our failures and negative characteristics (Roth, Snyder, and Pace, 1986). We tend to take credit for the positive outcomes of our behavior and to deny responsibility for the negative outcomes (Bradley, 1978). Additionally, we "enhance" our own contributions to the success of a group effort (Ross and Sicoly, 1979). There is evidence that we even "deflect" some appraisals, rather than reflect them. For example, African-American women who received negative feedback about themselves or their performance deflected these appraisals by attributing them to the prejudice of the source (Crocker et al., 1991). Thus, we tend to be less receptive to any information, including social appraisals, which are contrary to our existing self-attitudes. A strong self-attitude may even motivate us to attempt to change other people's unfa-

vorable appraisals of us (Hilton and Darley, 1985).

However, when we do not possess a strong conception of ourselves, we are more susceptible to outside appraisals. For example, whenever we go through major role transitions, such as entering school, beginning a new job, getting married, or taking on any new role, we have only a weak self-identity about these roles. Therefore, during such periods, we may be especially vulnerable to social influence.

Self-Fulfilling Prophecy

The attitudes of others toward us sometimes lead them to have unrealistic expectations for us. Such false expectations can then influence their behavior toward us and, in turn, our own behavior in such a way that a self-fulfilling prophecy is set in motion. A **self-fulfilling prophecy** is a false definition of the situation that creates conditions that make it come true. Another's false expectations about us can lead us to adopt the expected attributes and behavior. In Chapter 3, "Socialization over the Life Course," we discussed an example of self-fulfilling prophecy when we noted that teachers' differential expectations for the academic success of their students had some effect on their treatment of the students and the subsequent success of those students.

The self-fulfilling-prophecy effect was also demonstrated in a study in which the researchers gave male college students a folder of information about a female student on campus (Snyder, Tanke, and Berscheid, 1977). Each woman's folder contained a photograph, supposedly of her but really of another woman who was either very attractive or unattractive. The photos were randomly assigned to the folders. Hence, the real attractiveness of the women was unrelated to the attractiveness as perceived by the men. The women did not know that the men had seen false photographs. After looking over the contents of his folder, each man telephoned the woman it described and talked with her for ten minutes. The conversations were tape-recorded and later played for judges who had not seen the materials in the folders.

The judges rated the men who talked to the "attractive" women as being more warm than those who talked to the "unattractive" women. Moreover, the judges rated the women whose folders contained an attractive photograph as more friendly, likable, and sociable in their conversations with the men than the women whose folders contained an unattractive photograph. Apparently, the men's misperceptions of the women's attractiveness affected the men's behavior toward the women in a way that elicited a confirming response from the women.

The study we have just described indicates that three stages are necessary to produce a self-fulfilling prophecy (Hamilton, Sherman, and Ruvolo, 1990). First, an expectancy must be activated. In this study, the researchers activated the men's expectations by presenting the false photographs. (Of course, real photographs might also have activated expectancies, but the researchers manipulation of the photographs makes it more clear what that expectancy was.) Second, the activation of the stereotype must affect how the perceiver behaves toward the target. In this study, the judges' ratings of the telephone conversations indicated that the men who believed they were talking to attractive women were warmer in their responses than those who believed they were talking to unattractive women. Third, the perceiver's behavior must affect the target's behavior. In our

example, the women who were falsely perceived as attractive acted differently (more friendly, sociable, and likable) than those perceived as unattractive. The study shows that the effects of expectancies on behavior can be very subtle. Face-to-face interaction was not necessary to produce behavioral confirmation of the perceivers' expectancies. Other studies show that nonverbal behaviors such as interpersonal spacing, eye contact, and speech characteristics can elicit self-fulfilling prophecies (Word, Zanna, and Cooper, 1974; Neuberg, 1989).

Lee Jussim (1990) has suggested that others' expectations can be confirmed for any of three reasons, only one of which is the self-fulfilling prophecy. Besides self-fulfilling prophecies, he says, a second type of appraisal error that accounts for the confirmation of expectancies is *perceptual bias:* appraisers sometimes select, interpret, and remember behaviors consistent with their appraisals. For example, the self-fulfilling prophecy would suggest that a child viewed by his teacher as the "class clown" will be treated by the teacher in ways that actually lead to an increase in the kinds of behavior we would expect from a class clown. The perceptual bias explanation would suggest that the teacher may observe an increase in the child's clowning behavior not because the frequency of such behavior has increased, but rather because she is paying more attention to and remembering the kinds of behavior that confirm her assessment.

Jussim suggests that the third reason that our behavior sometimes confirms expectancies is that the expectancies are "accurate" assessments of our conduct. The teacher may notice clowning behavior by the student she thinks of as the class clown not because of an appraisal error but because he actually exhibits clowning behavior. The problem for social psychologists is to determine which combination of these possible explanations accounts for a particular case.

For example, a student may initially perform very poorly on class tests. Her performance (along with other factors, such as her race and gender) may cause her teacher to appraise her as a "low achiever." The teacher may subsequently give the student little encouragement to improve her performance. But suppose that later the student performs very well on a standardized test. How would the teacher react? Does he attribute the good test performance to a fluke, or does he change his appraisal of the student? And how does the student react to her performance on the standardized test and to her teacher's appraisal or reappraisal? The self-fulfilling prophecy is just part of a larger question concerning how social appraisals affect self-attitudes and behavior.

IMPRESSION MANAGEMENT

We have ideas about who and what we are — ideas that we seek to present to others. We are concerned with the ideas that others develop about us. Only by influencing others' ideas can we hope to predict or control what happens to us. The process of tailoring our presentations to different audiences is fundamental to social interaction. Erving Goffman (1959) terms it **impression management** when we seek to manipulate others' perceptions of us.

So, although the attitudes that others have of us — or at least our perception of those attitudes — affect our self-attitudes, we do not just sit by and passively wait for others to express their judgments of us. We often actively cultivate behaviors in others that substantiate our self-attitudes (Fazio, Effrein, and Falander, 1981; Swann and Read, 1981b). For example, a man who thinks of himself as an intimidating figure may validate this self-attitude by inducing others to cower and grovel in his presence. And individuals who conceive of themselves as unlovable often sustain this conception by causing lovers to reject them.

Although nearly every behavior we engage in reveals information about us, some of our behaviors do not entail impression management — in which the goal is to influence how others perceive us. Impression management does not necessarily imply conscious deception. Frequently, it involves merely bringing our actual attributes or accomplishments to the attention of others. For example, we may perform deeds that normally win approval or inspire confidence in ourselves (Schlenker and Leary, 1982; Schlenker and Weigold, 1992).

When we encounter someone for the first time and expect to have future dealings with him or her, we start structuring the person's view of us; in fact, we attempt to shape the person's definitions of the situation. Consider how the skilled waitress accomplishes this:

> The skilled waitress tackles the customer with confidence and without hesitation. For example, she may find that a new customer has seated himself before she could clear off the dirty dishes and change the cloth. He is now leaning on the table studying the menu. She greets him, says, "May I change the cover, please?" and, without waiting for an answer, takes his menu away from him so that he moves back from the table, and she goes about her work. The relationship is handled politely but firmly, and there is never any question as to who is in charge. (Whyte, 1946: 132–133)

If we are to elicit the responses we desire from others, we must take steps to fashion the meanings that others employ within the situation. Some spheres, such as criminal law, seem to be more susceptible to impression management than others. Seymour Wishman (1981), a prominent and successful criminal lawyer, describes how he has represented hundreds of people accused of crimes. Most of his clients, he claims, have been not merely guilty but guilty of atrocities — sons who hatcheted fathers, strangers who murdered strangers, and lovers who knifed lovers — and he says that he fully expects some of them to go out and commit new outrages. The heart of Wishman's courtroom effort rests on impression management. Consider his staging of anger. Wishman observes, "I'm sure I'm not the first trial lawyer who knew exactly when he was going to 'lose' his temper, what he would do while his temper was 'lost,' and how long it would be before he recovered it" (1981: 25).

But impression management is not restricted to such obvious arenas as the courtroom. Teachers, for example, often attempt to present themselves as knowledgeable, judges as objective and neutral, and clergy as moral and altruistic (Buss and Briggs, 1984). Goffman (1981) also finds expressions of impression management in spheres that we often overlook. Take such common "response cries" as "Good God," "wow," "oops," and "whee." These responses, Goffman argues, are more than emotional ventings. A man reading the evening newspaper groans "Good God!" in an implicit appeal to his wife to ask him to elaborate.

We are motivated to present ourselves in ways that yield enhanced levels of self-esteem and social approval. Consequently, we strive to associate ourselves with desirable images and to dissociate ourselves from undesirable ones; this is the association principle. We can see the association principle at work in these fans' efforts to bask in the reflected glory of their team's victory. All of us use such indirect image management tactics at one time or another to influence other people's images of ourselves by presenting information about something with which we are associated (rather than by directly presenting information about ourselves).

Barry R. Schlenker (1980) asserts that we strive to associate ourselves with desirable images and to dissociate ourselves from undesirable ones; Schlenker terms this the "association principle." We can see the association principle at work in the nearly universal tendency of ordinary people to seek to bask in the reflected glory of the highly successful; an example is the common boast about shaking hands with a famous entertainment or sports celebrity. The same principle evidently motivates college students to wear more school-identifying apparel such as sweatshirts and school buttons on a Monday following a Saturday football victory than on one following a loss.

These techniques are characterized by indirect rather than direct tactics of self-presentation. All of us employ them to influence other people's images of ourselves through the presentation of information about something with which we are associated (rather than through the direct presentation of information about ourselves). Individuls differ in the degree to which they tend to observe and control their self-presentations. (See the box "Self-Monitoring.")

Front

Central to the process of impression management is **front** — the expressive equipment that we intentionally or unwittingly use in presenting ourselves to others (Goffman, 1959; Ball, 1966). Front consists of setting, appearance, and manner.

Setting refers to the spatial and physical items of scenery (props) that we employ in staging our performances. Consider, for example, the carefully laid out office of the typical physician. Patients are herded together in a waiting room and impersonally distributed on couches and chairs along the walls. The arrangement immediately and forcefully conveys the difference in status and power setting patients apart from doctor. A receptionist or nurse acts as a gatekeeper, regulating access to the physician's special chambers. The waiting room often has plush carpet and is well furnished with couches, chairs, large lamps, and tables with "appropriate" magazines — all signaling luxury and the special status of the doctor. In

SELF-MONITORING

According to psychologist Mark Snyder (1974, 1987), individuals differ strikingly in the extent to which they observe and control their self-presentations. Some people are intensely concerned with the situational appropriateness of their behavior. These individuals, termed "high self-monitors" by Snyder, are actors on a social stage, more concerned with playing a role than with presenting a true picture of the self. They are especially sensitive to how they express and present themselves in various social settings — at parties, job interviews, professional meetings, and chance encounters. They agree with such statements as "In different situations and with different people, I often act like a very different person" and "I may deceive people by being friendly when I really dislike them."

In contrast, "low self-monitors" have less concern for the situational appropriateness of their presentations and expressive behavior. They pay less attention to the behavioral cues afforded by others, and they monitor and control their own presentations to a lesser extent. They agree with such statements as "At parties and social gatherings, I do not attempt to do or say things that others will like" and "My behavior is usually an expression of my true inner feelings, attitudes, and beliefs."

Low self-monitors have a firmer, more single-minded idea of what their "self" should be. They strive for congruence between "who they are" and "what they do." In contrast, high self-monitors present many "selves," fitting the "self" of the moment to the dictates of the situation. Self-monitoring individuals are more likely to laugh at a comedy when watching it with friends who are laughing at it than when watching it alone. But low-self-monitoring individuals show less difference in the two situations; their expression is internally controlled by their experience more than by their sensitivity to situational factors.

Snyder suggested the existence of only one kind of high self-monitor — people who pay attention to the behavioral cues of others *and* control their self-presentations. More recent research indicates that there are really *two* kinds of high self-monitors (Lennox and Wolfe, 1984; Lennox, 1988). The researchers find evidence that high self-monitors do not always meet both of Snyder's criteria. Some high self-monitors pay particular attention to the behavior cues of others: "The slightest look of disapproval in the eyes of a person with whom I am interacting is enough to make me change my approach." "I try to pay attention to the reactions of others to my behavior in order to avoid being out of place." Other high self-monitors actively try to affect the application of social standards by modifying their self-presentations: "I have the ability to control the way I come across to people, depending on the impression I wish to give them." "I would probably make a good actor." The researchers characterize the motivation behind these two different behavior patterns as "getting along" versus "getting ahead."

due course the patient is ushered into an office or examining room to await an audience with the physician. The office exudes luxury; shelved medical books and framed diplomas convey a scientific mystique and competence; family portraits communicate trustworthiness by telegraphing that the occupant is a pillar of "proper" community life. The examining room features medical paraphernalia — an aseptic table, stainless-steel pans and trays, bottles and vials enclosing colored liquids, gauze, hypodermic syringes, and other "equipment." These arrangements arouse awe and de-fine the situation as one in which the patient should honor and defer to the physician (Goffman, 1959).

Appearance refers to personal items that serve to identify an individual (Stone, 1970). Clothing, insignia, titles, and grooming are all elements of appearance. The doctor's white lab coat, stethoscope, and black bag provide cues to his or her identity; the title "Doctor" (linked with the last name or simply used by itself) establishes a social rank eliciting deference and social distance. Likewise, used-car sellers aim to present a favorable image by not assuming the look of a con man (by avoiding villainous mustaches, loud clothes, and other stereotyped "con-man" attributes). They must also try not to dress too expensively (Davidson, 1975).

Manner refers to those expressions that reveal the performer's style of behavior, emotion, and disposition (Hochschild, 1979; Thoits, 1989). Some physicians may display a brusque, coldly professional, businesslike manner: the conventional greeting, "How are you?" (the conventional answer, "Fine") as you step into the office, quickly followed by "What's the trouble?" as you seat yourself. Other doctors project a warm, kind, sympathetic manner (more chitchat between the "How are you?" and the "What's the trouble?"). But whatever the manner, the physician sets the tone for the ensuing interaction. Used-car sellers, in contrast, notoriously "come on" as cheerful,

smiling, friendly "good guys." Mourners at funerals look sad (whether sad or not) because to laugh or crack jokes would elicit disapproval.

In sum, in presenting ourselves to others, we employ front. We use a variety of expressive equipment — setting, appearance, and manner — to publicize the meanings that we wish to convey. (Before reading further, look at the Student Observations: "Front.")

Regions: Front-stage and Backstage

Part of impression management consists of manipulating **regions** — places separating front-stage from backstage performances. Some of our behavior occurs *front-stage*, before an audience. Other behavior occurs *backstage*. Here, away from our audience, we may engage in performances that we seek to screen from the audience's view because

---

STUDENT OBSERVATIONS

Front

This year I have been interviewing with several companies for a job after I graduate. Before the interviews, I took my parents' advice and "cleaned up" my appearance. I used to have hair all the way down my back, a beard, and an earring. Now, I'm clean-shaven, with a "GQ" haircut and no earring. I changed my appearance in an effort to look like the ideal character these companies would want to hire — an example of using front to manage impressions.

This also illustrates that impression management is not always successful. The last interview I had was with a very large advertising firm. I really wanted to get a job with the company. However, when I got to the interview, the interviewer had long hair and an earring. I didn't get a callback.

It's funny — I don't think of my father as the type of person who would be "fake," but the other day we noticed something he did without even thinking about it: a case of using front for impression management. Dad has very eclectic musical taste, including some selections that may not be in keeping with his image as head of a department at a prestigious private university. The other night, a few of his colleagues were coming over, and I noticed that he put the "undesirable" selections inside the cabinet, while leaving his Chopin and *Parkening Plays Bach* out for the visitors to see. When I raised the issue with him, he admitted that this was an obvious case of trying to present a not-necessarily-accurate image of himself to his guests, and he laughed at himself, but he left the undesirables in the cabinet. I think this was a case of using setting, displaying a particular selection of musical choices, to manage the impressions of his colleagues. My dad hoped the Chopin would suggest that he's a calm, cultural guy — the image he wanted to present to his colleagues — rather than the wild-and-crazy-kind-of-guy image that Meatloaf would portray.

they contradict the impressions we are attempting to convey (Goffman, 1959).

We engage in front-stage behavior in our living rooms, where we entertain guests. Here we display our best behavior and present ourselves as respectable, upstanding, proper, good people. But backstage in our kitchens or bedrooms—areas commonly off-limits to guests—we may criticize or ridicule outsiders, wage hard-fought family squabbles, "let down our hair," and generally live a somewhat cluttered and disorderly existence.

Although backstage performances would discredit the front-stage performance if the audience ever saw them, they may be essential for successful front-stage behavior. Restaurants seal off the dirty work of food preparation (the gristle, grease, and foul smells of spoiled food) from the appetizing and enticing front-stage atmosphere. Furthermore, in the backstage region the tensions built up front-stage can be released. Teachers can laugh about the stupidity of their students, students can ridicule their teachers, doctors can make jokes about human suffering and death, and prostitutes can mock their "johns."

Role Distancing

Sometimes we are uncomfortable when our behavior threatens to create an impression in others that contradicts our own self-attitudes. Indeed, when we must undertake roles that contradict our self-attitudes, we may attempt to display behavior that suggests our detachment from the role as well as our lack of personal involvement and reflects the role's low salience among our self-identities. Goffman (1961b) calls such behavior **role distancing**.

Researchers Allen Smith and Sherryl Kleinman (1989) did an interesting study of medical students that illustrates the idea of role distancing. They observed and interviewed students in their first three years of training at a major medical school in the Southeast. Their study focused on the problem of the intimate feelings and behavior associated with the physical contacts inherent in

medicine. These feelings are considered natural responses to the same kind of contact when it occurs in personal relationships, but they are considered *inappropriate* in the professional doctor-patient relationship. A conflict results: doctors are supposed to be caring, but they are supposed to show a *detached* concern. Smith and Kleinman's interviews revealed, for example, that during their medical training, students had difficulty performing autopsies and examinations:

> I did my autopsy 10 days ago. That shook me off my feet. Nothing could have prepared me for it. The person was my age.... She just looked (pause) asleep. Not like the cadaver. Fluid, blood, smell. It smelled like a butcher shop. And they handled it like a butcher shop. The technicians. Slice, move, pull, cut . . . all the organs, insides, pulled out in 10 minutes. I know it's absurd, but what if she's not really dead? She doesn't look like it. [Second-year female]

> When you listen to the heart you have to work around the breast, and move it to listen to one spot. I tried to do it with minimum contact, without staring at her tit . . . breast.... The different words (pause) shows I was feeling both things at once. [Second-year male]

> One patient was really gross! He had something that kept him standing, and coughing all the time. Coughing phlegm, and that really bothers me. Gross! Just something I don't like. Some smelled real bad. I didn't want to examine their axillae. Stinking armpits! It was just not something I wanted to do. [Second-year female] (Smith and Kleinman, 1989: 58–59)

How did students manage their uncomfortable and "inappropriate" responses? They did so by distancing themselves from intimate or personal roles, favoring the more appropriate impersonal role of the physician. They did this to impress patients, faculty, and other students. The students accomplished this through several techniques. One technique was to define their physical contacts with patients differently than the contacts they had in their personal lives. Their contacts with cadavers or patients were defined as an analytic problem or a complex intellectual puzzle and were described using impersonal medical jargon and machine metaphors:

> The patient is really like a math work problem. You break it down into little pieces and put them together. The facts you get from a history or physical, from the labs and chart. They fit together, once you begin to see how to do it. . . . It's an intellectual challenge. [Third-year female]

> When we were dissecting the pelvis, the wrong words kept coming to mind, and it was uncomfortable. I tried to be sure to use the right words, penis and testicles (pause) not cock and balls. Even just thinking. Would have been embarrassing to make that mistake that day. School language, it made it into a science project. [First-year female]

> You can't tell what's wrong without looking under the hood. It's difficult when I'm talking with a patient. But when I'm examining them it's like an automobile engine. . . . There's a bad connotation with that, but it's literally what I mean. [Third-year male] (Smith and Kleinman, 1989: 61)

A second role-distancing technique used by the medical students involved humor. Through shows of joking, sarcasm, and sullenness the students demonstrated their efforts to distance themselves from the intimate identities that could result from their physical contact with others:

> The way we talk. Before we wouldn't talk about the penis or vagina. Now we do casually, with folks in medicine. And we say more about what's happening with us sexually. Lots of comments about ejaculation, orgasms, getting it back in less than 20 minutes, that kind of thing. Some of it is serious learning conversation. Sometimes it's just joking, banter. [Second-year female] (Smith and Kleinman, 1989: 63–64)

The students learn from the faculty that joking is an acceptable way to talk about uncomfortable encounters in medicine. Joking is a backstage behavior done primarily in hallways or in physicians' workrooms, away from the public ear. Joking also contributes to the social bonds among the medical personnel, both students and faculty.

A third role-distancing technique used by the students was to simply avoid the kinds of contact that would create the unwanted discomfort. They did so by (1) covering "personal" body parts and (2) abbreviating parts of the physical examination:

> We did make sure that it was covered. The parts we weren't working on. The head, the genitals. All of it really. It is important to keep them wrapped and moist, so they wouldn't get moldy. That made sense. But when the cloth slipped, someone made sure to cover it back up, even if just a little (pubic) hair showed. [First-year female]

> If you skip the genitals or rectal, and you note "exam deferred" in the chart, there's no problem. Sometimes they [the faculty] tell you to go ahead and do it, but there's no problem. So long as they don't think you just forgot. Just say "pelvic deferred." [Third-year female] (Smith and Kleinman, 1989: 64–65)

Smith and Kleinman observed that the students sometimes took their newly acquired impersonal behavior home with them from the hospital. This created the opposite problem of behaving impersonally in a situation where intimate behavior is more appropriate:

> I have learned enough to find gross problems. And they taught us that breast cancer is one of the biggest threats to a woman's health. OK. So I can offer my expertise. But I found myself examining her, right in the middle of making love. Not cool! [Second-year male] (Smith and Kleinman, 1989: 65–66)

Role distancing is not to be equated with distancing one's self from another *person*. We distance ourselves from *role expectations*. Depending upon the nature of those expectations, role distancing may result in either less or greater involvement with others. For example, a teacher or professor may have to distance herself from her teaching role in order to maintain the proper perspective as a parent when her children request help with their homework.

GENDER DIFFERENCES IN THE PROCESSES AFFECTING SELF-ATTITUDES

We've covered a lot of ground since we last paused to reflect. Let's summarize now. We began the chapter with a discussion of the components of our self-attitudes: self-identities, self-esteem, and self-efficacy. We showed that our self-attitudes are influenced by our positions in the social structure — our social class, race, and gender, for example. We gave attention to three processes through which the influence of social structure operates: self-reflection, social comparison, and social influence. Finally, we discussed impression management, the process involving our own efforts to shape others' perceptions of ourselves.

In conclusion, let us suggest that the relative importance of these processes probably differs from one situation to another and from one person to another. What we don't know is just how or why it differs. Some researchers suspect that the processes for men and women differ — that women's self-attitudes are more affected by social influence than men's, while men's are affected more by social comparisons. This belief has been bolstered by observations that women are more interested in preserving harmony in relationships, while men are more interested in competing with others to distinguish themselves. These gender differences were emphasized in our earlier discussions of Carol Gilligan's developmental theory in Chapter 2, "Early Socialization," and of the communication process in Chapter 5, "Communication."

Some research supports the conclusion that there are gender differences in the processes affecting self-attitudes. For example, one study of 514 undergraduates in introductory sociology courses at a Midwestern university found that when the subjects were asked to judge the importance of the three processes for "feeling good about yourself," the responses of men and women differed (Schwalbe and Staples, 1991). Although both men and women rated social influence (what others think of them) as the most important source of self-esteem, women rated social influence to be *more* important than men did. In contrast, men rated social comparison (how they compare to others) to be more important than did women. Men's and women's ratings of the importance of self-reflection (gaining knowledge of themselves by observing their own thoughts and behaviors) did not differ.

Although some other studies have found similar results (Rosenberg, 1986; Nolen-Hoeksema, 1990), still others have not (Hoelter, 1984; Schwalbe, Gecas, and Baxter, 1986; Alpert-Gillis and Connell, 1989) — perhaps because these studies examined gender differences in various settings. It appears that gender differences are greater in some settings than in others. We might expect, for example, that women's self-attitudes would be more affected by social influence processes than men's in a study of friendships but perhaps not in a study of men's and women's relationships at work. Research aimed at discovering the implications of gender differences in the sources of self-attitudes is continuing.

Summary

1. Just as we have attitudes about others, we have attitudes — schemas of beliefs and feelings — about ourselves. These self-attitudes affect our feelings toward ourselves and our interaction with others. We have multiple self-identities. Some are more important to us, more salient, than others.

2. Like social attitudes, self-attitudes have both belief and feeling components. Our evaluations of ourselves as good or bad are called self-esteem. We also judge ourselves in terms of our ability to control the environment — our potency or power — which is called internal or external locus of control. When we see our-

selves as being competent and being in control, we are said to have high self-efficacy.

3. Our positions in the social structure affect our self-attitudes. For example, there is a weak relationship between income, education, and occupational prestige, on the one hand, and class identity, or class consciousness, on the other, in the United States.

4. Three processes affect our self-attitudes: self-reflection, social comparison, and social influence. Self-reflection is the process of learning about our own internal characteristics by inferring them from our overt behavior or covert experiences. Social comparison involves comparing ourselves with others. Social influence is the process by which others' attitudes and actions influence our self-attitudes and behavior.

5. Others' attitudes toward us sometimes lead them to have false expectations for us. These false expectations can influence their behavior toward us and, in turn, our own behavior in such a way that a self-fulfilling prophecy is set in motion.

6. We do not simply sit by and passively wait for others to express their judgments of us. We often actively cultivate behaviors in others that support our self-attitudes. We have ideas about who we are, and we seek to present them to other people. In other words, we engage in impression management. When we must undertake roles that contradict our self-attitudes, we may attempt to display behavior which suggests our detachment from the role. Such behavior is called role distancing.

CHAPTER 8

ATTITUDES
AND BEHAVIOR

*I*n Chapter 6, "Social Attitudes and Attributions," and Chapter 7, "The Social Nature of Self," we discussed the sources and effects of the beliefs and feelings we have about other people and ourselves. Of course, we have attitudes about many other objects and events in our environment as well — abortion, smoking, recycling, interracial dating and marriage, skateboarding, fried food, politics, and so on. But why do social psychologists give attitudes so much attention? The reason for this is that many investigators have assumed that attitudes occupy a crucial position in our mental makeup and, as a result, have consequences for the way we act. Viewed from this perspective, attitudes serve as powerful energizers and directors of our behavior: they *ready* us for certain kinds of action. Indeed, many social psychologists are interested in attitudes because they assume that our attitudes serve as rather accurate *predictors* of our behavior (Kahle and Berman, 1979; Schuman and Johnson, 1976; Hill, 1981; Jaccard and Becker, 1985; McGuire, 1985).

There are all sorts of behaviors social psychologists would like to be able to predict: Whom will we vote for in the next election? Will we make a donation to a particular cause? Will we recycle our glass bottles and aluminum cans? Are we likely to commit crimes? Will we stop smoking? Will our marriage last? How many children will we have?

However, some research does not support the basic assumption that attitudes predict behavior. Indeed, many studies have revealed a lack of correspondence or a low correspondence between the two. A classic study by Richard T. LaPiere (1934) is frequently cited as providing a striking example of such a discrepancy. LaPiere accompanied a Chinese couple as they traveled throughout the United States, covering about 10,000 miles. He kept a list of hotels, auto camps, tourist homes, and restaurants that served the couple, and he took notes on their treatment. Only once were they denied service, and LaPiere judged that their treatment was above average in nearly half of the restaurants they visited. Several months later, he mailed questionnaires to the proprietors of the establishments asking if they would accept Chinese as guests. Approximately 92 percent indicated that they would *not* accept them; their statements were *clearly in contradiction to their actual behavior.*

Should we conclude that attitudes and behavior are unrelated? Critics have faulted LaPiere's study because his presence with the Chinese couple undoubtedly had a biasing effect (Linn, 1965). Also, whereas the couple dealt with waitresses and desk clerks, management most probably completed the questionnaires. Nevertheless, since LaPiere's study, many additional studies have also failed to discover a consistent relationship between people's attitudes and their behavior.

In one study undertaken just before the civil rights movement, Saenger and Gilbert (1950) compared the attitudes of white customers buying from African-American clerks with the attitudes of white customers buying from white clerks in a large New York department store. Customers were followed out of the store, where they were then interviewed. In both groups 38 percent either disapproved of African-American clerks or wanted them excluded from some departments in the store (e.g., the food department). Still, a number of customers who had insisted that they would not buy from black clerks were observed purchasing from them. Thus a considerable gap existed between what the customers said and what they did.

Saenger and Gilbert suggested a number of situational factors to account for the attitude-behavior discrepancy of the prejudiced customers. First, prejudiced individuals might have experienced conflicting motivations: their desire to avoid blacks and their desire to shop where it was most comfortable and convenient. To resolve their dilemma, they may have acted contrary to their prejudice but also completed their shopping as quickly as possible. Second, prejudiced individuals might have experienced a conflict between their own inclination to avoid black clerks and prevailing public opinion. That blacks served as clerks may have suggested to the prejudiced whites that the public approved of the blacks' presence (and, by the same token, that the public would disapprove of openly prejudiced behavior). Thus, because situational factors intervene, we cannot accurately predict the behavior of one person toward another solely on the basis of the actor's attitude toward the target person.

Social psychologists, then, have begun to view the relationship between attitudes and behavior in increasingly complex terms — as a relationship involving multiple factors and mediating variables. They no longer ask *whether* people's attitudes can be used to predict their actions, but *when*. In any event, attitudes offer a convenient starting point for examining our behavior. In this chapter we will discuss three social psychological theories that attempt to describe how attitudes and behavior are related.

The Reasoned Action Model

Martin Fishbein and Icek Ajzen (1975; Ajzen and Fishbein, 1980) have proposed a way of conceptualizing the relationship between attitudes and behavior. Their **reasoned action model** suggests that our behavior is best predicted by our **behavioral intentions** — our plans to perform a behavior. If you say that you intend to study in order to pass a test, you are more likely to study than if you do not intend to do so. Behavioral intentions, in turn, Fishbein and Ajzen suggest, are shaped by two factors: the individual's *attitude toward the specific behavior*, which consists of the person's beliefs and evaluations of the possible outcomes of the behavior, and the individual's *subjective norm*, which consist of the person's beliefs about whether significant others think he or she should or should not perform the behavior and the person's motivations to comply with their wishes. Figure 8-1 illustrates the reasoned action model.

ATTITUDE TOWARD A BEHAVIOR

The reasoned action model proposes that one of the two factors shaping our behavioral intentions is **attitude toward the behavior**. This idea represents an important departure from other attempts to predict and explain behavior on the basis of *attitudes toward individuals, objects, or policies*. Other researchers have assumed that the more favorable someone's attitude is toward a person or category of persons, the more likely that individual will be to act positively toward such persons. The more negative the social attitude, the more likely are

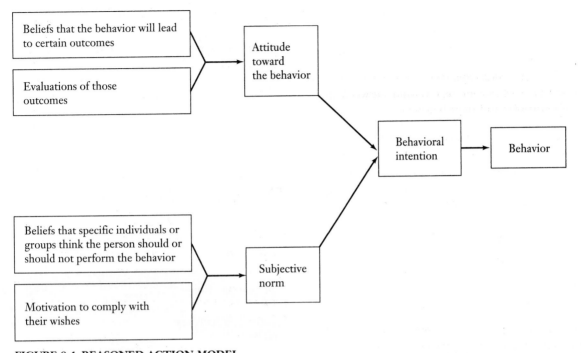

FIGURE 8-1 REASONED ACTION MODEL
Source: Icek Ajzen and Martin Fishbein, *Understanding Attitudes and Predicting Behavior,* © 1980, p.8. Adapted by permission of Prentice-Hall, Englewood Cliffs, NJ

negative behaviors toward the person or category of persons. But, according to Ajzen and Fishbein, many of these attempts to predict specific behaviors from general attitudes have failed. Since a general attitude *summarizes* a number of beliefs and feelings about a social identity (or object or policy), it is not surprising that it doesn't contain all the information needed to predict a *specific* behavior toward a representative of the social identity on a particular occasion. For example, your attitude toward members of another religion may not be a good predictor of whether you would share an office with someone of that religion. Your attitude toward abortion may not be a good predictor of your participation in a local pro-life or pro-choice demonstration.

Ajzen and Fishbein propose a method for increasing the predictability of behavior from attitudes. They stress that predictability will be greatest when the attitudes and behaviors are measured at the same level of generality. In other words, we should use general attitudes to predict general behaviors and specific attitudes to predict specific behaviors. Let's look at some studies that apply this principle.

General attitudes toward people, objects, or policies, according to Fishbein and Ajzen, can best predict *categories* of behavior. Behavioral categories consist of sets of actions rather than of a single action. A study by Weigal and Newman (1976) supports this idea. The researchers found that general attitudes best predicted categories of action, rather than specific actions. Here's how they conducted the study: The researchers gave subjects a sixteen-item scale to measure their general attitudes toward conservation and pollution. After a delay of at least three months, the researchers contacted the same subjects (three times over a five-month period) and asked them to participate in various environmental projects: signing and circulating petitions, working in a litter-pickup program and recruiting a friend to help, and participating for up to eight weeks in a recycling program. The researchers discovered that the correspondence between a subject's general attitude toward conservation and pollution and each of the individual behaviors was quite weak. In other words, the general attitude did not do a good job of predicting the individual behaviors, such as participation in the recycling program in week 5.

When the researchers grouped the individual behaviors into three kinds of environmental behavior — petition signing, litter pickup, and recycling — the correspondence between the general attitude and these somewhat more general measures of behavior was stronger. For example, each respondent received a score between 1 and 8 on recycling behavior (1 point for each week the subject participated in the program). Subjects' scores on the recycling-behavior measure were predicted more reliably from their general attitudes toward environmental quality than was their

participation in the recycling program during any particular week.

Finally, the researchers created an even more general index of environmental behavior by adding up all the scores from the individual behaviors in the three behavior categories (petition signing, litter pickup, and recycling). A person's score on this summary behavior measure was better predicted from his or her general environmental attitude than the individual behaviors or category behavior measures had been. So some evidence suggests that *general* attitudes can predict *general* patterns of relevant behaviors. It is likely, therefore, that if a person has a positive attitude toward the members of a particular social category, *in general* — that is, over many instances — her or his behavior toward those persons will probably be positive. Still, on specific occasions, the person's behavior toward a particular member of the category might be negative — contrary to her or his general attitude.

General attitudes can predict *general* patterns of relevant behaviors. These fans have a positive attitude about their team, and we can expect most of their behaviors to reflect this attitude. Nevertheless, it is possible that on specific occasions their behaviors may be contrary to the positive attitude. For example, they might criticize the coach or players.

Is it impossible, then, to predict specific behaviors from attitudes? According to Fishbein and Ajzen, it is not. When prediction of a specific behavior is the goal, they propose that we use an attitude measure that assesses the person's attitude *toward the behavior we are interested in predicting*. For example, your attitude about demonstrating for or against abortion is probably a better predictor of whether you would actually demonstrate than is your more general pro- or anti-abortion attitude.

The reasoned action model proposes two determinants of attitudes toward behavior, each focusing on the consequences of the behavior: (1) our evaluations of the consequences, either positive or negative, of our behavior and (2) our beliefs about the likelihood of each consequence. Ajzen and Fishbein approach the measurement of a person's salient beliefs about outcomes in the following manner: Initially, a list of outcomes is obtained by asking a sample of respondents the questions, "What do you see as the advantages of (the particular behavior)? What do you see as the disadvantages?" Next, for the most frequently mentioned outcome responses, individual respondents answer two sets of questions. First, the respondent *evaluates* each outcome on a 7-point, good-bad scale:

(A)

good						bad
+3	+2	+1	0	−1	−2	−3
extremely	quite	slightly	neither	slightly	quite	extremely

(the particular behavior)

Second, the respondent indicates, on a likely-unlikely scale, the *likelihood* that the behavior will result in each outcome:

(B)

likely						unlikely
+3	+2	+1	0	−1	−2	−3
extremely	quite	slightly	neither	slightly	quite	extremely

(the particular behavior)

To predict the respondent's attitude toward the specific behavior, each outcome evaluation (A) is weighted by the corresponding likelihood rating (B) (by multiplying them), and the products are summed over all outcomes. The larger this score is, the stronger the respondent's attitude toward the behavior is predicted to be. A positive score predicts a positive attitude toward the behavior, while a negative score predicts a negative attitude toward it. As Figure 8-1 indicates, attitude toward the behavior is one of two factors influencing our behavioral intentions and, ultimately, our behavior.

SUBJECTIVE NORMS

According to the reasoned action model, the second factor shaping our behavioral intentions is **subjective norms**—our beliefs about whether significant others think we should or should not perform the particular behavior. The more we believe that these important others think we should, the more we will intend to perform the behavior. On the other hand, when we believe that they think we should *not* perform a behavior, the greater the chance of our not intending to perform the behavior. Thus, whether a person's attitude (toward a behavior) is consistent with his or her behavioral intention is influenced by the person's beliefs about what others think he or she should do.

The reasoned action model suggests that, in forming a subjective norm, we take into account the normative expectations of significant others in our environment. That is, we consider whether *specific* individuals and groups (referents) think we should or should not engage in the behavior—these perceptions constitute our *normative beliefs*—and we use this information to arrive at the subjective norm. Clearly, some individuals and groups are more important (salient) to us than others. So the first task in forming subjective norms is to identify the most salient referents—specific persons and groups. This is done by asking a sample of respondents the questions, "Who are the groups or people who would approve of your doing (the particular behavior)? Who are the groups or people who would disapprove?" Next, for the individuals or groups most frequently mentioned, individual respondents are asked two sets of questions. First, the respondent indicates on a 7-point scale how each referent would feel about her or his performing the behavior:

(C)
I should   **I should not**
+3   +2   +1   0   −1   −2   −3
(the particular behavior)

Second, provide a measure of the respondent's motivation to comply with what each referent wishes, the respondent indicates how much she or he wants to do what each specific referent thinks the respondent should do:

(D)
Very much   **Not at all**
+3   +2   +1   0   −1   −2   −3

To predict the respondent's subjective norm, each normative belief (C) is weighted by the corresponding importance rating (D), and the products are summed over all referents. The larger this score is, the stronger the respondent's subjective norm is expected to be. A positive score would predict a subjective norm favoring the relevant behavior; a negative score would predict an unfavorable subjective norm. In Chapter 7, "The Social Nature of Self," the components we have just

discussed were referred to as reflected appraisals by significant others — an example of the social influence process. Figure 8-1 illustrates how subjective norms, along with attitude toward the behavior, influence behavioral intentions and, ultimately, behavior.

AN EXAMPLE

Let's look at an example of how the reasoned action model works. Suppose Samantha, having discovered that she is pregnant, must decide whether to have an abortion. The reasoned action model says that whether Samantha has an abortion will be a function of her behavioral intention, which, in turn, will be determined by her attitude toward having an abortion and her subjective norm about going through with an abortion.

Let's look first at Samantha's *attitude* toward having an abortion. The model says that her attitude is a function of a small number of salient beliefs about the likelihood of various consequences of having an abortion, weighted by her evaluation of these consequences (Fishbein and Ajzen, 1975). Table 8-1 shows how these elements might combine to determine Samantha's attitude toward having an abortion. Samantha believes that she will very probably feel guilty about having an abortion, a pretty negative outcome for her. But she also believes that, by having an abor-

TABLE 8-1   ATTITUDE AS THE PRODUCT OF BELIEF LIKELIHOODS AND EVALUATIONS*

Belief	Likelihood	Evaluation	Product
Having an abortion will:			
1. Make me feel guilty	+3	−2	−6
2. Save parents' embarrassment	+3	+3	+9
3. Save relationship with boyfriend	+2	+3	+6
4. Interfere with rights of the fetus	+1	−3	−3
5. Involve a medical procedure	+3	−1	−3
			+3

*Both likelihood and evaluation are measured on a +3 to −3 scale.

TABLE 8-2 SUBJECTIVE NORM AS THE PRODUCT OF BELIEF LIKELIHOODS AND MOTIVATIONS*

Significant others	Normative belief	Motivation	Product
1. Parents	+3	+3	+9
2. Boyfriend	+3	+3	+9
3. Best female friend	+3	+1	+3
4. Favorite aunt	-2	+3	-6
5. Church	-2	+1	-2
			+13

*Both normative belief and motivation are measured on a +3 to -3 scale.

tion, she would save her parents the embarrassment of having an unwed mother in the family. This is a very positive outcome for her. She believes that there is a pretty good probability that, by having an abortion, she will save her relationship with her boyfriend, which she desperately wants to do. Yet she also has some doubts about whether abortion is the right course to take. She believes that the fetus should have some rights, too, and realizes that its "right to life" conflicts with her own interests. Finally, she is a little fearful of medical procedures in general, so she does not look forward to the prospect of undergoing an abortion. As Table 8-1 shows, the reasoned action model would conclude from this information that Samantha's overall attitude toward having an abortion is weakly positive.

Now, what about Samantha's *subjective norm* about having an abortion? The people and institutions whose opinions on abortion Samantha cares about most are her parents, boyfriend, best female friend at college, favorite aunt, and church. She knows that her parents strongly support a woman's right to choose an abortion. She believes they would be slightly less in favor of an abortion for their own daughter, but she still thinks they would approve strongly. She is very motivated to do what her parents think is right on this issue. She cares most of all about her boyfriend's opinion, since she thinks he is the other person most affected by her decision. Samantha knows that he

feels very strongly that she should have an abortion so that they both can finish school. Samantha gives less importance to her best female friend's opinion, which she knows is also that she definitely should have the abortion. Samantha knows that her favorite aunt and her church would have moderately strong misgivings about her undergoing an abortion. She cares as much about her aunt's feelings on this as she does about her parents', but she cares much less about the church's position, which seems quite impersonal to her now that she is faced with this difficult decision. Overall, Samantha feels that the important people and institutions in her life would approve of her having an abortion in this situation. This is illustrated in Table 8-2.

The reasoned action model would predict that Samantha's behavioral intentions about having an abortion would be the sum of her attitude and her subjective norm about this behavior: (+3) + (+13) = +16. From this calculation, we would predict that Samantha would intend to get an abortion.

According to the reasoned action model, behavior is the result of an interaction between the strength of the person's attitude and social pressure to act in a specific way. When the attitude is strong, it takes considerable pressure in the opposite direction to contribute to contrary behavior. When the attitude is weak, it is hard to predict what the person will do when confronted with weak social pressure to act in a way inconsistent with the attitude, but he or she is likely to conform to strong social pressure, even if it is contrary to the attitude. When our attitudes are congruent with social pressure, our attitudes and behavior are likely to be consistent; when attitudes and social pressure are not congruent, the relationship between attitudes and behavior is harder to predict (Warner and DeFleur, 1969; Schuman and Johnson, 1976; Schutte, Kendrick, and Sadalla, 1985; Rabow, Neuman, and Hernandez, 1987; Grube and Morgan, 1990).

EVALUATION OF THE MODEL

Fishbein and Ajzen's reasoned action theory has been widely used in social psychology. The model's appeal lies, partly, in its simplicity. It uses only a small number of variables to explain all kinds of behavior. Although the individual components in the model differ in their explanatory power (Vallerand et al., 1992), the model has successfully predicted exercise, dating, and studying behaviors (Bentler and Speckart, 1981); weight loss, consumer choices, and women's occupational choices (Ajzen and Fishbein, 1980; Lane, Mathews, and Presholdt, 1988); smoking (Fishbein, 1980); the use of various contraceptive techniques (Pagel and Davidson, 1984); whether women breast- or bottle-fed their babies (Manstead, Proffit, and Smart, 1983); whether alcoholics signed up for a treatment program (McArdle, 1972); women's use of mammography (Montano and Taplin, 1991) and breast self-exams (Lierman et al., 1990); other health behaviors (Ried and Christensen, 1988; Brubaker and Wickersham, 1990; DeVellis, Blalock, and Sandler, 1990); use of dental floss (Toneatto and Binik, 1987); participation in continuing-education programs (Pryor, 1990); and junior high school girls' enrollment in elective physical science courses (Koballa, 1988).

The model does have limitations however (Liska, 1984). All of us can probably think of situations in which we *intended* to do something but failed to follow through — our behavior didn't, as the model predicts, match our intentions. Several factors can interfere with our behaving in accord with our attitudes. Such factors sometimes prevent us from acting as we intend to. Let's look at three such factors: past behavior, self-identity, and self-efficacy.

Past Behavior

One factor is a person's past behavior. People who intend to do something they have done previously may be more likely to go ahead with it than people who intend to do something for the first time. For example, Ajzen and Madden (1986) concluded that college students' previous class attendance was the single best predictor of their future class attendance, no matter what their atti-

This person *intends* to diet and lose weight but falls back into established eating patterns. The influence of prior behavior on subsequent behavior can be explained psychologically and situationally. Psychologically, we are creatures of habit; we tend to repeat the way we did something previously. And the same situational factors that caused our prior behavior continue to operate and thus may explain why our current behavior does not always match our current intentions.

tudes or intentions about attending class. Similarly, another study showed that how a woman fed her first child influenced how she fed her second, irrespective of her attitude and subjective norms (Manstead, Proffit, and Smart, 1983). Researchers also found that whether a person had donated blood in the past was a better predictor of making blood donations in the next four months than the person's stated intentions about doing so (Bagozzi, 1981; Charng, Piliavin, and Callero, 1988). The influence of prior behavior on subsequent behavior can be explained psychologically and situationally. Psychologically, we are creatures of habit; we tend to repeat the way we did something previously. And the same situational factors that caused our prior behavior continue to operate and thus may explain why our current behavior does not always match our current intentions.

Self-Identity

A second factor that may influence the relationship between our intentions and our behavior is self-identity (Charng, Piliavin, and Callero, 1988). People who intend to behave in a manner consistent with a specific self-identity may be more likely to do so than people who intend to act inconsistently in relation to it. For example, Granberg and Holmberg (1991) found that when people intended to vote in a way that was consistent with their party identification, they did, but there was less consistency between their intentions and behavior when their intentions conflicted with their political identity. In Sweden and the United States, 96 percent voted as they intended when their intentions matched their party allegiance. However, among voters who intended to "cross over" and vote in a way not implied by their political identity, only 83 percent in the United States and 78 percent in Sweden showed consistency between their voting intentions and their voting behavior.

Self-Efficacy

Ajzen and Madden (1986) have suggested that another variable—perceived control over outcomes —also contributes to the relationship between intentions and behavior, and they propose that this variable be added to the model. As we discussed in Chapter 7, "The Social Nature of Self," people differ in the degree to which they feel they have control over the good and bad things that happen to them. Some persons, characterized as having "high self-efficacy," feel that they pretty much control their positive outcomes. Others, characterized as having "low self-efficacy," believe that they cannot attain positive consequences—either because they do not have the requisite attributes (e.g., ability, discipline, determination) or because the consequences are controlled by the external environment and they don't have much to do with it.

Several researchers believe that intentions better predict the behavior of high-self-efficacy persons—those believing that they can control their behavior to produce successful consequences—than that of low-self-efficacy persons. These researchers emphasize self-efficacy related to *specific* *behaviors*, rather than to *global* self-efficacy. They note that we feel more in control of some aspects of our behavior than others, and they suggest that our intentions do a better job of predicting our behavior when we feel we are in control of our behavioral outcomes (Sheppard, Hartwick, and Warshaw, 1988; Netemeyer, Burton, and Johnson, 1991). For example, most people probably feel they have more control of such behaviors as voting, attending a movie, and going to buy groceries than they do of behaviors such as getting a bank loan (since the banker's cooperation is required) or quitting smoking (since much willpower is required). Thus, we might expect that the former behaviors would be better predicted by intentions than the latter for most people. Of course, there are individual differences in self-efficacy with respect to any specific behavior. Thus, among female students who felt that they could successfully control their weight if they tried, the intention to lose weight resulted in actual weight loss more often than it did for their peers who felt that their efforts would probably not be successful (Schifter and Ajzen, 1985).

Despite these limitations, the theory of reasoned action has clarified the role of attitudes in determining behavior. Research inspired by the theory has helped explain why many studies find only weak relationships between attitudes and behavior. The attitude-behavior relationship is stronger when the measure of attitude focuses on the specific behavior and its outcomes, rather than on the object of the behavior (e.g., another person). The relationship is also stronger when the person believes that (1) he or she can control the behavior to produce successful outcomes (high self-efficacy), (2) the behavior is consistent with his or her relevant social identities, and (3) most of the significant others favor his or her performing the behavior (when the subjective norm, in other words, is positive). Researchers are already at work on revised versions of the theory, called "planned behavior theory" and "the theory of self-regulation," which specify the role of perceived control and emotion in the relationship between intentions and behaviors (Bagozzi, 1992).

Balance and Cognitive Dissonance Theories

Underlying much social psychological theory and research is the notion that people strive to maintain **attitude consistency:** they organize their attitudes in a harmonious manner so that the attitudes are not in conflict with each other. Thus civil rights activists do not ordinarily endorse or contribute to the Ku Klux Klan; Christian Scientists do not usually enroll in medical schools; and liberal and radical reformers seldom support or vote for conservative Republicans. At the core of the concept of attitude consistency is the assumption that people experience inconsistency as an uncomfortable state, one that they are impelled to eliminate or reduce.

The basic prediction derived from the principle of attitude consistency is that people typically seek to reconcile their conflicting attitudes—that the direction of attitude change will be from a state of inconsistency toward a state of consistency. Behavior may either help resolve or cause conflict among attitudes. Suppose that you strongly support abortion laws that protect a woman's right to terminate an unwanted pregnancy. Indeed, your feelings are so ardent that you have recently begun to campaign for pro-choice political candidates and to raise funds to support a local abortion clinic. Suppose, too, that your best friend vigorously opposes abortion, believing it to be an act of murder. How can you maintain deep and abiding ties with a person whose opinions about abortion are the opposite of your own? To resolve the inconsistency, you may decide that you do not like your friend that much (a change in the feeling component of the attitude); or you may attempt to delude yourself into believing that your friend is not really opposed to abortion (a change in the belief component); or you may decide that you really do not feel so strongly about abortion legislation after all (another atti-

---

STUDENT OBSERVATION

Attitude Consistency

I used to smoke pot on a recreational basis. We would smoke at parties and concerts, and I enjoyed it. Two years ago, I started dating a girl with conservative attitudes. It was clear that she disapproved of pot smoking. During the time we dated, I never smoked, even when she wasn't around. When a situation arose in which I formerly would have smoked, I would tell myself that I didn't want to anymore—that I was past that.

As soon as my girlfriend and I broke up last semester, I began smoking a little pot again. I realized that while we were dating, I had convinced myself that I didn't want to smoke, because otherwise our differing attitudes about pot would have created a distressing situation for me. I had changed my behavior to make our attitudes more consistent.

tude change) and may stop your campaigning and fund-raising (behavior change). In any event, the chances are that you will alter one of your attitudes or behaviors so as to bring about consistency. (Before reading further, look at the Student Observation: "Attitude Consistency.")

There are several theories of attitude consistency. We shall review two of the most influential here: balance theory and cognitive dissonance theory.

BALANCE THEORY

The initial formulation of the principle of attitude consistency came from Fritz Heider's **balance theory** (1946, 1958). Three elements in attitude change concerned Heider: (1) the person who is the focus of attention, labeled P; (2) some other person, labeled O; and (3) an impersonal entity—an object, idea, or event—labeled X. The theory suggests that P strives to maintain consistency, or **balance,** among the attitudes connecting the elements P, O, and X.

Heider's theory can be applied to the abortion example we gave above. In the example, you would be P, your friend would be O, and support for abortion legislation would be X. We can diagram the situation according to Heider's balance theory as follows:

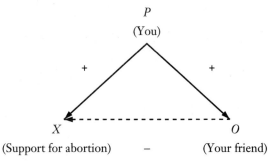

P
(You)

+   +

X   O
(Support for abortion)   –   (Your friend)

Since you favor abortion, the link between you and abortion has a positive value, indicated by a plus sign (+). Further, since you and your friend have a close, friendly relationship, the link between you and your friend has a positive value (+). Finally, since your friend opposes abortion, the link between your friend and abortion has a

negative value, indicated by a minus sign (−). In mathematics, the multiplication of two positives and one negative produces a negative:

$$+ \cdot + \cdot - = -$$

Heider terms a minus state, such as the one here, **imbalance**. This state is characterized by stress, discomfort, and unpleasantness. Hence, according to balance theory, you will be motivated to reduce the imbalance.

One way you may accomplish this, in the example, is to change *your* attitude toward abortion (and stop campaigning and fund-raising):

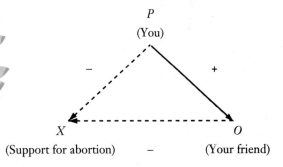

P
(You)

–   +

X   O
(Support for abortion)   –   (Your friend)

In this case you are multiplying two negatives and one positive, which in mathematics gives you a positive:

$$+ \cdot - \cdot - = +$$

Since the sign is positive, balance has been restored.

Instead of changing your attitude toward abortion, you may reject your friend:

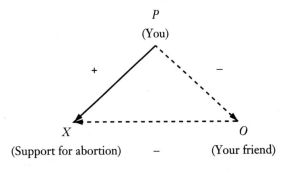

P
(You)

+   –

X   O
(Support for abortion)   –   (Your friend)

In this case you also have restored balance:

$$+ \cdot - \cdot - = +$$

Observe that a balanced state exists when there are either no negatives or two negatives; an imbalanced state exists when there are one or three negatives (see Figure 8-2).

Balance theory suggests that there are various ways to restore balance to an imbalanced configuration of attitudes. The theory predicts that people will change as few affective relations as possible to achieve a balanced configuration. Balance pressures seem to be stronger when we like, rather than dislike, the other person. Apparently, when we dislike someone, we do not care as much whether we agree or disagree with her or him. It is easy enough to end the relationship so that no configuration is left to be balanced. Such situations have been called "nonbalanced" rather than "imbalanced" (Newcomb, 1968).

Balance theory suggests that inconsistent attitudes generally do not pose a problem for us *unless* they are somehow brought together within the

same context. Suppose that you have a positive attitude toward a professor of yours and also toward the idea of pro-choice legislation. These two attitudes remain unrelated unless the professor expresses a position on abortion legislation. Should the professor support pro-choice legislation, your two attitudes are congruent—in harmony or agreement. But if the professor opposes such legislation, your two attitudes are incongruent—out of harmony or agreement with each other.

A degree of complexity is added to balance theory if we recognize that all our attitudes are not equally strong or intense (Osgood and Tannenbaum, 1955). It is possible to assign different weights to attitudes, depending on *how strongly they are evaluated*. We might develop a measure, for example, in which attitude objects are evaluated on a scale running from *good* to *bad*, or $+3$ (maximum positive evaluation) to -3 (maximum negative evaluation).

The recognition that we do not feel equally strongly or intensely about all issues allows us to predict the direction and degree of attitude

FIGURE 8-2 HEIDER'S BALANCED AND IMBALANCED STATE

A balanced state exists when there are no negatives or two negatives; an imbalanced state exists when there are one or three negatives. An imbalanced state is one characterized by discomfort and unpleasantness. Accordingly, the individual is under pressure to reduce imbalance, which means changing one's attitude toward either the person or the impersonal entity (object, idea, or event). The arrows indicate the direction of the relationships.

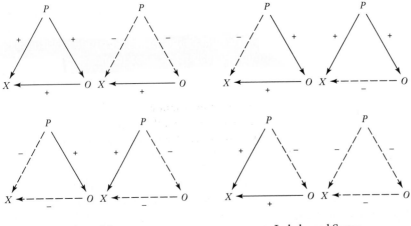

Balanced States   Imbalanced States

STUDENT OBSERVATION

Balance Theory

I have never used marijuana in my life. When I was in high school, none of my friends ever smoked pot. Our group called those who did "potheads" or "druggies," and we all had a strong dislike for those people. When I came to college, I pledged a fraternity which has some members who smoke pot and I became good friends with several of these brothers. For a short time, I experienced a state of "imbalance" as described by Heider's balance theory. I felt stress, discomfort, and unpleasantness while in the presence of my friends smoking pot. My attitude toward smoking pot quickly changed. I felt that these friendships were more important than insisting that all my friends share my high moral standards. Although I still do not use marijuana myself, it no longer bothers me if my friends choose to use the drug. This is an excellent example of the balance theory of attitude consistency at work.

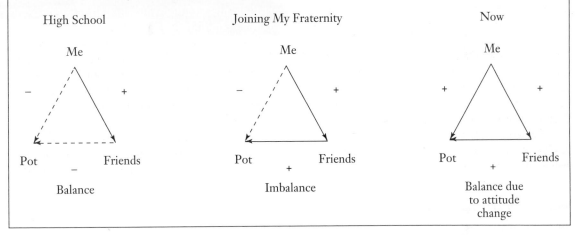

change. When two attitudes are in conflict, the stronger one is less likely to change. Suppose you like a professor at the highest scale value of $+3$ and you learn that she or he opposes legislation permitting abortion, a position you dislike at the relatively moderate level of -1. Balance theory's prediction is that your attitude toward abortion would be more likely to "give" than your attitude toward the professor. Inasmuch as extreme attitudes are more resistant to change than neutral ones, there would be a greater shift in the milder attitude. (Before reading further, look at the Student Observation: "Balance Theory.")

COGNITIVE DISSONANCE THEORY

Few theories in social psychology have had the impact of Leon Festinger's **cognitive dissonance**

theory (Festinger, 1957). Although interest in it has waned in recent years, from its initial formulation in 1957, it stimulated a vast amount of controversy, research, and theoretical development. The theory has shown considerable versatility, resilience, and predictive ability (Greenwald, 1975; Kiesler and Pallak, 1976; Fazio, Zanna, and Cooper, 1977, 1979; Croyle and Cooper, 1983). The theory proposes that we strive to maintain **consonance**, or consistency, among attitudes and to avoid **dissonance**, or inconsistency, which produces psychological tension.

Festinger developed his theory as a tool for interpreting some bizarre rumors surfacing after an earthquake in India. Included among the rumors were the following: "There will be a severe cyclone in the next few days"; "There will be a severe earthquake on the lunar eclipse day";

"A flood is rushing toward the province." The rumors arose in an area where people experienced tremors but not personal injury or destruction of property. The prevalence of the rumors in this area seemingly contradicted the prevalent psychological notion that people seek to avoid unpleasant things, such as anxiety and the prospect of pain. Moreover, comparable data revealed that people in an actual disaster setting—an area of death and destruction—did not create rumors predicting further disaster.

Festinger hypothesized that the rumors in the undamaged community derived from cognitive dissonance. The people had a strong and persistent fear reaction to the tremors; yet in the absence of destruction, they could see nothing to fear. The *feeling* of fear in the absence of an adequate reason for fear was dissonant—inconsistent or out of balance. But the rumors of impending disaster offered explanations consonant with being afraid; the rumors functioned to justify fear and thus to reduce dissonance. The people, then, undertook to reduce dissonance by *adding* new beliefs; the fear-justifying rumors added new beliefs consistent with being afraid.

The Behavior-Attitude Link

The reasoned action model, discussed earlier, specifies the conditions under which our *attitudes determine our behavior*. Cognitive dissonance theory grew out of an attempt to show that we sometimes change attitudes to make them consistent with our behavior. We can think of many examples of instances in which a person's *behavior influences his or her attitudes*. What about the person who resents and resists others' efforts to prevent him from driving after having a couple of drinks but who, after causing an accident in which someone is injured, not only refrains from drinking and driving himself but also becomes a strong advocate of the buddy system? And how about the person who is afraid her neighborhood will deteriorate if Hispanics move in but subsequently who becomes good friends with her new Hispanic neighbors and changes her mind? Surely you've encountered someone who, having lost many

pounds through a long and difficult process of dieting and exercise, becomes an extremely vocal critic of the diet and exercise habits of friends who haven't shed their extra pounds. Studies have found, for example, that although attitudes toward divorce do not predict subsequent marital dissolution, marital dissolution affects attitudes toward divorce significantly—those who are divorced have more positive attitudes toward it (Thornton, 1985; Amato and Booth, 1991).

Returning to Festinger's initial study, we see that dissonance was reduced by *adding* beliefs that were consistent with being and acting afraid. Still another method for reducing dissonance is to *change* certain beliefs. Festinger illustrates this method of dissonance reduction with the example of smokers who believe that cigarette smoking causes cancer. Such people experience dissonance.

The most efficient way to reduce dissonance would be to stop smoking, but for many smokers this behavioral change would be the most difficult solution. Instead, they undermine the other belief—that cigarette smoking causes cancer. Thus they may belittle the evidence that links smoking to cancer. Festinger (1957) cites a survey which found that 29 percent of nonsmokers, 20 percent of light smokers, but only 7 percent of heavy smokers believed that a relationship had been established between smoking and lung cancer. Or dissonance-experiencing smokers might switch to filter-tipped cigarettes, deluding themselves that the filter traps all the cancer-producing materials. Or they might convince themselves that cigarette smoking is worth the price: "I'd rather have a short, enjoyable life than a long, unenjoyable one." In employing any of these approaches, smokers seek to reduce dissonance by reducing the absurdity involved in making themselves cancer-prone (Aronson, 1969). It is interesting to note in this context that alcohol also reduces the unpleasant feelings associated with attitude conflict, an effect possibly reinforcing alcohol consumption (Steele, Southwick, and Critchlow, 1981). (See the box "When Prophecy Fails," for a description of a doomsday cult's change in beliefs to reduce dissonance after the world was not de-

WHEN PROPHECY FAILS

Some years ago the following story appeared in a Midwestern newspaper:

> Prophecy from Planet.
> Clarion Call to City: Flee that Flood.
> It'll Swamp Us on Dec. 21,
> Outer Space Tells Suburbanite
> Lake City will be destroyed by a flood from Great Lake just before dawn, December 21, according to a suburban housewife, Mrs. Marion Keech, of 847 West School Street. . . . It is the purport of many messages she has received by automatic writing, she says. . . . The messages, according to Mrs. Keech, are sent to her by superior beings from a planet called "Clarion." These beings have been visiting the earth, she says, in . . . flying saucers. . . . Mrs. Keech reports she was told the flood will spread to form an inland sea stretching from the Arctic Circle to the Gulf of Mexico. At the same time, she says, a cataclysm will submerge the West Coast from Seattle, Washington, to Chile in South America. (Festinger, Riecken, and Schachter, 1956: 30–31)

Mrs. Keech told her friends about the message and attracted a small following of believers. Leon Festinger, Henry W. Riecken, and Stanley Schachter (1956), three social psychologists, joined the movement for research purposes, concealing their identity as social scientists. Many of the members of the doomsday sect made considerable financial sacrifices in committing themselves to the group, re-signing from jobs and giving away their belongings. Thus, according to the researchers, the way was prepared for a monumental example of cognitive dissonance between prophecy and outcome.

Mrs. Keech set the hour (midnight, December 21) for the arrival of a visitor from outer space who would escort group members to safety by means of a flying saucer. But, at the appointed hour, nothing happened. When the visitor failed to arrive and the earth was not destroyed, the believers became intensely confused, apprehensive, and despairing. They checked and rechecked their watches in disbelief. Two facts were in dissonance: the members believed in their prophet, and her prophecy had failed.

About five hours later, Mrs. Keech called the members together and announced that she had received a message: God had saved the world from destruction because of the faith spread throughout the world by the believers' actions. In recounting this message, Mrs. Keech offered her followers a way to reduce their cognitive dissonance. Instead of rejecting their prophet, they altered the other cognition — the doomsday belief. Members thus reinterpreted the events and redirected their cause, finding a justification for their considerable commitment and investment. This example illustrates how attitudes can be resistant to change even in the face of strong disconfirming evidence.

stroyed as the cult's members had believed it would be. See also the Student Observations: "Cognitive Dissonance.")

Commitment

Subsequent research has led to various modifications of Festinger's original theory. One of the most notable has been proposed by Jack W. Brehm and A. R. Cohen (1962). According to these researchers, the theory of cognitive dissonance holds only under certain conditions. Two key conditions are commitment and internal attribution. **Commitment** is a state of being bound to or locked into a position or a course of action. It implies that people, by closing the door to alternative behaviors, have to "live with" their decisions. Consequently, they need to reduce any dissonant elements deriving from their irreversible commitments.

Suppose that Mike, a high school senior, praises Ivy League schools and ridicules the scholastic attributes of state universities. Later, he learns not only that Ivy League schools are far more expensive than he had anticipated but that the state university will give him a scholarship. Mike decides to go to the state university and turns down offers from the Ivy League schools he applied to. By his actions, Mike has *committed*

STUDENT OBSERVATIONS

Cognitive Dissonance

Today I went to the auto show at the fairgrounds arena. It cost $5 to get into the show. Once inside, the patrons could see all the cars with one exception. Curtained off from the other cars was John Lennon's limousine. You had to pay another 50 cents to view the car. Well, like the other suckers, I paid my 50 cents and saw the car. We were all raving about it. Yet if I were to be honest, the car really was not all that special and a number of other cars on the floor actually topped it. But we had paid 50 cents to see it. To admit that we were fools for having paid an extra 50 cents would have been a difficult solution to our cognitive dissonance. So instead, having paid 50 cents to see the car, we brought our cognitions into balance by redefining the car as the greatest.

For spring break this year, I went to Key West, and I was completely obsessed with getting a savage tan. Only one other girl, Cynthia, of the five I went down with was as obsessed as I was. We were all supposed to come back to campus on Saturday so that we could rest for a day before starting back to class, but since we had two cars, Cynthia and I decided to stay an extra day to get more sun. The extra day turned out to be very cloudy, but admitting that the day was a total waste would have been a difficult solution to our cognitive dissonance. Instead, we brought our cognitions into balance by deciding that we got just as much sun when it was cloudy as we would have on a gorgeous day.

himself to attend a state university. Dissonance theory predicts that he will reduce dissonance by bringing his attitudes into line with his behavior: Mike's attitude toward state universities will become more favorable; conversely, his attitude toward Ivy League schools may become more negative (Sherwood, Barron, and Fitch, 1969). We cannot expect such a result if Mike feels that he can change his decision at any time. The absence of commitment would reduce the dissonance he is experiencing, and, therefore, less attitude change would be expected.

Internal-External Attributions

For individuals to experience dissonance, they must believe they acted *voluntarily;* otherwise, they will not feel responsible for the outcomes of their decisions. In other words, they must make an *internal attribution* regarding the causes of the event (Goethals, Cooper, and Naficy, 1979). If, in contrast, they are *compelled* to act contrary to their beliefs, they can avoid dissonance by reasoning, "I was forced to do this; I really did not have any choice." Thus, they make an *external attribution* for the causes of the event. If Mike feels that he is

being forced to attend the state university, he presumably will experience less dissonance — and thus less pressure to change his attitudes about state universities — than if he feels that he is making a free choice (Sherwood, Barron, and Fitch, 1969). Such a lack of choice probably explains why some American soldiers in Vietnam never really supported the war in which they were fighting. Although they were behaving contrary to their beliefs, these soldiers did not experience dissonance because they felt compelled to fight.

Several factors influence whether we attribute our actions to internal or external sources. Let's examine a few: reward, threat, perceived responsibility, and effort.

Reward. One surprising aspect of dissonance theory is that it makes a prediction that is contradictory to common sense: The less the reward for engaging in behavior contrary to an attitude (low external attribution), the greater will be the resultant attitude change. Presumably, people seduced by a large reward to act in a way conflicting with their attitudes can deny responsibility by saying, "How could I refuse a reward of that size?"

These predictions are illustrated by a classic experiment of Festinger and J. Merrill Carlsmith (1959). The researchers asked subjects to perform a very boring task for two hours. Afterward, most of the subjects were instructed by the experimenter to tell the subjects who replaced them that the experiment had been fun and exciting; others, members of a control group, also performed the task but were not asked to lie. Some of the subjects who lied were paid $1 for their compliance, while other "liars" received $20. Subjects were next referred to the psychology department office, where they evaluated the experiment. The evaluations were actually part of the experiment, although the subjects were led to believe that the experiment was finished.

Among other questions included in the evaluation, the students were asked to indicate the degree to which they had enjoyed the task they had performed and whether they would like to participate in a similar experiment again. The ratings of the control group indicated that the task was indeed unpleasant. Subjects who were paid $1 rated the task more positively than those paid $20. These findings support dissonance theory. The subjects who received only $1 found it necessary to rationalize their falsehood; for a trivial sum they had lied, and hence they undertook to resolve their dissonance by coming to believe that they really had liked the dull task. In contrast, the subjects who received $20 experienced little dissonance and thus had little reason to alter their

Some American soldiers in Vietnam did not support the war in which they fought. Because of the draft, many were in the military service against their wills. Under these conditions, dissonance would not be expected to produce pro-war attitude change.

unfavorable attitudes toward the boring task. In fact, other research suggests that when offered a large payment for engaging in an activity, we infer that the activity must be difficult, tedious, risky, or unpleasant in some way (Freedman, Cunningham, and Krismer, 1992).

Threat. Do greater threats, like greater rewards, produce less dissonance and, consequently, less attitude change? We sometimes try to induce people to engage in behavior that they dislike by threatening them with punishment. The severity of the threatened punishment can vary substantially—a verbal reprimand, the silent treatment, a fine, a blow, jail, termination of the relationship, even death. But, although the most severe punishments may increase the chances that the person will engage in the disliked behavior, they may also decrease the possibility that the negative attitude will change.

Two experiments examined this hypothesis (Aronson and Carlsmith, 1963; Freedman, 1965). In both studies, children were threatened with either mild or severe punishment if they played with a toy they rated as very desirable. None of the children played with the toy, as even the threat of mild punishment was severe enough to induce compliance. In the first study, the children subsequently rerated the desirability of the toy; in the second study, the children were given the opportunity to play with the toy several weeks later. Under conditions of mild threat (low external attribution), the children reduced their evaluation of the toy more and were less likely to play with it later than under severe threat (high external attribution). The researchers interpreted their findings as suggesting that the children in the mild threat condition experienced greater dissonance, which they reduced by subsequently devaluating the toy and refusing to play with it.

Perceived responsibility. Punishment, as we all know, is not always an effective deterrent to behavior. Here, the critical question is whether the person who has acted feels responsible for the punishment he or she subsequently receives—in other words, whether the person makes an internal or external attribution of responsibility. When we *choose* an attractive course of action that turns out badly, we feel responsible for the outcome, and this creates dissonance. For example, you may volunteer to stuff envelopes for a political candidate you really believe in, only to find out that the task is really boring and that nobody seems particularly grateful for your help. You experience dissonance because you chose to do the job and then you ended up hating it. You may reduce the dissonance by changing your opinion about the task—perhaps deciding that, although you didn't enjoy doing it, without your help and that of the other volunteers, the candidate, who is really worthy, would probably not be elected (Scher and Cooper, 1989).

Effort. Cognitive dissonance partly explains why some patients benefit from psychotherapy. Social psychologists Danny Axsom and Joel Cooper (1985; Axsom, 1989) observed that the effort involved in therapy, plus the decision to undergo the effort (internal attribution), leads to positive outcomes through the reduction of cognitive dissonance. For example, people in weight therapy programs apparently respond positively to the programs partly to justify the expenditure of effort. Not losing weight after undergoing highly effortful sessions would seem absurd. Losing weight justifies the effort. Some weight-loss programs take this a step further by having clients at the beginning of the program put up money that is refunded if they meet their weight-loss goals but forfeited if they fail to do so.

Bem's Challenge

According to dissonance theory, the greater the dissonance we experience, the greater the subsequent consistency between an originally discrepant attitude and behavior. When we engage in behavior that we feel is contrary to our attitudes, we experience stress that can be relieved by changing our attitudes to be more consistent with our behavior.

A challenge to dissonance theory comes from Daryl Bem (1972). His *self-perception theory*, which we discussed in Chapter 7, "The Social Nature of

Self," proposes that many cases of attitude-behavior inconsistency are not stressful. Instead, Bem argues, many of our expressions of attitude are rather casual verbal statements. On many topics, we don't have strong feelings one way or the other. Yet when someone is asked for an opinion and wants to be cooperative (or not to appear uninformed), the person offers an opinion anyway. Not really knowing what her or his attitude is, Bem suggests, the person simply infers it from her or his own behavior and the associated circumstances. For example, if someone asks you your opinion of a specific television program, you think for a minute and conclude that because you almost never watch it — and there's no particular reason you couldn't if you wanted to — you must not like the program. If your subsequent behavior appears to contradict your stated opinion, you can quite easily "change your attitude" about the program without experiencing much stress.

Research suggests there is some validity to *both* cognitive dissonance and self-perception theories (Chaiken and Baldwin, 1981; Wood, 1982; Tybout and Scott, 1983). Which theory is correct hinges on the strength of the attitude. For weakly held attitudes, self-perception theory works quite well. On the other hand, when we do have strong attitudes, contradictory behavior can be stressful, producing changes that may include attitude change. Of course, it is also true that strong attitudes (that is, those supported by information about the attitude object, one's personal experience, or one's vested interest) discourage contradictory behavior in the first place (Zanna, Olson, and Fazio, 1980; Davison et al., 1985; Kallgren and Wood, 1986).

Self-Concept and Dissonance

Elliot Aronson (1968, 1969) and others (Baumeister and Tice, 1984) have suggested a still further refinement in dissonance theory. Festinger, Aronson asserts, mislocated the source of dissonance. What is critical, he argues, and Festinger overlooks it, is the conflict between people's self-attitudes and their attitudes about a behavior that violates these self-attitudes. According to this view, dissonance does not arise between just any two attitudes; rather, it occurs when our behavior threatens to diminish the positive feelings we have about ourselves.

Aronson suggests that in the boring-task experiment, the dissonance did not occur, as Festinger and Carlsmith insisted, between the belief "I believe the task is dull" and the belief "I said the task was interesting." Instead, the belief "I am a good and decent human being" and the belief "I have committed an indecent act; I have misled a person" were dissonant. Some research tends to confirm this alternative view of dissonance (Nel, Helmreich, and Aronson, 1969; Steele and Liu, 1983).

Research into attitude consistency theories, especially cognitive dissonance theory, makes several contributions to our understanding of the relationship between attitudes and behavior. First, it reverses the direction of assumed influence between the two components. Whereas the reasoned action model views attitudes as influencing behavior, cognitive consistency theories view behavior as having a major impact on attitudes. Second, not all inconsistencies between attitude and behavior are stressful enough to force a change in attitude (or behavior) in order to establish a consistent relationship. The stress is greater when: (1) the person's attitude is strong, (2) the person believes he or she is committed to the behavior, and (3) the person feels responsible for his or her own behavior, which is likely when the person has expended effort without substantial reward or threat (external attribution is low).

Affect Control Theory

David Heise's **affect control theory** (also referred to as ACT) concentrates on how attitudes toward self, others, and behaviors relate to interpersonal behaviors (Heise, 1979; Smith-Lovin and Heise, 1988). In the tradition of the symbolic interaction perspective, affect control theory emphasizes that culture and social situations are important determinants of social behavior. The theory offers a model of attitudes which suggests that the meanings we assign to identities and behaviors shape our social interactions.

THE MEANING OF SOCIAL EVENTS: EVALUATION, POTENCY, AND ACTIVITY

A key feature of affect control theory is its emphasis on the shared nature of meanings for identities and behaviors. Indeed, it is because we share these meanings with other members of our culture that interaction and communication are possible. (We discussed the importance of shared meanings in Chapter 5, "Communication.") Affect control theory conceptualizes meaning in a specific, measurable way (Smith-Lovin, 1990). The theory suggests that we tend to think about people and behaviors in terms of how *good*, how *powerful*, and how *lively* they are.

These sentiments—goodness, powerfulness, and liveliness—correspond to the three dimensions of affective meaning discovered by Charles Osgood and his colleagues (1957, 1975): evaluation, potency, and activity. The researchers employed a measurement procedure called the *semantic differential*. Subjects were given a list of 7-point adjective scales such as the following.

```
happy  ___  ___  ___  ___  ___  ___  ___  sad
good   ___  ___  ___  ___  ___  ___  ___  bad
warm   ___  ___  ___  ___  ___  ___  ___  cold
strong ___  ___  ___  ___  ___  ___  ___  weak
lively ___  ___  ___  ___  ___  ___  ___  quiet
young  ___  ___  ___  ___  ___  ___  ___  old
```

Subjects were also given a list of items and were asked to indicate on each scale where these items fell. The items rated were identities and objects such as mother, robber, professor, boulder, and rose. For example, subjects rated whether mothers were more "happy" or more "sad," more "good" or more "bad," more "warm" or more "cold," and so on.

The researchers found that respondents' ratings of many of the identities and objects tended to cluster around three underlying dimensions: *evaluation* (good-bad), *potency* (strong-weak), and *activity* (lively-quiet). For example, if respondents rated mothers as "good," they also tended to view mothers as "nice," "kind," and "happy." If they saw an identity as "powerful," they also tended to see it as "strong" and "big." In other words, most of the meaning in any concept seems to be summarized by its evaluation, potency, and activity dimensions. Indeed, these three dimensions subsequently have been found to underlie reactions to many types of concepts in a variety of cultures. Of the three, evaluation was the most important dimension of meaning, with potency of secondary and activity of lesser importance. Perhaps this accounts for the greater attention paid to the measurement of evaluation (social esteem and prejudice and self-esteem) in studies of social attitudes and self-attitudes.

Affect control theory uses the semantic differential methodology to measure meaning. According to the theory, our attitudes toward something (a self-identity, another's identity, or a behavior) consist of the particular **EPA profile** — the particular combination of meanings on the basis of evaluation, potency, and activity — that the identity or behavior has for us. These meanings are part of our culture. Studies on a variety of topics show a surprising degree of agreement about the affective meanings associated with social identities and behaviors (Smith-Lovin, 1990). Despite different backgrounds, U.S. respondents largely agree that mothers are nicer than children, physicians have more power than patients, and children are livelier than most other identities, and that love is more powerful than hate. Table 8-3 contains the average ratings of a few social identities and behaviors on the three dimensions.

Affect control theory assumes that we have **fundamental sentiments** about identities and behaviors. Fundamental sentiments can be thought of as the *usual meanings* — as measured by evaluation, potency, and activity — that an identity or behavior has for us. These are the meanings we bring to a situation. Because affect control theory proposes that these meanings are cultural, or shared, it measures fundamentals by averaging the ratings across a large number of respondents from a single culture.

TABLE 8-3 RATINGS OF SELECTED IDENTITIES AND BEHAVIORS ON
EVALUATION (E), POTENCY (P), AND ACTIVITY (A) DIMENSIONS*

Stimulus	Male raters			Female raters		
	E	P	A	E	P	A
Mother	2.52	1.50	−0.13	2.33	1.90	0.04
Mafioso	−1.78	2.09	0.31	−1.57	1.80	0.21
Physician	1.90	1.85	0.36	1.57	1.68	−0.46
Patient	0.07	−1.72	−0.78	0.26	−1.55	−0.97
Child	1.42	−1.48	2.31	1.94	−1.10	2.52
Cripple	−0.14	−1.62	−1.03	0.32	−1.04	−1.13
Love	2.87	2.62	0.50	2.89	2.67	0.48
Hate	−2.50	0.38	0.77	−2.77	0.09	0.77
Rescue	2.77	2.78	2.03	2.41	1.76	1.22
Nag	−1.81	−0.72	0.76	−1.54	−0.17	0.59
Tease	−1.01	−0.02	1.48	−0.46	0.14	1.68
Soothe	1.73	1.09	−1.26	2.00	1.49	−1.02

*E: good-bad; P: powerful-weak; A: lively-quiet.
Scales range from +4 to −4, with a 0 midpoint indicating neutral. Good, powerful, and lively are the positive ends of the scales.
Source: Adapted from L. Smith-Lovin, 1990, "Emotion as the confirmation and disconfirmation of identity: An affect control model." In T. D. Kemper (ed.), *Research Agendas in the Sociology of Emotion.* NY: SUNY Press, p. 240, Table 9-1.

Exceptions to the shared nature of such meanings do occur. Sometimes, subcultures develop unique meanings for identities or behaviors central to their groups. For example, homosexual identities may have different meanings within the gay subculture than they do among the heterosexual population, and law enforcement officers have different meanings for their professional identities than does the population as a whole. Subcultures may even develop new labels for identities to reflect their differences from mainstream society; for example, the use of the term "pig" by gang members conveys a more negative evaluation and less potency than the term "police officer." Subcultural differences in the meanings of identities and behaviors can cause the members of different subcultures to view the same situation quite differently because they expect different behaviors from others and perform different behaviors themselves.

When subcultures are expected to have different meanings for a set of concepts, it is necessary to obtain separate measures of fundamental sentiments for each subculture. For example, using affect control theory to study the interactions of police officers and gang members, we would need to measure fundamental sentiments separately for the two groups. Males and females have been found to give different ratings (indicating that they have different meanings) for a large number of identities and behaviors, hence their ratings are often reported separately. For example, in Table 8-3, females rate children and cripples as more positive than males do, and males rate mothers as less powerful than females do.

DEFINITION OF THE SITUATION

When we enter a new situation, we scan the environment for cues that will tell us how to "make sense" of it. Social psychologists would say that we are attempting to develop a definition of the situation — a best guess about the nature of the reality we are encountering. In other words, we

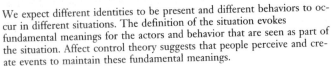

We expect different identities to be present and different behaviors to occur in different situations. The definition of the situation evokes fundamental meanings for the actors and behavior that are seen as part of the situation. Affect control theory suggests that people perceive and create events to maintain these fundamental meanings.

are answering the question, "What's going on here?" A **definition of the situation** is a mental schema of a situation — the meaning we give to an entire situation — including who should be there and what behaviors are expected. We expect different identities to be present and different behaviors to occur in different situations, for example, a birthday party, a camping trip, a business transaction, a chance encounter with an old friend, and a job interview.

When we enter a situation, we use such cues as appearance and behavior to figure out what identities we and others occupy, such as host or guest, doctor or patient, professor or student, lover or friend, boss or employee. Physical settings also suggest some situation definitions (and corresponding identities) and make others seem unlikely. For example, we discussed in Chapter 5, "Communication," how a church might suggest that the situation is a worship service, a wedding, or a funeral, with the corresponding identities of worshipper, clergy, bride and groom, organist, wedding guests, grieving family, or funeral attendees. A church would not be likely to suggest situation definitions such as a robbery, a keg party, a football game, or a camping trip.

Of course, some identities are less situation-specific than others. A husband and wife, for example, might interact in a theater, a drugstore, an apartment, a shopping mall, or a church. In still other settings, individual actors — through their chosen identities, actions, and physical props — may transform the definition of a situation. For example, a person with a gun can transform a routine banking situation with managers, tellers, and customers into a robbery with robber and hostages (Goffman, 1974; Smith-Lovin, 1990).

A definition of the situation leads us to expect and perform some behaviors and not others. Certain behaviors seem appropriate and likely for a bride at a wedding, a fan at a basketball game, or a student in a social psychology class, while others seem inappropriate and unlikely. How we define the situation shapes how we recognize the social events that occur within it. Who is doing what to whom? We perceive social events when one identity acts upon another, such as when the host is ignoring me, the guest; the doctor is patronizing me, the patient; the professor is intimidating me, the student; I, the student, am flattering the professor; he, a roommate, is sympathizing with his roommate; she, a sister, is defending her brother.

A definition of the situation evokes fundamental meanings for the actors and behaviors that are seen as part of the situation. Affect control theory suggests that *people perceive and create events to maintain these fundamental meanings* (Smith-Lovin, 1990).

SOCIAL EVENTS AND TRANSIENT SENTIMENTS

Affect control theory assumes that we have fundamental sentiments about identities and behaviors, which, having been stored in memory, we attempt to control or confirm. But when we experience actual social events, which link actor, behavior, and object, the experience can produce *momentary* sentiments about identities and behaviors — feelings that may differ from our fundamental sentiments. These momentary sentiments resulting from events are called **transient sentiments**. Such sentiments make the identities and behaviors in the situation seem better or worse, stronger or weaker, livelier or quieter than we usually expect. ACT researcher Lynn Smith-Lovin gives the following example:

Suppose I attend a party and think that the Host is ignoring me, her Guest. Hosts and Guests normally are viewed as pleasant people, with the Host adjudged somewhat more powerful and lively than the Guest. When rated by female undergraduates on a scale ranging from −4 to +4, Host has an evaluation (goodness) of 1.5, a potency (powerfulness) of 1.2, and an activity (liveliness) of 0.5; Guest has an evaluation of 1.7, potency of 0.0, and activity of −0.2 (Heise and Lewis, 1988: 97–98). The unpleasant and inappropriate act of Ignoring (with an evaluation of −1.8, potency of −0.2, and activity of 0.2) damages the reputation of both Host and Guest. A Host who has Ignored a Guest loses goodness and power, though not liveliness . . . the Host and Guest have both lost status as a result of the Ignoring. The theory suggests that this event is unlikely, since it does not maintain and support the identities of the interactants. But such a behavior might be produced accidentally (if the Host is busy with other party arrangements, or if the Guest comes in a back way) or because of some mood left over from another interaction (the Host is depressed because of a rejection by her boyfriend) or because the Host temporarily defines the Guest as Obnoxious. (1990: 241)

Perceiving an event, such as a host ignoring a guest, generates new, transient feelings about identities — feelings that may not be the same as the perceiver's fundamental sentiments associated with the identities. Affect control theory uses mathematical equations, estimated from large numbers of events, to predict how specific events will produce transient sentiments and how these feelings will affect subsequent events. The affect control theory equations support the traditional balance theory notion that doing good acts to a good other or bad acts to a bad other enhances the actor's evaluation, while doing good to a bad other or bad to a good other (as in the host-ignores-guest example) damages the actor's reputation. The object of an act is also affected by it. In the host-guest example, the guest also suffers from having been ignored. The victim of a negative act loses evaluation — an effect that corresponds to the unjust, but common phenomenon of *derogating the victim*. Potency is also reduced by being the object of another's inappropriate, unpleasant action.

The difference between a transient feeling for an identity or a behavior and the fundamental sentiment for the identity or behavior is called a **deflection** in affect control theory. When deciding how to act toward another identity, we choose behaviors that minimize deflections. This is consistent with the control principle just discussed. When deflections occur, we choose behaviors that will reduce them and will restore our fundamental sentiments about the identities and behaviors involved in the interaction. (See the Student Observation: "Transient Sentiments.")

Events that produce large deflections are seen as unlikely (Heise, 1987). For example, very large discrepancies between transients and fundamentals occur when people in positive identities engage in extremely negative behaviors toward one another. Such events strike us as improbable.

STUDENT OBSERVATION

Transient Sentiments

This summer I attended the wedding of a close friend from high school. The ceremony was beautiful, and the reception afterward was one of the fanciest I had ever attended. But something didn't seem quite right. After several hours, I finally pinpointed the source of my uneasiness — the bride and groom had not been seen together for several hours. I eventually located my friend, the bride, and pulled her aside. "Where is Randy?" I had to know. She looked at me with tears in her eyes and said, "He's driving me crazy. Everything he does makes my skin crawl." Needless to say, this was a transient sentiment created by the stress and strain of the wedding. The transient sentiment was very different from her fundamental sentiment about the man she loved and wanted to be with for the rest of her life. Thus, my friend was experiencing deflection. Our goal is usually to minimize deflection, and that's just what this couple did. They found each other, attributed their irritability to nervousness, and from then on were able to enjoy their special day. Thank goodness that transient sentiment didn't last!!

Heise and MacKinnon (1987) have shown that perceived likelihoods of events decline as more affective deflection is produced. For example, the thought of a father killing his daughter seems so unlikely that we find it almost unbelievable. Similarly, events in which people with negative identities engage in extremely positive behaviors also seem unlikely. For example, it strikes us as so unlikely that a gangster would save a baby that we try to think of alternative interpretations of the behavior, such as kidnapping, that better fit the gangster's negative image.

CONTROL OF MEANINGS: DEFLECTION REDUCTION

It should be obvious by now that affect control theory's name is based partly on its heavy emphasis on *affect*, or feelings, as measured by evaluation, potency, and activity. But why "control"? Affect control theory says that we strive to maintain the fundamental meanings we have for identities and behaviors. We have seen that social events (one person acting toward another) can produce transient sentiments that differ from fundamentals. So what form do our strivings to maintain fundamentals (and minimize deflections)

take? Affect control theory suggests two major techniques that we use to control meanings. One is behavioral: by engaging in certain behaviors, we create acts that confirm our fundamental sentiments and minimize deflections. The other technique is cognitive: when events don't "make sense" to us, given the identities and behaviors we recognize as part of the definition of the situation, we sometimes redefine the situation, reinterpreting who the identities are or what behaviors have been engaged in. Redefinition can enable us to maintain fundamentals and minimize deflections. We'll discuss each of these techniques for controlling meaning in more detail below.

Behavior Change: Creating New Events

According to affect control theory, people construct social events to *confirm* their fundamental sentiments about themselves and others. When events create transient sentiments that differ from our fundamental sentiments about people and behaviors, we are likely to generate new events to *restore* the fundamental meanings. Thus, we attempt to manage social life in ways that *control* the meanings of identities and social behaviors. We do this by creating new events that, when cognitively processed, will return the evaluation, potency, and activity meanings of the identities and behaviors to their original — fundamental — meanings.

Let's use Smith-Lovin's host-guest example to illustrate how we might control meanings by creating new events:

> If the Guest points out the event as Ignoring and the Host accepts this account of what has transpired, the Host is likely to produce a restorative act: a behavior that, when processed, will move impressions back in line with fundamental meanings. Or she may expect the Guest to repair the situation with such an act. Possibilities for the Host include Appreciate, Soothe, and Apologize To; the Guest might Excuse or Caution the Host to restore her view of the occasion. (1990: 242)

Affect control theory produces these predictions about alternative restorative acts with a computer program called INTERACT, which simulates what, according to the theory, happens in our minds (Heise and Lewis, 1988). Because the theory says that we store (in our minds) much cultural information in terms of EPA profiles for actions and identities, the computer program has access to a dictionary of fundamental sentiments (ratings for many behaviors and identities provided by a sample of undergraduate students). The program solves for the EPA profile of the behavior that would return the identities of the actor and object to their positions before the event. Then the program searches a dictionary of EPA profiles for the behaviors that most closely match the profile produced by the equation. Affect control theory says we do something similar to this in our minds. The resulting behaviors are the ones the theory predicts would be most likely in the next event involving the same actor and object (Heise, 1987; Smith-Lovin, 1987).

Cognitive Change: Redefining the Situation

Sometimes events cause so much change in our transient sentiments that no new event could possibly restore our original sentiments about the participants in the scene. Smith-Lovin (1990)

notes that "grandfather rapes the granddaughter" is an example of an event that produces massive deflections. After this action, no subsequent action can restore our original view of the relationship. So what do we do? Affect control theory says that transient sentiments that cannot be restored to fundamental sentiments through action may lead to *redefinition of the situation*.

In such cases, where actions don't make sense for the original identities involved, we search for a new view of the situation that does make sense of the events. A grandfather who rapes a granddaughter no longer fits our cultural view of what a grandfather is. We may come to think of him as a rapist or child molester — both identities are nasty and active enough to commit such a heinous act.

In sum, affect control theory suggests two ways to reduce deflection: Usually, we create events, choosing behaviors that confirm or restore the identities of the interactants. But when deflections are so large that new events can't restore fundamental sentiments, we redefine the situation, reinterpreting behaviors or reidentifying identities, to make sense of what has occurred.

PROBLEMATIC INTERACTION: WHERE DEFINITIONS OF THE SITUATION DIFFER

If all of us are going around trying to minimize deflections, then why do deflections occur? Why aren't we able to minimize deflections and keep interaction flowing smoothly? Smith-Lovin's guest-host example suggests one answer. Sometimes we accidentally produce events that cause deflections. The host may not have intended to ignore the guest, but because she was busy with another guest, was distracted by an argument with her lover, or simply didn't notice the guest's arrival, she ignored the guest. Attitudes and behaviors, according to ACT, are more likely to be consistent when we act intentionally.

Deflections are also likely when the two interactants in a situation don't share the same definitions of it. If one person, for example, thinks of the situation as "co-worker discussing a project with another co-worker," while the other person thinks of it as "subordinate discussing a project with the boss," then events that confirm identities for the first person are likely to cause deflections for the second and vice versa. If one person sees a behavior as "impressing" while the other sees it as "showing off," then the two participants will have different transients. Subsequent events are likely to confirm one person's meanings while disturbing the other's. We would expect the course of interaction resulting from such a situation to differ from that resulting from one in which the participants shared definitions of the situation. An impressive feature of affect control theory is its ability to predict likely events involving interactants with different definitions of the situation.

Whether we are able to maintain our fundamental meanings also hinges on other persons' availability as resources for our interaction. For example, power is confirmed by acting toward powerful others. A woman whose fundamental identity is powerful but who is at home all day with only a young infant to interact with may experience deflection, since actions toward the powerless infant do not confirm her powerful identity.

THE AFFECT CONTROL MODEL OF BEHAVIOR

Suppose an event occurs that creates a transient self-esteem for a person that is lower than her fundamental — or usual — self-esteem, for example, she is embarrassed. The prediction from affect control theory is that the embarrassed person will be nice to a good other. The embarrassed person has to generate especially positive transient evaluations in order to reconfirm her fundamentally good identity, and acting nice to someone good does this. But suppose the embarrassed woman interacts with a bad other. Acting nice toward a disvalued person generates a negative transient evaluation, and the embarrassed person needs no more of that. The behavior-object consistency principle requires a bad act toward the disvalued other, producing a *positive*

transient evaluation. However, affect control theory also predicts that bad acts create a *negative* transient evaluation — whether the object of the act is evaluated positively or negatively — so the net prediction of the combined effects is that the embarrassed woman will act neutrally toward the disvalued other.

Social psychologists Beverly Wiggins and David Heise (1987) designed an experiment to test these affect control theory predictions. The researchers found that the predictions — that an embarrassed person would act positively toward a positively evaluated other and neutral toward a negatively evaluated other — were supported. Subjects were randomly assigned to experimental conditions. All were told that the purpose of the experiment was to study the communication styles of different kinds of people. Half the subjects were told that they would be interacting with a delinquent; the other half learned that their interaction partner would be another university student.

Subjects were taken into the experimental room and seated next to the student/delinquent, who was already busily filling out a form. The experimenter introduced the two and handed the subject a pen and a questionnaire like the one the student/delinquent was completing. The experimenter explained that he had to leave but would return later with the envelopes containing discussion topics and that, in the meantime, his secretary would look in to answer questions and collect the questionnaires.

Videotaping had begun the moment the subject entered the experimental room. A few seconds after the experimenter left, the student/delinquent accomplice asked the subject, "What time is it?" The subject's videotaped response to this question was used as a measure of how nice or nasty the subject's behavior was toward the other *before* a temporary change in the subject's self-esteem was introduced.

The secretary subsequently entered and was pleasant and helpful toward half of the subjects and critical toward the remaining subjects. Upon the secretary's exit, the student/delinquent, who had not spoken since his earlier question, asked, "What are we supposed to do now?" When the subject had responded, he asked, "How long do you think we'll have to wait?" The subject's videotaped responses to these questions were the behaviors of interest in the experiment, as they represented behaviors toward a valued (other student) or disvalued (delinquent) other *after* a positive or negative experience (being complimented or embarrassed by the secretary).

Twelve judges viewed the videotapes of the subjects' responses and rated the subjects' behaviors toward the (unseen) student/delinquent on the following scales: good/nice vs. bad/awful, friendly/helpful vs. unfriendly/unhelpful, big/powerful vs. little/powerless, fast/young/noisy vs. slow/old/quiet.

Note that the judges did not see the entire scene—they saw only the subject. Neither did they know what had happened to the subject or the identity of the person the subject was responding to. They saw only the short clips of the subject's responses to the other person's questions. This was to ensure that the judges' ratings were not based on how they thought the subject *should* react in the situation.

The judges' ratings showed that, before the interaction with the secretary, subjects treated the student or delinquent somewhat positively. However, *after* the interaction with the secretary, some of the subjects' treatment of the student or delinquent changed. As affect control theory predicts, embarrassed subjects acted positively toward the other student and neutral toward the delinquent. Subjects who were treated nicely by the secretary acted nicer toward the student than toward the delinquent, but with less of a difference, also as ACT predicts. The study provides support for the notion that our self-attitudes—both fundamental and transient—and our attitudes toward others do, in fact, determine our behavior. (See "Controversy About Low Self-Esteem.")

Affect control theory provides a model of how events are shaped by the affective (EPA) meanings we have for self and other: we choose behaviors that will confirm our own and others' identities.

The theory specifies how events produce momentary changes in feelings about these identities, and it predicts what kinds of events will restore fundamental meanings.

The experiment conducted by Wiggins and Heise demonstrates that a person's fundamental sentiments toward her or his salient identities are only *part* of what determines the person's behavior. Behavior is also shaped by the transient sentiments for self and others created by recent events. In other words, the difference between fundamental and transient sentiments (deflection), not fundamentals alone, is critical to ACT's predictions. According to ACT, our attitudes and behaviors will be most consistent (that is, deflections will be minimized) when (1) we act intentionally, (2) we share definitions of the situation and meanings for salient identities and behaviors with the persons we interact with, and (3) our potential interaction partners are people whose identities allow us to confirm our own identities through interaction.

ACT is a recently developed theory incorporating important features from some of the other theories discussed in this chapter. ACT recognizes, as does Ajzen and Fishbein's reasoned action theory, that attitudes toward specific behavior must be an important part of any theory of attitudes and behavior. ACT incorporates the traditional consistency theory notion that doing good acts to good others makes us feel more positive, while doing good acts to bad others or bad acts to good others makes us feel more negative. ACT also recognizes the importance of self-identities and the sociological notion that we have multiple identities and behave within a context of social institutions and interpersonal relationships affecting our behavior.

In summary, attitudes shape our behavior, but research has shown that the relationship between attitudes and behavior is reciprocal; that is, each influences the other. Nevertheless, considerable evidence suggests that the relationship between attitudes and behavior is not always strong. Social psychologists have come to see the strength of the

CONTROVERSY ABOUT LOW SELF-ESTEEM

There is some disagreement among social psychologists as to whether people basically strive to *enhance* or to *maintain* their self-attitudes (Tessor and Campbell, 1983; Swann, 1983, 1985, 1987; Tessor, 1988; Robinson and Smith-Lovin, 1992). Our discussion of self-presentation in previous chapters might seem to suggest that we all attempt to make the best possible impression. Indeed, most of us think very well of ourselves, and our self-presentational efforts reflect this high self-esteem. But what about people with low self-esteem? Do their self-presentational efforts reflect their negative images of themselves, or do they attempt to present themselves to others in a more positive light than they see themselves? Do they prefer the company of others who provide information overestimating their self-worth or that of others who gave them feedback more consistent with their negative self-conceptions?

Psychologist William Swann and his colleagues developed an extensive research program to examine the question of whether people with low self-esteem basically strive to enhance or to maintain their negative self-attitudes. They found that persons with either high *or* low self-esteem experienced positive feedback as pleasing and negative feedback as uncomfortable. However, persons with high self-esteem were more likely to say the positive feedback was *accurate*, while persons with low self-esteem rated the negative feedback as more accurate (Swann et al., 1987). And even people whose global self-esteem was high sought out unfavorable feedback pertaining to areas in which their self-views were negative (Swann, Pelham, and Krull, 1989). The researchers also found that people with strong self-attitudes were more likely to prefer relationships with others who saw them as they saw themselves, even if this didn't make them feel good (Swann and Pelham, 1990). They conclude that the desire for a stable identity seems to be an important motivation determining our cognitive reactions to events as well as our active creation of new events. Thus, we seek to *maintain* our identities, even when they are negative.

Other evidence suggests that we are not particularly threatened by negative feedback about identities that are not salient to us. Even if we possess some negatively evaluated identities, if they are not very salient, we can compensate for them and maintain a positive *global* self-esteem by bolstering other positively evaluated identities (Greenberg and Pyszczynski, 1985; Steele, 1988). For example, it may not bother me that I am a "lost cause" as a cook, because this identity is not very salient for me and I feel that I am good at other things that are more salient, such as being a writer, teacher, daughter, and wife.

These studies imply that although maintaining negative identities is distressing for the individuals involved, such people actively seek out feedback that confirms their negative self-views, and they discount positive feedback as inaccurate (Swann and Pelham, 1990; Robinson and Smith-Lovin, 1992). This suggests that improving the self-esteem of people with chronically low self-esteem may be a very difficult task. These people will reject as inaccurate any information designed to foster their sense of self-worth. They will also choose interaction partners who reflect their low opinions of themselves.

relationship between attitudes and behavior as dependent on many factors, such as self-efficacy, subjective norms, commitment, self-attitudes, and transient sentiments.

Summary

1. Fishbein and Ajzen's reasoned action model suggests that our behavior is best predicted by our behavioral intentions, which, in turn, are shaped by (1) our attitudes toward the behavior — how positively or negatively we evaluate the expected consequences of performing the behavior and how likely we think each outcome is, and (2) our subjective norms regarding a specific behavior — whether we believe specific significant others think that we should or should not perform the behavior and how motivated we are to do as each of them would

like us to. The relationship between attitudes and behavior is stronger when the measure of attitude focuses on the specific behavior and its outcomes rather than on the object of the behavior (another person). The relationship is also stronger when the person believes that (1) he or she can control the behavior to produce successful outcomes (high self-efficacy); (2) the behavior is consistent with his or her relevant social identities; and (3) others favor his or her performing the behavior (favorable subjective norms).

2. Attitude consistency theories — balance theory and, particularly, cognitive dissonance theory — suggest that behavior may influence attitudes as well as attitudes influence behavior. They also recognize that not all inconsistencies between attitude and behavior are sufficiently stressful to motivate a change in attitude (or behavior) in order to establish a consistent relationship. The relationship between attitudes and behavior is strongest when the person's attitude is strong, the person feels committed to the behavior, and the person feels responsible for her or his behavior.

3. Affect control theory (ACT) argues that while a person's fundamental sentiments toward his or her salient identities constitute part of what determines the person's behavior, we must also look at the transient sentiments for self and others that have been created by recent events. In other words, the difference between fundamental and transient sentiments (deflection), not the fundamentals alone, is critical to ACT's predictions. According to ACT, our attitudes and behaviors will be most consistent with each other (that is, deflections will be minimized) when (1) our actions are deliberate, rather than accidental; (2) we share definitions of the situation and meanings for salient identities and behaviors with the persons with whom we interact; and (3) we have as potential interaction partners people whose identities allow us to confirm our own identities through interaction.

PART THREE

FORMS OF
SOCIAL
INTERACTION

CHAPTER 9

PERFORMANCE, CONFORMITY, AND COOPERATION

*I*n social life, we are often interested in **performance** — how well an individual's behavior meets a quantitative or qualitative standard. We speak of academic performance, athletic performance, job performance, and even sexual performance. *Any* behavior can be compared to a standard.

Of particular interest to social psychologists has been how the presence and behavior of other people influence our performance on a task. Consider these examples:

- You have been playing racquetball with a friend for about half an hour, and your performance has been mediocre. Then you notice that several people have stopped to watch you through the glass that is the back wall of the court. Does your performance improve, deteriorate, or remain relatively unaffected?

- You are typing a paper on a computer in a computer lab. You are alone and have been producing about one page every ten minutes. Then three students join you in the lab and begin typing papers. You are in a position to observe the rates at which they type their papers. Does your "production rate" increase, decrease, or stay about the same?

- You are at a basketball game with several friends. You are all sitting together in the student section. When your team makes a good play, you are on your feet, clapping and cheering the players on. But you notice that your cheering efforts pale in comparison to those of your friends and the other students around you. Even on unspectacular plays, they scream at the top of their lungs, jump up and down, whistle, wave their arms, stomp, and generally go crazy. Does your own cheering become more enthusiastic, become less enthusiastic, or stay about the same?

Audience and Coaction Effects on Performance

These examples illustrate two types of tasks. In the racquetball example, an individual's behavior is being observed by others who are not performing the same task. This type of task is an **audience task**. In the typing and basketball-game examples, several people are performing the same task but have little interaction with one another. This type of task is a **coaction task**. Eating in a fast-food restaurant can be either an audience task or a

270

coaction task. If other people are watching you eat but not eating themselves, they are acting as an *audience*; if they are engaged in the same task— eating— they are *coactors*. Taking an exam can be either type of task. Other students may be taking the test along with you (coaction), or, having completed their own tests, they may be watching you complete yours so that the professor can begin the lecture (audience). Almost any behavior can occur in the context of either kind of task.

Note that in a coaction task a person's outcome is *independent* of the other coactors'. For example, if a woman happens to be bowling alongside others but isn't comparing her score to theirs, then her outcome is independent. She and the others are coactors. But if she is keeping score and trying to do better than the others, then she is *competing*. This is a different type of task entirely— one that we will discuss in Chapter 12, "Aggression and Conflict."

The study of how we perform in the presence of others *in comparison to* our performance when we are alone dates back to the turn of the century. In 1898, Norman Triplett, a bicycling enthusiast, noticed that cyclists rode faster when they were riding with other cyclists (coaction) or were paced by a person on a motor-driven cycle (audience) than when the cyclists were racing against the clock (alone). Conducting what many regard as the first social psychological laboratory experiment, he had forty children play simple games (e.g., pulling on a fishing line) in pairs or alone. Like the cyclists, the children performed better when they played the games in pairs (coaction). One of the first studies of the effects of an audience occurred in an exercise laboratory (Meumann, 1904). Using an ergograph— a device measuring how far an individual can move a weight— the researcher observed that with practice a person typically reached a performance level that remained relatively constant across time. But the researcher noted that when he was present, the person moved the weight a greater distance.

The same effect has been observed in animals and insects. For example, one study involved the number of balls of dirt that ants excavated as they built their tunnels (Chen, 1937). In some cases the researcher had an ant work alone, while in other cases the ant worked with other ants. The results of the study showed that the individual ants removed more balls of dirt when working with others than when working alone.

SOCIAL FACILITATION AND SOCIAL INHIBITION

As the above discussion shows, we sometimes perform better in audience or coaction tasks than we do when we are alone. This is called **social facilitation**— the enhancement of performance when others are present. Undoubtedly, you have also experienced situations in which you felt that the presence of others was detrimental to your performance and you could have performed better if you were left alone. When the presence of others decreases performance, the effect is called **social inhibition**.

Early social psychologists quickly discovered that the presence of others can sometimes cause social facilitation while at other times it can cause social inhibition. In one early study of an audience task (Travis, 1925), college students were asked to hold a pointer over a small target attached to a rotating disk. When they performed the task before an audience of advanced undergraduates, their tracking of the target was better than when they performed alone. But another study (Pessin and Husband, 1933) found that an audience *slowed* the learning of both a maze task and a nonsense-syllable task. After subjects had learned the tasks, however, they performed *better* in front of an audience.

Similar inconsistent results were obtained in early studies involving coaction tasks. In one such study (Allport, 1920), student subjects were asked to work at several tasks, while others sitting at the same table were doing the same thing. Subjects were told not to compare their scores with one another's, nor would the researcher make any such comparisons. For simple tasks (e.g., writing down as many thoughts as possible associated with a given word or performing multiplications),

The presence of others sometimes facilitates and other times inhibits our performance.

subjects performed better in the coaction setting than they did when alone. In performing more complex tasks (thinking up arguments to refute an opinion expressed in philosophical works), the subjects produced *more* in the coaction situation than they did when alone, but their performance tended to be lower in *quality*. (Before reading further, look at the Student Observations: "Social Facilitation" and "Social Inhibition.")

COMPETENCE: ITS CONDITIONAL EFFECT

So why does the presence of others have these contradictory effects? Researcher Robert Zajonc (1965) has provided an answer. Zajonc focused on the distinction between the original *learning* of a behavior and the subsequent *performance* of that behavior. He proposed that the presence of others — as audience or coactors — facilitates the performance of well-learned behaviors ("simple" tasks) but inhibits the conduct of novel, unpracticed behaviors ("complex" tasks).

In one study testing Zajonc's hypothesis, researchers observed people playing pool in a college student-union building (Michaels et al., 1982). The researchers began by secretly recording the scores of players who were identified as either above-average or below-average players. Then four confederates approached the players and watched them during several more rounds of pool. When good players were watched by the confederates, their accuracy increased 71 to 80 percent. In contrast, when poor players were being watched, their accuracy dropped 25 to 36 percent.

In another study, the researchers sought to distinguish between the effects of the "mere presence" of another person and the effects of another person who is closely monitoring our behavior (Schmitt et al., 1986). Forty-five undergraduates reported for a "sensory deprivation" experiment. When the students arrived for the study, the experimenter explained that they would first undertake a brief session in which they were to answer questions presented on a small computer. For this session, each student was assigned to one of three conditions: (1) Some students were left alone for the entire session; (2) some were in a room with another person (presumably another subject who was further along in the study) who faced in the opposite direction and wore earphones and a blindfold; and (3) some had the experimenter constantly looking over their shoulders. Using the keyboard, each student answered questions that involved, for example, a well-learned task (typing his or her name) and a much more difficult task (typing the letters of his or her name in reverse order).

As the studies discussed earlier would lead us to expect, subjects responded more quickly on the well-learned task when another person was present and did better on the difficult task when they were alone. Furthermore, on both the well-learned and the difficult tasks, subjects performed more quickly when the experimenter was looking over their shoulders than when another person was in the room but not attending to the subject. Thus, it appears that the attention of another person has a greater influence on our behavior than another person's mere presence.

EXPLANATIONS

A comprehensive review of research in this area lends considerable support to Zajonc's proposal (Bond and Titus, 1983). On the other hand, there has been considerable controversy over the explanations for social facilitation and social inhibition (Geen, 1989). Particular attention has been given to three explanations:

STUDENT OBSERVATION

Social Facilitation

My roommate and I both enjoy exercising and have memberships at the same health club. Our busy schedules usually make it impossible for us to go together, but occasionally we do go at the same time. I find that on these occasions, I invariably exercise harder than when I am there on my own. My roommate's presence definitely leads to *social facilitation*. I exercise harder and take fewer breaks because I want to impress her with my performance (and I want her to assume that it is my normal workout level — which it definitely is not). I'm pretty sure that exercising together has the same effect on her as well.

STUDENT OBSERVATION

Social Inhibition

It was in middle school that I first started playing sports. I played on both the basketball and softball teams. I can remember so vividly how nervous I would get when my father came to my games. I knew he had gotten off work early especially to come and watch me play. I wanted to perform well and not let him down. Unfortunately, I consistently performed worse when he attended my games. In one softball game, I was pitching and walked in a run. I had to ask my dad to leave. After he left, my performance level went back up, and I was able to finish the game without allowing another run. As much as I appreciated his taking an interest in me, it was, nevertheless, apparent that his presence worsened my performance — an example of *social inhibition*.

Alertness: Zajonc proposed that the mere presence of others raises the performer's level of arousal. This arousal is basically an increased state of alertness. Given the primary significance of social stimuli in our lives, such alertness attunes us to the chance that we may be called upon to behave quickly—sometimes in novel or unique ways. Thus, arousal facilitates performance provided the task calls for a well-learned response.

Evaluative motivation: A second explanation is that the presence of others motivates the performer because she or he has learned that others are evaluating the performance. We want to look good in public and avoid a performance damaging to our public image. (See the Student Observation: "Evaluative Motivation.") Such anticipations, elicited by the presence of others, enhance our performance on well-learned, simple tasks but retard it on complex tasks that we are still learning.

Distraction: A third explanation proposes that others' presence distracts the performer because she or he is in conflict over whether to pay attention to the task or to the others. This conflict may be overcome with increased effort, again depending on the nature of the task. On well-learned, simple tasks, this effort can offset the effects of distraction and facilitate performance. But while we are learning more complex tasks, the effects of distraction cannot be countered by increased effort. Therefore, the distraction will inhibit performance.

There is really no reason to choose among these three explanations. In any specific situation, one or any combination of them may account for social facilitation or social inhibition.

Coaction Effects on Conformity

We have been discussing how the presence of others (as audience or coactors) affects the quantity or quality of an individual's performance. Situations involving *coaction tasks* allow us to expand our focus: as all those present are performing the same task, we can also look at whether an individual's behavior meets a standard set by the behaviors of the other coactors. Social psychologists refer to the standard set by the coactors as a *norm* and to subsequent norm-matching behavior as **conformity,** which is behavior in accordance with norms set by others.

In judging the quality or quantity of a *performance*, we compare the behavior to standards that

---

STUDENT OBSERVATION

Evaluative Motivation

*M*y best friend/roommate smokes cigarettes. When we are in the apartment together, it seems that she lights up every twenty to thirty minutes. But when we are on campus, or at a fraternity/ sorority function where smoking is less common, she refrains from smoking, even though I can tell she is having a "nic-fit." I believe this has to do with the *evaluative motivation* that affects conformity. My friend is afraid that others will evaluate her negatively and like her less if she lights up a cigarette when no one else is smoking.

I have also noticed this in other people at bars in Chapel Hill. Early in the evening, when alcohol consumption is just beginning, people are conscious of others around them and conform to others' norms by not smoking. But as the night goes on and there is plenty of alcohol in everyone's system, smoking tends to increase. I have even noticed some people smoking whom I have been around lots of times and had thought didn't smoke. This may have to do with the fact that alcohol temporarily impairs our evaluative motivation so that conforming is not as relevant to us anymore. Or maybe it's that late-night norms change, and we are evaluatively motivated to conform to what others are doing—by lighting up.

may or may not be set by the coacting individuals. Judgments about *conformity*, on the other hand, are made by comparing the individual's behaviors to the standard set by the behaviors of the other coactors. Thus, the two judgments are unrelated. A behavior may be judged as a *high*-quality performance and *high* conformity or as a *high*-quality performance and *low* conformity. Conversely, behavior judged to be *low* performance may be *high* conformity or *low* conformity. If coactors set a standard of low-quality (or low-quantity) performance and we match that standard, our behavior will be low performance and high conformity.

NORM FORMATION

Social psychologists not only study how the standards set by others can influence the behavior of an individual but also want to know something about the *origins* of the standards themselves. When do the different behaviors of several individuals converge to form a common standard or norm? In Chapter 4, "Social Relationships and Groups," we noted that we negotiate an internal culture — norms and roles that emerge as a result of our interactions with other participants in relationships and groups. These negotiations are also influenced by external culture — norms and roles that originate outside the relationship or group. In the present discussion, we want to focus attention on the fact that normative behavior is sometimes created in even more minimal social situations by mere coaction, that is, by the presence of others performing the same task.

In a pioneering study, Muzafer Sherif (1936) investigated norm formation within a laboratory setting, using students as subjects. His experiment used an optical illusion, the so-called *autokinetic effect*. If a small, fixed spot of light is briefly exposed in a darkened room, it appears to move and may appear to move erratically in all directions. People differ in their estimates of how far the spot "moves." Sherif found that when he tested subjects alone, each evolved a characteristic range for the reported movements. This range functioned as a reference point for the individual in comparing and judging each successive movement.

Sherif then brought together subjects who had established very *different* ranges as reference points in their solitary sessions. In a coaction task, each person was again exposed to the light and asked to report aloud on his or her appraisal of the light's movement. The coacting subjects soon converged toward a common standard of apparent movement — a norm. Later, when individual sessions were resumed, this norm persisted; individuals did not return to the ranges they had evolved in the initial solitary sessions.

Sherif also discovered that the coacting individuals were not necessarily aware of the fact that they were being influenced by others, or that they and the other individuals were converging toward a common norm. In fact, most of the subjects reported not only that their judgments were made before the others spoke but also *that they were not influenced by the others* (Sherif and Sherif, 1969). Hence, situational factors influence perception, although we are not necessarily aware of such influences. This finding has been experimentally confirmed by other researchers (Schofield, 1975; Moscovici and Personnaz, 1980; Sorrentino, King, and Leo, 1980).

It appears, especially in ambiguous situations such as the one Sherif produced using the autokinetic effect, that the formation of a common standard results from the need for information to solve a problem. With no other reliable basis of information available, we turn to coacting others to help us define reality.

Researchers have shown that group norms may eventually take on a life of their own. The norm remains unchanged even though the individuals change. In experiments (Jacobs and Campbell, 1961; MacNeil and Sherif, 1976), a common standard was established in the manner described in the Sherif study. Then one coactor was removed and replaced by a new subject. The new subject gradually shifted his or her position in the direction of the common norm. Eventually all the original coactors were replaced with new subjects. But the common norm either remained unchanged or changed very slowly.

Thus, social interaction — even minimal interaction, such as the presence of coactors — can re-

Is the man lying here injured, intoxicated, or sleeping? Does he need help? The passers-by in the photo seem to have concluded that he does not—perhaps by observing the reactions of coactors. In ambiguous situations the formation of a common standard results from the need for information to solve a problem. With no other reliable basis of information available, we turn to coacting others to help us define reality.

sult in the establishment of social norms that serve as standards for subsequent behavior. Especially in ambiguous situations, the formation of a common standard results from the need for information to solve a problem. But, what happens when other information is available and it conflicts with that provided by coactors?

CONFORMITY WHEN CONFLICTING INFORMATION IS AVAILABLE

A very different kind of experimental manipulation of coaction was devised by Solomon Asch (1952). The Asch studies have attracted considerable attention, and other social psychologists have developed variations on them. In his research, Asch seated several students (usually seven to nine) side by side. Unlike Sherif, he did not present his subjects with an ambiguous situation. Instead, subjects were asked to match lines of the same length from two sets of cards displayed at the front of the room. One card had a single line (the standard). The other card had three lines: one was the same length as the standard, and the other two were clearly shorter or longer.

Asch had the subjects give their answers aloud. Except for one person, the "critical" subject, the coactors were all confederates of Asch who unanimously provided incorrect answers on certain trials. Asch interpreted this unanimity as the common standard, or norm. Despite the fact that the correct answer was obvious, nearly one-third of all the critical subjects' judgments contained errors identical with, or in the direction of, the rigged errors of the majority. Further, 74 percent of the subjects conformed on at least one of the trials.

Why did some subjects conform to the majority opinion even though it contradicted the evidence of their own eyes? In follow-up interviews with the subjects, Asch observed that three different kinds of reactions had contributed to their conformity:

Distortion of judgment: Most of the subjects who yielded to the majority had concluded that their own perceptions were inaccurate. Lacking confidence in their own observations, they reported not what they saw but what they felt must be correct. (See the Student Observation: "Distortion of Judgment.")

Distortion of perception: A number of subjects said that they were *not* aware that their estimates had been distorted by the majority. They came to perceive the rigged majority estimates as the correct estimates. These subjects had *internalized* the norms of the group.

Distortion of action: A number of subjects frankly admitted that they had not reported what they in fact had seen. They said that they had yielded so as not to appear different or stupid to other performers. These subjects had *complied* with the common standard, but their behavior change was not accompanied by private acceptance.

Asch's study shows that even in an unambiguous situation in which our physical senses are providing information that doesn't match what the coacting others are saying, there is considerable pressure to conform. Thus, we may find ourselves joining our co-workers in criticizing the boss, even though we haven't observed the behaviors they are complaining about. Or we might follow several other drivers onto a road marked "Closed."

TYPES OF CONFORMITY AND NONCONFORMITY

Social psychologists frequently distinguish two types of conformity (Nail, 1986; Levine and Russo, 1987). In some instances, our conformity tends to be situation-specific. We may, for example, conform to others' positions *only when the others are present.* When they are present, we do as they do or expect. When they are not present, and when they have no way to learn about our behavior, we do something different. Such conformity is called *compliance:* we go along with what others want or expect, but only to get the rewards they offer if we do or to avoid the punishment they might impose if we don't. For example, a teenager might comply with his peers' expectations about drinking and smoking pot when he is with them because to do otherwise would result in their criticism, but the same teenager might never drink or smoke alone.

In other cases, our conformity tends to be less situational. We conform whether the others are present or not. Such conformity is called *conversion* or *internalization.* When we have internalized, or been converted, we are just as likely to conform in others' absence as in their presence because we are doing what *we* think is right or want to do. For example, a person who has internalized her group's taste in music will listen to that kind of music whether her friends are present or not.

STUDENT OBSERVATION

Distortion of Judgment

On a homework assignment in second grade, this question appeared: "How many classrooms are there in the entire school?" I sat there and counted them all in my head and arrived at the correct number of rooms. After discussing the answer with several of my classmates, I learned that they had all arrived at the same answer — one different from mine. I changed my answer to match theirs. Why did I conform to the majority opinion even though it contradicted the evidence of my own estimation? The answer is *distortion of judgment.* Because these classmates were considered "brains" of the class, I assumed they were correct. Lacking confidence in my own observation, I concluded that my perception was inaccurate, so I reported not what I saw but what I felt must be correct.

Mark Snyder's (1987) personality concept of *self-monitors*, which we discussed in Chapter 7, "The Social Nature of Self," is relevant here. Remember that high self-monitors show more situation-specific behavior; they monitor the situation closely to get clues about what is expected, and they adapt their behavior to what others expect. In contrast, low self-monitors tend to display greater consistency in their behavior across situations; they act in accordance with internal standards. High self-monitors, then, are likely to conform to the expectations of others. The type of conformity they exhibit is *compliance*. Low self-monitors are less likely to conform to the expectations of others unless they have *internalized* those expectations.

Similarly, social psychologists distinguish two types of nonconformity — *not* conforming to the standards set by others. In some cases, we may differ from others' positions whether the others are present or not. In other words, their presence does not affect our performance: our nonconformity is consistent. Such nonconformity is called *independence*. The nonconforming individuals are motivated to do their "own thing." In other cases, we may differ from others' positions only when the others are present. Otherwise, we conform. This kind of nonconformity for the sake of being different is called *counterconformity*.

FACTORS AFFECTING CONFORMITY

Since the early Sherif and Asch studies demonstrated how strong the tendency was for individuals to conform to standards set by others, many other studies have looked at the various factors affecting conformity. One question these studies asked was: Just why do we conform?

Characteristics of the Individual

Motivation. Some people have a negative attitude toward conformity. They attribute a person's conformity to his or her being mindless or spineless. Research by Ellan Langer and her associates does suggest that we sometimes conform without thinking about the implications of our conformity

(Langer, Chanowitz, and Blank, 1985). Yet other research indicates that if we are asked our opinions before we are given the chance to think, we simply express our own views and conform *less* (Tetlock, Skitka, and Boettger, 1989). Social psychologists have identified two motivational factors that account for much of our conformity — evaluative motivation and informational motivation (Kaplan, 1987; Kaplan and Miller, 1987; Forsyth, 1990).

Sometimes we conform because we seek the rewards provided by the others and want to avoid the punishments they would impose for our failure to conform. For example, we may want the

Conformity is often evaluatively motivated: we are concerned with appearing to be like others in order to be liked. This is especially true when our bonds to the group are expressive, that is, when being with others is its own reward.

approval of others and certainly want to avoid their rejection. In such instances, we are most concerned with appearing to be like others *in order to be liked*. Social psychologists would describe us as being *evaluatively motivated*. Earlier we noted that this motivation is also an explanation of social facilitation.

An individual's evaluative motivation is affected by the bonds between the individual and the coacting others (Hogg and Turner, 1987). The bonds can be expressive (being with others is its own reward) or instrumental (being with others is the means to a goal). The stronger these bonds, the greater the likelihood of the individual's conformity. These bonds increase conformity because they increase evaluative motivation. For example, the stronger the bonds, the more important it is to us that the others like us and the more we believe that our conformity will bring their acceptance.

In other instances, we conform to others' positions because of the information the others' responses provide. We are more concerned with *being right* than with being similar to the group in order to be liked. This kind of motivation is called *informational motivation*. For example, suppose you are walking along a sidewalk and come to a construction site. There's a tunnel for pedestrians to walk through, but nobody is using it and you observe several people walking *around* the tunnel, even though they have to walk in the street to do so. Are you likely to use the tunnel or go around it? It would not be surprising if you choose to walk around the tunnel, reasoning that the other people must know something you don't know (that there is a big puddle inside the tunnel, perhaps). If you conform to the actions of the other pedestrians for this reason, we would say you are informationally motivated.

Social psychological research shows that we are more likely to conform when uncertain about our own positions (Campbell, Tesser, and Fairey, 1986). Uncertainty is more probable when the task we are presented with is ambiguous (as in Sherif's autokinetic situation) or difficult. Ambiguity and difficulty increase our informational

motivation to conform. In contrast, the more clear the sensory information available to us for determining an answer, the less likely we will be to conform.

The effects of task difficulty and ambiguity have been demonstrated by a number of researchers. In a study using procedures similar to Asch's, some subjects were asked to judge the length of the lines while the cards were still in front of them, while others made their judgments after the cards had been removed for a few seconds. When the subjects no longer had the information in front of them, they were less certain and conformed more (Deutsch and Gerard, 1955). In another variation of the study, the researchers distributed rulers to some subjects (Luchins and Luchins, 1961). These subjects, able to validate their opinions objectively, conformed much less frequently than the subjects who had to rely solely on their vision. Using a different type of task, other researchers asked subjects to count slow or fast clicks. When the clicks came faster, the task was more difficult, and more people conformed (Coleman, Blake, and Moulton, 1958).

Although the two motivations for conformity — evaluative and informational — can operate separately, in most situations we are concerned *both* with *being liked* and with *being right* (Insko et al., 1985).

Gender.   Many early experiments on conformity showed females to be more conforming than males (Crutchfield, 1955; McGuire, 1985). This finding was consistent with then-prevailing stereotypes about men and women, and for almost twenty years, it went largely unchallenged. But, as attitudes about women began to change, the research was reexamined and a different conclusion reached (Eagly and Carli, 1981; Eagly, 1983; Becker, 1986).

A closer look at the studies that found male-female differences revealed that females may have complied more because the tasks employed in the experiments favored men's interests and expertise (Goldberg, 1974, 1975). To test this idea, researchers presented subjects with a series of items to determine whether men or women were more knowledgeable about each (Sistrunk and McDavid, 1971). On some items, the sexes were equally knowledgeable (neutral items); on others, males were more likely to be knowledgeable (masculine items); on still others, females were more knowledgeable (feminine items). The researchers used these items in a conformity experiment and found that on masculine items, women did conform more than men. But they also discovered that on feminine items, men conformed more than women. On neutral items there were no differences. Another study found that although the areas about which the two sexes are knowledgeable have changed somewhat, each sex is still more likely to conform when the task involves an area about which they are less knowledgeable (Karabenick, 1983).

Still another study (Feldman-Summers et al., 1980) concluded that both sexes complied more on male-related items when the influence source was male and more on female-related items when the influence source was female. Other differences in compliance may result from the different interactional concerns of men and women. We noted in Chapter 5, "Communication," that some researchers believe women to be more concerned with social harmony and men to be more concerned with "besting" others. Psychologist Alice Eagly (1978, 1983, 1987) has suggested that females may comply in some conformity experiments in order to preserve social harmony. Men, on the other hand, disagree with others so that they can distinguish themselves from the rest of the group (Maslach, Santee, and Wade, 1987). But at the level of actual conversion, women conform no more than men.

Status. Research suggests that status affects conformity (Kipnis, 1976). Several studies of juries have shown that individuals with high occupational statuses — professionals and white-collar workers — are more likely than those with lower statuses to be chosen as forepersons, to direct the discussion, and to influence the final vote (Strodtbeck, James, and Hawkins, 1957;

Strodtbeck and Hook, 1961; Gerbasi, Zuckerman, and Reis, 1977). Similarly, a study requiring subjects to perform a simple perceptual task found more conformity to a physician than to a postal clerk (Moore and Krupat, 1971).

The notion that "number two tries harder" may apply to status and conformity. Some studies indicate that those who are second in command conform the most (Harvey and Consalvi, 1960). This may be partly because "number twos" value the group more, since they are striving to be in a leadership position, and partly because as lower-level leaders they feel it is their duty to act as models of group norms (Homans, 1974). Other studies have found that those with the lowest status within the group conform the most (Montgomery, 1971). These persons may be attempting to gain status and avoid total rejection by the group.

Characteristics of the Group

Size of the majority. Asch conducted many variations of his basic experiment. Some were concerned with the size of the majority facing the lone naive respondent. In one variation, instead of a group of six people giving the wrong answer, there was only one. When the lone confederate responded incorrectly, the naive respondents usually did not conform. Out of twelve trials, the mean number of conforming responses was 0.33. (Most of the naive respondents didn't conform on any trials, and those who did never conformed more than once.) When Asch increased the majority to two, the rate of conformity rose to a mean of 1.53 conforming responses in twelve trials. With a majority of three, the rate of conformity climbed considerably, to a mean of 4.0 conforming responses in twelve trials.

But Asch found that there was a limit to the effect of majority size. He tested naive respondents with majorities that were as large as fifteen, but above a majority size of three, the addition of more group members did not significantly affect conformity.

Research has also indicated that the effect of majority size on conformity depends on other factors. One experiment found that the number of individuals in the majority was less significant than the person's perception of the number of separate or independent entities urging a position (Wilder, 1977). For example, an individual faced with three individuals may categorize them as a single group — conservatives, administrators, students, or radicals. The opinion of six separate individuals, the researcher found, led to more conformity than did two groups of three; and the opinion of two groups of three led to more conformity than one group of six.

In addition, another study found that majority size has a greater effect on conformity when the task is easy than when it is difficult (Campbell and Fairey, 1989). If a task is easy, the majority has little information to provide. Thus, the only motivation for conforming to the group's judgment is evaluative, and conformity depends on the pressure that the majority can exert on the individual through rewards and punishments (acceptance and rejection). Often, the larger the majority, the greater the pressure. In contrast, when a task is more difficult, the individual looks to others more for information to ease the task. Under these conditions, the number of people in the majority has little to do with conformity. Two or three people can supply the information the individual needs. Adding more people may not contribute to the information necessary to make the decision.

Unanimity of the majority. In another variation of Asch's group-pressure experiment, one of the confederates breaks with the majority. This results in a substantial drop in subjects' conformity (Allen and Levine, 1971; Morris and Miller, 1975). (Asch himself observed a decline from 32 percent conformity to 6 percent under these conditions.) The nonconformity of one other person emboldens the subject to stick to his or her judgment. Indeed, one study has revealed that the planted deviant need not give the correct answer (Allen and Levine, 1971). Even when the nonconformist's answer was more incorrect than that of the majority, the amount of conformity among subjects was greatly reduced.

In the study, the researchers employed three experimental conditions: (1) All four confederates unanimously answered incorrectly; (2) one of the confederates gave the correct answer, but the other three gave the wrong one; and (3) one of the confederates, with a "severe visual handicap," dissented from the group but did so correctly only 40 percent of the time. (The latter confederate wore eyeglasses with extremely thick lenses and indicated in response to a question by the experimenter before the experiment began that he could not easily read a legible sign on the wall.) Having social support made a considerable difference. And it made the most difference when the subject had valid support, that is, when the subject believed that the dissenting confederate gave the right answer and was capable of seeing the card sets.

Timing of dissent. These studies suggest that almost any form of social support can help us resist social pressure to conform. There is some evidence that support received early is more helpful than support received later. In one study, each naive respondent was the fifth person in a five-person group (Morris, Miller, and Spangenberg, 1977). The other four participants were confederates. The experimenters looked at differences in rates of conformity depending upon whether the confederate who broke with the majority and gave the correct answer was in the first, second, third, or fourth position. Conformity was reduced the most when the dissenting confederate was in the first position. Early social support for dissent appears to neutralize some of the group's informational influence by confirming the subject's view of reality.

Cultural Factors

Conformity to standards set by others is a necessary fact of social life and, therefore, is found in all cultures. Yet cultural values may affect conformity to some degree. When Stanley Milgram (1961) performed several variations of the Asch experiment (using tones of varied lengths, rather than lines) in France and Norway, he found consistent differences between French and Norwegian subjects. The French were more likely to stick with their own positions, while the Norwegians conformed more often. These observations are consistent with the French culture's stress on individualism and the Norwegian's on group harmony. Similarly, twelve-year-olds raised in the former Soviet Union were more likely to conform to peer pressure than were Israeli children (Shouval et al., 1975). Soviet child-rearing practices, the investigators point out, stressed discipline and obedience more than did Israeli practices. The study also found that children raised in individual family settings conformed less than those raised in collective settings, which emphasize group identity more.

Replicating Asch's line-judging study using Japanese college students, another researcher found that 26 percent of the subjects resisted group pressure and did not conform on any trials (Frager, 1970). This is very close to the percentage of subjects remaining independent in Asch's study with American students. But this study also showed something that previous research with American respondents had not. Some of the Japanese students gave the *wrong* answer even on trials in which none of the confederates did so and thus there was no pressure to conform. We can only guess why the Japanese students exhibited this counterconformity. Perhaps they felt their free will was being challenged, and they responded incorrectly in order to assert their freedom.

In summary, conformity is affected by many factors, including individual characteristics such as motivation, gender, and status; task characteristics such as majority size, majority unanimity, and timing of dissent; and cultural factors favoring individualism or group harmony. (The role of

BINGE EATING AMONG COLLEGE WOMEN

Bulimia is an eating pattern in which individuals engage in extensive binge eating followed by induced vomiting to prevent weight gain. It is practiced almost exclusively by women. Our national obsession with dieting and thinness, it has been argued, has helped to increase the incidence of bulimia as one method of remaining thin. Medical experts agree that bulimia poses a serious threat to both physical and psychological health.

Christian Crandall (1988) proposes that conformity plays a key role in bulimia. Crandall argues that social pressure in friendship groups is an important mechanism by which binge eating is acquired and spread. If eating, dieting, and losing weight are important to the members of such groups as athletic teams, cheerleading squads, and sororities, then the group will develop norms defining how much, when, and with whom (1988: 590). The stresses of college life may increase students' susceptibility to the pressures to conform to such group norms.

To test his proposal, Crandall studied bulimia among women in college sororities. He collected information on such behaviors as binge eating, vomiting, and restrictive dieting. Although few of the women reported severe cases of bulimic behavior, milder forms, especially binge eating, were reported by many of them.

The results of Crandall's study indicated that norms involving binge eating differed among sororities. For example, in one sorority, the more binge-eating symptoms a woman reported, the more popular she was. In another sorority, women who engaged in moderate binge eating were the most popular. Crandall continued to gather this information over an academic year. He found that as friendship groups within the sororities became more cohesive, women's eating patterns became more similar to those of their friends.

This is an example of conformity that, though it produces popularity, has potentially negative effects. You can probably think of others—for example, conformity to drug and alcohol use or to unsafe sex. But conformity can be positive. In some environments, conformity could *decrease* binge eating and drug and alcohol use, as well as increase academic success, safe driving, and healthy exercise habits.

social norms in conformity is explored in the box "Binge Eating Among College Women.")

MINORITY INFLUENCE AND SOCIAL CHANGE

You might ask why the pressures to conform exerted by majorities don't bring all minorities, especially those low in power and prestige, into line. Given our tendency to conform to standards set by the majority, how is it ever possible for the status quo to change?

The answer is that social influence is not limited to the impact of a majority on a minority. A minority that firmly and resolutely pursues its ends can considerably influence a majority, even when the minority displays no obvious advantages such as wealth or recognized positions of power. Historical figures such as Galileo, Abraham Lincoln, and Sigmund Freud steadfastly advanced a minority position and eventually induced the majority to adopt their beliefs. In recent decades, committed minorities advocating such causes as environmental protection and the elimination of racial and sexual prejudice have influenced the majority position; they have brought about *social change*. Social influence, then, is a process involved in both social control and social change.

Numerous experiments have demonstrated the ability of a minority to influence a majority (Moscovici and Faucheux, 1972; Bray, Johnson, and Chilstrom, 1982; Maass and Clark, 1984; Moscovici, 1985; Levine and Russo, 1987). A minority commonly finds itself in conflict with some majority standard for behavior. French social psychologist Serge Moscovici (1976) notes that if the minority is to challenge the majority, it needs to exhibit internal consensus and consistency over time in its promotion of an alternative norm (e.g., regarding air pollution, women's rights, abortion, or the employment of migrant workers). The consistency with which the minority promotes its program is critical because the majority interprets consistency as an expression of certainty and confidence (Moscovici, Lage, and Naffrechoux, 1969; Nemeth and Wachtler, 1973, 1974, 1983; Mos-

covici and Lage, 1976; Wolf, 1979; Maass and Clark, 1984). However, should the majority perceive the minority as too rigid, it finds it easy to discount the minority's opinions (Mugny, 1975, 1982, 1984; Papastamou and Mugny, 1985). Under these circumstances, the majority may simply define the minority as dogmatic and narrow-minded.

In addition, the more similar the minority is to the majority on other characteristics, the more difficult it is for the majority to attribute the minority's position to idiosyncratic personal characteristics. For example, supporters of the environmental movement once were perceived to be mostly "little old ladies in tennis shoes" — birdwatchers who were oblivious to the realities of the world. As support for the movement has grown among people of all ages and walks of life, it has become more difficult for opponents of the movement to characterize supporters as being part of an unrealistic fringe, a group not to be taken seriously. Similarly, it is easier for the majority to dismiss the disagreement of a lone minority member as a product of the person's idiosyncrasy (perhaps a lack of familiarity with the task, a visual problem, or pigheadedness). But the majority often has more difficulty discounting two or more minority members who support one another.

Several studies suggest that majorities seem more effective in producing *compliance* — public conformity — while minorities are more successful in generating *conversion* — private conformity (Moscovici, 1980; Nemeth, 1986; Maass, West, and Cialdini, 1987). Social psychologists Maass and Clark (1983) demonstrated this effect in a study of attitudes about gay rights. Initially, several hundred undergraduate students completed a questionnaire about their attitudes toward gay rights, including such issues as homosexual marriages, job protection, and adoption by gay couples. Next, the researchers scored the responses to the questionnaire, giving each respondent a score indicating whether the person was "pro," "con," or neutral on the gay rights issue. Then they selected about 400 of the respondents whose attitudes were near neutral to be subjects in an experiment.

Each subject read what was purported to be a summary of a sixty-minute group discussion of gay rights held by five undergraduates like themselves. In all cases, a majority of four members of the fictitious group favored one position, and a minority of one favored the other. The number of arguments put forth by both the majority and the minority was the same (eight). For half of the subjects, the majority was pro on gay rights and the minority con. For the other half of the subjects, this was reversed: the majority was con and the minority was pro. This was the manipulated, or independent, variable in the study. The dependent variables were public and private conformity — compliance and conversion.

When asked to publicly state their views after reading the summary of the group discussion, subjects tended to conform to the majority position whether it was pro or con. But when their private beliefs were measured later, these tended to shift toward the minority position, again whether it was pro or con. The majority was more effective in producing *compliance* (public conformity), while the minority was more successful in generating *conversion* (private conformity). Moscovici (1980) suggests that this is because we don't think much about majority positions — we just go along. We give more thought to consistently expressed minority positions; consequently, they have more effect on our private beliefs.

These studies show that minority influence can be powerful. When it occurs, it may be more likely than majority influence to produce conversion — private acceptance. Sufficient influence by the minority can bring about a change in the norms of the group. This constitutes social change.

CONFORMITY AND INDIVIDUALITY

At first glance this strong tendency for members of a society or group to go along with expectations about how they should behave in various situations may appear to conflict with our respect for individuality, independence, and creativity. Why can't we all just "do our own thing" and "be ourselves"? There is a good reason for the existence of so much conformity. Without it, social life would be impossible. Consider the resultant chaos if every semester, for each new class you entered, no norms were in effect. You, the professor, and other members of the class would have to negotiate such matters as when and where the class would be held, how long it would last, what the format of the class would be, whether there would be exams, and, if so, how they would be graded. Settling those issues might well take most of the term, leaving little time for accomplishing any learning. Would any of us risk the danger of driving to the grocery store if we couldn't assume the existence of widely followed traffic regulations? Think about what you would do if you were invited to dinner at the White House and knew that you would be the only guest who had never been there before. You'd probably start trying to find out what the norms governing dinner at the White House are — what you should wear, how you should act. It helps us in most situations to have norms that make interaction with others predictable and allow us to take many things for granted. Norms enable us to assume that others will behave a particular way and to know what is expected of us.

This is not to say that conformity is always good. Some norms seem to have no obvious practical purpose. For example, a survey indicated that 45 percent of American women wear uncomfortable shoes because they look good (20 percent of men did so). And norms are not always fair. Some norms place an unfair burden on people with certain physical characteristics. Consider the American norm that says a person should be thin because, according to our social attitudes, "thin is beautiful and fat is ugly, lazy, slothful." Obese individuals are often judged harshly because of this norm. Other norms stigmatize individuals on the basis of gender. In the business world, managers are expected to be direct, authoritative, and witty. But some of those attributes traditionally have been seen as unbecoming when displayed by females, making it difficult for women to be judged as good managers.

Cooperative Tasks

Thus far we have discussed behavior that occurs in the context of observing others — audience tasks — and behaviors that take place in the context of others who are engaged separately in the same kind of behavior — coaction tasks. Now we want to focus on tasks in which the *collective* activities of several individuals affect the outcomes (rewards and costs) for each of the individuals. Such activities are called **cooperative tasks.** It is important to note that the same behavior can occur in any of the three contexts. For example, you may be seated at your kitchen table stuffing envelopes for a fund-raiser while your three roommates watch (audience task). Or you may be engaged in the same behavior while your roommates also stuff envelopes. If each person has a stack of 100 envelopes to stuff, you are engaged in a coaction task: you are doing the same thing as the others, but working independently; the speed and quality of your envelope stuffing does not affect your roommates' outcomes, nor does their speed and quality affect yours. If, however, you and your roommates are working from a common stack of 400 envelopes, the speed and quality with which each person stuffs *does* affect the others. If the common goal is to correctly stuff all the envelopes as quickly as possible, then one person's sloppy or efficient work will affect the others. In this last situation, you are involved in a *cooperative task.*

EFFECTS ON CONFORMITY AND PERFORMANCE

Earlier in this chapter we discussed the Sherif studies in which several people were given a coaction task in which they made individual judgments in the presence of one another. What would happen if we asked these people to discuss their individual judgments and to arrive at a single, *collective*

decision — a cooperative task? What impact would this have on their collective judgment? To answer, we'll look at two areas of research: group polarization and groupthink.

Group Polarization

It has long been thought that groups tend to be more conservative than their individual members — that groups have a dampening impact on boldness, creativity, innovation, and daring. William H. Whyte, in his book *The Organization Man* (1956), which became a bible of the business world, suggests that the administrator who wants conservative advice should ask a committee, rather than individuals, for recommendations. Yet, as often happens with common-sense knowledge, this prediction is contradicted by an impressive body of social psychological evidence.

Research on this topic originated in James Stoner's (1961) unpublished master's thesis at the Massachusetts Institute of Technology. His study revealed that people tend to make more daring decisions when in groups than when alone — a phenomenon termed the *risky shift.* Experiments studying the risky shift generally begin by having subjects individually read about a hypothetical case of a person who must choose between two alternatives — one that is safe but unattractive and one that is attractive but exposes the person to a much higher possibility of failure.

Subjects are presented, for instance, with the case of an electrical engineer who has a secure job with a modest, but adequate, income. He is offered another position at a considerably larger salary with a small, newly founded company that has an uncertain future. Subjects are asked the lowest probability of success in the new venture that they would consider acceptable before they would recommend that the engineer take the new job: 1 chance in 10, 3 in 10, 5 in 10, 7 in 10, or 9 in 10. After the pretest, subjects discuss the issue as a group and arrive at a decision. Results vary somewhat owing to the type of risk item employed or the social setting, but there is an overwhelming tendency (over the diverse conditions of more than a hundred experiments) for riskier choices to be made in the group condition than in the solitary one.

On some tasks, however, people in a group shift not toward a risky but toward a *cautious* direction. For instance, when experimental tasks involve the alternative of divorce (a culturally disfavored option) as a solution to marital discord, a cautious shift occurs. Thus we observe not only risky-shift effects but also cautious-shift effects in group behavior.

Social psychologists call both phenomena *choice shifts*. People tend to shift in social situations toward the dominant position in a given reference group, whether risky or cautious. Consequently, group discussion *polarizes* individual judgment. It enhances the tendency of group members to shift toward the extreme of the already preferred position — a tendency known as the **group polarization** phenomenon (Myers and Lamm, 1976). Norris R. Johnson (1974; Johnson, Stemler, and Hunter, 1977) says that crowd behavior is a good illustration of group polarization: the average response of group members becomes even more extreme, although shifting in the same dominant direction, than it was in the precrowd context. Group members apparently perceive a norm, and group consensus regarding it, as more extreme than it actually is. Because of their bonds to the group, the individuals conform to what they believe to be the group's norm (Mackie and Cooper, 1984).

Several explanations for group polarization have been suggested. A review of published research supports two main explanations (Isenberg, 1986). The *persuasive arguments* explanation emphasizes informational motivation. People listen to the arguments of the discussants, and they shift their opinions in the direction of the position that has the most persuasive arguments. Group members tend to discuss the information and opinions they have in common, rather than unshared information (Stasser, Taylor, and Hanna, 1989). Thus, discussion tends to amplify, or polarize, the original position of the majority. Those who are exposed to mostly risky arguments shift in that direction and become more risk taking. Those who hear mostly conservative arguments shift in that direction and become more cautious.

On the other hand, the *social comparison* explanation emphasizes evaluative motivation. People are interested in making a favorable impression within the group. During discussion, some individuals learn that others have more extreme views than they do. In order to make a favorable impression within the group — to appear as confident and at least as bold as other group members — these individuals shift their positions to even more extreme positions than those of the others.

STUDENT OBSERVATION

Risky Shift

I am currently working with a group on an entry for the American Advertising Federation competition. Our "client" is Visa, and we have been instructed by Visa to specifically target our campaign to four-year college students.

Initially, our campaign followed this guideline, but many group members, including myself, felt that parents of college students needed to be included. If I had had to make this decision on my own, I probably would have chosen to abide by the rule instead of taking the risk — I would have settled for the safe but unattractive alternative. However, as a group we decided to "go for it" and incorporate parents as another target market. We chose the attractive alternative but, as a result, may have increased our chances of failure (losing the competition). Thus, I engaged in a phenomenon called *risky shift*. I made a more daring decision as part of the group than I would have made alone.

Other individuals have more extreme positions before the discussion. Yet they initially express more moderate positions for fear of being rejected and labeled "extremist" or "radical." When they discover their real opinions are closer to the opinions expressed by other group members, they appear to "shift" to more extreme positions, feeling they will then be accepted. (Before reading further, look at the Student Observation: "Risky Shift.")

Groupthink

On January 28, 1986, the space shuttle *Challenger* was launched from Kennedy Space Center. The temperature that morning was in the mid-20s, well below the previous low temperatures at which the shuttle engines had been tested. Seventy-three seconds after launch, the *Challenger* exploded, killing all seven astronauts aboard and becoming the worst disaster in space-flight history.

The presidential commission that investigated the accident pointed to a flawed decision-making process as a primary contributory cause. The decision to launch was made the night before the launch in the Level I flight-readiness review meeting. Early in the evening, members of the top-level decision-making group were informed that engineers from the private supplier of the solid rocket booster engines would *not* recommend a launch below 53 degrees Fahrenheit. But the group did not meet with the engineers to review their data and concerns.

How could such seemingly competent individuals go so wrong? Irving Janis (1989), a Yale social psychologist, says that the answer is groupthink. **Groupthink** refers to a decision-making process occurring within highly cohesive groups in which the members are so preoccupied with maintaining group consensus that their critical abilities become ineffective. Insulated from outside opinions, the group has strong, directive leaders. Under circumstances of external threat, a hidden agenda emerges which stipulates that group members must, at all costs, maintain friendly relations with one another. Individuals begin to place a premium on unanimity and concurrence, each of which interferes with their capacity for critical thinking. Group members, consequently, are willing to sanction policies that entail excessive risk taking (Hart, 1990). Let's apply Janis's model to the decision to launch the ill-fated *Challenger* (Moorhead, Ference, and Neck, 1991). Janis identified eight symptoms, or characteristics, of groupthink. We'll ignore one of Janis's symptoms — illusion of morality — because it did not appear to play a role in this particular decision.

1 *An illusion of invulnerability:* The solid rocket joint problem that destroyed *Challenger* was discussed often at flight-readiness review meetings prior to flight. However, a mentality of overconfidence existed due to the space program's extraordinary record of success. Since 1967, when a flash fire in the capsule of *Apollo I* killed three astronauts, NASA had a string of fifty-five successful missions, including putting men on the moon and launching *Skylab* and the shuttle. This background of success gave group members the confidence to lower their standards and take more risks.

2 *Rationalization:* The engineers who recommended against launching *Challenger* presented evidence showing that in the coldest previous launch (30 degrees), the joint in question had experienced serious erosion, and they pointed out that no data existed as to how the joint would perform at colder temperatures. NASA officials put forth numerous technical rationalizations faulting the engineers' analysis, including the opinion that the engineers' data were *inconclusive*. Under normal conditions, the engineers would have had to prove the shuttle boosters' *readiness* for launch; instead, they found themselves being required to prove that the boosters were *unsafe*.

3 *Negative stereotypes of opponents*: NASA officials felt that the engineers opposing the launch did not understand the launch decision. In fact, they denigrated and badgered the engineers and their information and opinions.

4. *Pressure on dissent:* NASA officials pressured the engineers and the top management of their company to change their position after the original recommendation that the launch not take place. It was this pressure that the top managers were responding to when they overruled their engineering staff and recommended launch.

5. *Self-censorship:* The cohesiveness of the group became such an overriding consideration that individuals censored their own divergent opinions. Individuals who had misgivings were reluctant to express them lest they look like they were not part of "the team." One vice president of the engineering company, who had originally presented information *against* the launch, was later asked by NASA why the company had changed its recommendation. He defended the recommendation to launch using NASA's own rationalizations.

6. *Illusion of unanimity:* Group members shared an illusion of unanimity concerning the majority view. Falsely assuming that anyone who remained silent was in agreement with the majority opinion, group members focused on points of convergence rather than fully examining points of divergence. None of the decision-making officials ever openly sided with the engineers in the discussion about the *Challenger* launch. The absence of expressions of dissenting opinions may have been amplified by the fact that the Level I meeting was a teleconference linking participants at three different locations, thus minimizing the role that body language might have played in evidencing dissension.

7. *Mindguarding:* Several top managers shielded the group from adverse information that might have destroyed the majority view of the facts regarding the decision. They became, in effect, self-appointed "mindguards." These managers knew that just five months earlier, the rocket casings had been ordered redesigned to correct a flaw, but they withheld this information at the meeting, as well as other technical details concerning the history of the joint problem.

Janis offers several suggestions for combating groupthink: First, the leader should encourage dissent by having each group member air objections and doubts. Second, the leader should initially remain impartial in discussion, stating her or his preferences only after other group members have expressed their views. Third, the group should divide into subgroups that discuss issues independently before coming together to hammer out a group decision. Fourth, at each meeting, at least one person should be assigned to play the role of devil's advocate to challenge the group's ideas. Fifth, outside experts holding different views should be invited to present their views to the group. And sixth, after a tentative group decision has been reached, the group should hold a "second-chance" meeting at which each member can express any lingering doubts before the group reaches a final decision. These suggestions are designed to counter premature conformity and the low performance it sometimes generates. (Attempts to improve decision making among group members in a legal setting are discussed in the box "Jury Decisions.")

EFFECTS ON COOPERATIVE RESPONSE AND PERFORMANCE

Thus far we have discussed the impact of cooperative tasks on performance and conformity. The effects of cooperative tasks on individual behavior can also be considered in terms of whether the individual makes the **cooperative response** — the one maximizing collective rewards. The task in team sports is a cooperative task. All team members either win or lose as a result of their collective action. Putting out a school newspaper is a cooperative task. All the staff members either succeed or fail (the paper gets to the students or it doesn't) as a result of their collective action. A family vacation is a cooperative task. All members of the family either go on the vacation or stay at home as a consequence of their collective action.

But will all the group members faced with a cooperative task make the *cooperative response*? Will the strong-forward on the basketball team

JURY DECISIONS

The right of trial by a jury of one's peers is one of the oldest and most cherished rights of United States citizens. Because of the critical role juries play in the U.S. system of justice, they have come under increasing public and scientific scrutiny. In recent years, significant changes have been made in the way that juries deal with certain crimes and civil litigations. Let's take at look at three of these changes.

VOIR DIRE

The selection of jury members has customarily involved verbal or written questioning of prospective jurors to uncover any biases or prejudices that may stand in the way of their reaching a verdict that is fair and impartial. The process is called *voir dire*.

Recently a number of social scientists have assisted defense attorneys in selecting jurors by drawing up a "jury profile" favorable to acquittal. The defense lawyers exercise their twenty peremptory challenges to eliminate potential jurors lacking the desired characteristics. Proponents of scientific jury selection argue that biases are already introduced in jury decisions by unfair publicity, regional prejudices, and unrepresentative jury rosters. Scientific jury selection is necessary to counter these forces so that a defendant can receive fair treatment. Opponents of this system of jury selection argue that it is really jury rigging, since it creates an unrepresentative jury by excluding certain types of people and produces lenient rather than fair verdicts.

UNANIMITY

Another change in the jury process has involved replacing the unanimous verdict with decision rules that permit a verdict when two-thirds of the jurors agree. This change also makes a difference in jury outcomes. Robert D. Foss (1981) finds that juries that are required to reach unanimity rather than a specified quorum (e.g., concurrence among ten of twelve jurors) not only take longer to decide a case but are more likely to hang (be incapable of reaching a verdict). At first, the extent of disagreement in both types of juries is basically the same. But within fifteen minutes, disagreements in quorum juries drop to virtually half the level found in unanimous juries. Seemingly, jurors are less contentious in quorum juries and more opinionated in unanimous juries. Foss speculates that in quorum juries the members know that one or two of their number cannot block a verdict. Consequently, the members work toward consensus, even if one or two jurors remain steadfast in a contrary view. In contrast, differences among jurors in unanimous juries are more likely to build into sharp opposition, so that polarization ensues. Further, Foss conjectures, jurors in quorum juries may be less insistent in their views because they lack the power to block a consensus verdict.

JURY SIZE

A third change in the jury system involves the size of the jury. The twelve-person jury has been replaced in some states by juries as small as six. In the case of *Williams* v. *Florida* (1970), the nation's highest court said that six-person juries could achieve the functions of a jury no less successfully than could twelve-person juries.

The Supreme Court upheld these changes in the structure of juries not on the basis of legal or historical analysis but on the grounds that social scientists have found that size has no effect on the verdict produced by a jury (Saks, 1977). However, social scientists have accused the Supreme Court of misreading and misinterpreting their research findings (Gerbasi, Zuckerman, and Reis, 1977; Wrightsman, 1978). For instance, with respect to jury size, social psychologist Michael J. Saks (1977) has found that large juries, compared to small juries, spend more time deliberating, communicate more, recall testimony better, better represent the community, and tend to produce more consistent verdicts.

play his best? Will the editorial writer complete her job by the deadline? Will the teenage son arrange for a pet-sitter for the family's dog and two cats? What factors influence whether individuals facing a cooperative task will behave cooperatively or uncooperatively?

Social Loafing

Every summer, hundreds of bubbly teenagers bounce into Chapel Hill, North Carolina, for the cheerleader camp at the University of North Carolina. Walking across campus, you notice groups of young women, all dressed in their distinctive school colors, practicing their yells and gymnastic moves in formal sessions headed by university cheerleaders or on informal romps through the university and community. One thing you always notice about these teens is the noise. After all, their ability to yell and clap — to arouse the enthusiasm of the fans, one key to the success of an athletic team — is the source of their social identity as "good cheerleaders."

Enter two social psychologists — Charles Hardy and Bibb Latané (1986). They asked the cheerleaders at the camp to "give us a hand for about 20 minutes so that we might measure how loud you cheer." Almost all agreed, and later they were ushered, two at a time, into a small room where they donned earphones and blindfolds and completed a series of thirty-two trials of shouting and clapping. For each trial, a tape-recorded voice heard through their individual earphones announced who was to perform ("A alone," "B alone," or "A and B together"). Actually, when cheerleader A heard that both partners were to shout or clap together, cheerleader B heard that only A was to perform. Therefore, cheerleader A believed that she was performing as part of a group. This was made possible by having all cheerleaders hear the prerecorded sound of six people shouting and clapping — just loud enough to keep each cheerleader from hearing her partner perform or *not* perform. Thus, on some trials cheerleaders believed they shouted or clapped alone, while on other trials they thought they did so as part of a group.

Using a sound level meter, the researchers found that the cheerleaders produced prodigious quantities of noise, especially when shouting. The average shout, from a distance of 4 feet, was 101 decibels, comparable to the loudness on a New York City subway platform. However, cheerleaders who thought they were cheering as a member of a group produced only 92 percent as much noise as cheerleaders cheering alone. Previous research by Bibb Latané and his associates had also revealed that when people work on a cooperative task, they work less hard than they do when working individually (Latané, Williams, and Harkins, 1979a, b; Williams, Harkins, and Latané, 1981). Latané called this process **social loafing**.

Initial evidence for social loafing came before World War I from the work of a French agricultural engineer named Max Ringelmann (Kravitz and Martin, 1986). He tested individuals singly and collectively in a rope-pulling task. When they were working in groups, a division of labor did not typically result and performance depended on the sum of individual efforts. We might expect that three individuals could pull three times as much as one person and that eight could pull eight times as much. Yet, whereas persons individually averaged 130 pounds of pressure when tugging on a rope, groups of three averaged 352 pounds (only two-and-a-half times the solo rate) and groups of eight only 546 pounds (less than four times the solo rate).

Some psychologists have speculated that faulty coordination is the source of this group inefficiency. But when Alan G. Ingham and his associates (1974) replicated Ringelmann's work with blindfolded subjects who *believed* they were pulling with others, the subjects also pulled less when in the group setting than when alone. They pulled at only 90 percent of their individual rate when pulling with "another person" and at only 85 percent when they believed two to six others were pulling with them. Other researchers have observed similar effects with cognitive tasks such as solving mazes (Jackson and Williams, 1985) and reacting to proposals (Brickner, Harkins, and Ostrom, 1986).

But wait a minute! We said earlier that the presence of others would facilitate the performance of simple, well-learned tasks. The cheerleading and rope-pulling behaviors were well learned and simple. So why did performance levels decrease instead of increase when subjects believed that they were working with others? One possibility is that the cheerleading and rope-pulling situations were *cooperative* tasks. The examples of social facilitation we discussed earlier involved others acting as an *audience* or as *coactors*. Why should cooperative tasks inhibit performance of even simple, well-learned behaviors? Let's see if we can answer that question.

Social Dilemmas

Lowered performance can result from situations in which members of a group must choose between the *noncooperative response* of maximizing their personal interests and the *cooperative response* of maximizing the group's collective welfare — situations called **social dilemmas** (Komorita and Barth, 1985; Hechter, 1987; Sell, 1988; Coleman, 1990). Take the choice confronting a soldier in a foxhole at the outset of a battle. To win the battle, most of the soldiers will have to leave their foxholes and assault the enemy position. But if a particular soldier joins the assault force (the cooperative response), he risks being captured, wounded, or killed. The safest course for each soldier is to remain in the foxhole and not assault the enemy position (the noncooperative response). But if all soldiers make this choice, the battle will be lost and everyone in the unit will be killed or taken prisoner.

Free-rider effect.   In certain social dilemma situations, some members of the group can and will provide for the public good, making others' contributions unnecessary (Kerr, 1983). This "let George do it" approach is termed the **free-rider effect** — the tendency to make a noncooperative response based on the reasoning that others will cooperate for the collective welfare, making one's own cooperation unnecessary.

The free-rider effect inclines individuals to resist appeals to unite with others for the public good (Olson, 1965). This was seen, for example, in the Three Mile Island area after the serious nuclear accident in 1979, in which radiation leaked from the Unit 2 reactor. Although some area residents became active politically, the vast majority, while agreeing with the goals of the citizen protest groups, contributed neither time nor money to the movement. Instead, they became free riders on the efforts of others (Walsh and Warland, 1983). Similarly, every year, we are confronted with campaigns to raise funds for public radio and television. The success of a local station depends on such public support but not on any particular person's support. Even the nonsupporting public can have access to the station. But when too many of us decide to withhold our donations, the station goes off the air and the

---

STUDENT OBSERVATION

Free-Rider Effect

The free-rider effect is the tendency to make a noncooperative response based on the reasoning that others will cooperate for the collective welfare, so one's own cooperative response is unnecessary. An example of this effect occurred just the other night. A group of friends went out to eat at a nearby restaurant. The dinner was good and the company pleasant. The bill arrived at the table, and we divided it into separate payments. Then came time to chip in for the tip. Everyone put down at least a dollar or more, except for Steve. He felt that everyone else had more than covered the waitress's tip, so he left without making a contribution.

public good goes "down the tubes." Still, some people fail to donate to public radio and television, assuming that others will provide the necessary funds. (See the Student Observation: "Free-Rider Effect.")

Sucker effect. There is another side to the free-rider effect. In many group settings, there is not only the possibility that we can free-ride on other people's contributions but also the danger that other people may free-ride on our contributions. This can lead to the **sucker effect** — the tendency to make a noncooperative response based on the reasoning that if one cooperates, others will take advantage of one's contribution and refrain from cooperating (Jackson and Harkins, 1985). We are usually reluctant to "play the sucker," and to avoid this possibility, we may reduce our own contributions to the group. An individual may reason that if she goes to great effort and expense to make a special cake for the office party, others will feel free to make no contribution but will come to enjoy her cake. She may therefore decide *not* to go to the trouble of baking and instead bring a bag of storebought cookies to the party.

Social fences and social traps. Each of these cases (social loafing, free-rider effect, and sucker effect) is characterized by an incentive *not* to do something that, when done by too few people, results in a poorer state of affairs than would be the case if everyone had done it. Another example would be the prototypical citizen considering whether to shovel the snow from his sidewalk after a blizzard. Each resident realizes that shoveling the snow from her or his sidewalk will not, by itself, improve the situation, since the neighbors' sidewalks will still be unnavigable. Consequently, none of the residents shovel his or her snow, and all of them remain confined to their houses. This type of social dilemma is called a *social fence* because it blocks positive action.

A second type of social dilemma involves an incentive to *do* something that, when done by many, leads to disaster. Such a dilemma is known as a *social trap*. Garrett J. Hardin (1968) offers the example of the "tragedy of the commons," in which the long-run consequences of self-interested individual choice result in social disaster. In a situation where a number of herders share a common pasture, each individual may reason that he or she will realize a benefit by adding one additional cow to graze in the pasture. But should each person follow this course, the commons will soon be overgrazed and each will be a loser. Hardin had in mind the problem of population growth, but the notion can also be applied to other types of problems, such as congestion and misuse of resources. The traffic jams that we endure at 7:30 A.M. and 5:30 P.M. arise because most of us arrive at our offices between 8 and 9 A.M. and leave around 5 P.M. We may squander fossil fuels by driving alone rather than carpooling, or by driving at 65 miles per hour rather than 55, or by maintaining our thermostats at 72 degrees rather than 68 in the winter. If only a few of us enjoy these immediate benefits, the long-term costs may be minimal. However, if enough people go for the short-term benefits, the resources will be overused and we will collectively pay for the disasters that none of us caused individually. (See the Student Observation: "Social Trap.")

Social psychologists most often use laboratory experiments to study social traps. A common example attempts to simulate the tragedy of the commons by giving a group of four or five people the chance to draw as many tokens as they want from a pool of available tokens. However, they are informed that after each round of "harvesting," the pool is replenished in direct proportion to the number of tokens remaining in the pool. Conservative removal of only a small number of tokens (the cooperative response) ensures continued replenishment of the pool; significant withdrawal (the noncooperative response) causes the eventual disappearance of the pool. Despite this information, some group members choose to draw out all the tokens (Brewer and Kramer, 1986; Schroeder, Irwin, and Sibicky, 1988).

Conditional effects. So, at least sometimes, cooperative tasks inhibit performance or cooperative responses by producing social loafing, the free-rider effect, or the sucker effect. But obvi-

STUDENT OBSERVATION

Social Trap

A rather extreme example of a social dilemma known as a *social trap* occurred in my country [South Africa] a while back. A small eight-seat airplane crashed into some hills shortly after takeoff, seriously injuring several passengers. An investigation revealed that the luggage on board had been way over the weight limit, probably causing the crash. Evidently, a number of self-interested passengers had decided to sneak extra luggage on board, thus putting their own short-term gains ahead of the long-term safety of the group. Note that many of them had the same idea and together precipitated the accident. The limited power of the plane was overextended, and the group suffered as a whole, although no one individual bears responsibility.

ously this is not *always* the outcome (Coleman, 1988; Williams and Karau, 1991). Many observers and participants in sports believe that sports teams, which are engaged in a cooperative tasks, sometimes *enhance* individual performance.

A member of a team might cooperate and might even give extra effort (the famous 110 percent!) despite knowing that he or she will receive the same rewards as teammates who don't try as hard. Similarly, soldiers and members of extremist political groups sometimes risk extreme costs, even death, to further the goals of the group. We call such people "martyrs" if we share their political views; if not, we call them "zealots" or "terrorists."

So, like audience and coactor tasks, cooperative tasks sometimes inhibit and sometimes facilitate cooperative performance. Given the existence of social dilemma problems, what mechanisms are available to group members for encouraging one another to choose the cooperative response — supporting the interests of the group — rather than to act selfishly? Hardin suggested that social controls restrict individual actions deemed detrimental to the common good. Government frequently serves this function by regulating access to critical resources. But there are other measures as well (Conlon and Barr, 1989).

Let's begin by looking more closely at the situations we have been discussing. What features distinguish them, and how are they likely to discourage the high-performance or cooperative re-

sponse? We will examine three features: (1) group task structure, (2) group reward structure, and (3) group communication and normative pressure.

Group Task Structure

Task structure has to do with the features of a task itself, including whether performers act simultaneously or at different times, whether they perform the same or different responses, and how group performance is measured. These aspects of task structure have been shown to affect the likelihood of group members making cooperative responses.

Simultaneous-unitary-additive tasks.   First, the group response in these situations involves group members performing similar activities, frequently at the same time. "Group performance" is measured in terms of the sum of the performances of the individual members. The group's outcome (reward or cost) is dependent on this measure of group performance. For example, in the cheerleading experiment participants who thought they were in a group all yelled and clapped at the same time, while the measure of their group performance was the recordings on the sound level meter. This kind of task is called a *simultaneous-unitary-additive task*. It is a **simultaneous task** because the group members perform at the same time, a **unitary task** because their responses are the same, and an **additive task** because the performance of the group is measured in terms of the sum of the members' responses. For example, the profits of an insurance company may be partly contingent on the performances of members of a typing pool who sit at computer terminals retrieving and revising policyholders' records. Members of rowing teams and forwards in rugby's scrummage also perform simultaneous-unitary-additive tasks.

Studies suggest that this kind of task decreases the chances of high-performance or cooperative responses. Why? The major culprit appears to be *anonymity* — the lack of identifiability of individual performances. Anonymity may encourage noncooperative responses because there is little chance of being held accountable for one's deviation. All three characteristics of the task contribute to this anonymity. The members of the group are doing the same activity at the same time, and this often makes it difficult to distinguish the level of performance of any one member. Individual performances are further masked by the measure of group performance — the sum of individual performances. So, if anonymity is the culprit, cooperative responding should be increased by altering the task structure to increase identifiability (Harkins, 1987; Sell and Wilson, 1991).

Divisible and sequential tasks. Identifiability is greater in tasks in which group members are performing different, as opposed to similar, activities. **Divisible tasks** are those in which members perform different, although complementary, activities. Sociologists refer to taking a task, breaking it into subtasks, and assigning them to different group members as a *division of labor*. The next time you are flying on a commercial airplane, notice the divisible tasks performed by the ground and flight crews — the ticket agents, baggage handlers, food handlers, flight attendants, pilots, and navigator. Sports such as baseball, football, lacrosse, and basketball involve some tasks that are divisible. In most of these sports, it's the offensive task that is particularly divisible; in baseball, it's the defense.

Successful football teams often take steps to highlight and make visible the individual contribution of every player to the outcome of a play. The coaching staff screens and grades each play and computes the average performance of each individual. Teammates know one another's scores, and the scores influence which players start the next game. At weekly press luncheons, coaches announce "lineman of the week" honors and award decals to adorn players' helmets, signifying superior performance to the player, his teammates, and fans. The success of football teams using these techniques suggests that identifiability and individual reward may be effective deterrents to social loafing (Szymanski and Harkins, 1987).

STUDENT OBSERVATION

Group Task Structure

I am currently working on a group project in one of my economics classes. As long as I can remember, I have always hated group projects because there is such a great temptation either to free-ride on the others or not to be suckered by others free-riding on me. The result has always been a rather poor group performance and an average grade. However, understanding the dilemma that these group projects pose, the professor has structured the group assignment so that the task is *divisible* and the presentation is *sequential*. In effect, each member must contribute to the written report by investigating one aspect of the group topic and must also give a five-minute oral report on that subtopic during the presentation. This makes the individual performance of each group member more identifiable both by members of the group and, more importantly, by the professor. Indeed, the sequential-divisible-additive task structure is, I believe, responsible for the progress our group has already made, with the due date still three and a half weeks away.

Identifiability is also greater in tasks in which group members perform activities *sequentially*, as opposed to simultaneously. Take, for example, intercollegiate wrestling or tennis. Each team member performs the same activity, and each member's winning of a match is cumulated to determine the team's performance; they are engaged in a unitary-additive task. But, unlike the case in sports such as football and basketball, team members perform sequentially rather than simultaneously. Think about it. Is it harder for a wrestler or tennis player to be anonymous than it is for a football or basketball player? Identifiability may be increased even more by combining a sequential task with a divisible task. Track and gymnastics are sports examples. The assembly line also illustrates the sequential-divisible task. (See the Student Observation: "Group Task Structure.")

Nonadditive tasks. And what about alternatives to additive tasks: tasks in which the performances of group members are not masked by the sum or average of their performances? One alternative is the **disjunctive task**, in which the group's performance is judged in terms of the *best* individual performance. Quiz teams are frequently involved in a disjunctive tasks. Any one member of the team can answer a question correctly and score a point for the team. This is also true for "boardroom brainstorming" or best-ball golf. The disjunctive task increases the identifiability of the *most cooperative* group member.

Do you think a disjunctive task will affect the performances of less cooperative members — those who loaf or excessively consume? Probably not. But there is another kind of task, known as a **conjunctive task**, in which the group's performance is judged in terms of the *worst* individual performance. So the question is: Does this kind of task affect performance? It certainly eliminates the anonymity of the worst offender. This is one approach to dealing with students who have poor academic records. They are grouped with other students, and the performance of the whole group is graded on the basis of the student whose perfor-

mance is poorest. The theory is that this conjunctive task will focus attention on the least productive student. Over time, other group members will be motivated to influence the student to be more cooperative — to perform better academically. They *may* provide the student with academic assistance and/or informal sanctions (approval and disapproval) for the student's academic performance. However, this is a very big "may." Although group members are *motivated* to influence the student to be more cooperative, they may not have the *expertise* to accomplish their goal. For example, their assistance may be too chaotic (confusing the student) or their sanctions too negative (alienating the student).

Obviously, group reward may not be an all-or-none situation. The *amount* of reward available to a group may depend on the proportion of group members who perform at a designated level. In such cases, an individual's cooperative response will increase his or her own share of the resulting group benefits. When the individual concludes that he or she can make a *unique* contribution to a group effort and that failure to work with the rest of the group may spoil the whole group's outcome, the individual is more likely to cooperate (Harkins and Petty, 1982; Stroebe and Frey, 1982; Brickner, Harkins, and Ostrom, 1986).

Reward Distribution

One of the explanations for the lack of cooperative responding by some group members is the anonymity provided by some group task structures. The *reward structure* is undoubtedly another explanation.

Equality. All the cooperative situations we have discussed so far share a common reward structure. Whatever the outcome (reward or cost) of the group's performance, it is shared equally by all group members, regardless of other factors. This type of reward distribution is called **equality**. Equality is based on the credo "All for one and one for all — share and share alike." Equal distribution has the advantage of being relatively easy to implement because it requires neither compli-

Performance is enhanced when individual contributions to a group product are identifiable. Although this quilt was a joint effort, each quilter signed the square she contributed, making her contribution identifiable and probably enhancing the quality of her work.

cated formulas nor worries about ascertaining the respective contributions of group members (Elliott and Meeker, 1984). Consequently, it tends to prevent within-group conflict and contributes to a high level of harmony and satisfaction among group members, especially when they do not know their individual performance levels (Bickman and Rosenbaum, 1977).

But does equality encourage *non*cooperation? Equality means that a group member's reward has little to do with his or her individual performance, especially in larger groups, where each person's response is, in a sense, "diluted" by many others. The *difference* between the individual's reward for cooperating and that for not cooperating is minimal, because the reward distribution offers no incentive to cooperate. If a user of some resource (gasoline, water, grazing land) will continue to have access to the resource whether she uses excessive or conservative amounts (as long as most members of the group conserve), why shouldn't she use excessive amounts (the noncooperative choice)? If a worker is going to get a job whether he pays union dues or not (as long as most members pay dues), why shouldn't he decline to pay the dues? One answer, of course, is guilt. A person who receives the same amount of reward as other members of the group without assuming the cost that they do *may* feel troubled. If so, one way to alleviate the guilt would be to assume the cost of cooperation—conserve, pay dues, increase production. But others will be content to continue their lack of cooperation and enjoy the equal benefits.

Equity.   Can group benefits be distributed another way? Rewards could be distributed proportionally among members relative to their cooperative inputs—conservation, payment of dues, productivity. Those who conserve, pay dues, or produce would receive a greater proportion of the group's benefits than those who don't. This type of reward distribution is called **equity**. Students working together on a class project may be graded according to the amount of information each provided for the group's paper. Water users may be charged in direct proportion to the amount of water they use instead of the usual flat rate. Nonunion employees can be prevented from enjoying the benefits provided by the labor union by creating a closed shop or union fee (all workers would be required to join the union or pay the union fee as a condition of employment). The existence of an equitable reward distribution is obviously contingent on a high level of identifiability. Group members must be in a position to identify the performance levels of each member in order to determine the distribution of rewards.

Unequal-unequitable. But rewards that are distributed unequally are not always equitable. Some group members can receive greater rewards than other members for a similar level of cooperation. Students may make similar contributions to a group project but receive different grades from their professor. Football players may make similar contributions to their team's success, but quarterbacks and running backs receive more public attention and higher salaries.

When both the performance and the rewards of group members are identifiable, group members can compare their rewards with those of other group members. Discovering that our colleagues are receiving greater rewards than we are *for the same level of cooperation* can be a source of dissatisfaction—a feeling of injustice or another form of the "sucker effect." The amount of the discrepancy sometimes may be great enough to cause the withdrawal of our cooperation, especially if an alternative (noncooperative) response will earn us some reward (Marwell and Schmitt, 1975). For example, a baseball pitcher may refuse to sign a contract with his current team because the salary offered to him is lower than that of another player whose contribution to the team's success is the same as or lower than his own.

How can the withdrawal of cooperation be avoided under these circumstances? In some cases, the group can establish an *internal* reward system (that is, sanctions to enforce the group's norms) to *compensate* for the inequitable method of distributing rewards to group members. For instance, members who are overrewarded could give some of their rewards to underrewarded members, and underrewarded members could be compensated with other kinds of rewards, such as social approval. There is some evidence that such a system can maintain cooperation (Marwell and Schmitt, 1975). But there are several considerations with this possibility: (1) Does the group have a reward that can be distributed compensatively? Money may be transferable; grades are not. Group friendships may not be strong enough to make social approval a viable reward. (2) Will this "solution" to the noncooperation problem be obvious to most groups? (3) Will the internal reward system be effective in maintaining cooperation? A reward-transfer solution may cost the overrewarded members too much. Once the amount of the transfer is subtracted from the member's reward, the balance may be less than the reward she or he would receive for an alternative (noncooperative) behavior.

Gender differences. Men and women apparently differ in the ways that they allocate rewards between themselves and others (Major and Deaux, 1982; Major and Adams, 1983), although in some cases the sex difference is very small (Stockard, van de Kragt, and Dodge, 1988). When asked to split rewards between themselves and a partner whose performance is inferior to their own, women tend to allocate the rewards equally, whereas men tend to allocate the rewards equitably. When the partner's performance is superior to their own, both women and men tend to divide the rewards equitably, but women generally take fewer rewards for themselves than do men. Even when their own performance is equal to that of a partner, women take fewer rewards for themselves than do men. This pattern holds regardless of the sex of the partner.

Various explanations have been suggested for these differences. One explanation is that women, by virtue of their socialization, show greater concern than do men for maintaining good relations with a partner and emphasize harmony among people rather than end results (Kahn et al., 1980; Gilligan, 1982*a*). Another explanation is that women have a tendency to be more tolerant in their judgment of individual differences (Stake and Katz, 1982). Still another explanation is that women attribute different motivations than do men to slower workers; for instance, women are more likely to view slower workers as being more conscientious or as working under internal constraints such as poor training or lower ability (Stake, 1985).

Communication and Normative Pressure

Another feature commonly found by studies of cooperation in social dilemmas is the lack of communication between group members. Many social dilemmas involve group members who are extended in time and space. In one experiment, group members were faced with a resource conservation dilemma. The researchers discovered that when the group members had the opportunity to discuss their dilemma before choosing to cooperate or to serve their self-interest, they made significantly more cooperative choices than (1) members of groups with no prior discussion or (2) members of groups who engaged in discussion about a topic irrelevant to the dilemma (Dawes, McTavish, and Shaklee, 1977). As is common in social psychology, this study raised more questions than it answered. For example, *why* did communication among group members alter their cooperation?

One possible answer is that the content of communication among group members may make members aware of group goals and the performance standards necessary to achieve those goals. Research indicates that groups working toward challenging performance goals perform better than groups working without explicit goals (Weldon, Jehn, and Pradhan, 1991). Informal sanctions are sometimes employed to support cooperative choices. Group members might discuss how angry they would be at a noncooperator. Such a discussion may then lead members to commit themselves to cooperate (Orbell, van de

Kragt, and Dawes, 1988). Such commitments probably do much to decrease the sucker effect and, instead, enhance the trust that group members have in one another. Members who trust their colleagues to cooperate are more likely to cooperate themselves (Jackson and Harkins, 1985).

The likelihood that a sanction system will evolve depends on several factors. First, each individual's behavior must be identifiable. Second, the social dilemma facing the group members must be serious enough (that is, the consequences of noncooperation by an individual member must be very positive for the individual and very negative for the group) to warrant the costly time and effort required to develop and maintain an effective sanction system (Yamagishi, 1988). Third, the particular sanctions have to be effective. There is no guarantee that any individual member will be affected by social approval or anger. (The box "The Bank Wiring Observation Room Group" examines how one group of workers enforced the group's standards.)

Another reason why communication among group members may alter their cooperation is that it can create or enhance a group identity and cohesive bonds based on a shared problem or "common fate." The group identity reduces the psychological distance among individual members and increases their perceived responsibility for one another. It also increases the perceived efficacy of their *collective* action. The salience of a group identity increases the likelihood that the individual members will constrain their self-interests and, instead, make cooperative choices. But there is also the risk that communication will uncover existing social attitudes that could increase the *differentiation* and *competition* among individuals. (The effects of competition on performance are discussed in the box "Cooperation versus Competition.")

The Discontinuity Effect

We'll conclude our discussion of cooperation with the observation, made by social psychologists Chester Insko, John Schopler, and their col-

THE BANK WIRING OBSERVATION ROOM GROUP

How do groups enforce their norms? As part of a series of studies at the Western Electric Company's Hawthorne Works in Chicago, a group of researchers tried to answer this question. They examined a group called the "Bank Wiring Observation Room Group" (Roethlisberger and Dickson, 1939). The group was composed of fourteen men who were engaged in making parts of switches for telephone equipment. Nine workers connected wires to terminals, three soldered the connections, and two inspected the finished product.

The wages of an individual worker were made up of two parts. One part was an hourly wage based largely on the worker's own past record of productivity. The other part was a percentage of the wages *the group* earned for their total productivity. If a worker increased his outputs while the other workers did not, it would have little effect on his earnings. On the other hand, if all the other workers increased their outputs while he held his constant, his wages would increase. Under these wage conditions, the researchers expected the group to increase their total production.

However, this proved not to be what happened. The workers had developed their own standards as to the right amount of output to achieve in a given day. This was their definition of "doing a fair day's work for a fair day's pay." They worked hard in the morning until their production standard was in sight. Then they took it easy in the afternoon. As quitting time approached, more time was devoted to conversation, games, and equipment care.

The group had methods of enforcing their production norm. Ridicule was one method. A worker who worked too fast was called "rate buster" or "speed king." If he worked too slowly, he was called a "chiseler." He was cutting down the earnings of the group. Nonconforming workers were also likely to be "binged"—given a sharp blow on the upper arm. As a result of this enforcement, the average hourly output of the workers changed little from week to week.

This is an example of how group enforcement can increase individual conformity to group norms. Support for group norms and the enforcement of those norms is strongest when individuals do *not* have an independent, noncooperative response available. Such a situation maximizes their dependence on the collective behavior of the group for outcomes.

leagues (1990), that a person may face the choice of whether to cooperate as an individual (interindividual choice) or as a member of a group (intergroup choice). The research we have discussed in this chapter has focused on interindividual choice—an individual's choice between cooperating with other individuals or going it alone. In intergroup choice, a member of a group must decide whether to cooperate with *another group*. This might occur, for example, if a feminist group and a gay group are deciding whether to join forces in support of a political candidate.

Insko and his colleagues have found that when a person is acting as a member of a group, the likelihood that she or he will cooperate is even lower than it is when the person is acting as a single individual. This is called the **discontinuity effect**. The researchers offer two explanations for

this effect: (1) People hold general beliefs that intergroup relations are marked by ingroup-outgroup differences, and characterize members of the outgroup as having negative characteristics (untrustworthy, unfriendly, aggressive, and so on). Most beliefs about interindividual relations are not so negative. (2) The presence of other group members provides social support for each member's acting in a manner consistent with immediate self-interest. In other words, to be noncooperative is to be conforming.

Summary

1. Social psychologists are interested in how the presence and behavior of other people influence the individual's performance on tasks.

COOPERATION VERSUS COMPETITION

The reward structure of a classroom may be either competitive or cooperative. In most classrooms students compete for a limited number of high grades. Grading "on the curve" is a competitive reward structure. In contrast, few classrooms are organized so that a student succeeds only if the other members of the class (or subgroup) succeed. This would be a cooperative reward structure.

Does the traditional competitive structure create better academic performances by increasing the individuals' "competitive juices" so that they want to be the best in the class? Or does it lead to poorer academic performances by (1) motivating students to interfere with the performances of other students and (2) leading students with a history of poor performance to give up? Research has found that a competitive reward structure produces less attraction and friendly behavior among students than a cooperative structure (Johnson, Johnson, and Maruyama, 1984). But how do cooperation and competition affect academic success? A review of more than 120 studies, including many in educational settings, concluded that students generally perform *poorer* under competition than they do under cooperation (Johnson et al., 1981).

But we should be careful about predicting how cooperation and competition will affect performances *in any specific situation*. Remember, the relative effects of cooperative and individual tasks depend on several factors — identifiability, reward distribution, and communication. The same can be said about cooperative and competitive tasks. For example, the authors of the review mentioned above conclude that competition can increase academic performance when the competition is *between small groups* whose members are themselves cooperating with one another.

Another factor that has a tremendous effect on the comparative advantages of cooperation and competition is the opportunity for interference. Some situations allow competing individuals to interfere with one another's performance. Other situations require the individuals to compete separately without any such interference. Competitive sports differ in amount of interference permitted. Tennis, wrestling, boxing, and auto racing allow interference; gymnastics, swimming, golf, and track do not. The competition among salespersons or vice presidents can involve either considerable interference or none. So can the competition for the attention of a third party, such as that among siblings for their parents' attention or between two males for the attention of a female. When interference opportunities are *not* available, an individual must rely on maximizing performance as the only way to compete successfully.

But we have noted that cooperation also has its interference costs. These sometimes come in the form of poor coordination between individuals. The quarterback can make a perfect pass, but the flanker might drop it. Or costs may come in the form of social loafing. Whether a cooperative or competitive task fosters higher performance depends on the interference opportunities existing in each.

When performing in an audience or coaction task, we sometimes perform *better*, and other times *worse*, than when performing the same behavior alone. The presence of others generally facilitates the performance of well-learned or simple behaviors but inhibits the performance of novel, unpracticed behaviors or complex tasks.

2. Conformity is behavior in accordance with norms. Factors affecting conformity include individual factors such as the need for information to solve a problem, social approval, gender, and status; task characteristics such as the size of the majority, unanimity of the majority, and timing of dissent; and cultural factors. A number of experiments have demonstrated the ability of a minority to influence the majority.

3. Cooperative tasks — those in which the collective activities of several individuals affect the outcomes (rewards and costs) of each of the individuals — sometimes lead to group polarization and groupthink. A number of studies have identified the tendency for individuals to perform less well on a cooperative task than

they do individually; this is the social loafing phenomenon.

4. When faced with social dilemmas we are apparently sometimes motivated to withhold our own cooperative responses, assuming that others will provide for the public good (the free-rider effect) or fearing that if we make the cooperative response, others will take advantage of our contributions and refrain from cooperating (the sucker effect). Tasks that mask individuals' contributions especially decrease cooperation. The reward structure of a task also affects cooperation. Equitable reward distributions appear to increase our motivation to cooperate. Communication also appears to improve cooperation.

5. A person is more likely to cooperate as an individual with other individuals than as a group member with other groups — a tendency called the discontinuity effect. Social psychologists hypothesize that this is partly due to people's tendency to negatively stereotype outgroups and thus to distrust them. In addition, when an individual is making a choice as a member of a group, other group members may provide support for his or her noncooperative response.

CHAPTER 10

HELPING AND REWARD EXCHANGE

You have just been to a late movie. You walk the two blocks to the lot where you parked your car — only to find that it has a flat tire. You have never fixed a flat by yourself. Several people walk by and seem to notice your ineptness at removing the tire, but they continue on to their own cars. Finally, an older man stops and asks if he can assist you. On receiving your relieved "Yes!" he changes your tire and sends you on your way.

You have to get to your bank to deposit a check from your parents. If you don't do it before 3 P.M., a check you just wrote will bounce. You ask your roommate to drive you to the bank. He does, and you deposit the check. When you both return to the apartment, he says the phone bill needs to be paid but he is "a little short." He asks if you could pay his share until he gets a paycheck next Friday. That evening you mail a check to the telephone company.

This chapter will focus on situations similar to these examples. In the first example, one person engages in behavior that benefits another person. For want of a more technical term, let's call such behavior **helping**. We concluded our last chapter with a discussion of cooperative responses, and it may seem as if we are continuing that discussion here. But, although the concepts are similar, there

is a distinction between cooperative responses and helping. A cooperative response is a behavior engaged in by one person that, *in combination with the behaviors of others*, produces benefits for *all those involved*. In contrast, helping is a behavior engaged in by one person that produces benefits for *another person*. In the flat-tire example, if you had been accompanied by a friend, you and your friend might have *cooperated* in fixing the tire.

In the second example, two people perform helping behaviors for each other. In this case, each performs a behavior that benefits the other. This exchange of benefits is called **reward exchange**. What distinguishes reward exchange from individual helping behavior is that in reward exchange the behavior of *each* individual provides benefits for the *other*. We'll begin our discussion with a focus on individual helping behavior.

Helping Behavior

In the early hours of a March morning in 1964, Kitty Genovese was returning home from a night job when a male assailant attacked and stabbed her. In response to her screams, at least thirty-eight residents in the respectable New York City neighborhood looked out their windows and witnessed the attack. A number shouted, "Leave the girl alone!" At first, the attacker ran away, but he returned and stabbed the young woman again. Once more there was a commotion and the assailant fled, only to come back a third time and complete the murder. No one went to the woman's assistance or called the police until after she was dead. Then one person called the police, but only after he first checked with a friend by telephone about the advisability of doing so. The case attracted national attention. News and other media commentators branded the incident "a national disgrace" and spoke of "the dehumanization of society," "a case of moral callousness," "the cold society," "apathy," "indifference," and "a loss of human decency and compassion."

Happenings such as the Genovese case are not unique to New York City. Newspapers throughout the nation periodically report similar incidents. In Columbus, Ohio, a man punched a woman several times in the face and made off with her wallet. The attack took place in a downtown bank parking lot in clear view of at least a half-dozen witnesses. The onlookers did nothing. Indeed, they quickly left the scene lest they be asked to identify the assailant (*Columbus* [Ohio] *Dispatch*, July 25, 1981). And in New Bedford, Massachusetts, when a young mother of two entered a bar to buy cigarettes, a man grabbed her, stripped off her clothes, and raped her on the barroom floor. Other male patrons then lifted her onto a pool table and raped her repeatedly, to the cheers and applause of onlookers. Although the assault lasted for more than an hour, none of the at least fifteen other male customers came to her aid or called the police (*Newsweek*, March 21, 1983: 25).

Probably no one incident has led social psychologists to pay as much attention to a single aspect of social behavior as Kitty Genovese's murder. Like many others, social psychologists wonder why people may fail to assist an individual in an emergency. Is it simply that apathy and alienation are so rampant in contemporary society that people are insensitive, indifferent, and un-

concerned with the misfortunes of others? This explanation appears to be refuted by examples of heroic behavior in response to emergencies. On one local television news program, the authors saw two reports of such cases: one was about a person who waded into a swollen river to save the life of a rafter clinging to a tree branch, and the other was about two men who chased a purse-snatcher, one of whom was struck during the chase by a car driven by the snatcher's accomplice. And in our everyday lives, we observe people donating their time, effort, and limited resources for the benefit of others. Analysis of national survey data indicates that about half of all Americans performed some kind of volunteer work in the past twelve months (Clary and Snyder, 1991). So why is it that people sometimes do help others but other times don't?

THE GOOD SAMARITAN: THE HELPFUL PERSONALITY

Many psychologists have been interested in identifying *traits* — relatively enduring ways in which individuals differ. Traits refer to descriptive characteristics: an individual may be more or less passive, more or less cooperative, more or less adventurous, and so on. We infer people's traits, as we do their motives, from their behavior in various environmental settings.

Comparing 231 Gentiles who saved Jews in Nazi Europe with 126 nonrescuers, researchers found that rescuers not only had stronger beliefs in equity, greater empathy, and feelings of responsibility for others but also were distinguished by a sense of self-competence (Oliner and Oliner, 1988). They viewed themselves as being in control of their lives and were inclined to take calculated risks. Moreover, the rescuers had to have at their disposal the wherewithal to put their values and sense of competence into action. They may have been expert skiers who could escort Jews across the Alps to Switzerland, or they may have had a large home or estate where they could hide Jews. Other studies have confirmed the importance of *self-efficacy* — feelings of competence or being in control — as a determinant of helping (Peterson, 1983; Midlarsky, 1984; Batson et al., 1986).

Often the rescuers of Jews initially made only a small commitment, such as to hide a person for a day or so. However, once they took the first step, they began to define themselves differently, as persons who help others. For instance, Raoul Wallenberg, the Swedish diplomat who used his position to save hundreds of Hungarian Jews, started by rescuing a Hungarian-Jewish business partner. Soon Wallenberg was manufacturing passes that made Jews eligible for Swedish citizenship and hence exempt from German capture. As Wallenberg's involvement grew, he exposed himself to considerable risk by providing passes to Jews waiting in line for deportation trains (Goleman, 1985). It appears that after small and sometimes reluctant helping efforts, the individual incorporates helping as part of his or her self-image. By coming to see himself or herself as the kind of person who helps, the individual increases the likelihood that he or she will engage in helping behavior (Smith and Shaffer, 1986).

Not all psychologists accept the notion that human behavior is sufficiently consistent and stable to warrant conceiving of it in terms of "helping personalities." On the contrary, a person who engages in helping behavior on one occasion may not do so on another occasion (Hampson, 1984; Romer, Gruder, and Lizzadro, 1986). Instead, such behavior is largely a function of the specific situations in which people find themselves.

John M. Darley and C. Daniel Batson (1973) have reached somewhat similar conclusions on the basis of a study in which they tested the influence of religiosity on helping. The subjects were students at Princeton Theological Seminary. None of the religious variables predicted whether or not a seminarian would help the victim (a confederate of the experimenters who sat slumped motionless in an alleyway, coughing and groaning with his head down and eyes closed). Nor did it matter that some of the young men were on their way to deliver a lecture on the biblical parable of the good Samaritan. Indeed, Darley and Batson report that one seminarian literally stepped over the victim as he hurried to give his lecture.

URBAN AND RURAL DIFFERENCES: ENVIRONMENTAL EFFECTS ON HELPING

While psychologists have looked at personality for explanations of helping, sociologists have looked at the environment. Sociologists ask, for example: "Who is more likely to come to the aid of another person — residents of small towns or those who live in urban centers?" The folklore of small towns would have you believe that small-town residents are more likely to help others, even strangers. But is the folklore true? And if it is, what is it about small towns and cities that creates the difference in their residents' helpfulness? Is it the people themselves? Or does it have something to do with their environment?

In a nutshell, research supports this folklore. An examination of all the research to date indicates that people in small towns are more helpful to strangers than are those in larger communities (Steblay, 1987). It also shows that the size of the town in which a person grew up is unrelated to helping. Instead, the *current* environment, the one in which help is needed, affects the likelihood of helping behavior. In fact, persons from small-town backgrounds may be *less* likely to respond helpfully in an urban environment than those with city backgrounds (Holahan, 1977).

One of the best studies of the urban-rural difference in helping behavior was conducted in several large cities and small towns in Australia (Amato, 1983). To ensure that the results of the study would not be restricted to just one kind of helping behavior, five different situations were studied: (1) witnessing a man with a bandaged leg fall to the ground and cry out in pain, (2) overhearing a salesclerk give obviously wrong directions to someone, (3) receiving a request to donate money to the Multiple Sclerosis Society, (4) being asked by a student pedestrian to write down one's favorite color as part of a school project, and (5) seeing a pedestrian inadvertently drop an envelope on the sidewalk.

Of the five helping behaviors, the study found that the percentage of people performing four of the behaviors was greater in small towns than in large cities. For example, nearly half of those in small towns stopped to help the man with the bloody, bandaged leg; in large urban areas, only about 20 percent gave him assistance. The one exception involved the pedestrian dropping an envelope. For some reason, only a small percentage of people helped in this situation, *regardless* of where they lived. So even though the *overall* likelihood of being helped is greater in smaller towns than in larger cities, it appears that in a particular situation the likelihood may depend partly on the type of helping behavior in question.

Social psychologists have proposed some possible explanations for why residents of communities of different sizes are differentially responsive to helping situations. Does urban life make for greater anonymity (low identifiability) that allows people to hide their inactivity in a large crowd? Do urbanites face a daily diet of stimulus overload — exposure to a high density of heterogeneous people — that makes them insensitive to the needs of others? Hopefully, future research will provide answers to these questions.

STEPS INVOLVED IN HELPING

Social psychologists Bibb Latané and John M. Darley launched a research program exploring the *situational* factors that influence helping behavior. Latané and Darley (1970) proposed several steps bystanders use in deciding whether to intervene in an emergency. For purposes of our discussion, we will make some adjustments in their proposal and apply the revision to *all* helping behavior, both in emergency and in nonemergency situations. We'll examine five steps: (1) noticing the event, (2) interpreting the situation as one in which help is needed, (3) assessing whether help is deserved, (4) determining responsibility for helping, and

(5) deciding what to do. Figure 10-1 illustrates the decision process linking these steps.

Noticing the Event

The first step in helping occurs when our attention is drawn to a particular event. Do we notice the person slumped in the doorway, the child crying in the middle of the shopping mall, a friend's feeling depressed, a request to give blood to the Red Cross? We can't help if we don't notice the event.

This may explain the differences in helping among urban and rural residents. Urbanites face a daily diet of stimulus overload, including a high density of heterogeneous people. To cope with this information overload, city residents may limit the amount of information they attend to. Both experimental and survey research supports this proposal. In an experiment involving college students, some participants were required to do two tasks at once, while others were required to do the tasks one at a time (Weiner, 1976). When a young woman unexpectedly came into the participant's room and tripped and fell, participants working on the two tasks simultaneously (high overload) were less likely to offer her help than were those working on the tasks sequentially (low overload). In a survey of residents in cities and towns in Holland, it was found that information load was the only factor explaining the differences in helping between big-city and small-town residents (Korte, Ypma, and Toppen, 1975).

Curiously, one study indicated that even a difference in noise levels can affect helping (Mathews and Canon, 1975). In a laboratory setting, noise decreased the likelihood that students would help a person who dropped some papers on the floor. In the presence of regular room noise, 72 percent of the students helped pick up the papers; only 37 percent did so when a very loud noise was present. The researchers took the same idea outside the laboratory where they had a man wearing a cast on his arm drop some of the books he was carrying. When only typical street noises were present, 80 percent of the passersby helped

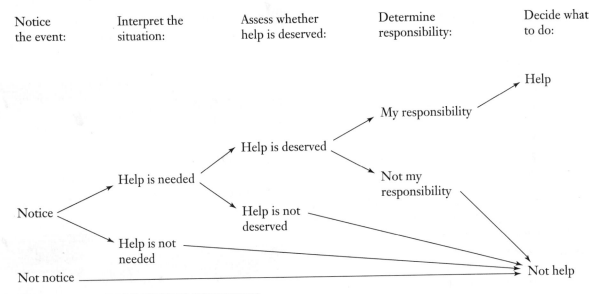

FIGURE 10-1 STEPS INVOLVED IN HELPING

pick up his books; when a noisy lawn mower was operating nearby, only 15 percent helped. The researchers thought that either the noise distracted the passersby, so they didn't notice the event, or the cost of having to listen to the noise while helping the man was too great. What do you think?

Interpreting the Situation: Is Help Needed?

Many emergencies begin as *ambiguous* events. A man staggering about may be having a heart attack, experiencing the onset of a diabetic episode, or simply suffering from drunkenness. What appears to be smoke pouring from a building may be an indication of fire or may be merely steam. Within such settings, people may have considerable difficulty in interpreting an event.

To explore subjects' reactions to ambiguous events, Latané, Darley, and their colleagues undertook experiments in a number of different contexts. In one experiment, heavy smoke filtered into the room where the subjects were working (Latané and Darley, 1968). In another, subjects overheard a person having an epileptic seizure in an adjoining room (Darley and Latané, 1968). In still another, subjects overheard a woman experi-

menter fall and cry out for help (Latané and Rodin, 1969). The researchers varied the conditions under which subjects learned of the emergency: each subject was either alone, with another naive subject, or with a passive, nonreacting person (a confederate of the researchers).

When confronted with an ambiguous event, individuals observe the reactions of other bystanders and are powerfully influenced by them. If others take the event calmly, without apparent concern or anxiety, a bystander is led to interpret the situation as "not serious" and thus as not requiring personal action. For example, in the Latané and Darley (1968) experiment in which smoke filtered into the workroom, 75 percent of the subjects who were alone reported the smoke, compared with 38 percent of the pairs in the naive condition, and only 10 percent of the pairs in the passive-confederate condition. Thus we take cues from the behavior of others in the social situation; if no one else is helping, we have doubts about whether the victim actually needs help. In everyday life, we may assume that someone else has already called the police or the hospital.

Since social reality is often ambiguous, we rely to some extent on other people's reactions to define the meaning for us. This is analogous to our discussion in the previous chapter on conformity in ambiguous situations. On the basis of our observations of what other people say and do—whether they are responsive or unresponsive to a stimulus—we conclude that the situation is one that either merits or does not merit our intervention.

In light of these considerations, it is perhaps not surprising that experimental evidence shows that helping is much more likely to occur in *unambiguous* situations, especially in emergencies (Shotland and Huston, 1979). Russell D. Clark and Larry E. Word (1972, 1974) set up an "emergency" that was designed to be less ambiguous than the events provided by Latané and his associates. In a room adjoining the subjects' workroom, a maintenance worker (a confederate) climbed a metal ladder, fell off, and pulled the ladder over on top of himself. He grunted heavily and exclaimed, "Oh, my back; I can't move!" He continued groaning with each breath; then he gave a cry for help. In *all* conditions—whether subjects were alone, with other naive subjects, or with confederates of the researchers—100 percent of the subjects went to the aid of the victim. In a second experiment, Clark and Word staged the same fall in an ambiguous manner, without any verbal cues of injury. Under these circumstances, only 30 percent of the subjects helped.

In another unambiguous situation, Irving M. Piliavin, Judith Rodin, and Jane Allyn Piliavin (1969) found that help was forthcoming in sixty-two out of sixty-five trials (95 percent) involving a faked emergency on a New York subway train. Shortly after entering the train, a young man with a cane staggered forward and collapsed. As in the Clark and Word experiments, this emergency was unambiguous; indeed, it was not only heard but seen.

Assessing Who's at Fault: Is Help Deserved?

Is it as simple as that? All we have to do is clearly see that someone is in trouble, and we'll go to his or her aid? Not quite. Once we've identified a problem that seems to call for helping, we may want to know whose fault it was. In a variation of

the subway experiment, Piliavin and his colleagues altered the characteristics of the person needing help. For the young man with a cane, they substituted an apparently drunk young man (smelling of liquor and carrying a liquor bottle). Bystanders came to the aid of the drunk victim in only 50 percent of the trials, compared with 95 percent of the trials involving the man with the cane.

Bernard Weiner (1980; Schmidt and Weiner, 1988) points out that bystanders typically make inferences (attributions) regarding the causes of a person's difficulties. Persons assumed to be ill (which might have been inferred from the cane carried by the man in the original subway experiment) are usually viewed as having little personal control over their misfortunes. In contrast, drunkenness is perceived as personally controllable. Consequently, illness is more likely than drunkenness to elicit sympathy in bystanders and to result in their rendering assistance. But drunkenness typically triggers feelings of disgust. Presumably a drunk is seen as less deserving of help because he or she is at least partly responsible for the difficulty. Consequently, the drunk is helped less often.

Unfortunately, it appears that helping is often inhibited by our tendency to reason that *most* victims deserve their suffering, at least to some degree. Melvin J. Lerner (1980*a*) proposes that we rely heavily on the **just-world hypothesis**. Lerner suggests that we have a need to believe that we live in a just world—one in which people get what they deserve and deserve what they get. In such a world, deserving people are rewarded and the undeserving are punished.

The just-world concern is not always translated into helping behavior. Another way of reestablishing justice is by persuading ourselves that the victim deserves to suffer (Wyer, Bodenhausen, and Gorman, 1985). We blame a seemingly innocent victim in order to convince ourselves that there is no injustice in the victim's suffering, that the victim got exactly what was deserved. This is called *derogating the victim*. We assume that responsibility lies in some bad quality within the victim. In other words, we *infer* an internal attri-

---

STUDENT OBSERVATION

The Just-World Hypothesis

I believe that many rape trials illustrate the operation of the *just-world hypothesis*. Often, a victim is put on trial herself, as jurors decide whether or not she "deserved" to be raped. The just-world hypothesis asserts that we live in a fair and just world where people deserve what they get and get what they deserve. Therefore, if a woman is raped and the society we live in is just, then she must have deserved to be raped. If she had a promiscuous reputation or if she wore alluring clothes, then she must "have asked for it." In essence, she was bad, so she must suffer.

The hypothesis further asserts that if other people (including the rape victim) suffer unfairly, then there is a possibility that each of us (the jurors) could also suffer unjustly, and this is not acceptable, so we must believe that the world is just. These feelings lead jurors to assume that the victim deserved to be raped as a way of denying the possibility that they themselves could also suffer unjustly. By believing that suffering is only for those who deserve it, then suffering can be avoided by being "good."

---

bution for the victim's suffering. Consequently, we lower our opinion of the victim. This kind of reasoning is most likely when we believe that the victim's suffering will continue and that we are powerless to help (Lerner and Simmons, 1966; Lincoln and Levinger, 1972).

In a test of the hypothesis, Lerner showed subjects a televised session in which a supposed victim (actually a confederate) received painful electric shocks for incorrect responses in a "learning" experiment (Lerner and Simmons, 1966). In one condition, subjects saw the victim willingly enter the room where the experiment was to be held. In another, the "martyr condition," the victim at first refused to enter the room. She reluctantly agreed only after being told that as a result of her refusal, the subjects would not receive course credit for participating in the experiment. In a third condition, the confederate received no shocks; all her responses were correct and she was rewarded for them. Later, subjects were asked to rate the confederates on their general attractiveness.

The confederate in the martyr condition was judged *least* attractive. To justify her misfortune (the shocks), especially when she appeared to be so noble, the subjects devalued her; in effect, she was seen as deserving her suffering. In contrast, the confederate who had been rewarded was judged most attractive; in effect, she was defined

in positive terms to justify her good fortune. A number of other studies have been interpreted as supporting the just-world hypothesis (Simons and Piliavin, 1972; Apsler and Friedman, 1975).

There may be occasions, however, in which dismissing the misfortune of others as the product of their own misdoings becomes difficult. When we perceive the victim as being similar to us — perhaps in age, race, or other attributes — we feel it disconcerting to fault the person. To do so would be much like devaluing or blaming ourselves. Accordingly, we assign less responsibility for their own victimization to people who are similar to us than to people who are dissimilar. A review of studies found that subjects did, in fact, help similar others significantly more than they helped dissimilar others (Dovidio, 1984). (Before reading further, look at the Student Observation: "The Just-World Hypothesis.")

Determining Responsibility to Help

Even when we've decided that someone needs and deserves help, we don't always help the person. Before we actually help, we must decide that it is our *personal responsibility* to help. Let's look at several factors that affect this decision.

Cultural norms of sympathy and responsibility. Among the factors influencing the likelihood of our engaging in helping behavior are the norms of our society that prescribe helping others. Sociologist Candace Clark (1987) suggests that **sympathy norms** not only prescribe that we should care about others but also specify how we should respond to their problems, depending on the nature of the difficulty and the person's relationship to us. Clark gathered data from several sources: (1) she observed sympathy interactions in natural settings such as hospitals, funeral homes, and offices; (2) she conducted intensive interviews in which she asked people to describe specific instances in which they experienced either the presence or the absence of sympathy interactions; and (3) she conducted a survey that asked respondents about their sympathetic reactions to vignettes depicting others' plights.

Clark discovered that sympathy norms obligate us in three ways: First, they obligate us to be empathetic — to search for information about another's problem (putting ourselves in the other's situation). Second, they prescribe that we feel sympathy toward others, that is, care about the welfare of others. Although a minimum level of sympathy is owed to strangers, people involved in our close relationships are due a greater latitude of sympathy. For example, we are expected to feel sympathetic toward strangers in a disaster, but our friends and loved ones should be able to count on our sympathies for their *minor* problems as well as for their disasters. Third, we are obligated to display sympathy appropriate to the person and the plight — through facial expressions, postures, tone of voice, words, and actions.

This is not to say that sympathy norms require us to be indiscriminately sympathetic. The sympathy due another is not constant; rather, it may

Sympathy norms obligate us to be empathetic, to feel sympathy toward others, and to display sympathy — through facial expressions, postures, tone of voice, words, and actions — appropriate to the person and the plight. Major problems are expected to elicit sympathy even for strangers, but we are expected to display sympathy even for the *minor* problems of friends and loved ones.

increase, decrease, and even be extinguished altogether. Clark says these changes are determined by a "sympathy account," in which a person can earn sympathy credits or debits. Her research found evidence of four rules guiding our concern for others:

1. *Do not make false claims to sympathy.* That is, do not falsely manipulate others' sympathy by pretending to need it, by exaggerating claims, or by courting disaster with the intent to gain others' sympathy. People interviewed by Clark felt "conned," "taken advantage of," or "betrayed" when others violated this rule. False claims draw on a person's sympathy account to a point where she or he "cries wolf" once too often, the account becomes bankrupt, and we judge the person to have become less deserving of our sympathy.

2. *Do not claim too much sympathy.* Even when legitimate grounds exist, one can claim "too much" sympathy. People tend to lose patience when others expect too much sympathy. In such cases, the troubled person's repeated claims may fall on deaf ears. A teacher in her thirties, beset by a sympathy seeker, explained:

> Every time I see her, I think, "Here we go again!" She's like a broken record. "Sam did this to me; Sam didn't do that for me." I'm sorry, but a lot of us have been through divorces and survived. She's gone completely overboard. (Clark, 1987: 305)*

What is defined as "too much" is related to the duration of one's problem. Problems that are over quickly, such as a painful shot for the flu, should be expected to elicit minimal sympathy. Intermediate-range problems, such as the flu itself, warrant more sympathy. But if the problem persists over a long duration — as in the case of a chronic illness, unemployment, or a sequence of different problems — sympathy will begin to diminish. A victim of severe or enduring problems is expected to deflect some of the sympathy offered by others: "I'm

doing okay. It could have been worse. At least we are still alive and have each other. And I'm sure we will be stronger for it." This is particularly true when the person offering sympathy has his or her own problems to worry about.

3. *Claim some sympathy.* Clark's interviewees indicated that one must claim or accept some sympathy from time to time. This rule applies to the person who gives sympathy without accepting it. If we do not claim some sympathy, we appear too lofty or too self-possessed. If we both give and receive sympathy, we will be defined as members of the group — friends or intimates. If not, we will soon find our sympathy accounts closed! A young female editor who rarely claimed sympathy described a time when she needed it:

> I was so surprised — shocked — at the reaction of my colleagues last week. I had to give a big presentation that lasted two days. I've done shorter ones before, but this was frightening. I found myself getting nervous and tried to talk to my friends about it. They just said, "Oh, you'll do okay. You always do." Not an ounce of sympathy! And these were "near" friends, too, not just people I know. (Clark, 1987: 309)*

4. *Reciprocate to others for the gift of sympathy.* One is expected to repay another's sympathy with gratitude, deference, or reciprocal sympathy. If we fail to repay our debts to others when suitable occasions arise, our sympathy accounts will be diminished or closed altogether. As a 70-year-old retired secretary put it:

> I was by her side at her mother's funeral. Where was she when my brothers died? I don't count her as part of the family any more. (Clark, 1987: 312)*

The type of return expected for sympathy received varies with the relative status of donor and recipient. "Equals" usually give equal gratitude or sympathy for sympathy received. On the other hand, this is seldom true among people of different statuses. Their exchanges are expressions of their unequal status. A superior who gives sympathy to a subordinate expects deference, not sympathy, in exchange. A subordinate who gives sympathy to a superior does not expect much of any kind of return. (Before reading further, see the Student Observation: "Sympathy Norms.")

Another norm related to helping is the **norm of social responsibility**. This norm prescribes that we should help others who are in need and who are dependent on us. There is less evidence for this norm than there is for the sympathy norms identified by Clark. One reason for this may be that social psychologists have looked for a *general* norm of social responsibility that regulates our helping behavior across many different kinds of situations. Maybe they should take a lesson from Clark. She increased our understanding of sympathy norms by recognizing that there are several sympathy norms — not a single, general norm — and that specific conditions determine how these norms operate. We are more sympathetic in some situations and toward some people

than others. The same may be true of social responsibility. Social psychologists who have looked more closely at the normative factors influencing helping in different situations have discovered a number of specific responsibility norms that identify when and whom we are expected to help. We'll discuss the results of some of their studies in the next three subsections: diffusion of responsibility, sex-role expectations, and relationship expectations.

Diffusion of responsibility. The probability that an individual will help in an emergency decreases as the number of strangers who witness the emergency increases (Howard and Crano, 1974; Mynatt and Sherman, 1975; Latané and Nida, 1981). When others are present, **diffusion of responsibility** may occur. Both the obligation to assist and the potential blame for not acting are spread around. Something like this apparently occurred in the Kitty Genovese murder: each observer, seeing lights and figures in nearby apartment-house windows, knew that others were also watching. But when only one bystander is present in an emergency, help must come from the bystander if it is to come at all, so the pressures to intervene are focused on an individual.

Diffusion of responsibility seemingly accounts for the outcome in the Darley and Latané (1968) experiment in which subjects overheard a person

---

STUDENT OBSERVATION

Sympathy Norms

Recently, one of my friends subtly reminded me of one of the sympathy norms discussed in the text — "Do not claim too much sympathy." I tend to take most of my problems to this friend rather than to my other friends, and I often exaggerate how bad a problem really is. Well, a couple of weeks ago we were talking and she told me about one of her old friends who was coming to visit from New England. She was not particularly looking forward to seeing him, and she explained that he constantly complains about his problems and makes her tired of hearing about them. Her friend had violated a sympathy norm, and she was explaining the adverse effect the violation had. I realized that if I kept up my own complaints, I too would be violating the norm about claiming too much sympathy. Whether she was trying to drop a hint to me or not, I drew the conclusion that my friend definitely operates according to this sympathy norm.

STUDENT OBSERVATION

Diffusion of Responsibility

Recently, while traveling home on Interstate 85, I came upon a car with its hazard lights flashing and hood up. A middle-aged man wearing blue jeans and a polo shirt stood in front of the car, staring under the hood. No one had stopped to help him. As I passed, I thought that I really should stop to see if I could get some assistance for him. However, my thoughts quickly turned to the "worst-case scenario": What if this man plans to harm the person who stops to help him? There was no way I was stopping with such thoughts racing through my mind. To make my conscience feel better for not stopping to help, I told myself that there were plenty of other motorists on the highway and one of them would stop to help the man. In social psychological terminology, I *diffused the responsibility* for helping onto the other motorists. Consequently, I will never know how long the man was stranded by the side of the road.

---

having an epileptic seizure. Whereas 85 percent of the subjects who were alone reported the seizure, only 31 percent of those who thought four other people were present did so. In sum, Latané and Darley (1970) conclude that safety does not necessarily lie in numbers. A "surplus" of helpers reduces responsibility; this finding is known as the *bystander effect.* (See the Student Observation: "Diffusion of Responsibility.")

There are exceptions to the bystander effect. Most research conducted on the bystander effect has involved individuals who were strangers at the time of the emergency. In such settings, group cohesiveness is usually low. However, if bystanders are cohesive — if they know one another and have ties with one another — they are *more* likely to intervene when they are part of a larger group rather than a smaller one (Rutkowski, Gruder, and Romer, 1983). Apparently, cohesiveness increases responsiveness to social responsibility norms that prescribe helping. Thus, *social cohesiveness* tends to cancel the negative effect of diffusion of responsibility in a group of bystanders.

Some situations may require that more than a single bystander intervene for helping to be successful. The *need for multiple intervenors* may also cancel the negative effect of diffusion of responsibility in a group of bystanders. For example, one study simulating a rape found that groups of males were more likely to intervene than were individual males (Harari, Harari, and White, 1985).

Diffusion of responsibility can also be reduced by having people *commit themselves in advance* to assist another person under given circumstances. For instance, Thomas Moriarty (1975) found that bystanders at a public beach more readily intervened to stop the theft of a portable radio from an unattended beach blanket if they had previously agreed to watch the victim's belongings. Similarly, individuals in two midtown Manhattan Automat cafeterias who were asked to watch another person's suitcase intervened substantially more often to stop the theft of the suitcase than those who were not asked. In addition, if bystanders expect to have *future face-to-face interaction* with a person in distress, they are more likely to provide help than if they do not expect future interaction (Gottlieb and Carver, 1980). Indeed, even *informal social contact* seems to activate a latent sense of obligation. "Familiar strangers" — for instance, the person one sees at the bus stop every day without ever exchanging a word — have been known to act with extraordinary kindness in a crisis (Cunningham, 1984).

Sex-role expectations. Who helps more — men or women? If you combined the results of all the studies noted in this chapter (and others we could have included), you would find that men are more likely than women to engage in helping behavior (Eagly and Crowley, 1986). Interesting? Are you somewhat skeptical? Well, perhaps you should be. Let's take another look at some of the results.

Men acted more frequently than women to help an individual when:

• The individual was a stranded motorist and the help involved changing a tire or mechanical work (West, Whitney, and Schnedler, 1975).

• The individual was a workman with a severely bleeding leg (Shotland and Heinold, 1985).

• The individual was a man with a cane (or brown paper bag) who fell in a subway car and suffered a bleeding mouth (Piliavin and Piliavin, 1972).

• The individual was a woman who dropped her groceries (Wispé and Freshley, 1971).

• The stranger needing help was a woman.

• Women perceived the situation as more dangerous than men did.

• No direct request for help was made.

• An audience witnessed the helping.

Women provided help more frequently than men when:

• A friend needed a personal favor, emotional support, or counseling about personal problems (Aires and Johnson, 1983; Johnson and Aires, 1983; Berg, 1984).

• A friend needed "someone to talk to" (Otten, Penner, and Waugh, 1988).

Men and women did not differ in giving help to a man having an epileptic seizure (Darley and Latané, 1968) and in intervening to keep a drunk person from driving (Rabow et al., 1990).

Most of the studies of helping in emergencies that required physical intervention used only men as subjects (e.g., Latané and Rodin, 1969). The few studies focusing more on empathic responses in nonemergency situations, such as donations, used women (Toi and Batson, 1982).

Some social psychologists propose that results like these—along with other sex differences that we discussed elsewhere in the text—can best be interpreted as the result of sex roles (Eagly and Crowley, 1986). Most people in our society expect men and women to behave differently. When it comes to helping expectations, men are not expected to give *more* help than women—just *different types* of help. Whereas men are expected to give help that is heroic and chivalrous, women are expected to give help that is nurturant and caring. These gender-specific helping norms are reflected even in children's books (Barnett, 1986) and in the helping behavior of fourth-graders (Larrieu and Mussen, 1986). The selection of men or women as subjects for studies of specific types of helping behavior indicates that social psychologists themselves believe that the helping behaviors of men and women are different.

Much of the research reviewed in this chapter has involved a stranger in distress who needs the helper's physical assistance and/or places the helper in danger. On the other hand, what about helping people we know—doing personal favors for friends or providing advice about personal matters? Are women more likely than men to give these kinds of help? They are, as we shall see in the following discussion.

Relationship expectations. Gender roles are not the only source of helping expectations. Naturally, the most explicit expectations are associated with people in occupations that are sometimes called the "helping professions"—social workers, physicians and nurses, day-care workers, people at information desks. More implicit (and possibly less consensual) expectations of helping are associated with individuals we identify as "people like us," "friends," or "family." Social psychologists are just beginning to illuminate helping behavior in these kinds of relationships. The results of their research can be summarized as follows: (1) Among people without a previous relationship, individuals help others who are similar to themselves more often than they help those dissimilar to themselves. (2) People help friends more than strangers. (3) The closeness of kinship is related to both willingness to provide aid and expectations that aid will be given (Dovidio, 1984; Cunningham, 1986; Dovidio et al., 1991). Let's look at two recent studies.

Men and women in our society are expected to give *different types* of help. Whereas men are expected to give help that is heroic and chivalrous, women are expected to give help that is nurturant and caring.

Researcher Paul Amato (1990) — whose Australian study of urban-rural differences in helping behavior was discussed earlier — asked two groups of respondents in the United States to describe helping behaviors in which they had engaged during the previous week or two. The first group consisted of university students; the second, of the students' nonstudent friends and family members. From the pool of 793 helping episodes described by these individuals, Amato grouped similar types of episodes into categories of helping behavior. The following are a few examples:

1. Donated money to a charitable organization that gives assistance to needy people.
2. Donated blood or any other medical item.
3. Looked after a sick friend or relative.
4. Had a talk with a friend or relative about a personal problem he or she was experiencing.
5. Looked after a person's plants, mail, or pets while the person was away.
6. Gave directions to a stranger.
7. Helped someone pick up items that he or she had dropped.

Several results emerged from Amato's study. First, half of the helping reported by both groups was provided to friends and family. Not surprisingly, the only difference between the two

groups was that the students were more likely to report helping roommates and classmates, while the nonstudents were more likely to report helping co-workers, customers and clients, and organizations. Only about 10 percent of the reported helping behavior involved strangers. Second, *females reported significantly more helping behavior than did males*. (Amato did not separate the helping of strangers from his general measure of helping, so it is impossible to tell whether males were more likely to help strangers — as is suggested by the studies discussed earlier.) Third, factors other than gender were more powerful predictors of helping behavior. *Receiving* help was a very important predictor of *giving* help, at least when the help involved friends and relatives. And the larger a person's network of social contacts (relatives, friends, neighbors, co-workers, club and church associates), the more frequently the person engaged in helping. Evidently, the more fully one participates in social life, the more assistance one provides to others.

Researchers Alice and Peter Rossi (1990) have noted that we are so embedded in our own kinship system that we take its rules for granted. As part of a study of Boston families spanning several generations, the Rossis undertook an empirical study of kinship norms. They asked the 1,380 respondents to read vignettes describing crisis or celebratory events and to indicate on a scale of 0 (no obligation) to 10 (very strong obligation) how strongly they would feel obligated to perform the gesture in the question.

The Rossis concluded that the kind of response being asked about — giving money or comfort, giving gifts or visiting — didn't matter much, especially when the sense of obligation was strong. When we feel a strong obligation to visit someone, we are also likely to feel an obligation to give gifts, money, or comfort. Yet the type of kinship mattered a great deal in the respondents' obligation ratings. The strongest obligation for all four types of responses was found in ratings involving parents and children. A somewhat less, but still strong, obligation applied to kin connected to the respondents through a child, a parent, or a spouse. For example, respondents felt strong obligations to provide comfort in crises to siblings and grandchildren, to provide financial aid and gifts to children-in-law and siblings, and to pay visits on special occasions to grandchildren and parents-in-law. More distant kin — aunts and uncles, nieces and nephews, and cousins — evoked roughly the same level of obligation as did friends and neighbors. At the bottom of the obligation hierarchy were ex-spouses. Other research supports these findings (Waite and Harrison, 1992).

The Rossis discovered in their study that kinship norms are modified by gender. The respondents generally felt more *obligated* toward female kin than toward male kin. It also appears that we *feel closer* to female kin and to kin who are connected to us through our female relatives. When respondents were asked to indicate the extent to which a variety of relatives, friends of parents, and teachers were particularly important to them while growing up, they more often cited as "very important" grandmothers and aunts than they did grandfathers and uncles. This was especially true for maternal aunts (mother's sisters) and the maternal grandmother (mother's mother). Father's brothers and father's father were the least likely to be cited as "very important" in the early lives of respondents, and these same kin evoked the lowest obligation ratings in the study. Greater obligations were also felt toward widowed and

unmarried persons, especially women, than toward married persons of the same kin type. Gender of the *respondent* did not matter for close, primary kin — that is, men and women felt equally obligated to close relatives — but women showed higher obligation levels toward secondary and distant kin than did men. The results are summarized in Figure 10-2.

Thus far, the study had revealed the obligations people *felt* to help family members. But did these obligations result in actual helping behavior? To find out, the Rossis focused on help given to and received by parents and their adult children. They selected a variety of types of help that they felt were relevant to parents and adult children as well as to men and women. They asked each respondent to answer "yes" or "no" to whether they had given each kind of help "over the past year or so."

Table 10-1 shows the percentage of the respondents who reported having given each type of help. The table distinguishes the gender of the parent and the adult child. The percentage rates range from a low of 9 percent of daughters who reported that they gave money to their fathers to a high of 89 percent of daughters who reported that they gave a special gift to their mothers. With the exception of financial help and job leads, the highest percentages of helping behavior occur between mothers and daughters. Women are both the greater providers and the greater beneficiaries of intergenerational helping behavior. The types of help parents and their adult children gave one another were somewhat different. The parents more frequently gave their children financial aid, while the adult children more frequently gave their parents health care, comfort, and (in the case of sons) repairs.

The Rossis found that several factors (in addition to gender) affected intergenerational helping behavior. First, greater geographic distance between parents and adult children reduced their helping behavior. More interestingly, this applied not only to "hands-on" help (domestic chores, homewatching) but also to "long-distance" help that could be provided by mail or telephone (fi-

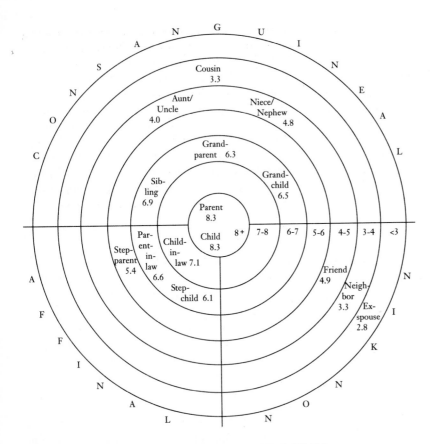

FIGURE 10-2 LAYERING OF NORMATIVE OBLIGATION
Mean ratings of financial aid obligations by type of relationship. Consanguineal
relationships are "blood" relationships; affinal relationships are ties through marriage;
the nonkin relationships included in the study were friends, neighbors, and ex-spouses.
The rings, or layers, in the diagram represent the strength of the obligations we feel
toward the types of relationships listed there. The closer the relationship is to the
middle of the circle, the stronger the obligation for providing help – in this case,
financial assistance. The number next to each relationship is the average obligation
rating the Rossis' respondents gave when asked to indicate on a scale of 0 (no
obligation) to 10 (very strong obligation) how strongly they would feel obligated to
provide financial assistance to a person in that relationship to them. [Reprinted with
permission from Alice S. Rossi and Peter H. Rossi, *Of Human Bonding: Parent-Child
Relations Across the Life Course* (New York: Aldine de Gruyter, 1990, p. 175). Copyright
© 1990 Walter de Gruyter, Inc., New York.]

nancial aid, advice). Second, the higher the income of parents, the more extensive was the help
they gave to adult children, especially low-income
children, unattached daughters, and daughters
low on "drive." Third, as parents aged beyond 40,
the help they gave their adult children steadily
declined. Simultaneously, the help they received

from their adult children remained steady or actually increased in the case of financial aid and
health care, particularly that received by elderly
mothers.

The ideas discussed throughout this section on
responsibility are explored further in the box
"Helping in Drunk-Driving Situations."

Deciding What to Do: To Help or Not to Help?

We may have noticed a situation, decided that help is needed, and believe that we should help. Now we are faced with a final step in our decision making. Do we help or not? Let's examine some of the factors affecting this final decision.

Mood. One factor influencing whether or not we assist others in need of help is how we feel at the time (Carlson and Miller, 1987; Carlson, Charlin, and Miller, 1988; Salovey, Mayer, and Rosenhan, 1991). Research shows that positive emotions or "good moods" induce helpful behaviors. When experimental subjects are led to believe that they have done well on tasks requiring motor-coordinating, creative, or problem-solving abilities, they are more likely to volunteer, work, or sacrifice for the benefit of others. Other studies reveal that generosity is fostered by positive-emotion imagery, induced by thinking "happy" thoughts, reading "elation" statements, or listening to radio broadcasts containing "good news." Still other studies demonstrate that good for-

TABLE 10-1   PERCENTAGES OF PARENTS AND ADULT CHILDREN GIVING HELP

Type of help	Daughter to mother	Son to mother	Daughter to father	Son to father
Advice	77	72	45	56
Comfort	79	67	47	45
Health care	49	36	34	33
Repairs	50	61	40	54
Home sitting	41	40	37	37
Chores	59	48	48	36
Special gift	89	76	76	60
Job leads	14	14	11	18
Financial aid	19	21	9	13

	Mother to daughter	Mother to son	Father to daughter	Father to son
Advice	69	57	60	64
Comfort	62	45	46	33
Health care	35	26	32	20
Repairs	46	39	41	33
Home sitting	42	33	34	26
Chores	42	44	36	23
Special gift	81	65	62	48
Job leads	22	20	18	30
Financial aid	42	34	43	39

Source: Adapted and used by permission from Alice S. Rossi and Peter H. Rossi, *Of Human Bonding: Parent-Child Relations Across the Life Course* (New York: Aldine de Gruyter, 1990, p. 394). Copyright © 1990 Walter de Gruyter, Inc., New York.

HELPING IN DRUNK-DRIVING SITUATIONS

Intervening to prevent a person from driving under the influence of alcohol can avert potential harm to the driver and innocent bystanders. Such interventions have been studied by a number of researchers as a kind of helping behavior. A recent study by Rabow, Newcomb, Monto, and Hernandez (1990) illustrates a number of the points we have been discussing about helping behavior.

The researchers chose college students for their study because college students report both high rates of drunk driving (Rabow et al., 1987) and rates of intervening in drunk-driving situations that are comparable to national rates for all adults (Rabow and Hernandez, 1986). The researchers asked the respondents a number of questions about the most recent situation they had encountered (if any) involving a potential drunk driver. Respondents were also asked whether they had friends or family members who had been hurt or killed in an alcohol-related accident, how many other drunk-driving situations they had been involved with in the past year, and whether they felt a moral obligation to intervene in drunk-driving situations.

In this study, 51 percent of the respondents reported that they had intervened to keep a drunk from driving in the past year. These researchers found that perceiving the potential driver as dangerous and in need of help and feeling competent to help or intervene were important predictors of the respondents' decision to intervene. The rates of helping by males and females did not differ.

Knowing others who had been killed or injured because of drunk driving did not influence respondents' decisions about helping. Nor did the person's sense of moral obligation predict helping. The researchers suggest that the latter finding indicates that situational factors are more important than personal factors in determining helping — at least *this kind* of helping.

Helping was more likely to occur among those who knew and liked each other. The researchers suggest that feelings of similarity and "we-ness" are related to helping: "Friends don't let friends drive drunk." Unlike the experimental studies of stranger intervention in emergencies (discussed earlier in the chapter), this study found that the number of others in the situation did not reduce the likelihood of helping. In fact, the larger the number of others in the situation and the larger the number of others in the situation who were *known* by the respondent, the more likely the respondent was to see the situation as potentially dangerous and to intervene. This supports the findings of Rutkowski, Gruder, and Romer (1983) indicating that when bystanders are cohesive — when they know and have ties with one another — they are *more* likely to intervene when they are part of a larger group.

tune — such as finding a quarter in a phone booth or being given a packet of stationery — enhances the likelihood that shoppers or individuals at home will help others. Perhaps not surprisingly, sunny days encourage helping behavior; cloudy days and bad weather discourage it. However, a good mood may actually *decrease* helping behavior if giving help would detract from the person's positive feelings. (Before reading further, look at the Student Observation: "Effect of Positive Mood on Helping.")

The influence of negative mood on helping also varies with the circumstances. "Bad moods" sometimes increase helping, sometimes decrease it, and sometimes have no significant effect. Guilt induced by doing harm increases helping behaviors. When we are feeling guilty, helping seems to function as self-therapy or image repair. Under some conditions, the tendency to help is increased by feelings of sadness (Schaller and Cialdini, 1988), because people anticipate that helping will relieve their negative feelings (Cialdini et al., 1987).

But in many settings, negative moods — such as unhappiness, sadness, or envy — curtail helping tendencies. For example, the experience of being competent or incompetent and successful or unsuccessful affects our feelings (Staub, 1978). People who fail on a task may become preoccupied with how others evaluate them, engage in self-criticism, and become susceptible to negative thoughts. Consequently, their attention turns inward, away from happenings in the outer world. They do not feel "free" to attend to others, nor do they experience the ease or comfort necessary to move outward in the direction of other people. For instance, students who have done poorly on an exam or have been rejected in an interpersonal relationship report that they often watch television or engage in other "time-out" and withdrawing activities; it is as if some inner, self-correcting system operates, with time, to effect recuperation. When a negative mood produces an inward, self-absorbed focus, helping is generally inhibited (Carlson and Miller, 1987).

Others' reactions. We have already discussed how others' reactions can shape our definitions of situations as ones requiring helping, or not requiring it, and how the presence and reactions of others can lead to diffusion of responsibility—reducing our own feelings of responsibility to help. Even after we have decided that someone needs help and that we have some responsibility for providing it, our concern with how others will evaluate us may either enhance or inhibit helping (Schwartz and Gottlieb, 1980). Typically, we assume that others will view our intervention as appropriate, and consequently we conclude that they will evaluate our helping in a positive fashion. But when cues in the situation imply that others consider helping to be inappropriate, we fear that our helping actions will appear foolish or that our assistance will be judged incompetent (Staub, 1978; Latané and Nida, 1981).

Leonard Bickman and Dennis P. Rosenbaum (1977) have investigated the impact that verbal communication between bystanders has on people's reporting of crime. They found that one bystander can influence another bystander's decision making by uttering a few comments. In an experiment undertaken in a field setting, weekday shoppers in a supermarket checkout line witnessed a "shoplifter" stealing a number of items. A confederate-bystander discouraged a bystander from reporting the thief by observing, "Say, look at her. She's shoplifting. She put that into her purse. But it's the store's problem. They have security people here." In contrast, reporting was encouraged when the confederate-bystander said, "Say, look at her. She's shoplifting. She put that into her purse. We saw it. We should report it. It's our responsibility." In addition to helping a bystander define whether or not a particular incident constitutes a crime, such comments can suggest the appropriate course of action and consequently have a strong impact on a person's tendency to report a crime to the proper authorities.

Rational motives. Some social psychologists believe that we help others (or don't) for the same reason that we engage in any other behavior (or don't)—the expectation that we will realize some gain or avoid some loss. We may help others in

---

STUDENT OBSERVATION

Effect of Positive Mood on Helping

Last year, on the day before Spring Break, I remember being in a really good mood. I had just aced an exam, and I couldn't wait to get to the beach (the weather was looking great!). On my way out of Chapel Hill, I stopped at Hardee's to grab a bite to eat. While I was waiting in line, an elderly lady approached me. She said that she hadn't had anything to eat and asked me for some money. Because I was in a good mood, I felt generous—I wanted to help the lady. As a result, I gave her some money. Thus, my positive emotional state, or *good mood*, induced a helping behavior.

order to gain material benefits, social approval, and honor or to escape group sanctions, social disapproval, and ostracism (Baumann, Cialdini, and Kenrick, 1981; Cialdini et al., 1987; Dovidio et al., 1991). According to this *rational choice,* or *cost-reward, analysis of helping,* whether we help in a situation depends on our assessment of costs relative to rewards: (1) *costs* associated with *helping* (effort, embarrassment, possible distasteful experiences, and potential bodily harm), (2) *rewards* associated with *not helping* (benefits derived from continuing other activities), (3) *rewards* associated with *helping* (praise from oneself, the victim, and others), and (4) *costs* associated with *not helping* (self-blame and potential censure from others) (Piliavin, Rodin, and Piliavin, 1969; Piliavin, Piliavin, and Rodin, 1975). The cost-reward model hypothesizes that individuals' decisions to help or not help will be motivated by their desire to incur as few net costs (costs minus rewards) as possible.

Costs of helping. In real-life situations offering help may result in negative outcomes — possible retaliation from a criminal if we intervene in a crime, days spent in court testifying if we report a robbery to the police, possible exposure to AIDS if we stop to help a bleeding accident victim. The cost of helping plays a major part in discouraging helping behaviors.

A large number of studies have demonstrated that as costs for helping increase, helping decreases. In these studies, several kinds of costs have been examined: effort and time (Darley and Batson, 1973), money expended or forgone (Bleda et al., 1976), potential embarrassment to the helper (Edelman et al., 1984), aversion to a physical stigma (Edelman et al., 1983), fear of disapproval (Midlarsky and Hannah, 1985), unfamiliarity with the helping task (Ladd, Lange, and Stremmel, 1983), and pain (Batson et al., 1983). Of the various kinds of costs and rewards associated with helping and not helping, *costs for helping* seem to be the most important factor affecting helping behavior (Dovidio, 1984). *Indirect* helping, such as calling on a third party for assistance, is also more likely when costs for direct helping are high than when they are low.

We are more likely to help if the costs of helping are low.

Rewards for not helping. Rewards for *not* helping include such things as having money to spend on something that brings us pleasure because we *didn't* donate, spending time in an enjoyable way because we *didn't* spend time volunteering, or accomplishing an errand because we *didn't* stop to help the person with the flat tire. In addition, we *avoid* the possible embarrassment that would occur if our attempts to assist someone were rejected or viewed as inept. These rewards are also factored into our decisions about whether to help.

Rewards for helping. Conversely, as the perceived rewards for helping increase, actual helping increases. Praise, for example, facilitates helping (Deutsch and Lamberti, 1986). We are also more likely to help when it is possible to get feedback about the effectiveness of helping (Smith, Keating, and Stotland, 1989) and when helping seems to be improving the needy person's condition (Utne and Kidd, 1980). Thus, the chances that we will donate money to a charity organization providing food supplies to starving families in another country might be increased if the organization promises to send us quarterly reports on the situation there. And the likelihood that we will be persuaded to make a subsequent donation to the same group would probably be greater if its reports indicate that previous donations have really made a difference in the lives of the targeted families.

Costs of not helping. In addition to incurring costs when we help someone, we may also incur costs for *not* helping. We may, for example, be criticized by others for our failure to help, or we may blame ourselves for not behaving as we believe we *should*. Another cost for *not* helping is having to watch, or even simply being aware of, the victim's continued suffering.

Generally, as costs for *not* helping decrease, helping behavior also decreases. For example, subjects asked to make a telephone call for a person in need were less likely to help when costs of *not* helping were lowered by (1) giving the subject an easy way to escape the situation (Batson et al., 1981), (2) decreasing the likelihood of future contact with the victim (Toi and Batson, 1982), (3) giving the subject a justification for not helping (Batson et al., 1988), and (4) eliminating the possibility that the subject would be negatively evaluated by others for not helping (Batson et al., 1986).

Altruistic motive. Other social psychologists ask, "Is helping always and exclusively motivated by the prospect of some benefit for ourselves?" Advocates of *altruism* do not deny that much of what we do, including much that we do for others, is motivated by self-interest. But they also claim that, at least under some circumstances, we are capable of a very different form of motivation, one concerned with the welfare of others, not just of ourselves. Such motivation has the ultimate goal of benefiting someone else (Batson and Oleson, 1991).

Why should an individual engage in behavior that benefits another when this behavior provides no tangible self-benefit and might even demand great self-sacrifice (Etzioni, 1988; Batson, 1990)? The answer is *empathy*. Empathy leads us to take another person's perspective and to view the

world as he or she sees it. By assuming the perspective of a person in need, we increase the likelihood that we will recognize the need and then act to reduce it (Batson et al., 1988; Batson, 1990). Although we often help others for whom we feel little empathy, research suggests that we do so only when it is in our own best interests (Batson and Oleson, 1991).

Some researchers argue that we have a remarkable capacity for becoming involved and invested in the welfare of others, that is, for empathy. Social psychologists Daniel Batson and Kathryn Oleson illustrate this point by urging us to reflect on our capacity to feel empathy for characters in novels, in movies, and on television. "We have known these characters only for minutes, and we know they are fictitious. Still, we find ourselves churning inside when they are in danger, yearning when they are in need, weeping over their losses and successes" (Batson and Oleson, 1991: 81).

Some sociobiologists, such as Edward O. Wilson (1978), have suggested that our empathetic emotions have a genetic base. The altruistic impulse, they claim, springs from genetic pre-programming designed to protect the species. In support of their position, these sociobiologists point to studies showing that empathetic concerns with others' needs appear, apparently spontaneously, very early in childhood (Grusec, 1991; Eisenberg and Fabes, 1991). A study conducted by psychologists in Canada and Great Britain on altruism among pairs of identical and fraternal twins estimated that about half of the altruism scores were due to genetic influences and the other half to environmental factors (Zuckerman, 1985). But most social psychologists have preferred to look to social and psychological factors as motivational sources of helping. They argue that even if there is a genetic basis for empathy, human culture largely affects whom we define as kin and nonkin — and therefore to whom we apply our empathetic concerns — and what form our helping takes (Fiske, 1991).

Research suggests that *both* motivations — rational and altruistic — may shape helping behavior. Many volunteers report both rational and altruistic motives for volunteering, for example (Anderson and Moore, 1978; Pearce, 1983; Piliavin and Callero, 1991). In addition, other social psychologists argue, even the most unselfish act can produce a psychological reward for the actor or confirm her or his self-identity as a helping person (Clary and Snyder, 1991).

Empathy itself may create the opportunity for psychological rewards. When we are empathically in tune with another person, we experience emotional distress through imagined participation in that person's plight. But when we help the person with whom we empathize, we can also share vicariously in the joy of the person's relief (Smith, Keating, and Stotland, 1989). For example, in explaining her involvement in church activities to transport and hide illegal immigrants from Guatemala and El Salvador, a mother with two young children says, "I'm a mother and I would want another mother to shelter my children from a war" (King, 1985: 6). By assisting another person, thereby reducing the person's suffering, we simultaneously reduce our *own* empathetic distress (Schaller and Cialdini, 1988; Dovidio et al., 1991).

Another source of psychological reward has to do with personal values, norms, and self-identity. Through socialization and moral development we build up internalized standards for behavior, which we experience as obligations to act in certain ways (Alper, 1985; Grusec, 1991). We feel good about ourselves when we act in accordance with these principles and bad when we act contrary to them.

In sum, our self-reflections have motivating properties. We experience positive self-evaluation, various forms of self-reward, and positive emotions when we act in accordance with internalized norms; we experience negative self-evaluation, various forms of self-punishment, and negative emotions (including guilt) when we deviate from these standards. To one degree or another, most of us have internalized a humanistic value system that leads to a concern for others' welfare and a sense of obligation toward people in need. If this humanistic value system is part of a religious ideology, these psychological rewards may be coupled with the belief that self-gain need not derive only from worldly motivations. The belief that God will reward or punish us can have powerful motivating properties.

Similarly, when we have come to think of ourselves as kind and thoughtful people, acting in accordance with this self-concept is psychologically rewarding and acting contrary to it is punishing. We noted in Chapter 7, "The Social Nature of Self," that if we perceive that we have taken an action without the external coercion of a large reward, we are likely to attribute to ourselves a predisposition toward the action and to act in ways consistent with that predisposition. If we voluntarily help someone and perceive that we will not gain from this action, we are likely to attribute our action to our sense of moral obligation and responsibility to others. This view of ourselves will motivate us to perform future helping actions (Callero, 1985; Charng, Piliavin, and Callero, 1988; Piliavin and Charng, 1990). Thus, even the most seemingly "altruistic" action may result both from one's concern for a needy other *and* from a more rationally or egoistically motivated need to act in accordance with one's values or self-concept (Clary and Snyder, 1991).

Reward Exchange

As Amato's study of helping in relationships and the Rossis' study of helping among family members indicate, helping in the context of ongoing social relationships is often *reciprocal*. In other words, unlike emergency situations, in which we help a person whom we may never see again and from whom we don't expect repayment for the good deed (except perhaps gratitude), ongoing relationships more frequently involve *reward exchange* than they do *individual helping*.

The reciprocal nature of reward exchange is illustrated by Peter Blau's (1955) classic study of a federal law enforcement agency in Chicago. Blau spent several months at the agency—which consisted of sixteen agents, one supervisor, and a clerk—observing and taking notes. The agency's task was to investigate businesses suspected of violating federal law. Each case was assigned to a single agent, who was expected to make all the decisions concerning it. Processing a case involved auditing the books and records of the firm, interviewing the employer and a sample of employees, weighing the evidence of legal violation, and taking appropriate action. An explicit rule prohibited consulting with other agents about a case, although consultation with the supervisor was allowed. Agents were periodically rated by the supervisor on the quality of their performance.

The supervisor at the agency told Blau, "They [the agents] are not permitted to consult other agents. If they have a problem, they take it up with me" (Blau, 1955: 99). But Blau observed that this was not what actually happened. Agents consulted with their colleagues about cases several times an hour. Not surprisingly, the agents were reluctant to reveal to their supervisor their inability to solve a problem for fear that their ratings would be adversely affected. Their need for getting advice without exposing their difficulties to the supervisor led agents to consult one another, in violation of the official rule. One agent would take a problem to another agent and ask him what he thought. The second agent would stop his own work, think about the problem, and offer the first agent advice. The advice-giving agent helped the advice-seeking agent. Observing more closely, however, Blau noted that the advice-giving agent gained something from the interaction — approval or prestige. In Blau's words:

A consultation can be considered an exchange of values; both participants gain something, and both have to pay a price. The questioning agent is enabled to perform better than he could otherwise have done, without exposing his difficulties to the supervisor. By asking for advice, he implicitly pays his respect to the superior proficiency of his colleague. This acknowledgement of inferiority is the cost of receiving assistance. The consultant gains prestige, in return for which he is willing to devote some time to the consultation and permit it to disrupt his own work. The following remark of an agent illustrates this: "I like giving advice. It's flat-tering, I suppose, if you feel that the others come to you for advice."

The expert whose advice was often sought by colleagues obtained social evidence of his superior abilities. This increased his confidence in his own decisions, and thus improved his performance as an investigator. . . . The role of the agent who frequently solicited advice was less enviable, even though he benefitted most directly from this unofficial practice. Asking a colleague for guidance was less threatening than asking the supervisor, but the repeated admission of his inability to solve his own problems also undermined the self-confidence of an agent and his standing in the group. The cost of advice became prohibitive if the consultant, after the questioner had subordinated himself by asking for help, was in the least discouraging — by postponing a discussion or by revealing his impatience during one. To avoid such rejections, agents usually consulted a colleague with whom they were friendly, even if he was not an expert. (1955: 99, 104–106, 108–111, 113)*

Blau's observations reveal a situation in which two individuals are providing benefits for each other — one giving advice, the other giving approval. Each individual behaves in a manner that rewards the other. Such reciprocal helping is called reward exchange.

SOCIAL EXCHANGE THEORY

The theory explicitly designed to understand exchange behaviors is called *social exchange theory* (Thibaut and Kelley, 1959; Blau, 1964; Homans, 1974; Emerson, 1981; Cook, 1987; Coleman, 1990). Social exchange theorists use a rational cost-reward analysis of social exchange similar to the one discussed previously in connection with helping behavior. A *reward* is anything that benefits a person. A *cost* is anything a person would rather avoid. Since most behaviors have both rewards and costs associated with them, exchange theorists summarize these outcomes using the concept of **profits** — rewards minus costs. In addition, exchange theorists emphasize that behavior occurs in the context of **alternative sources** of rewards. Each person has the choice of obtaining rewards through the actions of one or more others as well as through his or her own actions. This is a choice similar to the social dilemma we discussed in the previous chapter. But, while the social dilemma involved the choice between cooperating or not cooperating with others, in social exchange the choice is whether to exchange rewards with one person or another or possibly with no one.

Dependence

The main prediction of exchange theory is that the likelihood that we will engage in exchange behavior toward a particular other increases with our "dependence" on that particular person. **Dependence** on another person is the degree to which that person can provide us with profits, relative to alternative sources. Our dependence is greater when (1) our profit is high (that is, the value of the rewards provided by the other person is high and the costs are low) and (2) alternative sources of the rewards are scarce (that is, we can't obtain the profits from other persons or ourselves).

Let's return to Blau's example to illustrate these concepts. Why did the agents choose to engage in an exchange of advice and approval?

They had other alternatives. Each agent could have done his own work independently. Or an advice-seeking agent could have asked for his supervisor's advice instead of going to another agent. Why did the agents choose to exchange advice for approval with one another instead of choosing one of these other alternatives?

First, let's look at the advice-seeker's alternatives and their consequences. The advice-seeking agent would consider the rewards and the costs of each alternative to arrive at the net profit value of each one. As researchers, we might ask the advice-seeker to rate the value of each reward and cost on a scale ranging from $+10$ (highest reward) to -10 (highest cost). The best alternative would be the one producing the greatest rewards and the lowest costs — in other words, the greatest *profit*. An analysis of the advice-seeker's situation is presented in Table 10-2.

From the table's assessment of the alternatives, we can see why the advice-seeking agent would choose to give approval to the other agent for his advice. Choosing between giving approval for advice from another agent and doing his own work, the agent decided that receiving advice and giving up some social status was more valuable (profit $= +5$) than remaining independent but doing a lower-quality job (profit $= 0$). Changing the reward and cost values associated with the different behavioral alternatives could produce a different behavioral choice. For example, Blau's descrip-

| TABLE 10-2 | ASSESSMENT OF THE ADVICE-SEEKER'S CHOICES |

Behavioral alternatives	Rewards	Reward value	Costs	Cost value	Profit
1. Ask other agent for advice.	Receive advice and do better job.	$+8$	Lower social status	-3	$+5$
2. Do own work.	Remain independent.	$+6$	Lower job quality	-6	0
3. Ask supervisor for advice.	Receive advice and do better job.	$+8$	Lower job ratings	-10	-2

TABLE 10-3   ASSESSMENT OF THE ADVICE-GIVER'S CHOICES

Behavioral alternatives	Rewards	Reward value	Costs	Cost value	Profit
1. Give advice to other agent.	Approval, higher social status	+6	Time away from own work, interruptions	−2	+4
2. Do own work.	Freedom from interruptions	+2	No acknowledgment of superior performance	−6	−4

tion notes that the cost of advice sometimes increased — when an advice-giver became less receptive or more impatient, for example, in response to the advice-seeker's request for help. The increase in cost decreased the likelihood of going to (and giving approval to) a particular agent for advice. On the other hand, the cost of asking for advice could also be reduced — for example, by consulting with a more friendly agent who required less subordination. The reduced cost would increase the likelihood that an exchange would be established as long as rewards (quality of the advice) remain about the same.

When faced with the choice between seeking advice from another agent or seeking it from his supervisor, the agent in our example decided that the consequences of seeking advice from a fellow agent were less costly. The rewards were similar for both alternatives (+8), but the cost of lower job ratings was greater (−10) than that of lower social status (−3). The comparison might have been different. For example, the advice of other agents could be made less valuable by a change in agency procedures that reduced their expertise in comparison to that of the supervisor.

And what about the advice-giver? According to Blau's description, an assessment of his alternatives would look something like the analysis presented in Table 10-3. Blau's description contains less information about the choices of the advice-giver. The information available suggests that he valued approval from colleagues very highly (+6) and that the increase in confidence that the ap-proval provided even increased his job performance. Because the agent could give advice and do his own job well, the costs of providing advice were low (−2). On the other hand, the consequences might have been different. Suppose, for example, that the advice-giver's performance had been lowered by spending time helping others. This would increase the costs associated with giving advice. Anything that alters the balance between the rewards and costs associated with various alternatives could change the likelihood that the exchange would occur.

The example we have been using involves exchanging status for information. However, people exchange many kinds of rewards. One analysis proposed six basic types of rewards: money, goods, services, information, status, and love (Foa and Foa, 1974). There are also many kinds of costs, including loss of rewards and even loss of the *opportunity* to achieve the rewards that would have accrued had the individual chosen another alternative. One of the major problems social psychologists encounter is how to compare dependencies derived from different kinds of rewards and costs (Gray and Tallman, 1987; Lawler and Bacharach, 1987; Molm, 1988).

Dependence Imbalance

Dependence on another person involves our expectation that that person will provide us with greater profits than we can get from alternative sources. But the dependencies of two persons who are contemplating or engaged in an exchange are not always equal. When they are not, we say that the exchange is characterized by **dependence imbalance**. We'll use Blau's example of the federal agents to illustrate. Keep in mind that dependencies are affected by both profits *and* alternatives.

We have noted that Blau's description of the exchange tells us less about the advice-giver than about the advice-seeker. So let's concentrate on filling in the information about the former. For the advice-giver, offering advice was very rewarding ($+6$) and not very costly (-2). This high profit (rewards minus costs = $+4$) contributes to his dependence on the advice-seeker. The dependence of the advice-giver will be lowered, however, if the profits associated with giving advice decrease. This will occur if his rewards decrease or if his costs increase.

For example, if the advice-seeker takes much longer each time he asks for advice (and gives approval), this will make advice-giving more costly to the advice-giver. The more time he spends giving advice, the less time the advice-giver has to spend on his own work. The advice-giver's dependence on the other agent, exchange theorists would say, has been lowered by the decrease in profit. As a result, the dependencies of the two agents on each other have become imbalanced. The dependence of the advice-seeker is greater than that of the advice-giver. In this example, the inequity is due to a difference in the two agents' profits — a *profit imbalance* or *inequity* (Michaels and Wiggins, 1976).

But there is another possible source of dependence imbalance. Let's add to the scenario. Suppose a new agent is assigned to the office. His inexperience makes him willing to exchange his approval for the other agent's advice. The advice-giver is now even *less* dependent on his original exchange partner because he can receive the approval he wants from an alternative source. The dependence of the original advice-seeker is again greater than that of the advice-giver. Dependence imbalance has been further increased because of a difference in the original agents' alternatives — an *alternatives imbalance*.

Reactions to Dependence Imbalance

Dependence imbalance can produce several reactions. How would it affect the advice-approval exchange of our federal agents? Let's find out by continuing with our three-agent dependence imbalance scenario.

Decrease or terminate the exchange. The immediate result of a dependence imbalance — whether due to differences in profits or in alternatives — is that the less dependent person tends to decrease his or her participation in the exchange. As a consequence, the exchange partner might follow suit, depending on whether she or he can find an alternative source of rewards.

In our example, the advice-giver would lower the amount or frequency of giving advice to the original advice-seeker. In response to the decrease in advice received, the advice-seeker might look for alternative sources of advice. *If* an alternative source of advice can be found, the dependencies of both members of the original exchange would be lowered but more equitable. Because each agent's dependency on the other has been lowered, advice-approval exchanges between the two are likely to occur less frequently or might cease altogether.

Decrease dependence imbalance. On the other hand, *if* a profitable alternative is not available, the more dependent person will remain highly dependent and will attempt to restore equity to the original exchange relationship. For example, since getting advice from his supervisor is still very costly, the advice-seeking partner might try to reestablish the original exchange relationship by increasing the advice-giver's dependence on him. He could provide the advice-giver with a greater amount of approval, higher-quality approval, or another kind of valuable reward (e.g., buying him drinks or praising him to the supervisor) to compensate for the cost to the advice-giver of being taken away from his own work to give his advice. Or, in order to reduce the rewards the advice-giver is receiving from his alternative source, the advice-seeker could attempt to denigrate the value of the new agent's approval by portraying him as someone with undesirable traits: "Why do you want to associate with him? I heard that nobody in his old agency trusted him."

If equity is successfully restored at a high-dependence level, advice-approval exchanges are likely to continue. But efforts to restore dependence equity may fail. If the alternative source is more attractive, the less dependent person will reject the more dependent person's attempts to maintain the exchange relationship and the original exchange will cease.

Do nothing. Exchange sometimes occurs in spite of a dependence imbalance. However, the more dependent person will have to make the *same* level of contribution to the exchange in order to receive *fewer* rewards. In contrast, the less dependent person will make a lower contribution and still receive the same rewards. The more dependent person, though disadvantaged, will participate in an imbalanced exchange when he or she is unsuccessful at restoring the partner's dependence on him or her and when alternatives are not readily available (Skvoretz and Willer, 1991). In our example, this may be the situation in which the advice-seeker finds himself when the new agent offers approval to the advice-giver.

But why doesn't the *less dependent* person completely terminate the exchange relationship? Why continue to participate? Because she or he can get something for nearly nothing. And equally important, this partner's lower contributions to the original relationship may allow the exchange of her or his resources for rewards in an alternative relationship. *If* simultaneous participation in both exchanges is possible, it will increase the likelihood that the original exchange will continue in spite of the dependence imbalance. On the other hand, the less dependent person may not be able to participate in both exchanges at once. For example, the alternative partner may require that their exchange be an *exclusive* one. Under these circumstances, the less dependent person will

have to choose between the exchange relationships, and the person's dependence on the alternative partner could influence her or him to terminate the original exchange relationship.

This could very easily apply to our advice-giver. He is in a position to extract more approval for each bit of advice he gives to the more dependent advice-seeker, thus increasing his own profit in the exchange. Decreasing the time involved in giving advice to this original partner (without losing approval) leaves him with more time to give advice to the second agent in exchange for the latter's approval (or to devote to his own work). If the dual exchanges are possible, the likelihood that the advice-giver will maintain the original — now imbalanced — exchange relationship will increase. Otherwise, the original advice-approval exchange will probably cease.

It might be interesting for you to apply the same analysis to a "love triangle" with which you are familiar. The addition of a third party in a romantic relationship creates a dependence imbalance. To analyze the outcome according to social exchange theory, you would need to answer a number of questions: How dependent were the original partners on each other? Who was the third party, and how did he or she affect the dependence equity? What was the reaction to the imbalance, and what factors influenced the particular reaction?

TRUST

So far, our discussion of exchange might seem to depict humans as self-centered and uncaring — qualities you probably didn't expect to find in a chapter about helping behavior. However, Peter Blau (1964) notes that social exchange involves *trust*, which is frequently viewed as one of the more noble human features. Social exchange, Blau argues, differs in important ways from strictly economic exchange. The most important difference is that social exchange entails *unspecified* obligations. Economic transactions specify the exact quantities to be exchanged; social exchange, in contrast, involves the underlying principle that when one person does another a favor, there is a general expectation of some future return but its exact nature is definitely *not* stipulated in advance.

Exchange theory proposes that relationships endure only as long as the rewards exchanged are approximately equivalent. This is not to say that the profits in every individual transaction need to be equivalent. Rather, there must be an equivalence in exchange over the long term. *Tit-for-tat exchanges* are those in which *each instance* of one person's rewarding another is reciprocated. In such exchanges one person provides a reward for another and must trust the other only to reciprocate on the next turn. Each person's behavior in the exchange can function as a reward for the other's behavior. In the example we have been discussing, one agent's approval is a reward for the other agent's advice, and vice versa.

Although dependence certainly provides the opportunity and motivation for social exchange, it does not ensure it. Even in tit-for-tat exchanges, things can go wrong. For example, our advice-seeking agent, perhaps in an attempt to signal that he could use some advice, may give approval to the advice-giver at a time when the latter has chosen to do his own work. Here, the advice-seeking agent has in essence rewarded the other agent for doing his own work rather than for giving advice. Consequently, he has inadvertently decreased the future likelihood of the behavior (advice giving) he wished to produce.

In contrast, the advice-seeker could have withheld his approval until the other agent stopped his own work to offer his advice; this is a tit-for-tat strategy, or *contingent exchange*. By making his approval contingent on the other's advice, the advice-seeker might have increased his chances of receiving advice in the future (Molm, 1987). Whether the advice-seeking agent will use contingent exchange will depend on several factors. For example, he may or may not have learned contingent-exchange skills before entering this particular exchange relationship (Molm and Wiggins, 1979). Or even if he has already acquired the skills, he may be too dependent on the advice-

giver to risk alienating him by withholding his approval.

When trust is absent, two persons may become locked into a pattern of *no* exchange: unwilling to "take the first step," each withholds the reward the other wants. If neither party is offering the reward he or she possesses, then there is no opportunity for either one to use the contingent-exchange strategy. Exchange can be established only if one party breaks the pattern by offering a reward *unilaterally*. This may not only signal the party's desire to reestablish the exchange relationship but also indicate a degree of trust, which eases the transition to a renewed exchange of rewards (Boyle and Lawler, 1991).

Many exchange relationships require more trust than do simple tit-for-tat exchanges because the rewards exchanged on any single occasion are not equivalent. In his study of the federal agents, Blau kept track of who consulted whom over a period of several months. He found that many of the consultation partnerships consisted of two agents of roughly equal expertise who would more or less take turns at giving and receiving advice. Thus, on any single occasion the advice-giver might benefit less than the advice-seeker, but in the long run the two agents would give and receive about equally often, so the rewards exchanged balanced out.

When trust is well established, an exchange may evolve into an *expansive exchange* in which a mental ledger is kept of the rewards each person has given to the other over a period of time (Matthews and Shimoff, 1979). One person's helping another on several occasions may go unreciprocated. Thus, you may do three favors for your roommate, without reciprocation, before needing to ask for some favors in return. But the exchange continues only as long as the books balance over the long haul. You can see why an expansive exchange requires more trust than a tit-for-tat exchange. (See the Student Observation: "Expansive Exchange.")

Some research suggests that in certain relationships we actually stop keeping an exchange ledger altogether (Clark and Reis, 1988). In some cases,

STUDENT OBSERVATION

Expansive Exchange

*M*y roommates and I have an expansive exchange regarding rides to and from campus. If any one of us needs a ride, she can ask a roommate. The roommate almost always agrees. One roommate may be asked to drive another to or from campus several times before she herself asks for a ride. Her actions, in other words, may go unreciprocated for a while, but she trusts the others to return the favor when asked. So all of us place trust in one another, believing that our favors will be reciprocated when we ask, no matter how long the delay before a favor is needed. In essence, our trust replaces the need to keep a mental list of how many times we have driven one another to or from campus. However, if one roommate were to refuse to give a ride to another for no apparent valid reason, the expansive exchange would break down.

the focus may shift away from what one receives in an exchange and center, instead, on the needs of the other person or on the relationship as a whole—what's good for *us*? This distinction is similar to the distinction between rational and altruistic motives for helping behavior.

When well-established trust is expected, it becomes *in*appropriate to keep track of each other's rewarding behaviors. Roger Brown (1986) points out, for example, that among Japanese friends, it is considered inappropriate to suggest "splitting the check" at a restaurant, because this implies an unwillingness to take turns and thus an unwillingness to sustain trust and enter into a real friendship. Similarly, among Americans, even when we do split a check, it is considered inappropriate to insist on doing so too exactly: "Let's see, I owe you fourteen dollars and thirty-two cents." To reciprocate too quickly and too exactly is also seen as inappropriate when trust is expected, since it makes a social exchange seem too much like an economic one. For example, your feelings would probably suffer if you gave a close friend a lovely sweater and a couple of days later the friend gave *you* a sweater of the same quality and value.

Some researchers argue that trust in expanded relationships requires more than reciprocity— even expanded reciprocity (Haas and Deseran, 1981). They suggest that these relationships depend partly on symbolic exchanges of gestures that indicate commitment to the relationship. A symbolic gesture is a reward intended more to establish trust and strengthen a relationship than to provide a benefit to the person receiving the reward. Often the *cost to the giver* is more important in indicating commitment to the relationship than is the benefit to the receiver. Common symbolic gestures in American society include offers of food and drink, birthday and wedding gifts, love tokens (e.g., wedding rings), and attendance at formal ceremonies. The greater the cost to the giver, the stronger the indication of the giver's commitment to the relationship.

The presence of alternative sources of rewards is always a basis for *dis*trust. In our discussion of cooperative behavior in Chapter 9, "Performance, Conformity, and Cooperation," we noted the free-rider and sucker effects—the former involving the untrustworthiness of others and the latter our own distrust. We discussed how the task and reward structures of groups can supply both the opportunity and the motivation to create an informal sanction system that may provide an additional incentive for members to cooperate, thus increasing trust.

SHARED REWARD VALUES

One problem in predicting how people will respond in an exchange is determining the values

When trust is well established, an exchange may evolve into an *expansive exchange* in which a mental ledger is kept of the rewards each person has given to the other over a period of time. One person's helping another on several occasions may go unreciprocated, but the exchange continues only as long as the books balance over the long haul. This requires more trust than a tit-for-tat exchange.

that the participants attach to the rewards and costs involved. In our example of the federal agents, we had to guess at how much value the agents attached to the advice and approval they were exchanging. We noted how various circumstances—for example, the addition of another agent willing to give approval—might change the values of advice and approval for the agents.

Another important issue is whether the participants *agree* about the values of the rewards. When they do agree, the calculations that each partner makes should also make sense to the other. If we agree, for example, that your borrowing my lawn mower has a value of 6 (a cost of − 6 for me and a reward of + 6 for you) and that your clipping my hedge has a value of 12 (a reward of + 12 for me, and a cost of − 12 for you), an exchange in which you clip my hedge every other time you borrow my lawn mower will probably satisfy both of us. If, on the other hand, *you* value borrowing

my lawn mower at + 6 and clipping my hedge as − 12, but *I* value lending my lawn mower at − 10 and getting my hedge clipped at + 12, then what seems a reasonable exchange for you — one hedge clipping for every two lawn mower loans — will not seem equitable to me.

Of course, we would rarely discuss our expectations in such explicit terms. It would seem unfriendly in a social, as opposed to an economic, exchange to do so. Therefore, the exchange might go on for a while with you being satisfied and me beginning to feel taken advantage of before something happens to make our dependencies more equitable. I might, for example, bring the exchange to an end by making excuses about why you can't borrow my mower. Or I might start asking to borrow your trimmer on the weeks you don't clip my hedge. Perhaps noticing that I act a bit "funny" when you don't clip my hedge, you might realize that I expect more. You'd then have to decide whether to adjust your own values or find another neighbor whose value on loaning her mower was lower.

The suggestion that we make these mental calculations of rewards, costs, profits, and alternatives in our relationships with others — especially in those with friends, relatives, and lovers — may strike you as unappealing or even offensive. You might say, "Surely we don't have to agree on the values of the gifts we give and the things we do for the people we love! We do nice things because of the way we *feel* about them! There's no need to agree on values if you're not keeping score!" But Arlie Russell Hochschild's (1989) observations of two married couples (the Delacortes and the Shermans) suggest that even spouses can be viewed as exchange partners with value norms, that is, shared definitions about the values of the rewards they exchange. Both the Delacortes and the Shermans have such norms, though the norms of the two couples differ. In the following description, Hochschild uses the words "gratitude" and "gift" to indicate what we have been calling "reward."

The Delacortes — Frank and Carmen

In Frank's social world, the older gender rules hold: the wife of an adequate man should not *need* to work. But to support a family in the urban working class in the early 1980s, men like Frank in fact do need a wife's salary. Frank's economic circumstances erode the rules on which he bases his identity as a man, and make him, as a man, vulnerable to insult. Frank feels grateful, then, that his wife gives him the real gift of working without complaining about it.

For her part, Carmen feels *her* job is to care for the home and children; she expects Frank to do the outside chores and to help some, when she asks, with the inside ones. Like most working mothers, Carmen averaged fifteen hours longer each week than Frank did — it added up to an extra month a year. But as a traditional, Carmen could not formally define her "double day" as a problem. Like a number of traditional women in my study, Carmen found a way around her dilemma. She claimed incompetence. She did not drive, so Frank had to shop with her. She did not have a mechanical sense, so

Frank had to get money from the automatic teller. In this way, Carmen got relief from her burdens but clung to her traditional notion of womanhood. . . . Carmen . . . [saw] Frank's help at home as a continual series of "gifts."

The Delacortes agreed on certain ritually symbolic extras, for which they felt a certain ritual gratitude. Frank occasionally brought flowers to Carmen. From time to time Carmen troubled to bake an apple pie, because it was Frank's favorite dessert. The roses and the pie were their private extras, symbols of other private gifts. . . .

The Shermans — Michael and Adrienne

Michael Sherman is a thoughtful, upper-middle-class engineer and in the eight years of marriage he has gradually at his wife's urging "converted" from traditional to egalitarian gender rules. His wife, Adrienne, is a college professor. By the time their twins were born, their understanding was that both would give priority to the family and would take whatever cuts in income and career they had to.

. . . When Michael bathed the twins, he was helping Adrienne; he was doing what a good father and a good man does. Adrienne was not grateful for Michael's help because she expected it. . . .

For his part, Michael was grateful because, despite their egalitarianism, Adrienne had for six years in good spirit moved from city to city, disrupting her professional training in order to follow him.

. . . Although Adrienne wanted her husband to treat her work as just as important as his, her salary was half of his. This piece of economic reality undermined her cultural claim to an equal part in the "class-making" of the family. Adrienne was grateful, then, when Michael honored her work despite the wage gap. . . . On one occasion, Michael brought the children to a conference at which she was giving a talk. As she rose to give her talk, she saw in the audience her beaming husband and two squirming children . . . she felt Michael had given her a great gift. (1989: 99–101)*

Although the two couples have very different ideas about what a marriage should be like, as

*Reprinted with permission from A. R. Hochschild, "The Economy of Gratitude," in *The Sociology of Emotions: Original Essays and Research Papers* (Greenwich, CT: JAI Press, Inc., 1989).

A husband who does more housework than his father did — and more than he himself used to do — may feel that he has made a substantial contribution to his wife. However, his wife may see the matter differently. If she works outside the home and still does most of the housework, she may welcome her husband's contribution but feel that it is less than she would like. Shared values for rewards are not "givens"; we cannot assume that all exchange relationships are based on them.

couples, the Delacortes and the Shermans share, *within* their own marriages, definitions of the values of the rewards they exchange. Each couple shares the definition of a gift and the corresponding feelings of gratitude. What one spouse felt was a gift, the other felt was a gift. Seldom was a gift "mis-received."

It is precisely because the values of the infinite variety of benefits we can exchange are not givens that disagreement between exchange partners is possible. Through interaction and negotiation, we may be able to arrive at shared definitions of what these commodities are worth. But not all exchange partners come to share such value norms. Hochschild continues:

> Take the example of housework in a two-job marriage. A husband does the laundry, makes the bed, washes the dishes. Relative to his father, his brother and several men on the block this husband helps

more at home. He also does more than he did ten years ago. All in all he feels he has done more than his wife could reasonably expect, and with good spirit. He has given her, he feels, a gift. She should, he feels, be grateful. However, to his wife the matter seems different. In addition to her eight hours at the office, she does 80% of the housework. Relative to all she does, relative to what she wants to expect of him, what she feels she deserves, her husband's contribution seems welcome, but not extra, not a gift. So his gift is "mis-received." For each partner has perceived this gift through a different cultural prism. (1989: 95–96)*

Hochschild's observations show that shared values for rewards are not "givens"; we cannot

*Reprinted with permission from A. R. Hochschild, "The Economy of Gratitude," in *The Sociology of Emotions: Original Essays and Research Papers* (Greenwich, CT: JAI Press, Inc., 1989).

assume that all exchange relationships are based on them. The partners in some exchange relationships share values; others do not. It seems reasonable to assume that partners with shared values function more smoothly than those with different values. Whether partnerships without shared values dissolve completely depends on the availability of alternative sources of rewards.

CULTURAL NORMS

Earlier in this chapter, we discussed norms in American culture which prescribe that we should help others who are in need and who are dependent on us—sympathy norms and the norm of social responsibility. Additional norms—those of reciprocity and equity—relate to our discussion of social exchange.

Norm of Reciprocity

Sociologist Alvin Gouldner (1960) proposed that much social exchange is regulated by a **norm of reciprocity**. The norm of reciprocity stipulates that (1) people should help those who have helped

them and (2) people should not injure those who have helped them. More broadly, social psychologists have viewed the norm of reciprocity as embodying the expectation that people return good for good and evil for evil. Thus, besides its positive form, the norm of reciprocity has a negative component guiding retaliation. Although people differ in their feelings regarding retaliation, negative reciprocity is embodied in the ancient code "A tooth for a tooth and an eye for an eye." (See the Student Observations: "The Norm of Reciprocity.")

People do not like to be in the debt of others. While reciprocal exchanges breed cooperation and good feelings, gifts that cannot be reciprocated breed discomfort, distress, and ultimately dislike. It is not surprising, therefore, that being unable to reciprocate a favor, or accepting assistance outside an ongoing relationship characterized by mutual cooperation and help, tends to reduce both our overall social esteem *and* our self-esteem (Staub, 1978). People often will fail to ask for help or will even refuse help that is offered if they feel that they cannot reciprocate (DePaulo

STUDENT OBSERVATIONS

The Norm of Reciprocity

Writing for the *Daily Tar Heel* [UNC's student newspaper] while leading an active social and academic life can be difficult at times. Last year one of my co-workers asked me to write for him on several occasions—when he had exams, papers, or social obligations. I always took on the extra work. But one day when I had two midterms to study for, I asked him nicely to work for me and he refused. The next time he needed a day off, he asked another writer instead of me to cover for him. I guess he thought that because he violated the *norm of reciprocity*, he shouldn't ask me for help again (or maybe he was just embarrassed). In any case, I doubt that I would have agreed to help him after he didn't help me.

I was struck by how relevant this norm has been in my interpersonal relationships. I was recently involved in a relationship in which I received most of the effort and caring without reciprocating. I was honest in telling my partner that I was not ready to give a lot of time or emotion to the relationship, but he persisted. He continued to offer his time, feelings, support, and gifts on a regular basis. I came to the point where the guilt and distress I felt because of this inequity forced me to make a change in the relationship. After reevaluating the relationship and imagining being without him, I discovered I was ready to give more of myself to make it work. It was a scary choice for me, but (obviously, I think) the correct one.

and Fisher, 1980). In accordance with the norm of reciprocity we feel that favors *should be* reciprocated. Accepting help thus obligates us to reciprocate, and obligations — especially those that are unclear — are uncomfortable. We may suspect that the cost of accepting help will eventually be greater than the benefit received; hence, we are reluctant to take on such obligations.

Profit Equity Norm

Is there a norm in our society supporting profit equity as the expected outcome of social exchanges? Psychologist J. Stacy Adams (1965) and sociologist George C. Homans (1974) both say yes. In the previous chapter, we discussed how the distribution of rewards among group members affected the members' performance and cooperation. The more the distribution was based on equity, the greater the likelihood of high performance and cooperation. Some evidence even suggests that people in our culture share the belief that we should receive returns (rewards) equal to what we put forth (costs) — that the resources we expend on behalf of others should equal the resources others expend on our behalf. We define a situation as "fair" or "just" when each person receives as much as others who provided the same input. We feel that a person who invests more deserves more, while a person who invests less deserves less. This shared belief — that the profits (rewards minus costs) of parties to an exchange should be equal — is called the **equity norm** or the **distributive justice norm** (Wrightsman, 1987). Note that it is the *profits, not the rewards*, that should be equal according to the equity norm. Profits take into account the balance of rewards *and* costs; both are crucial to determining equity. For example, a $20 donation from a poor widow is valued more than a $20 donation from a millionaire.

It seems to be important to people that they maintain equity (a proper ratio between their own inputs and their own outcomes), both in their own eyes and in the eyes of others. In general, people who receive greater amounts of help return greater amounts of help, and those who receive

more valuable help tend to give more valuable help in return (DePaulo, Brittingham, and Kaiser, 1983). Research supports the propositions (1) that people *believe* they would experience distress in an inequitable relationship and (2) that people participating in inequitable relationships actually *experience* distress. These propositions appear to be true for both the victims and the beneficiaries of an inequity. Those who receive less than they deserve often feel anger or depression; those who receive more feel guilt (Walster, Walster, and Berscheid, 1978; Hegtvedt, 1990; Mikula, Petri, and Tanzer, 1990; Sprecher, 1992).

But equity ultimately lies in the eye of the beholder. As Aesop observed, "The injuries we do and those we suffer are seldom weighed on the same scales." Thus people are *more* distressed by inequity when they are victims than when they are the harm doers. Those who benefit from inequity are more tolerant of inequity than those who suffer from it (Blumstein and Weinstein, 1969; Walster, Berscheid, and Walster, 1973). And those who suffer from inequity are quicker to demand a fair distribution of resources than those who do not suffer (Leventhal and Lane, 1970).

As we discussed earlier, reactions to inequity include (1) decreasing the exchange or terminating the relationship altogether, (2) restoring equity, and (3) doing nothing — letting the inequity continue. Although, as we discussed, a number of factors affect the likelihood of these reactions, research indicates that people *believe* they would probably behave so as to restore equity to the relationship (Sprecher, 1992). This is further evidence of the equity norm.

Summary

1. Some research suggests that those likely to help others have stronger beliefs in equity, greater empathy, and a sense of self-efficacy. Other studies indicate that helping is not so much a personality trait as it is a situationally determined trait.

2. Five steps involved in deciding whether to help in a particular situation are (1) noticing the

event, (2) interpreting the situation as one in which help is needed, (3) assessing whether help is deserved, (4) determining responsibility for helping, and (5) deciding what to do and how to do it. At each step of this decision process, situational factors may influence the outcome. For example, many emergencies and other helping opportunities are *ambiguous* events. In such events we observe the reactions of others and are powerfully influenced by them. Helping is often inhibited by our tendency to reason that most victims deserve their suffering, at least to some degree.

3. Cultural norms such as sympathy norms and the norm of social responsibility influence whether we decide that helping is our personal responsibility. When others are present, diffusion of responsibility may occur: the obligation to help and the potential blame for not helping are spread around — making helping less likely, especially when the costs of helping are high. In our society, men and women are expected to give different types of help. Although we are expected to help strangers on occasion, the expectation that we help friends and family members is stronger. Several other factors affect the likelihood of helping — good moods, rewards and costs of helping, and empathy.

4. Reward exchange is reciprocal helping. The likelihood that an individual will engage in exchange behavior with another person increases with his or her dependence on that other person. Dependence is the degree to which the other person provides the individual with valued rewards at costs lower than he or she can get via other alternatives (either personally or through third parties). An imbalance in the dependencies of the parties to an exchange will lead to efforts to reestablish the balance of the dependencies.

5. Since there is no way to ensure an appropriate return for a favor, social exchange requires trusting others to discharge their obligations. Typically, however, exchange relations evolve slowly, starting with minor transactions requiring little trust. Participants in an exchange may disagree about the values of the rewards and costs involved. When reward values are not shared, one or both partners may view the exchange as inequitable. Some social psychologists propose that most of us share beliefs that (1) people should help those who have helped them and (2) the profits of parties to an exchange should be equal.

CHAPTER 11

CLOSE RELATIONSHIPS: INTERPERSONAL ATTRACTION AND INTIMACY

*T*hink for a moment about what matters most to you in life. What gives your life meaning and brings you happiness? For many of us, the answer to this question involves our relationships with friends, lovers, and family – *primary relationships* (Caldwell and Peplau, 1982; Astin, 1985). Clearly, we recognize that all primary relationships are not the same. Social psychologists would say that the *bonds* in some relationships are more intense than the bonds in others. You might say that some of your relationships are "closer" or "more intimate" than others. But what do we mean when we say that we have a "close" or "intimate" relationship with someone? And what factors influence how we become involved in, and maintain or dissolve, such relationships? Let's see if social psychology can help answer these questions. In this chapter, we'll discuss the characteristics and types of close relationships, the factors affecting our initial attraction to another person, and the life course of close relationships.

Characteristics of Close Relationships

What makes a relationship *close* or *intimate*? According to James Averill (1985), society provides us with a set of criteria against which to match our experiences. We use these cultural scripts to decide whether we are "in love," whether another person is "just a friend" or "a close friend," and so on. Social psychologists have identified a number of characteristics that we use to distinguish close from less close relationships. These include certain intimate behaviors as well as intimate feelings. Let's begin our discussion with three kinds of intimate behaviors: companionship, self-disclosure, and helping.

INTIMATE BEHAVIORS

Companionship

One of the most obvious benefits of close relationships is the companionship that they provide (Hays, 1988; Allan, 1989). Being with certain others, spending time with them, and sharing activities and pastimes are valued for their own sake. Shared activities can be active or passive and can involve special events or quite ordinary interactions with others to whom we feel close. Such activities offer "amongst other things, a distraction from the more serious matters of life, a sense of involvement and participation in the social realm and a means of expressing one's character and individuality" (Allan, 1989). Most of us take the benefits of companionship for granted, but studies have shown that their significance becomes apparent when our opportunities for such interaction are restricted (McKee and Bell, 1986).

When respondents are asked to define friendship, studies show that *companionship*, or the enjoyment of each other's company, consistently emerges as a key feature (Weiss and Lowenthal, 1975; Crawford, 1977; Davis and Todd, 1982; Hays, 1988). We derive satisfaction from our interactions with partners in close relationships, in and of themselves. In other words, our bonds to these others are expressive bonds. Interactions with friends tend to revolve around leisure activities such as eating, drinking, and talking and are less task-oriented than those involving colleagues or kin (Argyle and Furnham, 1982). While friends can, and often do, serve instrumental purposes — helping us repair a car, study for an exam, make a decision — this is not the primary reason for our association with them. "Individuals can be useful because they are friends, but not friends because they are useful" (Allan, 1979).

Self-Disclosure

Social scientists find that communication plays a critical part in primary relationships, underlying and supporting most other processes and outcomes. **Self-disclosure** is the act of revealing one's "real" self to another person. Typically, it involves telling another about oneself. Through self-disclosure we express feelings, perceptions, fears, and inner doubts to a partner. We hope that the partner will respond in an *emotionally supportive* manner, that is, in an understanding and car-

One of the most obvious benefits of close relationships is the companionship they provide. Being with certain others, spending time with them, and sharing activities and pastimes are valued for their own sake. Interactions with friends tend to revolve around leisure activities and are less task oriented than those involving colleagues or kin.

ing way. Mutual self-disclosure can encourage relationship growth. Through self-disclosure partners in a relationship reveal their areas of vulnerability to each other. Partners must strategically manage their communications to protect each other's discovered vulnerabilities (Rawlins, 1983a, b). This promotes the development of *trust* between the parties — belief by one person in the integrity of another person. By the same token, trust fosters self-disclosure, for trust implies that individuals believe that other people are genuinely interested in their welfare and that these others are honest when revealing their future intentions. Not surprisingly, self-disclosure is significantly associated with relationship satisfaction (Jorgensen and Gaudy, 1980; Hendrick, 1981).

Self-disclosure is used strategically both to develop relationships and to discourage them or shape them into one form rather than another (Baxter and Wilmot, 1985; Duck, 1986). Self-disclosure implies that in some situations we can choose how much or how little we divulge to another. In brief, we can voluntarily alter the degree of openness we maintain in the course of a social relationship. For example, if a person reciprocates a particularly personal self-disclosure, the individual is presumably confirming his or her desire to develop the relationship further, since the option existed of not revealing the information. On the other hand, a person can discourage or limit a relationship by *not* reciprocating a self-disclosure, as this indicates that he or she doesn't desire the level of intimacy offered by the other person.

Social psychologists have repeatedly found that increased self-disclosure by one party increases self-disclosure by the other party; this is sometimes called the *dyadic effect* (Berg and Archer, 1982; Cunningham, Strassberg, and Haan, 1986; Derlega and Berg, 1987). Although the effect is firmly documented, social psychologists have three somewhat different explanations for it.

Social exchange theorists note that self-disclosure is positively related to *liking* (Worthy, Gary, and Kahn, 1969; Archer and Burleson,

1980). Mutual disclosure spirals upward as a relationship develops, with people disclosing more about themselves at each encounter. Presumably, by disclosing personal information to others, we reveal to them that we value and trust them. A second approach (Walster, Berscheid, and Walster, 1973; Davidson, Balswick, and Halverson, 1983), suggests that the *norm of reciprocity* obligates us to exchange comparable behaviors and maintain equity in a relationship. A third approach takes its cue from Sherif's experiments with the autokinetic phenomenon and Asch's work with distortions of judgments in group settings (see Chapter 9, "Performance, Conformity, and Cooperation"). The exchange of disclosures is seen as occurring because the partner who first provides a disclosure is defining for the other partner what constitutes appropriate behavior in an otherwise ambiguous situation (Rubin, 1975). An *emergent norm* is fashioned, establishing situational demands affecting disclosure response. Thus we may make self-disclosures not because of a feeling of attraction for the other party or because of a felt obligation to reciprocate but because we perceive the situation as calling for this type of behavior (Lynn, 1978).

It should be noted that not all self-disclosures are good for relationships. Through a partner's disclosures, a person may learn that the partner is not as "right" for her or him as the person once thought. Further, there are taboo topics that people tend to recognize and respect; past relationships and the state of the current relationship are two potentially dangerous themes (Baxter and Wilmot, 1985).

Most friendship interactions, research suggests, do not involve highly intimate disclosures. Among college students, for example, superficial conversation is the most frequent kind of interaction engaged in with friends (Hays, 1984, 1985; Duck and Miell, 1986; McCarthy, 1986). Several studies have examined the content of conversation between close friends. Middle-aged adults reported that their most common topics of conversation with friends were daily activities, community affairs, family activities, family problems, reminiscences, and work (Aries and Johnson, 1983).

Helping

Besides supplying companionship and fostering self-disclosure and trust, close relationships provide practical support. Our friends, lovers, and kin help us move furniture, feed our pets and water our houseplants when we are away, loan us their trucks, run errands for us, tell us about good prices on items we need, and so on. Close relations comprise, in this sense, part of the resources we rely on to manage our day-to-day affairs (Allan, 1979; Litwak, 1985; Wellman, 1985; Willmott, 1987; Rossi and Rossi, 1990).

There is substantial concern in close relationships about "using" or "taking advantage of" those who help us. As noted in Chapter 10, "Helping and Reward Exchange," we worry about whether it is appropriate to ask for assistance from a particular person unless the help is part of an ongoing exchange of favors or we have some way to repay the person in the future. This concern reflects the fact that even close relationships are not exempt from the pressure to maintain some sort of balance in exchanges; that is, they are subject to the norm of reciprocity. If requests for assistance are too one-sided, the relationship may be terminated, either abruptly or gradually as the feeling of "being used" intensifies (Wiseman, 1986; Willmott, 1987). This is unusual, however. Since we are sensitive to the need for balance, if our needs seem greater than those of our partner, we will often refuse assistance, even when offered, to avoid becoming too indebted or being judged as abusing the relationship.

In general, we depend on friends for fairly mundane favors that do not greatly inconvenience them. Such favors usually can be reciprocated easily and do not entail high levels of obligation. This does not mean that such help is unimportant. Limited though it may be, such support often helps us meet our objectives and cope with the demands others make upon us. The closer the

friendship is regarded as being, the less concern there usually is about asking for help. This is because trust in the relationship is well established.

INTIMATE FEELINGS

You may be thinking, "Finally, here's a section I know something about. We've all liked some people and loved others. I know what it's like to feel these emotions. What can social psychology have to add that I don't already know?" You might be very surprised. The study of intimate feelings — indeed, the study of all emotions — has received much attention in recent years by social psychologists.

Liking and Loving

Liking, as social psychologists use the term, is having a positive attitude toward a person. As we discussed in Chapter 6, "Social Attitudes and Attributions," having a positive attitude toward a person means that we evaluate the person as good and that we have a mental schema associating the person with characteristics that, overall, we view as positive.

All of us are familiar with the notion of *love*. Yet if letters to "Dear Abby" and "Ann Landers" are any indication, it seems that a good many Americans, particularly teenagers, are uncertain about what love is supposed to feel like and how they can recognize the experience within themselves. Common questions include: "How can I be sure that I'm in love?" "How can I tell if my partner loves me?" "What can I do to get my partner to be more committed to our relationship?" Social scientists and laypeople alike recognize that the intense emotion of love entails more than the mild feelings of liking. However, social psychologists have had difficulty specifying how these two essential relationships differ.

In our everyday lives we readily distinguish between friends and lovers and value each differently (Davis, 1985). A study examining undergraduates' and other adults' accounts of "falling in love" and "becoming friends" found that descriptions of the two kinds of relationships differed (Aron et al., 1989). Falling in love was more likely to be preceded by the respondent's discovery that the other person liked him or her, the recognition of the other's desirable characteristics, and special processes such as "being ready for love." In their descriptions of becoming friends, the respondents gave more emphasis to being similar to the other and being conveniently near the other person. Another study found that whether a person becomes friends with an ex-lover when a romantic relationship ends depends not so much on what things were like in the relationship as on whether the two were friends before they became romantically involved (Metts, Cupoch, and Bejlovec, 1989).

A 1970 study by Zick Rubin also suggests that love is not just an intense form of liking. In addition to having a positive attitude about the other, a person in *love* has a powerful desire to be with and be cared about by the partner (*needing*) and shows a high degree of *concern* about the partner's needs (*caring*). Rubin developed measures of liking and loving that reflect these differences. The liking scale asks about the degree to which you respect, admire, and have confidence in the other person. The loving scale asks about need, caring, trust, and tolerance.

A study by Steck and colleagues (1982) indicates that the four components of Rubin's love scale — need, caring, trust, and tolerance — are not equally important as indicators of love. These researchers made up a number of patterns of responses to the love scale and asked undergraduates to rate the degree of love they thought each pattern expressed. For example, one pattern revealed that the person responding to the scale had agreed strongly with the need items and only mildly with the care items. Another pattern suggested that a different person had strongly agreed with the care items and only mildly with the need items. These two patterns would yield the same score on the love scale. However, the raters indicated that care plays a more important role in judgments of love than does need. In other words,

they rated the person who indicated strong care and mild need as more in love than the person indicating strong need and mild care. Trust was not a particularly important factor for judgments of love, but it was as important as care for judgments of friendship. Judgments of liking were not very different from judgments of love, perhaps indicating that Rubin's differentiation of the two concepts is clearer than the difference in people's minds.

Types of Love

Some social psychologists have found it useful to differentiate between types of love. Elaine (Walster) Hatfield and her colleagues (Berscheid and Walster, 1974; Walster and Walster, 1978; Hatfield, 1988) were among the first to do so. They identified two types: companionate love and passionate love. *Passionate love* is a "wildly emotional state" (Walster and Walster, 1978: 2). Intense and usually highly sexual, it entails extreme absorption in, acute longing for and dependency on, and strong bodily sensations in response to a loved one. *Companionate love* is the steadier, less intense affection we feel for those with whom our lives are closely connected.

The major differences between the two types of love are *emotional intensity* and *stability*. Passionate love is very intense: "The highs are higher and the lows are lower" (Brehm, 1985: 92). The love relationship is often the primary focus in life. It may be hard for a person to work or even to enjoy the company of others because she or he is always thinking about the partner. In companionate love, the attachment is strong, but it is calmer and steadier — more relaxed — tending not to "overshadow all other joys" (Brehm, 1985: 93). As you may imagine, the emotional intensity of passionate love can be exhausting, and at some point the realities of the world are likely to intrude on a person's single-minded concentration on her or his lover. Hence the common wisdom that "mad, passionate love" tends to wane over time (Huston, 1973; Traupmann and Hatfield, 1981). Companionate love is based on more definite, less fragile attachments to the partner — such as the trust, respect, and admiration measured by Rubin's liking scale.

Both types of love relationships can involve sexuality — or not. Passionate love often includes intense sexual experiences, but romantic lovers may have little or no sexual interaction. Nevertheless, passionate love almost always involves sexual *attraction* to the partner. Companionate love, on the other hand, can be experienced with or without sexual feelings and behavior. Some companionate relationships are characterized by sexual attraction and frequent sexual interaction and others, such as close friendships, by none.

Sternberg's Triangular Theory of Love

Robert Sternberg (Sternberg and Grajek, 1984; Sternberg, 1986, 1988) has suggested that love has three basic components, which, when combined in different proportions, produce eight types of love. The three basic components of love are intimacy, passion, and commitment. *Intimacy* is emotional closeness — a feeling of bondedness to the other person. It usually comprises concern for the partner's welfare, as well as mutual understanding and support. Intimacy is expressed through self-disclosure, emotional support, and practical helping. *Passion* refers to the arousal of physical attraction and sexual drives. It is expressed through such actions as kissing, touching, and sexual intercourse. *Decision/commitment* involves the short-term decision that one loves the other person and the long-term promise to maintain the relationship. It is demonstrated by such actions as saying "I love you," becoming engaged, getting married, and sticking with the relationship through hard times.

Sternberg's (1986) triangular theory of love is diagrammed in Figure 11-1. *Nonlove*, or the absence of love, occurs when all three basic components are absent, as is the case in casual interac-

FIGURE 11-1 STERNBERG'S TRIANGULAR THEORY OF LOVE

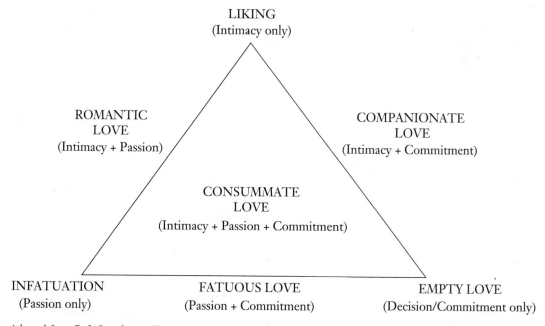

Adapted from R. J. Sternberg, "Triangulating Love," in R. J. Sternberg and M. L. Barnes (eds.), *The Psychology of Love* (New Haven, CT: Yale University Press, 1988), p. 122. © Copyright 1988 by Yale University. All rights reserved. Reprinted by permission.

tions between acquaintances or in instrumental interactions. *Liking*, which characterizes many close friendships, involves relatively high levels of intimacy but low levels of passion and commitment. *Infatuation* is experienced when passion is high but intimacy and commitment are low. Love at first sight is an example of infatuation. *Empty love* is characterized by high commitment in the absence of intimacy and passion. A marriage in which the partners don't feel intimacy or passion but stay together "for the sake of the children" is an example of empty love.

Romantic love is the combination of intimacy and passion without commitment. *Companionate love* consists of intimacy and commitment without passion, such as in long-term friendships or marriages in which passion has declined over time. *Fatuous love* involves commitment and passion without intimacy. Finally, there is *consummate love*, the combination of all three components.

According to Sternberg, the types of love, such as the passionate love and companionate love described by Walster, need not be "all-or-nothing" propositions. The triangular theory stresses that love consists of several ingredients and that these can be combined in different proportions to produce different experiences of love. Sternberg's research indicates that when there is a good match between the partners' love, the two tend to feel satisfied with their relationship. When there is a mismatch, dissatisfaction is more likely. For example, relationship problems are likely if both partners feel the same level of passion for each other but one wants more intimacy and commitment than the other.

The Sociology of Emotion

Some social psychologists do not agree with the common-sense notion of emotions as simply internal states. Emotions, they argue, do *not* arise exclusively within our bodies. They are *not biological givens* and are *not private, inner,* or *deep.* Instead, emotions are *social* in two ways: They arise out of social interaction and are given meaning by shared, cultural definitions (McCarthy, 1989).

This explains why two persons may experience the same event yet feel different emotions.

According to the two-stage theory of emotion, an emotion includes an internal state of arousal *and* a reflexive process of emotional identification. Morris Rosenberg (1990) suggests one reason cognitive factors play such a large part in emotional identification is that the internal state of arousal is often ambiguous. We must use additional information to decide *what* we are feeling. Rosenberg identifies three cognitive factors that may affect our emotional identification: causal assumptions, social consensus, and cultural scenarios.

We employ *causal assumptions* to help us decide which emotion we are feeling. In the course of socialization, we come to view emotions within a causal framework. That is, we learn that certain events are expected to produce certain emotions and that particular emotions produce specific behaviors. In our culture, for example, an insult is expected to lead to anger; a compliment, to pleasure; a threat, to fear; and sexual attraction, to intimacy. In addition, anger may lead to aggression and fear to withdrawal. By undergoing these experiences ourselves, observing others in similar situations, and talking about such situations with others, as well as through movies, television, and other mass media, we learn to accept our culture's emotion logic. We come to see particular emotions not just as typical, or usual, responses but as *logically necessary* outcomes and causes of events.

Another basis for inferring the nature of an internal state of arousal is other people's responses — *social consensus.* If everyone around us is fleeing in panic, we may conclude that we, too, are afraid. If everyone treats two partners as a couple, they may conclude that they are in love. Even a single other person can influence what inferences an individual makes about the nature of his or her internal state.

We sometimes identify our emotional experiences by matching our thoughts, feelings, and behaviors with an *emotional template,* or *cultural scenario,* provided by our society. For example, an

American person and a Japanese person may feel very different emotions in response to the same situation. An event that makes the Japanese person feel ashamed, for example, might make the American feel angry. This is because the Japanese and American cultures have different rules specifying when these emotions are appropriate. Emotions, then, including liking and loving, are our reactions to experiences. We react reflexively by taking our own feelings as objects and comparing them to the emotion scripts our culture provides. This allows us to label our emotions — to "know"

what we are feeling. Cultural scripts may change over time. (See, for example, the box "Jealousy in American Culture.")

COMMITMENT

A person's **commitment** to a relationship is the probability that he or she will try to maintain the relationship — it is what we called a "bond" in Chapter 4, "Social Relationships and Groups." When we say people are committed to a relationship, we mean that they are likely to stay in the

JEALOUSY IN AMERICAN CULTURE

That emotions are social as well as psychological phenomena is illustrated by a study conducted by Gordon Clanton (1989), which shows that patterns of emotional experience change in response to cultural changes. Clanton studied *jealousy* — a protective reaction to a perceived threat to a valued relationship. He identified approximately 80 articles about jealousy by examining an index of almost 200 popular magazines from 1945 to 1985.

From the end of World War II until the late 1960s, Clanton found that virtually all the articles in popular magazines agreed that a certain amount of jealousy was natural. It was seen as a normal accompaniment of love, an inevitablity, a proof of love, and a good ingredient for marriage. Women were advised to avoid situations that might make their husbands jealous but to interpret their husbands' expressions of jealousy as evidence of love. They were also warned to keep their own jealous feelings "under control" and to avoid "unreasonable" jealousy, characterized by suspicion, hostility, accusations, and threats. The focus was on episodes of "normal" jealousy, which show that love is alive. The conclusion was, therefore, that jealousy should not threaten the quality of the relationship.

By about 1970, magazine articles began to question the appropriateness of jealous feelings in love relationships. According to the new view, jealousy was *not* natural, *not* evidence of love, and *not* good

for relationships. Rather, it was evidence of a defect such as low self-esteem, insecurity, or excessive possessiveness. Thus, jealousy was seen as *bad* for relationships, and various prescriptions for eradicating traces of jealousy from one's personality were offered by advice-givers of all sorts.

Clanton argues that the new view of jealousy that arose in the 1970s was a by-product of a change in the meaning of love relationships in the United States. Indeed, researchers Francesca Cancian and Steven Gordon (1988) report that their analysis of magazine articles shows that the meaning of love did change during this period of time. Before the 1960s, articles suggested to women that love was signified by self-sacrifice — that they should suppress their individual interests in favor of their husbands' interests or for "the relationship." By the late 1960s, love had come to imply self-fulfillment and marriage was viewed as a partnership in self-development. As a result of these and other manifestations of concern for personal freedom in love relationships, jealousy came to be viewed by many as a personal defect — as inappropriate and undesirable.

Clanton suggests that while many people still hold the view that jealousy is a personal defect, "commitment" is making a comeback. He believes that as AIDS and other developments make our culture more conservative about sex, jealousy will, to some degree, come back into fashion.

relationship "through thick and thin," "for better or worse." Commitment helps us understand why some relationships endure and others do not. In the words of one man married for more than twenty years:

> Commitment implies a willingness to be unhappy for a while. I wouldn't go on for years and years being wretched in my marriage. But you can't avoid troubled times. You're not going to be happy with each other all the time. That's when commitment is really important. (Lauer and Lauer, 1985: 25)

Commitment indicates that the partners in a relationship have been able to negotiate a balance of long-term and short-term interests that is beneficial to both — relative to other available options. Commitment helps explain why people stay in relationships that might be, for the moment, not particularly rewarding. In addition to assessing current outcomes, a person also takes into account the past history of the relationship, his or her investments in it, and what the alternatives seem to be.

Cognitive consistency researchers suggest that the more freely, publicly, and frequently someone acts in a particular way, the more committed that person becomes to the action and to the attitudes it implies. Thus, by freely acting as though she or he is part of a relationship and by thinking positively about the partner, the person will become more committed to this line of action and way of thinking. If this seems a little too magical to be true, recall our discussion of Bem's self-perception theory in Chapter 8, "Attitudes and Behavior." What happens, in effect, is that we observe our own behavior and the associated circumstances in order to interpret our internal states. We reason that if we stay with a romantic partner even though we are perfectly free to leave, we must be staying because we want to do so. Acting as though we are committed to a relationship also indicates to others that we are unavailable and is likely to reduce their interest in us. This increases our commitment by reducing the alternatives available to us.

Societies increase commitment to certain roles by constraining the options available to individuals. For example, the marital role is more difficult to leave than the friendship role, partly because our society regulates marriage and divorce. Consequently, the costs of divorce are higher than the costs of ending a friendship. Burke and Reitzes (1991) have pointed out that we are also committed to maintaining certain *identities* and that we act to sustain and support those identities. This view emphasizes that we are active agents who make our own decisions. We might, for example, remain in a relationship with fewer rewards than we would like because to end it would destroy others' views of us and, ultimately, our views of ourselves as "devoted spouses."

So why don't all committed relationships last forever? In spite of elaborate and expensive wedding ceremonies, joint bank accounts, public identification as a couple, and children, many marriages still end in divorce. When an individual is committed to a relationship, the person looks ahead to continuously being with the partner. When things are going well, this expectation of future involvement is pleasantly anticipated. But when things are going badly, every negative aspect of the relationship has not only an existence in the present but also a potential existence in the future. The person may begin to worry that "giving in" on some trivial point will be an indication to the partner of the person's willingness to surrender on other, more important issues. Consider this example:

> There is an old story about a marriage breaking up because the husband couldn't stand the way his wife squeezed the toothpaste tube in the middle instead of, like him, rolling it up from the bottom. This sounds ridiculous, but in the context of the present discussion maybe there is a great deal of wisdom about human behavior in the story. Every morning that husband had to think about facing that squashed toothpaste tube for every coming morning of his life. And, standing in the bathroom, only half-awake, he may have thought "First the toothpaste . . . then what?" (Brehm, 1985: 194).

In addition to considering "What makes relationships close?" and "What's the difference between love and liking?" social psychologists have sought the answers to such questions as: "What are the forms that our close relationships take?" "How do we come to choose some individuals over others as the objects of our affection?" "How do close relationships change?" These questions will be the focus of the remainder of this chapter.

Types of Close Relationships

There are several kinds of primary relationships in which intimacy or closeness is often expressed: same-sex and other-sex friendships, romances, marriages, parent-child relationships, and other familial or kin relationships. Of these, the types most often studied are same-sex friendships and heterosexual romantic relationships and marriages.

FRIENDSHIP

Friendship is distinguished from some other types of primary relationships by its *voluntary* nature. We choose our friends but not our relatives, for example. Friendships are not supported by institutional structures, blood ties, or social arrangements. A friendship survives only through the special efforts its members make to continue the relationship. This makes friendships more vulnerable and less stable than other primary relationships, but this voluntary quality is highly valued. When a friend helps us out in a difficult time, we are especially touched because we know he or she *chose* to help us (Ridgeway, 1983).

Throughout our lives, friends reinforce, shape, and sometimes challenge our identities. They do this in numerous and subtle ways — through disclosure and emotional support, through humor (perhaps kidding us about trying to appear to be something that *they* think we are not). When a person voluntarily spends time with others, he or she grows to identify with them to some degree. If

the person's status changes significantly, the change is likely to be reflected in his or her self-concept and may result in the person's replacing some friendships with others that are more congruent with the new identity and support it more effectively. For example, numerous studies indicate that when adolescents enter the courtship scene, their friendships alter dramatically. They give up their same-sex group or gang for friends who are couples (Griffin, 1985; Coffield, Borrill, and Marshall, 1986). In contrast, when people divorce, their ties with friends who are couples tend to weaken (this is discussed further later in the chapter).

Because friendship groups focus on their members' unique characteristics and concerns, they tend to develop highly specialized group cultures — the internal cultures, or idiocultures, we discussed in Chapter 4, "Relationships and Groups." These consist of jokes, rituals, and special concerns relevant only to the specific people who are members. Because the group culture is so specialized, it cannot easily accommodate new members. If a new person is added to a friendship group, considerable restructuring will be necessary to take into account the unique concerns of the new member. Because this seriously disrupts the group, friendship groups do not experience as much membership turnover as some other groups do. Instead of recruiting new members when old members are lost, most friendship groups simply shrink or disband. Friendship groups would be less rewarding to us if we felt that we could easily be replaced in them by others.

Men's Friendships

On the whole, men appear likely to be involved in relationships whose basis is sociability and enjoyment. Often these relationships are focused on specific tasks and activities. Nevertheless, men do develop close relationships based on shared action. Men express intimacy by exchanging favors, engaging in competitive action, joking, sharing accomplishments, and including one another in activities. Most of these relationships are likely to involve little self-disclosure of personal worries.

Men's friendships are often based on the sociability and enjoyment of joint tasks and activities.

British social psychologist Graham Allan has suggested that such patterns of friendship seem quite well adapted to the demands of men's roles in modern industrial societies:

> Men are supposed to be strong and self-sufficient, able to get along well with a range of others, yet not become dependent on them. At least some of their careers demand mobility, so that the capacity to generate (and, of course, break off) ties with others has some utility. Furthermore, in some respects, there is a tension between cooperation and competition, friendliness and self-interest within the occupational sphere, so that a form of friendship which entails strong elements of nonintimate fellowship appears well-suited. (1989: 72)

Gender stereotypes apparently not only shape the friendships that men have but also help sustain the notions of maleness (Allan, 1989; Swain, 1989). The emphasis in male friendships is on doing things, often in groups rather than in dyads. Relationships tend to be limited to particular con-

texts, helping to structure the setting so that disclosure of intimate matters is unlikely. Kidding and needling are frequent in such interactions, reinforcing the moratorium on self-disclosure. Making verbal disclosures and touching sometimes occur but only in particular circumstances. Otherwise, these behaviors are seen to be *unmasculine* (Swain, 1989). *Homophobia* — the irrational fear or intolerance of homosexuality — is a socially determined prejudice much like sexism or racism. Fear of being labeled "homosexual" ensures that heterosexual males maintain "appropriate" male behavior (Lehne, 1989).

Women's Friendships

Some research suggests that females develop fewer informal contacts and relationships than males do. Women's friendships are oriented less around specific activities than are men's, with talk playing a larger role in female friends' interactions (Baxter and Wilmot, 1986; Hays, 1988). Women tend to emphasize emotional sharing, trusting, and confiding in their interactions with friends more than do males. Most studies of self-disclosure indicate that females self-disclose more than males. Males appear to disclose less than females in same-sex encounters but not in interactions with females (Derlega et al., 1985; Reis, Senchak, and Solomon, 1985). This would contribute to an overall difference in self-disclosure between men and women, since both males and females tend to interact more with same- than opposite-sex others.

The differences between men's and women's friendships have led to debates about which type of friendship is "better." On the one hand, some argue that our culture defines close or intimate relationships in terms of self-disclosure and thus that women's friendships are better than men's, since women disclose more in same-gender relationships than men do. Others react to this "feminine definition" of closeness by arguing that men's friendships can be as close as women's but that males show closeness in different ways, such as through shared activities. Thus, sociologist Francesca Cancian (1986) argues that although women in our society verbally express feelings of affection more than men do, this does *not* mean that women are more loving or caring. She main-

tains that men are equally loving and caring but that they express these feelings nonverbally through behaviors such as doing favors or sharing activities. Other researchers believe that each gender fails to fully understand, and thus tends to devalue, the other gender's style of expressing care (Swain, 1989).

These different styles result partly from the way males and females are socialized (see our discussion in Chapters 2 and 3) *and* partly from the different social worlds they inhabit as adults. Boys tend to have larger friendship networks than do girls, but girls tend to disclose more about themselves—their feelings, anxieties, concerns—than do boys (Maccoby and Jacklin, 1974; Hess, 1979; Dickens and Perlman, 1981). Boys' relationships with their peers are based on shared activities. Girls' peer relationships focus on the relationships themselves. Verbally communicating and disclosing self-information plays a far larger part in girls' relationships than in those of boys.

In adulthood, males generally lead more public lives than females. Their work and leisure activities bring them into contact with a relatively wide range of others with whom they are required to develop cordial, though not necessarily close, relationships. Women, on the other hand, especially those whose traditional roles exclude work outside the home and whose greater domestic and child-care responsibilities leave less time for activities outside the home, generally have less opportunity to develop such extensive social networks. Instead, in their family responsibilities, they are expected to devote much of their time and energy to serving the needs of a relatively small number of others. We'll see examples of these points later in the discussion of specific types of close relationships.

Some researchers have noted that our culture tends to idealize men's friendships and trivialize women's. Think of all the books and movies that portray the adventures of male buddies: the men are shown doing things together. At the same time, popular images of women's friendships show housewives idly gossiping over the fence or

Women's friendships are oriented less around specific activities than are men's, with talk—emotional sharing, trusting, and confiding—playing a larger role.

chatting over coffee or tea, situations reflecting the low level of esteem in which these relationships are held. Indeed, the movie *Thelma and Louise* generated much controversy by showing females in the traditionally male roles of buddies sharing a sometimes-violent adventure.

Cross-Sex Friendships

Researchers have paid little attention to cross-sex friendships — platonic relationships between men and women. The sex segregation of occupational and social structures may make it less likely that men and women will meet and interact under conditions that facilitate friendship.

Social norms often discourage cross-sex friendships, implying that such relationships are a threat to marital relationships (Lampe, 1985). Studies have shown that married and romantically involved couples, especially those in the middle class, tend to socialize primarily with other couples (Allan, 1989). However, this does not mean that the friendship ties among the four individuals in a two-couple relationship are equally strong. Culturally, the expectation seems to be that the closest relationships will occur between the two males and between the two females rather than across gender boundaries. Separate conversations more commonly develop within the same-sex pairings than between the male and female of different couples. Similarly, it is more common for the two females or the two males in a couple friendship to socialize with each other without their partners than it is for the male and female of different couples to do so.

Sociologist Bert Adams (1985) argues that we are socialized extensively regarding how to behave in same-gender friendships but not cross-gender friendships. Our cross-gender socialization is so focused on romantic relationships that opposite-gender friendships are frequently judged to include some level of sexual interest. Because of the possibility of sexual involvement, social pressure and control are often exerted to a greater degree on cross-gender than on same-gender friendships. Cross-gender friendships are more likely to develop when the potential sexuality of the relationship

is neutralized by some factor of the situation (Bell, 1976). For example, in the couple relationships mentioned above, the presence of both couples sustains the asexual definition of the friendship ties. Likewise, in friendships between opposite-sex colleagues, the work setting clearly defines the scope of the relationship. Another situational factor that neutralizes sexual implications of cross-sex friendship is a large age difference, especially if the female is much older than the male.

Adams (1985) suggests that cross-gender friendships will become more common as younger cohorts experience less gender segregation in such institutions as school and work, since this would provide males and females with more opportunities to meet socially and would decrease the controls exerted over their contacts. Others argue that as long as gender shapes social experience to such a large degree, it is unlikely that there will be radical shifts in friendship patterns (Allan, 1989). Those taking the second position argue that there is little evidence that cross-gender friendships are becoming more socially legitimized. Such relationships continue to be viewed as different from same-gender friendships and are not supported by social organizations the way same-gender friendships are. Which position does your own experience support? (Before reading further, look at the Student Observation: "Cross-Sex Friendships.")

ROMANTIC AND MARRIAGE RELATIONSHIPS

Romantic relationships differ from friendships in that *sexuality* is involved, either actually or potentially. In our culture, romantic relationships also are expected to be *exclusive*. That is, in general, we are expected to be romantically involved with only one partner at a time. This is not an expectation of friendships. In most instances, one friendship is not lessened by the existence of others. In romantic relationships, progressive commitment is expected, along with an evolving emphasis on sexual exclusivity. For example, once two people have dated a certain number of times, they often find

---

STUDENT OBSERVATION

Cross-Sex Friendships

My mother has had a very close male friend who went to both high school and college with her. Although they both now have their own families, they remain close friends and contact each other frequently. Our society, however, tends to view cross-sex relationships primarily in terms of romantic relationships, so people often think that cross-sex friendships involve some sexual interest. For example, when my father and my mother's friend were first introduced, my father was a bit leery of the relationship. He felt that my mother's friend must have had more than friendship on his mind all these years. But as my father grew to know him better, he realized that theirs was a very special friendship — one that just happened to cross gender barriers. My mother is still very close to her friend, and as a result, the two families are now close as well.

---

themselves "going steady" by default. Other males respect the male partner's "territory" and don't ask the female out. When a romantic relationship does *not* develop greater exclusivity and commitment over time, we often judge it to be "going nowhere."

Marriage changes a romantic couple's relationship — even if the partners lived together before marrying — by increasing expectations for exclusivity and commitment (Arond and Pauker, 1987). As we noted in Chapter 3, "Socialization over the Life Course," marriage is a *rite of passage* meant to change how the partners see themselves and how others see them. One change occurring with marriage is the activation of a host of beliefs about wives' and husbands' roles. One husband, for example, noted that before his wedding, he and his partner ate out regularly and enjoyed this practice. He expected it to continue. His wife, however, felt that married people ought to eat at home. Another new husband surprised both himself and his wife by becoming extremely angry when his wife disagreed with his choice of presidential candidates (Arond and Pauker, 1987).

The Development of Romantic-Feeling Norms

Many ideas about love and romantic relationships start to take shape in early adolescence. Although we do not have much information about the

specifics of this process, one study, conducted by researchers Robin Simon, Donna Eder, and Cathy Evans (1992), examined the peer culture of adolescent girls to see if they had developed norms involving romantic love. All the girls studied attended a middle school (Grades 6, 7, and 8) in a Midwestern community; most were white and middle class. The researchers gathered data over a three-year period, using a variety of methods that included participant observation, audio and audiovisual recording, and in-depth group interviews. Three female researchers observed ten adolescent peer groups during lunch periods twice a week, over time spans ranging from five months to two years.

Romantic love, the researchers found, was a frequent topic of conversation among the female students, beginning in the seventh grade. Most conversations about romance took place when boys were absent. The researchers concluded that the girls not only had acquired cultural knowledge about romantic love but also had developed several feeling and expression norms in response to their own concerns about romance. Four "love norms" were identified, although at least one was still in the process of being negotiated:

1. *One should have romantic feelings only for someone of the opposite sex.* This was the most basic norm concerning the object of romance. By the time

the girls had become actively interested in romance, a norm of heterosexuality had developed among the groups. This is reflected in the words of a seventh-grader, as described by the researcher:

> Sally . . . was going on and on about how somebody would sign her letters "love you queerly." She said, "I always sign my letters 'love you dearly but not queerly.'" (Simon, Eder, and Evans, 1992: 36)

Group members frequently teased one another about behaviors that could be interpreted as homosexual, such as close physical contact between friends. For example, they distinguished between a "friendship" hug and a "romantic" hug. And girls who did not express romantic interest in boys or who had gender-atypical interests often were the targets of gossip. The researchers summarized the opinion of a seventh-grader:

> Sandy said her sister is extremely different from her and has absolutely no interest in boys — she considers boys pests. Sandy referred to her sister as a tomboy. [Her sister was interested in sports and in becoming a mechanic.] She said that since her sister is a tomboy, if she liked boys then she would be queer, but on the other hand, if she liked girls then she would really be queer. (Simon, Eder, and Evans, 1992: 35)

2. *One should not have romantic feelings for a boy who is already attached.* As long as romantic activities consisted of only talking about the objects of their affections, this norm had little significance. It was not uncommon for many group members to like the same boy. But once a group member was actively pursuing a boy or had formed a relationship with him, it was no longer acceptable for other girls to express romantic feelings for him. Acceptable contact with the boy was limited to behavior that promoted their friend's romantic interests, such as serving as an intermediary. Violation of this norm subjected girls to the negative label "flirt."

3. *One should have romantic feelings for only one boy at a time.* In some groups, this exclusivity norm appeared to reflect the girls' awareness of the societal norm of monogamy; in others, its function was to avoid creating jealousy among the boyfriends. Even though the girls knew that they should have romantic feelings for only one boy at a time, they sometimes found themselves feeling multiple attractions. Those who did faced criticism, as shown in the researchers' summary of a situation involving eighth-graders:

> I heard Karla being teased when a specific boy walked by. Her friends were saying that she had a crush on him and once they yelled it at the boy. Karla acted rather embarrassed and angry about this. . . . They said that they had seen her walking with him in the halls. After a long pause Karla asked Laura rather indignantly, "How could I like him when I'm already going with somebody?" Effie said, "Two-timing." Karla was embarrassed and seemed rather mild in her denial. (Simon, Eder, and Evans, 1992: 41)

4. *One should always be in love.* Although romantic relationships should be important, they should not be everything in life. This belief was held less widely than those discussed above; thus it was less normative. It was still a matter of negotiation within many of the groups. However, for some girls, the onset of their first romantic attraction was the beginning of a continuous state of being in love — despite many changes in the object of affection. For example, one of the researchers, noticing that a girl had "I love" written on her hand, asked her about it. Although the girl's romantic feelings had no particular target, she explained that she was ready to add the name of a boy as soon as a suitable target was found. One way for the girls to remain continuously in love was to "recycle" boys with whom they had had a previous relationship. (See the Student Observation: "Romantic-Feeling Norms.")

Group members also had mixed attitudes about the importance of relationships with boys relative

---

STUDENT OBSERVATION

Romantic-Feeling Norms

*T*he fourth norm of romantic love states that "one should always be in love." My freshman roommate lived by this rule. She seemed to be in a perpetual state of "love." Practically every week there was a new man to occupy her. She studied and made pretty good grades, but her main purpose seemed to be to find a boyfriend. When she needed a fellow, she often recycled guys she had dated previously. We talked several times about her feelings of needing to be in love all the time. She always protested that she was not continually in search of love. But she also said that she felt more negatively about herself when she had no immediate romantic prospect and that, in order to be self-confident, she needed someone to emphasize her good qualities (hence, a boyfriend).

---

to their other interests. Some girls thought they could not live without boys; others believed that doing their schoolwork and learning about themselves were more important. In discussing this issue, the girls sometimes exchanged negative labels, calling each other "boy-crazy" (or "slut" when more serious) or "lesbies."

Gender Differences in Heterosexual Romantic Relationships

We have just discussed some of the differences between men's and women's styles of intimacy, especially in relation to companionship, self-disclosure, and support. Because of these differences, heterosexual romantic relationships, like cross-gender friendships, often bring together two partners who don't communicate closeness the same way. The exclusivity of romantic relationships sometimes intensifies the problems caused by these differences.

Our culture has traditionally prescribed different sexual roles for males and females. In the 1950s the prescription was that love, sex, and marriage should always go together. But a double standard existed in terms of how this prescription was applied to males and females. Women were expected to remain virgins until they married; premarital sexual experiences for females were strongly condemned.

More recently, attitudes toward premarital sexuality have changed. Premarital sexual activity is more acceptable now, as long as it occurs within the context of a close relationship (Sprecher, 1989). Still, premarital sexuality is not uniformly accepted. A 1987 Gallup Poll found that 46 percent of Americans still disapprove of sex before marriage, while 48 percent think it is acceptable (Gallup, 1988). Opinions about premarital sexuality vary by age. Of those over age fifty, 65 percent disapprove of premarital sex, compared with 27 percent of those under age thirty. College-educated persons and those with higher incomes and white-collar occupations are more accepting of premarital sex than persons with less education, lower incomes, and blue-collar occupations (Gallup, 1988). Men tend to be more approving of premarital sex than do women (Sprecher, 1989).

Since the 1950s, premarital sexual activity has increased, especially among women. Virginity at marriage has become the exception rather than the rule (Williams, 1989). In a 1988 study, 80 percent of nineteen-year-old females and 88 percent of nineteen-year-old males reported that they had had intercourse (Johnson, 1989). Despite these changes in behavior, the double standard has not totally disappeared (Christopher and Frandsen, 1990). Men are still seen as the initiators of sex — the ones with power.

Some researchers argue that our culture expects women to be more expressive than men (Dosser, Balswick, and Halverson, 1986). Still others suggest that inexpressiveness is not learned by males as an end in itself but as a means for them to assume and maintain positions of power. In other words, men use inexpressiveness in conversations with women to indicate that the interaction is to proceed by *their* rules, according to *their* timetable (Sattel, 1990). Even with other men they hide emotion "to *consolidate* power, to make the effort appear effortless, to guard against showing the real limits of one's potential and power by making it *all* appear easy" (Sattel, 1990: 380).

In Western societies, the widely accepted ideology about love has been dubbed "romanticism." **Romanticism** consists of two basic beliefs: "Love conquers all," and "One should marry for love" (Brehm, 1985). Several studies of American college students indicate that, at least among that age group, males tend to be more romantic than females, endorsing such statements as "True love lasts forever," "True love comes but once," and "Love conquers all" (Peplau, 1983; Brehm, 1985; Sprecher and Metts, 1989). Women are more likely to say that we can each love many people, economic security is as important as passion, and some disillusionment often accompanies long-term relationships. The most common explanation given for this gender difference in romanticism is that females need to pick their mates more carefully because they are choosing a "provider and protector" (Buehler and Wells, 1981). Researchers have also asked people about their specific romantic experiences. Females usually report having been in love more frequently than males (Dion and Dion, 1973). However, males report falling in love earlier than do females (Kanin, Davidson, and Scheck, 1970; Huston et al., 1981).

Homosexual Romantic Relationships

In many respects, intimate homosexual relationships are similar to heterosexual ones. Letitia Peplau (1981) surveyed gay men, lesbians, and heterosexual men and women. The homosexual respondents were volunteers, recruited from homosexual organizations, advertisements, and informal social networks. To compare homosexuals and heterosexuals on attitudes and values, Peplau matched a sample of homosexual respondents

with a sample of heterosexual respondents on the basis of similarities in age, education level, and length of current romantic relationship. Heterosexuals and homosexuals, she found, differ little in their orientation toward love relationships, leading her to conclude that differences in values were linked more to *gender* than to *sexual orientation*. Blumstein and Schwartz (1983) reached a similar conclusion — that gender is a more important determinant of the nature of couple relationships than is sexual orientation — in a study of married heterosexual couples, unmarried heterosexual cohabitants, gay male couples, and lesbian couples.

That lesbian couples consist of two *women* and gay male couples consist of two *men* is important because of the differences in gender socialization: "Males are socialized to engage in sexual behavior both with and without affection while women are more expected to combine the two. As a result, when two men enter a partnership, nonexclusiveness can be expected, while when two women enter a partnership, exclusiveness could be expected" (Harry, 1983: 226). Among lesbians, sexual relationships usually arise out of a developing affectionate relationship; among gay men, affection often develops from a sexual relationship. Studies done in the early 1980s revealed that about 40 to 50 percent of gay men were partners in stable relationships at any given time, as compared with about 75 percent of lesbians (Bell, Weinberg, and Hammersmith, 1981; Harry, 1983). These studies also indicated that, following a breakup, gay men tended to go through long periods of nonexclusive sexual activity, while lesbians tended to find a new partner quickly. More recent studies suggest that casual sexual contacts among homosexual males have decreased due to a fear of contracting AIDS (Quadland and Shattis, 1987).

Homosexual relationships do differ from heterosexual relationships in two important ways. First, homosexuals are much less likely to adopt traditional masculine and feminine roles in their relationships and are more likely to be egalitarian. Some researchers have suggested that this is because the partners in homosexual couples are more likely than those in heterosexual couples to have similar incomes (Blumstein and Schwartz, 1983; Harry, 1983). Second, homosexual relationships, on the average, tend to last for a shorter time—although this, too, may be changing as a result of the AIDS crisis. The shorter duration of homosexual relationships may stem partly from the fact that homosexual partnerships are not reinforced by societal expectations of permanence but, rather, must endure substantial social disapproval.

FAMILY AND KIN

We have been discussing friendships, romantic relationships, and marriages. These relationships are characterized by a high degree of choice. While we *choose* our friends and lovers, our kin are defined in terms of a number of cultural rules, based on a combination of biological and legal concepts—ties through blood and marriage. According to these rules, certain people are our relatives—aunts, uncles, sisters, brothers, in-laws, cousins. A number of aspects of our relationships with kin are *obligatory*. For example, the norms of our culture specify that parents and children and grandparents and grandchildren should have *some* relationship. A father who never sees his child and who doesn't check on how the child is doing would be judged a bad father by most people. Most of us would feel some obligation to help a sibling who was in trouble—but less obligation to help a cousin with the same problem.

Allan (1979) suggests that interaction with kin is not considered social in the same sense that interaction with friends is. Interaction with kin is a way of expressing concern and interest; such interaction is not engaged in simply for enjoyment, as interaction often is with friends. While we may enjoy our visits with kin a great deal, there is nonetheless a strong element of obligation involved.

Often our interaction with relatives is a way of expressing concern and interest and is not engaged in simply for enjoyment, as interaction usually is with friends. While we may enjoy our visits with kin a great deal, there is nonetheless a strong element of obligation involved.

Support for this proposal comes from Alice and Peter Rossi (1990), who have noted that we are so embedded in our society's kinship system that we take its rules for granted. As part of a study of Boston families spanning several generations, the Rossis undertook an empirical study of kinship norms. In Chapter 10, "Helping and Reward Exchange," we reported on their findings about the norms that specify the strength of our obligations to help various relatives. They found strong evidence of the existence of obligation norms.

While geographic separation often ends a friendship, this is not so with relationships between parents and children and between siblings. These relationships endure even when a comparatively limited amount and range of contact is involved. One study found, for example, that about 50 percent of American adults reported seeing and talking to their siblings at least once a month, and about two-thirds considered at least one of their siblings to be among their closest friends (White and Riedmann, 1992). Another study found that support from parents to their children declines as the children enter their forties. Nevertheless, the parents continue to be viewed as valued and dependable sources of support should a need for help arise (Cooney and Uhlenberg, 1992).

Let's examine in greater depth how close relationships develop. George Levinger (1980) has suggested that it is useful to look at relationships in terms of five general phases of development. This approach is called the *ABCDE model of relationship development* because of the five phases it incorporates: *a*ttraction, *b*uilding, *c*ontinuation, *d*eterioration, and *e*nding. Not every close relationship goes through all five phases, of course. But all do begin with attraction, which may explain why social psychologists have given so much attention to this topic.

Factors Affecting Initial Attraction

Attraction to strangers is the starting point for many primary relationships (Duck, 1986). What causes us to be attracted (and attractive) to other people? Of all the strangers with whom we come into contact, why do we prefer some to others? It may seem that common-sense knowledge can adequately explain attraction with little need for social psychological study. But a little reflection reveals numerous examples in which common-sense explanations lack reliability. Indeed, common-sense knowledge is often contradictory: "Opposites attract," yet "Birds of a feather flock together." "Absence makes the heart grow fonder," yet "Out of sight, out of mind." "True love never dies," yet "Love is like linen, often changed." "There's no fool like an old fool," yet "Love, like wine, is best when aged." Clearly we cannot rely on common-sense knowledge for an understanding of social attraction. Research has shown that proximity, familiarity, arousal, physical attractiveness, similarity, complementary needs, and social exchange are key determinants of social attraction.

PROXIMITY

Proximity—nearness in physical space—has a considerable influence on our friendship choices. Various studies reveal that students typically develop closer friendships with those who share their classes, who sit near them, or who live near them (Segal, 1974).

These findings suggest that proximity plays a critical part in attraction by providing the *opportunity* for people to interact with one another: persons who are physically closer are more available than those farther away. Proximity acts as a physical screen in determining the probability of initial contact. Obviously, we cannot like or be friends with someone we have never met. Once people are in contact with one another, other factors determine the course of the relationship. For instance, an equal status ranking among the parties facilitates friendship; an unequal status ranking impedes friendship (Schutte and Light, 1978).

However, although proximity provides the opportunity for people to interact, it does not guarantee attraction. It is possible that the interaction may be negative. In such cases, proximity may breed contempt rather than attraction. Police records reveal that aggravated assault and murder occur most frequently among family members, neighbors, and acquaintances. Although proximity may be a necessary condition for attraction, it also may function as a condition for hatred.

Take the case of "environment spoiling." We may dislike another because of the unpleasant things he or she does. For instance, in a suburban setting, a dog might be allowed to bark without control, music might be played too loudly at night, the other party might not mow her lawn or might complain about the state of one's own lawn, and so on. If events of this sort occur frequently enough, they can lead to disliking even in the absence of face-to-face contact. Since we cannot easily avoid such experiences in a neighborhood setting, proximity can directly affect the formation of negative relationships. (Before reading further, look at the Student Observation: "Proximity.")

FAMILIARITY

One of the reasons that proximity may increase liking—over and above the obvious fact that it offers an opportunity for liking—is that it increases familiarity. Proximity increases the chances of being exposed to another person. And there is some evidence that mere exposure, in and of itself, can enhance liking.

The *familiarity*, or *mere exposure effect*, has been demonstrated by Robert Zajonc and his associates. In one study (Moreland and Zajonc, 1982), the researchers showed college students pictures of faces. Subjects saw some of the faces as many as twenty-five times and others only once or twice. Afterward, the subjects were asked to indicate how much they thought they would like each of the persons pictured. The more often the subjects had seen the same person's face, the more they said that they thought they would like the person. The same result has been found for repeated exposure to actual people (Saergert, Swap, and Zajonc, 1973).

As is true of proximity, there are definite limits to familiarity's effect on liking. For example, repeated exposure to a person who is initially perceived as positive, or at least neutral, increases liking. However, repeated exposure to a person who is initially perceived as strongly negative does not have this effect (Perlman and Oskamp, 1971).

AROUSAL

Writing *The Art of Love* in first-century Rome, the poet Ovid noted that an excellent time for a man to arouse romantic passion in a woman was while

---

STUDENT OBSERVATION

Proximity

Living in Granville Towers [a dormlike apartment complex] during my freshman year provided me with an excellent example of the impact of proximity on initial attraction. I lived on one end of a thirty-room hall that was divided in the middle by a set of elevators. Because I had to pass all the rooms on my end of the hall each time I used the elevator, I had an excellent opportunity to interact with the people on that half of the floor often. My best friends were the people in my suite and the one across the hall, but I knew and was friendly with all of the people on my half of the floor (except for two, who constantly complained about the noise). However, I can recall only three of the people who lived on the other side of the elevators. In fact, I always felt very out of place "hanging out" on their side of the elevators, even though this was only nine or ten doors away from my own room. This illustrates how architectural decisions and perceived distances affect potential friendships.

watching gladiators disembowel one another in the arena. Presumably the emotions of fear and repulsion excited by the grisly scene were somehow converted into romantic interest. Studies of "falling in love" suggest that there may be some truth to Ovid's observation. Social psychologists such as Zick Rubin (1977) and Ellen Berscheid and Elaine (Walster) Hatfield (Berscheid and Walster, 1974) assert that passionate love, like other emotional states, requires arousal and then the assignment of a label to that arousal. Intense attraction, they suggest, is most likely to occur when people are in situations in which they experience physiological arousal, such as during an exciting football game, the bombardment of a city, or a frightening storm.

An experiment by Donald G. Dutton and Arthur R. Aron (1974) helps our understanding of this matter. These researchers undertook their study near two footbridges that cross the Capilano River in North Vancouver, Canada. The first bridge, suspended 230 feet above the rushing rapids, tended to tilt, sway, and wobble and had low handrails of wire cable; in brief, the bridge had many arousal-inducing features. The second bridge, farther upriver, was a solid wood structure only 10 feet above a small, shallow stream.

An attractive female experimenter approached men who had crossed either of the bridges and explained that she was doing a project for her psychology class on "the effects of exposure to scenic attractions on creative expression." The men were asked to complete a questionnaire with a number of brief "filler items" and write a short dramatic story based on a picture she showed them. When the subjects had completed their questionnaires, the woman gave each man her name and telephone number and told him to call if he desired more information about the study.

As revealed by the content of their stories, the men who had been on the frightening suspension bridge were more sexually aroused than the men who had been on the solid bridge. Additionally, half of the men on the high-fear bridge called the young woman, ostensibly to find out more about her study. (In contrast, only 13 percent of those on the low-fear bridge called her.) Presumably, the men on the rickety bridge had relabeled their inner stirrings of fear as the product of sexual arousal and romantic attraction. This sort of labeling is encouraged by the cultural script that portrays falling in love as entailing such symptoms as a pounding heart, shortness of breath, and trembling hands (also the physical symptoms of fear). In sum, according to this view, love does not exist unless we define our inner feelings of arousal as love. Consequently, it is easy for people to follow the romantic clues that abound in their environment and decide that they are "in love."

Not all researchers accept the notion that love is physiologically indistinguishable from other arousal states, such as fear. Michael R. Liebowitz (1983), a clinical psychiatrist, believes that love has a unique chemical basis, which is associated with phenylethylamine (a compound related to the amphetamines).

Studying patients who have a history of roller-coaster love affairs, Liebowitz finds that the individuals often have a craving for chocolate after a breakup. Chocolate has a high supply of the mood-altering chemical phenylethylamine. Perhaps, reasons Liebowitz, the brain pours out its own chemical correlate to amphetamine—phenylethylamine—when the person is in love and halts production of the substance in a breakup, leaving the person to suffer from its absence. Chocolate binges may simply be an attempt at self-medication.

PHYSICAL ATTRACTIVENESS

If we ask people about the importance of various factors that might affect their attraction to another person, most will tell us that the person's physical attractiveness is not very important (Simenquer and Carroll, 1982). However, when we examine how people actually respond to others, we discover that physical attractiveness plays a major role.

Social psychologists find that we prefer the companionship and friendship of attractive people to that of unattractive people (Reis, Nezlek, and

Wheeler, 1980; Marks, Miller, and Maruyama, 1981; Hatfield and Sprecher, 1986). Likewise, even when appearance has no conceivable tie to the requirements of a job, people with good looks are more likely to be hired, even by experienced personnel officers. And when television technicians pan a football crowd, they stop and focus the camera on an attractive person. Apparently the advantages of being attractive start early. Newborn infants who are independently judged as attractive are held, cuddled, and kissed more than less attractive babies (Berscheid, 1982).

A study of clients of a commercial dating service confirms the importance of physical attractiveness. As part of the normal procedures of the dating service, clients had access to detailed files about other clients. Each file contained a photograph, background information, and answers to open-ended questions about interests, hobbies, ideals, and relationship goals. Clients screened prospective partners on the basis of this information. The dating service had each client select five people he or she would like to date and another five he or she would definitely not be interested in dating. To assess physical attractiveness for purposes of the study, research assistants evaluated the photos of all clients. The researchers concluded that physical attractiveness was a major factor in partner selection, since both males and females wanted to date the more attractive people and rejected the less attractive people (Green, Buchanan, and Heuer, 1984). A study of a video dating service (Woll, 1986) replicated these results, finding that physical attractiveness is an important factor in men's and women's initial screenings of prospective dates.

In *hypothetical* situations, research shows that we think in terms of idealized visions and prefer a date or mate of considerable physical attractiveness. Very simply, physical beauty seems to be rewarding for both sexes, both as an individual experience and for the reflected status it brings. But the supply of unusually beautiful or handsome partners is limited. Real-life situations generally confirm the *matching hypothesis of mate selection*, which holds that we tend to acquire partners who

have a degree of physical attractiveness similar to our own (Berscheid et al., 1971; Murstein, 1972; Feingold, 1988). Hence, although we strongly prefer physically attractive individuals as dates (and also like them more), in actual practice, we tend to settle for persons as dates whose attractiveness is very similar to our own. (See the Student Observation: "The Dating Game.")

Some evidence indicates that being *similar* in physical attractiveness affects the progress and quality of a relationship. One researcher (Folkes, 1982*b*) studied clients of a professional dating service that supplied its clients with background information about prospective dates, plus a photo and a five-minute videotape of each (in the latter, the prospective date responded to interview questions). If the client was interested in dating someone, the service asked that person for permission to release his or her name to the interested client. The researcher asked judges to rate the physical attractiveness of the clients on the basis of the same photos and videotapes that the clients saw. He measured the progression of the relationship on a five-step scale:

1. One client interested in meeting, but the other does not allow release of his or her name.
2. Potential partner does allow release of name.
3. The two clients have telephone contact.
4. The clients have one date.
5. The clients have two or more dates.

The research indicated that the more similar couples were in physical attractiveness, the more their relationship progressed.

ATTITUDE SIMILARITY

A good deal of research reveals that we tend to like others whose attitudes are similar to our own. In experiment after experiment, subjects say that they like people whom the experimenter suggests are close to them in beliefs and attitudes. In fact, the greater the proportion of similar attitudes held by two people, the greater their attraction to

---

STUDENT OBSERVATION

The Dating Game

*L*ast year Ted, my brother, was in eighth grade. He was friendly during the year with Kris. Both shared similar interests and he felt quite comfortable with her. So he asked Kris to the May Dance, and Kris gave him an affirmative response. Well, Ted's friends quickly heard that he was taking Kris to the dance and really gave the poor kid a rough time. They made all kinds of derogatory remarks about Kris. That same evening Ted came home from school and started sobbing uncontrollably. He told mom that he wasn't going to go to the dance, but mom insisted that since he had asked Kris, he had to follow through on it. Well, he took Kris to the dance, but he wouldn't even talk to her in the halls thereafter. Apparently, Ted's classmates had let him know that Kris was at a lower level in the peer group's erotic-popularity hierarchy than he was.

Well, another dance has now rolled around. Ted has had a "crush" on one girl since both were in seventh grade. She is a petite number, a real "all-American girl." She ranks at the very top of the erotic-popularity hierarchy. For the past four weeks Ted has been putting the "moves" on her, and the other day he asked her to go to the May Dance with him. She outright refused. I had guessed as much before he asked her, as Ted is somewhat lower in the ranking system.

Yesterday some of Ted's classmates were telling him, "You ought to ask Dot to the May Dance." But Ted told me last evening that he didn't care that much for Dot. Today Ted learned that the kids in study hall had "polled" one another and decided that he ought to ask Dot to the dance. And another girl informed Ted that she had talked with Dot and that Dot had said that if Ted asked her, she "probably" would go with him. So Ted now has asked Dot, and they're going to the dance together.

All of this seems very interesting to me. Certain patterns seem to be at work in the dating game at the junior high school. The students have pretty well arrived at some sort of erotic hierarchy—the relative physical attractiveness and popularity of their peers. On the basis of this informal hierarchy, they engage in "matchmaking." If you violate the ranking system, you are punished: the girl is likely to refuse to go out with you if she is ranked higher; if she is ranked lower, your peer group bugs you to death. It seems to me that this arrangement gives a new twist to the matching hypothesis of mate selection. The theory says that we tend to choose partners whose physical attractiveness is similar to our own. But such selection is not merely a function of one's own behavior—translating one's own options into reality. It is also a product of the behavior of one's group, which brings pressure on individuals to date and mate with others of like ranking. We also see from the experience of my brother how one's clique or network operates to "arrange" certain pairings. This arrangement smooths the way for the "coupling" of a boy and a girl and saves each from the embarrassment of rejection. Mate selection is clearly a social, or group, happening.

---

each other tends to be (Gonzales et al., 1983) and the longer their friendships are likely to last (Griffin and Sparks, 1990). Conversely, people are less favorable toward others who disagree with them. Studies of marriages also point to the impact of **homogamy**—the tendency of "like to marry like." More than a hundred studies have been conducted on homogamy. They have dealt with such diverse characteristics as age, race, religion, nationality, social class, social attitudes,

education, previous marital status, intelligence, neuroticism, emotional stability, deafness, health, and physical height. With few exceptions, people who are similar marry more often than would be expected by chance. (Homogamy appears most influential in the realm of social variables. The evidence is less clear with regard to various psychological and personality components.)

Unlike physical appearance, attitudes are not so apparent when people first meet. It may take several episodes of interaction for one person to get to know very much about another person's attitudes and beliefs. To test the hypothesis that people who discover that their attitudes are similar will like each other more than those who discover that their attitudes are dissimilar, Theodore Newcomb (1956, 1961, 1963) acquired a large house at the University of Michigan and offered male undergraduates free housing in return for participating in his study. Before the students arrived, Newcomb asked them to fill out various questionnaires about their attitudes and values. He assigned roommates so that some had very similar and others dissimilar attitudes. Over the next sixteen weeks, Newcomb studied the development of friendships among the group.

At first, roommates were most attracted to each other, irrespective of similarity in attitudes and values (proximity and familiarity effects!). But, with the passage of time, similarity in attitudes and values increasingly became a factor in attraction. Shared attitudes toward other group members, and similarity between the attitudes an individual held toward himself and the attitudes held toward him by another, assumed critical importance. Knowing the degree of similarity that existed among the men *before* they moved into the house enabled Newcomb to predict who would be attracted to whom by the end of the period. Evidently it took the men a certain amount of time to learn who held values similar and dissimilar to their own. By the end of the semester, roommates whose attitudes were similar before they met were more likely to like each other and be friends than were those whose attitudes were initially dissimilar. Neimeyer and Mitchell (1988) found similar effects.

Milton Rosenbaum (1986) has proposed an alternative explanation for the relationship between similarity and attraction. He argues that similarity doesn't increase attraction but, rather, that dissimilarity causes repulsion. Dissimilar attitudes and other negative factors are especially important in the early stages of relationships (Byrne, Clore, and Smeaton, 1986). We tend to avoid, or at least not to seek out, interaction with others

having these characteristics. There is evidence that if people have dissimilar attitudes when they first meet, their attraction tends to decrease over time (Neimeyer and Mitchell, 1988). As relationships develop, similar attitudes and other positive factors may become more important as we make decisions about increasing relationship closeness.

Why should this be so? Why should similarity lead to liking—or dissimilarity to disliking? A number of explanations have been advanced by social psychologists. Some researchers have suggested that this is partly because people who experience a like world are able to *communicate more effectively* with one another (Padgett and Wolosin, 1980). We may also be attracted to others who are similar to us because we *assume they will like us*. And being liked can, in turn, produce liking for the would-be friend. Researchers find, for instance, that if people believe a stranger will like them, they like the stranger (McWhirter and Jecker, 1967). Others argue that the perception of similarity is rewarding because it provides us with independent evidence of the correctness of our interpretations of social reality. The individual feels that his or her *point of view is validated* and that he or she can confidently and effectively cope with the environment. Similarity, then, reinforces people's "need for competence" and, in doing so, feeds attraction. In contrast, dissimilar attitudes are presumed to threaten the person's view of the world, leading to dislike and avoidance (Byrne, Clore, and Smeaton, 1986; Rosenbaum, 1986).

Although similarity usually leads to liking, there are some circumstances that cause similarity to be threatening. If someone similar to us suffers an unfortunate outcome or is shown to possess an important flaw, we may worry about our own vulnerability. This may make us uncomfortable around the person and lead us to avoid him or her. This outcome was illustrated by a study in which subjects read a questionnaire supposedly completed by another student whose attitudes were either very similar or dissimilar to their own (Novak and Lerner, 1968). For half of the subjects in the similar and dissimilar conditions, the other person was portrayed as "disturbed." The disturbed other wrote at the end of the questionnaire: "I don't know if this is relevant or not, but last fall I had a kind of a nervous breakdown and I had to be hospitalized for a while. I've been seeing a psychiatrist ever since. As you probably noticed, I'm pretty shaky right now." For the other half of the subjects in both conditions, this information was not presented. Among subjects who evaluated a "normal" other, similarity of attitudes increased liking. For those who evaluated a "disturbed" other, similarity *decreased* liking.

COMPLEMENTARY NEEDS/ROLE COMPATIBILITY

People with some personality traits "rub us the wrong way," whereas we feel comfortable with individuals who exhibit certain other traits. Robert F. Winch (1958) formulated a theory of attraction based on this everyday observation. Instead of stressing the similarities between people, Winch emphasizes differences. He focuses on the role of **complementary needs** in producing attraction. This term refers to two different personality traits that are the counterparts of each other and provide a sense of completeness when they are joined. They mutually supply each other's lack.

Winch notes that many of our needs are met in a complementary manner. People possessing a strong desire for recognition may love and be loved by deferential people who prefer to bask in the achievements of others. Within such relationships, each person's needs are satisfied. People with a nurturance need (a need to sympathize with or help others in difficulty) find fulfillment with people who have a succorance need (a need to be helped and taken care of). Dominant people find a complementary relationship with submissive people. Talkative people are attracted to taciturn people.

The theory of complementary needs appeals to common sense — the notion that "opposites attract" — and we can all think of examples that seem to substantiate the theory (the domineering male and the mousy wife, or vice versa), but actual studies have produced mixed findings. While a number support the theory (Kerckhoff and Davis, 1962; Becker, 1964; Rychlak, 1965), others fail to confirm it (Levinger, Senn, and Jorgensen, 1970; Meyer and Pepper, 1977; Fishbein and Thelen, 1981; Antill, 1983). One problem is that some of our personality needs are complemented by similarity rather than by contrast. For instance, a quiet, thoughtful, introverted person usually prefers a similar companion rather than a loud, active extrovert.

Bernard Murstein (1967, 1972, 1976) suggests a somewhat different version of the theory, for which there is more research support. He stresses

---

STUDENT OBSERVATION

Complementary Needs

I recently ran into an old girlfriend and discovered something about my preferences in women. Although Ann and I went together for nearly a year and seemed to care a good deal for each other, something was wrong with the relationship. I'm very outgoing, extroverted, talkative, and aggressive. In many ways, Ann shared these characteristics, although to a somewhat lesser extent. I think this was part of the difficulty. I'm now going with Marie, and we plan to get married in June. Marie is quiet, retiring — even shy. We seem to complement each other in this respect, whereas Ann and I always seemed to be engaged in an underlying tussle to see who would be out front and in command of the relationship. We just didn't seem to find a good fit, whereas Marie is no rival for me. She welcomes my taking the lead in the world and prefers a more dependent role. Of interest, Ann is now going with a guy who strikes me as being on the passive side.

the part that **role compatibility** plays in interpersonal attraction—how well both partners fulfill the role expectations of each other and how mutually gratifying their role "fit" is. This version of the theory stresses complementarity of personal resources and role expectations rather than personality needs. For instance, a man who defines his primary family role as that of "provider" may be more comfortable with a spouse who wants to be "provided for," as opposed to a spouse for whom earning an income is also important. A bedroom athlete is likely to be attracted to a lusty, passionate partner rather than a cool, cerebral one with little "animal" sensuousness. Thus, according to Murstein, the essential determinant of marital adjustment is the degree to which each spouse fulfills the other's expectations of the ideal husband or wife. (Before reading further, look at the Student Observation: "Complementary Needs.")

SOCIAL EXCHANGE

On the basis of the principles of social exchange theory, Peter M. Blau (1964) suggests that we usually end up with the friends, lovers, and marriage partners that we "deserve." If we want to reap the benefits of associating with others, we must offer them enough to entice them to enter into and maintain a relationship with us. The more individuals have to offer, the greater will be the demand for their company. Consequently, we will have to provide such people with more benefits if we hope to win their friendship. The principle of supply and demand ensures that we will get partners only as desirable as we are ourselves.

A major advantage of social exchange theory is that it enables us to identify unifying principles that underlie the other factors of attraction. Take physical beauty, discussed earlier in the chapter. Suppose a physically unattractive man desires a woman who has the asset of beauty (Murstein, 1972). Other things being equal, she would gain less profit from the relationship than he would; therefore, he reasons that his suit is likely to be rejected. Moreover, rejection would constitute a cost to him, since he would lose in self-esteem. If

he should try to date a woman less attractive than he is, on the other hand, he feels confident of success; the cost is low, because he risks little chance of rejection. But the reward in such a conquest is also low. He can obtain the greatest reward at the least cost when he directs his efforts toward a woman approximately equal to him in physical attractiveness—thus the proposition that people tend to select partners of physical attractiveness comparable to their own. An exception to this tendency occurs when one person provides beauty in exchange for a *different* resource, such as financial support.

Social exchange theory is also helpful in explaining other factors in attraction. People who are geographically close (proximity) are more likely to interact because of the low cost of initiating the interaction. People whose attitudes and values are similar can offer each other the reward of attitudinal validation and social support also at low cost. And the participants in complementary relationships also offer each other high rewards at low cost to themselves.

The Life Course of Close Relationships

We have discussed the factors that increase the probability that an individual will find another person attractive and desire to establish a relationship with him or her. If the other person also finds the individual attractive, then the stage is set for the development of a relationship between the two. From the point of initial attraction, however, relationships take different forms and follow different courses of development.

BUILDING CLOSE RELATIONSHIPS

When two people meet and are attracted to one another, a primary relationship may, or may not, develop. People do not go on to develop a primary relationship with every attractive person they meet. Reasons for the failure to move from attraction to relationship include lack of interest (e.g., being married or engaged, having too little time or too many commitments), inappropriateness (e.g., not wanting to date the boss or to develop a relationship with a co-worker), and incompetence (e.g., feeling unable to carry out one's wishes to develop a relationship due to shyness or lack of social skills).

Relationships do not develop simply because two people find each other attractive. People have to *do* something to create a relationship. What a person does is reveal information about herself or himself and attempt to detect information about the other person. Using the processes described in Chapter 6, "Social Attitudes and Attributions," the person revises and reevaluates her or his initially sketchy model of the other person. Using the process of self-presentation described in Chapter 7, "The Social Nature of Self," the person strategically reveals personal information to make the partner like her or him. Initial moves toward a relationship may be tentative and deliberately ambiguous to minimize risks of rejection and allow time to resolve uncertainty about the desirability of the other as a friend or romantic partner.

Cultural Rules

Relationship development is also affected by cultural views about the nature of various relationships and the rules for conducting them. There exist, in effect, social blueprints for a "good marriage," a "close friendship," and an "extramarital affair." Thus we all know the difference between a friendship and an extramarital affair. We know that one is "approved" while the other is not. We compare our developing relationships to such cultural blueprints and make judgments: "We have a very strong friendship." "I guess it wasn't a good marriage after all." "The relationship wasn't going anywhere." "The relationship was too intense." Our feelings about a relationship — that it is going well or going badly — depend to some degree on what we expect of such relationships. Our expectations derive in part from cultural blueprints (Duck, 1986; Sabatelli and Pearce, 1986).

Our execution of the cultural rules of relationships will likely affect our partners' view of our skills and intentions. One study identified forty-three friendship rules, such as "Trust and confide in the other," "Show emotional support," "Don't criticize the friend in public," "Don't nag," and "Respect privacy" (Argyle and Henderson, 1984). Some rules were particularly central in that breaking them dissolved the friendship. Others were used to distinguish ordinary friendships from high-quality ones. Some people are more skilled at following relationship rules for friendships than are others, and such skills tend to run in families (Burns and Farina, 1986). We learn friendship skills, it appears, from our parents.

Quantity and Quality of Interaction

As interpersonal relationships progress from initial acquaintance to close friendship, the amount of interaction (breadth) and the intimacy level (depth) increase. Hays (1984, 1985) asked first-term university students to complete an extensive checklist of the types of interaction they had engaged in within newly forming friendships at three-week intervals during their first semester. In the early stages of friendships, the *quantity* of interaction between the partners accounted for most of the variance in the students' ratings of friendship strength. However, as the friendships progressed, *intimacy* level, rather than quantity of interaction, became more important as a predictor of perceived friendship strength. Other researchers have also found increasingly intimate interaction between friends as relationships develop (Berg, 1984; Duck and Miell, 1986). Several studies suggest that the progression to close friendship occurs quickly (Hays, 1984, 1985; Berg and Clark, 1986).

Among university students, the period between the third and sixth weeks of a relationship appears to be particularly important as a friendship-building phase. This period serves as an exploratory time, during which potential friends get to know each other and sample the possibilities of a relationship before evolving more stable patterns of interaction. They seek out one another for activities and share growing amounts of information with each other. One student observed: "We have become closer. We increasingly spend more time together. I also can tell her things that I may not have felt comfortable telling her three weeks ago" (Hays, 1985: 920). After an initial flurry that peaks at about six weeks, the rate of interaction drops off to some extent. It seems that as the school term progresses, students have less free time to devote to their friends. And they may also form other friendships that compete for their time.

Intimate interactions create a climate of trust, stable expectations, and practices within which intimate interactions are more likely. They thereby increase feelings of being understood, supported, and cared for. One study suggests that as perceived understanding — the feeling of being understood — increases, so does satisfaction with communication with the partner and satisfaction with the relationship (Cahn, 1990). This was especially true in closer relationships and those that had lasted longer. When partners sense that they mutually foster these feelings in each other, they become more committed to the relationship (Reis and Shaver, 1988). For example, as a woman pays

Intimate interactions create a climate of trust, stable expectations, and practices within which intimate interactions are more likely. They increase feelings of being understood, supported, and cared for, thereby increasing satisfaction with the relationship.

more attention to and shares more activities with her new romantic partner, she spends less time with old friends; she adjusts her lifestyle around being with her new partner. Researchers have found that as young couples move from occasional dating through various stages to becoming engaged and married, they tend to withdraw from other social networks (Johnson and Leslie, 1982; Milardo, Johnson, and Huston, 1983). This binding together of the routines of partners' everyday lives contributes to the development of a sense of interdependence and commitment.

Partners communicate their growing attachment to each other through *tie signs* — behaviors indicating that they are a couple. We noted, for example, in Chapter 5, "Communication," that lovers sit closer to each other than do friends and that they gaze at each other more. Partners may put their arms around each other while walking down the street, hold hands, dress alike, or wear wedding rings to communicate their "we-ness." These displays reassure the partners and tell the outside world, too, that they want to be considered a couple.

Exchange, Closeness, and Commitment

Research indicates that the greater were college students' ratings of the amount of benefits received from interacting with friends, the higher were their ratings of friendship closeness (Hays, 1985). Dyads with declining benefit ratings did not progress to close friendship. When asked to list the types of benefits received from their friendships, respondents identified companionship, having a confidant, emotional support, information exchange, material or task assistance, and increased self-esteem. Companionship was the benefit most often cited. However, having a confidant and emotional support were more often cited as benefits for close friends than for nonclose, suggesting that these are the critical factors that make a friendship "close" (Hays, 1988, 1989).

Some research suggests that in close relationships rewards may be a more important element than costs. A study of heterosexual dating relationships found that increases over time in rewards led to corresponding increases in satis-faction and commitment, whereas variations in costs did not significantly affect either (Rusbult, 1980, 1983; Rusbult, Johnson, and Morrow, 1986). And a study of long-term friendships among college students showed that benefit scores, not cost or benefit-minus-cost scores, are the best predictor of the current and long-term status of relationships (Hays, 1985). In other words, relationships become close because of in-creasing benefits — sometimes in spite of increas-ing costs.

Evidence suggests that the norms of exchange governing friendships change as friendships be-come closer. As we noted in Chapter 10, "Help-ing and Reward Exchange," in casual friendships, a norm of reciprocity — a fairly immediate "pay-back" of benefits — is expected. Closer friends do not expect this immediate tit-for-tat reciproca-tion but assume that an eventual balance will be reached in the long term, a condition referred to as exchange expansion.

The prevalence of exchange expansion in close relationships may account for recent findings sup-porting the idea that absolute reward levels pre-dict relationship satisfaction and stability better than either equity (equality of the partners' ratios of rewards to costs) or equality (equality of the partners' rewards) (Cate et al., 1982; Lloyd, Cate, and Henton, 1984; Michaels, Edwards, and Acock, 1984, 1986; Cate, Lloyd, and Henton, 1985). Researchers studying relationships over a three-month period found that equity became *less* predictive of changes in satisfaction, while abso-lute rewards became *more* predictive (Cate, Lloyd, and Long, 1988). Possibly, we are concerned with the fairness of the reward distribution early in a close relationship but become less concerned as the relationship develops. Other research suggests that if later in the relationship reward levels drop, we may again return to a tit-for-tat exchange of both positive and negative behaviors (Filsinger and Thoma, 1988).

As relationship researcher Steve Duck notes: "Relationships have their permanence *in the mind*, on the basis of beliefs, not just of behaviour. They survive distance, climate, revolt, pestilence, and

Acts of God, as long as we both *think* they have" (1986: 91). The exchange of benefits characteris-tic of close relationships is not based on an ac-counting system that "begins each day as a blank tablet." Instead, the exchange becomes an un-challenged and comfortably predictable aspect of our lives derived from the assumption that most of our future interactions will be supported on the foundations of today's. Our interdependencies with our partners may become taken for granted precisely because they are built into the routines of our lives. Disruption of these taken-for-granted routines may partly account for the severe distress that often accompanies the breakdown of rela-tionships. (See the box "Successful Marriages.")

CONTINUATION: CHANGE AND ADAPTATIONS

A relationship exists when the partners think they have one and represent that belief in their behav-ior toward each other. The beliefs and behaviors that constitute a relationship are always evolving. To continue to exist, relationships require ongo-ing interaction between the partners. Each inter-action between the partners not only *expresses* the degree and type of relationship the individuals have but also *affects* the relationship, serving to maintain, strengthen, or weaken the partners' bonds (Baxter and Wilmot, 1986; Hays, 1988).

The existence of culturally prescribed scripts may facilitate relationship development. For ex-ample, some evidence suggests that, in our cul-ture, getting married may have a romanticizing effect, as a couple at this point focus on their relationship. This romanticism quickly dissipates "after the honeymoon" as the couple turn their attention to mundane matters. (See the box "When the Honeymoon Is Over.")

Third-Party Influences

Relationships are affected by the environment in which they develop — including other people. Sometimes environmental factors facilitate the development of relationships, and other times they interfere. A couple's bonds may be rein-forced by others' approval and acknowledgment

SUCCESSFUL MARRIAGES

More than a million couples each year end their marriages by divorce. Even so, there are a good many Americans whose marriages endure. In recent years, a number of social scientists have turned their attention to the study of happy marriages to identify the ingredients that make for marital success. Jeanette Lauer and Robert Lauer (1985) surveyed 300 happily married couples, asking them why their marriages survived. The most frequently given reason was having a positive attitude toward one's spouse. The partners commonly said, "My spouse is my best friend" and "I like my spouse as a person." One woman observed, "I would want to have him as a friend even if I weren't married to him" (Lauer and Lauer, 1985: 24).

Yet the couples studied were hardly blind to each other's faults. They recognized flaws in their mates and acknowledged that they had had their share of rough times. But they felt that their mates' likable qualities outweighed the deficiencies and the difficulties. In one way or another, many individuals indicated that marriage sometimes demands that you grit your teeth and remain on track despite the difficulties.

Among the external factors affecting marital satisfaction is the presence of children. Children tend to lower marital satisfaction, especially for women, by reducing the partners' interaction and creating dissatisfaction with finances and the division of labor (Abbott and Brody, 1985; Schumm and Bugaighis, 1986; White, Booth, and Edwards, 1986).

Studies of marital partners' discussions of relationship problems tend to show sex differences, with wives being more likely to express their negative feelings directly and to be more critical (Hahlweg, Revenstorf, and Schindler, 1984). Researchers interpret this as fitting with females' overall greater emotional expressiveness (Balswick, 1986; Noller and Fitzpatrick, 1990). Gottman and Levenson (1988) suggest that women are also better able to function in the context of high negative affect. In contrast, men are likely to attempt to play a reconciling role during low levels of marital conflict but to withdraw during high conflict. Christensen and Heavey (1990) found that the husband was particularly likely to withdraw if the wife raised the issue in question. This response may make wives believe that their husbands are minimizing the difficulties in the relationship. The wives may respond by increasing their negativity in an effort to gain their husbands' attention (Notiaius and Pellegrini, 1987).

A number of studies suggest that harmonious couples have learned a different form of interaction than dissatisfied couples (Jacobson, Waldron, and Moore, 1980; Koren, Carlton, and Shaw, 1980; Grigg, Fletcher, and Fitness, 1989). Satisfied partners tend to reciprocate each other's rewarding behavior, but they tend not to react in kind when a partner acts in an unrewarding fashion. In contrast, unhappy partners react unpredictably when one of them acts positively but tend to reciprocate negative actions.

of the couple's "oneness." A number of studies have found that partners' contact with and liking for each other's friends and family is positively associated with romantic involvement (Parks, Stan, and Eggert, 1983; Felmlee, Sprecher, and Bassin, 1990). At the same time, romantically involved couples tend to withdraw from other, less close relationships (Surra, 1985, 1988). This finding is explained by noting that the partners' romance demands more of their time, attention, and emotional energy.

Do the actions and reactions of third parties affect whether romantic relationships survive or

falter? Does opposition to a romance strengthen it? A 1972 study suggested that parental opposition *increased* romantic involvement — a condition called the "Romeo and Juliet effect" (Driscoll, Davis, and Lipetz, 1972). However, subsequent research has not supported this finding. A 1986 study, for example, provided evidence that parents' actions to show approval or disapproval of their children's dates, as well as their children's efforts to influence their opinions about the dating partner, increase as the dating relationship becomes more serious (Leslie, Huston, and Johnson, 1986). However, whether the dating relation-

WHEN THE HONEYMOON IS OVER

More than fifty years ago, noted sociologist Willard Waller (1938) wrote, "It has been said that marriage is the remedy for the disease of love, a remedy which operates by destroying the love." Researcher Ted Huston and his colleagues tested Waller's notion of the fading of romance in marriage by looking at a sample of 100 newlywed couples through the first two and a half years of their marriages (Huston, McHale, and Crouter, 1986). Reporting on their findings for the first year studied, the researchers note that the couples did become less satisfied with the quality of their interactions with each other.

According to the researchers, the most striking change occurring over the first year of marriage was a general decline in emotional responsiveness. While the rate of pleasing behaviors (such as "Spouse approved of or complimented partner," "Spouse did or said something to make partner laugh," "Spouse said 'I love you,'" and "Shared physical affection") remained positive, the rate declined over the first year of marriage by about 40 percent overall.

On the other hand, rates of negative behaviors (such as "Spouse seemed bored or uninterested," "Spouse showed anger or impatience," and "Spouse criticized or complained") were very low and did not increase over the year of the study.

The researchers were somewhat surprised to find that the couples in their study who had lived together before marriage experienced the same decline in romantic feelings and positive interaction as those who did not live together until after marriage. They had suspected that cohabitors would have gone through the process of declining romanticism much earlier and would not show the same pattern as the other couples. The researchers suggest two possible explanations: (1) The cohabiting couples in their study may not have lived together long enough for the expected decline in romanticism to take place, or (2) the act of marriage itself is, in our culture, so significant an event and so imbued with romance that it may have a romanticizing effect both on those who have cohabited and on those who have not.

ship progressed or declined was affected very little by the parents' approval or disapproval.

A number of studies suggest that whether we perceive others as supportive of our relationships is more important than their actual supportive or interfering actions. For adolescent dating relationships and friendships, as well as college dating relationships, perceived support from one's own and the partner's network was positively associated with relationship stability (Parks, Stan, and Eggert, 1983; Johnson and Milardo, 1984; Eggert and Parks, 1987). For example, one study showed that perceived lack of support for a relationship from family and friends and disliking of the partner's family and friends were significant predictors of the rate of breakup for romantic relationships over a twelve- to thirteen-week period (Felmlee, Sprecher, and Bassin, 1990).

Life Course Changes

Relationships also can be altered substantially by changes in the life of one (or both) of the parties.

For example, as an elderly parent becomes increasingly infirm, the adult child's relationship with the parent must change. Similarly, when a married couple has a child, the relationship between the two partners is altered. If one partner in a relationship wins a million dollars, loses a job, or suffers a severe injury, the relationship between the parties will probably require some adjustments.

As noted in Chapter 3, "Socialization over the Life Course," our concerns and behaviors change as we pass through culturally defined, age-graded statuses. Research on friendship indicates that what we look for in friendship varies through life, as do our opportunities for making friends (Dickens and Perlman, 1981). Teenagers search for a group of friends and for sexual partners. Later, most of us become committed to one romantic partner and our networks of casual friends shrink and stabilize. If we marry and have children, our friendships are affected by the networks of people marriage and children bring us into contact with, as well as by our career development. When children have left home and work demands subside, many persons increase their involvement in the community and develop new friendships.

DETERIORATION AND ENDING

Earlier in this chapter, we discussed the concept of commitment. Relationships deteriorate when commitment declines: (1) the reward-cost balance of maintaining the relationship declines, (2) the social costs of terminating the relationship are reduced, (3) the attractiveness of alternative relationships increases, and/or (4) the centrality of the relationship to the self-concept declines (Drigotas and Rusbult, 1992). At times, a person considering a divorce may be convinced that the marriage is terrible and that any alternative is better. At other times, the existence of remaining marital rewards may make the costs of terminating the relationship seem too high. The decision process of making such appraisals and reappraisals is likely to be difficult and distressing. These appraisals of rewards and costs are strongly linked to self-appraisals, which in turn are linked to one's relationships with kin, friends, and the larger community. Whether one finally decides to end a marriage may hinge on the extent to which one defines oneself as an independent individual or as a member of the relationship (Levinger, 1983).

Unlike romantic relationships and marriages, which often end with an emotional and protracted breakup, friendships are more likely to end by a gradual "fading away" (Hays, 1988). The ending of a friendship does not call for negotiation, since there are no formal ties to be severed or public announcements of a change in status to be made. Consequently, it can be difficult to distinguish temporary downswings in a friendship from absolute declines. This confusion may result in regret when, in hindsight, we realize that a friendship has dissolved (Rose, 1984; Hays, 1988).

Responses to Relationship Dissatisfaction

How do people respond when they become dissatisfied with a relationship? Psychologist Caryl Rusbult and her colleagues propose that there are four alternative responses a dissatisfied partner may make (Rusbult, Zembrodt, and Gunn, 1982; Rusbult and Zembrodt, 1983). The first, *exit*, entails formally separating from the other person (e.g., moving out of a joint residence, deciding to be "just friends," or getting a divorce). The second, *voice*, involves active verbal attempts to resolve difficulties (e.g., asking a partner what is troubling him or her, compromising, or seeking help from a therapist or member of the clergy). The third, *loyalty*, implies remaining passively loyal to the relationship or waiting for conditions to improve. And the fourth, *neglect*, entails passively allowing the relationship to atrophy, (e.g., ignoring the partner, refusing to discuss problems, treating the partner badly, or just letting things fall apart).

Three conditions influence which response an individual will make: (1) the degree of satisfaction with the relationship prior to the emergence of problems, (2) the magnitude of a person's investment of resources in the relationship, and (3) the quality of the best available alternative to the relationship. In cases in which prior satisfaction is high, voice and loyalty tend to be the responses. Similarly, greater prior investment in the relationship encourages voice and loyalty. More attractive alternatives promote exit and hamper loyalty behaviors.

It should be noted that two partners may not use the same criteria in judging the reward-cost balance of the relationship. One may have more or better alternatives than the other, and the relationship may be more central for one partner's self-concept than the other's. It is entirely possible for one partner to believe that the relationship has become unrewarding while the other believes that it is as good as ever. Furthermore, unlike the creation and maintenance of a relationship, which requires the participation of *both* partners, its dissolution can be undertaken by the actions and decisions of only *one* partner.

Uncoupling

Like establishment and growth, the deterioration and ending of a close relationship is not an *event* but, rather, a *process*. Sociologist Diane Vaughan

(1986) calls this process "uncoupling." Her studies of cohabitors, homosexual couples, and married couples who had ended their relationships indicated that, in some ways, the process of ending an intimate relationship is almost a mirror image of the process of developing one. As intimacy develops, for example, partners focus on the positive characteristics of the relationship and of each other. As a relationship dissolves, partners tend to recall and emphasize the negative characteristics. As relationships develop, partners spend more and more time together; as they deteriorate, partners spend less and less time together. Partners in developing relationships increasingly base their self-identities on the relationship; partners in dissolving relationships often begin identifying with someone or something outside the relationship. And, finally, while partners in developing relationships are optimistic about the fact that their relationship will last, those in collapsing relationships tend to be pessimistic, believing that their relationship will end.

In other ways, however, the dissolution process is *not* just a reversal of the development process. It is not possible to withdraw the partners' intimate knowledge of one another or to erase their shared memories. The interdependence of partners in close relationships is great; each person is vitally affected by the other. Each person must live with the consequences of his or her own behavior *and* the other's behavior. Because of this high degree of interdependence, close relationships can be very rewarding or very frustrating. Likewise, their demise can be very disruptive and distressing.

Although both partners go through the same steps in exiting a relationship, they may experience them on very different schedules (Vaughan, 1986). The *initiator* — the person who first becomes unhappy or dissatisfied with the relationship — may try to change the situation by expressing small complaints or renegotiating the rules of the relationship. If such attempts fail (and barriers to leaving seem low and attractive alternatives exist), the initiator may decide that the relationship cannot be saved and begin the process of leaving the relationship — emotionally, psychologically, and socially. The initiator may

make considerable efforts to protect the other partner from hurt, while convincing the partner that ending the relationship would be best for both of them. The process of recognizing dissatisfaction, deciding how to deal with it, and trying to protect the partner (while also desperately maneuvering an escape) involves, according to Vaughan, considerable external and internal conflict and emotional trauma.

The "partner left behind" may first deny the initiator's hints of dissatisfaction. When the initiator makes clear that he or she wants to leave the relationship, the partner left behind must go through the same uncoupling process — recognizing dissatisfaction, trying to change things to save the relationship, and finally withdrawing emotionally and psychologically from the relationship and establishing a new self-identity. The partner left behind may not go through the stressful uncoupling process until after the separation or divorce has occurred.

Responses to Dissolution

Given the importance we attribute to primary relationships, it is not surprising that their dissolution is disruptive and disturbing to us. The amount of disruption experienced upon the dissolution of a primary relationship depends on the degree of interdependency the relationship involved. One study of mid-life divorce found that men were more likely than women to report negative feelings about the divorce (Levinger, 1983). The researchers note that most of the women in the study perceived the disintegration of their marriages as having been a long, slow process, while most of the men perceived it as an abrupt event of relatively short duration. They suggest that the women had begun to disengage themselves from their marriages years earlier and hence had already adjusted to some degree to the dissolution of the relationship.

Gunhild Hagestad and Michael Smyer (1982) assert that there are at least three aspects of the marriage relationship that have to be "undone" in divorcing: love for the partner, attachment to established routines, and attachment to the marital role. An individual must decide that he or she does not love the partner, does not want to share the routines of life with that person, and does not want to be that person's spouse.

Steve Duck (1986) suggests that when we leave a relationship, we go through a grave-dressing phase: Once the relationship is dead, we have to bury it. We do this, he says, by constructing an account of the relationship's history—how it was born, what it was like, and why it died. The parties put their accounts forward so that other people can "see" them; each party hopes that people accept his or her version and show support by being sympathetic and understanding. One way of doing this is through gossip about the ex-partner (La Gaipa, 1982).

Accounts for relationship failures are intended to let the parties leave a relationship with "social credit" for developing new relationships. It is socially acceptable for someone to have been "let down" or "faced with unreasonable odds or an unreasonable partner" or even to have "tried hard to make things work out, but without success." For a person to cheerfully admit ending the relationship because she or he "got bored" is less socially acceptable and implies that the person might be something of a risk in future relationships. There is also evidence that having a publicly acceptable story helps a person get over the loss of a relationship (McCall, 1982).

The ending of a relationship can affect persons other than the two partners. The ending of a marriage in divorce, for example, obviously affects the relationships of the partners with their children, their in-laws, and their friends. Studies of

CHILDREN AND DIVORCE

Divorce is a process of changing a relationship that inevitably "affects the entire family system and the functioning and interactions of the members within that system" (Heatherington, Cox, and Cox, 1982: 233). The experience of divorce affects different members of the family differently. How do separation and divorce affect children?

Researchers disagree about how negative the consequences of family disruption are for children. Psychologists Judith Wallerstein and Sandra Blakeslee (1990) have conducted longitudinal research on the children of divorced families which suggests that the consequences are quite damaging. Divorce, they note, has both economic and emotional consequences for children. Children whose parents are divorced almost always have less money to live on than they would have had if their parents had stayed together. They often feel that they have "lost" their fathers, who become physically separated from the family and may become disinterested and detached as well. They may also feel that they have "lost" their mothers, who become preoccupied with supporting the family and managing the household alone or who are busily pursuing their "second chance." Despite these findings, Wallerstein and Blakeslee conclude that living in an intact family characterized by unresolved tension and conflict can cause more problems for children than living in a divorced family.

A less pessimistic view of the way children are affected by divorce is taken by sociologists Paul Amato and Bruce Keith (1991), who reviewed and analyzed virtually all existing studies of children's postdivorce adjustment. Like Wallerstein and Blakeslee they conclude that in general, children of divorced families are less well adjusted than those from intact families. Amato and Keith note that the difference is modest and that other factors affecting the child's development will be much more important. Nevertheless, say Amato and Keith, in choosing to divorce, parents are not condemning their children to a disastrous and disappointing life. They may be preventing more damaging experiences that would occur in an unhappy family life. Which situation is worse remains a matter of debate.

Divorce is, of course, not the only example of a relationship change that affects other members of the family. Children are affected when a divorced parent begins to develop new romantic relationships or remarries. The effects can be positive or negative. And children *affect* such relationships as well as being affected by them.

the social networks of divorced spouses have indicated that the men have fewer kin ties and the women have fewer friends (Marsden, 1987; Milardo, 1987). Relationships with joint friends tend to dissolve upon separation or divorce. After divorce, women's networks tend to return to the size and composition that they were before marriage (Acock and Hurlbert, 1990; Hurlbert and Acock, 1991). And, of course, children's relationships with their parents, grandparents, and other relatives are profoundly affected by divorce. The effect of divorce on children has been a topic of interest to social psychologists. See the box "Children and Divorce" for a summary of recent findings.

We have noted that close relationships take different forms and follow different courses of development. While these relationships involve many positive forms of behavior—companionship, self-disclosure, and helping—they do not preclude negative ones. As this chapter suggests, relationship partners do not always agree about the course the relationship should take. Their negotiations—whether aimed at establishing, maintaining, or dissolving a relationship—may involve conflict and aggression, the topic of the next chapter.

Summary

1. The intimate behaviors of companionship, self-disclosure, and helping characterize close relationships. Social psychologists have many views of intimate feelings, including the view that emotions are social constructions that arise out of social interaction and are given meaning by shared, cultural definitions.

2. Commitment is the likelihood of staying in a relationship. This concept explains why people might remain in relationships that, for the moment, are not particularly rewarding. In addition to assessing the current rewards, a person also takes into account the past history of the relationship, his or her investments in it, and what the alternatives seem to be.

3. Men's friendships tend to be based largely on companionship. Women's friendships emphasize emotional sharing, trusting, and confiding. Some evidence indicates that our culture discourages cross-sex friendships in a number of ways. Family and kin relationships have an obligatory quality that is absent from friendships and romantic relationships.

4. Many norms about romantic relationships develop in adolescent peer groups. Heterosexual romantic relationships bring together two partners whose styles of closeness differ. Homosexual romantic relationships are similar to heterosexual ones in many ways. A number of studies have concluded that gender is a much more important determinant of the nature of a couple's relationship than is sexual orientation.

5. Attraction to strangers is the starting point of most close relationships. A number of factors cause us to be attracted, and attractive, to others: proximity, familiarity, arousal, physical attractiveness, similar attitudes, complementary needs/role compatibility, and social exchange.

6. Relationship development is affected by cultural views about the nature of various relationships and the rules for conducting them. The quality of interaction is more important than the quantity in intimate relationships. How rewarding we find interaction with a partner—rather than the costs involved or the rewards minus cost—is the best predictor of satisfaction with, and commitment to, the relationship. As relationships become closer, we move away from the norm of immediate reciprocity (a tit-for-tat exchange) to a more expansive exchange norm, in which the benefits the partners provide each other should equal out over the long run.

7. Romantic relationships and marriages often end with an emotional and protracted breakup period, since formal ties have to be severed and official changes in status made. This is not true of friendships, which are more likely to end by a gradual fading away. When people become dissatisfied with a relationship, they respond through one of four ways: exit, voice, loyalty, or neglect.

CHAPTER 12

AGGRESSION AND CONFLICT

People are more likely to be killed, physically assaulted, hit, beaten up, slapped, or spanked in their own homes by other family members than anywhere else, or by anyone else, in our society. Some observers . . . have proposed that violence in the family is more common than love. (Gelles and Cornell, 1990: 11)

Most women who get raped are raped by people they already know—like the boy in biology class, or the guy in the office down the hall, or their friends' brother. The familiarity is enough to make them let down their guard, sometimes even enough to make them wonder afterward whether they were "really raped." What people think of as "real rape"—the assault by a monstrous stranger lurking in the shadows—accounts for only 1 out of 5 attacks. (Gibbs, 1991: 48)

Black-clad German skinheads from both parts of the newly united country parade through the streets of Dresden to mourn their hero Rainer Stonntag, killed by a gang of pimps in a dispute over turf. Silent onlookers and 1,500 police watch as the 2,000 neo-Nazis raise their arms and shout, "Sieg heil!" and "Foreigners out!" (Nelan, 1991: 36)

On March 3, 1991, police cars chased a motorist through the night, cornering his car in a Los Angeles suburb and surrounding the driver as he stepped into

the street. A sergeant fired a 50,000-volt stun gun at the unarmed black man, then three officers took turns kicking him and hitting him in the head, neck, kidneys and legs with their truncheons. Eleven other policemen looked on as a hovering helicopter bathed the scene in a floodlight. When the beating was over, the victim, Rodney King, had suffered 11 skull fractures, a crushed cheekbone, a broken ankle, internal injuries, a burn on his chest, and some brain damage. (Prud'homme, 1991: 16)

Terror, violence, and aggression seem everywhere about us. War, internal strife, violent repression, terrorism, and rampant crime haunt people on all continents. The United States is no exception. Each year more than 50,000 people are murdered or commit suicide in the United States. The average American's chances of having his or her life end in homicide are 1 in 150. Much of the homicide takes place within families. (Before reading further, look at the box "Family Violence.")

In this chapter, we will first define aggression and examine some of the factors thought to influence it. Then we will discuss conflict, which is reciprocal aggression.

FAMILY VIOLENCE

The problem of family violence has long been neglected by both society and the academic community. Indeed, the view that the family is and ought to be a warm unit has contributed to a perceptual blackout on family violence. Yet the family is the most frequent arena for violence of all types, including homicide (Goodstein and Page, 1981; Bowker, 1983; Gelles and Straus, 1988; Gelles and Cornell, 1990).

SPOUSE ABUSE

Although researchers disagree about whether women engage in as much or less aggression than men, they do agree that the violence by husbands and wives is *qualitatively* different (Kurz, 1991; Straus, 1991). Women are more likely to report that they have slapped, kicked, bitten, hit, or thrown something at their spouses. Men are more likely to report having choked or beaten their wives (Gelles and Straus, 1988).

Richard Gelles and Murray Straus asked women respondents how they reacted to the most recent incidence of violence. The most frequently reported responses included crying, yelling, and cursing (55 to 37 percent). Only about one in four women hit the attacker back. One explanation for the low incidence of counterviolence by wives is that such behavior can produce more intensive aggression by husbands, whose superior physical strength and willingness to use it eventually might prove decisive.

Women were least likely to respond to their husbands' violence by seeking help from others, particularly the police. One possible explanation for this is that calling the police or seeking the intervention of a social agency does not guarantee that a woman will receive meaningful assistance (Ford, 1983; Sherman and Bouza, 1984). Much official acceptance exists regarding family violence, encompassed in the belief that such matters are "private affairs."

Even when women do enter official complaints with the law, husbands are seldom detained by the police. Consequently, the men are free to return and inflict even greater suffering on the women. Research indicates that husbands arrested and held for abusing their wives are less likely to be the source of further complaints than are those who were simply warned (Shermand and Berk, 1984). Other research suggests that it is the personal humiliation of arrest that confers its deterrent effect (Williams and Hawkins, 1989).

Therefore, many battered wives remain in violent relationships, passively submitting to their husbands' violence without seeking help from outsiders. A woman's passive response (such as, crying or complying with her husband's wishes) may lead to a temporary reduction in her husband's violence. But research suggests that such relationships become increasingly negative, involving a progressive escalation of violence and submission (Wiggins, 1983; Denzin, 1984).

Social Definitions of Aggression

Social psychologists typically refer to the intentional harm done by one person to another as **aggression.** Both social psychologists and society in general differentiate among the types of harmful behavior according to motive, legitimacy, and content.

We distinguish harmful behavior on the basis of the *motive,* or *intent,* of the behavior. In some cases, the *only* intent of aggression is to harm or otherwise injure another party ("hostile aggres-

sion"). In other cases, harming another party is only a secondary objective carried out to gain some primary objective ("instrumental aggression"). For example, harming another in order to indicate that the other party's behavior was wrong is referred to as *punishment* or *sanction.* Harming another in order to get the party to yield his or her position or change his or her behavior is called *coercion* (Felson and Tedeschi, 1991).

Distinctions are also drawn on the basis of the *legitimacy* of the aggression. Harmful behavior that is consistent with social norms is called *disci-*

CHILD ABUSE

"Child abuse" is a catchall term referring to non-accidental physical attack on or injury to children (including emotional injury) by individuals caring for them. Child abuse is found among families from all social, religious, economic, educational, and racial backgrounds. Although it is difficult to generalize about parents who abuse children, a number of facts, nonetheless, stand out. Abusing parents demand a great deal from their children, far more than the children can understand or respond to:

Henry J., in speaking of his sixteen-month-old son, Johnny, said, "He knows what I mean and understands it when I say 'come here.' If he doesn't come immediately, I go and give him a gentle tug on the ear to remind him of what he's supposed to do." In the hospital it was found that Johnny's ear was lacerated and partially torn away from his head. (Steele and Pollock, 1968: 110)

Frequently, abusive parents feel insecure and unsure of being loved, and look to the child as a source of reassurance, comfort, and affection:

Kathy made this poignant statement: "I have never felt really loved all my life. When the baby was born, I thought he would love me; but when he cried all the time, it meant he didn't love me, so I hit him." Kenny, age three weeks, was hospitalized with bilateral subdural hematomas [multiple bruises]. (Steele and Pollock, 1968: 110)

Many child abusers were raised in the same authoritarian style that they later re-create with their own children (Herrenkohl, Herrenkohl, and Toedler, 1983; Egeland, Jacobvitz, and Papatola, 1987; Egeland, Jacobvitz, and Sroufe, 1988).

PARENT ABUSE

Researchers find that between 5 and 12 percent of children have engaged in violent behavior toward their parents (Peek, Fisher, and Kidwell, 1985; Agnew and Huguley, 1989). Sons are slightly more likely to be abusive than daughters, with the difference between the sexes in the rate of violence increasing with age. Mothers are the more likely victims of their children's violence, but fathers are the more likely victims of older male children (Agnew and Huguley, 1989).

Social psychologists are uncertain as to the causes of parent abuse. One explanation for the abuse of elderly parents is the dependence of the victim. Dependence generates resentment in the caretakers and does not provide protection against abuse. Violence may be the way that people attempt to influence others' behavior when they lack other resources for doing so. And although social psychologists are inclined to believe that children learn their violent responses toward their parents from being victims themselves of abuse, evidence does not support this view (Pillemer and Suiter, 1988).

pline or self-defense; that which is contrary to social norms is termed abuse or brutality. One person's failure to help another who has already been harmed is identified as neglect when the person has some legitimate responsibility for the other. For example, parents' treatment of their children is sometimes referred to as child abuse or child neglect.

Other distinctions are drawn on the basis of the content of the aggression; for example, aggression can be physical or psychological. Criminologists usually use the word "violence" when referring to acts resulting in physical harm—murder, armed robbery, extortion, kidnapping, rape, assault and battery, aggravated assault, and arson (Powitzky, 1990).

In this text, the word "aggression" is used in reference to harmful behavior regardless of its particular intent, its legitimacy, or its content.

Explanations of Aggression

Why would someone intentionally harm another? The answer to this question involves three broad

The black leader H. Rap Brown once observed, "Violence is as American as cherry pie." Many Americans believe that violence remains our number-one problem.

explanations of aggression, which are considered in this section. First, we will take a detailed look at aspects of the *situation* in which the aggression occurs. Then we will look at several proposals regarding the role that *emotional arousal* plays in aggression. Finally, we will examine the proposition that current aggression is the result of *past learning*.

SITUATIONAL EXPLANATIONS

Do some aspects of the person's environment increase the likelihood of aggression? How can the behavior and characteristics of the target contribute to the aggression? And do social norms operating in the situation affect the likelihood of aggression?

Interference

For over fifty years, the *frustration-aggression hypothesis* has been a popular explanation for aggressive behavior (Dollard et al., 1939; Berkowitz,

1989). According to the original version of the theory, frustration produces aggression; aggression *never* occurs without prior frustration. The term "frustration" refers to the interference with or blocking of the attainment of some goal or reward. For instance, frustration might arise from interference with the satisfaction of some biological need (say, for food, water, sex, or sleep) or social need (for recognition, love, or security).

A classic study testing the frustration-aggression hypothesis was carried out by Kurt Lewin and his associates (Barker, Dembo, and Lewin, 1941). The experimenters allowed one group of children to play with a number of attractive toys. Another group was allowed to look at the toys but not play with them—a frustrating situation. Later, when the children in the second group were permitted to play with the toys, they smashed them on the floor, threw them against the wall, and engaged in other destructive activities. In contrast, the first group of children, who had not been frustrated, played quietly and constructively.

Attack

Subsequent research has explored another cause of aggression. In laboratory experiments, subjects receiving verbal abuse and insults, as well as shocks, have acted aggressively (in ways such as delivering shocks to other persons). Such results indicate that in certain social conditions, we strike at an available target, inflicting harm because we ourselves have experienced a psychological or physical attack.

Both interference (frustration) and attack are negative events—in essence, harmful. In interference, our access to something we define as positive (a reward, benefit, or goal) is blocked. In attack, we are presented with something we define as negative. Although both events are harmful, social psychologists distinguish between the two because research findings suggest that their effects on aggression may not be identical. Attack appears to cause *more* aggression than does interference with an ongoing task (Geen, 1968; Gentry, 1970).

Attributions About Others

The *amount* of aggression produced by interference or attack is influenced by several factors. One of these is our perception of the *reason* for the interference or attack. Was the slap on your back meant as a greeting or a sign of affection, or was it intended to hurt you? Did the child hit you in the stomach to get your attention or to hurt you? Was the intent of the "hard foul" in the basketball game to stop the player from scoring or to injure him?

In Chapter 6, "Social Attitudes and Attributions," we referred to the individual's assessment of the causes of others' behavior as "causal attribution." We distinguished between attributing the cause of a behavior to environmental or situational circumstances (external attribution) and attributing the cause to a characteristic of the other person (internal attribution). Interference or attack will produce less aggression if we make an external attribution of the harm done to us than if we make an internal attribution. For example, a man will display more aggression toward a person who harms him (through either interference or

attack) when he perceives the person's behavior as being intentional rather than accidental. In other words, we become more aggressive ourselves when we interpret others' behavior as "aggression." Indeed, the perception of the opponent's intent is *sometimes* more important in causing counteraggression than is the amount of harm done by the aggression (Maselli and Altrocchi, 1969; Greenwell and Dengerink, 1973; Kulik and Brown, 1979).

In one study (Kulik and Brown, 1979), students were asked to make telephone appeals for a charity. Interference was created by having all their appeals refused by potential donors (actually confederates of the researchers). However, in half of the cases, potential donors offered an external reason for refusing (e.g., "I just lost my job"); in the other half of the cases, they offered an internal reason (e.g., "Charities are a rip-off"). The students exposed to external reasons directed less verbal aggression toward the potential donors than did those exposed to internal reasons.

Hans Toch's (1991) observations of the accounts offered by violent offenders to explain their violent behavior suggest that the offenders tailored their accounts to affect the attributions of their audience. When faced with officials who are in a position to punish them, some highlight their own irrationality, sometimes "proving" it with displays of rage. These offenders are attempting to get others to attribute their violence to uncontrollable urges ("The devil made me do it," or "The dirtbag asked for it when he gave me the finger"). A rapist may try to persuade jurors to attribute his violence to the victim's low-cut blouse or miniskirt. However, these "official" or "public" accounts are not presented to audiences of peers who share the offenders' value of violence. Here accounts are unnecessary because the distinction between legal and illegal violence is blurred. Similarly, college men may confuse "rape" and "scoring," or civilians killed in war become "collateral damage."

While external attributions for interference or attack tend to reduce counteraggression, research indicates that the amount of a person's aggression is affected by *when* the person acquires the attributional information (Johnson and Rule, 1986). The findings suggest that if a person understands the explanation for her or his being harmed by the other *before* actually being harmed, the chances are the person will be less aggressive. Learning the information afterward doesn't seem to have the same effect on the mitigation of aggression.

Still another factor appears to operate among those who encounter attack and interference on a routine basis. Sociologists Barbara Stenross and Sherryl Kleinman (1989) suggest that responding aggressively is work; they call it "emotional labor." Because aggression is work, we sometimes actually provide an attacker with a ready-made account for the attack that will justify our *not* responding with counteraggression. Stenross and Kleinman studied interactions between criminal suspects and detectives during police interrogations. The suspects frequently verbally abused the detectives. To respond to numerous such attacks in a day's work would be very taxing to the detectives. Therefore, the detectives interpreted the suspects' abusive behavior as part of a "who-done-it game" played between criminals and detectives. This ready-made attribution reduced the detectives' counteraggression, saving them the emotional work involved.

Aggression Cues

Whether or not interference or attack leads to aggression depends on the presence of situational cues that suggest an aggressive response. For example, Berkowitz (1981) found that the mere presence of guns can have an aggressive influence on behavior; he terms this the "weapons effect." He disputes the claim of the National Rifle Association that "guns don't kill people; people kill people." His research and that of his associates suggest that the weapon itself acts as a stimulant to violence.

In one experiment, Berkowitz had frustrated and angry subjects deliver shocks to their partners as a way of evaluating the partner's unimaginative ideas for an advertising campaign. One group of subjects worked individually at a table with nothing on it but the telegraph key that sent the shocks. A second group worked at the same table, but for this condition the experimenters also placed badminton rackets and shuttlecocks on the table. Finally, a third group was tested under similar circumstances, except that the badminton equipment was replaced by a 12-gauge shotgun and a snub-nosed .38 revolver. The presence of the weapons had a decided effect on aggression. Those subjects in the weapons group administered more shocks to their partners and held the key down longer for each shock than did the subjects in the other two groups. Berkowitz concludes that "the finger pulls the trigger; but the trigger may also be pulling the finger" (1981: 11).

Desmond Ellis and his associates (Ellis, Weiner, and Miller, 1971) performed a similar study which found that the effect of weapons might sometimes *inhibit* rather than *facilitate* the expression of aggression. In part of the experiment, the partner was a policeman (a confederate of the researchers). Half of the subjects involved were confronted with a pistol, bullet clip, and blackjack belonging to the policeman. He had removed these from his person "for reasons of comfort while sitting down to write the essay." The other half of the subjects saw the policeman in uniform but with no weapons on his person, since he was "going off duty." In the first part of each session, the policeman gave the subject electric shocks indicating the policeman's evaluation of an essay written by the subject. In the second part, the roles were reversed, and the subject was given the opportunity to evaluate the policeman's essay in the same manner. The study found that the subjects gave *fewer* shocks to the policeman when his weapons were present than when they were absent. The results of the study did not support the view that weapons *generally* facilitate the expression of aggression. Instead, under some conditions, the presence of weapons apparently inhibits aggressive behavior.

Much is made of the proposition that weapons — at least those in the possession of an "instigator" — inhibit aggression. It is argued that the gun worn by the police officer on the street inhibits violence, particularly if the officer is convincing in his or her willingness to use it. The same is said about guns used by criminals. In this view, the threat represented by the presence of a gun will deter the victim from counteraggressing. In turn, this will reduce the probability that the possessor of the gun will escalate her or his aggression to physical attack. The criminal's use of a gun may also give the victim a socially acceptable excuse (attribution) for not retaliating when faced with an intended robbery or assault: "Only a fool attacks a man with a gun." Perceived cowardice gives way to perceived prudence.

There is some evidence to support this proposition. This research uses data from interviews of representative national samples (National Crime Survey) as well as reported crimes (FBI's Supplementary Homicide Reports). It indicates that the criminal's being in possession of *lethal* weapons, such as guns and knives, does lower the likelihood that the victim will attack the criminal. However, the presence of less lethal weapons, such as blunt objects or broken bottles, *increases* the probability that the victim will attack (Kleck and McElrath, 1991). Thus, the lethality of the weapon appears to be an important determinant of whether the instigator's possession of a weapon will facilitate or inhibit aggression.

Relative Social Status

Whether interference or attack results in aggression may also depend on the social status of the source of the frustration. But what effect would status have? There are two possibilities: (1) A person's status within a group might protect him or her from aggression if that person interferes with the immediate goal of the group — a phenomenon called **idiosyncrasy credit**. The rationale is that lower-status group members fear the high-status person's counteraggression. (2) On the other hand, the opposite might be true. Instead of protecting the person, his or her high status might make that person more susceptible to the others' aggression; this is called **status liability**. The rationale here is that a person who has obtained large rewards and high status for his or her past achievements should have to pay a com-

parably high cost for his or her current interference. Which hypothesis do you think is most likely true?

An experiment showed that status *does* influence the aggressive reactions to frustration but that the direction of the effect depends on the level of frustration (Wiggins, Dill, and Schwartz, 1965). Subjects participated in groups of four, but each subject was in a cubicle that did not allow him to see or communicate with the others. Each group competed against other groups in solving five tasks of varying degrees of difficulty and of varying natures (e.g., a logic and math test and a synonym-antonym test). On each task, a score was obtained for each group member, and these scores were combined to obtain the group's score. The winning group would receive $50. "Status" was manipulated in terms of a group member's past contribution to the group score. We say "manipulated" because, on the first three tasks, each group was shown by the researcher scores that included a score for "member C," but there was no such member. For some groups, the fictitious member C was the top scorer (high status), while in other groups C was among the average scorers (medium status).

On the fourth task, the group members were told that C had violated a task rule and that points would have to be removed from the group's score. For some groups, this meant they could not win the competition (high interference); for other groups, it meant they still had a chance (medium interference); and for still others, it had very little effect on the group score (low interference). After completing all the tasks, group members were asked to indicate how they would distribute the $50 among themselves should they win the competition. The measure of aggression was the proportion they awarded to the fictitious member C — the lower the proportion, the greater the aggression.

Among the groups for whom member C was the source of only medium or low interference, C received a larger share of the $50 when C had high status than when C had medium status. In other words, C's status was protective as long as

STUDENT OBSERVATION

Status Liability

Status has never worked to my advantage when I have caused interference with the immediate goal of a group. It has always been a liability for me in these situations. Most recently, I was helping a group of friends cook a Chinese dinner. I am half Chinese and have watched my mother cook Chinese food all my life, so I was pretty confident that I was the expert in the group—I had the highest status. However, something went terribly wrong, and our stir fry turned out to be a stir *flop*! My status as an ethnic expert was a liability, as my friends thought I should have known better and prevented the mess-up. Needless to say, I felt really horrible and at that moment wished I were a Scandinavian.

C's interference did not eliminate the group's chances of winning. But among the groups for whom C was the source of high interference, C received a smaller share of the $50 when C had high status. The effects of status had reversed themselves: when the cooperation of the high-status C was no longer useful (because the level of C's interference was enough to eliminate the group's chances of winning), status now increased—rather than decreased—C's susceptibility to aggression. So in some instances, status is a "credit"; in others, it is a "liability." (Before reading further, look at the Student Observation: "Status Liability.")

Deindividuation and Institutional Norms

Crowd violence has intrigued laypeople and social psychologists alike. Crowds gathered at the site of a suicide threat have often taunted and urged the victim to jump (Mann, 1981). And any number of observers have documented the savage cruelty of the lynch mob (Cantril, 1941). Or take the episode that occurred after midnight on June 27, 1981, in New York City's Times Square. A twenty-six-year-old man was mugged and then mugged again, stripped of his clothes, and chased naked through the square by a jeering mob, who threw bottles at him. Attempting to elude his attackers, the man fled for safety into a subway station, where he jumped onto the tracks and died of electrocution. His death was just another bit of "fun" and excitement for the shadowy figures,

drug peddlers, con artists, vagrants, flower peddlers, prostitutes, tourists, and others who haunt Times Square in the early-morning hours (Barbanel, 1981).

One factor that makes individuals susceptible to aggressive and violent behavior in crowd settings is **deindividuation**—a psychological state of diminished self-awareness. Deindividuation may lessen our sense of personal responsibility, thus making aggression more likely. *Anonymity* contributes to deindividuation.

In a laboratory study, Philip C. Zimbardo (1969) produced anonymity in half of the subjects by dressing them in hoods, never using their names, and conducting the experiment in the dark. The other half of the subjects, in the *identifiability* condition, were greeted individually, given large name tags, and encouraged to use one another's names. The procedure entailed administering shocks to a target person. Total duration of electric shocks delivered by the subjects who felt anonymous was twice as long as the duration of shocks delivered by subjects whose individuality was emphasized.

Presumably anonymity draws attention to the group as a whole and reduces the reflexive thinking about ourselves that *might* otherwise lead us to define shocking someone as undesirable. We become less aware of our usual thoughts, moods, bodily states, and other internal processes (Diener, 1979; Prentice-Dunn and Rogers, 1980, 1982; Mann, Newton, and Innes, 1982). Deindividuation may also play a role in social loafing and the denial of help in emergency situations (that is, diffused responsibility), both of which were discussed in previous chapters.

Institutional roles can also offer the anonymity that promotes deindividuation. Deindividuation (reduced reflexivity) minimizes whatever personal standards of behavior the role players have. Therefore, if the role they are asked to assume prescribes aggressive behavior, deindividuation increases the likelihood that the role players will perform the prescribed aggression. A good deal of aggression occurs within institutional contexts. People — ordinary people — commit aggressive and even violent acts as part of "doing their job."

This is **institutional aggression**. It can be seen most clearly in the case of the military, the police, and certain sports. A freshman linebacker for the Ohio State football team says, "When I hit somebody and I see him hurting, just grimacing, it sends something through me that's hard to explain. A bolt. A charge. You play to hurt somebody. You've got to be clean, but you play to put them out of the game" (Harden, 1984: B1). The incident of police violence in Los Angeles that we cited at the beginning of this chapter is also an example of institutional aggression. Taking roles within institutional settings, people come to see themselves as being absolved of personal responsibility for their acts. They make external attributions for their negative behavior, viewing themselves as "pawns" rather than as "originators of behavior." If they place any blame at all, they pin it on the role requirements of the institution,

Institutional roles can offer the anonymity that promotes deindividuation, thereby minimizing whatever personal standards of behavior the role players have. Deindividuation increases the likelihood that role players will perform aggressive acts prescribed by the role expectations associated with their identities. In institutional contexts ordinary people commit aggressive and even violent acts as part of "doing their job."

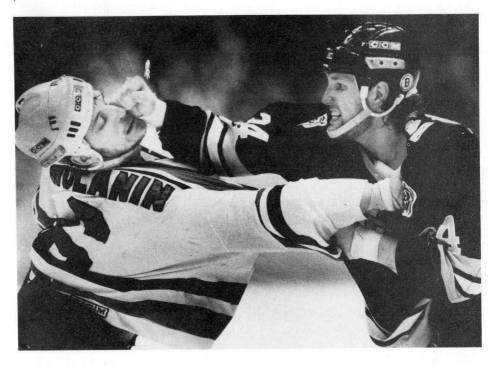

excusing themselves by the rationalization, "If I don't do it, someone else will" (De Charms, 1968; Kipnis, 1974).

Prisons are a common setting for institutional aggression. To investigate the consequences of being a prisoner or a prison guard, Philip C. Zimbardo and his associates (Haney, Banks, and Zimbardo, 1973; Zimbardo, Haney, and Banks, 1973) converted the basement of the Stanford University psychology building into a mock prison. Some seventy-five male student volunteers were given intensive clinical interviews and personality tests, and on the basis of the results, twenty-one were selected for their maturity and stability. About half of these were assigned randomly to serve as "guards," half as "inmates." To enhance the realism of the experiment, the prisoners were unexpectedly picked up at their homes by city police in a squad car. Each subject was charged with a felony, told of his constitutional rights, spread-eagled against the car, searched, and handcuffed; then he was delivered to the station for fingerprinting and preparation of an information file.

At the mock prison each man was stripped naked, skin-searched, and sprayed for lice; issued a uniform, bedding, soap, and a towel; and placed in a 6- by 9-foot barred cell with two other "convicts." The prisoners were required to obtain permission from the guards to perform routine activities such as writing a letter, smoking a cigarette, or using the toilet.

"Guards" worked on three eight-hour shifts and went home when off duty. Although instructed not to use physical violence, they were given considerable latitude to improvise and develop strategies for maintaining "law and order" in the prison. They wore khaki uniforms and carried billy clubs, whistles, and handcuffs as symbols of power.

Over the six-day experiment as the guards behaved more aggressively, the prisoners became more passive. As the guards fell into their roles, they became increasingly authoritarian. They made the prisoners obey petty, meaningless, and even inconsistent rules. They forced the prisoners to undertake tedious and useless work (moving cartons back and forth and picking thorns out of their blankets after the guards had dragged the blankets through thorn bushes). They made the prisoners sing songs, laugh, or refrain from smiling on command. They regularly called prisoners out of their cells to count them, and they encouraged the prisoners to curse and vilify one another publicly during some of the counts. One guard said later:

> I was surprised at myself. . . . I made them call each other names and clean the toilets out with their bare hands. I practically considered the prisoners cattle, and I kept thinking: I have to watch out for them in case they try something. (Zimbardo, Haney, and Banks, 1973: 42)

In this instance, even *playing* the role of a guard in a prison environment significantly impacted the aggressive behavior of the "guards" toward men *playing* the role of prisoner. The guards' aggressive behavior arose out of an institutional environment that condoned this behavior while weakening possible inhibitions of individual participants through deindividuation. What would otherwise have been termed "pathological" behavior became "appropriate" in the prison.

Deindividuation itself is *behavior-neutral*. That is, it is simply the shutting-down of the reflexivity process. People are not attending to themselves. Instead, they are focusing their attention outward, on other group members or environmental objects. It is information from these sources that influences our choice of behavior in a given situation. In the prison situation, institutional roles suggested aggression. In a hospital situation, institutional roles might be more likely to promote helping behavior (Johnson and Downing, 1979). (Before reading further, look at the Student Observation: "Deindividuation.")

Cultural Norms

Whether or not an individual displays aggression toward the source of interference or attack depends largely on the extent to which his or her cultural norms *permit* aggression. In some societies, such as the Kwakiutl Indians of the Pacific

STUDENT OBSERVATION

Deindividuation

When I was younger, I played Little League baseball and was the only girl on my team. I got along really well with the guys on an individual basis. Everyone used to go to practice early to play around. One day, before practice, one of the boys began to throw rocks and mud at me because I had "stolen his position." He encouraged the others to join in and eventually most of the guys were doing it, including my brother. The coach arrived in a minute or two, which broke things up. I was very upset and hurt that they would all allow this to happen — even the ones who did not throw rocks joined in the cheering. I asked my brother and a few of the guys I was closest to how they could just stand there and let that happen, and they all replied that everyone else was doing it and why did I have to single them out? *Deindividuation* (along with peer pressure) allowed the boys to partake in this aggressive behavior without feeling that any one of them could be singled out for questioning or reprimand. Not one of them felt he had to take responsibility for his action because each reasoned that he was just one of many doing the same thing.

Northwest, aggressive behavior is viewed as the mark of a "real man" and hence is encouraged and rewarded. Among some groups within the United States — sailors, marines, lumberjacks, longshoremen, and oil-field workers — a macho-male subculture actively fosters violent interpersonal aggression; the man who exclaims, "I don't believe in fighting" wins no popularity contest. But in other societies, such as the Zuñi Indians of the American Southwest, aggression is viewed as an evil force that disrupts group harmony. And some groups in the United States define overt aggression and fighting as sinful or, at least, as ungentlemanly and uncivilized (Westie, 1964).

Cultural norms specify what kinds of interference or attack deserve an aggressive response, as well as what kinds of people are appropriate targets of what kinds of aggression by what kinds of people. For example, a parent's spanking of her eight-year-old child for disobedience may be seen as acceptable in the United States. But change any one of these components, and the aggression may be contrary to our norms: a parent shouldn't *shoot* the child; a *stranger* (or teacher) shouldn't spank the child; a parent shouldn't spank a *baby*; a parent shouldn't spank her eight-year-old child for *not being a good athlete*.

Obeyesekere (1975) presents an interesting analysis of sorcery, which he interprets as a cul-

turally prescribed alternative to other forms of aggression, such as murder or institutional punishment. Data were gathered at three sorcery shrines in Sri Lanka. Sorcery shrines are believed to be presided over by powerful deities. The clients consult the ritual priest of the shrine, who enlists the aid of the deity in order to cause death or harm to the "enemy." Researchers gathered most of the data from the priests, who elicited the information from clients as a matter of routine. The sixty days of fieldwork produced 803 cases of sorcery. The largest proportion of the cases involved disputes over theft and damage done to property. In two-thirds of the cases, the enemy was known to the client. In almost all the observed cases, people practiced sorcery as a retaliation for an actual wrong done to them. Sorcery was seen as an alternative to using more confrontational methods (verbal and physical aggression) or official channels to seek redress when the enemy was too powerful. Obeyesekere interprets these results as indicating that the Sri Lanka culture uses sorcery to "channelize aggression" in a socially acceptable manner.

EMOTIONAL AROUSAL

Our discussion thus far has focused on the impact of situational conditions on expressions of aggression — such conditions as interference and attack, status of and attributions about the source, aggression cues, and institutional and cultural norms. But what about the role played by emotions such as anger? Aversive events such as interference and attack do sometimes create a heightened emotional arousal that may be defined as "anger." Anger, then, may or may not produce aggression, depending on the situational conditions. And sometimes, the emotional arousal produced by aversive conditions is defined as some *other* emotion — fear, anxiety, depression, and so forth.

There are also occasions on which we direct our aggression toward others *without* experiencing anger or any other emotion. For example, it is common advice that parents should spank their children only after they have "cooled off," that is, when they are not angry. Boxers, soldiers, muggers, and even attorneys frequently aggress toward "adversaries," not because they are angry but in order to obtain championships, territory, money, or justice. Social psychologists sometimes distinguish between anger-caused and anger-free aggression by using the terms *hostile aggression* and *instrumental aggression.*

Displacement and Catharsis: Frustration-Aggression Theory

The earliest theory to make proposals about emotional anger was frustration-aggression theory. According to frustration-aggression theorists, aversive events such as interference and attack activate an emotion of anger — an aggressive drive. Presumably anger remains a motivating force until it is discharged through aggressive behavior. Consequently, the anger may become "free-floating," that is, detached from the source of interference or injury and discharged onto some other person, group, or object. Frustration-aggression theorists term this process **displacement**. Displacement (also called "scapegoating") has been a popular explanation for racism, anti-Semitism, and other kinds of prejudice. Hitler and Goebbels allegedly gave the German people — who were frustrated by their defeat in World War

I, plagued by poverty and wild inflation, and exasperated by the problems of life in general — Jews, Reds, and international bankers as targets to vent their rage on. And in ancient Rome, the Christian minority was allegedly "thrown to the lions" at public circuses to divert popular attention from the problems, failures, and corruption of the Roman state. (See the Student Observation: "Displacement.")

Still another process closely associated with the frustration-aggression hypothesis is **catharsis** — a purging and lessening of aggressive energy by discharging it through aggressive behavior. According to this view, anger is depicted as blocked energy in a hydraulic system. To feel better, the enraged person should vent the anger fully and forthrightly. The notion of catharsis has wide popularity. Many of us have experienced a sense of relief after engaging in some aggressive behavior (perhaps an emotional outburst): "I just had to get that out of my system," or "Gee, I'm glad I let off steam." Since the frustration-aggression theory postulates that all forms of aggression are functionally equivalent, one type of aggressive response can be substituted for another. Presumably we can drain off our aggressive energies by fantasizing physical assaults or by watching someone who is behaving violently (as when we watch a boxing match or a football game).

However, experimental evidence contradicts the popular notion. Although some researchers have found that aggressive behavior lowers subsequent aggression (Manning and Taylor, 1975), such behavior often produces a rise in aggression (Geen, Stonner, and Shope, 1975).

Letting rage out is rarely cathartic and usually produces more anger, not less, by functioning as a rehearsal for future outbursts (Tavris, 1983). As individuals recite their grievances, their emotional arousal builds up again. It makes them feel as angry as they did when the infuriating event first happened, all the while more deeply entrenching the angry attitudes. For instance, a study of laid-off aerospace engineers in San Diego showed that men who were invited to ventilate their anger became more hostile toward the company or their

---

STUDENT OBSERVATION

Displacement

One of the great things about where I work is that we can all have a lot of fun. Working in a busy restaurant is stressful, and it is good to know that we can still joke around. However, last week one of my fellow waitpersons, Joe, got in trouble with my boss for no apparent reason. Joe has been on the job for only a few months, so he doesn't understand that my boss comes down on everyone now and then. He's just trying to keep us under his thumb, and we all know it. Anyway, a few minutes later, I was talking to Joe and joking with him when he absolutely went berserk. Joe, normally a friendly and amusing fellow, started yelling at me in front of the entire restaurant. I didn't find out until later that my boss had "chewed him out." Nevertheless, I was embarrassed and angry, but I just walked away. Joe had *displaced* his anger toward our boss onto me, an innocent bystander. The story doesn't end here. That night, when I got home, I started to harp on my roommate for silly things like talking on the phone too loud and standing in front of the TV. She began to get angry, but then I realized I was *displacing* my hurt and anger from work onto her. I apologized and told her about my experience at work. She understood and a vicious cycle was stopped.

---

supervisors than did men who were asked to evaluate their own performance. And third-grade children instructed to express anger toward a child who had frustrated them ended up liking that child less than did children not encouraged to express anger.

Excitation Transfer Theory: The Pornography Case

Excitation transfer theory (Zillman, 1984) proposes that emotional arousal created in one situation can be transferred to emotions produced in a subsequent situation. There is a tendency to misattribute the cause of one's *accumulated* emotions to the most plausible *current* source. The behavior normally resulting from the emotion attributed to the current source is thus exacerbated by the emotions carried over from other sources. A number of social psychologists have demonstrated that people respond more aggressively to aversive stimuli if aroused by vigorous exercise or environmental stressors such as loud noise, overcrowding, and high temperature (Griffitt and Veitch, 1971; Zillmann, Katcher, and Milavsky, 1972; Baron and Bell, 1976; Donnerstein and Wilson, 1976; Mann, 1981).

When viewed from this perspective, heightened arousal of any sort serves to exaggerate *any* behavior already prevalent at the time. For example, pornography may create sexual arousal that gets transferred to an "angry" emotion aroused by current aversive events. Thus, the emotional arousal created by pornography carries over to intensify aggressive behavior beyond that which would have resulted from the current aversive event alone. Let's look more closely at social psychologists' attempts to examine this proposal.

Social psychologists typically study the relationship between sexual arousal and aggression by exposing some subjects to a sexually arousing stimulus such as an erotic film or written passage. Other subjects watch a neutral film or read a neutral passage. All the subjects are then provided with an opportunity to act aggressively against someone else, generally a confederate who makes a preset number of errors in a guessing game. For each error, the subject administers an electric shock to the other party, the intensity of which is determined by the subject. (Unknown to the subject, the wires do not carry an actual electric shock but simply lead to a recording device.) The average intensity level of the shock that the subject administers over several trials is taken as an index of the subject's level of aggression.

In general, exposure to nonviolent erotic material seems not to increase aggressive reactions (Smeaton and Byrne, 1987; Smith and Hand, 1987). Yet some studies suggest that, among men *already angered* by a female confederate's shocking them, exposure to *highly erotic*, but nonviolent, stimuli (especially depictions of precoital and coital activity) increased their aggressive behavior (Meyer, 1972; Zillmann, Hoyt, and Day, 1974; Donnerstein and Hallam, 1978).

Initial research showed that men typically become more aggressive toward women after viewing sexual *violence* (Donnerstein, 1980; Donnerstein and Berkowitz, 1981). Males who watch films depicting sexual violence administer more electric shocks to their female partners than men who watch nonviolent sexual films. And when they have been previously angered, the men are even more willing to administer shocks to women.

Other research also suggests that pornographic films depicting sexual assault help justify aggression, reduce men's sensitivity to rape, and lower men's inhibitions against sexual aggression. Men who have watched such films more easily attribute responsibility for the assault to the woman, shifting the responsibility for rape to the victim (Donnerstein and Berkowitz, 1981).

For instance, when researchers showed sexually violent films to young men and then asked the men to judge a simulated rape trial, the subjects were less likely to vote for conviction than were subjects who had not seen the films (Donnerstein and Linz, 1984). Similarly, after viewing sexually violent films in which a rape victim appears to enjoy the attack, the young men were more likely to believe that a woman who was raped wanted to be and that hitchhikers or provocatively dressed women *deserve* to be raped. The researchers conducting these studies concluded that watching sexual violence had caused the men to become more calloused toward women (Malamuth and Briere, 1986).

However, recent research has suggested some limitations to this interpretation. In the studies described above, subjects were asked to watch brief stag films depicting a variety of sexual activities and then, almost immediately, were requested to shock a woman or express opinions about sexual violence. How do you think the *subjects* interpreted this sequence of events? At a minimum they must have thought that the researchers saw some connection between the two events. Could these observations have affected their aggressive responses?

To deal with this problem, some researchers disguised the connection between the two events. In one such experiment, Malamuth and Ceniti (1986) had one researcher ask subjects to view a film depicting sexual violence and a *second* researcher administer the shock-learning portion of the study. Linz, Donnerstein, and Penrod (1988), also trying to disguise the connection between the two events, had a second researcher phone subjects at home to ask them to participate in a study in the law school. When they arrived, the subjects were asked to act as jurors in a rape case. Under these conditions, both studies found that prior exposure to the films had no effect on aggression toward another woman or evaluation of the rape victim.

Thus, although excitation transfer appears to apply in some situations of aggression (exercise and environmental stressors), social psychologists are as yet unable to demonstrate that it applies to most instances of viewing pornography. Sexual violence is explored in greater detail in the box "The Social Definition of Rape." The effects of rape and other violent crimes are discussed in the box "Victimization."

Reflexivity: Symbolic Interaction Theory

In Chapter 2, "Early Socialization," we discussed symbolic interaction theory. There we focused on the theory's ideas about the development of the *self*, or the capacity to engage in *reflexive behavior*—the capacity to look at one's own behavior and, in doing so, to react to what one sees. In Chapter 11, "Close Relationships," we discussed Morris Rosenberg's (1990) proposal that reflexive behavior is implicated in our perceptions of our

THE SOCIAL DEFINITION OF RAPE

The definition and attribution of rape is a matter of social debate. In a telephone poll of 500 American adults, just over 50 percent of the respondents said they would not classify as rape a situation in which "a man uses emotional pressure, but no physical force, to get a woman to have sex" (Gibbs, 1991). One in three respondents said it was not rape if "a married man has sex with his wife even though she does not want him to." In the same survey, over 50 percent of older respondents (fifty years of age or older) said they believe a woman who is raped is partly to blame if she (1) is under the influence of drugs or alcohol, (2) dresses provocatively, or (3) agrees to go to the man's room or home. A smaller percentage of younger respondents share these beliefs. For example, only 20 percent of the eighteen- to thirty-year-old respondents believed that a woman is partly to blame if she agrees to go to the man's room or home. These age differences may suggest that as younger people grow older, they will either (1) hold raped women more responsible or (2) maintain their current beliefs, thus changing the distribution of beliefs among all adults.

Women who press rape charges are as much on trial as their alleged rapists. Researchers who observed thirty-seven Indianapolis sexual assault trials and interviewed 360 jurors found that jurors — both male and female — admit to being influenced by a victim's character, appearance, reputation, and life style (Brozan, 1985). They treat more seriously the rape of a woman who seems chaste or is conventional in her life style. They are more likely to exonerate men charged with raping women who reputedly are sexually active outside marriage or women who knew their assailants. A woman becomes suspect if mention is made that she uses birth control pills, has an illegitimate child, has a child with a different last name than her own, or shares the same address as a boyfriend. And jurors judge harshly such behaviors as going to a bar alone, accepting a ride with a male stranger, drinking, keeping late hours, or using marijuana.

Accused men are usually placed in one of two categories. If the men come across as losers, are scruffy, lack a job, or are unmarried, jurors tend to be biased against them. If the men are attractive, have a girlfriend, or are married, jurors find it difficult to believe that they would commit rape. But in fact these characteristics are not good predictors of who is or is not a likely rapist.

own emotions and in our "emotional reactions" to these perceptions. The emotional *response* is a mixture of physiological sensation (nonreflexive process) and interpretation of the sensation (reflexive process). Rosenberg proposes that the reflexive process involving emotions can be broken down into three parts: emotional identification, emotional display, and emotional experiences. We'll use these distinctions in our discussion of aggression.

Emotional identification. Symbolic interaction theory focuses on how we interpret our physiological sensations, relying partly on information from our environment. We do not simply "feel" angry; we also "think" we are angry — a cognitive process. Reflexive interpretation is particularly important when our physiological sensations are ambiguous. Sometimes we are uncertain whether what we feel is anger or not. According to some researchers, anger has some of the same physiological symptoms as joy, excitement, fear, anxiety, and jealousy (Tavris, 1983). We have to interpret these symptoms before we can decide that we are, in fact, angry.

Rosenberg proposes that we have been socialized to use cultural scenarios (such as "aggression schemas" or "scripts") in interpreting our emotions. For example, we learn to expect causal connections between events and our internal reactions. We expect certain things to cause us to feel angry — for example, an insult. Therefore,

VICTIMIZATION

We become victims in many ways. We can have a serious accident; contract a terrible disease; be assaulted, raped, robbed, or abducted; experience a tornado, earthquake, or fire; or bear the impact of a technological disaster. When we become victims, we must deal not only with any physical injury that may ensue but also with the psychological toll produced by the event. Much of the psychological toll derives from the shattering of a number of basic assumptions we hold about ourselves and the world. Prior to victimization, most of us go about our daily activities imbued with an "illusion of invulnerability" — the notion that "it can't happen to me." But after victimization, we become preoccupied with the fear that misfortune will recur; we worry, for instance, about being raped or robbed again or suffering a recurrence of disease. In brief, once victimized, we find it easy to see ourselves in the role of victim again, perceiving the world as "senseless" and ourselves as weak, helpless, needy, frightened, and out of control. Joe Phillips, a 6-foot-5-inch, 326-pound nosetackle for the San Diego Charges, described his feelings as he was recovering from an assault by three men:

> I feel like there's a part of me that isn't there anymore. . . . It's pretty horrific, really. I don't have the same personal security I once had. I have this feeling that it's a stark reality that I could get beaten again. (*Sports Illustrated*, September 30, 1991)

Even the threat of victimization may limit people's freedom, keeping them off the streets at night — whether or not they have actually been victimized (Riger and Gordon, 1981; Warr, 1985).

someone who has been insulted tends to interpret her or his emotion as anger.

We also have learned that anger causes us to behave in a certain way — for example, to strike someone (Perinbanayagam, 1989). Thus, a person who strikes someone is inclined to interpret his or her antecedent emotion as anger: "I struck him because I was angry." On the other hand, if the person is motivated to *not* behave this way (maybe because striking someone would cause the victim to strike back, terminate a friendship, or result in being fired), the person is more inclined to interpret his or her emotion as something other than anger — fear, for example. When we experience ambiguous internal sensations, we use our cultural knowledge about the causes and effects of events such as being insulted or striking someone to identify our sensations as "anger." (See the Student Observation: "Emotional Identification.")

Emotional display. Emotional display is an example of impression management. It consists of both the exhibition and the concealment of emotions for purposes of affecting the attitudes and behavior of others. Therefore, role-taking — mentally looking at our own behavior choices from another person's point of view — is a key part of the reflexive process. For example, a boy is angered by being battered by a male schoolmate. Should he express his anger through fighting back or not?

Quickly, he reflects on how others would react to his aggression and to his supporting accounts. He believes that his father would approve, especially if the boy labeled the schoolmate "a bully" and said, "I was only defending myself." He believes that his friends would also support his aggression, but only if he changed his story. He could call the schoolmate "dogmeat" and say, "He messed with me once too often and had to be taught a lesson." But what about the schoolmate? How is he going to react? Will he be intimidated enough by the counteraggression not to retaliate? In balance, the victim decides to exhibit his anger by fighting back.

However, if the victim were a girl (or the bully schoolmate were a girl), the results of the reflexive thinking might be different. Because our culture provides different scripts and different expectations for females, a female victim might have concealed her anger or defined her emotion as something other than anger.

In addition to concealing the emotions we define ourselves as feeling, we sometimes *pretend to feel* emotions that we believe we are not feeling. For example, if we are in a restaurant, we may feign or exaggerate our anger in order to obtain better service from a waiter. In sum:

> Expressions of anger have important social functions in the interactions of the two parties. Anger is an emotion that expresses a judgment that one has been treated unfairly, but it also conveys the notion that the angered person is the victim and the target of anger is the oppressor in the relationship. The intensity of anger conveys the degree of unjust harm experienced by the angered party. Anger has the function of drawing the other person's attention to the issues of concern to the angered party. Anger also shows a commitment to resolving the grievance. And, of course, anger is a type of threat, since we believe it is frequently associated with aggression. (Tedeschi, 1991: 5-6)

Emotional experience. Finally, Rosenberg proposes that we try to shape our own emotions. Whereas emotional display includes deciding what emotion to show, emotional experience involves deciding what emotion to feel. We try to accomplish this by controlling our reflexive thinking or even the stimulus events that cause such cognitions. The chief way to do so is through selective attention and selective exposure. For example, you might cognitively control your anger toward a lover who has rejected you. You could intensify your anger by thinking about the betrayal or reduce it by shifting your thoughts intentionally to future alternatives. Behaviorally, you could pursue further interaction with your former lover (venting your hostility) or avoid places you know she or he frequents.

LEARNING AGGRESSION: SOCIAL LEARNING THEORY

According to social learning theorists, our *current* aggressive behavior in response to current environmental events such as interference, attack, or "aggressive cues" is a result of *past* learning. Our learning of aggression proceeds in the same manner as our learning of other kinds of behavior — even behavior as different from aggression as helping behavior. We discussed social learning theory quite extensively in Chapter 2, "Early So-

---

STUDENT OBSERVATION

Emotional Identification

*A*s I read about Morris Rosenberg's idea that emotional identification is largely determined by cognitive factors, "because the internal state of arousal is often ambiguous," I couldn't help thinking about students at bars here in Chapel Hill. Most of us drink for the emotional arousal that alcohol causes, and we label this arousal a "high" or a "buzz" and experience it as pleasant or fun. But I wonder how a person would feel about the buzz if he had never experienced it before, didn't know what was causing it, and had had no exposure to people talking about it positively. Say, if the person were sitting in class, listening intently to a lecture, and suddenly couldn't think straight. If his handwriting went all to hell and he fell off his chair. And imagine how he'd feel if he realized that he was smiling vacuously at nothing at all. I think I would be frightened — afraid that my brain was melting down or something. But when I drink a beer or three and feel the same buzz beginning, I am hardly afraid; I look forward to the sensation because I have labeled it positively. Being drunk isn't the same thing, really, as having an emotional response to a situation, but the idea that both are merely internal states of arousal to which we apply labels is an appealing one.

cialization," so we will only review it here, high-lighting how it has been used to explain aggressive behavior.

Imitation

Albert Bandura (1973, 1983) is the name that social psychologists most often associate with the application of social learning theory to the study of aggression. Bandura proposed that the most important mechanism for a child's initial learning of aggressive behavior is *observational learning* (imitation). Children observe other people being aggressive or controlling their aggression, and they imitate them. You might remember our discussion of Bandura's classic study, which involved children learning to attack a large, inflated Bobo doll by observing an adult act aggressively toward the doll. The probability that an observing child would imitate the adult's aggression was affected by what happened to the adult after he or she attacked the doll. The likelihood of the child's aggression increased when the adult was given soft drinks and candy, while it decreased when the adult was spanked with a magazine by another adult.

Media violence. Bandura's study raises the question of whether media violence increases the aggressiveness of viewers. Violence on television and in movies has become increasingly common (Comstock, 1982). In laboratory experiments, subjects who view aggression usually display more aggressive behavior than control groups who do not.

Studies measuring both the amount of time individuals spend watching violence on television and their own aggressiveness find that the two are related. We can't conclude from these studies that watching violence *causes* aggression. It may be that persons who are inclined to be aggressive choose to watch violent programs (Friedrich-Cofer and Huston, 1986). Field studies of the effects of exposure to violent films and television shows have produced mixed results. So the debate rages on. Some social psychologists have con-cluded that we have not convincingly demon-strated that watching violence in the media causes aggression (Freedman, 1984, 1986). Others argue that even if the effects are weak, the social impli-cations are great (Rosenthal, 1986). This is an area of research that is likely to continue to receive the attention of social psychologists.

Discriminative stimuli. The children in Ban-dura's study learned to attack a Bobo doll. Did they learn to attack only Bobo dolls, or did they learn to attack other objects (including other peo-ple) as well? Does it seem reasonable to you that they would be more likely to attack some things rather than others? In the jargon of social learning theory, what is the *discriminative stimulus* eliciting the aggression? Experiments by Leonard Berk-owitz and his associates supply clues about how observational learning affects the targets of ag-gression. In some of these experiments, subjects watched a seven-minute violent film clip from *Champion* (Geen and Berkowitz, 1967). Then they were told that they could give electric shocks to an individual (a confederate of the experimenter) who had previously insulted and angered them within the experimental setting. Berkowitz varied the nature of the target person by varying his name: one-third of the subjects were told that the person who had angered them and to whom they could apply shocks was Bob Kelly; one-third, that it was Bob Dunne; and the other third, that it was Bob Riley. In the movie *Champion*, a boxer named Midge Kelly is given a bloody beating by another boxer named Dunne.

Berkowitz expected that after witnessing the boxing film, subjects would administer more shocks to Bob Kelly than to the other confeder-ates. This proved to be true. When the confeder-ate's last name was the same as that of the victim in the film, subjects gave him an average of 5.4 shocks. When the confederate was called Riley, a name not mentioned in the film, they gave him 4.4 shocks. Thus subjects made the strongest at-tack on a target with the *same* last name as the target in the movie.

On the basis of other research (Berkowitz, 1965; Berkowitz and Knurek, 1969; Berkowitz, 1973), Berkowitz concludes that persons with characteristics an angry individual has previously learned to dislike are also especially apt to be victimized. As children grow up, the significant people in their environment may repeatedly respond negatively toward members of given groups. For example, they may make unpleasant remarks or otherwise display distaste whenever they encounter or talk about Jews or blacks. Thus if a category of persons — Jews, blacks, women — is culturally defined in negative terms, it becomes easier to attack individuals within that category.

Reinforcement and Punishment Contingencies

Whereas Bandura proposed that imitation was the most important way to initially learn aggressive behavior, he suggested that the continued performance of such behavior was a function of reinforcement and punishment contingencies. When a particular aggressive behavior is rewarded, an individual is more likely to repeat that aggressive behavior in the future; when it is punished, the individual is less likely to repeat it. A reward can be a *positive reinforcer* (something added to the person's environment), such as the verbal approval of a friend or parent. Such approval could be expected in subcultures that have norms favoring aggression — male teenage gangs, military units, and even some sports teams. Similarly, a child may be able to gain her or his parent's attention or compliance to a demand by banging on the parent's arm or leg.

Other rewards are *negative reinforcers*. Here, aggressive behavior is rewarded by the *removal* of an aversive (painful) stimulus such as an insult, a demand, or an attack by another person. If a victim can hurt an "attacker" enough, the attacker may withdraw his or her insults, demands, attack, or presence altogether. A child may learn to terminate a sibling's physical assault by retaliatory violent acts. Reinforcement contingencies also affect the discriminative stimuli that elicit aggres-

sive behavior — stimuli that signal when and against whom we act aggressively. For example, most children tend to be more aggressive away from home than at home and more aggressive toward their peers than toward parents.

Although it is distressing to think that our society promotes aggression by rewarding aggressive behavior, this also suggests that aggression might be controlled by societal efforts to withhold such rewards. Social groups can increase the costs for aggressive conduct and the rewards for nonaggressive alternatives.

Conflict

The unidirectional view of aggression we have been discussing — that the actions of one person cause another person to behave aggressively — dominates the thinking of many people in public life. Whether the conflict involves warfare among nations, strife between racial groups, disagreement among politicians, controversies among scientists, or whatever, one party typically views the other as the "aggressor." Depending on the observer's bias, one side in the dispute (the "bad-guy villain") is seen as motivated by ignoble, evil, and illegitimate aims; the other ("the good-guy hero"), by noble, morally correct, and legitimate aims. The "good guys" may be forced to engage in aggression to ensure that the "bad guys" are held in check — that "law and order" prevails.

This one-sided view of aggression focuses on frustration (and its source) as the "cause" and on aggression as the "effect." If blame must be fixed, it is usually assigned to the source of the frustration. But for social psychologists, the unidirectional aggression model provides an incomplete account of the processes underlying social conflict. A better model would focus on the intentional *exchange* of harmful behavior (or reciprocal aggression). In previous chapters, we have referred to reward exchange — the reciprocal exchange of benefits between parties. Here we are going to discuss the reciprocal exchange of *harm-*

ful behaviors between parties — an exchange called **conflict** (Blalock, 1989).

COMPETITION

Competition is a situation in which people perceive themselves as having incompatible objectives or goals, so the success of one party means the failure of other parties. Each party, therefore, perceives that the other can interfere with his or her own goal attainment. In fact, the parties may actually behave in a manner that does interfere with each other's goal — reciprocal interference. Thus, competition (1) produces the perception of the opportunity for interference and (2) increases the likelihood of actual interference, which makes our earlier discussion of interference and aggression pertinent to the discussion of competition and conflict. Under competitive conditions, people may have to contend against one another in order to be among the few to achieve their goals. In some cases, they will engage in social conflict, with each side harming the other in an attempt to eliminate, or at least neutralize, the other's interference.

Although competition produces losers and may lead to competitors being harmed, our society and its institutions promote the advantages of competition — the achievement of excellence, the best products at the lowest cost, character building, cohesion building, generation of revenues. However, the ideology supporting socially approved competition usually includes some restrictions on the extreme survival-of-the-fittest style of competition. All competitors are said to begin the competition with an "equal opportunity," although (as we will discuss in a later chapter) there are many interpretations of just what this means. And during the competition, there are forms and levels of interference and conflict that are socially unacceptable.

Cases of Competition

Competition in marriage. Donald Peterson received these accounts when he asked wives and husbands to write about "significant" interactions in their daily lives:

> I asked Jim if he would do the dishes — to get them out of the way — while I fixed the handle of the teapot so we could have some tea. Negative vibrations from Jim, who immediately suggested we do the dishes together, implying that I should wash. I asked if he would like to wash them and he said, "Well, I would if it were just the dinner dishes, but there's all that other stuff in the sink." I had been cooking all afternoon for a camping trip and Jim didn't like the way I left pans and things around. General manifestations of disgust from both participants at this point.

> I came home from work and went to sit on Bert's lap. I kissed him and began to tell him something that had happened to me during the day. Bert said it was time for the news. End of encounter. (1983: 371)

Peterson calls these two events examples of "illegitimate demand" and "rebuff" and says they are two types of events that commonly initiate conflict within marriages. They feature competition — mutual interference of interests and, in all probability, of values as well — a difference of opinion over the legitimacy of the expectations each spouse holds of the other.

Competition in industry. We are generally aware of the disputes between labor and management over wages, benefits, and profit sharing. But another source of dispute has more recently drawn the public's attention — the protection of the health and safety of workers. Examples of diseases associated with unhealthy working conditions are black lung disease among coal miners and cancer among workers exposed to radiation or chemicals. Many jobs are associated with particularly unsafe working conditions. Ditchdiggers are killed when the unsupported walls of the ditches in which they are working collapse. Construction workers die or receive serious injuries in falls from scaffolds. Machine operators can lose a hand or a foot. Fire fighters die or receive serious burns due to defective protective equipment.

The federal government joined the labor-management dispute in 1970 and 1971 when it created the Occupational Safety and Health Administration (OSHA). Several barriers separate the various players in this dispute (Ritzer and Walczak, 1986). All involve competition. First, on the one side is management's desire to keep costs down and profits up, as well as its desire to control what goes on in the workplace. Opposed to this is the workers' desire to improve their working conditions, particularly in regard to health and safety, and to maximize their control of the workplace. Management and OSHA disagree about who should decide when there is enough evidence to prove that particular work conditions are hazardous to workers. And *within* OSHA some believe the focus of the government should be on treatment, while others believe it should be on prevention.

Competition in sales and service.   If you have ever negotiated the price of a car with an automobile salesperson, you will immediately recognize your relationship with the salesperson as one involving a clash of interests — competition. You want to minimize the cost of the car you will buy; the salesperson wants to maximize the cost because his or her income derives from the sales price. But you are not the only two parties involved. The third party is the automobile agency, and ultimately it is the agency (not the salesperson) and you who decide whether the car transaction occurs. Although this sometimes creates a clash of interests between the salesperson and the agency (the salesperson may be willing to make the sale at a particular price, only to have the agency ask for more), the salesperson may try to use a "weak alliance" as a way of reducing your perceptions of the clash of interest between you and him or her. The salesperson may present himself or herself as representing *your* interests in the negotiation with the agency.

Service-for-pay transactions may also involve a similar clash of interests. The client usually wants more or better service for a given price than the service provider is willing to offer. Take the prostitute-"john" relationship, for example. To the prostitute, "time is money." Therefore, the john who wants to enjoy himself as long as he can is causing the prostitute to lose considerable income. Yet the prostitute knows that if the john feels he has been cheated, he may "stiff" (refuse to pay for services) or physically assault her. At the same time, the john knows that the prostitute may try to "rip him off" by obtaining his money without providing the service. This relationship is also affected by the prostitute's clashing interests with both her pimp (or madam) and the police. In the case of the former, there is the problem of how to divide the money earned by the prostitute. In the case of the latter, there is the problem of how to avoid detection and arrest or, if arrested, how to avoid a large fine or jail sentence.

Competition in sports.   Sports competition has features that distinguish it from the other cases of competition we have just mentioned. In sports, people agree to engage in competition in which the primary goal is to win the competition itself. Success is measured by directly comparing the achievements of those who perform the same activity rather than by obtaining a scarce resource or establishing a set of dominant values. A time limit is usually established for a particular competition, after which a renewal of the competition gives the previous loser another opportunity to become a future winner.

In unorganized sports (e.g., pickup games), the participants negotiate their own rules (norms) and penalties of play. In organized sports, the rules, ideologies, and rituals are established by a superordinate authority — a governing or sanctioning body such as the National Collegiate Athlete Association or a high school athletic association. The rules not only identify how the competition is to be conducted but also place limits on the expression of aggression and conflict and establish penalties for those who violate such rules. Officials of the authority (referees and umpires) enforce these rules during competition.

The term "sportsmanship" generally refers to behavior that is consistent with these rules.

Competitions often conclude with ritualistic ceremonies in which competitors congratulate one another on a "good game." Such rituals are meant to erase lingering hostilities and renew the normative bonds between competitors who share a commitment to their sport.

Sportsmanship is supported by an ideology that is meant to place some limits on the goal of winning *at any cost*. "It isn't whether you win or lose, it's how you play the game." This means that (1) if you lose, you can take pride in having played by the rules, and (2) if you win by being too aggressive or breaking other rules, your victory will be tarnished or forfeited. On the other hand, competitors are frequently reminded that sportsmanship can also be carried too far, as when it jeopardizes the chances of success. In such instances, competitors are accused of not taking the game seriously or lacking the "killer instinct."

Sports competitions are sometimes concluded with ritualistic ceremonies. Opposing competitors may slap hands and congratulate each other on a "good game." Such rituals are meant to erase lingering hostilities and renew the normative bonds between competitors who share a commitment to their sport.

However, the existence of rules, ideology, and ritual directed at controlling conflict only points to the fact that while competition in sports sometimes produces (even requires) cooperation and positive bonds, it can also result in conflict.

INITIAL CONFLICT AND ITS ALTERNATIVES

Just as aggression is not the only response to frustration, conflict is but one of several alternative responses to competition. Most other alternative responses attempt the direct reduction of competition itself. To illustrate just one set of alternatives to conflict, let's use a modification of Dean Pruitt and Jeffrey Rubin's (1986) example.

A Hypothetical Example

For months Peter Colger has been anticipating two weeks of vacation at a quiet mountain lodge where he can hunt, fish, and hike to lofty scenic overlooks. Now his wife, Mary, has rudely challenged his dream. She has told him that she finds the mountains boring and wants to go instead to Ocean City, Maryland, a busy seaside resort that Peter dislikes intensely. Peter and Mary must decide how to respond to this clash of interests.

Inaction or withdrawal. In response to their dispute Peter and Mary can resort to *inaction*; in other words, they can do nothing. Withdrawal might occur following a brief bout of conflict. It may occur in the hope that the issue will simply go away (to each person that means the other gives in) before the dispute or conflict erupts again and leads to irreparable damage to their relationship. If it doesn't go away, at least the withdrawal period will give them a chance to cool off before resuming their dispute. But the opposite may occur, since Peter and Mary may interpret each other's inaction as a lack of willingness to even discuss the matter. Inaction may give each partner more time to rationalize his or her own position. Peter and Mary might also decide to *permanently* withdraw; that is, they might decide neither to reopen their dispute nor to take a vacation this year.

Compromise. Peter and Mary could compromise. In *compromise*, the parties search for the middle ground by gradually diluting their objectives until they are no longer incompatible. For example, Peter and Mary could spend half their vacation in the mountains and the other half at the seashore. Or they could spend this year's entire vacation in the mountains and next year's at the seashore.

Bridging, cost cutting, and logrolling. The resolution to the dispute can take several forms *if* the dispute can be divided into several subissues. This is the case with Peter and Mary, who not only disagree as to whether they will spend their vacation in the mountains or at the seashore but also disagree as to whether they will stay in a hotel or a cottage, hike or socialize, fish or swim, take the children or leave them with the grandparents, be isolated or be among people, and eat out or fix their own meals.

In *bridging*, the parties agree on which issues are most important, disregard the others, and find a way to reduce the incompatibility of the important goals. For example, Peter and Mary may agree that fishing (Peter) and swimming (Mary) are the most important goals. They may be able to achieve both by vacationing at either an inland lake with a nice beach or a location at the seashore with a reputation for good fishing.

In some instances, the most important issue is not which of two activities the parties will perform (e.g., hike or socialize). Instead, the issue is whether the parties will perform a given activity *or not* (e.g., socializing with strangers). One party may not want to do that particular activity. *Cost cutting* involves finding a way that both parties can achieve their interests by reducing the one party's suffering. For example, Peter and Mary can go either to the mountains or to the seashore as long as they can rent a house that is located within a community where Mary can find people to talk to and that has a quiet area where Peter can isolate himself.

Logrolling is yet another alternative in disputes that can be divided into several subissues. In this solution, the parties yield on an equal number of issues. For example, Peter and Mary could each yield to the other on three of the six issues. (See the Student Observation: "Logrolling.")

Compensation. The dispute could be resolved through *compensation* if the dispute, rather than being divided, can be expanded to include a second dispute. In this solution, one party yields to the other party in the first dispute in exchange for the other's yielding in the second dispute. For example, Mary may yield in the couple's vacation dispute and spend the two weeks in the mountains if Peter yields in their dispute over buying her a new car.

STUDENT OBSERVATION

Logrolling

When I was in high school, the issue of when I was and was not allowed to go out socially was a big source of disagreement between my mother and me. Specifically, my mother did not want me to go out on weeknights, and she wanted me to be in by 12:30 on weekends (because she did not like to go to sleep until I arrived home and she did not want to be up past 12:30). This produced something of a conflict ritual between us. Every Friday night as I was getting ready to leave, she would say, "Be back by 12:30!" and I would always respond with something like, "None of my friends have a curfew. Why do you treat me like such a baby?" There would be an argument, and I would leave with no resolution and often came home after the 12:30 curfew. Additionally, every time I wanted to go out on a weeknight for some reason other than to study, we would have a big argument about that. By my senior year, my mother finally decided that we were arguing too much and that she was being manipulated too often, so she decided that we should come to some agreeable compromise and not discuss the issue any further. The way we reached that resolution was through *logrolling*. We decided that my staying home on weeknights was more important to my mother (so that my grades would not suffer) and that having no curfew on weekends was more important to me. Therefore, I stopped asking to go out on weeknights, but I was allowed to come home when I wanted on weekends. My mother and I each yielded on one issue.

Expanding the pie. It may be possible to resolve the dispute by *expanding the pie*, which consists of increasing the resources such that the parties' goals are no longer incompatible. For example, Peter and Mary might solve their problem by convincing their employers to extend their vacation time another two weeks. This way, each party can get two weeks in the environment of choice.

Yielding. Of course, the dispute could be resolved by *yielding*; that is, one party can simply submit to the demands of the other. This surrender can involve total capitulation or, if the issue is divisible, partial capitulation, in which the party gives in on one or more subissues. For example, Peter and Mary can go to the seashore as Mary wished or just forgo Peter's fishing until another time.

Conflict. In most of the above cases, the disputants' reactions reduce or eliminate their competition. But there is an alternative approach. People like Peter and Mary can resort to *conflict* (which Pruitt and Rubin call "contending"). The conflict can include making threats; imposing sanctions, which may involve physical assault (and which, it is understood, will be withdrawn if the other concedes); and one party's taking preemptive actions that would commit both parties to a particular decision without the other's consent (e.g., making reservations, arranging to have friends join them).

Deterrence: The Relative Cost of Conflict

A variety of forces come into play in influencing the alternative responses to a dispute. Our major interest is in those factors that influence the choice of conflict as a means of resolving the dispute. To what degree are the parties willing to expend resources and energy to defeat or neutralize each other? For example, are they committed to engaging in physical conflict, psychological threats, and name-calling, or will they limit themselves to verbal debate? A variety of factors determine whether disputants will choose conflict or another alternative, but most of these factors can be reduced to a single consideration: What will it cost? Individuals or groups often minimize or contain conflict because they feel that the expenditure of greater resources or energy "just isn't worth it." In other words, as the disputants appraise the situation, the costs of conflict outweigh the gains to be derived from it (Brockner, Shaw, and Rubin, 1979).

The parties to a dispute may impose self-contained limits on conflict lest it imperil other rewarding aspects of their relationship. Thus many husbands and wives "pull their punches" in a marital disagreement because they recognize that they wish to continue living together. They do not want to jeopardize the broader companionship, the security, or the sexual and affectional aspects of the marriage.

The *relative* capabilities of the competing parties to punish each other play a role in whether either party will initiate conflict. If *both* parties have a great capacity to punish each other, then each party will hesitate to actually initiate conflict because (1) each fears retaliation due to the opponent's capacity and (2) each does not expect the opponent to attack due to the party's own capacity. The combination of these factors would lead both parties to respond to their competition in some manner other than conflict.

In contrast, if the parties' capacities to punish each other are *unequal*, the outcome will be quite different. It is probably obvious that the person who has the higher capacity to punish his or her opponent may choose to use it. After all, the major cost of doing so — retaliation — is minimal. But what will the low-capacity person do? Their opponent's initiation of conflict is unpreventable, and retaliation to the low-capacity person's initiation is probable. You might feel that this should be enough to deter the low-capacity person from initiating conflict. Or you might think that the person would actually initiate conflict as a means of communicating resolve and avoiding intimidation. If the latter is true, the parties' unequal capacities to punish each other will increase the likelihood that both will choose to engage in conflict to resolve their dispute. There is some evidence to support this position (Lawler and Bacharach, 1987).

Conflict Rituals

Once parties are involved in a conflict, they sometimes express their conflict in a style typical of

The parties to a dispute may impose self-contained limits on conflict lest it imperil other rewarding aspects of their relationship. Thus many husbands and wives "pull their punches" in a marital disagreement because they do not want to jeopardize the marriage.

their relationship. Social psychologists call these characteristic conflicts **conflict rituals**. For example, a father and his daughter have a ritual that begins when she comes home and is upset because she had to meet an 11 P.M. curfew. (She is fifteen going on twenty.) When she confronts her father, she starts talking about her grievance: "Girls my age don't have to be in until midnight"; "I won't have any friends"; "You don't trust me." Her father (who is forty going on eighty) is intent on being a responsible father, and that responsibility includes setting hours for her to be home at night. Each time he is confronted by his daughter, he responds by saying, "Ginny's parents make her be in at eleven, too"; "Let's find you some new friends"; "Trust is something you earn." With this, she begins to cry and rushes off to her room. Her father reacts by saying, "Oh, let her cry. She'll get over it." This ritual gets played out in a similar fashion about every two weeks. (Before reading further, look at the Student Observation: "Conflict Ritual.")

FACTORS AFFECTING ESCALATION AND DEESCALATION

Conflict can be the source of further conflict. For example, an argument may be followed by personal insults that are followed, in turn, by a fistfight. The conflict-spiral model describes the dynamic, interactive process by which individuals or groups become caught in an upward spiral of hostilities.

Hans Toch's (1969) investigation of episodes of conflict between police and civilians indicates that conflict spirals were common features of such interactions. He found that much of the violence began with the police officer's questioning the civilian ("What is your name?" or "What are you doing?"), making demands, or touching the civilian and the civilian's subsequent failure to comply. Police officers tended to respond aggressively to (1) the civilian's verbal aggression toward the officer — for example, calling the officer a derogatory name or using other profanities, (2) the civilian's physical aggression toward the officer, or

---

STUDENT OBSERVATION

Conflict Ritual

Every morning my brother and mother go through the same routine. My brother is supposed to be up at 6:45 A.M. and be ready to leave at 7:30 so that my mother can be at work by 8 and he can get to school early. And every morning it's the same old thing: "Chad, it's time to get up," my mother yells. While my mother goes about her own morning duties, Chad comes downstairs and says something like, "Are my blue jogging pants clean?" Mama always responds by saying, "No, go look downstairs and see if you can find anything else to wear." Chad goes to look and then comes stomping back upstairs grumbling, "There's nothing for me to wear; I guess I can't go to school." Like he really cares if he goes or not; he's just trying to lay a guilt trip on my mother. My mother's response is always, "I told you to get your clothes ready last night. If there was something you wanted to wear today I would have washed it. Now go find something to wear, it is fifteen minutes after seven." A few minutes later the shower can be heard running, and by this time my mother is furious. When Chad gets out of the shower, the war is on: "I am not taking you to school anymore; you can ride the bus from now on. If you miss it, then that's just tough; you can stay home all day, and I'm not going to come and get you either." Chad responds, "I can't go to school dirty and naked. I didn't have time to take a shower last night." My mother screams, "I told you to get your things together for school last night. If you hadn't been playing with that stupid Nintendo, you would've had plenty of time to take a shower." This is an example of a conflict ritual. No matter how much my mother threatens my brother, he does the same thing every morning, and my mother's responses are always the same.

(3) the civilian's physical aggression toward another police officer. From this point on, aggression begot aggression. For example, Toch found that (1) the police officer's threat or attempts to arrest the civilian, (2) the officer's physical aggression toward the civilian, (3) the officer's aggression toward another civilian, and (4) the civilian's own previous aggression toward the police all precipitated more violence by the civilian.

On the basis of his interviews, Toch concluded that the civilian responds aggressively in order to avoid (or protect herself or himself from) the negative situation of being controlled by others. On the other hand, the police officer responds aggressively in order to avoid the loss of his or her authority as a police officer. In other words, being controlled by others is perceived as harmful to the civilian, and losing control of others is harmful to the police officer — each interferes with the other's goals. From a similar analysis of civilian encounters that ended in murder, sociologist David Luckenbill (1977) concluded that the encounters also took the form of escalating action-reaction, in which each opponent sought to establish or maintain face *at the other's expense* when confronted with adversity.

If conflict can escalate, it can also deescalate. With the recognition that the findings of social science might be used to solve social problems, social psychologists became interested in whether their research could be useful in evaluating proposals to reduce social conflict. One area that has drawn particular attention is interracial conflict. Social psychologists have provided evidence suggesting several factors that might reduce such conflict and others that would not. They believe that such factors, though most often discussed in the context of interracial conflict, might have similar effects on conflict between any parties (Worchel, 1986).

Contact

"Bring ethnic and racial groups into contact with one another, and their prejudices will wither away." This folk wisdom is widely accepted in the United States; indeed, Americans have an almost mystical faith in "getting to know one another" as a solution to racial difficulties. Yet social psychologists usually point to an early series of ingenious field studies whose results refute this belief.

Muzafer Sherif and his associates (Sherif et al., 1961) undertook these studies to investigate conditions that cause and reduce intergroup conflict. The subjects, boys eleven and twelve years old, did not know one another at the beginning of the experiment. They were healthy, socially well adjusted, and somewhat above average in intelligence. They came from stable, middle-class, white Protestant families. Thus, the researchers ruled out any group behavior caused by differences in family, religious, ethnic, or socioeconomic backgrounds.

In stage 1 of the study, the boys were assigned to one of two groups and taken in separate buses to a summer camp run by the researchers. They were settled in cabins at a considerable distance from each other and were unaware of the other group's existence. The boys in each group camped out together, cooked meals, worked on improvements for their swimming place, canoed, and played various organized and informal games. Gradually group bonds evolved and each group developed its own recognized status hierarchy, individual role assignments, norms (regarding cursing, toughness, and rowdy behavior), name (one group called itself the "Rattlers," the other the "Eagles"), jargon, special jokes, secrets, and preferred places.

In stage 2, the Rattlers and the Eagles "discovered" each other's existence and challenged each other to competitive sports. The experimenters arranged a tournament during which cumulative scores were recorded for each group. The events included baseball, touch football, a tug-of-war, skits, and a treasure hunt. In the course of the week, good sportsmanship gradually gave way to accusations, friction, name calling, scuffling, and fighting. Eagles and Rattlers raided each other's cabins, causing some destruction. Interviews and observations at the end of the second stage revealed that hostile attitudes and negative stereotypes had developed toward the outgroup, while ingroup cohesiveness had increased.

In stage 3, the experimenters undertook to unite the warring groups. Following the common-sense notion that "contact breeds friendliness," Sherif and his associates mixed Eagles and Rattlers together for pleasant social contacts: attending movies, eating meals, shooting fireworks on the Fourth of July, and the like. But far from reducing conflict, these situations served as new occasions for the rival groups to call names and attack each other. In the dining-hall line they shoved and scuffled, and at meals they started "garbage wars," throwing paper and food.

So the study found that simple contact is not the panacea for reducing social conflict. Once you stop to think about it, this finding is not particularly surprising, as contact is a necessary ingredient for both the deescalation and the escalation of conflict. What is more important are the conditions under which contact occurs.

Cooperation

If competition can produce conflict, why can't cooperation reduce it? Sherif and his colleagues found that the method most effective in reducing the conflict between the Rattlers and the Eagles was suggested by a corollary to the researchers' hypothesis of the cause of the original conflict. Their hypothesis was that conflict develops from mutually incompatible goals. If this is true, then it must also be true that shared, compatible goals should decrease conflict. Accordingly, *superordinate goals* were introduced into the intergroup situation. They involved a number of urgent and "naturally" occurring situations that made it necessary for the boys of both groups to come together and jointly tackle the problem. For example, it was arranged for the camp truck to break down when it was taking both groups on a camping trip. All the boys were needed to push the truck up the hill and get it started again.

Gradually the series of activities requiring interdependent action reduced conflict and hostility between the groups. Interviews with the boys

confirmed a change in attitudes as well. From choosing their best friends almost exclusively in their own group, many shifted to listing some boys in the other group. Further, group stereotypes became more positive.

Helping behavior. Could the conflict have been reduced equally well by one group's assisting the other group in achieving something from which only the *latter* benefits? In the terms of Chapter 10, "Helping and Reward Exchange," can helping behavior reduce conflict as much as cooperation can? Stephen Worchel (1984) performed a study designed to answer this question. In the first stage of his study, Worchel assigned groups to either cooperate or compete on a series of tasks. In the second stage, one group offered either to help the other group solve a problem or to work cooperatively with the other group on the task. In the helping offer, the helping group would contribute its expertise without sharing in the eventual reward. The cooperative offer involved willingness to share the work on the task as well as the eventual reward.

Worchel's study found that cooperation during the second stage increased the attraction toward the initiating group whether the interaction during the previous stage was cooperative or competitive. However, helping during the second stage increased attraction only if the groups had been cooperating during the first stage. Helping during the second stage *reduced* the attraction toward the initiating group when the helping was preceded by competitive interaction — the condition of real interest.

Why doesn't helping behavior reduce conflict in the same fashion as cooperation? Worchel suggests that helping could establish a relationship of unequal status between the helper and the recipient, that is, a power hierarchy. The helper demonstrates competence and power, while the recipient demonstrates helplessness by accepting help. This is a situation that the recipient would just as soon avoid.

Whether helping gets interpreted this way depends partly on the conditions preceding the helping behavior. Previous competition and associated conflict may have already established who is the more powerful. If this is the case, one party's receiving help from the other would only exacerbate the inequality in status. As noted in Chapter 10, "Helping and Reward Exchange," a norm of reciprocity exists that makes us obligated to those who help us. It appears that being obligated to a former "enemy" is especially uncomfortable.

What if the recipient of help could return the favor, creating a reward exchange and thereby reducing the effects of unequal status? Research shows that in situations in which each party's behavior can benefit the other (i.e., equal status), one party's unilateral initiative of helping can reduce the established conflict in the relationship (Boyle and Lawler, 1991).

Equal-status cooperation. Cooperative tasks do not ensure equal status and power. Even among cooperating individuals there can be inequalities in competence and power. Social psychologists believe that the chances that coop-

eration will decrease conflict are greater when the previous disputants are of equal status in pursuing their common goals. One technique they like to point to involves forming racially mixed teams within classrooms. For example, Eliot Aronson and his associates (Aronson et al., 1978) developed a technique they called the "Jigsaw method," in which students from different racial and ethnic groups are assigned to a single group and given a group problem to solve. Each group member possesses a different piece of information necessary to solve the problem. Thus, each student is of equal importance (i.e., equal status) in *this aspect* of his or her contribution to solving the group's problem. Reviews of research on simple techniques such as the Jigsaw method indicate that this type of equal-status cooperation reduced racial and ethnic hostility and increased cross-racial and cross-ethnic friendships (Johnson, Johnson, and Maruyama, 1984; Miller and Davidson-Podgorny, 1987).

Of course, just having a different piece of information does not make the students "equal" — just more equal or less unequal. Students may still

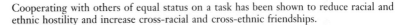

Cooperating with others of equal status on a task has been shown to reduce racial and ethnic hostility and increase cross-racial and cross-ethnic friendships.

perceive status inequalities on the basis of other characteristics, such as reading, writing, and speaking abilities (*specific status characteristics*) and race or sex (*diffuse status characteristics*). Although these characteristics may be irrelevant for the task at hand, they may form the basis for students' expectations of competence on a particular task. These sources of status inequality are more difficult to change than is the possession of a particular piece of information (Cohen, 1984).

Common threat.   One source of conflict-reducing cooperation of special interest to social psychologists concerns the response to an external threat that is menacing both parties to the conflict. The external threat may cause the disputants to set aside their differences and work together to overcome their common threat. The camp study by Sherif and his associates also suggests this possibility. An outside group came to the camp to compete against the Rattlers and Eagles. As the Rattlers and Eagles combined their efforts to compete against the outside group, the conflict between the two camp groups decreased. However, this was not the only important finding of this part of the study. After the outside group left the camp, the Rattlers and Eagles resumed their original conflict.

The lesson to be learned here is that if the causes of conflict reduction are withdrawn and the *causes of the original conflict remain unchanged*, the conflict is going to escalate again. In addition, in most situations it is not practical to introduce a common external threat as a method of reducing conflict between two parties, since this method often requires deliberate efforts to increase conflict with a third party.

Cooperation outcome.   The assumption behind most of the conclusions about the conflict-reducing features of cooperation we have been discussing is that cooperation is successful in achieving the shared goal. For example, in the Sherif studies, cooperation between members of the Rattlers and the Eagles achieved some successes: their arrival at their camping sight, the resumption of water to the camp, and the delivery of supplies to their outpost.

But Worchel and his colleagues asked whether cooperation would reduce conflict if the cooperation results instead in failure (Worchel, Andreoli, and Folger, 1977). To answer this question, the researchers conducted an experiment wherein, during the first stage, the subjects in each experimental session were assigned to one of two groups. The groups were given several tasks to perform in order to win money. Each pair of groups performed under one of three conditions: (1) competition—only the winning group received money, (2) cooperation—the performance of both groups determined if they both won or lost, and (3) independence—each group's winning or losing depended on its performance alone. In the second stage of the study, the groups were brought together to work cooperatively on a series of tasks. Half of the combined groups were told that their efforts had been successful on each trial; the other half were told that their combined efforts had failed.

As other studies had found, the first-stage competition produced least attraction for the "outgroup" of the three conditions. And the second-stage cooperation, *regardless of outcome*, increased intergroup attraction when the groups' first-stage relationship was cooperation or independence. But if the first-stage relationship was competition (the case of real interest), the outcome of the groups' subsequent cooperation determined their intergroup attraction. Success brought an increase in intergroup attraction; failure brought a decrease. According to the researchers' interpretation of the results, when a cooperative endeavor between groups ends in failure, the groups will look for someone or something to blame the failure on. Given their history of hostility and negative social attitudes, groups who have previously been in competition and conflict will have a ready-made scapegoat in their competitors.

Social Attitudes

As competition produces conflict, the disputants develop negative attitudes and attributions about each other. Each perceives the other as having at least some negative characteristics that constitute the basis for a negative evaluation of the adversary — characteristics such as unreasonable, self-centered, uncaring, cruel, or immoral. Each blames the other for their escalating conflict. Such negative attitudes and attributions provide additional bases for even more conflict.

How can the process through which such negative social attitudes and attributions escalate conflict be minimized or even reversed? Several social psychologists propose that one answer lies in reducing the salience of social categories (Tajfel, 1981; Miller and Brewer, 1986; Wilder, 1986). In Chapter 4, "Relationships and Groups," we discussed the kinds of activities that bond people to others in relationships and groups, increasing their feelings of "we-ness." We noted that feelings of we-ness also produce feelings of "they-ness" toward others who are not members of the group. To avoid the consequences of negative social categories, bonding activities would have to be reversed, thereby decategorizing members of relationships and groups.

Differentiation. Social psychologists use the term **differentiation** when referring to the perception of *intracategory differences* (Miller and Brewer, 1986). Differentiation occurs when we learn information that is unique to one or more individual members of a social category, allowing us to draw distinctions among the members of that category. Differentiation decreases one's negative attitude toward a member of a negatively evaluated social category by taking that person "out of the category."

But responses to the individual may become more positive *without* being generalized to the remaining members of the social category. The individual is viewed as an "exception to the rule" because of some unusual ability, greater effort, favorable treatment by others (e.g., affirmative action), or other circumstances:

For example, when a white (who is unfamiliar with blacks) first meets a black person, "blackness" (an attribute associated with a superordinate category)

may be the most salient feature, and the one that becomes most strongly associated with relevant behavioral episodes. With increasing familiarity, the black person becomes "individuated" and is encoded under more specific categories (Artist, Scientist, Extrovert, etc.), with "blackness" losing its salience. The interesting implication, however, is that as the person loses his or her "blackness" s/he is less likely to be stored under the category Black People, and his/her counter-stereotypic attributes may therefore become isolated from the stereotypic category. — [One of us (MR) had an experience with a southern colleague at a conference, who expressed less than flattering sentiments toward Blacks; when MR asked him about his obviously intelligent and scholarly co-author, who was black, he responded, "I never think of him as black!"] (Rothbart and John, 1985: 93)

So factors such as equal-status cooperation may decrease the conflict between the *participating* members of different social categories, but the likelihood that this conflict reduction will generalize to nonparticipating members is quite small.

Goodness of fit. Are there any conditions that would make it more likely that a decrease in negative attitude toward particular representatives of a social category will generalize to the whole social category? One of the ideas that social psychologists have been exploring is limited differentiation, or "*overall goodness of fit.*" In Chapter 6, "Social Attitudes and Attributions," we noted that social categories are mostly schemas composed of several associated characteristics. For example, "Duke University students are wealthy, loud, and egocentric; drink too much; are politically conservative; wear yuppie clothes; major in business or prelaw; and hate the University of North Carolina." This is a social schema shared by many University of North Carolina (UNC) students and a source of conflict between students from the two schools, especially during athletic events.

Let's stipulate that a UNC student works on a Special Olympics project with a Duke student who fails to conform to the egocentric characteristic of the stereotype and does not possess most of the other characteristics. As discussed earlier, the UNC student not only may cognitively differentiate that student from other Duke students but also may have a positive attitude schema toward that particular student. This differentiation would lead to continued positive interaction between the Duke and the UNC student. But it would have little effect on the UNC student's negative attitude toward Duke students in general. The reason may be that the particular Duke student is so totally different from the UNC student's stereotype of Duke students.

Let's look at a second scenario. What would happen if the Duke student were more typical of the stereotype? In the case of high typicality, or "goodness of fit," let's say that the Duke student is typical of the stereotype except for the absence of the egocentric characteristic. Faced with this situation, the UNC student possesses little information on which to differentiate this Duke student from Duke students in general. It is unlikely that the UNC student will develop a less negative attitude toward this particular Duke student than he holds toward Duke students in general. But if the UNC student does, the chance of that attitude generalizing to other Duke students is greater. Here, the result is just the opposite of our first scenario.

The lesson is that differentiation will result in reducing negative attitudes between the immediate disputants, but too much differentiation will have little effect in reducing the negative attitudes toward other members of the stereotyped category. On the other hand, too little differentiation will not allow the disputants to escape the baggage of each other's negative stereotypes. Somewhere in between there may be an optimum point where conditions favor the reduction in negative attitudes between both the immediate disputants *and* the social categories they represent. If such a point does exist, social psychologists have yet to find it.

Entrapment

When people defend their positions against attack, their commitment to their positions is strengthened (Staw and Ross, 1987). In turn, their increased commitment may lead to a situation in which the parties expend more of their time, energy, money, and other resources in the conflict than seems appropriate or justified by external standards. This form of conflict escalation is called **entrapment** (Brockner and Rubin, 1985; Pruitt and Rubin, 1986).

Allan Teger's (1980) studies of "dollar auctions" illustrate the entrapment process. Several research participants are told by the researcher that he will auction off a dollar bill to the highest bidder. The participants are to offer bids, as you would in a regular auction, and the highest bidder will receive the dollar for her or his bid. But what's different about this auction is that the second-highest bidder is also required to pay the auctioneer the amount he or she bid—but gains no dollar in return. Participants typically begin the auction with very low bids, but then the bids begin to climb. When the bids approach one dollar, the number of bidders typically decreases to just two. But Teger has found that bidding often goes beyond one dollar, sometimes as high as twenty dollars. Why? Because the higher a person's bid, the more the person stands to lose if he or she is not the highest bidder. So the person keeps raising his or her bid in order to minimize how much money is lost. Apparently, participants feel that there is some degree of winning in being the bidder to lose less money:

> Although a player in the Dollar Auction game is continually restrained from further participation because of the amount of money that he or she has already committed, this restraint is offset by the desire to win that rotten dollar bill, the hope or belief that such victory lies just a bid or two away, and the conviction that the money already spent needs to be justified by even more expenditure. (Pruitt and Rubin, 1986: 123)

Later we will discuss how a third party can help reduce overcommitment and its entrapment effects.

Issue Proliferation

When parties are actively engaged in an ongoing dispute, they often compound the conflict by introducing new issues. One of these new disputed issues can be the conflict itself. For example, one party may complain about the intimidation, threats, or force the other party used in an effort to get him or her to yield. Of course, other types of responses to the original dispute can also become issues that escalate the conflict. Inaction or withdrawal may become a source of complaint. For example, a husband may respond to a dispute with his wife by stating, "There's nothing wrong — I'm not upset. I think you are exaggerating things." His wife may take issue with his response: "You don't care enough about me, my feelings, or our relationship to try and resolve the problem."

Other issues that may have previously been ignored or suspended can surface in the context of an ongoing conflict. Consider, for example, a couple fighting over the woman's having had dinner with a male friend. She may respond with (1) "I didn't like it when you had lunch with your secretary," (2) "You *always* find fault with everything I do," or (3) "I wouldn't have had dinner with him if you hadn't scheduled a meeting at our usual dinnertime." Any one of these responses introduces to the dispute an additional issue that can escalate the conflict. Of course, the man in this example can escalate the conflict even more by complaining that she is compounding their problem by bringing up irrelevant issues.

Issue proliferation does create at least one opportunity for deescalating conflict. Earlier, we explained that parties can take two issues of dispute and use one party's yielding on one issue as compensation for the other party's yielding on the second issue. In the example we used, the wife yielded to her husband's wish to vacation in the mountains, while he yielded to her wish to purchase a new car. The couple above may be able to deescalate their conflict by agreeing that neither partner will dine alone with persons of the opposite gender.

Third-Party Allies or Mediators

Conflicts are not always restricted to two parties. At times three or more parties have an interest in a competitive outcome. By forming an alliance with one or more others, people can combine their resources in order to advance their own individual interests — to the disadvantage of those excluded from the alliance. Alternatively, third parties can mediate the conflict. Thus, third parties can contribute to either the escalation or the deescalation of conflict (Simmel, 1902).

Coalitions and escalation. A **coalition** consists of two or more parties who coordinate their efforts in order to achieve their ends against the opposition of one or more competing parties. In Chapter 4, "Social Relationships and Groups," we noted that, in triads, a third person can increase conflict by acting as an opportunist — strategically taking the side of the person with the best offer — or by trying to "divide and conquer" — instigating conflict between the other two parties in order to prevent their forming a coalition against him or her. Similarly, by combining their efforts, a number of parties can determine the allocation of rewards within a group or force their will upon other group members. Coalition formation occurs at all levels of social interaction — among family members, politicians, special-interest groups, ethnic groups, cartel participants, nations, and blocks of nations (Komorita and Tumonis, 1980). The resources that parties may pool include status, expertise, special abilities, votes, money, natural resources, weapons, and troops.

Social psychologists commonly study coalition behavior by confronting two or more individuals with a game situation in which the players must try to maximize their share of the rewards. A number of studies have employed the popular board game Parcheesi. In such a game, no single player enjoys dictatorial or veto power and no single alternative will maximize the payoff to all participants. Researchers focus on the processes by which potential coalition partners offer various divisions of the winnings to form a successful coalition. They hope to identify the conditions under which coalitions are likely to form and, consequently, how they are likely to affect the outcomes of conflict.

In some coalition studies, the players are assigned unequal resource units at the beginning of the game. For instance, 16 resource units may be distributed among four players as follows: A has 7 units, B has 5 units, C has 3 units, and D has 1 unit. The quota needed to win the game is 9 units. The general form for symbolizing this type of arrangement is $Q:A$-B-C-D. Q refers to the quota necessary to win; A, B, C, and D designate the resources held by the four players, with individual A being the strongest, B the second strongest, and so on. Substituting resource units for the symbols, we arrive at 9:7-5-3-1. Thus individuals A and C (7 units and 3 units, respectively) can form a coalition to win the game; so can individuals B, C, and D (5 units, 3 units, and 1 unit, respectively).

Studies of coalition formation have found that coalitions seem to contain only the minimum resources necessary to win — *the cheapest winning solution* (Gamson, 1961, 1964). The idea is to form a coalition with just enough resources to be successful, not a great deal more. Forming a coalition with people who bring more resources than needed for success is disadvantageous because these others will have to be paid off in proportion to their contributions. Thus, in the above example, a coalition between B, C, and D is the most likely, since these three players bring just enough resources to win the game.

In addition, coalition formation apparently follows the rule that *smaller is better* (Nicholson, Cole, and Rocklin, 1986). Although people whose resources are so minimal that they are no help in achieving success are rarely chosen for coalition membership, the person who has just enough to tip the coalition's balance of resources to the winning quota is typically the most valued partner. We seem to count on the fact that such weak individuals will realize that success can be attained only through coalition with those who are more powerful, and we hope that they will be satisfied with only a small fraction of the total payoff because they realize that they are contributing only a small part of the total resources. In this sense, *weakness is strength* in coalition formation. Conversely, *strength is weakness*. Stronger individuals are not valued coalition members because their greater resources entitle them to a bigger share of the payoff, and we fear that they may attempt to

exploit the weaker members (Komorita and Ellis, 1988).

As with many other aspects of behavior, women and men differ in their coalition behavior. Women don't always form the cheapest winning solution, and they are likely to divide up payoffs based on equality rather than equity, are less likely to exclude a powerful person from the coalition, and refrain more often from taking full advantage of the weakness of others. Some researchers have proposed that women strive to maintain smooth intergroup relations, while men strive to maximize payoffs. Thus, men's and women's reactions to conflict situations may differ.

Mediators and deescalation. As an alternative to contributing to the escalation of conflict by participating as a coalition member, a third party can be involved in the deescalation of conflict by participating as a mediator. It is often hard for a mediator to keep from acting (or being treated) like a coalition member. The impartiality of a mediator is difficult to maintain. But given this risk, third parties can facilitate the reduction of conflict by performing several important functions.

A third party may be in a position to determine whether something constructive can emerge from encouraging communication between the disputants. Although most of us like to believe that communication will reduce most disputes, under some conditions the opposite is true. If conflict is intense, encouraging people to communicate with each other may result (after only a brief respite) in an escalation of their conflict — heaping insult and abuse on top of insult and abuse. A mediator who is aware of the present state of the conflict might keep the disputants separate and, instead, convey messages (carefully edited) back and forth while educating the disputants about how effective communication should occur. When the intensity of the conflict has been reduced and the communication skills of the disputants have been increased, the parties can be brought together to begin the task of seeking solutions to their differences. The mere presence of the mediator in the negotiations may inhibit the expression of conflict.

Negotiations often take place in a setting that itself can become a barrier to the negotiations. Location, the size and shape of the table, seating arrangements, the way each party is addressed, time constraints, other attendees, and the agenda all represent potential issues of dispute that may prevent the parties from even beginning their negotiations over "the real issues." Of course, the mediator is the first aspect of the setting that has to be negotiated. Typically, one or both of the disputants want to mend their own fences without the intervention of a third party. The threat of a third party may either contribute to the proliferation of the conflict or hasten a resolution in order to avert such intervention. However, if a mediator is acquired, she or he can assume responsibility for advising or deciding the remaining aspects of the negotiation setting.

A third party can guide the disputants through the analysis of the issues that separate them. Attempts can be made to break one large issue into smaller subissues. If successful, this would increase the opportunities to use the conflict reduction alternatives we discussed earlier—bridging, cost cutting, and logrolling. A mediator may be able to counter many of the other factors that escalate conflict by promoting cooperation and emphasizing common interests, depolarizing the issues, suggesting ways to circumvent the entrapment of previous commitments, and keeping issues from proliferating.

Concessions, no matter how trivial, are frequently interpreted by each disputant as a sign of weakness. And the perception of weakness is something neither side wants to convey; it is better to look tough and unyielding. Herein lies a problem. How can a disputant make necessary concessions without appearing to yield and giving the opponent the impression that he or she will make further concessions? A third party can help overcome this problem by allowing the disputants to make concessions without taking responsibility for them. Thus, a disputant can save face by saying that his or her concession was due to the request of the third party and that it was given in the spirit of cooperation and fair-mindedness rather than in response to the demands of the opponent.

In sum, we have been discussing some the factors affecting whether initial conflict will escalate or deescalate. Several factors may lead to the reduction of conflict, while others escalate it. Once conflict has started, deescalation may be difficult. We like to think that all differences can be resolved through negotiation, but negotiation and compromise are not always possible.

Summary

1. Interference and attack increase the likelihood of aggression, although the amount of aggression is influenced by (1) the perceived reason for the interference or attack and (2) the presence of situational cues that suggest an aggressive response. A high-status group member who interferes with the group's goal may be protected from aggression as long as the interference does not eliminate the group's chances to achieve its goal. But if the interference does eliminate the group's chances, the person's high status may *increase* the aggression directed at him or her.

2. The combination of institutional norms advocating aggression and deindividuation can increase aggression. Cultural norms specify what kinds of interference or attack deserve an aggressive response, as well as what kinds of people are appropriate targets of what kinds of aggression by what kinds of people.

3. Several theories suggest that emotional anger may instigate aggressive behavior. Frustration-aggression theory proposes that anger instigated by one party can be discharged onto another party (displacement), purging the aggressor of his or her aggressive energy (catharsis). Excitation transfer theory proposes that emotional arousal created in one situation can be transferred to emotions produced in a second situation. Symbolic interaction theory

proposes that reflexive behavior is involved in our perceptions of our own emotions and in our "emotional reactions" to these perceptions. Social learning theory proposes that aggression, like any behavior, is a result of past learning.

4. Conflict—reciprocal aggression—is one of several responses to competition. One of the major factors influencing the choice of conflict as a means of resolving the dispute is its relative cost. Factors reducing the likelihood of conflict escalation include (1) equal-status exchange, (2) cooperation, particularly if the cooperation is successful in achieving the shared goal, and (3) differentiation among members of negative social categories.

5. When people defend their positions against attack, their commitment to their positions is strengthened. Individuals in such situations often compound conflict through issue proliferation, the introduction of new issues that become additional sources of conflict.

6. Conflict is not always restricted to two parties. Additional parties may (1) participate in the formation of coalitions to escalate conflict or (2) participate as mediators in efforts to deescalate conflict.

CHAPTER 13

SOCIAL POWER: BEHAVIOR AND ATTITUDE CHANGE

Kim is unhappy with the division of household chores between herself and her husband, Gene. Although they both work full-time, Kim spends more than twice as many hours per week doing household work — cooking and cleaning — than Gene does. Kim has tried to talk to Gene about this a couple of times, but he has become defensive and says she's "nagging." How can Kim get Gene to share the housework more equally?

Nick has had some personal problems this semester and has missed quite a few classes. Now that midterms are approaching, he realizes that he needs to borrow class notes from someone. He knows a fellow student, Bob, in his chemistry class — not well, but they've talked a little during intramural soccer games. How can Nick get Bob to lend him the class notes he needs?

Susan has recently been promoted to a supervisory position at the firm where she works. As the supervisor of sixteen artists, Susan's responsibility is to see that their work matches clients' specifications and that it is done on time. Susan's own performance ratings — and thus her future raises and promotions — depend on clients' satisfaction. How can Susan get the artists in her unit to do their best work?

In everyday life, we often attempt to change another person's (or group of persons') attitudes or behavior. In addition, others attempt to get us to comply with *their* wishes. When a person successfully overcomes another's resistance to changing his or her attitudes or behavior, we say that person has *power*. We will use "power" as a very general term encompassing such concepts as influence, authority, persuasion, and leadership.

The resolutions to the conflicts discussed in Chapter 12, "Aggression and Conflict," are determined, at least partly, by power. The use of power is not limited to resolving disputes between two superpower nations, labor and management, a husband and wife, or even a professor and student. Much of our everyday lives involve seeking things we value — goods, services, information, security, love, and so on. Most significantly, we can acquire these valued things only through the actions of others. Thus, to achieve our goals, it is essential that we be able to influence other people's conduct. In other words, we must have social power.

Power can be good or bad. "Good power" is the magic engine that propels us to the promised land; in the hands of the blessed, it can end tyranny and usher in an age of justice and freedom. "Bad power" is the soulless machine that subjects us to misery and suffering; in the hands of the unworthy, it breeds oppression and exploitation. Indeed, the recurrent rallying cry crossing the ages of time has been "Power to the people." It has found expression in the question: "Shall pow-

Resolutions to conflicts are determined, at least partly, by power.

er be the servant of the people (translated: 'me and my group') or the slave of selfish interests (translated: 'them and their group')?" In truth, of course, power usually serves someone's interest and advances some goal. Even in a democracy, the majority's interest is often advanced at the expense of the minorities'. Ignoring the abuse of power will not make it go away. Social psychology tries to do its part to increase our awareness and understanding of power so that we can protect ourselves against the abuses.

The Nature of Social Power

Social power is a process of social interaction in which one party produces intended changes in another party's attitudes or behavior, even in the face of the other's resistance. Although we commonly equate power with big organizations — big government, big business, big unions, and so on — in reality it pervades all human interaction,

finding expression in one-to-one, family, and couple relationships. Thus, our definition uses the word "party" to refer to one person or group, small or large. The party who causes the change is called the *source* (of power); the party who is changed is referred to as the *target* (of power). Although people often talk about "John's power" or "IBM's power," we want to emphasize that *both* parties — source and target — play a role in social power. The target may eventually yield to *or* continue to resist the source's attempts to change the target's behavior. Both parties may attempt to change each other's behavior.

When most people think of power, they probably think of a person "having" power over another. This suggests two things about the way they view power. First, they see power as "potential" power rather than as "actual" or "exercised" power. Social psychologists, including the authors of this text, disagree about whether social power should be defined in terms of potential or actual power. To spare you the controversy, we will discuss the entire process of social power, including both potential and actual power, later in the chapter.

Most of our discussion of social power in this chapter will focus on an individual as the source of power. The target of the power will be another person or a group of people. Consider this hypothetical situation: The members of a campus sorority are meeting to discuss how they can be more successful in next year's rush. The result of this year's rush was unsatisfactory, as the members had been able to pledge only a small proportion of the women given invitations. Although several of the members make one or two suggestions, most of the suggestions — usually opposing ideas — come from two members. Liz proposes that their sorority should have a "dry rush" because it would give the rushees the idea that the sorority is "out front" on the alcohol-abuse issue. Meg disagrees because she thinks only a minority of college students are really interested in being out front on this issue. Meg proposes that the sorority should combine its rush with a fraternity's rush so that rushees will be attracted by the promise of social opportunities. Liz disagrees, arguing that the fraternity would be too dominant in the operation of the joint rush. Liz suggests that each first- and second-year member "adopt" a rushee in order to develop ties of friendship with the sorority. Meg opposes this suggestion because she thinks it is discriminatory. If some members are going to be required to devote a lot of their valuable time to this enterprise, then *all* members should be required to do so. In the end, the members adopt all of Liz's suggestions.

Liz has social power over the members of her sorority. Social psychologists refer to power over the members of one's group as **leadership**. Like power between two individuals, leadership is a negotiated exchange. The source (leader) and the targets have some power over each other — though it may be unbalanced — and this power arrangement is (re)negotiated over time. Liz's power may not extend to other domains (maintenance of the sorority house, dues, or quiet hours).

In fact, social psychologists think it is particularly difficult for a person to have leadership in domains involving group tasks (*task leadership*) at the same time that she or he has leadership in domains involving personal relations among group members (*socioemotional leadership*). Solving group tasks may involve disagreements that create tension or even hostility among the group members.

Power Resources

The process of social power begins with control over valued resources. What resources might contribute to one party's ability to change another party's conduct? Social psychologists suggest that the specific resources involved can be organized into "classes." We will use a classification first advanced by John R. P. French and Bertram Raven (1959) and subsequently modified by Raven (1990) and others (Podsakoff and Schriesheim, 1985; Yukl and Falbe, 1991). According to these social psychologists, there are six classes of resources that may be available to the parties in an interaction: (1) reward, (2) coercive, (3) expert (influence), (4) informational (persuasion), (5) personal, and (6) normative (authority).

REWARD AND COERCIVE RESOURCES

To say that a person has **reward resources** is simply to say that the person has the ability to provide another party with rewards. The reward may be impersonal (e.g., financial benefits, promotions, or help with a task) or personal (e.g., love, esteem, or acceptance). A mother may have enough money to give her child $5 for each A on his report card. A wife may have a hug to give her husband for washing the dishes. A politician may have a patronage job to give a constituent for helping the politician get elected.

There are two ways for one party to demonstrate her or his access to and willingness to use a reward resource to another party. The first is the actual use of the reward — such as giving the target person money, help, or love — *after* the person "complies." For example, a woman may give her lover a big kiss or a backrub after he cooks her a special meal. As we noted in Chapter 2, "Early Socialization," using a reward in this manner creates a *social contingency*. Of course, the two parties must agree on the value of the reward. A nice backrub from one's lover might be a highly valued reward; a backrub from one's boss might not be. We discussed shared reward values in more detail in Chapter 10, "Helping and Reward Exchange."

The second way for a party to indicate that she or he has rewards is to promise a reward *before* the target complies. Thus, a husband may promise to take his wife to a restaurant tomorrow if she'll make his favorite dessert tonight. This is using a reward as an *incentive*. As we discussed in Chapter 5, "Communication," for a promise — whether conveyed through words or a gesture (such as a seductive smile) — to be effective, it must be understood by *both* persons as a symbol of the actual reward to follow. Without this shared understanding, the symbolic promise of reward will not be understood as "reward to follow" and the value of the reward resource will be reduced.

To have **coercive resources** is to have the ability to harm or punish another. Thus, the use of coercive resources combines the intent to harm a target (aggression) with the intent to change the target's behavior (power). As with rewards, the punishment may be impersonal (spankings, fines, or dismissals) or personal (hate or rejection). Most frequently, coercion is used to *stop* somebody from doing something. A sister punches her brother for making uncomplimentary comments about her looks. A husband gives his wife the silent treatment for a comment she made at a party. A driver receives a ticket and fine for speeding.

Just as promises can symbolize rewards, *threats of punishment* can symbolize actual punishments (e.g., a disgusted look or shaken fist). Such actions are meant to intimidate. As symbols, their contribution to power depends on both persons' understanding that the threat means that the source has

Threats of punishment can symbolize actual punishments, showing that a source has access to punishers and is willing to use them.

access to punishers and is willing to use them. If the target has (1) never before confronted the threat and thus doesn't know its meaning or (2) learned from past experience that the threatened punishment is seldom delivered, the threat will not be an effective source of power.

Guilt

In some forms of coercion the source creates conditions that produce psychological distress for the target. Fear of punishment is one kind of psychological distress; guilt — "psychological blackmail" — is another. The target can escape psychological distress by complying with the request of the source. Let's examine two methods for making a person feel guilty: receiving a reward and committing a wrong.

Receiving a reward.   One way to make a target feel guilty is to reward the target before he or she responds. Does this sound risky? It is, but it sometimes works. The source strategically rewards the target in order to increase the target's liking of the source and feelings of obligation to the source for giving the target something he or she values. This is called *ingratiation.* Consequently, the target will feel indebted to the source and will feel guilty if he or she does not repay the source with something the source values. The debt may be paid by fulfilling the source's next request. For example, it is a familiar practice in the business world to wine and dine prospective clients and even give them gifts. The assumption is that the recipient will feel obligated to reciprocate the favor by complying with the other person's wishes. You might correctly recognize this as an example of the norm of reciprocity in social exchange, which we discussed in Chapter 10, "Helping and Reward Exchange." Here, complying with a request (one kind of reward) is exchanged for the reward the source pro-

vided before the target responded. Of course, we sometimes decide that it is better to reject an offered reward than to accept "the strings attached" to it. (Before reading further, look at the Student Observation: "Guilt Through Reward.")

Committing a wrong.   Common sense tells us that when we commit a wrong, we feel guilty. We seek to atone — to balance the scales, so to speak — by complying with another person's wishes, especially if doing so entails performing a good act. Two social psychologists, J. Merrill Carlsmith and Alan E. Gross (1969), decided to test whether in fact this common-sense notion is true. The researchers told each subject that they were conducting a "learning" experiment. Subjects were instructed to throw a switch whenever the "learner" (the experimenters' accomplice) made a mistake. Carlsmith and Gross told half of the subjects that when they closed the switch the learner received a painful shock. The other half were told nothing; they merely heard a buzzer sound when they threw the switch. After the experiment was completed, the learner (the confederate) asked the subject to participate in a telephone campaign to get signatures on a petition to save the redwood trees in northern Cali-

---

STUDENT OBSERVATION

Guilt Through Reward

*A*t the hospital where I am employed, it is fairly difficult to get a weekend off when you are scheduled to work. It is interesting to observe how people approach their fellow employees about this and how they present their requests. Some people outright plead with the other person to trade a weekend with them. There is no question about their motives. However, others are more subtle. For instance, "Jim" is always wanting weekends off. He is an attractive guy and uses this to his advantage; he usually tries to get one of the women in the office to work for him. Jim targets a woman and starts complimenting her on her work, appearance, and so on. Then he asks for her advice on both work and personal situations. This process establishes a relationship between Jim and the woman, making her feel that Jim values her opinion as a worker and a friend. Once the woman defines herself as Jim's friend, he requests that she work his weekend shift. Willing to help a friend, she accepts. Jim is apparently quite successful at getting others to see themselves as his "special friends," so he gets many weekends off.

fornia. Of those who had only heard the buzzer, 25 percent complied. In contrast, 75 percent, or three times as many, of those who thought they had administered shocks complied—presumably to lessen their feelings of guilt.

Social psychologists have found a similar effect operating in many different kinds of transgressions: ruining an experiment, breaking an experimenter's machine, causing someone to forfeit green stamps, scattering a graduate student's index cards, breaking a camera, littering, and lying (see Grasmick, Bursik, and Kinsey, 1991). Under such experimental conditions, people who felt guilty agreed to sign a petition, donate blood, and volunteer to serve in future experiments for no pay.

But someone other than the injured party may be the beneficiary of a person's guilt feelings. Research has demonstrated that even when the request is made by someone who lacks knowledge of the target's transgression, the guilty target is more likely to comply (Freedman, Wallington, and Bless, 1967). Indeed, evidence suggests that a person who does harm may be even more inclined to help someone *other than* the victim. (For an example, see the Student Observation: "Guilt and Compliance.") Continued contact with the victim apparently results in uncomfortable feelings of obligation or serves as an unpleasant reminder of the harm the target inflicted (Carlsmith and Gross, 1969). Further, as we discussed in Chapter 10, guilt does not merely make people more compliant with requests for help; guilty people may *seek out* ways to lessen their guilt by voluntarily engaging in a good deed.

Emotional Contrast

Reward and coercive resources are sometimes used simultaneously. When used together, each of the two kinds of resources provides an "emotional contrast" for the other, making both appear more extreme—the reward looks better, the coercion looks worse. As a consequence, the likelihood of the target's compliance is greater than it would be if the source used only one kind of resource.

There is no better illustration of this than the "good cop, bad cop" strategy of influence. Organizational psychologists Anat Rafaeli and Robert Sutton (1991) examined the use of this strategy by two different types of sources: criminal investigators in three agencies in Israel and bill collectors from a large U.S. collection facility that specialized in obtaining overdue credit card payments. "Good cop" referred to the source's (interrogator's or bill collector's) efforts to convey positive and supportive feelings, such as warmth, friendliness, approval, respect, empathy, and sympathy, to a target (suspect or debtor). "Bad cop" referred to the source's efforts to convey negative and unsupportive emotions, such as coldness, disapproval, lack of respect, and hostility.

The researchers found that sources used these contrasting routines in several different ways. In some situations, one person played the good cop,

STUDENT OBSERVATION

Guilt and Compliance

This semester I was solicited on the phone by a man selling light bulbs for the Handicapped People of America. Being a college student whose financial assets are budgeted, I politely turned him down. I felt bad about not buying the light bulbs from such a good cause. Well, the next day, those $10-T-shirt-selling people came by my room selling T-shirts for the Ronald McDonald House. Because I felt guilty about not buying the light bulbs, I gave in very quickly to the appeal to buy a T-shirt—and I felt much better about myself.

another the bad cop. This was done either sequentially or simultaneously. An interview with
an interrogator illustrates the simultaneous use of
the routine:

> Whenever we did the good guy, bad guy thing, we'd
> plan and coordinate. The good guy would say,
> "C'mon leave him alone, let him calm down. He
> didn't mean it. Just did something stupid. He looks
> like a good guy to me. I think we should help him."
> Then the bad guy would say, "What's wrong with
> him. He's a piece of shit. I don't think we should
> help him. We'll get it out of him in time." (Rafaeli
> and Sutton, 1991: 759)

In other variations, one person played the good
cop in contrast to a *hypothetical* bad cop based on
the source's suggestions or the target's own expectations of what the typical interrogator or bill
collector was like. This is illustrated by a quote
from a bill collector:

> If you don't pay me today, you are going to have to
> start dealing with the collection agency. I'd better
> warn you – those folks are bloodthirsty. (Rafaeli and
> Sutton, 1991: 760)

In the final routine, the investigator or bill
collector played *both* the good cop and the bad,
alternating between a pleasant, friendly demeanor
and a harsh, demanding one. Some sources reported that they were initially unsuccessful in
their directives when they were consistently pleasant; they found they were more effective if they
shocked the target by turning nasty after being
nice and only then returned to being nice again.

Rafaeli and Sutton propose three explanations
for the effect of the "good cop, bad cop" strategy
on compliance: (1) Targets may comply to escape
the fear they feel during interactions with the bad
cop. Complying with the good cop's wishes is the
best alternative. (2) Targets may feel pressure to
reciprocate the kindness of the good cop by complying with his wishes. (We discussed this explanation in more detail earlier.) (3) Targets may
come to trust the good cop to *minimize* the costs

of their compliance. Friendliness creates the impression that "he'll give me a break."

EXPERT RESOURCES

Rather than administering rewards or punishments to the target directly, a source may *show
the target what to do* in order to receive rewards
or to avoid or escape punishments, including rewards and punishments from a third party. In
other words, the source has specialized knowledge, competence, skill, or experience – **expert
resources** – that can help the target get rewards
or avoid or escape punishments, but the source
does not administer the rewards or punishments.
The resource offered is a service rather than an
outcome.

The target accepts the expert's directive not
necessarily because it makes a lot of sense, but
because the target believes in the source's expertise. We frequently take medication prescribed by
a doctor, for example, without knowing much
about what it is or how it works; we simply trust
that the doctor knows what's best for us. In fact,
research suggests that people do not even pay
much attention to the reasons supporting a directive when the directive comes from a very competent source (Sternthal, Phillips, and Dholakia,
1978; Romer, 1979; McGuire, 1985).

The expert's power may be increased if his or
her "good advice" helps the target achieve desirable outcomes. The target will then feel indebted
to the source and be inclined to "pay back" the
expert by complying with future directives. So
expert power may be based on a combination of
two factors – expected rewards for the target and
a sense of obligation to the source. Expert power
depends on two characteristics of the source: expertise and trustworthiness.

Expertise

Expertise is established through experience and
through symbols of expertise. If a target complied
with the advice of a particular expert in the past
and the outcome was a positive one, the target's

past rewards will make compliance with the expert's future directives more likely. Family physicians usually have credibility based on their patients' personal experiences with their medical directives. In laboratory studies, social psychologists have shown that group leadership can develop the same way. If compliance with a particular member's directive produced external rewards for the group (e.g., solved the problem facing the group), then the advice giver's expert power will increase (Griffith and Gray, 1985).

If an expert is known to have followed her or his own directives, resulting in outcomes similar to those sought by the target, the expert will appear more credible. For example, we are more influenced by those who are paid more than we are on a common task than we are by those who earn less than we do (Stewart and Moore, 1992). The expert's own success will have a greater impact on the expert's credibility if the target believes the expert to be similar to himself or herself. The same reasoning applies to the target's observations of the consequences of *other people's* compliance with the expert's directives. If other people receive the desired consequences by following the expert's advice, the expert's credibility will be enhanced — and more so if these people are similar to the target.

But what if we have little or no experience with the particular person giving the directive and haven't had the opportunity to observe his or her behavior? For example, how would a woman react if she (or her physician) moves and she is faced with an unfamiliar physician? Or what if we have experience with the person but not with the consequences of her or his directives within a particular domain? For example, how would a man react if his physician gave him advice about dealing with a delinquent child or offered a tip on the stock market? If we have little or no experience with following a particular person's directives, we have to rely on our *impressions* of the person's expertise. If we feel that the person "does not know what he is talking about," then the person will probably not influence our behavior.

Sources often rely on symbols of expertise to influence others' impressions of their expertise. As with all symbols, to be effective and contribute to power, symbols of expertise must be understood by both parties. So what kinds of symbols typically convey the message that a person is "an expert"? Certain personal characteristics are often thought to be associated with expertise. Being older, being highly educated, having higher social status, or seeming "intelligent" are symbols of expertise (in some domains) to many (but not all) people. Titles, such as "Professor" or "Doctor," and uniforms, such as a physician's white coat or an airline pilot's jacket, are frequently used symbols of expertise. Sometimes all a person has to go on is the expert's claim, "Oh, I know all about that!" or "Mother Mary Francis — Palm Reader Supreme!"

An expert who gives personal advice will often be judged according to the amount of time or attention she or he gives the target (Gergen, 1971). For example, although a man may believe that an expert "knows her business," he may feel that she doesn't know (or care) enough about his individual case to be helpful. Some experts are aware of this and carefully cultivate a style in which they ask questions and attend to a target's individual characteristics. This leads the target to raise his or her assessment of the source's expertise, and it increases the probability that the target will comply with the source's directives. Another symbol of expertise is the ability to make the target wait (see the box "The Power to Make Us Wait").

Of course, we may be faced with more than one symbol of expertise, and one may conflict with another. A directive may come from a source who possesses two characteristics symbolizing expertise — one symbol that suggests expertise regarding the particular task facing the target and another that suggests (more indirectly) a general expertise. Let's say a very young sociology professor tells you that government welfare programs for the poor contribute positively to the country's productivity. Would you adopt his opinion (or

THE POWER TO MAKE US WAIT

Do you remember the last time you had to wait to obtain services or advice, perhaps from your college adviser, your physician, or a banker or at a restaurant, travel agency, or social services office? Did you feel that you had very little control over the situation or that you were deliberately kept waiting? Social psychologist Barry Schwartz (1974) examined waiting experiences and drew several interesting conclusions.

The ability to make others wait reflects power. People who have the resources to affect others' compliance also have the resources to make others wait. In general, the more powerful a person is, the more that person can regulate others' access to him or her: "Get an appointment"; "Take a number"; "I'll be through in a minute." The powerful can even ask the less powerful to cancel a previous commitment so as not to "keep the boss waiting."

Having to wait reflects dependence. An expert who has a monopoly on a service needed by a target can make the target wait. The enormous waiting lines confronting clients of public (people-serving) bureaucracies (e.g., public hospitals or state colleges and universities) are the result of the monopolization of the services they offer or impose.

Waiting can dramatize power differences. One person may keep another waiting in order to reaffirm a power advantage: "I'll just let him cool his heels. That'll show him who is boss!"

Waiting can be a coercive resource. When was the last time you were kept waiting by a friend? Did it make you angry? Did you respond by keeping your friend waiting the next time? Making a person wait can be a form of punishment.

Waiting can be used by the subordinate as passive pressure. Although the powerless lack important resources to resist the compliance pressures of the powerful, one thing they may be able to do without significant retaliation is keep their superiors waiting. The next time you are in a department store, watch how slowly some clerks respond to irritating customers.

---

at least change in that direction)? You might be inclined to because, after all, he is a professor of sociology and sociologists know something about poverty, welfare, and productivity. But he is so young! What could anyone that young know about such a complex problem? The two symbols are inconsistent because you perceive that one indicates high expertise and the other indicates low expertise. So what would you do? If you don't know, don't feel too badly because social psychologists aren't sure either. Some predict that you would respond to the most relevant symbol (professor of sociology) and change your opinion; others predict that you would respond to the more general symbol (young age); and still others predict that you would respond to a the combination of the symbols and adopt a compromise position of some kind (Berger and Fisek, 1970; Zeldich, Lauderdale, and Stublarec, 1980).

Trustworthiness

Thus far, we have discussed whether an expert appears to know what she or he is talking about — expertise. But "knowing" is not necessarily "giving it to us straight." The expert may have excellent information but have ulterior motives for giving the target biased or deceptive advice. So, in addition to assessing the expert's expertise, we also want to assess the expert's **trustworthiness**.

Again, experience (our own or others') is the most reliable indicator of trustworthiness. Of course, even experiences can be staged to make "experts" look more expert than they really are. Bogus faith healers frequently plant confederates in the audience who pretend to be "miraculously" cured. Advertisers select consumers who they feel typify the target audience to present testimonials on their satisfaction with the advertiser's product. Manufacturers often attempt to win the seal of approval from independent product-testing agencies to substantiate their product claims. And politicians running for office commonly solicit the endorsement of prestigious individuals. These are all efforts to increase power by convincing potential targets that the source is trustworthy.

Particularly important in assessing trustworthiness is the target's perception of whether the expert has an ulterior motive for her or his advocacy. How much of a payoff will the expert receive? If the expert is seen as arguing *against* his or her own best interests (contrary to what is expected), the expert will be perceived as more trustworthy and thus will become more powerful (Kaplowitz et al., 1991). Social psychologists found that when a criminal argued in *favor* of more individual freedom and against greater police power, he produced little attitude change in his listeners. But when he argued in favor of a stronger police force, he produced considerable attitude change (Walster et al., 1966). Similar effects may result from Budweiser's "Know when to say when" campaign.

Likewise, the effectiveness of conflict mediators is dependent on their having no vested interest in the outcome of the mediation. Lawyers who use expert witnesses try to promote the appearance of the witnesses' disinterest or lack of bias. They make it a matter of public knowledge that such witnesses are paid a fee regardless of the outcome of the trial.

Similarly, perceptions of bias are reduced by the expert's appearing to be less directive. The expert's acknowledgement that there is an alternative position to the one which he or she is advocating may enhance his or her trustworthiness (McGuire, 1985). An expert is more effective when he or she seems to present only "neutral facts" to the target, presumably leaving the target free to draw independent conclusions (Thistlethwaite and Kamenetzky, 1955). Of course, this is tricky, because if the source's directive is *too* subtle, the target may not be influenced at all. In this case, the source would appear trustworthy but would still be ineffective.

Sometimes the people we like the most—those who know us the best—are not to be trusted when it comes to giving particular kinds of advice. Consider the father who tells his child to stay in school, explaining that things will get better, or the boyfriend who tells his troubled girlfriend that she is the best person he knows. The child and the girlfriend may discount the advice of these sources because each perceives the expert to be biased. They know the parent and the boyfriend love them and want them to feel better; thus these sources aren't trusted to give unbiased advice.

It is important to note that once the expert's directive is followed, the symbol of expertise or trustworthiness is tested. If compliance does not produce the expected outcome, both the symbol and the expert identified by the symbol lose some of their credibility and power.

INFORMATIONAL RESOURCES

Do you have a place on your campus that is designated as a kind of open forum, a place where anyone can go to speak his or her mind to those pausing to listen? On the University of North Carolina campus, this place is called "the Pit" (a sunken brick terrace bordered by steps). The point of having such a place is to create an opportunity for people to present information, often with the aim of changing the attitudes or behavior of those willing to listen. But most of the speakers will not be able to pressure their listeners by using any of the resources we have discussed so far. They will not be able to affect the listeners' rewards or punishments (either directly or indirectly via their expertise). So, if a speaker is able to change the conduct of a listener without access to these resources, what is the source of the speaker's power? We often try to influence other people by giving them information or logical arguments that we think will suggest the "right" course of action to them—the one we prefer. The ability to communicate information to another person is called **informational resources**.

We use informational resources every day to

persuade others to act a certain way. For example, a woman might present arguments to a friend about why he should come with her to dinner at a new restaurant that is currently her favorite. She would do this by providing him with information about how good the food is, how many choices are offered, how attractive the decor is, and how reasonable the prices are. In political campaigns candidates make speeches and buy advertisements giving potential voters information about the good things they will do if elected and the bad things their opponents will do or have done.

Channels of Information

A person's ability to persuade another party by using informational resources is partly determined by access to a forum for presenting his or her case. Let's call this part of informational resources the source's *channel of information*. In addition to using the face-to-face channel provided by everyday encounters and public forums such as UNC's "Pit," a source can transmit information visually and verbally through television, videos, and movies; verbally through radio, audios, and telephone; or in writing through newspapers, pamphlets, signs, and letters.

What kind of channel is best? The answer depends on the kind of conduct the source wants to change. A *behavior* change is hard to accomplish without face-to-face contact and the use of a model. Thus a visual channel is usually more effective. Visual channels are also more effective if the change is a rather simple one (Andreoli and Worchel, 1978). More complex directives are frequently best communicated in writing so that targets can absorb the information at their own pace (Chaiken and Eagly, 1976).

Individuals with access to the mass media have a special advantage in any society. Much attention has been paid to the media's role in *agenda setting* — focusing the public's attention on certain issues and thereby elevating public concern about those issues. Experiments have demonstrated that viewers' priorities can be *changed* by varying the amount of coverage given to particular issues.

One experiment manipulated the amount of coverage given to particular issues in television newscasts. The more coverage an issue received, the higher its importance rating as given by subjects twenty-four hours later. In addition, subjects tended to base their judgments of the President's performance on his handling of the issues that were covered most in the newscasts they viewed during the experiment (Iyengar and Kinder, 1987).

But what about the information itself? A person's social power depends not only on access to the right channel of information but also on *skill in conveying the information*. Both the content and its presentation are important. Let's begin with the content of the information.

Information Content

Basically, *content* consists of the arguments that the communicator offers to encourage the target to change his or her position or behavior to that advocated by the communicator. Arguments can appeal to thinking (cognition) or to emotion.

Cognitive appeals. Some cognitive appeals focus on presenting "good reasons," or justifications, for the source's claims and on offering disclaimers to discount the target's counterarguments. For example, a frequently used justification is that the target's compliance with the source's directive will result in greater social esteem or self-esteem: "If you study harder and get better grades, your family will feel proud." The implication, is "If you don't, your family will feel ashamed." Disclaimers discount the possibility of negative outcomes of compliance, such as being caught: "Let's have a party at your house. Your parents will never find out."

Other cognitive appeals concentrate on image making. The source may attempt to cast herself or himself in a particular image (*impression management*) or cast the target in such an image ("*altercasting*"). For example, a husband may want his wife to let him select their vacation location ("Let me do it; I've read all about those places") yet want her to fix dinner ("No, you better do it — you're the expert"). Adults often attempt to get children's compliance by altercasting. "Be a good girl" means that if you comply, you are a good girl, and if you don't, you're a bad girl. Similar appeals cast the target as a "mature person," "believer," or "real friend" in order to exact compliance. The point of all such arguments is to make compliance appear to be *consistent* with the target's self-attitude.

Another kind of cognitive appeal relies on repetition to produce recognition. Political campaigns, as well as other advertisers, for example, frequently bombard targets with repeated "thirty-second" messages of low intensity. We encounter ten to twenty-five such messages per hour on commercial radio or television (Baumgardner et al., 1983). Obviously, the information presented must be simple. It frequently attempts to associate a "new" person or product with an *existing* attitude of the audience (anticrime, pro-life, nationalism, democracy, antitax). During the next political campaign, count the number of times you see the same ad for a particular candidate and note the simplicity of the message.

Emotional appeals. Emotional appeals are arguments designed to arouse feelings of pride, love, nostalgia, pity, or concern. The most thoroughly studied of emotional appeals are *fear appeals*. Rather than attempting to get targets to comply as a result of intensive thinking, fear appeals seek an emotional response by providing information suggesting that impending danger or harm will result from following or failing to follow a given course of action. Communicators have successfully used fear appeals to influence a great many behaviors, including terminating cigarette smoking, getting vaccinations, and wearing auto seat belts (Rogers, 1983). Yet evidence suggests that the effects of fear appeals are short-lived — that is, that they wear off over time — or may even boomerang (Janis and Feshbach, 1953; Leventhal, 1970; McGuire, 1985). The anxiety that fear appeals cause may lead people to propose

counterarguments, suppress their thoughts about the danger, or think up elaborate rationalizations for why the threat does not apply to them. Thus, to be effective, such appeals may have to be repeated (Rogers, 1983).

Fear appeals work better, however, if targets believe that the threat is *real*, that it affects *them*, and that they can cope with the anxiety the appeal induces by taking positive actions (McGuire, 1985). They work best when the appeal comes from a highly credible source (Hewgill and Miller, 1965) and when they are combined with a cognitive appeal containing specific recommendations for reducing the threat — for example, telling people to stop smoking *and* showing them how to do it (Smith, 1982). The "how-to's" must be easily "do-able," and evidence must be provided that compliance will eliminate the threat (Bettinghaus and Cody, 1987; Tanner, Day, and Crask, 1989; Tanner, Hunt, and Eppright, 1991). Appeals that enhance *self-efficacy* are particularly effective (Maddux and Rogers, 1983; Bennett, Spoth, and Borgen, 1991; Maibach, Flora, and Nass, 1991).

Although appeals to positive emotions have been the subject of less research than fear appeals, it is clear that positive emotions also arouse target responsiveness. Positive appeals avoid the complication associated with negative appeals of having the target try to escape the situation (McGuire, 1985). Studies suggest, for example, that "warmth commercials" — those focusing on love, pride, affection, sympathy, and comfort — result in positive attitudes toward the product and an increased intention to purchase (Bettinghaus and Cody, 1987). You've probably felt a bit "mushy" after watching a commercial in which a Hallmark card expresses just the right sentiment and brings tears to the eyes of someone's grandmother, best friend, or grumpy old music teacher. And haven't you felt that you ought to call your mom or dad after watching one of those "reach out and touch someone" commercials?

Emotions can be aroused by verbal and visual associations. Commercials telling us that "nothin'

Fear appeals seek an emotional response by providing information suggesting that impending danger or harm will result from following or failing to follow a given course of action.

says lovin' like something from the oven" do both: they verbally associate the product with caring for another person, and they show us those yummy, warm cinnamon rolls that we associate with comfort and happiness. In a "greeting card" commercial run by a major beer company during the holidays, we see a wonderful, snowy scene and hear pleasant music. That's it. There's no plug for the product, just a "signature" from the company at the end. Associations work for negative emotions too. In political advertisements, we see candidate A looking attractive and competent, but we're shown a photo or clip of the opponent, candidate B, looking dull and clumsy; and the background music differs, depending on whether the announcer is talking about the "preferred"

candidate or the opponent. (Before reading further, see the box "Image Is Everything.")

Information Presentation

In addition to considering information content, social psychologists have also examined the effectiveness of various *ways of presenting* information.

Foot-in-the-door technique. The *foot-in-the-door technique* is based on the idea that to get a person to comply with a large request, we should get the person to comply with a smaller one first. The theory is that compliance breeds compliance. Suppose you'd like to convince a friend to stop smoking. In all probability, you will not be able to change your friend's attitude or behavior by ask-

IMAGE IS EVERYTHING

Political campaigns attempt to influence voters' candidate choices. To do this, they rely heavily on projecting a particular image of the candidate. Television ads have become critically important to political campaigns. These ads incorporate both visual and audio channels of communication, which, when combined creatively, can produce an emotional appeal that is nearly impossible to achieve with words alone (Trenholm, 1989). Consider the following ad, which was seen by viewers watching CBS's *Monday Night at the Movies* on an evening in 1964:

> We hear birds chirping and see a little girl standing in a field of flowers, picking petals from a daisy, one at a time. The little girl counts, "One, two, three, four, five, six, six, eight, nine, nine . . ." The camera zooms in for a close-up of the little girl's face as she looks up toward the sky and continues to zoom in on her eyes as an announcer counts, "Ten, nine, eight, seven, six, five, four, three, two, one, zero." An atomic bomb explodes. We hear the explosion and see a mushroom cloud billowing fire and smoke. Then we hear candidate Lyndon Johnson's voice: "These are the stakes: to make a world in which all God's children can live, or go into the dark. We must either love each other or we must die." The words "Vote for President Johnson on November 3" appear on the screen while an announcer says, "Vote for President Johnson on November third. The stakes are too high for you to stay home" (adapted from Devlin, 1986).

Like other Johnson campaign ads run that year, this one, often referred to as the "daisy spot," portrayed Johnson's opponent, Barry Goldwater, as someone who might plunge America into nuclear war. The daisy ad was clearly a fear appeal.

Political ads can also be used to change the candidate's image, creating a personal resource in the form of increased liking and respect. In 1972, for example, political commercials for presidential candidate Jimmy Carter often showed him at home, dressed in jeans and a casual shirt. While Carter made "suitably presidential" comments about issues of national importance, the biggest impact of the commercials was in creating an image of the candidate as a competent "grass-roots" leader untarnished by Washington politics. The campaign also used effective slogans emphasizing that Carter was the candidate who could build a government "as good as its people," fostering Carter's image as a leader who was still close to his Georgia roots (Woodward and Denton, 1988). Thus, character is an important issue in a campaign, addressing the candidate's fitness to make decisions on yet unknown problems.

Ads attempt to influence our views of a candidate's image by associating the candidate with desirable values or characteristics. In the 1992 presidential campaign, ads and news clips showing the Democratic candidate Bill Clinton jogging were common, perhaps to create the image of the "pudgy" candidate as physically fit and vital. Similarly, the candidate was shown on the job with blue-collar workers to demonstrate his or her understanding of the problems of average working Americans. George Bush was shown buying socks at Sears for his grandchildren—an attempt to change his image as a president who was out of touch with the average American's life style and problems. Of course, there are limits on the effectiveness of advertising in changing the candidate's image. In the words of media consultant Jill Buckley, "It is a very hard job to turn a turkey into a movie star; you try instead to make people like the turkey" (quoted in Sabato, 1981: 144).

ing your friend to stop today. However, you might begin by convincing him to refrain from smoking while in the car with you.

The major limitation to this technique is that it won't work if the first request is too small or too big. For the foot-in-the-door technique to suc-

ceed, the first request must be of sufficient magnitude to commit the person to further compliance (Seligman, Bush, and Kirsch, 1976) but not so big that the person refuses (Snyder and Cunningham, 1975). Gradual changes are the key. This strategy has been used to get people to give to charity

(Pliner et al., 1974); to donate blood, kidneys, and bone marrow (Saks, 1978; Schwarzwald, Bizman, and Raz, 1983); and to generate attachment to cult religions (Lofland, 1981).

J. L. Freedman and S. C. Fraser (1966) demonstrated this effect in a safe-driving campaign. Experimenters visited homemakers and asked the women to sign a petition that was to be sent to their state senator supporting safe-driving legislation. The vast majority complied. A few weeks later another experimenter visited the petition signers. This time the women were asked to place a large, unattractive "Drive Carefully" sign in their front yards. Of these women, 55 percent complied. In contrast, only 17 percent of a control group composed of women who had not previously been approached agreed to put the signs in their yards. Thus, convincing the women to comply with a small initial request more than tripled their compliance with a much larger request.

One explanation for why the foot-in-the-door technique works is that people who agree to the small request become committed to the issue or the behavior or simply to the idea of taking some action. Any of these commitments would probably make a person more likely to agree to future requests. Another explanation is based on Daryl Bem's (1972) self-perception theory, which we described in Chapter 7, "The Social Nature of Self." According to this theory, we observe our own actions and draw inferences (make attributions) regarding our internal states. Thus, in the safe-driving experiment, the women who agreed to sign the petition observed themselves taking action on a good cause without much external pressure. Perhaps they inferred from this that they actually felt strongly about the cause or were the sort of people who become involved with such causes. In other words, compliance with the small request may have changed the women's self-perceptions slightly. As a consequence, they became more disposed to comply with the second, larger request.

Low-ball technique.   A variation of the foot-in-the-door technique is a method that salespeople

and researchers call the *low-ball technique*. This technique involves making a request and, after the target has agreed, changing the conditions of the deal. Assume, for example, that your social psychology professor calls you and asks you to participate in a study. *After you agree*, the professor tells you that the study is scheduled for 7 A.M. Would you tell the professor to forget it or, since you have already agreed to participate, reluctantly show up for the study?

Social psychologist Robert Cialdini and his associates (1978) compared this request with one in which students were told from the outset that the study would be scheduled for 7 A.M. The researchers found that the first approach was much more successful. When students were told as part of the initial request that the study would be conducted at 7 A.M., only 25 percent agreed to participate and showed up on time. When the time wasn't mentioned until after the students had agreed to participate, 55 percent decided to stay in the study and almost all showed up on time. An automobile salesperson might use a similar approach by first securing an agreement from a customer to purchase a car and then increasing the cost of the vehicle.

The technique appears to work because once we have made an initial commitment to a course of action, we are reluctant to back out—even if the other party changes the rules of the game (Burger and Petty, 1981). The low-ball technique is often effective, but because it is deceptive, it has been made illegal in several industries, including automobile sales. (See the Student Observation: "Low-Ball Technique.")

Door-in-the-face technique.   Another presentation strategy is much the reverse of the foot-in-the-door technique. The *door-in-the-face technique* involves first making a large request, which we expect will be refused, and then following with a smaller request that is closer to what we really want anyway. Following this strategy, a son who hopes to get $300 from his father for a spring break trip should first ask his father for $500 (or $300 and the use of the family car), knowing that

---

STUDENT OBSERVATION

Low-Ball Technique

A suite-mate and I have a class together. Before our midterm examination she asked to borrow my notes for a certain day she had missed. I agreed and started to take the notes for that particular day out of my notebook to give her. When she realized that I was not going to give her my notebook, she asked to borrow the whole thing because there were a few other days she had missed as well. I was on the spot. Had she asked for the entire notebook in the beginning, I probably would not have lent it to her. Since she originally asked for one day's notes, however, and I had agreed to this request, I felt obligated to comply when she increased her request. This is an example of the low-ball technique.

---

his father will think he's insane. Once the refusal is made, the son should *reluctantly* lower his request. The idea is to ask for an outrageous amount to begin with so that when you reduce your demands, you appear to be compromising and your smaller request seems more reasonable.

Research has found that this technique, like the foot-in-the-door technique, is often effective for securing others' compliance. In one illustrative study, subjects were asked to volunteer time for a good cause (Cialdini et al., 1975). Some were first asked to volunteer for a large number of hours — two hours a week for several weeks as camp counselors for a group of delinquent boys. Almost all refused, as the experimenter expected. When they did, he immediately suggested that maybe they would agree to volunteer for a much smaller amount of time — a single day as chaperons on a bus trip to the zoo with the same boys. Other subjects were asked to volunteer for only the smaller amount of time, with no mention of the larger request. Among the subjects who had first turned down the large request, 51 percent agreed to the smaller request. In contrast, only 17 percent of the subjects in the small-request-only condition agreed to volunteer. An impressive difference!

We associate the door-in-the-face technique with bargaining. We often ask for more than we expect to get so that we have "room to negotiate." You might have received requests for donations

from groups who seem to be aware of this technique. Many organizations have learned that people are more willing to give $25 when they have already turned down a request for $100. There does seem to be one limitation on the door-in-the-face technique. It is less effective when too much time elapses between the requests (Cann, Sherman, and Elkes, 1975; Dillard, Hunter, and Burgoon, 1984). The passing of time reduces the perception of concession and reasonableness on which the effect hinges.

Both the foot-in-the-door and the door-in-the-face techniques involve efforts to alter targets' self-attitudes. The first technique begins by asking the target to make such a small change that it only minimally conflicts with the target's self-image. This sets up a series of small attitude changes. By the time the communicator makes the final pitch, it is almost consistent with the target's revised self-attitude. The door-in-the-face technique tries to get the target to view compliance with the final (and real) request as consistent with the target's view of himself or herself as a reasonable person who does not *always* say "no." (See the Student Observation: "Door-in-the-Face Technique.")

That's-not-all technique. A variation of the door-in-the-face technique is the *that's-not-all technique.* This involves making a large request and, *before the target refuses*, improving the deal by

---

STUDENT OBSERVATION

Door-in-the-Face Technique

My parents love to come to North Carolina to have little "family reunions" with me two or three times a year. We usually meet in the mountains now because, while I love my family dearly, I have always had a miserable time when they come to Chapel Hill. This semester, however, it seems that my mom and dad were so set on coming here for "Parents' Weekend" that they used the door-in-the-face technique to secure my compliance. Thus, early in October they called me to ask about coming up for my twenty-first birthday, which fell one week after Parents' Weekend and represented perhaps the single worst time in my college career for a parental visit. After I politely said "no," my mom replied, "Well, honey, we miss you so much. How about if we come up the week before and stay for Parents' Weekend?" At this point I really felt there was no way for me to refuse and be consistent with my self-schema that I am a good son and not unconditionally negative. I reluctantly agreed.

In talking to my parents this past weekend, I found out not only that they were aware that I would refuse their first request but also that they did not really want to be around for my "coming of age." Though they called it a "guilt trip," their technique was a perfect execution of the door-in-the-face technique. I was quite surprised that my parents would employ such sociological chicanery on me. Next time, however, I will be ready.

---

lowering the original request or throwing in some additional benefit. In one study demonstrating the effectiveness of this approach, social psychologist Jerry Burger (1986) held a psychology club bake sale on campus. At random, half of the potential customers who approached the table and inquired about prices were told that a package of one cupcake and two cookies was 75 cents. In this control condition, 40 percent of the customers made a purchase. In the that's-not-all condition, potential customers were first told that the price of a cupcake was 75 cents; a moment later, they were told that they would actually get not only the cupcake but also two cookies for the 75-cent price. When the information was presented this way, 73 percent of the customers made a purchase. Presenting the cookies as "a special deal" seemed to add to the attractiveness of the product.

In summary, foot-in-the-door, low-ball, door-in-the-face, and that's-not-all techniques are ways of presenting information that are designed to overcome our resistance to a communicator's requests. The content of the information a communicator presents may be designed to influence our thinking, or feeling, or both. Of course, a communicator must have access to an effective channel of communication to get his or her message across.

PERSONAL RESOURCES

Have you ever observed the behavior of a young teenager who idolizes a rock star or some other famous person? Even though the celebrity does not control any reward, coercive, expert, or informational resources, he or she has the power to influence the teenager's behavior. When compliance to a person's directives is its own reward, we say the person has **personal resources**. Adults, as well as young teenagers, are subject to this kind of power. For example, good-looking people are used to advertise clothes because potential buyers admire the models and want to look like them. We realize that we won't *become* Liz Taylor by wearing her perfume, Cheryl Tiegs by eating her brand of yogurt, Jaclyn Smith by wearing the K-Mart clothes she designs and models, or Burt Reynolds by using Quaker State oil in our cars, but it pleases us to "be like" the people we admire, even in these small ways. Why do you think advertisers use professional basketball players and movie stars to convey antidrug messages? Those individuals are not experts on drug abuse. (Indeed, the ones who might be considered experts are not chosen for such ads!) Celebrities are chosen as spokespersons for this message because they have personal resources that can encourage compliance "as its own reward." (Recall our discussion of expressive bonds in Chapter 4, "Social Relationships and Groups"—the type of bond one person feels for another that "is its own reward." The concepts of personal resources and expressive bonds are closely related.)

Compliance can bring the source and target closer together (at least in the eyes of the target). Sometimes becoming more *similar to* a particular person is very satisfying. For this to be so, the parties must initially be dissimilar. One's admiration of, or attraction toward, a dissimilar other makes one try to emulate that person (Chaiken, 1979). Directives from that person are hardly necessary. All the source has to do is model the behavior he or she wants the target to adopt and the target will do the rest. Thus, the advertisers show us that Michael Jordan drinks Gatorade, wears Nikes and Hanes underwear, and eats Wheaties, knowing that many of us "wanna be like Mike."

When personal resources are involved, the target follows the directives of the source because of the unique qualities of the source—who she or he is as a person. What are these unique qualities? They can be anything and depend entirely on the target's perception! What is an admirable quality to one person is an abominable quality to another (remember the different reactions of you and your parents to your favorite rock star). One person's hero is another person's geek. The important distinction is between power that rests on the source's ability to affect outcomes, directly or indirectly, for the target (reward, coercive, or expert resources) and power that rests on the personal qualities of the source (personal resources).

Personal power also has a negative form (Raven, 1988). The source's efforts to change the conduct of another person may produce an effect, but it may be the *opposite* of the intended effect. This is especially likely when the source is *disliked*. If a disliked or disvalued source is aware of the target's attitude, the source may try to minimize the association between himself or herself and the message. Research suggests that a disliked source's power can be more effective if the source communicates through channels that minimize his or her personal impact—for example, through a written, rather than a videotaped or an audiotaped, message (Chaiken and Eagly, 1983). Of course it is not unusual for one person to advocate a change in the conduct of another by noting that a disliked third party advocates the opposite conduct. Would you be inclined to change your hair style, for example, if a friend told you that your current hair style made you look like Bart Simpson? (Before reading further, look at the Student Observation: "Personal Resources.")

NORMATIVE RESOURCES

Normative resources derive from a rule or an agreement (a norm) among a group of persons which recognizes that one party has a right to command (authority) while other parties have the responsibility to obey. Group members may vary in their support of such norms. Those who support the norm comply because of their commitment to it: "It's the American way." "It's my duty (or my job)." Even members whose support of the norm is weak are "encouraged" to comply by rewards and punishments dealt out by norm supporters. Thus, the compliance of supporters is affected by normative resources, while the compliance of nonsupporters is affected by reward and coercive resources.

The authority of a person in a leadership position depends on the support of most of the targets. But lack of support for the *person* in a position may not necessarily undermine the support for the *position* itself (Evans and Zelditch, 1961). This is because the position of power is part of an organization to which targets are committed. Targets' attitudes toward the position are

---

STUDENT OBSERVATION

Personal Resources

*J*ust recently I was in a drugstore trying to decide on a hair color. I'm a brunette turned blonde who can't afford a professional job every time my brown hair begins to grow out. Therefore, I rely heavily on the hair-coloring section of the store. In pursuit of the best decision, I found myself remembering the hair color commercials for the various brands. I could picture Linda Evans and Cybill Shepherd each discussing how her own brand of hair color was best.

Then I found myself comparing the two stars. I most identified with Cybill. She's younger than Linda, she's a beautiful woman, and I know a lot about her. People also tell me I have her nose. Plus, I enjoyed watching *Moonlighting* better than *Dynasty*. Needless to say, I bought Cybill Shepherd's brand of hair color—because, "I'm worth it!" Thus I followed the "directives" of the advertisement because of the person I believe Cybill Shepherd to be. Being like Cybill was my reward for buying her product. The ad relied on Cybill's personal resources to influence my purchase decision.

---

often strong because they include attitudes toward other aspects of the organization.

Formal organizations—universities, corporations, governments, military units, churches, or sports teams—rely heavily on power based on normative resources. The position holder usually has access to titles and symbols—such as uniforms and offices—which identify him or her as the holder of the position. Organizational rules specify for each position the domain of activities over which the position holder is to have power and the resources available to the position holder to exact compliance. For example, university rules specify that professors have limited powers over students in their classes. Professors are given the power to require students' class attendance and exam taking and to enforce the honor code, but they do not have the power to require a dress code or particular political opinions. Their resources are pretty much limited to passing or failing a student.

In contrast to the limited authority of university professors, the power of military officers is based on broad normative resources. Their authority covers many aspects of their soldiers' lives, and military regulations give them the power to reward and punish behavior in these domains. Soldiers are supposed to follow directives (orders) *immediately* regardless of the expertise or personal

qualities of the officer. The symbols of the officer's normative resources are the indicators of rank worn on the shoulders or sleeves of his or her uniform. Soldiers are exposed to an intensive training program in order to establish this unquestioning compliance to superiors' directives. This extreme level of obedience to authority (normative resources) is intended to produce positive military outcomes—to save the lives of friendly forces and to win military objectives—but the actual outcomes, like those involving other types of power resources, can be negative.

This was highlighted by the massacre at the Vietnamese village of My Lai, which occurred during the Vietnam War. American soldiers under the command of Lieutenant William Calley landed near the village in helicopters. The troops moved into the village, rounding up men, women, children, and infants. One American soldier gave this account:

We made them squat down and Lieutenant Calley came over and said, "You know what to do with them, don't you?" And I said yes. So I took it for granted that he just wanted us to watch them. And he left, and came back about ten or fifteen minutes later and said, "How come you ain't killed them yet?" And I told him that I didn't think you wanted us to kill them, that you just wanted us to guard them. He said, "No. I want them dead." (*New York Times*, November 25, 1969: 16)

The Americans then backed away about 15 feet and fired their automatics into the group of villagers. The following exchange occurred between one American soldier and Mike Wallace of CBS News:

Q: How do you shoot babies?

A: I don't know. It's just one of those things.

Q: How many people would you imagine were killed that day?

A: I'd say about three hundred and seventy. (*New York Times*, November 25, 1969: 16)

Lieutenant Calley was later brought to trial and convicted for having ordered the death of the civilians. In his trial, Calley did not deny that he had personally ordered the slayings; rather, the defense insisted that Calley was acting in accordance with what he saw as his duty in carrying out orders from legitimate authorities.

The Process of Social Power

Now you know how some social psychologists conceptualize the kinds of resources that may be available to us in our attempts to change the behavior of others and our efforts to resist others' attempts to change our behavior. Resources are only a part, though a very important part, of the process of social power. There are four aspects of the process. First, there is power potential — the control of valuable resources by source and target. This aspect is called the **power structure**. The second aspect of the power process involves the *use* of these resources in the source's attempts to change the target's behavior and the target's efforts to resist. (Note that there may be several attempts and efforts before the issue of the target's compliance is resolved.) This aspect of the power process is called **power strategies**. The third aspect of the power process consists of **pow-er outcomes**. Possible outcomes include the compliance of the target — the intended change in the target's behavior — partial compliance, noncompliance, or reactance (in which the target not only resists the power attempt but behaves in a manner *contrary* to the source's desires).

In the process of social power one party (or both) uses resources to influence the other (or each other). Therefore, one of the possible consequences of social power is the *redistribution* of resources among parties: one party gains resources while the other loses resources. Thus, not only is the target's behavior changed, but the power structure may also change. We'll refer to this aspect of the power process as the **revised power structure**. From here, the process of social power can either stop or begin again with another round of power strategies.

POWER STRUCTURE AND RATIONAL CHOICE

To describe the process of social power, we are going to rely heavily on social exchange theory (Molm, 1990). Let's look at the first aspect of the process of social power — the power structure, which consists of the resources possessed by the source and the target. What matters most, according to social exchange theory, is the degree to which the source and target are *dependent* on one another for the resources each possesses. *Dependence* on another person refers to our expectations that the person will provide us with greater *profit* (rewards are high while costs are low) than we can get from alternative sources.

Power Structure

The likelihood that an individual will engage in exchange behavior — in this case, interactions involving social power — with a particular person increases with the individual's *dependence* on that particular person. This is true for both source and target. In other words, the more dependent you are on another person, the greater the likelihood that you will participate in the process of social power with that person, as either a source or a target.

Dependence imbalance. Of course, the source and the target may not be equally dependent on each other. When they are not, social exchange theory refers to this condition as *dependence imbalance*. Either the source or the target may be more dependent — whichever one has fewer resources, resources that are less valued by the other, or resources that the other can obtain from another source.

For example, suppose a supervisor, Beth, feels that it's important for all the analysts who work for her to "dress professionally." She makes this well known to her staff members and most comply, hoping that they'll please the supervisor (or at least avoid her disapproval) and that, perhaps, they'll be rewarded with bigger pay raises. One particular analyst, Dave, does not comply. His attire is *far* from professional, ranging from jeans to cutoff shorts and T-shirts with holes in them. Dave clearly doesn't care how he looks. He's Beth's best programmer, however. He's assigned all the toughest problems and always comes through. He's frequently consulted by the other analysts on their projects as well. He may be a slob, but he's the "brain" of the unit. Can Beth get Dave to comply with her standards for office attire? Let's analyze Beth's and Dave's dependencies to find out.

Beth controls Dave's work assignments, job performance reviews, and pay raises. Pay raises, unlike fashion, are highly valued by Dave, who knows that his skills are valuable and who, despite his appearance, could easily find another job at his current salary. Dave, on the other hand, is responsible for the high performance of Beth's entire unit. She realizes that if she lost Dave, he'd be hard to replace and the efficiency of her unit would drop dramatically. So, will Beth attempt to improve Dave's appearance by offering him a larger pay raise if he dresses more professionally? She might, but to Dave, the costs of changing his personal habits are very high. He's just not "in-

to" clothes, shopping, and the discomfort of dressing more professionally. Beth's authority to give raises doesn't cover the amount he'd ask for to make such a change. Will she threaten to lower his pay or fire him? Not likely. The costs to *her* are too high if he decides to quit, which is likely since he can easily get another job. In this situation, Beth is more dependent on Dave than vice versa. There is a dependence imbalance that favors Dave, so Beth is unlikely to get her way.

This example also illustrates that the values assigned to the resource and compliance involved in a potential social power exchange may be different for the source and the target. In this case, Beth sees her request that the staff dress professionally as entailing only modest costs, as do the other analysts in the office. For Dave, however, dressing professionally would entail *great* costs; he doesn't want to think about clothes, spend time or money buying them, or give up his comfortable rags. Unless Beth "puts herself in Dave's shoes" — mentally, that is — she may not understand his resistance to her directive. She may think, for example, that he deliberately dresses the way he does to show that she can't tell him what to do.

Strength and balance. Social exchange theory draws our attention to *bilateral* social power — social interaction in which *both* parties have some capacity to produce intended changes in each other's behavior. In other words, each party is both source and target. What distinguishes one power structure from another is the *strength* and *balance* of the social power of the individuals involved. We have already noted that the strength of social power is a function of dependence (rewards, costs, profits, and alternatives) and that balance is a function of the relative dependencies of the parties involved.

When we compare the dependencies of interaction partners, there are several patterns we might observe. The dependencies may be strong and quite similar — *strong* and *balanced*. According to social exchange theory, we would expect such power structures to produce considerable bilateral social power, that is, an exchange of power. Another power structure may be characterized by *weak* and *balanced* dependencies, with neither person particularly dependent on the other. Social exchange theory predicts that weak dependencies produce little social power, since neither party has much to gain from interaction. If a power structure is characterized by dependencies that are dissimilar, or *imbalanced*, one person is more dependent than the other. Social exchange theory proposes that the *least* dependent person is in the best position to exercise power, either as a source attempting to change the target's behavior or as a target resisting the source's attempts. (For an example, see the Student Observation: "Dependence Imbalance.")

Other kinds of imbalance. Thus far we have discussed power imbalance in terms of the inequality of the strengths of the parties' dependencies (dependence imbalance). But there are two other ways to think about the balance of power between parties. Instead of assessing the power balance within a single exchange, we can view power balance in the context of several episodes. The power structure within a marriage may have evolved to a point where the husband has power over his wife in a greater number of areas ("domains" in social exchange terminology). For ex-

ample, he determines whether she may work outside the home, where she lives and vacations, what kind of car she drives, what TV programs she watches (when he is around), and how often they have sex. She has the power over her husband in the domains of what he eats (at least at home), how often they go to church, and how often they visit her parents. The husband's power is more comprehensive than that of the wife, because he controls more domains than she does. There is a *domain imbalance*. Most parent-child relationships are characterized by a domain imbalance.

Social exchange theorists sometimes think of power imbalance in terms of differences between two parties in the *number of persons* over which each has power. For example, in a large family, the mother may have power over the younger children, while the father has power over the older children as well as the mother. A college student may have some power over a small number of professors, but most professors have some power over a larger number of students. The husband's and the professor's power are more extensive than those of their counterparts. There is a *targets imbalance*.

Thus, when comparing the power structures of two parties, we need to take into account all these aspects of power: (1) the strength of the power (that is, resources, value, and best alternative),

---

STUDENT OBSERVATION

Dependence Imbalance

It seems I have more power in my relationship of seventeen months with my girlfriend. I am dependent on her for little: my social life is exciting, many activities keep me busy, I get good grades, and I receive a lot of support and affection from my family and close friends. I am not dependent on my girlfriend for fun, status, knowledge, self-esteem, or security (reward, expert, and personal resources). However, she goes to a school where there is not much to do, struggles with her grades, and has family problems. She is more dependent on me for things to do, status, help with schoolwork, and affection (reward, personal, and expert resources). Whenever we have a conflict, it has less emotional effect on me and I usually get my way — just as social exchange theory would predict.

(2) the comprehensiveness of the domains, and (3) the number of targets. The parties' power structures may be more imbalanced on some of these aspects than others. Think of a relationship in which you feel that one person has more power than the other person. To which aspect of the power structure can the more powerful party's advantage be attributed?

Rational Choice

Social exchange theorists believe that to understand social power — to predict or explain who will influence whom — we must first calculate the dependencies of the source and the target. While the participants in social power may not think of it in those terms, they may also engage in a series of calculations to decide which persons they will try to influence, whether to comply or resist, and how much of a certain resource they are willing to give for a particular amount of compliance or vice versa.

According to this view, both source and target are engaged in a *rational choice* decision-making process that determines the effects of the power structure on the power process — the actual exchange of resources for compliance. The source's resources are evaluated by the target, who decides their value and balances this against the costs of compliance and noncompliance. The target's compliance is evaluated by the source, who decides its value and balances this against the resources it will cost to obtain the compliance. Both source and target calculate their profits (rewards minus costs) from a potential exchange. They may also calculate the profits of alternative exchanges, and they are likely to choose the alternative providing the highest profit (Raven, 1990).

Limited Effects of Structural Power

How much influence will the power structure have on the source's attempts to influence the target's behavior and the target's efforts to resist? This depends partly on how well each party can assess his or her own and the other's dependencies. Such information is seldom "total," and even

if it were, social psychologists are not sure exactly how we combine the information in order to make our decisions (Heimer, 1988; Kruglanski, 1989; Tallman and Gray, 1990; Payne, Bettman, and Johnson, 1992).

In many cases, we must make our decisions about whether or not to attempt to influence others, or whether to comply or resist, even though we have *incomplete* information about our own dependencies on those others. For example, a college student may have little experience with a new roommate and be unsure just what resources the roommate controls. Sometimes, we may have *too much* information. For instance, a man's experiences with a neighbor may be very inconsistent or he may have many alternatives. There is some evidence that we do not seek out complete information about all of our alternatives before we act. Instead, we respond after finding an alternative that is "good enough" — one that simply meets our current needs or, even better, one that offers a greater profit than did a previous choice (Janis and Mann, 1977).

Sometimes, we have *inaccurate* information about our own and others' dependencies. As we have emphasized, it is not so much actual resources that count in human affairs as people's *beliefs* about these resources, particularly their beliefs regarding the availability of resources and the willingness of various parties to commit them to the encounter. Consequently, the *appearance of power* can be as useful as the real thing. Each party, in order to get the other to act in accordance with her or his wishes, may attempt to create a self-image (impression management) and an image of the other (altercasting). Some of these impressions may be inaccurate.

If we have several opportunities to engage in exchange we may not always choose the best or better alternative. Instead, research suggests, that we choose our partners in *proportion* to the frequency with which they have rewarded us in the past (Hamblin, 1979; Rachlin et al., 1986; Gray and Tallman, 1987). In other words, we may alternate the targets of our power attempts, targeting the best alternative more often than the next best alternative.

Profits are probably not a simple function of subtracting the value of costs from the value of rewards. Some evidence suggests that costs are a more important factor than rewards in determining choices (Gray and Tallman, 1987; Lopes, 1987). And some consideration has to be given to the *likelihood*, or probability, of the reward and cost in addition to their value. A person may have a good idea that the target *can* comply with his or her directive, but what is the likelihood that the target *will?* In order to estimate this, the person might take the target's perspective, through role-taking. But we do not all respond to the same likelihood in the same manner. Some of us are more willing to pursue a course of action even though the likelihood of its success is very low. Our experiences can actually teach us to take (or not take) risks (Osborn and Jackson, 1988; Larrick, Morgan, and Nisbitt, 1990; Thaler and Johnson, 1990).

Finally, a choice may also entail "irrational" aspects. One of the more common irrational aspects involves the use of, and reaction to, coercion. A source may use coercion for the personal satisfaction it provides, as when she or he feels a good deal of hostility toward the target. Or the source may feel that the use of coercion demonstrates "toughness" or "manliness."

POWER STRATEGIES IN DIFFERENT CONTEXTS

The *power structure* consists of the resources controlled by the source and target. The actual *uses* of resources in the source's attempts to change the target's behavior (as well as the target's efforts to resist) are referred to as *power strategies*. These strategies may differ in terms of the different resources involved — reward, informational, normative, and so on. In this section, we will consider the use of power strategies in three different contexts: laboratory experiments, families, and formal organizations. Our focus will be on how the various contexts affect our choice of power strategies

(Cody, McLaughlin, and Schneider, 1981; O'Hair, Cody, and O'Hair, 1991).

Power in Laboratory Experiments

Let's begin by looking at some laboratory experiments of power strategies involving social contingencies that were conducted by social psychologist Linda Molm (1990). Social contingency strategies apply reward or coercive resources *after* the target behaves. A source can use a social contingency strategy *only* if the target first performs the intended behavior. For example, a child must say "Da-Da" at least once before the parent can establish a contingency between the utterance and their hugs. You must express one opinion before your professor can institute a contingency between your expression of opinion and her or his compliments. In Molm's experiments each subject could make his or her rewarding of the other (that is, giving the other money) contingent on the other's having given the subject money previously. Subjects could use punishment (taking money away) contingently as well.

Molm's results indicate that the power structure is only weakly related to the use of social contingency strategies, whether the strategies involve reward or punishment (coercion). In other words, although people who have access to the most resources are, structurally, in the best position to use social contingencies to alter another's behavior to their advantage, they *do not always* do so.

Molm offers two explanations for this "discrepancy" between structural power and power use. First, those in advantage in the power structure may not be aware of their power advantage, or they may not know how to use the opportunities it provides to establish social contingencies. These are things that must be *learned*. Second, those with an advantage in the power structure may not have to actually use their resources (through social contingencies) to achieve the target's compliance (the power outcome). The disadvantaged target may accurately analyze the power structure and decide that his or her best alternative is to comply with the source's directives. And this may occur without the source's applying social contingency strategies. As a result, the advantaged source gains the target's compliance without expending resources and, instead, can "bank" the resources or use them to gain compliance from other targets. On the other hand, the disadvantaged target must strategically use his or her limited resources to compensate for the source's power structure advantage. A social contingency strategy may be the target's only method of achieving a degree of power, even though, as Molm's experiment shows, it does not guarantee success.

Molm and her colleague, Mark Hedley (1992), also address the question of whether men or women with *equivalent power* use social contingencies differently. The results of their experiments show that when men and women with the same level of power are compared, there are few differences in their use of contingencies as a power strategy. While there may be an association between gender and the use of power strategies in many situations in real life, the researchers conclude that these differences are probably due to structural differences — differences in the positions men and women hold and the power structure associated with these positions — not to gender per se.

Power in Families

Another setting in which social psychologists have studied power is the family. The power structure of the family is partly based on normative resources. In a **patriarchal power structure**, the husband/father has the normative resources. If the wife/mother has the claim to the normative resources, the family has a **matriarchal power structure**. State laws are the source of some of the normative power in families. Not so long ago in the United States, husbands were given very comprehensive power over their wives (and the law held husbands responsible for their wives' deviant conduct). Even today, vestiges of this very pervasive right still remain. For example, husbands, by law, have the right to decide where the family will live. A wife is legally required to follow her husband if he moves; otherwise, she is considered to have deserted him, as she is if *she* moves and her husband refuses to follow. Laws also give parents power over their children, allowing parents to use most resources, except those that are considered abusive.

Marital power. The power structure of spouses includes not only normative resources, of course, but others as well. For example, some studies suggest that white-collar husbands have more power than blue-collar husbands, even though white-collar husbands espouse a more egalitarian relationship than their blue-collar counterparts (Blood and Wolfe, 1960; Gillespie, 1971). The explanation for this finding is that white-collar husbands have higher occupational status and education — more resources. When wives are employed, they too have more power (Lee and Peterson, 1983; Szinovacz, 1987; Blumstein and Schwartz, 1991; White, 1991). And the higher their incomes and ownership of property, the greater their power.

One of the criticisms of this research is its narrow focus on economic resources. Some researchers have argued, for example, that although women's power may not be the same as men's power, which tends to be primarily economic and normative, women do, in fact, have a great deal of power in the family context (Kranichfeld, 1987). According to this argument, women's power is based on their roles as "nurturers and kinkeepers." Their power is of "low visibility" but is very fundamental and pervasive in that it largely determines family cohesion and socialization.

This is the marital power structure, but what about the actual use of power strategies? Sociologist Judith Howard and her colleagues (Howard, Blumstein, and Schwartz, 1986) studied the power strategies used by partners in three types of couples: ninety-eight heterosexual married couples and cohabitors, seventy-five male homosexual couples, and sixty-two lesbian couples, all in the Seattle, San Francisco, and New York City areas. During interviews, respondents were asked: "When your partner wants you to do something you do not want to do, how often does [he or she] do each of the following?" Respondents answered using a 9-point scale from "always" to "never" for numerous strategies the researchers had selected from prior studies of intimate couples.

Through a statistical analysis of the responses, the researchers organized twenty-one strategies into six categories, (see Table 13-1). In terms of the resource categories we discussed in the first section of the chapter, three of the researchers' categories can be viewed as relying largely on coercive resources—bullying, supplication, and disengagement. Manipulation strategies involve the use of reward resources, while bargaining strategies involve a combination of reward and informational resources. Autocratic strategies combine expert and normative resources.

The researchers examined associations between the use of these power strategies and various characteristics of the partners involved. They were particularly interested in whether sex had an effect on the choice of power strategies—either the sex of the source, the sex of the target, or the combined sexes of the partners (that is, male and female in heterosexual couples, two gay males, or two lesbian women). The study indicated that

sexual orientation had *no* effect on the choice of power strategies. Homosexual and heterosexual partners used the various strategies with about equal frequencies.

When the researchers examined the effect of the *sex of the source*, they found only one difference between men and women: men used disengagement more often. The *sex of the target* had the greatest effect on the choice of power strategies. The respondents, both men and women, used manipulation and supplication strategies more often on male partners than on female partners.

In addition, the findings indicated that the use of manipulation and supplication strategies was influenced by other characteristics of the targets. Respondents who had relatively higher incomes or greater physical attractiveness than their partners were more likely to be the targets of their partners' manipulation and/or supplication strategies. This result is somewhat surprising. If we assume that being male, having a higher income, and being more physically attractive represent structural advantages in a relationship, we might expect that the partner with these advantages would be the more likely *source* of power attempts. But this study suggests that the structurally ad-

---

TABLE 13-1   POWER STRATEGIES AMONG INTIMATE COUPLES

Manipulation strategies:	Supplication strategies:
Flattery	Pleading
Behaving seductively	Crying
Reminding of past favors	Acting ill
Dropping hints	Acting helpless
Bullying strategies:	Autocratic strategies:
Making threats	Insisting
Insulting	Claiming great knowledge
Being violent	Asserting authority
Ridiculing	
Disengagement strategies:	Bargaining strategies:
Sulking	Reasoning
Try to make feel guilty	Offering to compromise
Leaving the scene	Offering a trade-off

Source: Adapted from Judith A. Howard, Philip Blumstein, and Pepper Schwartz, "Sex, Power, and Influence Tactics in Intimate Relationships," *Journal of Personality and Social Psychology,* vol. 51, 1986, Table 1, p. 105.

Researchers have found gender differences in the use of power strategies. Men tend to use disengagement more frequently than women do. Both men and women use manipulation and supplication more often on male partners than on female partners.

vantaged partner is more likely to be the target of power attempts — at least, those involving manipulation and supplication — by the disadvantaged partner. This finding is similar to those of Molm's laboratory experiments, which indicated that the structurally disadvantaged (more dependent) partner used power strategies more often than did the advantaged (less dependent) partner.

So how might we explain these results? Consider this: Being disadvantaged in a relationship does not mean that one does not attempt to change the partner's behavior. But a "weak" partner will use only "weak" strategies. Compared

with bullying (insults and violence) and autocratic strategies (insisting and asserting authority), manipulation (flattery) and supplication (crying) are weaker strategies — strategies that rely heavily on impression management and altercasting. The use of "strong" strategies, such as bullying, might threaten the relationship on which the disadvantaged partner is more dependent.

On the other hand, the advantaged partner may not need to use special power strategies in order to influence the behavior of the disadvantaged partner. In exchange terms, the advantaged partner derives power primarily from being less dependent on the relationship. Alternative relationships are more available to this partner. The less dependent partner doesn't have to look far for a power strategy; the *implicit* threat to leave the relationship is a powerful resource. The more dependent partner perceives this threat and tries to please the advantaged partner by anticipating or quickly complying with his or her requests.

Parental power. The power relations between parents and their offspring have also been a subject of social psychological attention. Psychologist Donna Baumrind studied many parent-child relationships and identified three broad styles of parenting that are distinguished partly in terms of the resources the parents use to control their children's behavior, in other words, in terms of the power strategies they employ. In the **permissive** style the parents rely largely on reasoning and explanations — informational resources — to persuade their children to behave in a certain manner (Baumrind, 1971; LeMasters and Defrain, 1989). The focus is on providing the children with information (particularly the reasons for doing one thing as opposed to another) but allowing the children to make their own decisions. Parents using this style tend not to use other resources to impose adult control. An alternative parenting style is **authoritarian**. Parents using this style typically require strict obedience and rely on a combination of normative, reward, and coercive resources. Children are told what to do without extensive explanation. Instead, reasons tend to be of the "because I told you to" or "because if you don't, you're grounded" variety. A third parenting style is **authoritative**. Parents using this style rely on a combination of expert, informational, reward, and coercive resources. Unlike the authoritarian parent, who requires unquestioning obedience to the adult authority, the authoritative parent takes into account the child's explanation for noncompliance. Coercion may be used to exert adult control if other strategies are unsuccessful, but when it is, the parents also explain to the child why he or she is being punished.

Most research suggests that the authoritative style, when used consistently, is the most effective (Baumrind, 1971; McDonald, 1977; Dornbusch et al., 1987; Coombs and Landsverk, 1988; Dishion, Reid, and Patterson, 1988; Paikoff, Collins, and Laursen, 1988; Henry, Wilson, and Peterson, 1989). It is interesting to note that coercion is part of both the authoritarian and the authoritative styles. As part of the authoritarian style, research suggests, coercion is not particularly effective in the long run. Frequent use of coercive strategies may diminish the parents' personal resources. Children just try to avoid parents who use this style. But as part of the authoritative style, coercion's potentially negative effects appear to be canceled by other resources. Research suggests that when occasional punishment is combined with rewards from an emotionally close parent, its effects are not so negative.

Personal resources, some researchers argue, comprise the crucial ingredient to successful parental strategies (Gecas and Seff, 1991). Parents whose children perceive them as following their own advice, for example, are particularly influential (Schumm et al., 1986). The emotional bonds between parents and children encourage children to model their behavior after that of the parents (Lueptow, 1980; Smith and Self, 1980; Korman, 1983). Research has focused on the significance of the close contact with and nurturing by the parent to develop the emotional bonds that make modeling effective (Ainsworth, 1973; Steinberg, 1987).

The establishment of emotional bonds and personal resources is especially significant when children become adolescents. It is at this point that the "battle" of control and autonomy (depending on whose perspective you take) starts in earnest. Some parents try to maintain at least partial control over most of the behaviors they have controlled in the past, including general appearance and demeanor. Others "fall back" and defend their control over only what they consider to be the most important aspects of the adolescent's behavior, such as school performance, drug use, premarital sex, and delinquency. Parental control over adolescent behavior is usually diminished because of teenagers' access to alternative sources of some important resources. For example, many teenagers have part-time jobs, which give them an alternative source of money, and strong peer groups may provide teenagers with an alternative source of emotional support. Therefore, the amount of parental control hinges on the type of resources still available to parents.

Studies have found that the choice of parenting strategies is related to several factors. First, parents choose strategies according to their *effectiveness*, continuing to use strategies that work and abandoning those that don't (Marwell and Schmitt, 1969). Parents learn that to be effective their strategies may have to change with the circumstances, such as the child's level of development, the locale, and the specific behavior they are trying to influence. For example, strategies which work with a very young child may not work when she gets older; strategies which work at home may not work at the grocery store (where there's a larger audience) or at grandma's house (where the child more often gets his way); and strategies that are successful in getting the child to brush her teeth may not keep her from hitting her playmates. Second, parents' choices of strategies are affected by *family structure*. In the period immediately following divorce, for example, many custodial mothers become punitive, using coercion to attempt to control their children in the father's absence. This strategy is often ineffective and may result in a "reciprocal aggravation cycle" (Peterson and Cleminshaw, 1980). The punishment doesn't produce the behavior the mother desires, so she punishes again, and so on. In response to the ineffectiveness of the coercive parenting strategy, many single mothers eventually adopt a permissive parenting style (Dornbusch et al., 1987).

As we noted in Chapter 3, "Socialization over the Life Course," some researchers suggest that social class differences in parenting styles are a result of differences in the kinds of jobs held by parents (Kohn and Schooler, 1969; Ellis, Lee, and Petersen, 1978). Lower-class parents tend to have jobs that are closely supervised, in which control is a result of reward and coercion more than of information and persuasion. Middle-class parents more often confront the opposite situation. Thus, parents use the style at home that they experience on their jobs.

Power of children. Children, too, have power, but social psychologists have given little attention to it. Power in the parent-offspring relationship is reciprocal. Not only do children have resources that enable them to resist their parents' attempts to influence them (autonomy), but they also have resources that provide them with some control

over the behavior of their parents. For example, a little girl may resist her parents' attempts to get her to stop sucking her thumb by crying whenever they even mention the topic, or a little boy may get a parent to buy him a toy by having a tantrum in the toy store. Parents tend to have control over more domains of their children's behavior than vice versa, creating a domain imbalance that favors the parents.

One study of sixth-, ninth-, and twelfth-graders and their parents (Cowan, Drinkard, and McGavin, 1984) found that children used more "indirect," or weak, strategies such as flattering, sulking, and crying in their attempts to influence their parents. This reflected, the researchers argue, the children's greater dependence in the parent-child relationship. In their interactions with same-sex peers—which the researchers assumed were characterized by more balanced dependencies—the children used more "direct," or strong, strategies such as asking, demanding, arguing, threatening, and engaging in physical violence.

Siblings also attempt to control one another's conduct. Limited research suggests that the resources used by one sibling to control another

In their interactions with same-sex peers — which are characterized by more balanced dependencies — children use more "direct," or strong, strategies such as asking, demanding, arguing, threatening, and engaging in physical violence.

sibling are related to both sex and birth order (Sutton-Smith and Rosenberg, 1970; Haefner, Metts, and Wartella, 1989). For example, firstborns, particularly females, are frequently appointed as "second in command" by their parents. To achieve control of their younger siblings' behavior, older sisters rely principally on their designated authority and reasoning (normative and informational resources). Should this fail, they threaten "to tell mother" — a kind of indirect coercion. Older males tend to use more physical attacks (direct forms of coercion). Younger siblings rely more on psychological coercion, such as evoking guilt or obligations and threatening to cry. Perhaps due to their smaller size and physical strength, younger siblings' physical attacks are usually a form of sabotage, in which the younger sib damages or hides the property of the older sib. Very few studies have looked at sibling power, so social psychologists have much to learn about the power strategies of children.

Power in Organizations

Social psychologists have given considerable attention to power in formal organizations. One important feature of such organizations is their specification of normative resources. Organizational rules specify (though sometimes unclearly) both the resources available to each position holder and the domains of behavior that he or she can legitimately control. For example, a supervisor's power may apply only to the domain of his employees' productivity and not to the domains involving their physical appearance, religious practices, or taste in music. (For employees in higher levels of an organization or in positions directly involving the public, the number and variety of domains regulated by the organization tend to increase.) The supervisor customarily has authority over only the on-the-job behaviors of the employees. Of course, even on the job, employees may try to keep some of their work behavior beyond the eyes of the supervisor. The resources available to the supervisor may include all forms except the most intimate of rewards or the most physical of punishments.

Effects of power structure on power outcomes. Are normative resources the most important aspect of the organization's power structure when it comes to actually influencing employees' behavior? Let's examine the results of one study that looked at this question *from the point of view of the employees* (Yukl and Falbe, 1991). The study involved 195 employees of 3 companies: a pharmaceutical company, a chemical and manufacturing company, and a financial services company. The employees were asked questions about their managers and about their peers. They were given descriptions of several kinds of resources and were asked how important each was in determining the influence of their managers and peers on their work. Here are the descriptions used by the researchers (the resource labels are our own):

- Can do things to help you get ahead in your organization (reward resource)
- Could get you into trouble by complaining to management about you (coercive resource)
- Has expertise to make good decisions about the work (expert resource)
- Has information you need to do your job effectively (expert resource)
- Has ability to use facts and logic to present a persuasive case (informational resource)
- Has personal qualities that make him or her easy to like (personal resource)
- Has an attitude of enthusiasm and optimism that is contagious (personal resource)
- Has authority to give you tasks or assignments (normative resource)

The employees reported that the most important resource affecting the influence of *their managers* was the manager's normative resources — the authority to give tasks and assignments. On the other hand, the two resources of *least* importance for the manager's influence were (1) personal resources — an attitude of enthusiasm and optimism that is contagious and (2) expert resources — information needed to do the work effectively. In the view of most employees, their managers are not experts in terms of knowing the employee's job as well as or better than the employee does. The employees' reports of their *peers'* influence on their work were quite different. The most important resource among peers was a personal resource — personal qualities making the peer easy to like. The least important were reward, coercive, and normative resources.

Supervisors' power strategies. But what about the actual use of these resources? What factors influence the particular power strategies employed by supervisors in organizations? Researchers have observed that supervisors are economical. If the employee can be counted on to do her or his job without the "expenditure" of the supervisor's resources, the supervisor will not use *any* resource to sustain this compliance (Kipnis, 1976). This is another case in which the *less* dependent person does not have to use *explicit* power strategies to gain the compliance of the more dependent person. If the supervisor suspects that the worker's continued compliance is in doubt, the supervisor will often use reward resources to strengthen the compliance (Kipnis, 1976).

A supervisor will most often rely on normative resources to change a worker's behavior, unless conditions call for the use of an alternative resource. One of the major conditions affecting a supervisor's choice of alternative resources is his or her perception of the cause of the worker's unsatisfactory performance (attribution). If the supervisor attributes the worker's unsatisfactory performance to a lack of motivation, he or she will most likely use *informational resources* in attempting to improve the performance (Kipnis, 1974). If the supervisor attributes the unsatisfactory performance to incompetence, he or she will probably use *expert resources*, concentrating on training the worker.

If the supervisor perceives that the worker is deliberately rejecting orders (and therefore questioning the authority of the supervisor or even the organization), he or she will attribute the worker's insubordination to a willful, voluntary resistance

(poor attitude). As a result, the supervisor might use *coercion* to change the behavior of the non-compliant worker. In this situation, the supervisor might also provide rewards to compliant workers who are present (Goodstadt and Kipnis, 1970; Goodstadt and Hjelle, 1973; Kipnis, 1984).

Effects of supervisors' power strategies on power outcomes. Which types of resources are likely to be *most effective* for the supervisors? It seems that the most effective are *expert* and *personal* resources, which tend to be positively associated with employees' job performance, satisfaction with their work, and satisfaction with their supervisors (Rahim, 1989). A supervisor's expert power might come from previous personal experience in the positions that she or he now supervises. How does a supervisor obtain personal resources? One way to do this is by *not* using official normative resources. The supervisor's position gives her or him the right to enforce some company rules that are not directly related to production (e.g., those pertaining to talking among co-workers, length of breaks, arriving late or leaving early, smoking, tidiness, nonbusiness phone calls, and dress). By not exercising the authority to enforce some of these rules, the supervisor may gain the obligation and perhaps the appreciation of the employees and thus may become better liked — a personal resource (Blau, 1964). However, supervisors using this strategy must be careful not to create the impression that they are lax, irresponsible, or easily taken advantage of.

Supervisors' use of *coercive* and *normative* resources is frequently associated with low employee performance and greater dissatisfaction (Podsakoff and Schriesheim, 1985; McGee, Goodson, and Cashman, 1987). A disadvantage of coercion is that once a supervisor has employed it, her or his subsequent efforts to use other resources (e.g., informational resources) will be less effective (Kipnis, 1976; Kipnis and Schmidt, 1985). When employees are equally or more highly educated or skilled than their supervisor, almost any resource the supervisor uses will be *ineffective* (Abdalla, 1987). (Before reading further, look at the Stu-

---

STUDENT OBSERVATION

Coercive Resources and Power Outcomes

My supervisor at work provides an excellent example of a manager whose power is due to his coercive resources. Everyone at the hotel listens to him and obeys him because they know that he can punish them, either by firing them or by reducing the hours they are scheduled to work. I believe that he has to resort to coercive resources because he is lacking in other areas. He rarely uses reward resources, as he seems to not believe in giving raises. He is low in expert resources because he very often contradicts himself and loses much of his credibility. The employees don't like the manager very much, but he has power over them in the form of the ability to punish them. This tends to make the employees dissatisfied with their work, and performance levels are low. This is one reason that our turnover rate is so high. I have seen other work environments, and this is the only one I've experienced in which power is based on coercive resources. It has an obvious effect on the employees, and the company's morale is very low. People do not take much pride in their work, and are quick to move to new opportunities.

---

dent Observation: "Coercive Resources and Power Outcomes.")

Subordinates' power strategies.   Subordinates can be sources as well as targets of power. Since we have concentrated thus far on the supervisor as the source, let's now consider a study that focused on the subordinate as the source and the supervisor as the target (Schriesheim and Hinkin, 1990). Student, clerical, and secretarial workers at a Southern university were administered a questionnaire asking them to indicate the tactics they used to influence their bosses. The analysis of their responses revealed eight distinct tactics. The following list identifies the tactics and presents a representative behavior of each one:

- *Exchange of benefits:* "Offered an exchange (e.g., if you do this for me, I'll do something for you)." (reward resource)
- *Ingratiation:* "Acted in a friendly manner prior to asking for what I wanted." (reward resource)
- *Assertiveness:* "Expressed my anger verbally." (coercive resource)
- *Sanction:* "Threatened to give him or her an unfavorable performance evaluation." (coercive resource)

- *Blocking:* "Threatened to stop work." (coercive resource)
- *Rationality:* "Explained the reasons for my request." (informational resource)
- *Upward appeal:* "Made a formal appeal to higher levels to back up my request." (normative resource)
- *Coalitions:* "Mobilized other people in the organization to help me influence him or her." (normative resource)

Although this study does not tell us how effective these strategies are in influencing supervisors' behavior, it does show that subordinates are active power users. In some ways, the power strategies subordinates use on supervisors are different from those used by supervisors on subordinates. For one thing, subordinates do not use coercive strategies (assertiveness or sanctions) as often as supervisors do (Kipnis, Schmidt, and Wilkinson, 1980). Also, they do not use personal strategies (attraction and modeling) at all. And they use normative strategies that may be different from the normative strategies used by supervisors. They appeal to someone "over the supervisor's head" or create an apparent consensus by mobilizing a coalition of other organization members who share their views.

POWER OUTCOMES

So what will be the outcome of a particular power structure and particular power strategies? Will the target comply with the source's directive?

Conversion

Some resources are more effective at bringing about *immediate* compliance; others are better at producing *long-term* compliance — sometimes referred to as **conversion**, or **internalization** — a process in which the target adopts the source's directives as his or her own. Social psychologists believe that, in general, informational resources are not the most effective method for achieving immediate compliance, particularly when considerable resistance is involved (Petty and Cacioppo, 1986). This is because informational resources must meet the resistance of the target's current attitudes and behaviors head-on, taking "the central route." The information must be compelling enough to overcome the target's inattention, lack of involvement, incomprehension, and denial. Other resources are more effective at achieving immediate compliance because they involve less reorganization of the target's attitudes. Most do not elicit a lot of issue-related thinking; they take a "peripheral route." They require only that the target recognize the symbols linking the source with the resource: dad has to be associated with money; the professor has to be associated with grades.

On the other hand, if informational resources *are* successful in overcoming a target's attitudes (your professor's lectures converted you to a political liberal), the resulting compliance is more likely to persist over time. The information becomes part of the target's revised attitude. The target will continue to comply because the ongoing compliance is consistent with (supported by) his or her new attitude.

Inoculation

The target's attitude may also provide resistance to subsequent social pressures to change his or her conduct. One key to the target's future compliance is how he or she processes counterarguments. Thus, when stating a case for a particular position the original source of information may present some of "what the other side thinks." For example, a mother may tell her teenage daughter, "Your boyfriend is going to put pressure on you to have sex. He's going to tell you it is just another expression of love. But here is what's wrong with this kind of argument. . . ." Recent antidrug ads aimed at young children portray a father and son role-playing a dealer-child interaction. The father, pretending to be a dealer, gives his son the arguments a dealer might present: "Try it, I won't charge you this time," or "What's the matter? Are you scared?" The child "just says 'no'" and is praised by his father for handling the situation correctly.

When a source provides counterarguments intended to influence a target to resist subsequent social pressure to change, social psychologists say the source is using **inoculation**. The term suggests that such situations are similar to the medical procedure of exposing the body to a weakened form of a disease, enabling it to resist a stronger form.

Future Social Pressure

When resources other than informational ones are used to establish compliance, the continuation of compliance is more dependent on the *consistency* of future social pressures. Continued compliance is more likely if the original source is present to continue her or his reward and punishment of the target's conduct or if the source has lieutenants or collaborators to consistently perform the rewards and punishments (or informers to report the target's conduct).

If the source or her or his representatives are not present, continued compliance is dependent on the target's being in an environment where new social pressures are consistent with compliance. For example, although rewards and punishments may produce the compliance of criminals while in prison, once they leave prison, they face the *in*consistent social pressures of a new environment that often does not sustain their compliance.

Denigration of the Target

The absence of power renders individuals vulnerable to the wishes and dictates of others, but the possession of power may present problems. Research by social psychologist David Kipnis (1984) shows that the use of power may lead to the *denigration of the target*. This may result whether the source is a dominant family member, an executive who manages a business, or a political leader who governs a nation.

Kipnis distinguished among three types of tactics: *soft tactics* — ingratiating, flattering, and pleading behaviors; *rational tactics* — explaining, discussing, and compromising behaviors; and *strong tactics* — ordering, threatening, and angry behaviors. He found that the use of strong tactics was most likely to set in motion a train of events leading to the denigration of the target. First, when the tactics result in success, the source concludes that he or she controls the other person. When the same tactics succeed time after time, the notion is reinforced and strengthened. Second, the source begins to devalue the individuals he or she controls. By making other people do what he or she wants, the source attributes their behavior, no matter how well they do their tasks, to his or her orders rather than to their own drive and abilities. Consequently, the source does not give them credit for what they accomplish. Third, the source finds it increasingly easy to exploit the less powerful.

We can see, then, that power strategies differ not only in their long-term and short-term effectiveness in obtaining the target's compliance but also in their effects on the source's and target's perceptions of each other and of their relationship. In choosing power strategies, we should be aware of all these potential power outcomes.

REVISED POWER STRUCTURE

Power outcomes also have consequences for the ongoing power structure. A particular outcome may produce a redistribution of resources, increasing or decreasing dependencies and potentially changing the power balance. An initial power imbalance — in which one party is less dependent, and therefore more powerful, than the other — can result in the redistribution of "welfare" and power.

The social power of individuals, simultaneously exercised in an exchange, usually comes at some cost to *each* party, but the costs may be greater to the less powerful party. Compliance may cost the less powerful person money, labor, recreation opportunities, social status, self-esteem, or happiness. As a result, the person becomes "poorer." She or he will also become less powerful if compliance involves the expenditure of resources the person could have used in future power negotiations (e.g., money, labor, or social status). At the same time, the more powerful person experiences fewer losses and greater gains, thus contributing to his or her general welfare. This person's power may also increase if he or she can use some of these rewards as resources in future power negotiations. Thus, when parties of unequal power engage in exchange, the balance of power may become more and more disparate.

We have observed that power generally implies resistance (competition and possibly conflict) — clashing interests and social values. Within this context, power determines whose will shall prevail. More particularly, it provides an answer to the distributive question, "Who shall get what, when, and how?" (Lasswell, 1936). In other words, power largely decides who will be advantaged and who disadvantaged, who will be the haves and who the have-nots.

Power enables some individuals or groups to impose limits on the ability of others to compete and negotiate; one party can screen others off from access to knowledge, skills, and resources. In brief, some individuals or groups can control the flow of good things to themselves by continuously imposing their definitions of the situation in the arena of social interaction. They define what is possible, what is rational, what is real, and what is right. Power also allows some individuals or groups to make their advantage self-perpetuating.

Thus advantage becomes hereditary in fact, if not by law. Even when positions are theoretically open to all on the basis of merit (when academic degrees, scientific training, and special aptitudes as measured by standardized tests are the qualifications for offices), some people have a head start in the race for the good things. The disadvantaged seldom possess the resources for meeting the expense of long preparation or the connections and kinship that set them promptly on the right road. Thus many members of minority groups have come to realize that equality of opportunity does not produce equality of results. This will be the topic of Chapter 14, "Inequality and Discrimination."

Summary

1. Social power is a process of social interaction in which one party (the source) produces intended changes in another party's (the target's) attitudes or behavior, even in the face of the target's resistance. The process of social power involves four aspects: (1) the power structure — the control of valuable resources by source and target; (2) power strategies — the use of these resources in the source's attempts to change the target's behavior and the target's efforts to resist; (3) power outcomes — the target's eventual compliance, partial compliance, noncompliance, or reactance; and (4) the revised power structure — the resulting redistribution of resources.

2. The power structure is based on the control of valuable resources by the source and target. Resources may be organized into six classes: reward, coercive, expert, informational, personal, and normative.

3. Social exchange theory draws our attention to bilateral social power — social interaction in which both parties have some capacity to produce changes in each other's behavior. What distinguishes one power structure from another is the strength and balance of the dependencies of the individuals involved.

4. Power strategies are the actual uses of resources in the source's attempts to change the target's behavior (as well as the target's efforts to resist). Research found that the likelihood of using power strategies is greater for the structurally disadvantaged (more dependent) person than for the advantaged (less dependent) person. However, the disadvantaged person most often uses "weak" strategies involving impression management and altercasting rather than "strong" strategies such as threats or violence.

5. Different strategies have different outcomes. Some are more effective at bringing about immediate compliance (e.g., using reward and coercive resources); other are more effective at achieving long-term compliance (e.g., using informational resources). Although the use of reward and coercive resources may bring about immediate compliance, it may lead to the source's denigration of the target. Power outcomes also may have consequences for the ongoing power structure. An initially imbalanced power structure can cause a redistribution of resources, resulting in a revised power structure that is even more imbalanced.

PART FOUR

THE STRUGGLE
OVER SOCIAL
DEFINITIONS

CHAPTER 14

INEQUALITY AND DISCRIMINATION: THE EXAMPLES OF RACISM AND SEXISM

*U*nfortunately, discrimination is a topic with which I am very familiar. I am a black female. When I was in elementary school, my family moved to a very conservative, rich neighborhood in Connecticut. We were the only black family living in the neighborhood, and apparently some of the other families were not happy about our being there. At school, the kids would call my brother and me "nigger." One morning my family woke up to find the word "nigger" written on both of the garage doors to our house and crosses painted on the lower-story windows. This incident upset my mother greatly. She was afraid, but at the same time she did not want to "give in" and crumble under pressure when white people tried to make things difficult for us because we were black.

My being here at Carolina is the result of discrimination of sorts. When I applied to UNC my grades were not great, but I did have some athletic ability. I had no extracurricular activities because I spent all my time in sports practice. I was not admitted when I initially applied. Instead, I was "wait listed." When I found this out, I wrote back to admissions to tell them that my stepmother just won the distinguished alumni award the previous year and would love for me to be a part of Carolina. (I wrote a lot of baloney.) I was accepted a week later. The next year, my little sister,

Gael, applied to Carolina. (You need to know that Gael is white. I'm half white and half black, which at most schools counts as black.) Gael's SAT's were much better than mine and so were her grades. She had all A's and B's in honors courses. She also had a list a mile long of impressive extracurricular activities. And she wasn't admitted. Once I found out that Gael was turned down, I knew that I was admitted because I am black — I could help UNC's minority enrollment figures look better. I probably also was accepted at other good schools because I am black. I was glad when I was admitted to Carolina — I really wanted to come here — but at the same time it is definitely *not* fair. I think discrimination for or against someone because of their race or sex is ugly and wrong. Something must be done about it, and affirmative action is not the answer. I now feel that race should not even be included on college applications — to ensure that everyone's opportunity truly is equal.

I recently discovered an incident of what seems to be sex discrimination that surprised me. My fiancé works for a nearby daily paper. One of his co-workers has a master's degree from Harvard in journalism. Both she and my fiancé have been on the job, their first since graduating, for about a year. A while back, they were talking, and he discovered that their salaries were the same, even though she has a higher degree — he has only a bachelor's. Recently, the position of bureau chief came open, and he got the job. It surprised him that he got the promotion. He thought his co-worker would get it because their experience is the same and she has the higher degree. Of course, I do not know for sure why she was overlooked for the promotion, but I believe it was because she is a female. My fiancé agrees that she is not given the more serious assignments and therefore lacks some hard-core experience. It seems that even her extra two years of education are not helping her to be treated equally.

In Chapter 13, "Social Power: Behavior and Attitude Change," we discussed the process of social power. Whether the process entails one party trying to change the behavior of another or two parties trying to change each other's behavior, the outcome is affected by the power structure of the relationship — who has the control over resources and who is most dependent — as well as by the actual use of power strategies. Often, the exchange of resources affects the power structure, allowing one party to preserve a power advantage.

In this chapter, we will continue our discussion of social power, but with a particular focus on how people's membership in groups and social categories affects their social power. Resources and their associated power are distributed unequally among groups in the United States, as the student observations above indicate. Moreover, the norms and arrangements of our society operate to "institutionalize" inequality. They perpetuate the privileges of some social categories and the disadvantages of others.

Inequality in American Society

Some people have more resources and power than others. When social psychologists compare the resources possessed by different individuals in the United States, they frequently focus on resources affecting our capacity to earn a living — education, occupational prestige, and income. Their ranking of people on these bases is called **stratification**. A person's location in the stratification hierarchy is called his or her **socioeconomic status (SES)**.

A person's SES affects his or her **life chances** — opportunities to experience the good things in life, such as survival, health, justice, and happiness. For example, the lower a person's SES, the lower his or her life expectancy, that is, the greater the chance of infant mortality, or of death due to occupational hazard, or of a briefer life span. Lower SES is also positively related to higher rates of certain cancers and mental disorders, as well as to fewer visits to dentists (Goodman et al., 1983; National Center for Health Statistics, 1983; Findlay, 1986). In addition, the lower their SES, the more likely a couple are to divorce (Raschke, 1987). And the lower a person's SES, the greater his or her chances of either being a victim of a crime or being arrested, convicted, and given a longer sentence after conviction (Petersilia, 1985; Welch, Spohn, and Gruhl, 1985; Humphrey and Fogarty, 1987).

But the socioeconomic resources of education, occupational prestige, and income are not the only resources distinguishing individuals from one another. Power is also a function of other personal characteristics: age, sex, sexual orientation, race, religion, marital status, physical attributes, and mental capacities. These characteristics function as symbols for other resources. For example, being white and being male are power resources in American society because white males hold such a large proportion of power positions that many of us have come to associate these characteristics with power. It isn't necessary for us to believe that white males *should* have more power; it is only necessary that we believe they *do*. Such a belief would affect how we act toward a person in that social category. Similarly, old age can be a symbol of wisdom or of helplessness; youth, a symbol of health and vitality or of inexperience. In other words, our stereotypes of social categories attribute characteristics to members of these categories that may symbolize power resources. (See the Student Observations: "Social Identities as Power Resources" and the box "Unequal Justice.")

Characteristics such as race, sex, sexual orientation, and age not only are power resources in

STUDENT OBSERVATIONS

Social Identitites as Power Resources

As a woman, I am a fighter for equal rights in the labor force, home, and so on. This is why I am totally shocked by my recent behavior. I am a member of a campus organization that has been trying to earn money for a trip. One of our fund-raisers includes a sponsored T-shirt drive: we ask local businesses to contribute money in return for having their names displayed on the T-shirts. I devoted one day to visiting as many businesses in town as possible, and in each place I asked to see the manager. When the manager wasn't in, I simply asked, "When will *he* be back?" After a few times, I finally heard myself! I could not believe that *I* assumed the manager would be a male! I was infuriated with myself. I then realized how I have been brainwashed, or socialized, into automatically thinking that a male would be in charge of managing a business. This shows that the traditional stereotype of women as being in the lower ranks of the work force is still alive and well — even, unfortunately, among those of us who advocate equal rights.

I work at the planetarium on campus at night and on weekends, when it is staffed by students only. At these times, I am in charge of all the other students at the planetarium. Patrons often come in with questions, problems, or other concerns. The other day, a patron asked one of the other students a question that I would need to handle. The student pointed to where I was discussing something with another employee and told the patron, "Just ask that person in charge, over there." The patron walked over to us and promptly asked the other student (who was male) his question. The student worker told the patron that I would help him. The male patron looked surprised that I was in charge. Apparently, his stereotypes led him to assume that a male would be in charge and that females would be in subordinate positions.

their own right but may also affect our access to important socioeconomic resources. People of a particular age, sex, race, religion, or physical capacity may have greater access to higher levels of education, occupations of greater prestige, and higher incomes than their counterparts. Race and sex are master statuses, that is, statuses that affect our own attitudes and behavior as well as how others see and treat us, no matter what other social positions we may hold. Perhaps for this reason, they are the social categories to which social psychologists have devoted the most research. Consequently, the effects of race and sex on inequality (unequal access to socioeconomic resources) will be the focus of this chapter. When we discuss race, we will usually compare whites and African-Americans, to the exclusion of other racial and ethnic groups in American society. Again, this is because the preponderance of research is on whites and African-Americans.

Of course, inequality affects other social categories as well. During recent decades the Spanish-speaking population of the United States has grown substantially. In 1990 there were 22 million Hispanics in this country. Like African-Americans, they are underrepresented in high-skill, high-income jobs, and the poverty rate among Hispanics is three times the rate among non-Hispanic whites. Hispanics are far less likely than other Americans to complete high school or attend college. Their dropout rate is twice that of blacks and three times that of whites (U.S. Bureau of the Census, 1992*a*). Similarly, the nearly 2 million Native Americans living in the United States have the lowest per capita income and educational level, accompanied by the highest illiteracy and infant mortality rates, of any ethnic group in the country.

Even "model minorities" such as Asian-Americans, who have largely achieved upward mobility, experience some discrimination. Evidence suggests that despite their high level of academic success, they may encounter discrimination when applying to the nation's most prestigious univer-

UNEQUAL JUSTICE

RACE AND THE DEATH PENALTY

- Of the 144 executions since the 1976 reinstatement of the death penalty in the United States, only one white person has been executed for the killing of a black. This occurred in 1991.

- In those 144 killings, 86 percent of the victims were white, although roughly half of all murder victims in the United States are black.

- Of the 16,000 executions in U.S. history, only thirty cases involved a white sentenced for killing a black. (Smolowe, 1991: 68)

In many of the thirty-six states that have capital-punishment statutes, the decision concerning who shall live and who shall die often has disturbingly little to do with the seriousness of the crime (Smolowe, 1991). More pertinent factors commonly are the race of the victim and the competence of the defense counsel. Murderers of whites are four times as likely to receive the death penalty as murderers of blacks. The race of the defendant, many legal experts believe, also plays a role. Although only 12 percent of the U.S. population is black, blacks constitute 50 percent of death-row inmates.

Whether a person convicted of murder receives the death penalty depends on a number of discretionary stages: whether the prosecutor decides to seek the death penalty, whether the jury recommends it, and whether a judge gives it. In some parts of the United States, white district attorneys, white juries, and white judges make these decisions. When justice depends on such factors as the race of the victim and the race of the accused, justice is assuredly *not* equal.

DOES SEX AFFECT SENTENCING?

A common finding in studies of criminal court outcomes is a "sex effect," whereby women receive more lenient treatment than men (Daly, 1987*a*). Court officials also distinguish between "familied" and "nonfamilied" defendants. The court views familied defendants (either males or females with family responsibilities) to be more deserving of leniency than nonfamilied defendants. This is partly because court officials believe that familied defendants are constrained by the responsibilities they have for the welfare of others (Daly, 1987). It is also because jailing a familied defendant may entail the social costs of punishing innocent family members and placing a burden on society to support them.

Kathleen Daly (1987b) suggests that the greater leniency toward women in some sentencing decisions results from the sexes' different family roles. Women *care* for others, while men *provide* for others. Court officials associate more costs with removing the mother's caring from the family than with removing the father's economic support. Loss of economic support is more easily compensated for by state supports than is loss of caretaking. Thus women are accorded more leniency for being familied than are men.

Daly argues that the assertion that women are treated more leniently than men in the criminal courts is misleading. She suggests that the court views defendants not as individuals but as members of familial social groups. Class, race, and sex differences in treatment arise partly, she says, because the court considers the social costs of punishing familied dependents with caretaker or economic provider roles. She suggests that this raises legal, moral, and practical questions for the legal ideal of "equal treatment."

---

sities (Lindsey, 1987; Bunzel, 1988). After college, they are again discriminated against in the business world, as employers are reluctant to promote them to managerial positions (McLeod, 1986; J. Schwartz, 1987). We do not intend to imply that socioeconomic inequality based on these social identities is unimportant. Instead, we hope our thorough discussion of the effects of race and

sex will suggest to readers how similar social psychological processes might affect other social identities as well.

Our discussion will focus on the answers to three questions: (1) How are race and sex related to socioeconomic inequality? (2) Are the socioeconomic inequalities between African-Americans and whites and between males and females best explained by equity or discrimination? (3) What are Americans' attitudes toward the various remedies for discrimination that are being proposed or tried?

SOCIOECONOMIC INEQUALITY: RACE AND SEX DIFFERENCES

We'll begin with the questions: "How much socioeconomic inequality is there in the United States?" and "How are race and sex related to socioeconomic inequality?" We'll examine each of the three socioeconomic resources.

Education

The proportion of African-Americans twenty-five years or older who completed less than eight years of school is about twice that of whites. And the proportion of African-Americans with four or more years of college is only half that of whites. Among African-Americans, the median number of school years completed is the same for males and females (12.4 years). Among whites, there is only one significant sex difference: more males have completed four or more years of college than have females (25 percent versus 19 percent, respectively) (U.S. Bureau of the Census, 1992a).

Employment and Occupational Prestige

Fifty-five percent of black adults and 63 percent of white adults are employed (U.S. Bureau of the Census, 1992a). Most of this difference is attributable to the difference in employment among males. The difference between the percentages of employed white and African-American women is small, less than 1 percent. Yet the proportion of African-Americans who are unemployed (have no job but have made specific efforts to find one) is more than twice that of whites. The percentage of African-Americans not in the labor force (those who report that they are currently not looking for a job) is slightly higher than that of whites, due entirely to the difference among males (U.S. Bureau of the Census, 1992a).

Differences in employment status between the sexes are greater than those between the races. The percentage of employed females is lower than that of employed males, although the difference is greater among whites than among African-Americans. The proportion of females of both races not in the labor force (not seeking a job) is over 40 percent, reflecting societal norms that historically have prescribed that males should be the providers for their families and that females should care for the household and children (U.S. Bureau of the Census, 1992a).

Not only are the employment rates of African-Americans and females lower than those of their white or male counterparts, but blacks and women who work are overrepresented in lower-prestige jobs. Thus, while white males are overrepresented in jobs such as airline pilots, sales engineers, fire-fighting supervisors, and electrician supervisors, black males are disproportionately represented in jobs such as stevedores, garbage collectors, longshore equipment operators, and baggage porters. Similarly, white women are overrepresented in jobs such as dental hygienists, secretaries, dental assistants, and occupational therapists, while African-American women dominate such low-prestige occupations as private household workers, cooks, housekeepers, and welfare aides (National Committee on Pay Equity, 1987). Thus, compared with whites, blacks hold lower-prestige jobs. Similarly, compared with men, women hold lower-prestige jobs.

Income

Among Americans employed year-round and full-time during 1991, the median income for white workers was $26,502; for African-Americans, it was $20,823 (U.S. Bureau of the Census, 1992b). The ratio of the median incomes, or **earnings ratio**, of African-Americans to whites was .79. In other words, for every dollar earned by whites, African-Americans were paid 79 cents. The earnings ratio of women to men in 1991 was .70 — women made about 70 cents for each dollar earned by men. The income differentials between blacks and whites and between women and men are primarily attributable to the disproportionately high incomes of white males (U.S. Bureau of the Census, 1992a).

Let's stop for a moment to make sure you

understand the concept of earnings ratio. An earnings ratio gives the amount that one group earns relative to each dollar earned by another group. So, the *higher* the earnings ratio, the *more equal* are the incomes of the two groups. Social psychologists sometimes also refer to the earnings *gap* or income *difference* between two groups. The *larger* the gap or difference, the *smaller* the earnings ratio will be. Both concepts measure the relative incomes of groups but do so in different ways. In the examples above, we see that the earnings ratio of blacks compared with whites is slightly *higher* than the earnings ratio of women compared with men (.79 versus .70). Thus, the earnings gap between blacks and whites is slightly *smaller* than the gap between men and women.

Poverty

Clearly, some Americans are richer, and some are poorer, than others. But what is the relationship between this income gap and how people live? When we talk about "the poor," whom do we mean? The categories "poor" and "nonpoor" are socially defined. The official definition—the one used by government programs—is established by the federal government's Social Security Administration. The agency computes the cost of a basic nutritionally adequate diet for a family of a given size and then multiplies that figure by three, because research has found that poor people spend about one-third of their incomes on food. Anyone whose income falls below this figure is defined by the government as being "below the poverty level."

In 1990, one in ten white Americans fell below the poverty level, compared with one in three African-Americans. Nevertheless, even though the poverty rate for whites was lower than that for African-Americans, 65 percent of poor persons in 1990 were white because whites make up a larger

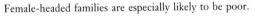
Female-headed families are especially likely to be poor.

proportion of the U.S. population. The poverty rate for children in 1990 was 15 percent among whites and 44 percent among African-Americans (U.S. Bureau of the Census, 1992a).

In addition, more women, both black and white, had incomes below the poverty level than did men (about 15 percent versus about 11 percent, respectively). The main source of this sex difference is single-parent families. Among female-headed single-parent families, the poverty rate was about 33 percent, while it was only about 12 percent among male-headed single-parent families (of which there are few). Female-headed families account for over half of all poor families in America (U.S. Bureau of the Census, 1991c).

This information reveals considerable inequality in the distribution of socioeconomic resources in the United States. Both race and sex affect the acquisition of socioeconomic resources. For each resource, whites as a group have "more" than African-Americans. And men as a group have "more" than women.

Inequality: Equity or Discrimination

Most Americans support income inequality (Kluegel and Smith, 1986). This is a reflection of the equity norm, which we discussed in Chapter 10, "Helping and Reward Exchange." The equity norm is a widely accepted distribution rule that is strongly associated with ideas of social justice and fairness in the United States (Ritzman and Tomaskovic-Devey, 1992). The gist of the norm is that rewards should be based on contributions: Those who contribute more are entitled to receive higher rewards. There is consistent strong evidence that in the United States support for the equity norm is quite strong among individuals of all social classes (Shepelak and Alwin, 1986; Shepelak, 1987). Other studies also suggest that, despite the strong acceptance of the equity norm, Americans are somewhat uneasy with the inequalities which currently exist in the United States (Hochschild, 1981; Della Fave, 1986a). For example, Jennifer Hochschild (1981) found that even

among those most strongly favoring equity, there was strong support for the notion that people who are poverty stricken should be helped. In this view, although rewards should, generally, be based on contributions, no one should be too poor to afford the necessities of life.

The important question, then, is not whether some individuals have higher SES than others. Americans approve of the general principle of socioeconomic inequality. Rather, the question of interest is whether the inequality is seen as fair or just. Our judgments about fairness seem to be affected by what we see as the *causes* of inequality.

CAUSES OF INEQUALITY

We have already noted that African-Americans and women, as groups, tend to have lower SES than white males. Americans disagree about whether this inequality is the result of *equity*— unequal rewards based on unequal contributions — or **discrimination** — actions which produce unequal outcomes for categories of people on the basis of *socially disapproved criteria*. Notice that according to our definition, whether an action resulting in unequal outcomes constitutes discrimination or not depends on whether the outcomes are based on socially *approved* or *disapproved* criteria. Discrimination is *socially defined*.

Equity

According to the equity explanation, compared with white males, a smaller proportion of African-Americans and females acquire the capabilities and qualifications for higher paying jobs. Economists call these acquired capabilities and qualifications **human capital**. Human capital explanations suggest that differences in incomes between the races and the sexes result from blacks' and females' having fewer qualifications and capabilities when compared with white males.

Research suggests that Americans view differences in human capital — such as years of education, or time, effort, and money invested in work — as legitimate bases for distributing outcomes. A 1980 national survey showed that a large majority of Americans believe that income differences *should* reflect differences in the type of job one holds (93 percent) and one's productivity on the job (83 percent) (Kluegel and Smith, 1986). On the other hand, only 27 percent of Americans feel that education should influence the incomes of people *with the same job*. These data suggest that Americans feel very strongly that pay should reflect the quality (productivity) and value (type of job) of job contributions. Even criteria that are normally associated with job performance, such as education, are not seen by most Americans as legitimate criteria for determining pay if other factors suggest that they do not affect the actual performance of workers. Thus, socially approved criteria for determining pay, according to American norms, are those which affect the *actual performance of workers*. Inequality based on such socially approved criteria would not, according to our definition, constitute discrimination.

Discrimination

An alternative explanation suggests that differences in the investment in human capital do not account for the inequality in incomes between the races and the sexes. Proponents of this view argue that even African-Americans and women *with the same human capital — the same capabilities and qualifications as their white or male counterparts —* have lower incomes. Thus, they conclude, race or sex directly — not human capital — is the cause of the income gap.

Americans' attitudes about basing income on such criteria as race and sex are reflected in U.S. laws. Laws currently make it illegal for employers to base the hiring or salaries of their employees on race or sex. The law recognizes such behavior as "job discrimination," suggesting that race and sex are *illegitimate* criteria for the distribution of income. The U.S. government has continued to broaden its definition of discrimination to include other illegal criteria for determining income (e.g., age and certain disabilities), as well as outcomes other than income (e.g., access to housing and public facilities). Federal and state laws generally indicate that Americans disapprove of using race

and sex as criteria on which employment, income, housing, and other opportunities and compensation are distributed.

It is important to note that to be considered discrimination, the differential treatment of persons based on their race or sex must be *externally* based — for example, caused by the employer's actions — and *not* due to choices made by the individuals themselves. If women apply only for low-paying jobs, for example, this is not considered to be job discrimination. However, as we shall discuss later in the chapter, the job choices of women and African-Americans may be influenced by prior socialization that constitutes discrimination because it operates to their disadvantage in later life.

CONFOUNDED CRITERIA: PERFORMANCE, RACE, AND SEX

It is clear that norms in our society strongly suggest that race and sex are illegitimate criteria for determining income and that productivity and performance are legitimate criteria. Yet a problem arises in applying these norms to everyday interactions. Sometimes it is very difficult to separate legitimate criteria from illegitimate criteria because they are associated with one another, either in statistical facts or in stereotypes held by Americans.

Statistical Facts

Legitimate and illegitimate criteria for income inequality may themselves be associated statistically. Staying in school longer to obtain advanced degrees is an example of investing in human capital because higher education provides people with the greater knowledge, skills, and credentials that qualify them for well-paying jobs. But the proportion of both African-Americans and women, as previously noted, who complete four or more years of college is smaller than the proportion of whites and males who do. This is a *statistical fact*. It does not mean that if you compare the college records of a particular African-American and a particular white, you will find that the white completed college while the African-

American did not. The same can be said for a comparison of a man and a woman. Nor does it mean that most whites have completed four or more years of college while most African-Americans have not. The statistical fact is that the proportion of African-Americans who complete four or more years of college is *smaller* than the proportion of whites who do.

Work experience is another kind of human capital that increases people's qualifications by adding to their job skills, expanding their network of clients and colleagues, and familiarizing them with related jobs so that they can organize and manage them. The job careers of a *greater proportion* of African-Americans than of white Americans traditionally have been characterized by frequent job changes punctuated by periods of unemployment or part-time employment. And, compared with men, a *greater proportion* of women either have not entered the labor force or, if they did, have left it, either temporarily or permanently, to raise children.

In short, there are important statistical differences between the races and sexes in human capital. *As groups*, African-Americans and females tend to have less education, fewer work hours, and fewer work years invested. There are other differences between groups that may confuse the distinction between legitimate and illegitimate criteria for treating members of groups differently. Take, for example, the use of physical size requirements as qualifications for certain jobs. Many police departments set minimum height requirements for police officers. People may not be barred from these jobs *explicitly* because of their race or sex, but the height requirement effectively bars many members of some groups — Asian-Americans and women — because they are, on average, shorter than white males.

In order to determine whether a particular action constitutes discrimination, we must discover whether the action is based on illegitimate or legitimate criteria. When the legitimate criteria — such as education, experience, or height — are statistically associated with the illegitimate criteria of race or sex, this can be difficult. We must determine, first, whether the criterion being applied is actually related to job performance. Whether a criterion such as height, or even work experience, is legitimate or illegitimate depends on whether, in the particular case being evaluated, the criterion is *actually related to job performance*. If not, the data discussed above suggest that most Americans would disapprove of the use of that criterion to determine pay. Second, even if the criterion in question *is* related to job performance in the case being evaluated, paying workers less because they are members of social categories that, statistically, are less qualified with respect to that criterion — are shorter or less well educated, for example — is discriminatory. To avoid discrimination, we must show that the *particular individuals* being evaluated fall short of what is considered to be acceptable on the criterion. In brief, it is not acceptable to base individual judgments on statistical associations.

Stereotypes

In Chapter 6, "Social Attitudes and Attributions," we noted that many people associate different characteristics with being African-American or white, male or female, and that they evaluate members of one group more positively than members of the other. We defined a **stereotype**, you may recall, as a schema of beliefs that attributes a set of characteristics to *most or all* members of a social identity. Although stereotypes may be necessary, we noted, they are not necessarily accurate. By definition, they are generalizations that ignore some potentially significant information — the fact that many members of a social identity do *not* conform to the stereotype. (See the Student Observations: "Stereotypes.")

Some of the characteristics included in our stereotypes of racial and sex identities may be related to our judgments about people's qualifications for specific jobs. For example, according to popular stereotypes, women are more emotional and gentle than men — too emotional to make major rational-economic decisions and too gentle to handle tough job situations. Similarly, African-Americans are believed to be less motivated and

STUDENT OBSERVATIONS

Stereotypes

While shopping for Christmas gifts during Thanksgiving break, I was asked by a clerk whether I was home from college. I said "yes," and she asked which school I attended. I told her "Carolina," and she asked, "East Carolina?" I said, "No. North Carolina," and she asked "State?" I finally got specific: "No. UNC–Chapel Hill. The Tarheels, you know." She looked shocked. I guess she thought a black female, like myself, could not get accepted at UNC. You can probably guess what she asked next: "Oh, are you an athlete?" I did not even dignify her question with an answer. I left the store. Later I felt terrible about how I handled the situation, but also for her. She obviously believes that the only black females at UNC are athletes. It's sad that even today, some people still view black women as lazy, dumb, pregnant dropouts. I was so embarrassed by the situation that I'm afraid I didn't respond in a way that might have changed the clerk's stereotype.

Last Saturday after work I was talking to Rita, one of my co-workers, about some of the other girls at work. Rita told me that one of the "relish girls" — young (fourteen- to sixteen-year-old) girls who pass the relish trays at the restaurant — had quit because she was pregnant. She made me guess which girl it was. My guesses were all young black girls, revealing my stereotype of young blacks. I never did guess the name of the girl who quit. She turned out to be white — the boss's fourteen-year-old daughter. My stereotype was so strong that I never would have guessed the correct name.

---

less committed than whites — too unmotivated or uncommitted to contribute to a high-quality product.

Job discrimination, as suggested earlier, occurs when equal access to jobs or to compensation is denied on the basis of characteristics of a person that are *unrelated* to job performance. Therefore, the key to determining if stereotypes cause discrimination is to establish whether the stereotypical characteristic attributed to someone (1) is really a characteristic of the person and (2) is relevant to job qualifications. To determine this, we must conduct a three-part analysis. First, we need to know whether the characteristic attributed to the social identity is actually descriptive of it. For example, are women really more emotional and less rational than men? If not, paying a woman less than a man because you *believe* women are more emotional and less rational would be discrimination.

Second, even if women are more emotional and less rational than men, before discrimination can be ruled out, we must know whether the *particular* woman in question is more emotional and less rational. Even if women in general are more emotional than men, the particular woman applying for a job may be very unemotional. If we deny an unemotional, rational woman a job because we *assume* she is emotional — simply because she is a woman and we believe women to be more emotional than men — then discrimination has occurred.

Third, even if the first two conditions are true — that is, women are generally more emotional than men, and the particular woman applying for a job is more emotional than the average man — denying her the job or paying her less than we pay men for the same job may still constitute discrimination. This is because for some jobs, one's emotionality is an irrelevant qualification. Does emotionality reduce a plumber's productivity, a doctor's competence, a police officer's effectiveness, the quality of a potter's wares?

This kind of mental analysis — in which an employer asks and answers all these questions before making a decision — often does not occur. (See the

Some of the characteristics included in our stereotypes of racial and sex identities may be related to our judgments about people's qualifications for specific jobs. For example, according to popular stereotypes, women are more emotional and gentle than men. Some employers conclude that these qualities make women unsuited to particular jobs.

box "Sex Discrimination: Does It Happen Only to *Other* Women?") Our stereotypes about social identities encourage us to make assumptions and uninformed judgments. We tend to assume that we know how a person *is* because we have mental schemas for *types* of people. We fit the particular person into a type and assume that he or she possesses certain characteristics.

In Chapter 6, we discussed the *ultimate attribution error* — our tendency to explain the successes of ingroup members and failures of outgroup members in terms of *internal causes* (causes having to do with the person) and to explain the failures of ingroup members and successes of outgroup members in terms of *external causes* (causes outside

the person's control). For example, Jessica is a member of the outgroup when Paul, who is making the judgment, uses different social identities to describe himself and Jessica. Because in our society positions of power are held primarily by white males, both African-Americans and females are outgroup members to the white males who generally make important decisions about jobs, raises, school admissions, and so on.

If the people in power positions — who tend to be white males — make the ultimate attribution error, they are likely to explain the failures of African-Americans and women in terms of negative characteristics of those social identities. Conversely, they are likely to see the successes of

SEX DISCRIMINATION: DOES IT HAPPEN ONLY TO *OTHER* WOMEN?

According to a recent review, a large number of experimental studies have demonstrated that a job applicant's sex — quite apart from qualifications — has an effect on hiring recommendations (Olian, Schwab, and Haberfeld, 1988). When this happens, men are favored. Could job discrimination happen to you, your wife, or your girlfriend?

One recent study suggests that it could. Female college graduates in business were found to earn less than their male counterparts in their first full-time jobs after graduation (Fuller and Schoenberger, 1991). This is in spite of the fact that, as a group, the women had higher academic achievement, more internship experience, and more sought-after college majors. Moreover, the salary gap between the men and women *widened* over time.

African-Americans and women as either (1) exceptions to the rule; (2) the result of a special advantage, such as affirmative action; or (3) the result of situational factors. This pattern of attributions reinforces negative stereotypes of, and discrimination toward, outgroup members.

AMERICANS' BELIEFS ABOUT DISCRIMINATION

So are income inequalities between the races and the sexes based on equity (differences in legitimate criteria that affect job performance) or on discrimination (illegitimate criteria)? Before we answer this question, let's examine what Americans *believe* the answer to be. In a 1991 survey, 40 percent of respondents said that they believe blacks' worse jobs, income, and housing are due mainly to discrimination (NORC, 1991). On the other hand, a 1989 survey found that 52 percent of blacks and 56 percent of whites agreed that "discrimination has unfairly held down blacks, but many of the problems that blacks in this country have today are brought on by blacks themselves" (ABC/*Washington Post*, 1989). Kluegel and Smith's (1986) national survey also provides insight into what Americans believe. The researchers asked respondents two questions about African-Americans and women. The first was, "How much discrimination do you feel there is against blacks and other minorities [women] in any areas of life that *limits* their chances to get ahead?" The second was, "How much preferen-

tial treatment for racial minorities [women] is there that *improves* their chances to get ahead?"

A majority of respondents believed that there is "some" discrimination against both racial minorities and women that limits their chances to get ahead and that there is "some" preferential treatment for both racial minorities and women that improves their chances to get ahead. Thus, these respondents use external attributions, at least partly, to explain *both* successes and failures. Only a small percentage of respondents felt that there is "just a little" discrimination or "none at all" toward racial minorities and women.

But, as we might expect, the respondents' own social identities affected their opinions about the relative amounts of discrimination and preferential treatment that racial minorities and women receive. African-Americans were more likely than whites to believe that there is "a lot" of discrimination toward blacks and toward women and that there is "just a little" preferential treatment for racial minorities and women. On the other hand, the responses of men and women were very similar.

More recent studies have also addressed beliefs about race and sex discrimination. A 1991 telephone survey asked a national sample of respondents, "In general, do you think blacks have as good a chance as white people in your community to get any kind of job for which they are qualified, or don't you think they have as good a chance?" Twenty-three percent of whites and 58 percent of blacks said that blacks do *not* have as good a chance as whites to get jobs for which they are qualified, showing that blacks perceive more discrimination against their racial group than whites do (Gallup and Newport, 1991). This is consistent with the findings of other studies showing that a majority of whites attribute blacks' lower SES to internal causes, such as lack of effort and low aspirations, while a majority of African-Americans attribute blacks' lower SES to external causes, such as discrimination (Bobo, 1989).

In another national survey, 64 percent of respondents said they believe that women face some or a lot of discrimination in employment (CBS/ *New York Times*, 1991). A survey of women found that 71 percent feel that job discrimination is a major problem facing women today (Yankelovich Clancy Shulman, 1992).

EVIDENCE OF DISCRIMINATION

Americans believe that discrimination toward blacks and women limits these groups' chances to get ahead, but does the evidence indicate that discrimination *actually* occurs? For example, does discrimination explain the income inequalities between African-Americans and whites or between men and women? Discrimination is hard to prove because one has to *disprove* the alternative equity explanation, which views differences in human capital and qualifications as the source of income inequality. One has to show that people who have different incomes have the *same* (not different) *qualifications*.

Education

For example, we may agree that one qualification that should affect the amount of money a person earns is level of education. We have already noted that, as groups, African-Americans and whites differ in their levels of education. However, some individual African-Americans and whites have the same educational level. To determine whether it is level of education or something else — discrimination, perhaps — that accounts for the lower incomes of African-Americans, we can compare African-Americans and whites who have the *same* level of education to see if their incomes differ. Table 14-1 shows the results of such a comparison.

Table 14-1 includes only those Americans who are employed year-round and full-time. A greater percentage of African-Americans are part-time workers, so any income inequality between the races may be due to differences in their levels of employment. Therefore, if we exclude part-time workers from our comparison and look only at year-round, full-time workers, we eliminate this source of income inequality.

In Table 14-1 workers are divided into three education classifications. Within each classification (that is, for individuals having similar education), the incomes of African-American and white workers are compared, using earnings ratios. The ratios compare the amount made by African-American workers in a particular education category with each dollar made by white workers with the same education level.

TABLE 14-1   AFRICAN-AMERICAN/WHITE EARNINGS RATIOS, BY EDUCATION AND AGE, 1989*

Education	Age of worker		
	18–35	35–54	55+
Less than 4 yr. high school	.664	.796	.861
4 yr. high school–3 yr. college	.811	.825	.792
4 yr. or more college	.840	.865	.821

* For year-round, full-time workers.
Source: U.S. Bureau of the Census, machine-readable *Current Population Survey*, 1990.

As you can see in the table, when workers with similar education levels are compared, African-American/white earnings ratios range from a low of .664 for young workers with fewer than four years of high school to a high of .865 for middle-aged workers with four or more years of college. So even when the human-capital variable of level of education is removed by comparing workers with similar education levels, African-American workers make, *at best*, only about 87 cents for each dollar earned by white workers.

Occupation

But we would have even better evidence if we also took into account the *kinds of jobs* held by the individuals. Let's do this in comparing the in-comes of men and women. Besides differing in their levels of education, men and women differ substantially in the kinds of jobs they hold. In Table 14-2, we again look only at American workers who are employed year-round and full-time. This eliminates differences in the incomes of males and females that may be attributable to the greater percentage of women than men who work in part-time jobs. Next, we separate workers by type of job, dividing them into five classifications. In each job classification, we further separate the workers into the three education classifications used in Table 14-1. In addition, we divide the workers into two age groups, to roughly control for job experience. Then we calculate female/male earnings ratios for the workers within each

TABLE 14-2   FEMALE/MALE EARNINGS RATIOS BY OCCUPATION, EDUCATION, AND AGE, 1989*

	Age of worker	
Occupation/education	18–35	35–54
Executive, managerial, and professional specialty:		
Less than 4 yr. high school	†	.640
4 yr. high school–3 yr. college	.800	.668
4 yr. or more college	.777	.655
Technical, sales, and administrative support:		
Less than 4 yr. high school	.785	.708
4 yr. high school–3 yr. college	.755	.603
4 yr. or more college	.782	.574
Service:		
Less than 4 yr. high school	.804	.679
4 yr. high school–3 yr. college	.669	.494
4 yr. or more college	.653	.440
Precision production, craft, and repair:		
Less than 4 yr. high school	†	.665
4 yr. high school–3 yr. college	.753	.619
4 yr. or more college	†	†
Operators, assemblers, inspectors, transportation and material moving:		
Less than 4 yr. high school	.734	.663
4 yr. high school–3 yr. college	.696	.635
4 yr. or more college	†	†

* For year-round, full-time workers.
† Number of workers too small to draw reliable estimates
Source: Adapted from U.S. Bureau of the Census, *Current Population Reports*, series P-60, no. 168, September 1990. Washington, D.C.: Government Printing Office, pp. 53–54, table 16.

age, education, and job classification. Thus, we are comparing only male and female full-time workers in the same age category who have similar jobs and similar educations.

Among middle-aged workers (thirty-five to fifty-four years old), the earnings ratios range from a low of .440 (for workers in service occupations with four or more years of college) to a high of .708 (for workers in technical, sales, and administrative support jobs with less than four years of high school). The earnings ratio for all middle-aged workers is .635, which means that the average female worker earns less than 64 cents for every dollar earned by the average male worker in this age group.

Is the situation any better for younger (under age thirty-five) female workers? Their earnings ratios range from a low of .653 (for those in service occupations with four or more years of college) to a high of .804 (for those in service jobs with less than four years of high school). The earnings ratio for all young workers is .787, which means that the average young female worker earns less than 79 cents for every dollar earned by the average young male worker in the same job category and with the same education. So although young women's incomes are still below those of men their age, the earnings gap between young women and men is smaller than the gap between middle-aged women and men. This may mean that the earnings gap is getting *smaller* over time or that the gap *increases* as women stay in the labor force longer.

Note that for both age categories, the earnings gap between women and men is *greatest* among those who have made the greatest investment in human capital as measured by education level. Women who have four or more years of college make even *less* relative to males with similar jobs and education levels than do women with less education. This strongly suggests that differences in human capital do not account for all, or even most, of the income differential between the sexes.

Experience and Performance

So does this prove sex discrimination, or are there other factors that may explain the income in-

equality? Some would argue that the type of analysis we have just completed fails to adequately control for education and job type. Even within a job classification, for example, men and women might have very different jobs, and this might account for some of the difference in their incomes.

To address this kind of criticism, some researchers have studied *individuals* within a single firm. Such studies allow the researchers to take into account very precise measures of education level, job type, job tenure, tenure with the company, and even performance (as measured by the firm's own performance appraisal system).

For example, in a study of one large, successful firm with roughly 100 manufacturing operations in 30 states, researchers compared 5,550 men and 840 women in high-level jobs — professional, managerial, sales, and technical jobs (Gerhart and Milkovich, 1989). The ratio of women's salaries to men's, overall, was .84 in 1980; in 1986, it was .88 — the highest ever found in such a study. According to the researchers, the high ratio may be due to the study's exclusive focus on high-level jobs and the success of the company during this period. Within job levels the salary ratios were higher, ranging from .93 to .95.

But even taking into account detailed measures of job level, experience, and performance ratings, the researchers noted that males' higher salaries could not be accounted for entirely by human-capital factors. This suggests that some discrimination was occurring. Women's salaries did grow faster than men's during the six years the firm was studied. Women's higher salary growth, the researchers found, resulted partly from their higher performance ratings, even though women received a smaller payoff for performance than men did in terms of both income and promotions. The researchers suggest that women may be held to higher standards than men.

Working Conditions

To conclude that pay differentials between men and women are the result of discrimination, we must eliminate the possibility that women's jobs are lower-paid than men's due to differences in undesirable working conditions. If workers are compensated for bad or unpleasant working conditions by higher pay, and if men's jobs entail more of these undesirable conditions, then this would account for at least part of the differences in income between men and women. This would be an equity explanation. Randall Filer (1989) has argued that both men and women assess the undesirable and desirable features of jobs but that they use different criteria in making job choices. Men, Filer believes, attach more value to a job's wages and benefits, while women most value its interpersonal and nonwage aspects. This, Filer suggests, is why we find more women concentrated in lower-paying jobs than men.

In a recent study, Jerry Jacobs and Ronnie Steinberg (1990) assessed whether unpleasant working conditions account for the lower pay associated with jobs held primarily by women. The researchers found that jobs dominated by men were more likely than those dominated by women

to involve work in hot or cold conditions, exposure to fumes, risk of injury, strenuous physical activity, and slightly more stress. Yet jobs dominated by women not only were more likely to be noisy but also were more likely to involve cleaning others' dirt, to entail working with difficult clients and sick or dying patients, and to offer less autonomy and more repetition. Women's jobs, Jacobs and Steinberg concluded, involve somewhat *different*, but not necessarily fewer, undesirable working conditions than jobs dominated by men. Furthermore, their data indicate that (except for health workers who work with sick and dying patients and construction and trade workers whose jobs expose them to high risks of injury) *neither male nor female* workers are compensated for holding jobs with these undesirable characteristics. Workers in such jobs actually make less than workers in other jobs that have similar requirements but do not involve unpleasant working conditions. Thus it appears that the un-

Neither male nor female workers are compensated for holding jobs with undesirable working conditions. Thus it appears that the undesirable qualities of jobs do *not* account for male-female wage differentials.

desirable qualities of jobs do *not* account for male-female wage differentials, so discrimination remains a possibility.

COMPARABLE WORTH

The problem of determining whether discrimination is the cause of income inequality becomes more difficult when one cannot compare similarly qualified workers of different races and sexes. Many occupations, as previously noted, are so totally dominated by workers of a particular race or sex that no *within*-occupation comparisons are possible. In addition, workers in female-dominated occupations are paid less than workers in male-dominated occupations. If over 90 percent of low-paying jobs such as typists, secretaries, elementary school teachers, and seamsters are held by women, how can we determine whether their income is even partly the result of discrimination? One cannot reasonably compare women in these occupations with men in the same jobs because there are too few men in such positions.

The alternative is to compare women in low-status jobs with men in other jobs requiring "comparable" qualifications. But such a comparison is more difficult to make than it initially appears. First, we would need a set of standard qualifications by which most jobs can be compared—for example, education, skill, complexity, decision-making responsibility, supervisory role, and risk. Next, we would have to award points to each job for how well it meets each of these qualifications. Finally, we would have to compare the incomes of men and women (or African-Americans and whites) in jobs with the same point totals. Through this procedure, we establish **comparable worth**.

Americans are generally supportive of the notion of comparable worth. In a 1987 national survey 87 percent favored "paying women equal pay for comparable but different work" (Harris, 1987). According to its supporters, comparable worth is a necessary tool for dealing with income discrimination. But its detractors argue that it is impossible to develop a procedure for adequately specifying the various qualifications for different jobs. For example, the jobs of female secretaries and male plumbers, they assert, have too few qualifications in common for us to compare them.

Others argue that job qualifications are established by the powerful—in other words, by white men—in order to maintain their power (Acker, 1989; Steinberg, 1990). Some research indicates that white men perceive their common interests and cooperate to preserve their control over privileged positions and opportunities (Cohn, 1985; Bergmann, 1986; Reskin, 1988). In this view, white men make and enforce hiring and advancement rules intentionally to protect and benefit their own group (Jackall, 1988; Lewis, 1989). This may explain the lack of progress in efforts to revise wages according to comparable worth. It would cost employers $150 billion yearly, experts estimate, to raise women's wages to the levels of men's for jobs of comparable worth (Lewin, 1984).

Institutional Racism and Sexism

Discrimination may be individual or institutional. An individual may be the source of discrimination. For example, you may be one of many managers of a company who are responsible for recommending pay raises for subordinates. If you routinely recommend higher wages for white workers than you do for equally qualified African-American workers, then you *as an individual* are discriminating on the basis of race. On the other hand, if most of the company's managers routinely do the same thing, it is probably *the company* that is discriminating on the basis of race. The pervasiveness of the discrimination throughout the company suggests that the company has a policy of racial discrimination. **Institutional discrimination** occurs when the policies and programs of an institution systematically produce greater negative outcomes for members of one social category than for members of another. Of course, such policies tend to benefit members of a particular group. They may even be *established* by members of that group deliberately, in order to benefit themselves and other group members.

The group advantaged by institutional discrimination is called the **dominant group**; the disadvantaged group is called the **minority group**.

Institutional racism is institutional discrimination on the basis of race. Similarly, **institutional sexism** is institutional discrimination on the basis of sex. Both encompass the social arrangements and enduring patterns employed by a dominant group to oppress and exploit members of a minority group. Is it true that, in the United States, social arrangements ensure that critical decisions are made, issues defined, and resources allocated for the advantage of whites and the disadvantage of African-Americans and Hispanics? The findings of many sociologists support this view (Wilson and Aponte, 1985; Allen and Farley, 1986; Dreeben and Gamoran, 1986; Braddock and McPartland, 1987; Pettigrew and Martin, 1987). Toxic waste dumps, for example, usually are located in areas where residents are predominantly nonwhite (Williams, 1987). Not only are the *benefits* of business and production (such as jobs and incomes) unequally distributed, with the majority going to whites, but so also are the *costs* of production (such as toxic wastes and job hazards), of which nonwhites bear a disproportionate burden (Haar and Fessler, 1986).

A number of scholars argue that organizations not only mirror society's racial, ethnic, and sex inequality but also *create* inequality (Miller, 1986;

Martin and Chernesky, 1989; Martin, 1992). They do this by creating ideologies, norms, and practices that produce and reproduce inequality in the activities and social relationships that occur within their walls. To illustrate how institutional racism and sexism actually work, we will examine several examples in more detail — institutional discrimination on the job, in schools, and in the home. (Before reading further, look at the Student Observation: "Racism.")

INSTITUTIONAL DISCRIMINATION IN JOBS

Ample evidence supports the fact that in the United States the incomes of African-Americans are lower than those of whites and the incomes of women are lower than those of men. White males are the economically advantaged group. Racism and sexism in structure, stereotypes, and social interaction on the job are implicated in income differentials by race and sex.

Structure and Job Discrimination

The structural aspect most responsible for income discrimination is the unequal distribution of jobs, or job segregation. **Segregation** is the physical and social separation, by custom or law, of people from different social categories. It is much easier to justify paying white men more than African-Americans and white women if they have different

---

STUDENT OBSERVATION

Racism

*L*ast fall when my roommate and I moved back into the dorm, we met our new RA, Amy. She has a great personality, and we hit it off well from the start. Later, though, we found out something we hadn't expected. One day my roommate came into the room and said, "Oh my gosh, Amy has a black boyfriend!" Obviously, this was an issue because Amy is white. Yes, I was surprised. I don't think of myself as prejudiced. One of my very best friends is black, and I don't believe that I treat him or think of him differently than my white male friends. Still, although I hate to admit it now, I did find myself having reservations about Amy's character after I found out her boyfriend was black. I guess my racist feelings ran deeper than I thought. I had come to think of having blacks as friends as acceptable but felt very differently about a white person having a black as a romantic partner. After thinking this through, I realized that Amy is still the great person I thought she was from the start. My later negative judgments of her resulted from *my* racist feelings.

jobs. Income inequality can then be presented as the result of the differential value of the jobs rather than of race or sex.

As we noted earlier, judgments of comparable worth for different jobs held by men and women are much more difficult than judgments of comparable pay for the same job. For example, if women cannot observe men at work, they cannot determine if men's work is more skilled, difficult, or demanding than their own. And when women's access is restricted to a limited number of occupations, the oversupply of workers in these occupations provides another justification for lower pay for women.

Within the labor market. Job segregation by race and sex occurs at several levels. First, there is unequal distribution within the entire labor market. The races and sexes are disproportionately represented in different occupations (Reskin and Roos, 1987). It has been argued that white men, white women, minority men, and minority women form four different labor markets, with white men being the most advantaged group (Miller, 1986). White men predominate as managers, officials, and proprietors; white women, as clerical workers; African-American men, as laborers and operators of industrial equipment; and African-American women, as private household and service workers (Carlson, 1987). Although this is changing somewhat for some occupations — more women and African-Americans are going into professional, technical, craft, and clerical occupations — the races and sexes remain unequally distributed among *most* occupations.

Frequently, in the changes that *do* occur, women and African-Americans move into occupations being abandoned by white males because of declining rewards, status, or opportunities (Reskin and Roos, 1990). The white males remaining in these occupations may resist the entry of women and African-Americans because it signals a continuing decline in their positive job outcomes, such as pay and status (Bergmann, 1986). Their worries are not unfounded. The greater the percentage of females or nonwhites in an occupation, the less the average pay, even when occupational skills and requirements are taken into account (Strober and Arnold, 1987; England and Dunn, 1988).

Job segregation is not merely the result of past events. Even relatively new occupations are stratified internally. For example, although occupations related to computers would seem to offer opportunity for both sexes, these jobs are segregated into men's and women's work. Men domi-

Job segregation is not merely the result of past events. Even relatively new occupations are segregated by race and sex. For example, occupations related to computers are segregated into men's and women's work. Men dominate the "head-work" computer occupations (computer scientists and programmers), while women dominate the routine computer jobs (data-entry and equipment operators).

nate the "head-work" computer occupations, such as computer scientists and programmers, while women dominate the routine computer jobs, such as data-entry and equipment operators (Glenn and Tolbert, 1987).

Within organizations. Jobs within organizations are also distributed unequally among members of different races and sexes. A study of 393 establishments over a twenty-year period found that a large majority of jobs were completely sex-segregated: over 93 percent of the jobs contained *only* men or *only* women (Bielby and Baron, 1986). And many more women than men were found to hold jobs that were "dead ends," or not in job ladders (Baron, Davis-Blake, and Bielby, 1986).

Thus, one form of job segregation occurs when *different work* is done by members of different races or sexes. Another form occurs when the members of one race or sex hold jobs in which they supervise workers of another race or sex who are doing *similar work*. White males predominate in supervisory positions (Morrison and Von Glinow, 1990). Many men supervise women; few women supervise men. A third form of job segregation occurs when members of different races or sexes do *identical work* in jobs given different job titles; thus they do not appear to be doing equal work. For example, a woman's job may be labeled "Technician I" and a man's "Assembler I," although an observer would be unable to discern a difference in their work activities (Acker, 1989). All these forms of job segregation are accompanied by differential compensation that almost always favors white men (Baron and Newman, 1990; Blum, 1991).

Stereotypes and Job Discrimination

Job segregation, like income inequality, is often justified ideologically through race- and sex-related stereotypes. As we discussed in Chapter 6, "Social Attitudes and Attributions," the attitudes of Americans include schemas involving sex, race, personal traits (personality and physical characteristic) and role expectations (occupation and family). For example, because employers tend to think of a woman's income as a "second income" for her household, they often assume that women applicants need the job less and are less interested in it than men. They also assume that women would not want to travel on the job, would be absent more than men due to sickness or childcare demands, would keep the job only briefly (because they're likely to get married or have children), are not physically strong enough for it, and are more emotional than men (Reskin and Hartmann, 1986; Eagly, Makhijani, and Klonsky, 1992).

While the proportion of whites who believe that African-Americans are innately inferior has declined, many whites who control jobs still view blacks as responsible for their concentration in lower-paying jobs. Such whites reason that blacks are less motivated to work hard and are less dependable (Braddock and McPartland, 1987; Kluegel, 1990). This is an example of "turning the equity norm around" (Della-Fave, 1986*b*; Ritzman and Tomaskovic-Devey, 1992). According to the equity norm, individuals should be rewarded according to their contributions. Therefore, the turned-around reasoning goes, if women and blacks are, as groups, rewarded less than white males, it must be because they are less worthy. A number of studies show, for example, that both males and females attribute less worth to work performed by females (Major, McFarlin, and Gagnon, 1984; Deaux, 1985; McArthur, 1985).

Employers' stereotypes are not the only ones affecting workers. Co-workers may base efforts to protect "their turf" on stereotypes. For example, one study found that women prison guards were viewed by male guards as violating the job's masculinity requirements (Zimmer, 1987). The male guards' believed that their job required stereotypically masculine characteristics — being tough, in control, macho. These beliefs were called into question by the entry of the women guards. To protect their own advantages — including their images of themselves as masculine — some of the male guards excluded the women guards in their interactions and undermined their authority among the inmates.

Social Interaction and Job Discrimination

The members of an advantaged group often act, intentionally or not, in ways that will preserve for their group the jobs that are less repetitive, boring, place-bound, and physically abusive. Both supervisors and employees can serve as **gate-keepers** — those who control the decision-making process by which individuals are admitted to scarce positions and offices of power, privilege, and status within a society or an organization.

Networks. Selective word-of-mouth recruiting is an example of gatekeeping (Collinson, Knights, and Collinson, 1990). When an organization has a job opening, for example, those in power, who tend to be white males, may pass this information on to white males in other departments of the organization or to acquaintances or friends outside the organization — the "old boys' network." The individuals who do this may or may not *intend* to ensure that other members of their own group are more likely to be recruited. But intentional or not, that is the effect. By passing on job information to others *like themselves*, they preserve the advantage of their group (Braddock and McPartland, 1987; Mueller, Parcel, and Tanaka, 1989).

Recruitment. Personnel officers can serve as gatekeepers by steering African-American and women applicants away from higher-paying jobs dominated by white males. The gatekeeper may justify this by arguing — and may even believe — that minority applicants are better suited to and would be happier in other jobs. Research indicates that interviewers of black job applicants use non-verbal cues that are perceptibly more cold than those used with white applicants (Pettigrew and Martin, 1987). Interviewees pick up on such cues, and we might expect that their own behavior is affected by them.

Work assignments. Barbara Reskin and Irene Padavic's (1988) study of several power plants

shows how the attitudes of gatekeeper supervisors can influence the sex segregation of jobs. During a seven-week strike by unionized workers, strikers were replaced with nonunion workers including, for the first time, a significant number of women who filled men's jobs. Plant supervisors — all males — were responsibile for assigning the new workers to particular jobs. For several jobs, sex was a criterion for assignments. For example, the supervisors assigned 41 percent of the women and only 2 percent of the men to jobs involving plant cleaning and food preparation. On the other hand, they assigned 13 percent of the men and only 4 percent of the women to security jobs. When asked how they felt about the employment of women, only a minority of the supervisors said they were neutral. Over half anticipated problems, based on their stereotypic beliefs that women are not strong enough and do not want to get dirty.

The belief that putting women and men together causes the "problem of sexual relationships" is common among the gatekeepers for many jobs, including those on construction sites, at coal mines, on ships, and in other military units (Burrell and Hearn, 1989; Acker, 1990). One solution to this problem — which feminists note is, curiously, thought to be caused by the *women* — is to segregate women into different jobs, often at lower pay (Crull, 1987). When women do encounter men in the workplace, overt and sexual harassment, as well as isolation, may occur, especially for women in traditionally male jobs (Baker, 1978; Crull, 1987). The effect (and perhaps the intent) of these responses is the same — to keep women "in their place." This issue is explored further in the box "Sexual Harassment."

Subordinate reactions. African-Americans and women who breach the wall of job segregation and become supervisors of white men may also face problems resulting from reactions to their race or sex. Minority supervisors are often viewed first as blacks or women (a status inferior to that of a white male) and only second as a supervisor (a status superior to the employee's). Such supervisors may be viewed as "uppity blacks" or "queen

SEXUAL HARASSMENT

In 1991, the nation witnessed an important event that brought the issue of sexual harassment to the public's attention in a forceful way. That event was the televised congressional hearing on charges of sexual harassment against a nominee for Supreme Court Justice, Clarence Thomas. Though Thomas denied the charges and was eventually confirmed, many believed his accuser, Anita Hill, an attorney and Thomas's former employee, who underwent a grueling interrogation by the all-male congressional committee.

According to a 1992 survey of American adults, 32 percent of women interviewed said they had been sexually harassed on the job (Morin, 1992). Half of all men and women questioned said that they knew someone who had been the victim of sexual harassment.

Sexual harassment has been defined as actions and practices by a person or group of people at work that are directed at one or more workers and that are repeated and unwanted, interfering with job performance or creating an unpleasant working environment. The two key components of this definition are that sexual harassment is unwanted and that it affects one's job. It may take many forms. It can be a look, a "friendly" pat or squeeze, suggestive remarks, an off-color joke, persistent requests for a date, brushing against the person's body, leering, a pinch, pornographic pictures left in the person's desk or work area, a proposition, threat of rape, or rape. Women experience these kinds of unwanted sexual advances everywhere they go. But when a woman worker is harassed at her workplace, her livelihood is at stake.

Sexual harassment appears to take two forms: "quid pro quo" and "hostile environment." *Quid pro quo* means "one thing in return for another" — continued employment for sex, for example. According to researcher Peggy Crull (1987), quid pro quo harassment is usually directed at women who fill subordinate positions and take orders from men. This type of harassment gives men power over their female employees. If the woman is not cooperative, she may get a poor recommendation or a negative evaluation in her record, or she may lose a raise, promotion, or even her job. Harassment in these jobs often takes the form of hints and requests for dates, which, when rejected, are followed by work retaliation.

Hostile environment is anything that is perceived as an expression of hostility by the person experiencing it. Hostile environment is often perpetrated by a co-worker who views women as threats to his own power. This type of harassment tends to be more overtly hostile; the point seems to be to humiliate the woman rather than to gain sexual favors (Cockburn, 1985, 1991).

Cynthia Cockburn (1991) describes the case of a woman manager, recruited to a very senior position in an organization. The woman viewed herself as very direct and tough. She claimed that sexual harassment was much ado about nothing. Rather, she saw it as "sexual innuendo — infinitely childish, you just ignore it." Yet she admitted that the men saw her as a huge threat when she first took the position and that they made her feel very uncomfortable for the first six months. She took an aggressive approach and was not afraid to take on high-ranking males. And then, one day, as she walked up the stairs to a top-level meeting with her male colleagues, one of them covertly pinched her bottom. "I couldn't *believe* it," she said. "I was so stunned that I didn't even react." Later, of course, she felt mortified that she had not said or done something on the spot. Long after the event occurred, it bothered her. The pinch, in this case, was a controlling gesture to remind her that "you're only a woman and that's the way I see you."

Initially, most women ignore offensive behavior, hoping the harasser will get the message that they are not interested. They feel guilty and ashamed, often wondering what they have done to make the harasser think they would comply. Most victims say they feel alone, frightened, and angry. Co-workers often are not supportive, assuming that "she's asking for it" or "she's trying to sleep her way to the top" (Clarke, 1982). This situation may have changed somewhat in the wake of the Thomas hearings. As a result of the media attention given to the hearings, many people discovered that sexual harassment is a common problem and became more willing to label certain behaviors "sexual harassment."

bees" and may have trouble gaining the compliance of their subordinates. The subordinates may feel freer to express opinions contrary to those of minority supervisors, and the supervisors may be given little leeway for mistakes, being criticized with a vengeance when they err (Pringle, 1989).

Organizational authority, it appears, is neither sex- nor race-neutral. Rather, authority on the job is confounded with race and sex in ways that profoundly affect interactional encounters (Acker, 1990; Fenstermaker, West, and Zimmerman, 1991). One study of managers in large businesses found that the women promoted to middle-management positions by male supervisors were the less aggressive, less threatening women, who didn't "rock the boat" or "make waves" (Harlan and Weiss, 1981). However, these middle-management positions were dead ends for the women because supervisors wanted more aggressive and dynamic people for top management positions.

In Chapter 5, "Communication," we discussed the double bind that women face because characteristics associated with femininity — and thus appropriate for their sex — conflict with characteristics seen as important for leadership. Women who exhibit behavior seen as appropriate for white male leaders are evaluated negatively (Taps and Martin, 1990). African-Americans face much the same problem. If they don't use the white male leadership style, they are viewed as incompetent. If they do use it, they are viewed as pushy and threatening.

We do not mean to suggest that white males *always* have an advantage when it comes to higher-status, higher-paying jobs. In some instances, it may be to the advantage of a particular organization and its employees to have more African-Americans or white women in such positions — for example, organizations whose principal clients are African-Americans or women. Race or sex stereotypes may factor into such staffing decisions. For example, an abortion clinic may give its higher-status physician jobs to women not only because it believes its female clients would feel more comfortable with female physicians but also because it believes that women are more sensitive and caring than men. Organizations doing busi-

ness with the federal government are certainly sensitive to the government's affirmative action criteria for awarding contracts. Still, the economic advantages of white males are often supported by structural features of many organizations, such as white male dominance of top positions, stereotypes that equate being white and male with job qualifications, and interaction patterns that preserve white male dominance.

AFFIRMATIVE ACTION

Title VII of the Civil Rights Act of 1964 is the legal foundation of efforts to eliminate discrimination based on race, sex, religion, and ethnic origin. Since it became law, a debate has persisted over exactly how to accomplish the act's intent. Much of the debate has focused on the term **affirmative action**.

In addition to ending discriminatory practices by employers, affirmative action policies require that steps be taken to overcome the effects of past discrimination — deficiencies in human capital and qualifications. Some supporters of affirmative action maintain that compensatory practices are necessary because of the continuing effects of previous discrimination. Special programs, they argue, must also be designed to improve the qualifications of women and minorities:

> For a while, a policy of equal opportunity appeared to be the answer to the racial and sex injustices of American society. But the policy of equal opportunity operates fairly only in a system that does not distinguish between groups either *de jure* or *de facto*, either intentionally or unintentionally, either blatantly or subtly. If racism and sexism exist in America, then equal opportunity is not a feasible policy for American institutions.
>
> That racism and sexism do persist has been documented countless times in a number of ways. Overt and blatant prejudice is no longer acceptable in most circles, but it takes more than a few decades to dismantle the structures that have so relentlessly and so systematically put some groups at a disadvantage relative to others. Imbalances continue, even when they are not intended or attended.
>
> Given the unjust realities of the past, it is not enough to wait passively for a better society. Institu-

tions must go out of their way to assure that their practices are fair. That is why affirmative action can potentially assure a more equitable and efficient society than does a policy of so-called equal opportunity. (Blanchard and Crosby, 1989: vii)

Challenges to Affirmative Action

Of course, affirmative action programs have had their critics — among them social scientists who support the antidiscrimination goals of these programs. Let's look at some of their concerns.

Ineffectiveness of current programs.   Some critics argue that evidence of the continuing effects of previous discrimination indicates that present efforts to implement affirmative action are ineffective. Thus, according to sociologist William J. Wilson (1987), affirmative action programs have helped middle-class African-Americans but not poorer African-Americans. For example, increasing African-Americans' opportunity to attend traditionally white universities does not help the poorer members of the population, many of whom lack academic qualifications or have conflicting economic responsibilities to their families.

Minorities admitted to universities or given jobs through affirmative action programs frequently have large attrition rates. Whether individuals admitted to school or hired for a job under affirmative action are successful depends on policies and practices *throughout* an organization, many of which may be unrelated to admissions, hiring, or promotion. Practices that have "worked" for whites and males may place a burden on racial minorities and women. For example, women or racial minorities who enter a profession dominated by white males may find themselves isolated from the support network that their majority colleagues take for granted. Male professionals may, for example, exclude a female colleague from their lunches together because they want to be able to "talk with the guys" and not have to "be careful what they say." But some of the talk at such gatherings is about work and the office. The men come to understandings and pass

on job-related information from which their female colleague is excluded.

Current affirmative action policies do not affect such practices. Some critics argue that they should. Others call for changes in affirmative action programs that would take into account the life styles of minority employees (Feagin, 1987). New practices may include flexible work schedules, work at home, paternity and maternity leave, and on-site child care.

Reinforce stereotypes.   Still other critics of affirmative action have expressed concerns that such programs may actually *reinforce existing stereotypes* of minorities and women. According to this argument, the existence of affirmative action programs suggests to some that women and minorities are unqualified for certain jobs; otherwise, they wouldn't have to depend on affirmative action.

There is some experimental support for this hypothesis (Summers, 1991). Affirmative action does require that race and sex be noticed and taken into account in recruiting, admissions, and hiring and in promotion decisions. Critics who believe that affirmative action programs may reinforce stereotypes have argued that calling attention to categorization schemas will delay the ultimate goal of a society in which opportunities and evaluations are not allocated on the basis of race and sex. In the context of our discussion of social stereotypes (Chapter 6, "Social Attitudes and Attributions"), "affirmative action appointee" becomes an identifying label from which some people infer other characteristics. For example, African-Americans may be described as seeking special treatment through affirmative action because they are lazy or unwilling to work hard. This is reflected in one white male's comment: "I have nothing against blacks generally, but this one was clearly hired under affirmative action" (Dovidio, Mann, and Gaertner, 1989).

Negative self-expectations.   Another concern about affirmative action is that being a beneficiary of it can affect a person's self-attitude by forming negative self-expectations (Heilman, Simon, and

Repper, 1987). (See the discussion in Chapter 7, "The Social Nature of Self.") Social psychologist Rupert Nacoste (1989) has found that some students who believed they were selected to participate in a study under a preferential procedure displayed greater self-doubt than other students in the study. Nacoste asked male and female students to complete a "creativity test." Before taking the test, half the students were informed that they had been selected for the study in order to include enough students of their own sex — the "affirmative action" condition. In contrast, the other half were told that their scores on a previous creativity test caused them to be selected — the "merit" condition. The two groups were asked to estimate how well they would do on the creativity test. They were then given the test.

Although the actual test performance of the two groups did not differ, some of the students who thought they had been selected on the basis of affirmative action gave lower performance estimates than did the students who thought they were chosen on the basis of merit. The students who rated themselves lower believed that affirmative action was *unfair*, whereas students who believed that affirmative action was *fair* did not rate themselves lower. Thus, the high attrition among some affirmative action appointees may possibly be traced to the belief, held by both the appointees and their colleagues, that their race or sex, not their job-related qualifications, was the decisive factor in their admission, hiring, or promotion.

Definitions of Affirmative Action

But do the concerns about affirmative action programs prove decisively that such programs are failures? The answer, we believe, depends partly on which definition of affirmative action you are assessing. Affirmative action has come to mean many things to many people. Table 14-3 shows the results of several national public opinion polls conducted between 1985 and 1992. At least 80 percent of the respondents favored affirmative action programs that give *equal opportunities* to minorities and women, even programs offering special training and advice. Moreover, two out of three respondents favored affirmative action programs that were *unspecified* except for excluding rigid quotas. A higher proportion of African-Americans supported such programs than did whites.

On the other hand, respondents split about evenly in their support or opposition to programs that set hiring goals or give a preference to women or African-Americans. This result is hard to interpret because some respondents may have thought the question referred to programs that set goals or gave preference to *equally qualified* women or African-Americans, while others may have thought the programs involved *less qualified* women and African-Americans. Support for affirmative action programs falls to about one in three respondents when quotas are mentioned. Respondents' opinions about quotas were more uncertain than their opinions about other aspects of affirmative action programs. Some Americans are opposed to affirmative action under any circumstances. In a 1991 survey, 34 percent of whites and 22 percent of blacks agreed that "minorities and women are not entitled to any special consideration" (Harris, 1991).

INSTITUTIONAL DISCRIMINATION IN SCHOOLS

Schools, hospitals, banks, factories, businesses, and other institutions do not have to be staffed by prejudiced people for discrimination to occur in these environments. For example, employers in every organization set the qualifications that job candidates need in order to be considered for job openings. These qualifications usually include formal education and previous job experience. When these standards are applied to all job applicants, regardless of race, creed, color, or sex, they are, in themselves, nondiscriminatory. However, if members of certain racial or ethnic groups or of a particular sex lack equal opportunities to attain the required level of education or gain the necessary job experience, they obviously will be at a disadvantage in the job market (Braddock and McPartland, 1987; Tienda and Lii, 1987).

In Chapter 3, "Socialization over the Life

TABLE 14-3 PUBLIC ATTITUDES ABOUT AFFIRMATIVE ACTION, 1985–1992 (IN PERCENT)

Affirmative action programs	Favor	Oppose	Don't know
Giving equal opportunity in employment and education (1985)	85	14	1
Whites (1991)	76	22	2
Blacks (1991)	96	3	1
Giving special training and advice:			
1985	82	17	1
1991	78	20	2
Not having rigid quotas:			
All respondents (1985)	75	21	4
All respondents (1987)	69	25	6
All respondents (1991)	75	22	3
African-American respondents (1988)	66	18	16
White respondents (1988)	55	24	21
In employment for blacks, provided no rigid quotas (1988)	74	17	9
In business for blacks, provided no rigid quotas (1990)	68	18	14
Using hiring goals (1986)	46	36	18
Giving preference in hiring and promotion:			
To women (1992)	52	37	11
To blacks (1992)	49	41	10
Including the use of racial quotas (1986)	33	49	18
Including quotas for minorities in colleges and graduate programs (1985)	28	46	26

Source: Data are from a variety of polls conducted by Louis Harris and Associates, Hart and Teeter Research Companies, CBS/*New York Times*, Yankelovich Clancy Shulman, and the Roper Organization.

Course," we discussed the beginnings of race and sex discrimination during childhood. Female and African-American children are encouraged to pursue traditional sex and race roles through socialization by family, peers, media, and schools. Here, we'll expand our discussion of institutional discrimination in schools. Clearly, some of the difference between blacks and whites, males and females, in life chances begins with differential treatment in schools.

As we noted earlier in this chapter, the number of years of schooling completed by African-Americans as a group is less than that completed by whites. African-Americans are twice as likely as whites to complete less than eight years of schooling and are only half as likely as whites to complete at least four years of college. Although the years of school completed by males and females

differ only slightly, schools reinforce traditional sex roles in many ways that restrict the achievement potential of women. Some of these educational inequalities are probably due to institutional discrimination, occurring in the same forms as are found in jobs: structure, stereotypes, and social interaction.

Structure

Segregation of children in schools according to their race or sex is a form of institutional discrimination. It maintains prejudice and prevents the kinds of intergroup contact that might weaken stereotypes. On May 17, 1954, the U.S. Supreme Court ruled in *Brown* v. *Board of Education* that mandatory school segregation on the basis of race was unconstitutional. Still, many aspects of American life remain, for all practical purposes, racially segregated, including American schools. Nearly forty years after the *Brown* decision, a majority of African-American students attend predominantly black schools (Orfield, 1987).

Sex segregation in schools takes a different form from racial segregation. In preschool, boys and girls usually line up separately. In later grades, they may have recess or physical education at different times. Sex is often the basis for creating separate teams for spelling bees and other activities. This kind of separation reinforces the idea that sex can be used to divide people. It isolates the sexes from each other and reinforces sex stereotypes. At the college level, white male domination of faculty positions means that women and blacks have few role models (Sadker and Sadker, 1985).

Stereotypes

In recent decades African-American militancy has challenged and undermined the more traditional, blatant, and overt expressions of white dominance. Consequently, covert and subtle mechanisms now predominate in the establishment and maintenance of white advantage. Among these mechanisms are the expectancy effects or self-fulfilling prophecies we discussed in Chapter 3, "Socialization over the Life Course," and Chapter 7, "The Social Nature of Self." These are false definitions of a situation that create conditions that make it come true. For example, teachers give students in what they perceive as low-ability groups less chance to perform, either by allowing them less time to answer, interrupting them more frequently, or supplying them with the answer (Allington, 1980). On the other hand, research shows that teachers seem to prepare more thoroughly for, care more about, and be more interested in their "high-ability" classes (Evertson, 1982).

Self-fulfilling prophecies based on negative stereotypes concerning women's abilities and competence may operate to restrict women's achievement. Throughout elementary school, high school, and college, females get less attention from teachers in class (Hall and Sandler, 1982; Sadker and Sadker, 1985). By the end of their teen years, girls are more likely to be under-achievers than boys (Greenberg, 1985) and are less likely to see themselves as "college material" even when they get the same grades as boys (Cordos, 1986). Many teachers seem to have a stereotype that includes the belief that girls are less competent at math than boys. Although this belief is not true, it affects teachers' interactions with students. Boys are more likely to be encouraged to take advanced math courses than are equally skilled girls because they are expected to enter occupations such as engineering and physics (Sabers, Cushing, and Sabers, 1987; Wentzel, 1988). Even when they are good at math, women come to see math as a male domain and often fail to develop a sense of self-competence in math-related fields, thereby restricting their access to careers that value these skills (Singer and Stake, 1986).

Social Interaction

Another of the mechanisms through which institutional racism is expressed is gatekeeping. Most gatekeepers are white males. They are usually professionals with experience and credentials in the fields they monitor. They are found in schools and colleges, in real estate offices, in employment agencies, and in the hiring offices of businesses and government. Even when white gatekeepers are well intentioned — dedicated to objective, nonprejudiced hiring and sympathetic to the American democratic creed — ethnics, Chicanos, and African-Americans frequently find themselves victimized in their encounters with "the Man" (white, Anglo-Saxon Protestants — WASPs — who have power and influence). What actually occurs in such interactions to produce this effect? School counseling interviews provide insight into the gatekeeping process (Erickson, 1975).

In their interactions, students and counselors rely heavily on a variety of implicit cues. They communicate not only verbally but nonverbally through gestures, tone of voice, and figurative meanings and by what is left unsaid. Seldom do white counselors directly tell African-American students *not* to continue their education. but this message may be communicated *indirectly*, as the following exchange reveals:

White counselor: As far as next semester . . . why don't we give some thought to what you'd like to take there. . . . *(Leans forward)* Do you plan on continuing along this P.E. major?

African-American student: Yeah, I guess so. I might as well keep it up . . . my P.E., and *(Shifts in chair)* I wanna go into counseling too, see . . . you know, to have two-way . . . like equal balance.

White counselor: I see, Ah . . . What do you know about counseling?

African-American student: Nothing. *(Smiles and averts eyes, then looks up)*

White counselor: Okay . . .

African-American student: *(Shifts in chair, smiles and averts eyes)* I know you have to take psychology courses of some sort . . . and counseling.

White counselor: *(Leans back)* Well . . . *(Student stops smiling, looks directly at counselor and sits almost immobile while counselor talks and shifts in chair repeatedly)* it's this is a. . . . It'll vary from different places to different places. . . . But essentially what you need. . . . First of all you're gonna need state certification . . . state teacher certification . . . in other words you're gonna have to be certified to teach in some area . . . English or history, or whatever happens to be your bag . . . P.E. Secondly, you're gonna have to have a Master's Degree . . . in counseling . . . which as you know is an advanced degree. *(Short laugh)* That's what you have to do to get a counseling . . . to be a counselor. (Erickson, 1975: 54)*

On first sight, this exchange may appear fairly straightforward. Yet the white counselor and the African-American student had different reactions when they viewed a tape of the interview sep-

arately. The counselor's impression was relatively positive:

Right now we both seem to be concentrating on giving information. . . . He on the other hand is concentrating . . . on accepting the information and putting it together . . . he's got aspirations for the future. P.E. and uh . . . uh counseling . . . he's a little bit ahead of himself as far as the counseling . . . as the year progressed, I guess I got the question so often that it became one of my favorite topics an' I was ready to uh numerate . . . essentially what he did was he started me off on my information. (Erickson, 1975: 54–55)*

The African-American student interpreted the interchange negatively. When asked whether the counselor's information was satisfactory, he responded, "Not especially." When asked to explain, the student observed:

Well . . . well I couldn't really say, but I wasn't satisfied with what he wanted to push. . . . I guess he didn't think I was qualified, you know. That's the way he sounded to me. . . . This guy here seems like he was trying to knock me down, in a way, you know. Trying to say no. . . . I don't think you can handle anything besides P.E. You know he just said it in general terms, he just didn't go up and POW like they would in the old days, you know. This way they just try to use a little more psychology . . . they sugar-coat it this way. (Erickson, 1975: 55)*

Although the counselor did not specifically discourage the African-American student about becoming a counselor, his hesitant and roundabout talk about certification and requirements achieved the same end. Whether they do it intentionally or unintentionally, white counselors often "cool out" minority students.

Other research indicates that the unconscious operation of the stereotype that women do not

---

* From Frederick Erickson, "Gatekeeping and the Melting Pot Interaction in Counseling Encounters," *Harvard Educational Review*, 1975 45:1, pp. 44–70. Copyright © 1975 by the President and Fellows of Harvard College. All rights reserved.

need to be serious about or prepared for careers results in "counseling them out of" mathematics and preparation for engineering courses (Marini and Brinton, 1984). Even in college, women are more likely than men to be belittled or ignored in the classroom (Hall and Sandler, 1982). The climate is particularly bad for black women, who may be seen as less competent both because they are black and because they are female (Benokraitis and Feagin, 1986). Women apparently internalize the lower expectations for their performance held by teachers and school counselors. After four years of college, many women's ambitions have decreased (Vollmer, 1986; Bush, 1987).

RACIAL DESEGREGATION OF SCHOOLS

Institutional sexism in schools has received little attention compared with institutional racism, especially in its most radical form, racial segregation. In 1954, relying in part on testimony given by social scientists, the nation's highest court ruled school segregation unconstitutional. Writing for the unanimous court, Chief Justice Earl Warren gave the reasons for the decision:

> Does segregation of children in public schools solely on the basis of race, even though the physical facilities and other "tangible" factors may be equal, deprive the children of the minority group of equal educational opportunities? We believe that it does. . . . To separate them from others of similar age and qualifications solely because of their race generates a feeling of inferiority as to their status in the community that may affect their hearts and minds in a way unlikely ever to be undone. (*Brown* v. *Board of Education of Topeka*, 1954)

To enforce the Supreme Court's desegregation ruling, federal courts have ordered busing, reassigned students to different schools, specified the location of new schools, and redrawn school district boundaries. These measures have sometimes been supplanted by (or been combined with) "magnet schools" and voucher systems. The purpose of magnet schools is to distribute, and desegregate, students according to their special interests or talents — for example, science, mathe-

matics, art and music, and vocational education. In voucher systems each family within a school district receives money vouchers that entitle the school-age children to a year of education at the school of their choice.

Underlying both the magnet-school and voucher-system plans is the assumption that both white and minority parents want their children to attend the best schools. Thus, proponents of these programs argue that desegregation will result from the parents' acting in their own self-interest. But self-interest may not be the strongest motivation operating. It appears that much of the conflict over desegregation is racially motivated, that is, seen in terms of ingroups and outgroups. This is supported by research showing that many whites who were not personally affected by busing — because there were no blacks in their school district or because they had no children — opposed it because it signaled a displacement of whites by blacks (Bobo, 1988). Despite all these programs aimed at desegregating schools, many public schools are not racially balanced. And even in racially mixed schools, interracial interaction may be minimal.

Self-Esteem

In its landmark 1954 decision, the Supreme Court relied on the argument that psychological damage to the self-esteem of black children results from segregation. This notion grew out of the work of Kenneth and Mamie Clark (1939, 1947, 1950), who, finding that African-American preschool children preferred white dolls to black dolls, concluded that the white-doll choice reflected black self-hatred. Numerous subsequent studies appeared to confirm the existence of low self-esteem in African-American children (Goff, 1949; Morland, 1962; McCarthy and Yancey, 1971; Porter, 1971; Zirkel, 1971).

In the 1970s, however, investigators began to observe that the levels of self-esteem among African-American children and adolescents were either higher than or no different from those among white youngsters (Rosenberg and Simmons, 1972; Yancey, Rigsby, and McCarthy, 1972; Paton, Walberg, and Yeh, 1973; Cummings, 1975; Wylie, 1979; Phillips and Zigler, 1980; Hoelter, 1983). Indeed, some research has suggested that African-American children in all-black schools, especially in the South, showed the highest self-esteem of all schoolchildren (Simmons et al., 1978; Drury, 1980).

Social scientists now recognize that a variety of factors may blunt the impact of the negative racist feedback directed toward minority groups. First, African-Americans do not necessarily judge themselves by the standards of the white society; the assessments of African-Americans are much more important to them. Second, the existence of racist institutions allows African-Americans to blame the system rather than themselves should they be unable to realize American goals of success. Third, an increase in African-American militancy has enhanced feelings of black dignity, pride, and unity.

Academic Achievement

During the 1950s the scientific community was pervaded by the rather naive optimism that school desegregation would almost automatically improve the academic performance of African-Americans. In 1966 the voluminous Coleman Report appeared, apparently offering research support for the Supreme Court's conclusion. The study, funded by Congress, was based on tests and surveys of 645,000 pupils and 60,000 teachers in 4,000 schools. The data gathered by sociologist James S. Coleman and his associates seemed to show that the level of academic performance of blacks rose as the proportion of white students in a school increased.

Social scientists assumed that this was due to the higher levels of educational motivation in predominantly white student bodies. This is the "lateral transmission of values" hypothesis. According to this notion, black students, when immersed within predominantly white schools, acquire the achievement-related values held by whites.

But some black leaders have insisted that it is not the presence of white children per se that leads to higher achievement by black children; it is the quality of the education provided *because*

white children are there that makes the difference (Bell, 1980). Other research has found that the higher standards to which teachers and administrators hold predominantly white classes cause the progress (Patchen, 1982; Dreeben and Gamoran, 1986). Still other research suggests that the effects of school desegregation are conditional. For example, when desegregation begins at kindergarten age, the effects are apparently positive; in contrast, students desegregated in secondary school are far less likely to experience positive outcomes (Crain and Mahard, 1983). In sum, there is more to effective integration than mixing together children from different racial backgrounds (Epstein, 1985).

Schools do more than teach academic skills; they also socialize youngsters for membership in the larger society. Desegregation brings children of different races together so that they can learn to coexist. Studies show that desegregation of schools contributes to desegregation in later life — in college, in neighborhoods, and on the job (Braddock, 1985; Stephan, 1986, 1990; Armor, 1989). One of the long-term effects of racial segregation is its tendency to become self-perpetuating. School segregation gives birth to and nurtures avoidance learning, which in turn maintains the separation of blacks and whites in later life. Consequently, minority members who have been educated in segregated schools generally move into segregated niches in adult society (Hallinan and Williams, 1987).

Institutional discrimination in schools is only one source, albeit an important source, of the unequal distribution of races and sexes in occupations and jobs, as well as the resulting inequality of incomes. Another important source of inequality between the sexes is the institutional division of labor in the traditional American family.

INSTITUTIONAL DISCRIMINATION IN THE HOME

With respect to power, privilege, and status, men have traditionally enjoyed advantages relative to women. Thus, women possess less power over their communities and in human affairs, earn less money, and experience more difficulty becoming eminent than men. The distributive question of who shall get what, when, and how has been answered mainly in favor of males: it is men who attain top political office and obtain the best jobs, while escaping from menial household labor. It is even men who schedule sexual intercourse and who traditionally have most of the orgasms in heterosexual sex.

Sexual Property

Within the Western world, male dominance has involved the notion of sexual property, namely, the tenet that men "own" female sexuality. All too frequently, men appropriated women for their beds and pressed them into service in their fields and kitchens. Many women exchanged sexual and domestic services for male financial support. A sexual double standard, however, traditionally permitted men considerable sexual latitude outside the home, a right withheld from women. Indeed, marital "swinging" is often referred to as "wife swapping" (as opposed to "husband-and-wife swapping"), clearly suggesting that a husband owns his wife's sexuality. Feminists note that a woman's virginity has long been defined as the property of her father and her sexuality as the property of her husband. In the context of this definition, society has viewed rape less as a crime perpetrated by a man against a woman than as a crime perpetrated by one man against another man. (Before reading further, look at the Student Observations: "Sexual Property" and "'Sex Bait.'")

The view of wives as sexual property is part of the legacy of the past. Until the twentieth century, English and American common law viewed a woman as entering "civil death" upon marriage. She lost her legal identity—indeed, her social identity—since she had to forsake her own name for that of her husband. In the eyes of the law, women became "incorporated and consolidated" with their husbands. The common-law doctrine of *femme couverte* held that a married woman was covered, or veiled, by her husband's name and authority. A wife could not own property in her own right or sign a contract; she was not allowed to sue or testify against her husband. Her husband had claim to all her property, inherited or earned. In the view of the court, he was legally liable for criminal acts committed by her in his presence. He could, and in a few states still can, require his wife to submit to sexual intercourse against her will and to live wherever he chose.

Primary Household Laborer, Secondary Wage Earner

Women traditionally have provided unpaid child-rearing and domestic services. Although most

---

STUDENT OBSERVATION

Sexual Property

Tonight my boyfriend, Fred, and I went with another couple to a campus bar to drink and dance. When we left, about midnight, Jan (my girlfriend) and I walked out ahead of the two guys. As we passed the bar, another guy reached out and pinched me. I slapped his hand and quickened my pace. Fred came up to the guy and said, "Hey, that's my girl. What do you think you're doing pinching her?" A big argument developed between Fred and the guy on the bar stool. The guy said that he didn't mean any harm but that I had a "damn cute butt." Well, Fred is a big guy, 6 feet 8 inches tall. The other guy, eventually intimidated, backed down and apologized to Fred for pinching me. None of the guys ever thought that maybe he should be apologizing to me. After all, I was the one who was molested, but the apology was offered to Fred. It was Fred who was "wronged," not me. By pinching me, the other guy had "violated" Fred's property—me. Within our society, women are often considered to be *sexual property*.

STUDENT OBSERVATION

"Sex Bait"

I'm in dental hygiene. A few years ago there were some guys in the program, but now all the dental hygiene students are women. My boyfriend made an interesting observation about us today. He said, "You know, Jinny, all the dental hygienists are cute. Not one of them is ugly." And he's right. The other day a dentist in the clinic was talking with a number of us during a break, and he made a remark that angered me at the time. He said that dentists want attractive dental hygienists because they bring the guys in and the guys are also more likely to come back again. I guess what made me mad is that dental hygienists perform a necessary and useful health function. It's degrading that we are used for sexist purposes, almost as if we were "sex bait."

men in American society have always belonged to the wage sector of the economy, most women were until recently left out of the wage economy altogether. Since household labor and child care typically take place outside the arena of trade and the marketplace, they are not considered "real work." This situation reflects a sexist value system. In a society where money defines worth, women's domestic labor is belittled because it does not yield a monetary return. Household work is devalued because it is private, unpaid, commonplace, done by women, and mingled with love and leisure (Daniels, 1987). Most Americans view household labor as the primary responsibility of the woman, although the man is expected to "help out." If a wife participates in paid labor, her income is seen as "secondary," since the primary responsibility for financially supporting the family falls to the husband (Thompson and Walker, 1991).

Traditionally, the American family system has operated to bind women to their reproductive function. Motherhood has been central to our society's definition of the adult female — the notion that a woman must have children and rear them well. American family patterns have implied that sex is inevitably connected with reproduction (the availability of contraception and abortion notwithstanding). Additionally, the motherhood mandate has ordained that the woman who bears a child must also be the person primarily responsible for his or her rearing. Each woman raises one man's children in an individual household

viewed as private property and private space. This situation has led to the slow development of institutions providing child-care services outside the home.

Women traditionally have provided unpaid child-rearing and domestic services. In a society where money defines worth, women's domestic labor is belittled because it does not yield a monetary return. Most Americans view household labor as the primary responsibility of the woman, although the man is expected to "help out."

Wives' wage labor. The Western definition of marriage as an institution in which the husband provides for his "dependents" has contributed to sexist patterns. Wage labor for women has been viewed as a premarital pastime, a marital supplement, or a threat to the husband's provider role. This view persists despite women's entry into the labor force in unprecedented numbers. Although women's earnings are comparatively low, their financial contribution is becoming an increasingly important component of total household income. (Many women are, moreover, the sole supporters of their families.)

Thus, the wife's income is the one that frequently makes the difference between middle-income and low-income status or that catapults the family into affluence (Townsend, 1985). As of 1991, more than 58 percent of American wives (with husbands present) were in the labor force, up from 30 percent in 1960. Two of three wives with children worked, including 57 percent of those with children younger than three and 60 percent of those with children younger than six (U.S. Bureau of the Census, 1992*a*).

Husbands' domestic labor. Studies show that husbands whose wives work in the wage economy do not engage in more work around the house than do husbands whose wives stay at home (Berk, 1985; Pleck, 1985; Warner, 1986; Kamo, 1988). One survey found that only 14 percent of husbands in two-earner families perform as much as half the housework, and 60 percent do less than a quarter (Townsend, 1985). (See the box "Excuses of a Male Chauvinist Husband.")

Hence, working wives typically must perform two jobs, while their husbands do one. Even if a husband is unemployed, he does much less housework than a wife who puts in a forty-hour week (Blumstein and Schwartz, 1983). And young, educated professional men — yuppies — who claim to support sexual equality are no more likely to do the dishes or change diapers than their blue-collar counterparts (Coleman, 1991; Blumstein and Schwartz, 1991). Not surprisingly, nearly half of working women report difficulty in keeping up with housework, and more than a third feel guilty about work left undone. Half say they have too little time for themselves (Townsend, 1985).

EXCUSES OF A MALE CHAUVINIST HUSBAND

I am willing to share the housework. I'm just not good at it. Why don't we each do what we're best at?

Meaning: You grocery shop, cook, do dishes, clean the house, and do the laundry. I'll bring in the money and maybe help out by changing light bulbs and moving furniture.

I'm willing to help out, but first you'll have to show me over how to do it.

Meaning: Every time I do it, first you'll have to show me over again. And don't plan to read or watch television, because I'll annoy the hell out of you until you find it easier to do it yourself.

I just hate this work. You don't mind it as much as I do.

Meaning: This is crap work. It degrades someone of my intelligence, but it's okay for women.

Gee, we used to be so happy! (When it is the husband's turn to do a task.)

Meaning: *I* used to be so happy before *you* got on this women's liberation kick.

I'm willing to help share the housework. But you can't make me do it on your schedule. That wouldn't be fair.

Meaning: I'll never get around to doing it, so just make up your mind that if you want it done, you had better do it yourself.

Source: Adapted from Pat Mainardi, "The Politics of Housework," in Leslie B. Tanner (ed.), *Voices from Women's Liberation*. New York: New American Library, 1970, pp. 336–342.

Attitudes toward mothers' wage labor. The participation of women in the work force — even mothers with young children — has grown quickly over the past two decades. All Americans do not agree with this change, however. Table 14-4 shows the results of a 1988 national survey of adults. Although two out of every three respondents said that wives should work full-time before they have children and again after the children leave home, 20 percent thought wives should stay home or only work part-time. Seventy-eight percent of the respondents said that mothers of children under school age should stay home or work only part-time; 56 percent responded similarly when asked about mothers of school-age children. While about half of the respondents agreed that being a housewife is as fulfilling as working for pay, one in three saw disadvantages to working outside the home (family life suffers; the woman is not filling the wife's job or is not doing what she really wants). So anywhere between 20 and 80 percent of the respondents, depending on the circumstances, believed that wives should not hold full-time jobs. All of this results in resistance to change in the division of paid labor by sex (Thompson and Walker, 1991).

The entry of women into the wage sector of the economy has constituted one of the most significant social and demographic developments of recent decades. A number of factors have contributed to the expansion of the female work force. Economists point to the shift from a manufacturing to a service economy, a shift accompanied by greater demand for white-collar workers. Demographers cite the increasing availability of new contraceptive methods and legal abortions and the trend toward later marriage and smaller families — all increasing the number of years women can spend in the labor force. And sociologists note such factors as the increased educational attainment of women (educated women are more likely to enter the wage economy), changing societal attitudes toward careers for women outside the home, and legislation that has ended or curtailed some job discrimination barriers. Still, women's participation in the wage economy is hampered by the burden of child care and household labor.

Parental Leave and Child Care

Two types of programs that remove *some* obstacles to women's participating in the labor force on a more equal footing with men are parental leaves and child care. These may occur as a policy of

TABLE 14-4   ATTITUDES TOWARD WOMEN IN THE LABOR FORCE (IN PERCENT)

Do you think that women should work outside the home full-time, part-time, or not at all under these circumstances . . .*	Full-time	Part-time	Stay home
After marrying and before there are children	66	15	5
When there is a child under school age	10	30	48
After the youngest child starts school	31	45	11
After the children leave home	63	17	4

Do you agree or disagree . . .	Agree	Disagree	Other†
A husband's job is to earn money; a wife's job is look after home and family.	27	50	23
All in all, family life suffers when the woman has a full-time job.	34	48	18
A job is alright, but what most women really want is a home and children.	33	37	31
Being a housewife is just as fulfilling as working for pay.	51	22	27

* Percentages do not total to 100% because respondents who couldn't choose or gave no answer are not included in table.
† Includes respondents who neither agreed nor disagreed, couldn't choose, or gave no answer.
Source: General Social Survey, 1988.

employers and/or the government. About 61 percent of our nation's employers, mostly large corporations, provide for flexible work schedules, flexible leaves, and part-time work — policies that assist parents of young children (Hayghe, 1988). About 2 percent of the nation's employers sponsor day-care facilities for their employees' children, and another 9 percent provide some financial assistance or informational referral in helping parents find alternative child care. For these employees, parental leave and child care represent fringe benefits, like health insurance, vacation time, and retirement funds.

However, a large majority of women are without such benefits, and more women might join the labor force if they could obtain them. Thus, there has been increasing pressure for the establishment of government support for such benefits (Harris, 1987). In 1993 the U.S. Congress passed the nation's first family-leave bill, which grants large numbers of employees the right to limited leave without pay for family emergencies. Most European countries have state-subsidized and regulated systems of care for preschool and after-school care (Hewlett, 1986). There is growing public support for the government to act, and an increasing number of politicians describe such programs in terms of a "good investment" — putting more people to work to make the United States more productive and competitive. Others, however, feel strongly that a woman's place is in the home, making sure that her family receives proper care (which only she can provide).

Even these programs may not be enough to give women fully equal opportunity to succeed in the workplace. For example, family-leave policies may guarantee that women don't lose their jobs when they must care for a sick child, and the more generous of such programs even provide some pay. But these policies would not eliminate the stereotype that women are more likely than men to be absent from work in order to care for children. As long as employers have such stereotypes, women as a group are likely to suffer socioeconomic consequences. Yet, if women have a disproportionate responsibility for domestic and child-care duties, how can we expect them to be as productive as the men who do not? (And even if women are as productive, how can we expect employers to believe it?) Until men and women share household and child-care duties more equitably, women's access to socioeconomic rewards will be adversely affected. (Before reading further, look at the Student Observation: "Child Care as a Source of Equality in the Workplace.")

A FINAL WORD ABOUT INEQUALITY IN THE UNITED STATES

We began our discussion by examining evidence showing that socioeconomic inequality results partly from race and sex discrimination — actions that produce greater negative outcomes for one category of people than another on the basis of socially disapproved criteria. Prejudice accounts for some, but not all, discriminatory behavior. Once a group has a structural advantage — such as white males' dominance of managerial positions — the members' actions may *inadvertently* protect their group's advantage and, in the process, discriminate against women and other racial groups. Americans' strong belief in the equity norm would seem to preclude basing socioeconomic rewards on race, sex, ethnicity, or other factors unrelated to job performance. However, our tendency to "turn-around" the equity norm and *legitimate* inequality by assuming that unequal socioeconomic rewards *reflect* differences in contributions undermines the actual operation of equity.

Socioeconomic inequality is a result of the unequal power of groups. Power not only provides an answer to the distributive question of who shall get what, when, and how. It also answers the question of whose social values shall govern human affairs. That is to say, power determines which individual or group will make its behavioral preferences the operating normative rules for others. Power decides which party will be able to translate its social values into the accepted standards for defining the situation and which can

---

STUDENT OBSERVATION

Child Care as a Source of Equality in the Workplace

*M*y Aunt Ann and my Aunt Karen have a lot in common. Both graduated from Georgia Tech with a degree in computer science, both obtained good jobs with respectable corporations when they graduated, and both have two young children. Karen is now a manager with her company and makes about $60,000 a year. Her company has on-site, free child-care facilities, where her two children have been cared for since they were infants. Because of this facility, Karen missed very little work as a result of her children's births. Conversely, Ann is still a technical writer and makes $25,000 a year. Her company has no child-care facilities. The cost of sending her two children to day care would have amounted to at least half of her salary. In addition, Ann felt uncomfortable about leaving her children at a place where she would not be nearby in order to check on them throughout the day. Therefore, she left work for five years (until both of her children were of school age). Upon her return to work, she found that several of her male counterparts had received promotions while she was gone. If her company had child care like Karen's, perhaps she, too, would have been on a more equal footing with her male co-workers. This exemplifies the effect that child care can have on sexual equality in the workplace.

---

make these standards stick through the manipulation of rewards, penalties, and other resources. This will be the topic of Chapter 15, "Deviance and Stigmatization." How some groups work to bring about change in the society's power structure will be discussed in Chapter 16, "Collective Action and Social Movements."

Summary

1. Resources and power are distributed unequally among individuals in the United States. A person's location in the stratification hierarchy of power and resources is measured by three characteristics: education, income, and occupational prestige. Some Americans are more likely than others to fall at the low end of the three indicators of socioeconomic status. African-Americans are only half as likely as whites to have completed four or more years of college. Middle-aged women (thirty-five to fifty-four) earn only 64 cents for each dollar earned by males in this age category. African-Americans are three times as likely as whites to have incomes below the poverty level.

2. The human-capital explanation for the lower incomes of African-Americans and females is that members of these social categories have fewer acquired capabilities and qualifications. For example, African-Americans and females are less likely to have completed four years of college than are whites and males. Discrimination is another explanation for the lower incomes of African-Americans and females. A comparison of African-Americans and whites with similar education levels shows that, even with this human-capital factor held constant, African-Americans earn substantially less than whites do. A comparison of males and females with similar education levels *and* occupations shows that women make much less than men, even with these human-capital factors controlled.

3. Institutional discrimination refers to the policies and programs that systematically deny opportunities and equal rights to members of particular groups. Racism and sexism in structure, stereotypes, and social interaction on the job are implicated in the lower incomes of African-Americans and women. The goal of affirmative action is to ensure equal opportunity for minorities. Public support for affirmative action programs nevertheless remains

high. Support is lowest when quotas are mentioned, but even here opposition does not exceed 50 percent.

4. Segregation, stereotypes, and social interaction also operate to discriminate against African-American and female children in schools. Efforts to reduce institutional discrimination include attempts to racially desegregate American schools. But studies do not find consistent support for the positive impact of desegregation on African-American children's self-esteem or academic achievement.

5. The socioeconomic inequality of men and women results partly from the sexual division of labor in the traditional American family. Women's increasingly large role in the wage economy is affected by the burden of child care and household labor. Programs to alleviate women's disproportionate burden, such as family-leave policies and child-care benefits, have been slow to develop.

CHAPTER 15

DEVIANCE AND STIGMATIZATION

*A*s an Italian-American, I am accustomed to certain norms that are different from those of the larger culture. For example, my family has wine at dinner every night, and I have been expected to drink my share ever since I was seven years old. Once, when I was ten, my family went out to dinner and my grandmother poured wine into a glass for me. When the manager saw me drinking, he came over and told my family that if I continued to drink the wine, he would ask us to leave. This illustrates how a custom of a *subculture* may be viewed as deviant by the dominant culture.

Last summer, I worked on repairing the homes of the poor deep in Appalachia in Matewan, West Virginia. In the hollows of the mountains, I experienced a very different subculture. As I worked at the site, I noticed several "deviant" behaviors, as judged by the norms I was accustomed to. For example, it seemed common for fourteen-year-old girls to date forty-year-old men — a practice often judged unacceptably different by the larger culture. Not only is smoking and growing marijuana considered deviant in our society, but it is also illegal. But in this poverty-stricken Appalachian subculture, marijuana was smoked routinely. No one seemed to worry about being "caught." Also, marijuana was grown in flower boxes in people's front yards, along with the marigolds. Although I thought such acts were deviant, I now realize that they were accepted by the subculture in this part of Appalachia.

Passing, deliberately concealing a stigmatized attribute, has become a difficult part of my everyday life. The fear of my parents' and friends' rejection and their labeling me as a "freak" causes me to conceal the fact that I am a lesbian. I have finally accepted my sexuality, but I cannot deal with the world's reaction and the limits that society might place upon me because of it. While I have other gay friends who know who I really am, I continually employ several techniques to conceal my sexuality. For example, I talk about guys that "look good" and go out on a date every once in a while to appear as what our society considers normal. Passing takes a great deal of effort for me and is often very frustrating. Sometimes I wonder how long people will believe these acts of concealment.

This chapter is an extension of our discussion in Chapter 14, "Inequality and Discrimination." There we discussed how race and sex are sometimes used as criteria for deciding a person's socioeconomic success. Members of our society indicate their *disapproval* of this unequal treatment by calling it "discrimination." As we discussed in Chapter 6, "Social Attitudes and Attributions," *any* diversity within a group of people can be a source of prejudice and unequal treatment: weight (slim or overweight), visual ability (sighted or blind), marital and parental status (married or divorced, parent or stepparent), sexual orientation (heterosexual, homosexual, or bisexual), military participation (soldier or conscientious objector), source of property (buying or stealing).

In Chapter 14, we discussed how the negative treatment of members of a social category is "justified" by their being in possession of less human capital. In this chapter, we will focus our attention on how negative treatment is justified by attributions of "deviance" or "criminality." Just as members of our society disagree about whether unequal treatment associated with race and sex is justified, they also disagree about whether particular types of diversity are deserving of the label "deviant" and, consequently, of negative treatment.

The Social Definition of Deviance

Deviance, as the term is used by social psychologists, consists of characteristics, behaviors, or attitudes that are defined as *undesirably different* from those prescribed by the norms of the group (Stafford and Scott, 1986). Group norms provide the baseline against which deviation is defined, measured, and sanctioned. A group's norms can define *any* characteristic as deviant.

This view differs from the **absolutist view of deviance**, which views deviance as residing in the nature of an act itself; that is, deviance is intrinsic to certain actions. According to the absolutist view, what is deviant is decided not by the social customs of a particular group. Instead, right and wrong exist independently of these arbitrary, human-created social judgments. Standards of right and wrong apply to all cultures at all points in history. According to this view, deviant behavior is something abnormal or wrong that should be corrected—punished, treated, or controlled.

In contrast, the **culturally relative view of deviance**—which is accepted by most social psychologists—recognizes that judgments of right and wrong, normal and abnormal, vary from place to place, from culture to culture, and from one historical time period to another. What one group, in one culture, at one point in time regards as sinful or even criminal behavior may be perfectly acceptable to or even expected by another group or at another time or place. A young gang member who wears a ring through his nose is considered deviant in American culture, but in many African tribes a young male with a ring through his nose is simply conforming to cultural expectations. Public, nonviolent political protest is accepted as a basic right by most Americans, but a majority of Iranians believe in legally prohibiting such protests. Thus, whether a behavior is "normal" or "deviant" depends on the point of view of the group whose norms we judge the behavior against. Deviance is not inherent in behavior but is a judgment made by some about the actions and characteristics of others.

Situation and timing sometimes determine whether a behavior is judged acceptable or deviant (Maines, 1987). For example, whether drinking is defined as "problem drinking" depends partly on *when* we drink (Reese and Katovich, 1989). Drinking early in the morning, during working or parenting hours, all weekend, or too early or late in life may be interpreted as "problematic" or even as alcoholism. In contrast, having one or two drinks after work, at a party, or before bedtime is viewed as "social drinking." Similarly, in most modern societies, killing an unarmed person during an argument is usually regarded as murder, while killing an enemy in war is doing one's duty.

Even a behavior that a group defines as "good" may be considered deviant if practiced in excess. For example, although tidiness is deemed "good" in American culture, it is possible to be "too tidy," and an excessively tidy person will probably be thought of as fanatical or obsessed—certainly as undesirably different, or deviant.

Conceptions of right and wrong are also relative in that they change over time. Consider cigarette smoking, for example, which has undergone a number of changes in acceptability in the United States since 1800 (Troyer and Markle, 1983). In the 1870s many groups strongly condemned cigarette smoking. This was partly because the practice was most common among urban immigrants, who not only had lower social status but also had other habits considered deviant by the larger society, such as heavy drinking. Gradually, the attitudes of Americans toward smoking changed, and by the end of World War

Sometimes *timing* determines whether a behavior is judged acceptable or deviant. For example, whether drinking is defined as "problem drinking" depends partly on *when* we drink. Drinking during working hours is often interpreted as "problematic" or as a sign of alcoholism.

II, it was considered acceptable behavior. In the 1960s, as evidence associating smoking with serious illnesses mounted, attitudes began to change again. By the 1980s, smoking began to be increasingly prohibited in public places as groups began campaigns to protect nonsmokers from cigarette smoke. Smoking is now once again becoming a practice most common among the lower social classes — a fact that may contribute to its loss of popularity among the general American public (Graham, 1987).

It is important to note that neither the commonness nor the rarity of a behavior determines whether the behavior is considered to be deviant. Many uncommon acts are not deviant, and some deviant acts are quite common. For example, winning the Miss USA Pageant is uncommon but not deviant, because it is not negatively evaluated by most Americans. Yet failing to come to a full stop for a stop sign is common but deviant (even illegal), because it violates a formal written norm of the society and may be punishable by fines, loss of driving privileges, or jail, depending on the number and severity of prior driving offenses.

DEVIANCE AND STIGMATIZATION

All of us occasionally deviate from societal norms, at least in minor ways. Some kinds of deviance are quite ordinary, yet disapproved nonetheless. We may burp audibly, utter a remark everyone considers gross, display emotion inappropriately, be "too skinny," or show up in formal dress at a party where everyone else is in jeans. We are likely to feel uncomfortable or embarrassed when we make such social gaffes, primarily because we realize that others are evaluating us negatively on the basis of our behavior.

Each of us can probably remember many instances in which we felt at least momentarily stigmatized by our deviant status. Perhaps we have or can remember having acne as a teenager, along with the feeling that others must be disgusted by our appearance. Perhaps we have a slight speech impediment or an occasional stammer. Or we have experienced the "shame" of having an alcoholic mother or a retarded brother. Some of us may recall instances where we were caught cheating or lying, where it seemed, at least for a while, that our basic integrity was at stake. Perhaps we come from the "wrong side of the tracks" or a city, country, or region that is deprecated in many jokes. Perhaps we remember acquiring nicknames that hurt—"tubby," "four-eyes," "baldy," or "tanglefoot." On occasion we have undoubtedly expressed an opinion that turned out to be at odds with the clear consensus of a group we were anxious to impress, an opinion whose expression seemed to invite derision or scathing disbelief. (Jones et al., 1984: 5)

When we violate norms, our identities, at least momentarily, become tarnished. Among social psychologists, the process by which negatively evaluated attributes cause a person's identity to be discredited or spoiled is referred to as **stigmatization** (Goffman, 1963b).

Some forms of deviance cause a person's identity to fall into disrepute only briefly. Other deviant acts may lead to the application of a "deviant" label not just to the act itself but to the *person*. In effect, some persons are assigned a *deviant social identity*, such as troublemaker, liar, addict, or unbeliever. For example, a man who interrupts, apologizes, and is excused once might find less forgiveness if he interrupts too often. Friends and associates may start to view him as a "jerk" or an "ass." Similarly, a woman who regularly trips over things might be thought of as a "klutz"; a man who regularly spills ketchup on his tie may be termed a "slob"; and someone who belches repeatedly might be labeled a "geek." Like other social identities, such deviant identities can negatively affect how others view and react to those so labeled. (See the Student Observation: "Stigmatized Identities.")

In some cases, a discredited behavior (or other attribute) may become the most important component in a person's social identity. Such persons are perceived not only as having committed deviant *acts* but as being deviant *persons*. Their social identities are profoundly and often permanently changed—spoiled. They become, in the minds of others, epileptics, handicapped, blind, homosexuals, illiterate, murderers, rapists, thieves, child molesters, delinquents, drug addicts, alcoholics, or mentally ill. Such deviant identities may become *master statuses* that profoundly shape others' perceptions of the persons so labeled (Becker, 1963; Goffman, 1963b). On the basis of master statuses, we tend to attribute to the person a wide range of imperfections (Goffman, 1963b). In other words, stigmatization involves the activation of negative stereotypes for deviant identities (Barbarin, 1986; Crocker and Lutsky, 1986). Thus, one generally negative identity comes to dominate all the person's interactions.

Let's now turn to a discussion of several characteristics and behaviors stigmatized by American society: physical disabilities, homosexuality, juvenile delinquency, and white-collar crime. Social definition of these varied attributes as undesirab-

---

STUDENT OBSERVATION

Stigmatized Identities

This past summer I worked as a lifeguard at the local country club. A fourteen-year-old named Bob also worked at the club, and he often came over to the pool to chat and to help me do some jobs that took more than one person. He was a really nice kid and everybody seemed to like him. One day, my boss came over to the pool and told me that Bob would not be coming over to the pool anymore unless I specifically needed him to help me do something. I asked why. My boss said that Bob had told some of the members' children at the pool that he was on probation and was working to pay back some of the money he was fined by the courts. Needless to say, the kids at the pool told their parents, and their parents told my boss they didn't want Bob around their kids. My boss really had no choice. Bob's identity was stigmatized, so he wasn't allowed to associate with the "conventional" children at the pool.

ly different illustrates the social construction of deviance.

Physical Disability

What do criminals and persons with physical disabilities have in common? Not much, according to popular definitions. We tend to view criminals as "morally defective" but the disabled as "unfortunate." Both identities, however, are *undesirably different* and thus, according to the social psychological definition, are deviant. How is this way of viewing physical disability useful? The social psychological treatment of physical disability as deviance emphasizes that the disabled are *stigmatized* in ways that have profound implications for their identities and social interactions.

Your negative feelings about criminals are probably pretty definite. If you are a nondisabled person, you may have ambivalent — a mixture of positive and negative — feelings toward persons with physical disabilities or may even deny that you have any negative feelings at all. This is a common reaction. When the stigmatized person cannot be held responsible for his or her condition, any negative feelings that we may have come into conflict with our societal norms of fairness and sympathy. Thus, we may feel both positive (friendly, sympathetic, accepting) and negative (hostile, denigrative, rejecting) feelings toward the stigmatized person. To complicate matters further, we may conceal our negative feelings in order to support our own and others' view of ourselves as tolerant and caring.

Despite norms which specify that we should feel sympathy for and not reject those with physical disabilities, there is evidence that physical deviance generates powerfully negative reactions. For example, persons with physical deformities — missing limbs, obesity, burn scars, and the like — are often referred to as "disgusting," "nauseating," "offensive," "gross," "sickening," or "revolting" (Jones et al., 1984). Our interactions with others, especially with strangers, are strongly influenced by appearance. Recall the discussion in Chapter 6, "Social Attitudes and Attributions,"

about the importance of physical attractiveness stereotypes in shaping our responses to others. We might reasonably expect that persons with physical disabilities that are viewed as extremely unattractive — "gross" or "revolting" — would be the targets of much negative stereotyping. If "what is beautiful is good," then "what is revolting" is surely bad.

Physically deviant people are clearly disadvantaged both by the immediate negative reactions they elicit and by the longer-term consequences of coping with the avoiding and rejecting behaviors of others. In addition to encountering physical barriers — such as the lack of wheelchair access or the absence of signing interpreters — those with physical disabilities face *social* barriers as well. Historically, laws restricted people with handicaps who "constitute a disgusting sight" from appearing in public, and many disabled people report reactions from "normal" people suggesting that the disabled should not be "out in public." A man with spina bifida confided to a researcher that another man had said to him, "When I was young, we kept people like you in institutions" (Gardner, 1991).

Even when others are sympathetic to the plight of disabled persons, they may be uncomfortable interacting with them. Informants with disabilities reported to one researcher that their interactions with "normals" often were characterized by awkward solemnity, artificial levity, fixed stares directed elsewhere, and avoidance of common, everyday words that suddenly were taboo (Davis, 1961). Normals often take great pains to disguise their awareness of the disability. The disabled person is then obligated to disguise his or her awareness of the normal's disguise. All this posturing interferes with the smooth flow of interaction:

> I get suspicious when somebody says, "Let's go for a uh, ah [imitates confused and halting speech] push with me down the hall," or something like that . . . it means that they're aware, really aware, that there's a wheelchair here, and that this is probably uppermost with them. (Davis, 1961: 123)

Persons with disabilities often feel that their physical and social environments are more disabling than their medical conditions (Albrecht, 1994). Disability activists distinguish between three interrelated concepts: impairments, disability, and handicap. *Impairments* are bodily disturbances resulting from birth, injury, or disease. Examples include deafness, loss of a limb, paralysis, or brain damage. A *disability* is a restriction resulting from an impairment that prevents an individual from performing an activity in the manner considered "normal." Examples include difficulties with such tasks as reading, using the toilet, preparing meals, speaking, or walking. A *handicap* is the social disadvantage individuals experience as a result of an impairment or a disability. The term "handicap" is in disfavor with some disability activists because it suggests that the problem resides in the individual, not in society. This reaction to the term is reflected in a statement by a nurse who has difficulty keeping a job because of rare epileptic seizures: "I'm not handicapped. Society handicaps me" (Albrecht, 1994).

Social psychologists have offered two explanations for the stigmatization of the disabled (Jones et al., 1984). The first derives from the norm of social responsibility which requires that we help those who are dependent. We discussed this norm in Chapter 10, "Helping and Reward Exchange." People with disabilities represent a cost to us in that they obligate us to provide help. This obligation may become a serious threat when our association with the person is ongoing, as with a neighbor, relative, or co-worker. In such cases, an initial commitment to help may imply continued obligations. How can we offer help today and refuse tomorrow? This may explain why people are more reluctant to help a permanently disabled person than someone with a temporary impairment, such as a broken leg.

Second, physically disabled persons confront those without disabilities with a direct challenge to their conception of the world as a just place (Jones et al., 1984). As noted in Chapter 10, the just-world hypothesis sometimes leads us to

Why do we stigmatize physically disabled persons? Social psychologists suggest that the disabled represent a cost to us because we feel an obligation to help them, and that they threaten our view of the world as fair.

blame victims for their own misfortune. We want to believe that the world is just because this view enables us to confront our physical and social environments as stable and orderly. Rather than abandoning the notion that the world is fair when confronted with the unfortunate circumstances of physically disabled persons, normals may attribute qualities to the victim that make his or her misfortune seem deserved. Because belief in a just world is so important to all facets of our lives, the non-disabled may be tempted to view the disabled person as evil or immoral, or at least foolish, and therefore deserving of her or his fate. By *blaming the victim*, the nondisabled are able to preserve their view of the world as just while accounting for the disabled person's misfortune.

Homosexuality: Difference or Deviance?

Physical disability is not the only form of diversity that evokes "deviant" labels and stigmatization. There is variety in human sexual behavior, not only among societies but also among subcultures within the same society. Almost any sexual behavior you can think of is condoned somewhere in the world at the same time that it is condemned somewhere else. Even within any subculture, the same sexual behavior may be condoned in one situation while condemned in another. For example, a pat on the buttocks is condemned when the parties are strangers or co-workers, but it is condoned when the parties are married (although maybe not even then, if the behavior takes place in public).

In some cases, disapproved sexual behaviors are criminalized. If authorities define certain sexual behaviors as a threat to society, they may pass legislation establishing specific penalties for these behaviors. In our society, for example, sexual assault (rape) and sexual abuse of children are crimes. There are national debates over whether premarital sex (fornication), pornography, homosexuality, and prostitution should be legal or criminalized.

Within the United States, reactions to homosexuality vary. For example, a 1992 opinion poll asked Americans whether "homosexuality should be considered an acceptable alternative lifestyle or not," 38 percent said it should and 57 percent said it should not (Hugick, 1992). When the same poll asked whether "homosexual relations between consenting adults should or should not be legal," 48 percent said such relations should be legal and 44 percent said they should be illegal. In fact, private, consensual, same-sex acts between adults are illegal in about half of the states and legal in the other half (Rivera, 1991).

Public support for gay rights has increased over the past two decades, but the issue continues to divide the country. In 1977, only 56 percent of Americans polled supported gay rights in the workplace. In a 1992 Gallup Poll, 74 percent of Americans endorsed the concept that homosex-

uals should have equal rig[...] portunities (Hugick, 1992). [...] about specific occupation[...] supported gay job rights. F[...] 82 percent of the 1992 respo[...] should be hired as salespers[...], fewer thought gays should be allowed to be members of the armed forces (57 percent), doctors (53 percent), or elementary school teachers (41 percent).

In most places, homosexuals can be denied private employment. They are denied security clearances. During his presidential campaign, Bill Clinton received death threats for his support of lifting the ban on gays in the military. Many professional and occupational licensing requirements have "good character" clauses that allow discrimination against gays. A number of public school teachers were dismissed when their homosexuality became known. Homosexuals have no legal right to marry (although some churches perform religious ceremonies for them), and the homosexuality of a parent is a serious disadvantage in child custody proceedings. Homosexuals from other countries can be denied entry to the United States and can be deported even if they have been in this country many years.

Although some cities and states have passed legislation prohibiting discrimination on the basis of sexual orientation, movements to void such laws are growing. In 1992, initiatives banning civil rights protections designed specifically for homosexuals passed in Colorado and in Tampa, Florida, and others were narrowly defeated in Oregon and in Portland, Maine (Carper, 1992). Oregon's measure would also have required schools, public colleges, and all other branches of state government to "assist in setting a standard for Oregon's youth that recognizes homosexuality as abnormal, wrong, unnatural, and perverse . . . and to be discouraged and avoided." In addition to institutionalized discrimination, homosexuals face growing antigay violence (Herek, 1991; *New York Times*, March 20, 1992).

Thus, homosexuality is at the center of a national debate on sexual behavior. The debate fo-

488

on whether homosexuality is *deviant* behavior — which should be punished, outlawed, or at least disapproved — or whether it constitutes a *different but acceptable* alternative sexual life style. Social psychology cannot tell us which side of the deviance versus alternative-life style controversy we should agree with, but it can examine societal reactions to homosexuality and the impact of stigmatization on homosexuals themselves.

What is homosexuality? Even the question of who is and who is not homosexual, or what is or is not homosexual behavior, is controversial. Americans disagree about the defining features of homosexuality. A person may be classified as "homosexual" according to some of these features but not according to others. Consider, for example, Bill, a married construction worker in his mid-forties, who fits our masculine stereotype, thinks of himself as masculine — even macho — and unquestionably considers himself to be heterosexual. Bill has no friends who are gay, and he ridicules the homosexual subculture. However, on two occasions — both when he was in his twenties — Bill had a sexual encounter with a man. Is Bill a homosexual?

Contrast Bill with an adolescent girl, Tammy, who is viewed by others as "a tomboy." Tammy is sexually and romantically attracted to women and thinks of herself as a homosexual. She has fantasized about, but never actually had, sexual contact with a woman. Many of her friends are gay, and she shuns the heterosexual dating subculture, although she occasionally has intercourse with a close male friend. Is Tammy a homosexual?

There is no single formula for determining the categorization of sexual orientation (Klein, Sepekoff, and Wolf, 1985; Berkey, Perelman-Hall, and Kurdek, 1990). If the members of your social psychology class were to categorize Bill and Tammy on the basis of the descriptions we provided, some would probably say that both are homosexuals; others would say that neither is a homosexual; some would say that Bill is but Tammy is not; others would say that Tammy is but Bill is not; and still others would admit that they aren't sure.

Even lesbians and gay males seem to differ in the criteria they use to classify themselves as homosexual. Lesbians tend to give same-sex affectional orientations more weight, while gay men view sexual behavior and sexual fantasy as more central to their self-identities as gay (Gonsiorek and Weinrich, 1991).

Stereotypes of homosexuals. According to common American stereotypes, homosexuals are believed to have confused gender identities, in which male homosexuals are effeminate and female homosexuals are masculine. In fact, one study showed that most people cannot easily distinguish homosexuals and heterosexuals on the basis of appearance and mannerisms. Videotaped interviews with homosexual and heterosexual men and women were shown to male and female raters, who were asked to identify the homosexuals (Berger et al., 1987). Less than 20 percent of the raters were able to identify homosexuals at better than chance levels.

Part of the American stereotype of homosexuals includes the notion that they are transvestites, or cross-dressers. Despite the stereotype, most American homosexuals do not cross-dress, and many transvestites are heterosexual. This is not the case in some other cultures, where homosexuals *are* more likely to cross-dress and to engage in androgynous gender behavior (Jackson, 1989).

Reactions to homosexuality in other cultures. Different reactions to homosexuality among cultures illustrate that each culture maintains its own way of interpreting the range of sexual behavior — defining some patterns as "normal," ignoring other patterns, and stigmatizing still others. Whether homosexuality is deviance or not depends on the norms of the society and the symbolic meaning attached to sexual behaviors in a particular culture.

Among Melanesians, for example, homosexual behavior has a different meaning from the one it has in Western societies. It is viewed not only as natural and normal but as *necessary*. Melanesian culture *prescribes* homosexual behavior, while Western cultures generally forbid it. Ritualized homosexual behavior is a means by which Melanesian boys are incorporated into the adult society of men. Melanesians also believe homosexuality encourages a boy's growth, finishing off his growth in puberty:

> Semen is also necessary for young boys to attain full growth to manhood. . . . They need a boost, as it were. When a boy is eleven or twelve years old, he is engaged for several months in homosexual intercourse with a healthy older man chosen by his father. (This is always an in-law or unrelated person, since the same notions of incestuous relations apply to little boys as to marriageable women.) Men point to the rapid growth of adolescent youths, the appearance of peach fuzz beards, and so on, as the favorable results of this child-rearing practice. (Schieffelin, 1976: 124)

The men and boys involved in these relationships are all expected to marry and to father children. They do not think of themselves as homosexuals, nor do they engage in homosexual behavior outside this narrowly defined relationship. The homosexual behavior is seen as a helpful and honorable means of passing on strength to younger men and boys. Thus, it is clear that whether homosexuality is considered deviant is a matter of social definition. Such social definitions are culturally and historically relative.

Crime

A **crime** is an act that violates a criminal code enacted by an officially constituted political authority. In common terms, crimes are acts that violate laws — a distinctive set of formal norms. In literate societies laws are written down and have an enforcement mechanism attached, along with specific penalties for violation. The Federal Bureau of Investigation (FBI) publishes an annual document called the Uniform Crime Reports that summarizes crime statistics from across the country (FBI, 1986). These reports also reflect the social definition of crime. In them, the FBI distinguishes between Part I offenses and Part II offenses. Part I offenses are defined as the more serious offenses and include both violent crimes (murder, rape, aggravated assault, and robbery) and property crimes (burglary, larceny-theft, motor vehicle theft, and arson). Part II offenses are defined as less serious and include such behavior as forgery, fraud, embezzlement, vandalism, gambling, public drunkenness, and disorderly conduct.

At first glance, it appears that crimes are dangerous acts. But many criminologists argue that the acts labeled as "crimes" are not the only acts that endanger us, nor are they the acts that endanger us the most. Criminal justice expert Jeffrey Reiman explains:

> We have a greater chance . . . of being killed or disabled, for example, by an occupational injury or disease, by unnecessary surgery, or by shoddy emergency medical services than by aggravated assault or even homicide! . . .
>
> Similarly, the general public loses more money *by far* . . . from price-fixing and monopolistic practices and from consumer deception and embezzlement than from all the property crimes in the FBI's Index combined . . . although the individuals responsible for these acts take more money out of the ordinary citizen's pocket . . . they rarely show up in arrest statistics and almost never in prison populations. . . . The criminal justice system does not simply *reflect* the reality of crime; it has a hand in *creating* the reality we see. (Reiman, 1990: 44–45)

Crime is a reality that takes shape as it is filtered through a series of human decisions — from the lawmakers who determine which behaviors should be labeled "criminal" to the law enforcers who decide which individuals the labels will be applied to. Decisions about what to label and treat as "crime" are not determined by objective dangers. Thus, to understand the reality of crime, we must examine the social processes that shape those decisions. Reiman offers us another example of turning the equity norm on its head:

> If people believe . . . that the criminal justice system simply *reacts* to the gravest threats to their well-being — they come to believe that whatever is the

target of the criminal justice system must be the greatest threat to their well-being. In other words, if people believe that the most drastic of society's weapons are wielded by the criminal justice system *in reaction to* the gravest dangers to society, they will believe the reverse as well: that those actions that call forth the most drastic of society's weapons *must be those* that pose the gravest dangers to society. . . . People come to believe that prisoners must be criminals *because* they are in prison. . . . (1990: 45–46)

We will examine some of the social processes that shape decisions about what we consider "crime" by focusing on two types of crime—juvenile delinquency and white-collar crime.

Juvenile delinquency. Although misbehavior by children and adolescents has apparently been common throughout human history, "juvenile delinquency" is a relatively modern concept (Gibbons and Krohn, 1986). The term was introduced after the establishment of the first juvenile court and of procedures for treating young offenders *differently* from adults. Until the late nineteenth century, deviant behavior by youths was usually considered to be a family matter. Nevertheless, if serious or persistent cases of deviance became a matter of community concern, public reprimands, whippings, and even capital punishment were administered to children (Reid, 1988). Children over the age of seven were considered old enough to know right from wrong and to understand the consequences of their actions. Consequently, although they were not considered adults, they were held legally responsible for their law-violating behavior.

As we discussed in Chapter 3, "Socialization over the Life Course," during the last part of the nineteenth century, the concept of adolescence developed, identifying the period of life between childhood and adulthood. In effect, this "stage" of the life course was created to reflect growing social agreement that adolescents were somehow different from both children and adults. Child-labor and compulsory-education laws were enacted, restricting the participation of children and

adolescents in the labor force and requiring that they attend school until reaching a certain age. At the same time, public sentiment grew for laws that held juveniles somewhat accountable for their behavior but less accountable than adults. States passed laws legally defining adulthood and applied the term "juvenile" to persons under the legal age of adulthood. In 1899, the first juvenile court was established, creating special legal procedures to deal with law violations by children and youths. Juvenile court systems were established in all the states.

In the United States, delinquency statutes vary from state to state, and from locale to locale. Each state has designated a specific age as the dividing line between juvenile and criminal offenders. Typically, the minimum age for delinquency is set at seven years, reflecting the historical assumption that children younger than seven are not capable of criminal intent. The upper age boundary is defined by state laws legally defining adulthood. Exceptions to these definitions may be made when the juvenile court refers an offender to criminal court to stand trial as an adult.

Juvenile delinquency includes acts that, if committed by an adult, would be crimes. Generally, juveniles who commit such offenses are treated less harshly by the justice system than adults who commit the same crimes. In addition, other activities that are not legally prohibited for adults are considered illegal when engaged in by juveniles. For example, being truant from school, running away from home, smoking, drinking, and violating curfew are illegal only because of the age status of the juvenile offenders. Such acts are called *status offenses*. Thus, like other forms of deviance, juvenile delinquency is socially defined.

Federal and state statutes dealing with juvenile delinquency are based on cultural values and assumptions regarding adolescents, specifically, their capabilities, their relationship to adults, and the state's appropriate role in regulating their lives. In the United States, adults, particularly parents, are given the right and responsibility to make decisions for adolescents. The state is assumed to have an interest in the welfare of juveniles, including the right and responsibility to intervene if parents fail to meet their obligations. In this sense, the state is seen as a substitute parent and is required to act "in the best interests of the child."

The youngsters officially labeled "delinquent" (such as juvenile defendants in court cases or wards of juvenile training schools) are disproportionately lower-class and African-American males. Some researchers argue that official statistics exaggerate social class and racial differences because they reflect discrimination on the basis of social class and race by the police and courts.

To test this possibility, self-reports have been used in some studies of delinquent behavior. Such studies ask respondents to indicate how often they have committed each of a list of delinquent acts. Most self-report studies suggest that nearly all juveniles engage in at least some delinquent behavior at some time. Only a small fraction of young people who admit committing offenses are caught by the police. Some juveniles engage in

repetitive, serious forms of misconduct, while others participate only in relatively innocuous kinds of misbehavior (Elliott and Ageton, 1980; Hindelang, Hirschi, and Weis, 1981; Elliott and Huizinga, 1983; Gibbons and Krohn, 1986). In addition, numerous studies indicate that the police use extensive discretion when arresting people and that social status, race, and gender are all factors influencing their decisions (Sampson, 1986; Fagan, Slaughter, and Hartstone, 1987; Corley, Cernkovich, and Giordano, 1989).

White-collar crime. Think of a crime — any crime. Picture the first crime that comes into your mind. What do you see? You're probably imagining a robbery or a physical attack by one person on another. What does the criminal look like? Most likely, you haven't pictured a person wearing a suit and tie. In fact, you're probably looking at a young, tough, lower-class male.

Criminologists have come to define **white-collar crime** as "a violation of the law committed

Only a small fraction of young people who admit committing offenses are caught by the police. The youngsters officially labeled "delinquent" are disproportionately lower-class and African-American males. Numerous studies indicate that the police use extensive discretion when arresting people and that social status, race, and gender are all factors influencing their decisions.

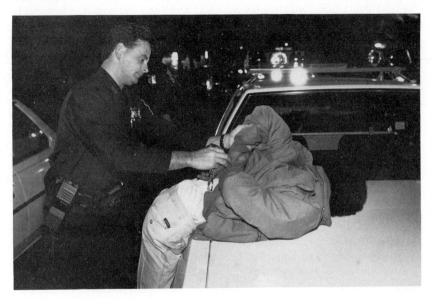

by a person or group of persons *in the course of an otherwise respected and legitimate occupation or financial activity*" (Sutherland, 1949; Coleman, 1985). Thus, if an executive bribes a public official to secure favors for his corporation, a white-collar crime has been committed. If the same executive murders his wife, the act is not a white-collar crime but a violent crime committed by a man with a respectable job. The activities of people or organizations that make money *exclusively* through illegal means—the business activities of drug rings, phony stock companies, land swindlers, and so forth—are not considered to be white-collar crimes. Criminologists distinguish two varieties of white-collar crime: occupational and organizational crime.

Occupational crimes are work-related crimes committed by individual organization members for personal gain. For example, the embezzlement of funds by a bank employee, the pilferage of office supplies by a worker, tax evasion, and the accepting of a bribe are crimes committed in an occupational setting for personal gain. In the government sector, occupational crimes include making special deals for government contracts, selling immunity, and engaging in a conflict of interest. In the professions, occupational crime occurs, for example, when a physician provides unnecessary medical procedures, when a lawyer talks a client into pursuing legal action that will bring lucrative fees to the lawyer but have little chance of success for the client, and when an auditor files fraudulent financial statements in order to keep a firm's business. There are also more blatant cases, such as

Medicaid and Medicare fraud. (Before reading further, see the Student Observation: "Occupational Crime" and the box "The Savings and Loan Scandal" for examples of occupational crime.)

Organizational crimes are committed with the support and encouragement of a formal organization and are intended, at least partly, to advance the goals of that organization. Victims of organizational crimes may be the owners of the organization (such as stockholders), the workers, the customers or consumers, and the general public. Examples of organizational crime include the falsification of drug test reports by a pharmaceutical company in order to cover up negative side effects of a drug it manufactures, rigging of bids by a weapons manufacturer in order to procure a government contract, violations of state safety laws by a construction firm in order to meet a deadline, violations of emissions regulations by a factory, fraud and false advertising by a health-food chain, attempts to control the marketplace by airline companies, and violations of civil liberties (such as harassment and illegal surveillance) by the police. Consider the following example of organizational crime.

The deaths and injuries caused by industries frequently result from corporate acts that are criminal in nature. Every year, because of corporate disregard for safe working conditions, hundreds of thousands of American workers become disabled or die from occupational diseases (Simon and Eitzen, 1986). For example, in the United States, over 4 million workers have been heavily

---

STUDENT OBSERVATION

Occupational Crime

My father worked in an office in New York City before he retired. I remember when it came time for school to begin again, he would bring bags of pens, paper, and notebooks home with him. I never thought about where my father was getting all the school supplies, and I certainly never thought that he was stealing them. Now, however, I realize that my father was committing an occupational crime. He was taking home with him supplies intended for office use. By doing this, he avoided spending his own money and thus gained at the expense of the company he worked for.

THE SAVINGS AND LOAN SCANDAL

In 1990, Americans became aware of the financial failure of savings and loan companies across the country, which would cost taxpayers billions of dollars. Although part of the failure was caused by bad loans, a large part was the result of crime. Kitty Calavita and Henry Pontell (1991) studied "collective embezzlement" both in the savings and loan institutions and in the insurance industry. *Collective embezzlement*, according to their definition, is the siphoning off of company funds for personal use by members of top management. These white-collar criminals do not act alone; they operate within networks of co-conspirators inside and outside the institutions they run. Collective embezzlement ranges from outright looting of an institution's cash or other resources to engaging in business practices whose sole purpose is the generation of personal profits for management, despite negative effects on the health of the institution itself.

The sources of collective embezzlement, according to Calavita and Pontell, can be traced to two factors: opportunity and risk. *Opportunity* exists in the very setup of thrifts and insurance companies, which are entrusted to handle and manage other people's money. Embezzlers have access to this money through their management positions within the institutions. The amounts of money involved are unique to financial institutions. Unlike manufacturing institutions, from which consumers receive products for their money, financial institutions give consumers only a "promise" of a future service. Thrift and insurance managers do not need to actu-

ally produce anything immediately in exchange for the capital of their customers. They are, therefore, unburdened by the costs of the production process that limit the expansion possibilities of manufacturing institutions. As a result, opportunities for embezzlement are almost infinitely expanded.

While opportunities for fraud in the thrift and insurance industries are extensive, the *risks* involved in such fraud remain relatively minor. Much of this low risk can be "credited" to inadequate government regulation, based on faith in free-market practices. According to free-market theorists, government regulation stifles competition among institutions, thereby reducing their efficiency and fitness. In fact, competition may reduce the fitness of a financial institution, for weak institutions often offer the most competitive deals (e.g., low interest rates on loans and high rates on savings) in an effort to attract new money. This may only compound their solvency problems.

The savings and loan debacle emphasizes the role that public trust plays in the operation of financial institutions. People need to "trust" these institutions with their money; otherwise, they will invest it elsewhere. The dilemma for government regulators is that while they must not allow embezzlers to jeopardize public faith in the integrity of the institutions, revelations of criminality might erode the very trust they want to protect. If regulators close an insolvent institution, government insurance funds will have to cover the losses. The huge sums involved are a disincentive to close such institutions.

exposed to asbestos. About 1.6 million of these are expected to die of lung cancer — more than the total U.S. loss of lives during World War II and subsequent wars (Balkan, Berger, and Schmidt, 1980). As early as 1920, asbestos-industry top executives knew that workers exposed to asbestos were in danger of contracting several fatal diseases. Yet workers were not informed of these dangers until the late 1970s.

Before 1920, evidence began appearing in medical journals that exposure to asbestos dust

causes debilitating, often fatal, diseases. By 1918, insurance companies had decided that it was too expensive and risky to insure asbestos workers, and four states already had enacted workers' compensation laws that included the disease of asbestosis (Ermann and Lundman, 1982). Corporate memos and other documents indicate that while executives at the Johns-Manville Corporation — one of the oldest and largest manufacturers of asbestos in the United States — knew about this information, they did nothing to warn or protect the company's workers. To the contrary, company executives *suppressed* research on the dangers of working with asbestos, instructed company physicians not to tell workers when their chest X-rays showed symptoms of asbestosis, and quietly settled workers' claims out of court. This cover-up continued for forty years (Calhoun and Hiller, 1988).

Johns-Manville's medical director, Kenneth Wallace Smith, went along with the company policy of not informing employees that their routine physical examinations revealed asbestosis. He explained his actions this way:

> Eventually, compensation will be paid to each of those men. But, as long as a man is not disabled it is felt he should not be told of his condition so that he can live and work in peace and the company can benefit by his many years of experience. (Ermann and Lundman, 1982: 73)

Profit is the most obvious explanation for the company's blatant disregard for its workers' safety. For example, in 1972, it would have cost Johns-Manville $12 million to install dust control equipment and $5 million a year to maintain it. Paying workers' compensation cost the company only $1 million a year. In short, it was not "cost-effective" to protect workers.

Workers are not the only victims of white-collar crime. Millions of serious injuries are caused each year by unsafe consumer products. A number of cases have received substantial publicity: Firestone's cover-up of defects in its Firestone 500 tire, Richardson-Merrell Company's falsification of tests required by the Food and Drug Administration, Beech-Nut Nutrition Corporation's sale of phony apple juice for babies, and Cordis Corporation's sale of faulty cardiac pacemakers (Coleman, 1985; Welles, 1988; Allen, 1988). In addition, corporations also violate laws designed to protect the environment and public health. Before reading further, see the box "Organizational Crime in the 1980s and 1990s."

Although determining exactly how many people are killed and injured each year as a result of white-collar crimes may be impossible, the claim that such crimes are harmless, nonviolent offenses can hardly be taken seriously. Yet Americans appear reluctant to treat white-collar crime as serious deviance.

Our reluctance to define white-collar offenses as crime, some researchers argue, stems partly from our stereotypes of the "typical crime" and "typical criminal" (Reiman, 1990). These stereotypes, which are strengthened by the media's portrayal of crime as violent acts committed by lower-class persons, keep us from defining as murder a mine or factory disaster in which workers die, even if someone is responsible for the unsafe conditions. The typical criminal, we reason, *wants* to harm his or her victim. A company executive, on the other hand, would prefer that none of the firm's workers is harmed. The executive who violates safety regulations to maximize profits is seen as just doing her or his job. If workers die as a result, we may think the executive is a callous individual but not a murderer. She or he is not the typical criminal and has not committed the typical crime.

There is some evidence that public concern about white-collar crime is increasing. Respondents in a number of studies have rated white-collar offenses as being as serious as street crimes (Geis, 1984). In 1985, a Chicago judge gave the most severe sentence ever (25 years) to three company executives for their failure to correct unsafe plant conditions that resulted in the death of an employee. The employee died after inhaling cyanide poison. During the trial, evidence was presented showing that employees were not warned that they were working with dangerous substances and that safety precautions had been deliberately ignored. In his opinion, the judge observed, "This is not a case of taking a gun and shooting someone. It is more like leaving a time bomb in an airport. The bomb kept ticking . . . until Stefan Golab [the employee] died." Although the defense attorneys shook their heads in disbelief and the wife of one executive shrieked in horror at the judge's statement, 80 percent of the *Detroit Free Press* readers who responded to a poll the day after

ORGANIZATIONAL CRIME IN THE 1980s AND 1990s

Recent examples of organizational crime include the following:

- The Beech-Nut Nutrition Corporation marketed phony apple juice for babies. The product it sold as 100 percent apple juice actually contained little, if any, apple juice. The company was indicted in 1986 (Buder, 1987; Welles, 1988).

- Motorola, a major U.S. defense contractor, pleaded guilty to defrauding the Pentagon of at least $5 million on Navy weapons contracts from 1982 to 1984 (*Columbus*, [Ohio] *Dispatch*, March 26, 1988: 3).

- The Hertz Corporation charged its rental-car customers and their insurance agents more for repairs to damaged cars than the company actually paid. The scam produced a $13-million gain for the company over seven years, until discovery in 1985 (Levine, 1988).

- The Cordis Corporation sold cardiac pacemakers that it knew were faulty, and it filed false quality-assurance reports with the Food and Drug Administration from 1980 to 1985 (Allen, 1988).

- E. F. Hutton and Company (now part of Shearson Lehman Hutton, Inc.) pleaded guilty in 1988 to laundering money for organized crime figures and for business people trying to hide income from the Internal Revenue Service (*Wall Street Journal*, May 17, 1988: 16).

- The tanker Exxon *Valdez* ran aground on a reef off the coast of Alaska in March 1989, dumping 11 million gallons of crude oil and fouling 700 miles of shoreline. In 1991, Exxon agreed to pay $1 billion in criminal and civil fines rather than face trial. A federal judge later refused to accept this amount. At the time this book went to print, the case was still being settled (*Wall Street Journal*, April 25, 1991: A3).

- In 1991, the Food and Drug Administration seized all of the Citrus Hill orange juice stored in a Minneapolis warehouse. The maker of Citrus Hill, Procter & Gamble, had advertised the juice as "pure squeezed" and "fresh," despite the fact that the juice was made from concentrate. (Ingersoll and Swasy, 1991).

- A 1992 investigation revealed that Sears' automobile repair services were routinely overcharging customers and charging for unnecessary repairs. Sears admitted no wrongdoing, but agreed to an $8-million settlement (Faison, 1992).

- In 1992, nine U.S. airlines—including American, Delta, and United—were charged with price-fixing. At the time this book went to print, a class-action lawsuit was pending and the airlines were denying that they had acted unlawfully, but most of the airlines involved had agreed to settlements totaling $458 million (McDowell, 1992).

the verdict said that the murder charge was not too harsh for negligent employers (Thio, 1988). The murder convictions were later overturned on appeal (Frank, 1988).

STIGMATIZING EFFECTS OF CAUSAL ATTRIBUTIONS

In Chapter 6, "Social Attitudes and Attributions," we noted that people's causal explanations, or *attributions*, about behaviors and events can strongly affect their reactions to them. For example, we are likely to react more negatively to someone who

we believe is *responsible* for his or her physical deviance (such as an obese person) than to someone who we believe is an *innocent victim* (such as a person disabled in an automobile accident). We make attributions about all kinds of behavior all the time.

Not surprisingly, scientific theories *reflect* cultural values about deviance. The scientists who have studied deviance have, for the most part, grounded their investigations in the assumption that deviance is, by definition, pathological — that deviants, by virtue of some mental, physical, or social defect, are not like the rest of us (Farrell and

Swigert, 1988). Early physicians and psychologists hoped to identify the causes of deviance by searching for abnormal mental and physical characteristics among deviant populations. On the other hand, early sociologists doubted the biological origin of deviance and focused instead on abnormal social conditions, such as rapid social change, urbanization, and weak social ties.

Both scientific and popular views of deviance have, in many instances, moved away from purely moral or criminal judgments of deviance and toward conceptions of deviance as symptoms of physical or emotional illness (Archer, 1985). This trend—referred to as the **medicalization of deviance**—has led to the replacement of criminal punishments by medical interventions for many forms of deviance. The transition from a "badness" to a "sickness" explanation has occurred for hyperactivity in children, alcoholism, substance abuse, mental illness, and homosexuality.

Our causal attributions about such conditions have profound effects on our reactions to those labeled as "having" these conditions. To the degree that scientific theories influence public opinion, they can also *affect* the degree to which a particular behavior, attribute, or life style is seen as deviant and, in turn, can strongly affect the self-conceptions and life chances of those labeled "deviant" (Archer, 1985). The degree of stigma attached to an attribute derives at least partly from the causes we use to explain it.

For example, if a stigmatized attribute, such as mental illness, is seen as genetically determined, we are likely to view the attribute as unchangeable. This will affect how we view and behave toward persons with this attribute, making us more likely to segregate them from ourselves, institutionalizing them perhaps. We will not hold such persons morally responsible for their condition but may, nevertheless, experience great discomfort when required to interact with them. We may also stigmatize members of such persons' families, believing that they share the "defect" to some degree. If, on the other hand, we believe that mental illness is induced by environmental factors, such as stress, we may view affected persons quite differently. We are likely to believe that their condition is correctable if the right treatments or medications can be found. Even then, we may stigmatize the victims, perhaps attributing their environmentally induced illness to a "weakness" or "defect" in their characters. (Before reading further, look at the Student Observation: "Attributions About Deviance.")

CONFLICT AND POWER INEQUALITY: WHOSE DEFINITION PREVAILS?

Why are some behaviors socially defined as deviant while other behaviors are simply viewed as different? According to **conflict theory**, definitions of deviance depend on the relative *power* of

---

STUDENT OBSERVATION

Attributions About Deviance

Deviance is an attitude, a behavior, or a characteristic that is considered undesirably different according to a society's norms. In American society, homosexuality is considered deviant, so homosexuals are persecuted. Recently, scientists have tried to find a biological explanation for homosexuality. In other words, they are trying to medicalize this deviant behavior by suggesting that it is a physical or emotional illness. My brother was gay, but I never attributed his sexual orientation to a biological mishap or emotional trauma. I considered it merely his preference, like someone preferring rock music over country. There was nothing abnormal about my brother, in my eyes, except that he was extremely intelligent. People's personal lives are their business, and I do not understand what is so terrible about homosexuality. Scientists need to stop wasting money trying to find a cure for homosexuality and focus their efforts on finding a cure for AIDS, a true illness, which my brother had and died from.

groups to enforce their norms and apply them to people outside the group. This view maintains that what constitutes deviance and the severity of punishments for it are determined by the segments of society wielding greater power (Quinney, 1981; Kennedy, 1990). Thus, a burglar who steals a $200 television set may receive a prison sentence, whereas a savings and loan executive who knowingly defrauds consumers of millions of dollars may be given a small fine, a short sentence, or probation or may be required to perform community service as punishment.

Definitions of deviance, according to conflict theory, are often surrounded by conflicts based on economic and class interests. Despite the general language of our laws calling for equal treatment and fairness for everyone, in practice — according to this view — the laws favor the rich and the powerful over the poor and the weak. For example, vagrancy laws in the United States reflect the desire of the influential middle and upper classes to make their streets safe and peaceful by controlling others whom they view as criminals, undesirables, or nuisances.

Effects of Negative Social Definitions

We have chosen for special attention in this chapter four characteristics that some people define as undesirably different and a basis for discrimination — physical disability, homosexuality, juvenile delinquency, and white-collar crime. Most of us have ambivalent reactions toward persons with physical disabilities, but we stigmatize them nevertheless. Members of our society disagree, sometimes violently, about whether homosexuality is morally wrong and should be prohibited and punished or whether it is an acceptable form of sexual expression and should be permitted. Juvenile delinquency illustrates that we apply norms differently depending upon such characteristics as age. Some behaviors are crimes only when committed by juveniles and not when engaged in by adults. Other behaviors are serious crimes if committed by an adult but are treated much less harshly when committed by a juvenile. And white-collar crime illustrates that the harmfulness or serious-

ness of an offense does not necessarily determine our reaction to it. Despite the cost and harmfulness of white-collar offenses, we, as a society, react less strongly in terms of prohibiting and punishing these offenses than we do in regard to less harmful and less costly street crimes.

We have noted that the dominant culture of a society defines what behaviors are acceptable (and rewarded), different (and tolerated), and deviant or criminal (and discouraged or punished). Social psychologists also note that the designation of particular persons as deviant — criminals, perverts, crazy, handicapped — affects their subsequent behavior. Persons who are stigmatized may react by engaging in repair work, offering accounts for their behavior. Alternatively, they may attempt to hide their deviance or at least minimize its effect on social interactions. Labeling theory also points out that stigmatization may have the unintended effect of perpetuating deviant behavior. Let's turn to a discussion of these three kinds of effects.

REPAIR WORK: ACCOUNTS

Efforts to restore identities tarnished by deviant acts involve letting others know the reasons, or motives, for our behaviors. If we can't offer satisfactory explanations, our identities remain suspect and our standing within the group may drop. To explain our motives when our actions are seen as deviant, we learn a *vocabulary of motives* — sociologist C. Wright Mills's term for the sets of explanations regarded as appropriate reasons by particular groups in particular situations. Our vocabulary of motives frequently consists of **accounts** — explanations for our behavior (Riordan, Marlin, and Kellogg, 1983; Semin and Manstead, 1983; Snyder and Higgins, 1989).

Accounts for Everyday Deviance

Obviously, there is no need for accounts when we engage in routine, common-sense behavior, because its appropriateness is settled in advance by cultural definitions. But when our behavior is questionable, we may provide accounts for what we and others probably regard as inept, wrong, or unwelcome actions. Accounts are some of the communication strategies we use to enact, support, and challenge our own and others' public images, or face. In Chapter 5, "Communication," we discussed such strategies, which are called *facework*. Let's review the four forms of accounts: excuses, justifications, concessions, and refusals.

Excuses are statements that deny responsibility for the negative consequences of an action but admit that the behavior was reprehensible. For example, a young girl might excuse herself by saying, "I know I promised to call, but I didn't have time. John was in a hurry." *Justifications* are statements that admit responsibility for an action but reinterpret it in a more socially acceptable manner. For example, a young boy might justify his action by saying, "I had to hit him to protect myself!" (See the box "Accounts in Traffic Court.")

Concessions are statements that neither deny responsibility nor attempt to justify conduct; instead, they simply confess or admit that the behavior was inappropriate. Concessions are often accompanied by apologies, expressions of remorse, offers to make restitution, and so on (Schlenker and Darby, 1981; Darby and Schlenker, 1982). For example, a man might concede, "I acted foolishly; I'm sorry." *Refusals* are statements which deny that the questionable act was committed and reject the other party's right of reproach. For example, a woman might say, "How can you criticize *my* reaction after the way *you* behaved?!"

Accounts are extremely common because they act as a social lubricant that is vital to the smooth operation of our daily lives (Snyder, Higgins, and Stucky, 1983). When we accept other people's accounts or they accept ours, interaction can proceed "normally." Sometimes we are virtually obligated to offer an account, and if we fail to, others may do so for us: "They're late because he's been having trouble sleeping ever since the baby started crying through the night." Not offering a "proper excuse" is viewed as too much of a threat to the ongoing social fabric for most people to let it pass. Accordingly, "white lies"—in which we

ACCOUNTS IN TRAFFIC COURT

What kinds of accounts work in traffic court? In assessing traffic-court cases in the Greater Los Angeles area, Cody and McLaughlin (1988) compared reactions to the basic forms of oral accounts used by the plaintiff. Of the 375 cases studied, 74 involved a guilty plea, and virtually all the people making such pleas were penalized.

Most of the other accused individuals ($n = 134$) used some type of *excuse* to claim that they were not responsible. Seventy-five percent of these were penalized. Four kinds of excuses were observed: (1) lack of knowledge ("I didn't know it was illegal"); (2) mitigating circumstances ("I couldn't see the sign because a tree obstructed my view"); (3) appeal to illness or impairment ("I was feeling dizzy"); and (4) denial of intention ("I didn't mean to screech my tires when I accelerated"). Of these, the denial-of-intention excuses were most effective (only 30 percent were penalized). The other excuses were considered "lame," and 70 to 80 percent were penalized.

Three types of *denials* or *refusals* were observed: (1) challenge to the authority of the police officer ("The officer ticketed the wrong person"), of which 91 percent were penalized; (2) denial of definition of the offense ("The officer claims that the light was red when I went through it, but I know it was still yellow"), of which 81 percent were penalized; and (3) logical proofs ("Your Honor, the photographs and diagrams I have submitted will show that I could not have been going 47 miles per hour, as charged, when the officer stopped me"), of which 25 percent were penalized.

A judge in a traffic court must decide whether an accused person is guilty as charged or whether there is "reasonable doubt" of his or her guilt. Cody and McLaughlin's data indicate that logical proofs are the best method for raising doubts about guilt. Second in effectiveness were excuses that denied the intention of committing the error.

withhold the true reasons for an action in order to give a "better" reason — are a standard of everyday interaction: "Sorry, I can't make it to the meeting. I have a previous engagement" (Folkes, 1982*a*).

Techniques of Neutralization

Some researchers have suggested that juvenile delinquents develop a distinct set of accounts for their violation of social norms — much the same as the ones more conventional members of society use to excuse or justify their behavior when it violates norms (Sykes and Matza, 1957; Matza, 1964, 1974). Such **neutralization techniques** allow the teenagers to release themselves temporarily from normative constraints. By accepting these accounts for their own behavior, they neutralize any definition of themselves as deviant or criminal. Neutralization techniques include the following:

- *Denial of responsibility*: Delinquents employing this technique of neutralization define delinquent acts as "accidents" or as events caused by forces beyond their control (e.g., unloving parents, bad companions, drunkenness).

- *Denial of injury*: To rationalize their behavior, delinquents may deny its harmfulness. For example, stealing a car becomes "borrowing," while fights become "private quarrels" that should be of no concern to the community.

- *Denial of victim*: Delinquents often claim that their victim deserved what he or she got (e.g., when a homosexual or a homeless person is beaten) or that there is no victim (e.g., when the victim is a corporation).

- *Condemnation of condemnors*: Delinquents may shift blame from their own acts by pointing out that the police are corrupt, teachers unfair, or parents self-absorbed. By questioning the motives of others, delinquents take the focus off their own behavior.

- *Appeal to higher loyalties*: Delinquents may justify their behavior by pointing out the dilemma between being loyal to their peer group and abiding by society's rules. You can't "rat on a friend" or "chicken out on your buddies." These excuses stress that the delinquent behavior is motivated by fine and noble sentiments.

White-collar criminals also employ techniques of neutralization. For example, a physician justifies claiming Medicaid reimbursements for services she did not perform by telling herself that her false claims really do not harm anyone. Similar justifications are used by those involved in price-fixing and by workers whose theft from their employers has been uncovered: "It's not really hurting anybody — the store can afford it" (Zeitlin, 1971). According to one study of embezzlers (Cressey, 1971), embezzlers often rationalize their criminal behavior by telling themselves that they are "borrowing" the money and will soon return it. Other common justifications used by business criminals are that the law they are violating is unnecessary or unjust or that criminal behavior is necessary in order to survive. A common rationalization for employee theft is that the stolen property is a "justified addition to inadequate wages." Another popular neutralization technique is to tell oneself, "Everybody else is doing it."

PASSING AND COVERING

Some stigmatized conditions don't easily lend themselves to accounts. The person, for example, whose stigma consists of deafness or paralysis, will find it difficult to account for this disapproved condition. The stigma is permanent, not a temporary, excusable condition. Some people engage in an alternative form of facework by attempting to *conceal* their deviance in order to avoid the negative consequences of stigmatization.

Goffman (1963*b*) distinguishes between two types of concealment: passing and covering. Passing involves deliberate concealment of the stigmatized attribute, while covering consists of strategies to keep the stigma from dominating particular interactions. For example, some observers have noted that deaf people often cover their stigma, or at least minimize the disruption to ongoing interaction, by refraining from interrupting the conversation to request repetition; instead, they pretend to be following the conversation when, in fact, they are not (Higgins, 1980). Physically disabled people may use humor to show themselves as gifted social interactants or to let a "normal" person know that they do not take offense at the normal's uneasiness (Davis, 1961). For example, a paraplegic might refer to the normal as a "good-legger" or a "dirty normal" to show good humor and put the normal at ease. Others cover by making sure that when they meet new people they are in the company of a "highly presentable normal companion," recognizing that the presence of the normal third party eases interaction.

Passing is an option for individuals whose stigmatized attribute is easily concealed, such as alcoholics, homosexuals, prostitutes, ex-convicts, former mental patients, and light-skinned minorities. Passing may be a deliberate response to anticipated negative reactions to detection or an unintended consequence of the stigma's going unnoticed by unsuspecting others. Third parties may support the deviant's efforts to pass. Caregivers of persons with Alzheimer's disease, for example, may become partners in passing, helping preserve the public face of the afflicted family member and of the family or couple as a collective unit (Blum, 1991). Alternatively, they may help cover by monitoring the actions of the person with Alzheimer's in order to prevent or smooth over troublesome behavior that might occur in the person's interactions with outsiders.

Both passing and covering are associated with difficulties and strains. First, a successful passer must face prejudice against persons "of the kind he can be revealed to be" (Goffman, 1963: 42). For example, the homosexual who passes may have to listen to offensive "fag" jokes. Second, the passer must be continually concerned with maintaining his or her disguise. Passing alcoholics, for example, often make elaborate plans and arrangements to conceal their drinking. Third, of course, the passer always faces the danger of discovery. Discovery adds the discredit of deceit to the disgrace of the stigmatized condition. Those from

whom the stigma was concealed are likely to feel resentment.

Most of us are aware of what our friends, family members, religious leaders, co-workers, and so forth, think about homosexuals, and we know how they would react to us if they knew we were homosexual. In fact, to avoid direct rejection and other severe consequences, such as the loss of employment, homosexuals often hide this aspect of themselves from others. This is a form of passing.

The term "coming out" is used in the homosexual world to refer to the acceptance of a homosexual identity for oneself. It is also used to refer to making one's homosexual identity public, as in "coming out of the closet." Moreover, it sometimes refers to participation in the homosexual subculture. When a person is faced with the realization that some of his or her behavior qualifies as homosexual and that, therefore, he or she probably *is* a homosexual, it is not surprising that the person might seek out homosexual others. If the identity a person is coming to accept for himself or herself is negatively valued by the larger culture, the person will probably feel isolated or excluded from normal sources of social support. Consequently, he or she might seek such support from others with the same devalued identity. If the person's contacts with other homosexuals are positive, this can help the individual redefine the homosexual identity as a positive one, raise self-esteem, and encourage further contact (Cass, 1990). (See the Student Observation: "Homosexuality: Coming Out.")

Positive reactions from others and experience in the homosexual subculture can encourage homosexuals to risk revealing their homosexuality to selected others and can help them neutralize the negative stereotype of homosexuals (Jacobs and Tedford, 1980; D'Augelli, 1987; D'Augelli and Hart, 1987; Schmidt and Kurdek, 1987). Large urban areas, such as New York City and San Francisco, have large, well-developed, politically organized gay communities. Most other areas of the United States have homosexual subcultures that are smaller and less visible to outsiders. Gay

---

STUDENT OBSERVATION

Homosexuality: Coming Out

Last Christmas my sister surprised me by telling me that she is gay — something only one other member of our family knows. My sister has known for several years that she was gay, but she has only recently begun to "come out" about it. She is still afraid to tell our other family members, but she and I talk a lot about her partner and their relationship. She also has started going out to gay clubs, which is a sign that she is becoming more comfortable with her homosexuality. These are normal steps for someone learning to deal with being gay in a very homophobic society. My sister has learned to accept being gay within herself and has begun to tell the people she trusts most. She has also started becoming part of the homosexual subculture.

---

bars have traditionally provided a place where homosexuals can meet others, can relax and enjoy themselves without having to hide their sexual orientation, and can keep up with news in the gay community (Bell and Weinberg, 1978). More recently, other types of gay organizations, such as employee groups, have developed to fight for gay rights and also help homosexuals define a positive homosexual identity. For example, a gay church has developed rituals that transform its members' homosexual identities into positive, powerful ones consistent with their religious identities (Smith-Lovin and Douglass, 1990).

SELF-FULFILLING PROPHECIES: UNINTENDED EFFECTS OF DEVIANT LABELS

Labeling theory focuses on the effects of stigmatized social identities. The theory is not particularly interested in explaining the behavior that initially evokes the deviant identity — behavior that the theory calls **primary deviance**. Instead, it examines the impact the deviant label has on the behavior of others toward the labeled person and on his or her subsequent behavior. Labeling someone with a stigmatized identity evokes in others a schema of beliefs about how the labeled person will behave. Frequently, the label leads us to expect the person to engage in behaviors consistent with the stigmatized identity.

For example, a person identified as "handicapped" is expected to be unable to do some of the things that "normal" people do as they go about attending school, working at a job, or raising a family. As a result, the person may not be given the same opportunities to excel in these areas. If, for example, workers rush to their blind co-worker's aid each time she attempts to operate the copy machine, it is unlikely that she will master this aspect of her job. As a result, she may become increasingly dependent and remain incompetent. According to labeling theory, these characteristics, which were brought about by others' reactions to the person's stigmatized identity, are called **secondary deviance**. The process of creating secondary deviance involves the *self-fulfilling prophecy* we have referred to several times in other chapters.

We usually attribute secondary deviance — in the above example, increased dependence and incompetence — to the person's deviant status rather than recognizing it as an outcome of the restriction of opportunity produced by social reactions. The labeled person may begin to apply the stigmatized identity to himself or herself; in other words, it may become part of the person's self-identity. Acceptance of a stigmatized label as part of one's self identity magnifies the probability of behavior consistent with the label. Thus, self-identification as deviant may have the unintended consequence of causing a person to adopt a deviant life style.

Labeling and Delinquency

Let's look at how labeling theory is applied to juvenile delinquency. According to the theory, youths may initially violate the law for a number of reasons, such as poor family relationships, peer pressure, or learning experiences. This *primary deviance* — first or early acts of deviance, which are not integrated as part of the actor's self-concept — may remain hidden or be detected. If detected, a number of different social responses — by others such as parents, teachers, the police, courts, and correctional agencies — become possible. The behavior might be ignored or excused, or it might be defined as deviant. If it is defined as deviant, a negative label might be conferred on the youth — "troublemaker," "juvenile delinquent," "thief," "junkie," or "criminal."

The way these labels are applied often has serious consequences. Parents may consider young people labeled this way to be unmanageable and a bad influence on their siblings. Teachers may view them as disruptive or a lost cause, thus reducing their chances of doing well in school. Eligibility for employment may also be adversely affected. Because of the "criminal" label, legitimate opportunity structures may be shut to the delinquent. This may cause a self-fulfilling prophecy, since the social responses to the offenders limit their options and thrust them more deeply into delinquent roles. As the negative feedback of others continues, these young people may come to accept the "delinquent" label that others have applied to them. Thus, they may *come to regard themselves* as "criminals," "troublemakers," or "no good." Once this happens, behavior appropriate to those deviant roles becomes more probable. Such behavior, or *secondary deviance*, is caused by the earlier social responses identifying the actor as a deviant.

Although it is an interesting proposal, empirical support for the notion that labeling promotes delinquency is inconsistent. A few studies have shown that youths who have been in the juvenile justice system are the most likely to have delinquent self-concepts (Ray and Downs, 1986).

However, most studies have not indicated that delinquent self-concepts increase *after* police contact (Jensen, 1980; Thomas and Bishop, 1984). It is conceivable that youths with more delinquent self-concepts have a higher arrest rate because they engage in more frequent or more serious delinquent behavior (Farrington, 1989). The notion that juvenile justice processing amplifies delinquent self-labels is unsupported by most research (Anson and Eason, 1986).

Labeling and White-Collar Crime

From a strict labeling theory point of view, white-collar crime may not be serious deviance because outsiders do not regard it as such. From a less strict perspective, white-collar crime *is* deviance because it violates societal norms — in this case, laws. Yet because community reaction is weak (especially when compared with the response to street crimes) and penalties are less probable and, if imposed, less severe, white-collar criminals often do not develop deviant self-identities. Instead, they view themselves as honest, law-abiding citizens. What they do, they see as routine business practice — *technically* illegal, perhaps, but not really wrong, since business success "demands" violations of these laws. The defendants in a number of well-known cases of white-collar crime almost invariably testified that they came to a new job, where they found law violation an established way of doing business, and simply entered into it as they did into other aspects of the job. Almost all denied that personal benefits came from participating in the criminal conspiracy.

White-collar crimes are routine, taken for granted, prevalent, and ideologically supported. To many in the business community, some kinds of violations are seen as essential. Those who violate the law do not lose status among their peers; in fact, they are considered foolish if they *don't* violate the law. Some violations are probably so common that law-abiding behavior puts a businessperson at a tremendous competitive disadvantage.

Thus far, we have been discussing the process

of stigmatizing and criminalizing behavior that is viewed as deviant. Particular attention was given to (1) individual attributes that a significant number of people in the United States define as deviant, (2) actions toward people who are viewed as deviant, and (3) those people's reactions to the actions of others. Now we want to focus on social psychological theories that attempt to explain the causes of behavior viewed by some as deviant — particularly criminalized behavior, since this is the form of deviance that has been given the most attention by sociologists and social psychologists. As in the first part of this chapter, we will limit our discussion of criminalized behavior to juvenile delinquency and white-collar crime. We will continue to refer to them as criminal*ized* behavior to remind you that we are talking about socially defined behavior. But rather than focusing on why some behaviors are defined as deviant, we will discuss why some people engage in these behaviors. We'll organize our discussion around two types of explanations: motivation and group influences.

Motivational Explanations of Criminalized Behavior

Social psychologists have offered an array of motives for criminalized behavior, and most believe that no single motive can explain all, or even most, of such behavior. Many different behaviors are defined as criminal and different behaviors may be caused by different motivations. Even if we were to focus our attention on a single behavior — say stealing cars — the motivations for doing so may vary from person to person. A person's gender or socioeconomic status may influence his or her particular motivation. Therefore, it is not surprising that several motivational explanations for criminalized behavior have been proposed. For purposes of illustration, we will examine only five of the most prominent ones suggested by social psychologists: deprivation, identity anxiety, thrill, competition, and fear of punishment.

DEPRIVATION

Deviance may be generated when adverse circumstances interfere with a person's efforts to live up to social expectations. In this view, such conditions cause profound deprivation and frustration. This explanation, which has been called strain theory, was developed by sociologist Robert Merton (1938, 1957). American society, Merton speculated, emphasizes the cultural value of success. From preschool to college, our teachers urge us to achieve scholastically and to have high ambitions for our futures. The books, magazines, and newspapers we read, along with the television and movies we watch, frequently portray success stories that encourage us to strive for success. Even the games and sports we play and watch promote the value of winning. So pervasive is the cultural value of success that people of *all classes* are expected to be ambitious, have high aspirations, and make something of themselves. The cultural *goal* of success is freely available to all Americans, regardless of their social class.

Not only does our culture have norms emphasizing the value of success — particularly financial success — but also it defines, regulates, and controls the acceptable means of achieving these goals. In our society, the legitimate means to success include good education, lucrative job, hard work, thrift, and personal sacrifice. Many Americans have access to both the legitimate means to success and the resulting success goals. However, for some, access to legitimate means is restricted. Some may not be able to get a good education or job; for others, hard work and personal sacrifice do not bring success. Such limited access to approved means or goals causes deprivation and frustration, which Merton proposed results in several alternative responses:

- Some people continue to pursue the success goal through legitimate means despite the frustration.
- Others accept the goal and the legitimate means but attempt to change the conditions creating

deprivation (through, for example, social movements — a topic we will give greater attention in the following chapter).

- Some people give up on both the success goal and the legitimate means, withdrawing into such personal or social alternatives as addictions or religious cults.
- Others give up on achieving the success goal but maintain a ritualistic adherence to the legitimate means. For example, they may believe that education and hard work themselves are the important goals.
- Still others adhere to the prescribed success goal but pursue it using illegitimate means. In other words, they use *deviant* means of achieving legitimate goals.

What factors influence whether an individual is likely to experience frustration? The legitimate means of achieving success — such as obtaining a good job — are, Merton noted, *not* equally available to all social classes. Our society is structured so that the lower social classes have less opportunity than the higher social classes to attain commonly shared goals for success. For example, finding a good job is easier if you are a middle-class young man who has graduated from good schools, wears nice clothes, displays middle-class manners and ways of interacting, and possesses friends able to provide job opportunities or references. Lower-class people, then, experience frustration because of the inconsistency between the high success aspirations society has encouraged and the relative lack of opportunities to realize them. To resolve this dilemma, some lower-class people resort to *illegitimate* — disapproved or deviant — means of achieving success.

Merton's explanation was developed to explain why lower classes have higher rates of delinquency and crime than the middle and upper classes. Lower-class youths, according to this view, are the most vulnerable to pressures promoting deviance that arise from discrepancies between aspirations and opportunities for achievement. Lower-class youths are disadvantaged, sociologist Albert

Cohen (1955, 1965) argues, because in such settings as schools, middle-class standards of "good" behavior are defined as the legitimate means to success. Since many lower-class youths have not been socialized by their families to meet middle-class standards of neatness, ambition, verbal skills, long-range goals, and good manners, they have less chance of doing well than their middle-class peers. Most lower-class youths accept, at least to some degree, the goals of the general culture of being successful at school, jobs, and so forth, but many, having repeatedly met with failure, start believing that they have few prospects.

Sociologist Robert Agnew (1985) suggests that frustration may be produced by factors other than the blockage of success goals. Specifically, Agnew notes that the inability to escape a painful, aversive, or unpleasant situation is as frustrating as the lack of opportunity to achieve success. Adolescents who experience school as unpleasant but are not allowed to quit or adolescents whose parents are abusive but who don't run away because they fear they can't fend for themselves will probably experience extreme frustration. Strain from the inability to escape such aversive situations, Agnew suggests, is a major cause of delinquency. He notes that this modification — the recognition of alternative sources of frustration — allows strain theory to account not only for lower-class but also for middle-class delinquency, since frustration caused by being stuck in aversive situations may be experienced by adolescents of all classes.

IDENTITY ANXIETY

Official statistics tell us that young people account for more arrests than their numbers in the population lead us to expect. Victim surveys generate similar findings for crimes in which the age of the assailant can be determined. Comparisons for "Part I offenses" — including murder, non-negligent manslaughter, forcible rape, robbery, aggravated assault, burglary, larceny-theft, motor-vehicle theft, and arson — show that while youths fifteen to eighteen years old make up about 6 percent of the U.S. population, they make up about 25 percent of arrests for Part I offenses. In contrast, adults forty-five and over, although comprising 30 percent of the population, account for only 6 percent of arrests for Part I offenses. The peak age for property crime is generally about sixteen; for violent crime it is about eighteen (Federal Bureau of Investigation, 1986).

A model proposed by David Matza (1964) may partially explain these age-crime relationships as well as the higher rates of delinquent behavior among male adolescents. Matza's model suggests that delinquency results from two adolescent identity anxieties, gender and membership, each associated with a "loosening of social controls" that tends to occur during adolescence. Adolescents seek to abandon their old identities as children and to establish new self-identities that correspond to their greater biological maturity. Adolescents in this anxious state take their cues from other, similarly anxious youths. Males, in particular, develop and promote a "masculine" identity—a tough, rebellious front that makes them more accepting of delinquency than the larger culture.

Most of these teens, Matza argues, are not really as committed to this delinquent subculture as they appear. That is, they haven't completely abandoned conventional norms and values, but

their peer group encourages them to act as though they have. (The dynamics of this peer group influence are similar to the group polarization effect we discussed in Chapter 9, "Performance, Conformity, and Cooperation.") This difference between appearance and reality explains how delinquents can **drift** back and forth between conventional and delinquent behavior—for example, they may participate in conventional family activities and attend church and school but also commit delinquent acts such as smoking, drinking, and vandalism. (See the Student Observation: "Drift.")

As adolescent males mature, Matza asserts, physiological changes reduce their masculinity anxiety. Simultaneously, most form attachments to conventional groups and institutions (marriage, jobs), which resolve their membership anxiety and reassert social control. This concept of *maturational reform* is consistent with the observation that relatively few juveniles become adult criminals (Gottfredson and Hirschi, 1986; Cohen and Land, 1987).

THRILLS, KICKS, AND EXCITEMENT

Albert Cohen (1955) suggests that lower-class young men may establish groups—delinquent

---

STUDENT OBSERVATION

Drift

When I was in high school, I was very close to a group of guys in my class. These boys were the "rebels" of our school; they drank, smoked, sneaked out of their houses late at night, and sometimes went on minor sprees of vandalism. All of them had been arrested at least once for crimes such as shoplifting, possession of marijuana, and status offenses like underage drinking. These guys talked tough, scared the socks off me on some of the delinquent escapades to which I was invited (I recall one climb to the top of an electrical tower to spray paint some obscenity on the roof of our school), and generally made me feel quite prissy, though I wasn't the straightest of girls in our school. However, these boys also went to church every Sunday (no matter how hung-over they were), attended school, made relatively good grades, and at least pretended to follow most of their parents' rules. It amazed me that they could behave in such completely different ways at different times. My friends were not really committed to the delinquent subculture; they had not completely abandoned conventional norms and values. In short, my friends *drifted* back and forth between delinquent and conventional behavior.

subcultures — whose rules for achievement differ from those of the middle-class schools they attend. Sometimes the rules of these groups prescribe behavior in deliberate defiance of middle-class standards — a counterculture. To many observers, such behavior may seem to be negative and pointless. For example, delinquent youths may steal something that they don't really want or may destroy property "just for the hell of it." In this view, the juveniles are seeking "opportunities for excitement, autonomy, and sense of action." Other sociologists have elaborated on this thesis (Katz, 1988; Sato, 1988).

Some controversy exists among social psychologists as to whether this thrill-kicks-excitement motivation is found (1) primarily among those adolescents experiencing the strains of deprivation, that is, lower-class adolescents, or (2) among people of all classes in the course of pursuing leisure activities. Cohen, for one, argued that the thrill explanation for delinquency should account for the class differential in delinquency rates. Thrills, kicks, and excitement, in his view, are the lower-class adolescent's alternative (and often illegitimate) means of achieving the status that he or she is denied through legitimate means. This interpretation is common among researchers restricting their study of delinquency to lower-class adolescents. For example, sociologist Elijah Anderson (1976) suggests that the thrill-seeking activities of black youths in Philadelphia can be understood in terms of the youths' irregular work careers.

Other researchers, however, note that adolescents of all social classes engage in thrill-seeking behavior (Katz, 1988). In this view, the boredom of conformity to the conventional norms of institutions such as schools, the family, jobs, and the church is in no way restricted to lower-class adolescents. Adolescents from families of all social classes question the purpose of many of these norms, which may seem irrelevant to their current

Some researchers believe that adolescents of all social classes engage in thrill-seeking behavior. Thus, many acts of theft and vandalism are not aimed at economic gain but are engaged in for the "fun of it."

lives. One response to this boredom is thrill-seeking behavior. Thus, many acts of theft and vandalism are not aimed at obtaining a materially improved life style.

According to the thrill-seeking hypothesis, the targets of much deviant behavior are the conventions that are both boring and constraining to adolescents. The more illegitimate and risky the behavior involved, the greater the thrill and the greater the prestige accorded by one's peers. Thrill and prestige are heightened by "getting away with" rule violations. Such behavior may boost youths' feelings of self-control. The specific forms of thrill seeking vary considerably, reflecting both the opportunities of the situation and the creativity of the participants.

For most adolescents, thrill seeking eventually gives way to the "routine seeking" of adult life — family and jobs. However, the poor socioeconomic backgrounds of some adults may make it difficult for them to achieve the rewards of a nice family and a good job. This deprivation may become the motivation to continue their criminalized thrill-seeking behavior as adults.

"CULTURE OF COMPETITION" AND PROFIT

White-collar crimes challenge some of the traditional theories about the causes of criminal activity, especially those that define *poverty* or deprivation as an important cause. Some criminologists believe that white-collar crime, rather than being promoted by deprivation, or a "culture of poverty," is promoted by a "culture of competition."

In societies whose economies are based upon the principles of industrial capitalism, the culture of competition defines the competitive struggle for personal gain as a positive, rather than a negative or selfish, activity. Great importance is given to wealth and success if they are achieved competitively. Competition is thought to build the character of the competitors and to produce the maximum economic value for society as a whole. Ivan Boesky, honored commencement speaker at the School of Business Administration of the Uni-versity of California at Berkeley in 1985, reflected this view when he proclaimed, "Greed is all right, by the way. I want you to know that. I think greed is healthy. You can be greedy and still feel good about yourself" (quoted in Thio, 1988: 440). Boesky was later convicted of Wall Street insider trading.

The culture of competition promotes a view of competitive economic struggles as fair and equitable battles in which the most capable and hardest-working individuals are the most successful. This implies that the poor deserve their inferior position because they are lazy or incompetent. Thus, the culture of competition not only provides a strong desire for wealth but also contributes to a pervasive fear of failure. While ethical prescriptions regulate the competitive struggle, those who are willing to violate ethical standards often enjoy a competitive edge over those who will not. Malcolm X described this perspective in his autobiography when he noted, "Full-time hustlers never can relax to appraise what they are doing and where they are bound. As is the case in any jungle, the hustler's every waking hour is lived with both the practical and subconscious knowledge that if he ever relaxes, if he ever slows down, the other hungry, restless foxes, ferrets, wolves, and vultures out there with him won't hesitate to make him their prey" (1965: 109).

FEAR OF PUNISHMENT

The deprivation, identity-anxiety, thrill, and competition explanations specify motives thought to increase the likelihood of criminalized behavior. Yet another motivational explanation focuses on the notion that the fear of punishment *deters* crime. As we discussed earlier, labeling theory proposes that applying a deviant label to a person may actually *increase* the likelihood that the person will engage in behaviors expected of the deviant role (secondary deviance). Other theories propose that punishment, if it occurs in a particular manner and in combination with rewards for alternative behavior, will *decrease* deviance. Two quite different lines of research based on this viewpoint have involved studies of parental discipline and criminal prosecution.

Parental Discipline

Delinquency is related to two identifiable parenting styles according to psychologist Gerald Patterson and his colleagues (Patterson, 1982; Patterson, Dishion, and Bank, 1984; Snyder and Patterson, 1987). A lax disciplinary style, they argue, is the most likely to result in delinquency. In the lax, or permissive, style, parents allow much problematic behavior to occur without taking disciplinary action. Unpunished, the antisocial behaviors continue to occur.

Also problematic is the "enmeshed" style. Parents with this child-rearing style regard an unusually large number of minor behaviors as problematic and use inconsistent and coercive strategies to deal with them. For example, such parents issue increasingly numerous commands and threats but fail to back them up consistently (perhaps because they don't have the energy to apply punishment to every behavior they view as problematic). In many instances, therefore, the antisocial behavior is unpunished.

But coercion, even if used consistently, may actually *increase* the likelihood of antisocial behavior by establishing a pattern of family interactions that exacerbates the aggressive behavior of all family members. For example, Mike reacts to his sister Julie's locking the bathroom door by yelling for her to get out. She screams back at him to "buzz off." He responds by banging on the door. Julie screams louder for him to go away. The father yells at them both to "shut up." Mike and Julie keep up the banging and yelling. Eventually, someone "wins" this escalating confrontation when the father resolves the conflict — for example, by ordering Mike to go to his room or Julie to unlock the door immediately. Thus, children learn that harsh tactics work in social interactions.

Patterson and his colleagues suggest that faulty socialization in the family fosters poor interpersonal, academic, and work skills in children. These deficiencies subsequently "turn off" outsiders, whose rejection in turn restricts the child's opportunity to acquire the skills necessary to adjust and achieve in society. Rejected by mainstream society, such children are drawn to other socially disabled children. The association with similar others increases opportunities for socially disabled children to acquire, perform, and perfect antisocial behavior. Researchers suggest that parents should be taught better ways of interacting with their children and that children should be given direct help with academic problems and social skills (Kazdin, 1987; Patterson, DeBaryshe, and Ramsey, 1989).

Criminal Prosecution

Proponents of deterrence as a crime control strategy believe swift, certain, and severe legal punishments have the greatest chance of deterring crime, especially when applied to offenses that are rational or calculated and when backed up by extralegal sanctions such as public opinion (Ellis, 1987). But, research support for deterrence theory is mixed. Several studies of domestic violence indicate that arresting the offender deters future violence more than do less severe forms of punishment, such as ordering the offender to stay away from the victim for eight hours (Sherman and Berk, 1984; Berk and Newton, 1985). In contrast, other studies of released prisoners have found that the more severe the punishment they have experienced (e.g., the longer their sentences), the *greater* the likelihood that they will commit crimes again (Gibbs, 1975).

Studies focusing on the *certainty* of punishment have found that the more certain the punishment for crimes such as assault, rape, robbery, and auto theft, the lower the rates of these offenses (Tittle, 1969; Bailey, Martin, and Gray, 1974). However, according to other studies, the certainty of punishment deters economic crimes only, such as robbery and auto theft, but not violent crimes, such as homicide and assault (Geerken and Gove, 1977; Meier, Burkett, and Hickman, 1984).

One study found that juvenile delinquents in six U.S. cities, who had been convicted of felonies and serious misdemeanor offenses, did not reduce their propensity to commit subsequent crimes as a function of their *perception* of the certainty or severity of punishment (Schneider, 1990). In fact, those who believed they would be punished more severely and those who perceived a higher likelihood of being caught actually committed *more* crimes during the two- to three-year follow-up period.

Still other research suggests that two factors other than deterrence may play an important role in determining whether juveniles commit crimes. One study found that *lack of criminal opportunities* was far more important than the threat of punishment in discouraging people from breaking the law (Piliavin et al., 1986). Fear of *informal sanctions* from parents, peers, and teachers may also be a more important factor in preventing juvenile delinquency than is perceived severity of legal punishment (Tittle, 1980; Paternoster and Iovanni, 1986). In addition, informal sanctions may *increase* delinquency. Because juveniles often commit crimes in groups, peer pressure to commit a delinquent act can outweigh the deterrent effect of the law (Siegel and Senna, 1988). (We'll discuss this further in a subsequent section of this chapter.) Rewards and incentives for engaging in criminalized behavior, as well as *legal* alternatives, are factors overlooked by deterrence theory (Akers, 1990).

Criminal prosecution may be an ineffective deterrent to organizational crime. Criminal fines are often trivial for corporations in relation to their ability to pay and to the profits gained from the criminal violations. Because organizational offenses are often carried out collectively, culpability is difficult to assign to individuals. In addition, harsh punishments directed at a corporation frequently result in spillovers, affecting the innocent as well as the guilty.

These difficulties have led us to develop a system of social control for organizational crime that stresses civil or administrative proceedings (Shapiro, 1990). Such strategies try to induce conformity by setting up economic incentives for obeying the law. Injunctive proceedings aim at stopping the illicit activities and warning of-

fenders against committing future violations. They may also be used to freeze assets, compel restitution, reorganize a firm, or take other corrective action. Thus, upper-status offenders are underrepresented among the ranks of criminals at least partly because other legal options divert them from the criminal process.

But some researchers argue that white-collar offenses will continue to be common until they are explicitly treated as crimes (Geis, 1984; Michalowski and Kramer, 1987; Klepper and Nagin, 1989). This, they argue, will require a change in public attitudes; "a deepening sense of moral outrage" (Nader and Green, 1982: 53).

Group Influences on Criminalized Behavior

The focus of most motivational explanations of criminalized behavior is on the individual. This is not to deny that social conditions give rise to some of these motives — for example, the unequal opportunities that produce deprivation and frustration. To provide some balance to our discussion, let's now turn our attention to explanations that focus on how interactions in relationships and groups influence criminalized behavior. We will discuss two theories: social control and differential association.

SOCIAL BONDS AS SOCIAL CONTROL

The idea of social control assumes that people are inclined to act deviantly and will do so unless properly controlled. Social control is believed to deter deviance; the absence of social control, to cause it. The chief architect of **social control theory** is Travis Hirschi. According to Hirschi (1969), deviance occurs when the individual's bonds to conventional society — attachments to persons who accept conventional norms, commitments to conventional goals and rewards, involvement with conventional activities, and possession of conventional beliefs — are inadequate.

Parental Bonds

A number of studies have used supervision as a measure of parental bonds. Juveniles who believe that their parents are aware of their activities and their companions are less likely to engage in delinquent acts than those who believe that their actions will go unsupervised. Youths who participated in supervised social activities were less likely to engage in delinquency than those who were involved in unsupervised peer-oriented activities (Agnew and Peterson, 1989). Do you think these results have implications for youths with single parents or working mothers? Let's see.

Single-parent families.   A recent review of fifty studies indicates that children from *single-parent families* are somewhat more likely to engage in delinquent behavior than children from intact families (Wells and Rankin, 1991). But the same review found two important qualifications: (1) The relationship between single-parent families and delinquency was stronger for *minor* forms of delinquency (such as status offenses) and weakest for *serious* forms (such as theft and interpersonal violence). (2) When *self-report* measures of delinquency are used, the differences between single-parent and intact families are smaller than the differences found when *official* delinquency statistics are used as the measure of delinquency. Some researchers speculate that this is not because children from single-parent homes engage in more delinquency. Instead, it is because agents of the criminal justice system, assuming that parents in such households cannot be counted on for supervision, may be more likely to take official action against children from single-parent households.

Other studies suggest that children from conflict-free single-parent homes are less likely to be delinquent than are children from conflict-ridden "intact" homes. Extensive research reviews have concluded that it is parental conflict, or the absence of supportive parent-child relationships, rather than parental absence that causes delinquency (Emery, 1982; Gove and Crutchfield, 1982; Hanson et al., 1984; Van Voorhis et al., 1988; Rankin and Wells, 1990).

Working mothers and supervision.   Research on the effects of maternal employment on juvenile delinquency shows that employed mothers are no likelier than other mothers to have delinquent children (D'Amico, Haurin, and Mott, 1983; Hayes and Kamerman, 1983; Rutter and Giller, 1984). One exception is the work of Laurence Steinberg (1986) on "latchkey" children. Steinberg has found that children without supervision after school are more prone to commit *minor* delinquent acts than children with some sort of adult supervision. Lack of supervision seems to increase susceptibility to peer pressure. Even if the working parent simply telephones the child after school, delinquency is apparently less likely.

Gender differences.   Some researchers have found that social control theory's predictions apply more to female than to male delinquency (Krohn and Massey, 1980; Rosenbaum and Lasley, 1990). One study (Hill and Atkinson, 1988) tested the hypothesis that boys and girls are subjected to different parental expectations and levels of control. After collecting self-report measures of delinquency from 3,000 youths, age fourteen to eighteen, the researchers found evidence suggesting that girls were subject to more parental control than boys. But boys and girls differed more in the *type* of control exerted over them than the *degree* of control. Boys reported receiving more emotional support from their fathers and being subjected to more rules regarding their appearance. Girls reported receiving more emotional support from their mothers and being subjected to more rules about curfews.

Among the boys in the sample, those who had strong support from their fathers and were subject to appearance rules were less likely to engage in delinquent acts. Among the girls, those who received strong support from their mothers and were subject to curfew rules were less likely to engage in delinquent acts.

Attachment to School

Indicators of attachment to and involvement in school, such as grade point average, educational aspirations, and time spent on homework, consistently have been found to be negatively related to delinquency (Krohn and Massey, 1980; Wiatrowski, Griswold, and Roberts, 1981). Students who like school are less likely to perform delinquent acts (Rankin, 1980; Wiatrowski, Griswold, and Roberts, 1981). Students who drop out of school are subsequently more likely to engage in crime (Thornberry, Moore, and Christenson, 1985).

The findings that weak parental and school attachments and involvements are related to delinquency seem to provide strong support for Hirschi's model of social bonding. However, a longitudinal study by Robert Agnew (1985) suggests that the relationship may not be a simple one. Agnew observed not only that teenagers who have weak bonds to society are likely to be delinquent but that being delinquent weakens the individual's bonds. In other words, weak bonds and delinquency influence each other (Liska and Reed, 1985).

Marriage and Work Bonds

What about crime beyond juvenile delinquency? What are the chances that delinquent juveniles will continue their criminal careers as adults? Moreover, do some people start their criminal careers only when they are adults?

A study by Robert Sampson and John Laub (1990) offers answers to these questions. Their study examined a large sample of white males from childhood to age thirty-two. The researchers found that men who engaged in antisocial behavior during childhood had substantially more arrests as adults, indicating that childhood antisocial behavior is a good predictor of adult crime. Yet this prediction is hardly perfect. Some males who exhibited antisocial behavior during childhood did *not* have an arrest record as adults, while others who did not exhibit childhood antisocial behavior *did* have adult arrest records.

How can we account for these changes between childhood and adulthood? Sampson and Laub believe that social control theory offers a possible explanation. The researchers predicted that changes strengthening social bonds to society in adulthood would lead to less crime, whereas changes weakening social bonds would lead to more crime. Parents, school, and peer groups, as previously noted, are the primary sources of social bonds during childhood and adolescence. During young adulthood, marriage and work are the dominant sources. Thus, if social control theory is correct, attachment to job and spouse should decrease criminal behavior and lack of attachment should increase it.

The researchers found that social control theory's predictions were supported. For example, among males who earlier had been in a correctional school, those who, as young adults, indicated attachments to either their jobs or their spouses had lower arrest records than those who were "disattached." Similarly, among young adults who were never in correctional school as juveniles, those without adult bonds to spouse or job had higher arrest records than those with these bonds. The trajectories of crime from childhood to adulthood, Sampson and Laub concluded, are systematically modified by social bonds to society's agents of informal social control.

Self-Control: An Expanded Theory

Travis Hirschi and Michael Gottfredson have recently expanded control theory. The expanded theory, which they call "self-control theory," suggests that individual differences in the tendency to commit criminal acts result from differences in *self-control* (Gottfredson and Hirschi, 1990). Limited self-control means being impulsive, risk taking, adventuresome, and self-centered and having a here-and-now orientation (Mak, 1990).

Thus, the theory focuses on the thrill-seeking motivation we discussed earlier. Males, the researchers suggest, as a group, have lower self-control than females and are thus more likely to engage in delinquency and crime.

What causes individuals to lack self-control? The answer, according to Gottfredson and Hirschi, is weak social bonds, which, in turn, result from inadequate child-rearing practices.

Children who are not attached to their parents, who are poorly supervised, whose parents who do not punish deviant behavior, and whose parents are criminal or deviant themselves, the researchers argue, are most likely to develop poor self-control. (This notion is supported by the research of Gerald Patterson and his colleagues, which we discussed earlier.)

DIFFERENTIAL ASSOCIATION

Originally Hirschi had proposed that social bonds of any kind would protect against delinquency. Consistent with this prediction, studies have found that youths who eventually become delinquent (as measured by official contact with juvenile court) had been neither liked nor accepted by their peers prior to their delinquency (Roff and Wirt, 1984; Elliott, Huizinga, and Ageton, 1985; White, Padina, and LaGrange, 1987).

But what about the idea that delinquents are likely to have bonds to *delinquent* peer groups? Even Hirschi's own research indicated that associating with delinquent peers *increased* the probability of delinquent behavior. When deviates are rejected by conventional groups, they tend to turn to alternative, deviant groups for support. Besides providing normative support (shared beliefs about the acceptability of the "deviant" acts), such groups also offer more technical support for deviant behavior. For example, a prostitution ring may give new members information about how to spot a dangerous trick, what areas of town the vice squad is least likely to cover, and how much to charge for various services.

Differential association theory argues that we learn deviant behavior the same way we learn conventional behavior. The term "differential" emphasizes the significance of the ratio of deviant to conventional contacts. We become deviant when exposed to an *overabundance* of deviant behavior patterns, compared with conventional behavior patterns.

Differential association theory also suggests that our associations with some groups influence us more than our associations with other groups do. A group's influence tends to be greater when (1) we experience the association with the group early in life, (2) we are more emotionally attached to the group, or it has greater prestige, and (3) we have more frequent and longer associations with group members. Each of these factors increases the probability that we will adopt the group's definitions.

Differential Association and Juvenile Delinquency

There is substantial support for differential association theory. A number of studies suggest that involvement in delinquency is related to delinquent companions (Akers et al., 1979; Orcutt, 1983; Matsueda and Heimer, 1987; Jackson, 1989b; Smith, Visher, and Jarjoura, 1991). A smaller number of longitudinal studies also indicate that a juvenile's association with delinquent peers seems to come before, rather than after, his or her own delinquent behavior (Ginsberg and Greenley, 1978; Kandel, 1978; Andrews and Kandel, 1979; Huba and Bentler, 1982, 1983).

Other studies suggest that the concept of differential association is useful because delinquent behavior, like any behavior, is shaped by the reactions of others to it (Burgess and Akers, 1966; Akers, 1977, 1985, 1990). Social behavior, these researchers note, is learned through direct modeling of others' behavior and by differential reinforcement—the balance of rewards and punishments for deviant and conforming behavior. Youths who receive more rewards than punishments from their associates for conforming behavior will remain nondelinquent, while those who receive an excess of rewards over punishments for delinquency will become delinquent. A longitudinal study of cigarette smoking among junior and senior high school students, for example, found that reinforcement of smoking by parents and friends increased adolescent smoking (Krohn et al., 1985). Studies of adolescent drug and alcohol use have produced similar findings (Kandel, 1984, 1986; Sebald, 1986). (Differential

Delinquent behavior, like socially approved behavior, is learned through direct modeling of others' behavior and by differential reinforcement.

reinforcement, you may recall, is a component of social learning theory, which we discussed in detail in Chapter 2, "Early Socialization.")

Differential Association and White-Collar Crime

Juveniles are not the only ones influenced by groups. Just as adolescent peer groups may influence juvenile delinquency, occupational subcultures play a critical role in determining opportunities for white-collar crime. For example, police subcultures often work to silence objections to corrupt activities among officers, thereby expanding opportunities for illicit gain. Most of the neutralization techniques that people use to justify white-collar crimes are learned within the occupational subculture. Police subcultures often distinguish between "clean" and "dirty" payoff money, thereby implying that there is nothing wrong in accepting at least some payoffs.

In one study of a police department, the researchers observed that the instructors in the police academy encouraged recruits to lie in some situations but strongly discouraged it in others

(Hunt and Manning, 1991). In the same department, veteran officers approvingly noted that it took rookies only a few months to learn not only where to hide when they left their beats during inclement weather but also what to say if questioned by supervisors. Workers in many offices and factories clearly distinguish between which property it is permissible to steal (e.g., paperclips, pads, and pens) and which it is not (e.g., personal computers, chairs, and desks). Many politicians regard the swapping of political favors for campaign contributions or personal rewards as a normal part of their jobs. Thus, the amount and nature of occupational crime seems to be regulated in large part by the norms of informal work groups.

According to Diane Margolis (1979) much of organizational crime, which has the support and encouragement of the organization, is part of a socialization process that produces a "moral numbness" in corporate managers. By frequently transferring young executives from one geographic area to another, an organization weakens outside ties while making managers more dependent on the corporation. Long work hours also strain outside ties, disrupting commitments to family, friends, community, and other interests that could exert conflicting pressures on managers. The outcome of this process, Margolis argues, is the creation of executives who display a narrow, pragmatic approach to work and act in the best interests of the corporation with little thought of the moral implications of their actions. By prescribing customary responses to situations and by teaching employees to direct their attention to certain aspects of their environment while ignoring others, a corporation may encourage unethical or illegal activities by making them seem to be a normal part of the daily routine (Kramer, 1982; Braithwaite, 1985).

Deviant or illegal acts are often parceled out among a number of positions in an organization so that no one person has complete information about or overall responsibility for the action (Ermann and Lundman, 1982). Thus, employees can rationalize that they are just doing their jobs. Should they have second thoughts about their roles in an illegal activity, they must also consider that they are small cogs in a big machine and can easily be replaced. Those who raise questions are often told to "be part of the team or go look for

another job" (Clinard and Yeager, 1980: 67). (See the Student Observation: "Moral Numbness and White-Collar Crime.")

We have discussed the contributions of a number of social psychological theories to the study of deviance. Some theories focus on the process of defining attributes as deviant; others address the process causing behavior so defined. No one perspective seems to provide an adequate explanation of the phenomenon, even when a single type of deviance is examined. Deviance is a multifaceted phenomenon. It is unrealistic to expect a single perspective to account for all these facets or all the many varieties of behavior that are defined as deviant. Still, the theories inform our view of deviance. They point to commonalities among very different types of behavior, such as physical disability, homosexuality, juvenile delinquency, and white-collar crime. They also lead us to discover differences among behaviors that have in common a negative societal reaction.

Summary

1. Social psychologists consider behaviors and attitudes to be deviant when they are defined as

---

STUDENT OBSERVATION

Moral Numbness and White-Collar Crime

I read a book this summer that illustrated the role of differential association in white-collar crime. In *The Firm*, by John Grisham, the main character was hired by a very prestigious law firm and was given many fringe benefits. He had to work hard in order to keep up with the expected work load; in the process, he began to lose contact with his wife and family and began to associate more with friends from work. He did not mind being overworked because the amount of money and fringe benefits were so great. He was slowly sucked into the firm and began to depend on his co-workers for advice and encouragement.

After he was totally dependent on the firm, the managers began to ask him to commit some illegal acts. One thing that he was "advised" to do was to pad many bills to increase the amount of time charged to each case. It did not seem very wrong to him to do this because everyone else in the firm was doing it and the extra money it brought in wasn't bad either. The managers hoped to create a moral numbness in him by keeping him wrapped up in the firm and in his new success. By enticing him to participate in increasingly corrupt activities, they hoped to trap him so that when he found out that the whole firm was actually a mob organization, he would be unable to leave or to even consider turning the firm in. Sorry, but you'll have to read the book to find out what happened.

undesirably different from those prescribed by the norms of a group. This view sees deviance as culturally relative, recognizing that judgments of right and wrong vary from one group, place, and time period to another.

2. The designation of particular persons as deviant affects their subsequent behavior — repair work, passing, covering, and self-fulfilling prophecy.

3. Some efforts to explain criminalized behavior have focused on the individual's motivation for such conduct: deprivation, identity anxiety, boredom and thrill seeking, competition, and the absence of fear of punishment. Each of these motivations may account for some criminalized behavior; but alone, each is an incomplete explanation.

4. Social control theory proposes that deviance occurs when the individual's bonds to conventional society are inadequate. Research indicates that children from single-parent families are somewhat more likely to engage in delinquent behavior, particularly minor forms of delinquency that reach the juvenile courts. Moreover, employed mothers are no more likely than other mothers to have delinquent children. Success in school is negatively related to delinquency. Attachment to job and spouse decreases the likelihood of adult crime.

5. Differential association theory argues that we learn deviant behavior the same way we learn conventional behavior. We become deviant when we are exposed to an overabundance of criminalized behavior patterns, compared with conventional behavior patterns, and when we receive an excess of rewards over punishments for delinquency. Occupational subcultures play a critical role in determining opportunities for white-collar crime.

CHAPTER 16

COLLECTIVE ACTION AND SOCIAL MOVEMENTS

*W*e began this book with an emphasis on our society's culture, its institutions, and the socialization process by which we come to adopt its norms and institutions as our own. In Chapter 14, "Inequality and Discrimination," we noted that individuals and groups differ in social power and that these differences affect the distribution of resources and well-being. Power also determines which individual or group will make its behavioral preferences the operating normative rules for others, as we discussed in Chapter 15, "Deviance and Stigmatization." The task of this chapter, the concluding one, is to focus your attention on how groups may attempt to "turn the tables" on society and institutions by working to bring about social change. Consider the following example.

Homosexuals, like members of some other stigmatized groups, have organized to try to change society's negative reaction to them. Homosexuality was once a seldom-discussed topic. Now there are gay organizations in many colleges, gay associations, gay political groups, gay magazines and newspapers, gay churches, and gay business groups. These changes are due, at least partly, to collective action on behalf of homosexuals—a gay rights movement that has advocated and continues to advocate for change in the form of increasing social acceptance of homosexuals as

well as the elimination of institutional and individual discrimination against them.

Some scholars suggest that several things contributed to the development of the gay rights movement (Clinard and Meier, 1989). First, the Kinsey Report on human sexuality noted in 1948 and 1953 that millions of American men and women were exclusively or sometimes homosexual. This report gained much attention, possibly making many homosexuals aware for the first time that they were not alone. Second, the increase in sexual permissiveness in American society since the 1960s has produced a growing tolerance for various kinds of sexual behavior. Third, the success of the black civil rights movement in the 1960s encouraged homosexuals, along with other oppressed minorities, to fight for equality and respect. Many observers suggest that the event that precipitated the gay rights movement was the "Stonewall Rebellion," which occurred in 1969. After numerous unprovoked raids by the police on the Stonewall, a gay bar in New York City, the patrons decided to fight back.

Unlike other organizations of deviants, such as Alcoholics Anonymous, Synanon (for drug addicts), and Weight Watchers, homosexual organizations don't try to change the behavior of their members. Rather, their goal is to reduce the social and legal stigma surrounding homosexuality—in

Homosexuals, like members of some other stigmatized groups, have organized to try to change society's negative reaction to them. Their goal is to ensure that homosexuals are not discriminated against because of their sexual orientation and to reduce the social and legal stigma surrounding homosexuality — in other words, to redefine the norms of the society so that homosexuality is no longer considered deviant.

other words, to redefine the norms of the society so that homosexuality is no longer considered deviant. Like the "Black Is Beautiful" theme of the 1960s' civil rights movement, yearly Gay Pride celebrations illustrate that one of the movement's goals is to help gay people form a positive self-identity.

The gay rights movement has achieved many victories. In 1973, the American Psychiatric Association deleted homosexuality from its list of psychiatric disorders and urged "all mental health professionals to take the lead in removing the stigma of mental illness that has long been associated with homosexual orientation" (American Psychological Association, 1975). Many states have decriminalized private, adult, consensual sex

regardless of the gender of the partners. In some cities, school boards have banned discrimination in the hiring of gay teachers, and several court decisions upheld the rights of homosexuals to teach. A number of large corporations have announced their willingness to hire homosexuals, and a few have made gay partners eligible for benefits, such as health insurance, usually reserved for heterosexual spouses (Stewart, 1991). President Bill Clinton proposed lifting the ban on gays in the military (although he ultimately compromised with opponents and supported a policy that allows homosexuals to serve in the military only if they do not disclose their sexual orientation).

The movement has also suffered setbacks. In 1992, several states and communities passed legislation prohibiting or rescinding civil rights protections designed specifically for homosexuals, and similar legislation was narrowly defeated in other communities (Carper, 1992). One of the defeated measures, in Oregon, would also have required schools, public colleges, and all other branches of state government to promote the view that homosexuality is "abnormal, wrong, unnatural, and perverse." Homosexuals also face growing antigay violence (*New York Times*, March 20, 1992). Statistics compiled by victim assistance agencies in five cities (New York, San Francisco, Chicago, Boston, and Minneapolis) show that incidents of violence against gays — including harassment, threats, physical assaults, vandalism, arson, police abuse, and murder — increased by nearly a third from 1990 to 1991.

The Nature of Collective Action

Movements such as the gay rights movement have played a significant role in American history and continue to be an important part of life in America today. All of us have been affected by changes brought about by the labor movement, the black civil rights movement, the peace movement, and the women's movement. And today's news is shaped by actions inspired by the environmental movement, the clash between the pro-life and pro-choice movements, and the continuing struggle of blacks, women, the disabled, and homosexuals to be protected from discrimination.

ACTIONS, COLLECTIVES, AND GOALS

Social psychologists use the term **collective action** in reference to specific actions by several people—a collective—oriented toward a specific goal involving social change. Let's take a closer look at three of the components in this definition: actions, collectives, and goals.

Kinds of Actions

There are four types of collective action: (1) *civil actions*, such as talking to officials, conducting letter-writing campaigns, or holding a news conference; (2) *protest actions*, such as demonstrating or marching; (3) *obstruction actions*, such as holding sit-ins and picketing; and (4) *violent actions*, such as rioting and engaging in terrorism.

The kinds of collective actions a movement utilizes are affected by several factors. One collective may imitate the successful tactics of another collective. Collectives use those tactics that "work" and give up upon those that don't. One collective may have greater access to a particular tactic than another collective. A middle-class group, for example, may differ from a working-class or deprived group in its access to authorities and financial resources (McCarthy and Zald, 1987*a*). Because of the resources available to them, members of a middle-class group can rely on civil and protest actions in their efforts to produce change. In contrast, the poor, who lack such resources, may have to rely on obstruction and violent strategies.

Kinds of Collectives

The word "collective" in the definition of collective action indicates that the actions involve the behavior of more than a single person. Several kinds of collectives may participate in collective action: organizations, identity groups, and crowds. A collective may consist of a *single* organization or a whole *network* of organizations. Some organizations may be formed for the purpose of pursuing social change; for example, the NAACP exists to promote the civil rights of African-Americans. Organizations whose primary goal is social change are called *social movement organizations* (SMOs). Other organizations may have primary goals unrelated to social change but later adopt an interest in the specific social change goals—for example, the black churches whose members joined many civil rights demonstrations, and the many Catholic and Protestant churches that are active in mobilizing support for the pro-life movement (McCarthy, 1987). If representatives of several SMOs periodically interact or cooperate to sponsor collective action, the organizations are said to have formed a network.

Not all collectives are organizations. A collective may be comprised of an *identity group*—a category of individuals identified (by others and themselves) as members of the same group, such as women, feminists, men, blacks, whites, gays, straights, students, or faculty. As we discussed in Chapter 4, "Social Relationships and Groups," the members of an identity group do not necessarily engage in sustained interaction with one another, but they do share a common identity or group consciousness. The interpersonal contact among members of an identity group may consist of *informal networks*, which are webs of social relationships tying an individual directly to some individuals and indirectly, through these others, to still more people.

A third type of collective is a *crowd*. Crowds are people who come together for a limited amount of time, sharing a particular focus. The people who gather for a demonstration, for example, constitute a crowd. Participation in crowds may be influenced, to some degree, by membership in a social movement organization or an interaction network, but such influence is limited as crowds are usually diverse and fluid in their actions, responding to specific events as they occur. Thus, a social movement organization may call a crowd together, but whether the organization maintains control of the event will depend on other factors. You may be more familiar with crowds unrelated to social movements; for example, the people who gather to watch a football game constitute a crowd. Like the SMOs that sponsor collective actions, the university sponsoring a football game also has limited control over crowd behavior.

Over time, collectives go through peaks and valleys in regard to the kinds and numbers of actors involved in them (Tarrow, 1989; Lofland and Johnson, 1991). For example, a collective may begin with the actions of an identity group or impromptu crowd, which spur the development of an SMO, which in turn sponsors additional collective action and recruits greater public participation. Over time, the participation of the public and even more committed SMO members may wane — a process called *demobilization* — leaving only the SMO leaders and a few highly committed members to carry out collective action aimed at social change. These core members and professionals may remain poised to initiate a new surge of the movement, ready to call the public back to action in response to a significant event.

Kinds of Goals

All collective action is oriented toward the goal of social change. This goal can take three different forms: escaping the dominant culture, changing the dominant culture, or resisting a change in the dominant culture.

The goal of some collective action is to *escape the dominant culture*. In other words, the goal of such actions is to deviate from the dominant culture without experiencing the prescribed negative sanctions. The examples that most often spring to mind are actions involving the attempts of religious minorities to escape the influence or persecution of a dominant religious culture. The dominant culture labels these religious minorities "cults." Cults rely largely on legal, nonviolent behavior to achieve their escapist goals. Other collectives with escapist goals, however, rely on illegal, violent behavior. Criminal collectives, which the dominant culture labels "gangs," for example, seek to escape the sanctions of the dominant legal authorities.

Other collective action is aimed at *changing,*

rather than escaping, the dominant culture. Civil and economic rights movements are usually "reform" movements that focus on expanding the culture to create equal opportunities for minorities. The environmental movement seeks to halt or reverse the environmental damage that results from the dominant "business as usual" approach.

Again, these movements differ in the types of collective action they emphasize. For example, the gun control and Mothers Against Drunk Driving (MADD) campaigns rely primarily on civil activities such as lobbying and letter writing. Civil rights and pro-life movements rely most often on protest and obstruction activities, such as demonstrations and sit-ins, as well as legal action. The environmental group Greenpeace receives a lot of public attention for its obstruction strategies. Most of these social movements include fringe groups whose strategies extend to violent activities, particularly the destruction of property. The white supremacy movement, which has a history of violence against persons and property, now includes some SMOs that rely more exclusively on protest actions such as demonstrations and marches.

Many reform movements are opposed by "countermovements" whose goal it is to *resist changes* in the dominant culture. For example, the pro-life movement (a reform movement) is opposed by the pro-choice movement (the dominant countermovement). The gun-control lobby is opposed by the pro-gun lobby, centered in the National Rifle Association. The gun movements square off using civil actions, while the abortion movements go head to head using protest actions.

Thus, collective actions can involve three general goals — escaping the dominant culture, changing the dominant culture, and resisting a change in the dominant culture. At times, all three of these goals operate simultaneously. For example, the black civil rights movement, with its change-the-dominant-culture goal, was and is opposed by the white supremacy movement's resist-the-change goal. And within the civil rights movement, there were escapist campaigns — efforts to create all-black communities — aimed at allowing blacks to escape the disadvantages experienced by African-Americans in white-controlled communities.

CAMPAIGNS AND MOVEMENTS

Attempts by citizens to exercise power over society or its institutions vary in complexity. The more complex the attempt, the harder it is to observe the phenomenon. Even if you have not been on campus or in your community very long, you have probably observed some instances of collective action — specific actions by several people oriented toward a specific goal involving social change. For example, you may have observed or participated in a demonstration or sit-in. You may also have observed a **collective campaign** — a *chain* of collective actions oriented toward specific goals involving social change. Whereas collective *action* refers to a single occurrence of collective action aimed at change — a single demonstration, for example — a collective campaign consists of several incidents of collective action aimed at the same change. Three of the most recent campaigns on the authors' university campus have involved efforts to build an African-American cultural center, efforts to eliminate discrimination on the basis of sexual orientation, and efforts to improve the wages and benefits of university housekeepers. Each campaign has consisted of several demonstrations, meetings with university officials, and an exchange of editorials (pro and con) in the campus newspaper.

Social movements are usually made up of several collective campaigns carried out by a number of different collectives oriented toward general goals of social change. In other words, several collective actions make a collective campaign, and several campaigns make a social movement. Movements themselves vary in duration, the kinds of collective action involved, and the degree of organization among collective actors. Let's emphasize the distinction between a "simple" campaign and a "complex" social movement with a few examples.

In July 1987, as a result of the closing of two emergency shelters for the homeless, a collective campaign was organized in Portland, Maine. Homeless protestors organized an occupation of City Hall. After threats of arrest, the protestors proceeded to a nearby park and established a "tent city." Participants organized security patrols, job and clothing banks, and shower facilities and even conducted their own surveys counting the city's homeless population. The homeless protestors abandoned the encampment more than a month later — only after the city agreed to open several year-round shelters, provide the homeless with representation on a variety of city boards, and liberalize welfare requirements. The protest also led to the development of a loosely organized homeless grievance committee, which continued to represent the homeless (Wagner and Cohen, 1991). Even this relatively small-scale collective campaign illustrates a number of kinds of collective action.

Sociologist Pamela Oliver (1989) does an excellent job of defining a social movement. She encourages us to view social movements as complex phenomena encompassing organizations, informal groups, crowds, group consciousness, and the interactions among all these elements. Social movements, she contends, are not static things but are "chains of reactions as actions of one kind in one place by one entity influence actions of other kinds in other places by other entities" (Oliver, 1989: 26). In this view, social movements "are not at all like armies at war with hierarchical command and a centralized leadership. They are not like organizations, not even very informal ones. They are more like networks. They are made up of lots of smaller collective units, each acting autonomously in accord with their own internal logic" (Oliver, 1989: 4). Because the different parts of a movement *influence* each other, no one organization or entity is likely to *control* the movement.

Oliver explains her idea of a social movement by using the example of the black civil rights movement of the 1950s and 1960s, a very large and complex movement that illustrates many of the features of social movements. Many organizations played important roles in this movement — the National Association for the Advancement of Colored People (NAACP), the Student Nonviolent Coordinating Committee (SNCC), the Congress of Racial Equality (CORE), the Southern Christian Leadership Conference (SCLC), and the Black Panthers. These organizations, their leaders, and their members engaged in collective actions such as filing lawsuits, organizing sit-ins and boycotts, and making speeches. Other organizations, such as black churches, whose primary purpose for existing had little to do with the movement, often mobilized mass support for these activities. Thus, people who were not members of "movement organizations" often participated in collective events such as boycotts, marches, rallies, demonstrations, and sit-ins.

Another aspect of the movement was the riots in Northern cities. The riots were neither planned nor encouraged by black movement organizations. In fact, existing civil rights organizations and their leaders universally *opposed* the riots. Although organizations neither started nor controlled the riots, these classic crowd actions were an integral part of the black movement in the 1960s. Whites viewed the riots as yet another, particularly frightening, demonstration of black unrest and generally conceded social benefits in response. Oliver says of the riots:

> They were clearly sparked by the climate of protest created by the civil rights demonstrations and they in turn altered the course of the organized parts of the movement. More militant leaders and organizations were created or rose in prominence as a consequence of the riots, and existing organizations altered their rhetoric and moved their bases of operations north to address the issues raised by the riots. (1989: 3)

Finally, people were changed by the civil rights movement. Active participants were changed by their experiences, often undergoing a progressive commitment to change. And, Oliver notes, nonactivists and even those who opposed the movement were changed as well:

> The movement raised the pride and consciousness of the mass of nonactivist blacks in important and enduring ways. Not only did the majority of blacks feel proud of the movement, their collective sense of culture and group pride rose. This shift in consciousness began with the period of black protests during World War II and continued with the postwar anticolonial struggles in Africa, but was accelerated by the movement activities of the 1950s and 1960s. Rising consciousness led millions of blacks to change the ways they dealt with whites in interpersonal encounters, a change that had a big effect on the perceptions and behavior of many whites. (1989: 3)

Oliver's description of the civil rights movement illustrates that social movements are characterized by a variety of actions, actors, issues, and goals. It also illustrates the *complexity* of the interrelationships among these components. In a social movement the actions of one collective may cause *re*actions. A particular collective action often creates a new event to which the collective reacts. For example, an SMO may sponsor a crowd to stage a sit-in to which the police respond with clubs and tear gas. The crowd's reaction may then shift from sit-ins to violence. Similarly, if the sit-ins prove to be successful in gaining an audience with the authorities, the sponsoring SMO may drop the crowd/sit-in tactic and adopt a representatives/lobbying tactic.

In addition, when one collective engages in a particular collective action (demonstration, sit-in, riot), other collectives may adopt the tactic — a process referred to as *diffusion* (Pitchner, Hamblin, and Miller, 1978; McAdam, 1983). The mass media can be particularly significant in stimulating diffusion and other reactions by disseminating information over great geographic and social distances. In contrast, the interpersonal communication of information requires organizational and informal networks to be in place.

The actions and reactions within the social movement are, largely, what give it *movement*. These chains of action and reaction are outside the control of any person or organization. Instead, movements are shaped by complex interactions of collective entities whose intentions may be quite divergent. "Each event in a social movement," Oliver explains, "is like throwing a rock into a pond, creating ripples which eventually damp out and become imperceptible."

The Origins of Collective Action

How do collective actions begin? We will answer this question by focusing on two general factors: (1) People feel discontented due to their position in the social order. (2) They define undesirable conditions as a social problem worthy of change.

DISCONTENT

Let's begin with the idea that discontent with existing social arrangements must become strong enough to motivate people to fight for change. Two sources of discontent are clashing socioeconomic interests and clashing values.

Clashing Socioeconomic Interests

Some collective actions are aimed at change designed to resolve clashing socioeconomic interests. Thus, the goal of some social movements is the redistribution of resources so that the "have-nots" get a bigger slice of the pie while the "haves" get a smaller slice. One social movement that arose from clashing socioeconomic interests is the labor movement, which was increasingly successful in the United States during the first half of this century but lost some of its power during the last half. Initially, the goal of the labor movement was to improve the socioeconomic conditions of industrial workers in general. However, gains were achieved primarily by white males, while groups such as African-Americans and white women remained disadvantaged (as we discussed in Chapter 14, "Inequality and Discrimination").

Of course, those who are better off socioeconomically have a stake in consolidating their power, privilege, and status by solidifying existing social arrangements. As a result, directed, conscious, deliberate social change occurs only when people make it happen through collective action. To be successful, social movements must overcome the resistance and opposition of those who benefit from the status quo.

Relative deprivation. Social psychologists use the term **relative deprivation** to refer to a state of mind in which a gap exists between what people seek and what seems attainable (Gurr, 1970; Folger, Rosenfield, and Robinson, 1983). Relative deprivation may occur under a variety of conditions. One of these is *rising expectations*. As a group experiences improvements in its conditions of life, it may also experience a rise in its expectations. But the expectations may rise more rapidly than the actual improvements, leading to dissatisfaction.

It was rising expectations, rather than despair, that bred the black protest and ghetto riots of the 1960s (Abeles, 1976). Blacks were led to believe that they were going to be much better off in the very near future. The early successes of the civil rights movement made it seem probable that blacks would rapidly gain a fair share of America's good things. As it turned out, many blacks found themselves in the position of the underprivileged urchin who has his nose pressed against the bakery window, longing for the goodies inside. Previously, segregation had barred blacks from entering the store at all. Now they could walk in like any other customers, but they had no money with which to buy the goodies. Thus the new expectations went unfulfilled or were perceived as being fulfilled too slowly. Perhaps the closest a society can come to social dynamite is the situation brought on by raising people's expectations for a new day and then delivering crumbs. Such feelings may be individual (when an individual compares his or her situation with that of others), fraternal (when an individual compares the situation of his or her group as a whole with that of an outgroup), or both (Guimond and Dubé-Simard, 1983). (See the Student Observation: "Relative Deprivation.")

Sociologist James Davies (1962, 1969, 1974) notes that relative deprivation may be fostered under still another condition—that characterized by his "rise-and-drop," or "J-curve," hypothesis. He shows that rebellions and revolutions are likely to occur when a prolonged period of objective economic and social improvement is followed by a short period of reversal. People fear that the ground they gained with great effort will be lost, and their mood becomes revolutionary. Although people may be objectively better off at the time of the reversal than they were a short time before, they *feel* deprived in relation to their expectations (see Figure 16-1).

Factors inhibiting relative deprivation. Social scientists have wondered why those who come out on the poor end of the unequal distribution of resources don't more often challenge the injustice of their circumstance. One reason is, of course, that they may perceive their situation as hopeless and therefore do not try to change it. But more often their failure to demand equity results from the absence of feelings of relative deprivation (Moore, 1991). But why wouldn't a deprived group *feel* deprived?

One reason might be that the disadvantaged lack information about the benefits received by other people and hence *do not perceive the inequality* of their situation. This is one effect of job segregation, which we discussed in Chapter 14, "Inequality and Discrimination." For example, although women earn lower wages than men with similar education, training, and experience (England et al., 1988), they tend to compare themselves not to men but to other women in similar occupations (Major and Forcey, 1985). Therefore, they may be unaware of the income gap that exists. Alternatively, a disadvantaged person may believe that his or her *group* is discriminated against but may also believe that he or she has *personally* escaped discrimination. There is some evidence that many women in the United States have this view (Crosby et al., 1986).

A second reason that a disadvantaged group might not experience the feeling of deprivation is that its members may believe that their disadvantaged state is deserved or fair. Thus, although they realize that they are treated unequally, they *do not perceive the inequity* of their situation. Some researchers suggest that the perception of fairness depends on whether the individual attributes her or his condition to internal or external factors (Della Fave, 1980; Stolte, 1983; Shepelak, 1987). This explanation proposes that poor people will be more likely to believe that inequalities are just if they attribute the cause of their disadvantage to themselves, that is, to their own lack of ability, education, or effort.

STUDENT OBSERVATION

Relative Deprivation

Two weeks ago, I accepted a job with a large accounting firm. I will not graduate until May, but I already have the job search behind me. Because I am in the Masters in Accounting (MAC) program, I had high expectations about my chance of getting a job. Last year the placement rate for the MAC program was about 85 percent, compared with less than 50 percent for the campus in general. I have friends in other majors who do not have jobs yet. They do not seem to be upset because they were not expecting to have a job at this point. However, those in the MAC program who do not yet have jobs are very upset and frustrated. They are viewing themselves relative to the others in the MAC program who do have jobs. Because they were expecting to get a job early, they are more frustrated than my other friends who were not expecting to get one. My MAC friends are experiencing *relative deprivation*.

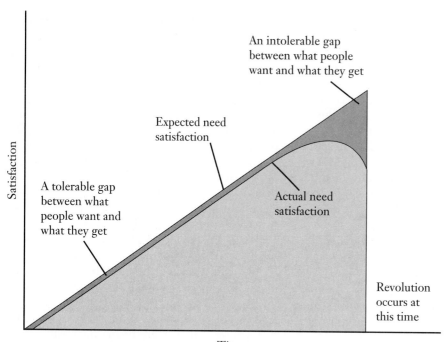

FIGURE 16-1 THE J-CURVE HYPOTHESIS
This graph illustrates Davies's theory that revolutions are most likely to occur when a period of economic and social progress is succeeded by sharp reversals, fueling fears that all gains will be lost. (Adapted from J. C. Davies, "Toward a Theory of Revolution," *American Sociological Review*, 1962, 27, 6, figure 1.)

In addition, people who experience prolonged disadvantage may develop self-attitudes that reflect and justify their inferior standing. Groups with a long history of being disadvantaged may come to devalue their own investments. This is an example of "turned-around" reasoning based on the equity norm, as we discussed in Chapter 14. Because we believe so strongly that rewards should be based on inputs or contributions, we assume that they are. Thus, we conclude that if we receive less — less pay, for example — it must be because our work is not as worthy. Women may be aware of the income gap between themselves and men, for instance, but consider the gap legitimate because they devalue their own work (Major and Deaux, 1982).

A third reason that oppressed groups don't always challenge their situation is that they claim "relative *advantage*" (Wolf, 1990). In order to cope with their disadvantaged situation, some groups make comparisons with groups they perceive as being even worse off than themselves. These comparisons support not only a sense of advantage but also a sense of contentment with their lot. Disadvantaged groups may even compare themselves with the dominant group and stress the domains in which they perceive themselves to be superior. For example, while black slaves in the South were well aware of the power that white slave owners had over them, many slaves perceived that they had the advantage of relatively deep religious beliefs, compared with the superficial religiosity of many whites. Such comparisons give oppressed groups a sense of dignity and honor, even in the face of negative evaluations by dominant people. The slaves' belief that their rewards would be forthcoming in heaven (where their white masters were unlikely to be in residence) supported accommodation to the unjust system of slavery.

Clashing Values

As we discussed in Chapter 15, "Deviance and Stigmatization," some groups are able to make their behavioral preferences the operating norms for others. These more powerful groups control the rewards and the penalties of others. Since values are often invested with "gut-level" emotion, many people do not take kindly to having their behavior regulated by what they define as unacceptable, even "immoral," standards. For example, many young people find themselves in a conflict of values with their elders about marijuana usage or premarital sex. As viewed by many older Americans, smoking pot and having premarital sex are dangerous, insidious problems; viewed from the perspective of pot users or sexually active singles, it is the "uptight" standards of older Americans that are the "real" problem. Likewise, the issue of abortion involves debate over the morality of the act, the question of the origin of human life, and the specific ways in which legal abortions should be funded. Women's rights groups and their right-to-life opponents wage a struggle on these questions. The same can be said of the environmental movement and its economic-development opposition. Whose morality shall prevail becomes a contestable matter (Offe, 1985).

The change pursued by social movements, then, is not neutral. Generally, some groups perceive that their fortunes would be improved by a proposed change; others feel threatened. People want many different things in life. Their definitions of situations tend to vary with their places in the social order. Those whose interests are served by the existing arrangements or whose social values prevail may enter the public arena to block or

The change pursued by social movements is not neutral. Generally, the members of one group feel that their lives would be improved by change, while those in an opposing group feel threatened by change. The emotional reactions of these pro-life and pro-choice demonstrators illustrates their intense involvement in the issue of whose morality shall prevail.

curtail change that they define as imperiling "the good life."

DEFINING THE SITUATION AS A SOCIAL PROBLEM

How is it that some issues of discontent provide the focus or fuel for collective action while others do not? Ordinarily, individuals make their way through life assuming that "nothing unusual is happening." But from time to time, for whatever reasons, they begin to label a situation as outside the "normal" province of everyday life. Sometimes, this results from a change in the situation. War, economic crises, geographic and social mobility, catastrophes, Supreme Court decisions, and technological change disrupt people's traditional or anticipated ways of life.

In other instances, it is people's *perceptions* of the situation that change, rather than the situation itself. Something changes the way they look at the situation, and they no longer take it for granted. Instead, they begin defining the circumstances as extraordinary or problematic. Whatever the cause, the situation comes to be viewed as a **social problem** — an undesirable condition that a collective believes (1) applies to a large number of people in society and (2) is attributable to an external cause.

It appears that conditions are unlikely to be perceived as social problems if they do not affect a large number of people. The more people they affect, the more likely they are to be publicly debated and defined as a problem that society should address. When people perceive a situation as a social problem, they usually see the condition as a consequence of forces external to themselves (Ferree and Miller, 1985). If they attribute their dissatisfaction to internal forces, such as their own shortcomings or bad luck, or if they believe the situation is hopelessly uncontrollable, they will not be inclined to define the problem as a *social* problem. Episodes of robbery, mugging, financial loss, illness, and death also involve suspending the customary definitions associated with everyday life, but the private and individual character of these episodes leads people to label them as "personal" tragedies rather than "social" problems (Lofland, 1981).

Sometimes a problem is defined *out* of existence as a *social* problem by redefining its causes. For example, a problem may be redefined as a medical condition or an illness requiring professional treatment. By attributing the cause of the problem to internal factors, the problem is personalized, weakening its status as a social problem. Within our society, this has been true for some forms of "mental illness," alcoholism, hyperactivity in children (hyperkinesis), and child abuse. Such an orientation *individualizes* the problem. The relevance of social or economic conditions (external factors) is downgraded, and the behavior is attributed to more or less random individual pathology (internal factors). Individualizing the problem tends to remove it from the realm of political discussion.

Among the factors that may bring about the perception of a situation as problematic are long-term causes such as a history of clashing interests and values. Other causes are more immediate but are interpreted in the context of the more long-term problem: Rosa Parks's refusal to sit in the back of a bus; the acquittal of four Los Angeles police officers who were videotaped beating Rodney King; a company's decision to build a new plant opposed by environmentalists. These more immediate causes are sometimes referred to by social psychologists as *precipitating incidents*. In many ways they are like the "last straw" — the one that "breaks the camel's back" — since these events confirm and dramatize people's collective view of the social problem, providing a focus for collective discontent.

Thus, a social problem is a matter of social definition (Blumer, 1971). People *attribute* problem status to certain circumstances or behaviors and assign an unfavorable meaning to them. Indeed, people can even define a nonexistent condition as a social problem. In colonial times, many inhabitants of Salem, Massachusetts, believed in witches and actively hunted them down. And some 200,000 to 500,000 witches, 85 percent of whom were women, were executed in Europe between the fourteenth and seventeenth centuries (Ben-Yehuda, 1980).

Conflict over the Definition

This means, of course, that disagreement about social problems is common. One group may define a condition as a social problem, while another group does not. In some cases, the initiative is taken by persons who wish to define as deviant a previously nondeviant activity. The temperance movement, which criminalized alcohol consumption during Prohibition, is an example. In other cases, members of a stigmatized group may confront their labelers in an effort to destigmatize their identities. Political movements to destigmatize marijuana use, prostitution, heroin use (in Britain), and homosexuality are examples of such initiatives.

Conflict may result from the fact that what is a problem to some is a benefit to others. For example, discrimination against minorities and women means favored treatment of majority males. Thus, negotiations over what is problematic and what should be done about it are often passionate.

Conflicting groups often define their opponents as "the cause" of the social problem — as deviants, even enemies — and characterize them in negative terms (Blain, 1988). For example, in the dominant group's view the "cranks" who advocate equal rights legislation are the problem; the opposing group views discrimination against disadvantaged groups (by the dominant group) as the problem. Political scientist Murray Edelman (1988) notes that political enemies are often portrayed in *contradictory* but uniformly negative terms:

> Members of the group in question are aloof and clannish and they insist on entering social circles where they are not welcome. They are less intelligent, lower on the scale of evolution, or farther from God's grace than others and are shrewd, dangerously resourceful, and uncanny in their talent for besting others unless kept in their place by force. They are ill-favored physically, behave like one or another animal, and smell bad, and they display superior sexual attractions and physical talents that make them seductive. They are weak, self-effacing, and cowardly and they are domineering, with a gift for attack or a talent for ruthless tactics. (1988: 74)

The discontent that launches a social movement can arise from situations that the public experiences either directly or indirectly (Neuman, 1990). When the public doesn't have direct information about a situation or an event, its perception of the situation as problematic or not is frequently shaped largely by the media or some authoritative source. If nothing else, the media and authorities often have the power to tell people what to think about. This is called *agenda setting* — focusing the public's attention on certain issues and thereby elevating public concern about those issues and creating a climate for collective action.

Interpretation by the Media

As we noted in Chapter 13, "Social Power: Behavior and Attitude Change," the public's perception of important problems is strongly affected by the amount of news coverage given to various issues. This is not simply a reflection of the media's coverage of problems *already* important to the public. Experiments demonstrated that viewers' priorities could be *changed* by varying the amount of coverage given to particular issues (Iyengar and Kinder, 1987), illustrating that the media can, under the right circumstances, have an agenda-setting effect.

During a conversation about a particular situation, have you ever heard someone say, "All I know is what I saw on TV"? Many of the situations we make judgments about are not ones we observe directly. This may be because they happen in parts of the world distant from our own (e.g., poverty in Appalachia or the nuclear accident at Chernobyl) or because we were simply not present to observe them (e.g., a police officer's shooting of a suspect in a nearby neighborhood). We also make judgments about situations we are not trained to observe — the effects of acid rain or depletion of the ozone layer, for example. We rely on the media for our information about such situations. In reporting "the facts," the media frequently also suggest how we should think about and interpret an issue or event and what should be done about it.

The media have the power to encourage public attention to an issue or to promote a group that is working for a particular cause (Graber, 1984). Social movements often need publicity to reach their goals, so media publicity can be crucial for success. Media decisions may or may not be politically motivated. A reporter may want to trigger social action or simply to produce an exciting story that will appeal to media audiences and enhance his or her professional status. But intentionally or unintentionally, journalists may write stories that arouse public reaction or influence authorities.

Sociologists William Gamson and Andre Modigliani (1989) have provided an interesting example of how the media's presentation of information about an issue is not neutral but, rather, suggests an interpretation. They studied the media's treatment of two events dealing with the issue of nuclear power — the accidents at nuclear plants at Three Mile Island, Pennsylvania, and in Chernobyl, Ukraine, formerly part of the Soviet Union. The Three Mile Island accident involved a relatively small release of radiation. The Chernobyl accident involved a fire and an explosion that released radioactivity into the environment, causing disease, death, and long-term pollution of the land. The researchers examined the coverage of three major television networks (ABC, CBS, and NBC) and three major news magazines (*Time*, *Newsweek*, and *U.S. News & World Report*), as well as editorial cartoons and syndicated columns.

Gamson and Modigliani's analysis, which covered the period before, during, and after each event, revealed that the media treated the nuclear power issue in seven different ways. The re-

searchers called the different interpretations "media packages":

- The *progressive package* framed the nuclear power issue in terms of our society's commitment to technological development and economic growth.
- The *energy-independence package* suggested that to rely on foreign suppliers for alternative sources of energy such as oil would make the United States vulnerable to political blackmail.
- The *soft-paths package* counseled us to change our life styles in order to conserve energy and protect the earth's ecology.
- The *public-accountability package* implied that the nuclear industry is motivated to protect its own interests (profits) rather than the public interest.
- The *not-cost-effective package* insinuated that unsolved problems and delays make nuclear power much more expensive than first expected.
- The *runaway package* proposed that we have unleashed nuclear power but can no longer control it.
- The *devil's bargain package* was a combination of a pro-nuclear package (either progressive or energy independence) and the anti-nuclear runaway package. In essence, its message implies that while we haven't figured out how to control nuclear power, we have to utilize it in order to continue economic growth and avoid the potential blackmail of foreign suppliers of oil.

The researchers also found that these media packages, or interpretations, were not evenly distributed over the time period studied. *Before* the Three Mile Island and Chernobyl accidents, the media generally presented pro-nuclear packages — progressive and energy independence. *Immediately after* each accident, the media dropped the pro-nuclear position in favor of the runaway package. *As time passed*, the message again shifted to a more ambivalent position — the devil's bargain package. Clearly, these messages suggest to the public how an event should be interpreted. The media may have a large impact on whether or not an issue becomes defined as a social problem, and hence the object of collective action.

Interpretation by Authorities

Because social movements are actions aimed at changing the existing social order, authorities often care about their success. If the authority is threatened by the social movement *or* believes that the change pursued by the movement would enhance his or her power, the authority may intervene to affect the outcome.

Authorities may affect social movements by using informational resources to influence the public's acceptance of their policies. Engineering such approval entails a kind of political impression management in which the authority attempts to shape the public's definition of a situation as a social problem or as not a problem. By inducing people to share his or her view of reality, an authority can persuade them to act in the manner he or she prescribes. Political impression management is largely a matter of controlling the flow of information, which authorities, as powerholders, are especially able to do.

Authorities can upstage their opponents through news conferences, press briefings, public speeches, and television interviews. In some instances, the credibility of the information may be enhanced by providing the information indirectly through news leaks, trial balloons, and off-the-record confidences. Efforts are made to project the authority as a wise, able, and deliberate person capable of heroic feats, baffling successes, and near miracles. Whereas the authority is cast in heroic terms, the leaders of discontented groups are portrayed as incompetents, villains, hypocrites, scoundrels, or worse yet, atheistic communists.

Authorities particularly try to take advantage of the television news, which devotes only brief coverage to each news story. Rather than taking time to develop the history behind a social problem and the future outcomes of possible solutions, the media focus on the current positions of "traditional news sources." A statement by an authority or her or his representative is always regarded as newsworthy, regardless of its content (Edelman, 1988). Such statements can be effective because of the expert resources of authorities: they are perceived by much of the public as possessing problem-solving skills that the public lacks.

Authorities are not in complete control of information. Much of the information provided by authorities is in turn processed by journalists. This is one reason that some authorities try to limit freedom of the press. Journalists select the happenings that they will portray and translate them into public events for a mass constituency. Consequently, events are filtered through a set of "news gates." The journalists can put a better or worse face on the information they are transmitting.

Studies indicate that media disclosures of wrongdoings by authorities have limited effects on the general public but are influential in changing the attitudes of policy makers (Protess et al., 1987). Although the media regularly expose the misconduct and blunders of public officials, for the most part they display a favorable attitude toward authorities (Graber, 1984; Senter, Reynolds, and Gruenenfelder, 1986). American political symbols and rituals, such as the presidency, the courts, elections, and patriotic celebrations, are usually treated with respect, perpetuating public support for authority.

The Public's Influence

Both the media and the authorities attempt to shape the public's attitudes toward issues and events. But doesn't the reverse also seem plausible? Doesn't public opinion also influence the media and authorities?

Researcher William Gonzenbach (1992) conducted a study to see which direction the influence flows. Public attitudes toward the drug issue — attitudes about drugs as a social problem — were measured by compiling monthly national polls that asked very similar versions of the question, "What do you think is the most important problem facing the country today?" The media's drug agenda was measured by the monthly frequency of drug stories in the *New York Times*. And the authorities' drug agenda was measured by the President's monthly public proclamations about the drug issue. The study covered seventy months, from January 1985 to October 1990.

The results of the study indicated that increases or decreases in the amount of attention given to the drug issue by the *Times* and the President were reflected in subsequent public attitudes about the importance of drugs as a problem. In other words, the greater the coverage of the drug problem in the *Times* or in the President's speeches, the more likely Americans were to mention drugs as the most important problem facing the country. However, the study also indicated that both the *Times* and the President followed public attitudes. In other words, the greater the public concern about drugs, the more likely the topic was to be covered in the *Times* and, even more, by the President. As we discussed in Chapter 13, "Social Power," power is usually a two-way street. Thus, Gonzenbach concludes, the media and authorities such as the President do, to some extent, set the public agenda. However, the public agenda also filters into the press's and authorities' agendas.

The Influence of Social Movement Organizations

Some social scientists view social discontent as more or less a given and thus as endemic within all modern societies. Yet there are relatively few social movements. Consequently, these researchers do not believe that social discontent is a *sufficient* condition for energizing and activating collective action. Instead, they argue, discontent must be coupled with resources devoted to a group's collective interests. In this view, the rise and growth of social movements depends largely on the recruitment of participants and on the bonds or cohesion of individual actors to the collective actor or action. In other words, social movements depend on the mobilization of resources for collective ends (Zald and McCarthy, 1987*a*).

Resource mobilization is the process by which resources are devoted to collective action. According to those who emphasize resource mobilization, collective action is seldom a viable option for discontented people because they lack the *resources* to challenge the status quo (Weitzer, 1991). Resources include human skills, such as leadership to represent the movement, personal resources to attract new members and legitimate the movement, expertise to achieve the movement's goals, and time to do the work of the movement. They also include tangible assets, such as money, equipment, weapons, access to channels of communication, and secure headquarters. When discontented people do mobilize, it is often with the infusion of outside help from those with organizational experience and through the exploitation of other institutional resources (mailing or telephone lists of sympathetic groups, informal networks, support from leaders of sympathetic organizations, publicity from the mass media, and so on).

One of the ways that social movement organizations mobilize resources for collective action is through efforts to manipulate the public's definition of the situation as a social problem. Social movements tend to develop an **ideology** — a set of shared definitions that provide interpretations and solutions to what is felt to be an unsatisfactory social condition (Ferree and Miller, 1985). An ideology may be shared by members of any kind of collective — a social movement organization, a crowd, or an identity group. When we share a belief in a social movement's ideology, our bonds to the collective are said to be normative. As we discussed in Chapter 4, "Social Relationships and Groups," normative bonds provide one basis for our desire and efforts to be a member of a group — to commit ourselves to the group. Once an ideology is developed, it may even attract members to a movement who do not directly experience the discontent that precipitated the movement.

Sociologists David Snow and his colleagues (Snow et al., 1986) have identified five kinds of attitudes among social movement ideologies: (1) a negative attitude toward a set of circumstances —

in other words, the identification of the circumstances as a social problem; (2) the attribution of blame for the social problem to external sources (one exception may be some religious movements that emphasize personal responsibility for problems); (3) negative stereotypes of the persons believed to be responsible for the social problem; (4) belief in the efficacy of the social movement to solve the social problem; and (5) a positive attitude toward "standing up" and doing something about the social problem. In short, an ideology puts forth a simplified set of beliefs about a social problem, specifying what or who caused it (who the villains are) and what the movement can do about it — a rationale for collective activity designed to produce change (Oberschall, 1973).

Snow and his colleagues were particularly interested in **consensus-building**, a process in which a social movement organization attempts to recruit members by increasing the consistency between its own ideology and the attitudes of segments of the public. For example, if people do not believe that the social movement can alleviate the relevant social problem, they are unlikely to be recruited to the movement. The SMO, therefore, must convince the public that its approach to the problem will be effective.

To find out how SMOs go about consensus-building, Snow and his colleagues conducted field research on two religious movements, the European peace movement, and several neighborhood campaigns (e.g., a campaign against the location of a Salvation Army shelter for the homeless). The researchers identified four methods used by the SMOs to align their ideologies with the attitudes of segments of the public: bridging, amplifying, grafting, and converting.

Bridging. In *bridging*, the SMO appealed to segments of the public (or other SMOs) that already had attitudes or an ideology *somewhat* consistent with its own. The appeals focused on attitudes shared by the different actors and gave minimal attention to attitudes *not* held in common, which were potential sources of internal conflict. Bridging techniques emphasized contact,

informational resources, and the encouragement of members of the public segments to align themselves with the ideologically consistent SMO, that is, to form a coalition. The bridging was carried out through networks, the mass media, the telephone, and, most recently, computerized direct mail for the purpose of soliciting cash contributions or a vote. Are you on one of these mailing lists yet? (Before reading further, look at the Student Observation: "Bridging.")

Amplifying or agenda setting. To align the public's attitudes with its own, the SMO also used *amplifying*. This involved elevating the *salience* of attitudes among the public that were consistent with the SMO's ideology. In these cases, the public already possessed relevant attitudes but failed to associate the attitude with the particular problem at hand. For example, in the neighborhood campaign that opposed the Salvation Army shelter for the homeless, the SMO activists appealed to the public's "family values." They repeatedly portrayed the shelter as a threat to women and children. This is the same agenda-setting process used by the media and authorities.

Grafting. In the alignment method of *grafting* the SMO *expanded* its own ideology to include some aspects of the public's attitudes. In doing this, the SMO tried to portray itself as being in sync with the problems and goals of particular segments of the public. For example, a local peace campaign — largely composed of white middle-class persons — attempted to enlarge its participation base by mobilizing racial and ethnic minorities. The SMO attempted to increase its attractiveness to these groups by calling itself the Peace and Justice Coalition and adding another goal to its ideology, namely, to nonviolently confront all forms of discrimination and oppression. (Before reading further, look at the Student Observation: "Grafting.")

Converting. The method of *converting* (which Snow and his colleagues call "transforming") involved the SMO's efforts to *change* the public's

STUDENT OBSERVATION

Bridging

This summer I joined the Sierra Club. I joined because I support conservation and environmental awareness and because I wanted *Sierra*, the club's fine magazine. Recently, however, I have found myself on a number of mailing lists and have experienced the consensus-building technique of *bridging* as a result. Bridging is the process in which social movement organizations (SMOs) appeal to segments of the public having attitudes or an ideology somewhat consistent with their own; they focus on shared attitudes and minimize attitudes not held in common. I have received a number of mailings from organizations requesting my help, usually monetary, for some cause. Some organizations, such as the National Wildlife Federation (NWF), have goals very close to those of the Sierra Club. The NWF is more concerned with preserving wildlife than entire ecosystems, but the same basic idea of environmental awareness underlies them both. The NWF did not have to do much to minimize unshared attitudes between itself and the Sierra Club because there are not many. On the other hand, I also received a mailing from an organization called the Southern Legal Defense Fund, whose main purpose was to help defend victims of violent racism. It emphasized its respect for equal rights for all people, highlighting concerns of the environmental movement. Both groups attempted to bridge the gap between their goals and the Sierra Club's (and hence my) goals in order to enlist my help with their SMOs.

attitudes to be more consistent with the ideology of the SMO. In grafting, the SMO changes; in converting, the effort is directed at changing the public. For example, Mothers Against Drunk Driving (MADD) has tried to redefine the personal misfortune of the loss of a loved one in an accident involving alcohol as a social problem — an injustice requiring an increase in the penalties for drunk driving.

Successful consensus-building depends heavily on informational resources. Recall, for example, our discussion of the foot-in-the-door technique in Chapter 13, "Social Power." The idea is to get a

STUDENT OBSERVATION

Grafting

Grafting is a method of consensus-building, or recruiting members by increasing the consistency between an SMO's own ideology and the attitudes of segments of the public. Grafting includes expanding the SMO's own ideology to include some aspects of the public's attitudes. An antiwar group that I was involved with during my freshman year of college in Illinois used grafting to align itself with various groups on campus in order to recruit members and support during the Persian Gulf War. For example, my committee enlarged its participation base by gaining support from the environmental group on campus. In order to do this, my group voted to include damage to the environment in Iraq and at home caused by the military-industrial complex as a form of violence that we felt was intolerable. We began a big publicity campaign, had forums and speakers about the projected environmental damage from the war, and attended meetings of the environmental group in the hopes that the group would formally pledge its support to our coalition. It worked — we made ourselves more attractive to this group, which formally stated its belief in our cause and a good portion of its members attended our functions.

person to comply with a large request by first getting him or her to comply with a smaller one. Compliance with the small request may increase the person's commitment to the actions involved because the individual infers personal responsiblility for his or her own actions (an internal attribution). This applies to participation in collective action. Many social movement organizations attempt to increase our commitment to their cause by first asking us to take a small step—to make a small donation, sign a petition, send a postcard to the President voicing our concern. If we agree, we may later be asked to make a larger donation for a "special effort," to become a member of a telephone network, or to volunteer our time. The more we see ourselves working for the movement's cause, the more committed we are likely to become to it. Similarly, if a person can be drawn to a demonstration by an SMO's message, she or he may become somewhat committed to the issue surrounding the demonstration.

Excessive use of consensus-building methods also has its limitations, from the SMO's perspective. Too much bridging may result in the public's being inundated with a barrage of similar appeals from the SMOs in the network. This may produce a kind of "public desensitization" to the social problem. Too much amplifying may invite effective competition from opposing movements: "*We* support family values (education, individual freedom, social responsibility) more than *they* do." Too much grafting may result in the trivialization of the movement's goals: "They're trying to do something *for everybody*." And converting may require too large a proportion of the movement's resources, at least in terms of time and effort, if nothing else. Converts may be lost to "backsliding," especially if countermovements—protest or "anti" movements that arise in response to the social change advocated by another movement—are investing their resources toward reclaiming those who are not strongly committed (Mottl, 1980).

An ideology may function to induce members to prepare for collective action by convincing them that potential costs will be small relative to anticipated benefits. For example, an ideology may espouse the belief that the opponent will be defeated rather easily because of the movement's own superior courage, organization, moral superiority, or supernatural support. As the conflict wears on, however, and the opponent's strengths become more obvious, these beliefs may become discredited and be replaced by others emphasizing the negative consequences of defeat, the desperate and treacherous nature of the opponent's actions, or the importance of sacrifices already made. If conflict continues, a movement may find it impossible to engineer credible shifts in ideology (Blalock, 1989).

Factors Affecting Participation in Collective Action

Under what conditions will we engage in collective action to bring about social change? After all, we do not participate in most collective actions. There is no simple answer to this question. Two facts account for this: (1) Each person's participation is influenced by *several* factors. (2) The factors influencing one person's participation may not be the same as those influencing another person's participation. In other words, the factors affecting participation in collective action *vary* from one person to another. You should remember these two facts as we discuss the many conditions influencing participation in collective action.

THREE EARLY EXPLANATIONS OF CROWD BEHAVIOR

Earlier in this chapter you were introduced to the *crowd*—a collective of people who come together for a limited amount of time, sharing a particular focus. "Crowd" is a wide-ranging concept that refers to all sorts of human assemblages: audiences, rallies, mobs, riots, and panics. Crowds can be engaged in a demonstration organized by an SMO or can consist of football fans led by team cheerleaders. Crowds frequently occur more spontaneously, going beyond the control of the event's sponsors (such as an SMO or university).

For example, a crowd's action may shift from an organized demonstration to "spontaneous" collective violence.

Crowd behavior has long intrigued social psychologists (Ross, 1908). Three explanations of crowd behavior dominated the thinking of social psychologists until the 1980s. These explanations focused on emotional arousal, convergent predispositions and emergent norms.

Emotional Arousal

No work on crowds has commanded greater attention than that of Gustave Le Bon (1896). In colorful and imaginative terms, Le Bon painted a picture of the crowd as characterized by a collective mind that overpowers and submerges the individual. His **contagion theory** assumes that the crowd assimilates its members, producing a psychic unity that alters the individual's normal emotions, thoughts, and conduct: "He [the individual] is no longer himself but has become an automaton who has ceased to be guided by his will." The sentiments and ideas of the participants all take the same direction, so people's conscious personalities vanish. This is Le Bon's "law of the mental unity of crowds."

Le Bon was originally trained as a physician. Impressed with the involuntary manner in which people contract a disease from one another, he advanced the notion that a similar mechanism operates within the crowd. Excitability and the mob-mind effect spread like an infectious disease.

People immersed in a crowd "lose themselves" and their sense of personal responsibility. They become engulfed in a wave of collective excitement in which the will of the collectivity is stronger than their own. Anonymity—not being easily identified as individuals—provides crowd members with a euphoric and exultant feeling of invincible power. This formulation by Le Bon finds expression in the contemporary social psychological concept of *deindividuation*, which we first discussed in Chapter 12, "Aggression and Conflict." Under some circumstances, deindividuation is thought to reduce moral restraints and to unleash a contagion of random, irrational, and destructive behavior.

Convergent Predispositions

The spread of an infectious disease is a good analogy for the contagion theory, whereas the heart-surgery ward of a hospital can be used to illustrate **convergence theory**. The patients on the ward share a common problem, but not because they have infected one another. Rather, they select themselves out of the public at large by virtue of their common complaint and assemble on the ward with a common purpose. Contagion theorists suggest that "normal, decent people" are *transformed* under crowd influence. In contrast, convergence theorists argue that a crowd consists of a highly unrepresentative group of people who come together *because* they share certain predispositions (Milgram and Toch, 1969). According to this view, the task for social psychologists is to identify classes or categories of "crowd-prone" people.

Hostile mobs are commonly cited as cases of convergence. For angry, aggression-prone individuals, a crowd functions as an attracting magnet. It supplies them with a pretext to translate their hidden and often destructive impulses into overt behavior. In his early study of a Leeville, Texas, lynching, Hadley Cantril (1941) notes that poor whites and men who had police records composed the crowd of lynchers. According to Cantril, the aggravated state of relations between poor whites and blacks and the lack of commitment to lawful procedures among criminal elements provided a reservoir of people who were ready for a lynching on a minimum of provocation. Convergence also occurs among teenagers who assemble for a rock concert and among sports fans who turn out to root for the home team.

Emergent Norm

"Unanimity," "uniformity," "oneness," and "similarity" are words used by both contagion and convergence theorists to describe crowds. **Emergent-norm theory**, developed by sociologists Ralph Turner and Lewis Killian (1972), challenges this imagery. It emphasizes the *differences* in motives, attitudes, and behaviors that characterize crowd members. It points out that crowds contain core activists, cautious activists, passive supporters, opportunistic yielders, passersby, the curious, the unsympathetic, and dissenters. The problem, then, is not to explain the "crowd mind"; rather, it is to explain how the *illusion* of uniformity and unanimity develops (McPhail and Wohlstein, 1983).

The view of people in crowds as impulsive, unpredictable creatures who cannot control their own behavior is overly simplistic, Turner and Killian argue. In emergent-norm theory, Turner and Killian employ concepts derived from the study of small groups. They take their cue from the work of Muzafer Sherif (1936) with the autokinetic phenomenon and the work of Solomon Asch (1952) with distortions of judgment in group settings (both studies are described in Chapter 9, "Performance, Conformity, and Cooperation"). Turner and Killian stress the part norms play in crowd behavior. They argue that collective behavior typically entails an attempt to define an am-

biguous situation. In ambiguous circumstances, people search for cues to appropriate and acceptable behavior. Like the participants in the Sherif experiments, who developed group norms that were different from the standards they had adopted when they were alone, crowd members evolve new standards in ill-defined settings (e.g., they might develop the norm that one should chant, throw bottles, loot, burn, harass police, or whatever). In the fashioning of emergent norms, the behavior of a few conspicuous and active members becomes perceived as the dominant course of action.

Once it has been formulated, crowd members undertake to enforce the new norm, convert others to it, inhibit behavior contrary to the norm, and institute restraining action against dissenters. Although people may not necessarily share the belief or emotion themselves, because of the norm they experience social pressures against

These demonstrators may have planned to use this tactic to block the shipment of nuclear waste on their local highways, *or* it may have developed spontaneously, with some group members following the lead of a few and then urging still others to join in. According to the emergent-norm theory of collective action, responses such as this are often the result of individuals' attempts to define an ambiguous situation. The behavior of a few active and conspicuous members may become perceived as the appropriate response.

nonconformity. And when dissenters remain silent, they provide passive support for the emergent norm and contribute to the illusion of unanimity.

REWARDS AND COSTS: INSTRUMENTAL BONDS

During the 1980s social psychologists began to expand their explanations of participation in crowds and other kinds of collectives. By now, you should be quite familiar with the rational choice explanation of behavior, as we have used it to explain, at least partly, social behavior such as cooperation, helping, exchange, and power. Once one recognizes that all these kinds of social behaviors are involved in collective action, it becomes obvious that the expectation of rewards and costs can also be used to explain, in part, why we participate in collective action on some occasions but not others (Oliver, 1980; Aguirre, 1984; Klandermans and Oegema, 1987; Blalock, 1989; McPhail, 1991; Wiltfang and McAdam, 1991).

What Do We Get?

Our participation in a collective action may be an example of a *cooperative response* — an action maximizing *collective* rewards. In other words, all participants are either rewarded or not as a result of their collective action. Some people participate in collective action because they see their needs inextricably tied to others' needs. For example, black Americans who believe their chances in life depend more on what happens to black people as a group than on themselves as individuals are more likely to belong to national organizations working to improve the conditions of black Americans (Ellison and London, 1992).

As we discussed in Chapter 9, "Performance, Conformity, and Cooperation," getting people to cooperate can be a difficult task. Some people may expect to receive rewards as a result of the performances (collective action) of others. In such a situation, three types of problems can arise: (1) Some people will not perform at their highest level but, instead, will expect others to contribute

more to the collective action — the social loafing effect. (2) Some members of the public will choose not to participate at all in collective action, reasoning that others will cooperate for the collective good and thus make their own participation unnecessary — the free-rider effect. (3) Still others will not participate because they reason that if they participate, others will not, thereby taking advantage of their contributions — the sucker effect. Each of these effects helps to explain the fact that collective action is not an everyday occurrence.

To overcome individuals' susceptibility to the social loafing, free-rider, and sucker effects, social movement organizations sometimes work to limit the benefits of collective action to their members. Labor unions provide a good example of such efforts. Unions would probably be ineffective at attracting members who were willing to pay dues, lose wages during strikes, and engage in other forms of collective action if the benefits of such actions were shared equally by nonmembers. Thus, unions try to negotiate for some benefits that are awarded only to union members, giving individuals an incentive to join together in collective action.

What Do They Get?

Rational choice does not preclude participating in collective action to benefit others (Muller and Opp, 1986; Gibson, 1991). The participation of white students and professionals in the black civil rights movement illustrates this point. So, although social movements often advocate changes that would benefit the weaker groups in the society, the relatively well-to-do also participate. Weaker groups, (e.g., children, whales, dogs and cats, and the poor) may be represented by supporters of a social movement who do not stand to benefit from its success (McCarthy and Zald, 1987b). For example, in 1984 and 1985 a vigorous movement developed around the goal of stopping or limiting the use of animals for medical research. It was not merely a movement of "pet lovers" but developed an elaborate ideology about the relation of humans to other species (Zald,

1987). To achieve its goals, the movement's followers used a number of tactics, such as rallies, lobbying, illegal rescues of research animals, and even the bombing of medical laboratories.

When the participants in collective action are motivated to benefit others, their participation can be thought of as *helping behavior*. We may participate in collective behavior so that others will receive the long-term benefits. We ourselves receive only the immediate satisfaction of seeing ourselves as kind and thoughtful persons for having helped others (Zald and McCarthy, 1987a). As discussed in Chapter 10, "Helping and Reward Exchange," many factors influence whether we will help others. For example, the likelihood of our helping others is greater when we (1) perceive the problem as unambiguous (those in need require our help); (2) view those in need as not responsible for their problems (they deserve our help); and (3) have a special responsibility to help those in need (other people are not available to

help or those in need of help include our friends, family members, or "people just like us"). All these elements find expression in a movement's ideology.

What Does It Cost Me?

The likelihood that we will engage in a particular collective action — donate money, demonstrate, take a leadership role — is increased if we expect that our costs will not be too out of line with our rewards. For example, if you expect that participation in a sit-in entails the risk that you will be expelled from school, lose your job, or be physically beaten, you may decide against taking part in the sit-in. Activists are overwhelmingly people whose work schedules provide considerable control over daily time — students, retired people, housewives, and lawyers (Flacks, 1990; Wiltfang and McAdam, 1991). Such people can participate in collective action and still meet the demands of school, work, and family.

Some types of collective action are more costly to participants than are others. Participants in sit-ins, for example, are more likely than those in marches or rallies to be arrested or involved in physical violence.

In his analysis of different kinds of protest actions in Washington, D.C., between 1961 and 1983, sociologist Kevin Everett (1992) found that the frequency of different actions had shifted away from sit-ins and pickets and toward marches and rallies. He explained this shift in terms of the cost of sit-ins and pickets to participants and ultimately to the SMOs involved. Everett found that the likelihood of arrest was greater in sit-ins (71 percent of all sit-ins involved one or more arrests) as was that of physical violence (29 percent involved violence).

Social psychologists would be quick to point out that this does not mean that arrest and violence will *always* deter participation in collective action. Cognitive dissonance theory (Chapter 8, "Attitudes and Behavior") proposes that sometimes the greater the cost of our behavior, the greater the likelihood of our repeating that behavior *if* we take personal responsibility for that particular behavior (as opposed to being forced to do it). Whether repressive consequences do deter our participation in collective actions probably depends on other factors as well (Opp and Roehl, 1990). Repressive consequences may be viewed as yet another illustration of the immorality of those supporting the dominant culture, that is, as just another reason why change must occur. Then too, there are social reactions to one's being repressed. Some of these reactions may support continuing the protest in the same manner. Such reactions are particularly common among those who shared the repression or those who joined the protest because they were moved by seeing someone else treated repressively. Other reactions may entail additional negative sanctions for being involved in the protest, such as being shunned by one's friends or being threatened with the loss of one's job. Whether or not we participate in a particular collective action is influenced by all the expected and resulting rewards and costs. (See the Student Observations for a case involving a cost for participating in a social movement and another involving a cost for *not* participating.)

THE ROLE OF EXPRESSIVE BONDS

Expressive bonds are another important source of bonding and commitment to social movements. As discussed in Chapter 4, "Social Relationships and Groups," expressive bonds are based on our attraction to a group's other members.

Two kinds of expressive bonds can increase our commitment to social movements: bonds to informal groups within the organization and bonds to the social movement organization itself. Both kinds can constitute *social incentives* for participation in collective action.

Expressive Bonds to Friends

One of the most powerful ways a person can become bonded to a social movement organization is through a network of personal friends (Kendrick, 1991). Many people are drawn into collective action through friends who are already active in the movement. Although we tend to explain "conversion" to social movements on purely ideological grounds, in most cases, "the truth" is communicated within the context of a preexisting social relationship. In his autobiography, Malcolm X (1964) describes his conversion to the Black Muslims. His initial contact with the movement came through his brother, who visited him in prison, introduced him to Black Muslim ideology, and led him through the first stages of the commitment process.

Recruitment to other religious groups, such as the Nichiren Shoshu Buddhist movement, the Moonies, and Hare Krishna, and to political movements, such as NOW, Right to Life, and the Lesbian-Gay Alliance, reveals somewhat similar patterns (Lofland, 1966; Snow, Zurcher, and Ekland-Olson, 1980; Stark and Bainbridge, 1980). Conversion is not merely a product of prior susceptibility to a movement or its ideology. Rather, interpersonal relationships frequently play a critical part. Two factors seem particularly important: First, individuals typically have links to one or more movement members or sympathizers

STUDENT OBSERVATIONS

The Cost of Participating

When I was a senior in high school, Hurricane Hugo struck Charlotte and school was canceled for a week. To make up for this lost time, the school board decided that we would not have the previously scheduled Spring Break. As you can imagine, this severely angered many students. In reaction, students decided to "boycott" fouth-period classes. The cost of participating in this protest was, for me, quite high. Seniors with two or fewer excused absences did not have to take the exam in my fourth-period class. Even in the face of pressure from my peers to participate in the collective action, the cost of having to take the exam was too high for me, so I decided not to join the boycott and went to class. This shows how the costs of collective action can be out of line with the rewards, thus deterring participation. (However, my fourth-period teacher sympathized with our plight and let those of us who showed up to class go to the demonstration!)

The Cost of Not Participating

When the local school board decided to vote on a 4 percent decrease (or increase, I never found out which) of the school budget, the student body arose in outrage. To get the money they needed for something, the members of the board proposed to cut late busing and freshman sports and to institute mandatory student activity fees. They decided to vote on this issue over the spring holiday so that their normally sparse audience would be even smaller. They got more than they bargained for from the students.

Save Our School (SOS) was born. This social movement was made up of the student body — everyone. Its purpose was to promote student participation in township politics. Those who did not proudly wear their SOS button and show up at the seemingly endless school board meetings were regarded as enemies.

I like to get perspective before I support or join a cause. However, in this case it was virtually impossible to do so. Public sentiment looked disdainfully on those who hesitated in their support. In the eyes of the great number of SOS members, the social problem was the school board's lack of compassion toward student issues, and they set about mobilizing students, parents, and faculty against the board. The usually bland school board meetings (25 people maximum) grew to shouting matches of 300 people or more and were moved to the school auditorium.

I'm afraid that I disappointed myself in the whole two-month affair. I never found a definitive view or even the motive of the "other" side. I wore my button, if only to avoid being harassed, but I tried to take a passive role.

I can't see now that the whole movement was very effective. I still don't know the entire story, but the next year we had late busing and freshman sports. That's probably all SOS wanted anyway.

through a preexisting or emergent interpersonal bond. Second, individuals commonly lack ties to other social networks that are antagonistic to the movement and its ideology. Once individuals move into a proselytizing network, their relationships become "encapsulated" by movement members, and they are increasingly exposed to broadened socialization messages.

It is also true, however, that recruitment to a religious or social movement may occur in the absence of preestablished social ties. For instance, one study found that about 42 percent of the initial contacts between members of the Hare Krishna movement and later converts took place in public places (Rochford, 1982). Within modern societies some people actively search for "meaningful encounters," "identity change," and "creative-transformation experiences" (Richardson, 1985). In his study of conversion to the Divine Light Mission, James V. Downton (1979) portrays recruits as actively seeking new ways to live and new interpretations of life. In her study of the Moonies, Eileen Barker (1984) concludes that most recruits are not coerced to join the movement by devious manipulations but, rather, are predisposed to accept the social and religious messages of the Unification Church by their traditional religious and family backgrounds. In sum, human beings are hardly passive subjects recruited and converted by external powers over which they lack control. (See the box "Religious Cults.")

Of course, participation in collective action creates opportunities to develop new friendships with other activists. Once these friendship networks are in place, participation in the SMO and its collective actions becomes a means of supporting and receiving the support of one's friends. Thus, individuals' expressive bonds to friendship networks within the movement may cultivate instrumental bonds to the SMO, since the SMO is instrumental in maintaining the friendship network. A person's participation in the SMO and the collective action it sponsors may be enhanced by the SMO's contribution to maintaining his or her friendship network. This can be particularly important in movements engaged in a protracted struggle, when weariness and competing commitments may lead to demobilization. Friends may reinforce one another's commitment to the movement. Therefore, SMOs may devote a portion of their resources toward sustaining friendship networks, even though these may be bonded only tenuously to the movement. (Before reading further, look at the Student Observation: "Expressive Bonds to Friends.")

Expressive Bonds to the Organization

Participation in an SMO may be an end in itself. In other words, participants may have expressive bonds to the organization. This is the case when membership or participation in the organization is a salient part of the person's self-identity: "I am a member of Greenpeace, and that is important to me."

One probable source of expressive bonds to an SMO is the performance of organizational roles. The more that members are involved in taking on organizational roles, the more they will identify with the organization and participate in its actions. Some SMOs are organized hierarchically, with their few formal roles held by the same individuals over a long period of time. Leadership in the SMOs involved in the black civil rights movement and the labor movement tends to be structured in this manner.

In contrast, other movements invite widespread participation by creating many organizational roles at the grass-roots level. The meetings of these organizations are, like town meetings, open to all and operated very democratically. Even the role of moderator may be rotated among the regular participants. SMOs involved in the peace movement in the late 1980s were structured according to this model (Downton and Wehr, 1991). One would expect that the expressive bonds of the "average participant" to these SMOs would be greater than those to SMOs organized more hierarchically. Thus, many social movement organizations are actually federations of small, local groups, which are better able to maintain expressive bonds than larger, more centralized organizations would be.

INFLUENCES OVER THE LIFE-COURSE: THE EXAMPLE OF 1960s ACTIVISTS

In Chapter 3, "Socialization over the Life-Course," we discussed how people learn and adapt to a sequence of changes from life to death. The life-course perspective can be applied to ac-

RELIGIOUS CULTS

Two explanations for participants' strong bonding to cults have been offered. One suggests that cults recruit and maintain members through "brainwashing," or coercive persuasion. The other argues that the brainwashing model ignores the voluntary aspects of participation in cults. Let's examine these two models.

THE BRAINWASHING MODEL

Although cult leaders deny that they practice brainwashing, a number of individuals who have studied cults compare their techniques with brainwashing methods — isolation, forced confession, and sensory deprivation (Lifton, 1979). Whatever they are labeled, the groups' recruitment and indoctrination procedures seek to bring about fundamental behavioral change. Some adherents and ex-members describe constant exhortation, training to arrive at exalted spiritual states, altered consciousness, and automatic submission to directives. Some cults require long hours of prayer, chanting, meditation, marathon encounter groups, psychodrama, and guided fantasy (Singer, 1979).

More recent cults have had particular appeal to youths. Many of them find that in the cults there are friends and fellowship for the friendless; a sense of belonging to something larger than oneself; the ego boost that comes to the possessor of special knowledge; ready-made decisions about careers, dating, sex, and marriage; and easy answers to complicated problems (Singer, 1979, Paloutzian, 1981; Levine, 1984).

The process of persuading cult members to relinquish their involvement with a cult has frequently involved coercive "deprogramming." The convert may be abducted from the cult, physically detained, and subjected to forcible "therapy." Supporters of this approach assert that devotees have lost their faculties for critical reasoning and consequently are incapable of leaving a cult without assistance from outside the cult.

THE RATIONAL CHOICE MODEL

Critics of the brainwashing, or coercive persuasion, model argue that most conversions are voluntary and occur in the absence of confinement or severe stress (Robbins and Anthony, 1980; Barker, 1984; Robbins, 1988). They note that only a small minority of those who join such groups actually stay for lengthy periods of time (Bird and Reimer, 1982). Accordingly, for many of these individuals departure is not a particularly disturbing event; indeed, the time they spend in the cult is often a rather benign, even therapeutic, experience, particularly if it compels them to come to terms with themselves (Galanter, 1983; Levine, 1984; Wright, 1987). Leaving a cult has been compared to leaving a marriage, and some researcher suggest that similar departure strategies, sanctions for departure, and aspects of adjustment are involved (Wright, 1991).

Opponents of deprogramming view it as a threat to religious liberty and protest the labeling of certain religious practices as "bizarre" and "psychopathic." They argue that medicalization is an effort by authorities to suppress deviance by attributing it to a mental aberration with psychiatric causes (Wright, 1991). And on a practical level, they suggest that deprogramming often does not work. It operates against the possibility that cult members will resolve their conflicts, leave the group, and rejoin the larger society on their own. Deprogramming can drive young adults back into the cult or into a pattern of later "cult hopping" (Levine, 1984; Richardson, van der Lans, and Derks, 1986).

tivists in social movements to help us answer two questions: (1) What factors affect the probability of our becoming committed to a social movement? (2) What are the probable long-term consequences of this commitment? Although these are interesting questions, social psychologists in the United States have paid scant attention to them. The only research of any substance has

STUDENT OBSERVATION

Expressive Bonds to Friends

*M*y Uncle Bob has always been an animal rights activist, and for the past seven years he has been very active with People for the Ethical Treatment of Animals (PETA). He spends a great deal of time and money with this social movement organization. He flies all over the country to participate in protests against testing on animals, writes to members of Congress, donates money to animal shelters, and educates children about PETA's activities. Bob's girlfriend, Chris, recently joined PETA. Although she had always liked animals, she had never been particularly concerned about animal rights. Since joining PETA, however, she has become sensitive to its cause and is becoming very attached to the organization. She joined PETA because of her bond to Bob and is committed to it because of him. This exemplifies the role that expressive bonds to friends play in commitment to social movement organizations.

been the study of activists of the turbulent 1960s, when the issues focused primarily on black civil rights and the Vietnam War.

Two studies provide some information about the backgrounds of these activists. Social psychologists Jack Whalen and Richard Flacks (1989), themselves activists, conducted life-history interviews with eighteen former leftist college students who had participated in political protests from 1967 to 1971 at the University of California at Santa Barbara and its surrounding community. The researchers compared the life patterns of the activists with those of fifteen nonactivist students at the same university. The second study was conducted by Margaret and Richard Braungart (1990). These researchers compared the life patterns of thirteen left-wing (members of the Students for a Democratic Society) and eleven right-wing (members of Young Americans for Freedom) activist leaders from the 1960s.

Parental Socialization

In the 1960s, a popular explanation for student activism was that left-wing activists were rebelling against their parents. However, the results of the studies by Whalen and Flacks and Braungart and Braungart indicated that this assumption was incorrect. Instead, the student activists, on both the left and the right, reflected the political orientations of their parents. Compared with the families

of nonactivists, activists' families were more likely to be members of minority groups, with the leftists predominantly Jewish and the rightists predominantly Catholic.

The parents of left-wing activists were more likely to hold jobs in the public sector (as educators and civil servants) or to be active in trade unions. These parents shared their children's liberal-leftist views. These families promoted an ideology that said (1) you should devote your life, in some way, to social betterment and (2) you are a person of outstanding potential, who ought to fulfill your unique promise in a significant way. In contrast, the parents of right-wing activists were more likely to have occupations in the private sector (in small businesses, as salespersons, and as journalists). Although the effects of parental socialization were stronger for left-wing than right-wing activists, parents of *both* groups stressed strong values and standing up for one's beliefs.

Opportunity Structures

Parents are, of course, not the only source of political activism. All the activists studied by Whalen and Flacks and Braungart and Braungart were college students in the 1960s. In college young people are relatively free of adult constraints and are encouraged to increase (among other things) their individual and political awareness. Not all students take advantage of these opportunities. Students from politically oriented families probably do. Political groups are available, and direct contact with these groups is possible. A person's network of friends may encourage affiliation with a particular political group.

Political groups offered 1960s students (newly separated from their parents) a source of identity and support, as well as the now familiar "we versus they" perspective. Collective participation gave them not only a sense of power and accomplishment but also feelings of love and community. While the activists were in college, political groups, friends, and professors had an impact on their politics — not changing their political orientations but reinforcing and amplifying the views already held.

The Legacy of Commitment

But what about *after* the 1960s? What was the legacy of this activism? In addition to the two studies just discussed, two others offer information to help us answer this question. The first study compared 212 activists in the 1964 Mississippi Freedom Summer project (a civil rights program in the deep South) with 118 people who were accepted for the project but did not participate in it (McAdam, 1989). Both groups were largely white, Northern college students. The second study compared three groups of former students enrolled at Florida State University during the early 1960s: (1) civil rights activists, (2) members of student government, and (3) non-activists (Fendrich and Turner, 1989). Data were gathered in 1971 on ninety-five former students and again in 1986 on eighty-five of them.

In the 1970s and 1980s, the popular belief was that the 1960s left-wing activists had abandoned their political attitudes and activism in favor of life styles more consistent with those of their right-wing counterparts, becoming materialistic and seeking jobs in corporations and finance. A few probably did. But again, research finds this popular belief to be generally false. The leftists' careers of activism were sustained for many years. Their incomes remained low, as they did not have jobs that promised regular advancement. Most acti-

vists did not marry or have children until well into their thirties, choosing instead to live among other activists while moving from one collective campaign to another. In their thirties, their lives did begin to change. Many married, had children, and chose an occupation. But they chose mates with similar political attitudes and occupations with obvious links to their more activist pasts, (e.g., a doctor in public health, a liberal minister, a historian). Although they no longer saw themselves as committed to "the Cause," they still found satisfaction in their participation within the traditional political process (usually the Democratic party) and the "small victories." In other words, they were much like their parents were at the same age.

What about the right-wing activists of the 1960s? What have their lives been like since then? Most married earlier than the leftists, but again their mates were of similar political persuasion. They began their careers earlier, although they, too, pursued occupations linked to their activist past (law, publishing, government, and political consulting). Most remained politically active, though like the leftists, they became less radical and more involved in the traditional political process — in this case, the Republican party. Thus, it appears that differential childhood socialization resulted in two types of political attitudes and activism, which, although modified, continued to be reflected throughout the life course.

We have covered a lot of material in trying to answer the question, "What are the factors influencing our participation in collective action?" We began by saying that many factors are involved and that the particular combination of factors varies from one participant to the next. Among these factors are the following: discontent with existing social arrangements, who wins the struggle to define unacceptable conditions as a social problem, the success of social movement organizations in mobilizing resources, the rewards and costs of participation, a network of personal friends who are participants, an expressive bond to an SMO, parental socialization, and a legacy of prior participation. Think of an opportunity you have had to participate in a collective action, campaign, or social movement. How well do these factors explain whether you participated or not?

The Power of Opposing Forces

The question of why we participate in social movements — whether a single collective action or an entire collective campaign — is only one of the questions that interest social psychologists. An equally important question involves collective *inter*action. How do opposing forces interact with one another?

All social movements interact with the protectors of the dominant culture, that is, the authorities whose power is invested in the status quo. We noted in Chapter 13, "Social Power," that *authority* is a kind of power based on normative resources — a rule or an agreement (a norm) among a group of persons which recognizes that one party has a right to command while other parties have the responsibility to obey. As a result, the authority's initial response to a social movement may be to ignore it. Authorities also often control reward and coercive resources. Many authorities have the right and resources to punish those who do not follow their directives; for example, coercion can take the form of police dogs, stun guns, tear gas, pistol-whippings, beatings, fines, jail, deportation, and even execution. Alternatively, authorities may appoint members of the opposition to token leadership positions within the establishment as a reward for their "cooperation" — a process called *cooptation*. For example, a leader of the environmental movement might be appointed to the President's cabinet; a children's rights advocate, to a judgeship; or a student leader for a homosexual rights group, to the chancellor's advisory committee.

INTERACTIONS BETWEEN MOVEMENTS AND COUNTERMOVEMENTS

A social movement may be opposed not only by authorities but also by a countermovement allied with authorities. The collective actions comprising a social movement and a corresponding countermovement are often aimed at confronting, neutralizing, discrediting, or even destroying each other. The movements are engaged in *social conflict* (Zald and Useem, 1987).

The actions of a movement and a countermovement strongly influence each other's reactions (Staggenborg, 1989). First, a countermovement is likely to emerge if the social movement appears to be gaining momentum — mobilizing public resources, gaining media attention, winning concessions from authorities. A movement may act as a collective *model* that suggests to the opposition that collective action works. Second, rather than imitate a successful strategy of the movement, the countermovement may devise new ways to counter (neutralize) the opposing group's strategy (McAdam, 1983). For example, if a movement is particularly successful at attracting media attention by creating large demonstrations, the countermovement may learn methods that will increase the likelihood of violent confrontation; although this may still attract the media, it will have a negative effect on the public. In response, the movement might undertake special training for its demonstrators in nonviolent strategies. Third, as one movement wins the victory of mobilizing resources or achieving a specific goal, the opposing movement may intensify its efforts (e.g., use more obstructive or violent actions) or shift its attention to another goal. For example, once the pro-choice forces won the support of the Supreme Court, the pro-life forces turned their attention to Congress and state legislatures and used obstructive sit-ins with increasing frequency. Fourth, even though one movement may have won the current battle, the continued presence of the countermovement may prevent its demobilization.

Because the public may be turned off by obstructive and violent actions, the conflict between movements more often resembles a debate than a battle. Both sides rely on informational and expert resources to gain the support of uncommitted elites and members of the public. Each side tries to paint the other as unjust and evil. For example, both the pro-choice and the pro-life forces attempt to portray the other as antifamily. The pro-choicers are stereotyped as baby killers (through, for example, the display of pictures and sounds of fetuses) who are interested in putting their jobs ahead of their families. On the other hand, the pro-lifers are also stereotyped as antifamily — as women exploiters who are not interested in the future *quality* of life of the fetus.

Countermovements have special problems. Social movements are trying to change the dominant culture, while countermovements are defending it. This allows the social movement to portray itself as the "agent of change" and to cast the countermovement as the "defender of the imperfect past or the unfair status quo." The countermovement tries to manage impressions so that the social movement is discredited and the countermovement is portrayed as a revisionist movement rather than as a defender of the past. For example, the pro-nuclear power countermovement became a pro-energy movement. After the legalization of abortion in 1973, the abortion movement became the pro-choice movement.

In impression management efforts, leaders are often singled out for personal attack. Men may be portrayed as womanizers or draft dodgers, women as former alcoholics or mental patients, and both as tax evaders or past drug users. Some members of a movement may specialize in gathering information that can be used in these kinds of attacks. The leaders singled out for this treatment frequently respond by describing it as "dirt gathering," "character assassination," or "negative campaigning," arguing that "the debate should be restricted to issues, rather than personal attacks."

INTERACTIONS WITHIN SOCIAL MOVEMENTS

As we noted in the beginning of the chapter, many social movements involve a number of collectives, sometimes even two or more SMOs. The SMOs have the same general goals but may prefer different targets, strategies, or participants. In some instances, the SMOs have always been different SMOs; in other cases, they began as a single SMO but *fractionalized*, or split into sub-groups, as a result of differences within the group. The SMOs within a network may on some occasions cooperate with one another but on other occasions compete and engage in intense social conflict (Zald and McCarthy, 1987b).

Competition and conflict among SMOs within a social movement is very similar to the conflict between a social movement and its corresponding countermovement. SMOs often compete for the same resources — the same private organizations and foundations, authorities, and members of the public. For example, the authors are on the direct mailing lists of a large number of environmental SMOs. Some supporters have the resources (time, money, and so on) to participate in several SMOs of a social movement and are willing to do so. SMOs may try to facilitate this inclusive participation by specializing in different strategies or targets, for example, civil, protest, or obstructive forms of collective action.

Legitimation is a more exclusive resource, and therefore it leads to more competition and conflict. SMOs may compete with one another for leadership of the movement. Only one SMO can be "out front" in a particular social movement. Ideologically, SMOs may try to portray each other in terms of negative stereotypes. Some are defined as "radicals"; others, as "in bed with the enemy." When one SMO claims legitimacy through a protest action, another may try to portray the protest as illegitimate by suggesting that it was the work of "agitators" or "outsiders" (Turner, 1969).

Competition within social movements has its advantages and disadvantages. The disadvantage is that movement supporters are divided, and no one group may be powerful enough to produce the desired social change. In other words, the movement's effectiveness may be diminished by infighting among collective actors. Nevertheless, conflict may work to the advantage of some movement organizations. Those favoring more moderate civil or protest strategies may be able to use the obstructive and violent strategies of other SMOs as a threat in their negotiations with the people in power: "You had better deal with us, because you won't want to have to deal with them." Does this remind you of the "good cop–bad cop" example in Chapter 13, "Social Power"?

Sometimes the SMOs of a social movement will cooperate with each other. Cooperation may be based on very informal arrangements among the SMOs in a loose network or may take the form of a formal federation in which each SMO gives up some rights to the new federation. Cooperation is fostered by the organizations' shared goals, enemies, and participants (that is, overlapping membership). Some researchers argue that the likelihood of cooperation is increased when the entire social movement is on the verge of collapse (Staggenborg, 1986). Then, collective action by a coalition of SMOs may seem like the only way to maintain a viable movement. Others believe that coalitions of SMOs are most likely

when the movement seems to be on the verge of reaching its goals (Zald and Garner, 1987). Then, they argue, the costs of investing in the coalition seem small compared with the potential benefits of success.

Outcomes

So what are the outcomes of collective action? There are certainly winners and losers, but sometimes it is difficult to tell which is which. The process of social change often involves "two steps forward, and one step back" (Blumer, 1971; Spector and Kitsuse, 1987).

A selective process takes place: many budding social problems are choked off; others are avoided or ignored or have to fight their way to respec-

A problem must acquire a certain degree of "respectability" if it is to secure consideration in recognized public arenas such as the media and government. Until a movement gains respectability, those advocating change are often viewed as "crackpots" or "subversives." The animal rights movement once faced this barrier, but it is now gaining respectability.

tability (e.g., racism and sexism); while still others are rushed along the road to legitimacy by strong and influential backing (e.g., the energy crisis). If a social problem acquires legitimacy, its sponsors are no longer considered simply "protest groups" but become bona fide "spokespeople" for a constituency.

BECOMING OFFICIAL PUBLIC POLICY

If a social problem manages to secure social legitimacy, it enters a new stage in its career. This consists of hammering out an official plan of action, commonly by legislative committees and executive boards. Diverse interests and views result in maneuvering, diplomacy, and bargaining. Compromises, concessions, trade-offs, deference to high-status public figures, responses to power, and assessments of what is practical and workable all play a part. This is a defining and redefining process that alters the collective picture of the social problem. The restructuring of a social problem as it passes through successive phases of the collective process may make it unrecognizable to its early sponsors.

Although protest groups may regard gaining official attention as their "finest hour," such attention often represents the beginning of the end of their control over the issues they raise (Spector and Kitsuse, 1987). Official agencies may capture and monopolize the problem, neutralizing or eliminating the original protesters. It becomes a matter of the agencies' own vested interests to stimulate a widespread belief among the discontented that solutions to the social problem are finally in place and that substantial progress is being made toward eliminating the problem. "Success" is defined in the short-run terms of official public policy—the enactment of a law or regulatory statute.

However, the proposed solution may not accomplish its long-term goal. So-called antidiscrimination laws may not eliminate or even reduce discrimination; in fact, the legislation may even exacerbate the social problem. As we discussed in Chapter 14, "Inequality and Discrimi-

nation," affirmative action legislation may *lower* the status and efforts of those it is intended to help. But effectiveness is something that only time can demonstrate. In the meantime, the public's attention may shift to other social problems.

Of course, legislation and other official action are not necessarily doomed to failure. For example, in 1977 federal regulations were signed that prohibited discrimination against persons with disabilities in any program or activity receiving federal financial assistance. Some observers believe that these regulations gave the disabled movement focus, ensuring that the regulations were enforced (Johnson, 1983). The regulations also provided federal funds for teaching people with disabilities their rights. The training workshops became a means of movement recruitment. The movement successfully lobbied for passage of a 1992 law prohibiting discrimination against the disabled in employment.

When a social movement is successful in bringing about the change it desires, the movement may dissolve. However, new issues may be raised, and the movement may focus on new aspects of the problem (Zald and Garner, 1987). For example, after the suffrage movement won the vote for American women, most suffrage organizations disbanded, but the National Woman's Party began to fight for the equal rights amendment, beginning a new cycle of the women's movement (Rupp and Taylor, 1987). Positive outcomes can also mobilize countermovement opposition and, in turn, revitalize a movement. For example, the antiabortion countermovement kept the prochoice movement mobilized after the 1973 legalization of abortion (Staggenborg, 1989).

WHY DO MANY SOCIAL MOVEMENTS FAIL?

Social psychologist Donald Campbell (1975, 1983) argues that planned social change is difficult because the cultural norms supporting existing social arrangements are very powerful. Indeed, a number of psychological processes set the stage for us to resist social change. Research suggests that people tend to believe that social change is more rapid than it really is (Silka, 1989). We tend, for example, to believe in "the good old days," viewing past times as happier, safer, and better in many ways than the present. Our nostalgia about the past leads us to distrust change because we imagine it to be for the worse. Similarly, our tendency to believe we live in a "just world," in which things are as they should be and life is fair, leads us to distrust social change (Lerner, 1980b).

It appears that people may resist change when its effects cannot be known with certainty. We prefer unpleasant, but familiar, realities to some possible disaster that might result from changing present policy. Although we may support change *in principle*, we are slow to support specific proposals for bringing the change about. Thus, there is strong American support for revising the welfare system, but support for specific proposals for revising it are weaker. Similarly, between 1983 and 1986 the Irish public supported legalization of divorce "in certain circumstances" by a two-to-one margin, yet a 1986 referendum on a constitutional amendment allowing legal divorce for couples demonstrating irreconcilable differences over a minimum of five years was defeated (Darcy, Laver, and Engstrom, 1987). Consider the implications of this resistance to change for discussions in this country about health care reform, reducing the drug problem, the deficit, unemployment, and so on.

CAN SOCIAL MOVEMENTS SUCCEED?

Can ordinary people join together in collective action to successfully bring about social change? Can social movements succeed? Despite the pressures to resist change, intentional change, brought about by social movements, does occur. In this chapter we have provided numerous examples of change brought about by the efforts of collective actors: voting rights for women and blacks, public school integration, the legalization of abortion in the United States, the removal of legal prohibitions against homosexual relations in a number of states. Yet none of these movements has been entirely successful in bringing about the

full range of social change its proponents desire. Indeed, the movements are still active, working toward additional changes.

Psychologist Karl Weick (1984) suggests that citizens should seek to bring about large-scale changes by breaking them into smaller discrete problems to be tackled one at a time. He calls this the "strategy of small wins." There are numerous psychological reasons, Weick argues, why social change is more effectively pursued in local, brief, focused efforts with specific, concrete, and limited objectives. People perform best, according to Weick, when they are only moderately aroused. People who are not aroused are not motivated to perform well. People who are too highly aroused, as might occur when tackling too large a problem, are unable to concentrate and are vulnerable to discouragement when they meet with failure along the way. If a movement focuses on limited goals, it avoids raising the participants' arousal levels too high, and the odds of success improve, thereby motivating continuation of the effort to bring about change. Another reason that the strategy of small wins is successful, Weick argues, is that people with power give little thought to the long-term implications of isolated requests for small change. In contrast, larger-scale changes attract the attention of the public and lead to political counterpressures.

Political scientists David Palatz and Robert Entman (1981) note that the media are more favorable to those pursuing a strategy of small wins, that is, those working within established rules toward discrete, incremental goals. They argue that groups pursuing more radical objectives through unconventional methods usually find their activities distorted or condemned by the media. This kind of publicity tends to isolate the groups from the public, "encouraging them to moderate their ways until they either fade from sight or shade into the establishment" (Palatz and Entman, 1981: 146).

An example of the effectiveness of the strategy of small wins is the relatively recent reduction of the use of male-oriented language in the media. Feminists attempted to increase the public understanding of the importance of language in shaping thought through small-scale lobbying efforts at the local level. As a result, many authors and editors now accept that using masculine pronouns and male characters to "stand for" both men and women inappropriately influences our thinking about the importance of men and women in our society. Through the accumulation of many local publishing decisions, great progress toward removing the male bias in language use was made in only a few years. In contrast, the movement's attempts to bring about wider-scale social change in the form of the equal rights amendment have, thus far, failed.

Summary

1. Collective action refers to actions by several people oriented toward a specific goal involving social change. A collective campaign is a chain of collective actions. A social movement is usually made up of several collective campaigns that share the same general goal of social change.

2. A social problem is a matter of social definition; thus disagreements about social problems are common. One group may define a condition as a social problem, while another group does not. Groups influencing the definition of social problems include the media, authorities, the public, and social movement organizations.

3. There is no simple answer to the question, "Under what conditions will we engage in collective action to bring about social change?" The reasons for this are (1) each person's participation is influenced by several factors and (2) the factors affecting participation vary from one person to another. People may participate in collective action because of (1) instrumental bonds, whereby their costs are not too far out of line with the benefits received by themselves or those whom they support, and/or (2) expressive bonds, whereby they have friendships with other participants or participation is important to their self-identities. Studies of the movement activists of the turbulent 1960s show that the views of both leftists and rightists were at least partly a reflection of the political orientations of their parents, political groups, friends, and professors.

4. The actions of a social movement and countermovement strongly influence one another. Their collective actions are often aimed at confronting, neutralizing, discrediting, or even destroying each other. Although the SMOs within a social movement sometimes cooperate with one another, they frequently engage in competition and conflict similar to the conflict between the social movement and its corresponding countermovement.

5. A problem must acquire a certain degree of respectability if it is to secure consideration in recognized public arenas. A selective process takes place in social interaction, whereby many budding social problems are choked off, others are avoided, others are ignored, others have to fight their way to respectability, and others are rushed along the road to legitimacy by strong and influential backing. If a social problem manages to secure social legitimacy, it enters the policy-making phase. The restructuring of a social problem as it passes through successive phases of this process may make it unrecognizable to its early sponsors.

absolutist view of deviance The view that deviance is intrinsic to certain actions. In this view, right and wrong exist independently of arbitrary, human-created social judgments.

accounts Explanations that we offer for our behaviors. Accounts take four forms: excuses, justifications, concessions, and refusals.

additive task A task in which the performance of the group is measured in terms of the sum of the members' responses.

affect control theory (ACT) David Heise's theory offering a model of attitudes which suggests that the meanings we assign to identities and behaviors shape our social interactions. The theory uses the concepts of fundamental sentiments, transient sentiments, and deflection to describe the relationship between attitudes and behaviors.

affirmative action A government policy aimed at ending discriminatory practices by employers, as well as requiring them to take additional steps necessary to overcome the effects of past discrimination and give minorities "equal opportunity."

age grading The classification of individuals into age categories which divide the life course into meaningful stages and establish timetables for life events.

ageism Society's denial of privileges to a category of people because of their age.

agents of socialization The individuals, groups, and institutions that play a part in the transmission of culture to the new generation.

aggregate A unit of two or more persons whose interaction is minimal.

aggression Intentional harm done by one party to another.

alternative sources All the sources of rewards available to a person.

anticipatory socialization A phase of socialization in which individuals fantasize about, experiment with, and try on the behaviors associated with role expectations for future roles.

attitude consistency The organization of attitudes in a harmonious manner so that attitudes are not in conflict with each other (inconsistency or imbalance). Attitude consistency theories suggest that we strive to maintain consistency and to avoid inconsistency, which is experienced as an uncomfortable psychological state.

attitude toward the behavior In the reasoned action model, the behavioral-intention factor consisting of a person's beliefs and evaluations of the possible outcomes of the behavior. It is estimated by summing the person's evaluations of the consequences of the behavior, weighted by the likelihood of each consequence.

audience task A task involving performance in the presence of others who are observing the behavior but not performing the same task.

authoritarian parenting style A style of parenting in which parents rely on a combination of normative, reward, and coercive resources to produce their children's strict obedience.

authoritative parenting style A style of parenting in which parents rely on a combination of expert, informational, reward, and coercive resources to persuade their children to behave in a certain manner, taking into account the child's explanation for noncompliance.

backchannel feedback Any subtle vocal or nonverbal response that a listener makes while a speaker is talking that signals to the speaker whether he or she is keeping the listener's interest and being understood.

balance Balance theory's term for attitude consistency.

balance theory The original formulation of attitude consistency theory, developed by Fritz Heider, which focused on three elements: (1) the person who is the focus of attention, P; (2) some other person, O; and (3) an impersonal entity, X. The theory posits that P strives to maintain consistency among the attitudes connecting these elements, that is, P's attitude toward O, P's attitude toward X, and P's perception of O's attitude toward X.

behavioral intentions Our plans to perform a behavior. In the reasoned action model, behavioral intention is a function of the person's attitude toward the behavior and his or her subjective norm regarding it.

behavioral perspective An approach to social psychology proposing that our social behavior can best be understood by focusing on directly observable behavior and the environment that causes our behavior to change.

biological maturation The more or less automatic unfolding of biological potential in a set, predictable sequence.

birth cohort A category of people who were born in the same year or period and who age together.

body language The nonverbal communication of meaning through physical movements and gestures.

bonding The effort or desire to maintain a relationship.

catharsis A lessening of aggressive energy (anger) by discharging it through aggressive behavior.

civil inattention Form of body language in which we give others enough visual notice to signal to them that we recognize their presence, but then we quickly withdraw visual contact to show that we pose no threat to them and that we do not wish to interact with them.

coaction task A task involving performance in the presence of others with whom one has little interaction but who are performing the same task.

coalition An alliance of two or more parties who coordinate their efforts in order to achieve their ends against the opposition of one or more competing parties.

coercive resources Resources characterized by one party's ability to harm or punish another party.

cognitive dissonance theory An attitude consistency theory, formulated by Leon Festinger, focusing on the impact of behavior on attitudes. If we are committed to a behavior and choose it freely, we are likely to adjust other attitudes or behaviors to be consistent with it.

cognitive perspective An approach to social psychology proposing that our social behavior can best be understood by focusing on how we mentally structure and process information coming from the environment.

cohesion The effort or desire to be a member of a group.

collective action The body of actions by several people oriented toward a specific goal involving social change.

collective campaign A chain of collective actions oriented toward specific goals involving social change.

commitment A state of being bound to or locked into a position or course of action. Commitment to a relationship is the likelihood that a person will try to maintain a relationship in the future.

communication The process by which people interact and interpret their interactions.

comparable worth The value of one occupation in terms of another. Points are awarded to each job for the skills and requirements involved so that very dissimilar jobs can be compared.

compartmentalization A strategy of role-strain resolution in which the roles are kept separate in time or space so that the different behaviors required by the roles do not cause conflict.

competition A situation in which people perceive themselves as having incompatible objectives or goals, so the success of one party means the failure of other parties.

complementary needs Two different personality traits that are the counterparts of each other, thus providing a sense of completeness when they are joined.

concepts Mental representations, or ideas, of things in our environment.

conflict The exchange of intentional harmful behavior (that is, reciprocal aggression).

conflict rituals Conflicts in which the parties express their conflict in a style typical of their relationship.

conflict theory A perspective which argues that what is considered deviant depends on the relative power of groups to enforce their norms and apply them to others. According to this view, crime and other forms of deviance are defined by the segments of society that have greater power.

conformity Behavior in accordance with norms or standards set by others.

conjunctive task A task in which the group's performance is judged in terms of the *worst* individual performance.

conscience The internal operation of ethical or moral principles that control or inhibit the actions and thoughts of an individual.

consensus-building The process in which a social movement organization attempts to recruit members by increasing the consistency between its own ideology and the attitudes of segments of the public.

consonance Cognitive dissonance theory's term for attitude consistency.

contagion theory of crowds The view that a crowd assimilates its members, producing a psychic unity that alters the individual's normal emotions, thoughts, and conduct.

contested mobility A model of intergenerational mobility which posits that higher-income occupations go to those who demonstrate the appropriate skills in competition with others.

convergence theory of crowds The view that a crowd consists of a highly unrepresentative grouping of people who come together because they share certain predispositions.

conversion A process in which the target adopts the source's directives as his or her own. Conversion is effective in producing the target's long-term compliance to a source's directives.

cooperative principle The assumption that speakers are trying to be (1) informative (but not overly informative), (2) truthful, (3) relevant, and (4) clear (unambiguous and brief). We use this assumption to decipher the meaning intended by a speaker.

cooperative response The response among a number of choices that maximizes the collective rewards.

cooperative task A task in which the collective activities of several individuals affect the outcomes (rewards and costs) for each individual.

crime An act that violates a criminal code enacted by an officially constituted political authority.

culturally relative view of deviance A view of deviance which recognizes that judgments of right and wrong vary with social context—time, place, and group. What is sinful or criminal to one group, in one place, or at one point in time may be acceptable to another group or at another time or place. This view is accepted by most social psychologists.

culture The aggregate of things that a given social unit has created and to which the unit's members attach similar meanings: their beliefs, values, norms, knowledge, language, and patterns of behavior and interaction, as well as the physical objects they produce.

definition of the situation The meaning we give to an entire situation, including who should be there and what behaviors are expected.

deflection In affect control theory, the difference between a transient sentiment and a fundamental sentiment for an identity or behavior. According to ACT, we construct and interpret events to minimize deflections.

deindividuation A psychological state of diminished self-awareness.

dependence The degree to which a particular person can provide us with profits, relative to alternative sources. Dependence is greater when profit is high and alternative sources of the rewards are scarce.

dependence imbalance The condition in which the dependencies of the two parties in an exchange are unequal.

dependent variable The factor that is affected—that occurs or changes—because of manipulation of or changes in another factor (the independent variable). The dependent variable is the variable a researcher wishes to explain.

deviance A condition encompassing behaviors, attitudes, or characteristics that are defined as undesirably different from those prescribed by the norms of a group.

differential association theory A theory of deviance proposing that we learn deviant behavior the same way we learn conventional behavior: we are socialized to accept the definitions of a particular group of people, and we come to adopt the standards of that group as our own.

differentiation The perception of differences among those in a social category.

diffusion of responsibility A process in which the obligation to help in an emergency and the potential blame for not helping are spread among observers.

discontinuity effect The tendency to make a noncooperative response more readily in intergroup relations than in interindividual relations.

discrimination Any action that produces greater negative outcomes for one category of people than another on the basis of socially disapproved criteria. According to American norms, race and sex are not legitimate criteria for treating people differently.

disjunctive task A task in which the group's performance is judged in terms of the *best* individual performance.

displacement The detachment of anger from the frustrating source and the discharge of that anger in aggression toward some other party.

dispositional identities Beliefs linking ourselves with character traits and behavioral tendencies.

dissonance Cognitive dissonance theory's term for attitude inconsistency.

distributive justice norm See **equity norm**.

divisible task A task in which the members perform different, although complementary, activities.

dominant culture The culture of the group whose values, norms, traditions, and outlooks are imposed on the society as a whole.

dominant group The group advantaged by institutional discrimination.

drift The back-and-forth shifting between delinquent and conventional behavior that characterizes many adolescents.

earnings ratio The ratio of one social category's earnings to another's earnings. The ratio gives the earnings of the first group for every dollar earned by the second group. Typical comparisons involve African-Americans to whites and females to males.

emergent-norm theory of crowds The view that a crowd consists of people with different motives, attitudes, and behaviors, who, faced with an ambiguous situation, evolve a group norm that gives them the illusion of uniformity and unanimity.

empty-nest stage The period of family life experienced by parents when the last child leaves home. It was once assumed that parents, especially mothers, would feel lonely and useless at this time.

entrapment An escalation of conflict involving the parties' increasing commitment to their positions and increasing expenditure of their resources in the conflict.

EPA profile The meaning of an identity or a behavior as measured on three basic dimensions: evaluation (E), potency (P), and activity (A).

equality A reward distribution in which all group members share equally in the rewards or costs.

equity A reward distribution in which rewards or costs are distributed among members in proportion to their cooperative inputs.

equity norm The cultural expectation that the profits (rewards minus costs) of parties in an exchange should be equal; also called the *distributive justice norm*.

ethnocentrism The tendency to view our own group as the center of everything and to judge all other people with reference to it.

evaluations (of a social identity) Our feelings that the social identity is good or bad, pleasant or unpleasant—a group to be liked or disliked. Evaluation is one dimension of the feeling component of attitudes.

expectancy effect See **self-fulfilling prophecy**.

experiment A method of study in which the investigator manipulates or varies one or more factors (termed the independent variables) and measures other factors (termed the dependent variables).

expert resources Resources characterized by one party's ability to show another what to do in order to receive rewards or to avoid or escape punishments.

expressive bonds Attachments to another person or group that are based on our attraction to particular others. Relationships and groups based on expressive bonds are called *primary* relationships or groups.

external attributions Beliefs that assign responsibility for an individual's behavior (or outcomes resulting from the behavior) to environmental or situational circumstances.

external culture Culture that originates *outside* the relationship or group. Relationships based primarily on external culture are called *role relationships*.

facework A descriptive term for the communication strategies we use to enact, support, or challenge our own and others' public images ("faces").

field experiment An experiment in which a researcher introduces an independent variable into a natural setting to determine its impact on behavior.

field research A method of study in which the investigator undertakes intensive observation and recording of people's behavior in a natural setting.

free-rider effect The tendency to make a noncooperative response based on the reasoning that others will cooperate for the collective welfare, making one's own cooperative response unnecessary.

front The expressive equipment—setting, appearance, and manner—we intentionally or unintentionally use in presenting ourselves to others.

fundamental attribution error Our tendency to overestimate the extent to which the actions of other people derive from their underlying personality. In other words, our tendency to make internal attributions for much of other people's behavior.

fundamental sentiments In affect control theory, the usual meanings—as measured by evaluation, potency, and activity—that an identity or a behavior has for us. These meanings, stored in memory, are the ones activated by a definition of a situation.

gatekeepers Those who control the decision-making process by which individuals are admitted to scarce positions and offices of power, privilege, and status within a society.

group Two or more people linked by a social relationship who are interdependent with respect to their environment and who are identified as "one."

group polarization The tendency of group members to shift toward the extreme of an already preferred position.

groupthink A decision-making process occurring within highly cohesive groups in which the members are so preoccupied with maintaining group consensus that their critical abilities become ineffective.

halo effect The tendency to assume that a person possessing one good quality will also have other good qualities.

helping Behavior engaged in by one person that produces benefits for another.

homogamy The tendency of "like to marry like." People who are similar marry more often than would be expected by chance.

human capital The acquired capabilities and qualifications increasing a person's attractiveness as a job candidate.

identities Social categories applied to persons or settings.

ideology A set of shared definitions that provide interpretations and solutions to what is felt to be an unsatisfactory social condition.

idiosyncrasy credit The protection from others' aggression that a person's status affords if that person should interfere with the immediate goal of the group.

imbalance Balance theory's term for attitude inconsistency.

implicit personality theories Schemas about types of people whose identities are defined in terms of personality traits.

impression management Process in which a person attempts to manipulate others' perceptions of himself or herself.

independent variable The factor that is assumed to cause or determine changes in another variable (the dependent variable) that the research wants to explain; the factor manipulated in an experimental setting.

informational resources Resources characterized by one party's ability to communicate information to another party.

ingroup A social unit that we either belong to or identify with.

inoculation The provision of counterarguments intended to influence a target to resist subsequent social pressure to change.

institutional aggression Aggression in an institutional context, performed as part of "doing one's job."

institutional discrimination Discrimination that occurs when the policies and programs of an institution systematically produce greater negative outcomes for one category of people than another on the basis of socially disapproved criteria.

institutional racism Institutional discrimination based on race.

institutional sexism Institutional discrimination based on sex.

instrumental bonds Attachments to another person or group that are based on our need of others to achieve certain goals. Relationships and groups based on instrumental bonds are called *secondary* relationships or groups.

interactionist perspective An approach to social psychology proposing that social behavior can be understood by focusing on individuals as active agents who negotiate with others to construct their social interactions.

internal attributions Beliefs that assign responsibility for an individual's behavior (or outcomes resulting from the behavior) to the stereotypic characteristics of the social identity.

internal culture Culture that emerges as a result of the interactions among members of the relationship or group. Relationships based primarily on internal culture are called *personal* relationships.

internalization The process whereby an individual incorporates within his or her personality the standards of behavior prevalent within a group or the larger society. See also **conversion.**

interpersonal spacing Nonverbal communication of meaning through the distances and angles at which people position themselves relative to others.

intra-role conflict A type of role strain in which the expectations associated with a single role contain inconsistencies.

just-world hypothesis The belief that we live in a just world — one in which people get what they deserve and deserve what they get.

kinesics See **body language.**

labeling theory A theory which stresses that social groups create deviance by applying labels to particular people. Eventually, these individuals begin to believe that the label is accurate, assume it as a personal identity, and enter into a deviant or criminal career.

laboratory experiment An experiment in which specially constructed facilities are employed to facilitate determining the relationship between independent and dependent variables.

leadership One person's power over the members of his or her group.

life chances A person's opportunities to experience the good things in life, such as survival, health, justice, and happiness.

life course The socially patterned sequence of changes in roles that defines the human journey from life to death.

linguistic universals Features that are common to all languages.

linkage The connection between a group, a subgroup, and an individual.

locus of control The propensity to explain most events in terms of oneself (internal) or one's environment (external).

matriarchal power structure The power structure of a family in which the wife/mother has the normative resources.

medicalization of deviance The trend toward conceptions of deviance as symptoms of physical or emotional illness.

minority group The group disadvantaged by institutional discrimination. See also **oppression bonds.**

negotiation The bargaining process through which we settle on the terms of a transaction or an agreement.

network A web of social relationships centering on a single individual and tying him or her directly to some people and indirectly, through these people, to still others.

neutralization techniques Accounts that enable individuals to violate important normative standards but to neutralize any definition of themselves as deviant or criminal.

norm of reciprocity The cultural expectation that (1) people should help those who help them and (2) people should not harm those who have helped them.

norm of social responsibility The cultural expectation that people should help those who are in need and who depend on them.

normative bonds Attachments to a group that are based on the group's norms. Groups based primarily on normative bonds are called *reference groups*.

normative resources Resources that derive from a rule or an agreement among a group of persons which recognizes that one party has a right to command while other parties have the responsibility to obey.

norms Standards for behavior that members of a social unit share, to which they are expected to conform, and that are enforced by positive and negative sanctions.

observational learning A type of learning in which individuals reproduce the actions, attitudes, or emotional responses displayed by real-life or symbolized models.

occupational careers Patterned paths of mobility within an organization.

occupational crimes Work-related crimes committed by individual organization members for personal gain.

operant conditioning A type of learning in which the association between a behavior and the environmental change it produces affects the *future* probability of that behavior.

oppressed group See **oppression bonds**.

oppression bonds Attachments to another person or group that are based on common oppression by a different person or group. Groups based primarily on oppression bonds are called *minority* or *oppressed* groups.

organizational crimes Crimes committed with the support and encouragement of a formal organization and intended, at least partly, to advance the goals of that organization.

organizational socialization The process by which a person learns the values, norms, and required behaviors that permit him or her to participate as a member of an organization.

outgroup A social unit that we do not belong to or identify with.

paralanguage The nonsemantic aspects of speech — the stress, pitch, and volume of speech — by which we communicate meaning.

participant observation A procedure for gathering data in which the researcher spends a good deal of time in a natural setting, noticing, watching,

and at times interacting with the people he or she is studying.

patriarchal power structure The power structure of a family in which the husband/father has the normative resources.

performance How well a person's behavior meets a quantitative or qualitative standard.

permissive parenting style A style of parenting in which parents rely largely on reasoning and explanations — informational resources — to persuade their children to behave in a certain manner.

person-attitude A schema that applies to only a single, unique individual.

personal relationship See **internal culture**.

personal resources Resources that derive from one party's attraction to another because of the latter's personal qualities.

perspective A set of the most basic assumptions supporting a particular approach to social psychology.

pervasiveness (of a social attitude) The degree to which a social attitude is shared by members of a social group or groups.

power outcomes The results of the social power process, including compliance, partial compliance, noncompliance, or reactance to a power structure and power strategies.

power strategies The ways that resources are used in the source's attempts to change the target's behavior and the target's efforts to resist.

power structure The control of valuable resources by source and target.

prejudice Negative evaluation of a social identity.

primacy effect The tendency for impressions to be most influenced by the earliest information received.

primary deviance The first or early acts of deviance, which are not integrated as part of the actor's self-image.

primary groups or **relationships** See **expressive bonds**.

profit The difference between the rewards and costs of a behavior.

proxemics See **interpersonal spacing**.

reasoned action model Fishbein and Ajzen's theory proposing that behavior is best predicted by a person's behavioral intention, which, in turn, is a function of both the person's attitude toward the behavior and his or her

subjective norm regarding the behavior.

recency effect The tendency for impressions to be most influenced by the latest information received.

reference group See **normative bonds**.

reflected appraisals Self-appraisals based on how we believe others see us.

reflexive behavior Behavior in which we act toward ourselves, taking ourselves as an object. We can look at our own behavior from our own or others' points of view. Reflexivity allows us to observe, plan, guide, and respond to our own behavior.

regions Places separating front-stage performances (behavior in front of an audience) from backstage performances (behavior away from the audience). We manipulate regions as part of our efforts to manage impressions.

relative deprivation A state of mind in which a gap exists between what people seek and what seems attainable.

research methods Procedures for acquiring and analyzing information.

resource mobilization The process by which resources are devoted to collective action.

revised power structure The control of valuable resources by source and target which results from power outcomes.

reward exchange Reciprocal helping, in which each person's behavior produces benefits for the other person.

reward resources Resources characterized by one party's ability to provide another party with rewards.

rites of passage Public ceremonies or rituals marking the transition from one role to another.

rituals Social acts of symbolic significance that are performed on certain occasions prescribed by tradition.

role The set of normative expectations that apply to the behavior of a specific category of people in a particular situation.

role ambiguity A type of role strain in which the expectations associated with a role are unclear.

role compatibility Fulfilling the role expectations of both partners in a relationship.

role conflict A type of role strain in which the expected behavior in one role is contrary to the behavior expected of the same person in a different role.

role discontinuity A type of role strain in which expectations associated with an old role conflict with expectations associated with a new role.

role dissensus A type of role strain in which the expectations held by various others for a single role contain inconsistencies.

role distancing Behavior that suggests detachment from a particular role. A form of impression management.

role identities Beliefs linking ourselves with social categories, group membership, and social roles.

role overload A type of role strain in which a person has to meet too many role demands at once.

role priorities Rankings of roles so that a person can give priority to one role over others and reduce involvement with lower-priority roles; used as a strategy of role-strain resolution.

role relationship See **external culture**.

role strain Difficulty experienced by an individual in meeting the requirements of a role or roles.

role-taking Reflexive behavior in which a person looks at his or her own behavior from the point of view of another person.

romanticism A widely accepted ideology about love that includes the beliefs "Love conquers all" and "one should marry for love."

schema A set of beliefs linking one concept to several others. When the beliefs are about a social identity, the schema is sometimes called a *stereotype*.

secondary deviance Deviant behavior that is caused by earlier social responses identifying the actor as deviant.

secondary groups or **relationships** See **instrumental bonds**.

segregation The physical and social separation of people from different social categories on the basis of custom or law.

self The capacity for reflexive action — to observe, plan, guide, and respond to our own behavior.

self-attitude The schema of beliefs and feelings a person has about himself or herself.

self-concept See **self-attitude**.

self-disclosure The act of revealing one's "real" self to another.

self-efficacy The sense of being competent and in control.

self-esteem Evaluation of oneself as good or bad, better or worse, acceptable or unacceptable.

self-fulfilling prophecy A false definition of the situation that creates conditions that make it come true.

self-identities The characteristics we associate with ourselves.

self-identity saliency The rank of a particular self-identity on a person's hierarchy of self-identities. The more salient a particular identity is in our hierarchy of identities, the more frequently we will draw on that identity in our perceptions of our environment and our behavior toward it.

self-reflection The process of coming to know our own internal characteristics by inferring them from our overt behavior or covert experiences.

self-schema See **self-attitude**.

sex roles Role expectations that differ by gender.

sexism Inequality between the sexes, characterized by social behavior, arrangements, and patterns by which members of one gender group realize more benefits and fewer burdens than members of the other gender group.

significant other A person who is important to us and who, therefore, has considerable influence on our self-attitudes.

significant symbol A symbol whose meaning is shared by the parties in question.

simultaneous task A task in which the responses of the group members are performed at the same time.

social attitudes Beliefs and feelings about persons or social identities.

social change A basic alteration in the behavior patterns, culture, or structure of a society.

social cognition The mental process by which we interpret the sensations that reach us from the social environment in terms of other information we have stored in memory.

social comparison The process of comparing ourselves with others.

social contingency A behavior-altering association between a person's behavior and a subsequent change in the conduct of another person or a social group.

social control theory A theory of deviance which posits that deviance occurs in the absence of an individual's bonds to conventional society —

attachments to persons who accept conventional norms, commitments to conventional goals and rewards, involvement with conventional activities, and possession of conventional beliefs.

social dilemmas Situations in which members of a group are faced with a conflict between the noncooperative response of maximizing their own personal interests and the cooperative response of maximizing the group's collective interests.

social distance A subjective sense of being set apart from a particular outgroup.

social esteem Positive evaluation of a social identity.

social facilitation The enhancement of performance in the presence of others.

social identities Concepts or categories that differentiate several people on the basis of similarities and differences in one or more characteristics.

social influence The process by which others' attitudes and actions influence our attitudes and behavior.

social inhibition The decline of performance in the presence of others.

social interaction Any process directed toward, or influenced by, another person or persons.

social learning theory A theory focusing on social contingencies and observational learning as the primary sources of all changes in behavior, including socialization.

social loafing The tendency for people working on a cooperative task to work less hard than they do individually.

social movement Several collective campaigns carried out by a number of different collectives oriented toward general goals of social change.

social power A process of social interaction in which one party produces intended changes in another party's attitudes or behavior, even in the face of the other's resistance.

social problem An undesirable condition that a collective believes applies to a large number of people in society.

social psychology The study of the behavior, thoughts, and feelings of an individual or interacting individuals and of their relationships with larger social units.

social relationship Social interaction

between two people that is characterized by a relatively stable set of expectations and pattern of interaction.

social survey A method of obtaining information using questions in an interview or written questionnaire.

socialization The process by which we learn, through interaction with other people, the ways of thinking, feeling, and acting that are essential for effective participation with a particular group of people; the process by which new members of a society or group are instilled with the fundamental elements of the group's culture.

socioeconomic status (SES) A person's location in the stratification hierarchy.

sponsored mobility A model of intergenerational mobility which posits that social institutions steer younger members toward occupations in the same social class as their parents.

stage model of development A model of learning which proposes that development is not a continuous process but occurs in a series of sequential periods, or stages, that differ markedly from one another. Individuals are thought to pass through these stages in a particular order, although some individuals advance further than others in the series of stages.

status liability The susceptibility to others' aggression that a person's status causes should that person interfere with the immediate goal of the group.

stereotype A schema of beliefs that attributes a set of characteristics to most or all members of a social identity.

stigmatization The process by which negatively evaluated attributes cause a person's identity to become negatively evaluated.

stratification The ranking of people on the basis of particular power resources—income, education, and occupational prestige.

structural perspective An approach to social psychology proposing that our social behavior can best be understood by focusing on how our behavior and views are shaped by the multiple and changing roles prescribed by our society.

subculture The culture of a group of people whose perspective and life style differ significantly from those of the dominant culture and who identify themselves as different.

subjective norm In the reasoned action model, the behavioral-intention factor consisting of a person's beliefs about how significant others would feel about his or her performing a specific behavior. It is estimated by adding up the person's assessment of each other person's evaluation, weighted by his or her own motivation to comply with the others' wishes.

sucker effect The tendency to make a noncooperative response based on the reasoning that if one cooperates, others will take advantage of one's contribution and refrain from cooperating.

symbol An object or action that, by social convention, stands for something else.

symbolic interaction theory A theory which focuses on how individuals interpret and give meanings to their social interactions.

sympathy norms Cultural expectations prescribing that we should care about others and specifying how we should respond to their problems, depending on the nature of the difficulty and the person's relationship to us.

theory A set of ideas that summarizes, organizes, and explains observations parsimoniously, or efficiently.

trajectory The history or path taken by each of a person's roles over the life course.

transient sentiments In affect control theory, the momentary feelings—based on evaluation, potency, and activity—resulting from an interpersonal event. These momentary sentiments may differ from the fundamental sentiments we have for the identity or behavior.

transitions The major shifts or changes in the stages of a role.

trustworthiness The component of a source's credibility whereby the target perceives the source as neither biased nor deceptive in his or her directives.

ultimate attribution error A bias favoring internal attributions to explain the success of ingroups and failure of outgroups, on the one hand, and external attributions to explain the failure of ingroups and success of outgroups on the other.

unitary task A task in which the responses of the members are the same.

values The ethical principles to which members of a group feel a strong commitment and which they employ in judging behavior.

white-collar crime A violation of the law committed by a person or group of persons in the course of an otherwise respected and legitimate occupation or financial activity.

REFERENCES

Note: The bracketed number(s) at the end of each reference indicate the chapter(s) in which the reference is cited in this text.

Abbey, A. 1982. Sex differences in attributions for friendly behavior: Do males misperceive females' friendliness? *Journal of Personality and Social Psychology,* 42:830–838. [5]

Abbott, D. A., and Brody, G. H. 1985. The relation of child age, gender, and number of children to the marital adjustment of wives. *Journal of Marriage and the Family,* 47:77–84. [11]

ABC/*Washington Post.* 1989. Question id: USABCWP.89RACE. R22 GB(W). (October 1989) Roper Center POLLS [computer file]. [14]

Abdalla, I. A. 1987. Predictors of the effectiveness of supervisory social power. *Human Relations,* 40:721–739. [13]

Abeles, R. P. 1976. Relative deprivation, rising expectations, and black militancy. *Journal of Social Issues,* 32:119–137. [16]

Achenbach, T., and Edelbrock, C. 1981. Behavioral problems and competencies reported by parents of normal and disturbed children aged 4 through 16. *Monographs of the Society for Research in Child Development,* 45 (Serial No. 188). [7]

Acker, J. 1989. *Doing Comparable Worth: Gender, Class, and Pay Equity.* Philadelphia: Temple University Press. [14]

Acker, J. 1990. Jobs, hierarchies, and sexuality: Some further thoughts on gender and organizations. *Gender and Society,* 4:139–158. [14]

Acock, A. C., and Hurlbert, J. S. 1990. Social network analysis: A structural perspective for family studies. *Journal of Social and Personal Relationships,* 7:245–264. [11]

Adams, J. S. 1965. Inequality in social exchange. In Berkowitz, L. (ed.), *Advances in Experimental Social Psychology,* vol. 2. New York: Academic Press. [10]

Adams, R. G. 1985. People would talk: Normative barriers to cross-sex friendships for elderly women. *Gerontologist,* 25:605–611. [11]

Adelmann, P. K., Antonucci, T. C., Crohan, S. E., and Coleman, L. M. 1989. Empty nest, cohort, and employment in the well-being of midlife women. *Sex Roles,* 20:173–189. [3]

Adler, P. A., and Adler, P. 1988. Intense loyalty in organizations: A case study of college athletes. *Administrative Science Quarterly,* 33:401–417. [4]

Agnew, R. 1985. Social control theory and delinquency: A longitudinal test. *Criminology,* 23:47–61. [15]

Agnew, R., and Huguley, S. 1989. Adolescent violence toward parents. *Journal of Marriage and the Family,* 51:699–711. [12]

Agnew, R., and Peterson, D. 1989. Leisure and delinquency. *Social Problems,* 36:332–348. [15]

Aguirre, B. 1984. Conventionalization of collective behavior in Cuba. *American Journal of Sociology,* 90:541–566. [16]

Ainsworth, M. 1973. The development of infant-mother attachment. In Caldwell, B., and Ricuitti, H. (eds.), *Review of Child Development Research,* vol. 3. Chicago: University of Chicago Press. [13]

Aires, E. J., and Johnson, F. L. 1983. Close friendship in adulthood: Conversational content between same-sex friends. *Sex Roles,* 9:1183–1196. [10]

Ajzen, I., and Fishbein, M. 1980. *Understanding Attitudes and Predicting Social Behavior.* Englewood Cliffs, NJ: Prentice-Hall. [8]

Ajzen, I., and Madden, T. J. 1986. Prediction of goal-directed behavior: Attitudes, intentions, and perceived behavior control. *Journal of Experimental Social Psychology,* 22:453–474. [8]

Akers, R. 1990. Rational choice, deterrence and social learning theory in criminology: The path not taken. *Journal of Criminal Law and Criminology,* 81:653–676. [15]

Akers, R. L. 1985. *Deviant Behavior: A Social Learning Approach* (3rd ed.). Belmont, CA: Wadsworth. [15]

Akers, R. L., Krohn, M. D., Lanza-Kaduce, L., and Radosevish, M. J. 1979. Social learning and deviant behavior: A specific test of a general theory. *American Sociological Review,* 44:636–655. [15]

Albin, R. S. 1981. How court testimony goes awry. *New York Times* (March 17):16. [6]

Albrecht, G. L. (1994). The social experience of disability. In Calhoun, C., and Ritzer, G. (eds.), *Social Problems.* New York: McGraw-Hill. [15]

Aldous, J. 1987. New views on the family life of the elderly and near-elderly. *Journal of Marriage and the Family,* 49:227–234. [3]

Alexander, K. L., and Entwisle, D. R. 1988. Achievement in the first two years of school: Patterns and processes. *Monographs of the Society of Research in Child Development,* 53:2 (entire issue). [3]

Alishio, K. C., and Schilling, K. 1984. Sex differences in intellectual and ego development in late adolescence. *Journal of Youth and Adolescence,* 13: 213–225. [3]

Allan, G. 1979. *A Sociology of Friendship and Kinship.* London: Allen & Unwin. [11]

Allan, G. 1989. *Friendship: Developing a Sociological Perspective.* San Francisco: Westview Press. [11]

Allen, M. 1988. Cordis admits it hid defects of pacemakers. *Wall Street Journal* (September 1):2–22. [15]

Allen, R. L., Dawson, M. C., and Brown, R. E. 1989. A schema-based approach to modeling an African-American racial belief system. *American Political Science Review,* 83: 421–441. [7]

Allen, V. L., and Levine, J. M. 1971. Social support and conformity: The role of independent assessment of reality. *Journal of Experimental Social Psychology,* 7:48–58. [9]

Allen, V. L., and Wilder, D. A. 1975.

Categorization, belief similarity, and intergroup discrimination. *Journal of Personality and Social Psychology*, 32: 971–977. [4]

Allen, W. R., and Farley, R. 1986. The shifting social and economic tides of black America, 1950–1980. *American Review of Sociology*, 12:277–306. [14]

Allington, R. 1980. Teacher interruption behaviors during primary grade oral reading. *Journal of Educational Psychology*, 72:371–377. [14]

Allport, F. H. 1920. The influence of the group upon association and thought. *Journal of Experimental Psychology*, 3:159–182. [9]

Alper, J. 1985. The roots of morality. *Science 85* (March):70–76. [10]

Alpert-Gillis, L., and Connell, J. 1989. Gender and sex-role influences on children's self-esteem. *Journal of Personality*, 57:97–114. [7]

Amato, P. R. 1983. Helping behavior in urban and rural environments: Field studies based on a taxonomic organization of helping episodes. *Journal of Personality and Social Psychology*, 45:571–586. [10]

Amato, P. R. 1990. Personality and social network involvement as predictors of helping behavior in everyday life. *Social Psychology Quarterly*, 53: 31–43. [10]

Amato, P. R., and Booth, A. 1991. The consequences of divorce for attitudes toward divorce and gender roles. *Journal of Family Issues*, 12:306–322. [8]

Amato, P. R., and Keith, B. 1991. Parental divorce and adult well-being: A meta-analysis. *Journal of Marriage and the Family*, 53:43–58. [11]

American Psychological Association. 1975. Minutes of the council of representatives. *American Psychologist*, 30: 633. [16]

Andersen, S., and Ross, L. 1984. Self-knowledge and social inference: 1. The impact of cognitive/affective and behavioral data. *Journal of Personality and Social Psychology*, 46: 280–293. [7]

Anderson, E. 1976. *A Place on the Corner.* Chicago: University of Chicago Press. [15]

Anderson, J., and Jay, S. 1985. The diffusion of medical technology: Social network analysis and policy research. *Sociological Quarterly*, 26:49–64. [4]

Anderson, J. C., and Moore, L. 1978. The motivation to volunteer. *Journal of Voluntary Action Research*, 7:51–60. [10]

Anderson, N. H. 1981. *Foundations of Information Integration Theory.* New York: Academic Press. [6]

Anderson, S. A., Russell, C. S., and Schumm, W. R. 1983. Perceived marital quality and family–life cycle categories: A further analysis. *Journal of Marriage and the Family*, 45: 227–239. [3]

Andreoli, V. A., and Worchel, S. 1978. Effects of media, communicator, and position of message in attitude change. *Public Opinion Quarterly*, 42:59–70. [13]

Andrews, K. H., and Kandel, D. B. 1979. Attitudes and behavior: A specification of the contingent consistency hypothesis. *American Sociological Review*, 44:298–310. [15]

Anson, R., and Eason, C. 1986. The effects of confinement on delinquent self image. *Juvenile and Family Court Journal*, 37:39–47. [15]

Antill, J. K. 1983. Sex role complementarity versus similarity in married couples. *Journal of Personality and Social Psychology*, 45:145–155. [11]

Anyon, J. 1980. Social class and the hidden curriculum of work. *Journal of Education*, 162:67–92. [3]

Apsler, R., and Friedman, H. 1975. Chance outcomes and the just world: A comparison of observers and recipients. *Journal of Personality and Social Psychology*, 31:887–894. [10]

Aquilino, W. S. 1991. Predicting parents' experiences with coresident adult children. *Journal of Family Issues*, 12: 323–342. [11]

Archer, D. 1985. Social deviance. In Lindzey, G., and Aronson, E. (eds.), *The Handbook of Social Psychology*, Vol. 2 (3rd ed.). New York: Random House. [15]

Archer, D., and Akert, R. M. 1977. Words and everything else: Verbal and nonverbal cues in social interpretation. *Journal of Personality and Social Psychology*, 35:443–449. [5]

Archer, R. L., and Burleson, J. A. 1980. The effects of timing of self-disclosure on attraction and reciprocity. *Journal of Personality and Social Psychology*, 38:120–130. [11]

Argyle, M., Alkema, F., and Gilmour, R. 1971. The communication of friendly and hostile attitudes by verbal and nonverbal signals. *European Journal of Social Psychology*, 1:385–402. [5]

Argyle, M., and Furnham, A. 1982. The ecology of relationships: Choice of situation as a function of relationship. *British Journal of Social Psychology*, 21:259–262. [11]

Argyle, M., and Henderson, M. 1984. The rules of friendship. *Journal of Social and Personal Relationships*, 1: 209–235. [11]

Aries, E. J. 1987. Gender and communication. In Shaver, P., and Hendrick, C. (eds.), *Sex and Gender*. Newbury Park, CA: Sage, pp. 149–176. [5]

Aries, E. J., and Johnson, F. L. 1983. Close friendship in adulthood: Conversational content between same-sex friends. *Journal of Sex Roles*, 9:1183–1197. [11]

Armor, D. J. 1989. After busing: Education and choice. *Public Interest*, 95:24–37. [14]

Aron, A. R., Dutton, D., Aron, E. N., and Iverson, A. 1989. Experiences of falling in love. *Journal of Social and Personal Relationships*, 6:243–257. [11]

Arond, M., and Pauker, S. L. 1987. *The First Year of Marriage.* New York: Warner Books. [11]

Aronson, E. 1968. Dissonance theory: Progress and problems. In Abelson, R., Aronson, E., McGuire, W., Newcomb, T., Rosenberg, M., and Tannenbaum, P. (eds.), *Theories of Cognitive Consistency: A Sourcebook.* Chicago: Rand McNally. [8]

Aronson, E. 1969. The theory of cognitive dissonance: A current perspective. In Berkowitz, L. (ed.), *Advances in Experimental Social Psychology*. New York: Academic Press. [8]

Aronson, E., and Carlsmith, J. M. 1963. The effect of the severity of threat on the devaluation of forbidden behavior. *Journal of Abnormal and Social Psychology*, 66:584–588. [8]

Aronson, E., Stephan, W., Sikes, J., Blaney, N., and Snapp, M. 1978. *Cooperation in the Classroom.* Beverly Hills, CA: Sage. [12]

Asch, S. E. 1946. Forming impressions of personality. *Journal of Abnormal and Social Psychology*, 41:258–290. [6]

Asch, S. E. 1952. *Social Psychology.* Englewood Cliffs, NJ: Prentice-Hall. [9, 16]

Asch, S. E., and Zukier, H. 1984. Thinking about persons. *Journal of Personality and Social Psychology*, 46: 1230–1240. [6]

Ashmore, R. D., and Del Boca, F. K. (eds.). 1986. *The Social Psychology of Female-Male Relations.* New York: Academic Press. [6]

Astin, A. 1985. *The American Freshman: National Norms.* Los Angeles: UCLA Graduate School of Education. [11]

Aston, J. Z. 1984. Political hostage taking in Western Europe. *Conflict Studies*, 157:1–21. [12]

Athay, M., and Darley, J. M. 1982. Social roles as interaction competencies. In Ickes, W., and Knowles, E. (eds.), *Personality, Roles, and Social Behavior.* New York: Springer-Verlag. [4]

Attorney General's Commission on Pornography. 1986. *Final Report.* Washington, DC: U.S. Department of Justice. [12]

Averill, J. 1985. The social construction of emotion, with special reference to love. In Gergen, K. J., and Davis, K. E. (eds.), *The Social Construction of the Person.* New York: Springer-Verlag. [7, 11]

Axsom, D. 1989. Cognitive dissonance and behavior change in psychotherapy. *Journal of Experimental Social Psychology*, 25:234–252. [8]

Axsom, D., and Cooper, J. 1985. Cognitive dissonance and psychotherapy: The role of effort justification in inducing weight loss. *Journal of Experimental Social Psychology*, 21:149–160. [8]

Azmitia, M. 1992. Expertise, private speech, and the development of self-regulation. In Diaz, R. M., and Berk, L. E. (eds.), *Private Speech: From Social Interaction to Self-Regulation.* Hillsdale, NJ: Erlbaum. [2]

Babbie, E. 1992. *The Practice of Social Research* (6th ed.). Belmont, CA: Wadsworth. [1]

Backman, C. W., and Secord, P. F. 1962. Liking, selective interaction, and misperception in congruent interpersonal relations. *Sociometry*, 25: 321–335. [7]

Bagozzi, R. P. 1981. Attitudes, intentions, and behavior: A test of some key hypotheses. *Journal of Personality and Social Psychology*, 41:607–627. [8]

Bagozzi, R. P. 1992. The self-regulation of attitudes, intentions, and behavior. *Social Psychology Quarterly*, 55:178–204. [8]

Bailey, W., Martin, J. D., and Gray, L. 1974. Crime and deterrence: A correlational analysis. *Journal of Research in Crime and Delinquency*, 11:124–143. [15]

Baker, P. 1984. Age differences and age changes in the division of labor by sex: Reanalysis of White and Brinherhoff. *Social Forces*, 62:808–814. [3]

Baker, S. 1978. Women in blue-collar and service occupations. In Stromberg, A., and Harkness, S. (eds.), *Working Women: Theories and Facts in Perspective.* Palo Alto, CA: Mayfield. [14]

Baldwin, J. D., and Baldwin, J. I. 1986. *Behavior Principles in Everyday Life* (2nd ed.). Englewood Cliffs, NJ: Prentice-Hall. [2]

Baldwin, J. M. 1897. *Social and Ethical Interpretations in Mental Development.* New York: Macmillan. [1]

Balkan, S., Berger, R. J., and Schmidt, J. 1980. *Crime and Deviance in America: A Critical Approach.* Belmont, CA: Wadsworth. [15]

Ball, D. 1966. An abortion clinic ethnography. *Social Problems*, 14:293–301. [7]

Ball-Rokeach, S. J., Rokeach, M., and Grube, J. W. 1984. *The Great American Values Test: Influencing Behavior and Belief through Television.* New York: Free Press. [1]

Balswick, J. 1986. *The Inexpressive Male.* Lexington, MA: Lexington Books. [11]

Bandura, A. 1965. Influence of models' reinforcement contingencies on the acquisition of imitative responses. *Journal of Personality and Social Psychology*, 1:589–595. [2]

Bandura, A. 1971. *Psychological Modeling: Conflicting Theories.* Chicago: Aldine-Atherton. [1]

Bandura, A. 1973. *Aggression: A Social Learning Analysis.* Englewood Cliffs, NJ: Prentice-Hall. [12]

Bandura, A. 1981. Self-referent thought: The development of self-efficacy. In Flavell, J., and Ross, L. (eds.), *Development of Social Cognition.* New York: Cambridge University Press. [7]

Bandura, A. 1983. Psychological mechanisms of aggression. In Geen, R., and Donnerstein, E. (eds.), *Aggression: Theoretical and Empirical Reviews*, Vol. 1. New York: Academic Press. [12]

Bandura, A., and Jourden, F. J. 1991. Self-regulatory mechanism governing the impact of social comparison on complex decision making. *Journal of Personality and Social Psychology*, 60: 941–951. [7]

Bandura, A., and Walters, R. H. 1959. *Adolescent Aggression.* New York: Ronald. [1]

Bandura, A., and Walters, R. H. 1963. *Social Learning and Personality Development.* New York: Holt, Rinehart & Winston. [1]

Bannai, H., and Cohen, D. A. 1985. The passive-methodical image of Asian American students in the school system. *Sociology and Social Research*, 70:79–81. [6]

Baptist, B. 1984. Football makes it all happen. *Columbus Dispatch* (March 5):C-1. [4]

Barbanel, J. 1981. A block on 42nd St. in Manhattan is netherworld. *New York Times* (July 6):11. [12]

Barbarin, O. A. 1986. Family experience of stigma in childhood cancer. In Ainlay, S. C., Becker, G., and Coleman, L. M. (eds.), *The Dilemma of Difference: A Multidisciplinary View of Stigma.* New York: Plenum. [15]

Barker, E. 1984. *The Making of a Moonie.* New York: Basil Blackwell. [16]

Barker, R. G., Dembo, T., and Lewin, K. 1941. Frustration and regression: An experiment with young children. *University of Iowa Studies in Child Welfare*, 18:1–314. [12]

Barnett, M. A. 1986. Sex bias in helping behavior presented in children's picture books. *Journal of Genetic Psychology*, 147:343–351. [10]

Baron, J. N., Davis-Blake, A., and Bielby, W. T. 1986. The structure of opportunity: How promotion ladders vary within and among organizations. *Administrative Science Quarterly*, 31:248–273. [14]

Baron, J. N., and Newman, A. E. 1990. For what it's worth: Organizations, occupations and the value of work done by women and nonwhites. *American Sociological Review*, 55:155–175. [14]

Baron, N. S. 1992. *Growing Up with Language: How Children Learn to Talk.* New York: Addison-Wesley. [2]

Baron, R. A. 1977. *Human Aggression.* New York: Plenum. [12]

Baron, R. A., and Bell, P. A. 1976. Aggression and heat: The influence of ambient temperature, negative affect, and a cooling drink on physical aggression. *Journal of Personality and Social Psychology*, 33:245–255. [12]

Baron, R. A., and Bell, P. A. 1977. Sexual arousal and aggression by males: Effects of type of erotic stimuli prior to provocation. *Journal of Personality and Social Psychology*, 35:79–87. [12]

Barranti, C. C. R. 1985. The grandparent-grandchild relationship: Family resource in an era of voluntary bonds. *Family Relations*, 34:343–352. [3]

Basow, S. A. 1986. *Gender Stereotypes*. Pacific Grove, CA: Brooks/Cole. [3]

Batson, C. D. 1990. How social an animal? The human capacity for caring. *American Psychologist*, 45:336–346. [10]

Batson, C. D., Bolen, M. H., Cross, J. A., Neuringer-Benefiel, H. E. 1986. Where is the altruism in the altruistic personality? *Journal of Personality and Social Psychology*, 50:212–220. [10]

Batson, C. D., Duncan, B., Ackerman, P., Buckley, T., and Birch, K. 1981. Is empathetic emotion a source of altruistic motivation? *Journal of Personality and Social Psychology*, 40:290–302. [10]

Batson, C. D., Dyck, J. L., Brandt, J. R., Batson, J. G., Powell, A. L., McMaster, M. R., and Griffitt, C. 1988. Five studies testing two new egoistic alternatives to the empathy-altruism hypothesis. *Journal of Personality and Social Psychology*, 55:52–77. [10]

Batson, C. D., and Oleson, K. C. 1991. Current status of the empathy-altruism hypothesis. In Clark, M. S. (ed.), *Prosocial Behavior: Vol. 12. Review of Personality and Social Psychology*. Newbury Park, CA: Sage, pp. 62–85. [10]

Batson, C. D., O'Quin, K., Fultz, J., Vanderplas, M., and Isen, A. 1983. Influence of self-reported distress and empathy on egoistic versus altruistic motivation to help. *Journal of Personality and Social Psychology*, 45:706–718. [10]

Baumann, D. J., Cialdini, R. B., and Kenrick, D. T. 1981. Altruism as hedonism: Helping and self-gratification as equivalent responses. *Journal of Personality and Social Psychology*, 40:1039–1046. [10]

Baumeister, R. F., and Tice, D. M. 1984. Role of self-presentation and choice in cognitive dissonance under forced compliance: Necessary or sufficient causes? *Journal of Personality and Social Psychology*, 46:5–13. [8]

Baumgardner, M. H., Leippe, M. R., Ronis, D. L., and Greenwald, A. G. 1983. In search of reliable persuasion effects: II. Associative interference and persistence of persuasion in a message-dense environment. *Journal of Personality and Social Psychology*, 45:524–537. [13]

Baumrind, D. 1971. Harmonious parents and their preschool children. *Developmental Psychology*, 4:99–102. [13]

Baumrind, D. 1985. Research using intentional deception: Ethical issues revisited. *American Psychologist*, 40:165–174. [1]

Bavelas, J. B. 1983. Situations that lead to disqualification. *Human Communication Research*, 9:130–145. [5]

Bavelas, J. B. 1985. Situational theory of disqualification: Using language to "leave the field." In Fargas, J. (ed.), *Language in Social Situation*. New York: Springer. [5]

Bavelas, J. B., Black, A., Chovil, N., and Mullet, J. 1988. Equivocation as a solution to conflicting interpersonal goals. Paper presented at the 9th Annual Conference on Discourse Analysis, Temple University, Philadelphia. [5]

Bavelas, J. B., and Chovil, N. 1986. How people disqualify: Experimental studies of spontaneous written disqualification. *Communication Monograph*, 53:70–74. [5]

Baxter, L. A., and Wilmot, W. W. 1985. Taboo topics in close relationships. *Journal of Social and Personal Relationships*, 2:253–269. [5, 11]

Baxter, L. A., and Wilmot, W. W. 1986. Interaction characteristics of disengaging, stable, and growing relationships. In Gilmour, R., and Duck, S. W. (eds.), *The Emerging Field of Personal Relationships*. Hillsdale, NJ: Erlbaum. [11]

Beach, B. A. 1988. Fitting families and research strategy: The case of home-working families. *Journal of Contemporary Ethnography*, 17:309–325. [4]

Bechtold, A., Naccarato, M. E., and Zanna, M. P. 1986. Need for structure and the prejudice-discrimination link. Paper presented at the annual meeting of the Canadian Psychological Association, Toronto, Ontario. [6]

Becker, B. J. 1986. Influence again: Another look at studies of gender differences in social influence. In Hyde, J. S., and Linn, M. C. (eds.), *The Psychology of Gender: Advances through Meta-Analysis*. Baltimore, MD: Johns Hopkins University Press. [9]

Becker, F. D. 1973. Study of spatial markers. *Journal of Personality and Social Psychology*, 26:439–445. [5]

Becker, G. 1964. The complementary needs hypothesis: Authoritarianism, dominance, and other Edwards Personality Preference Schedule scores. *Journal of Personality*, 32:45–56. [11]

Becker, H. S. 1963. *Outsiders*. New York: Free Press. [15]

Becker, H. S. 1982. *Art Worlds*. Berkeley: University of California Press. [3]

Beckman, L. 1970. Effects of students' performance on teachers' and observers' attributions of causality. *Journal of Educational Psychology*, 61:76–82. [6]

Behrend, D. A., Rosengren, K. S., and Perlmutter, M. 1992. The relation between private speech and parental interactive style. In Diaz, R. M., and Berk, L. E. (eds.), *Private Speech: From Social Interaction to Self-Regulation*. Hillsdale, NJ: Erlbaum. [2]

Bell, A. P., and Weinberg, M. S. 1978. *Homosexualities: A Study of Diversity among Men and Women*. New York: Simon & Schuster. [15]

Bell, A. P., Weinberg, M. S., and Hammersmith, S. K. 1981. *Sexual Preference: Its Development in Men and Women*. Bloomington: University of Indiana Press. [11]

Bell, D. A., Jr. 1980. A reassessment of racial balance remedies—I. *Phi Delta Kappan*, 62:177–179. [14]

Bell, J. E., and Eisenberg, N. 1985. Life satisfaction in midlife childless and empty-nest men and women. *Lifestyles*, 7:146–155. [3]

Bell, R. 1976. Swinging: Separating the sexual from friendship. In Galzer-Malbin, N. (ed.), *Old Family/New Family: Interpersonal Relationships*. New York: Van Nostrand. [11]

Belsky, J., Lang, M. E., and Huston, T. L. 1986. Sex typing and division of labor as determinants of marital change across the transition to parenthood. *Journal of Personality and Social Psychology*, 50:517–522. [3]

Belsky, J., Lang, M. E., and Rovine, M. 1985. Stability and change in marriage across the transition to parenthood: A second study. *Journal of Marriage and the Family*, 47:855–865. [3]

Bem, D. 1967. Self-perception: An alternative interpretation of cognitive dissonance phenomena. *Psychological Review*, 74:183–200. [7]

Bem, D. 1972. Self-perception theory. In Berkowitz, L. (ed.), *Advances in Experimental Social Psychology*, Vol. 6. New York: Academic Press. [8, 13]

Bem, S. 1981. The BSRI and gender schema theory: A reply to Spence and Helmreich. *Psychological Review*, 88:269–371. [7]

Bengston, V. L., Cutler, N. E., Mangen, D. J., and Marshall, V. W. 1985. Generations, cohorts and relations between age groups. In Binstock, R. H., and Shanas, E. (eds.), *Handbook of Aging and Social Sciences*. New York: Van Nostrand Reinhold, pp. 304–338. [3]

Benin, M. H., and Nienstedt, B. C. 1985. Happiness in single- and dual-earner families: The effects of marital happiness, job satisfaction, and life cycle. *Journal of Marriage and the Family*, 47:975–984. [4]

Bennett, N. A., Spoth, R. L., and Borgen, F. H. 1991. Bulimic symptoms in high school females: Prevalence and relationship with multiple measures of psychological health. *Journal of Community Psychology*, 19:13–28. [13]

Benokraitis, N. V., and Feagin, J. R. 1986. *Modern Sexism: Blatant, Subtle, and Covert Discrimination*. Englewood Cliffs, NJ: Prentice-Hall. [14]

Bentler, P. M., and Speckart, G. 1981. Attitudes "cause" behaviors: A structural equation analysis. *Journal of Personality and Social Psychology*, 40: 226–238. [8]

Ben-Yehuda, N. 1980. The European witch craze of the 14th to 17th centuries: A sociologist's perspective. *American Journal of Sociology*, 86:1–31. [16]

Berardo, D. H., Shehan, C. L., and Leslie, G. R. 1987. A residual of tradition: Jobs, careers, and spouses' time in housework. *Journal of Marriage and the Family*, 49:381–390. [3]

Berardo, F. M., and Vera, H. 1981. The groomal shower: A variation of the American bridal shower. *Family Relations*, 30:395–401. [3]

Berg, J. H. 1984. The development of friendship between roommates. *Journal of Personality and Social Psychology*, 46:346–356. [10, 11]

Berg, J. H., and Archer, R. L. 1982. Responses to self-disclosure and interaction goals. *Journal of Experimental Social Psychology*, 18:501–512. [11]

Berg, J. H., and Clark, M. S. 1986. Differences in social exchange between intimate and other relationships: Gradually evolving or quickly apparent. In Derlega, V. J., and Winstead, B. A. (eds.), *Friendship and So-cial Interaction*. New York: Springer-Verlag. [11]

Berger, G., Hank, L., Ravzi, T., and Simkins, L. 1987. Detection of sexual orientation by heterosexuals and homosexuals. *Journal of Homosexuality*, 13:83–100. [15]

Berger, J., Cohen, B. P., and Zelditch, M., Jr. 1972. Status characteristics and social interaction. *American Sociological Review*, 37:241–255. [1]

Berger, J., and Fisek, M. H. 1970. Consistent and inconsistent status characteristics and the determination of power and prestige orders. *Sociometry* 33:278–304. [13]

Berger, J., Fisek, M. H., and Norman, R. Z. 1989. The evolution of status expectations: A theoretical extension. In Berger, J., Zelditch, M., and Anderson, B. (eds.), *Sociological Theories in Progress: New Formulations*. Newbury Park, CA: Sage. [1]

Berger, J., Wagner, D. G., and Zelditch, M., Jr. 1985. Expectation states theory: Review and assessment. In Berger, J., and Zelditch, M. (eds.), *Status, Rewards, and Influence: How Expectations Organize Behavior*. San Francisco: Jossey-Bass. [1]

Berglas, S., and Jones, E. 1978. Drug choice as a self-handicapping strategy in response to noncontingent success. *Journal of Personality and Social Psychology*, 36:405–417. [5]

Bergmann, B. 1986. *The Economic Emergence of Women*. New York: Basic Books. [14]

Berk, L. E. 1992. Children's private speech: An overview of theory and the status of research. In Diaz, R. M., and Berk, L. E. (eds.), *Private Speech: From Social Interaction to Self-Regulation*. Hillsdale, NJ: Erlbaum. [2]

Berk, R. A., and Newton, P. J. 1985. Does arrest really deter wife battery? An effort to replicate the findings of the Minneapolis spouse abuse experiment. *American Sociological Review*, 50:253–262. [15]

Berk, S. F. 1985. *The Gender Factory: The Apportionment of Work in American Households*. New York: Plenum. [14]

Berkey, B. R., Perelman-Hall, T., and Kurdek, L. A. 1990. The multidimensional scale of sexuality. *Journal of Homosexuality*, 19:67–87. [15]

Berkman, L., and Breslow, L. 1983. *Health and Ways of Living: The Al-ameda County Study*. New York: Oxford University Press. [4]

Berkowitz, L. 1965. Some aspects of observed aggression. *Journal of Personality and Social Psychology*, 2:359–369. [12]

Berkowitz, L. 1973. Works and symbols as stimuli to aggressive responses. In Knutson, J. F. (ed.), *The Control of Aggression*. Chicago: Aldine. [12]

Berkowitz, L. 1981. How guns control us. *Psychology Today*, 15:11–12. [12]

Berkowitz, L. 1989. Frustration-aggression hypothesis: Examination and reformulation. *Psychological Bulletin*, 106:59–73. [12]

Berkowitz, L., and Frodi, A. 1979. Reactions to a child's mistakes as affected by his/her looks and speech. *Social Psychology Quarterly*, 42:420–425. [6]

Berkowitz, L., and Knurek, D. A. 1969. Label-mediated hostility generalization. *Journal of Personality and Social Psychology*, 13:200–206. [12]

Berman, W. H., and Turk, D. C. 1981. Adaptation to divorce: Problems and coping strategies. *Journal of Marriage and the Family*, 43:179–189. [3]

Bernard, J. 1986. The good provider role. In Skolnick, A. S., and Skolnick, J. H. (eds.), *Family in Transition: Rethinking Marriage, Sexuality, Childrearing, and Family Organization*. Boston: Little, Brown. [3]

Bernard, L. C. 1980. Multivariate analysis of new sex role formulations and personality. *Journal of Personality and Social Psychology*, 38:323–336. [7]

Bernstein, B. 1971. *Class, Codes, and Control*, Vol. 1. London: Routledge & Kegan Paul. [3]

Bernstein, B. 1977. *Class, Codes, and Control*, Vol. 3 (rev. ed.). London: Routledge & Kegan Paul. [3]

Bernstein, B. 1981. Codes, modalities, and the process of culture reproduction: A model. *Language in Society*, 10:327–363. [3]

Berscheid, E. 1982. America's obsession with beautiful people. *U.S. News & World Report* (January 11):59–61. [11]

Berscheid, E., Dion, K., Walster, E., and Walster, G. W. 1971. Physical attractiveness and dating choice: A test of the matching hypothesis. *Journal* of *Experimental Social Psychology*, 7: 173–189. [11]

Berscheid, E., and Walster, E. 1974. A little bit about love. In Huston, T. L. (ed.), *Foundations of Interpersonal Attraction*. New York: Academic Press. [11]

Bettinghaus, E. P., and Cody, M. J. 1987. *Persuasive Communication* (4th ed.). New York: Holt, Rinehart & Winston. [13]

Bettman, J. R., and Weitz, B. 1983. Attributions in the board room: Causal reasoning in corporate annual reports. *Administrative Science Quarterly*, 28:165–183. [7]

Bickman, L., and Rosenbaum, D. P. 1977. Crime reporting as a function of bystander encouragement, surveillance, and credibility. *Journal of Personality and Social Psychology*, 35: 577–586. [9, 10]

Bielby, W. T., and Baron, J. N. 1986. Men and women at work: Sex segregation and statistical discrimination. *American Journal of Sociology*, 91:759–799. [14]

Billig, M., and Tajfel, H. 1973. Social categorization and similarity in ingroup behaviour. *European Journal of Social Psychology*, 3:27–52. [4]

Bird, F., and Reimer, B. 1982. Participation rates in new religious movements and para-religious movements. *Journal for the Scientific Study of Religion*, 21:1–14. [16]

Blain, M. 1988. Fighting words: What we can learn from Hitler's hyperbole. *Symbolic Interaction*, 11:257–276. [16]

Blalock, H. M., Jr. 1989. *Power and Conflict: Toward a General Theory*. Newbury Park, CA: Sage. [12, 16]

Blanchard, F. A., and Crosby, F. J. 1989. *Affirmative Action in Perspective*. New York: Springer-Verlag. [14]

Blau, P. M. 1955. *The Dynamics of Bureaucracy*. Chicago: University of Chicago Press. [10]

Blau, P. M. 1964. *Exchange and Power in Social Life*. New York: Wiley. [1, 10, 11, 13]

Blau, P. M., and Scott, W. 1962. *Formal Organizations*. San Francisco: Chandler. [4]

Blazer, D. 1982. Social support and mortality in an elderly community population. *American Journal of Epidemiology*, 115:684–694. [4]

Bleda, P. R., Bleda, S. T., Byrne, D., and White, L. A. 1976. When a bystander becomes an accomplice: Situational determinants of reaction to dishonesty. *Journal of Experimental Social Psychology*, 12:9–25. [10]

Blood, R. O., and Wolfe, D. M. 1960. *Husbands and Wives*. New York: Free Press. [13]

Blum, L. 1991. *Between Feminism and Labor: The Significance of the Comparable Worth Movement*. Berkeley: University of California Press. [14]

Blum, L., and Smith, V. 1988. Women's mobility in the corporation: A critique of the politics of optimism. *Signs*, 13(3):528–545. [3]

Blum, N. S. 1991. The management of stigma by Alzheimer's family caregivers. *Journal of Contemporary Ethnography*, 20:263–284. [15]

Blumer, H. 1971. Social problems as collective behavior. *Social Problems*, 18:298–306. [16]

Blumstein, P., and Schwartz, P. 1983. *American Couples: Money, Work, Sex*. New York: Morrow. [11, 14]

Blumstein, P., and Schwartz, P. 1991. Money and ideology: Their impact on power and the division of household labor. In Blumberg, R. L. (ed.), *Gender, Family, and Economy: The Triple Overlap*. Newbury Park, CA: Sage. [13, 14]

Blumstein, P. W., and Weinstein, E. A. 1969. The redress of distributive injustice. *American Journal of Sociology*, 74:408–418. [10]

Blyth, D. A., and Traeger, C. 1988. Adolescent self-esteem and perceived relationships with parents and peers. In Salzinger, S., Antrobus, J., and Hammer, M. (eds.), *Social Networks of Children, Adolescents, and College Students*. Hillsdale, NJ: Erlbaum. [7]

Bobo, L. 1988. Group conflict, prejudice, and the paradox of contemporary racial attitudes. In Katz, P. A., and Taylor, D. A. (eds.), *Eliminating Racism: Profiles in Controversy*. New York: Plenum. [14]

Bobo, L. 1989. Worlds apart: Blacks, whites, and explanations of racial equality. Paper presented at the meetings of the Midwest Political Science Association, Chicago. [14]

Boden, D., and Zimmerman, D. H. (eds.). 1991. *Talk and Social Structure: Studies in Ethnomethodology and Conversation Analysis*. Berkeley: University of California Press. [5]

Bond, C. F., and Titus, L. J. 1983. Social facilitation: A meta-analysis of 241 studies. *Psychological Bulletin*, 94: 265–292. [9]

Booth, A., and Edwards, J. N. 1985. Age at marriage and marital stability. *Journal of Marriage and the Family*, 47:67–75. [3]

Borland, D. C. 1982. A cohort analysis approach to the empty-nest syndrome among three ethnic groups of women: A theoretical position. *Journal of Marriage and the Family*, 44:117–28. [3]

Bornstedt, G. W., and Felson, R. B. 1983. Explaining the relations among children's actual and perceived performances and self-esteem: A comparison of several models. *Journal of Personality and Social Psychology*, 45: 43–56. [7]

Borresen, C. R. 1982. An exploratory survey of the development of a Vietnamese stereotype. *Psychological Reports*, 50:159–165. [6]

Bosma, H., and Jackson, S. (eds.). 1990. *Coping and Self-Concept in Adolescence*. New York: Springer-Verlag. [7]

Boulding, K. E. 1962. *Conflict and Defense*. New York: Harper & Row. [12]

Bowker, L. H. 1983. *Beating Wife-Beating*. Lexington, MA: Lexington Books. [12]

Boyle, E. H., and Lawler, E. J. 1991. Resolving conflict through explicit bargaining. *Social Forces*, 69:1183–1204. [10, 12]

Braddock, J. H., II 1985. School desegregation and black assimilation. *Journal of Social Issues*, 41:9–22. [14]

Braddock, J. H., II, and McPartland, J. M. 1987. How minorities continue to be excluded from equal employment opportunities: Research on labor market and institutional barriers. *Journal of Social Issues*, 43:5–39. [14]

Bradley, G. W. 1978. Self-serving biases in the attribution process: A reexamination of the fact or fiction question. *Journal of Personality and Social Psychology*, 36:56–71. [7]

Braithwaite, J. 1985. White collar crime. In Turner, R. H., and Short, J. F., Jr. (eds.), *Annual Review of Sociology*, 11:1–25. [15]

Braungart, M. M., and Braungart,

R. G. 1990. The life-course development of left- and right-wing youth activist leaders from the 1960s. *Political Psychology*, 11:243–282. [16]

Braungart, R. G. 1975. Youth and social movements. In Dragastin, S., and Elder, G., Jr. (eds.), *Adolescence in the Life Cycle*. Washington, DC: Hemisphere. [3]

Bray, J., and Berger, S. 1990. Noncustodial father and paternal grandparent relationship in stepfamilies. *Family Relations*, 39:414–419. [3]

Bray, R. M., Johnson, D., and Chilstrom, J. T., Jr. 1982. Social influence by group members with minority opinions: A comparison of Hollander and Moscovici. *Journal of Personality and Social Psychology*, 43:78–88. [9]

Brehm, J. W., and Cohen, A. R. 1962. *Explorations in Cognitive Dissonance.* New York: Wiley. [8]

Brehm, S. S. 1985. *Intimate Relationships.* New York: Random House. [11]

Bretl, D. J., and Cantor, J. 1988. Portrayal of men and women in U.S. television commercials: Recent content analysis and trends over fifteen years. *Sex Roles*, 18:545–609. [3]

Brewer, M. B., and Kramer, R. M. 1985. The psychology of intergroup attitudes and behavior. *Annual Review of Psychology*, 37:515–521. [6]

Brewer, M. B., and Kramer, R. M. 1986. Choice behavior in social dilemmas: Effects of social identity, group size, and decision framing. *Journal of Personality and Social Psychology*, 50:543–549. [9]

Brickner, M. A., Harkins, S. G., and Ostrom, T. M. 1986. Effects of personal involvement: Thought provoking implications for social loafing. *Journal of Personality and Social Psychology*, 51:763–769. [9]

Bridges, W. P., and Villemez, W. J. 1986. Informal hiring and income in the labor market. *American Sociological Review*, 51:574–582. [4]

Brigham, J. C., Maass, A., Snyder, L. D., and Spaulding, K. 1982. Accuracy of eyewitness identifications in a field setting. *Journal of Personality and Social Psychology*, 42:673–681. [6]

Brockner, J., and Rubin, J. Z. 1985. *The Social Psychology of Conflict Escalation and Entrapment.* New York: Springer-Verlag. [12]

Brockner, J., Shaw, M. C., and Rubin,

J. Z. 1979. Factors affecting withdrawal from an escalating conflict: Quitting before it's too late. *Journal of Experimental Social Psychology*, 15:492–503. [12]

Brody, C. J., and Steelman, L. C. 1985. Sibling structure and parental sex-typing of children's household tasks. *Journal of Marriage and the Family*, 47:265–273. [3]

Broman, C. L., Neighbors, H. W., and Jackson, J. S. 1988. Racial group identification among black adults. *Social Forces*, 67:146–158. [7]

Brooks-Gunn, J. 1991. How stressful is the transition to adolescence for girls? In Colten, M., and Gore, S. (eds.), *Adolescent Stress: Causes and Consequences.* New York: Aldine de Gruyter. [7]

Brown, B. L. 1980. Effects of speech rate on personality attributions and competency evaluations. In Giles, H., Robinson, W. P., and Smith, P. (eds.), *Language: Social Psychological Perspectives.* Oxford: Pergamon, pp. 293–300. [5]

Brown, J. D., and Gallagher, F. M. 1992. Coming to terms with failure: Private self-enhancement and public self-effacement. *Journal of Experimental Social Psychology*, 28:3–22. [7]

Brown, R. 1986. *Social Psychology, The Second Edition.* New York: Free Press. [4, 10]

Brozan, N. 1985. Jurors in rape trials studied. *New York Times* (June 17):20. [12]

Brubaker, R. G., and Wickersham, D. 1990. Encouraging the practice of testicular self-examination: A field application of the theory of reasoned action. *Health Psychology*, 9:154–163. [8]

Bruner, J. 1983. *Child's Talk.* New York: Norton. [2]

Bryan, L. R., Coleman, M., Ganong, L. H., and Bryan, S. H. 1986. Person perception: Family structure as a cue for stereotyping. *Journal of Marriage and the Family*, 48:169–174. [6]

Buder, L. 1987. Beech-Nut is fined on fake juice sale. *New York Times* (Novermber 14):1. [15]

Buehler, C. J., and Wells, B. L. 1981. Counseling the romantic. *Family Relations*, 30:452–458. [11]

Bumpass, L., Sweet, J., and Martin, T. C. 1990. Changing patterns of remarriage. *Journal of Marriage and the Family*, 52:747–756. [3]

Bunzel, J. H. 1988. Choosing freshmen: Who deserves the edge? *Wall Street Journal* (February 1):22. [14]

Burger, J. M. 1986. Increasing compliance by improving the deal: The that's-not-all technique. *Journal of Personality and Social Psychology*, 51:277–283. [13]

Burger, J. M., and Petty, R. E. 1981. The low-ball compliance technique: Task or person commitment. *Journal of Personality and Social Psychology*, 40:492–500. [13]

Burgess, R. L., and Akers, R. L. 1966. A differential association-reinforcement theory of criminal behavior. *Social Problems*, 14:128–147. [15]

Burgess, R. L., and Huston, T. L. 1979. *Social Exchange in Developing Relationships.* New York: Academic Press. [11]

Burgoon, M., and Miller, G. R. 1985. An expectancy interpretation of language and persuasion. In Giles, H., and St. Clair, R. (eds.), *Recent Advances in Language, Communication, and Social Psychology.* Hillsdale, NJ: Erlbaum, pp. 199–229. [5]

Burke, P. J., and Reitzes, D. C. 1991. An identity theory approach to commitment. *Social Psychology Quarterly*, 54:239–251. [11]

Burns, G. L., and Farina, A. 1984. Social competence and adjustment. *Journal of Social and Personal Relationships*, 1:99–114. [11]

Burrell, G., and Hearn, J. 1989. The sexuality of organization. In Hearn, J., et al. (eds.), *The Sexuality of Organization.* London: Sage, pp. 1–28. [14]

Burton, L. M., and Bengston, V. L. 1985. Black grandmothers: Issues of timing and continuity of roles. In Bengston, V. L., and Robertson, J. F. (eds.), *Grandparenting.* Beverly Hills, CA: Sage. [3]

Bush, D. M. 1987. The impact of family and school on adolescent girls' aspirations and expectations: The public-private split and the reproduction of gender inequality. Paper presented at the annual meeting of the American Sociological Society, Chicago. [14]

Buss, A. 1980. *Self-Consciousness and Social Anxiety.* San Francisco: Freeman. [7]

Buss, A., and Briggs, S. 1984. Drama and the self in social interaction. *Journal of Personality and Social Psychology*, 47:1310–1324. [7]

Button, G. 1987. Moving out of closings. In Button, G., and Lee, J. (eds.), *Talk and Social Organization.* Clevedon, England: Multilingual Matters Ltd. [5]

Button, G., and Lee, J. (eds.). 1987. *Talk and Social Organization.* Clevedon, England: Multilingual Matters Ltd. [5]

Bynum, T. S, Greene, J. R., and Cullen, F. T. 1986. Correlates of legislative crime control ideology. *Criminal Justice Policy Review*, 1:253–267. [6]

Byrne, D., Clore, G. L., and Smeaton, G. 1986. The attraction hypothesis: Do similar attitudes affect anything? *Journal of Personality and Social Psychology*, 51:1167–1170. [11]

Cahn, D. D. 1990. Perceived understanding and interpersonal relationships. *Journal of Social and Personal Relationships*, 7:231–244. [11]

Calavita, K., and Pontell, H. 1991. Other people's money revisited: Collective embezzlement in the savings and loan and insurance industries. *Social Problems*, 38:94–112. [15]

Caldwell, M. A., and Peplau, L. A. 1982. Sex differences in same-sex friendship. *Sex Roles*, 8:721–732. [11]

Calhoun, C., and Hiller, H. 1988. Coping with insidious injuries: The case of Johns-Mansville Corporation and asbestos exposure. *Social Problems*, 35:162–181. [15]

Callero, P. L. 1985. Role-identity salience. *Social Psychology Quarterly*, 48:203–215. [10]

Campagna, D. S., and Poffenberger, D. L. 1988. *The Sexual Trafficking in Children: An Investigation of the Child Sex Trade.* Dover, MA: Auburn House. [15]

Campbell, D. T. 1975. On the conflicts between biological and social evolution and between psychology and moral tradition. *American Psychologist*, 30:1103–1126. [16]

Campbell, D. T. 1983. The two distinct routes beyond kin selection to ultrasociality: Implications for the humanities and social sciences. In Bridgeman, D. L. (ed.), *The Nature of Prosocial Behavior.* New York: Academic Press. [16]

Campbell, J. D., and Fairey, P. J. 1989. Informational and normative routes to conformity: The effect of faction size as a function of norm extremity and attention to the stimulus. *Journal of Personality and Social Psychology*, 57:457–468. [9]

Campbell, J. D., Tesser, A., and Fairey, P. J. 1986. Conformity and attention to the stimulus: Some temporal and contextual dynamics. *Journal of Personality and Social Psychology*, 51:315–324. [9]

Cancian, F. M. 1986. The feminization of love. *Signs: Journal of Women in Culture and Society*, 11:692–709. [11]

Cancian, F. M., and Gordon, S. 1988. Changing emotion norms in marriage: Love and anger in U.S. women's magazines since 1900. *Gender and Society*, 2:308-342. [11]

Cann, A., Sherman, S. J., and Elkes, R. 1975. Effects of initial request size and time of a second request on compliance: The foot in the door and the door in the face. *Journal of Personality and Social Psychology*, 32:774–782. [13]

Cantril, H. 1941. *The Psychology of Social Movements.* New York: Wiley. [12, 16]

Caporael, L. 1981. The paralanguage of caregiving: Baby talk to the institutionalized aged. *Journal of Personality and Social Psychology*, 40:876–884. [5]

Caporael, L., and Culbertson, G. H. 1986. Verbal response modes of baby talk and other speech at institutions for the aged. *Language and Communication*, 6:99–112. [5]

Cappella, J. N. 1985. Controlling the floor in conversation. In Siegman, A. W., and Feldstein, S. (eds.), *Multichannel Integrations of Nonverbal Behavior.* Hillsdale, NJ: Erlbaum, pp. 69–103. [5]

Carley, K., and Palmquist, M. 1992. Extracting, representing, and analyzing mental models. *Social Forces*, 70:601–636. [6]

Carlsmith, J. M., and Gross, A. E. 1969. Some effects of guilt on compliance. *Journal of Personality and Social Psychology*, 11:232–239. [13]

Carlson, M., Charlin, V., and Miller, N. 1988. Positive mood and helping behavior: A test of six hypotheses. *Journal of Personality and Social Psychology*, 55:211–229. [10]

Carlson, M., and Miller, N. 1987. Explanation of the relationship between negative mood and helping. *Psychological Bulletin*, 102:91–108. [10]

Carlson, S. M. 1987. *Beyond "Occupational Segregation": Contradictory Labor Market Practices and Their Race/Sex Distributional Consequences in the Post-War United States.* Ann Arbor, MI: University Microfilms International. [14]

Carper, A. 1992. Gays win some, lose some. *Newsday* (November 5):29. [15]

Carver, C., and Humphries, C. 1981. Havana daydreaming: A study of self-consciousness and the negative reference group among Cuban Americans. *Journal of Personality and Social Psychology*, 40:545–552. [4]

Cash, T., and Janda, L. H. 1984. The eye of the beholder. *Psychology Today*, 18(December):46–52. [6]

Cash, T., Kehr, J., Polyson, J., and Freeman, V. 1977. Role of physical attractiveness in peer attribution of psychological disturbance. *Journal of Counseling Psychology*, 45:987–993. [6]

Cass, V. C. 1990. The implications of homosexual identity formation for the Kinsey model and scaling of sexual preference. In McWhirter, D. P., Sanders, S. A., and Reinisch, J. M. (eds.), *Homosexuality/Heterosexuality: Concepts of Sexual Orientation.* New York: Oxford University Press. [7, 15]

Cate, R. M., Lloyd, S. A., and Henton, J. M. 1985. The effect of equity, equality, and reward level on the stability of students' premarital relationships. *Journal of Social Psychology*, 125:715–721. [11]

Cate, R. M., Lloyd, S. A., Henton, J. M., and Larson, J. H. 1982. Fairness and reward level as predictors of relationship satisfaction. *Social Psychology Quarterly*, 45:171–181. [11]

Cate, R. M., Lloyd, S. A., and Long, E. 1988. The role of rewards and fairness in developing premarital relationships. *Journal of Marriage and the Family*, 50:443–452. [11]

CBS/New York Times. 1991. Question id: USCBSNYT.090991.R29. (September 1991) Roper Center POLLS [computer file]. [14]

Chaiken, S. 1979. Communicator physical attractiveness and persuasion. *Journal of Personality and Social Psychology*, 3:1387–1397. [13]

Chaiken, S., and Baldwin, M. W. 1981. Affective-cognitive consistency and the effect of salient behavioral information on the self-perception of attitudes. *Journal of Personality and Social Psychology*, 41:1–12. [8]

Chaiken, S., and Eagly, A. H. 1976.

Communication modality as a determinant of message persuasiveness and message comprehensibility. *Journal of Personality and Social Psychology*, 34: 605–614. [13]

Chaiken, S., and Eagly, A. H. 1983. Communication modality as a determinant of persuasion: The role of communicator salience. *Journal of Personality and Social Psychology*, 45: 241–256. [13]

Charng, H. W., Piliavin, J. A., and Callero, P. L. 1988. Role-identity and reasoned action in the prediction of repeated behavior. *Social Psychology Quarterly*, 51:303–317. [8, 10]

Cheepen, C. 1988. *The Predictability of Informal Conversation*. New York: Pinter. [5]

Chen, S. C. 1937. Social modification of the activity of ants in nest-building. *Physiological Zoology*, 10:420–436. [9]

Cherlin, A. J. 1981. *Marriage, Divorce, and Remarriage: Social Trends in the United States*. Cambridge, MA: Harvard University Press. [3]

Cherlin, A. J., and Furstenberg, F. F., Jr. 1986. *The New American Grandparent: A Place in the Family, a Life Apart*. New York: Basic Books. [3]

Chesser, B. J. 1980. Analysis of wedding rituals: An attempt to make weddings more meaningful. *Family Relations*, 29:204–215. [3]

Chomsky, N. 1968. *Language and Mind*. New York: Harcourt. [2]

Chomsky, N. 1975. *Reflections on Language*. New York: Pantheon. [2]

Christensen, A., and Heavey, C. L. 1990. Gender and social structure in the demand/withdraw pattern of marital conflict. *Journal of Personality and Social Psychology*, 59:73–81. [11]

Christopher, F. S., and Frandsen, M. M. 1990. Strategies of influence in sex and dating. *Journal of Social and Personal Relationships*, 7:89–105. [11]

Cialdini, R. B., Cacioppo, J. T., Bassett, R., and Miller, J. A. 1978. Low-ball procedure for producing compliance: Commitment, then cost. *Journal of Personality and Social Psychology*, 36:463–476. [13]

Cialdini, R. B., Schaller, M., Houlihan, D., Arps, K., Fultz, J., and Beaman, A. 1987. Empathy-based helping: Is it selflessly or selfishly motivated? *Journal of Personality and Social Psychology*, 52:749–758. [10]

Cialdini, R. B., Vincent, J. E., Lewis, S. K., Catalan, J., Wheeler, D., and Darby, B. L. 1975. Reciprocal concessions procedure for inducing compliance: The door-in-the-face technique. *Journal of Personality and Social Psychology*, 31:206–215. [13]

Clanton, G. 1989. Jealousy in American culture, 1945–1985: Reflections from popular literature. In Franks, D. D., and McCarthy, E. D. (eds.), *The Sociology of Emotions: Original Essays and Research Papers*. Greenwich, CT: JAI Press. [11]

Clark, C. 1987. Culture and sympathy. *American Journal of Sociology*, 93:290–321. [10]

Clark, E. V. 1976. From gesture to word: On the natural history of deixis in language acquisition. In Bruner, J. S., and Gartner, A. (eds.), *Human Growth and Development*. Oxford: Clarendon Press. [2]

Clark, H. H. 1985. Language use and language users. In Lindzey, G., and Aronson, E. (eds.), *The Handbook of Social Psychology* (3rd ed.). New York: Random House, pp. 179–231. [5]

Clark, H. H., and Clark, E. V. 1977. *Psychology and Language*. New York: Harcourt Brace Jovanovich. [5]

Clark, K. B. 1947. Racial identification and preference in Negro children. In Newcomb, T. M., and Hartley, E. L. (eds.), *Readings in Social Psychology*, New York: Holt. [14]

Clark, K. B. 1950. Emotional factors in racial identification and preference in Negro children. In Grossack, M. (ed.), *Mental Health and Segregation*. New York: Springer. [14]

Clark, K. B., and Clark, M. P. 1939. Development of consciousness of self and the emergence of racial identification in Negro preschool children. *Journal of Social Psychology*, 10:591–599. [14]

Clark, M. S., Milberg, S., and Erber, R. 1984. Effects of arousal on judgments of others' emotions. *Journal of Personality and Social Psychology*, 46: 551–560. [6]

Clark, M. S., and Reis, H. T. 1988. Interpersonal processes in close relationships. *Annual Review of Psychology*, 39:609–672. [10]

Clark, P. G., Siviski, R. W., and Weiner, R. 1986. Coping strategies of widowers in the first year. *Family Relations*, 35:425–430. [3]

Clark, R. D., III, and Word, L. E. 1972. Why don't bystanders help? Because of ambiguity? *Journal of Personality and Social Psychology*, 24: 392–400. [10]

Clark, R. D., III, and Word, L. E. 1974. Where is the apathetic bystander? Situational characteristics of the emergency. *Journal of Personality and Social Psychology*, 29:279–287. [10, 11]

Clarke, E. 1982. *Stopping Sexual Harassment: A Handbook* (2nd ed.). Detroit: Labor Education and Research Project. [14]

Clary, E. G., and Snyder, M. 1991. A functional analysis of altruism and prosocial behavior: The case of volunteerism. In Clark, M. S. (ed.), *Prosocial Behavior: Vol. 12. Review of Personality and Social Psychology*. Newbury Park, CA: Sage, pp. 119–148. [10]

Clausen, J. 1986. *The Life Course: A Sociological Perspective*. Englewood Cliffs, NJ: Prentice-Hall. [3]

Clayman, S. 1989. The production of punctuality: Social interaction, temporal organization, and social structure. *American Journal of Sociology*, 95:659–691. [5]

Clemens, A., and Axelson, L. 1985. The not-so-empty-nest: The return of the fledgling adult. *Family Relations*, 34:259–264. [3]

Clifford, M. M., and Walster, E. 1973. The effect of physical attractiveness on teacher expectation. *Sociology of Education*, 46:248–258. [6]

Clinard, M. B., and Meier, R. F. 1989. *Sociology of Deviant Behavior* (7th ed.). Chicago: Holt, Rinehart & Winston. [16]

Clinard, M. B., and Yeager, P. C. 1980. *Corporate Crime*. New York: Free Press. [15]

Cockburn, C. 1985. *Machinery of Dominance: Women, Men, and Technical Know-How*. London: Pluto Press. [14]

Cockburn, C. 1991. *In the Way of Women: Men's Resistance to Sex Equality in Organizations*. Ithaca, NY: ILR Press. [14]

Cody, M. J., and McLaughlin, M. L. 1985. Models for the sequential construction of accounting episodes: Situational and interactional constraints on message selection and evaluation. In Street, R. L., and Cappella, J. N. (eds.), *Sequence and Pattern in Communicative Behaviour*. London: Arnold. [5]

Cody, M. J., and McLaughlin, M. L. 1988. Accounts on trial: Oral arguments in traffic court. In Antiaki, C. (ed.), *Analyzing Everyday Explanation: A Casebook of Methods*. London: Sage, pp. 113–126. [15]

Cody, M. J., McLaughlin, M. J., and Schneider, M. J. 1981. The impact of relational consequences and intimacy on the selection of interpersonal persuasion tactics: A reanalysis. *Communication Quarterly*, 29:91–106. [13]

Coffield, F., Borrill, C., and Marshall, S. 1986. *Growing Up at the Margins*, Milton Keynes, England: Open University Press. [11]

Cogle, F. L., and Tasher, G. E. 1982. Children and housework. *Family Relations*, 31:395–399. [3]

Cohen, A. K. 1955. *Delinquent Boys*. New York: Free Press. [15]

Cohen, A. K. 1965. The sociology of the deviant act: Anomie and beyond. *American Sociological Review*, 30:5–14. [15]

Cohen, C. E. 1981. Person categories and social perception: Testing some boundaries of the processing effects of prior knowledge. *Journal of Personality and Social Psychology*, 40:441–452. [6]

Cohen, E. G. 1984. The desegregated school: Problems of status power and interethnic climate. In Miller, N., and Brewer, M. B. (eds.), *Groups in Contact: The Psychology of Desegregation*. Orlando, FL: Sage. [12]

Cohen, L. E., and Land, K. C. 1987. Age structure and crime. *American Sociological Review*, 52:170–183. [15]

Cohen, S., and McKay, G. 1984. Social support, stress, and the buffering hypothesis: A review of naturalistic studies. In Baum, A., Singer, J., and Taylor, S. (eds.), *Handbook of Psychology and Health*, Vol. 4. Hillsdale, NJ: Erlbaum. [4]

Cohen, S., and Symes, S. L. (eds.). 1985. *Social Support and Health*. New York: Academic Press. [4]

Cohen, S., and Wills, T. 1985. Stress, social support, and the buffering hypothesis. *Psychological Bulletin*, 98:310–357. [4]

Cohn, R. M. 1978. The effects of employment status change on self-attitudes. *Social Psychology*, 41:81–93. [7]

Cohn, S. 1985. *The Process of Occupational Sex-Typing: The Feminization of Clerical Labor in Great Britain*. Philadelphia: Temple University Press. [14]

Colclough, G., and Beck, E. M. 1986. The American educational structure and the reproduction of social class. *Sociological Inquiry*, 56:456–473. [3]

Coleman, J. F., Blake, R. R., and Moulton, J. S. 1958. Task difficulty and conformity pressures. *Journal of Abnormal and Social Psychology*, 57:120–122. [9]

Coleman, J. S. 1961. *The Adolescent Society*. New York: Free Press. [3]

Coleman, J. S. 1966. *Equality of Educational Opportunity*. Washington, DC: U.S. Government Printing Office. [14]

Coleman, J. S. 1975. Racial segregation in the schools: New research with new policy implications. *Phi Delta Kappan*, 57:75–82. [14]

Coleman, J. S. 1976. Response to Professors Pettigrew and Green. *Harvard Educational Review*, 46:217–224. [14]

Coleman, J. S. 1988. Free riders and zealots: The role of social networks. *Sociological Theory*, 6:52–57. [9]

Coleman, J. S. 1990. *Foundations of Social Theory*. Cambridge, MA: The Belknap Press of Harvard University Press. [10]

Coleman, J. S., Kelley, S. D., and Moore, J. 1975. *Trends in School Segregation, 1968–1973*. Washington, DC: Urban Institute. [14]

Coleman, J. W. 1985. *The Criminal Elite: The Sociology of White Collar Crime*. New York: St. Martin's Press. [15]

Coleman, M. T. 1991. The division of household labor: Suggestions for future empirical consideration and theoretical development. In Blumberg, R. L. (ed.), *Gender, Family, and Economy: The Triple Overlap*. Newbury Park, CA: Sage. [14]

Collinson, D. L., Knights, D., and Collinson, M. 1990. *Managing to Discriminate*. New York: Routledge. [14]

Colten, M., Gore, S., and Aseltine, R. 1991. Stress and disorder in high school aged youth. In Colten, M., and Gore, S. (eds.), *Adolescent Stress: Causes and Consequences*. New York: Aldine de Gruyter. [7]

Compas, B., and Wagner, B. 1991. Psychosocial stress during adolescence: Intrapersonal and interpersonal processes. In Colten, M., and Gore, S. (eds.), *Adolescent Stress: Causes and Consequences*. New York: Aldine de Gruyter. [7]

Comstock, G. 1982. Violence in television content: An overview. In Pearl, D., Bouthilet, L., and Lazar, J. (eds.), *Television and Behavior: Ten Years of Scientific Progress and Implications for the Eighties: Vol. II. Technical Reviews*. Rockville, MD: National Institute of Mental Health. [12]

Conlon, E. J., and Barr, S. H. 1989. A framework for understanding group feedback. In Lawler, E. J., and Markovsky, B. (eds.), *Advances in Group Processes*, Vol. 6. Greenwich, CT: JAI Press. [9]

Cook, K. S. 1987. Emerson's contributions to social exchange theory. In Cook, K. S. (ed.), *Social Exchange Theory*. Newbury Park, CA: Sage. [10]

Cooley, C. H. 1902. *Human Nature and the Social Order*. New York: Scribner. [1, 2]

Cooley, C. H. 1909. *Social Organization*. New York: Scribner. [4]

Coombs, R. H., and Landsverk, J. 1988. Parenting styles and substance use during childhood and adolescence. *Journal of Marriage and the Family*, 50:473–482. [13]

Cooney, T. M., and Uhlenberg, P. 1992. Support from parents over the life course: The adult child's perspective. *Social Forces*, 71:63–84. [11]

Cordos, C. 1986. Tent tilt: Boys outscore girls on both parts of the SAT. *APA* (June):30–31. [14]

Corley, C., Cernkovich, S., and Giordano, P. 1989. Sex and the likelihood of sanction. *Journal of Criminal Law and Criminology*, 80:540–553. [15]

Corsaro, W. A. 1979. Young children's conception of status and role. *Sociology of Education*, 52:46–59. [2]

Corsaro, W. A. 1985. *Friendship and Peer Culture in the Early Years*. Norwood, NJ: Ablex. [3]

Corsaro, W. A. 1988. Routines in the peer culture of American and Italian nursery school children. *Sociology of Education*, 61:1–14. [3]

Corsaro, W. A. 1992. Interpretive reproduction in children's peer cultures. *Social Psychology Quarterly*, 55:160–177. [2, 3]

Corsaro, W. A., and Eder, D. 1990. Children's peer cultures. *Annual Review of Sociology*, 16:197–200. [3]

Corsaro, W. A., and Rizzo, T. 1988. *Discussione* and friendship: Socialization processes in the peer culture of Italian nursery school children. *American Sociological Review*, 53:879–894. [2]

Corsaro, W. A., and Rizzo, T. 1990. Disputes in the peer culture of American and Italian nursery-school children. In Grimshaw, A. D. (ed.), *Conflict Talk: Sociolinguistic Investigations of Arguments in Conversations*. New York: Cambridge University Press. [2]

Coser, R. L., and Rokoff, G. 1982. Women in the occupational world: Social disruption and conflict. In Kahn-Hut, R., Daniels, A. K., and Colvard, R. (eds.), *Women and Work*.

New York: Oxford University Press. (First published in 1971 in *Social Problems*, 18:535–554.) [3]

Couch, C. 1987. *Researching Social Processes in the Laboratory*. Greenwich, CT: JAI Press. [1]

Coulter, J. 1989. *Mind in Action*. Atlantic Highlands, NJ: Humanities Press International. [1]

Coupland, N., Giles, H., and Weimann, J. M. (eds.), 1991. *"Miscommunication" and Problematic Talk*. Newbury Park, CA: Sage. [5]

Coverman, S., and Sheley, J. F. 1986. Change in men's housework and child-care time, 1965–1975. *Journal of Marriage and the Family*, 48:413–422. [3]

Cowan, C. P., Cowan, P. A., Heming, G., Garrett, E., Coysh, W., Curtis-Boles, H., and Boles, A. 1985. Transition to parenthood: His, hers, and theirs. *Journal of Family Issues*, 6:461–481. [3]

Cowan, C. P., Cowan, P. A., Heming, G., and Miller, N. B. 1991. Becoming a family: Marriage, parenting, and child development. In Cowan, P. A., and Hetherington, M. (eds.), *Family Transitions*. Hillsdale, NJ: Erlbaum. [3]

Cowan, G., Drinkard, J., and McGavin, L. 1984. The effects of target, age, and gender on use of power strategies. *Journal of Personality and Social Psychology*, 47:1391–1398. [13]

Cowan, P. A., and Cowan, C. P. 1988. Changes in marriage during the transition to parenthood: Must we blame the baby? In Michaels, G. Y., and Goldberg, W. A. (eds.), *The Transition to Parenthood: Current Theory and Research*. New York: Cambridge University Press. [3]

Cowan, P. A., and Cowan, C. P. 1990. Becoming a family: Research and intervention. In Sigel, I., and Brody, G. (eds.), *Family Research*, Vol. 1. Hillsdale, NJ: Erlbaum. [3]

Craig, R. T., Tracy, K., and Spisak, F. 1986. The discourse of requests: Assessment of a politeness approach. *Human Communication Research*, 12:437–468. [5]

Crain, R. L., and Mahard, R. E. 1983. The effect of research methodology on desegregation-achievement studies: A meta-analysis. *American Journal of Sociology*, 88:839–854. [14]

Crandall, C. S. 1988. Social conta-

gion of binge eating. *Journal of Personality and Social Psychology*, 55:588–598. [9]

Crawford, M. 1977. What is a friend? *New Society*, 20:116–117. [11]

Cressey, D. T. 1971. *Other People's Money: A Study in the Social Psychology of Embezzlement*. Belmont, CA: Wadsworth. [15]

Crocker, J., and Lutsky, N. 1986. Stigma and the dynamics of social cognition. In Ainlay, S. C., Becker, G., and Coleman, L. M. (eds.), *The Dilemma of Difference: A Multidisciplinary View of Stigma*. New York: Plenum. [15]

Crocker, J., Voelkl, K., Testa, M., and Major, B. 1991. Social stigma: The affective consequences of attributional ambiguity. *Journal of Personality and Social Psychology*, 60:218–228. [7]

Crosby, F., Bromley, S., and Saxe, L. 1980. Recent unobtrusive studies of black and white discrimination and prejudice: A literature review. *Psychological Bulletin*, 87:546–563. [6]

Crosby, F., Clayton, S., Alksins, O., and Hemker, K. 1986. Cognitive biases in the perception of discrimination: The importance of format. *Sex Roles*, 14:637–646. [16]

Croyle, R. T., and Cooper, J. 1983. Dissonance arousal: Physiological evidence. *Journal of Personality and Social Psychology*, 45:782–791. [8]

Crull, P. 1987. Hidden aspects of women's work. In Bose, C., and Feldberg, R. (eds.), *Hidden Aspects of Women's Work*. New York: Praeger. [14]

Crutchfield, R. A. 1955. Conformity and character. *American Psychologist*, 10:191–198. [9]

Cummings, S. 1975. An appraisal of some recent evidence dealing with the mental health of black children and adolescents, and its implications for school psychologists and guidance counselors. *Psychology in the Schools*, 12:234–238. [14]

Cunningham, J. A., Strassberg, D. S., and Haan, B. 1986. Effects of intimacy and sex-role congruency of self-disclosure. *Journal of Social and Clinical Psychology*, 4:393–401. [11]

Cunningham, M. R. 1986. Levites and brother's keepers: Sociobiological perspective on prosocial behavior. *Humbodt Journal of Social Relations*, 13:35–67. [10]

Cunningham, S. 1984. Genovese: 20 years later, few heed a stranger's cries. *APA Monitor* (May):30. [10]

Cupach, W. R., Metts, S., and Hazelton, V., Jr. 1986. Coping with embarrassing predicaments: Remedial strategies and their perceived utility. *Journal of Language and Social Psychology*, 5:181–200. [5]

Curran, D. 1983. Judicial discretion and defendant's sex. *Criminology*, 21:41–58. [14]

Curtiss, S. 1977. *Genie: A Psycholinguistic Study of a Modern Day "Wild Child."* New York: Academic Press. [2]

Cutrona, C. 1982. Transition to college: Loneliness and the process of social adjustment. In Peplau, L. A., and Perlman, D. (eds.), *Loneliness: A Sourcebook of Current Theory, Research and Therapy*. New York: Wiley-Interscience. [4]

Daly, K. 1987a. Structure and practice of familial-based justice in a criminal court. *Law and Society Review*, 21:267–290. [14]

Daly, K. 1987b. Discrimination in the criminal courts: Family, gender, and the problem of equal treatment. *Social Forces*, 66:152–175. [14]

D'Amico, R. J., Haurin, R. J., and Mott, F. L. 1983. The effects of mothers' employment on adolescent and early adult outcomes of young men and women. In Hayes, C. D., and Kamerman, S. B. (eds.), *Children of Working Parents*. Washington, DC: National Academy Press, pp. 130–219. [15]

Daniels, A. K. 1987. Invisible work. *Social Problems*, 34:403–415. [14]

Danziger, N. 1983. Sex-related differences in aspirations of college students. *Sex Roles*, 9:683–695. [3]

Darby, B. W., and Schlenker, B. R. 1982. Children's reactions to apologies. *Journal of Personality and Social Psychology*, 43:742–753. [15]

Darcy, R., and Laver, M. 1987. Referendum dynamics and the Irish divorce amendment. *Public Opinion Quarterly*, 54:1–20. [16]

Darley, J. M., and Batson, C. D. 1973. From Jerusalem to Jericho: A study of situational and dispositional variables in helping behavior. *Journal of Personality and Social Psychology*, 27:100–108. [10]

Darley, J. M., Fleming, J. H., Hilton,

J. L., and Swann, W. B., Jr. 1988. Dispelling negative expectancies: The impact of interaction goals and target characteristics on the expectancy confirmation process. *Journal of Experimental Social Psychology*, 24:19–36. [6]

Darley, J. M., and Latané, B. 1968. Bystander intervention in emergencies: Diffusion of responsibility. *Journal of Personality and Social Psychology*, 8:377–383. [10]

Darley, J. M., and Schultz, T. R. 1990. Moral rules: Their content and acquisition. *Annual Review of Psychology*, 41:525–556. [2]

D'Augelli, A. R. 1987. Social support patterns of lesbian women in a rural helping network. *Journal of Rural Community Psychology*, 8:12–21. [15]

D'Augelli, A. R., and Hart, M. M. 1987. Gay women, men, and families in rural settings: Toward the development of helping communities. *American Journal of Community Psychology*, 15:79–93. [15]

Davidson, B. 1975. King of the iron merchants. *New York Times Magazine* (March 2):12, 32–37. [7]

Davidson, B., Balswick, J., and Halverson, C. 1983. Affective self-disclosure and marital adjustment: A test of equity theory. *Journal of Marriage and the Family*, 45:93–102. [11]

Davies, J. C. 1962. Toward a theory of revolution. *American Sociological Review*, 27:5–19. [16]

Davies, J. C. 1969. The J-curve of rising and declining satisfactions as a cause of some great revolutions and a contained revolution. In Graham, H. D., and Gurr, T. R. (eds.), *The History of Violence in America*. New York: Bantam. [16]

Davies, J. C. 1974. The J-curve and power struggle theories of collective violence. *American Sociological Review*, 39:607–610. [16]

Davies, M., and Kandel, D. B. 1981. Parental and peer influence on adolescents' educational plans: Some further evidence. *American Journal of Sociology*, 87:363–387. [3]

Davis, F. 1961. Deviance disavowal: The management of strained interaction by the visibly handicapped. *Social Problems*, 9:120–123. [15]

Davis, K. 1949. *Human Society*. New York: Macmillan. [2, 3]

Davis, K. E. 1985. Near and dear: Friendship and love compared. *Psy-*chology Today*, 19(February):22–30. [11]

Davis, K. E., and Todd, M. J. 1982. Friendship and love relationships. In Davis, K. E. (ed.), *Advances in Descriptive Psychology*, Vol. 2. Greenwich, CT: JAI Press, pp. 79–112. [11]

Davison, A. R., Yantis, S., Norwood, M., and Montano, D. E. 1985. Amount of information about the attitude object and the attitude-behavior consistency. *Journal of Personality and Social Psychology*, 49:1184–1198. [8]

Dawes, R. M., McTavish, J., and Shaklee, H. 1977. Behavior, communication, and assumptions about other people's behavior in a common dilemma situation. *Journal of Personality and Social Psychology*, 35:1–11. [9]

Deaux, K. 1981. Sex: A perspective on the attribution process. In Harvey, J. H., Ickes, W., and Kidd, R. (eds.), *New Directions in Attribution Research*, Vol. 3. Hillsdale, NJ: Erlbaum. [6]

Deaux, K. 1985. Sex and gender. *Annual Review of Psychology*, 36:49–81. [2, 14]

Deaux, K., and Emswiller, T. 1974. Explanations of successful performance on sex-linked tasks: What is skill for the male is luck for the female. *Journal of Personality and Social Psychology*, 29:80–85. [6]

Deaux, K., and Lewis, L. L., 1984. Structure of gender stereotypes: Interrelationships among components and gender labels. *Journal of Personality and Social Psychology*, 46:991–1004. [6]

De Charms, R. 1968. *Personal Causation*. New York: Academic Press. [12]

DeCotiis, T., and Summers, T. 1987. A path analysis of a model of the antecedents and consequences of organizational commitment. *Human Relations*, 40:445–470. [4]

DeFreitas, G. 1991. *Inequality at Work: Hispanics in the U.S. Labor Force*. New York: Oxford University Press. [14]

DeJong, W. 1980. The stigma of obesity: The consequences of naive assumptions concerning the causes of physical deviance. *Journal of Health and Social Behavior*, 21:75–87. [6]

Del Boca, F. K., Ashmore, R. D., and McManus, M. A. 1986. Gender-related attitudes. In Ashmore, R. D., and Del Boca, F. K. (eds.), *The Social Psychology of Female-Male Relations: A*Critical Analysis of Central Concepts*. New York: Academic Press. [6]

Della Fave, L. R. 1980. The meek shall not inherit the earth: Self-evaluation and the legitimacy of stratification. *American Sociological Review*, 45:955–971. [16]

Della Fave, L. R. 1986a. The dialectics of legitimation and counternorms. *Sociological Perspectives*, 29:435–460. [14]

Della Fave, L. R. 1986b. Toward an explanation of the legitimation process. *Social Forces*, 65:476–500. [14]

Demetras, M. J., Post, K. N., and Snow, C. E. 1986. Feedback to first language learners: The role of repetitions and clarification questions. *Journal of Child Language*, 13:275–292. [2]

Demo, D. H., and Hughes, M. 1990. Socialization and racial identity among black Americans. *Social Psychology Quarterly*, 53:364–374. [7]

Denzin, N. K. 1984. Toward a phenomenology of domestic, family violence. *American Journal of Sociology*, 90:483–513. [12]

Denzin, N. K. 1986. Postmodern social theory. *Sociological Theory*, 4:194–204. [1]

DePaulo, B. M., Brittingham, G. L., and Kaiser, M. K. 1983. Receiving competence-relevant help: Effects of reciprocity, affect, and sensitivity to the helper's nonverbally expressed needs. *Journal of Personality and Social Psychology*, 45:1045–1060. [10]

DePaulo, B. M., and Coleman, L. M. 1986. Talking to children, foreigners and retarded adults. *Journal of Personality and Social Psychology*, 51:945–959. [5]

DePaulo, B. M., and Fisher, J. D. 1980. The costs of asking for help. *Basic and Applied Social Psychology*, 1:23–25. [10]

DePaulo, B. M., Rosenthal, R., Eisenstat, R. A., Rogers, P. L., and Finkelstein, S. 1978. Decoding discrepant nonverbal cues. *Journal of Personality and Social Psychology*, 36:313–323. [5]

Derlega, V. J., and Berg, J. H. (eds.). 1987. *Self-Disclosure: Theory, Research, and Therapy*. New York: Plenum. [11]

Derlega, V. J., Winstead, B. A., Wong, P. T. P., and Hunter, S. 1985. Gender effects in an initial encounter: A case where men exceed women in disclosure. *Journal of Social and Personal Relationships*, 2:25–44. [11]

Dermer, M., and Thiel, D. L. 1975. When beauty may fail. *Journal of Personality and Social Psychology*, 31:1168–1176. [6]

Deutsch, F. M., and Lamberti, D. M. 1986. Does social approval increase helping? *Personality and Social Psychology Bulletin*, 12:149–157. [10]

Deutsch, M., and Gerard, H. 1955. A study of normative and informational social influences upon individual judgment. *Journal of Abnormal and Social Psychology*, 51:629–636. [9]

DeVellis, B. M., Blalock, S. J., and Sandler, R. S. 1990. Predicting participation in cancer screening: The role of perceived behavioral control. *Journal of Applied Social Psychology*, 20:639–660. [8]

Devine, P. G., Sedikides, C., and Fuhrman, R. W. 1989. Goals in social information processing: The case of anticipated information. *Journal of Personality and Social Psychology*, 56:680–690. [6]

Devlin, L. P. 1986. An analysis of presidential television commercials, 1952–1984. In Kaid, L. L., Nimmo, D., and Sanders, K. R. (eds.), *New Perspectives on Political Advertising*. Carbondale: Southern Illinois University Press. [13]

Dewey, J. 1922. *Human Nature and Conduct: An Introduction to Social Psychology*. New York: Holt. [1]

Dickens, W. J., and Perlman, D. 1981. Friendship over the life cycle. In Duck, S. W., and Gilmour, R. (eds.), *Personal Relationships: 2. Developing Personal Relationships*. New York: Academic Press. [11]

Diener, E. 1979. Deindividuation, self-awareness, and disinhibition. *Journal of Personality and Social Psychology*, 37:1160–1171. [12]

Diener, E., and Crandall, R. 1978. *Ethics in Social and Behavioral Research*. Chicago: University of Chicago Press. [1]

Dillard, J. P., Hunter, J. E., and Burgoon, M. 1984. Sequential-request persuasive strategies: Meta-analysis of foot-in-the-door and door-in-the-face. *Human Communication Research*, 10:461–488. [13]

Dion, K. 1972. Physical attractiveness and evaluations of children's transgressions. *Journal of Personality and Social Psychology*, 24:207–213. [6]

Dion, K., and Berscheid, E. 1974. Physical attractiveness and peer perception in children. *Sociometry*, 37:1–12. [6]

Dion, K., Berscheid, E., and Walster, E. 1972. What is beautiful is good. *Journal of Personality and Social Psychology*, 24:285–290. [6]

Dion, K. L., and Dion, K. K. 1973. Correlates of romantic love. *Journal of Consulting and Clinical Psychology*, 41:51–56. [11]

Dishion, T. J., Reid, J. B., and Patterson, G. R. 1988. Empirical guidelines for a family intervention for adolescent drug use. In Coombs, R. H. (ed.), *The Family Context of Adolescent Drug Use*. New York: Haworth. [13]

Dix, T. H., and Grusec, J. E. 1985. Parental attribution processes in the socialization of children. In Sigel, I. E. (ed.), *Parental Belief Systems: The Psychological Consequences for Children*. Hillsdale, NJ: Erlbaum, pp. 201–233. [3]

Dix, T. H., Ruble, D. N., Grusec, J. E., and Nixon, S. 1986. Social cognition in parents: Inferential and affective reactions to children of three age levels. *Child Development*, 57:879–894. [3]

Dollard, J., Miller, N., Doob, L., Mowrer, O. H., and Sears, R. R. 1939. *Frustration and Aggression*. New Haven, CT: Yale University Press. [12]

Donnerstein, E. 1980. Aggressive erotica and violence against women. *Journal of Personality and Social Psychology*, 39:269–277. [12]

Donnerstein, E., and Berkowitz, L. 1981. Victim reactions in aggressive erotic films as a factor in violence against women. *Journal of Personality and Social Psychology*, 41:710–724. [12]

Donnerstein, E., Donnerstein, M., and Evans, R. 1975. Erotic stimuli and aggression: Facilitation or inhibition. *Journal of Personality and Social Psychology*, 32:237–244. [12]

Donnerstein, E., and Hallam, J. 1978. Facilitating effects of erotica on aggression against women. *Journal of Personality and Social Psychology*, 36:1270–1277. [12]

Donnerstein, E., and Linz, D. 1984. Sexual violence in the media: A warning. *Psychology Today*, 18(January):14–15. [12]

Donnerstein, E., and Wilson, D. W. 1976. Effects of noise and perceived

control on ongoing and subsequent aggressive behavior. *Journal of Personality and Social Psychology*, 34:774–781. [12]

Donohue, W. 1985. Ethnicity and mediation. In Gudykunst, W., Stewart, L., and Ting-Toomey, S. (eds.), *Communication, Culture and Organizational Processes*. Beverly Hills, CA: Sage. [5]

Dornbusch, S. M., Carlsmith, J. M., Bushwall, S. J., Ritter, P. L., Leiderman, H., Hastorf, A. H., and Gross, R. T. 1985. Single-parents, extended households, and control of adolescents. *Child Development*, 56:326–341. [3]

Dornbusch, S. M., Mont-Reynaud, R., Ritter, P. L., Chen, Z., and Steinberg, L. 1991. Stressful events and their correlates among adolescents of diverse backgrounds. In Colten, M., and Gore, S. (eds.), *Adolescent Stress: Causes and Consequences*. New York: Aldine de Gruyter. [7]

Dornbusch, S. M., Ritter, P. L., Leiderman, P. H., Roberts, D. F., and Fraleigh, M. J. 1987. The relation of parenting style to adolescent school performance. *Child Development*, 58:1244–1257. [13]

Dosser, D., Balswick, J., and Halverson, C. 1986. Male inexpressiveness and relationships. *Journal of Social and Personal Relationships*, 3:241–256. [11]

Doval, B. 1990. A dialogized version of Piaget's theory of egocentric speech. In Doval, B. (ed.), *Conversation Organization and Its Determinants*. Norwood, NJ: Ablex. [2]

Dovidio, J. F. 1984. Helping behaviors and altruism: An empirical and conceptual overview. In Berkowitz, L. (ed.), *Advances in Experimental Social Psychology*, Vol. 17. New York: Academic Press. [10]

Dovidio, J. F., and Gaertner, S. L. (eds.). 1986. *Prejudice, Discrimination, and Racism*. New York: Academic Press. [6]

Dovidio, J. F., Mann, J., and Gaertner, S. L. 1989. Resistance to affirmative action: The implications of aversive racism. In Blanchard, F. A., and Crosby, F. J. (eds.), *Affirmative Action in Perspective*. New York: Springer-Verlag. [14]

Dovidio, J. F., Piliavin, J. A., Gaertner, S. L., Schroeder, D. P., and Clark, R. D. 1991. The arousal: Cost-reward model and the process of intervention: A review of the evidence. In Clark, M. (ed.), *Prosocial Behavior*. Newbury Park, CA: Sage, pp. 86–118. [10]

Dowd, J. J. 1991. Social psychology in a postmodern age: A discipline with a subject. *American Sociologist*, 22:188–209. [1]

Downton, J. V., Jr. 1979. *Sacred Journeys*. New York: Columbia University Press. [16]

Downton, J. V., Jr., and Wehr, P. E. 1991. Peace movements: The role of commitment and community in sustaining membership participation. *Research in Social Movements, Conflicts, and Change*, 13:113–134. [16]

Draughn, P. S. 1984. Perceptions of competence in work and marriage of middle-age men. *Journal of Marriage and the Family*, 46:403–409. [3]

Dreben, E. K., Fiske, S. T., and Hastie, R. 1979. The independence of evaluative and item information: Impression and recall order effects in behavior-based impression formation. *Journal of Personality and Social Psychology*, 37:1758–1768. [6]

Dreeben, R., and Gamoran, A. 1986. Race, instruction, and learning. *American Sociological Review*, 51:660–669. [14]

Drew, P. 1987. Pro-faced receipts of teases. *Linguistics*, 25:219–253. [5]

Drigotas, S., and Rusbult, C. 1992. Should I stay or should I go? A dependence model of breakups. *Journal of Personality and Social Psychology*, 62:62–87. [11]

Driscoll, R., Davis, K. E., and Lipetz, M. E. 1972. Parental interference and romantic love: The Romeo and Juliet effect. *Journal of Personality and Social Psychology*, 24:1–10. [11]

Drucker, P. F. 1972. *Concept of the Corporation* (rev. ed.). New York: John Day Company, p. 88. [15]

Drury, D. W. 1980. Black self-esteem and desegregated schools. *Sociology of Education*, 53:88–103. [14]

Duck, S. W. 1986. *Human Relationships: An Introduction to Social Psychology*. London: Sage. [11]

Duck, S. W., and Miell, D. E. 1986. Charting the development of personal relationships. In Gilmour, R., and Duck, S. W. (eds.), *The Emerging Field of Personal Relationships*. Hillsdale, NJ: Erlbaum, pp. 133–143. [11]

Dugger, K. 1990. Social location and gender-role attitudes: A comparison of black and white crime. In Lorber, J., and Farrell, S. A. (eds.), *The Social Construction of Gender*. New York: Sage. [6]

Dullea, G. 1982. On the pressures and politics of waiting in line. *New York Times* (February 11):17. [4]

Duncan, S., Jr. 1972. Some signals and rules for taking speaking turns in conversations. *Journal of Personality and Social Psychology*, 23:283–292. [5]

Dunn, J. 1987. The beginnings of moral understanding: Development in the second year. In Kagan, J., and Lamb, S. (eds.), *The Emergence of Morality in Young Children*. Chicago: University of Chicago Press. [2]

Dunn, J. 1988. *The Beginnings of Social Understanding*. Oxford: Basil Blackwell. [3]

Durkheim, E. 1954. *The Elementary Forms of the Religious Life*. Translated by J. W. Swain. New York: Free Press. [4]

Durkin, K. 1985. *Television, Sex Roles, and Children: A Developmental Social Psychological Account*. Philadelphia: Taylor and Francis. [3]

Dutton, D. G., and Aron, A. P. 1974. Some evidence for heightened sexual attraction under conditions of high anxiety. *Journal of Personality and Social Psychology*, 30:510–517. [11]

Duval, T. S., Duval, V. H., and Mullis, J. P. 1992. Effects of self-focus, discrepancy between self and standard, and outcome expectancy favorability on the tendency to match self to standard or to withdraw. *Journal of Personality and Social Psychology*, 62:340–348. [7]

Eagly, A. H. 1978. Sex differences in influenceability. *Psychological Bulletin*, 85:86–116. [9]

Eagly, A. H. 1983. Gender and social influence: A social psychological analysis. *American Psychologist*, 38:971–981. [9]

Eagly, A. H. 1987. *Sex Differences in Social Behavior: A Social-Role Interpretation*. Hillsdale, NJ: Erlbaum. [9]

Eagly, A. H., and Carli, L. L. 1981. Sex of researchers and sex-typed communications as determinants of sex differences in influenceability: A meta-analysis of social influence studies. *Psychological Bulletin*, 90:1–20. [9]

Eagly, A. H., and Crowley, M. 1986. Gender and helping behavior: A meta-analytic review of the social psychological literature. *Psychological Bulletin*, 100:283–308. [10]

Eagly, A. H., and Karau, S. J. 1991. Gender and the emergence of leaders: A meta-analysis. *Journal of Personality and Social Psychology*, 60:685–710. [5]

Eagly, A. H., Makhijani, M. G., and Klonsky, B. G. 1992. Gender and the evaluation of leaders: A meta-analysis. *Psychological Bulletin*, 111:3–22. [5, 6, 11]

Ebaugh, H. 1988. *Becoming an Ex: The Process of Role Exit*. Chicago: University of Chicago Press. [3]

Eccles, J. S., Jacobs, J. E., and Harold, R. D. 1990. Gender-role stereotypes, expectancy effects, and parents' socialization of gender differences. *Journal of Social Issues*, 46:183–201. [3]

Eckert, P. 1988. Adolescent social structure and the spread of linguistic change. *Language in Society*, 17:183–208. [3]

Eckert, P. 1990. Cooperative competition in adolescent "girl talk." *Discourse Process*, 13:1. [3]

Edelman, M. 1988. *Constructing the Political Spectacle*. Chicago: University of Chicago Press. [16]

Edelman, R. J. 1985. Social embarrassment: An analysis of the process. *Journal of Social and Personal Relationships*, 2:195–213. [5]

Edelman, R. J., Childs, J., Harvey, S., Kellock, I., and Stain-Clark, C. 1984. The effect of embarrassment on helping. *Journal of Social Psychology*, 124:253–254. [10]

Edelman, R. J., Evans, G., Pegg, I., and Tremain, M. 1983. Responses to physical stigma. *Perceptual and Motor Skills*, 57:294. [10]

Eder, D. 1990. Serious and playful disputes: Variation in conflict talk among female adolescents. In Grimshaw, A. (ed.), *Conflict Talk: Sociolinguistic Investigations of Arguments in Conversation*. Cambridge, England: Cambridge University Press. [5]

Edinger, J. A., and Patterson, M. L. 1983. Nonverbal involvement and social control. *Psychological Bulletin*, 93:30–56. [5]

Egeland, B., Jacobvitz, D., and Papatola, D. 1987. Intergenerational continuity of abuse. In Gelles, R. J., and Lancaster, J. B. (eds.), *Child Abuse and Neglect: Biosocial Dimensions*. Hawthorne, NY: Aldine de Gruyter. [12]

Egeland, B., Jacobvitz, D., and Sroufe, L. A. 1988. Breaking the cycle of abuse. *Child Development*, 59:1080–1088. [12]

Eggert, L. L., and Parks, M. R. 1987. Communication network involvement in adolescents' friendships and romantic relationships. In McLaughlin, M. L. (ed.), *Communication Yearbook*, Vol. 10. Newbury Park, CA: Sage, pp. 283–322. [11]

Ehrensaft, D. 1987. *Parenting Together*. New York: Free Press. [4]

Eisenberg, N., and Fabes, R. A. 1991. Prosocial behavior and empathy: A multimethod developmental perspective. In Clark, M. S. (ed.), *Prosocial Behavior: Vol. 12. Review of Personality and Social Psychology*. Newbury Park, CA: Sage, pp. 34–61. [10]

Ekman, P. 1980. *The Face of Man: Expressions of Universal Emotion in a New Guinea Village*. New York: Garland STPM Press. [5]

Ekman, P., Friesen, W., and Bear, J. 1984. The international language of gestures. *Psychology Today*, 18(May): 64–69. [5, 11]

Ekman, P., Friesen, W., O'Sullivan, N., Chan, A., Diacoyanni-Tarlatzis, I., Heider, K., Krause, R., LeCompte, W. A., Pitcairn, T., Ricci-Bitti, P. E., Scherer, K., Tomita, M., and Tzavaras, A. 1987. Universals and cultural differences in the judgments of facial expressions of emotion. *Journal of Personality and Social Psychology*, 53:712–717. [5, 11]

Elder, G. H., Jr. 1974. *Children of the Great Depression*. Chicago: University of Chicago Press. [3]

Elder, G. H., Jr. 1975. Age differentiation and the life course. In Inkeles, A., Coleman, J., and Smelser, N. (eds.), *Annual Review of Sociology*, Vol. 1. Palo Alto, CA: Annual Reviews. [1]

Elder, G. H., Jr. 1978. Approaches to social change and the family. *American Journal of Sociology*, 84(suppl): 170–199. [3]

Elder, G. H., Jr. 1985. Perspectives on the life course. In Elder, G. H., Jr. (ed.), *Life Course Dynamics*. Ithaca, NY: Cornell University Press. [3]

Elder, G. H., Jr. 1987. Families and lives: Some developments in life-course studies. In Hareven, T. K., and Plakans, A. (eds.), *Family History at the Crossroads*. Princeton, NJ: Princeton University Press. [3]

Elliott, D. S., and Ageton, S. S. 1980. Reconciling race and class differences in self-reported and official estimates of delinquency. *American Sociological Review*, 45:95–110. [15]

Elliott, D. S., and Huizinga, D. 1983. Social class and delinquent behavior in a national youth panel, 1976–1980. *Criminology*, 21:149–177. [15]

Elliott, D. S., Huizinga, D., and Ageton, S. 1985. *Explaining Delinquency and Drug Use*. Beverly Hills, CA: Sage. [15]

Elliott, G. C., and Meeker, B. F. 1984. Modifiers of the equity effect: Group outcome and causes for individual performance. *Journal of Personality and Social Psychology*, 46:586–597. [9]

Ellis, D. 1991. The two sides of warspeak. *Time* (February 25):13. [5]

Ellis, D. P. 1987. *The Wrong Stuff*. Ontario: Collier Macmillan Canada. [15]

Ellis, D. P., Weiner, P., and Miller, L. 1971. Does the trigger pull the finger? An experimental test of weapons as aggression-eliciting stimuli. *Sociometry*, 34:453–466. [12]

Ellis, G., Lee, G., and Petersen, L. 1978. Supervision and conformity: A cross-cultural analysis of parental socialization. *American Journal of Sociology*, 84:386–403. [13]

Ellison, C. G., and London, B. 1992. The social and political participation of black Americans: Compensatory and ethnic community perspectives revisited. *Social Forces*, 70:681–701. [16]

Emerson, R. M. 1962. Power-dependence relations. *American Sociological Review*, 27:31-41. [1]

Emerson, R. M. 1981. Social exchange theory. In Rosenberg, M., and Turner, R. H. (eds.), *Social Psychology: Sociological Perspectives*. New York: Basic Books. [10]

Emery, R. E. 1982. Interparental conflict and the children of discord and divorce. *Psychological Bulletin*, 92: 310–330. [15]

England, P., and Dunn, D. 1988. Evaluating work and comparable worth. *Annual Review of Sociology*, 14:227–248. [14]

England, P., Farkas, G., Stanek Kilbourne, B., and Dou, T. 1988. Explaining occupational sex segregation and wages: Findings from a model with fixed effects. *American Sociological Review*, 53:544–558. [16]

Epstein, C. F. 1988. *Deceptive Distinctions: Sex, Gender, and the Social Order*. New York: Russell Sage Foundation. [5]

Epstein, J. L. 1985. After the bus arrives: Resegregation in desegregated schools. *Journal of Social Issues*, 41: 23–44. [14]

Erickson, F. 1975. Gatekeeping and the melting pot. *Harvard Educational Review*, 45:44–70. [3, 14]

Erickson, F. 1979. Talking down: Some cultural sources of miscommunication in interracial interviews. In Wolfgang, A. (ed.), *Nonverbal Behavior*. New York: Academic Press. [5]

Erikson, E. 1950. *Childhood and Society*. New York: Norton. [2]

Erikson, E. 1959. Identity and the life cycle. *Psychological Issues*, Monograph 1, Vol. 1. New York: International University Press. [7]

Ermann, M. D., and Lundman, R. J. 1982. *Corporate Deviance*. New York: Holt, Rinehart & Winston. [15]

Etzioni, A. 1988. *The Moral Dimension: Toward a New Economics*. New York: Free Press. [10]

Evans, W. M., and Zelditch, M., Jr. 1961. A laboratory experiment on bureaucratic authority. *American Sociological Review*, 26:883–893. [13]

Everett, K. D. 1992. Professionalization and protest: Changes in the social movement sector, 1961–1983. *Social Forces*, 70:957–975. [16]

Evertson, C. 1982. Differences in instructional activities in higher and lower achieving junior high English and math classes. *Elementary School Journal*, 82:329–350. [14]

Fader, S. 1984. Finding "hidden jobs." *Working Women* (June):42–45. [4]

Fagan, J., Slaughter, E., and Hartstone, E. 1987. Blind justice? The impact of race on the juvenile justice process. *Crime and Delinquency*, 33: 224–258. [15]

Fagot, B. I., Hagan, R., Linebach, M. D., and Kronsberg, S. 1985. Differential reactions to assertive and communicative acts of toddler boys and girls. *Child Development*, 56: 1499–1505. [3]

Faison, S. 1992. Sears will pay $8 million to settle repair complaints. *New York Times* (September 3):D5. [15]

Fantz, R. L. 1967. Visual perception and experience in early infancy: A look at the hidden side of behavior development. In Stevenson, H. W., Hess, E.

H., and Reingold, H. L. (eds.), *Early Behavior: Comparative and Developmental Approaches*. New York: Wiley. [2]

Farrell, R. A., and Swigert, V. L. (eds.). 1988. *Social Deviance* (3rd ed.). Belmont, CA: Wadsworth. [15]

Farrington, D. 1989. Early predictors of adolescent aggression and adult violence. *Violence and Victims*, 4:79–100. [15]

Fazio, R. H., Effrein, E., and Falander, V. 1981. Self–perceptions following social interaction. *Journal of Personality and Social Psychology*, 41:232–242. [7]

Fazio, R. H., Zanna, M. P., and Cooper, J. 1977. Dissonance and self-perception: An integrative view of each theory's proper domain of application. *Journal of Experimental Social Psychology*, 13:464–479. [8]

Fazio, R. H., Zanna, M. P., and Cooper, J. 1979. On the relationship of data to theory: A reply to Ronis and Greenwald. *Journal of Experimental Social Psychology*, 15:70–76. [8]

Feagin, J. R. 1987. Changing back Americans to fit a racist system. *Journal of Social Issues*, 43:85–89. [14]

Feather, N. T., and Simon, J. G. 1975. Reactions to male and female success and failure in sex-linked occupations: Impressions of personality, causal attributions, and perceived likelihood of different consequences. *Journal of Personality and Social Psychology*, 31:20–31. [6]

Federal Bureau of Investigation. 1986. *Crime in the United States: Uniform Crime Reports, 1985.* Washington, DC: U.S. Government Printing Office. [15]

Federbush, M. 1974. The sex problem of school math books. In Stacy, J., et al. (eds.), *And Jill Came Tumbling After: Sexism in American Education*. New York: Dell. [3]

Feingold, A. 1988. Matching for attractiveness in romantic partners in same-sex friends: A meta-analysis and theoretical critique. *Psychological Bulletin*, 104:226–235. [11]

Feldman-Summers, S., Montano, D. E., Kasprzyk, D., and Wagner, B. 1980. Influence attempts when competing views are gender related. *Psychology of Women Quarterly*, 5: 311–320. [9]

Felmlee, D., Sprecher, S., and Bassin, E. 1990. The dissolution of intimate relationships: A hazard model. *Social Psychology Quarterly*, 53:13–30. [11]

Felson, R. B. 1981. Social sources of information in the development of self. *Sociological Quarterly*, 22:69–80. [7]

Felson, R. B. 1985. Reflected appraisal and the development of self. *Social Psychology Quarterly*, 48:71–78. [7]

Felson, R. B., and Reed, M. 1986. The effects of parents on the self-appraisals of children. *Social Psychology Quarterly*, 49:302–308. [7]

Felson, R. B., and Tedeschi, J. T. 1991. A theory of coercive actions: An integration of research on conflict, influence, aggression, and violent crime. Paper presented at the Conference on Social Interactionist Approaches to Aggression and Violence, State University of New York at Albany (April). [12]

Fendrich, J. M., and Turner, R. W. 1989. The transition from student to adult politics. *Social Forces*, 67: 1049–1057. [16]

Fenstermaker, S., West, C., and Zimmerman, D. H. 1991. Stalking gender inequality: New conceptual terrain. In Blumberg, R. L. (ed.), *Gender, Family and Economy: The Triple Overlap*. Beverly Hills, CA: Sage. [14]

Fernald, A. 1985. Four-month old infants prefer to listen to motherese. *Infant Behavior and Development*, 8: 181–195. [5]

Ferree, M. M. 1987. Family and job for working-class women: Gender and class systems seen from below. In Gerstel, N., and Gross, H. E. (eds.), *Families and Work*. Philadelphia: Temple University Press. [14]

Ferree, M. M., and Miller, F. D. 1985. Mobilization and meaning: Toward an integration of social psychological and resource perspectives on social movements. *Sociological Inquiry*, 55:38–61. [16]

Festinger, L. 1957. *A Theory of Cognitive Dissonance*. New York: Harper & Row. [8]

Festinger, L., and Carlsmith, J. M. 1959. Cognitive consequences of forced compliance. *Journal of Abnormal and Social Psychology*, 58:203–210. [8]

Festinger, L., Riecken, H. W., Jr., and Schachter, S. 1956. *When Prophecy Fails*. Minneapolis: University of Minnesota Press. [8]

Filer, R. 1989. Occupational segregation, compensating differentials, and

comparable worth. In Michael, R. T., Hartmann, H. I., and O'Farrell, B. (eds.), *Pay Equity: Empirical Inquiries*. Washington, DC: National Academy Press, pp. 153–171. [14]

Filsinger, E. E., and Thoma, S. J. 1988. Behavioral antecedents of relationship stability and adjustment: A five-year longitudinal study. *Journal of Marriage and the Family*, 50:785–795. [11]

Findlay, S. 1986. Cancer risk higher for poor. *USA Today* (October 7):1D. [14]

Fine, G. A. 1979. Small groups and culture creation: The idioculture of Little League baseball teams. *American Sociological Review*, 44:733–745. [4]

Fine, G. A. 1987. *With the Boys: Little League Baseball and Preadolescent Culture*. Chicago: University of Chicago Press. [3]

Fine, M. 1986. Perceptions of stepparents: Variations in stereotypes as a function of current family structure. *Journal of Marriage and the Family*, 48:537–543. [6]

Finkelhor, D., and Yllo, K. 1985. *License to Rape: Sexual Abuse of Wives*. New York: Holt, Rinehart & Winston. [12]

Fishbein, M. 1980. A theory of reasoned action: Some applications and implications. In Howe, H., and Page, M. (eds.), *Nebraska Symposium on Motivation*, Vol. 27. Lincoln: University of Nebraska Press. [8]

Fishbein, M., and Ajzen, I. 1975. *Belief, Attitude, Intention, and Behavior: An Introduction to Theory and Research*. Reading, MA: Addison-Wesley. [8]

Fishbein, M. D., and Thelen, M. H. 1981. Psychological factors in mate selection and marital satisfaction: A review. *JSAS: Catalog of Selected Documents in Psychology*, vol. 11. Greenwich, CT: Johnson Associates Inc. in cooperation with the American Psychological Association. [11]

Fishman, P. M. 1978. Interaction: The work women do. *Social Problems*, 25:397–406. [5]

Fishman, P. M. 1980. Conversational insecurity. In Giles, H., and Robinson, W. P. (eds.), *Language: Social Psychological Perspectives*. New York: Pergamon. [5]

Fiske, A. P. 1991. The cultural relativity of selfish individualism: Anthropological evidence that humans are inherently sociable. In Clark, M. S.

(ed.), *Prosocial Behavior: Vol. 12. Review of Personality and Social Psychology.* Newbury Park, CA: Sage, pp. 176–214. [10]

Fiske, S. T., and Taylor, S. E. 1991. *Social Cognition.* New York: McGraw-Hill. [1, 6, 7]

Flacks, R. 1990. Social bases of activist identity: Comment on Braungart article. *Political Psychology,* 11:283–292. [16]

Fletcher, G. J. O., and Ward, C. 1988. Attribution theory and processes: Cross-cultural perspective. In Bond, M. H. (ed.), *The Cross-Cultural Challenge to Social Psychology.* Newbury Park, CA: Sage. [7]

Foa, U. G., and Foa, E. B. 1974. *Societal Structures of the Mind.* Springfield, IL: Charles C. Thomas. [10]

Fogarty, M., Rapaport, R., and Rapaport, R. 1971. *Sex, Career and Family.* Prepared jointly by Political and Economic Planning and the Tavistock Institute. London: Allen & Unwin. [5]

Folger, R., Rosenfield, D., and Robinson, T. 1983. Relative deprivation and procedural justifications. *Journal of Personality and Social Psychology,* 45:268–273. [16]

Folkes, V. S. 1982*a*. Communicating the reasons for social rejection. *Journal of Experimental Social Psychology,* 18:235–252. [15]

Folkes, V. S. 1982*b*. Forming relationships and the matching hypothesis. *Personality and Social Psychology Bulletin,* 8:631–636. [11]

Ford, D. A. 1983. Wife battery and criminal justice: A study of victim decision-making. *Family Relations,* 32:463–475. [12]

Forsyth, D. R. 1990. *Group Dynamics.* Pacific Grove, CA: Brooks/Cole. [9]

Foss, R. D. 1981. Structural effects in simulated jury decision-making. *Journal of Personality and Social Psychology,* 40:1055–1062. [9]

Fox, M. F., and Hesse-Biber, S. 1984. *Women at Work.* Palo Alto, CA: Mayfield. [3]

Frager, R. 1970. Conformity and anti-conformity in Japan. *Journal of Personality and Social Psychology,* 15:207–210. [9]

Frank, N. 1988. Unintended murder and corporate risk-taking: Defining the concept of justifiability. *Journal of Criminal Justice,* 16:17–24. [15]

Frankfort-Nachmias, C., and Nachmias, D. 1992. *Research Methods in the Social Sciences* (4th ed.). New York: St. Martin's Press. [1]

Franklin, B. 1969. Operant reinforcement of prayer. *Journal of Applied Behavior Analysis,* 2:247. Submitted by B. F. Skinner. [1]

Freedman, J. L. 1965. Long-term behavioral effects of cognitive dissonance. *Journal of Experimental Social Psychology,* 1: 145–155. [8]

Freedman, J. L. 1984. Effect of television violence on aggressiveness. *Psychological Bulletin,* 96:227–246. [12]

Freedman, J. L. 1986. Television violence and aggression: A rejoinder. *Psychological Bulletin,* 100:372–378. [12]

Freedman, J. L., Cunningham, J., and Krismer, K. 1992. Inferred values and the reverse-incentive effect in induced compliance. *Journal of Personality and Social Psychology,* 62: 357–368. [8]

Freedman, J. L., and Fraser, S. C. 1966. Compliance without pressure: The foot-in-the-door technique. *Journal of Personality and Social Psychology,* 4:195–202. [13]

Freedman, J. L., Wallington, S. A., and Bless, E. 1967. Compliance without pressure: The effect of guilt. *Journal of Personality and Social Psychology,* 7:117–124. [13]

French, J. R. P., and Raven, B. H. 1959. The bases of social power. In Cartwright, D. (ed.), *Studies in Social Power.* Ann Arbor: University of Michigan Press. [13]

Friedrich-Cofer, L., and Huston, A. C. 1986. Television violence and aggression: The debate continues. *Psychological Bulletin,* 100:364–371. [12]

Fuller, R., and Schoenberger, R. 1991. The gender salary gap: Do academic achievement, internship experience, and college major make a difference? *Social Science Quarterly,* 72:715–726. [14]

Furrow, D., and Nelson, K. 1986. A further look at the motherese hypothesis: A reply to Gleitman, Newport, and Gleitman. *Journal of Child Language,* 13:163–176. [2]

Gaesser, D. L., and Whitbourne, S. K. 1985. Work identity and marital adjustment in blue-collar men. *Journal of Marriage and the Family,* 47:747–751. [3]

Galanter, M. 1983. Unification church ("Moonie") dropouts: Psychological readjustment after leaving a charismatic religious group. *American Journal of Psychiatry,* 140:984–989. [16]

Gallup, G., Jr. 1983. *The Gallup Poll: Public Opinion 1982.* Wilmington, DE: Scholarly Resources. [3]

Gallup, G., Jr. 1988. Gallup poll shows more Americans say premarital sex is wrong, reversing trend of last twenty years. *Family Planning Perspectives,* 20:180–181. [11]

Gallup, G., Jr., and Newport, F. 1991. Blacks and whites differ on civil rights progress. *Gallup Poll Monthly* (August):54–64. [14]

Gamson, W. A. 1961. A theory of coalition formation. *American Sociological Review,* 26:373–382. [12]

Gamson, W. A. 1964. Experimental studies of coalition formation. In Berkowitz, L. (ed.), *Advances in Experimental Social Psychology,* Vol. 1. New York: Academic Press. [12]

Gamson, W. A., and Modigliani, A. 1989. Media discourse and public opinion on nuclear power: A constructionist approach. *American Journal of Sociology,* 95:1–37. [16]

Gardner, C. B. 1991. Stigma and the public self. *Journal of Contemporary Ethnography,* 20:251–262. [15]

Gardner, R., Lalonde, R., Nero, A., and Young, M. 1988. Ethnic stereotypes: Implications of measurement strategy. *Social Cognition,* 6:40–60. [6]

Garfinkel, H. 1964. Studies of the routine grounds of everyday activities. *Social Problems,* 11:225–250. [1]

Garfinkel, H. 1967. *Studies in Ethnomethodology.* Englewood Cliffs, NJ: Prentice-Hall. [1, 7]

Gaskell, J. 1985. Course enrollment in the high school: The perspective of working-class females. *Sociology of Education,* 58:48–59. [3]

Gecas, V. 1979. The influence of social class on socialization. In Burr, W. R., et al. (eds.), *Contemporary Theories about the Family,* Vol. 1. New York: Free Press. [3]

Gecas, V. 1981. Contexts of socialization. In Rosenberg, M., and Turner, R. H. (eds.), *Social Psychology: Sociological Perspectives.* New York: Basic Books. [3]

Gecas, V. 1982. The self concept. In

Turner, R., and Short, J. (eds.), *Annual Review of Sociology*, 8:1–33. [7]

Gecas, V. 1989. The social psychology of self-efficacy. *Annual Review of Sociology*, 15:1291–316. [7]

Gecas, V., and Schwalbe, M. L. 1986. Parental behavior and adolescent self-esteem. *Journal of Marriage and the Family*, 48:37–46. [7]

Gecas, V., and Seff, M. A. 1990. Social class and self-esteem: Psychological centrality, compensation, and the relative effects of work and home. *Social Psychology Quarterly*, 53:165–173. [7]

Gecas, V., and Seff, M. A. 1991. Families and adolescents. In Booth, A. (ed.), *Contemporary Families: Looking Forward, Looking Back*. Minneapolis, MN: National Council on Family Relations. [13]

Geen, R. G. 1968. Effects of frustration, attack, and prior training in aggressiveness upon aggressive behavior. *Journal of Personality and Social Psychology*, 9:316–321. [12]

Geen, R. G. 1989. Alternative conceptions of social facilitation. In Paulus, P. B. (ed.), *Psychology of Group Influence*. Hillsdale, NJ: Erlbaum. [9]

Geen, R. G., and Berkowitz, L. 1967. Some conditions facilitating the occurrence of aggression after the observance of violence. *Journal of Personality*, 35:666–676. [12]

Geen, R. G., Stonner, D., and Shope, G. L. 1975. The facilitation of aggression by aggression: Evidence against the catharsis hypothesis. *Journal of Personality and Social Psychology*, 35:721–726. [12]

Geerken, M. R., and Gove, W. R. 1977. Deterrence, overload, and incapacitation: An empirical evaluation. *Social Forces*, 56:424–447. [15]

Geis, G. 1984. White-collar and corporate crime. In Meier, R. F. (ed.), *Major Forms of Crime*. Beverly Hills, CA: Sage. [15]

Geis, M. L. 1987. *The Language of Politics*. New York: Springer-Verlag. [5]

Gelles, R. J., and Cornell, C. P. 1990. *Intimate Violence in Families*. Newbury Park, CA: Sage. [12]

Gelles, R. J., and Straus, M. A. 1988. *Intimate Violence*. New York: Simon & Schuster. [12]

Gentry, W. D. 1970. Effects of frustration, attack, and prior aggressive training on aggression and vascular processes. *Journal of Personality and Social Psychology*, 16:718–725. [12]

Gerbasi, K. C., Zuckerman, M., and Reis, H. T. 1977. Justice needs a new blindfold: A review of mock jury research. *Psychological Bulletin*, 84: 323–345. [9]

Gergen, K. J. 1971. *The Concept of Self*. New York: Holt, Rinehart & Winston. [7, 13]

Gergen, K. J. 1991. *The Saturated Self: Dilemmas of Identity in Contemporary Life*. New York: Basic Books. [1]

Gergen, K. J., and Wishnov, B. 1965. Others' self-evaluations and interaction anticipation as determinants of self-presentation. *Journal of Personality and Social Psychology*, 2:348–358. [7]

Gerhart, B. A., and Milkovich, G. T. 1989. Salaries, salary growth, and promotions for men and women in a large, private firm. In Michael, R. T., Hartmann, H. I., and O'Farrell, B. (eds.), *Pay Equity: Empirical Inquiries*. Washington, DC: National Academy Press. [14]

Gewirtz, J. L. 1990. Social influence on child and parent via stimulation and operant-learning mechanisms. In Lewis, M., and Feinman, S. (eds.), *Social Influence and Socialization in Infancy*. New York: Plenum. [2]

Gibbons, D. C., and Krohn, M. D. 1986. *Deviant Behavior* (4th ed.). Englewood Cliffs, NJ: Prentice-Hall. [15]

Gibbons, F. X., Gerrard, M., Lando, H. A., and McGovern, P. G. 1991. Social comparison and smoking cessation: The role of the "typical smoker." *Journal of Experimental Social Psychology*, 27:239–258. [7]

Gibbons, F. X., and McCoy, S. B. 1991. Self-esteem, similarity, and reactions to active versus passive downward comparison. *Journal of Personality and Social Psychology*, 60:414–424. [7]

Gibbs, J. 1986. Assessment of depression in urban adolescent females: Implications for early intervention strategies. *American Journal of Psychiatry*, 6:50–56. [7]

Gibbs, J. P. 1975. *Crime, Punishment and Deterrence*. New York: Elsevier. [15]

Gibbs, N. 1991. When is it rape? *Time*, 137(June 3):48–54. [12]

Gibson, M. L. 1991. Public goods, alienation, and political protest: The sanctuary movement as a test of the public goods model of collective rebellious behavior. *Political Psychology*, 12:623–651. [16]

Gillespie, D. 1971. Who has the power? The marital struggle. *Journal of Marriage and the Family*, 33:445–458. [13]

Gilligan, C. 1982a. *In a Different Voice: Psychological Theory and Women's Development*. Cambridge, MA: Harvard University Press. [2, 9]

Gilligan, C. 1982b. Why should a woman be more like a man? *Psychology Today*, 16(June):68–77. [2]

Ginsberg, I. J., and Greenley, J. R. 1978. Competing theories of marijuana use: A longitudinal study. *Journal of Health and Social Behavior*, 19:22–34. [15]

Givens, D. 1983. *Love Signals: How to Attract a Mate*. New York: Crown. [5]

Glassner, B., Ksander, M., Berg, B., and Johnson, B. 1983. A note on the deterrent effect of juvenile vs. adult jurisdiction. *Social Problems*, 31: 219–221. [15]

Glenn, E., and Tolbert, C. 1987. Technology and emerging patterns of stratification for women of color: Race and gender in computer work. In Wright, B. (ed.), *Women, Work and Technology*. Ann Arbor: University of Michigan Press. [14]

Glenn, N. D. 1991. Quantitative research on marital quality in the 1980's: A critical review. In Booth, A. (ed.), *Contemporary Families: Looking Forward, Looking Back*. Minneapolis, MN: National Council on Family Relations. [3]

Glenn, N. D., and McLanahan, S. 1982. Children and marital happiness: A further specification of the relationship. *Journal of Marriage and the Family*, 44:63–72. [3]

Glenn, N. D., and Weaver, C. N. 1981. The contribution of marital happiness to global happiness. *Journal of Marriage and the Family*, 43: 161–168. [4]

Glenn, N. D., and Weaver, C. N. 1988. The changing relationship of marital status to reported happiness. *Journal of Marriage and the Family*, 50:317–324. [4]

Goethals, G. R., Cooper, J., and Naficy, A. 1979. Role of foreseen, foreseeable, and unforeseeable behavioral consequences in the arousal of cognitive dissonance. *Journal of Personality and Social Psychology*, 37: 1179–1185. [8]

Goff, R. 1949. *Problems and Emotional Difficulties in Negro Children.* New York: Columbia University Press. [14]

Goffman, E. 1955. On facework: An analysis of ritual elements in social interaction. *Psychiatry*, 18:213–231. [5]

Goffman, E. 1959. *The Presentation of Self in Everyday Life.* Garden City, NY: Doubleday. [4, 5, 7, 11]

Goffman, E. 1961a. *Asylums.* New York: Doubleday Anchor. [3]

Goffman, E. 1961b. *Encounters.* Indianapolis: Bobbs-Merrill. [4, 7]

Goffman, E. 1963a. *Behavior in Public Places.* New York: Free Press. [1]

Goffman, E. 1963b. *Stigma: Notes on the Management of Spoiled Identity.* Englewood Cliffs, NJ: Prentice-Hall. [5, 15]

Goffman, E. 1967. *Interaction Ritual.* Garden City, NY: Doubleday. [1]

Goffman, E. 1971. *Relations in Public.* New York: Basic Books. [1, 5]

Goffman, E. 1974. *Frame Analysis: An Essay on the Organization of Experience.* New York: Harper & Row. [8]

Goffman, E. 1981. *Forms of Talk.* Philadelphia: University of Pennsylvania Press. [1, 4, 5, 7]

Goldberg, C. 1974. Sex roles, task competence and conformity. *Journal of Psychology*, 86:157–164. [9]

Goldberg, C. 1975. Conformity to a majority as a function of task type and acceptance of sex-related stereotypes. *Journal of Psychology*, 89:25–37. [9]

Goleman, D. 1984. Order found in the development of emotions. *New York Times* (June 19):C1, C8. [2]

Goleman, D. 1985. Great altruists: Science ponders soul of goodness. *New York Times* (March 5):19, 22. [10]

Gonsiorek, J. C., and Weinrich, J. D. 1991. The definition and scope of sexual orientation. In Gonsiorek, J. C., and Weinrich, J. D. (eds.), *Homosexuality: Research Implications for Public Policy.* Newbury Park, CA: Sage. [15]

Gonzales, M. H., Davis, J. M., Loney, G. L., KuKens, C. K., and Junghans, C. M. 1983. Interactional approach to interpersonal attraction. *Journal of Personality and Social Psychology*, 44:1192–1197. [11]

Gonzenbach, W. J. 1992. A time-series analysis of the drug problem, 1985–1990: The press, the president, and public opinion. *International Jour-*

nal of Public Opinion Research, 4: 126–147. [16]

Goodman, A. B., Siegel, C., Craig, T. J., and Lin, S. P. 1983. The relationship between socioeconomic class and prevalence of schizophrenia, alcoholism, and affective disorders treated by inpatient care in a suburban area. *American Journal of Psychiatry*, 140:166–170. [14]

Goodstadt, B. E., and Hjelle, L. A. 1973. Power to the powerless: Locus of control and the use of power. *Journal of Personality and Social Psychology*, 27:190–196. [13]

Goodstadt, B. E., and Kipnis, D. 1970. Situational influences on the use of power. *Journal of Applied Psychology*, 54:201–207. [13]

Goodstein, R. K., and Page, A. W. 1981. Battered wife syndrome: Overview of dynamics and treatment. *American Journal of Psychiatry*, 138: 1036–1044. [12]

Goodwin, C. 1987a. Forgetfulness as an interactive resource. *Social Psychology Quarterly*, 50:115–131. [5]

Goodwin, C. 1987b. Unilateral departure. In Button, G., and Lee, J. (eds.), *Talk and Social Organization.* Clevedon, England: Multilingual Matters Ltd. [5]

Goodwin, C., and Heritage, J. 1990. Conversation analysis. *Annual Review of Anthropology*, 19:283–307. [5]

Goodwin, M. H. 1980. Directive/response speech sequences in girls' and boys' task activities. In McConnell-Ginet, S., Borker, R., and Furman, N. (eds.), *Women and Language in Literature and Society.* New York: Praeger. [5]

Goodwin, M. H., and Goodwin, C. 1987. Children's arguing. In Phillips, S. U., Steele, S., and Tanz, C. (eds.), *Language, Gender, and Sex in Comparative Perspective.* New York: Cambridge University Press, pp. 200–248. [3]

Gordon, L. 1986. College student stereotypes of blacks and jews on two campuses: Four studies spanning 50 years. *Sociology and Social Research*, 70: 200–201. [6]

Gottfredson, M., and Hirschi, T. 1986. The true value of lambda would appear to be zero: An essay on career criminals, criminal careers, selective incapacitation, cohort studies, and related topics. *Criminology*, 24: 213–234. [15]

Gottfredson, M., and Hirschi, T.

1990. *A General Theory of Crime.* Stanford, CA: Stanford University Press. [15]

Gottlieb, J., and Carver, C. S. 1980. Anticipation of future interaction and the bystander effect. *Journal of Experimental Social Psychology*, 16:253–260. [10]

Gottman, J. M., and Levenson, R. S. 1988. The social psychophysiology of marriage. In Noller, P., and Fitzpatrick, M. A. (eds.), *Perspectives on Marital Interaction.* Clevedon, England, and Philadelphia: Multilingual Matters Ltd., pp. 182–202. [11]

Gouldner, A. W. 1960. The norm of reciprocity: A preliminary statement. *American Sociological Review*, 25: 161–178. [10]

Gouldner, H. P. 1978. *Teacher's Pets, Troublemakers and Nobodies: Black Children in Elementary School.* Westport, CT: Greenwood Press. [3]

Gove, W. R., and Crutchfield, R. D. 1982. The family and delinquency. *Sociological Quarterly*, 23:301–319. [15]

Graber, D. A. 1984. *Mass Media and American Politics* (2nd ed.). Washington, DC: CQ Press. [16]

Graham, H. 1987. Women's smoking and family health. *Social Science and Medicine*, 25:47–56. [15]

Granberg, D., and Holmberg, S. 1991. The intention-behavior relationship among U.S. and Swedish voters. *Social Psychology Quarterly*, 53:44–54. [8]

Granovetter, M. S. 1973. The strength of weak ties. *American Journal of Sociology*, 78:1360–1380. [4]

Granovetter, M. S. 1982. The strength of weak ties: A network theory revisited. In Collins, R. (ed.), *Sociological Theory 1983.* San Francisco, CA: Jossey-Bass, Chap. 7. [4]

Grasmick, H. G., Bursik, R. J., and Kinsey, K. A. 1991. Shame and embarrassment as deterrents to noncompliance with the law: The case of an antilittering campaign. *Environment and Behavior*, 23:233–251. [13]

Gray, L. N., and Tallman, I. 1987. Theories of choice: Contingent reward and punishment applications. *Social Psychology Quarterly*, 50:16–23. [10, 13]

Green, R. 1978. Sexual identity of 37 children raised by homosexual or transsexual parents. *American Journal of Psychiatry*, 135:692–697. [15]

Green, S. K., Buchanan, D. R., and Heuer, S. K. 1984. Winners, losers, and choosers: A field investigation of dating initiation. *Personality and Social Psychology Bulletin*, 10:502–511. [11]

Greenberg, J., and Pyszczynski, T. 1985. Compensatory self-inflation: A response to the threat to self-regard of public failure. *Journal of Personality and Social Psychology*, 49:273–280. [8]

Greenberg, S. 1985. Educational equity in early educational environments. In Klein, S. (ed.), *Handbook for Achieving Sex Equity through Education*. Baltimore, MD: Johns Hopkins University Press. [14]

Greenwald, A. G. 1975. On the inconclusiveness of "crucial" cognitive tests of dissonance versus self-perception theories. *Journal of Experimental Social Psychology*, 11:490–499. [8]

Greenwald, A. G. 1980. The totalitarian ego: Fabrication and revision of personal history. *American Psychologist*, 35:608–616. [7]

Greenwald, A. G. 1982. Is anyone in charge? Person-analysis versus the principle of personal unity. In Suls, J. (ed.), *Psychological Perspectives on the Self*. Hillsdale, NJ: Erlbaum. [7]

Greenwell, J., and Dengerink, H. A. 1973. The role of perceived versus actual attack in human physical aggression. *Journal of Personality and Social Psychology*, 26:66–71. [12]

Greer, D. 1983. Spectator booing and the home advantage: A study of social influence in the basketball arena. *Social Psychology Quarterly*, 46:252–261. [4]

Grice, H. P. 1975. Logic and conversation. In Cole, P., and Morgan, J. L. (eds.), *Syntax and Semantics: 3. Speech Acts*. New York: Academic Press. [5]

Grice, H. P. 1978. Some further notes on logic and conversation. In Cole, P. (ed.), *Syntax and Semantics: 9. Pragmatics*. New York: Academic Press. [5]

Griffin, C. 1985. *Typical Girls? Young Women from School to the Job Market*. London: Routledge & Kegan Paul. [11]

Griffin, E., and Sparks, G. G. 1990. Friends forever: A longitudinal exploration of intimacy in same-sex friends and platonic pairs. *Journal of Social and Personal Relationships*, 7:29–46. [11]

Griffith, W. I., and Gray, L. N. 1985. A note on the "social law of effect": Expanding the model. *Social Forces*, 63:1030–1037. [13]

Griffitt, W., and Veitch, R. 1971. Hot and crowded: Influence of population density and temperature on in-

terpersonal affective behavior. *Journal of Personality and Social Psychology*, 17:92–98. [12]

Grigg, F., Fletcher, G. J., and Fitness, J. 1989. Spontaneous attributions in happy and unhappy dating relationships. *Journal of Social and Personal Relationships*, 6:61–68. [11]

Grube, J. W., and Morgan, M. 1990. Attitude–social support interactions: Contingent consistency effects in the prediction of adolescent smoking, drinking, and drug use. *Social Psychology Quarterly*, 53:329–339. [8]

Grusec, J. E. 1991. The socialization of altruism. In Clark, M. S. (ed.), *Prosocial Behavior: Vol. 12. Review of Personality and Social Psychology*. Newbury Park, CA: Sage, pp. 9–33. [10]

Guimond, S., and Dubé-Simard, L. 1983. Relative deprivation theory and the Quebec Nationalist movement: The cognition-emotion distinction and the personal-group deprivation issue. *Journal of Personality and Social Psychology*, 44:526–535. [16]

Gurr, T. R. 1970. *Why Men Rebel*. Princeton, NJ: Princeton University Press. [16]

Haar, C. M., and Fessler, D. W. 1986. *The Wrong Side of the Tracks*. New York: Simon & Schuster. [14]

Haas, D. F., and Deseran, F. A. 1981. Trust and symbolic exchange. *Social Psychology Quarterly*, 44:3–13. [10]

Haefner, M. J., Metts, S., and Wartella, E. 1989. Siblings' strategies for resolving conflict over television program choice. *Communication Quarterly*, 37:223–230. [13]

Hagestad, G. O. 1986. The aging society as a context for family life. *Daedalus*, 115:119–139. [3]

Hagestad, G. O., and Smyer, M. A. 1982. Types of divorce and their consequences. In Duck, S. W. (ed.), *Personal Relationships: 4. Dissolving Personal Relationships*. New York: Academic Press. [11]

Hahlweg, K., Revenstorf, D., and Schindler, L. 1984. Effects of behavioural marital therapy on couples' communication and problem-solving skills. *Journal of Consulting and Clinical Psychology*, 52:553–566. [11]

Hall, E. T. 1966. *Hidden Dimension*. Garden City, NY: Doubleday. [5]

Hall, J. A. 1978. Gender effects in decoding nonverbal cues. *Psychological Bulletin*, 85:845–857. [5]

Hall, J. A. 1984. *Nonverbal Sex Differ-

ences: Communication Accuracy and Expressive Style*. Baltimore, MD: Johns Hopkins University Press. [5]

Hall, P. M. 1987. Interactionism and the study of social organization. *The Sociological Quarterly*, 28:1–22. [4]

Hall, R. H. 1986. *Dimensions of Work*. Beverly Hills, CA: Sage. [3]

Hall, R. M., and Sandler, B. R. 1982. A chilly climate in the classroom. Washington, DC: Project on the Status and Education of Women, Association of American Colleges. [14]

Hallinan, M. T., and Williams, R. A. 1987. The stability of students' interracial friendships. *American Sociological Review*, 52:653–664. [14]

Halloran, R. 1982. Army special forces try to rebuild image by combining brains and brawn. *New York Times* (August 21):7. [16]

Hamblin, R. L. 1979. Behavioral choice and social reinforcement: Step function versus matching. *Social Forces*, 57:1141–1156. [13]

Hamilton, D. L., Sherman, S. J., and Ruvolo, C. M. 1990. Stereotype-based expectancies: Effects on information processing and social behavior. *Journal of Social Issues*, 46(2):35–60. [7]

Hampson, R. B. 1984. Adolescent prosocial behavior: Peer-group and situational factors associated with helping. *Journal of Personality and Social Psychology*, 46:153–162. [10]

Haney, C., Banks, C., and Zimbardo, P. G. 1973. Interpersonal dynamics in a simulated prison. *International Journal of Crime and Penology*, 1:69–97. [12]

Hanson, C., Henggeler, S., Haefele, W., and Rodick, J. D. 1984. Demographic, individual, and familial relationship correlates of serious and repeated crime among adolescents and their siblings. *Journal of Consulting and Clinical Psychology*, 52:528–538. [15]

Harari, H., Harari, O., and White, R. V. 1985. The reaction to rape by American male bystanders. *Journal of Social Psychology*, 125:653–658. [10]

Harden, M. 1984. Is this youth or brutality? *Columbus Dispatch* (September 12):B-1. [12]

Hardin, G. J. 1968. The tragedy of the commons. *Science*, 162:1243–1248. [9]

Hardy, C., and Latané, B. 1986. Social loafing on a cheering task. *Social Science*, 71:165–172. [9]

Haring-Hidore, M., Stock, W. A., Okum, M. A., and Witter, R. A.

1985. Marital status and subjective well-being: A research synthesis. *Journal of Marriage and the Family*, 47: 947–953. [4]

Harkins, S. G. 1987. Social loafing and social facilitation. *Journal of Experimental Social Psychology*, 23:1–18. [9]

Harkins, S. G., and Petty, R. E. 1982. Effects of task difficulty and task uniqueness on social loafing. *Journal of Personality and Social Psychology*, 43:1214–1229. [9]

Harlan, A., and Weiss, C. 1981. *Final Report from "Moving Up: Women in Managerial Careers."* Working paper number 86, Center for Research on Women, Wellesley College, MA. [14]

Harper, R. G. 1985. Power, dominance, and nonverbal behavior: An overview. In Ellyson, S. L., and Dovidio, J. F. (eds.), *Power, Dominance and Nonverbal Behavior*. New York: Springer-Verlag, pp. 29–48. [5]

Harrington, R., Fudge, H., Rutter, M., Pickles, A., and Hill, J. 1990. Adult outcomes of childhood and adolescent depression. *Archives of General Psychiatry*, 47:465–473. [7]

Harris, L. 1981. *Aging in the Eighties: America in Transition*. Washington, DC: National Council on Aging. [3]

Harris, L. 1987. *Inside America*. New York: Vintage. [3]

Harris, L. 1991. The Harris Poll (May). *World Opinion Update*, 15(6):72. [14]

Harris, L., and Associates. 1987. Harris Study Number 883013. Institute for Research in Social Science [computer file]. [14]

Harrod, W. J. 1980. Expectations from unequal rewards. *Social Psychology Quarterly*, 43:126–130. [14]

Harry, J. 1983. Gay male and lesbian relationships. In Macklin, E. D., and Rubin, R. H. (eds.), *Contemporary Families and Alternative Lifestyles: Handbook on Research and Theory*. Beverly Hills, CA: Sage. [11]

Hart, P. 1990. *Groupthink in Government: A Study of Small Groups and Policy Failure*. Rockland, MA: Swets and Zeitlinger. [9]

Harvey, O. J., and Consalvi, C. 1960. Status and conformity pressures in informal groups. *Journal of Abnormal Social Psychology*, 60:182–187. [9]

Hass, R. G. 1984. Perspective taking and self-awareness: Drawing an E on your forehead. *Journal of Personality and Social Psychology*, 46:788–798. [2]

Hatfield, E. 1988. Passionate and companionate love. In Sternberg, R. J., and Barnes, M. L. (eds.), *The Psychology of Love*. New Haven, CT: Yale University Press. [11]

Hatfield, E., and Sprecher, S. 1986. *Mirror, Mirror . . . : The Importance of Looks in Everyday Life*. Albany: State University of New York Press. [11]

Hawley, W. D. 1979. Getting the facts straight about the effects of school desegregation. *Educational Leadership*, 36:314–321. [14]

Hayes, C. D., and Kamerman, S. B. (eds.) 1983. *Children of Working Parents*. Washington, DC: National Academy Press. [15]

Hayghe, H. V. 1988. Employers and childcare: What roles do they play? *Monthly Labor Review* (September): 38–44. [14]

Hays, R. B. 1984. The development and maintenance of friendship. *Journal of Social and Personal Relationships*, 1: 75–98. [11]

Hays, R. B. 1985. A longitudinal study of friendship development. *Journal of Personality and Social Psychology*, 48:909–924. [11]

Hays, R. B. 1988. Friendship. In Duck, S. W. (ed.), *Handbook of Personal Relationships: Theory, Research, and Interventions*. New York: Wiley, pp. 391–408. [11]

Hays, R. B. 1989. The day-to-day functioning of close versus casual friendships. *Journal of Social and Personal Relationships*, 6:21–37. [11]

Heath, S. 1983. *Ways with Words*. Cambridge, England: Cambridge University Press. [5]

Heatherington, E. M., Cox, M., and Cox, R. 1982. Effects of divorce on parents and children. In Lamb, M. (ed.), *Nontraditional Families*, Hillsdale, NJ: Erlbaum. [11]

Hechter, M. 1987. *Principles of Group Solidarity*. Berkeley: University of California Press. [9]

Hegtvedt, K. 1990. The effects of relationship structure on emotional responses to inequity. *Social Psychology Quarterly*, 53:214–218 [10]

Heider, F. 1946. Attitudes and cognitive organization. *Psychology*, 21:107–122. [1, 8]

Heider, F. 1958. *The Psychology of Interpersonal Relations*. New York: Wiley. [1, 6, 8]

Heilman, M. E., Block, C. J., Martell, R. F., and Simon, M. C. 1989. Has anything changed? Current character-

izations of men, women, and managers. *Journal of Applied Psychology*, 74: 935–942. [5]

Heilman, M. E., Simon, M. C., and Repper, D. P. 1987. Intentionally favored, unintentionally harmed? Impact of sex-based preferential selection on self-perceptions and self-evaluations. *Journal of Applied Psychology*, 72:62–68. [14]

Heimer, C. A. 1988. Social structure, psychology, and the estimation of risk. *Annual Review of Sociology*, 14:491–519. [13]

Heise, D. R. 1979. *Understanding Events: Affect and the Construction of Social Action*. New York: Cambridge University Press. [8]

Heise, D. R. 1987. Affect control theory: Concepts and model. *Journal of Mathematical Sociology*, 13(1–2):1–33. [8]

Heise, D. R., and Lewis, E. 1988. *Introduction to INTERACT*. National Collegiate Software Clearinghouse, Box 8101, North Carolina State University, Raleigh, NC 27695. [8]

Heise, D. R., and MacKinnon, N. J. 1987. Affective bases of likelihood judgments. *Journal of Mathematical Sociology*, 13(1–2):133–151. [8]

Hendrick, S. S. 1981. Self-disclosure and marital satisfaction. *Journal of Personality and Social Psychology*, 40: 1150–1159. [11]

Henley, N. M., and Kramarae, C. 1991. Gender, power, and miscommunication. In Coupland, N., Giles, H., and Wiemann, J. M. (eds.), *Miscommunication and Problematic Talk*. Newbury Park, CA: Sage. [5]

Henry, C. S., Wilson, S. M., and Peterson, G. W. 1989. Parental power bases and processes as predictors of adolescent conformity. *Journal of Adolescent Research*, 4:15–32. [13]

Herek, G. M. 1991. Stigma, prejudice, and violence against lesbians and gay men. In Gonsiorek, J. C., and Weinrich, J. D. (eds.), *Homosexuality: Research Implications for Public Policy*. Newbury Park, CA: Sage. [15]

Heritage, J. 1984a. *Garfinkel and Ethnomethodology*. Cambridge, England: Polity Press. [5]

Heritage, J. 1984b. A change of state token and aspects of its sequential placement. In Atkinson, J., and Heritage, J. (eds.), *Structures of Social Action: Studies in Conversation Analysis*. Cambridge, England: Cambridge University Press. [5]

Heritage, J., and Greatbatch, D. 1991. On the institutional character of institutional talk: The case of news interviews. In Boden, D., and Zimmerman, D. H. (eds.), *Talk and Social Structure: Studies in Ethnomethodology and Conversation Analysis*. Berkeley: University of California Press. [5]

Herrenkohl, E. C., Herrenkohl, R. C., and Toedler, L. J. 1983. Perspectives on the intergenerational transmission of abuse. In Finkelhor, D., Gelles, R. J., Hotaling, G., and Straus, M. A. (eds.), *The Dark Side of Families: Current Family Violence Research*. Newbury Park, CA: Sage. [12]

Hess, B. B. 1979. Sex roles, friendship and the life course. *Research on Aging*, 1:494–515. [11]

Hetherington, E. 1989. Coping with family transitions: Winners, losers, and survivors. *Child Development*, 60: 1–14. [3]

Hewgill, M. A., and Miller, G. R. 1965. Source credibility and response to fear arousing communications. *Speech Monographs*, 32:95–101. [13]

Hewitt, J. P. 1984. *Self and Society: A Symbolic Interactionist Social Psychology*. Boston: Allyn & Bacon. [4]

Hewlett, S. A. 1986. *A Lesser Life: The Myth of Women's Liberation in America*. New York: Warner Books. [14]

Higgins, E. T., and Bargh, J. A. 1987. Social cognition and social perception. *Annual Review of Psychology*, 38: 369–425. [6]

Higgins, P. C. 1980. *Outsiders in a Hearing World: A Sociology of Deafness*. Beverly Hills, CA: Sage. [15]

Hill, G. D., and Atkinson, M. 1988. Gender, familial control, and delinquency. *Criminology*, 26:127–149. [15]

Hill, J. 1988. Adapting to menarche: Familial control and conflict. In Gunnar, M., and Collins, W. (eds.), *21st Minnesota Symposium on Child Psychology: Development in the Transition to Adolescence*. Hillsdale, NJ: Erlbaum. [3]

Hill, R. J. 1981. Attitudes and behavior. In Rosenberg, M., and Turner, R. (eds.), *Social Psychology: Sociological Perspectives*. New York: Basic Books. [8]

Hillenbrand, B. 1992. America in the mind of Japan. *Time* (February 10): 20–23. [6]

Hilton, J. L., and Darley, J. M. 1985. Constructing other persons: A limit on the effect. *Journal of Experimental Social Psychology*, 21:1–18. [7]

Hindelang, M. J., Hirschi, T., and Weis, J. G. 1981. *Measuring Delinquency*. Beverly Hills, CA: Sage. [15]

Hirschi, T. 1969. *Causes of Delinquency*. Berkeley: University of California Press. [15]

Hochschild, A. R. 1979. Emotion work, feeling rules, and social structure. *American Journal of Sociology*, 85:551–575. [7]

Hochschild, A. R. 1989a. The economy of gratitude. In Franks, D. D., and McCarthy, E. D. (eds.), *The Sociology of Emotions: Original Essays and Research Papers*. Greenwich, CT: JAI Press. [10]

Hochschild, A. R. 1989b. *The Second Shift*. New York: Viking Penguin. [4]

Hochschild, J. 1981. *What's Fair?* Cambridge, MA: Harvard University Press. [14]

Hodge, R. W., and Treiman, D. J. 1968. Class identification in the United States. *American Journal of Sociology*, 73:535–547. [7]

Hoelter, J. W. 1983. Factorial invariance and self-esteem: Reassessing race and sex differences. *Social Forces*, 61: 834–846. [14]

Hoelter, J. W. 1984. Relative effects of significant others on self-evaluation. *Social Psychology Quarterly*, 47: 255–262. [7]

Hoelter, J. W., and Harper, L. 1987. Structural and interpersonal family influences on adolescent self-conception. *Journal of Marriage and the Family*, 49:129–139. [7]

Hogg, M. A., and Abrams, D. 1988. *Social Identifications: A Social Psychology of Intergroup Relations and Group Process*. New York: Routledge. [4]

Hogg, M. A., and Turner, J. C. 1987. Social identity and conformity: A theory of referent information influence. In Doise, W., and Moscovici, S. (eds.), *Current Issues in European Social Psychology*, Vol. 2. New York: Cambridge University Press. [9]

Holahan, C. J. 1977. Effects of urban size and heterogeneity on judged appropriateness of altruistic responses: Situational vs. subject variables. *Sociometry*, 40:378–382. [10]

Holtgraves, T. 1992. Linguistic realization of face management: Implications for language production and comprehension, person perception, and cross-cultural communication. *So-cial Psychology Quarterly*, 55:141–159. [5]

Holtz, R., and Miller, N. 1985. Assumed similarity and opinion certainty. *Journal of Personality and Social Psychology*, 48:890–898. [4]

Homans, G. C. 1974. *Social Behavior: Its Elementary Forms* (rev. ed.). New York: Harcourt. (First published in 1961.) [1, 9, 10]

Homans, G. C. 1974. *Social Behavior: Its Elementary Forms*. New York: Harcourt. [9, 10]

Horn, J. C., and Meer, J. 1987. The vintage years. *Psychology Today*. 21: 76–90. [3]

Hornstein, G. 1985. Intimacy in conversational style as a function of the degree of closeness between members of a dyad. *Journal of Personality and Social Psychology*, 49:671–681. [5]

House, J., and Kasper, G. 1981. Politeness markers in English and German. In Coulmas, F. (ed.), *Conversational Routine: Explorations in Standardized Communication Situations and Prepatterned Speech*. The Hague: Mouton, pp. 157–158. [5]

House, J. S., Landis, K. R., and Umberson, D. 1988. Social relationships and health. *Science*, 241:540–545. [4]

House, J. S., Robbins, C., and Metzner, H. 1982. The association of social relationships and activities with mortality: Perspective evidence from the Tecumseh Community Health Study. *American Journal of Epidemiology*, 116:123–140. [4]

Hovland, C. I., Janis, I. L., and Kelley, H. H. 1953. *Communication and Persuasion*. New Haven, CT: Yale University Press. [1]

Hovland, C. I., Lumsdaine, A. A., and Sheffield, F. D. 1967. The effects of presenting "one side" versus "both sides" in changing opinions on a controversial subject. In Rosnow, R. L., and Robinson, E. J. (eds.), *Experiments in Persuasion*. New York: Academic Press. [13]

Howard, J. A., Blumstein, P., and Schwartz, P. 1986. Sex, power, and influence tactics in intimate relationships. *Journal of Personality and Social Psychology*, 51:102–109. [13]

Howard, J. A., and Pike, K. C. 1986. Ideological investment in cognitive processing: The influence of social statuses on attribution. *Social Psychology Quarterly*, 49:154–167. [6]

Howard, W., and Crano, W. D. 1974.

Effects of sex, conversation, location, and size of observer group on bystander intervention in a high risk situation. *Sociometry*, 37:491–507. [10]

Huba, G. J., and Bentler, P. M. 1982. A developmental theory of drug use: Deprivation and assessment of a causal modeling approach. In Bates, P. B., and Brim, O. G., Jr. (eds.), *Life-Span Development and Behavior*. New York: Academic Press, pp. 147–203. [15]

Huba, G. J., and Bentler, P. M. 1983. Causal models of the development of law abidance and its relationship to psychosocial factors and drug use. In Laufer, W. S., and Day, J. M. (eds.), *Personality Theory, Moral Development and Criminal Behavior*. Lexington, MA: Heath, pp. 165–215. [15]

Hugick, L. 1992. Public opinion divided on gay rights. *Gallup Poll Monthly* (June):2–6. [15]

Hull, J. B. 1982. Female bosses say biggest barriers are insecurity and "being a woman." *Wall Street Journal* (November 2):29. [3]

Humphrey, J., and Fogarty, T. 1987. Race and plea bargained outcomes: A research note. *Social Forces*, 66: 176–182. [14]

Humphreys, L. 1970. *Tearoom Trade: Impersonal Sex in Public Places*. Chicago: Aldine. [1]

Humphreys, L., and Miller, B. 1980. Identities in the emerging gay culture. In Marmor, J. (ed.), *Homosexual Behavior: A Modern Reappraisal*. New York: Basic Books. [7]

Hunt, J., and Manning, P. K. 1991. The social context of police lying. *Symbolic Interaction*, 14:51–70. [15]

Hurh, W., and Kim, K. C. 1989. The "success" image of Asian Americans: Its validity, and its practical and theoretical implications. *Ethnic and Racial Studies*, 12:512–538. [6]

Hurlbert, J., and Acock, A. C. 1990. The effects of marital status on the form and composition of social networks. *Social Science Quarterly*, 71: 163–174. [11]

Huston, T. L. 1973. Ambiguity of acceptance, social desirability, and dating choice. *Journal of Experimental Social Psychology*, 9:32–42. [11]

Huston, T. L., McHale, S. M., and Crouter, A. C., 1986. When the honeymoon's over: Changes in the marriage relationship over the first year. In Gilmour, R., and Duck, S. W. (eds.), *The Emerging Field of Personal*

Relationships. Hillsdale, NJ: Erlbaum. [11]

Huston, T. L., Surra, C. A., Fitzgerald, N. M., and Cate, R. M. 1981. From courtship to marriage: Mate selection as an interpersonal process. In Duck, S. W., and Gilmour, R. (eds.), *Personal Relationships: 2. Developing Personal Relationships*. New York: Academic Press. [11]

Inbau, F., and Reid, J. 1962. *Criminal Interrogation and Confessions*. Baltimore, MD: Williams & Wilkins. [4]

Ingersoll, B., and Swasy, A. 1991. FDA puts squeeze on P&G over Citrus Hill labeling. *Wall Street Journal* (April 15):B1. [15]

Ingham, A. G., Levinger, G., Graves, J., and Peckham, V. 1974. The Ringelmann effect: Studies of group size and group performance. *Journal of Experimental Social Psychology*, 10: 371–384. [9]

Insko, C. A., Schopler, J., Hoyle, R. H., Dardis, G. J., and Graetz, K. A. 1990. Individual-group discontinuity as a function of fear and greed. *Journal of Personality and Social Psychology*, 58:68–79. [9]

Insko, C. A., Smith, R. H., Alicke, M. D., Wade, T. J., and Taylor, S. 1985. Conformity and group size: The concern with being right and the concern with being liked. *Personality and Social Psychology Bulletin*, 11: 41–50. [9]

Isenberg, D. J. 1986. Group polarization: A critical review and meta-analysis. *Journal of Personality and Social Psychology*, 50:1141–1151. [9]

Iyengar, S., and Kinder, D. R. 1987. *News That Matters: Television and American Opinion*. Chicago: University of Chicago Press. [13, 16]

Jaccard, J., and Becker, M. A. 1985. Attitudes and behavior: An information integration perspective. *Journal of Experimental Social Psychology*, 21: 440–465. [8]

Jackall, R. 1988. *Moral Mazes: The World of Corporate Managers*. New York: Oxford University Press. [14]

Jackson, J. M., and Harkins, S. G. 1985. Equity in effort: An explanation of the social loafing effect. *Journal of Personality and Social Psychology*, 49: 1199–1206. [9]

Jackson, J. M., and Williams, K. D. 1985. Social loafing on difficult

tasks: Working collectively can improve performance. *Journal of Personality and Social Psychology*, 49: 937–942. [9]

Jackson, P. 1989a. *Male Homosexuality in Thailand: An Interpretation of Contemporary Thai Sources*. Elmhurst, NY: Global Academic. [15]

Jackson, P. 1989b. Theories and findings about youth gangs. *Criminal Justice Abstracts* (June):313–327. [15]

Jacobs, J. A., and Steinberg, R. J. 1990. Compensating differentials and the male-female wage gap: Evidence from the New York State comparable worth study. *Social Forces*, 69:439–468. [14]

Jacobs, J. A., and Tedford, W. H. 1980. Factors affecting self-esteem of the homosexual individual. *Journal of Homosexuality*, 5:373–382. [15]

Jacobs, L., Berscheid, E., and Walster, E. 1971. Self-esteem and attraction. *Journal of Personality and Social Psychology*, 17:84–91. [7]

Jacobs, R. C., and Campbell, D. T. 1961. The perpetuation of an arbitrary tradition through several generations of a laboratory microculture. *Journal of Abnormal and Social Psychology*, 62:649–658. [9]

Jacobson, N. S., Waldron, H., and Moore, D. 1980. Toward a behavioral profile of marital distress. *Journal of Consulting and Clinical Psychology* 48:696–703. [11]

James, W. 1890. *Principles of Psychology*, 2 vols. New York: Holt. [1]

Janis, I. L. 1989. *Crucial Decisions: Leadership in Policymaking and Crisis Management*. New York: Free Press. [9]

Janis, I. L., and Feshbach, S. 1953. Effects of fear-arousing communications. *Journal of Abnormal and Social Psychology*, 48:78–92. [13]

Janis, I. L., and Mann, L. 1977. *Decision Making: A Psychological Analysis of Conflict Choice and Commitment*. New York: Free Press. [13]

Jefferson, G. 1984. Notes on a systematic deployment of the acknowledgement tokens "yeah" and "mm hm." *Papers in Linguistics*, 17:197–206. [5]

Jefferson, G. 1985. An exercise in the transcription and analysis of laughter. In Van Dijk, T. (ed.), *Handbook of Discourse Analysis*, Vol. 3. London: Academic Press. [5]

Jefferson, G. 1987. On exposed and

embedded correction in conversation. In Button, G., and Lee, J. (eds.), *Talk and Social Organization*. Clevedon, England: Multilingual Matters Ltd. [5]

Jencks, C., Bartlett, S., Corcoran, M., Crouse, J., Eaglesfield, D., Jackson, G., McClelland, K., Mueser, P., Olneck, M., Schwartz, J., Ward, S., and Williams, J. 1979. *Who Gets Ahead? The Determinants of Economic Success in America*. New York: Basic Books. [3]

Jensen, G. F. 1980. Labeling and identity. *Criminology*, 18:121–129. [15]

Johnson, D. W., Johnson, R. T., and Maruyama, G. 1984. Goal interdependence and interpersonal attraction in heterogeneous classrooms: A meta-analysis. In Miller, N., and Brewer, M. (eds.), *Groups in Contact: The Psychology of Desegregation*. New York: Academic Press. [9, 12]

Johnson, D. W., Maruyama, G., Johnson, R., Nelson, D., and Skon, L. 1981. Effects of cooperation, competition, and individualistic goal structure on achievement: A meta-analysis. *Psychological Bulletin*, 89:47–62. [9]

Johnson, F. L., and Aires, E. J. 1983. Conversational patterns among same-sex pairs of late-adolescent close friends. *Journal of Genetic Psychology*, 142:225–238. [10]

Johnson, J. 1989. Childhood is not safe for most children, Congress is warned. *New York Times* (October 2): A-12. [11]

Johnson, M. P., and Leslie, L. 1982. Couple involvement and network structure: A test of the dyadic withdrawal hypothesis. *Social Psychology Quarterly*, 45:34–43. [11]

Johnson, M. P., and Milardo, R. M. 1984. Network interference in pair relationships: A social psychological recasting of Slater's theory of social regression. *Journal of Marriage and the Family*, 46:893–899. [11]

Johnson, N. R. 1974. Collective behavior as group-induced shift. *Sociological Inquiry*, 44:105–110. [9]

Johnson, N. R., and Feinberg, W. E. 1977. A computer simulation of the emergence of consensus in groups. *American Sociological Review*, 42:505–521. [16]

Johnson, N. R., Stemler, J. G., and Hunter, D. 1977. Crowd behavior as "risky shift": A laboratory experiment. *Sociometry*, 40:183–187. [9]

Johnson, R. A. 1983. Mobilizing the disabled. In Freeman, J. (ed.), *Social Movements of the 60s and 70s*. New York: Longman. [16]

Johnson, R. D., and Downing, L. L. 1979. Deindividuation and valence of cues: Effects on prosocial and antisocial behavior. *Journal of Personality and Social Psychology*, 37:1532–1538. [12]

Johnson, T. E., and Rule, B. G. 1986. Mitigating circumstance information, censure, and aggression. *Journal of Personality and Social Psychology*, 50: 537–542. [12]

Johnson, T. J., Feigenbaum, R., and Weiby, M. 1964. Some determinants and consequences of the teacher's perception of causation. *Journal of Educational Psychology*, 55:237–246. [6]

Jones, E. E., Farina, A., Hastorf, A. H., Markus, H., Miller, D. T., and Scott, R. A. 1984. *Social Stigma*. New York: Freeman. [15]

Jones, M. 1991. Stereotyping Hispanics and whites: Perceived differences in social roles as determinants of ethnic stereotypes. *Journal of Social Psychology*, 131:469–476. [6]

Jones, S. E., and Yarbrough, A. E. 1985. A naturalistic study of the meanings of touch. *Communication Monographs*, 52:19–56. [5]

Jorgensen, S. R., and Gaudy, J. C. 1980. Self-disclosure and satisfaction in marriage: The relation examined. *Family Relations*, 29:281–287. [11]

Judd, C. M., and Park, B. 1988. Outgroup homogeneity: Judgments of variability at the individual and group levels. *Journal of Personality and Social Psychology*, 54:778–788. [6]

Jussim, L. 1990. Social reality and social problems: The role of expectancies. *Journal of Social Issues*, 46:9–34. [3, 7]

Kadushin, C. 1969. The professional self-concept of music students. *American Journal of Sociology*, 75:389–403. [7]

Kagan, J. 1984. *The Nature of the Child*. New York: Basic Books. [2]

Kahle, L. R., and Berman, J. J. 1979. Attitudes cause behavior: A cross-lagged panel analysis. *Journal of Personality and Social Psychology*, 37: 315–321. [8]

Kahn, A., O'Leary, V., Krulewitz, J.

E., and Lamm, H. 1980. Equity and equality: Male and female means to a just end. *Basic and Applied Social Psychology*, 1:173–197. [9]

Kalab, K. 1987. Student vocabularies of motive: Accounts for absence. *Symbolic Interaction*, 10:71–83. [5]

Kallgren, C. A., and Wood, W. 1986. Access to attitude-relevant information in memory as a determinant of attitude-behavior consistency. *Journal of Experimental Social Psychology*, 22: 328–338. [8]

Kalmuss, D. S., and Straus, M. A. 1982. Wife's marital dependency and wife abuse. *Journal of Marriage and the Family*, 44:277–286. [12]

Kamhi, A. G. 1986. The elusive first word: The importance of the naming insight for the development of referential speech. *Journal of Child Language*, 13:155–161. [2]

Kamo, Y. 1988. Determinants of the household division of labor: Resources, power, and ideology. *Journal of Family Issues*, 9:177–200. [14]

Kandel, D. B. 1978. Convergence in prospective longitudinal surveys of drug use in normal populations. In Kandel, D. B. (ed.), *Longitudinal Research on Drug Use*. New York: Wiley. [15]

Kandel, D. B. 1984. Marijuana users in young adulthood. *Archives of General Psychiatry*, 41:200–209. [15]

Kandel, D. B. 1986. Process of peer influences in adolescence. In Silberseisen, R. K., Eyferth, K., and Rudinger, G. (eds.), *Development as Action in Context*. Berlin: Springer-Verlag. [15]

Kandel, D. B., and Davies, M. 1982. Epidemiology of depressive mood in adolescents. *Archives of General Psychiatry*, 39:1205–1212. [7]

Kandel, D. B., and Davies, M. 1986. Adult sequelae of adolescent depressive symptoms. *Archives of General Psychiatry*, 43:255–262. [7]

Kanin, E. J., Davidson, K. D., and Scheck, S. R. 1970. A research note on male-female differentials in the experience of heterosexual love. *Journal of Sex Research*, 6:64–72. [11]

Kanter, R. M. 1977. *Men and Women of the Corporation*. New York: Basic Books. [2]

Kaplan, M. F. 1987. The influencing process in group decision making. In Hendrick, C. (ed.), *Review of Personality and Social Psychology: Group*

Processes, vol. 8, Newbury Park, CA: Sage, pp. 189–212. [9]

Kaplan, M. F., and Miller, C. E. 1987. Group decision-making and normative versus informational influence: Effects of type of issue and assigned decision rule. *Journal of Personality and Social Psychology*, 53:306–313. [9]

Kaplowitz, S. A., Fink, E. L., with Mulcrone, J., Atkin, D., and Dabil, S. 1991. Disentangling the effects of discrepant and disconfirming information. *Social Psychology Quarterly*, 54: 191–207. [13]

Karabenick, S. A. 1983. Sex-relevance of content and influenceability: Sistrunk and McDavid revisited. *Personality and Social Psychology Bulletin*, 9:243–252. [9]

Karlins, M., Coffman, T., and Walters, G. 1969. On the fading of social stereotypes: Studies in three generations of college students. *Journal of Personality and Social Psychology*, 13:1–16. [6]

Katovich, M. A. 1984. Symbolic interaction and experimentation: The laboratory as a provocative stage. In Denzin, N. K. (ed.), *Studies in Symbolic Interaction*. Greenwich, CT: JAI Press. [1]

Katriel, T. 1986. *Talking Straight: Durgri Speech in Israeli Sabra Culture*. London: Cambridge University Press. [5]

Katz, J. 1988. *Seductions of Crime: Moral and Sensual Attractions in Doing Evil*. New York: Basic Books. [15]

Kaye, K. 1982. Organism, apprentice, and person. In Tronick, E. Z. (ed.), *Social Interchange in Infancy: Affect, Cognition, and Communication*. Baltimore, MD: University Park Press. [2]

Kazdin, A. E. 1987. Treatment of antisocial behavior in children: Current status and future directions. *Psychological Bulletin*, 102:187–203. [15]

Kelley, H. H. 1972. *Causal Schemata and the Attribution Process*. Morristown, NJ: General Learning Press. [6]

Kendon, A., Harris, R. M., and Key, M. R. 1970. *Organization of Behavior in Face-to-Face Interaction*. The Hague: Mouton. [5]

Kendrick, J. R., Jr. 1991. Meaning and participation: Perspectives of peace movement participants. *Research in Social Movements, Conflicts, and Change*, 13:91–111. [16]

Kennedy, G. 1990. College students'

expectations of grandparent and grandchild role behaviors. *Gerontologist*, 30:43–48. [3]

Kennedy, L. W. 1990. *On the Borders of Crime: Conflict Management and Criminality*. New York: Longman. [15]

Kerckhoff, A. C., and Davis, K. E. 1962. Value consensus and need complementarity in mate selection. *American Sociological Review*, 27: 295–303. [11]

Kerner Commission. 1968. *Report of the National Advisory Commission on Civil Disorders*. New York: Bantam. [14]

Kernis, M. H., and Wheeler, L. 1981. Beautiful friends and ugly strangers: Radiation and contrast effects in perceptions of same-sex pairs. *Personality and Social Psychology Bulletin*, 7: 617–620. [6]

Kerr, N. L. 1983. Motivation losses in small groups: A social dilemma analysis. *Journal of Personality and Social Psychology*, 45:819–828. [9]

Kessler, R. 1979. Stress, social status, and psychological distress. *Journal of Health and Social Behavior*, 20:259–272. [7]

Kessler, R. C., and Neighbors, H. W. 1986. A new perspective on the relationships among race, social class, and psychological distress. *Journal of Health and Social Behavior*, 27:107–115. [7]

Kiesler, C., and Pallak, M. S. 1976. Arousal properties of dissonance manipulations. *Psychological Bulletin*, 83: 1014–1025. [8]

Kihlstrom, J. F., Cantor, N., Albright, J. S., Chew, B. R., Klein, S. B., and Niedenthal, P. M. 1988. Information processing and the study of the self. In Berkowitz, L. (ed.), *Advances in Experimental Social Psychology*, Vol. 21. New York: Academic Press. [7]

Killian, L. 1984. Organization, rationality and spontaneity in the civil rights movement. *American Sociological Review*, 19:770–783. [16]

King, K. P., and Clayson, D. E. 1988. The differential perceptions of male and female deviants. *Sociological Focus*, 21:153–164. [6]

King, W. 1985. Church members go on with sanctuary drive. *New York Times* (January 23):6. [10]

Kipnis, D. 1974. The powerholder. In Tedeschi, J. T. (ed.), *Perspectives on Social Power*. Chicago: Aldine. [12, 13]

Kipnis, D. 1976. *The Powerholders*. Chicago: University of Chicago Press. [13]

Kipnis, D. 1984. The view from the top. *Psychology Today*, 18 (December): 30–36. [13]

Kipnis, D., and Schmidt, S. M. 1985. The language of persuasion. *Psychology Today*, 19(April):40–46. [13]

Kipnis, D., Schmidt, S. M., and Wilkinson, I. 1980. Intraorganizational influence tactics: Explanations in getting one's way. *Journal of Applied Psychology*, 65:440–452. [13]

Klandermans, B., and Oegema, D. 1987. Potentials, networks, motivations, and barriers: Steps towards participation in social movements. *American Sociological Review*, 52:519–531. [16]

Kleck, G., and McElrath, K. 1991. The effects of weaponry on human violence. *Social Forces*, 69:669–692. [12]

Klein, F., Sepekoff, B., and Wolf, T. 1985. Sexual orientation: A multivariable dynamic process. *Journal of Homosexuality*, 12:35–49. [15]

Kleinke, C. L., Meeker, F. B., and LaFong, C. 1974. Effects of gaze, touch, and use of name on evaluation of "engaged" couples. *Journal of Research in Personality*, 7:368–373. [5]

Klepper, S., and Nagin, D. 1989. The deterrent effect of perceived certainty and severity of punishment revisited. *Criminology*, 27:721–746. [15]

Kluegel, J. R. 1990. Trends in whites' explanations of the black-white gap in SES. *American Sociological Review*, 55:512–525. [6, 7, 14]

Kluegel, J. R., and Smith, E. R. 1986. *Beliefs about Inequality: Americans' Views of What Is and What Ought to Be*. New York: Aldine de Gruyter. [6, 14]

Knapp, M. L., Stafford, L., and Daly, L. 1986. Regrettable messages: Things people wish they hadn't said. *Journal of Communication*, 36:40–58. [5]

Koballa, T. R. 1988. The determinants of female junior high school students' intentions to enroll in elective physical science courses in high school: Testing the applicability of the theory of reasoned action. *Journal of Research in Science Teaching*, 25: 479–492. [8]

Kochman, T. 1981. *Black and White Styles in Conflict*. Chicago: University of Chicago Press. [5]

Kohlberg, L. 1963. The development of children's orientations toward a moral order: I. Sequence in the development of human thought. *Vita Humana*, 6:11–33. [2]

Kohlberg, L. 1984. *The Psychology of Moral Development: Essays on Moral Development*, Vol. 2. San Francisco: Harper & Row. [2]

Kohn, M. L. 1959. Social class and parental values. *American Journal of Sociology*, 64:337–351. [3]

Kohn, M. L. 1976. Occupational structure and alienation. *American Journal of Sociology*, 82:111–130. [3]

Kohn, M. L. 1977. Reassessment, 1977. In Kohn. M. L., *Class and Conformity* (2nd ed.). Chicago: University of Chicago Press. [3]

Kohn, M. L. 1981. Personality, occupation, and social stratification: A frame of reference. In Treiman, D. J., and Robinson, R. V. (eds.), *Research in Social Stratification and Mobility: A Research Annual*, Vol. 1. Greenwich, CT: JAI Press. pp. 276–297. [3]

Kohn, M. L., and Schooler, C. 1969. Class, occupation and orientation. *American Sociological Review*, 34: 659–678. [13]

Kohn, M. L., and Schooler, C. 1978. The reciprocal effects of the substantive complexities of work and intellectual flexibility: A longitudinal assessment. *American Journal of Sociology*, 84:24–52. [3]

Kohn, M. L., and Schooler, C. 1983. *Work and Personality: An Inquiry into the Impact of Social Stratification*. Norwood, NJ: Ablex. [3]

Kollock, P., Blumstein, P., and Schwartz, P. 1985. Sex and power in interaction: Conversational privileges and duties. *American Sociological Review*, 50:34–46. [5]

Komorita, S. S., and Barth, J. M. 1985. Components of reward in social dilemmas. *Journal of Personality and Social Psychology*, 48:364–373. [9]

Komorita, S. S., and Ellis, A. L. 1988. Level of aspiration in coalition bargaining. *Journal of Personality and Social Psychology*, 54:421–431. [12]

Komorita, S. S., and Tumonis, T. M. 1980. Extensions and tests of some descriptive theories of coalition formation. *Journal of Personality and Social Psychology*, 38:256–268. [12]

Koren, P., Carlton, K., and Shaw, D. 1980. Marital conflict: Relations among behaviors, outcomes, and distress. *Journal of Consulting and Clinical Psychology*, 48:460–468. [11]

Korman, S. K. 1983. The feminist: Familial influences on adherence to ideology and commitment to a self-perception. *Family Relations*, 32: 431–439. [13]

Korte, C., and Milgram, S. 1970. Acquaintance networks between racial groups. *Journal of Personality and Social Psychology*, 15:101–108. [4]

Korte, C., Ypma, I., and Toppen, A. 1975. Helpfulness in Dutch society as a function of urbanization and environmental input level. *Journal of Personality and Social Psychology*, 32: 996–1003. [10]

Kovar, M. G. 1986. Aging in the eighties: Age 65 years and over and living alone, contacts with family, friends, and neighbors. *Advance Data from Vital and Health Statistics*, no. 116 (DHHS Publication No. PHS 86-1250). Washington, DC: National Center for Health Statistics. [3]

Kozma, A., and Stones, M. J. 1983. Prediction of happiness. *Journal of Gerontology*, 38:626–628. [3]

Kramer, R. 1982. Corporate crime: An organizational perspective. In Wickman, P. W., and Dailey, T. (eds.), *White Collar and Economic Crime: A Multidisciplinary and Crossnational Perspective*. Lexington, MA: Lexington Books. [15]

Kranichfeld, M. 1987. Rethinking family power. *Journal of Family Issues*, 8:42–56. [13]

Krauss, R. M., Apple, W., Morency, N., Wenzel, C., and Winston, W. 1981. Verbal, vocal, and visible factors in judgments of another's affect. *Journal of Personality and Social Psychology*, 40:312–320. [5]

Kraut, R. E., Lewis, S. H., and Swezey, L. W. 1982. Listener responsiveness and the coordination of conversation. *Journal of Personality and Social Psychology*, 43:718–731. [5]

Kravitz, D. A., and Martin, B. 1986. Ringelmann rediscovered: The original article. *Journal of Personality and Social Psychology*, 50:936–941. [9]

Krohn, M. D., and Massey, J. L. 1980. Social control and delinquent behavior: An examination of the elements of the social bond. *Sociological Quarterly*, 21:529–543. [15]

Krohn, M. D., Skinner, W., Massey, J. L., and Akers, R. L. 1985. Social learning theory and adolescent cigarette smoking: A longitudinal study. *Social Problems*, 32:455–471. [15]

Krosnick, J. A. 1989. Question wording and reports of survey results: The case of Louis Harris and Associates and Aetna Life and Casualty. *Public Opinion Quarterly*, 53:107-113. [1]

Krosnick, J. A., and Judd, C. M. 1982. Transition in social influence at adolescence: Who induces cigarette smoking? *Developmental Psychology*, 18:359–368. [3]

Kruglanski, A. W. 1989. The psychology of being "right": The problem of accuracy in social perception and cognition. *Psychological Bulletin*, 106:395–409 [13]

Kruttschnitt, C. 1984. Sex and criminal court dispositions: The unresolved controversy. *Journal of Research in Crime and Delinquency*, 21:213–232. [14]

Kruttschnitt, C., and Green, D. 1984. The sex-sanctioning issue: Is it history? *American Sociological Review*, 49: 541–551. [14]

Kübler-Ross, E. 1969. *On Death and Dying*. New York: Macmillan. [3]

Kulik, C. T., and Ambrose, M. L. 1992. Personal and situational determinants of referent choice. *Academy of Management Review*, 17:212–237. [7]

Kulik, J. A., and Brown, R. 1979. Frustration, attribution of blame, and aggression. *Journal of Experimental Social Psychology*, 15:183–194. [12]

Kurz, D. 1991. Corporal punishment and adult use of violence: A critique of "Discipline and deviance." *Social Problems*, 38:155–161. [12]

Labov, W. 1972. *Language in the Inner City: Studies of the Black English Vernacular*. Philadelphia: University of Pennsylvania Press. [5]

Ladd, G. W., Lange, G., and Stremmel, A. 1983. Children's helping behavior: Factors that mediate compliant helping. *Child Development*, 54: 488–501. [10]

LaFrance, M., and Ickes, W. 1981. Postural mirroring and interactional involvement: Sex and sex-typing effects. *Journal of Nonverbal Behavior*, 5:139–154. [5]

LaFrance, M., and Mayo, C. 1976. Racial differences in gaze behavior during conversation. *Journal of Personality and Social Psychology*, 33: 547–552. [5]

La Gaipa, J. J. 1982. Rules and rituals in disengaging from relationships. In Duck, S. W. (ed.), *Personal Relationships: 4. Dissolving Personal Relationships*. New York: Academic Press. [11]

Lamb, M. E., Easterbrooks, M. A., and Holden, G. W. 1980. Reinforcement and punishment among preschoolers: Characteristics, effects, and correlates. *Child Development*, 51: 1230–1236. [3]

Lambert, W. E., Hodgson, R. C., Gardner, R. C., and Fillenbaum, S. 1960. Evaluative reactions to spoken languages. *Journal of Abnormal and Social Psychology*, 60:44–51. [6]

Lampe, P. 1985. Friendship and adultery. *Sociological Inquiry*, 55:310–324. [11]

Landy, D., and Sigall, H. 1974. Beauty is talent: Task evaluation as a function of the performer's physical attractiveness. *Journal of Personality and Social Psychology*, 29:299–304. [6]

Lane, I. M., Mathews, R. C., and Presholdt, P. H. 1988. Determinants of nurses' intentions to leave their profession. *Journal of Organizational Behavior*, 9:367–372. [8]

Langer, E. J., Chanowitz, B., and Blank, A. 1985. Mindlessness-mindfulness in perspective: A reply to Valerie Folkes. *Journal of Personality and Social Psychology*, 48:605–607. [9]

LaPiere, R. T. 1934. Attitudes versus actions. *Social Forces*, 13:230–237. [8]

Larrick, R. P., Morgan, J. N., and Nisbett, R. E. 1990. Teaching the use of cost-benefit reasoning in everyday life. *Psychological Science*, 1: 362–370. [13]

Larrieu, J., and Mussen, P. 1986. Some personality and motivational correlates of children's prosocial behavior. *Journal of Genetic Psychology*, 147:529–542. [10]

Larson, R., and Asmussen, L. 1991. Anger, worry, and hurt in early adolescence: An enlarging world of negative emotions. In Colten, M., and Gore, S. (eds.), *Adolescent Stress: Causes and Consequences*. New York: Aldine de Gruyter. [7]

Lasswell, H. 1936. *Politics: Who Gets What, When, How*. New York: McGraw-Hill. [13, 14]

Latané, B., and Darley, J. M. 1968. Group inhibition of bystander intervention in emergencies. *Journal of Personality and Social Psychology*, 10: 215–221. [10]

Latané, B., and Darley, J. M. 1970. *The Unresponsive Bystander*. New York: Appleton-Century-Crofts. [10]

Latané, B., and Nida, S. 1981. Ten years of research on group size and helping. *Psychological Bulletin*, 89: 308–324. [10]

Latané, B., and Rodin, J. 1969. A lady in distress: Inhibiting effects of friends and strangers on bystander intervention. *Journal of Experimental Social Psychology*, 5:189–202. [10]

Latané, B., Williams, K. D., and Harkins, S. G. 1979a. Many hands make light the work: The causes and consequences of social loafing. *Journal of Personality and Social Psychology*, 37: 822–832. [9]

Latané, B., Williams, K. D., and Harkins, S. G. 1979b. Social loafing. *Psychology Today*, 13(October):104–110. [9]

Lau, R. 1984. Dynamics of the attribution process. *Journal of Personality and Social Psychology*, 46:1017–1028. [7]

Lauderdale, P., Parker, J., Smith-Cunnien, P., and Inverarity, J. 1984. External threat and the definition of deviance. *Journal of Personality and Social Psychology*, 46:1058–1068. [4]

Lauer, J., and Lauer, R. 1985. Marriages made to last. *Psychology Today*, 19(June):22–26. [11]

Lawler, E. J., and Bacharach, S. B. 1987. Comparison of dependence and punitive forms of power. *Social Forces*, 66:446–462. [10, 12]

Lawton, M. 1989. Environmental proactivity and affect in older people. In Spacapan, S., and Oskamp, S. (eds.), *The Social Psychology of Aging*. Newbury Park, CA: Sage. [7]

Leary, M. R., Wheeler, D. S., and Jenkins, T. B. 1986. Aspects of identity and behavioral preference: Studies of occupational and recreational choice. *Social Psychology Quarterly*, 49:11–18. [7]

Le Bon, G. 1896. *The Crowd: A Study of the Popular Mind*. London: Ernest Benn. [16]

Lee, B. A., Jones, S. H., and Lewis, D. W. 1990. Public beliefs about the causes of homelessness. *Social Forces*, 69:253–265. [6]

Lee, G. R. 1977. *Family Structure and Interaction*. Philadelphia: Lippincott. [3]

Lee, G. R., and Petersen, L. R. 1983. Conjugal power and spousal resources in patriarchal cultures. *Journal of Comparative Family Studies*, 14:23–28. [13]

Lee, V. E., and Bryk, A. S. 1986. Effects of single-sex secondary schools on student achievement and attitudes. *Journal of Educational Psychology*, 78: 381–395. [3]

Lee, V. L. 1988. *Beyond Behaviorism*. Hillsdale, NJ: Erlbaum. [2]

Leeds-Hurwitz, W. 1989. *Communication in Everyday Life*. Norwood, NJ: Ablex. [5]

Leffler, A., Gillespie, D. L., and Conaty, J. C. 1982. The effects of status differentiation on nonverbal behavior. *Social Psychology Quarterly*, 45: 153–161. [5]

Lehne, G. K. 1989. Homophobia among men: Supporting and defining the male role. In Kimmel, M. S., and Messner, M. A. (eds.), *Men's Lives*. New York: Macmillan. [11]

LeMasters, E. E., and DeFrain, J. 1989. *Parents in Contemporary America*. Belmont, CA: Wadsworth. [13]

Leming, M. R., and Dickinson, G. E. 1985. *Understanding Dying, Death, and Bereavement*. New York: Holt, Rinehart & Winston. [3]

Lennox, R. D. 1988. The problem with self-monitoring: A two-sided scale or a one-sided scale. *Journal of Personality Assessment*, 51:58–73. [7]

Lennox, R. D., and Wolfe, R. N. 1984. A revision of the self-monitoring scale. *Journal of Personality and Social Psychology*, 46:1348–1364. [7]

Leone, C., and Robertson, K. 1989. Some effects of sex-linked clothing and gender schema on the stereotyping of infants. *Journal of Social Psychology*, 129:609–619. [3]

Lerner, M. J. 1980a. *The Belief in a Just World: A Fundamental Delusion*. New York: Plenum. [10]

Lerner, M. J. 1980b. The desire for justice and reactions to victims. In Macaulay, J. R., and Berkowitz, L. (eds.), *Altruism and Helping Behavior*. New York: Academic Press. [16]

Lerner, M. J., and Simmons, C. 1966. Observer's reaction to the "innocent victim." Compassion or rejection? *Journal of Personality and Social Psychology*, 4:203–210. [10]

Lesko, N. 1988. *Symbolizing Society: Stories, Rites and Structure in Catholic High School*. Philadelphia: Falmer. [3]

Leslie, L., Huston, T. L., and Johnson, M. P. 1986. Parental reactions to dating relationships: Do they make a difference? *Journal of Marriage and the Family*, 48:57–66. [11]

Leventhal, G. S., and Lane, D. W. 1970. Sex, age, and equity behavior. *Journal of Personality and Social Psychology*, 15:312–316. [10]

Leventhal, H. 1970. Findings and theory in the study of fear communications. In Berkowitz, L. (ed.), *Advances in Experimental Social Psychology*, Vol. 5. New York: Academic Press. [13]

Lever, J. 1978. Sex differences in the complexity of children's play and games. *American Sociological Review*, 43:471–483. [3]

Levine, J. M., and Russo, E. M. 1987. Majority and minority influence. In Hendrick, C. (ed.), *Review of Personality and Social Psychology: Group Process*, Vol. 8. Newbury Park, CA: Sage, pp. 13–54. [9]

Levine, K., and Mueller, E. 1988. Communication. In Yawkey, T., and Johnson, J. (eds.), *Integrative Processes and Socialization: Early to Middle Childhood*. Hillsdale, NJ: Erlbaum. [2]

Levine, R. 1988. Hertz concedes it overcharged for car repairs. *New York Times* (January 26):1. [15]

Levine, S. V. 1984. Radical departures. *Psychology Today*, 18(August):21–27. [16]

Levinger, G. 1980. Toward the analysis of close relationships. *Journal of Experimental Social Psychology*, 16:510–544. [11]

Levinger, G. 1983. Development and change. In Kelley, H. H., Berscheid, E., Christensen, A., Harvey, J. H., Huston, T. L., Levinger, G., McClintock, E., Peplau, L. A., and Peterson, D. R. (eds.), *Close Relationships*. New York: Freeman. [11]

Levinger, G., Senn, D. J., and Jorgensen, B. W. 1970. Progress toward permanence in courtship: A test of the Kerckhoff-Davis hypothesis. *Sociometry*, 33:427–443. [11]

Levinson, R., Powell, B., and Steelman, L. C. 1986. Social location, significant others and body image among adolescents. *Social Psychology Quarterly*, 49:330–337. [7]

Lewin, K. 1935. *A Dynamic Theory of Personality*. New York: McGraw-Hill. [1]

Lewin, K. 1936. *Principles of Topological Psychology*. New York: McGraw-Hill. [1]

Lewin, K., Lippitt, R., and White, R. K. 1939. Patterns of aggressive behavior in experimentally created "social climates." *Journal of Social Psychology*, 10:271–299. [1]

Lewin, T. 1984. A new push to raise women's pay. *New York Times* (January 1):F1, F15. [14]

Lewis, M. 1989. *Liar's Poker: Rising Through the Wreckage of Wall Street*. New York: W. W. Norton. [14]

Liebowitz, M. R. 1983. *The Chemistry of Love*. Boston: Little, Brown. [11]

Lierman, L. M., Young, H. M., Kasprzyk, D., and Benoliel, J. Q. 1990. Predicting breast self-examination using the theory of reasoned action. *Nursing Research*, 39:97–101. [8]

Lifton, R. J. 1979. The appeal of the death trap. *New York Times Magazine* (January 7):26–31. [16]

Lin, N., Ensel, W. M., and Vaughn, J. C. 1981. Social resources and the strength of ties: Structural factors in occupational status attainment. *American Sociological Review*, 46:393–405. [4]

Lincoln, A., and Levinger, G. 1972. Observers' evaluations of the victim and the attacker in an aggressive incident. *Journal of Personality and Social Psychology*, 22:202–210. [10]

Lindsey, R. 1987. Colleges accused of bias to stem Asians' gain. *New York Times* (January 19):8. [14]

Linn, L. S. 1965. Verbal attitudes and overt behavior: A study of racial discrimination. *Social Forces*, 43:353–364. [8]

Linton, R. 1936. *The Study of Man*. New York: Appleton-Century-Crofts. [1]

Linville, P. W., and Jones, E. E. 1980. Polarized appraisals of out-group members. *Journal of Personality and Social Psychology*, 38:689–703. [4]

Linz, D. G., Donnerstein, E., and Penrod, S. 1988. Effects of long-term exposure to violent and sexually degrading depictions of women. *Journal of Personality and Social Psychology*, 55:758–768. [12]

Lippman, W. 1922. *Public Opinion*. New York: Harcourt. [6]

Liska, A. E. 1984. A critical examination of the causal structure of the Fishbein-Ajzen attitude-behavior model. *Social Psychology Quarterly*, 47:61–74. [8]

Liska, A. E., and Reed, M. D. 1985. Ties to conventional institutions and delinquency: Estimating reciprocal effects. *American Sociological Review*, 50:547–560. [15]

Little, C. B., and Gelles, R. J. 1975. The social psychological implications of forms of address. *Sociometry*, 38:573–586. [5]

Litwak, E. 1985. *Helping the Elderly*. New York: Guilford Press. [11]

Lloyd, S. A., Cate, R. M., and Henton, J. M. 1984. Predicting premarital relationship stability. *Journal of Marriage and the Family*, 46:65–70. [11]

Locksley, A., Oritz, V., and Hepburn, C. 1980. Social categorization and discriminatory behavior: Extinguishing the minimal intergroup discrimination effect. *Journal of Personality and Social Psychology*, 39:773–783. [4]

Lodge, M., McGraw, K., and Stroh, P., 1989. An impression-driven model of candidate evaluation. *American Political Science Review*, 83:399–419. [6]

Lofland, J. 1966. *Doomsday Cult*. Englewood Cliffs, NJ: Prentice-Hall. [16]

Lofland, J. 1981. *Doomsday Cult: A Study of Conversion, Proselytization, and Maintenance of Faith*. New York: Irvington. [13, 16]

Lofland, J., and Johnson, V. 1991. Citizen surges: A domain in movement studies and a perspective on peace activism in the 1980s. *Research in Social Movements, Conflicts, and Change*, 13:1–29. [16]

Loftus, E. F. 1979. *Eyewitness Testimony*. Cambridge, MA: Harvard University Press. [6]

Loftus, E. F. 1984. Eyewitnesses: Essential but unreliable. *Psychology Today*, 18(February):22–26. [6]

Longino, C. F., and Lipman, A. 1981. Married and spouseless men and women in planned retirement communities: Support network differentials. *Journal of Marriage and the Family*, 43:169–177. [3]

Longshore, D., and Prager, J. 1985. The impact of school desegregation: A situational analysis. *Annual Review of Sociology*, 11:75–91. [14]

Lopes, L. L. 1987. Between hope and fear: The psychology of risk. In Berkowitz, L. (ed.), *Advances in Experimental Social Psychology*, Vol. 20. New York: Academic Press. [13]

Lovdal, L. 1989. Sex role messages in television commercials: An update. *Sex Roles*, 21:715–727. [3]

Luchins, A. S. 1957. Experimental attempts to minimize the impact of first impressions. In Hovland, C. I. (ed.),

The Order of Presentation in Persuasion. New Haven, CT: Yale University Press. [6]

Luchins, A. S., and Luchins, E. H. 1961. On conformity with judgments of a majority or an authority. *Journal of Social Psychology*, 53: 303–316. [9]

Luckenbill, D. F. 1977. Criminal homicide as a situated transaction. *Social Problems*, 25:176–186. [12]

Luckenbill, D. F. 1986. Deviant career mobility: The case of male prostitutes. *Social Problems*, 33:283–296. [15]

Lueptow, L. B. 1980. Social structure, social change, and parental influences in adolescent sex-role socialization: 1964–1975. *Journal of Marriage and the Family*, 42:93–100. [13]

Luthans, F., Baack, D., and Taylor, L. 1987. Organizational commitment: Analysis of antecedents. *Human Relations*, 40:219–235. [4]

Lynn, S. J. 1978. Three theories of self-disclosure exchange. *Journal of Experimental Social Psychology*, 14: 466–479. [11]

Maass, A., and Clark, R. D., III. 1983. Internalization versus compliance: Differential processes underlying minority influence and conformity. *European Journal of Social Psychology*, 13: 197–215. [9]

Maass, A., and Clark, R. D. III. 1984. Hidden impact of minorities: Fifteen years of minority influence research. *Psychological Bulletin*, 95: 428–450. [9]

Maass, A., West, S. G., and Cialdini, R. B. 1987. Minority influence and conversion. In Hendrick, C. (ed.), *Review of Personality and Social Psychology: Group Process*, Vol. 8. Newbury Park, CA: Sage, pp. 55–79. [9]

Maccoby, E. E. 1990. Gender and relationships: A developmental account. *American Psychologist*, 45: 513–520. [5]

Maccoby, E. E., and Jacklin, C. N. 1974. *The Psychology of Sex Differences*, Stanford, CA: Stanford University Press. [11]

Maccoby, E. E., Snow, M. E., and Jacklin, C. N. 1984. Children's dispositions and mother-child interactions at 12 and 18 months: A short-term longitudinal study. *Developmental Psychology*, 20:459–472. [3]

MacDermid, S. M., Huston, T. L., and McHale, S. M. 1990. Changes in marriage associated with the transition to parenthood: Individual differences as a function of sex-role attitudes and changes in the division of household labor. *Journal of Marriage and the Family*, 52:475–486. [3]

Mackie, D., and Cooper, J. 1984. Attitude polarization: Effects of group membership. *Journal of Personality and Social Psychology*, 46:575–585. [9]

MacLeod, J. 1987. *Ain't No Makin' It: Leveled Aspirations in a Low-Income Neighborhood.* Boulder, CO: Westview. [3]

MacNeil, M. K., and Sherif, M. 1976. Norm change over subject generations as a function of arbitrariness of prescribed norms. *Journal of Personality and Social Psychology*, 34:762–768. [9]

Maddux, J. E., and Rogers, R. W. 1983. Protection motivation and self-efficacy: A revised theory of fear appeals and attitude change. *Journal of Experimental Psychology*, 19:469–479. [13]

Maibach, E., Flora, J. A., and Nass, C. 1991. Changes in self-efficacy and health behavior in response to a minimal contact community health campaign. *Health Communication*, 3:1–15. [13]

Mainardi, P. 1970. The politics of housework. In Tanner, L. B. (ed.), *Voices from Women's Liberation.* New York: New American Library. [14]

Maines, D. R. 1987. The significance of temporality for the development of sociological theory. *Sociological Quarterly*, 28:303–311. [15]

Maines, D. R., and Hardesty, M. J. 1987. Temporality and gender: Young adults' career and family plans. *Social Forces*, 66:104–120. [4]

Major, B., and Adams, J. B. 1983. Role of gender, interpersonal orientation, and self-presentation in distributive-justice behavior. *Journal of Personality and Social Psychology*, 45: 598–608. [9]

Major, B., and Deaux, K. 1982. Individual differences in justice behavior. In Greenberg, J., and Cohen, R. L. (eds.), *Equity and Justice in Social Behavior.* New York: Academic Press. [9, 16]

Major, B., and Forcey, B. 1985. Social comparisons and pay evaluations: Preferences for same sex and same job wage comparisons. *Journal of Experimental Social Psychology*, 21: 393–405. [16]

Major, B., McFarlin, D. B., and Gagnon, D. 1984. Overworked and underpaid: On the nature of gender differences in personal entitlement. *Journal of Personality and Social Psychology*, 47:1399–1412. [14]

Mak, A. 1990. Testing a psychosocial control theory of delinquency. *Criminal Justice and Behavior*, 17: 215–230. [15]

Malamuth, N. M., and Briere, J. 1986. Sexual violence in the media: Indirect effects on aggression against women. *Journal of Social Issues*, 42:75–92. [12]

Malamuth, N. M., and Ceniti, J. 1986. Repeated exposure to violent and nonviolent pornography: Likelihood of raping ratings and laboratory aggression against women. *Aggressive Behavior*, 12:129–137. [12]

Malamuth, N. M., Heim, M., and Feshbach, S. 1980. Sexual responsiveness of college students to rape depictions: Inhibitory and disinhibitory effects. *Journal of Personality and Social Psychology*, 38:399–408. [1]

Malcolm X. 1965. *The Autobiography of Malcolm X.* New York: Grove Press. [15, 16]

Maltz, D. N., and Borker, R. A. 1982. A cultural approach to male-female miscommunication. In Gumperz, J. J. (ed.), *Language and Social Identity.* New York: Cambridge University Press. [5]

Mancini, J., and Blieszner, R. 1991. Aging parents and adult children: Research themes in intergenerational relations. In Booth, A. (ed.), *Contemporary Families: Looking Forward, Looking Back.* Minneapolis: National Council on Family Relations. [3]

Mandell, N. 1988. The least-adult role in studying children. *Journal of Contemporary Ethnography*, 16:433–467. [2]

Mandell, N. 1991. Children's negotiation of meaning. In Waksler, F. C. (ed.), *Studying the Social Worlds of Children: Sociological Readings.* New York: Falmer Press. [2]

Mann, L. 1981. The baiting crowd in episodes of threatened suicide. *Journal of Personality and Social Psychology*, 41: 703–709. [12]

Mann, L., and Boyce, S. 1982. Fundamental frequency and discourse structure. *Language and Speech*, 25: 341–383. [2]

Mann, L., Newton, J. W., and Innes, J. M. 1982. A test between individuation and emergent norm theories of crowd aggression. *Journal of Personality and Social Psychology*, 42:260–272. [12]

Manning, S. A., and Taylor, D. A. 1975. Effects of viewed violence and aggression: Stimulation and catharsis. *Journal of Personality and Social Psychology*, 31:180–188. [12]

Manstead, A. S. R., Proffit, C., and Smart, J. L. 1983. Predicting and understanding mothers' infant-feeding intentions and behavior: Testing the theory of reasoned action. *Journal of Personality and Social Psychology*, 44:657–671. [8]

Margolis, D. R. 1979. *The Managers: Corporate Life in America*. New York: Morrow. [3, 15]

Marini, M. M., and Brinton, M. 1984. Sex typing in occupational socialization. In Reskin, B. F. (ed.), *Sex Segregation in the Workplace: Trends, Explanations, and Remedies*. Washington, DC: National Academy Press. [14]

Markides, K. C., and Cohn, S. F. 1982. External conflict/internal cohesion: A reevaluation of an old theory. *American Sociological Review*, 47: 88–89. [4]

Marks, G., Miller, N., and Maruyama, G. 1981. Effect of targets' physical attractiveness on assumptions of similarity. *Journal of Personality and Social Psychology*, 41:198–206. [11]

Markstrom-Adams, C. 1989. Androgyny and its relation to adolescent psychosocial well-being: A review of the literature. *Sex Roles*, 21:325–340. [7]

Markus, H., Smith, J., and Moreland, R. L. 1985. Role of the self-concept in the perception of others. *Journal of Personality and Social Psychology*, 49: 1494–1512. [7]

Markus, H., and Zajonc, R. 1985. The cognitive perspective in social psychology. In Lindzey, L., and Aronson, E. (eds.), *The Handbook of Social Psychology* (3rd ed.). New York: Random House. [1, 6]

Marsden, P. V. 1987. Core discussion networks of Americans. *American Sociological Review*, 52:122–131. [11]

Marsden, P. V., and Hurlbert, J. S. 1988. Social resources and mobility outcomes: A replication and extension. *Social Forces*, 66:1038–1059. [4]

Marsh, H. W., Barnes, J., and Hocevar, D. 1985. Self-other agreement on multidimensional self-concept ratings: Factor analysis and multitrait-multimethod analysis. *Journal of Personality and Social Psychology*, 49: 1360–1377. [7]

Martin, P. Y. 1992. Gender, interaction, and inequality in organizations. In Ridgeway, C. L. (ed.), *Gender, Interaction, and Inequality*. New York: Springer-Verlag. [14]

Martin, P. Y., and Chernesky, R. H. 1989. Women's prospects for leadership in social welfare: A political economy perspective. *Administration in Social Work*, 13:117–143. [14]

Marwell, G., and Schmitt, D. 1969. Childbearing experience and attitudes toward the use of influence techniques. *Journal of Marriage and the Family*, 31:779–782. [13]

Marwell, G., and Schmitt, D. R. 1975. *Cooperation: An Experimental Analysis*. New York: Academic Press. [9]

Maselli, M. D., and Altrocchi, J. 1969. Attribution of intent. *Psychological Bulletin*, 71:445–454. [12]

Maslach, C., Santee, R. T., and Wade, C. 1987. Individuation, gender role, and dissent: Personality mediators of situational forces. *Journal of Personality and Social Psychology*, 53:1088–1093. [9]

Mathews, K. E., and Canon, L. K. 1975. Environmental noise level as a determinant of helping behavior. *Journal of Personality and Social Psychology*, 32:571–577. [10]

Matsueda, R. L., and Heimer, K. 1987. Race, family structure in delinquency: A test of differential association and social control theories. *American Sociological Review*, 52: 826–840. [15]

Matthews, B. A., and Shimoff, E. 1979. Expansion of exchange: Monitoring trust levels in ongoing exchange relations. *Journal of Conflict Resolution*, 23:538–560. [10]

Mattlin, J., Wethington, E., and Kessler, R. 1990. Situational determinants of coping and coping effectiveness. *Journal of Health and Social Behavior*, 31:101–122. [7]

Matza, D. 1964. *Delinquency and Drift*. New York: Wiley. [15]

Matza, D. 1974. *Becoming Deviant*. Englewood Cliffs, NJ: Prentice-Hall. [15]

Maurice, S. 1985. Evaluative reactions to spoken languages: Attitudes of French Canadians. *McGill Student Journal of Psychology*, 1:84–97. [6]

Maynard, D. W., and Clayman, S. E. 1991. The diversity of ethnomethodology. In Scott, W. R., and Blake, J. (eds.), *Annual Review of Sociology*, 17:385–418. [1, 5]

Mazur, A., Rosa, E., Faupel, M., Heller, J., Leen, R., and Thurman, B. 1980. Physiological aspects of communications via mutual gaze. *American Journal of Sociology*, 86:50–74. [5]

McAdam, D. 1983. Tactical innovation and the pace of insurgency. *American Sociological Review*, 48:735–753. [16]

McAdam, D. 1989. The biographical consequences of activism. *American Sociological Review*, 54:744–760. [16]

McArdle, J. B. 1972. Positive and negative communications and subsequent attitude and behavior change in alcoholics. Unpublished doctoral dissertation, University of Illinois, Urbana. [8]

McArthur, L. 1985. Social judgment biases in comparable worth analysis. In Hartmann, H. I. (ed.), *Comparable Worth: New Directions for Research*. Washington, DC: National Academy Press. [14]

McCall, G. J. 1982. Becoming unrelated: The management of bond dissolution. In Duck, S. W. (ed.), *Personal Relationships: 4. Dissolving Personal Relationships*. New York: Academic Press. [11]

McCarthy, B. 1986. Dyads, cliques, and conspiracies: Friendship behaviours and perceptions within long-established social groups. In Gilmour, R. and Duck, S. W. (eds.), *The Emerging Field of Personal Relationships*. Hillsdale, NJ: Erlbaum, pp. 133–143. [11]

McCarthy, E. D. 1989. Emotions are social things: An essay on the sociology of emotions. In Franks, D. D., and McCarthy, E. D. (eds.), *The Sociology of Emotions: Original Essays and Research Papers*. Greenwich, CT: JAI Press. [11]

McCarthy, J. D. 1987. Pro-life and pro-choice mobilization: Infrastructure deficits and new technologies. In Zald, M. N., and McCarthy, J. D. (eds.), *Social Movements in an Organizational Society: Collected Essays*. New Brunswick, NJ: Transaction Books. [16]

McCarthy, J. D., and Yancey, W. L. 1971. Uncle Tom and Mr. Charley: Metaphysical pathos in the study of racism and personal disorganization. *American Journal of Sociology*, 76: 648–672. [14]

McCarthy, J. D., and Zald, M. N. 1987a. Resource mobilization and social movements: A partial theory. In Zald, M. N., and McCarthy, J. D.

(eds.), *Social Movements in an Organizational Society: Collected Essays*. New Brunswick, NJ: Transaction Books. [16]

McCarthy, J. D., and Zald, M. N. 1987*b*. Appendix: The trend of social movements in America: Professionalization and resource mobilization. In Zald, M. N., and McCarthy, J. D. (eds.), *Social Movements in an Organizational Society: Collected Essays*. New Brunswick, NJ: Transaction Books. [16]

McCauley, C., and Thangavelu, K. 1991. Individual differences in sex stereotyping of occupations and personality traits. *Social Psychology Quarterly*, 54:267–279. [6]

McClendon, M., and O'Brien, D. 1988. Question-order effects on subjective well-being. *Public Opinion Quarterly*, 52:351-364. [1]

McDonald, G. W. 1977. Parental identification by the adolescent: A social power approach. *Journal of Marriage and the Family*, 39:705–719. [13]

McDonald, K., and Parke, R. D. 1986. Parent-child physical play: The effects of sex and age on children and parents. *Sex Roles*, 15:367–378. [3]

McDougall, W. 1908. *An Introduction to Social Psychology*. London: Methuen. [1]

McDowell, E. 1992. 10 million air travelers may share in settlement. *New York Times* (June 24):D4. [15]

McGarrell, E. F., and Flanagan, T. J. 1987. Measuring and explaining legislator crime control ideology. *Journal of Research in Crime and Delinquency*, 24:102–118. [6]

McGee, G. W., Goodson, J. R., and Cashman, J. F. 1987. Job stress and job satisfaction: Influence of contextual factors. *Psychological Reports*, 61:367–375. [13]

McGrath, J. 1984. *Groups: Interaction and Performance*. Englewood Cliffs, NJ: Prentice-Hall. [4]

McGuire, W. J. 1985. Attitudes and attitude change. In Lindzey, G., and Aronson, E. (eds.), *Handbook of Social Psychology*, Vol. 2 (3rd ed.). New York: Random House. [6, 8, 9, 13]

McGuire, W. J., McGuire, C. V., Child, P., and Fujioka, T. 1978. Saliences of ethnicity in the spontaneous self-concept as a function of one's ethnic distinctiveness in the social environment. *Journal of Personality and Social Psychology*, 36:511–520. [7]

McGuire, W. J., McGuire, C. V., and Winton, W. 1979. Effects of household sex composition on the salience of one's gender in the spontaneous self-concept. *Journal of Experimental Social Psychology*, 15:77–90. [7]

McGuire, W. J., and Padawer-Singer, A. 1976. Trait salience in the spontaneous self-concept. *Journal of Personality and Social Psychology*, 33:743–754. [7]

McHale, S. M., and Huston, T. L. 1985. A longitudinal study of the transition to parenthood and its effects on the marriage relationship. *Journal of Family Issues*, 6:409–433. [3]

McKee, L., and Bell, C. 1986. His unemployment, her problem: The domestic and marital consequences of male unemployment. In Allen, S., Waton, A., Purcell, K., and Wood, S. (eds.), *The Experience of Unemployment*. Basingstoke, England: Macmillan. [11]

McLeod, B. 1986. The oriental express. *Psychology Today*, 20(July): 48–52. [14]

McLeod, J., and Kessler, R. 1990. Socioeconomic status differences in vulnerability to undesirable life events. *Journal of Health and Social Behavior*, 31:162–172. [7]

McPhail, C. 1991. *The Myth of the Maddening Crowd*. New York: Aldine de Gruyter. [16]

McPhail, C., and Wohlstein, R. T. 1983. Individual and collective behavior within gatherings, demonstrations and riots. In Turner, R. H., and Short, J. F. (eds.), *Annual Review of Sociology*, Palo Alto, CA: Annual Reviews, 9:579–600. [16]

McTear, M. 1985. *Children's Conversation*. Oxford: Basil Blackwell. [2]

McWhirter, R. M., and Jecker, J. D. 1967. Attitude similarity and inferred attraction. *Psychonomic Science*, 7:225–226. [11]

Mead, G. H. 1932. *The Philosophy of the Present*. Chicago: University of Chicago Press. [2]

Mead, G. H. 1934. *Mind, Self, and Other*. Chicago: University of Chicago Press. [1, 2]

Mead, G. H. 1938. *The Philosophy of the Act*. Chicago: University of Chicago Press. [2]

Mehrabian, A. 1972. *Nonverbal Communication*. New York: Aldine-Atherton. [5]

Meier, R. F., Burkett, S. R., and Hickman, C. A. 1984. Sanctions, peers, and deviance: Preliminary models of a social control process. *Sociological Quarterly*, 25:67–82. [15]

Menaghan, E. G., and Parcel, T. L. 1991. Determining children's home environments: The impact of maternal characteristics and current occupation on family conditions. *Journal of Marriage and the Family*, 53:403–416. [3]

Merton, R. K. 1938. Social structure and anomie. *American Sociological Review*, 3:672–682. [15]

Merton, R. K. 1957. *Social Theory and Social Structure*. Glencoe, IL: Free Press. [3, 15]

Merton, R. K. 1968. *Social Theory and Social Structure* (enlarged ed.). New York: Free Press. [6]

Mesler, M. 1989. Negotiated order and the clinical pharmacist: The ongoing process of structure. *Symbolic Interaction*, 12:139–157. [4]

Messick, D. M., and Mackie, D. M. 1989. Intergroup relations. *Annual Review of Psychology*, 40:45–81. [4]

Metts, S., Cupoch, W. R., and Bejlovec, R. A. 1989. "I love you too much to ever start liking you": Redefining romantic relationships. *Journal of Social and Personal Relationships*, 6:259–274. [11]

Meumann, E. 1904. Haus-und schularbeit: Experimente an kindern der volkschule. *Die Deutsche Schule*, 8:278–303, 337–359, 416–431. [9]

Meyer, J. P., and Pepper, S. 1977. Need complementarity and marital adjustment in young married couples. *Journal of Personality and Social Psychology*, 35:331–342. [11]

Meyer, T. P. 1972. The effects of sexually arousing and violent films on aggressive behavior. *Journal of Sex Research*, 8:324–333. [12]

Meyers, B. 1984. Minority group: An ideological formulation. *Social Problems*, 32:1–15. [4]

Michaels, J. W., Bloommel, J. M., Brocato, R. M., Linkous, R. A., and Rowe, J. S. 1982. Social facilitation and inhibition in a natural setting. *Replications in Social Psychology*, 2:21–24. [9]

Michaels, J. W., Edwards, J. N., and Acock, A. C. 1984. Satisfaction in intimate relationships as a function of inequality, inequity, and outcomes. *Social Psychology Quarterly*, 47:347–357. [11]

Michaels, J. W., Acock, A. C., and Edwards, J. N. 1986. Social exchange and equity determinants of relationship commitment. *Journal of Social and Personal Relationships*, 3:161–175. [11]

Michaels, J. W., and Wiggins, J. A. 1976. Effects of mutual dependency and dependency asymmetry on social exchange. *Sociometry*, 39:368–376. [10]

Michalko, R. 1982. Passing: Accomplishing a sighted world. *Reflections: Canadian Journal of Visual Impairment*. Quoted in Jones, E. E., et al. (eds.), 1984. *Social Stigma*. New York: Freeman. [15]

Michalowski, R., and Kramer, R. 1987. The space between laws: The problem of corporate crime in a transnational context. *Social Problems*, 34: 34–53. [15]

Middleton, D. 1983. Departing army chief's goal: Professionalism through loyalty to unit. *New York Times* (June 23):10. [4]

Midlarsky, E. 1984. Competence and helping: Notes toward a model. In Staub, E., Bar-Tal, D., Karylowski, J., and Reykowski, J. (eds.), *Development and Maintenance of Prosocial Behavior*. New York: Plenum. [10]

Midlarsky, E., and Hannah, M. E. 1985. Competence, reticence, and helping by children and adolescents. *Developmental Psychology*, 21:534–541. [10]

Mikula, G., Petri, B., and Tanzer, N. 1990. What people regard as unjust: Types and structures of everyday experiences in injustice. *European Journal of Social Psychology*, 47:133–149. [10]

Milardo, R. M. 1987. Changes in social networks of women and men following divorce: A review. *Journal of Family Issues*, 8:78–96. [11]

Milardo, R. M., Johnson, M. P., and Huston, T. L. 1983. Developing close relationships: Changing patterns of interaction between pair members and social networks. *Journal of Personality and Social Psychology*, 44: 964–976. [11]

Milgram, S. 1961. Nationality and conformity. *Scientific American*, 205: 45–51. [9]

Milgram, S. 1967. The small-world problem. *Psychology Today*, 1(May): 61–67. [4]

Milgram, S. 1974. *Obedience to Authority*. New York: Harper & Row. [1]

Milgram, S., and Toch, H. 1969. Collective behavior: Crowds and social movements. In Lindzey, G., and Aronson, E. (eds.), *The Handbook of Social Psychology*, Vol. 4 (2nd ed.). Reading, MA: Addison-Wesley. [16]

Miller, C. I. 1987. Qualitative differences among gender-stereotyped toys: Implications for cognitive and social development in girls and boys. *Sex Roles*, 16:473–487. [3]

Miller, J. 1986. *Pathways in the Workplace*. New York: Cambridge University Press. [14]

Miller, N., and Brewer, M. B. 1986. Categorization effects on ingroup and outgroup perception. In Dovidio, J., and Gaertner, S. (eds.), *Prejudice, Discrimination, and Racism: Theory and Research*. New York: Academic Press. [12]

Miller, N., and Davidson-Podgorny, G. 1987. Theoretical models of intergroup relations and the use of cooperative teams as an intervention of desegregated settings. In Hendrick, C. (ed.), *Review of Personality and Social Psychology: Group Process*, Vol. 9. Newbury Park, CA: Sage. [12]

Miller, N. E., and Dollard, J. 1941. *Social Learning and Imitation*. New Haven, CT: Yale University Press. [1]

Mills, C. W. 1940. Situated actions and vocabularies of motive. *American Sociological Review*, 5:904–913. [5]

Mirowsky, J., and Ross, C. 1991. Eliminating defense and agreement bias from measures of the sense of control: A 2x2 index. *Social Psychology Quarterly*, 54:127–145. [7]

Miyamoto, S., and Dornbusch, S. 1956. A test of interactionist hypotheses of selfconception. *American Journal of Sociology*, 61:399–403. [7]

Modgil, S., and Modgil, C. (eds.). 1987. *B. F. Skinner's Consensus and Controversy*. New York: Falmer Press. [2]

Molm, L. D. 1987. Linking power structure and power use. In Cook, K. S. (ed.), *Social Exchange Theory*. Newbury Park, CA: Sage. [10]

Molm, L. D. 1988. The structure and use of power: A comparison of reward and punishment power. *Social Psychology Quarterly*, 51:108–122. [10]

Molm, L. D. 1990. Structure, action, and outcomes: The dynamics of power in social exchange. *American Sociological Review*, 55:427–447. [13]

Molm, L. D., and Hedley, M. 1992. Gender, power, and social exchange. In Ridgeway, C. (ed.), *Gender, Interaction, and Inequality*. New York: Springer-Verlag. [13]

Molm, L. D., and Wiggins, J. A. 1979. A behavioral analysis of social exchange in the dyad. *Social Forces*, 57:1157–1179. [10]

Montano, D. E., and Taplin, S. H. 1991. A test of an expanded theory of reasoned action to predict mammography participation. *Social Science and Medicine*, 32:733–741. [8]

Montemayor, R. 1983. Parents and adolescents in conflict: All families some of the time, some families all of the time. *Journal of Early Adolescence*, 3:83–103. [3]

Montemayor, R. 1986. Family variation in parent-adolescent storm and stress. *Journal of Adolescent Research*, 1: 15–31. [3]

Montgomery, J. E. 1982. The economics of supportive services for families with disabled and aging members. *Family Relations*, 31:19–27. [3]

Montgomery, R. L. 1971. Status, conformity and resistance to compliance in natural groups. *Journal of Social Psychology*, 84:197–206. [9]

Moore, D. 1991. Entitlement and justice evaluations: Who should get more and why. *Social Psychology Quarterly*, 54:208–223. [16]

Moore, J. C., Jr., and Krupat, E. 1971. Relationships between source status, authoritarianism and conformity in a social influence setting. *Sociometry*, 34: 122–134. [9]

Moorhead, G., Ference, R., and Neck, C. 1991. Group decision fiascoes continue: Space shuttle *Challenger* and revised groupthink framework, *Human Relations*, 44:539-550. [9]

Moreland, R. L., and Zajonc, R. B. 1982. Exposure effects in person perception: Familiarity, similarity and attraction. *Journal of Experimental Social Psychology*, 18:395–415. [11]

Morgan, D. L., and Schwalbe, M. L. 1990. Mind and self in society: Linking social structure and social cognition. *Social Psychology Quarterly*, 53:148-164. [1, 6, 7]

Moriarty, T. 1975. Crime, commitment, and the responsive bystander: Two field experiments. *Journal of Personality and Social Psychology*, 31: 370–376. [10]

Morin, R. 1992. Attitudes changing on sexual harassment. *Raleigh News and Observer* (December 18):14A. [14]

Morland, J. K. 1962. Racial acceptance and preference of nursery school children in a southern city. *Merrill-*

Palmer Quarterly of Behavior and Development, 8:271–280. [14]

Morris, W. N., and Miller, R. S. 1975. The effects of consensus-breaking and consensus-preempting partners on reduction of conformity. *Journal of Personality and Social Psychology*, 11: 215–223. [9]

Morris, W. N., Miller, R. S., and Spangenberg, S. 1977. The effects of dissenter position and task difficulty on conformity and response to conflict. *Journal of Personality*, 45: 251–266. [9]

Morrison, A. M., and Von Glinow, M. A. 1990. Women and minorities in management. *American Psychologist*, 45:200–208. [14]

Morse, S., and Gergen, K. J. 1970. Social comparison, self-consistency, and the concept of the self. *Journal of Personality and Social Psychology*, 16: 148–156. [7]

Mortimer, J. T., Lorence, J., and Kumka, D. S. 1986. *Work, Family, and Personality: Transition to Adulthood.* Norwood, NJ: Ablex. [3]

Moscovici, S. 1976. *Social Influence and Social Change.* London: Academic Press. [9]

Moscovici, S. 1980. Toward a theory of conversion behavior. In Berkowitz, L. (ed.), *Advances in Experimental Social Psychology*, Vol. 13. New York: Academic Press. [9]

Moscovici, S. 1985. Social influence and conformity. In Lindzey, G., and Aronson, E. (eds.), *Handbook of Social Psychology*, Vol. 2. New York: Random House. [9]

Moscovici, S., and Faucheux, C. 1972. Social influences, conformity bias, and the study of active minorities. In Berkowitz, L. (ed.), *Advances in Experimental Social Psychology*, Vol. 6. New York: Academic Press. [9]

Moscovici, S., and Lage, E. 1976. Studies in social influence: Part III. Majority versus minority influence in a group. *European Journal of Social Psychology*, 2:149–174. [9]

Moscovici, S., Lage, E., and Naffrechoux, M. 1969. Influence of a consistent minority on the responses of a majority in a color perception task. *Sociometry*, 32:365–379. [9]

Moscovici, S., and Personnaz, B. 1980. Studies in social influence: V. Minority influences and conversion behavior in a perceptual task. *Journal of Experimental Social Psychology*, 16: 270–282. [9]

Moskos, C., Jr. 1969. Why men fight. *Transaction*, 7:13–23. [4]

Moskos, C., Jr. 1984. The sociology of combat. *Contemporary Sociology*, 13: 420–422. [4]

Mottaz, C. 1988. Determinants of organizational commitment. *Human Relations*, 41:467–482. [4]

Mottl, T. L. 1980. The analysis of countermovements. *Social Problems*, 27:620–635. [16]

Muehlenhard, C. L., and Linton, M. A. 1987. Date rape and sexual aggression in dating situations: Incidence and risk factors. *Journal of Counseling Psychology*, 34:186–196. [12]

Mueller, C. W., Parcel, T. L., and Tanaka, K. 1989. Particularism in authority outcomes of black and white supervisors. *Social Science Research*, 18:1–20. [14]

Mugny, G. 1975. Negotiations, image of the other and the process of minority influence. *European Journal of Social Psychology*, 5:209–229. [9]

Mugny, G. 1982. *The Power of Minorities.* New York: Academic Press. [9]

Mugny, G. 1984. The influence of minorities: Ten years later. In Tajfel, H. (ed.), *The Social Dimension: European Developments in Social Psychology*, Vol. 2. Cambridge, England: Cambridge University Press. [9]

Mullen, B., and Riordan, C. A. 1988. Self-serving attributions for performance in naturalistic settings: A meta-analytical review. *Journal of Applied Social Psychology*, 18:3–22. [7]

Muller, E., and Opp, K. 1986. Rational choice and rebellious collective action. *American Political Science Review*, 80:471–487. [16]

Murphy, J. W. 1989. *Postmodern Social Analysis and Criticism.* New York: Greenwood Press. [1]

Murstein, B. I. 1967. Empirical tests of role, complementary needs, and homogamy theories of marital choice. *Journal of Marriage and the Family*, 29:689–696. [11]

Murstein, B. I. 1972. Physical attractiveness and marital choice. *Journal of Personality and Social Psychology*, 22: 8–12. [11]

Murstein, B. I. 1976. *Who Will Marry Whom?* New York: Springer. [11]

Myers, D. G., and Lamm, H. 1976. The group polarization phenomenon. *Psychological Bulletin*, 83:602–627. [9]

Mynatt, C., and Sherman, S. J. 1975. Responsibility attribution in groups and individuals: A direct test of the diffusion of responsibility hypothesis. *Journal of Personality and Social Psychology*, 32:1111–1118. [10]

Nacoste, R. 1989. Affirmative action and self-evaluation. In Blanchard, F. A., and Crosby, F. J. (eds.), *Affirmative Action in Perspective.* New York: Springer-Verlag. [14]

Nader, R., and Green, M. 1982. Quoted in Geis, G., *On White-Collar Crime.* Lexington, MA: Lexington Books. [15]

Nagel, I., and Hagan, J. 1983. Gender and crime: Offense patterns and criminal court sanctions. In Tonry, M., and Morris, N. (eds.), *Crime and Justice: An Annual Review of Research*, Vol. 4. Chicago: University of Chicago Press, pp. 91–144. [14]

Nail, P. R. 1986. Toward an integration of some models and theories of social response. *Psychological Bulletin*, 100:190–206. [9]

Nakao, K., and Treas, J. 1990. Computing 1989 occupational prestige scores. Unpublished paper, NORC. Chicago. [14]

National Center for Health Statistics. 1983. *Health, United States, 1983* (DHHS Publication No. PHS 84-1232). Washington, DC: U.S. Government Printing Office. [14]

National Commission for the Protection of Human Subjects of Biomedical and Behavioral Research. 1979. *The Belmont Report: Ethical Principles and Guidelines for the Protection of Human Research Subjects* (1988-201-778/80319). Washington, DC: U.S. Government Printing Office. [1]

National Committee on Pay Equity. 1987. *Pay Equity: An Issue of Race, Ethnicity, and Sex.* Washington, DC: National Committee on Pay Equity. [14]

NBC/Wall Street Journal. 1991. Question id: USNBCWSJ.032991. R25. (March 1991) Roper Center POLLS [computer file]. [14]

Neimeyer, R. A., and Mitchell, K. S. 1988. Similarity and attraction: A longitudinal study. *Journal of Social and Personal Relationships*, 5:131–148. [11]

Nel, E., Helmreich, R., and Aronson, E. 1969. Opinion change in the advocate as a function of the persuasibility of his audience. A clarification of the meaning of dissonance. *Journal of Personality and Social Psychology*, 12:117–124. [8]

Nelan, B. W. 1991. Europe's racism. *Time*, 138(August 12):36–38. [12]

Nemeth, C. J. 1986. Differential contributions of majority and minority influence. *Psychological Review*, 93:23–32. [9]

Nemeth, C. J., and Wachtler, J. 1973. Consistency and modification of judgment. *Journal of Experimental Social Psychology*, 9:65–79. [9]

Nemeth, C. J., and Wachtler, J. 1974. Creating the perceptions of consistency and confidence: A necessary condition for minority influence. *Sociometry*, 37:529–540. [9]

Nemeth, C. J., and Wachtler, J. 1983. Creative problem solving as a result of majority and minority influence. *European Journal of Social Psychology*, 13:45–55. [9]

Netemeyer, R., Burton, S., and Johnson, M. 1991. A comparison of two models for the prediction of volitional and goal-directed behaviors: A confirmatory analysis approach. *Social Psychology Quarterly*, 54:87–100. [8]

Neuberg, S. L. 1989. The goal of forming accurate impressions during social interactions: Attenuating the impact of negative expectancies. *Journal of Personality and Social Psychology*, 56:374–386. [7]

Neuman, W. R. 1990. The threshold of public attention. *Public Opinion Quarterly*, 54:159–176. [16]

Newcomb, T. M. 1956. The prediction of interpersonal attraction. *American Psychologist*, 11:575–586. [7, 11]

Newcomb, T. M. 1961. *The Acquaintance Process*. New York: Holt, Rinehart & Winston. [7, 11]

Newcomb, T. M. 1963. Stabilities underlying changes in interpersonal attraction. *Journal of Abnormal and Social Psychology*, 66:376–386. [7, 11]

Newcomb, T. M. 1968. Interpersonal balance. In Abelson, R. P., Aronson, E., McGuire, W. J., Newcomb, T. M., Rosenberg, M. J., and Tannenbaum, P. H. (eds.), *Theories of Cognitive Consistency: A Source Book*. Chicago: Rand McNally. [8]

Nichols, J. G. 1975. Causal attributions and other achievement-related cognitions: Effects of task outcome, attainment value and sex. *Journal of Personality and Social Psychology*, 31:379–389. [6]

Nicholson, N., Cole, S. G., and Rocklin, T. 1986. Coalition formation in parliamentary situations as a function of simulated ideology, resources, and electoral systems. *Political Psychology*, 7:103–116. [12]

Nisbett, R. E., Caputo, C., Legant, P., and Marecek, J. 1973. Behavior as seen by the actor and as seen by the observer. *Journal of Personality and Social Psychology*, 35:250–256. [6]

Nolen-Hoeksema, S. 1990. *Sex Differences in Depression*. Palo Alto, CA: Stanford University Press. [7]

Noller, P., and Fitzpatrick, M. A. 1990. Marital communication in the eighties. *Journal of Marriage and the Family*, 52:832–343. [11]

NORC. 1991. Question id: USNORC. GSS91.R266A. (April 1991) Roper Center POLLS [computer file]. [14]

Notiaius, C. I., and Pellegrini, D. S. 1987. Differences between husbands and wives: Implications for understanding marital discord. In Hahlweg, K., and Goldstein, M. J. (eds.), *Understanding Major Mental Disorder: The Contribution of Family Interaction Research*. New York: Family Process Press, pp. 231–249. [11]

Novak, D. W., and Lerner, M. J. 1968. Rejection as a consequence of perceived similarity. *Journal of Personality and Social Psychology*, 9:147–152. [11]

Oberschall, A. 1973. *Social Conflict and Social Movements*. Englewood Cliffs, NJ: Prentice-Hall. [16]

Obeyesekere, G. 1975. Sorcery, premeditated murder and the canalization of aggression in Sri Lanka. *Ethnology*, 14:1–23. [12]

Ochs, E. 1988. *Language, Affect, and Knowledge*. Cambridge, England: Cambridge University Press. [2]

Ochs, E. 1991. Misunderstanding children. In Coupland, N., Giles, H., and Wiemann, J. (eds.), *Miscommunication and Problematic Talk*. Newbury Park, CA: Sage. [2]

Offe, C. 1985. New social movements: Challenging the boundaries of institutional politics. *Social Research*, 52:817–868. [16]

O'Hair, M. J., Cody, M. J., and O'Hair, D. 1991. The impact of situational dimensions on compliance-resisting strategies: A comparison of methods. *Communication Quarterly*, 39:226–240. [13]

O'Keefe, B. J. 1988. The logic of message design: Individual differences in reasoning about communication. *Communication Monographs*, 55:80–103. [5]

O'Keefe, B. J., and Shepherd, G. J. 1987. The pursuit of multiple objectives in face-to-face persuasive interactions: Effects of construct differentiation on message organization. *Communication Monographs*, 54:396–419. [5]

Olian, J. D., Schwab, D. P., and Haberfeld, Y. 1988. The impact of applicant gender compared to qualifications on hiring recommendations: A meta-analysis of experimental studies. *Organizational Behavior and Human Decision Processes*, 41:180–195. [14]

Oliner, S., and Oliner, P. 1988. *The Altruistic Personality: Rescuers of Jews in Nazi Europe*. New York: Free Press. [10]

Oliver, P. E. 1980. Rewards and punishments as selective incentives for collective action. *American Journal of Sociology*, 85:1356–1375. [16]

Oliver, P. E. 1989. Bringing the crowd back in: The nonorganizational elements of social movements. *Research in Social Movements, Conflicts, and Change*, 11:1–30. [16]

Olson, M. 1965. *The Logic of Collective Action: Public Goods and the Theory of Groups*. New York: Schocken. [9]

Opp, K., and Roehl, W. 1990. Repression, micromobilization, and political protest. *Social Forces*, 69:521–547. [16]

O'Rand, A. M., and Krecker, M. L. 1990. Concepts of the life cycle: Their history, meanings, and uses in the social sciences. *Annual Review of Sociology*, 16:241–262. [3]

Orbell, J. M., van de Kragt, A. J., and Dawes, R. M. 1988. Explaining discussion-induced cooperation. *Journal of Personality and Social Psychology*, 54:811–819. [9]

Orcutt, J. D. 1983. *Analyzing Deviance*. Homewood, IL: Dorsey. [15]

Orfield, G. 1987. School segregation in the early 1980s. Washington, DC: Joint Center for Political Studies. [14]

Orne, M. 1962. On the social psychology of the psychological experiment. *American Psychologist*, 17:776-783. [1]

Osborn, R. N., and Jackson, D. H. 1988. Leaders, riverboat gamblers, or purposeful unintended consequences in the management of complex dangerous technologies. *Academy of Management Journal*, 31:924–947. [13]

Osgood, C. E., May, W. H., and Miron, M. S. 1975. *Cross Cultural*

Universals of Affective Meaning. Urbana: University of Illinois Press. [8]

Osgood, C. E., Suci, G. C., and Tannenbaum, P. H. 1957. *The Measurement of Meaning*. Urbana: University of Illinois Press. [8]

Osgood, C. E., and Tannenbaum, P. H. 1955. The principle of congruity in the prediction of attitude change. *Psychological Review*, 62:42–55. [8]

Osherson, S., and Dill, D. 1983. Varying work and family choices: Their impact on men's work satisfaction. *Journal of Marriage and the Family*, 45:339–346. [3]

O'Sullivan, M., Ekman, P., Friesen, W., and Scherer, K. 1985. What you say and how you say it: The contribution of speech content and voice quality to judgments of others. *Journal of Personality and Social Psychology*, 48:54–62. [5]

Otten, C. A., Penner, L. A., and Waugh, G. 1988. That's what friends are for: The determinants of psychological helping. *Journal of Social and Clinical Psychology*, 7:34–41. [10]

Padgett, V. R., and Wolosin, R. J. 1980. Cognitive similarity in dyadic communication. *Journal of Personality and Social Psychology*, 39:654–659. [11]

Pagel, M. D., and Davidson, A. R. 1984. A comparison of three social-psychological models of attitude and behavioral plan: Prediction of contraceptive behavior. *Journal of Personality and Social Psychology*, 47:517–533. [8]

Paikoff, R. L., Collins, W. A., and Laursen, B. 1988. Perceptions of efficacy and legitimacy of parental influence techniques by children and early adolescents. *Journal of Early Adolescence*, 8:37–52. [13]

Palatz, D. L., and Entman, R. M. 1981. *Media Power Politics*. New York: Free Press. [16]

Pallas, A., Entwisle, D. R., Alexander, K. L., and Weinstein, P. 1990. Social structure and the development of self-esteem in young children. *Social Psychology Quarterly*, 53:302–315. [7]

Paloutzian, R. F. 1981. Purpose in life and value changes following conversion. *Journal of Personality and Social Psychology*, 41:1153–1160. [16]

Papastamou, S., and Mugny, G. 1985. Rigidity and minority influence: The influence of the social in social influence. In Moscovici, S., Mugny, G.,

and Van Avermaet, E. (eds.), *Perspectives on Minority Influence*. Cambridge, England: Cambridge University Press. [9]

Paradiso, L. V., and Wall, S. M. 1986. Children's perceptions of male and female principals and teachers. *Sex Roles*, 14:1–7. [3]

Parcel, T. L., and Menaghan, E. G. 1990. Maternal working conditions and child verbal ability: Studying the transmission of intergenerational inequality from mothers to young children. *Social Psychology Quarterly*, 53:132–147. [3]

Park, R. E. 1922. The *Immigrant Press and Its Control*. New York: Harper. [1]

Parks, M. R., Stan, C. M., and Eggert, L. L. 1983. Romantic involvement and social network involvement. *Social Psychology Quarterly*, 46:116–131. [11]

Parsons, T. 1959. The social class as a social system: Some of its functions in American society. *Harvard Educational Review*, 29:297–318. [3]

Pasley, K., and Ihinger-Tallman, M. 1988. *Remarriage and Stepparenting: Current Research and Theory*. New York: Guilford Press. [3]

Passuth, P. M. 1987. Age hierarchies within children's groups. In Adler, P. A., and Adler, P. (eds.), *Sociological Studies of Child Development*, Vol. 2. Greenwich, CT: JAI Press. [2]

Patchen, M. 1982. *Black-White Contact in Schools: Its Social and Academic Effects*. West Lafayette, IN: Purdue University Press. [14]

Paternoster, R., and Iovanni, L. 1986. The deterrent effect of perceived severity: A reexamination. *Social Forces*, 64:751–777. [15]

Paton, S. M., Walberg, H. J., and Yeh, E. G. 1973. Ethnicity, environmental control, and academic self-concept in Chicago. *American Educational Research Journal*, 10:85–99. [14]

Patterson, G. R. 1982. *Coercive Family Process*. Eugene, OR: Castalia Press. [15]

Patterson, G. R., DeBaryshe, B. D., and Ramsey, E. 1989. A developmental perspective on antisocial behavior. *American Psychologist*, 44:329–335. [15]

Patterson, G. R., Dishion, T. J., and Bank, L. 1984. Family interaction: A process model of deviance training. *Aggressive Behavior*, 10:253–267. [15]

Patterson, M. L. 1988. Functions of nonverbal behavior in close relationships. In Duck, S. W. (ed.), *Handbook*

of Personal Relationships. New York: Wiley. [5]

Payne, J. W., Bettman, J. R., and Johnson, E. J. 1992. Behavioral decision research: A constructive processing perspective. *Annual Review of Psychology*, 34:87–131. [13]

Pearce, J. L. 1983. Job attitude and motivation differences between volunteers and employees from comparable organizations. *Journal of Applied Psychology*, 68:646–652. [10]

Pearlin, L., and Johnson, J. 1977. Marital status, life-strains and depression. *American Sociological Review*, 42:704–715. [7]

Peek, C., Fisher, J. L., and Kidwell, J. S. 1985. Teenage violence toward parents: A neglected dimension of family violence. *Journal of Marriage and the Family*, 47:1051–1058. [12]

Pellegrini, R. J. 1971. Some effects of seating position on social perception. *Psychological Reports*, 28:887–893. [5]

Peplau, L. A. 1981. What homosexuals want in a relationship. *Psychology Today*, 15(March):28–29. [11]

Peplau, L. A. 1983. Roles and gender. In Kelley, H. H., Berscheid, E., Christensen, A., Harvey, J. H., Huston, T. L., Levinger, G., McClintock, E., Peplau, L. A., and Peterson, D. R. (eds.), *Close Relationships*. New York: Freeman. [11]

Peretti, P. O., and Sydney, T. M. 1985. Parental toy stereotyping and its effects on child toy preference and sex role typing. *Social Behavior and Personality*, 12:213–216. [3]

Perinbanayagam, R. S. 1989. Signifying emotions. In Franks, D. D., and McCarthy, E. D. (eds.), *The Sociology of Emotions: Original Essays and Research Papers*. Greenwich, CT: JAI Press. [12]

Perlman, D., and Oskamp, S. 1971. The effects of picture content and exposure frequency on evaluations in Negroes and whites. *Journal of Experimental Social Psychology*, 7:503–514. [11]

Pessin, J., and Husband, R. 1933. Effects of social stimulation on human maze learning. *Journal of Abnormal and Social Psychology*, 28:148–154. [9]

Pestello, F. G., and Voydanoff, P. 1991. In search of mesostructure in the family: An interactionist approach to division of labor. *Symbolic Interaction*, 14:105–128. [4]

Petersilia, J. 1985. Racial disparities in the criminal justice system: A summary. *Crime and Delinquency*, 31:15–34. [14]

Peterson, A., Kennedy, R., and Sullivan, P. 1991. Coping with adolescence. In Colten, M., and Gore, S. (eds.), *Adolescent Stress: Causes and Consequences*. New York: Aldine de Gruyter. [7]

Peterson, D. R. 1983. Conflict. In Kelley, H. H., et al. (eds.), *Close Relationships*. New York: Freeman. [12]

Peterson, G. W., and Cleminshaw, H. 1980. The strength of single-parent families during the divorce crisis: An integrative review with clinical implications. In Stinner, N., Chesser, B., DeFrain, J., and Knaub, P. (eds.), *Family Strengths, Positive Models for Family Life*. Lincoln: University of Nebraska Press. [13]

Peterson, L. 1983. Role of donor competence, donor age, and peer presence on helping in an emergency. *Developmental Psychology*, 19:873–880. [10]

Peterson, R. R. 1989a. Firm size, occupational segregation, and the effects of family status on women's wages. *Social Forces*, 68:397–414. [3]

Peterson, R. R. 1989b. *Women, Work, and Divorce*. Albany: State University of New York Press. [3]

Pett, M. A., and Vaughan-Cole, B. 1986. The impact of income issues and social status in post-divorce adjustment of custodial parents. *Family Relations*, 35:103–111. [3]

Pettigrew, T. F. 1979. The ultimate attribution error: Extending Allport's cognitive analysis of prejudice. *Personality and Social Psychology Bulletin*, 5:461–476. [6]

Pettigrew, T. F., and Martin, J. 1987. Shaping the organizational context for black American inclusion. *Journal of Social Issues*, 43:41–78. [14]

Petty, R. E., and Cacioppo, J. T. 1986. The elaboration likelihood model of persuasion. In Berkowitz, L. (ed.), *Advances in Experimental Social Psychology*, Vol. 19. New York: Academic Press. [13]

Pfeiffer, J. 1985. Girl talk, boy talk. *Science 85*, 6(February):58–63. [5]

Philips, S. 1990. The judge as third party in American trial-court conflict talk. In Grimshaw, A. (ed), *Conflict Talk: Sociolinguistic Investigations of Arguments in Conversations*. New York: Cambridge University Press. [5]

Phillips, D. A., and Zigler, E. 1980. Children's self-image disparity: Ef-

fects of age, socioeconomic status, ethnicity, and gender. *Journal of Personality and Social Psychology*, 39: 689–700. [14]

Piaget, J. 1954. *The Language and Thought of the Child*. New York: Meridian. [2]

Piliavin, I. M., Gartner, R., Thornton, C., and Matsueda, R. L. 1986. Crime, deterrence, and rational choice. *American Sociological Review*, 51:101–119. [15]

Piliavin, I. M., and Piliavin, J. A. 1972. Effects of blood on reactions to a victim. *Journal of Personality and Social Psychology*, 23:353–361. [10]

Piliavin, I. M., Piliavin, J. A., and Rodin, J. 1975. Cost, diffusion, and the stigmatized victim. *Journal of Personality and Social Psychology*, 32:429–438. [10]

Piliavin, I. M., Rodin, J., and Piliavin, J. A. 1969. Good Samaritanism: An underground phenomenon? *Journal of Personality and Social Psychology*, 13: 289–299. [10]

Piliavin, J. A., and Callero, P. L. 1991. *Giving Blood: The Development of an Altruistic Identity*. Baltimore, MD: Johns Hopkins University Press. [10]

Piliavin, J. A., and Charng, H. W. 1990. Altruism: A review of recent theory and research. *Annual Review of Sociology*, 16:27–65. [10]

Pillemer, K. A., and Suiter, J. 1988. Elder abuse. In Van Hasselt, V. B., Morrison, R. L., Bellack, A. S., and Hersen, M. (eds.), *Handbook of Family Violence*. New York: Plenum. [12]

Pillemer, K. A., and Wolf, R. S. (eds.). 1986. *Elder Abuse: Conflict in the Family*. Dover, MA: Auburn House. [3]

Pitchner, B. L., Hamblin, R. L., and Miller, J. L. L. 1978. The diffusion of collective violence. *American Sociological Review*, 43:23–35. [16]

Pitt-Rivers, J. 1967. Race, color, and class in Central America and the Andes. *Daedalus*, 96:542–559. [4]

Piven, F., and Cloward, R. 1977. *Poor People's Movements*. New York: Pantheon. [16]

Pleck, J. 1985. *Working Wives/Working Husbands*. Beverly Hills, CA: Sage. [14]

Pliner, P., Hart, H., Kohl, J., and Saari, D. 1974. Compliance without pressure: Some further data on the foot-in-the-door technique. *Journal of Experimental Social Psychology*, 10: 17–22. [13]

Podsakoff, P., and Schriesheim, C. 1985. Field studies of French and Raven's bases of power: Critique, reanalysis, and suggestions for future research. *Psychological Bulletin*, 97:387–411. [13]

Pomerleau, A., Bolduc, D., Malcuit, G., and Cossette, L. 1990. Pink or blue: Environmental gender stereotypes in the first two years of life. *Sex Roles*, 22:359–367. [3]

Porter, J. 1971. *Black Child, White Child: The Development of Racial Attitudes*. Cambridge, MA: Harvard University Press. [14]

Porter, N., and Geis, F. L. 1981. Women and nonverbal leadership cues: When seeing is not believing. In Mayo, C., and Henley, N. M. (eds.), *Gender and Nonverbal Behavior*. New York: Springer-Verlag, pp. 39–61. [5]

Powell, G. N. 1990. One more time: Do female and male managers differ? *Academy of Management Executives*, 4: 68–75. [5]

Powers, S., Hauser, S., and Kilner, L. 1989. Adolescent mental health. *American Psychologist*, 44:200–208. [3]

Powitzky, R. J. 1990. Correctional responses to violence and violent offender. In Hertzberg, L. J., Ostrum, G. F., and Field, J. R. (eds.), *Violent Behavior*, Vol. 1. Great Neck, NY: PMA Publishing. [12]

Prentice-Dunn, S., and Rogers, R. W. 1980. Effects of deindividuating situational cues and aggressive models on subjective deindividuation and aggression. *Journal of Personality and Social Psychology*, 39:104–113. [12]

Prentice-Dunn, S., and Rogers, R. W. 1982. Effects of public and private self-awareness on deindividuation and aggression. *Journal of Personality and Social Psychology*, 43:503–513. [12]

Press, J. J. 1968. Self and role in medical education. In Gordon, C., and Gergen, K. J. (eds.), *The Self in Social Interaction*. New York: Wiley. [7]

Pringle, R. 1989. *Secretaries Talk: Sexuality, Power, and Work*. New York: Verso. [14]

Protess, D. L., Cook, F. L., Krutin, T. R., Gordon, M. T., Leff, D. L., McCombs, M. E., and Miller, P. 1987. The impact of investigative reporting on public opinion and policy making. *Public Opinion Quarterly*, 51: 166–185. [16]

Prud'homme, A. 1991. Police brutality! *Time* (March 25):16. [12]

Pruitt, D. G., and Rubin, J. Z. 1986.

Social Conflict: Escalation, Stalemate, and Settlement. New York: Random House. [12]

Pryor, B. W. 1990. Predicting and explaining intentions to participate in continuing education: An application of the theory of reasoned action. *Adult Education Quarterly*, 40:146–157. [8]

Quadagno, J. 1980. *Aging, the Individual, and Society.* New York: St. Martin's Press. [3]

Quadagno, J. 1986. Aging. In Ritzer, G. (ed.), *Social Problems* (2nd ed.). New York: Random House. [3]

Quadland, M. C., and Shattis, W. D. 1987. AIDS, sexuality, and sexual control. *Journal of Homosexuality*, 13:13–42. [11]

Quarantelli, E., and Cooper, J. 1966. Self-conceptions and others: A further test of Meadian hypotheses. *Sociological Quarterly*, 7:281–297. [7]

Quinney, R. 1981. *Class, State and Crime.* 2nd ed. New York: Longman. [15]

Rabow, J., and Hernandez, A. C. R. 1986. College students do intervene in drunk driving situations. *Sociology and Social Research*, 70:224–225. [10]

Rabow, J., Neuman, C. A., and Hernandez, A. C. R. 1987. Cognitive consistency in attitudes, social support and consumption of alcohol: Additive and interactive effects. *Social Psychology Quarterly*, 50:56–63. [8]

Rabow, J., Neuman, C. A., Watts, R. K., and Hernandez, A. C. R. 1987. Alcohol-related hazardous behavior among college students. In Galanter, M. (ed.), *Recent Developments in Alcoholism*, Vol. 5. New York: Plenum, pp. 439–450. [10]

Rabow, J., Newcomb, M. D., Monto, M. A., and Hernandez, A. C. R. 1990. Altruism in drunk driving situations: Personal and situational factors in intervention. *Social Psychology Quarterly*, 3:199–213. [10]

Rachlin, H., Logue, A. W., Gibbon, J., and Frankel, M. 1986. Cognition and behavior in studies of choice. *Psychological Review*, 93:33–45. [13]

Rafaeli, A., and Sutton, R. I. 1991. Emotional contrast strategies as means of social influence: Lessons of criminal investigators and bill collectors. *Academy of Management Journal*, 34:749–775. [13]

Rahim, M. A. 1989. Relationships of leader power to compliance and satisfaction with supervision: Evidence from a national sample of managers. *Journal of Management*, 15:545–556. [13]

Ramirez, J., Bryant, J., and Zillmann, D. 1982. Effects of erotica on retaliatory behavior as a function of prior provocation. *Journal of Personality and Social Psychology*, 43:971–978. [12]

Rankin, J. 1980. School factors and delinquency. *Sociology and Social Research*, 64:420–434. [15]

Rankin, J., and Wells, L. E. 1990. The effect of parental attachments and direct controls on delinquency. *Journal of Research in Crime and Delinquency*, 27:140–165. [15]

Raschke, H. C. 1987. Divorce. In Burr, W. R., Hill, R., Nye, F. I., and Reiss, I. L. (eds.), *Handbook of Marriage and the Family.* New York: Free Press. [14]

Raven, B. H. 1974. The comparative analysis of power and power preference. In Tedeschi, J. T. (ed.), *Perspectives on Social Power*. Chicago: Aldine. [13]

Raven, B. H. 1988. French and Raven 30 years later: Power, interaction, and interpersonal influence. Paper presented at the International Congress of Psychology, Sydney, Australia (August). [13]

Raven, B. H. 1990. Political applications of the psychology of interpersonal influence and social power. *Political Psychology*, 11:493–520. [13]

Rawlins, W. 1983a. Negotiating close friendship: The dialectics of conjunctive freedoms. *Human Communication Research*, 9:255–266. [11]

Rawlins, W. 1983b. Openness as problematic in ongoing friendships: Two conversational dilemmas. *Communication Monographs*, 50:1–13. [11]

Ray, M., and Downs, W. 1986. An empirical test of labeling theory using longitudinal data. *Journal of Research in Crime and Delinquency*, 23:169–194. [15]

Razran, G. 1950. Ethnic dislike and stereotypes: A laboratory study. *Journal of Abnormal and Social Psychology*, 45:7–27. [6]

Reed, R. 1985. Little Rock a symbol again: The resegregation of schools. *New York Times* (March 27):1–7. [14]

Reese, W.A., II, and Katovich, M. A. 1989. Untimely acts: Extending the interactionists conception of deviance. *Sociological Quarterly*, 30:159–184. [15]

Reid, S. T. 1988. *Crime and Criminology* (5th ed.). New York: Holt, Rinehart & Winston. [15]

Reiman, J. 1990. *The Rich Get Richer and the Poor Get Prison: Ideology, Class, and Criminal Justice* (3rd ed.). New York: Macmillan. [15]

Reis, H. T. 1986. Gender effects in social participation: Intimacy, loneliness, and the conduct of social interaction. In Gilmour, R., and Duck, S. (eds.), *The Emerging Field of Personal Relationships.* Hillsdale, NJ: Erlbaum. [5]

Reis, H. T., Nezlek, J., and Wheeler, L. 1980. Physical attractiveness in social interaction. *Journal of Personality and Social Psychology*, 38:604–615. [11]

Reis, H. T., Senchak, M., and Solomon, B. 1985. Sex differences in the intimacy of social interaction: Further examination of potential explanations. *Journal of Personality and Social Psychology*, 48:1204–1217. [11]

Reis, H. T., and Shaver, P. 1988. Intimacy as an interpersonal process. In Duck, S. W. (ed.), *Handbook of Personal Relationships: Theory, Research and Interventions.* New York: Wiley. [11]

Reis, H. T., Wheeler, L., Kernis, M., Speigel, N., and Nezlek, J. 1985. On specificity in the impact of social participation on physical and psychological health. *Journal of Personality and Social Psychology*, 48:456–471. [4]

Reis, H. T., Wheeler, L., Speigel, N., Kernis, M. H., Nezlek, J., and Perri, M. 1982. Physical attractiveness in social interaction. II: Why does appearance affect social experience? *Journal of Personality and Social Psychology*, 43:979–996. [6]

Reskin, B. A., and Hartmann, H. I. (eds.). 1986. *Women's Work, Men's Work; Sex Segregation on the Job.* Washington, DC: National Academy Press. [6, 14]

Reskin, B. A., and Padavic, I. 1988. Supervisors as gatekeepers: Male supervisors' response to women's integration in plant jobs. *Social Problems*, 35:536–550. [14]

Reskin, B. A., and Roos, P. 1987. Sex segregation and status hierarchies. In Bose, C., and Spitze, G. (eds.), *Ingredients for Women's Employment Policy.* Albany: State University of New York Press. [14]

Reskin, B. A., and Roos, P. 1990. *Gender Queues, Job Queues: Explaining Women's Inroads into Male Occupations.* Philadelphia: Temple University Press. [14]

Rheingold, H. L., and Cook, K. V. 1975. The contents of boys' and girls' rooms as an index of parents' behavior. *Child Development*, 46:459–463. [3]

Rice, F. P. 1986. *Adult Development and Aging.* Boston: Allyn & Bacon. [3]

Rice, F. P. 1989. *Human Sexuality.* Dubuque, IA: William C. Brown. [3]

Richardson, J. T. 1985. The active vs. passive convert: Paradigm conflict in conversion/recruitment research. *Journal for the Scientific Study of Religion*, 24:163–179. [16]

Richardson, J. T., van der Lans, J., and Derks, F. 1986. Leaving and labeling: Voluntary and coerced disaffiliation from religious social movements. *Research in Social Movements*, 9:97–126. [16]

Richins, M. L. 1991. Social comparison and the idealized images of advertising. *Journal of Consumer Research*, 18:71–83. [7]

Ridgeway, C. L. 1983. *The Dynamics of Small Groups.* New York: St. Martin's Press. [11]

Ridgeway, C. L. 1987. Nonverbal behavior, dominance, and the basis of status in task groups. *American Sociological Review*, 52:683–694. [5]

Ridgeway, C. L. 1992. Introduction: Gender and the role of interaction in inequality. In Ridgeway, C. L. (ed.), *Gender, Interaction, and Inequality.* New York: Springer-Verlag. [5]

Ridgeway, C. L., and Diekema, D. 1992. Are gender differences status differences? In Ridgeway, C. L. (ed.). *Gender, Interaction, and Inequality.* New York: Springer-Verlag. [5]

Ried, L. D., and Christensen, D. B. 1988. A psychosocial perspective in the explanation of patients' drug-taking behavior. *Social Science and Medicine*, 27:277–285. [8]

Riger, S., and Gordon, M. T. 1981. The fear of rape: A study in social control. *Journal of Social Issues*, 37:71–92. [12]

Riley, M. W. 1987. On the significance of age in sociology. *American Sociological Review*, 52:1–14. [3]

Rindfuss, R. R., Swicegood, C. G., and Rosenfeld, R. A. 1987. Disorder in the life course: How common and does it matter? *American Sociological Review*, 52:785–801. [3]

Riordan, C. A., Marlin, N. A., and Kellogg, R. T. 1983. The effectiveness of accounts following transgressions. *Social Psychology Quarterly*, 46:213–219. [15]

Ritzer, G., and Walczak, D. 1986. *Working: Conflict and Change,* Englewood Cliffs, NJ: Prentice-Hall. [12]

Ritzman, R. L., and Tomaskovic-Devey, D. 1992. Life chances and support for equality and equity as normative and counternormative distribution rules. *Social Forces*, 70:745–763. [14]

Rivera, R. R. 1991. Sexual orientation and the law. In Gonsiorek, J. C., and Weinrich, J. D. (eds.), *Homosexuality: Research Implications for Public Policy.* Newbury Park, CA: Sage. [15]

Rizzo, T. A. 1989. *Friendship Development among Children in School.* Norwood, NJ: Ablex. [3]

Robbins, T. 1988. *Cults, Converts, and Charisma.* Newbury Park, CA: Sage. [16]

Robbins, T., and Anthony, D. 1982. Deprogramming, brainwashing, and the medicalization of deviant religious groups. *Social Problems*, 29:283–297. [16]

Robertson, J. F. 1978. Women in mid-life: Crisis, reverberations, and support networks. *Family Coordinator*, 27:375–382. [3]

Robinson, C., and Morris, J. T. 1987. The gender-stereotyped nature of Christmas toys received by 36-, 48-, and 60-month old children: A comparison between requested and nonrequested toys. *Sex Roles*, 15:21–32. [3]

Robinson, D. T., and Smith-Lovin, L. 1992. Selective interaction as a strategy for identity maintenance: An affect control model. *Social Psychology Quarterly*, 55:12–28. [1, 7, 8]

Rochford, E. B., Jr. 1982. Recruitment strategies: Ideology and organization in the Hare Krishna movement. *Social Problems*, 29:399–410. [16]

Rodin, J. 1987. Personal control through the life course. In Abeles, R. (ed.), *Life-Span Perspectives and Social Psychology.* Hillsdale, NJ: Erlbaum. [7]

Roethlisberger, F. J., and Dickson, W. J. 1939. *Management and the Worker.* Cambridge, MA: Harvard University Press. [9]

Roff, J. D., and Wirt, D. 1984. Childhood aggression and social adjustment as antecedents of delinquency. *Journal of Abnormal Child Psychology*, 12:111–126. [15]

Rogers, R. W. 1983. Cognitive and physiological processes in fear appeals and attitude change: A revised theory of protection motivation. In Cacioppo, J., and Petty, R. (eds.), *Social Psychophysiology.* New York: Guilford Press. [13]

Rogers, S. J., Parcel, T. L., and Menaghan, E. G. 1991. The effects of maternal working conditions and mastery on child behavior problems: Studying the intergenerational transmission of social control. *Journal of Health and Social Behavior*, 32:145–164. [3]

Romer, D. 1979. Internalization versus identification in the laboratory: A causal analysis of attitude change. *Journal of Personality and Social Psychology*, 37:2171–2180. [13]

Romer, D., Gruder, C. L., and Lizzadro, T. 1986. A person-situation approach to altruistic behavior. *Journal of Personality and Social Psychology*, 51:1001–1012. [10]

Ronis, D. L., and Lipinski, E. R. 1985. Value and uncertainty as weighting factors in impression formation. *Journal of Experimental Social Psychology*, 21:47–60. [6]

Roper Organization. 1985. Question id: USROPER.85-7.R45. (July 1985) Roper Center POLLS [computer file]. [14]

Rose, S. M. 1984. How friendships end: Patterns among young adults. *Journal of Social and Personal Relationships*, 1:267–277. [11]

Rosenbaum, J. L., and Lasley, J. 1990. School, community context, and delinquency: Rethinking the gender gap. *Justice Quarterly*, 7:493–513. [15]

Rosenbaum, M. W. 1986. The repulsion hypothesis: On the nondevelopment of relationships. *Journal of Personality and Social Psychology*, 51:1156–1166. [11]

Rosenberg, M. 1965. *Society and the Adolescent Self-Image.* Princeton, NJ: Princeton University Press. [7]

Rosenberg, M. 1975. The dissonant context and the adolescent self-concept. In Dragastin, S., and Elder, G. (eds.), *Adolescence in the Life Cycle: Psychological Change and Social Context.* Washington, DC: Hemisphere. [7]

Rosenberg, M. 1979. *Conceiving the Self.* New York: Basic Books. [7]

Rosenberg, M. 1981. The self-concept: Social product and social force. In Rosenberg, M., and Turner, R. H. (eds.), *Social Psychology: Sociological Perspectives.* New York: Basic Books. [7]

Rosenberg, M. 1986. Self-concept from middle childhood through adolescence. In Suls, J., and Greenwald, A. (eds.), *Psychological Perspectives on the*

Self, Vol. 3. Hillsdale, NJ: Erlbaum. [7]

Rosenberg, M. 1990. Reflexivity and emotions. *Social Psychology Quarterly,* 53:3–12. [7, 11, 12]

Rosenberg, M., and Pearlin, L. I. 1978. Social class and self-esteem among children and adults. *American Journal of Sociology,* 84:53–78. [7]

Rosenberg, M., and Simmons, R. G. 1972. *Black and White Self-esteem: The Urban School Child.* Washington, DC: American Sociological Association. [7, 14]

Rosenhan, D. L., Salovey, P., and Hargis, K. 1981. The joys of helping: Focus of attention mediates the impact of positive affect on altruism. *Journal of Personality and Social Psychology,* 40:899–905. [10]

Rosenthal, R. 1966. *Experimenter Effects in Behavioral Research.* New York: Appleton-Century-Crofts. [1]

Rosenthal, R. 1985. From unconscious experimenter bias to teacher expectancy effects. In Dusek, J. (ed.), *Teacher Expectancies.* Hillsdale, NJ: Erlbaum. [14]

Rosenthal, R. 1986. Media violence, antisocial behavior, and the social consequences of small effects. *Journal of Social Issues,* 42:141–154. [12]

Rosenthal, R., and Jacobson, L. 1968. *Pygmalion in the Classroom.* New York: Holt, Rinehart & Winston. [3]

Ross, E. A. 1908. *Social Psychology: An Outline and Source Book.* New York: Macmillan. [1, 16]

Ross, H., and Taylor, H. 1989. Do boys prefer Daddy or his physical style of play? *Sex Roles,* 20:23–31. [3]

Ross, L. 1977. The intuitive psychologist and his shortcomings: Distortions in the attribution process. In Berkowitz, L. (ed.), *Advances in Experimental Social Psychology,* Vol. 10. New York: Academic Press. [6]

Ross, M., and Sicoly, F. 1979. Egocentric biases in availability and attribution. *Journal of Personality and Social Psychology,* 37:322–336. [7]

Rossi, A. S. 1968. Transition to parenthood. *Journal of Marriage and the Family,* 30:26–39. [3]

Rossi, A. S. 1980. Aging and parenthood in the middle years. In Baltes, P. B., and Brim, O. G., Jr. (eds.), *Life-Span Development and Behavior,* Vol. 3. New York: Academic Press. [3]

Rossi, A. S., and Rossi, P. H. 1990. *Of Human Bonding: Parent-Child Relations across the Life Course.* New York: Aldine de Gruyter. [10, 11]

Roth, D. L., Snyder, C. R., and Pace, L. M. 1986. Dimensions of favorable self-presentation. *Journal of Personality and Social Psychology,* 51: 867–874. [7]

Rothbart, M., and John, O. P. 1985. Social categorization and behavioral episodes: A cognitive analysis of the effects of intergroup contact. *Journal of Social Issues,* 41:81–104. [12]

Rothbaum, F., Weisz, J., and Snyder, S. 1982. Changing the work and changing the self: A two-process model of perceived control. *Journal of Personality and Social Psychology,* 42: 5–37. [7]

Rotter, J. B. 1966. Generalized expectancies for internal versus external control of reinforcement. *Psychological Monographs,* 80 (1, Whole No. 609). [7]

Ruberman, W., Weinblatt, E., Goldberg, J., and Chaudhary, B. 1984. Psychosocial influences on mortality after myocardial infarction. *New England Journal of Medicine,* 311:552–559. [4]

Rubin, J. Z., Provenzano, F. J., and Luria, Z. 1974. The eye of the beholder: Parents' views on sex of newborns. *American Journal of Orthopsychiatry,* 44:512–519. [3]

Rubin, L. B. 1978. *Women of a Certain Age: The Midlife Search for Self.* New York: Harper & Row. [3]

Rubin, L. B. 1983. *Intimate Strangers: Men and Women Together.* New York: Harper & Row. [3]

Rubin, Z. 1970. Measurement of romantic love. *Journal of Personality and Social Psychology,* 16:265–273. [11]

Rubin, Z. 1975. Disclosing oneself to a stranger: Reciprocity and its limits. *Journal of Experimental Social Psychology,* 11:233–260. [11]

Rubin, Z. 1977. The love research. *Human Behavior,* 6(February):56–59. [11]

Rupp, L. J., and Taylor, V. 1987. *Survival in the Doldrums: The American Women's Rights Movement, 1945 to the 1960s.* New York: Oxford University Press. [16]

Rusbult, C. E. 1980. Commitment and satisfaction in romantic associations: A test of the investment model. *Journal of Experimental Social Psychology,* 16:172–186. [11]

Rusbult, C. E. 1983. A longitudinal test of the investment model: The development (and deterioration) of satisfaction and commitment in heterosexual involvements. *Journal of Personality and Social Psychology,* 45: 101–117. [11]

Rusbult, C. E., Johnson, D. J., and Morrow, G. D. 1986. Predicting satisfaction and commitment in adult romantic involvements: An assessment of the generalizability of the investment model. *Social Psychology Quarterly,* 49:81–89. [11]

Rusbult, C. E., and Zembrodt, I. M. 1983. Responses to dissatisfaction in romantic involvements: A multidimensional scaling analysis. *Journal of Experimental Social Psychology,* 19: 274–293. [11]

Rusbult, C. E., Zembrodt, I. M., and Gunn, L. K. 1982. Exit, voice, loyalty, and neglect: Responses to dissatisfaction in romantic involvements. *Journal of Personality and Social Psychology,* 43:1230–1242. [11]

Rush, M. C., and Russell, J. E. A. 1988. Leader prototypes and prototype-contingent consensus in leader behavior descriptions. *Journal of Experimental Social Psychology,* 24:88–104. [6]

Russell, D. E. H. 1982. *Rape in Marriage.* New York: Macmillan. [12]

Russell, J. E. A., Rush, M. C., and Herd, A. M. 1988. An exploration of women's expectations of effective male and female leadership. *Sex Roles,* 18:279–287. [5]

Rutkowski, G. K., Gruder, C. L., and Romer, D. 1983. Group cohesiveness, social norms, and bystander intervention. *Journal of Personality and Social Psychology,* 44:545–552. [10]

Rutter, D. 1987. *Communicating by Telephone.* Elmsford, NY: Pergamon. [5]

Rutter, M., and Giller, H. 1984. *Juvenile Delinquency: Trends and Perspectives.* New York: Guilford Press. [15]

Rychlak, J. F. 1965. The similarity, complementarity, or incomplementarity of needs in interpersonal selection. *Journal of Personality and Social Psychology,* 2:334–340. [11]

Sabatelli, R., and Pearce, J. 1986. Exploring marital expectations. *Journal of Social and Personal Relationships*, 3:307–322. [11]

Sabato, L. J. 1981. *The Rise of Political Consultants*. New York: Basic Books. [13]

Sabers, D., Cushing, D., and Sabers, D. 1987. Sex differences in reading and mathematics achievement for middle school students. *Journal of Early Adolescence*, 7:117–128. [14]

Sachs, H. 1990. *Lectures on Conversation 1964–1972*. Edited by G. Jefferson. Oxford: Basil Blackwell. [5]

Sadker, M., and Sadker, D. 1985a. Sexism in the schoolroom of the 80s. *Psychology Today*, 19(March):54–57. [3]

Sadker, M., and Sadker, D. 1985b. Striving for equity in classroom teaching. In Sargent, A. G. (ed.), *Beyond Sex Roles*. New York: West. [14]

Saenger, G., and Gilbert, E. 1950. Customer reactions to the integration of Negro sales personnel. *International Journal of Opinion and Attitude Research*, 4:57–76. [8]

Saergert, S., Swap, W., and Zajonc, R. B. 1973. Exposure, context, and interpersonal attraction. *Journal of Personality and Social Psychology*, 25:234–252. [11]

Saks, M. J. 1977. *Jury Verdicts: The Role of Group Size and Social Decision Rule*. Lexington, MA: Lexington Books. [9]

Saks, M. J. 1978. Social psychological contributions to a legislative subcommittee on organ and tissue transplants. *American Psychologist*, 33:680–690. [13]

Salovey, P., Mayer, J., and Rosenhan, D. 1991. Mood and helping: Mood as a motivator of helping and helping as a regulator of mood. In Clark, M. (ed.), *Prosocial Behavior*. Newbury Park, CA: Sage. [10]

Saluter, A. 1989. Marital status and living arrangements: March 1989. In Bureau of the Census, *Current Population Reports*, "Population Characteristics," Series P–20, no. 445. Washington, DC: U.S. Government Printing Office. [3]

Sampson, R. J. 1986. Effects of socioeconomic context of official reaction to juvenile delinquency. *American Sociological Review*, 51:876–885. [15]

Sampson, R. J., and Laub, J. H. 1990.

Crime and deviance over the life course: The salience of adult social bonds. *American Sociological Review*, 55:609–627. [15]

Sanbonmatsu, D., Kardes, F., and Sansome, C. 1991. Remembering less and inferring more: Effects of time of judgment on inferences about unknown attributes. *Journal of Personality and Social Psychology*, 61:546–554. [6]

Sato, I. 1988. Play theory of delinquency: Toward a general theory of "action." *Symbolic Interaction*, 11:191–212. [15]

Sattel, J. W. 1990. The inexpressive male: Tragedy or sexual politics? In Kimmel, M. S., and Messner, M. A. (eds.), *Men's Lives*. New York: Macmillan. [11]

Schafer, R., and Keith, P. 1985. A causal model approach to the symbolic interactionist view of the self-concept. *Journal of Personality and Social Psychology*, 48:963–969. [7]

Schaller, M., and Cialdini, R. B. 1988. The economics of empathetic helping: Support for a mood management motive. *Journal of Experimental Social Psychology*, 24:163–181. [10]

Scheflen, A. E., and Ashcraft, N. 1976. *Human Territories: How We Behave in Space and Time*. Englewood Cliffs, NJ: Prentice-Hall. [5]

Schegloff, E. 1979. Identification and recognition in telephone conversation openings. In Psathas, G. (ed.), *Everyday Language: Studies in Ethnomethodology*. New York: Irvington Press. [5]

Schegloff, E. 1987a. Analyzing single episodes of interaction: An exercise in conversation analysis. *Social Psychology Quarterly*, 50:101–114. [5]

Schegloff, E. 1987b. Recycled turn beginnings: A precise repair mechanism in conversation's turn-taking organization. In Button, G., and Lee, J. (eds.), *Talk and Social Organization*. Clevedon, England: Multilingual Matters Ltd. [5]

Scher, S. J., and Cooper, J. 1989. Motivational basis of dissonance: The singular role of behavioral consequences. *Journal of Personality and Social Psychology*, 56:899–906. [8]

Schieffelin, E. L. 1976. *The Sorrow of the Lonely and the Burning of the Dancers*. New York: St. Martin's Press. [15]

Schiffrin, D. 1990. The management of a cooperative self during argument: The role of opinion and stories. In Grimshaw, A. (ed.), *Conflict Talk: Sociolinguistic Investigations of Arguments in Conversations*. New York: Cambridge University Press. [5]

Schifter, D. E., and Ajzen, I. 1985. Intention, perceived control, and weight loss: An application of the theory of planned behavior. *Journal of Personality and Social Psychology*, 49:843–851. [8]

Schlenker, B. R. 1980. *Impression Management: The Self-concept, Social Identity, and Interpersonal Relations*. Monterey, CA: Brooks/Cole. [7]

Schlenker, B. R., and Darby, B. W. 1981. The use of apologies in social predicaments. *Social Psychology Quarterly*, 44:271–278. [15]

Schlenker, B. R., and Leary, M. 1982. Social anxiety and self-presentation: A conceptualization and model. *Psychological Bulletin*, 92:641–669. [7]

Schlenker, B. R., and Weigold, M., 1992. Interpersonal processes involving impression regulation and management. *Annual Review of Psychology*, 43:133–165. [7]

Schmidt, G., and Weiner, B. 1988. An attribution-affect-action theory of behavior: Replications of judgments of help-giving. *Personality and Social Psychology Bulletin*, 14:610–621. [10]

Schmidt, W. E. 1985. Jim Crow is gone, but white resistance remains. *New York Times* (April 6):1–7. [14]

Schmidtt, K. P., and Kurdek, L. H. 1987. Personality correlates of positive identity and relationship involvement in gay men. *Journal of Homosexuality*, 13:101–109. [15]

Schmitt, B. H., Gilovich, T., Goore, N., and Joseph, L. 1986. Mere presence and social facilitation: One more time. *Journal of Experimental Social Psychology*, 22:242–248. [9]

Schneider, A. L. 1990. *Deterrence and Juvenile Crime: Results from a National Policy Experiment*. New York: Springer-Verlag. [15]

Schneider, D. 1991. Social cognition. *Annual Review of Psychology*, 42:527–561. [6]

Schofield, J. W. 1975. Effects of norms, public disclosure, and need for approval on volunteering behavior consistent with attitudes. *Journal of*

Personality and Social Psychology, 33: 1126–1133. [9]

Schofield, J. W. 1982. *Black and White in School: Trust, Tension, or Tolerance?* New York: Praeger. [5]

Schopler, J., and Layton, B. 1972. Determinants of the self-attribution of having influenced another person. *Journal of Personality and Social Psychology*, 22:326–332. [6]

Schram, R. W. 1979. Marital satisfaction over the family life cycle. *Journal of Marriage and the Family*, 41:7–12. [3]

Schriesheim, C. A., and Hinkin, T. R. 1990. Influence tactics used by subordinates: A theoretical and empirical analysis and refinement of the Kipnis, Schmidt, and Wilkinson subscales. *Journal of Applied Psychology*, 75:246–257. [13]

Schroeder, D. A., Irwin, M. E., and Sibicky, M. E. 1988. Social dilemma: A unifying framework. Paper presented at the 11th International Conference on Groups, Networks, and Organizations, Nags Head, NC. [9]

Schuman, H., and Johnson, M. P. 1976. Attitudes and behaviors. *Annual Review of Sociology*, 2:161–207. [8]

Schuman, H., and Scott, J. 1989. Generations and collective memories. *American Sociological Review*, 54:359–381.[3]

Schumm, W. R., and Bugaighis, M. A. 1986. Marital quality over the marital career: Alternative explanations. *Journal of Marriage and the Family*, 48:381–387. [11]

Schumm, W. R., Bugaighis, M. A., Jurich, A. P., and Bollman, S. R. 1986. Example and explanation as predictors of adolescent compliance with parental instructions. *Journal of Social Behavior and Personality*, 1:465–470. [13]

Schutte, J. G., and Light, J. M. 1978. The relative importance of proximity and status of relationship choices in social hierarchies. *Social Psychology*, 41: 260–264. [11]

Schutte, N. S., Kendrick, K. T., and Sadalla, E. K. 1985. The search for predictable settings: Situational prototypes, constraint, and behavioral variation. *Journal of Personality and Social Psychology*, 49:121–128. [8]

Schwalbe, M. L., Gecas, V., and Baxter, R. 1986. The effects of occupational conditions and individual characteristics on the importance of

self-esteem sources in the workplace. *Basic and Applied Social Psychology*, 7:63–84. [7]

Schwalbe, M. L., and Staples, C. 1991. Gender differences in sources of self-esteem. *Social Psychology Quarterly*, 54:158–168. [7]

Schwartz, B. 1974. Waiting, exchange, and power. *American Journal of Sociology*, 79:841–870. [13]

Schwartz, B., and Barsky, S. 1977. The home advantage. *Social Forces*, 55:641–661. [4]

Schwartz, J. 1987. A "superminority" tops out. *Newsweek* (May 11):48–49. [14]

Schwartz, N., Strack, F., and Mai, H. 1991. Assimilation and contrast effects in part-whole question sequences. *Public Opinion Quarterly*, 55: 2-23. [1]

Schwartz, S. H., and Gottlieb, A. 1980*a*. Bystander anonymity and reactions to emergencies. *Journal of Personality and Social Psychology*, 39: 418-430. [1, 10]

Schwartz, S. H., and Gottlieb, A. 1980*b*. Participation in a bystander intervention experiment and subsequent everyday helping: Ethical considerations. *Journal of Experimental Social Psychology*, 16:161-171. [1]

Schwartz, S. H., and Gottlieb, A. 1981. Participants' post-experimental reactions and the ethics of bystander research. *Journal of Experimental Social Psychology*, 17:396-407. [1]

Schwarz, L. M., Foa, U. G., and Foa, E. B. 1983. Multichannel nonverbal communication: Evidence for combinatory rules. *Journal of Personality and Social Psychology*, 45:274–281. [5]

Schwarzwald, J., Bizman, A., and Raz, M. 1983. The foot-in-the-door paradigm: Effects of second request size on donation probability and donor generosity. *Personality and Social Psychology Bulletin*, 9:443–450. [13]

Sebald, H. 1986. Adolescents' shifting orientations toward parents and peers: A curvilinear trend over recent decades. *Journal of Marriage and the Family*, 48:5–13. [15]

Seeman, M., Seeman, T., and Sayles, M. 1985. Social networks and health status: A longitudinal analysis. *Social Psychology Quarterly*, 48:237–248. [4]

Segal, M. W. 1974. Alphabet and attraction: An unobtrusive measure of

the effect of proximity in a field setting. *Journal of Personality and Social Psychology*, 30:654–657. [11]

Seligman, C., Bush, M., and Kirsch, K. 1976. Relationship between compliance in the foot-in-the-door paradigm and size of first request. *Journal of Personality and Social Psychology*, 33:517–520. [13]

Seligmann, J. 1984. The date who rapes. *Newsweek* (April 9):91–92. [12]

Sell, J. 1988. Types of public goods and free-riding. In Lawler, E. J., and Markovsky, B. (eds.), *Advances in Group Processes*, Vol. 6. Greenwich: CT: JAI Press. [9]

Sell, J., and Wilson, R. 1991. Levels of information and contributions to public goods. *Social Forces*, 70:107–124. [9]

Seltzer, J. A., and Bianchi, S. M. 1988. Children's contact with absent parents. *Journal of Marriage and the Family*, 50:663–677. [3]

Semin, G. R., and Manstead, A. S. R. 1983. *The Accountability of Conduct: A Social Psychological Analysis*. London: Academic Press. [15]

Senter, R., Reynolds, L. T., and Gruenenfelder, D. 1986. The presidency and the print media: Who controls the news? *Sociological Quarterly*, 27:91–105. [16]

Shaffer, D. R., and Sadowski, C. 1975. This table is mine: Respect for marked barroom tables as a function of gender, of spacial marker, and desirability of locale. *Sociometry*, 38:408–419. [5]

Shapiro, S. P. 1990. Collaring the crime, not the criminal: Reconsidering "white-collar crime." *American Sociological Review*, 55:346–365. [15]

Shaver, P., Furman, W., and Buhrmester, D. 1985. Aspects of a life transition: Network changes, social skills and loneliness. In Duck, S. W., and Perlman, D. (eds.), *Understanding Personal Relationships*. London: Sage. [4]

Shepelak, N. J. 1987. The role of self-explanations and self-evaluations in legitimating inequality. *American Sociological Review*, 52:495–503. [14, 16]

Shepelak, N. J., and Alwin, D. 1986. Beliefs about inequality and perceptions of distributive justice. *American Sociological Review*, 51:30–46. [14]

Sheppard, B., Hartwick, J., and Warshaw, P. 1988. The theory of reasoned action: A meta-analysis of past research with recommendations for modifications and future research. *Journal of Consumer Research*, 15:325–343. [8]

Sherif, M. 1936. *The Psychology of Social Norms*. New York: Harper & Row. [9, 16]

Sherif, M., Harvey, O. J., White, B. J., Hood, W. R., and Sherif, C. W. 1961. *Intergroup Conflict and Cooperation: The Robber's Cave Experiment*. Norman: Institute of Group Relations, University of Oklahoma. [12]

Sherif, M., and Sherif, C. W. 1969. *Social Psychology*. New York: Harper & Row. [9]

Sherman, L. W., and Berk, R. A. 1984. The specific deterrent effects of arrest for domestic assault. *American Sociological Review*, 49:261–272. [12, 15]

Sherman, L. W., and Bouza, A. V. 1984. The need to police domestic violence. *Wall Street Journal* (May 22):30. [12]

Sherman, S. J., Judd, C. M., and Park, B. 1989. Social cognition. *Annual Review of Psychology*, 40:281–326. [6]

Sherwood, J. J., Barron, J. W., and Fitch, H. G. 1969. Cognitive dissonance: Theory and research. In Wagner, R. V., and Sherwood, J. J. (eds.), *The Study of Attitude Change*. Belmont, CA: Brooks/Cole. [8]

Shils, E. 1950. Primary groups in the American army. In Merton, R., and Lazarsfeld, P. (eds.), *Continuities in Social Research*. New York: Free Press. [4]

Shils, E., and Janowitz, M. 1948. Cohesion and disintegration in the Wehrmacht in World War II. *Public Opinion Quarterly*, 12:280–315. [4]

Shipp, E. R. 1985. Racism lingers in Mississippi despite gains. *New York Times* (April 2):1–12. [14]

Shotland, R. L., and Heinold, W. D. 1985. Bystander response to arterial bleeding: Helping skills, the decision-making process, and differentiating the helping response. *Journal of Personality and Social Psychology*, 49:347–356. [10]

Shotland, R. L., and Huston, T. L. 1979. Emergencies: What are they and do they influence bystanders to intervene? *Journal of Personality and Social Psychology*, 37:1822–1834. [10]

Shouval, R., Venaki, S. K., Bronfenbrenner, U., Devereux, E. C., and Kiely, E. 1975. Anomalous reactions to social pressures of Israeli and Soviet children raised in family versus collective settings. *Journal of Personality and Social Psychology*, 32:477–489. [9]

Shrauger, J., and Schoeneman, T. 1979. Symbolic interactionist view of self-concept: Through the looking glass darkly. *Psychological Bulletin*, 86:549–573. [7]

Shumaker, S., and Brownell, A. 1984. Toward a theory of social support: Closing conceptual gaps. *Journal of Social Issues*, 40:11–36. [4]

Siegel, L. J., and Senna, J. J. 1988. *Juvenile Delinquency* (3rd ed.). St. Paul, MN: West. [15]

Sigall, H., and Landy, D. 1973. Radiating beauty: The effects of having a physically attractive partner on person perception. *Journal of Personality and Social Psychology*, 28:218–224. [6]

Sigall, H., and Ostrove, N. 1975. Beautiful but dangerous: Effects of offender attractiveness and nature of the crime on juridic judgment. *Journal of Personality and Social Psychology*, 31:410–414. [6]

Signorielli, N. 1989. Television and conceptions about sex roles: Maintaining conventionality and the status quo. *Sex Roles*, 21:341–352. [3]

Silka, L. 1989. *Intuitive Judgments of Change*. New York: Springer-Verlag. [16]

Simenquer, J., and Carroll, D. 1982. *Singles: The New Americans*. New York: Simon & Schuster. [11]

Simmel, G. 1902. The number of members as determining the sociological form of the group. *American Journal of Sociology*, 8:1–46, 158–196. [12]

Simmel, G. 1971. *On Individuality and Social Forms*. Edited by D. Levine. Chicago: University of Chicago Press. [4]

Simmons, C., and Parsons, R. 1983. Developing internality and perceived competence: The empowerment of adolescent girls. *Adolescence*, 18:917–922. [3]

Simmons, R. G., and Blyth, D. A. 1987. *Moving into Adolescence*. New York: Aldine de Gruyter. [7]

Simmons, R. G., Brown, L., Bush, D. M., and Blyth, D. A. 1978. Self-esteem and achievement of black and white adolescents. *Social Problems*, 26:86–96. [14]

Simon, B., Glassner-Bäyerl, B., and Stratenwerth, I. 1991. Stereo-typing and self-stereotyping in a natural intergroup context: The case of heterosexual and homosexual men. *Social Psychology Quarterly*, 54:252–266. [4]

Simon, D. R., and Eitzen, D. S. 1986. *Elite Deviance* (2nd ed.). Boston: Allyn & Bacon. [15]

Simon, R. 1975. *Women and Crime*. Lexington, MA: Lexington Books. [14]

Simon, R. W., Eder, D., and Evans, C. 1992. The development of feeling norms underlying romantic love among adolescent females. *Social Psychology Quarterly*, 55:29–46. [3, 11]

Simons, C. W., and Piliavin, J. A. 1972. Effects of deception on reactions to a victim. *Journal of Personality and Social Psychology*, 21:56–60. [10]

Simpson, I. H., Stark, D., and Jackson, R. A. 1988. Class identification processes of married, working men and women. *American Sociological Review*, 53:284–293. [7]

Singer, E. 1981. Reference groups and social evaluations. In Rosenberg, M., and Turner, R. (eds.), *Social Psychology: Sociological Perspectives*. New York: Basic Books. [4]

Singer, J. M., and Stake, J. E. 1986. Mathematics and self-esteem: Implications for women's career choices. *Psychology of Women Quarterly*, 10:369–402. [14]

Singer, M. T. 1979. Coming out of the cults. *Psychology Today*, 12(January):72–82 +. [16]

Sistrunk, F., and McDavid, J. W. 1971. Sex variable in conforming behavior. *Journal of Personality and Social Psychology*, 17:200–207. [9]

Skinner, B. F. 1953. *Science and Human Behavior*. New York: Macmillan. [1, 2]

Skinner, B. F. 1957. *Verbal Behavior*. New York: Appleton-Century-Crofts. [1, 2]

Skinner, B. F. 1974. *About Behaviorism*. New York: Vintage. [1]

Skvoretz, J., and Willer, D. 1991. Power in exchange networks: Setting and structural variations. *Social Psychology Quarterly*, 54:224–238. [10]

Smeaton, G., and Byrne, D. 1987. The effects of R-rated violence and erotica, individual influences, and victim characteristics on acquaintance rape proclivity. *Journal of Research on Personality*, 21:171–184. [12]

Smetana, J., Yau, J., Restrepo, A., and

Braeges, J. 1991. Conflict and adaptation in adolescence: Adolescent-parent conflict. In Colten, M., and Gore, S. (eds.), *Adolescent Stress: Causes and Consequences.* New York: Aldine de Gruyter. [3]

Smith, A., and Kleinman, S. 1989. Managing emotions in medical school: Students' contacts with the living and the dead. *Social Psychology Quarterly,* 52:56–69. [7]

Smith, D., Visher, C., and Jarjoura, G. R. 1991. Dimensions of delinquency: Exploring the correlates of participation, frequency, and persistence of delinquent behavior. *Journal of Research in Crime and Delinquency,* 28:6–32. [15]

Smith, J. D., and Shaffer, D. R. 1986. Self-consciousness, self-reported altruism, and helping behaviour. *Social Behavior and Personality,* 14:215–220. [10]

Smith, K., Keating, J., and Stotland, E. 1989. Altruism revisited: The effect of denying feedback on a victim's status to empathic witnesses. *Journal of Personality and Social Psychology,* 57: 641–650. [10]

Smith, M. D., and Hand, C. 1987. The pornographic/aggression linkage: Results from a field study. *Deviant Behavior,* 8:389–399. [12]

Smith, M. D., and Self, G. D. 1980. The congruence between mothers' and daughters' sex-role attitudes: A research note. *Journal of Marriage and the Family,* 42:105–109. [13]

Smith, M. J. 1982. *Persuasion and Human Action.* Belmont, CA: Wadsworth. [13]

Smith, R. M., and Smith, C. W. 1981. Childrearing and single parent fathers. *Family Relations,* 30:411–417. [3]

Smith, T. W., and Sheatsley, P. B., 1984. American attitudes toward race relations. *Public Opinion,* 7(October/November):14–15, 50–53. [6]

Smith-Lovin, L. 1987. Impressions from events. *Journal of Mathematical Sociology,* 13(1–2):35–70. [8]

Smith-Lovin, L. 1990. Emotion as the confirmation and disconfirmation of identity: An affect control model. In Kemper, T. D. (ed.), *Research Agendas in the Sociology of Emotion.* Albany: State University of New York Press. [8]

Smith-Lovin, L., and Brody, C. 1989. Interruptions in group discussions: The effects of gender and group composition. *American Sociological Review,* 54:424–435. [5]

Smith-Lovin, L., and Douglass, W. 1990. An affect control analysis of two religious groups. In Franks, D., and Gecas, V. (eds.), *Social Perspectives in Emotion,* Vol. 1. Greenwich, CT: JAI Press. [15]

Smith-Lovin, L., and Heise, D. R. (eds.). 1988. *Analyzing Social Interaction: Advances in Affect Control Theory.* New York: Gordon Breach Science. [8]

Smith-Lovin, L., and Robinson, D. T. 1992. Gender and conversational dynamics. In Ridgeway, C. (ed.), *Gender, Interaction, and Inequality.* New York: Springer-Verlag. [5]

Smolowe, J. 1991. Race and the death penalty: A high-court move to halt repeated appeals stirs concern about an arbitrary process. *Time* (April 29):68. [14]

Smolucha, F. 1992. Social origins of private speech in pretend play. In Diaz, R. M., and Berk, L. E. (eds.), *Private Speech: From Social Interaction to Self-Regulation.* Hillsdale, NJ: Erlbaum. [2]

Snow, D. A., and Phillips, C. L. 1982. The changing self-orientations of college students: From institution to impulse. *Social Science Quarterly,* 63: 462–476. [7]

Snow, D. A., Rochford, E. B., Jr., Worden, S. K., and Benford, R. D. 1986. Frame alignment processes, micromobilization, and movement participation. *American Sociological Review,* 51:464–481. [16]

Snow, D. A., Zurcher, L. A., Jr., and Ekland-Olson, S. 1980. Social networks and social movements: A microstructural approach to differential recruitment. *American Sociological Review,* 45:787–801. [16]

Snow, M. E., Jacklin, C. N., and Maccoby, E. E. 1983. Sex-of-child differences in father-child interactions at one year of age. *Child Development,* 54:227–232. [3]

Snyder, C. R. 1985. The excuse: An amazing grace. In Schlenker, B. R. (ed.), *The Self and Social Life.* New York: McGraw-Hill. [5]

Snyder, C. R., and Fromkin, H. 1980. *Uniqueness: The Human Pursuit of Difference.* New York: Plenum. [7]

Snyder, C. R., and Higgins, R. L. 1989. Reality negotiation and excuse-making: President Reagan's March 4, 1987, Iran Arms Speech and other literature. In Cody, M. J., and McLaughlin, M. L. (eds.), *The Psychology of Tactical Communication.* Cleve-

don, England: Multilingual Matters Ltd. [15]

Snyder, C. R., Higgins, R. L., and Stucky, R. J. 1983. *Excuses: Masquerades in Search of Grace.* New York: Wiley-Interscience. [15]

Snyder, J., and Patterson, G. R. 1987. Family interaction and delinquent behavior. In Quay, H. C. (ed.), *Handbook of Juvenile Delinquency.* New York: Wiley. [15]

Snyder, M. 1974. Self-monitoring of expressive behavior. *Journal of Personality and Social Psychology,* 30:526–537. [7]

Snyder, M. 1987. *Public Appearances/Private Realities: The Psychology of Self-Monitoring.* New York: Freeman. [7, 9]

Snyder, M., and Cunningham, M. R. 1975. To comply or not comply: Testing the self-perception explanation of the "foot-in-the-door" phenomenon. *Journal of Personality and Social Psychology,* 31:64–67. [13]

Snyder, M., Tanke, E. D., and Berscheid, E. 1977. Social perception and interpersonal behavior: On the self-fulfilling nature of social stereotypes. *Journal of Personality and Social Psychology,* 35:656–666. [7]

Solomon, S., and Saxe, L. 1977. What is intelligent, as well as attractive, is good. *Personality and Social Psychology Bulletin,* 3:670–673. [6]

Sorrentino, R. M., King, G., and Leo, G. 1980. The influence of the minority on perception: A note on a possible alternative explanation. *Journal of Experimental Social Psychology,* 16: 293–301. [9]

Spector, M., and Kitsuse, J. I. 1987. *Constructing Social Problems* (2nd ed.). New York: Aldine de Gruyter. [16]

Speier, H. 1941. The social types of war. *American Journal of Sociology,* 46: 445–454. [4]

Spence, J., and Helmreich, R. 1978. *Masculinity and Femininity: Their Psychological Dimensions, Correlates, and Antecedents.* Austin: University of Texas Press. [7]

Spinetta, J. J., and Rigler, D. 1975. The child-abusing parent: A psychological review. *Psychological Bulletin,* 77:296–304. [12]

Spitz, R. D. 1945. Hospitalism. *Psychiatric Study of the Child,* 1:53–72. [2]

Spitz, R. D. 1946. Hospitalism: A follow-up report. *Psychiatric Study of the Child,* 2:113–117. [2]

Sprecher, S. 1988. Investment model, equity, and social support determinants of relationship commitment. *So-*

cial Psychology Quarterly, 51:318–328. [11]

Sprecher, S. 1989. Premarital sexual standards for different categories of individuals. Journal of Sex Research, 26:232–248. [11]

Sprecher, S. 1992. How men and women expect to feel and behave in response to inequality in close relationships. Social Psychology Quarterly, 55:57–69. [10]

Sprecher, S., and Metts, S. 1989. Development of the "romantic beliefs scale" and examination of the effects of gender and gender-role orientation. Journal of Social and Personal Relationships, 6:387–411. [11]

Stafford, M. C., and Scott, R. R. 1986. Stigma, deviance, and social control: Some conceptual issues. In Ainlay, S. C., Becker, G., and Coleman, L. M. (eds.), The Dilemma of Deviance: A Multidisciplinary View of Stigma. New York: Plenum. [15]

Staggenborg, S. 1986. Coalition work in the pro-choice movement: Organizational and environmental opportunities and obstacles. Social Problems, 33:374–390. [16]

Staggenborg, S. 1989. Organizational and environmental influences on the development of the pro-choice movement. Social Forces, 68:204–240. [16]

Stake, J. E. 1985. Exploring the basis of sex differences in third-party allocations. Journal of Personality and Social Psychology, 48:1621–1629. [9]

Stake, J. E., and Katz, J. F. 1982. Teacher-pupil relationships in the elementary school classroom: Teacher-gender and pupil-gender differences. American Educational Research Journal, 19:465–471. [9]

Staples, B. 1986. Just walk on by: A black man ponders his power to alter public space. Ms. (September):54, 88. [5]

Stark, R. S., and Bainbridge, W. S. 1980. Networks of faith: Interpersonal bonds and recruitments to cults and sects. American Journal of Sociology, 85:1376–1395. [16]

Stasser, G., Taylor, L. A., and Hanna, C. 1989. Information sampling in structured and unstructured discussion of three- and six-person groups. Journal of Personality and Social Psychology, 57:67–78. [9]

Staub, E. 1978. Positive Social Behavior and Morality: Social and Personal Influences, Vol. 1. New York: Academic Press. [10]

Staw, B. M., and Ross, J. 1987. Behavior in escalation situations: Antecedents, prototypes, and solutions. Research in Organizational Behavior, 9:39–78. [12]

Steblay, N. M. 1987. Helping behavior in rural and urban environments: A meta-analysis. Psychological Bulletin, 102:346–356. [10]

Steck, L., Levitan, D., McLane, D., and Kelley, H. H. 1982. Care, need, and conceptions of love. Journal of Personality and Social Psychology, 43:481–491. [11]

Steele, B. G., and Pollock, C. B. 1968. A psychiatric study of parents who abuse infants and small children. In Helfer, R. E., and Kempe, C. H. (eds.), The Battered Child. Chicago: University of Chicago Press. [12]

Steele, C. M. 1988. The psychology of self-affirmation: Sustaining the integrity of the self. In Berkowitz, L. (ed.), Advances in Experimental Social Psychology, Vol. 21. New York: Academic Press. [8]

Steele, C. M., and Liu, T. J. 1983. Dissonance processes as self-affirmation. Journal of Personality and Social Psychology, 45:5–19. [8]

Steele, C. M., Southwick, L. L., and Critchlow, B. 1981. Dissonance and alcohol: Drinking your troubles away. Journal of Personality and Social Psychology, 41:831–846. [8]

Steffensmeier, D. 1980. Assessing the impact of the women's movement on sex-based differences in the handling of adult criminal defendants. Crime and Delinquency, 26:344–357. [14]

Steinberg, L. 1986. Latchkey children and susceptibility to peer pressure: An ecological analysis. Developmental Psychology, 22:434–439. [15]

Steinberg, L. 1987. Recent research on the family at adolescence: The extent and nature of sex differences. Journal of Youth and Adolescence, 16:191–197. [13]

Steinberg, R. 1990. The social construction of skill: Gender, power, and comparable worth. Work and Occupation, 17:449–482. [14]

Stenross, B., and Kleinman, S. 1989. The highs and lows of emotional labor. Journal of Contemporary Ethnography, 17:435–452. [12]

Stephan, C. W., and Langlois, J. H. 1984. Baby beautiful: Adult attributions of infant competence as a function of infant attractiveness. Child Development, 55:576–585. [6]

Stephan, W. G. 1985. Intergroup relations. In Lindzey, L., and Aronson, E. (eds.), The Handbook of Social Psychology (3rd ed.). New York: Random House. [6]

Stephan, W. G. 1986. Effects of school desegregation: An evaluation 30 years after Brown. In Saks, M. J., and Saxe, L. (eds.), Advances in Applied Social Psychology, Hillsdale, NJ: Erlbaum, 3:181–206. [7, 14]

Stephan, W. G. 1990. School desegregation: Short-term and long-term effects. In Knopke, H. (ed.), Opening Doors: An Appraisal of Race Relations in America. Tuscaloosa: University of Alabama Press. [14]

Stern, M., and Karraker, K. 1989. Sex stereotyping of infants: A review of gender labeling studies. Sex Roles, 20:510–511. [3]

Sternberg, R. J. 1986. A triangular theory of love. Psychological Review, 93:119–135. [11]

Sternberg, R. J. 1988. Triangulating love. In Sternberg, R. J., and Barnes, M. L. (eds.), The Psychology of Love. New Haven, CT: Yale University Press. [11]

Sternberg, R. J., and Grajek, S. 1984. The nature of love. Journal of Personality and Social Psychology, 47:312–329. [11]

Sternthal, B., Phillips, L. W., and Dholakia, R. 1978. The persuasive effect of source credibility: A situational analysis. Public Opinion Quarterly, 42:285–314. [13]

Stewart, P. A., and Moore, J. C., Jr. 1992. Wage disparities and performance expectations. Social Psychology Quarterly, 55:78–85. [13]

Stewart, T. A. 1991. Gay in corporate America. Fortune (December):42–56. [16]

Stiles, W., Orth, J., Scherwitz, L., Hennrikus, D., and Vallbona, C. 1984. Role behaviors in routine medical interviews with hypertensive patients: A repertoire of verbal exchanges. Social Psychology Quarterly, 47:244–254. [4, 5]

Stockard, J., van de Kragt, A. J., and Dodge, P. J. 1988. Gender roles and behavior in social dilemmas: Are there sex differences in cooperation and in its justification. Social Psychology Quarterly, 51:154–163. [9]

Stokes, J., and Levin, I. 1986. Gender differences in predicting loneliness from social network characteristics. Journal of Personality and Social Psychology, 51:1069–1074. [4]

Stolte, J. F. 1983. The legitimation of structural inequality. *American Sociological Review*, 48:331–342. [16]

Stone, G. P. 1970. Appearance and the self. In Stone, G. P., and Faberman, H. A. (eds.), *Social Psychology through Symbolic Interaction*, Waltham, MA: Xerox. [7]

Stoner, J. A. F. 1961. A comparison of individual and group decisions involving risk. Unpublished master's thesis, School of Industrial Management, Massachusetts Institute of Technology, Cambridge. [9]

Straus, M. A. 1991. New theory and old canards about family violence research. *Social Problems*, 38:180–197. [12]

Street, R. L., Jr., and Brady, R. M. 1982. Speech rate acceptance ranges as a function of evaluative domain, listener speech rate, and interaction context. *Communication Monographs*, 49: 290–308. [5]

Street, R. L., Jr., and Buller, D. 1988. Patients' characteristics affecting physician-patient nonverbal communication. *Human Communication Research*, 15:60–90. [5]

Street, R. L., Jr., and Cappella, J. N. 1985. Sequence and pattern in communicative behavior: A review and commentary. In Street, R. L., Jr., and Capella, J. N. (eds.), *Sequence and Pattern in Communicative Behavior*. London: Arnold, pp. 243–276. [5]

Strober, M. H., and Arnold, C. L. 1987. The dynamics of occupational segregation among bank tellers. In Brown, C., and Pechman, J. A. (eds.), *Gender in the Workplace*. Washington, DC: The Brookings Institution. [14]

Strodtbeck, F. L., and Hook, L. H. 1961. The social dimensions of a twelve-man jury table. *Sociometry*, 24:397–415. [9]

Strodtbeck, F. L., James, R. M., and Hawkins, C. 1957. Social status in jury deliberations. *American Sociological Review*, 22:713–718. [9]

Stroebe, W., and Frey, B. S. 1982. Self-interest and collective action: The economics and psychology of public goods. *British Journal of Social Psychology*, 21:121–137. [9]

Stryker, S. 1980. *Symbolic Interactionism: A Social Structural Version*. Menlo Park, CA: Benjamin/Cummings. [1, 7]

Stryker, S. 1987. Identity theory: Developments and extensions. In Yardley, K., and Honess, T. (eds.), *Self and Identity: Psychosocial Perspectives*. New York: Wiley. [7]

Stryker, S. 1991. Exploring the relevance of social cognition for the relationship of self and society: Linking the cognitive perspective and identity theory. In Howard, J., and Callero, P. (eds.), *The Self-Society Dynamic: Affect, Action, and Social Cognition*. New York: Cambridge University Press. [7]

Stryker, S., and Statham, A. 1985. Symbolic interaction and role theory. In Lindzey, G., and Aronson, E. (eds.), *Handbook of Social Psychology*, Vol. 1 (3rd ed.). New York: Random House. [1]

Suls, J., Marco, C. A., and Tobin, S. 1991. The role of temporal comparison, social comparison, and direct appraisal in the elderly's self evaluations of health. *Journal of Applied Social Psychology*, 21:1125–1144. [7]

Summers, R. J. 1991. The influence of affirmative action on perceptions of a beneficiary's qualifications. *Journal of Applied Social Psychology*, 21:1265–1276. [14]

Surra, C. A. 1985. Courtship types: Variations in interdependence between partners and social networks. *Journal of Personality and Social Psychology*, 49:357–375. [11]

Surra, C. A. 1988. The influence of the interactive network on developing relationships. In Milardo, R. M. (ed.), *Families and Social Networks*. National Council on Family Relations Monograph Series. Newbury Park, CA: Sage, pp. 48–81. [11]

Surra, C. A. 1990. Research and theory on mate selection and premarital relationships in the 1980's. *Journal of Marriage and the Family*, 52:844–865. [11]

Sutherland, E. H. 1939. *Criminology* (3rd ed.). Philadelphia: Lippincott. [15]

Sutherland, E. H. 1949. *White Collar Crime*. New York: Dryden Press, p. 2. [15]

Sutton-Smith, B., and Rosenberg, B. G. 1970. *The Sibling*. New York: Holt, Rinehart & Winston. [13]

Swadesh, M. 1971. *The Origin and Diversification of Language*. Chicago: Aldine. [5]

Swain, S. 1989. Covert intimacy: Closeness in men's friendships. In Risman, B. R., and Schwartz, P. (eds.), *Gender in Intimate Relationships: A Microstructural Approach*. Belmont, CA: Wadsworth. [11]

Swann, W. B., Jr. 1983. Self-verification: Bringing social reality into harmony with self. In Suls, J., and Greenwald, A. (eds.), *Psychological Perspectives on the Self*, Vol. 2. Hillsdale, NJ: Erlbaum. [8]

Swann, W. B., Jr. 1985. The self as architect of reality. In Schlenker, B. R. (ed.), *The Self and Social Life*. New York: McGraw-Hill. [8]

Swann, W. B., Jr. 1987. Identity negotiation: Where two roads meet. *Journal of Personality and Social Psychology*, 53:1038–1051. [8]

Swann, W. B., Jr., and Ely, R. 1984. A battle of wills: Self-verification versus behavioral confirmation. *Journal of Personality and Social Psychology*, 46: 1287–1302. [7]

Swann, W. B., Jr., Griffin, J. J., Predmore, S. C., and Gaines, B. 1987. The cognitive-affective crossfire: When self-consistency confronts self-enhancement. *Journal of Personality and Social Psychology*, 52:881–889. [8]

Swann, W. B., Jr., and Pelham, B. W. 1990. Embracing the bitter truth: Positivity and authenticity in social relationships. Unpublished manuscript, University of Texas, Austin. [8]

Swann, W. B., Jr., Pelham, B. W., and Krull, D. S. 1989. Agreeable fancy or disagreeable truth? Reconciling self-enhancement and self-verification. *Journal of Personality and Social Psychology*, 57:782–791. [8]

Swann, W. B. Jr., and Read, S. J. 1981*a*. Acquiring self-knowledge: The search for feedback that fits. *Journal of Personality and Social Psychology*, 41:1119–1128. [7]

Swann, W. B., Jr., and Read, S. J. 1981*b*. Self-verification processes: How we sustain our self-conceptions. *Journal of Experimental Social Psychology*, 17:351–372. [7]

Sykes, G., and Matza, D. 1957. Techniques of neutralization: A theory of delinquency. *American Sociological Review*, 22:664–670. [15]

Szasz, T. S. 1989. Power and psychiatry. In Henslin, J. A. (ed.), *Deviance in American Life*. New Brunswick, NJ: Transaction Books. [15]

Szinovacz, M. E. 1987. Family power. In Sussman, M. B., and Steinmetz, S. K. (eds.), *Handbook on Marriage and the Family*. New York: Plenum. [13]

Szymanski, K., and Harkins, S. G. 1987. Social loafing and self-evaluation with a social standard. *Journal of Personality and Social Psychology*, 53: 891–897. [9]

Tajfel, H. 1970. Experiments in intergroup discrimination. *Scientific American*, 223:96–102. [4]

Tajfel, H. 1981. *Human Groups and Social Categories*. New York: Cambridge University Press. [12]

Tajfel, H., Billig, M. G., Bundy, R. P., and Flament, C. 1971. Social categorization and intergroup behavior. *European Journal of Social Psychology*, 1:149–178. [4]

Tallman, I., and Gray, L. N. 1990. Choices, decisions, and problem-solving. *Annual Review of Sociology*, 16:405–433. [13]

Tannen, D. 1990. *You Just Don't Understand: Women and Men in Conversation*. New York: Ballantine. [3, 5]

Tanner, J. F., Day, E., and Crask, M. R. 1989. Protection motivation theory: An extension of fear appeals theory in communication. *Journal of Business Research*, 19:267–276. [13]

Tanner, J. F., Hunt, J. B., and Eppright, D. R. 1991. The protection motivation model: A normative model of fear appeals. *Journal of Marketing*, 55:36–45. [13]

Taps, J., and Martin, P. Y. 1990. Gender composition, attributional accounts, and women's influence and likability in task groups. *Small Groups Research*, 21:471–491. [14]

Tarrow, S. 1989. *Democracy and Disorder: Protest and Politics in Italy 1965–1975*. New York: Oxford University Press. [16]

Tavris, C. 1983. *Anger: The Misunderstood Emotion*. New York: Simon & Schuster. [12]

Taylor, S. E., and Lobel, M. 1989. Social comparison activity under threat: Downward evaluation and upward contacts. *Psychological Review*, 89:155–181. [7]

Tedeschi, J. T. 1991. Grievances: Development and reactions. Paper prepared for the Symposium on Social Interactionist Approaches to Aggres-

sion and Violence, State University of New York at Albany (April). [12]

Teger, A. 1980. *Too Much Invested to Quit*. New York: Pergamon. [12]

Tessor, A. 1988. Toward a self-evaluation maintenance model of social behavior. In Berkowitz, L. (ed.), *Advances in Experimental Social Psychology*, Vol. 20. New York: Academic Press. [8]

Tessor, A., and Campbell, J. 1983. Self-definition and self-evaluation maintenance. Toward a self-evaluation maintenance model of social behavior. In Suls, J., and Greenwald, A. (eds.), *Psychological Perspectives on the Self*, Vol. 2. Hillsdale, NJ: Erlbaum. [8]

Teti, D. M., Lamb, M. E., and Elster, A. B. 1987. Long-range socioeconomic and marital consequences of adolescent marriage in three cohorts of adult males. *Journal of Marriage and the Family*, 49:499–506. [3]

Tetlock, P. E., and Boettger, R. 1989. Accountability: A social magnifier of the dilution effect. *Journal of Personality and Social Psychology*, 57:388–398. [6]

Tetlock, P. E., Skitka, L., and Boettger, R. 1989. Social and cognitive strategies for coping with accountability: Conformity, complexity, and bolstering. *Journal of Personality and Social Psychology*, 57:632–640. [9]

Thaler, R. H., and Johnson, E. J. 1990. Gambling with the house money and trying to break even: The effects of prior outcomes on risky choice. *Management Science*, 36:643–660. [13]

Thayer, L., and Schiff, W. 1977. Gazing patterns and attribution of sexual involvement. *Journal of Social Psychology*, 101:235–246. [5]

Thibaut, J. W., and Kelley, H. H. 1959. *The Social Psychology of Groups*. New York: Wiley. [1, 10]

Thio, A. 1988. *Deviant Behavior* (3rd ed.). New York: Harper & Row. [15]

Thistlethwaite, D. L., and Kamenetzky, J. 1955. Attitude change through refutation and elaboration of audience counterarguments. *Journal of Abnormal and Social Psychology*, 51:3–9. [13]

Thoits, P. 1989. The sociology of emotions. *Annual Review of Sociology*, 15:317–342. [7]

Thoits, P. 1991. On merging identity theory and stress research. *Social Psychology Quarterly*, 54:101–112. [7]

Thomas, C., and Bishop, D. 1984. The effect of formal and informal sanctions on delinquency: A longitudinal comparison of labeling and deterrence theory. *Journal of Criminal Law and Criminology*, 75:1222–1245. [15]

Thomas, J. 1984. Some aspects of negotiated order, loose coupling and mesostructure in maximum security prisons. *Symbolic Interaction*, 2:213–231. [4]

Thomas, W. I. 1931. The relation of research to the social process. In Swann, W. F. G., Cook, W. W., Beard, C. A., Clark, J. M., Llewellyn, K. N., Bentley, M., Schlesinger, A. M., Ogburn, W. F., and Thomas, W. I. (eds.), *Essays on Research in the Social Sciences*. Washington, DC: Brookings Institution. [1]

Thomas, W. I. 1937. *The Unadjusted Girl*. Boston: Little, Brown. [1]

Thomas, W. I., and Thomas, D. S. 1928. *The Child in America*. New York: Knopf. [3]

Thomas, W. I., and Znaniecki, F. 1918. *The Polish Peasant in Europe and America*. Boston: Badger. [1]

Thompson, L., and Walker, A. J. 1987. Mothers as mediators between grandmothers and their young adult granddaughters. *Family Relations*, 36:72–77. [3]

Thompson, L., and Walker, A. J. 1989. Gender in families: Women and men in marriage, work, and parenthood. *Journal of Marriage and the Family*, 51:845–871. [3]

Thompson, L., and Walker, A. J. 1991. Gender in families: Women and men in marriage, work, and parenthood. In Booth, A. (ed.), *Contemporary Families: Looking Forward, Looking Back*. Minneapolis, MN: National Council on Family Relations. [14]

Thornberry, T. P., Moore, M., and Christenson, R. L. 1985. The effect of dropping out of school on subsequent criminal behavior. *Criminology*, 23:3–18. [15]

Thornburg, H. D. 1981. The amount of sex information learning obtained during early adolescence. *Journal of Early Adolescence*, 2:171–183. [3]

Thornton, A. 1985. Changing attitudes toward separation and divorce: Causes and consequences. *American Journal of Sociology*, 90:856–872. [3, 8]

Thornton, A. 1989. Changing attitudes toward family issues in the United States. *Journal of Marriage and the Family*, 51:873–893. [3]

Thornton, B. 1984. Defensive attribution of responsibility: Evidence for an arousal-based motivational bias. *Journal of Personality and Social Psychology*, 46:721–734. [10]

Tienda, M., and Lii, D. 1987. Minority concentration and earnings inequality: Blacks and Hispanics, and Asians compared. *American Journal of Sociology*, 93:141–165. [14]

Ting-Toomey, S. 1986. Conflict communication styles in black and white subjective culture. In Kim, Y. (ed.), *Interethnic Communication: Current Research*. Newbury Park, CA: Sage. [5]

Tittle, C. R. 1969. Crime rates and legal sanctions. *Social Problems*, 16: 408–423. [15]

Tittle, C. R. 1980. *Sanctions and Social Deviance*. New York: Praeger. [15]

Toch, H. 1969. *Violent Men*. Chicago: Aldine. [12]

Toch, H. 1991. Good violence and bad violence: Self-presentations of aggression. Paper prepared for the Symposium on Social Interactionist Approaches to Aggression and Violence, State University of New York at Albany (April). [12]

Toi, M., and Batson, C. D. 1982. More evidence that empathy is a source of altruistic motivation. *Journal of Personality and Social Psychology*, 43: 281–292. [10]

Tolstoy, L. 1869/1957. *War and Peace*. Middlesex, England: Penguin. [4]

Toneatto, T., and Binik, Y. 1987. The role of intentions, social norms, and attitudes in the performance of dental flossing: A test of the theory of reasoned action. *Journal of Applied Social Psychology*, 17:593–603. [8]

Tourangeau, R., Rasinski, K., and Bradburn, N. 1991. Measuring happiness in surveys: A test of the subtraction hypothesis. *Public Opinion Quarterly*, 55:255-256. [1]

Townsend, B. 1985. Working women. *American Demographics*, 7:4–7. [14]

Tracy, D. M. 1987. Toys, spatial ability and science and mathematics achievement: Are they related? *Sex Roles*, 17:115–136. [3]

Tracy, K. 1990. The many faces of facework. In Giles, H., and Robinson, W. P. (eds.), *Handbook of Language and Social Psychology*. New York: Wiley. [5]

Traupmann, J., and Hatfield, E. 1981. Love: Its effects on mental and physical health. In March, J., Kiesler, S., Fogel, R., Hatfield, E., and Shanna, E. (eds.), *Aging: Stability and Change in the Family*. New York: Academic Press. [11]

Travers, J., and Milgram, S. 1969. An experimental study of the small-world problem. *Sociometry*, 32:425–443. [4]

Travis, L. E. 1925. The effect of a small audience upon eye-hand coordination. *Journal of Abnormal and Social Psychology*, 20:142–146. [9]

Trenholm, S. 1989. *Persuasion and Social Influence*. Englewood Cliffs, NJ: Prentice-Hall. [13]

Triandis, H., Lisansky, J., Setiadi, B., Chang, B. H., Marin, G., and Betancourt, H. 1982. Stereotyping among Hispanics and Anglos: The uniformity, intensity, direction, and quality of auto- and heterostereotypes. *Journal of Cross-Cultural Psychology*, 13: 409–426. [6]

Trimble, J. E. 1988. Stereotypical images, American Indians, and prejudice. In Katz, P. A., and Taylor, D. A. (eds.), *Eliminating Racism: Profiles in Controversy*. New York: Plenum. [6]

Trimboli, C., and Walker, M. B. 1982. Smooth transitions in conversational turn-taking: Implications for theory. *Journal of Social Psychology*, 117:305–306. [5]

Trimboli, C., and Walker, M. B. 1984. Switching phases in cooperative and competitive conversations. *Journal of Experimental Social Psychology*, 20:297–311. [5]

Triplett, N. 1898. The dynamogenic factors in pacemaking and competition. *American Journal of Psychology*, 4:400–408. [9]

Troll, L. E., and Bengtson, V. L. 1982. Intergenerational relations through the life span. In Wolman, B. B. (ed.), *Handbook of Developmental Psychology*. Englewood Cliffs, NJ: Prentice-Hall. [3]

Troyer, R. J., and Markle, G. E. 1982. Creating deviance rules: A macroscopic model. *Sociological Quarterly*, 23(Spring):157–169. [15]

Turner, J. H. 1988. *A Theory of Social Interaction*. Stanford, CA: Stanford University Press. [4]

Turner, R. H. 1969. The public perception of protest. *American Sociological Review*, 34:815–831. [16]

Turner, R. H. 1978. The role and the person. *American Journal of Sociology*, 84:1–23. [7]

Turner, R. H. 1990. Role change. *Annual Review of Sociology*, 16:87–110. [3]

Turner, R. H., and Killian, L. M. 1972. *Collective Behavior* (2nd ed.). Englewood Cliffs, NJ: Prentice-Hall. [16]

Tybout, A. M., and Scott, C. A. 1983. Availability of well-defined internal knowledge and the attitude formation process: Information aggregation versus self-perception. *Journal of Personality and Social Psychology*, 44: 474–491. [7, 8]

Ulbrich, P., Warheit, G., and Zimmerman, R. 1989. Race, socioeconomic status, and psychological distress: An examination of differential vulnerability. *Journal of Health and Social Behavior*, 30:131–146. [7]

U.S. Bureau of the Census. 1990. *Current Population Reports*, Series P-60, no. 168. Washington, DC: U.S. Government Printing Office. [14]

U.S. Bureau of the Census. 1991a. *Statistical Abstract of the United States: 1991*. Washington, DC: U.S. Government Printing Office. [3, 14]

U.S. Bureau of the Census. 1991b. Marital and living arrangements: March 1990. *Current Population Reports*, Series P-20. Washington, DC: U.S. Government Printing Office. [3]

U.S. Bureau of the Census. 1991c. *Current Population Reports*, Series P-60, no. 175. Washington, DC: U.S. Government Printing Office. [14]

U.S. Bureau of the Census. 1992a. *Statistical Abstract of the United States: 1992*. Washington, DC: U.S. Government Printing Office. [3, 14]

U.S. Bureau of the Census. 1992b. Unpublished March 1992 Current Population Survey data. [14]

U.S. Department of Health and Human Services. 1990. Advance reports of final marriage statistics, 1987. *Monthly Vital Statistics Report*, 38(12). Washington, DC: U.S. Government Printing Office. [3]

Utne, M. K., and Kidd, R. F. 1980. Equity and attribution. In Mikula, G. (ed.), *Justice and Social Interaction*. New York: Springer-Verlag. [10]

Vallerand, R., Deshaies, P., Cuerrier, J., Pellitier, L., and Mongeau, C. 1992. Ajzen and Fishbein's theory of reasoned action as applied to moral behavior: A confirmatory analysis. *Journal of Personality and Social Psychology*, 62:98–109. [8]

Van Creveld, M. 1982. *Fighting Power: German and U.S. Army Performance, 1939–1945.* Westport, CT: Greenwood Press. [4]

Van der Werff, J. 1990. The problem of self-conceiving. In Bosma, H., and Jackson, S. (eds.), *Coping and Self-Concept in Adolescence.* New York: Springer-Verlag. [7]

Vander Zanden, J. W. 1983. *American Minority Relations.* New York: Knopf. [4]

Vanfossen, B. E., Jones, J. D., and Spade, J. Z. 1987. Curriculum tracking and status maintenance. *Sociology of Education*, 60:104–122. [3]

Van Maanen, J. 1976. Breaking in: Socialization to work. In Dubin, R. (ed.), *Handbook of Work, Organization, and Society*, Chicago: Rand McNally. [3]

Van Voorhis, P., Cullen, F. T., Mathers, R. A., and Garner, C. C. 1988. The impact of family structure and quality on delinquency: A comparative assessment of structural and functional factors. *Criminology*, 26:235–261. [15]

Varca, P. 1980. An analysis of home and away game performance of male college basketball teams. *Journal of Sport Psychology*, 2:245–257. [4]

Vaughan, D. 1986. *Uncoupling: How Relationships Come Apart.* New York: Vintage. [11]

Vidich, A. J., and Bensman, J. 1960. *Small Town in Mass Society.* Garden City, NY: Doubleday. [1]

Vollmer, F. 1986. Why do men have higher expectancy than women? *Sex Roles*, 14:351–362. [14]

Vygotsky, L. 1978. *Mind in Society.* Cambridge, MA: Harvard University Press. [2]

Vygotsky, L. 1987. *The Collected Works of L. S. Vygotsky: Vol. 1, Problems of General Psychology.* New York: Plenum. [2]

Wagner, D., and Cohen, M. B. 1991. The power of the people: Homeless protesters in the aftermath of social movement participation. *Social Problems*, 38:543–561. [16]

Waite, L. J., and Harrison, S. C. 1992. Keeping in touch: How women in mid-life allocate social contacts among kith and kin. *Social Forces*, 70:637–655. [10]

Wall, H. M., and Barry, A. 1985. Student expectations for male and female instructor behavior. In Cheatham, R. E. (ed.), *Women in Higher Education: Traditions, Transitions and Revolutions.* Proceedings for Women in Higher Education Conferences. St. Louis, MO: Saint Louis University, Metropolitan College, and SAASS, Inc., pp. 283–291. [5]

Wallace, P. M., and Gotlib, I. H. 1990. Marital adjustment during the transition to parenthood: Stability and predictors of change. *Journal of Marriage and the Family*, 52:21–29. [3]

Waller, W. 1938. *The Family: A Dynamic Interpretation.* New York: Cordon. [11]

Wallerstein, J., and Blakeslee, S. 1990. *Second Chances: Men, Women, and Children a Decade after Divorce.* New York: Ticknor and Fields. [11]

Walsh, E. J., and Warland, R. H. 1983. Social movement involvement in the wake of a nuclear accident: Activists and free riders in the T.M.I. area. *American Sociological Review*, 48:764–780. [9]

Walster, E. 1965. Effects of self-esteem on romantic liking. *Journal of Experimental Social Psychology*, 1:184–197. [7]

Walster, E., Aronson, E., and Abrahams, D. 1966. On increasing the persuasiveness of a low prestige communicator. *Journal of Experimental Social Psychology*, 2:325–342. [13]

Walster, E., Berscheid, E., and Walster, G. W. 1973. New directions in equity research. *Journal of Personality and Social Psychology*, 25:151–176. [10, 11]

Walster, E., and Walster, G. W. 1978. *Love.* Reading, MA: Addison-Wesley. [11]

Walster, E., Walster, G. W., and Berscheid, E. 1978. *Equity: Theory and Research.* Boston: Allyn & Bacon. [10]

Warner, L. G., and DeFleur, M. L. 1969. Attitude as an interactional concept: Social constraint and social distance as intervening variables between attitudes and action. *American Sociological Review*, 34:153–169. [8]

Warner, R. 1986. Alternative strategies for measuring household division of labor: A comparison. *Journal of Family Issues*, 7:179–195. [14]

Warr, M. 1985. Fear of rape among urban women. *Social Problems*, 32:238–250. [12]

Watson, D. 1982. The actor and the observer: How are their perceptions of causality divergent? *Psychological Bulletin*, 92:682–700. [6]

Watson, J. B. 1914. *Behavior: An Introduction to Comparative Psychology.* New York: Holt, Rinehart & Winston. [1]

Watson, J. B. 1919. *Psychology from the Standpoint of a Behaviorist.* Philadelphia: Lippincott. [1]

Weary, G. 1980. Examination of affect and egotism as mediators of bias in causal attributions. *Journal of Personality and Social Psychology*, 38:348–357. [6]

Webster, M., Jr., and Driskell, J. E. 1983. Beauty as status. *American Journal of Sociology*, 89:140–165. [6]

Weick, K. E. 1984. Small wins: Redefining the scale of social problems. *American Psychologist*, 39:40–49. [16]

Weigal, R. H., and Newman, L. 1976. Increasing attitude-behavior correspondence by broadening the scope of the behavioral measure. *Journal of Personality and Social Psychology*, 33:793–802. [8]

Weimann, J. M. 1985. Interpersonal control and regulation in conversation. In Street, R. L., Jr., and Capella, J. N. (eds.), *Sequence and Pattern in Communicative Behavior.* London: Arnold, pp. 85–102. [5]

Weinberg, S. 1974. *Deviant Behavior and Social Control.* Dubuque, IA: William C. Brown. [7]

Weiner, B. 1980. A cognitive (attribution)-emotion-action model of behavior: An analysis of judgments of help-giving. *Journal of Personality and Social Psychology*, 39:186–200. [10]

Weiner, F. 1976. Altruism, ambiance, and action: The effects of rural and urban rearing on helping behavior. *Journal of Personality and Social Psychology*, 34:112–124. [10]

Weinrich, J. D., and Williams, W. L. 1991. Strange customs, familiar lives: Homosexualities in other cultures. In Gonsiorek, J. C., and Weinrich, J. D. (eds.), *Homosexuality: Research Implications for Public Policy.* Newbury Park, CA: Sage. [15]

Weiss, L., and Lowenthal, M. F. 1975. Life-course perspectives on friendship. In Lowenthal, M. F., Thurnher, M., and Chirivoga, D. (eds.), *Four Stages of Life.* San Francisco: Jossey-Bass. [11]

Weiss, R. 1973. *Loneliness: The Experience of Emotional and Social Isolation.* Cambridge, MA: MIT Press. [4]

Weitzer, R. 1991. Prostitutes' rights in the United States. *Sociological Quarterly,* 32:23–41. [16]

Weitzman, L. J. 1979. *Sex Role Socialization.* Palo Alto, CA: Mayfield. [3]

Weitzman, L. J., Birns, B., and Friend, R. 1985. Traditional and nontraditional mothers' communication with their daughters and sons. *Child Development,* 56:894–896. [3]

Weitzman, L. J., Eifler, D., Hokada, E., and Ross, C. 1972. Sex role socialization in picture books for preschool children. *American Journal of Sociology,* 77:1125–1144. [3]

Welch, S., Spohn, C., and Gruhl, J. 1985. Convicting and sentencing differences among black, Hispanic, and white males in six localities. *Justice Quarterly,* 2:67:77. [14]

Weldon, E., Jehn, K., and Pradhan, P. 1991. Processes that mediate the relationship between a group goal and improved group performance. *Journal of Personality and Social Psychology,* 61:555–569. [9]

Welles, C. 1988. What led Beech-Nut down the road to disgrace. *Business Week* (February 22):124–128. [15]

Wellman, B. 1985. Domestic work, paid work and net work. In Duck, S. W., and Perlman, D. (eds.), *Understanding Personal Relationships.* Beverly Hills, CA: Sage. [11]

Wells, L. E., and Rankin, J. H. 1991. Families and delinquency: A meta-analysis of the impact of broken homes. *Social Problems,* 38:71–93. [15]

Wells, W. D., and Siegal, B. 1961. Stereotyped soma-types. *Psychological Reports,* 8:77–78. [6]

Wentzel, K. R. 1988. Gender differences in math and English achievement: A longitudinal study. *Sex Roles,* 18:691–698. [14]

Werner, C. M., Brown, B. B., and Damron, G. 1981. Territorial marking in a game arcade. *Journal of Personality and Social Psychology,* 41:1094–1104. [5]

Wertsch, J. V. 1991. *Voices of the Mind: A Sociocultural Approach to Mental Action.* Cambridge, MA: Harvard University Press. [2]

West, C., and Frankel, R. 1991. Miscommunication in medicine. In Coupland, N., Giles, H., and Weimann, J. (eds.), *"Miscommunication" and Problematic Talk.* Newbury Park, CA: Sage. [5]

West, C., and Zimmerman, D. H. 1983. Small insults: A study of interruptions in cross-sex conversations between unacquainted persons. In Thorne, B., Kramarae, C., and Henley, N. (eds.), *Language, Gender, and Society.* Rowley, MA: Newbury House, pp. 102–117. [5]

West, S. G., Gunn, S. P., and Chernicky, P. 1975. Ubiquitous Watergate: An attributional analysis. *Journal of Personality and Social Psychology,* 32:55–65. [1]

West, S. G., Whitney, G., and Schnedler, R. 1975. Helping a motorist in distress: The effects of sex, race, and neighborhood. *Journal of Personality and Social Psychology,* 31:691–698. [10]

Westie, F. R. 1964. Race and ethnic relations. In Faris, R. E. L. (ed.), *Handbook of Modern Sociology.* Chicago: Rand McNally. [12]

Whalen, J., and Flacks, R. 1989. *Beyond the Barricades: The Sixties Generation Grows Up.* Philadelphia: Temple University Press. [16]

Whalen, M. R., and Zimmerman, D. H. 1987. Sequential and institutional contexts in calls for help. *Social Psychology Quarterly,* 50:172–185. [5]

Wheeler, L., and Miyake, K. 1992. Social comparison in everyday life. *Journal of Personality and Social Psychology,* 62:760–773. [7]

Whitbeck, L., Simons, R., Conger, R., Lorenz, F., Huck, S., and Elder, G., Jr. 1991. Family economic hardship, parental support, and adolescent self-esteem. *Social Psychology Quarterly,* 54:353–363. [7]

White, H. R., Padina, R., and LaGrange, R. 1987. Longitudinal predictors of serious substance use and delinquency. *Criminology,* 6:715–740. [15]

White, L. K. 1991. Determinants of divorce. In Booth, A. (ed.), *Contemporary Families: Looking Forward, Looking Back.* Minneapolis, MN: National Council on Family Relations. [13]

White, L. K., Booth, A., and Edwards, J. N. 1986. Children and marital happiness. *Journal of Family Issues,* 7:131–147. [11]

White, L. K., and Riedmann, A. 1992. Ties among adult siblings. *Social Forces,* 71:85–102. [11]

Whitley, B. E. 1988. Masculinity, femininity, and self-esteem: A multi-trait-multimethod analysis. *Sex Roles,* 18:419–431. [7]

Whyte, W. F. 1943. *Street Corner So-*

ciety. Chicago: University of Chicago Press. [1]

Whyte, W. F. 1946. When workers and customers meet. In Whyte, W. (ed.), *Industry and Society.* New York: McGraw-Hill. [7]

Whyte, W. H., Jr. 1956. *The Organization Man.* New York: Simon & Schuster. [9]

Wiatrowski, M. D., Griswold, D. B., and Roberts, M. K. 1981. Social control and delinquency. *American Sociological Review,* 46:525–541. [15]

Wicker, T. 1968. Introduction. *Report of the National Advisory Commission on Civil Disorders.* New York: Bantam. [14]

Wiggins, B. B., and Heise, D. R. 1987. Expectations, intentions, and behavior: Some tests of affect control theory. *Journal of Mathematical Sociology,* 13(1–2):153–169. [8]

Wiggins, J. A. 1983. Family violence as a case of interpersonal aggression: A situational analysis. *Social Forces,* 62:102–123. [12]

Wiggins, J. A., Dill, F., and Schwartz, R. D. 1965. On "status-liability." *Sociometry,* 28:197–209. [12]

Wilder, D. A. 1977. Perception of groups, size of opposition, and social influence. *Journal of Experimental Social Psychology,* 13:253–268. [9]

Wilder, D. A. 1986. Cognitive factors affecting the success of intergroup contact. In Worchel, S., and Austin, W. G. (eds.), *Psychology of Intergroup Relations.* Chicago: Nelson-Hall. [12]

Wilder, D. A., and Shapiro, P. 1984. Role of out-group cues in determining social identity. *Journal of Personality and Social Psychology,* 47:342–348. [4]

Williams, D. G. 1988. Gender, marriage, and psychological well-being. *Journal of Family Issues,* 9:452–468. [4]

Williams, I. 1990. Season of superheros, slides, and sleep. *Daily Tar Heel* (February 28):4. [6]

Williams, J. A., Vernon, J. A., Williams, M. C., and Malecha, K. 1987. Sex role socialization in picture books: An update. *Social Science Quarterly,* 68:148–156. [3]

Williams, J. E., and Best, D. L. 1990. *Measuring Sex Stereotypes: A Multinational Study.* Newbury Park, CA: Sage. [6]

Williams, K. D., Harkins, S. G., and Latané, B. 1981. Identifiability as a deterrent to social loafing: Two cheering experiments. *Journal of Personality and Social Psychology,* 40:303–311. [9]

Williams, K. D., and Karau, S. J. 1991.

Social loafing and social compensation: The effects of expectations of co-worker performance. *Journal of Personality and Social Psychology*, 61: 570–581. [9]

Williams, K. R., and Hawkins, R. 1989. The meaning of arrest for wife abuse. *Criminology*, 27:163–181. [12]

Williams, L. 1987. Race bias found in location of toxic dumps. *New York Times* (April 16):A20. [14]

Williams, L. 1989. Teen-aged sex: New codes amid old anxiety. *New York Times* (February 27):A1, B11. [11]

Willmott, P. 1987. *Friendship Networks and Social Support*. London: Policy Studies Institute. [11]

Wilson, E. O. 1978. *On Human Nature*. Cambridge, MA: Harvard University Press. [10]

Wilson, W. J. 1987. *The Truly Disadvantaged: The Inner City, the Underclass, and Public Policy*. Chicago: University of Chicago Press. [14]

Wilson, W. J., and Aponte, R. 1985. Urban poverty. *Annual Review of Sociology*, 11:231–258. [14]

Wiltfang, G. L., and McAdam, D. 1991. The costs and risks of social activism: A study of sanctuary movement activism. *Social Forces*, 69: 987–1010. [16]

Wiltfang, G. L., and Scarbecz, M. 1990. Social class and adolescent self-esteem: Another look. *Social Psychology Quarterly*, 53:174–183. [7]

Winch, R. F. 1958. *Mate Selection: A Study of Complementary Needs*. New York: Harper & Row. [11]

Wiseman, J. P. 1986. Friendship: Bonds and binds in a voluntary relationship. *Journal of Social and Personal Relationships*, 3:191–211. [11]

Wishman, S. 1981. A lawyer's guilty secrets. *Newsweek* (November 9):25. [7]

Wishner, J. 1960. Reanalysis of "impressions of personality." *Psychological Review*, 67:96–112. [6]

Wispé, L., and Freshley, H. 1971. Race, sex and sympathetic helping behavior: The broken bag caper. *Journal of Personality and Social Psychology*, 17: 59–65. [10]

Wolf, C. 1990. How minority groups react. *Symbolic Interaction*, 13:37–61. [16]

Wolf, S. 1979. Behavioral style and group cohesiveness as sources of minority influence. *European Journal of Social Psychology*, 9:381–395. [9]

Wolff, K. H. (trans. and ed.). 1950. *The Sociology of George Simmel*. New York: Free Press. [4]

Wolff, M. 1973. Notes on the behavior of pedestrians. In Birenbaum, A., and Sagurin, E. (eds.), *People in Places*. New York: Praeger. [5]

Woll, S. 1986. So many to choose from: Decision strategies in videodating. *Journal of Personal and Social Relationships*, 3:43–52. [11]

Wood, W. 1982. Retrieval of attitude-relevant information from memory: Effects on susceptibility to persuasion and on intrinsic motivation. *Journal of Personality and Social Psychology*, 42: 798–810. [8]

Woodward, G. C., and Denton, R. E., Jr. 1988. *Persuasion and Influence in American Life*. Prospect Heights, IL: Waveland Press. [13]

Worchel, S. 1984. The darker side of helping: The social dynamics of helping and cooperation. In Saub, D., Bar-Tal, D., Karylowski, J., and Reykowski, J. (eds.), *Development and Maintenance of Prosocial Behavior: International Perspectives*. New York: Plenum. [12]

Worchel, S. 1986. The role of cooperation in reducing intergroup conflict. In Worchel, S., and Austin, W. G. (eds.), *Psychology of Intergroup Relations*. Chicago: Nelson-Hall. [12]

Worchel, S., Andreoli, V. A., and Folger, R. 1977. Intergroup cooperation and intergroup attraction: The effect of previous interaction and outcome of combined effort. *Journal of Experimental Social Psychology*, 13:131–140. [12]

Word, C. O., Zanna, M. P., and Cooper, J. 1974. The nonverbal mediation of self-fulfilling prophecies in interracial interaction. *Journal of Experimental Social Psychology*, 10: 109–120. [7]

Worthy, M., Gary, A. L., and Kahn, G. M. 1969. Self-disclosure as an exchange process. *Journal of Personality and Social Psychology*, 13:59–63. [11]

Wright, S. A. 1987. *Leaving Cults: The Dynamics of Defection*. Washington, DC: Society for the Scientific Study of Religion. [16]

Wright, S. A. 1991. Reconceptualizing cult coercion and withdrawal: A comparative analysis of divorce and apostasy. *Social Forces*, 70:125–145. [16]

Wrightsman, L. S. 1978. The American trial jury on trial: Empirical evidence and procedural modifications. *Journal of Social Issues*, 34:137–164. [9]

Wyer, R. S., Jr., Budesheim, T., Shavitt, S., Riggle, E., Malton, R., and Kuklinski, J. 1991. Image, issues, and ideology: The processing of information about political candidates. *Journal of Personality and Social Psychology*, 61:533–545. [6]

Wyer, R. S., Jr., Bodenhausen, G. V., and Gorman, T. F. 1985. Cognitive mediators of reactions to rape. *Journal of Personality and Social Psychology*, 48:324–338. [10]

Wylie, R. 1979. *The Self-Concept* (rev. ed.). Lincoln: University of Nebraska Press. [14]

Yamagishi, T. 1988. Seriousness of social dilemmas and the provision of a sanction system. *Social Psychology Quarterly*, 51:32–42. [9]

Yancey, W. L., Rigsby, L., and McCarthy, J. D. 1972. Social position and self-evaluation: The relative importance of race. *American Journal of Sociology*, 78:338–359. [14]

Yankelovich Clancy Shulman. 1992. Question id: USYANKCS.92WOM. R28E. (February 1992) Roper Center POLLS [computer file]. [14]

Yarmey, A. D. 1979. *The Psychology of Eyewitness Testimony*. New York: Free Press. [6]

Yinger, J. 1965. *Toward a Field Theory of Behavior*. New York: McGraw-Hill. [7]

Young, R. 1991. Race, conceptions of crime and justice, and support for death penalty. *Social Psychology Quarterly*, 54:67–75. [6]

Youniss, J., and Smollar, J. 1985. *Adolescent Relations with Mothers, Fathers, and Friends*. Chicago: University of Chicago Press. [3]

Yukl, G., and Falbe, C. 1991. Importance of different power sources in downward and lateral relations. *Journal of Applied Psychology*, 76:416–423. [13]

Zajonc, R. 1965. Social facilitation. *Science*, 149:269–274. [9]

Zald, M. N. 1987. The future of social movements. In Zald, M. N., and McCarthy, J. D. (eds.), *Social Movements in an Organizational Society: Collected Essays*. New Brunswick, NJ: Transaction Books. [16]

Zald, M. N., and Garner, R. A. 1987. Social movement organizations: Growth, decay, and change. In Zald, M. N., and McCarthy, J. D. (eds.), *Social Movements in an Organizational Society: Collected Essays*. New

Brunswick, NJ: Transaction Books. [16]

Zald, M. N., and McCarthy, J. D. 1987*a*. Religious groups as crucibles of social movements. In Zald, M. N., and McCarthy, J. D. (eds.), *Social Movements in an Organizational Society: Collected Essays*. New Brunswick, NJ: Transaction Books. [16]

Zald, M. N., and McCarthy, J. D. 1987*b*. Social movement industries: Competition and conflict among SMOs. In Zald, M. N., and McCarthy, J. D. (eds.), *Social Movements in an Organizational Society: Collected Essays*. New Brunswick, NJ: Transaction Books. [16]

Zald, M. N., and Useem, B. 1987. Movement and countermovement interaction: Mobilization, tactics, and state involvement. In Zald, M. N., and McCarthy, J. D. (eds.), *Social Movements in an Organizational Society: Collected Essays*. New Brunswick, NJ: Transaction Books. [16]

Zanna, M. P., and Hamilton, D. L. 1977. Further evidence for meaning change in impression formation. *Journal of Experimental Social Psychology*, 13:224–238. [6]

Zanna, M. P., Olson, J. M., and Fazio, R. H. 1980. Attitude-behavior consistency: An individual difference perspective. *Journal of Personality and Social Psychology*, 38:432–440. [8]

Zarate, M. A., and Smith, E. R. 1990. Person categorization and stereotyping. *Social Cognition*, 8:161–185. [6]

Zarate, M. A., and Smith, E. R. 1992. Exemplar-based model of social judgment. *Psychological Review*, 99:3–21. [6]

Zeitlin, L. R. 1971. A little larceny can do a lot for company morale. *Psychology Today*, 14(June):22. [15]

Zelditch, M., Jr., Lauderdale, P., and Stublarec, S. 1980. How are inconsistencies between status and ability resolved? *Social Forces*, 58:1025–1043. [13]

Zelizer, V. A. 1987. *Pricing the Priceless Child: The Changing Social Value of Children*. New York: Basic Books. [3]

Zillmann, D. 1984. *Connections between Sex and Aggression*. Hillsdale, NJ: Erlbaum. [12]

Zillmann, D., Hoyt, J. L., and Day, K. D. 1974. Strength and duration of the effect of aggression, violence, and erotic communications on subsequent aggressive behavior. *Communication Research*, 1:286–306. [12]

Zillmann, D., Katcher, A. H., and Milavsky, B. 1972. Excitation transfer from physical exercise to subsequent aggressive behavior. *Journal of Experimental Social Psychology*, 8:247–259. [12]

Zillmann, D., and Sapolsky, B. S. 1977. What mediates the effect of mild erotica on annoyance and hostile behavior in males? *Journal of Personality and Social Psychology*, 35:587–596. [12]

Zimbardo, P. C. 1969. The human choice: Individuation, reason, and order versus deindividuation, impulse, and chaos. In Arnold, W., and Levine, D. (eds.), *Nebraska Symposium on Motivation*, Lincoln, NE: University of Nebraska Press, 17:237–307. [12]

Zimbardo, P. C. 1974. On the ethics of intervention in human psychological research: With special reference to the Stanford prison experiment. *Cognition*, 2:243–256. [1]

Zimbardo, P. C. 1977. *Shyness: What It Is, What to Do about It*. Reading, MA: Addison-Wesley. [7]

Zimbardo, P. C., Haney, C., and Banks, W. C. 1973. A Pirandellian prison. *New York Times Magazine* (April 8):38–60. [12]

Zimmer, L. 1987. How women reshape the prison guard role. *Gender and Society*, 1:415–431. [14]

Zimmerman, D. H., and Boden, D. 1991. Structure-in-action: An introduction. In Boden, D., and Zimmerman, D. H. (eds.), *Talk and Social Structure: Studies in Ethnomethodology and Conversational Analysis*. Berkeley: University of California Press. [5]

Zimmerman, D. H., and West, C. 1975. Sex roles, interruptions, and silences in conversation. In Thorne, B., and Henley, N. (eds.), *Language and Sex Differences and Dominance*. Rowley, MA: Newbury House. [5]

Zirkel, P. A. 1971. Self-concept and the "disadvantage" of ethnic group membership and mixture. *Review of Educational Research*, 41:211–225. [14]

Zube, M. 1982. Changing behavior and outlook of aging men and women: Implications for marriage in the middle and later years. *Family Relations*,

Zuckerman, D. 1985. Can genes help helping? *Psychology Today*, 19(March):80. [10]

Zuckerman, M., Depaulo, B. M., and Rosenthal, R. 1981. The verbal and nonverbal communication of deception. In Berkowitz, L. (ed.), *Advances in Experimental Social Psychology*, Vol. 14. New York: Academic Press. [5]

Zuckerman, M., Larrance, D. T., Spiegel, N. H., and Klorman, R. 1981. Controlling nonverbal displays: Facial expressions and tone of voice. *Journal of Experimental Social Psychology*, 17:506–524. [5]

Zurcher, L. A., Jr. 1977. *The Mutable Self*. Beverly Hills, CA: Sage. [7]

PHOTO CREDITS

NAME INDEX

SUBJECT INDEX